Florida
Statistical Abstract
2000

Thirty-fourth Edition

Bureau of Economic and Business Research
Warrington College of Business Administration

UNIVERSITY OF
FLORIDA

UNIVERSITY OF FLORIDA

Charles E. Young, Interim President

WARRINGTON COLLEGE OF BUSINESS ADMINISTRATION

John Kraft, Dean

BUREAU OF ECONOMIC AND BUSINESS RESEARCH

Stanley K. Smith, Director

PUBLICATION PRODUCTION STAFF

Janet J. Galvez, Editor in Chief
Susan S. Floyd, Senior Editor
Eve M. Irwin, Associate Editor
Dorothy A. Evans, Editorial Assistant

MARKETING AND DISTRIBUTION

Carol Griffen, Marketing Coordinator
Pamela Middleton, Circulation Manager

Order books from Bureau of Economic and Business Research
Warrington College of Business Administration
221 Matherly Hall, Post Office Box 117145
Gainesville, Florida 32611-7145
phone (352) 392-0171, ext. 219
fax (352) 392-4739
email: info@bebr.ufl.edu
http://www.bebr.ufl.edu

ISBN 0-930885-57-0
ISSN 0071-6022

Printed in the United States of America on acid-free paper

Cover photograph of the Bridge of Lions, St. Augustine, Florida.
Photograph by Clark Wheeler, Gainesville, Florida

CONTENTS

PREFACE

Since 1967 the *Florida Statistical Abstract* has provided a comprehensive collection of the latest statistics available on the social, economic and political organization of Florida. This thirty-fourth edition continues the tradition. Most of the data is at the county level, although the *Abstract* also includes information about Florida Metropolitan Statistical Areas, cities, planning districts, and other substate units along with comparisons of Florida with other Sunbelt and other populous states and the United States as a whole. This volume contains a selection of data collected by public and private entities. Agencies of the State of Florida and the Federal Government contribute the majority of the data. A listing of agencies by section is provided in the Explanatory Notes in the back of the volume.

Every effort is made to publish the most up-to-date figures possible; however, these data cover a wide range of activities reported for different time periods so uniformity is impossible. Statistics in this edition are generally for the most recent year or period available by the summer of 2000. Each table title states the time period for data shown in the table and exceptions are footnoted. Sources are given at the bottom of each table. Usually more statistical detail and a more comprehensive discussion of methods and definitions than can be included in the *Abstract* are available from the source. Data not released in either a printed or on-line publication by the time of printing are identified in the source notes as either "unpublished data," or as a "prepublication release," and may be accompanied by an Internet address. Data available both in print and either on line or on CD-ROM are identified by an Internet address or CD-ROM designation in the table source notation.

Each year all tables are reviewed: new tables of current interest are added, continuing series are updated or revised to reflect changes in source definitions or methods, and less timely data are eliminated. Some tables of "benchmark" data, although not timely, are repeated. The reader is encouraged to use tables in earlier editions of the *Abstract*.

Organization of the *Florida Statistical Abstract*. The *Abstract* is organized around five divisions, each of which is subdivided into sections. Table numbers correspond to the section numbers. The first division (Sections 1.00 through 7.00) generally includes tables presenting data on characteristics of the population: demographics, housing, education, income, employment, and welfare. Except for Section 8.00, which presents data on physical geography and the environment, the next three divisions (Sections 9.00 through 23.00) refer primarily to establishments engaged in economic, social, and political activities.

Establishments are classified in most sources according to the Standard Industrial Classification (SIC) system. Major industry divisions are assigned two-digit codes 01 through 99; subdivisions are classified by three- and four-digit codes. The U.S. Bureau of the Census recently developed the North American Industry Classification System (NAICS) and industries are in the process of being classified according to the new system. Tables throughout this and future editions of the *Abstract* will reflect these transitional changes. See the Glossary and the Appendix for more discussion about the 1997 economic censuses.

The last division of the *Abstract* contains tables of a comparative nature: economic and social trends. Time series showing the fluctuations of major economic indicators such as prices and employment are included in Section 24.00. Selected statistics of the economic, social, and physical environments of Florida, other Sunbelt and other populous states and the United States comprise Section 25.00.

Changes in this edition. Most notably, several new tables have been added to Sections 11.00 through 20.00 to reflect the NAICS industry changes stemming from the completion of the 1997 economic census conducted by the U.S. Census Bureau. Data from the 1997 economic census will continue to be released by the Census Bureau throughout the year. Establishment, employment, and payroll data are presented on most tables by kind of business, and where available, by county. Other new tables in this edition highlight high school competency testing and Florida Comprehensive Assessment Test (FCAT) results; occupation growth trends; and prisoner recidivism rates.

Abstract on CD-ROM. The *Florida Statistical Abstract* is available on compact disc (CD-ROM) and may be ordered by contacting the Bureau of Economic and Business Research, 221 Matherly Hall, P. O. Box 117145, Gainesville, Florida, 32611-7145, (352) 392-0171, ext. 219, or e-mail info@bebr.ufl.edu.

Bureau of Economic and Business Research. The Bureau's mission is twofold: (1) to produce, collect, analyze, and disseminate economic and demographic data on Florida; and (2) conduct applied research and publish findings on topics relating to the state's ongoing economic growth and development. The Bureau's activities are organized around four research programs: forecasting, population, survey, and policy studies.

Acknowledgments. Key production personnel for the 2000 edition of the *Florida Statistical Abstract* were Janet Galvez, Eve Irwin, Dorothy (Dot) Evans, and student statistical assistants Mike Barrett and Kristin Floyd. Janet provided organizational and technical expertise in automating the publication process. Eve coordinated all aspects of table production including page layout, quality control, and database, Internet, and electronic data transferals. Eve also paged and printed the final volume, prepared the *Abstract* on CD-ROM, and investigated the feasibility of CD-ROM-to-film production as a future direction for the publication process. Dot Evans prepared all of the charts and maps, updated the Census Index, performed text conversions, and assisted with data entry and proofing. As always, our student assistants are perhaps our most valuable assets, performing tedious tasks in order to produce a quality publication. Kristin performed data entry and quality control tasks, prepared much of the individual section contents, and proofed the volume. Mike was given the arduous responsibility of performing the final proof, providing a "fresh set of eyes" to the proofing process while cross-checking each table with its data source.

Carol Griffen prepared the cover layout, supplied data from the BEBR database, marketed the volume, and consulted with Eve on the CD-ROM-to-film process. June Nogle provided unpublished data from the BEBR Population Program and Chris McCarty supplied data from the BEBR monthly Florida Economic and Consumer Survey. Pamela Middleton coordinated the promotional mailings. Pam is also responsible for filling all in-coming order requests. Janet Fletcher and Janet Rose, assisted by students Brian Heckman and Doughty Pierce, prepared and mailed promotional materials. Clint Collins, Ken Sturrock, and Paul Simpson furnished invaluable computer support.

Outdoor and nature photographer, Clark Wheeler, took the cover photograph of the Bridge of Lions in St. Augustine, Florida. Suggestions for improving the coverage and presentation of data in the *Abstract* are always welcomed.

Gainesville, Florida   Susan S. Floyd
September 2000

Counties and Metropolitan Statistical Areas
Effective June 30, 1999 to present

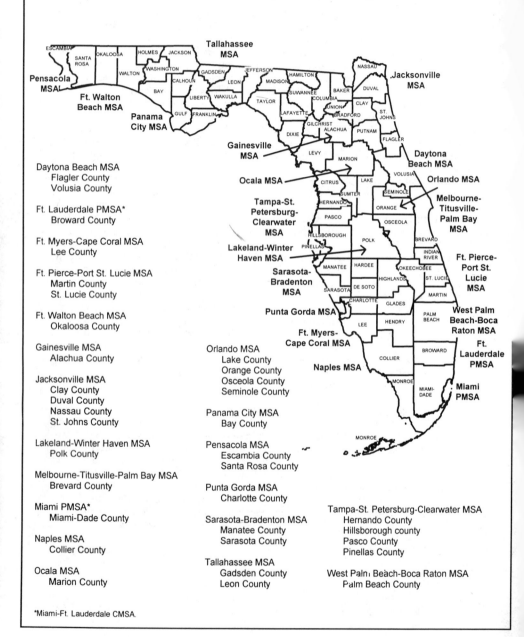

Daytona Beach MSA
  Flagler County
  Volusia County

Ft. Lauderdale PMSA*
  Broward County

Ft. Myers-Cape Coral MSA
  Lee County

Ft. Pierce-Port St. Lucie MSA
  Martin County
  St. Lucie County

Ft. Walton Beach MSA
  Okaloosa County

Gainesville MSA
  Alachua County

Jacksonville MSA
  Clay County
  Duval County
  Nassau County
  St. Johns County

Lakeland-Winter Haven MSA
  Polk County

Melbourne-Titusville-Palm Bay MSA
  Brevard County

Miami PMSA*
  Miami-Dade County

Naples MSA
  Collier County

Ocala MSA
  Marion County

Orlando MSA
  Lake County
  Orange County
  Osceola County
  Seminole County

Panama City MSA
  Bay County

Pensacola MSA
  Escambia County
  Santa Rosa County

Punta Gorda MSA
  Charlotte County

Sarasota-Bradenton MSA
  Manatee County
  Sarasota County

Tallahassee MSA
  Gadsden County
  Leon County

Tampa-St. Petersburg-Clearwater MSA
  Hernando County
  Hillsborough county
  Pasco County
  Pinellas County

West Palm Beach-Boca Raton MSA
  Palm Beach County

*Miami-Ft. Lauderdale CMSA.

Population

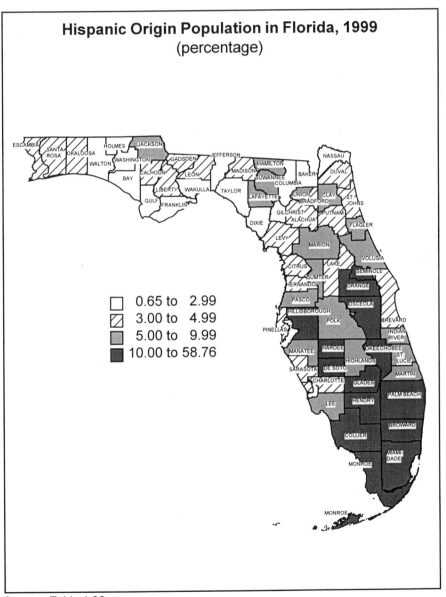

Hispanic Origin Population in Florida, 1999
(percentage)

Legend:
- 0.65 to 2.99
- 3.00 to 4.99
- 5.00 to 9.99
- 10.00 to 58.76

Source: Table 1.36

TABLES LISTED BY MAJOR HEADINGS

TABLES LISTED BY MAJOR HEADINGS

University of Florida   **Bureau of Economic and Business Research**

Table 1.10. CENSUS COUNTS: TOTAL, URBAN, AND RURAL POPULATION
IN FLORIDA, CENSUS YEARS 1830 TO 1990

Census year and date	Total Number	Change from preceding census Number	Change from preceding census Percent-age	Urban Number	Urban Per-cent-age of total	Rural Number	Rural Per-cent-age of total
Previous urban definition 1/							
1830 (June 1)	34,730	(X)	(X)	0	0.0	34,730	100.0
1840 (June 1)	54,477	19,747	56.9	0	0.0	54,477	100.0
1850 (June 1)	87,445	32,968	60.5	0	0.0	87,445	100.0
1860 (June 1)	140,424	52,979	60.6	5,708	4.1	134,716	95.9
1870 (June 1)	187,748	47,324	33.7	15,275	8.1	172,473	91.9
1880 (June 1)	269,493	81,745	43.5	26,947	10.0	242,546	90.0
1890 (June 1)	391,422	121,929	45.2	77,358	19.8	314,064	80.2
1900 (June 1)	528,542	137,120	35.0	107,031	20.3	421,511	79.7
1910 (April 15)	752,619	224,077	42.4	219,080	29.1	533,539	70.9
1920 (January 1)	968,470	215,851	28.7	353,515	36.5	614,955	63.5
1930 (April 1)	1,468,211	499,741	51.6	759,778	51.7	708,433	48.3
1940 (April 1)	1,897,414	429,203	29.2	1,045,791	55.1	851,623	44.9
1950 (April 1)	2,771,305	873,891	46.1	1,566,788	56.5	1,204,517	43.5
1960 (April 1)	4,951,560	2,180,255	78.7	3,077,989	62.2	1,873,571	37.8
Current urban definition 2/							
1950 (April 1)	2,771,305	873,891	46.1	1,813,890	65.5	957,415	34.5
1960 (April 1)	4,951,560	2,180,255	78.7	3,661,383	73.9	1,290,177	26.1
1970 (April 1)	6,791,418	1,839,858	37.2	5,544,551	81.6	1,244,892	18.3
1980 (April 1)	9,746,324	2,954,906	43.5	8,212,385	84.3	1,533,939	15.7
1990 (April 1)	12,937,926	3,191,602	32.8	10,970,445	84.8	1,967,481	15.2

(X) Not applicable.
1/ Figures have been adjusted to constitute a substantially consistent series based on incorporated places of 2,500 or more persons with additional areas defined as urban under special rules.
2/ The current urban definition defines the urban population as all persons living in urbanized areas and in places of 2,500 or more persons outside urbanized areas. An urbanized area comprises an incorporated place and adjacent densely settled surrounding area that together have a minimum population of 50,000. Population not classified as urban constitutes the rural population. Rural classification need not imply farm residence or a sparsely settled area because a small city is rural as long as it is outside an urbanized area and has fewer than 2,500 persons.

Source: U.S., Department of Commerce, Bureau of the Census, *1990 Census of Population: General Population Characteristics, Florida,* 1990 CP-1-11, and previous census editions.

Table 1.12. STATES: CENSUS COUNTS, APRIL 1, 1990, AND POPULATION ESTIMATES JULY 1, 1999, IN FLORIDA, OTHER STATES, AND THE UNITED STATES

State	Census April 1 1990 (1,000)	Esti-mates July 1 1999 (1,000)	Per-centage change 1990 to 1999	State	Census April 1 1990 (1,000)	Esti-mates July 1 1999 (1,000)	Per-centage change 1990 to 1999
Florida	12,938	15,111	16.8	Missouri	5,117	5,468	6.9
				Montana	799	883	10.5
Alabama	4,040	4,370	8.2	Nebraska	1,578	1,666	5.6
Alaska	550	620	12.6	Nevada	1,202	1,809	50.6
Arizona	3,665	4,778	30.4	New Hampshire	1,109	1,201	8.3
Arkansas	2,351	2,551	8.5	New Jersey	7,748	8,143	5.1
California	29,811	33,145	11.2	New Mexico	1,515	1,740	14.8
Colorado	3,294	4,056	23.1	New York	17,991	18,197	1.1
Connecticut	3,287	3,282	-0.2	North Carolina	6,632	7,651	15.4
Delaware	666	754	13.1	North Dakota	639	634	-0.8
District of				Ohio	10,847	11,257	3.8
Columbia	607	519	-14.5	Oklahoma	3,146	3,358	6.8
Georgia	6,478	7,788	20.2	Oregon	2,842	3,316	16.7
Hawaii	1,108	1,185	7.0	Pennsylvania	11,883	11,994	0.9
Idaho	1,007	1,252	24.3	Rhode Island	1,003	991	-1.3
Illinois	11,431	12,128	6.1	South Carolina	3,486	3,886	11.5
Indiana	5,544	5,943	7.2	South Dakota	696	733	5.3
Iowa	2,777	2,869	3.3	Tennessee	4,877	5,484	12.4
Kansas	2,478	2,654	7.1	Texas	16,986	20,044	18.0
Kentucky	3,687	3,961	7.4	Utah	1,723	2,130	23.6
Louisiana	4,222	4,372	3.6	Vermont	563	594	5.5
Maine	1,228	1,253	2.0	Virginia	6,189	6,873	11.0
Maryland	4,781	5,172	8.2	Washington	4,867	5,756	18.3
Massachusetts	6,016	6,175	2.6	West Virginia	1,793	1,807	0.7
Michigan	9,295	9,864	6.1	Wisconsin	4,892	5,250	7.3
Minnesota	4,376	4,776	9.1	Wyoming	454	480	5.7
Mississippi	2,575	2,769	7.5	United States	248,791	272,691	9.6

Note: Includes persons in the Armed Forces residing in each state. Some data may be revised.

Source: U.S., Department of Commerce, Bureau of the Census, Population Division, "State Population Estimate and Demographic Components of Population Change: April 1, 1990 to July 1, 1999," Internet site <http://www.census.gov/population/estimates/state/st-99-2.txt> (accessed 22 February 2000).

University of Florida   **Bureau of Economic and Business Research**

Table 1.19. COUNTIES: CENSUS COUNTS IN THE STATE AND COUNTIES OF FLORIDA, 1940 THROUGH 1990

County	1940	1950	1960	1970	1980	1990	Percentage change 1940-1950	1950-1960	1960-1970	1970-1980	1980-1990
Florida	1,897,414	2,771,305	4,951,560	6,791,418	9,746,961	12,938,071	46.1	78.7	37.2	43.5	32.7
Alachua	38,607	57,026	74,074	104,764	151,369	181,596	47.7	29.9	41.4	44.5	20.0
Baker	6,510	6,313	7,363	9,242	15,289	18,486	-3.0	16.6	25.5	65.4	20.9
Bay	20,686	42,689	67,131	75,283	97,740	126,994	106.4	57.3	12.1	29.8	29.9
Bradford	8,717	11,457	12,446	14,625	20,023	22,515	31.4	8.6	17.5	36.9	12.4
Brevard	16,142	23,653	111,435	230,006	272,959	398,978	46.5	371.1	106.4	18.7	46.2
Broward	39,794	83,933	333,946	620,100	1,018,257	1,255,531	110.9	297.9	85.7	64.2	23.3
Calhoun	8,218	7,922	7,422	7,624	9,294	11,011	-3.6	-6.3	2.7	21.9	18.5
Charlotte	3,663	4,286	12,594	27,559	58,460	110,975	17.0	193.8	118.8	112.1	89.8
Citrus	5,846	6,111	9,268	19,196	54,703	93,513	4.5	51.7	107.1	185.0	70.9
Clay	6,468	14,323	19,535	32,059	67,052	105,986	121.4	36.4	64.1	109.2	58.1
Collier	5,102	6,488	15,753	38,040	85,971	152,099	27.2	142.8	141.5	126.0	76.9
Columbia	16,859	18,216	20,077	25,250	35,399	42,613	8.0	10.2	25.8	40.2	20.4
De Soto	7,792	9,242	11,683	13,060	19,039	23,865	18.6	26.4	11.8	45.8	25.3
Dixie	7,018	3,928	4,479	5,480	7,751	10,585	-44.0	14.0	22.3	41.4	36.6
Duval	210,143	304,029	455,411	528,865	571,003	672,971	44.7	49.8	16.1	8.0	17.9
Escambia	74,667	112,706	173,829	205,334	233,794	262,798	50.9	54.2	18.1	13.9	12.4
Flagler	3,008	3,367	4,566	4,454	10,913	28,701	11.9	35.6	-2.5	145.0	163.0
Franklin	5,991	5,814	6,576	7,065	7,661	8,967	-3.0	13.1	7.4	8.4	17.0
Gadsden	31,450	36,457	41,989	39,184	41,674	41,116	15.9	15.2	-6.7	6.4	-1.3
Gilchrist	4,250	3,499	2,868	3,551	5,767	9,667	-17.7	-18.0	23.8	62.4	67.6
Glades	2,745	2,199	2,950	3,669	5,992	7,591	-19.9	34.2	24.4	63.3	26.7
Gulf	6,951	7,460	9,937	10,096	10,658	11,504	7.3	33.2	1.6	5.6	7.9
Hamilton	9,778	8,981	7,705	7,787	8,761	10,930	-8.2	-14.2	1.1	12.5	24.8
Hardee	10,158	10,073	12,370	14,889	20,357	19,499	-0.8	22.8	20.4	36.7	-4.2

Continued . . .

Table 1.19. COUNTIES: CENSUS COUNTS IN THE STATE AND COUNTIES OF FLORIDA, 1940 THROUGH 1990 (Continued)

County	1940	1950	1960	1970	1980	1990	Percentage change				
							1940-1950	1950-1960	1960-1970	1970-1980	1980-1990
Hendry	5,237	6,051	8,119	11,859	18,599	25,773	15.5	34.2	46.1	56.8	38.6
Hernando	5,641	6,693	11,205	17,004	44,469	101,115	18.6	67.4	51.8	161.5	127.4
Highlands	9,246	13,636	21,338	29,507	47,526	68,432	47.5	56.5	38.3	61.1	44.0
Hillsborough	180,148	249,894	397,788	490,265	646,939	834,054	38.7	59.2	23.2	32.0	28.9
Holmes	15,447	13,988	10,844	10,720	14,723	15,778	-9.4	-22.5	-1.1	37.3	7.2
Indian River	8,957	11,872	25,309	35,992	59,896	90,208	32.5	113.2	42.2	66.4	50.6
Jackson	34,428	34,645	36,208	34,434	39,154	41,375	0.6	4.5	-4.9	13.7	5.7
Jefferson	12,032	10,413	9,543	8,778	10,703	11,296	-13.5	-8.4	-8.0	21.9	5.5
Lafayette	4,405	3,440	2,889	2,892	4,035	5,578	-21.9	-16.0	0.1	39.5	38.2
Lake	27,255	36,340	57,383	69,305	104,870	152,104	33.3	57.9	20.8	51.3	45.0
Lee	17,488	23,404	54,539	105,216	205,266	335,113	33.8	133.0	92.9	95.1	63.3
Leon	31,646	51,590	74,225	103,047	148,655	192,493	63.0	43.9	38.8	44.3	29.5
Levy	12,550	10,637	10,364	12,756	19,870	25,912	-15.2	-2.6	23.1	55.8	30.4
Liberty	3,752	3,182	3,138	3,379	4,260	5,569	-15.2	-1.4	7.7	26.1	30.7
Madison	16,190	14,197	14,154	13,481	14,894	16,569	-12.3	-0.3	-4.8	10.5	11.2
Manatee	26,098	34,704	69,168	97,115	148,445	211,707	33.0	99.3	40.4	52.9	42.6
Marion	31,243	38,187	51,616	69,030	122,488	194,835	22.2	35.2	33.7	77.4	59.1
Martin	6,295	7,807	16,932	28,035	64,014	100,900	24.0	116.9	65.6	128.3	57.6
Miami-Dade	267,739	495,084	935,047	1,267,792	1,625,509	1,937,194	84.9	88.9	35.6	28.2	19.2
Monroe	14,078	29,957	47,921	52,586	63,188	78,024	112.8	60.0	9.7	20.2	23.5
Nassau	10,826	12,811	17,189	20,626	32,894	43,941	18.3	34.2	20.0	59.5	33.6
Okaloosa	12,900	27,533	61,175	88,187	109,920	143,777	113.4	122.2	44.2	24.6	30.8
Okeechobee	3,000	3,454	6,424	11,233	20,264	29,627	15.1	86.0	74.9	80.4	46.2
Orange	70,074	114,950	263,540	344,311	470,865	677,491	64.0	129.3	30.6	36.8	43.9

Continued . . .

Table 1.19. COUNTIES: CENSUS COUNTS IN THE STATE AND COUNTIES OF FLORIDA, 1940 THROUGH 1990 (Continued)

County	1940	1950	1960	1970	1980	1990	Percentage change				
							1940-1950	1950-1960	1960-1970	1970-1980	1980-1990
Osceola	10,119	11,406	19,029	25,267	49,287	107,728	12.7	66.8	32.8	95.1	118.6
Palm Beach	79,989	114,688	228,106	348,993	576,758	863,503	43.4	98.9	53.0	65.3	49.7
Pasco	13,981	20,529	36,785	75,955	193,661	281,131	46.8	79.2	106.5	155.0	45.2
Pinellas	91,852	159,249	374,665	522,329	728,531	851,659	73.4	135.3	39.4	39.5	16.9
Polk	86,665	123,997	195,139	228,515	321,652	405,382	43.1	57.4	17.1	40.8	26.0
Putnam	18,698	23,615	32,212	36,424	50,549	65,070	26.3	36.4	13.1	38.8	28.7
St. Johns	20,012	24,998	30,034	31,035	51,303	83,829	24.9	20.1	3.3	65.3	63.4
St. Lucie	11,871	20,180	39,294	50,836	87,182	150,171	70.0	94.7	29.4	71.5	72.3
Santa Rosa	16,085	18,554	29,547	37,741	55,988	81,608	15.3	59.2	27.7	48.3	45.8
Sarasota	16,106	28,827	76,895	120,413	202,251	277,776	79.0	166.7	56.6	68.0	37.3
Seminole	22,304	26,883	54,947	83,692	179,752	287,521	20.5	104.4	52.3	114.8	60.0
Sumter	11,041	11,330	11,869	14,839	24,272	31,577	2.6	4.8	25.0	63.6	30.1
Suwannee	17,073	16,986	14,961	15,559	22,287	26,780	-0.5	-11.9	4.0	43.2	20.2
Taylor	11,565	10,416	13,168	13,641	16,532	17,111	-9.9	26.4	3.6	21.2	3.5
Union	7,094	8,906	6,043	8,112	10,166	10,252	25.5	-32.1	34.2	25.3	0.8
Volusia	53,710	74,229	125,319	169,487	258,762	370,737	38.2	68.8	35.2	52.7	43.3
Wakulla	5,463	5,258	5,257	6,308	10,887	14,202	-3.8	0.0	20.0	72.6	30.4
Walton	14,246	14,725	15,576	16,087	21,300	27,759	3.4	5.8	3.3	32.4	30.3
Washington	12,302	11,888	11,249	11,453	14,509	16,919	-3.4	-5.4	1.8	26.7	16.6

Source: University of Florida, Bureau of Economic and Business Research, *The Urbanization of Florida's Population: An Historical Perspective of County Growth, 1830-1970*, and *Florida Estimates of Population, April 1, 1999*. Data from U.S. Bureau of the Census.

Table 1.20. COUNTIES: CENSUS COUNTS, APRIL 1, 1980 AND 1990, AND POPULATION ESTIMATES, APRIL 1, 1992 THROUGH 1999 IN THE STATE AND COUNTIES OF FLORIDA

(in thousands, rounded to hundreds)

County	Census 1980	Census 1990	Estimates 1992	1993	1994	1995	1996	1997	1998	1999	Percentage change 1990 to 1999
Florida	9,747.0	12,938.1	13,424.4	13,608.6	13,878.9	14,149.3	14,411.6	14,712.9	15,000.5	15,322.0	18.4
Alachua	151.4	181.6	186.2	190.7	193.9	198.3	202.1	208.1	211.4	216.2	19.1
Baker	15.3	18.5	19.2	19.5	19.7	20.3	20.7	21.1	21.1	21.9	18.4
Bay	97.7	127.0	131.3	134.1	136.3	139.2	142.2	144.6	147.5	150.1	18.2
Bradford	20.0	22.5	23.1	23.3	24.2	24.3	25.0	25.2	25.4	25.5	13.3
Brevard	273.0	399.0	417.7	427.0	436.3	445.0	450.2	458.0	465.8	474.8	19.0
Broward	1,018.3	1,255.5	1,294.1	1,317.5	1,340.2	1,364.2	1,392.3	1,423.7	1,460.9	1,490.3	18.7
Calhoun	9.3	11.0	11.8	11.5	11.6	12.0	12.5	12.9	13.6	14.1	28.2
Charlotte	58.5	111.0	118.7	121.7	124.9	127.6	129.5	131.3	133.7	136.8	23.2
Citrus	54.7	93.5	98.6	100.8	102.8	105.5	107.9	110.0	112.4	114.9	22.9
Clay	67.1	106.0	113.4	114.9	117.8	120.9	125.4	127.9	134.5	139.6	31.7
Collier	86.0	152.1	168.5	174.7	180.5	186.5	193.0	200.0	210.1	219.7	44.4
Columbia	35.4	42.6	45.2	46.4	48.9	50.4	52.6	53.7	55.4	56.5	32.6
De Soto	19.0	23.9	24.8	25.5	26.3	26.6	26.7	27.2	27.9	28.4	19.2
Dixie	7.8	10.6	10.9	11.8	12.2	12.4	12.6	13.0	13.2	13.5	27.3
Duval	571.0	673.0	693.5	701.6	710.6	718.4	728.4	741.5	753.8	762.8	13.4
Escambia	233.8	262.8	267.8	272.1	277.1	282.7	286.3	291.1	296.2	301.6	14.8
Flagler	10.9	28.7	32.0	33.5	35.3	37.0	39.1	41.2	43.4	45.8	59.6
Franklin	7.7	9.0	9.4	9.8	10.0	10.2	10.4	10.5	10.7	10.9	21.2
Gadsden	41.7	41.1	42.5	43.2	44.9	44.7	46.3	49.7	50.8	51.5	25.2
Gilchrist	5.8	9.7	10.2	10.7	11.5	11.9	12.2	12.5	13.1	13.4	38.7
Glades	6.0	7.6	8.1	8.3	8.4	8.6	9.4	9.6	9.9	9.9	30.0
Gulf	10.7	11.5	11.7	12.4	13.3	13.3	13.5	14.1	14.3	14.4	25.2
Hamilton	8.8	10.9	11.5	11.6	11.9	12.5	13.4	13.7	14.1	14.4	31.5

See footnote at end of table.

Continued . . .

University of Florida

Bureau of Economic and Business Research

Table 1.20. COUNTIES: CENSUS COUNTS, APRIL 1, 1980 AND 1990, AND POPULATION ESTIMATES, APRIL 1, 1992 THROUGH 1999 IN THE STATE AND COUNTIES OF FLORIDA (Continued)

(in thousands, rounded to hundreds)

County	Census 1980	Census 1990	Estimates 1992	1993	1994	1995	1996	1997	1998	1999	Percentage change 1990 to 1999
Hardee	20.4	19.5	21.1	22.0	22.5	22.9	22.5	22.4	22.8	22.6	15.9
Hendry	18.6	25.8	27.8	28.1	28.7	29.5	30.2	30.3	30.4	30.6	18.5
Hernando	44.5	101.1	108.1	111.7	114.9	117.9	119.9	122.1	125.0	127.4	26.0
Highlands	47.5	68.4	72.2	73.2	75.9	77.3	78.0	79.5	80.5	81.1	18.6
Hillsborough	646.9	834.1	854.0	866.1	879.1	892.9	910.9	928.7	942.3	967.5	16.0
Holmes	14.7	15.8	16.2	16.3	16.9	17.4	17.4	17.6	17.9	18.9	19.8
Indian River	59.9	90.2	94.1	95.6	97.4	100.3	102.2	104.6	106.7	109.6	21.5
Jackson	39.2	41.4	42.6	44.4	45.4	46.6	48.6	49.4	49.7	49.5	19.6
Jefferson	10.7	11.3	12.3	13.0	13.1	13.5	13.7	14.0	14.2	14.4	27.7
Lafayette	4.0	5.6	5.6	5.6	5.8	6.5	7.0	7.0	7.0	7.0	24.8
Lake	104.9	152.1	162.6	167.2	171.2	176.9	182.3	188.3	196.1	203.9	34.0
Lee	205.3	335.1	350.8	357.6	367.4	376.7	383.7	394.2	405.6	417.1	24.5
Leon	148.7	192.5	202.6	206.3	212.1	217.5	221.6	227.7	233.2	237.6	23.5
Levy	19.9	25.9	27.5	28.2	29.1	29.8	30.7	31.6	32.4	33.4	28.9
Liberty	4.3	5.6	5.5	5.7	6.5	6.9	7.4	7.7	7.7	8.0	44.5
Madison	14.9	16.6	17.0	17.3	17.8	18.3	18.7	19.0	19.3	19.6	18.5
Manatee	148.4	211.7	219.3	223.5	228.3	233.2	236.8	241.4	247.0	253.2	19.6
Marion	122.5	194.8	206.6	212.0	217.9	224.6	229.3	237.2	242.4	249.4	28.0
Martin	64.0	100.9	105.0	106.8	110.2	112.0	114.5	116.4	119.4	121.5	20.4
Miami-Dade	1,625.5	1,937.2	1,982.9	1,951.1	1,990.4	2,013.8	2,043.3	2,070.6	2,090.3	2,126.7	9.8
Monroe	63.2	78.0	81.0	81.8	82.3	83.4	83.8	84.7	85.6	87.0	11.5
Nassau	32.9	43.9	45.5	46.5	47.4	49.1	51.1	52.7	54.5	57.4	30.6
Okaloosa	109.9	143.8	150.0	154.5	158.3	162.7	165.3	171.0	175.6	179.6	24.9
Okeechobee	20.3	29.6	31.1	31.8	32.3	32.9	33.6	34.7	35.1	35.5	19.9

Continued . . . .

See footnote at end of table.

Table 1.20. COUNTIES: CENSUS COUNTS, APRIL 1, 1980 AND 1990, AND POPULATION ESTIMATES, APRIL 1, 1992 THROUGH 1999 IN THE STATE AND COUNTIES OF FLORIDA (Continued)

(in thousands, rounded to hundreds)

County	Census 1980	Census 1990	Estimates 1992	1993	1994	1995	1996	1997	1998	1999	Percentage change 1990 to 1999
Orange	470.9	677.5	712.6	727.8	740.2	759.0	777.6	803.6	824.1	846.3	24.9
Osceola	49.3	107.7	119.8	125.7	131.1	136.6	139.7	143.8	148.7	157.4	46.1
Palm Beach	576.8	863.5	897.0	918.2	937.2	962.8	981.8	1,003.8	1,020.5	1,042.2	20.7
Pasco	193.7	281.1	290.3	294.0	298.9	305.6	309.9	315.8	321.1	326.5	16.1
Pinellas	728.5	851.7	860.7	865.0	870.7	876.2	881.4	888.1	892.2	898.8	5.5
Polk	321.7	405.4	420.9	429.9	437.2	443.2	452.7	459.0	465.9	474.7	17.1
Putnam	50.5	65.1	67.8	67.6	69.0	69.5	70.3	70.2	71.5	72.9	12.0
St. Johns	51.3	83.8	88.4	91.2	94.8	98.2	101.7	106.0	109.9	113.9	35.9
St. Lucie	87.2	150.2	158.9	163.2	166.8	171.2	175.5	179.1	183.2	186.9	24.5
Santa Rosa	56.0	81.6	88.0	90.3	93.8	96.1	98.5	102.3	107.8	112.6	38.0
Sarasota	202.3	277.8	287.2	290.6	296.0	301.5	305.8	311.0	316.0	321.0	15.6
Seminole	179.8	287.5	305.9	310.9	316.6	324.1	329.0	337.5	345.2	354.1	23.2
Sumter	24.3	31.6	33.1	33.8	35.2	36.5	40.6	44.4	47.9	50.8	60.9
Suwannee	22.3	26.8	27.6	28.6	29.3	30.5	31.4	33.2	33.7	34.4	28.4
Taylor	16.5	17.1	17.4	17.4	17.5	18.3	19.0	19.2	19.5	19.8	15.9
Union	10.2	10.3	11.4	12.0	12.5	12.6	13.0	13.1	13.5	13.8	34.9
Volusia	258.8	370.7	384.0	390.1	396.6	403.0	407.2	413.7	420.4	426.8	15.1
Wakulla	10.9	14.2	14.7	15.4	16.4	17.0	18.0	18.7	19.8	20.6	45.4
Walton	21.3	27.8	29.7	30.6	31.9	33.4	34.3	36.1	38.3	40.5	45.8
Washington	14.5	16.9	17.4	17.6	18.1	19.0	19.8	20.1	21.3	22.2	30.9

Note: These are revised intercensal estimates that incorporate the effects of 1990 census counts, all revisions to 1990 census counts, and any changes that may have occurred in the underlying base data.

Source: University of Florida, Bureau of Economic and Business Research, Population Program, *Florida Estimates of Population, April 1, 1999*, and previous editions. Census data from U.S. Bureau of the Census.

Table 1.25. COUNTIES AND CITIES: CENSUS COUNTS, APRIL 1, 1990, AND POPULATION
ESTIMATES, APRIL 1, 1999, IN THE STATE, COUNTIES, AND MUNICIPALITIES
OF FLORIDA

Area	Census 1990	Estimates 1999	Area	Census 1990	Estimates 1999
Florida	12,938,071	15,322,040	Brevard (Continued)		
Incorporated	6,415,381	7,528,199	Satellite Beach	9,889	10,275
Unincorporated	6,522,690	7,793,841	Titusville	39,394	41,885
			West Melbourne	8,399	9,810
Alachua	181,596	216,249	Unincorporated	149,204	185,327
Alachua	4,547	6,305			
Archer	1,372	1,452	Broward	1,255,531	1,490,289
Gainesville	85,075	101,405	Coconut Creek	27,269	39,554
Hawthorne	1,305	1,394	Cooper City	21,335	28,730
High Springs	3,144	3,944	Coral Springs	78,864	111,724
LaCrosse	122	150	Dania	13,183	18,480
Micanopy	626	644	Davie	47,143	67,529
Newberry	1,644	2,601	Deerfield Beach	46,997	51,269
Waldo	1,017	1,049	Ft. Lauderdale	149,238	148,971
Unincorporated	82,744	97,305	Hallandale	30,997	31,504
			Hillsboro Beach	1,748	1,756
Baker	18,486	21,879	Hollywood	121,720	127,660
Glen Saint Mary	480	467	Lauderdale-by-the-Sea	2,990	3,798
Macclenny	3,966	4,417	Lauderdale Lakes	27,341	27,870
Unincorporated	14,040	16,995	Lauderhill	49,015	50,596
			Lazy Lake Village	33	35
Bay	126,994	150,119	Lighthouse Point	10,378	10,645
Callaway	12,253	14,418	Margate	42,985	50,727
Cedar Grove	1,479	3,255	Miramar	40,663	54,583
Lynn Haven	9,298	12,796	North Lauderdale	26,473	29,903
Mexico Beach	992	1,042	Oakland Park	26,326	28,236
Panama City	34,396	37,777	Parkland	3,773	13,219
Panama City Beach	4,051	5,174	Pembroke Park	4,933	4,784
Parker	4,598	5,084	Pembroke Pines	65,566	120,091
Springfield	8,719	9,359	Plantation	66,814	80,434
Unincorporated	51,208	61,214	Pompano Beach	72,411	74,403
			Sea Ranch Lakes	619	616
Bradford	22,515	25,500	Sunrise	65,683	78,413
Brooker	312	344	Tamarac	44,822	52,413
Hampton	296	315	Weston 1/	0	42,522
Lawtey	676	712	Wilton Manors	11,804	11,795
Starke	5,226	5,185	Unincorporated	154,408	128,029
Unincorporated	16,005	18,944			
			Calhoun	11,011	14,117
Brevard	398,978	474,803	Altha	497	633
Cape Canaveral	8,014	8,900	Blountstown	2,404	2,492
Cocoa	17,722	18,118	Unincorporated	8,110	10,992
Cocoa Beach	12,123	12,759			
Indialantic	2,844	2,969	Charlotte	110,975	136,773
Indian Harbour Beach	6,933	8,024	Punta Gorda	10,637	13,646
Malabar	1,977	2,544	Unincorporated	100,338	123,127
Melbourne	60,034	70,685			
Melbourne Beach	3,078	3,283	Citrus	93,513	114,898
Melbourne Village	591	620	Crystal River	4,050	4,375
Palm Bay	62,543	79,131	Inverness	5,797	6,956
Palm Shores	210	569	Unincorporated	83,666	103,567
Rockledge	16,023	19,904			

See footnotes at end of table.

Continued . . .

University of Florida   **Bureau of Economic and Business Research**

Table 1.25. COUNTIES AND CITIES: CENSUS COUNTS, APRIL 1, 1990, AND POPULATION
ESTIMATES, APRIL 1, 1999, IN THE STATE, COUNTIES, AND MUNICIPALITIES
OF FLORIDA (Continued)

Area	Census 1990	Estimates 1999	Area	Census 1990	Estimates 1999
Clay	105,986	139,631	Gadsden (Continued)		
Green Cove Springs	4,497	5,350	Greensboro	586	626
Keystone Heights	1,315	1,359	Gretna	1,981	2,874
Orange Park	9,488	9,802	Havana	1,717	1,816
Penney Farms	609	673	Midway	976	1,335
Unincorporated	90,077	122,447	Quincy	7,452	7,951
			Unincorporated	24,022	32,954
Collier	152,099	219,685			
Everglades	321	584	Gilchrist	9,667	13,406
Marco Island 1/	0	12,408	Bell	267	269
Naples	19,505	21,087	Fanning Springs (part)	230	250
Unincorporated	132,273	185,606	Trenton	1,287	1,374
			Unincorporated	7,883	11,513
Columbia	42,613	56,514			
Ft. White	468	567	Glades	7,591	9,867
Lake City	9,626	10,352	Moore Haven	1,432	1,478
Unincorporated	32,519	45,595	Unincorporated	6,159	8,389
De Soto	23,865	28,438	Gulf	11,504	14,403
Arcadia	6,488	6,498	Port St. Joe	4,044	4,098
Unincorporated	17,377	21,940	Wewahitchka	1,779	1,978
			Unincorporated	5,681	8,327
Dixie	10,585	13,478			
Cross City	2,041	2,069	Hamilton	10,930	14,376
Horseshoe Beach	252	220	Jasper	2,099	2,120
Unincorporated	8,292	11,189	Jennings	712	817
			White Springs	704	829
Duval	672,971	762,846	Unincorporated	7,415	10,610
Atlantic Beach	11,636	13,619			
Baldwin	1,450	1,590	Hardee	19,499	22,594
Jacksonville	635,230	719,072	Bowling Green	1,836	1,800
Jacksonville Beach	17,839	21,050	Wauchula	3,243	3,560
Neptune Beach	6,816	7,515	Zolfo Springs	1,219	1,241
			Unincorporated	13,201	15,993
Escambia	262,798	301,613			
Century	1,989	1,909	Hendry	25,773	30,552
Pensacola	59,198	60,994	Clewiston	6,085	6,364
Unincorporated	201,611	238,710	La Belle	2,703	3,185
			Unincorporated	16,985	21,003
Flagler	28,701	45,818			
Beverly Beach	314	322	Hernando	101,115	127,392
Bunnell	1,873	2,075	Brooksville	7,589	7,839
Flagler Beach (part)	3,818	4,448	Weeki Wachee	11	15
Marineland (part)	21	30	Unincorporated	93,515	119,538
Unincorporated	22,675	38,943			
			Highlands	68,432	81,143
Franklin	8,967	10,872	Avon Park	8,078	8,162
Apalachicola	2,602	2,852	Lake Placid	1,158	1,412
Carrabelle	1,200	1,412	Sebring	8,841	8,856
Unincorporated	5,165	6,608	Unincorporated	50,355	62,713
Gadsden	41,116	51,478	Hillsborough	834,054	967,511
Chattahoochee	4,382	3,922	Plant City	22,754	28,371

See footnotes at end of table.   Continued . . .

University of Florida   **Bureau of Economic and Business Research**

Table 1.25. COUNTIES AND CITIES: CENSUS COUNTS, APRIL 1, 1990, AND POPULATION
ESTIMATES, APRIL 1, 1999, IN THE STATE, COUNTIES, AND MUNICIPALITIES
OF FLORIDA (Continued)

Area	Census 1990	Estimates 1999	Area	Census 1990	Estimates 1999
Hillsborough (Continued)			Lake (Continued)		
Tampa	280,015	297,505	Minneola	1,515	3,902
Temple Terrace	16,444	20,574	Montverde	890	1,199
Unincorporated	514,841	621,061	Mount Dora	7,316	9,064
			Tavares	7,383	8,646
Holmes	15,778	18,899	Umatilla	2,350	2,513
Bonifay	2,612	2,831	Unincorporated	81,549	115,600
Esto	253	365			
Noma	207	249	Lee	335,113	417,114
Ponce de Leon	406	467	Cape Coral	74,991	96,760
Westville	257	324	Ft. Myers	44,947	47,068
Unincorporated	12,043	14,663	Ft. Myers Beach 1/	0	6,107
			Sanibel	5,468	6,012
Indian River	90,208	109,579	Unincorporated	209,707	261,167
Fellsmere	2,179	2,600			
Indian River Shores	2,278	2,790	Leon	192,493	237,637
Orchid	10	150	Tallahassee	124,773	145,610
Sebastian	10,248	15,707	Unincorporated	67,720	92,027
Vero Beach	17,350	17,907			
Unincorporated	58,143	70,425	Levy	25,912	33,408
			Bronson	875	930
Jackson	41,375	49,469	Cedar Key	668	769
Alford	482	589	Chiefland	1,917	2,038
Bascom	90	111	Fanning Springs (part)	263	452
Campbellton	202	248	Inglis	1,241	1,363
Cottondale	900	1,165	Otter Creek	136	136
Graceville	2,675	2,695	Williston	2,168	2,374
Grand Ridge	536	729	Yankeetown	635	623
Greenwood	474	667	Unincorporated	18,009	24,723
Jacob City	261	334			
Malone	765	2,174	Liberty	5,569	8,048
Marianna	6,292	6,672	Bristol	937	1,165
Sneads	1,746	2,254	Unincorporated	4,632	6,883
Unincorporated	26,952	31,831			
			Madison	16,569	19,632
Jefferson	11,296	14,424	Greenville	950	992
Monticello	2,603	2,920	Lee	306	346
Unincorporated	8,693	11,504	Madison	3,345	3,406
			Unincorporated	11,968	14,888
Lafayette	5,578	6,961			
Mayo	917	958	Manatee	211,707	253,207
Unincorporated	4,661	6,003	Anna Maria	1,744	1,881
			Bradenton	43,769	48,782
Lake	152,104	203,863	Bradenton Beach	1,657	1,698
Astatula	981	1,304	Holmes Beach	4,810	5,075
Clermont	6,910	8,861	Longboat Key (part)	2,544	2,647
Eustis	12,856	15,046	Palmetto	9,268	10,773
Fruitland Park	2,715	3,043	Unincorporated	147,915	182,351
Groveland	2,300	2,555			
Howey-in-the-Hills	724	825	Marion	194,835	249,433
Lady Lake	8,071	13,067	Belleview	2,678	3,562
Leesburg	14,783	15,624	Dunnellon	1,639	1,848
Mascotte	1,761	2,614	McIntosh	411	428

See footnotes at end of table.   Continued . . .

University of Florida   **Bureau of Economic and Business Research**

Table 1.25. COUNTIES AND CITIES: CENSUS COUNTS, APRIL 1, 1990, AND POPULATION
ESTIMATES, APRIL 1, 1999, IN THE STATE, COUNTIES, AND MUNICIPALITIES
OF FLORIDA (Continued)

Area	Census 1990	Estimates 1999	Area	Census 1990	Estimates 1999
Marion (Continued)			Nassau	43,941	57,381
Ocala	42,045	45,585	Callahan	946	1,056
Reddick	554	552	Fernandina Beach	8765	10890
Unincorporated	147,508	197,458	Hilliard	2,276	2,545
			Unincorporated	31,954	42,890
Martin	100,900	121,514			
Jupiter Island	549	561	Okaloosa	143,777	179,589
Ocean Breeze Park	519	487	Cinco Bayou	386	417
Sewalls Point	1,588	1,803	Crestview	9,886	14,252
Stuart	11,936	13,846	Destin	8,090	11,815
Unincorporated	86,308	104,817	Ft. Walton Beach	21,407	22,226
			Laurel Hill	543	600
Miami-Dade	1,937,194	2,126,702	Mary Esther	4,139	4,427
Aventura 1/	0	22,800	Niceville	10,509	11,954
Bal Harbour	3,045	3,231	Shalimar	341	660
Bay Harbor Islands	4,703	4,613	Valparaiso	6,316	6,716
Biscayne Park	3,068	3,035	Unincorporated	82,160	106,522
Coral Gables	40,091	42,012			
El Portal	2,457	2,485	Okeechobee	29,627	35,510
Florida City	5,978	6,181	Okeechobee	4,943	5,102
Golden Beach	774	845	Unincorporated	24,684	30,408
Hialeah	188,008	211,201			
Hialeah Gardens	7,727	17,859	Orange	677,491	846,328
Homestead	26,694	26,650	Apopka	13,611	22,724
Indian Creek Village	44	53	Bay Lake	19	24
Islandia	13	13	Belle Isle	5,272	5,704
Key Biscayne 1/	0	9,689	Eatonville	2,505	2,487
Medley	663	860	Edgewood	1,062	1,442
Miami	358,648	365,204	Lake Buena Vista	1,776	23
Miami Beach	92,639	94,012	Maitland	8,932	10,056
Miami Shores	10,084	10,170	Oakland	700	846
Miami Springs	13,268	13,295	Ocoee	12,778	22,746
North Bay	5,383	6,125	Orlando	164,674	184,639
North Miami	50,001	50,308	Windermere	1,371	1,802
North Miami Beach	35,361	36,982	Winter Garden	9,863	13,505
Opa-locka	15,283	15,475	Winter Park	22,623	24,967
Pinecrest 1/	0	17,894	Unincorporated	432,305	555,363
South Miami	10,404	10,546			
Sunny Isles Beach 1/	0	14,329	Osceola	107,728	157,376
Surfside	4,108	4,331	Kissimmee	30,337	41,248
Sweetwater	13,909	14,310	St. Cloud	12,684	18,263
Virginia Gardens	2,212	2,278	Unincorporated	64,707	97,865
West Miami	5,727	5,863			
Unincorporated	1,036,902	1,114,053	Palm Beach	863,503	1,042,196
			Atlantis	1,653	1,707
Monroe	78,024	87,030	Belle Glade	16,177	16,937
Islamorada 1/	0	7,639	Boca Raton	61,486	69,994
Key Colony Beach	977	1,084	Boynton Beach	46,284	55,483
Key West	24,832	27,698	Briny Breezes	400	400
Layton	183	204	Cloud Lake	121	136
Unincorporated	52,032	50,405	Delray Beach	47,184	53,589

See footnotes at end of table.

Continued . . .

University of Florida   **Bureau of Economic and Business Research**

Table 1.25. COUNTIES AND CITIES: CENSUS COUNTS, APRIL 1, 1990, AND POPULATION
ESTIMATES, APRIL 1, 1999, IN THE STATE, COUNTIES, AND MUNICIPALITIES
OF FLORIDA (Continued)

Area	Census 1990	Estimates 1999	Area	Census 1990	Estimates 1999
Palm Beach (Continued)			Pinellas (Continued)		
Glen Ridge	207	230	Kenneth City	4,345	4,375
Golf Village	184	189	Largo	65,910	68,372
Golfview	153	0	Madeira Beach	4,225	4,195
Greenacres City	18,683	25,609	North Redington Beach	1,135	1,195
Gulf Stream	690	714	Oldsmar	8,361	11,658
Haverhill	1,058	1,229	Pinellas Park	43,571	45,059
Highland Beach	3,209	3,477	Redington Beach	1,626	1,622
Hypoluxo	807	1,515	Redington Shores	2,366	2,360
Juno Beach	2,172	2,903	Safety Harbor	15,120	17,232
Jupiter	24,907	33,925	St. Petersburg	240,318	242,690
Jupiter Inlet Colony	405	416	St. Pete Beach	9,200	9,718
Lake Clarke Shores	3,364	3,656	Seminole	9,251	9,723
Lake Park	6,704	6,853	South Pasadena	5,644	5,870
Lake Worth	28,564	31,209	Tarpon Springs	17,874	20,588
Lantana	8,392	8,776	Treasure Island	7,266	7,355
Manalapan	312	317	Unincorporated	256,832	280,509
Mangonia Park	1,453	1,373			
North Palm Beach	11,343	12,582	Polk	405,382	474,704
Ocean Ridge	1,570	1,658	Auburndale	8,846	9,663
Pahokee	6,822	7,075	Bartow	14,716	15,187
Palm Beach	9,814	9,710	Davenport	1,529	2,122
Palm Beach Gardens	22,990	34,577	Dundee	2,335	2,640
Palm Beach Shores	1,035	1,037	Eagle Lake	1,758	1,895
Palm Springs	9,763	10,220	Ft. Meade	4,993	5,459
Riviera Beach	27,646	29,020	Frostproof	2,875	2,839
Royal Palm Beach	15,532	19,240	Haines City	11,683	13,834
South Bay	3,558	3,334	Highland Park	155	157
South Palm Beach	1,480	1,490	Hillcrest Heights	221	233
Tequesta Village	4,499	5,122	Lake Alfred	3,622	3,840
Wellington 1/	0	31,271	Lake Hamilton	1,128	1,155
West Palm Beach	67,764	81,132	Lake Wales	9,670	10,132
Unincorporated	405,118	474,091	Lakeland	70,576	77,487
			Mulberry	2,988	3,334
Pasco	281,131	326,492	Polk City	1,439	1,892
Dade City	5,633	6,165	Winter Haven	24,725	26,022
New Port Richey	14,044	14,674	Unincorporated	242,123	296,813
Port Richey	2,521	2,710			
Saint Leo	1,009	733	Putnam	65,070	72,883
San Antonio	776	896	Crescent City	1,859	1,825
Zephyrhills	8,220	9,080	Interlachen	1,160	1,453
Unincorporated	248,928	292,236	Palatka	10,444	10,874
			Pomona Park	726	791
Pinellas	851,659	898,784	Welaka	533	593
Belleair	3,963	4,114	Unincorporated	50,348	57,347
Belleair Beach	2,070	2,158			
Belleair Bluffs	2,234	2,190	St. Johns	83,829	113,941
Belleair Shore	60	62	Hastings	595	653
Clearwater	98,784	104,281	Marineland (part)	0	1
Dunedin	34,427	35,781	St. Augustine	11,695	12,681
Gulfport	11,709	11,967	St. Augustine Beach	3,657	4,320
Indian Rocks Beach	3,963	4,253	Unincorporated	67,882	96,286
Indian Shores	1,405	1,457			

See footnotes at end of table.

Continued . . .

University of Florida   **Bureau of Economic and Business Research**

Table 1.25. COUNTIES AND CITIES: CENSUS COUNTS, APRIL 1, 1990, AND POPULATION
ESTIMATES, APRIL 1, 1999, IN THE STATE, COUNTIES, AND MUNICIPALITIES
OF FLORIDA (Continued)

Area	Census 1990	Estimates 1999	Area	Census 1990	Estimates 1999
St. Lucie	150,171	186,905	Union	10,252	13,833
Ft. Pierce	36,830	38,401	Lake Butler	2,116	2,043
Port St. Lucie	55,761	83,254	Raiford	198	241
St. Lucie Village	584	610	Worthington Springs	178	211
Unincorporated	56,996	64,640	Unincorporated	7,760	11,338
Santa Rosa	81,608	112,631	Volusia	370,737	426,815
Gulf Breeze	5,530	6,189	Daytona Beach	61,991	65,102
Jay	666	692	Daytona Beach Shores	2,197	2,955
Milton	7,216	7,930	DeBary 1/	0	13,368
Unincorporated	68,196	97,820	DeLand	16,622	18,639
			Deltona 1/	0	61,191
Sarasota	277,776	321,044	Edgewater	15,351	18,507
Longboat Key (part)	3,393	4,048	Flagler Beach (part)	0	93
North Port	11,973	18,749	Holly Hill	11,141	11,383
Sarasota	50,897	51,659	Lake Helen	2,344	2,582
Venice	17,052	19,232	New Smyrna Beach	16,549	18,603
Unincorporated	194,461	227,356	Oak Hill	917	1,432
			Orange City	5,347	6,400
Seminole	287,521	354,148	Ormond Beach	29,721	35,620
Altamonte Springs	35,167	40,308	Pierson	1,148	1,226
Casselberry	18,849	24,727	Ponce Inlet	1,704	2,525
Lake Mary	5,929	10,222	Port Orange	35,399	45,282
Longwood	13,316	14,052	South Daytona	12,488	13,337
Oviedo	11,114	22,517	Unincorporated	155,978	108,570
Sanford	32,387	37,327			
Winter Springs	22,151	29,220	Wakulla	14,202	20,648
Unincorporated	148,608	175,775	St. Marks	307	300
			Sopchoppy	367	456
Sumter	31,577	50,823	Unincorporated	13,528	19,892
Bushnell	1,998	2,547			
Center Hill	735	775	Walton	27,759	40,466
Coleman	857	823	DeFuniak Springs	5,200	5,514
Webster	746	860	Freeport	843	1,242
Wildwood	3,560	4,109	Paxton	600	610
Unincorporated	23,681	41,709	Unincorporated	21,116	33,100
Suwannee	26,780	34,386	Washington	16,919	22,155
Branford	670	638	Caryville	631	327
Live Oak	6,332	6,630	Chipley	3,866	4,093
Unincorporated	19,778	27,118	Ebro	255	271
			Vernon	778	917
Taylor	17,111	19,836	Wausau	313	399
Perry	7,151	7,228	Unincorporated	11,076	16,148
Unincorporated	9,960	12,608			

(X) Not applicable.
1/ Not incorporated in 1990.
Note: Census counts include all adjustments made through September 30, 1999.

Source: University of Florida, Bureau of Economic and Business Research, Population Program, *Florida Estimates of Population, April 1, 1999.* Census data from U.S. Bureau of the Census.

Table 1.30. AGE, RACE, AND SEX: CENSUS COUNTS, APRIL 1, 1990, AND ESTIMATES, APRIL 1, 1999, BY AGE, RACE, AND SEX IN FLORIDA

Age	All races			White			Black 1/		
	Total	Male	Female	Total	Male	Female	Total	Male	Female
Census, 1990									
All ages	12,937,926	6,261,770	6,676,156	10,971,995	5,323,424	5,648,571	1,772,356	845,923	926,433
0-14	2,428,671	1,243,364	1,185,307	1,860,162	955,468	904,694	523,856	265,194	258,662
15-24	1,682,627	859,036	823,591	1,343,380	691,738	651,642	305,932	150,087	155,845
25-44	3,920,704	1,954,702	1,966,002	3,290,085	1,658,800	1,631,285	555,627	261,562	294,065
45-64	2,549,998	1,201,564	1,348,434	2,259,374	1,068,506	1,190,868	258,632	118,670	139,962
65-69	737,129	331,267	405,862	689,346	310,846	378,500	44,214	18,850	25,364
70-74	627,699	279,758	347,941	592,046	265,200	326,846	33,373	13,561	19,812
75-79	483,532	204,877	278,655	456,675	194,660	262,015	25,375	9,572	15,803
80-84	302,099	118,468	183,631	286,770	112,991	173,779	14,592	5,145	9,447
85 and over	205,467	68,734	136,733	194,157	65,215	128,942	10,755	3,282	7,473
Estimates, 1999									
All ages	15,322,040	7,445,679	7,876,361	12,905,318	6,272,864	6,632,454	2,136,839	1,037,200	1,099,639
0-14	2,905,719	1,482,845	1,422,874	2,217,689	1,133,490	1,084,199	622,226	315,813	306,413
15-24	1,839,790	945,526	894,264	1,439,454	740,509	698,945	354,649	180,846	173,803
25-44	4,288,294	2,163,095	2,125,199	3,548,944	1,800,545	1,748,399	638,448	314,478	323,970
45-64	3,472,839	1,675,229	1,797,610	3,048,913	1,483,051	1,565,862	369,732	167,958	201,774
65-69	722,377	329,042	393,335	668,168	306,159	362,009	49,175	20,710	28,465
70-74	725,947	316,862	409,085	682,752	299,593	383,159	39,640	15,770	23,870
75-79	622,936	261,172	361,764	591,753	249,475	342,278	28,885	10,730	18,155
80-84	426,539	168,539	258,000	407,075	161,796	245,279	18,168	6,193	11,975
85 and over	317,599	103,369	214,230	300,570	98,246	202,324	15,916	4,702	11,214

1/ "Black" reflects the self-identification of respondents in the 1990 census.
Note: Data for age and race categories have been modified by the U.S. Bureau of the Census to account for misreporting. As a result, these numbers may differ from those found in other publications.

Source: University of Florida, Bureau of Economic and Business Research, Population Program, *Florida Population Studies*, June 2000, Volume 33, No. 3. Bulletin No. 127, and unpublished data.

Table 1.31. AGE AND SEX: ESTIMATES BY SEX AND AGE GROUP AND MEDIAN AGE IN THE STATE AND COUNTIES OF FLORIDA APRIL 1, 1999

County	Total	Sex		Age						Median 1/
		Male	Female	0-14	15-24	25-44	45-64	65 and over	18 and over	
Florida	15,322,040	7,445,679	7,876,361	2,905,719	1,839,790	4,288,294	3,472,839	2,815,398	11,892,978	39.1
Alachua	216,249	107,152	109,097	39,794	55,044	66,145	35,391	19,875	169,380	28.5
Baker	21,879	11,582	10,297	4,794	3,728	7,159	4,231	1,967	15,919	32.0
Bay	150,119	73,868	76,251	31,684	19,863	44,483	34,162	19,927	112,508	36.3
Bradford	25,500	14,270	11,230	4,637	3,614	8,224	5,594	3,431	19,876	35.6
Brevard	474,803	232,677	242,126	87,185	54,415	134,224	112,030	86,949	371,053	39.9
Broward	1,490,289	717,010	773,279	283,822	152,163	438,175	335,093	281,036	1,159,921	39.8
Calhoun	14,117	7,519	6,598	2,478	2,164	4,438	2,979	2,058	11,066	36.0
Charlotte	136,773	65,699	71,074	17,804	11,808	27,705	35,040	44,416	115,151	52.1
Citrus	114,898	54,569	60,329	15,451	9,390	21,873	30,173	38,011	96,094	52.6
Clay	139,631	68,971	70,660	31,236	19,550	42,275	32,747	13,823	101,513	35.1
Collier	219,685	107,030	112,655	38,390	20,335	53,572	54,172	53,216	174,964	44.2
Columbia	56,514	29,101	27,413	12,209	8,159	15,996	12,588	7,562	41,617	35.6
De Soto	28,438	15,175	13,263	5,543	3,618	7,737	5,973	5,567	21,839	38.4
Dixie	13,478	6,972	6,506	2,492	1,753	3,413	3,246	2,574	10,467	39.5
Duval	762,846	373,297	389,549	172,240	105,355	244,784	155,660	84,807	562,790	33.5
Escambia	301,613	149,244	152,369	62,254	46,564	91,168	63,249	38,378	227,353	34.0
Flagler	45,818	21,880	23,938	6,472	4,179	9,423	12,164	13,580	37,964	49.9
Franklin	10,872	5,315	5,557	1,697	1,156	2,397	3,364	2,258	8,797	46.2
Gadsden	51,478	25,549	25,929	11,986	7,609	15,189	10,906	5,788	37,183	33.2
Gilchrist	13,406	7,069	6,337	2,550	2,628	3,450	2,971	1,807	10,221	34.3
Glades	9,867	5,238	4,629	1,612	1,303	2,679	2,346	1,927	7,853	40.3
Gulf	14,403	7,678	6,725	2,578	1,991	4,320	3,387	2,127	11,218	37.0

See footnotes at end of table.

Continued . . . .

Table 1.31. AGE AND SEX: ESTIMATES BY SEX AND AGE GROUP AND MEDIAN AGE IN THE STATE AND COUNTIES OF FLORIDA APRIL 1, 1999 (Continued)

County	Total	Sex		Age							Median 1/
		Male	Female	0-14	15-24	25-44	45-64	65 and over	18 and over		
Hamilton	14,376	8,066	6,310	2,649	2,533	4,759	2,892	1,543	11,015		33.2
Hardee	22,594	11,967	10,627	5,178	3,285	6,201	4,433	3,497	16,447		33.3
Hendry	30,552	15,806	14,746	8,191	4,547	8,775	5,767	3,272	20,939		30.8
Hernando	127,392	60,713	66,679	18,704	11,358	24,785	32,148	40,397	104,710		51.1
Highlands	81,143	38,151	42,992	11,951	6,892	14,158	18,077	30,065	66,872		54.5
Hillsborough	967,511	472,833	494,678	200,868	124,310	299,652	215,045	127,636	731,989		36.0
Holmes	18,899	9,892	9,007	3,401	2,790	5,315	4,390	3,003	14,722		37.3
Indian River	109,579	52,527	57,052	17,568	10,131	25,356	24,911	31,613	88,721		46.3
Jackson	49,469	26,231	23,238	8,656	7,715	15,320	11,129	6,649	38,822		35.8
Jefferson	14,424	6,489	7,935	2,882	1,995	4,200	3,284	2,063	10,929		36.5
Lafayette	6,961	3,990	2,971	1,188	1,110	2,457	1,370	836	5,491		33.8
Lake	203,863	97,303	106,560	32,914	18,166	44,083	49,064	59,636	165,013		47.8
Lee	417,114	200,957	216,157	69,509	39,742	101,524	103,433	102,906	335,235		44.6
Leon	237,637	114,650	122,987	42,485	60,075	70,991	45,246	18,840	186,191		29.4
Levy	33,408	15,871	17,537	6,033	3,789	7,981	8,151	7,454	26,147		42.5
Liberty	8,048	4,665	3,383	1,395	1,180	2,820	1,799	854	6,337		35.1
Madison	19,632	10,245	9,387	4,279	2,902	6,102	3,784	2,565	14,525		33.2
Manatee	253,207	120,386	132,821	41,464	23,997	60,382	59,013	68,351	204,478		45.2
Marion	249,433	119,537	129,896	43,687	26,280	56,367	59,943	63,156	197,160		44.5
Martin	121,514	59,090	62,424	18,166	10,846	29,908	28,764	33,830	99,892		46.2
Miami-Dade	2,126,702	1,028,757	1,097,945	466,434	272,363	621,960	476,636	289,309	1,578,816		35.9
Monroe	87,030	44,003	43,027	13,638	8,173	28,131	23,767	13,321	71,185		41.0
Nassau	57,381	28,384	28,997	12,451	7,540	16,611	14,510	6,269	42,422		36.4
Okaloosa	179,589	89,704	89,885	39,842	24,467	59,013	37,005	19,262	132,655		34.2

See footnotes at end of table.

Continued . . .

Table 1.31. AGE AND SEX: ESTIMATES BY SEX AND AGE GROUP AND MEDIAN AGE IN THE STATE AND COUNTIES OF FLORIDA
APRIL 1, 1999 (Continued)

County	Total	Sex		Age						Median 1/
		Male	Female	0-14	15-24	25-44	45-64	65 and over	18 and over	
Okeechobee	35,510	18,354	17,156	7,619	4,657	8,685	7,786	6,763	26,361	38.1
Orange	846,328	418,364	427,964	176,160	124,109	281,795	172,307	91,957	640,962	33.7
Osceola	157,376	77,263	80,113	33,291	20,286	45,803	36,602	21,394	118,265	36.7
Palm Beach	1,042,196	500,210	541,986	182,390	101,117	276,478	237,997	244,214	829,061	42.5
Pasco	326,494	154,439	172,055	48,758	29,684	68,944	74,726	104,382	268,580	49.2
Pinellas	898,784	425,327	473,457	139,480	86,852	234,748	216,892	220,812	733,427	44.2
Polk	474,704	229,587	245,117	92,224	56,385	120,700	107,495	97,900	365,121	40.0
Putnam	72,883	35,366	37,517	14,803	8,880	17,756	17,073	14,371	55,078	40.1
St. Johns	113,941	55,494	58,447	19,509	13,738	31,908	28,945	19,841	90,556	40.7
St. Lucie	186,905	90,678	96,227	34,411	19,993	47,457	43,822	41,222	146,020	41.8
Santa Rosa	112,631	56,500	56,131	23,793	14,496	36,205	25,737	12,400	84,223	35.4
Sarasota	321,044	150,657	170,387	41,898	25,305	68,757	80,780	104,304	271,258	51.0
Seminole	354,148	174,203	179,945	71,318	44,932	117,400	83,705	36,793	268,571	36.2
Sumter	50,823	27,178	23,645	8,139	6,707	12,631	11,921	11,425	40,776	41.7
Suwannee	34,386	16,681	17,705	6,519	4,785	8,281	8,480	6,321	26,263	40.0
Taylor	19,836	10,597	9,239	4,054	2,889	5,983	4,083	2,827	14,936	34.4
Union	13,833	9,003	4,830	2,095	2,006	5,749	2,785	1,198	11,248	34.6
Volusia	426,815	206,359	220,456	71,591	49,141	110,992	99,385	95,706	342,277	42.1
Wakulla	20,648	10,588	10,060	4,063	3,026	6,066	5,064	2,429	15,597	36.9
Walton	40,466	20,435	20,031	6,853	5,023	10,415	10,242	7,933	32,062	41.2
Washington	22,155	11,314	10,841	4,310	3,204	5,861	4,985	3,795	16,876	36.7

1/ Estimates based on Bureau of the Census modified age, race, and sex data.
Note: Detail may not add to totals because of rounding.

Source: University of Florida, Bureau of Economic and Business Research, Population Program, *Florida Population Studies*, June 2000, Volume 33, No. 3. Bulletin No. 127, and unpublished data.

Table 1.32. WHITE POPULATION: ESTIMATES BY SEX AND AGE GROUP IN THE STATE AND COUNTIES OF FLORIDA APRIL 1, 1999

County	Total	Sex		Age					
		Male	Female	0-14	15-24	25-44	45-64	65 and over	18 and over
Florida	12,905,318	6,272,864	6,632,454	2,217,689	1,439,454	3,548,944	3,048,913	2,650,318	10,285,844
Alachua	168,611	84,294	84,317	27,316	43,238	52,640	28,557	16,860	136,660
Baker	18,942	9,634	9,308	4,238	3,114	5,981	3,791	1,818	13,670
Bay	130,257	64,472	65,785	25,792	16,508	37,990	31,373	18,594	99,619
Bradford	20,240	10,575	9,665	3,787	2,587	5,817	4,900	3,149	15,661
Brevard	429,242	210,802	218,440	74,565	47,055	119,882	104,065	83,675	340,431
Broward	1,183,817	569,533	614,284	192,492	107,700	339,620	278,859	265,146	959,842
Calhoun	11,651	5,934	5,717	2,032	1,679	3,428	2,623	1,889	9,141
Charlotte	129,555	61,902	67,653	16,386	10,682	25,416	33,624	43,447	109,708
Citrus	111,472	52,975	58,497	14,567	8,861	21,027	29,463	37,554	93,750
Clay	128,672	63,693	64,979	27,788	17,886	38,747	30,910	13,341	94,618
Collier	208,658	101,592	107,066	34,970	18,870	50,128	52,038	52,652	167,847
Columbia	45,157	22,791	22,366	9,303	6,161	12,348	10,729	6,616	33,765
De Soto	23,271	11,944	11,327	4,416	2,629	5,815	5,162	5,249	18,062
Dixie	12,184	6,072	6,112	2,283	1,497	2,858	3,047	2,499	9,419
Duval	555,868	275,097	280,771	112,596	71,893	180,224	122,163	68,992	425,307
Escambia	229,461	114,759	114,702	40,898	33,808	70,101	51,917	32,737	180,472
Flagler	41,711	20,002	21,709	5,698	3,662	8,471	11,055	12,825	34,799
Franklin	9,552	4,672	4,880	1,357	934	1,995	3,143	2,123	7,880
Gadsden	21,005	10,731	10,274	3,912	2,239	6,198	5,406	3,250	16,475
Gilchrist	12,247	6,254	5,993	2,346	2,020	3,246	2,865	1,770	9,368
Glades	7,827	4,017	3,810	1,171	864	1,904	2,052	1,836	6,379
Gulf	11,391	5,824	5,567	2,014	1,510	3,026	2,962	1,879	8,883

Continued. . .

See footnote at end of table.

Table 1.32. WHITE POPULATION: ESTIMATES BY SEX AND AGE GROUP IN THE STATE AND COUNTIES OF FLORIDA APRIL 1, 1999 (Continued)

| County | Total | Sex | | Age | | | | | |
		Male	Female	0-14	15-24	25-44	45-64	65 and over	18 and over
Hamilton	8,610	4,687	3,923	1,361	1,319	2,809	1,971	1,150	6,853
Hardee	20,417	10,449	9,968	4,793	2,849	5,214	4,142	3,419	14,756
Hendry	25,160	12,733	12,427	6,743	3,485	6,966	4,994	2,972	17,309
Hernando	122,105	58,230	63,875	17,336	10,566	23,390	31,003	39,810	101,069
Highlands	73,402	34,415	38,987	9,517	5,497	12,081	16,856	29,451	62,045
Hillsborough	818,688	401,904	416,784	156,352	101,064	254,925	188,889	117,458	635,077
Holmes	17,290	8,696	8,594	3,202	2,313	4,660	4,180	2,935	13,390
Indian River	101,382	48,583	52,799	15,139	8,688	23,099	23,545	30,911	83,421
Jackson	35,076	17,823	17,253	5,871	4,932	10,220	8,758	5,295	27,907
Jefferson	8,442	3,996	4,446	1,400	980	2,380	2,272	1,410	6,725
Lafayette	5,920	3,189	2,731	1,049	856	1,925	1,275	815	4,621
Lake	186,654	89,076	97,578	27,752	15,580	39,471	45,915	57,936	153,822
Lee	387,095	186,533	200,562	60,304	34,836	93,181	98,040	100,734	316,096
Leon	174,278	85,466	88,812	28,037	39,756	54,085	36,994	15,406	140,415
Levy	29,527	14,180	15,347	4,999	3,144	6,855	7,451	7,078	23,503
Liberty	6,633	3,568	3,065	1,235	940	2,052	1,606	800	5,118
Madison	11,662	6,025	5,637	2,197	1,484	3,586	2,582	1,813	9,031
Manatee	232,022	110,222	121,800	35,114	20,710	54,128	55,218	66,852	190,687
Marion	218,179	104,837	113,342	34,800	21,483	47,602	54,387	59,907	176,349
Martin	113,588	54,668	58,920	15,936	9,440	27,141	27,624	33,447	94,602
Miami-Dade	1,601,458	777,028	824,430	314,280	189,392	465,279	377,144	255,363	1,232,482
Monroe	81,560	41,331	40,229	12,153	7,386	26,160	22,909	12,952	67,398
Nassau	52,165	25,898	26,267	11,015	6,691	15,149	13,595	5,715	38,930
Okaloosa	155,772	78,215	77,557	32,879	20,308	50,731	33,479	18,375	117,067

See footnote at end of table.

Continued. . .

Table 1.32. WHITE POPULATION: ESTIMATES BY SEX AND AGE GROUP IN THE STATE AND COUNTIES OF FLORIDA APRIL 1, 1999 (Continued)

| County | Total | Sex | | Age | | | | | |
		Male	Female	0-14	15-24	25-44	45-64	65 and over	18 and over
Okeechobee	32,234	16,289	15,945	6,885	3,996	7,432	7,329	6,592	24,005
Orange	687,458	341,428	346,030	130,858	97,219	231,109	145,377	82,895	535,443
Osceola	145,200	71,401	73,799	29,914	18,383	42,229	34,029	20,645	110,131
Palm Beach	899,419	430,733	468,686	139,106	80,496	232,242	212,510	235,065	736,335
Pasco	316,940	149,845	167,095	46,333	28,067	66,157	72,819	103,564	261,998
Pinellas	811,357	384,019	427,338	114,422	73,834	209,068	200,347	213,686	675,340
Polk	409,486	198,002	211,484	72,616	45,794	102,561	96,171	92,344	323,036
Putnam	59,495	29,050	30,445	10,830	6,650	14,495	14,663	12,857	46,446
St. Johns	105,505	51,514	53,991	17,182	12,459	29,565	27,414	18,885	84,866
St. Lucie	156,715	76,166	80,549	25,107	15,230	39,506	37,989	38,883	126,833
Santa Rosa	104,910	52,389	52,521	21,956	13,264	33,315	24,441	11,934	78,687
Sarasota	305,488	143,332	162,156	37,428	22,828	64,664	77,962	102,606	260,977
Seminole	317,501	156,632	160,869	61,208	39,380	105,527	76,868	34,518	243,921
Sumter	41,372	21,075	20,297	6,097	4,603	9,004	10,715	10,953	33,926
Suwannee	29,826	14,540	15,286	5,303	3,980	7,080	7,652	5,811	23,189
Taylor	15,622	8,009	7,613	3,130	2,064	4,343	3,544	2,541	11,855
Union	10,475	6,221	4,254	1,776	1,367	3,876	2,353	1,103	8,315
Volusia	385,819	186,657	199,162	61,152	41,411	98,320	92,620	92,316	313,461
Wakulla	17,856	9,008	8,848	3,464	2,472	5,059	4,644	2,217	13,562
Walton	36,873	18,352	18,521	6,175	4,463	9,106	9,580	7,549	29,311
Washington	17,891	8,881	9,010	3,356	2,398	4,335	4,353	3,449	13,778

Note: Detail may not add to totals because of rounding.

Source: University of Florida, Bureau of Economic and Business Research, Population Program, *Florida Population Studies*, June 2000, Volume 33, No. 3. Bulletin No. 127, and unpublished data.

Table **1.33.** BLACK POPULATION: ESTIMATES BY SEX AND AGE GROUP IN THE STATE AND COUNTIES OF FLORIDA
APRIL 1, 1999

County	Total	Sex		Age					
		Male	Female	0-14	15-24	25-44	45-64	65 and over	18 and over
Florida	2,136,839	1,037,200	1,099,639	622,226	354,649	638,448	369,732	151,784	1,406,452
Alachua	40,841	19,197	21,644	11,369	9,530	11,033	6,057	2,852	27,252
Baker	2,799	1,862	937	540	589	1,125	400	145	2,131
Bay	15,740	7,595	8,145	4,773	2,681	4,973	2,106	1,207	10,092
Bradford	5,019	3,551	1,468	809	988	2,304	646	272	4,020
Brevard	36,752	17,880	18,872	10,694	6,000	10,839	6,373	2,846	24,135
Broward	272,703	130,828	141,875	82,888	40,003	85,829	49,626	14,357	176,219
Calhoun	2,247	1,461	786	405	450	936	297	159	1,759
Charlotte	5,817	3,174	2,643	1,155	939	1,824	1,069	830	4,373
Citrus	2,568	1,214	1,354	676	421	592	500	379	1,736
Clay	7,643	3,775	3,868	2,537	1,196	2,438	1,083	389	4,702
Collier	9,423	4,706	4,717	3,022	1,192	2,921	1,809	479	6,002
Columbia	10,638	5,934	4,704	2,769	1,902	3,364	1,699	904	7,309
De Soto	4,869	3,070	1,799	1,059	941	1,829	735	305	3,562
Dixie	1,214	853	361	202	242	522	177	71	980
Duval	185,771	87,909	97,862	54,278	29,950	57,129	29,546	14,868	122,753
Escambia	61,592	29,431	32,161	18,654	10,597	17,671	9,471	5,199	39,714
Flagler	3,518	1,609	1,909	691	438	760	934	695	2,683
Franklin	1,231	598	633	327	213	368	201	122	843
Gadsden	29,961	14,553	15,408	7,959	5,285	8,843	5,370	2,504	20,328
Gilchrist	1,077	768	309	187	576	193	94	27	796
Glades	1,362	817	545	296	280	511	221	54	982
Gulf	2,842	1,751	1,091	536	462	1,217	387	240	2,199

See footnote at end of table.

Continued. . .

Table 1.33. BLACK POPULATION: ESTIMATES BY SEX AND AGE GROUP IN THE STATE AND COUNTIES OF FLORIDA APRIL 1, 1999 (Continued)

County	Total	Sex		Age					
		Male	Female	0-14	15-24	25-44	45-64	65 and over	18 and over
Hamilton	5,647	3,314	2,333	1,255	1,193	1,899	909	391	4,080
Hardee	1,932	1,351	581	340	395	872	251	74	1,506
Hendry	4,611	2,616	1,995	1,279	905	1,508	655	264	3,071
Hernando	4,436	2,083	2,353	1,190	681	1,111	947	507	3,011
Highlands	6,964	3,365	3,599	2,227	1,270	1,843	1,072	552	4,294
Hillsborough	129,656	61,976	67,680	40,024	20,119	37,722	22,404	9,387	83,144
Holmes	1,271	1,021	250	137	391	549	143	51	1,093
Indian River	7,443	3,587	3,856	2,232	1,329	2,007	1,217	658	4,787
Jackson	13,828	8,063	5,765	2,686	2,690	4,858	2,262	1,332	10,473
Jefferson	5,862	2,451	3,411	1,460	998	1,784	978	642	4,114
Lafayette	1,004	775	229	136	251	518	83	16	837
Lake	15,797	7,561	8,236	4,814	2,377	4,169	2,835	1,602	10,213
Lee	26,290	12,608	13,682	8,342	4,383	7,039	4,609	1,917	16,456
Leon	58,209	26,629	31,580	13,434	18,873	15,149	7,476	3,277	41,859
Levy	3,516	1,536	1,980	958	586	1,029	596	347	2,377
Liberty	1,344	1,052	292	148	225	735	185	51	1,161
Madison	7,820	4,136	3,684	2,051	1,394	2,458	1,174	743	5,382
Manatee	18,763	8,986	9,777	5,768	2,871	5,404	3,347	1,373	12,086
Marion	28,761	13,538	15,223	8,338	4,434	7,932	4,983	3,074	18,995
Martin	6,834	3,864	2,970	1,923	1,220	2,394	952	345	4,562
Miami-Dade	480,260	229,508	250,752	141,793	76,019	140,657	90,396	31,395	313,694
Monroe	4,454	2,230	2,224	1,253	647	1,501	709	344	3,029
Nassau	4,826	2,304	2,522	1,349	799	1,319	831	528	3,204
Okaloosa	17,312	9,131	8,181	5,330	3,132	5,852	2,301	697	11,087

Continued. . .

See footnote at end of table.

Table **1.33.** BLACK POPULATION: ESTIMATES BY SEX AND AGE GROUP IN THE STATE AND COUNTIES OF FLORIDA APRIL 1, 1999 (Continued)

County	Total	Sex		Age					
		Male	Female	0-14	15-24	25-44	45-64	65 and over	18 and over
Okeechobee	2,757	1,742	1,015	626	570	1,035	382	144	1,965
Orange	134,656	65,024	69,632	39,714	22,548	41,755	22,445	8,194	88,087
Osceola	8,866	4,247	4,619	2,664	1,446	2,487	1,664	605	5,691
Palm Beach	128,048	62,328	65,720	39,701	18,650	38,470	22,819	8,408	82,196
Pasco	6,558	3,261	3,297	1,788	1,145	1,780	1,227	618	4,382
Pinellas	72,735	34,167	38,568	21,321	10,821	20,631	13,613	6,349	47,848
Polk	59,875	28,974	30,901	18,312	9,644	16,455	10,202	5,262	38,378
Putnam	12,683	5,976	6,707	3,787	2,118	3,057	2,265	1,456	8,153
St. Johns	7,544	3,568	3,976	2,123	1,155	2,019	1,338	909	5,041
St. Lucie	28,043	13,506	14,537	8,720	4,466	7,264	5,400	2,193	17,715
Santa Rosa	5,108	2,823	2,285	1,319	796	1,874	728	391	3,558
Sarasota	13,152	6,224	6,928	3,936	2,109	3,314	2,303	1,490	8,524
Seminole	28,987	13,886	15,101	8,306	4,453	8,898	5,286	2,044	19,173
Sumter	8,991	5,847	3,144	1,956	2,025	3,447	1,110	453	6,506
Suwannee	4,322	2,040	2,282	1,162	768	1,141	769	482	2,904
Taylor	3,921	2,405	1,516	866	774	1,515	492	274	2,858
Union	3,190	2,641	549	308	611	1,783	395	93	2,781
Volusia	36,022	17,257	18,765	9,401	6,828	10,862	5,816	3,115	25,080
Wakulla	2,568	1,447	1,121	552	529	907	380	200	1,866
Walton	2,710	1,555	1,155	534	439	955	461	321	2,048
Washington	3,636	2,061	1,575	837	697	1,269	521	312	2,613

Note: Detail may not add to totals because of rounding.

Source: University of Florida, Bureau of Economic and Business Research, Population Program, *Florida Population Studies*, June 2000, Volume 33, No. 3. Bulletin No. 127, and unpublished data.

Table 1.36. HISPANIC ORIGIN POPULATION: ESTIMATES IN THE STATE AND COUNTIES
OF FLORIDA, APRIL 1, 1999

County	Total population	Hispanic origin population Number	As a percentage of total	County	Total population	Hispanic origin population Number	As a percentage of total
Florida	15,322,040	2,492,659	16.3	Lake	203,863	8,017	3.9
				Lee	417,114	31,370	7.5
Alachua	216,249	10,044	4.6	Leon	237,637	8,802	3.7
Baker	21,879	504	2.3	Levy	33,408	1,050	3.1
Bay	150,119	3,499	2.3	Liberty	8,048	296	3.7
Bradford	25,500	960	3.8	Madison	19,632	692	3.5
Brevard	474,803	22,396	4.7	Manatee	253,207	18,579	7.3
Broward	1,490,289	225,799	15.2	Marion	249,433	15,603	6.3
Calhoun	14,117	532	3.8	Martin	121,514	9,878	8.1
Charlotte	136,773	4,071	3.0	Miami-Dade	2,126,702	1,249,460	58.8
Citrus	114,898	3,460	3.0	Monroe	87,030	13,150	15.1
Clay	139,631	7,660	5.5	Nassau	57,381	697	1.2
Collier	219,685	37,882	17.2	Okaloosa	179,589	7,770	4.3
Columbia	56,514	1,588	2.8	Okeechobee	35,510	5,398	15.2
De Soto	28,438	5,160	18.1	Orange	846,328	148,656	17.6
Dixie	13,478	166	1.2	Osceola	157,376	36,547	23.2
Duval	762,846	34,240	4.5	Palm Beach	1,042,196	123,885	11.9
Escambia	301,613	12,217	4.1	Pasco	326,494	20,948	6.4
Flagler	45,818	2,953	6.4	Pinellas	898,784	38,427	4.3
Franklin	10,872	71	0.7	Polk	474,704	36,422	7.7
Gadsden	51,478	2,336	4.5	Putnam	72,883	2,749	3.8
Gilchrist	13,406	367	2.7	St. Johns	113,941	3,706	3.3
Glades	9,867	1,677	17.0	St. Lucie	186,905	13,743	7.4
Gulf	14,403	248	1.7	Santa Rosa	112,631	3,853	3.4
Hamilton	14,376	755	5.3	Sarasota	321,044	15,643	4.9
Hardee	22,594	6,619	29.3	Seminole	354,148	39,164	11.1
Hendry	30,552	9,676	31.7	Sumter	50,823	2,826	5.6
Hernando	127,392	5,562	4.4	Suwannee	34,386	2,847	8.3
Highlands	81,143	6,050	7.5	Taylor	19,836	301	1.5
Hillsborough	967,511	184,851	19.1	Union	13,833	944	6.8
Holmes	18,899	276	1.5	Volusia	426,815	28,484	6.7
Indian River	109,579	6,445	5.9	Wakulla	20,648	157	0.8
Jackson	49,469	2,489	5.0	Walton	40,466	1,031	2.5
Jefferson	14,424	194	1.3	Washington	22,155	277	1.3
Lafayette	6,961	540	7.8				

Note: Projections are based on Bureau of the Census modified age, race, and sex data.

Source: University of Florida, Bureau of Economic and Business Research, Population Program, *Florida Estimates of Population, April 1, 1999*, and unpublished data.

University of Florida   **Bureau of Economic and Business Research**

Table **1.37.** PERSONS AGED 65 AND OVER: CENSUS COUNTS, APRIL 1, 1990, AND ESTIMATES, APRIL 1, 1999, BY AGE IN THE STATE AND COUNTIES OF FLORIDA

County	65-69 Census 1990	65-69 Estimates 1999	70-74 Census 1990	70-74 Estimates 1999	75-79 Census 1990	75-79 Estimates 1999	80-84 Census 1990	80-84 Estimates 1999	85 and over Census 1990	85 and over Estimates 1999	65 and over (percentage) Census 1990	65 and over (percentage) Estimates 1999
Florida	737,129	722,377	627,699	725,947	483,532	622,936	302,099	426,539	205,467	317,599	18.2	18.4
Alachua	5,652	5,388	4,256	5,192	3,176	4,251	2,064	2,745	1,594	2,299	9.2	9.2
Baker	475	649	391	518	284	360	181	250	119	190	7.8	9.0
Bay	5,673	6,278	4,040	5,332	2,799	4,068	1,611	2,518	1,019	1,731	11.9	13.3
Bradford	962	920	689	906	501	757	344	466	228	382	12.1	13.5
Brevard	24,416	24,508	18,598	23,758	12,108	19,611	6,697	11,744	4,265	7,328	16.6	18.3
Broward	66,625	61,556	66,832	65,954	61,690	63,094	39,750	50,256	24,398	40,176	20.7	18.9
Calhoun	481	520	374	509	342	449	237	296	158	284	14.5	14.6
Charlotte	12,517	11,853	10,563	12,075	7,375	10,028	4,281	6,415	2,570	4,045	33.6	32.5
Citrus	10,174	10,293	8,313	10,380	5,785	8,531	3,066	5,336	1,807	3,471	31.2	33.1
Clay	3,225	4,248	2,248	3,520	1,628	2,746	994	1,717	846	1,592	8.4	9.9
Collier	11,975	14,633	9,810	14,618	6,649	11,803	3,894	7,578	2,128	4,584	22.7	24.2
Columbia	2,063	2,246	1,533	2,031	1,047	1,618	597	964	380	703	13.2	13.4
De Soto	1,495	1,463	1,323	1,575	934	1,267	523	756	317	506	19.2	19.6
Dixie	612	848	406	724	278	507	139	305	97	190	14.5	19.1
Duval	25,010	23,633	18,494	21,857	13,599	18,172	8,314	12,019	5,985	9,126	10.6	11.1
Escambia	11,247	10,772	8,189	10,022	5,770	8,271	3,450	5,287	2,488	4,026	11.9	12.7
Flagler	3,275	4,194	2,180	3,939	1,048	2,880	482	1,597	303	970	25.4	29.6
Franklin	492	697	449	583	291	430	192	314	164	234	17.7	20.8
Gadsden	1,574	1,588	1,353	1,442	1,069	1,169	647	845	509	744	12.5	11.2
Gilchrist	482	576	384	499	202	370	136	216	113	146	13.6	13.5
Glades	549	539	424	534	296	443	120	262	79	149	19.3	19.5
Gulf	601	643	449	538	338	444	224	280	136	222	15.2	14.8

Continued . . .

Table 1.37. PERSONS AGED 65 AND OVER: CENSUS COUNTS, APRIL 1, 1990, AND ESTIMATES, APRIL 1, 1999, BY AGE IN THE STATE AND COUNTIES OF FLORIDA (Continued)

County	65-69		70-74		75-79		80-84		85 and over		65 and over (percentage)	
	Census 1990	Esti-mates 1999	Census 1990	Esti-mates 1999	Census 1990	Esti-mates 1999	Census 1990	Esti-mates 1999	Census 1990	Esti-mates 1999	Census 1990	Esti-mates 1999
Hamilton	376	483	324	393	271	284	171	207	100	176	11.4	10.7
Hardee	1,028	867	792	978	558	778	353	501	214	373	15.1	15.5
Hendry	1,023	978	712	856	540	671	323	429	203	338	10.9	10.7
Hernando	11,953	11,339	9,332	11,541	5,635	9,161	2,508	5,236	1,522	3,120	30.6	31.7
Highlands	7,403	7,178	6,572	8,339	4,654	7,100	2,557	4,638	1,558	2,810	33.2	37.1
Hillsborough	34,478	34,877	27,070	33,166	19,750	27,488	11,931	18,101	8,217	14,004	12.2	13.2
Holmes	804	839	629	779	501	612	330	418	216	355	15.7	15.9
Indian River	8,260	7,961	7,086	8,688	4,676	7,483	2,787	4,622	1,642	2,859	27.1	28.9
Jackson	1,841	1,820	1,548	1,564	1,310	1,327	887	991	568	947	14.9	13.4
Jefferson	516	569	416	527	335	448	226	290	175	229	14.8	14.3
Lafayette	227	268	167	211	109	173	74	113	38	71	11.0	12.0
Lake	13,461	15,239	11,212	16,246	8,506	13,853	5,248	8,618	3,239	5,680	27.4	29.3
Lee	27,822	27,591	23,435	28,130	16,350	22,983	9,343	14,858	5,648	9,344	24.6	24.7
Leon	5,325	5,578	4,246	4,842	2,910	4,011	1,880	2,634	1,340	1,775	8.2	7.9
Levy	1,758	1,979	1,415	2,039	904	1,731	513	1,067	296	638	18.8	22.3
Liberty	197	285	176	229	123	149	75	112	50	79	11.2	10.6
Madison	662	644	603	642	490	532	336	391	228	356	14.0	13.1
Manatee	17,136	15,855	15,799	17,225	12,396	15,503	8,090	11,047	5,761	8,721	28.0	27.0
Marion	15,556	16,856	12,415	17,769	8,170	14,718	4,222	8,571	2,534	5,242	22.0	25.3
Martin	8,985	8,366	7,772	8,944	5,600	7,927	3,267	5,131	1,898	3,462	27.3	27.8
Miami-Dade	80,679	79,011	64,600	72,167	55,537	58,444	38,461	42,097	29,145	37,590	13.9	13.6
Monroe	4,665	4,028	3,475	3,644	2,285	2,888	1,251	1,798	671	963	15.8	15.3

Continued . . .

Table 1.37. PERSONS AGED 65 AND OVER: CENSUS COUNTS, APRIL 1, 1990, AND ESTIMATES, APRIL 1, 1999, BY AGE IN THE STATE AND COUNTIES OF FLORIDA (Continued)

County	65-69 Census 1990	65-69 Esti-mates 1999	70-74 Census 1990	70-74 Esti-mates 1999	75-79 Census 1990	75-79 Esti-mates 1999	80-84 Census 1990	80-84 Esti-mates 1999	85 and over Census 1990	85 and over Esti-mates 1999	65 and over (percentage) Census 1990	65 and over (percentage) Esti-mates 1999
Nassau	1,612	2,041	1,220	1,706	837	1,196	489	755	285	571	10.1	10.9
Okaloosa	5,345	6,331	3,615	5,133	2,151	3,965	1,215	2,253	916	1,580	9.2	10.7
Okeechobee	1,763	1,895	1,364	1,964	906	1,512	448	840	262	552	16.0	19.1
Orange	25,045	26,605	18,745	24,204	13,071	19,544	8,238	12,707	6,419	8,897	10.6	10.9
Osceola	4,886	6,099	4,028	5,341	2,811	4,511	1,678	3,028	1,436	2,415	13.8	13.6
Palm Beach	58,699	55,937	57,252	61,386	46,390	56,162	28,697	41,517	17,932	29,212	24.2	23.4
Pasco	27,031	23,530	26,172	26,724	19,440	25,058	11,358	18,034	6,501	11,036	32.2	32.0
Pinellas	59,240	49,582	55,480	53,121	46,573	49,387	33,313	36,786	26,278	31,936	25.9	24.6
Polk	25,097	25,304	20,281	26,200	14,753	21,681	8,810	13,919	5,746	10,796	18.4	20.6
Putnam	4,303	4,113	3,211	4,035	2,172	3,095	1,198	1,838	730	1,290	17.8	19.7
St. Johns	4,964	5,305	3,709	5,442	2,475	4,460	1,413	2,745	1,131	1,889	16.3	17.4
St. Lucie	11,312	11,317	9,133	11,454	6,088	9,526	2,989	5,723	1,762	3,202	20.8	22.1
Santa Rosa	3,037	4,178	1,956	3,423	1,412	2,434	753	1,372	559	993	9.5	11.0
Sarasota	25,967	24,186	23,807	26,379	18,835	24,131	12,058	16,876	8,471	12,732	32.1	32.5
Seminole	10,357	11,016	7,697	9,500	5,482	7,612	3,509	4,821	2,515	3,844	10.3	10.4
Sumter	2,540	3,200	2,056	3,183	1,339	2,514	717	1,527	382	1,001	22.3	22.5
Suwannee	1,400	1,677	1,080	1,621	893	1,335	639	892	477	796	16.8	18.4
Taylor	769	850	615	765	459	580	269	389	164	243	13.3	14.3
Union	279	374	216	316	131	237	76	156	62	115	7.5	8.7
Volusia	26,578	24,155	22,608	24,872	16,707	21,499	10,369	14,385	7,735	10,795	22.7	22.4
Wakulla	573	709	404	650	328	509	194	325	137	236	11.5	11.8
Walton	1,678	2,368	1,173	2,172	850	1,640	500	1,020	338	733	16.4	19.6
Washington	924	949	783	931	610	815	393	595	263	505	17.6	17.1

Source: University of Florida, Bureau of Economic and Business Research, Population Program, unpublished data. Census data from U.S. Bureau of the Census.

Table 1.38. AGE AND SEX PROJECTIONS: CENSUS COUNTS, APRIL 1, 1990, ESTIMATES APRIL 1, 1999, AND PROJECTIONS, APRIL 1, 2005, 2010, AND 2015 BY AGE AND SEX IN FLORIDA

Age	Census 1990	Estimates 1999	Projections 2005	Projections 2010	Projections 2015
Total	12,937,926	15,322,040	16,882,830	18,121,273	19,400,913
0-4	873,022	953,690	988,218	1,050,028	1,121,050
5-9	809,306	992,468	1,001,678	1,029,444	1,090,094
10-14	746,343	959,561	1,061,404	1,047,160	1,072,077
15-19	803,784	924,145	1,056,977	1,131,097	1,114,238
15-17	455,160	523,343	599,137	641,340	631,425
18-19	348,624	400,802	457,840	489,757	482,813
20-24	878,843	915,645	1,053,238	1,147,739	1,216,627
25-29	1,055,071	955,180	982,705	1,104,646	1,191,597
30-34	1,062,261	1,025,741	986,099	1,006,376	1,123,429
35-39	951,453	1,152,413	1,048,460	1,013,736	1,033,371
40-44	851,919	1,154,960	1,228,693	1,102,963	1,060,826
45-49	690,756	1,054,787	1,262,340	1,294,074	1,162,653
50-54	591,849	931,526	1,159,642	1,333,152	1,364,617
55-59	586,872	778,008	1,063,449	1,249,569	1,431,983
60-64	680,521	708,518	903,245	1,175,267	1,373,945
65-69	737,129	722,377	789,709	981,241	1,273,433
70-74	627,699	725,947	710,582	778,897	970,320
75-79	483,532	622,936	659,262	643,894	710,493
80-84	302,099	426,539	518,081	536,250	529,695
85 and over	205,467	317,599	409,048	495,740	560,465
Male	6,261,770	7,445,679	8,221,965	8,840,277	9,477,272
0-4	447,221	485,873	503,505	535,026	571,250
5-9	414,103	506,098	510,410	524,633	555,595
10-14	382,040	490,874	541,265	533,920	546,807
15-19	412,795	472,586	540,540	576,805	568,249
15-17	234,171	268,203	307,012	327,720	322,667
18-19	178,624	204,383	233,528	249,085	245,582
20-24	446,241	472,940	543,447	592,050	625,844
25-29	532,167	491,996	506,753	568,826	613,358
30-34	531,382	520,600	503,642	513,529	572,308
35-39	471,494	577,707	527,429	510,615	520,357
40-44	419,659	572,792	611,239	548,691	527,850
45-49	335,721	517,905	622,006	638,340	573,214
50-54	282,812	453,137	565,362	652,244	668,269
55-59	274,786	372,291	513,128	604,234	694,847
60-64	308,245	331,896	428,361	561,816	658,174
65-69	331,267	329,042	366,538	460,718	603,008
70-74	279,758	316,862	318,997	355,700	449,598
75-79	204,877	261,172	279,534	281,878	318,032
80-84	118,468	168,539	205,469	217,051	222,730
85 and over	68,734	103,369	134,340	164,201	187,782

See footnote at end of table. Continued . . .

University of Florida   **Bureau of Economic and Business Research**

Florida Statistical Abstract 2000

Table 1.38. AGE AND SEX PROJECTIONS: CENSUS COUNTS, APRIL 1, 1990, ESTIMATES
APRIL 1, 1999, AND PROJECTIONS, APRIL 1, 2005, 2010, AND 2015
BY AGE AND SEX IN FLORIDA (Continued)

Age	Census 1990	Estimates 1999	Projections 2005	Projections 2010	Projections 2015
Female	6,676,156	7,876,361	8,660,865	9,280,996	9,923,641
0-4	425,801	467,817	484,713	515,002	549,800
5-9	395,203	486,370	491,268	504,811	534,499
10-14	364,303	468,687	520,139	513,240	525,270
15-19	390,989	451,559	516,437	554,292	545,989
15-17	220,989	255,140	292,125	313,620	308,758
18-19	170,000	196,419	224,312	240,672	237,231
20-24	432,602	442,705	509,791	555,689	590,783
25-29	522,904	463,184	475,952	535,820	578,239
30-34	530,879	505,141	482,457	492,847	551,121
35-39	479,959	574,706	521,031	503,121	513,014
40-44	432,260	582,168	617,454	554,272	532,976
45-49	355,035	536,882	640,334	655,734	589,439
50-54	309,037	478,389	594,280	680,908	696,348
55-59	312,086	405,717	550,321	645,335	737,136
60-64	372,276	376,622	474,884	613,451	715,771
65-69	405,862	393,335	423,171	520,523	670,425
70-74	347,941	409,085	391,585	423,197	520,722
75-79	278,655	361,764	379,728	362,016	392,461
80-84	183,631	258,000	312,612	319,199	306,965
85 and over	136,733	214,230	274,708	331,539	372,683

Note: Medium projections are shown. High and low projections for total population are available from the Bureau of Economic and Business Research, University of Florida.

Source: University of Florida, Bureau of Economic and Business Research, Population Program, unpublished data. Census data from U.S. Bureau of the Census.

University of Florida   **Bureau of Economic and Business Research**

Table 1.39. MEDIAN AGE: CENSUS, APRIL 1, 1990, AND PROJECTIONS, APRIL 1
2005, 2010, AND 2015, IN THE STATE AND COUNTIES OF FLORIDA

County	Census 1990	Projections 2005	2010	2015	County	Census 1990	Projections 2005	2010	2015
Florida	36.3	41.1	42.4	43.5	Lake	44.5	50.2	52.5	54.9
					Lee	41.9	47.0	49.2	51.4
Alachua	28.2	28.7	28.8	29.3	Leon	28.7	30.0	30.4	31.1
Baker	30.1	32.8	33.4	34.0	Levy	38.4	45.3	47.4	49.5
Bay	33.1	38.1	39.1	39.8	Liberty	32.4	36.1	37.0	37.9
Bradford	33.5	36.9	37.8	38.4	Madison	32.2	33.8	34.3	34.5
Brevard	36.1	42.3	44.0	45.3	Manatee	43.0	47.4	49.5	51.5
Broward	37.6	41.5	42.6	43.5	Marion	39.8	47.2	49.6	51.8
Calhoun	33.4	37.4	38.5	39.5	Martin	44.3	48.3	50.4	52.5
Charlotte	53.5	53.2	55.0	56.8	Miami-Dade	34.0	37.0	37.4	37.5
Citrus	50.7	54.5	56.3	58.3	Monroe	38.7	42.8	44.1	44.8
Clay	31.9	36.8	38.0	39.1	Nassau	33.2	38.4	39.6	40.4
Collier	40.5	46.8	49.1	51.3	Okaloosa	31.4	35.4	35.9	36.3
Columbia	33.4	36.7	37.4	38.1	Okeechobee	34.1	40.2	41.5	42.6
De Soto	36.3	39.6	40.4	41.0	Orange	31.3	34.9	35.6	36.2
Dixie	36.7	41.1	42.5	43.9	Osceola	33.5	38.8	40.3	41.3
Duval	31.4	34.4	34.7	34.8	Palm Beach	39.7	44.8	46.7	48.5
Escambia	32.3	35.0	35.4	35.7	Pasco	47.9	50.8	52.7	55.0
Flagler	46.2	52.6	55.1	57.3	Pinellas	42.0	46.2	47.9	49.6
Franklin	38.9	50.3	53.1	55.6	Polk	36.3	42.4	44.1	45.5
Gadsden	31.6	34.6	35.8	36.8	Putnam	37.1	42.2	43.8	45.0
Gilchrist	33.4	35.4	36.4	37.1	St. Johns	36.9	43.1	45.2	46.7
Glades	39.7	41.8	43.2	44.4	St. Lucie	37.7	44.6	46.8	48.7
Gulf	35.6	37.2	37.9	38.4	Santa Rosa	32.4	37.4	38.8	39.9
Hamilton	30.7	34.4	35.5	36.5	Sarasota	48.9	53.1	55.2	57.3
Hardee	32.5	33.9	34.3	34.6	Seminole	33.2	38.0	39.2	39.9
Hendry	30.1	31.0	30.9	31.0	Sumter	40.0	44.4	47.1	49.6
Hernando	49.4	52.9	54.9	56.9	Suwannee	36.3	42.2	44.0	45.2
Highlands	51.3	56.2	57.8	59.7	Taylor	33.4	35.1	35.8	36.2
Hillsborough	32.9	37.8	38.8	39.5	Union	31.3	36.1	37.3	38.4
Holmes	35.5	39.0	40.2	41.4	Volusia	39.3	44.2	46.1	47.7
Indian River	43.9	48.5	50.6	52.6	Wakulla	34.1	38.3	39.3	40.0
Jackson	34.1	36.9	37.9	38.8	Walton	37.8	44.1	46.4	48.4
Jefferson	33.7	38.4	39.9	41.0	Washington	37.2	37.3	38.0	38.7
Lafayette	32.0	34.8	35.8	36.7					

Note: Projections are based on Bureau of the Census modified age, race, and sex data.

Source: University of Florida, Bureau of Economic and Business Research, Population Program, unpublished data. Census data from U.S. Bureau of the Census.

University of Florida   **Bureau of Economic and Business Research**

Table 1.40. MALE AND FEMALE PROJECTIONS: PROJECTIONS, APRIL 1, 2005, 2010, AND 2015, BY SEX IN THE STATE AND COUNTIES OF FLORIDA

County	2005 Total	2005 Male	2005 Female	2010 Total	2010 Male	2010 Female	2015 Total	2015 Male	2015 Female
Florida	16,882,830	8,221,965	8,660,865	18,121,273	8,840,277	9,280,996	19,400,913	9,477,272	9,923,641
Alachua	237,057	117,898	119,159	253,628	126,391	127,237	268,519	133,926	134,593
Baker	24,120	12,700	11,420	25,865	13,576	12,289	27,677	14,476	13,201
Bay	164,290	80,799	83,491	175,499	86,310	89,189	187,065	91,993	95,072
Bradford	27,094	15,097	11,997	28,207	15,666	12,541	29,359	16,250	13,109
Brevard	524,488	256,615	267,873	564,166	276,100	288,066	605,032	296,216	308,816
Broward	1,640,045	792,363	847,682	1,758,486	852,015	906,471	1,880,710	912,937	967,773
Calhoun	15,902	8,426	7,476	17,261	9,101	8,160	18,702	9,811	8,891
Charlotte	155,504	74,893	80,611	170,373	82,362	88,011	185,825	90,131	95,694
Citrus	129,496	61,610	67,886	141,305	67,479	73,826	153,463	73,551	79,912
Clay	161,743	79,816	81,927	179,465	88,443	91,022	197,901	97,396	100,505
Collier	262,929	127,691	135,238	297,826	144,635	153,191	334,310	162,450	171,860
Columbia	65,027	33,390	31,637	70,968	36,298	34,670	77,144	39,321	37,823
De Soto	31,690	16,957	14,733	33,732	17,922	15,810	35,841	18,930	16,911
Dixie	15,402	7,997	7,405	16,801	8,687	8,114	18,260	9,416	8,844
Duval	818,856	401,319	417,537	863,136	423,542	439,594	908,843	446,386	462,457
Escambia	321,850	159,786	162,064	338,077	167,951	170,126	354,749	176,340	178,409
Flagler	57,394	27,389	30,005	66,785	31,894	34,891	76,607	36,628	39,979
Franklin	11,921	5,777	6,144	12,761	6,170	6,591	13,624	6,575	7,049
Gadsden	56,816	28,182	28,634	61,116	30,268	30,848	65,624	32,449	33,175
Gilchrist	15,831	8,275	7,556	17,671	9,183	8,488	19,602	10,128	9,474
Glades	11,021	5,859	5,162	11,801	6,227	5,574	12,603	6,611	5,992
Gulf	16,670	9,392	7,278	17,510	9,801	7,709	18,373	10,225	8,148

Continued . . .

Table 1.40. MALE AND FEMALE PROJECTIONS: PROJECTIONS, APRIL 1, 2005, 2010, AND 2015, BY SEX IN THE STATE AND COUNTIES OF FLORIDA (Continued)

County	2005 Total	2005 Male	2005 Female	2010 Total	2010 Male	2010 Female	2015 Total	2015 Male	2015 Female
Hamilton	16,601	9,295	7,306	17,905	9,928	7,977	19,252	10,580	8,672
Hardee	23,247	12,235	11,012	23,627	12,399	11,228	23,998	12,569	11,429
Hendry	33,418	17,235	16,183	35,578	18,312	17,266	37,819	19,426	18,393
Hernando	146,263	69,861	76,402	161,713	77,561	84,152	177,619	85,506	92,113
Highlands	89,311	42,066	47,245	95,777	45,350	50,427	102,463	48,794	53,669
Hillsborough	1,054,305	515,788	538,517	1,124,015	550,236	573,779	1,196,542	585,939	610,603
Holmes	20,388	10,644	9,744	21,507	11,204	10,303	22,673	11,781	10,892
Indian River	122,699	58,849	63,850	133,140	64,054	69,086	143,971	69,498	74,473
Jackson	54,034	28,883	25,151	57,055	30,425	26,630	60,162	31,984	28,178
Jefferson	15,633	7,081	8,552	16,581	7,552	9,029	17,561	8,027	9,534
Lafayette	8,238	4,719	3,519	8,967	5,069	3,898	9,752	5,445	4,307
Lake	237,422	113,406	124,016	264,371	126,614	137,757	292,453	140,441	152,012
Lee	471,304	227,380	243,924	514,517	248,856	265,661	559,351	271,169	288,182
Leon	262,309	126,870	135,439	282,521	136,802	145,719	301,345	146,065	155,280
Levy	37,917	18,065	19,852	41,521	19,843	21,678	45,265	21,681	23,584
Liberty	9,256	5,272	3,984	10,206	5,741	4,465	11,199	6,233	4,966
Madison	21,192	11,039	10,153	22,380	11,642	10,738	23,607	12,253	11,354
Manatee	280,659	134,133	146,526	302,424	145,226	157,198	324,940	156,651	168,289
Marion	284,957	136,596	148,361	313,387	150,547	162,840	342,951	165,127	177,824
Martin	135,904	66,049	69,855	147,295	71,725	75,570	159,111	77,629	81,482
Miami-Dade	2,270,834	1,102,800	1,168,034	2,384,797	1,160,653	1,224,144	2,502,417	1,219,953	1,282,464
Monroe	92,744	46,350	46,394	97,321	48,390	48,931	102,096	50,592	51,504
Nassau	65,969	32,615	33,354	73,019	36,076	36,943	80,559	39,762	40,797
Okaloosa	201,373	100,158	101,215	218,726	108,562	110,164	236,713	117,318	119,395

Continued . . .

Table 1.40. MALE AND FEMALE PROJECTIONS: PROJECTIONS, APRIL 1, 2005, 2010, AND 2015, BY SEX IN THE STATE AND COUNTIES OF FLORIDA (Continued)

County	2005 Total	2005 Male	2005 Female	2010 Total	2010 Male	2010 Female	2015 Total	2015 Male	2015 Female
Okeechobee	38,666	19,924	18,742	41,018	21,029	19,989	43,486	22,215	21,271
Orange	965,909	476,612	489,297	1,061,559	523,452	538,107	1,160,984	572,091	588,893
Osceola	189,347	93,026	96,321	215,173	105,728	109,445	242,181	118,973	123,208
Palm Beach	1,159,707	558,246	601,461	1,253,000	605,129	647,871	1,349,535	653,490	696,045
Pasco	357,199	169,747	187,452	381,910	182,556	199,354	407,685	195,863	211,822
Pinellas	930,618	444,016	486,602	955,900	458,826	497,074	982,146	473,557	508,589
Polk	516,822	250,069	266,753	549,995	266,483	283,512	584,155	283,456	300,699
Putnam	77,860	37,768	40,092	81,788	39,705	42,083	85,919	41,748	44,171
St. Johns	349,400	164,796	184,604	371,702	176,333	195,369	394,697	188,239	206,458
St. Lucie	399,754	196,867	202,887	436,138	214,818	221,320	473,864	233,343	240,521
Santa Rosa	133,216	64,947	68,269	148,685	72,549	76,136	164,796	80,441	84,355
Sarasota	212,006	102,795	109,211	232,044	112,646	119,398	252,849	122,888	129,961
Seminole	131,380	65,759	65,621	146,379	73,046	73,333	162,014	80,638	81,376
Sumter	60,931	32,255	28,676	69,153	36,177	32,976	77,658	40,270	37,388
Suwannee	39,127	19,001	20,126	42,957	20,873	22,084	46,916	22,808	24,108
Taylor	21,738	11,733	10,005	22,415	12,067	10,348	23,119	12,422	10,697
Union	15,671	9,980	5,691	16,792	10,514	6,278	17,935	11,058	6,877
Volusia	465,286	225,474	239,812	496,059	241,016	255,043	528,278	257,213	271,065
Wakulla	24,644	12,766	11,878	27,447	14,140	13,307	30,368	15,565	14,803
Walton	47,752	23,939	23,813	53,672	26,776	26,896	59,825	29,731	30,094
Washington	24,674	12,625	12,049	26,698	13,626	13,072	28,851	14,694	14,157

Source: University of Florida, Bureau of Economic and Business Research, Population Program, Florida Population Studies, June 2000, Volume 33, No. 3. Bulletin No. 127, and unpublished data.

University of Florida　　　　　　　　　Bureau of Economic and Business Research

Table 1.41. AGE PROJECTIONS: PROJECTIONS, APRIL 1, 2005, 2010, AND 2015, BY AGE IN THE STATE AND COUNTIES OF FLORIDA

County	2005 Less than 18	2005 18-64	2005 65 and over	2010 Less than 18	2010 18-64	2010 65 and over	2015 Less than 18	2015 18-64	2015 65 and over
Florida	3,650,437	10,145,711	3,086,682	3,767,972	10,917,279	3,436,022	3,914,646	11,441,861	4,044,406
Alachua	50,105	165,426	21,526	52,413	177,188	24,027	55,066	184,975	28,478
Baker	6,308	15,503	2,309	6,612	16,599	2,654	6,968	17,525	3,184
Bay	39,679	101,812	22,799	40,911	108,802	25,786	42,598	113,648	30,819
Bradford	5,768	17,552	3,774	5,860	18,146	4,201	5,983	18,529	4,847
Brevard	108,289	318,655	97,544	110,794	344,375	108,997	115,106	361,738	128,188
Broward	360,140	984,953	294,952	375,046	1,060,628	322,812	389,051	1,112,578	379,081
Calhoun	3,262	10,214	2,426	3,475	10,980	2,806	3,693	11,674	3,335
Charlotte	23,551	83,347	48,606	24,601	91,945	53,827	25,693	97,165	62,967
Citrus	19,623	67,092	42,781	20,007	73,324	47,974	20,546	76,783	56,134
Clay	41,727	102,035	17,981	44,188	112,371	22,906	47,162	120,396	30,343
Collier	52,014	146,039	64,876	56,658	164,191	76,977	61,577	178,068	94,665
Columbia	16,537	39,534	8,956	17,578	42,956	10,434	18,795	45,563	12,786
De Soto	7,328	18,232	6,130	7,756	19,226	6,750	8,187	19,882	7,772
Dixie	3,306	8,958	3,138	3,556	9,590	3,655	3,799	10,125	4,336
Duval	210,307	517,564	90,985	216,561	546,840	99,735	224,322	567,132	117,389
Escambia	77,260	202,954	41,636	79,363	213,414	45,300	81,862	220,821	52,066
Flagler	9,056	30,662	17,676	9,800	35,421	21,564	10,692	38,897	27,018
Franklin	2,040	7,098	2,783	2,012	7,350	3,399	2,006	7,470	4,148
Gadsden	15,206	34,929	6,681	15,871	37,452	7,793	16,526	39,594	9,504
Gilchrist	3,700	10,002	2,129	4,109	11,069	2,493	4,532	11,967	3,103
Glades	2,102	6,770	2,149	2,169	7,249	2,383	2,258	7,601	2,744
Gulf	3,361	10,965	2,344	3,475	11,436	2,599	3,603	11,791	2,979

Continued . . .

Table 1.41. AGE PROJECTIONS: PROJECTIONS, APRIL 1, 2005, 2010, AND 2015, BY AGE IN THE STATE AND COUNTIES OF FLORIDA (Continued)

County	2005 Less than 18	2005 18-64	2005 65 and over	2010 Less than 18	2010 18-64	2010 65 and over	2015 Less than 18	2015 18-64	2015 65 and over
Hamilton	3,658	11,109	1,834	3,823	11,914	2,168	4,011	12,568	2,673
Hardee	6,268	13,367	3,612	6,281	13,540	3,806	6,271	13,572	4,155
Hendry	10,479	19,354	3,585	11,036	20,557	3,985	11,670	21,585	4,564
Hernando	24,390	76,293	45,580	25,338	84,644	51,731	26,497	89,719	61,403
Highlands	14,956	41,012	33,343	15,301	44,166	36,310	15,667	45,807	40,989
Hillsborough	246,718	663,868	143,719	251,983	708,232	163,800	260,173	739,472	196,897
Holmes	4,274	12,750	3,364	4,317	13,456	3,734	4,417	13,874	4,382
Indian River	22,332	65,214	35,153	23,099	71,110	38,931	24,147	74,799	45,025
Jackson	11,230	35,713	7,091	11,617	37,529	7,909	11,954	38,901	9,307
Jefferson	3,585	9,733	2,315	3,661	10,264	2,656	3,770	10,560	3,231
Lafayette	1,642	5,567	1,029	1,766	6,036	1,165	1,894	6,441	1,417
Lake	42,957	124,019	70,446	45,457	137,789	81,125	48,353	147,467	96,633
Lee	87,621	269,160	114,523	90,394	295,247	128,876	94,386	311,876	153,089
Leon	54,548	187,032	20,729	57,085	201,360	24,076	60,326	210,587	30,432
Levy	7,732	21,353	8,832	8,047	23,273	10,201	8,448	24,634	12,183
Liberty	1,937	6,318	1,001	2,127	6,874	1,205	2,328	7,316	1,555
Madison	5,384	13,104	2,704	5,558	13,938	2,884	5,814	14,627	3,166
Manatee	51,746	155,564	73,349	53,241	168,807	80,376	55,142	176,439	93,359
Marion	56,305	154,612	74,040	58,775	169,646	84,966	61,844	179,596	101,511
Martin	23,074	75,549	37,281	23,776	82,082	41,437	24,704	86,149	48,258
Miami-Dade	577,880	1,386,846	306,108	589,737	1,465,638	329,422	604,354	1,522,715	375,348
Monroe	16,339	62,712	13,693	16,542	65,881	14,898	16,997	67,725	17,374
Nassau	16,484	41,888	7,597	17,537	46,188	9,294	18,894	49,687	11,978
Okaloosa	51,033	127,698	22,642	53,792	139,196	25,738	57,099	148,496	31,118

Continued . . .

Table 1.41. AGE PROJECTIONS: PROJECTIONS, APRIL 1, 2005, 2010, AND 2015, BY AGE IN THE STATE AND COUNTIES OF FLORIDA (Continued)

County	2005 Less than 18	2005 18-64	2005 65 and over	2010 Less than 18	2010 18-64	2010 65 and over	2015 Less than 18	2015 18-64	2015 65 and over
Okeechobee	9,662	21,405	7,599	10,023	22,492	8,503	10,427	23,153	9,906
Orange	227,786	631,446	106,677	242,168	694,863	124,528	258,384	747,429	155,171
Osceola	45,098	118,131	26,118	49,183	134,250	31,740	53,865	147,506	40,810
Palm Beach	227,592	666,186	265,929	233,469	723,968	295,563	241,857	760,546	347,132
Pasco	61,155	185,428	110,616	62,671	199,595	119,644	64,301	206,875	136,509
Pinellas	164,510	546,167	219,941	160,729	566,261	228,910	158,614	568,747	254,785
Polk	113,779	294,065	108,978	116,148	312,857	120,990	119,388	324,433	140,334
Putnam	18,176	44,268	15,416	18,375	46,675	16,738	18,709	48,053	19,157
St. Johns	50,846	186,073	112,481	50,493	198,250	122,959	50,740	203,351	140,606
St. Lucie	91,277	265,646	42,831	94,657	290,000	51,481	99,448	308,887	65,529
Santa Rosa	25,560	84,142	23,514	26,993	93,578	28,114	28,846	100,640	35,310
Sarasota	43,081	122,216	46,709	44,379	134,762	52,903	46,513	143,063	63,273
Seminole	31,312	83,982	16,086	33,252	93,015	20,112	35,619	100,594	25,801
Sumter	11,589	35,015	14,327	12,771	38,870	17,512	13,988	41,821	21,849
Suwannee	8,744	22,878	7,505	9,297	24,897	8,763	9,891	26,460	10,565
Taylor	5,109	13,369	3,260	5,110	13,768	3,537	5,172	13,943	4,004
Union	2,703	11,411	1,557	2,771	12,092	1,929	2,866	12,615	2,454
Volusia	88,409	274,816	102,061	90,023	294,466	111,570	92,722	306,038	129,518
Wakulla	5,650	16,013	2,981	6,135	17,669	3,643	6,701	18,976	4,691
Walton	9,364	28,251	10,137	10,068	31,250	12,354	10,855	33,525	15,445
Washington	5,794	14,672	4,208	6,152	15,782	4,764	6,555	16,672	5,624

Source: University of Florida, Bureau of Economic and Business Research, Population Program, *Florida Population Studies*, June 2000, Volume 33, No. 3. Bulletin No. 127, and unpublished data.

Table 1.42. PERSONS AGED 65 AND OVER: PROJECTIONS, APRIL 1, 2005, 2010, AND 2015, BY AGE IN THE STATE AND COUNTIES OF FLORIDA

County	2005			2010			2015		
	65-74	75-84	85 and over	65-74	75-84	85 and over	65-74	75-84	85 and over
Florida	1,500,291	1,177,343	409,048	1,760,138	1,180,144	495,740	2,243,753	1,240,188	560,465
Alachua	10,654	8,011	2,861	12,533	7,994	3,500	16,211	8,291	3,976
Baker	1,302	755	252	1,469	875	310	1,845	959	380
Bay	12,560	7,922	2,317	14,414	8,425	2,947	18,158	9,174	3,487
Bradford	1,838	1,439	497	2,132	1,431	638	2,652	1,465	730
Brevard	50,070	37,058	10,416	57,586	37,789	13,622	72,598	39,782	15,808
Broward	130,082	115,937	48,933	155,026	112,695	55,091	201,513	117,854	59,714
Calhoun	1,174	896	356	1,414	936	456	1,742	1,058	535
Charlotte	24,637	18,558	5,411	28,769	18,428	6,630	36,321	19,192	7,454
Citrus	21,466	16,318	4,997	25,097	16,480	6,397	31,435	17,231	7,468
Clay	9,856	5,850	2,275	12,961	6,833	3,112	18,013	8,394	3,936
Collier	32,949	24,928	6,999	40,270	27,110	9,597	52,625	30,090	11,950
Columbia	4,819	3,150	987	5,797	3,344	1,293	7,535	3,720	1,531
De Soto	3,091	2,348	691	3,511	2,369	870	4,345	2,426	1,001
Dixie	1,746	1,110	282	2,020	1,248	387	2,485	1,355	496
Duval	45,306	33,960	11,719	52,080	33,339	14,316	67,151	34,101	16,137
Escambia	21,003	15,369	5,264	23,434	15,265	6,601	28,744	15,861	7,461
Flagler	9,384	6,486	1,806	11,399	7,336	2,829	14,881	8,302	3,835
Franklin	1,541	918	324	1,969	1,046	384	2,446	1,223	479
Gadsden	3,414	2,275	992	4,208	2,384	1,201	5,427	2,684	1,393
Gilchrist	1,200	721	208	1,428	795	270	1,889	884	330
Glades	1,095	831	223	1,268	823	292	1,541	858	345
Gulf	1,263	807	274	1,430	835	334	1,714	894	371

Continued . . .

University of Florida   Bureau of Economic and Business Research

41

Table 1.42. PERSONS AGED 65 AND OVER: PROJECTIONS, APRIL 1, 2005, 2010, AND 2015, BY AGE IN THE STATE AND COUNTIES OF FLORIDA (Continued)

County	2005			2010			2015		
	65-74	75-84	85 and over	65-74	75-84	85 and over	65-74	75-84	85 and over
Hamilton	1,013	598	223	1,242	674	252	1,619	752	302
Hardee	1,693	1,440	479	1,927	1,289	590	2,269	1,236	650
Hendry	1,905	1,258	422	2,217	1,251	517	2,668	1,316	580
Hernando	23,770	17,070	4,740	28,358	17,127	6,246	36,048	18,068	7,287
Highlands	15,628	13,711	4,004	17,649	13,508	5,153	21,478	13,677	5,834
Hillsborough	72,220	52,748	18,751	86,483	53,808	23,509	111,805	57,859	27,233
Holmes	1,754	1,176	434	1,999	1,208	527	2,470	1,316	596
Indian River	16,862	14,190	4,101	19,400	14,218	5,313	24,328	14,585	6,112
Jackson	3,591	2,379	1,121	4,272	2,398	1,239	5,410	2,567	1,330
Jefferson	1,190	849	276	1,445	881	330	1,900	955	376
Lafayette	570	351	108	621	398	146	782	459	176
Lake	34,310	28,194	7,942	40,699	29,811	10,615	51,771	32,136	12,726
Lee	58,055	43,718	12,750	68,876	44,066	15,934	88,261	46,499	18,329
Leon	11,080	7,400	2,249	13,779	7,632	2,665	19,153	8,265	3,014
Levy	4,293	3,531	1,008	5,110	3,699	1,392	6,519	3,957	1,707
Liberty	573	321	107	693	390	122	967	427	161
Madison	1,298	984	422	1,455	957	472	1,657	992	517
Manatee	33,330	28,904	11,115	38,944	28,222	13,210	49,853	28,929	14,577
Marion	36,799	29,259	7,982	43,722	30,356	10,888	55,949	32,366	13,196
Martin	17,590	14,883	4,808	20,565	14,828	6,044	26,021	15,357	6,880
Miami-Dade	154,165	109,455	42,488	172,352	109,121	47,949	208,863	113,438	53,047
Monroe	7,497	4,961	1,235	8,695	4,735	1,468	10,958	4,828	1,588
Nassau	4,349	2,465	783	5,516	2,785	993	7,497	3,241	1,240
Okaloosa	12,551	7,777	2,314	13,911	8,655	3,172	17,748	9,479	3,891

Continued . . .

Table 1.42. PERSONS AGED 65 AND OVER: PROJECTIONS, APRIL 1, 2005, 2010, AND 2015, BY AGE IN THE STATE AND COUNTIES OF FLORIDA (Continued)

County	2005			2010			2015		
	65-74	75-84	85 and over	65-74	75-84	85 and over	65-74	75-84	85 and over
Okeechobee	3,897	2,907	795	4,493	2,954	1,056	5,609	3,040	1,257
Orange	55,651	39,058	11,968	67,756	41,328	15,444	91,104	45,613	18,454
Osceola	13,436	9,238	3,444	17,105	10,232	4,403	23,654	11,798	5,358
Palm Beach	121,635	106,185	38,109	145,010	105,229	45,324	186,576	110,236	50,320
Pasco	49,736	45,790	15,090	57,721	43,865	18,058	72,362	44,503	19,644
Pinellas	98,123	85,850	35,968	110,127	79,466	39,317	135,967	78,327	40,491
Polk	52,394	41,804	14,780	60,428	41,801	18,761	75,503	43,090	21,741
Putnam	7,980	5,707	1,729	8,949	5,610	2,179	11,019	5,647	2,491
St. Johns	11,568	9,196	2,750	14,841	9,557	3,716	20,264	10,458	4,588
St. Lucie	23,860	18,085	4,764	28,263	18,403	6,237	36,506	19,452	7,315
Santa Rosa	9,361	5,316	1,409	11,768	6,323	2,021	15,484	7,651	2,666
Sarasota	51,286	44,850	16,345	59,684	43,716	19,559	74,343	44,776	21,487
Seminole	23,258	14,587	4,986	29,736	15,540	6,205	40,737	17,577	7,215
Sumter	7,373	5,350	1,604	9,134	6,047	2,331	11,961	6,877	3,011
Suwannee	3,679	2,803	1,023	4,428	3,031	1,304	5,656	3,343	1,566
Taylor	1,739	1,197	324	1,854	1,283	400	2,196	1,333	475
Union	840	528	189	1,044	619	266	1,397	718	339
Volusia	49,242	39,134	13,685	57,080	38,098	16,392	72,229	39,204	18,085
Wakulla	1,561	1,094	326	2,012	1,188	443	2,787	1,347	557
Walton	5,183	3,811	1,143	6,230	4,449	1,675	8,168	4,987	2,290
Washington	1,953	1,584	671	2,330	1,608	826	2,966	1,709	949

Source: University of Florida, Bureau of Economic and Business Research, Population Program, unpublished data.

University of Florida   **Bureau of Economic and Business Research**

Table 1.43. RACE: ESTIMATES, APRIL 1, 1999, AND PROJECTIONS, APRIL 1, 2005, 2010, AND 2015, BY RACE IN THE STATE AND COUNTIES OF FLORIDA

(rounded to thousands)

County	Estimates, 1999			2005			Projections 2010			2015		
	Total	White	Black	Total	White	Black	Total	White	Black	Total	White	Black
Florida	15,322	12,905	2,137	16,883	14,173	2,367	18,121	15,177	2,546	19,401	16,265	2,686
Alachua	216	169	41	237	184	45	254	196	48	269	207	51
Baker	22	19	3	24	21	3	26	23	3	28	25	3
Bay	150	130	16	164	143	17	175	152	18	187	163	19
Bradford	26	20	5	27	22	5	28	23	5	29	24	5
Brevard	475	429	37	524	474	40	564	510	43	605	547	45
Broward	1,490	1,184	273	1,640	1,273	323	1,758	1,341	363	1,881	1,434	385
Calhoun	14	12	2	16	13	2	17	14	3	19	16	3
Charlotte	137	130	6	156	147	7	170	160	8	186	175	9
Citrus	115	111	3	129	126	3	141	137	3	153	149	3
Clay	140	129	8	162	149	9	179	164	10	198	181	11
Collier	220	209	9	263	250	11	298	283	12	334	318	13
Columbia	57	45	11	65	52	12	71	57	12	77	63	13
De Soto	28	23	5	32	26	5	34	28	5	36	30	6
Dixie	13	12	1	15	14	1	17	15	1	18	17	2
Duval	763	556	186	819	595	199	863	625	209	909	658	218
Escambia	302	229	62	322	243	66	338	254	70	355	267	73
Flagler	46	42	4	57	52	4	67	61	5	77	70	6
Franklin	11	10	1	12	11	1	13	11	1	14	12	1
Gadsden	51	21	30	57	23	33	61	25	35	66	27	37
Gilchrist	13	12	1	16	15	1	18	16	1	20	18	1
Glades	10	8	1	11	9	2	12	9	2	13	10	2
Gulf	14	11	3	17	13	4	18	14	4	18	14	4

See footnote at end of table.

Continued . . .

Table 1.43. RACE: ESTIMATES, APRIL 1, 1999, AND PROJECTIONS, APRIL 1, 2005, 2010, AND 2015, BY RACE IN THE STATE AND COUNTIES OF FLORIDA (Continued)

(rounded to thousands)

County	Estimates, 1999			Projections 2005			Projections 2010			Projections 2015		
	Total	White	Black	Total	White	Black	Total	White	Black	Total	White	Black
Hamilton	14	9	6	17	10	6	18	11	7	19	12	7
Hardee	23	20	2	23	21	2	24	21	2	24	22	2
Hendry	31	25	5	33	28	5	36	30	5	38	32	5
Hernando	127	122	4	146	140	5	162	155	5	178	171	6
Highlands	81	73	7	89	81	7	96	88	7	102	94	7
Hillsborough	968	819	130	1,054	890	142	1,124	946	151	1,197	1,008	160
Holmes	19	17	1	20	19	1	22	20	1	23	21	2
Indian River	110	101	7	123	115	7	133	125	7	144	135	8
Jackson	49	35	14	54	38	15	57	40	16	60	43	16
Jefferson	14	8	6	16	9	6	17	10	6	18	11	6
Lafayette	7	6	1	8	7	1	9	8	1	10	8	1
Lake	204	187	16	237	219	17	264	245	17	292	271	19
Lee	417	387	26	471	438	29	515	479	31	559	520	33
Leon	238	174	58	262	192	64	283	207	68	301	221	72
Levy	33	30	4	38	34	4	42	37	4	45	41	4
Liberty	8	7	1	9	8	1	10	9	1	11	10	1
Madison	20	12	8	21	13	8	22	14	8	24	15	9
Manatee	253	232	19	281	258	20	302	278	21	325	298	23
Marion	249	218	29	285	250	31	313	276	33	343	302	36
Martin	122	114	7	136	127	7	147	138	7	159	150	8
Miami-Dade	2,127	1,601	480	2,271	1,678	536	2,385	1,736	580	2,502	1,822	603
Monroe	87	82	4	93	87	5	97	91	5	102	96	5
Nassau	57	52	5	66	61	5	73	67	5	81	74	6
Okaloosa	180	156	17	201	174	20	219	188	22	237	203	24

See footnote at end of table.

Continued . . .

Table 1.43. RACE: ESTIMATES, APRIL 1, 1999, AND PROJECTIONS, APRIL 1, 2005, 2010, AND 2015, BY RACE IN THE STATE AND COUNTIES OF FLORIDA (Continued)

(rounded to thousands)

County	Estimates, 1999			2005			Projections 2010			2015		
	Total	White	Black	Total	White	Black	Total	White	Black	Total	White	Black
Okeechobee	36	32	3	39	35	3	41	37	3	43	40	3
Orange	846	687	135	966	779	156	1,062	852	173	1,161	932	188
Osceola	157	145	9	189	174	11	215	198	12	242	223	14
Palm Beach	1,042	899	128	1,160	1,001	140	1,253	1,082	150	1,350	1,166	160
Pasco	326	317	7	357	346	7	382	370	8	408	395	8
Pinellas	899	811	73	931	837	77	956	857	81	982	880	82
Polk	475	409	60	517	447	63	550	477	66	584	507	69
Putnam	73	59	13	78	64	13	82	67	13	86	71	14
St. Johns	114	106	8	133	125	8	149	140	8	165	155	8
St. Lucie	187	157	28	212	179	30	232	197	32	253	215	34
Santa Rosa	113	105	5	131	122	6	146	136	7	162	151	7
Sarasota	321	305	13	349	333	14	372	354	14	395	376	15
Seminole	354	318	29	400	359	32	436	392	35	474	425	37
Sumter	51	41	9	61	50	10	69	58	11	78	65	12
Suwannee	34	30	4	39	34	4	43	38	5	47	42	5
Taylor	20	16	4	22	17	4	22	18	4	23	19	4
Union	14	10	3	16	12	3	17	13	3	18	14	3
Volusia	427	386	36	465	422	38	496	451	39	528	480	41
Wakulla	21	18	3	25	21	3	27	24	3	30	27	3
Walton	40	37	3	48	44	3	54	50	3	60	55	3
Washington	22	18	4	25	20	4	27	22	4	29	23	5

Note: Totals include other races not shown separately.

Source: University of Florida, Bureau of Economic and Business Research, Population Program, *Florida Population Studies*, June 2000, Volume 33, No. 3. Bulletin No. 127, and unpublished data.

Table 1.65. METROPOLITAN AREAS: CENSUS COUNTS, APRIL 1, 1980 AND 1990, AND POPULATION ESTIMATES, APRIL 1, 1999, IN THE STATE AND METROPOLITAN AREAS OF FLORIDA

Metropolitan area	Census 1980	Census 1990	Estimates 1999	Percentage change 1980-1990	Percentage change 1990-1999
Florida	9,746,961	12,938,071	15,322,040	32.7	18.4
Metropolitan areas, total	9,038,653	12,023,514	14,192,013	33.0	18.0
Daytona Beach	269,675	399,438	472,633	48.1	18.3
Flagler County	10,913	28,701	45,818	163.0	59.6
Volusia County	258,762	370,737	426,815	43.3	15.1
Ft. Lauderdale	1,018,257	1,255,531	1,490,289	23.3	18.7
Ft. Myers-Cape Coral	205,266	335,113	417,114	63.3	24.5
Ft. Pierce-Port St. Lucie	151,196	251,071	308,419	66.1	22.8
Martin County	64,014	100,900	121,514	57.6	20.4
St. Lucie County	87,182	150,171	186,905	72.3	24.5
Ft. Walton Beach	109,920	143,777	179,589	30.8	24.9
Gainesville	151,369	181,596	216,249	20.0	19.1
Jacksonville	722,252	906,727	1,073,799	25.5	18.4
Clay County	67,052	105,986	139,631	58.1	31.7
Duval County	571,003	672,971	762,846	17.9	13.4
Nassau County	32,894	43,941	57,381	33.6	30.6
St. Johns County	51,303	83,829	113,941	63.4	35.9
Lakeland-Winter Haven	321,652	405,382	474,704	26.0	17.1
Melbourne-Titusville-Palm Bay	272,959	398,978	474,803	46.2	19.0
Miami	1,625,509	1,937,194	2,126,702	19.2	9.8
Naples	85,971	152,099	219,685	76.9	44.4
Ocala	122,488	194,835	249,433	59.1	28.0
Orlando	804,774	1,224,844	1,561,715	52.2	27.5
Lake County	104,870	152,104	203,863	45.0	34.0
Orange County	470,865	677,491	846,328	43.9	24.9
Osceola County	49,287	107,728	157,376	118.6	46.1
Seminole County	179,752	287,521	354,148	60.0	23.2
Panama City	97,740	126,994	150,119	29.9	18.2
Pensacola	289,782	344,406	414,244	18.9	20.3
Escambia County	233,794	262,798	301,613	12.4	14.8
Santa Rosa County	55,988	81,608	112,631	45.8	38.0
Punta Gorda	58,460	110,975	136,773	89.8	23.2
Sarasota-Bradenton	350,696	489,483	574,251	39.6	17.3
Manatee County	148,445	211,707	253,207	42.6	19.6
Sarasota County	202,251	277,776	321,044	37.3	15.6
Tallahassee	190,329	233,609	289,115	22.7	23.8
Gadsden County	41,674	41,116	51,478	-1.3	25.2
Leon County	148,655	192,493	237,637	29.5	23.5
Tampa-St. Petersburg-Clearwater	1,613,600	2,067,959	2,320,181	28.2	12.2
Hernando County	44,984	101,115	127,392	127.4	26.0
Hillsborough County	646,939	834,054	967,511	28.9	16.0
Pasco County	193,661	281,131	326,494	45.2	16.1
Pinellas County	728,531	851,659	898,784	16.9	5.5
West Palm Beach-Boca Raton	576,758	863,503	1,042,196	49.7	20.7

Note: Data are for Metropolitan Statistical Areas (MSAs) and for Primary Metropolitan Statistical Areas (PMSAs) based on 1999 MSA designations. See Glossary for definitions and map at the front of the book for area boundaries.

Source: University of Florida, Bureau of Economic and Business Research, Population Program, *Florida Estimates of Population, April 1, 1999.* Census data from U.S. Bureau of the Census.

University of Florida   **Bureau of Economic and Business Research**

Table 1.66. PLANNING DISTRICTS: CENSUS COUNTS, APRIL 1, 1990, AND POPULATION ESTIMATES, APRIL 1, 1999, IN THE STATE, COMPREHENSIVE PLANNING DISTRICTS, AND COUNTIES OF FLORIDA

District and county	Census 1990	Estimates 1999	Percentage change 1990 to 1999	District and county	Census 1990	Estimates 1999	Percentage change 1990 to 1999
Florida	12,938,071	15,322,040	18.4	District 5	446,952	575,954	28.9
				Citrus	93,513	114,898	22.9
District 1	675,633	825,472	22.2	Hernando	101,115	127,392	26.0
Bay	126,994	150,119	18.2	Levy	25,912	33,408	28.9
Escambia	262,798	301,613	14.8	Marion	194,835	249,433	28.0
Holmes	15,778	18,899	19.8	Sumter	31,577	50,823	60.9
Okaloosa	143,777	179,589	24.9	District 6	1,994,559	2,463,333	23.5
Santa Rosa	81,608	112,631	38.0	Brevard	398,978	474,803	19.0
Walton	27,759	40,466	45.8	Lake	152,104	203,863	34.0
Washington	16,919	22,155	30.9	Orange	677,491	846,328	24.9
District 2	337,533	421,096	24.8	Osceola	107,728	157,376	46.1
Calhoun	11,011	14,117	28.2	Seminole	287,521	354,148	23.2
Franklin	8,967	10,872	21.2	Volusia	370,737	426,815	15.1
Gadsden	41,116	51,478	25.2	District 7	546,805	642,389	17.5
Gulf	11,504	14,403	25.2	De Soto	23,865	28,438	19.2
Jackson	41,375	49,469	19.6	Hardee	19,499	22,594	15.9
Jefferson	11,296	14,424	27.7	Highlands	68,432	81,143	18.6
Leon	192,493	237,637	23.5	Okeechobee	29,627	35,510	19.9
Liberty	5,569	8,048	44.5	Polk	405,382	474,704	17.1
Wakulla	14,202	20,648	45.4	District 8	2,178,551	2,445,996	12.3
District 3	354,196	434,171	22.6	Hillsborough	834,054	967,511	16.0
Alachua	181,596	216,249	19.1	Manatee	211,707	253,207	19.6
Bradford	22,515	25,500	13.3	Pasco	281,131	326,494	16.1
Columbia	42,613	56,514	32.6	Pinellas	851,659	898,784	5.5
Dixie	10,585	13,478	27.3	District 9	909,327	1,135,035	24.8
Gilchrist	9,667	13,406	38.7	Charlotte	110,975	136,773	23.2
Hamilton	10,930	14,376	31.5	Collier	152,099	219,685	44.4
Lafayette	5,578	6,961	24.8	Glades	7,591	9,867	30.0
Madison	16,569	19,632	18.5	Hendry	25,773	30,552	18.5
Suwannee	26,780	34,386	28.4	Lee	335,113	417,114	24.5
Taylor	17,111	19,836	15.9	Sarasota	277,776	321,044	15.6
Union	10,252	13,833	34.9	District 10	1,204,782	1,460,194	21.2
District 4	1,018,984	1,214,379	19.2	Indian River	90,208	109,579	21.5
Baker	18,486	21,879	18.4	Martin	100,900	121,514	20.4
Clay	105,986	139,631	31.7	Palm Beach	863,503	1,042,196	20.7
Duval	672,971	762,846	13.4	St. Lucie	150,171	186,905	24.5
Flagler	28,701	45,818	59.6	District 11	3,270,749	3,704,021	13.2
Nassau	43,941	57,381	30.6	Broward	1,255,531	1,490,289	18.7
Putnam	65,070	72,883	12.0	Miami-Dade	1,937,194	2,126,702	9.8
St. Johns	83,829	113,941	35.9	Monroe	78,024	87,030	11.5

Note: Data are for planning district boundaries as defined in May 1999. See map.

Source: University of Florida, Bureau of Economic and Business Research, Population Program, Florida *Estimates of Population, April 1, 1999.* Census data from U.S., Bureau of the Census.

University of Florida   **Bureau of Economic and Business Research**

Planning Districts

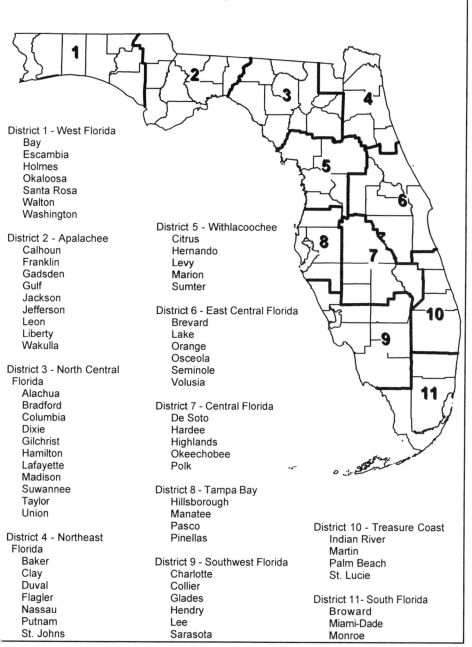

District 1 - West Florida
  Bay
  Escambia
  Holmes
  Okaloosa
  Santa Rosa
  Walton
  Washington

District 2 - Apalachee
  Calhoun
  Franklin
  Gadsden
  Gulf
  Jackson
  Jefferson
  Leon
  Liberty
  Wakulla

District 3 - North Central
Florida
  Alachua
  Bradford
  Columbia
  Dixie
  Gilchrist
  Hamilton
  Lafayette
  Madison
  Suwannee
  Taylor
  Union

District 4 - Northeast
Florida
  Baker
  Clay
  Duval
  Flagler
  Nassau
  Putnam
  St. Johns

District 5 - Withlacoochee
  Citrus
  Hernando
  Levy
  Marion
  Sumter

District 6 - East Central Florida
  Brevard
  Lake
  Orange
  Osceola
  Seminole
  Volusia

District 7 - Central Florida
  De Soto
  Hardee
  Highlands
  Okeechobee
  Polk

District 8 - Tampa Bay
  Hillsborough
  Manatee
  Pasco
  Pinellas

District 9 - Southwest Florida
  Charlotte
  Collier
  Glades
  Hendry
  Lee
  Sarasota

District 10 - Treasure Coast
  Indian River
  Martin
  Palm Beach
  St. Lucie

District 11- South Florida
  Broward
  Miami-Dade
  Monroe

Table 1.67. HEALTH DISTRICTS: CENSUS COUNTS, APRIL 1, 1990, AND POPULATION
ESTIMATES, APRIL 1, 1999, IN THE STATE, DEPARTMENT OF HEALTH
DISTRICTS, AND COUNTIES OF FLORIDA

District and county	Census 1990	Estimates 1999	Percentage change 1990 to 1999	District and county	Census 1990	Estimates 1999	Percentage change 1990 to 1999
Florida	12,938,071	15,322,040	18.4	District 6	1,045,761	1,220,718	16.7
District 1	515,942	634,299	22.9	Hillsborough	834,054	967,511	16.0
Escambia	262,798	301,613	14.8	Manatee	211,707	253,207	19.6
Okaloosa	143,777	179,589	24.9	District 7	1,471,718	1,832,655	24.5
Santa Rosa	81,608	112,631	38.0	Brevard	398,978	474,803	19.0
Walton	27,759	40,466	45.8	Orange	677,491	846,328	24.9
District 2	530,904	651,737	22.8	Osceola	107,728	157,376	46.1
Bay	126,994	150,119	18.2	Seminole	287,521	354,148	23.2
Calhoun	11,011	14,117	28.2	District 8	933,192	1,163,473	24.7
Franklin	8,967	10,872	21.2	Charlotte	110,975	136,773	23.2
Gadsden	41,116	51,478	25.2	Collier	152,099	219,685	44.4
Gulf	11,504	14,403	25.2	De Soto	23,865	28,438	19.2
Holmes	15,778	18,899	19.8	Glades	7,591	9,867	30.0
Jackson	41,375	49,469	19.6	Hendry	25,773	30,552	18.5
Jefferson	11,296	14,424	27.7	Lee	335,113	417,114	24.5
Leon	192,493	237,637	23.5	Sarasota	277,776	321,044	15.6
Liberty	5,569	8,048	44.5	District 9	863,503	1,042,196	20.7
Madison	16,569	19,632	18.5	Palm Beach	863,503	1,042,196	20.7
Taylor	17,111	19,836	15.9	District 10	1,255,531	1,490,289	18.7
Wakulla	14,202	20,648	45.4	Broward	1,255,531	1,490,289	18.7
Washington	16,919	22,155	30.9	District 11	2,015,218	2,213,732	9.9
District 3	411,498	500,994	21.7	Miami-Dade	1,937,194	2,126,702	9.8
Alachua	181,596	216,249	19.1	Monroe	78,024	87,030	11.5
Bradford	22,515	25,500	13.3	District 12	399,438	472,633	18.3
Columbia	42,613	56,514	32.6	Flagler	28,701	45,818	59.6
Dixie	10,585	13,478	27.3	Volusia	370,737	426,815	15.1
Gilchrist	9,667	13,406	38.7	District 13	573,144	746,409	30.2
Hamilton	10,930	14,376	31.5	Citrus	93,513	114,898	22.9
Lafayette	5,578	6,961	24.8	Hernando	101,115	127,392	26.0
Levy	25,912	33,408	28.9	Lake	152,104	203,863	34.0
Putnam	65,070	72,883	12.0	Marion	194,835	249,433	28.0
Suwannee	26,780	34,386	28.4	Sumter	31,577	50,823	60.9
Union	10,252	13,833	34.9	District 14	493,313	578,441	17.3
District 4	925,213	1,095,678	18.4	Hardee	19,499	22,594	15.9
Baker	18,486	21,879	18.4	Highlands	68,432	81,143	18.6
Clay	105,986	139,631	31.7	Polk	405,382	474,704	17.1
Duval	672,971	762,846	13.4	District 15	370,906	453,508	22.3
Nassau	43,941	57,381	30.6	Indian River	90,208	109,579	21.5
St. Johns	83,829	113,941	35.9	Martin	100,900	121,514	20.4
District 5	1,132,790	1,225,278	8.2	Okeechobee	29,627	35,510	19.9
Pasco	281,131	326,494	16.1	St. Lucie	150,171	186,905	24.5
Pinellas	851,659	898,784	5.5				

Note: See map of districts in Section 7.00.

Source: University of Florida, Bureau of Economic and Business Research, Population Program, *Florida Estimates of Population, April 1, 1999.* Census data from U.S. Bureau of the Census.

University of Florida   **Bureau of Economic and Business Research**

Table 1.69. POPULOUS CITIES: CENSUS COUNTS, APRIL 1, 1980 AND 1990
AND POPULATION ESTIMATES APRIL 1, 1999, IN THE 1999
MOST POPULOUS CITIES OF FLORIDA

City	Total population Census 1980	Census 1990	Estimates 1999	Rank 1980	Rank 1990	Rank 1999	Percentage change 1990 to 1999
Jacksonville (Duval)	540,920	635,230	719,072	1	1	1	13.2
Miami	346,865	358,648	365,204	2	2	2	1.8
Tampa	271,577	280,015	297,505	3	3	3	6.2
St. Petersburg	238,647	240,318	242,690	4	4	4	1.0
Hialeah	145,254	188,008	211,201	6	5	5	12.3
Orlando	128,291	164,674	184,639	7	6	6	12.1
Ft. Lauderdale	153,279	149,238	148,971	5	7	7	-0.2
Tallahassee	81,548	124,773	145,610	11	8	8	16.7
Hollywood	121,323	121,720	127,660	8	9	9	4.9
Pembroke Pines	35,776	65,566	120,091	34	21	10	83.2
Coral Springs	37,349	78,864	111,724	27	13	11	41.7
Clearwater	85,170	98,784	104,281	10	10	12	5.6
Gainesville	81,371	85,075	101,405	12	12	13	19.2
Cape Coral	32,103	74,991	96,760	41	14	14	29.0
Miami Beach	96,298	92,639	94,012	9	11	15	1.5
Port St. Lucie	14,690	55,761	83,254	72	27	16	49.3
West Palm Beach 1/	63,305	67,764	81,132	13	17	17	19.7
Plantation	48,501	66,814	80,434	20	18	18	20.4
Palm Bay	18,560	62,543	79,131	61	22	19	26.5
Sunrise	39,681	65,683	78,413	25	20	20	19.4
Lakeland	47,406	70,576	77,487	21	16	21	9.8
Pompano Beach	52,618	72,411	74,403	17	15	22	2.8
Melbourne	46,536	60,034	70,685	22	25	23	17.7
Boca Raton	49,447	61,486	69,994	18	24	24	13.8
Largo	57,958	65,910	68,372	14	19	25	3.7
Davie	20,515	47,143	67,529	58	32	26	43.2
Daytona Beach	54,176	61,991	65,102	16	23	27	5.0
Deltona 2/	(X)	(X)	61,191	(X)	(X)	28	(X)
Pensacola	57,619	59,198	60,994	15	26	29	3.0
Boynton Beach	35,624	46,284	55,483	35	34	30	19.9
Miramar	32,813	40,663	54,583	39	41	31	34.2
Delray Beach	34,329	47,184	53,589	36	31	32	13.6
Tamarac	29,376	44,822	52,413	45	36	33	16.9
Sarasota	48,868	50,897	51,659	19	28	34	1.5
Deerfield Beach	39,193	46,997	51,269	26	33	35	9.1

(X) Not applicable.
1/ Special census conducted since 1990.
2/ Not incorporated in 1990.
Note: Data are for the 35 most populous cities in the state. Changes in city populations include the effects of annexations.

Source: University of Florida, Bureau of Economic and Business Research, Population Program, *Florida Estimates of Population, April 1, 1999.* Census data from U.S. Bureau of the Census.

University of Florida   **Bureau of Economic and Business Research**

Table 1.72. COMPONENTS OF CHANGE: COMPONENTS OF POPULATION CHANGE IN THE STATE AND COUNTIES OF FLORIDA, APRIL 1, 1990 TO APRIL 1, 1999

County	Total population Census 1990	Total population Estimates 1999	Population change 1990 to 1999	Natural increase Number	Natural increase Per-centage	Net migration Number	Net migration Per-centage
Florida	12,938,071	15,322,040	2,383,969	418,994	17.6	1,964,975	82.4
Alachua	181,596	216,249	34,653	11,078	32.0	23,575	68.0
Baker	18,486	21,879	3,393	1,298	38.3	2,095	61.7
Bay	126,994	150,119	23,125	7,632	33.0	15,493	67.0
Bradford	22,515	25,500	2,985	596	20.0	2,389	80.0
Brevard	398,978	474,803	75,825	9,587	12.6	66,238	87.4
Broward	1,255,531	1,490,289	234,758	36,946	15.7	197,812	84.3
Calhoun	11,011	14,117	3,106	76	2.4	3,030	97.6
Charlotte	110,975	136,773	25,798	-7,358	0.0	33,156	100.0
Citrus	93,513	114,898	21,385	-6,665	0.0	28,050	100.0
Clay	105,986	139,631	33,645	7,417	22.0	26,228	78.0
Collier	152,099	219,685	67,586	6,591	9.8	60,995	90.2
Columbia	42,613	56,514	13,901	1,994	14.3	11,907	85.7
De Soto	23,865	28,438	4,573	986	21.6	3,587	78.4
Dixie	10,585	13,478	2,893	284	9.8	2,609	90.2
Duval	672,971	762,846	89,875	55,233	61.5	34,642	38.5
Escambia	262,798	301,613	38,815	14,868	38.3	23,947	61.7
Flagler	28,701	45,818	17,117	-1,099	0.0	18,216	100.0
Franklin	8,967	10,872	1,905	-62	0.0	1,967	100.0
Gadsden	41,116	51,478	10,362	2,747	26.5	7,615	73.5
Gilchrist	9,667	13,406	3,739	218	5.8	3,521	94.2
Glades	7,591	9,867	2,276	-29	0.0	2,305	100.0
Gulf	11,504	14,403	2,899	26	0.9	2,873	99.1
Hamilton	10,930	14,376	3,446	425	12.3	3,021	87.7
Hardee	19,499	22,594	3,095	2,174	70.2	921	29.8
Hendry	25,773	30,552	4,779	3,313	69.3	1,466	30.7
Hernando	101,115	127,392	26,277	-5,919	0.0	32,196	100.0
Highlands	68,432	81,143	12,711	-2,669	0.0	15,380	100.0
Hillsborough	834,054	967,511	133,457	55,909	41.9	77,548	58.1
Holmes	15,778	18,899	3,121	0	0.0	3,121	100.0
Indian River	90,208	109,579	19,371	-2,050	0.0	21,421	100.0
Jackson	41,375	49,469	8,094	617	7.6	7,477	92.4
Jefferson	11,296	14,424	3,128	316	10.1	2,812	89.9
Lafayette	5,578	6,961	1,383	218	15.8	1,165	84.2
Lake	152,104	203,863	51,759	-2,869	0.0	54,628	100.0
Lee	335,113	417,114	82,001	1,292	1.6	80,709	98.4
Leon	192,493	237,637	45,144	14,066	31.2	31,078	68.8

See footnotes at end of table.   Continued . . .

University of Florida   **Bureau of Economic and Business Research**

Table 1.72. COMPONENTS OF CHANGE: COMPONENTS OF POPULATION CHANGE IN THE STATE AND COUNTIES OF FLORIDA, APRIL 1, 1990 TO APRIL 1, 1999 (Continued)

County	Total population Census 1990	Total population Estimates 1999	Popula- tion change 1990 to 1999	Natural increase Number	Per- centage	Net migration Number	Per- centage
Levy	25,912	33,408	7,496	81	1.1	7,415	98.9
Liberty	5,569	8,048	2,479	236	9.5	2,243	90.5
Madison	16,569	19,632	3,063	435	14.2	2,628	85.8
Manatee	211,707	253,207	41,500	-1,584	0.0	43,084	100.0
Marion	194,835	249,433	54,598	27	0.0	54,571	100.0
Martin	100,900	121,514	20,614	-1,802	0.0	22,416	100.0
Miami-Dade	1,937,194	2,126,702	189,508	127,610	67.3	61,898	32.7
Monroe	78,024	87,030	9,006	1,791	19.9	7,215	80.1
Nassau	43,941	57,381	13,440	2,741	20.4	10,699	79.6
Okaloosa	143,777	179,589	35,812	12,097	33.8	23,715	66.2
Okeechobee	29,627	35,510	5,883	1,651	28.1	4,232	71.9
Orange	677,491	846,328	168,837	60,155	35.6	108,682	64.4
Osceola	107,728	157,376	49,648	8,386	16.9	41,262	83.1
Palm Beach	863,503	1,042,196	178,693	11,071	6.2	167,622	93.8
Pasco	281,131	326,494	45,363	-13,365	0.0	58,728	100.0
Pinellas	851,659	898,784	47,125	-25,622	0.0	72,747	100.0
Polk	405382	474704	69322	15213	21.9	54109	78.1
Putnam	65,070	72,883	7,813	1,241	15.9	6,572	84.1
St. Johns	83,829	113,941	30,112	1,910	6.3	28,202	93.7
St. Lucie	150171	186905	36734	3624	9.9	33110	90.1
Santa Rosa	81,608	112,631	31,023	6,273	20.2	24,750	79.8
Sarasota	277,776	321,044	43,268	-15,988	0.0	59,256	100.0
Seminole	287521	354148	66627	20070	30.1	46557	69.9
Sumter	31,577	50,823	19,246	-276	0.0	19,522	100.0
Suwannee	26,780	34,386	7,606	-46	0.0	7,652	100.0
Taylor	17111	19836	2725	442	16.2	2283	83.8
Union	10,252	13,833	3,581	-76	0.0	3,657	100.0
Volusia	370,737	426,815	56,078	-5,692	0.0	61,770	100.0
Wakulla	14202	20648	6446	647	10.0	5799	90.0
Walton	27,759	40,466	12,707	325	2.6	12,382	97.4
Washington	16,919	22,155	5,236	232	4.4	5,004	95.6

1/ Natural increase is calculated as the difference between the number of births and the number of deaths; net migration is calculated as the difference between total population change and natural increase.

Note: Vital statistics data for persons of unreported residence are included only in the entries for the state. For this reason, natural increase and net migration columns may not add to their state totals.

Source: University of Florida, Bureau of Economic and Business Research, Population Program, *Florida Estimates of Population, April 1, 1999*. Census data from U.S. Bureau of the Census.

University of Florida   **Bureau of Economic and Business Research**

Table 1.74. MIGRATION: STATE-TO-STATE MIGRATION FLOWS FOR FLORIDA
1990 AND 1996

State	1990	1996	Percentage change	State	1990	1996	Percentage change
From Alabama	11,443	11,727	2.5	From Indiana	11,292	10,956	-3.0
To Alabama	13,515	12,784	-5.4	To Indiana	8,971	7,539	-16.0
Net	-2,072	-1,057	(X)	Net	2,321	3,417	(X)
From Alaska	1,058	1,293	22.2	From Iowa	2,052	2,281	11.2
To Alaska	1,246	1,110	-10.9	To Iowa	2,037	1,565	-23.2
Net	-188	183	(X)	Net	15	716	(X)
From Arizona	4,046	4,233	4.6	From Kansas	2,581	2,755	6.7
To Arizona	3,702	5,426	46.6	To Kansas	2,075	2,212	6.6
Net	344	-1,193	(X)	Net	506	543	(X)
From Arkansas	2,610	2,663	2.0	From Kentucky	7,107	6,454	-9.2
To Arkansas	2,658	2,348	-11.7	To Kentucky	6,665	5,704	-14.4
Net	-48	315	(X)	Net	442	750	(X)
From California	24,697	20,295	-17.8	From Louisiana	6,686	5,905	-11.7
To California	18,766	16,426	-12.5	To Louisiana	6,180	4,472	-27.6
Net	5,931	3,869	(X)	Net	506	1,433	(X)
From Colorado	5,074	5,724	12.8	From Maine	4,175	3,498	-16.2
To Colorado	5,184	6,899	33.1	To Maine	2,097	2,403	14.6
Net	-110	-1,175	(X)	Net	2,078	1,095	(X)
From Connecticut	14,025	11,292	-19.5	From Maryland	11,943	12,618	5.7
To Connecticut	4,990	4,862	-2.6	To Maryland	6,940	6,683	-3.7
Net	9,035	6,430	(X)	Net	5,003	5,935	(X)
From Delaware	1,546	1,655	7.1	From Massachusetts	21,179	14,088	-33.5
To Delaware	977	911	-6.8	To Massachusetts	6,164	7,471	21.2
Net	569	744	(X)	Net	15,015	6,617	(X)
From District of Columbia	942	908	-3.6	From Michigan	17,711	15,712	-11.3
To District of Columbia	741	705	-4.9	To Michigan	10,947	10,329	-5.6
Net	201	203	(X)	Net	6,764	5,383	(X)
From Georgia	25,952	28,671	10.5	From Minnesota	3,477	4,066	16.9
To Georgia	32,032	38,393	19.9	To Minnesota	2,957	2,570	-13.1
Net	-6,080	-9,722	(X)	Net	520	1,496	(X)
From Hawaii	2,527	2,285	-9.6	From Mississippi	4,659	4,342	-6.8
To Hawaii	1,760	1,778	1.0	To Mississippi	4,455	4,314	-3.2
Net	767	507	(X)	Net	204	28	(X)
From Idaho	525	628	19.6	From Missouri	5,609	5,842	4.2
To Idaho	952	780	-18.1	To Missouri	4,636	4,545	-2.0
Net	-427	-152	(X)	Net	973	1,297	(X)
From Illinois	18,868	18,112	-4.0	From Montana	474	1,430	201.7
To Illinois	11,665	9,849	-15.6	To Montana	594	635	6.9
Net	7,203	8,263	(X)	Net	-120	795	(X)

See footnotes at end of table.

Continued . . .

University of Florida   **Bureau of Economic and Business Research**

Table 1.74. MIGRATION: STATE-TO-STATE MIGRATION FLOWS FOR FLORIDA
1990 AND 1996 (Continued)

State	1990	1996	Per-cent-age change	State	1990	1996	Per-cent-age change
From Nebraska	1,324	1,568	18.4	From Rhode Island	4,281	3,346	-21.8
To Nebraska	862	949	10.1	To Rhode Island	1,527	1,482	-2.9
Net	462	619	(X)	Net	2,754	1,864	(X)
From Nevada	1,880	2,226	18.4	From South Carolina	8,726	8,596	-1.5
To Nevada	2,748	3,275	19.2	To South Carolina	10,245	9,887	-3.5
Net	-868	-1,049	(X)	Net	-1,519	-1,291	(X)
From New Hampshire	5,681	3,471	-38.9	From South Dakota	586	472	-19.5
To New Hampshire	1,614	2,113	30.9	To South Dakota	440	442	0.5
Net	4,067	1,358	(X)	Net	146	30	(X)
From New Jersey	32,120	26,725	-16.8	From Tennessee	10,075	12,979	28.8
To New Jersey	9,585	9,324	-2.7	To Tennessee	12,400	13,262	7.0
Net	22,535	17,401	(X)	Net	-2,325	-283	(X)
From New Mexico	1,771	2,231	26.0	From Texas	23,693	21,532	-9.1
To New Mexico	1,682	1,941	15.4	To Texas	24,678	24,054	-2.5
Net	89	290	(X)	Net	-985	-2,522	(X)
From New York	71,586	61,722	-13.8	From Utah	867	1,358	56.6
To New York	21,103	18,990	-10.0	To Utah	1,141	1,313	15.1
Net	50,483	42,732	(X)	Net	-274	45	(X)
From North Carolina	15,295	16,789	9.8	From Vermont	1,725	1,349	-21.8
To North Carolina	19,204	23,851	24.2	To Vermont	797	915	14.8
Net	-3,909	-7,062	(X)	Net	928	434	(X)
From North Dakota	467	587	25.7	From Virginia	19,501	20,725	6.3
To North Dakota	321	320	-0.3	To Virginia	14,987	14,865	-0.8
Net	146	267	(X)	Net	4,514	5,860	(X)
From Ohio	21,803	20,816	-4.5	From Washington	3,536	4,237	19.8
To Ohio	16,175	13,004	-19.6	To Washington	4,214	4,567	8.4
Net	5,628	7,812	(X)	Net	-678	-330	(X)
From Oklahoma	3,324	3,133	-5.7	From West Virginia	2,999	2,803	-6.5
To Oklahoma	2,826	2,802	-0.8	To West Virginia	3,096	2,006	-35.2
Net	498	331	(X)	Net	-97	797	(X)
From Oregon	1,241	1,579	27.2	From Wisconsin	5,022	5,752	14.5
To Oregon	1,476	1,683	14.0	To Wisconsin	4,003	3,298	-17.6
Net	-235	-104	(X)	Net	1,019	2,454	(X)
From Pennsylvania	20,814	20,604	-1.0	From Wyoming	401	498	24.2
To Pennsylvania	12,596	10,293	-18.3	To Wyoming	454	398	-12.3
Net	8,218	10,311	(X)	Net	-53	100	(X)

(X) Not applicable.
Note: Data are based on individual income tax returns filed by citizens and resident aliens with the IRS and exclude migration exchanges with abroad.

Source: U.S., Department of the Treasury, Internal Revenue Service, unpublished data. Data prepared by University of Florida, Bureau of Economic and Business Research.

University of Florida   **Bureau of Economic and Business Research**

Table 1.75. MIGRATION: MIGRATION FLOWS IN THE STATE AND COUNTIES OF FLORIDA, 1993 THROUGH 1996

County	Net migration				In-migration				Out-migration			
	1993	1994	1995	1996	1993	1994	1995	1996	1993	1994	1995	1996
Florida 1/	108,462	101,017	87,668	116,784	429,374	437,102	418,838	444,531	320,912	336,085	331,170	327,747
Alachua	556	888	64	-530	11,176	12,178	11,844	11,432	10,620	11,290	11,780	11,962
Baker	54	112	163	97	936	951	996	1,140	882	839	833	1,043
Bay	1,179	1,450	1,318	879	9,384	10,488	10,448	9,303	8,205	9,038	9,130	8,424
Bradford	-78	60	160	219	1,123	1,139	1,233	1,142	1,201	1,079	1,073	923
Brevard	4,595	5,020	2,077	3,597	23,749	25,097	22,766	23,110	19,154	20,077	20,689	19,513
Broward	16,337	13,343	11,127	14,112	75,028	75,477	73,212	76,166	58,691	62,134	62,085	62,054
Calhoun	147	40	261	-96	584	489	681	493	437	449	420	589
Charlotte	3,214	3,533	2,184	2,791	8,985	9,670	8,330	9,165	5,771	6,137	6,146	6,374
Citrus	2,775	3,390	2,756	2,478	7,004	7,630	7,386	7,174	4,229	4,240	4,630	4,696
Clay	1,841	2,607	3,275	3,110	11,895	13,089	13,605	13,858	10,054	10,482	10,330	10,748
Collier	4,043	3,435	3,418	5,154	13,827	13,900	13,398	14,812	9,784	10,465	9,980	9,658
Columbia	879	791	730	730	2,945	3,149	3,087	3,305	2,066	2,358	2,357	2,575
De Soto	43	-96	-202	-65	1,752	1,580	1,372	1,520	1,709	1,676	1,574	1,585
Dixie	271	290	187	273	751	766	731	798	480	476	544	525
Duval	-2,063	126	7,370	860	38,968	41,658	45,950	41,358	41,031	41,532	38,580	40,498
Escambia	-863	-501	1,486	2,501	16,059	17,699	18,256	19,664	16,922	18,200	16,770	17,163
Flagler	1,619	2,184	1,661	2,183	3,208	3,716	3,402	4,105	1,589	1,532	1,741	1,922
Franklin	70	83	93	10	470	500	493	475	400	417	400	465
Gadsden	-76	131	91	-134	2,064	2,093	2,132	2,058	2,140	1,962	2,041	2,192
Gilchrist	255	292	365	291	850	936	964	991	595	644	599	700
Glades	134	-56	70	55	697	554	558	773	563	610	488	718
Gulf	54	228	5	89	683	813	735	761	629	585	730	672
Hamilton	11	175	252	-5	602	618	738	652	591	443	486	657
Hardee	-316	-429	-563	-235	1,491	1,376	1,175	1,264	1,807	1,805	1,738	1,499

See footnotes at end of table.

Continued . . .

Table 1.75. MIGRATION: MIGRATION FLOWS IN THE STATE AND COUNTIES OF FLORIDA, 1993 THROUGH 1996 (Continued)

County	Net migration				In-migration				Out-migration			
	1993	1994	1995	1996	1993	1994	1995	1996	1993	1994	1995	1996
Hendry	24	-497	-503	-146	2,783	2,460	2,171	2,180	2,759	2,957	2,674	2,326
Hernando	3,477	3,061	2,851	3,398	8,501	8,617	8,337	8,413	5,024	5,556	5,486	5,015
Highlands	1,347	1,390	918	875	5,196	5,215	4,568	4,575	3,849	3,825	3,650	3,700
Hillsborough	-1,476	1,378	1,220	5,656	45,410	47,724	47,378	49,492	46,886	46,346	46,158	43,836
Holmes	203	353	24	289	1,028	1,085	941	1,228	825	732	917	939
Indian River	1,494	1,557	833	2,035	5,762	6,022	5,518	6,506	4,268	4,465	4,685	4,471
Jackson	5	275	390	2	2,000	2,158	2,255	2,002	1,995	1,883	1,865	2,000
Jefferson	93	45	162	105	667	648	719	824	574	603	557	719
Lafayette	46	156	-61	-90	306	448	328	224	260	292	389	314
Lake	4,962	6,203	6,359	6,617	12,856	14,398	14,466	15,570	7,894	8,195	8,107	8,953
Lee	6,749	6,742	4,677	5,158	22,238	23,179	21,078	22,478	15,489	16,437	16,401	17,320
Leon	1,220	971	-1,541	-930	12,698	13,198	12,519	12,078	11,478	12,227	14,060	13,008
Levy	583	550	399	718	1,992	2,073	1,919	2,360	1,409	1,523	1,520	1,642
Liberty	129	59	27	117	326	288	318	358	197	229	291	241
Madison	87	-5	80	5	720	665	704	710	633	670	624	705
Manatee	3,268	4,133	2,864	3,112	16,490	17,338	16,983	15,204	13,222	13,205	14,119	12,092
Marion	5,452	5,415	4,231	5,049	14,048	14,473	13,625	14,601	8,596	9,058	9,394	9,552
Martin	1,957	1,721	2,149	2,199	8,372	8,516	8,496	9,012	6,415	6,795	6,347	6,813
Miami-Dade	-15,360	-21,363	-23,310	-24,237	46,606	44,799	42,084	41,481	61,966	66,162	65,394	65,718
Monroe	-509	-145	-592	-415	6,985	6,822	6,207	6,198	7,494	6,967	6,799	6,613
Nassau	697	724	972	1,320	3,599	3,596	3,738	4,151	2,902	2,872	2,766	2,831
Okaloosa	1,055	963	871	84	13,241	15,155	14,771	12,911	12,186	14,192	13,900	12,827
Okeechobee	-342	-142	-92	44	2,291	2,228	2,048	1,878	2,633	2,370	2,140	1,834
Orange	2,025	365	3,549	8,041	51,843	54,365	54,553	57,568	49,818	54,000	51,004	49,527

See footnotes at end of table.

Continued . . .

Table 1.75. MIGRATION: MIGRATION FLOWS IN THE STATE AND COUNTIES OF FLORIDA, 1993 THROUGH 1996 (Continued)

County	Net migration				In-migration				Out-migration			
	1993	1994	1995	1996	1993	1994	1995	1996	1993	1994	1995	1996
Osceola	1,535	2,601	2,831	3,026	11,217	12,794	12,569	13,905	9,682	10,193	9,738	10,879
Palm Beach	15,031	11,529	8,746	12,554	53,062	53,807	51,104	52,884	38,031	42,278	42,358	40,330
Pasco	6,369	6,335	6,334	6,840	20,864	21,821	21,661	21,226	14,495	15,486	15,327	14,386
Pinellas	5,616	7,823	4,701	5,022	43,358	46,811	44,813	41,335	37,742	38,988	40,112	36,313
Polk	4,325	4,564	3,358	4,470	21,403	22,415	21,175	22,299	17,078	17,851	17,817	17,829
Putnam	408	395	288	363	3,048	3,166	3,079	3,366	2,640	2,771	2,791	3,003
St. Johns	2,030	1,974	2,380	3,724	7,980	8,076	8,103	9,756	5,950	6,102	5,723	6,032
St. Lucie	2,469	2,316	2,379	2,557	11,120	11,520	11,049	11,374	8,651	9,204	8,670	8,817
Santa Rosa	2,683	3,368	2,842	3,072	9,350	10,443	9,878	10,444	6,667	7,075	7,036	7,372
Sarasota	4,924	5,351	3,404	4,574	18,460	19,159	18,168	18,084	13,536	13,808	14,764	13,510
Seminole	3,451	2,678	2,185	3,775	28,457	28,731	27,710	29,105	25,006	26,053	25,525	25,330
Sumter	571	680	371	1,384	2,065	2,319	2,172	3,072	1,494	1,639	1,801	1,688
Suwannee	460	496	773	654	1,801	2,150	2,129	2,028	1,341	1,654	1,356	1,374
Taylor	-55	57	104	-2	707	791	822	771	762	734	718	773
Union	23	33	209	90	544	558	652	629	521	525	443	539
Volusia	5,532	4,487	4,405	5,088	21,764	22,082	21,448	22,436	16,232	17,595	17,043	17,348
Wakulla	425	447	1,989	971	1,362	1,306	2,884	1,825	937	859	895	854
Walton	744	564	699	904	2,230	2,217	2,252	2,413	1,486	1,653	1,553	1,509
Washington	199	334	213	364	1,139	1,335	1,245	1,293	940	1,001	1,032	929

1/ County flow data will not add to state flow data due to the method in which the data are aggregated.
Note: Data are based on individual income tax returns filed by citizens and resident aliens with the IRS and exclude migration exchanges with abroad. Only returns for which the social security number matches from one year to the next are used. Data are affected by births, deaths, marriages, reporting error, and changes in tax filing status. IRS migration data tend to understate activity in Florida due to its large elderly population and foreign immigration. See Table 1.76 for migration exchanges with abroad.

Source: U.S., Department of the Treasury, Internal Revenue Service, unpublished data. Data prepared by University of Florida, Bureau of Economic and Business Research.

Table 1.76. MIGRATION: EXCHANGED MIGRANTS BY AREA OF EXCHANGE IN THE
COUNTIES OF FLORIDA, 1996

	In-migration Percentage from--				Out-migration Percentage from--			
County	Total	Other Florida counties	Other states 1/	Abroad	Total	Other Florida counties	Other states 1/	Abroad
Alachua	11,879	59.0	37.2	3.8	12,113	57.4	41.3	1.2
Baker	1,140	68.9	31.1	0.0	1,043	69.4	30.6	0.0
Bay	9,987	26.7	66.5	6.8	9,189	30.4	61.3	8.3
Bradford	1,142	76.4	23.6	0.0	923	77.4	22.6	0.0
Brevard	23,948	30.5	66.0	3.5	20,167	34.7	62.1	3.2
Broward	77,176	51.4	47.3	1.3	62,955	53.9	44.7	1.4
Calhoun	493	76.3	23.7	0.0	589	65.9	34.1	0.0
Charlotte	9,253	34.0	65.0	1.0	6,424	52.3	46.9	0.8
Citrus	7,239	40.3	58.8	0.9	4,756	52.8	45.9	1.3
Clay	14,450	52.8	43.1	4.1	11,062	56.5	40.7	2.8
Collier	15,025	34.4	64.2	1.4	9,734	43.9	55.3	0.8
Columbia	3,305	64.8	35.2	0.0	2,599	65.7	33.4	0.9
De Soto	1,520	55.7	44.3	0.0	1,585	55.2	44.8	0.0
Dixie	798	74.3	25.7	0.0	525	78.5	21.5	0.0
Duval	43,818	35.1	59.3	5.6	42,308	42.6	53.1	4.3
Escambia	21,035	21.9	71.6	6.5	18,127	30.3	64.4	5.3
Flagler	4,138	39.8	59.4	0.8	1,956	57.5	40.7	1.7
Franklin	475	51.6	48.4	0.0	465	63.2	36.8	0.0
Gadsden	2,075	72.9	26.3	0.8	2,192	72.9	27.1	0.0
Gilchrist	991	76.8	23.2	0.0	700	79.3	20.7	0.0
Glades	773	70.9	29.1	0.0	718	70.8	29.2	0.0
Gulf	761	51.9	48.1	0.0	672	66.2	33.8	0.0
Hamilton	652	60.4	39.6	0.0	657	64.2	35.8	0.0
Hardee	1,264	59.0	41.0	0.0	1,499	54.4	45.6	0.0
Hendry	2,180	66.5	33.5	0.0	2,348	50.0	49.1	0.9
Hernando	8,481	48.3	50.9	0.8	5,052	56.1	43.2	0.7
Highlands	4,600	47.5	52.0	0.5	3,750	51.7	47.0	1.3
Hillsborough	51,103	39.3	57.5	3.2	44,914	48.1	49.5	2.4
Holmes	1,228	64.7	35.3	0.0	939	62.0	38.0	0.0
Indian River	6,578	44.0	54.9	1.1	4,508	47.6	51.6	0.8
Jackson	2,039	60.2	38.0	1.8	2,000	54.3	45.7	0.0
Jefferson	824	74.0	26.0	0.0	719	69.8	30.2	0.0
Lafayette	224	77.2	22.8	0.0	314	73.9	26.1	0.0
Lake	15,662	55.1	44.4	0.6	9,024	57.3	41.9	0.8
Lee	22,705	29.7	69.3	1.0	17,492	44.5	54.5	1.0
Leon	12,391	55.9	41.6	2.5	13,151	57.6	41.3	1.1

See footnote at end of table.   Continued . . .

University of Florida   **Bureau of Economic and Business Research**

Table 1.76. MIGRATION: EXCHANGED MIGRANTS BY AREA OF EXCHANGE IN THE
COUNTIES OF FLORIDA, 1996 (Continued)

County	Total	In-migration Percentage from-- Other Florida counties	Other states 1/	Abroad	Total	Out-migration Percentage from-- Other Florida counties	Other states 1/	Abroad
Levy	2,360	70.5	29.5	0.0	1,642	71.0	29.0	0.0
Liberty	358	79.1	20.9	0.0	241	34.6	15.4	0.0
Madison	710	64.8	35.2	0.0	705	62.6	37.4	0.0
Manatee	15,348	43.6	55.4	0.9	12,204	51.1	48.0	0.9
Marion	14,772	44.7	54.2	1.2	9,623	51.4	47.9	0.7
Martin	9,101	53.4	45.6	1.0	6,863	59.4	39.9	0.7
Miami-Dade	43,756	37.3	57.5	5.2	67,524	61.9	35.4	2.7
Monroe	6,443	37.9	58.3	3.8	6,818	47.3	49.7	3.0
Nassau	4,214	52.8	45.7	1.5	2,861	52.0	46.9	1.0
Okaloosa	14,549	20.6	68.2	11.3	14,312	27.1	62.6	10.4
Okeechobee	1,878	60.8	39.2	0.0	1,834	52.2	47.8	0.0
Orange	59,082	48.7	48.7	2.6	50,686	56.5	41.3	2.3
Osceola	14,119	48.8	49.7	1.5	11,110	62.4	35.5	2.1
Palm Beach	53,886	40.3	57.9	1.9	40,903	45.6	53.0	1.4
Pasco	21,387	51.6	47.7	0.8	14,507	57.1	42.1	0.8
Pinellas	42,322	33.8	63.9	2.3	36,722	46.2	52.6	1.1
Polk	22,496	45.1	54.0	0.9	18,057	46.3	52.5	1.3
Putnam	3,412	63.1	35.6	1.3	3,041	63.4	35.3	1.2
St. Johns	9,853	53.1	45.9	1.0	6,112	59.1	39.5	1.3
St. Lucie	11,475	51.7	47.4	0.9	8,872	57.8	41.6	0.6
Santa Rosa	11,074	44.8	49.5	5.7	7,683	45.2	50.7	4.0
Sarasota	18,480	36.7	61.2	2.1	13,625	52.0	47.2	0.8
Seminole	29,490	57.4	41.3	1.3	25,675	64.4	34.3	1.3
Sumter	3,093	52.9	46.4	0.7	1,688	66.6	33.4	0.0
Suwannee	2,028	75.6	24.4	0.0	1,374	71.4	28.6	0.0
Taylor	771	60.3	39.7	0.0	773	66.4	33.6	0.0
Union	629	79.7	20.3	0.0	539	82.0	18.0	0.0
Volusia	22,759	41.7	56.9	1.4	17,540	46.1	52.8	1.1
Wakulla	1,825	80.8	19.2	0.0	854	69.1	30.9	0.0
Walton	2,433	52.5	46.7	0.8	1,509	57.2	42.8	0.0
Washington	1,293	73.3	26.7	0.0	929	71.0	29.0	0.0

1/ Includes the District of Columbia.

Source: U.S., Department of the Treasury, Internal Revenue Service, unpublished data. Data prepared by University of Florida, Bureau of Economic and Business Research.

University of Florida   **Bureau of Economic and Business Research**

Table 1.77. COUNTY RANKINGS AND DENSITY: POPULATION ESTIMATES, RANK
PERCENTAGE DISTRIBUTION, LAND AREA, AND DENSITY IN THE STATE
AND COUNTIES OF FLORIDA, APRIL 1, 1999

County	Number	Rank in state	Per-centage of state	Land area 1/ (square miles)	Persons per square mile	Rank in state
		Estimates			*Density*	
Florida	15,322,040	(X)	100.00	53,937.2	284	(X)
Alachua	216,249	20	1.41	874.3	247	20
Baker	21,879	52	0.14	585.3	37	52
Bay	150,119	25	0.98	763.7	197	27
Bradford	25,500	49	0.17	293.2	87	40
Brevard	474,803	8	3.10	1,018.5	466	11
Broward	1,490,289	2	9.73	1,208.9	1,233	2
Calhoun	14,117	60	0.09	567.4	25	60
Charlotte	136,773	27	0.89	693.7	197	25
Citrus	114,898	30	0.75	583.6	197	26
Clay	139,631	26	0.91	601.1	232	21
Collier	219,685	19	1.43	2,025.5	108	33
Columbia	56,514	38	0.37	797.2	71	42
De Soto	28,438	48	0.19	637.3	45	47
Dixie	13,478	62	0.09	704.1	19	63
Duval	762,846	7	4.98	773.9	986	5
Escambia	301,613	15	1.97	663.6	454	12
Flagler	45,818	42	0.30	485.0	94	36
Franklin	10,872	64	0.07	534.0	20	62
Gadsden	51,478	39	0.34	516.2	100	35
Gilchrist	13,406	63	0.09	348.9	38	49
Glades	9,867	65	0.06	773.5	13	66
Gulf	14,403	58	0.09	565.1	25	59
Hamilton	14,376	59	0.09	514.9	28	57
Hardee	22,594	50	0.15	637.4	35	53
Hendry	30,552	47	0.20	1,152.7	27	58
Hernando	127,392	28	0.83	478.3	266	18
Highlands	81,143	35	0.53	1,028.5	79	41
Hillsborough	967,511	4	6.31	1,051.0	921	7
Holmes	18,899	56	0.12	482.6	39	48
Indian River	109,579	33	0.72	503.3	218	23
Jackson	49,469	41	0.32	915.8	54	44
Jefferson	14,424	57	0.09	597.8	24	61
Lafayette	6,961	67	0.05	542.8	13	65
Lake	203,863	21	1.33	953.1	214	24
Lee	417,114	11	2.72	803.6	519	10
Leon	237,637	18	1.55	666.8	356	15

See footnotes at end of table.   Continued . . .

University of Florida   **Bureau of Economic and Business Research**

Table 1.77. COUNTY RANKINGS AND DENSITY: POPULATION ESTIMATES, RANK
PERCENTAGE DISTRIBUTION, LAND AREA, AND DENSITY IN THE STATE
AND COUNTIES OF FLORIDA, APRIL 1, 1999 (Continued)

County	Number	Estimates Rank in state	Per- centage of state	Land area 1/ (square miles)	Density Persons per square mile	Rank in state
Levy	33,408	46	0.22	1,118.4	30	55
Liberty	8,048	66	0.05	835.9	10	67
Madison	19,632	55	0.13	692.0	28	56
Manatee	253,207	16	1.65	741.2	342	16
Marion	249,433	17	1.63	1,579.0	158	30
Martin	121,514	29	0.79	555.7	219	22
Miami-Dade	2,126,702	1	13.88	1,944.5	1,094	4
Monroe	87,030	34	0.57	997.3	87	39
Nassau	57,381	37	0.37	651.6	88	38
Okaloosa	179,589	23	1.17	935.8	192	28
Okeechobee	35,510	44	0.23	774.3	46	46
Orange	846,328	6	5.52	907.6	932	6
Osceola	157,376	24	1.03	1,322.0	119	31
Palm Beach	1,042,196	3	6.80	1,974.2	528	9
Pasco	326,494	13	2.13	745.0	438	13
Pinellas	898,784	5	5.87	280.2	3,208	1
Polk	474,704	9	3.10	1,874.9	253	19
Putnam	72,883	36	0.48	722.2	101	34
St. Johns	113,941	31	0.74	609.0	187	29
St. Lucie	186,905	22	1.22	572.5	326	17
Santa Rosa	112,631	32	0.74	1,015.8	111	32
Sarasota	321,044	14	2.10	571.8	562	8
Seminole	354,148	12	2.31	308.2	1,149	3
Sumter	50,823	40	0.33	545.7	93	37
Suwannee	34,386	45	0.22	687.7	50	45
Taylor	19,836	54	0.13	1,042.0	19	64
Union	13,833	61	0.09	240.3	58	43
Volusia	426,815	10	2.79	1,105.9	386	14
Wakulla	20,648	53	0.13	606.7	34	54
Walton	40,466	43	0.26	1,057.7	38	50
Washington	22,155	51	0.14	579.9	38	51

(X) Not applicable.
1/ Land area figures represent the total area in the counties in 1990 and are not adjusted for lands which cannot be developed (government-owned parks or reserves) or are uninhabitable (swamps or marshes).

Source: University of Florida, Bureau of Economic and Business Research, Population Program, *Florida Estimates of Population, April 1, 1999.* Census data from U.S. Bureau of the Census.

University of Florida   **Bureau of Economic and Business Research**

Table 1.80. INSTITUTIONAL POPULATION: ESTIMATED NUMBER OF INMATES AND PATIENTS IN THE STATE, COUNTIES, AND MUNICIPALITIES OF FLORIDA, APRIL 1, 1999

County or city	Total	County or city	Total
Florida	92,178	Gilchrist	771
Incorporated	14,346	Glades	724
Unincorporated	77,832	Gulf	1,199
Alachua	1,785	Hamilton	1,796
Gainesville	1,306	Hardee	1,278
Unincorporated	479	Hendry	1,274
Baker	1,563		
Bay	966	Hernando	522
Panama City	176	Highlands	24
Unincorporated	790	Hillsborough	1,400
Bradford	3,627	Tampa	882
Starke	12	Unincorporated	518
Unincorporated	3,615		
		Holmes	1,313
Brevard	1,358	Indian River	391
Rockledge	16	Jackson	4,741
Titusville	48	Malone	1,282
Unincorporated	1,294	Marianna	288
Broward	1,674	Unincorporated	3,171
Cooper City	6		
Davie	14	Jefferson	899
Ft. Lauderdale	105	Lafayette	816
Hollywood	10	Lake	992
Lauderhill	47		
Oakland Park	8	Lee	634
Pembroke Pines	411	Cape Coral	30
Pompano Beach	132	Ft. Myers	97
Unincorporated	941	Unincorporated	507
Calhoun	1,282	Leon	1,481
Charlotte	1,276	Tallahassee	1,352
Punta Gorda	30	Unincorporated	129
Unincorporated	1,246	Levy	290
Citrus	116		
		Liberty	1,365
Collier	124	Madison	1,442
Columbia	1,913	Madison	42
Lake City	386	Unincorporated	1,400
Unincorporated	1,527		
		Manatee	384
De Soto	1,833	Bradenton	204
Dixie	927	Palmetto	25
Duval (Jacksonville)	490	Unincorporated	155
Escambia	1,926		
Pensacola	74	Marion	2,422
Unincorporated	1,852	Belleview	29
Franklin	190	Ocala	94
		Unincorporated	2,299
Gadsden	2,563		
Chatahoochee	1,398	Martin	1,421
Gretna	798	Stuart	83
Quincy	367	Unincorporated	1,338

Continued . . .

See footnote at end of table.

University of Florida **Bureau of Economic and Business Research**

Table 1.80. INSTITUTIONAL POPULATION: ESTIMATED NUMBER OF INMATES AND PATIENTS
IN THE STATE, COUNTIES, AND MUNICIPALITIES
OF FLORIDA, APRIL 1, 1999 (Continued)

County or city	Total	County or city	Total
Miami-Dade	8,853	Putnam	404
Miami	2,031	St. Lucie	175
North Miami	148	Ft. Pierce	102
Unincorporated	6,674	Unincorporated	73
Monroe	64	Santa Rosa	1,408
Nassau	48	Milton	36
Fernandina Beach	24	Unincorporated	1,372
Unincorporated	24		
Okaloosa	1,688	Sarasota	34
Okeechobee	1,484	Sarasota	16
		Unincorporated	18
Orange	2,682		
Eatonville	64	Seminole	221
Orlando	155	Casselberry	6
Winter Park	33	Sanford	87
Unincorporated	2,430	Unincorporated	128
Osceola	203		
		Sumter	5,072
Palm Beach	3,518	Taylor	1,149
Boca Raton	12	Union	3,925
Lantana	133	Raiford	20
West Palm Beach	230	Unincorporated	3,905
Unincorporated	3,143		
Pasco	737	Volusia	1,571
San Antonio	26	Daytona Beach	56
Unincorporated	711	Ormond Beach	6
		Unincorporated	1,509
Pinellas	1,084	Wakulla	787
Clearwater	60		
Largo	78	Walton	1,418
Pinellas Park	30	De Funiak Springs	40
St. Petersburg	230	Unincorporated	1,378
Unincorporated	686		
Polk	3,182	Washington	1,279
Bartow	335	Caryville	102
Lakeland	4	Vernon	40
Unincorporated	2,843	Unincorporated	1,137

Note: Inmates and patients residing in federal and state government-operated institutions and considered nonresidents of the local area for revenue-sharing purposes. Unless city data are specified separately for a county, county data are for unincorporated areas.

Source: University of Florida, Bureau of Economic and Business Research, Population Program, *Florida Estimates of Population, April 1, 1999.*

University of Florida   **Bureau of Economic and Business Research**

Table 1.81. HOMELESS POPULATION: ESTIMATED DAILY HOMELESS POPULATION
IN THE STATE AND COUNTIES OF FLORIDA, FISCAL YEAR 1997-98

District	Homeless coalition	County	Estimated daily homeless population
Florida			**52,557**
1	Escambia Coalition on the Homeless	Escambia, Santa Rosa	1,147
	Okaloosa Coalition on the Homeless	Okaloosa, Walton	512
2	Bay County Homeless and Hunger Coalition	Bay, Calhoun, Gulf, Holmes, Jackson, Washington	1,500
	Tallahassee Coalition for the Homeless	Leon, Franklin, Gadsden, Liberty, Jefferson, Madison, Wakulla, Taylor	1,530
3	District 3 Homeless Coalition	Alachua, Bradford, Columbia Dixie, Gilchrist, Hamilton, Lafayette, Levy, Putnam, Suwannee, Union	1,812
4	The Emergency Services and Homeless Coalition of Jacksonville	Baker, Clay, Duval, Nassau, St. Johns	3,119
5	Pinellas County Coalition for the Homeless	Pinellas	3,216
	Coalition for the Homeless of Pasco County	Pasco	558
6	Hillsborough County Homeless Coalition	Hillsborough	3,666
	Community Coalition on Homelessness	Manatee	1,202
7	Homeless Services Network of Orange County	Orange, Osceola, Seminole	5,600
	Coalition for the Hungry and Homeless of Brevard County	Brevard	2,503
8	District 8 Homeless Coalition	Charlotte, Collier, De Soto, Glades, Hendry, Lee, Sarasota	4,387
9	Homeless Coalition of Palm Beach County	Palm Beach	4,000
10	Broward Coalition for the Homeless	Broward	5,260
11	Miami-Dade County Homeless Trust	Miami-Dade, Monroe	5,200
12	Volusia/Flagler County Homeless Coalition	Flagler, Volusia	1,772
13	Mid-Florida Homeless Coalition	Citrus, Hernando, Lake, Marion, Sumter	2,610
14	Homeless Coalition of Polk County	Polk	1,114
15	Coalition for the Homeless of Indian River County	Indian River, Martin, Okeechobee, St. Lucie	1,849

Source: State of Florida, Department of Children and Families, *Annual Report on Homeless Conditions in Florida,* 1999, prepublication release.

University of Florida   **Bureau of Economic and Business Research**

Table 1.83. PLANNING DISTRICTS: POPULATION ESTIMATES, APRIL 1, 1999, AND PROJECTIONS SPECIFIED YEARS APRIL 1, 2005 THROUGH 2030, IN THE STATE AND COMPREHENSIVE PLANNING DISTRICTS OF FLORIDA

(in thousands, rounded to hundreds)

District	Estimates 1999	Projections 2005	2010	2020	2025	2030
Florida	15,322.0					
Low		15,708.7	16,373.4	17,901.2	18,697.4	19,429.2
Medium		16,882.8	18,121.3	20,725.0	22,014.1	23,198.0
High		17,892.9	19,716.5	23,411.2	25,197.4	26,835.8
District 1	825.5					
Low		821.0	818.9	784.8	750.9	704.0
Medium		911.9	980.6	1,125.9	1,198.1	1,264.5
High		1,013.4	1,166.8	1,513.4	1,704.1	1,902.4
District 2	421.1					
Low		412.3	404.5	368.0	340.2	305.6
Medium		467.1	502.5	571.6	605.4	636.3
High		527.2	612.0	797.0	898.3	1,003.3
District 3	434.2					
Low		433.0	429.7	403.8	382.0	354.0
Medium		482.9	518.8	588.4	622.7	654.0
High		538.0	619.2	795.2	890.7	990.2
District 4	1,214.4					
Low		1,210.7	1,209.4	1,164.9	1,118.1	1,052.9
Medium		1,339.2	1,438.8	1,649.7	1,754.5	1,850.9
High		1,483.5	1,703.6	2,201.8	2,476.1	2,761.9
District 5	576.0					
Low		583.3	587.8	563.0	532.2	487.6
Medium		659.6	727.1	869.7	941.0	1,006.6
High		746.6	890.6	1,221.7	1,407.4	1,602.6
District 6	2,463.3					
Low		2,490.4	2,509.0	2,431.6	2,326.6	2,172.0
Medium		2,782.3	3,037.6	3,578.9	3,848.1	4,096.2
High		3,114.8	3,657.0	4,899.0	5,588.8	6,310.6
District 7	642.4					
Low		639.4	638.1	619.8	601.3	575.7
Medium		699.7	744.1	837.3	882.9	924.6
High		767.4	866.1	1,084.3	1,201.8	1,322.3
District 8	2,446.0					
Low		2,397.0	2,371.2	2,270.2	2,190.3	2,087.5
Medium		2,622.8	2,764.2	3,062.4	3,209.3	3,343.5
High		2,871.1	3,208.0	3,949.5	4,347.7	4,756.5
District 9	1,135.0					
Low		1,141.1	1,143.1	1,089.1	1,029.8	946.1
Medium		1,283.5	1,401.8	1,652.3	1,777.5	1,892.8
High		1,444.8	1,702.7	2,295.6	2,626.8	2,974.6
District 10	1,460.2					
Low		1,479.3	1,495.2	1,474.7	1,434.2	1,370.5
Medium		1,630.3	1,765.4	2,050.6	2,191.9	2,321.8
High		1,803.1	2,084.0	2,717.2	3,064.8	3,425.2
District 11	3,704.0					
Low		3,660.6	3,640.5	3,516.3	3,405.5	3,256.3
Medium		4,003.5	4,240.6	4,737.9	4,983.1	5,207.0
High		4,384.8	4,925.4	6,117.7	6,760.1	7,419.9

Note: See footnote on Table 1.84.

Source: University of Florida, Bureau of Economic and Business Research, Population Program, *Florida Population Studies,* February 2000, Volume 32, No. 2. Bulletin No. 126.

University of Florida   **Bureau of Economic and Business Research**

Table 1.84. PROJECTIONS: POPULATION ESTIMATES, APRIL 1, 1999, AND PROJECTIONS
SPECIFIED YEARS APRIL 1, 2005 THROUGH 2030, IN THE STATE
AND COUNTIES OF FLORIDA

(in thousands, rounded to hundreds)

County	Estimates 1999	2005	2010	2020	2025	2030
Florida	15,322.0					
Low		15,708.7	16,373.4	17,901.2	18,697.4	19,429.2
Medium		16,882.8	18,121.3	20,725.0	22,014.1	23,198.0
High		17,892.9	19,716.5	23,411.2	25,197.4	26,835.8
Alachua	216.2					
Low		216.7	217.6	209.8	202.6	193.2
Medium		237.1	253.6	282.8	296.7	309.4
High		259.6	294.5	364.9	402.2	440.3
Baker	21.9					
Low		21.4	20.9	19.3	18.0	16.3
Medium		24.1	25.9	29.6	31.4	33.0
High		27.2	31.4	41.0	46.2	51.7
Bay	150.1					
Low		150.3	150.9	148.0	144.3	138.7
Medium		164.3	175.5	199.0	210.6	221.2
High		180.1	204.1	257.5	286.4	316.1
Bradford	25.5					
Low		24.7	24.1	22.6	21.6	20.4
Medium		27.1	28.2	30.6	31.8	32.8
High		29.6	32.7	39.3	42.9	46.5
Brevard	474.8					
Low		480.2	485.6	482.2	472.4	456.2
Medium		524.5	564.2	647.3	688.3	725.9
High		575.2	656.9	838.9	937.7	1,039.6
Broward	1,490.3					
Low		1,501.1	1,512.7	1,493.9	1,460.1	1,407.2
Medium		1,640.0	1,758.5	2,007.0	2,129.5	2,241.4
High		1,798.1	2,046.6	2,599.1	2,898.5	3,206.5
Calhoun	14.1					
Low		13.6	13.1	11.4	10.1	8.4
Medium		15.9	17.3	20.2	21.8	23.1
High		18.4	21.9	30.0	34.7	39.5
Charlotte	136.8					
Low		137.9	138.4	132.4	125.5	115.5
Medium		155.5	170.4	201.9	217.7	232.2
High		175.5	207.6	281.5	322.7	365.8
Citrus	114.9					
Low		114.8	114.7	108.8	102.7	94.2
Medium		129.5	141.3	166.1	178.4	189.7
High		146.1	172.1	231.2	264.1	298.4
Clay	139.6					
Low		143.6	146.1	142.8	136.4	126.5
Medium		161.7	179.5	217.1	235.9	253.4
High		182.7	219.2	303.4	350.8	400.6
Collier	219.7					
Low		225.8	228.0	211.4	191.4	163.0
Medium		262.9	297.8	372.5	410.1	445.2
High		305.5	380.1	557.4	659.4	768.4

See footnote at end of table.   Continued . . .

University of Florida   **Bureau of Economic and Business Research**

Table 1.84. PROJECTIONS: POPULATION ESTIMATES, APRIL 1, 1999, AND PROJECTIONS
SPECIFIED YEARS APRIL 1, 2005 THROUGH 2030, IN THE STATE
AND COUNTIES OF FLORIDA (Continued)

(in thousands, rounded to hundreds)

County	Estimates 1999	Projections 2005	2010	2020	2025	2030
Columbia	56.5					
Low		57.6	57.6	54.8	51.8	47.6
Medium		65.0	71.0	83.6	89.9	95.7
High		73.4	86.4	116.4	133.1	150.6
De Soto	28.4					
Low		29.0	29.0	28.3	27.5	26.4
Medium		31.7	33.7	38.0	40.2	42.1
High		34.7	39.2	49.2	54.6	60.1
Dixie	13.5					
Low		13.2	12.8	11.1	9.8	8.2
Medium		15.4	16.8	19.8	21.3	22.7
High		17.8	21.3	29.4	33.9	38.7
Duval	762.8					
Low		748.4	740.4	708.7	683.7	651.6
Medium		818.9	863.1	956.1	1,001.9	1,043.7
High		896.4	1,001.7	1,233.0	1,357.3	1,484.9
Escambia	301.6					
Low		294.1	289.8	275.5	265.0	251.8
Medium		321.9	338.1	372.0	388.7	403.9
High		352.2	392.1	479.2	526.0	573.9
Flagler	45.8					
Low		49.4	51.3	49.6	45.6	39.3
Medium		57.4	66.8	86.9	97.1	106.6
High		66.9	85.6	130.7	156.9	185.1
Franklin	10.9					
Low		10.6	10.3	9.5	8.8	8.0
Medium		11.9	12.8	14.5	15.4	16.2
High		13.4	15.5	20.1	22.7	25.3
Gadsden	51.5					
Low		50.3	49.5	45.9	42.9	39.0
Medium		56.8	61.1	70.2	74.7	78.8
High		64.0	74.3	97.5	110.2	123.4
Gilchrist	13.4					
Low		13.6	13.5	12.2	11.0	9.3
Medium		15.8	17.7	21.6	23.6	25.5
High		18.4	22.5	32.3	37.8	43.8
Glades	9.9					
Low		9.4	9.0	7.5	6.6	5.4
Medium		11.0	11.8	13.4	14.3	15.0
High		12.7	14.9	19.9	22.6	25.5
Gulf	14.4					
Low		14.2	13.2	10.7	9.2	7.5
Medium		16.7	17.5	19.3	20.1	20.9
High		19.2	22.1	28.3	31.7	35.2
Hamilton	14.4					
Low		14.2	13.6	11.6	10.2	8.4
Medium		16.6	17.9	20.6	22.0	23.3
High		19.2	22.7	30.6	35.0	39.6

See footnote at end of table.   Continued . . .

University of Florida   **Bureau of Economic and Business Research**

Florida Statistical Abstract 2000

Table 1.84. PROJECTIONS: POPULATION ESTIMATES, APRIL 1, 1999, AND PROJECTIONS
SPECIFIED YEARS APRIL 1, 2005 THROUGH 2030, IN THE STATE
AND COUNTIES OF FLORIDA (Continued)

(in thousands, rounded to hundreds)

County	Estimates 1999	Projections 2005	2010	2020	2025	2030
Hardee	22.6					
Low		20.5	19.0	15.7	13.9	12.1
Medium		23.2	23.6	24.4	24.7	25.0
High		26.1	28.4	33.3	35.7	38.3
Hendry	30.6					
Low		30.6	30.6	29.8	29.0	27.8
Medium		33.4	35.6	40.1	42.4	44.4
High		36.6	41.4	51.9	57.6	63.4
Hernando	127.4					
Low		129.8	131.6	127.6	121.5	112.4
Medium		146.3	161.7	194.2	210.4	225.3
High		165.2	197.4	271.1	312.4	355.8
Highlands	81.1					
Low		81.7	82.4	81.4	79.6	76.8
Medium		89.3	95.8	109.4	116.1	122.3
High		97.9	111.5	141.7	158.1	174.9
Hillsborough	967.5					
Low		964.5	966.0	944.7	919.3	882.7
Medium		1,054.3	1,124.0	1,270.8	1,342.8	1,408.5
High		1,155.2	1,306.9	1,643.5	1,824.8	2,011.3
Holmes	18.9					
Low		18.0	17.4	15.5	14.3	12.8
Medium		20.4	21.5	23.9	25.0	26.1
High		22.9	26.0	33.0	36.7	40.5
Indian River	109.6					
Low		108.7	108.0	101.6	95.5	87.4
Medium		122.7	133.1	155.2	166.2	176.2
High		138.4	162.0	215.8	245.7	276.8
Jackson	49.5					
Low		49.4	49.0	47.0	45.4	43.2
Medium		54.0	57.1	63.4	66.4	69.2
High		59.2	66.2	81.7	90.0	98.5
Jefferson	14.4					
Low		13.4	12.6	10.4	9.0	7.3
Medium		15.6	16.6	18.6	19.6	20.4
High		18.1	20.9	27.4	30.9	34.6
Lafayette	7.0					
Low		7.0	6.8	5.9	5.2	4.4
Medium		8.2	9.0	10.5	11.3	12.0
High		9.5	11.4	15.7	18.0	20.6
Lake	203.9					
Low		210.8	215.3	211.8	202.8	188.5
Medium		237.4	264.4	321.7	350.5	377.2
High		268.3	323.0	450.0	521.6	597.0
Lee	417.1					
Low		417.8	417.8	397.1	375.1	344.6
Medium		471.3	514.5	605.9	651.4	693.3
High		531.7	626.7	843.9	964.7	1,091.1

See footnote at end of table.

Continued . . .

University of Florida

Bureau of Economic and Business Research

Florida Statistical Abstract 2000

Table 1.84. PROJECTIONS: POPULATION ESTIMATES, APRIL 1, 1999, AND PROJECTIONS
SPECIFIED YEARS APRIL 1, 2005 THROUGH 2030, IN THE STATE
AND COUNTIES OF FLORIDA (Continued)

(in thousands, rounded to hundreds)

County	Estimates 1999	Projections 2005	2010	2020	2025	2030
Leon	237.6					
Low		232.0	228.5	208.4	193.3	174.7
Medium		262.3	282.5	319.8	337.8	354.3
High		295.3	342.7	442.8	497.0	553.2
Levy	33.4					
Low		33.6	33.7	32.2	30.5	28.1
Medium		37.9	41.5	49.2	53.0	56.5
High		42.8	50.6	68.5	78.5	89.0
Liberty	8.0					
Low		7.7	7.3	5.8	4.6	3.2
Medium		9.3	10.2	12.2	13.2	14.2
High		11.0	13.5	19.3	22.7	26.2
Madison	19.6					
Low		18.7	18.1	16.2	14.9	13.3
Medium		21.2	22.4	24.9	26.1	27.2
High		23.8	27.1	34.3	38.2	42.3
Manatee	253.2					
Low		257.0	260.4	259.5	254.7	246.3
Medium		280.7	302.4	348.2	370.9	391.7
High		307.8	352.3	451.5	505.6	561.3
Marion	249.4					
Low		252.8	254.8	245.3	233.0	215.1
Medium		285.0	313.4	373.7	403.9	431.7
High		321.7	382.2	521.4	599.2	681.0
Martin	121.5					
Low		120.4	119.5	112.1	105.4	96.4
Medium		135.9	147.3	171.4	183.3	194.4
High		153.2	179.2	238.3	271.0	305.2
Miami-Dade	2,126.7					
Low		2,074.8	2,044.4	1,943.2	1,869.2	1,776.7
Medium		2,270.8	2,384.8	2,623.9	2,741.8	2,849.5
High		2,485.2	2,765.9	3,380.7	3,710.4	4,048.5
Monroe	87.0					
Low		84.7	83.4	79.2	76.2	72.4
Medium		92.7	97.3	107.0	111.8	116.1
High		101.5	112.9	137.9	151.2	164.9
Nassau	57.4					
Low		58.5	59.4	58.0	55.3	51.2
Medium		66.0	73.0	88.2	95.7	102.6
High		74.5	89.1	123.3	142.2	162.1
Okaloosa	179.6					
Low		178.4	177.5	167.2	157.4	144.1
Medium		201.4	218.7	255.4	273.6	290.4
High		227.1	266.2	355.3	404.7	456.3
Okeechobee	35.5					
Low		35.4	35.2	34.2	33.2	31.8
Medium		38.7	41.0	46.1	48.5	50.8
High		42.4	47.7	59.5	65.9	72.4

See footnote at end of table.   Continued . . .

University of Florida   **Bureau of Economic and Business Research**

Table 1.84. PROJECTIONS: POPULATION ESTIMATES, APRIL 1, 1999, AND PROJECTIONS
SPECIFIED YEARS APRIL 1, 2005 THROUGH 2030, IN THE STATE
AND COUNTIES OF FLORIDA (Continued)

(in thousands, rounded to hundreds)

County	Estimates 1999	2005	2010	2020	2025	2030
			Proj	ections		
Orange	846.3					
Low		856.7	862.9	829.9	787.9	726.7
Medium		965.9	1,061.6	1,264.4	1,365.7	1,459.3
High		1,090.4	1,294.4	1,763.6	2,026.0	2,301.4
Osceola	157.4					
Low		162.7	164.8	153.6	139.4	118.8
Medium		189.4	215.2	270.5	298.3	324.3
High		220.1	274.7	405.0	480.0	560.3
Palm Beach	1,042.2					
Low		1,062.2	1,079.2	1,081.0	1,062.9	1,029.9
Medium		1,159.7	1,253.0	1,449.5	1,546.8	1,636.1
High		1,272.3	1,460.1	1,880.6	2,110.0	2,346.8
Pasco	326.5					
Low		326.8	328.4	322.9	314.9	302.9
Medium		357.2	381.9	434.0	459.6	482.9
High		391.5	444.3	561.7	625.0	690.1
Pinellas	898.8					
Low		848.7	816.4	743.1	701.4	655.6
Medium		930.6	955.9	1,009.4	1,036.0	1,060.4
High		1,016.6	1,104.5	1,292.8	1,392.3	1,493.8
Polk	474.7					
Low		472.8	472.5	460.2	447.1	428.6
Medium		516.8	550.0	619.4	653.4	684.4
High		566.3	639.3	800.6	887.5	976.6
Putnam	72.9					
Low		71.1	70.1	66.9	64.4	61.3
Medium		77.9	81.8	90.2	94.4	98.2
High		85.2	94.9	116.3	127.8	139.6
St. Johns	113.9					
Low		118.3	121.2	119.6	114.7	106.7
Medium		133.2	148.7	181.6	198.1	213.4
High		150.6	181.7	254.1	294.9	337.9
St. Lucie	186.9					
Low		188.0	188.5	180.0	170.4	156.8
Medium		212.0	232.0	274.5	295.6	315.1
High		239.2	282.7	382.5	438.1	496.4
Santa Rosa	112.6					
Low		116.7	119.2	117.4	112.5	104.6
Medium		131.4	146.4	178.3	194.4	209.3
High		148.5	178.9	249.5	289.3	331.3
Sarasota	321.0					
Low		319.6	319.3	310.9	302.2	289.8
Medium		349.4	371.7	418.5	441.6	462.7
High		382.8	432.0	541.0	599.8	660.4
Seminole	354.1					
Low		354.4	354.1	336.2	317.4	291.4
Medium		399.8	436.1	513.0	551.3	586.5
High		451.0	531.2	714.4	816.2	922.8

See footnote at end of table.   Continued . . .

University of Florida   **Bureau of Economic and Business Research**

Table 1.84. PROJECTIONS: POPULATION ESTIMATES, APRIL 1, 1999, AND PROJECTIONS SPECIFIED YEARS APRIL 1, 2005 THROUGH 2030, IN THE STATE AND COUNTIES OF FLORIDA (Continued)

(in thousands, rounded to hundreds)

County	Estimates 1999	Projections 2005	2010	2020	2025	2030
Sumter	50.8					
Low		52.3	53.0	49.1	44.5	37.8
Medium		60.9	69.2	86.5	95.3	103.4
High		70.8	88.3	129.5	153.2	178.4
Suwannee	34.4					
Low		34.7	34.9	33.5	31.7	29.2
Medium		39.1	43.0	51.0	55.1	58.8
High		44.2	52.4	71.2	81.6	92.6
Taylor	19.8					
Low		19.2	18.0	15.4	13.9	12.3
Medium		21.7	22.4	23.9	24.6	25.2
High		24.4	27.0	32.8	35.8	38.9
Union	13.8					
Low		13.4	12.7	10.7	9.3	7.7
Medium		15.7	16.8	19.1	20.3	21.4
High		18.1	21.2	28.3	32.2	36.3
Volusia	426.8					
Low		425.6	426.3	417.9	406.7	390.4
Medium		465.3	496.1	562.0	594.0	623.0
High		509.8	576.8	727.1	807.3	889.5
Wakulla	20.6					
Low		21.1	21.0	18.9	16.9	14.3
Medium		24.6	27.4	33.4	36.4	39.2
High		28.6	34.9	49.9	58.4	67.4
Walton	40.5					
Low		42.4	43.8	43.7	42.1	39.3
Medium		47.8	53.7	66.2	72.6	78.4
High		54.0	65.7	92.8	108.2	124.4
Washington	22.2					
Low		21.1	20.3	17.5	15.3	12.7
Medium		24.7	26.7	31.1	33.2	35.2
High		28.6	33.8	46.1	52.8	59.9

Note: The medium projection is the one we believe is most likely to provide an accurate forecast of future population. The high and low projections indicate the range in which future populations are likely to fall. They do not represent absolute limits to growth; for any county, the future population may be above the high projection or below the low projection. If future distributions of errors are similar to past distributions, however, future populations will fall between high and low projections in approximately two-thirds of Florida's counties. For a detailed description of projection methodology, see the source.

Source: University of Florida, Bureau of Economic and Business Research, Population Program, *Florida Population Studies,* February 2000, Volume 32, No. 2. Bulletin No. 126.

University of Florida   **Bureau of Economic and Business Research**

Florida Statistical Abstract 2000

Table 1.88. VETERANS: ESTIMATED NUMBER OF VETERANS IN CIVIL LIFE BY PERIOD
OF SERVICE IN FLORIDA AND THE UNITED STATES, JULY 1, 1997

(rounded to thousands)

Area	Total vet- erans	Total	World War I	World War II	Korea 1/	Viet- nam 1/	Per- sian Gulf 1/	Be- tween Korea and Viet- nam	Post- Viet- nam	Oth- er
								Peacetime veterans		
		War veterans								
Florida	1,686	1,315	1	560	239	432	85	158	202	11
United States	25,423	19,520	1	6,674	3,585	7,687	1,566	2,750	3,010	141

1/ No prior wartime service.

Source: U.S., Department of Veterans Affairs, *Annual Report of the Secretary of Veterans Affairs, Fiscal Year, 1997.*

Table 1.89. IMMIGRANTS: NEW ARRIVALS BY SPECIFIED PORT OF ENTRY IN FLORIDA
AND IN THE UNITED STATES, FISCAL YEARS 1997 AND 1998

Port of entry	1997	1998	Port of entry	1997	1998
All ports	380,719	357,037	Newark	13,184	4,341
Chicago	21,195	6,203	New York	92,768	21,538
El Paso	49,007	19,081	San Francisco	25,936	10,077
Los Angeles	51,586	15,881	Washington, D.C.	9,225	2,838
Miami	28,141	8,878	Other	89,677	268,200

Note: Data are for federal fiscal years ending September 30.

Table 1.90. IMMIGRANTS: NUMBER ADMITTED BY SPECIFIED COUNTRY OF BIRTH AND
RESIDENCE IN FLORIDA AND THE UNITED STATES, FISCAL YEAR 1998

Country of birth	Florida	United States	Country of birth	Florida	United States
Total 1/	59,965	660,477	Haiti	6,613	13,449
			Honduras	1,594	6,463
Canada	1,075	10,190	India	1,079	36,482
Colombia	3,452	11,836	Jamaica	4,795	15,146
Cuba	14,265	17,375	Mexico	2,788	131,575
Dominican Republic	1,483	20,387	Peru	1,937	10,154

1/ Only admissions of 1,000 or more immigrants to Florida are shown separately.
Note: Data are for fiscal year ending September 30.

Source for Tables 1.89 and 1.90: U.S., Immigration and Naturalization Service, Office of Policy and Planning Statistics Branch, *1998 Statistical Yearbook*, Internet site < http://www.ins.usdoj.gov/graphics/ aboutins/statistics/imm98.pdf> (accessed 18 August 2000)

University of Florida	**Bureau of Economic and Business Research**

Table 1.91. IMMIGRANTS: NUMBER ADMITTED BY COUNTRY OF BIRTH AND INTENDED
RESIDENCE IN SPECIFIED METROPOLITAN AREAS OF FLORIDA, FISCAL YEAR 1998

Country of birth	Ft. Lauder-dale	Miami	Orlando	Tampa-St. Peters-burgh-Clear-water	West Palm Beach-Boca Raton
All countries	9,954	29,242	3,799	4,155	4,951
Bangladesh	61	42	26	32	107
Canada	266	108	95	175	104
China, Peoples Republic	128	115	82	66	65
Columbia	680	2,033	205	194	181
Cuba	390	12,308	220	534	358
Dominican Republic	186	880	148	105	61
Ecuador	150	354	34	32	40
El Salvador	87	211	23	16	25
Germany	70	60	52	73	30
Guatemala	67	242	24	27	56
Haiti	1,496	2,799	339	102	1,335
Honduras	136	1,189	36	51	102
Hong Kong	29	36	14	2	16
India	171	114	150	176	100
Iran	63	62	50	30	18
Jamaica	2,105	1,331	277	118	621
Korea	23	15	25	49	21
Mexico	157	401	235	396	275
Nigeria	42	74	26	34	2
Pakistan	137	178	72	25	17
Peru	420	1103	100	98	96
Philippines	90	82	98	125	52
Poland	38	29	8	34	31
Russia	70	92	25	47	35
Taiwan	19	28	11	8	1
Ukraine	42	17	20	34	17
United Kingdom	197	92	141	134	85
Vietnam	36	16	116	129	37
Other	2,598	5,231	1,147	1,309	1,063

Note: Data are for fiscal year ending September 30 and include legalized aliens.

Source: U.S., Immigration and Naturalization Service, Office of Policy and Planning Statistics Branch,
1998 Statistical Yearbook, Internet site <http://www.ins.usdoj.gov/graphics/aboutins/statistics/imm98.
pdf> (accessed 18 August 2000)

University of Florida   **Bureau of Economic and Business Research**

Table 1.92. REFUGEES: CUBAN AND HAITIAN ENTRANTS BY AGE AND SEX ARRIVING IN FLORIDA FEDERAL FISCAL YEAR 1999

Age	Cuban and Haitian entrants 1/			Cuban entrants 1/			Haitian entrants			Cubans from Havana
	Total	Male	Female	Total	Male	Female	Total	Male	Female	
All ages	4,465	2,734	1,731	3,485	2,113	1,372	980	621	359	13,732
0-4	112	57	55	103	54	49	9	3	6	826
5-9	177	97	80	163	87	76	14	10	4	1,160
10-14	175	96	79	165	90	75	10	6	4	1,166
15-19	196	99	97	137	72	65	59	27	32	851
20-24	535	315	220	373	214	159	162	101	61	1,102
25-29	1,070	661	409	748	452	296	322	209	113	1,913
30-34	828	567	261	624	434	190	204	133	71	1,997
35-39	576	401	175	461	322	139	115	79	36	1,925
40-44	245	160	85	193	127	66	52	33	19	1,044
45-49	195	109	86	174	96	78	21	13	8	854
50-54	167	89	78	161	85	76	6	4	2	545
55-59	98	45	53	94	42	52	4	3	1	279
60-64	37	20	17	37	20	17	0	0	0	39
65 and over	54	18	36	52	18	34	2	0	2	31

1/ Excludes Cuban parolee arrivals from Havana (lottery).
Note: Historically, 85 percent of Cubans arriving in the United States remain in Florida.

Table 1.93. REFUGEES: ARRIVALS BY COUNTRY OF ORIGIN AND BY AGE IN FLORIDA FEDERAL FISCAL YEAR 1999

Country	Total	Less than 10 years	10-24	25-44	45-64	65 and over
Total	22,524	2,985	5,224	11,237	2,880	198
Bosnia	1,545	295	408	642	180	20
Cuba 1/	1,268	146	275	499	283	65
Serbia	656	131	255	184	79	7
Vietnam	328	38	83	155	47	5
Croatia	154	17	48	54	30	5
Sudan	67	21	20	23	2	1
Ukraine	56	10	12	20	9	5
Liberia	51	14	27	6	4	0
Russia	32	3	7	8	9	5
Haiti 1/	30	9	18	3	0	0
Iraq	22	8	1	11	2	0
Somalia	21	1	11	8	1	0
Iran	18	2	8	6	2	0
Afghanistan	13	6	4	3	0	0
Ethiopia	12	0	10	0	2	0
Uzbekistan	10	0	3	2	5	0
Other	18,241	2,284	4,034	9,613	2,225	85

1/ Refugees only. Cuban entrants, Cuba-Havana lottery entrants, and Haitian entrants are included in "other" and are shown separately on Table 1.92.

Source for Tables 1.92 and 1.93: State of Florida, Department of Children and Families, Refugee Programs Administration, *Florida's Refugee and Entrant Arrivals Statistical Report, Federal Fiscal Year 1999*, Internet site <http://www.state.fl.us/cf_web/refugee/pdf/rsr1999.pdf> (accessed 10 August 2000).

University of Florida					**Bureau of Economic and Business Research**

Table 1.94. REFUGEES: REFUGE AND ENTRANT ARRIVALS IN THE STATE AND COUNTIES OF FLORIDA, FEDERAL FISCAL YEARS 1995 THROUGH 1999

County	Total 1995 to 1999	1995	1999	County	Total 1995 to 1999	1995	1999
Florida	99,084	31,466	22,524	Lake	31	10	14
				Lee	249	52	62
Alachua	9	0	2	Leon	17	7	4
Baker	0	0	0	Levy	0	0	0
Bay	2	1	0	Liberty	0	0	0
Bradford	6	6	0	Madison	0	0	0
Brevard	31	11	4	Manatee	35	9	8
Broward	3,390	1,076	855	Marion	12	11	0
Calhoun	0	0	0	Martin	17	4	9
Charlotte	72	4	3	Miami-Dade	76,150	26,104	16,609
Citrus	3	3	0	Monroe	524	205	127
Clay	39	23	2	Nassau	4	0	0
Collier	551	159	143	Okaloosa	18	10	4
Columbia	0	0	0	Okeechobee	5	0	3
De Soto	0	0	0	Orange	1,969	467	524
Dixie	0	0	0	Osceola	80	15	31
Duval	4,254	603	1,139	Palm Beach	2,846	772	934
Escambia	119	42	20	Pasco	868	77	233
Flagler	19	3	6	Pinellas	2,761	437	657
Franklin	0	0	0	Polk	177	57	48
Gadsden	0	0	0	Putnam	4	3	0
Gilchrist	0	0	0	St. Johns	7	7	0
Glades	1	0	0	St. Lucie	75	15	35
Gulf	2	2	0	Santa Rosa	14	5	0
Hamilton	0	0	0	Sarasota	394	69	61
Hardee	5	1	4	Seminole	460	61	93
Hendry	66	28	9	Sumter	0	0	0
Hernando	26	4	12	Suwannee	8	2	3
Highlands	24	14	5	Taylor	0	0	0
Hillsborough	3,634	1,058	839	Union	0	0	0
Holmes	0	0	0	Volusia	70	22	9
Indian River	35	6	13	Wakulla	0	0	0
Jackson	0	0	0	Walton	1	1	0
Jefferson	0	0	0	Washington	0	0	0
Lafayette	0	0	0				

Source: State of Florida, Department of Children and Families, Refugee Programs Administration, *Florida's Refugee and Entrant Arrivals Statistical Report, Federal Fiscal Year 1999*, Internet site <http://www.state.fl.us/cf_web/refugee/pdf/rsr1999.pdf> (accessed 10 August 2000).

University of Florida   **Bureau of Economic and Business Research**

HOUSING

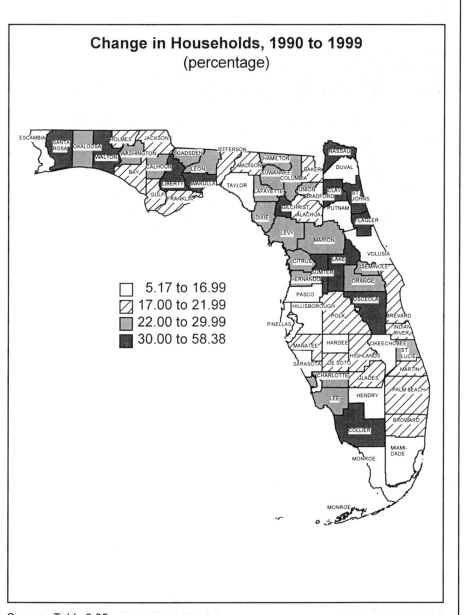

Change in Households, 1990 to 1999
(percentage)

- ☐ 5.17 to 16.99
- ▨ 17.00 to 21.99
- ▦ 22.00 to 29.99
- ▩ 30.00 to 58.38

Source: Table 2.05

SECTION 2.00
HOUSING

TABLES LISTED BY MAJOR HEADINGS

Table 2.01. STATES: ESTIMATES OF HOUSING UNITS AND HOUSEHOLDS IN FLORIDA
OTHER STATES, AND THE UNITED STATES, JULY 1, 1998

(in thousands)

State	Total housing units	Households Total	Persons per--	State	Total housing units	Households Total	Persons per--
Florida	7,007	5,881	2.48	Missouri	2,394	2,089	2.53
				Montana	383	346	2.47
Alabama	1,866	1,663	2.56	Nebraska	711	636	2.54
Alaska	248	215	2.78	Nevada	767	676	2.54
Arizona	2,006	1,762	2.60	New Hampshire	539	450	2.56
Arkansas	1,092	970	2.56	New Jersey	3,237	2,957	2.69
California	12,037	11,446	2.79	New Mexico	747	632	2.70
Colorado	1,722	1,561	2.49	New York	7,455	6,766	2.61
Connecticut	1,379	1,238	2.57	North Carolina	3,367	2,883	2.54
Delaware	326	284	2.54	North Dakota	293	247	2.48
District of				Ohio	4,682	4,285	2.55
Columbia	265	225	2.15	Oklahoma	1,459	1,288	2.52
Georgia	3,184	2,843	2.63	Oregon	1,401	1,286	2.50
Hawaii	440	401	2.87	Pennsylvania	5,229	4,593	2.54
Idaho	503	448	2.69	Rhode Island	431	376	2.53
Illinois	4,777	4,438	2.65	South Carolina	1,683	1,441	2.58
Indiana	2,503	2,231	2.57	South Dakota	322	277	2.55
Iowa	1,208	1,103	2.50	Tennessee	2,318	2,100	2.52
Kansas	1,130	999	2.55	Texas	7,808	7,113	2.71
Kentucky	1,664	1,497	2.56	Utah	731	677	3.06
Louisiana	1,806	1,599	2.66	Vermont	289	231	2.46
Maine	626	490	2.48	Virginia	2,837	2,579	2.55
Maryland	2,091	1,906	2.63	Washington	2,386	2,211	2.52
Massachusetts	2,568	2,349	2.52	West Virginia	794	716	2.48
Michigan	4,168	3,693	2.60	Wisconsin	2,279	1,973	2.58
Minnesota	2,021	1,791	2.58	Wyoming	213	185	2.54
Mississippi	1,106	997	2.68	United States	112,499	101,041	2.61

Note: Detail may not add to totals because of rounding. See Glossary for definition of household.

Source: U.S., Department of Commerce, Bureau of the Census, Population Division, *Estimates of Housing Units, Households, Households by Age of Householder, and Persons per Household: July 1, 1998*, released December 8, 1999, Internet site <http://www.census.gov/population/estimates/housing/sthuhh1.txt> (accessed 18 May 2000).

Florida Statistical Abstract 2000

Table 2.02. STATES: HOMEOWNERSHIP RATES IN THE STATE AND SPECIFIED METROPOLITAN STATISTICAL AREAS (MSAS) OF FLORIDA AND IN OTHER STATES AND THE UNITED STATES 1997, 1998, AND 1999

State and MSA	1997	1998	1999	State and MSA	1997	1998	1999
Florida	66.9	66.9	67.6	Michigan	73.3	74.4	76.5
				Minnesota	75.4	75.4	76.1
Metropolitan Statistical				Mississippi	73.7	75.1	74.9
Area 1/				Missouri	70.5	70.7	72.9
Ft. Lauderdale	67.8	68.3	71.7				
Jacksonville	67.4	67.5	66.5	Montana	67.5	68.6	70.6
Miami	52.7	53.1	53.7	Nebraska	66.7	69.9	70.9
Orlando	62.5	62.3	62.4	Nevada	61.2	61.4	63.7
Tampa-St. Petersburg-				New Hampshire	66.8	69.6	70.2
Clearwater	68.7	70.0	69.9				
West Palm Beach-				New Jersey	63.1	63.1	64.5
Boca Raton	69.2	69.5	73.7	New Mexico	69.6	71.3	72.6
				New York	52.6	52.8	52.8
Other states							
Alabama	71.3	72.9	74.8	North Carolina	70.2	71.3	71.7
Alaska	67.2	66.3	66.4	North Dakota	68.1	68.0	70.1
Arizona	63.0	64.3	66.3	Ohio	69.0	70.7	70.7
Arkansas	66.7	66.7	65.6	Oklahoma	68.5	69.7	71.5
California	55.7	56.0	55.7	Oregon	61.0	63.4	64.3
Colorado	64.1	65.2	68.1	Pennsylvania	73.3	73.9	75.2
Connecticut	68.1	69.3	69.1	Rhode Island	58.7	59.8	60.6
Delaware	69.2	71.0	71.6	South Carolina	74.1	76.6	77.1
Georgia	70.9	71.2	71.3	South Dakota	67.6	67.3	70.7
Hawaii	50.2	52.8	56.6	Tennessee	70.2	71.3	71.9
Idaho	72.3	72.6	70.3	Texas	61.5	62.5	62.9
Illinois	68.1	68.0	67.1	Utah	72.5	73.7	74.7
Indiana	74.1	72.6	72.9	Vermont	69.1	69.1	69.1
Iowa	72.7	72.1	73.9	Virginia	68.4	69.4	71.2
Kansas	66.5	66.7	67.5	Washington	62.9	64.9	64.8
Kentucky	75.0	75.1	73.9	West Virginia	74.6	74.8	74.8
Louisiana	66.4	66.6	66.8	Wisconsin	68.3	70.1	70.9
Maine	74.9	74.6	77.4	Wyoming	67.6	70.0	69.8
Maryland	70.5	68.7	69.6				
Massachusetts	62.3	61.3	60.3	United States	65.7	66.3	66.8

1/ Data for are based on 1990 metropolitan/nonmetropolitan definitions.

Note: Data are based on the American Housing Survey (AHS) conducted by the Bureau of the Census. Homeownership rates are computed by dividing the number of households that are owners by the total number of households.

Source: U.S., Department of Commerce, Bureau of the Census, *Housing Vacancies and Homeownership Annual Statistics: 1999,* Internet site <http://www.census.gov/hhes/www/housing/hvs/annual99/ann99tl4.html> (accessed 9 June 2000).

University of Florida   **Bureau of Economic and Business Research**

Table 2.05. HOUSEHOLDS AND AVERAGE HOUSEHOLD SIZE: ESTIMATES IN THE STATE
AND COUNTIES OF FLORIDA, APRIL 1, 1999

County	Households Esti-mates	Per-centage change 1990 to 1999	Average house-hold size	County	Households Esti-mates	Per-centage change 1990 to 1999	Average house-hold size
Florida	6,045,271	17.7	2.47	Lake	84,330	32.6	2.37
				Lee	173,944	24.1	2.36
Alachua	84,963	19.2	2.40	Leon	92,441	23.5	2.43
Baker	6,731	21.2	2.99	Levy	13,026	29.2	2.51
Bay	57,738	18.0	2.53	Liberty	2,484	45.6	2.69
Bradford	8,157	13.4	2.68	Madison	6,496	17.6	2.75
Brevard	191,348	18.6	2.44	Manatee	107,847	18.4	2.31
Broward	618,278	17.0	2.38	Marion	100,066	28.0	2.45
Calhoun	4,743	25.0	2.64	Martin	51,770	20.3	2.29
Charlotte	59,433	22.7	2.25	Miami-Dade	751,068	8.5	2.78
Citrus	49,843	22.8	2.27	Monroe	37,276	11.0	2.25
Clay	48,263	31.6	2.86	Nassau	21,191	30.9	2.68
Collier	89,380	44.9	2.40	Okaloosa	66,589	24.9	2.60
Columbia	20,172	29.2	2.67	Okeechobee	11,857	16.1	2.74
De Soto	9,835	19.6	2.62	Orange	321,269	26.1	2.57
Dixie	4,902	25.2	2.56	Osceola	56,594	44.6	2.71
Duval	291,877	13.5	2.54	Palm Beach	436,635	19.4	2.34
Escambia	112,993	14.6	2.56	Pasco	141,277	16.1	2.26
Flagler	18,815	58.4	2.42	Pinellas	400,325	5.2	2.19
Franklin	4,316	19.0	2.42	Polk	182,926	17.3	2.53
Gadsden	16,806	25.4	2.88	Putnam	28,058	11.9	2.55
Gilchrist	4,611	40.4	2.65	St. Johns	45,195	35.2	2.45
Glades	3,492	21.0	2.56	St. Lucie	71,820	23.5	2.56
Gulf	5,062	17.1	2.56	Santa Rosa	40,769	36.4	2.69
Hamilton	4,382	25.6	2.81	Sarasota	144,077	14.8	2.19
Hardee	6,994	9.4	2.95	Seminole	132,810	23.4	2.64
Hendry	9,792	16.5	2.99	Sumter	18,087	49.2	2.48
Hernando	52,862	25.0	2.38	Suwannee	12,907	28.6	2.61
Highlands	35,065	18.7	2.28	Taylor	6,977	9.0	2.67
Hillsborough	377,006	16.0	2.51	Union	3,414	28.4	2.90
Holmes	6,793	17.1	2.56	Volusia	175,930	14.7	2.34
Indian River	45,661	20.0	2.36	Wakulla	7,300	40.1	2.69
Jackson	17,344	19.9	2.56	Walton	15,873	40.5	2.44
Jefferson	4,777	20.0	2.78	Washington	8,017	24.4	2.55
Lafayette	2,192	27.4	2.74				

Source: University of Florida, Bureau of Economic and Business Research, Population Program, *Florida Population Studies,* January 2000, Volume 33, No. 1. Bulletin No. 125.

University of Florida   **Bureau of Economic and Business Research**

Table 2.10. HOUSE PURCHASE PRICE: COST OF A HOUSE IN THE COUNTIES OF FLORIDA
1998 AND 1999

(amounts in dollars)

County	1998	1999	Percent-age change	County	1998	1999	Percent-age change
Alachua	84,403	80,481	-4.6	Lee	89,453	84,590	-5.4
Baker	75,202	73,168	-2.7	Leon	84,786	81,869	-3.4
Bay	84,978	82,981	-2.4	Levy	78,553	74,191	-5.6
Bradford	77,516	74,041	-4.5	Liberty	74,556	71,817	-3.7
Brevard	89,637	88,840	-0.9	Madison	72,282	70,646	-2.3
Broward	110,479	117,696	6.5	Manatee	94,464	97,265	3.0
Calhoun	74,261	72,640	-2.2	Marion	82,681	81,405	-1.5
Charlotte	84,131	80,806	-4.0	Martin	94,755	94,235	-0.5
Citrus	79,968	76,300	-4.6	Miami-Dade	116,643	117,904	1.1
Clay	88,225	84,885	-3.8	Monroe	130,897	122,756	-6.2
Collier	109,653	101,814	-7.1	Nassau	83,475	79,382	-4.9
Columbia	80,051	77,626	-3.0	Okaloosa	87,192	83,946	-3.7
De Soto	76,718	73,835	-3.8	Okeechobee	82,982	78,646	-5.2
Dixie	75,528	71,814	-4.9	Orange	95,145	93,968	-1.2
Duval	90,398	89,381	-1.1	Osceola	88,467	85,427	-3.4
Escambia	79,275	79,210	-0.1	Palm Beach	103,926	115,227	10.9
Flagler	86,919	82,199	-5.4	Pasco	85,346	89,481	4.8
Franklin	82,729	79,401	-4.0	Pinellas	106,079	108,519	2.3
Gadsden	76,230	73,956	-3.0	Polk	88,229	87,508	-0.8
Gilchrist	77,618	72,602	-6.5	Putnam	79,995	76,491	-4.4
Glades	83,927	79,763	-5.0	St. Johns	91,451	88,339	-3.4
Gulf	76,953	73,234	-4.8	St. Lucie	83,715	80,358	-4.0
Hamilton	74,624	72,081	-3.4	Santa Rosa	80,200	81,276	1.3
Hardee	78,794	76,629	-2.7	Sarasota	97,821	98,078	0.3
Hendry	79,252	75,751	-4.4	Seminole	93,030	93,041	0.0
Hernando	83,389	79,756	-4.4	Sumter	78,968	74,690	-5.4
Highlands	80,337	79,300	-1.3	Suwannee	78,041	75,213	-3.6
Hillsborough	99,683	100,807	1.1	Taylor	75,092	72,376	-3.6
Holmes	74,074	71,610	-3.3	Union	75,265	73,006	-3.0
Indian River	86,687	81,277	-6.2	Volusia	87,553	83,971	-4.1
Jackson	73,982	72,031	-2.6	Wakulla	76,258	71,372	-6.4
Jefferson	77,390	74,896	-3.2	Walton	84,983	79,159	-6.9
Lafayette	75,651	72,559	-4.1	Washington	72,975	70,943	-2.8
Lake	91,517	88,478	-3.3				

Note: Data represent the cost of a house as measured by the Florida Price Level Index (FPLI) and are based on a sample of records for those single-family residential properties eligible for homestead exemption and which are between 1,200 and 1,600 square feet. The goal of this method is to provide data on homes that would fit on an "average" lot, eliminate upper and lower income levels, and guard against weekend homes and part-time residents. Excludes mobile homes. See discussion of FPLI on Table 24.80.

Source: State of Florida, Department of Education, Office of Education Budget and Management, unpublished data.

University of Florida   **Bureau of Economic and Business Research**

Table 2.20. NURSING HOMES: NUMBER, LICENSED BEDS, AND ROOM RATES IN THE STATE
AGENCY FOR HEALTH CARE ADMINISTRATION (AHCA) REGIONS, AND COUNTIES
OF FLORIDA, 1998

AHCA region and county	Number of homes	Licensed beds	Semi-private rooms	AHCA region and county	Number of homes	Licensed beds	Semi-private rooms
Florida	746	81,986	36,379	North region (Continued)			
				Taylor	1	120	57
North region	221	23,727	10,578	Union	0	0	0
Alachua	8	893	378	Volusia	32	3,453	1,525
Baker	2	188	82	Wakulla	1	120	47
Bay	9	854	320	Walton	2	217	98
Bradford	2	240	110	Washington	1	180	84
Calhoun	2	231	103				
Citrus	8	961	493	Central region	269	28,875	12,830
Clay	11	1,159	613	Brevard	20	2,411	1,086
Columbia	4	280	118	Hardee	2	99	56
Dixie	0	0	0	Highlands	5	598	265
Duval	34	3,920	1,648	Hillsborough	39	4,392	1,934
Escambia	14	1,688	736	Manatee	15	1,457	661
Flagler	3	248	107	Orange	36	4,153	1,993
Franklin	2	150	41	Osceola	9	973	387
Gadsden	2	180	83	Pasco	18	1,748	869
Gilchrist	2	180	79	Pinellas	94	9,383	3,891
Gulf	1	120	38	Polk	23	2,756	1,243
Hamilton	1	60	25	Seminole	8	905	445
Hernando	5	660	309				
Holmes	1	180	85	South region	256	29,384	12,971
Jackson	4	480	282	Broward	41	4,567	1,993
Jefferson	2	157	43	Charlotte	9	1,100	484
Lafayette	1	60	30	Collier	11	842	291
Lake	12	1,231	513	De Soto	1	118	110
Leon	8	941	478	Glades	0	0	0
Levy	1	180	81	Hendry	2	213	100
Liberty	0	0	0	Indian River	8	638	291
Madison	3	197	89	Lee	18	1,886	843
Marion	9	1,193	491	Martin	7	760	279
Nassau	2	240	113	Miami-Dade	59	8,289	3,548
Okaloosa	10	837	472	Monroe	3	360	175
Putnam	4	347	163	Okeechobee	2	179	85
St. Johns	4	310	192	Palm Beach	56	6,281	2,698
Santa Rosa	9	661	230	Sarasota	29	3,176	1,600
Sumter	1	210	38	St. Lucie	10	975	474
Suwannee	3	401	184				

Source: State of Florida, Agency for Health Care Administration, *1998 Guide to Nursing Homes in Florida,* Internet site <http://www.floridahealthstat.com/publications/Nursguide98/nhguide98.htm> (accessed 17 August 2000).

University of Florida   **Bureau of Economic and Business Research**

Table 2.21. HOME SALES: SALES AND MEDIAN SALES PRICE OF EXISTING SINGLE-FAMILY
HOMES IN SPECIFIED METROPOLITAN STATISTICAL AREAS (MSAS)
OF FLORIDA, 1998 AND 1999

MSA	Number of homes sold			Median sales price		
	1998 A/	1999	Per-centage change	1998 A/ (dollars)	1999 (dollars)	Per-centage change
Florida	140,321	149,532	6.6	99,800	106,900	7.1
Daytona Beach	5,907	6,851	16.0	81,100	85,500	5.4
Ft. Lauderdale 1/	11,179	11,999	7.3	129,800	136,700	5.3
Ft. Myers-Cape Coral	3,542	4,630	30.7	98,400	106,600	8.3
Ft. Pierce-Port St. Lucie 1/	3,128	3,303	5.6	86,300	89,100	3.2
Ft. Walton Beach	2,884	2,931	1.6	109,100	114,400	4.9
Gainesville	2,187	2,508	14.7	103,800	108,000	4.0
Jacksonville	10,093	11,692	15.8	97,300	99,400	2.2
Lakeland-Winter Haven	3,252	3,897	19.8	78,900	77,600	-1.6
Melbourne-Titusville-Palm Bay	4,411	5,079	15.1	85,700	88,800	3.6
Miami 1/	10,729	9,726	-9.3	122,400	133,800	9.3
Naples	1,901	2,690	41.5	175,400	201,300	14.8
Ocala	3,209	3,493	8.9	69,500	70,700	1.7
Orlando	19,139	20,945	9.4	96,000	103,300	7.6
Panama City 1/	1,419	1,549	9.2	94,900	99,400	4.7
Pensacola	3,884	4,328	11.4	93,400	99,600	6.6
Punta Gorda	(NA)	(NA)	(NA)	(NA)	(NA)	(NA)
Sarasota-Bradenton	7,280	7,551	3.7	119,100	129,400	8.6
Tallahassee	2,067	2,443	18.2	114,900	117,800	2.5
Tampa-St. Petersburg-Clearwater 1/	25,844	25,323	-2.0	88,000	94,200	7.0
West Palm Beach-Boca Raton	10,237	11,262	10.0	127,300	133,800	5.1

(NA) Not available.
A/ Revised.
1/ Due to periodic unavailability of data, figures are adjusted for comparison purposes. Florida includes other nonMSA areas.

Source: Florida Association of Realtors and University of Florida, Real Estate Research Center, unpublished data.

University of Florida   **Bureau of Economic and Business Research**

Table 2.30. PUBLIC LODGING: LICENSED LODGINGS, APARTMENTS, ROOMING HOUSES, RENTAL CONDOMINIUMS, AND TRANSIENT APARTMENTS IN THE STATE AND COUNTIES OF FLORIDA, FISCAL YEAR 1999-2000

County	Total licensed lodgings 1/ Number	Units	Apartment buildings Number	Units	Rooming houses Number	Units	Rental condominiums Number	Units	Transient apartment buildings 2/ Number	Units
Florida	31,726	1,395,619	18,359	919,306	394	5,430	6,896	83,377	1,372	16,545
Alachua	442	28,337	383	24,003	2	51	0	0	5	130
Baker	5	207	2	59	0	0	0	0	0	0
Bay	504	20,455	127	5,773	2	13	174	5,065	5	110
Bradford	28	763	12	371	1	2	0	0	2	9
Brevard	593	30,947	393	20,320	4	34	40	1,483	42	555
Broward	3,733	147,525	2,831	112,576	16	164	53	2,320	336	3,920
Calhoun	6	126	4	102	0	0	0	0	0	0
Charlotte	135	3,433	27	992	0	0	57	847	24	237
Citrus	74	2,083	31	827	4	37	3	138	11	88
Clay	60	6,359	44	5,124	0	0	3	21	1	13
Collier	297	19,510	125	9,713	2	35	83	3,140	5	54
Columbia	88	3,183	48	1,115	1	12	0	0	4	76
De Soto	18	402	12	255	1	19	0	0	0	0
Dixie	12	190	1	32	1	9	0	0	1	7
Duval	812	81,962	656	67,695	18	235	3	20	1	3
Escambia	397	20,306	185	12,411	3	6	127	1,652	3	34
Flagler	39	974	10	185	1	26	9	172	3	5
Franklin	226	1,278	4	121	1	3	201	678	1	7
Gadsden	28	898	15	644	2	16	0	0	1	5
Gilchrist	5	93	2	60	0	0	0	0	2	5
Glades	15	236	4	50	0	0	0	0	2	12
Gulf	86	539	4	127	0	0	70	301	4	31
Hamilton	16	460	7	148	0	0	0	0	1	20

See footnotes at end of table.

Continued . . .

Table 2.30. PUBLIC LODGING: LICENSED LODGINGS, APARTMENTS, ROOMING HOUSES, RENTAL CONDOMINIUMS, AND TRANSIENT APARTMENTS IN THE STATE AND COUNTIES OF FLORIDA, FISCAL YEAR 1999-2000 (Continued)

County	Total licensed lodgings 1/		Apartment buildings		Rooming houses		Rental condominiums		Transient apartment buildings 2/	
	Number	Units	Number	Units	Number	Units	Number	Units	Number	Units
Hardee	21	413	15	330	0	0	0	0	3	38
Hendry	32	705	15	274	0	0	1	25	0	0
Hernando	43	1,688	25	1,014	3	27	1	1	0	0
Highlands	129	3,592	73	1,686	2	10	4	212	24	428
Hillsborough	1,043	111,805	823	92,010	19	266	2	238	23	383
Holmes	12	302	7	109	0	0	0	0	0	0
Indian River	155	4,829	88	2,606	3	32	27	414	3	38
Jackson	37	1,406	22	684	0	0	1	10	0	0
Jefferson	18	430	10	237	2	11	0	0	1	1
Lafayette	4	73	1	36	0	0	0	0	1	4
Lake	334	7,699	135	5,107	11	117	129	497	12	146
Lee	697	30,814	282	15,405	4	34	186	6,338	58	361
Leon	440	27,586	373	21,585	4	346	1	30	5	669
Levy	58	928	15	320	2	20	8	136	8	38
Liberty	1	13	0	0	0	0	0	0	0	0
Madison	14	521	10	323	0	0	0	0	0	0
Manatee	393	16,484	153	11,136	2	43	120	1,721	49	555
Marion	219	9,889	131	6,067	2	36	2	28	10	53
Martin	124	4,795	78	2,863	2	46	10	308	9	353
Miami-Dade	6,670	226,585	6,030	175,157	111	1,296	56	2,681	7	318
Monroe	671	14,320	88	1,833	28	318	206	3,004	148	876
Nassau	80	3,537	23	832	1	25	26	1,085	1	2
Okaloosa	283	14,375	120	4,582	1	10	96	4,641	3	169
Okeechobee	28	600	9	174	1	14	0	0	8	65

Continued . . . .

See footnotes at end of table.

Table 2.30. PUBLIC LODGING: LICENSED LODGINGS, APARTMENTS, ROOMING HOUSES, RENTAL CONDOMINIUMS, AND TRANSIENT APARTMENTS IN THE STATE AND COUNTIES OF FLORIDA, FISCAL YEAR 1999-2000 (Continued)

County	Total licensed lodgings 1/		Apartment buildings		Rooming houses		Rental condominiums		Transient apartment buildings 2/	
	Number	Units	Number	Units	Number	Units	Number	Units	Number	Units
Orange	1,459	171,143	717	91,991	27	478	449	9,575	22	527
Osceola	3,480	46,877	107	10,897	8	99	3,216	9,810	18	856
Palm Beach	1,476	76,691	1,112	57,196	27	435	43	1,900	75	982
Pasco	254	9,946	123	6,693	2	38	80	976	6	72
Pinellas	2,144	89,498	1,378	63,102	16	179	120	4,998	230	2,074
Polk	1,069	26,186	400	15,726	28	509	492	2,725	36	471
Putnam	64	1,669	32	1,067	4	43	1	23	3	24
St. Johns	193	10,884	61	4,016	1	3	42	1,779	5	35
St. Lucie	144	5,870	67	2,555	2	31	13	560	23	193
Santa Rosa	194	3,002	47	1,678	1	3	134	476	0	0
Sarasota	544	19,653	245	10,513	6	69	124	3,721	88	947
Seminole	204	32,690	160	28,502	1	9	3	84	3	174
Sumter	37	1,314	17	461	4	20	4	262	4	24
Suwannee	24	569	9	244	0	0	3	3	1	13
Taylor	48	889	8	289	0	0	12	43	3	6
Union	2	80	2	80	0	0	0	0	0	0
Volusia	923	38,185	400	16,656	9	194	174	4,629	26	309
Wakulla	8	165	0	0	0	0	2	25	0	0
Walton	317	6,263	12	425	1	7	284	4,581	2	20
Washington	17	390	9	142	0	0	1	1	0	0

1/ Includes hotels and motels shown separately in Table 19.60.
2/ Apartments which rent for six months or less.
Note: Excludes 226 bed and breakfast facilities.

Source: State of Florida, Department of Business and Professional Regulation, Division of Hotels and Restaurants, *Master File Statistics: Public Lodging and Food Service Establishments*, Fiscal Year 1999-2000.

Table 2.36. MOBILE HOME AND RECREATIONAL VEHICLE TAGS: NUMBER SOLD IN THE STATE AND COUNTIES OF FLORIDA, FISCAL YEAR 1998-99

County	Mobile homes 1/	Real prop-erty 2/	Recrea-tional vehicles	County	Mobile homes 1/	Real prop-erty 2/	Recrea-tional vehicles
Florida	506,671	32,252	200,710	Lee	30,835	479	8,081
				Leon	8,539	946	2,200
Alachua	4,775	493	2,260	Levy	760	1,037	941
Baker	426	338	539	Liberty	148	42	125
Bay	3,225	844	3,040	Madison	1,161	166	276
Bradford	611	234	617	Manatee	23,505	1,241	4,889
Brevard	11,913	497	9,034	Marion	16,331	1,818	7,056
Broward	18,163	111	6,854	Martin	4,950	213	2,497
Calhoun	273	158	144	Miami-Dade	9,543	40	5,536
Charlotte	8,956	189	3,139	Monroe	1,596	130	2,534
Citrus	4,133	723	3,479	Nassau	1,244	733	1,103
Clay	1,429	984	2,235	Okaloosa	2,354	374	2,350
Collier	5,755	247	3,053	Okeechobee	1,624	160	2,316
Columbia	1,917	1,076	1,249	Orange	14,807	245	7,020
De Soto	1,778	95	1,242	Osceola	7,263	279	2,625
Dixie	178	273	367	Palm Beach	16,257	370	6,653
Duval	19,089	725	7,487	Pasco	26,046	1,452	11,610
Escambia	4,790	444	4,448	Pinellas	46,765	752	10,673
Flagler	1,124	116	1,061	Polk	44,880	1,821	10,799
Franklin	93	88	218	Putnam	1,543	995	1,813
Gadsden	818	487	333	St. Johns	2,675	1,043	2,262
Gilchrist	670	341	396	St. Lucie	14,286	135	2,884
Glades	423	124	327	Santa Rosa	1,941	655	2,644
Gulf	145	107	295	Sarasota	16,555	453	5,796
Hamilton	404	202	189	Seminole	3,862	89	3,161
Hardee	1,212	129	657	Sumter	2,631	404	1,858
Hendry	2,346	321	866	Suwannee	2,608	805	850
Hernando	4,761	695	2,721	Taylor	486	440	434
Highlands	10,831	207	2,914	Union	247	124	162
Hillsborough	33,640	1,116	11,727	Volusia	24,726	345	7,385
Holmes	521	207	259	Wakulla	423	377	496
Indian River	9,442	104	2,021	Walton	1,007	417	655
Jackson	1,637	406	671	Washington	539	347	341
Jefferson	433	306	236	Office agency	626	122	85
Lafayette	130	102	137	Refunds	0	0	1
Lake	17,867	714	6,384				

1/ Includes military mobile homes.
2/ Tags sold to mobile home owners who also own the land on which the mobile home stands. A real property tag is bought only once, not annually.

Source: State of Florida, Department of Highway Safety and Motor Vehicles, *Revenue Report, July 1, 1997 through June 30, 1998.*

University of Florida　　　　　　　　　**Bureau of Economic and Business Research**

VITAL STATISTICS
AND HEALTH

Resident Live Births by Age of Mother, 1999

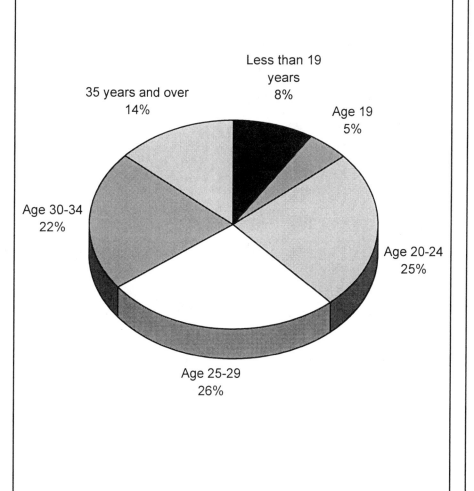

Less than 19
years
8%

35 years and over
14%

Age 19
5%

Age 30-34
22%

Age 20-24
25%

Age 25-29
26%

Source: Table 3.02

SECTION 3.00
VITAL STATISTICS AND HEALTH

TABLES LISTED BY MAJOR HEADINGS

Table 3.01. BIRTH AND DEATH RATES: RESIDENT LIVE BIRTH AND DEATH RATES BY RACE IN FLORIDA AND THE UNITED STATES, 1989 THROUGH 1999

	Birth rates						Death rates					
	Total		White		Nonwhite		Total		White		Nonwhite	
Year	Flor-ida	U.S.	Flor-ida	U.S.	Flor-ida	U.S.	Flor-ida	U.S.	Flor-ida	U.S.	Flor-ida	U.S.
1989	15.2	16.3	13.4	15.4	24.9	23.1	10.3	8.7	10.8	8.9	7.6	7.5
1990	15.1	16.7	13.4	15.8	24.3	19.0	10.1	8.6	10.6	8.9	7.2	7.4
1991	14.6	16.3	12.9	15.4	23.9	20.6	10.2	8.6	10.7	8.9	7.3	7.3
1992	14.2	15.9	12.6	15.0	23.2	20.5	10.3	8.5	10.8	8.8	7.3	7.2
1993	14.1	15.5	12.5	14.7	22.6	19.8	10.6	8.8	11.1	9.1	7.6	7.4
1994	13.7	15.2	12.2	14.4	21.6	19.0	10.5	8.8	11.1	9.1	7.5	7.3
1995	13.3	14.8	12.0	14.2	19.8	17.9	10.7	8.8	11.3	9.1	7.4	7.3
1996	13.1	14.7	11.8	14.1	19.5	18.3	10.5	8.7	11.2	9.1	7.0	7.1
1997	13.0	14.5	11.5	13.9	20.7	17.4	10.4	8.6	11.0	9.0	7.2	6.8
1998	13.0	14.6	11.5	(NA)	20.9	(NA)	10.4	8.7	11.0	9.1	7.2	9.2
1999	12.8	(NA)	11.3	(NA)	20.8	(NA)	(NA)	(NA)	(NA)	(NA)	(NA)	(NA)

(NA) Not available.
Note: Rates per 1,000 population based on July 1 population estimates for noncensus years. Some data are revised; some 1998 or 1999 data are preliminary.

Source: U.S., Department of Commerce, Bureau of the Census, *Statistical Abstract of the United States, 2000,* annual editions, and State of Florida, Department of Health, Office of Vital Statistics, Public Health Statistics Section, *Florida Vital Statistics Annual Report, 1999,* preliminary final, and previous editions.

Table 3.02. BIRTHS: NUMBER OF RESIDENT LIVE BIRTHS BY AGE OF MOTHER IN FLORIDA 1994 THROUGH 1999

Age of mother	1994	1995	1996	1997	1998	1999 A/
All ages	190,546	188,535	189,338	192,304	195,564	196,963
Less than 13	24	20	25	20	17	18
13	132	128	110	102	130	100
14	594	588	507	480	457	426
15	1,646	1,583	1,542	1,428	1,352	1,322
16	3,341	3,236	3,172	3,013	2,987	2,739
17	5,151	5,166	4,791	5,005	4,934	4,703
18	6,753	6,971	6,694	6,891	7,072	6,933
19	8,524	8,112	8,596	8,815	8,871	9,203
20-24	48,540	46,865	46,331	46,877	48,138	49,121
25-29	51,017	49,649	50,496	51,552	52,541	52,272
30-34	43,423	43,689	43,339	43,231	42,941	43,100
35-39	18,053	19,020	(NA)	(NA)	(NA)	(NA)
35-44	(NA)	(NA)	23,588	24,707	25,903	26,789
40 years and over	3,295	3,472	(NA)	(NA)	(NA)	(NA)
45 years and over	(NA)	(NA)	115	155	192	202
Age not stated	53	36	32	28	29	35
Less than 19 years, number	17,641	17,692	16,841	16,939	16,949	16,241
Percentage of total	9.3	9.4	8.9	8.8	8.7	8.2

(NA) Not available.
A/ Preliminary.

Source: State of Florida, Department of Health, Office of Vital Statistics, Public Health Statistics Section, *Florida Vital Statistics Annual Report, 1999,* preliminary final, and previous editions.

University of Florida   **Bureau of Economic and Business Research**

Table 3.03. BIRTHS: NUMBER AND RATES OF RESIDENT LIVE BIRTHS BY RACE
IN THE STATE AND COUNTIES OF FLORIDA, 1999

County	Number of births				Birth rates 1/			
	Total 2/	White 3/	Black	Other	Total 2/	White 3/	Black	Other
Florida	196,963	146,329	45,029	5,444	12.8	11.3	21.0	19.3
Alachua	2,389	1,558	738	93	11.0	9.2	18.0	13.5
Baker	391	331	59	1	17.7	17.4	20.4	7.1
Bay	1,959	1,570	315	63	13.0	12.0	20.0	15.2
Bradford	339	283	53	3	13.3	13.9	10.5	12.2
Brevard	4,741	3,930	655	152	9.9	9.1	17.7	17.2
Broward	21,033	13,452	6,928	641	14.1	11.3	25.2	18.8
Calhoun	129	107	21	1	9.1	9.1	9.3	4.5
Charlotte	957	861	85	11	6.9	6.6	14.6	7.9
Citrus	829	768	49	12	7.2	6.9	19.0	13.8
Clay	1,741	1,549	141	51	12.4	12.0	18.3	15.2
Collier	2,878	2,521	293	64	13.0	12.0	30.9	39.5
Columbia	755	594	153	8	13.3	13.1	14.2	10.7
De Soto	421	362	57	2	14.7	15.5	11.7	6.7
Dixie	182	167	15	0	13.4	13.6	12.5	0.0
Duval	12,113	7,417	4,175	518	15.8	13.3	22.4	24.2
Escambia	3,976	2,646	1,184	143	13.1	11.5	19.1	13.4
Flagler	340	286	52	2	7.3	6.8	14.6	3.4
Franklin	117	100	15	2	10.7	10.4	12.2	22.7
Gadsden	714	288	420	5	13.8	13.6	14.0	9.5
Gilchrist	157	152	5	0	11.6	12.4	4.5	0.0
Glades	75	56	8	11	7.6	7.2	5.7	15.7
Gulf	137	104	30	3	9.5	9.2	10.1	16.9
Hamilton	162	103	59	0	11.2	11.9	10.4	0.0
Hardee	445	417	27	1	19.7	20.5	13.5	3.9
Hendry	615	499	104	11	20.0	19.7	22.7	14.1
Hernando	1,065	974	73	18	8.3	7.9	16.4	20.7
Highlands	838	662	161	15	10.3	9.0	23.1	18.9
Hillsborough	14,444	11,057	2,932	434	14.9	13.4	22.5	22.5
Holmes	199	192	5	2	10.5	11.0	3.8	5.7
Indian River	1,017	848	150	18	9.2	8.3	20.2	23.7
Jackson	577	398	166	13	11.6	11.3	12.0	22.6
Jefferson	171	101	69	1	11.8	11.9	11.7	8.2
Lafayette	71	64	7	0	10.1	10.8	6.8	0.0
Lake	2,236	1,866	338	31	10.9	9.9	21.3	21.9
Lee	4,758	4,027	676	54	11.3	10.3	25.6	14.4
Leon	2,934	1,701	1,139	90	12.3	9.7	19.5	17.3

See footnotes at end of table.   Continued . . .

Table 3.03. BIRTHS: NUMBER AND RATES OF RESIDENT LIVE BIRTHS BY RACE
IN THE STATE AND COUNTIES OF FLORIDA, 1999 (Continued)

County	Number of births				Birth rates 1/			
	Total 2/	White 3/	Black	Other	Total 2/	White 3/	Black	Other
Levy	374	302	67	5	11.1	10.2	19.0	13.9
Liberty	82	72	9	1	10.1	10.8	6.5	14.3
Madison	201	92	108	1	10.2	7.8	13.8	6.5
Manatee	3,044	2,542	406	95	12.0	10.9	21.5	38.9
Marion	2,767	2,184	535	48	11.0	9.9	18.5	19.0
Martin	1,197	979	120	98	9.8	8.6	17.4	88.1
Miami-Dade	31,484	21,593	9,241	577	14.7	13.4	19.1	12.7
Monroe	802	688	90	22	9.2	8.4	20.2	21.7
Nassau	763	681	73	9	13.2	12.9	15.1	22.7
Okaloosa	2,274	1,904	293	77	12.6	12.2	16.8	11.7
Okeechobee	483	443	32	8	13.5	13.7	11.4	14.9
Orange	13,176	9,312	3,326	532	15.5	13.5	24.5	21.8
Osceola	2,355	2,079	213	63	14.8	14.2	23.8	18.8
Palm Beach	13,059	9,221	3,340	490	12.5	10.2	26.0	33.0
Pasco	3,501	3,295	127	76	10.7	10.4	19.3	25.2
Pinellas	9,257	7,418	1,478	358	10.3	9.1	20.3	24.2
Polk	6,594	5,178	1,316	100	13.8	12.6	21.9	18.6
Putnam	956	715	235	5	13.1	12.0	18.5	7.0
St. Johns	1,210	·1,076	113	21	10.5	10.1	15.0	23.5
St. Lucie	2,151	1,514	611	26	11.4	9.6	21.7	11.9
Santa Rosa	1,551	1,436	70	45	13.7	13.6	13.6	17.1
Sarasota	2,638	2,362	228	48	8.2	7.7	17.3	19.8
Seminole	4,445	3,656	624	164	12.5	11.4	21.4	21.2
Sumter	423	337	79	7	8.3	8.1	8.6	15.1
Suwannee	472	404	67	1	13.6	13.5	15.5	4.0
Taylor	241	193	46	2	12.1	12.3	11.5	6.7
Union	157	129	28	0	11.3	12.2	8.7	0.0
Volusia	4,449	3,704	668	77	10.4	9.6	18.5	15.4
Wakulla	272	230	41	1	13.1	12.8	15.7	4.3
Walton	445	395	43	7	10.9	10.6	15.9	8.0
Washington	235	184	45	6	10.6	10.3	12.3	9.5

1/ Rates per 1,000 population, July 1, 1999.
2/ Unknown race included in total only.
3/ Persons designating "Hispanic" as a race were counted as white.
Note: Data are for births occurring to residents of the specified area regardless of place of occurrence.

Source: State of Florida, Department of Health, Office of Vital Statistics, Public Health Statistics Section, *Florida Vital Statistics Annual Report, 1999*, preliminary final, and previous edition.

University of Florida   **Bureau of Economic and Business Research**

Table 3.04. BIRTHS: RESIDENT LIVE BIRTHS BY HISPANIC OR HAITIAN ORIGIN
IN THE STATE AND COUNTIES OF FLORIDA, 1999

County	Total births 1/	Hispanic or Haitian origin As a percent-age of total births	Hispanic origin	Haitian origin	NonHis-panic/ Haitian origin
Florida	196,963	23.8	41,467	5,505	149,829
Alachua	2,389	4.6	109	1	2,276
Baker	391	1.0	4	0	387
Bay	1,959	2.9	57	0	1,885
Bradford	339	1.5	5	0	334
Brevard	4,741	5.8	270	5	4,464
Broward	21,033	27.6	4,402	1,398	15,219
Calhoun	129	2.3	3	0	126
Charlotte	957	8.7	65	18	874
Citrus	829	2.8	21	2	806
Clay	1,741	4.4	72	5	1,664
Collier	2,878	45.6	1,123	190	1,563
Columbia	755	1.7	13	0	742
De Soto	421	27.8	116	1	304
Dixie	182	1.6	3	0	179
Duval	12,113	4.3	499	24	11,583
Escambia	3,976	2.1	83	1	3,889
Flagler	340	7.1	24	0	316
Franklin	117	0.9	1	0	115
Gadsden	714	15.1	108	0	604
Gilchrist	157	3.2	5	0	152
Glades	75	33.3	25	0	50
Gulf	137	1.5	2	0	134
Hamilton	162	8.0	13	0	149
Hardee	445	60.0	267	0	177
Hendry	615	40.7	250	0	362
Hernando	1,065	6.0	64	0	1,001
Highlands	838	21.8	178	5	655
Hillsborough	14,444	23.3	3,283	86	11,054
Holmes	199	1.0	2	0	196
Indian River	1,017	15.7	149	11	856
Jackson	577	2.4	14	0	563
Jefferson	171	1.2	2	0	169
Lafayette	71	15.5	11	0	60
Lake	2,236	11.5	245	13	1,976
Lee	4,758	17.0	699	110	3,946
Leon	2,934	3.0	85	2	2,841

See footnotes at end of table.   Continued . . .

University of Florida   **Bureau of Economic and Business Research**

Table 3.04. BIRTHS: RESIDENT LIVE BIRTHS BY HISPANIC OR HAITIAN ORIGIN IN THE STATE AND COUNTIES OF FLORIDA, 1999 (Continued)

County	Total births 1/	Hispanic or Haitian origin			NonHispanic/ Haitian origin
		As a percentage of total births	Hispanic origin	Haitian origin	
Levy	374	4.8	18	0	356
Liberty	82	3.7	3	0	79
Madison	201	1.5	3	0	198
Manatee	3,044	22.4	657	26	2,360
Marion	2,767	7.7	212	0	2,555
Martin	1,197	16.1	182	11	1,004
Miami-Dade	31,484	61.2	17,341	1,939	12,178
Monroe	802	23.6	177	12	611
Nassau	763	0.9	7	0	754
Okaloosa	2,274	4.9	112	0	2,161
Okeechobee	483	28.6	138	0	345
Orange	13,176	25.5	2,891	475	9,803
Osceola	2,355	34.5	795	18	1,541
Palm Beach	13,059	28.1	2,730	939	9,377
Pasco	3,501	8.7	300	4	3,195
Pinellas	9,257	8.4	769	5	8,475
Polk	6,594	16.4	1,012	70	5,510
Putnam	956	10.7	102	0	854
St. Johns	1,210	3.1	37	0	1,173
St. Lucie	2,151	18.4	279	117	1,755
Santa Rosa	1,551	2.3	35	1	1,515
Sarasota	2,638	9.1	237	2	2,399
Seminole	4,445	13.5	586	13	3,845
Sumter	423	9.7	41	0	382
Suwannee	472	9.1	43	0	429
Taylor	241	0.8	2	0	239
Union	157	1.3	2	0	155
Volusia	4,449	10.4	462	1	3,984
Wakulla	272	0.0	0	0	272
Walton	445	4.5	20	0	423
Washington	235	0.9	2	0	231

1/ Unknown origin included in total only.
Note: Data are for births occurring to residents of the specified area regardless of place of occurrence.

Source: State of Florida, Department of Health, Office of Vital Statistics, Public Health Statistics Section, *Florida Vital Statistics Annual Report, 1999*, preliminary final.

University of Florida   **Bureau of Economic and Business Research**

Table 3.05. BIRTHS: RESIDENT LIVE BIRTHS BY RACE AND BY EDUCATION OF MOTHER
IN THE STATE AND COUNTIES OF FLORIDA, 1999

County	Total 2/	White births 1/ Education of mother (percentage) 0-12 years	13-15 years	16 years and over	Total 2/	Nonwhite births Education of mother (percentage) 0-12 years	13-15 years	16 years and over
Florida	146,329	50.8	24.5	24.4	50,473	66.5	20.4	12.3
Alachua	1,558	30.2	30.1	39.6	831	56.2	30.2	13.6
Baker	331	74.6	16.3	8.2	60	83.3	15.0	0.0
Bay	1,570	55.5	25.0	16.9	378	64.3	24.6	6.1
Bradford	283	68.2	25.1	6.7	56	73.2	23.2	3.6
Brevard	3,930	44.4	31.1	24.2	807	59.1	25.0	15.9
Broward	13,452	39.4	26.2	33.7	7,569	59.7	22.2	16.4
Calhoun	107	64.5	18.7	16.8	22	68.2	22.7	9.1
Charlotte	861	59.2	25.8	14.8	96	46.9	40.6	12.5
Citrus	768	63.0	24.2	12.8	61	57.4	26.2	16.4
Clay	1,549	52.4	28.0	19.4	192	57.3	31.3	11.5
Collier	2,521	65.5	16.6	17.7	357	82.6	10.6	6.2
Columbia	594	65.0	22.2	12.6	161	75.8	18.0	5.6
De Soto	362	84.3	9.9	5.2	59	78.0	16.9	3.4
Dixie	167	75.4	20.4	4.2	15	100.0	0.0	0.0
Duval	7,417	48.3	25.2	25.6	4,693	61.0	23.8	11.7
Escambia	2,646	47.0	29.0	23.3	1,327	69.2	22.5	7.3
Flagler	286	46.5	37.1	16.1	54	68.5	20.4	11.1
Franklin	100	75.0	16.0	8.0	17	70.6	23.5	0.0
Gadsden	288	64.6	23.6	11.8	425	80.0	16.7	3.1
Gilchrist	152	71.7	21.1	7.2	5	100.0	0.0	0.0
Glades	56	76.8	19.6	3.6	19	84.2	15.8	0.0
Gulf	104	64.4	26.0	7.7	33	72.7	12.1	9.1
Hamilton	103	71.8	14.6	11.7	59	86.4	13.6	0.0
Hardee	417	87.8	7.9	4.1	28	75.0	21.4	0.0
Hendry	499	81.2	10.0	8.4	115	80.9	13.9	3.5
Hernando	974	59.5	28.5	11.9	91	74.7	13.2	12.1
Highlands	662	69.6	19.3	11.0	176	77.3	17.0	5.7
Hillsborough	11,057	51.0	23.2	25.6	3,366	66.2	19.4	14.3
Holmes	192	68.2	22.4	8.9	7	71.4	14.3	0.0
Indian River	848	55.1	25.1	19.6	168	73.2	19.0	7.7
Jackson	398	56.3	26.9	16.3	179	72.1	22.9	4.5
Jefferson	101	48.5	29.7	21.8	70	71.4	25.7	2.9
Lafayette	64	76.6	10.9	12.5	7	71.4	28.6	0.0
Lake	1,866	60.6	22.0	17.4	369	73.4	19.2	7.0
Lee	4,027	60.5	22.1	17.2	730	80.3	13.3	6.4
Leon	1,701	29.9	24.8	45.3	1,229	47.4	29.4	23.1

See footnotes at end of table.   Continued . . .

Table 3.05. BIRTHS: RESIDENT LIVE BIRTHS BY RACE AND BY EDUCATION OF MOTHER
IN THE STATE AND COUNTIES OF FLORIDA, 1999 (Continued)

County	Total 2/	White births 1/ Education of mother (percentage) 0-12 years	13-15 years	16 years and over	Total 2/	Nonwhite births Education of mother (percentage) 0-12 years	13-15 years	16 years and over
Levy	302	68.5	23.2	8.3	72	84.7	8.3	6.9
Liberty	72	76.4	11.1	11.1	10	80.0	20.0	0.0
Madison	92	57.6	30.4	12.0	109	76.1	20.2	3.7
Manatee	2,542	59.0	22.0	18.9	501	77.0	16.8	6.0
Marion	2,184	62.3	24.9	12.9	583	70.5	24.0	5.5
Martin	979	51.2	24.2	24.6	218	84.4	7.8	6.9
Miami-Dade	21,593	50.9	22.3	26.7	9,818	70.5	17.6	11.7
Monroe	688	44.0	29.5	25.4	112	68.8	22.3	8.0
Nassau	681	61.5	25.0	13.1	82	67.1	23.2	7.3
Okaloosa	1,904	48.4	31.3	20.1	370	63.0	27.8	8.9
Okeechobee	443	79.9	12.9	7.2	40	60.0	22.5	17.5
Orange	9,312	45.7	23.9	30.2	3,858	66.4	18.9	14.4
Osceola	2,079	55.7	27.9	16.3	276	56.5	26.8	16.7
Palm Beach	9,221	42.7	24.0	32.5	3,830	69.2	18.1	11.2
Pasco	3,295	57.7	25.9	16.1	203	57.1	21.7	20.7
Pinellas	7,418	48.6	26.0	25.1	1,836	69.2	19.2	11.2
Polk	5,178	67.0	19.9	12.8	1,416	74.6	17.9	7.3
Putnam	715	73.8	18.7	7.4	240	83.3	14.2	2.5
St. Johns	1,076	40.7	23.5	35.4	134	72.4	15.7	11.9
St. Lucie	1,514	59.1	26.8	14.1	637	76.6	17.0	6.4
Santa Rosa	1,436	47.3	28.4	24.1	115	58.3	26.1	15.7
Sarasota	2,362	47.4	27.2	25.4	276	73.2	15.9	10.9
Seminole	3,656	36.0	29.8	34.1	788	56.6	22.7	20.6
Sumter	337	78.9	14.8	6.2	86	83.7	14.0	2.3
Suwannee	404	69.6	19.1	11.4	68	76.5	20.6	2.9
Taylor	193	72.0	15.5	12.4	48	77.1	20.8	2.1
Union	129	63.6	22.5	14.0	28	82.1	17.9	0.0
Volusia	3,704	53.6	28.7	17.3	745	61.6	25.1	12.9
Wakulla	230	66.5	21.3	12.2	42	76.2	19.0	4.8
Walton	395	63.3	24.8	11.1	50	78.0	20.0	2.0
Washington	184	65.2	26.6	7.6	51	72.5	19.6	5.9

1/ Persons designating "Hispanic" as a race were counted as white.
2/ Unknown race included in total only.
Note: Data are for births occurring to residents of the specified area regardless of place of occurrence.

Source: State of Florida, Department of Health, Office of Vital Statistics, Public Health Statistics Section, *Florida Vital Statistics Annual Report, 1999*, preliminary final.

Table 3.06. TEENAGE BIRTHS: RESIDENT LIVE BIRTHS TO MOTHERS UNDER AGE 20 BY RACE IN THE STATE AND COUNTIES OF FLORIDA, 1999

County	Total	White Number	White Percentage of total teenage births	White As a percentage of all white births	Nonwhite Number	Nonwhite Percentage of total teenage births	Nonwhite As a percentage of all nonwhite births
Florida	25,435	15,819	62.2	10.8	9,616	37.8	19.1
Alachua	298	113	37.9	7.3	185	62.1	22.3
Baker	87	67	77.0	20.2	20	23.0	33.3
Bay	345	261	75.7	16.6	84	24.3	22.2
Bradford	76	62	81.6	21.9	14	18.4	25.0
Brevard	600	428	71.3	10.9	172	28.7	21.3
Broward	1,908	780	40.9	5.8	1,128	59.1	14.9
Calhoun	24	17	70.8	15.9	7	29.2	31.8
Charlotte	123	114	92.7	13.2	9	7.3	9.4
Citrus	136	127	93.4	16.5	9	6.6	14.8
Clay	232	196	84.5	12.7	36	15.5	18.8
Collier	399	338	84.7	13.4	61	15.3	17.1
Columbia	139	112	80.6	18.9	27	19.4	16.8
De Soto	103	87	84.5	24.0	16	15.5	27.1
Dixie	42	37	88.1	22.2	5	11.9	33.3
Duval	1,698	771	45.4	10.4	927	54.6	19.8
Escambia	646	326	50.5	12.3	320	49.5	24.1
Flagler	41	30	73.2	10.5	11	26.8	20.4
Franklin	31	28	90.3	28.0	3	9.7	17.6
Gadsden	161	41	25.5	14.2	120	74.5	28.2
Gilchrist	20	20	100.0	13.2	0	0.0	0.0
Glades	16	8	50.0	14.3	8	50.0	42.1
Gulf	25	17	68.0	16.3	8	32.0	24.2
Hamilton	36	19	52.8	18.4	17	47.2	28.8
Hardee	117	109	93.2	26.1	8	6.8	28.6
Hendry	117	96	82.1	19.2	21	17.9	18.3
Hernando	154	130	84.4	13.3	24	15.6	26.4
Highlands	136	107	78.7	16.2	29	21.3	16.5
Hillsborough	2,067	1,361	65.8	12.3	706	34.2	21.0
Holmes	44	41	93.2	21.4	3	6.8	42.9
Indian River	134	95	70.9	11.2	39	29.1	23.2
Jackson	96	51	53.1	12.8	45	46.9	25.1
Jefferson	24	8	33.3	7.9	16	66.7	22.9
Lafayette	21	20	95.2	31.3	1	4.8	14.3
Lake	349	273	78.2	14.6	76	21.8	20.6
Lee	707	520	73.6	12.9	187	26.4	25.6

See footnote at end of table.   Continued . . .

University of Florida   **Bureau of Economic and Business Research**

Table 3.06. TEENAGE BIRTHS: RESIDENT LIVE BIRTHS TO MOTHERS UNDER AGE 20 BY RACE
IN THE STATE AND COUNTIES OF FLORIDA, 1999 (Continued)

County	Total	White			Nonwhite		
		Number	Percent- age of total teenage births	As a per- centage of all white births	Number	Percent- age of total teenage births	As a per- centage of all nonwhite births
Leon	314	117	37.3	6.9	197	62.7	16.0
Levy	65	43	66.2	14.2	22	33.8	30.6
Liberty	17	16	94.1	22.2	1	5.9	10.0
Madison	40	14	35.0	15.2	26	65.0	23.9
Manatee	445	329	73.9	12.9	116	26.1	23.2
Marion	525	369	70.3	16.9	156	29.7	26.8
Martin	128	91	71.1	9.3	37	28.9	17.0
Miami-Dade	3,558	1,834	51.5	8.5	1,724	48.5	17.6
Monroe	60	52	86.7	7.6	8	13.3	7.1
Nassau	114	99	86.8	14.5	15	13.2	18.3
Okaloosa	335	261	77.9	13.7	74	22.1	20.0
Okeechobee	94	87	92.6	19.6	7	7.4	17.5
Orange	1,596	902	56.5	9.7	694	43.5	18.0
Osceola	286	241	84.3	11.6	45	15.7	16.3
Palm Beach	1,303	666	51.1	7.2	637	48.9	16.6
Pasco	448	414	92.4	12.6	34	7.6	16.7
Pinellas	1,161	745	64.2	10.0	416	35.8	22.7
Polk	1,230	873	71.0	16.9	357	29.0	25.2
Putnam	204	148	72.5	20.7	56	27.5	23.3
St. Johns	125	93	74.4	8.6	32	25.6	23.9
St. Lucie	330	186	56.4	12.3	144	43.6	22.6
Santa Rosa	190	171	90.0	11.9	19	10.0	16.5
Sarasota	285	212	74.4	9.0	73	25.6	26.4
Seminole	413	271	65.6	7.4	142	34.4	18.0
Sumter	77	53	68.8	15.7	24	31.2	27.9
Suwannee	90	73	81.1	18.1	17	18.9	25.0
Taylor	44	33	75.0	17.1	11	25.0	22.9
Union	29	20	69.0	15.5	9	31.0	32.1
Volusia	610	458	75.1	12.4	152	24.9	20.4
Wakulla	54	41	75.9	17.8	13	24.1	31.0
Walton	69	60	87.0	15.2	9	13.0	18.0
Washington	44	37	84.1	20.1	7	15.9	13.7

Note: Persons designating "Hispanic" as a race were counted as white.

Source: State of Florida, Department of Health, Office of Vital Statistics, Public Health Statistics Section, *Florida Vital Statistics Annual Report, 1999*, preliminary final.

University of Florida   **Bureau of Economic and Business Research**

Table 3.07. TEENAGE BIRTHS: RESIDENT LIVE BIRTHS TO MOTHERS AGED 15 THROUGH 19
IN THE STATE AND COUNTIES OF FLORIDA, 1999

County	Total	Unwed	Birthweight Under 1,500 grams	Birthweight Under 2,500 grams	No prenatal care 1/	One or more previous births	Birth rate 2/
Florida	24,900	82.1	2.1	10.1	6.6	21.6	54.7
Alachua	293	90.8	3.4	15.4	6.1	19.8	27.1
Baker	84	71.4	2.4	6.0	2.4	15.5	96.6
Bay	342	72.5	2.0	8.5	5.8	20.2	69.4
Bradford	75	76.0	1.3	12.0	1.3	16.0	99.9
Brevard	594	85.2	2.4	10.8	3.7	16.2	41.7
Broward	1,871	85.9	2.0	10.9	10.4	21.4	48.3
Calhoun	23	73.9	0.0	0.0	0.0	13.0	49.1
Charlotte	122	80.3	2.5	6.6	12.3	20.5	38.9
Citrus	134	84.3	0.7	11.9	3.7	14.2	52.0
Clay	228	71.5	1.3	8.8	2.2	16.7	41.9
Collier	393	78.4	1.8	6.9	10.4	22.6	73.8
Columbia	135	75.6	2.2	4.4	12.6	19.3	62.3
De Soto	99	68.7	2.0	10.1	17.2	32.3	126.4
Dixie	40	67.5	2.5	12.5	7.5	25.0	94.8
Duval	1,655	84.9	2.5	10.8	6.8	22.8	67.0
Escambia	631	81.6	2.2	11.1	4.3	23.5	57.9
Flagler	40	80.0	2.5	12.5	5.0	15.0	36.0
Franklin	30	63.3	0.0	10.0	3.3	23.3	101.7
Gadsden	159	91.2	2.5	15.7	3.8	25.8	85.1
Gilchrist	19	68.4	0.0	5.3	5.3	15.8	44.1
Glades	14	71.4	0.0	7.1	0.0	21.4	47.8
Gulf	25	68.0	8.0	12.0	4.0	16.0	57.5
Hamilton	36	77.8	0.0	13.9	0.0	13.9	72.4
Hardee	112	67.9	0.0	8.9	7.1	25.9	149.5
Hendry	114	70.2	3.5	12.3	11.4	23.7	103.5
Hernando	152	77.6	1.3	5.3	2.6	25.7	47.1
Highlands	134	74.6	1.5	9.7	7.5	21.6	72.8
Hillsborough	2,007	83.3	1.5	9.9	5.0	24.6	66.3
Holmes	44	59.1	2.3	9.1	6.8	27.3	76.5
Indian River	133	78.9	0.8	10.5	9.8	14.3	48.9
Jackson	95	64.2	2.1	9.5	2.1	17.9	59.7
Jefferson	24	87.5	8.3	12.5	8.3	4.2	48.3
Lafayette	20	60.0	0.0	5.0	5.0	5.0	98.0
Lake	346	80.1	2.6	9.5	7.2	18.5	72.6
Lee	699	83.8	1.3	9.0	7.3	23.9	68.0
Leon	301	87.0	1.3	10.6	3.0	23.6	22.5

See footnotes at end of table.   Continued . . .

University of Florida   **Bureau of Economic and Business Research**

Table 3.07. TEENAGE BIRTHS: RESIDENT LIVE BIRTHS TO MOTHERS AGED 15 THROUGH 19
IN THE STATE AND COUNTIES OF FLORIDA, 1999 (Continued)

County	Total	Unwed	Birthweight Under 1,500 grams	Birthweight Under 2,500 grams	No prenatal care 1/	One or more previous births	Birth rate 2/
Levy	62	80.6	3.2	8.1	3.2	22.6	61.2
Liberty	17	70.6	5.9	11.8	5.9	11.8	70.5
Madison	40	97.5	2.5	12.5	7.5	17.5	60.7
Manatee	434	78.6	1.6	8.8	7.1	23.5	71.2
Marion	515	78.1	2.9	10.1	5.4	19.2	73.8
Martin	122	82.0	3.3	6.6	12.3	16.4	43.6
Miami-Dade	3,463	84.1	2.5	10.2	5.2	21.3	50.3
Monroe	60	81.7	0.0	3.3	3.3	10.0	31.3
Nassau	113	73.5	2.7	10.6	1.8	17.7	57.1
Okaloosa	329	69.3	1.2	9.1	4.3	20.7	55.5
Okeechobee	91	71.4	1.1	5.5	3.3	25.3	78.2
Orange	1,564	85.2	2.3	12.2	8.4	22.3	54.0
Osceola	283	77.7	1.8	11.3	5.7	17.0	55.8
Palm Beach	1,278	84.8	2.4	9.9	12.1	24.2	49.2
Pasco	444	80.0	1.4	8.6	4.7	17.3	58.2
Pinellas	1,129	86.0	1.5	9.2	6.6	21.4	51.4
Polk	1,210	80.2	1.1	8.5	6.4	26.1	83.8
Putnam	201	74.6	3.5	10.0	6.5	21.4	84.5
St. Johns	123	81.3	2.4	8.1	5.7	23.6	35.7
St. Lucie	323	83.9	0.9	7.7	6.5	16.1	61.0
Santa Rosa	188	71.8	3.2	10.6	2.7	21.8	51.0
Sarasota	281	83.6	2.8	9.3	7.5	16.4	43.1
Seminole	409	81.2	2.2	10.5	4.9	19.1	35.3
Sumter	75	77.3	0.0	10.7	2.7	21.3	54.7
Suwannee	87	72.4	2.3	9.2	8.0	24.1	70.9
Taylor	44	72.7	2.3	11.4	0.0	15.9	70.0
Union	28	71.4	3.6	10.7	3.6	17.9	85.1
Volusia	598	80.6	2.8	13.4	4.5	19.7	49.6
Wakulla	54	79.6	5.6	14.8	5.6	14.8	74.0
Walton	69	69.6	0.0	10.1	2.9	17.4	57.3
Washington	43	67.4	2.3	14.0	2.3	18.6	58.0

1/ Third trimester or no prenatal care.
2/ Births to females aged 15-19 per 1,000 population.

Source: State of Florida, Department of Health, Office of Vital Statistics, Public Health Statistics Section, *Florida Vital Statistics Annual Report, 1999*, preliminary final.

Table 3.08. INFANT DEATHS: NUMBER AND RATE OF RESIDENT INFANT DEATHS BY RACE IN FLORIDA, 1987 THROUGH 1999

Year	Number of deaths			Mortality rate per 1,000 live births		
	Total 1/	White 2/	Non-white	Total 1/	White 2/	Non-white
1987	1,844	1,039	802	10.5	7.9	18.6
1988	1,949	1,167	782	10.6	8.5	17.0
1989	1,899	1,141	756	9.8	7.9	15.8
1990	1,909	1,121	786	9.6	7.5	16.0
1991	1,726	966	758	8.9	6.7	15.6
1992	1,685	987	695	8.8	6.9	14.4
1993	1,654	951	699	8.6	6.6	14.5
1994	1,540	927	611	8.1	6.5	12.9
1995	1,402	840	562	7.4	5.9	12.1
1996	1,405	821	583	7.4	5.8	12.4
1997	1,358	805	552	7.1	5.6	11.4
1998	1,415	850	562	7.2	5.8	11.4
1999	1,442	815	625	7.3	5.6	12.4

1/ Unknown race included in total only.
2/ Persons designating "Hispanic" as a race were counted as white.
Note: Infants are considered to be less than one year. Some data may be revised.

Table 3.09. ABORTIONS: REPORTED TERMINATIONS OF PREGNANCY IN FLORIDA 1987 THROUGH 1999

Year	Induced abor-tions 2/	Resident live births	Total known pregnancies 1/		Abortion rate per 100 preg-nancies
			Number	Rate per 100 women aged 15-44	
1987	52,697	175,072	229,387	9.0	23.0
1988	65,153	183,998	250,889	9.5	26.0
1989	62,626	192,887	257,315	9.5	24.3
1990	66,073	199,146	267,030	9.7	24.7
1991	71,254	193,717	266,663	9.6	26.7
1992	69,285	191,530	262,313	9.3	26.4
1993	70,069	192,453	263,969	9.3	26.5
1994	73,394	190,546	265,459	9.3	27.6
1995	74,749	188,535	264,815	9.0	28.2
1996	80,040	189,338	270,856	9.3	29.6
1997	81,692	192,304	275,519	9.3	29.7
1998	82,335	195,564	279,419	9.4	29.5
1999	83,971	196,963	282,513	9.4	29.7

1/ Includes induced abortions, total resident births, and total reported resident fetal deaths.
2/ Abortions have been legal in Florida since April 1972.
Note: Some data may be revised.

Source for Tables 3.08 and 3.09: State of Florida, Department of Health, Office of Vital Statistics, Public Health Statistics Section, *Florida Vital Statistics Annual Report, 1999*, preliminary final, previous editions, and unpublished data.

Table 3.10. ABORTIONS: REPORTED TERMINATIONS OF PREGNANCY IN THE STATE
AND COUNTIES OF FLORIDA, 1993 THROUGH 1999

County	1993	1994	1995	1996	1997	1998	1999 Number	Rate 1/
Florida	70,069	73,394	74,749	80,040	81,692	82,335	83,971	278.1
Alachua	2,684	2,473	2,552	2,454	2,473	2,250	2,161	364.2
Bay	82	65	0	0	0	0	0	0.0
Brevard	1,300	1,418	1,467	1,363	1,221	1,087	1,115	120.6
Broward	7,919	8,199	8,668	9,662	9,924	10,328	11,207	380.6
Charlotte	228	174	207	245	217	274	262	138.1
Collier	271	314	306	325	93	110	0	0.0
De Soto	1	0	0	0	0	0	0	0.0
Duval	5,973	5,451	4,671	5,363	6,264	6,368	6,269	362.2
Escambia	2,116	2,664	2,531	2,698	2,504	2,461	2,470	374.1
Hillsborough	5,524	5,541	5,425	5,711	5,849	5,744	6,544	309.9
Jackson	1	1	0	3	0	0	0	0.0
Lee	1,725	1,748	1,674	1,879	2,021	2,099	2,063	294.5
Leon	3,063	3,018	2,886	2,787	2,639	2,537	2,682	396.3
Manatee	0	1	0	0	0	0	0	0.0
Marion	2	0	1	0	2	168	573	138.7
Miami-Dade	18,046	18,180	20,612	22,254	21,862	22,163	22,343	499.3
Monroe	1	1	0	0	0	0	0	0.0
Okaloosa	515	0	0	0	0	0	0	0.0
Orange	4,447	7,063	7,226	8,559	10,173	10,300	9,341	468.3
Palm Beach	4,860	5,934	6,086	6,396	6,359	6,153	6,341	338.4
Pinellas	5,026	4,601	4,232	4,181	4,002	4,118	3,954	246.4
Polk	1,466	1,459	1,452	1,540	1,418	1,400	1,244	141.2
St. Lucie	1,069	509	352	421	577	678	835	248.8
Santa Rosa	0	1	0	0	0	0	0	0.0
Sarasota	1,934	2,011	1,896	1,938	1,986	1,910	1,914	409.6
Seminole	579	0	0	0	0	74	735	91.1
Volusia	1,237	2,568	2,505	2,261	2,108	2,113	1,918	244.5

1/ Rate per 10,000 female population aged 15-44, April 1, 1999.
Note: Only counties reporting induced terminations of pregnancy are shown.

Source: State of Florida, Department of Health, Office of Vital Statistics, Public Health Statistics Section, unpublished data.

University of Florida   **Bureau of Economic and Business Research**

Table 3.11. BIRTHS TO UNWED MOTHERS: RESIDENT LIVE BIRTHS AND BIRTHS TO UNWED MOTHERS BY AGE AND RACE OF THE MOTHER IN THE STATE AND COUNTIES OF FLORIDA, 1999

County	Total resident live births	Num-ber 1/	Births to unwed mothers				
			Percent-age of total	Age of mother		Race of mother	
				Under 20	20 and over	White 2/	Non-white
Florida	196,963	73,785	37.5	20,958	52,817	42,398	31,335
Alachua	2,389	898	37.6	271	627	341	557
Baker	391	165	42.2	63	102	113	52
Bay	1,959	722	36.9	253	469	477	242
Bradford	339	148	43.7	58	90	106	42
Brevard	4,741	1,640	34.6	512	1,128	1,140	498
Broward	21,033	7,062	33.6	1,643	5,419	2,895	4,162
Calhoun	129	52	40.3	18	34	35	17
Charlotte	957	312	32.6	99	213	265	47
Citrus	829	314	37.9	115	199	276	38
Clay	1,741	449	25.8	166	283	364	85
Collier	2,878	1,069	37.1	314	755	889	180
Columbia	755	329	43.6	105	224	211	118
De Soto	421	189	44.9	72	117	145	44
Dixie	182	77	42.3	29	48	65	12
Duval	12,113	4,651	38.4	1,448	3,202	1,815	2,834
Escambia	3,976	1,592	40.0	529	1,063	667	925
Flagler	340	122	35.9	33	89	77	45
Franklin	117	43	36.8	20	23	31	12
Gadsden	714	431	60.4	147	284	99	332
Gilchrist	157	45	28.7	14	31	40	5
Glades	75	40	53.3	12	28	26	14
Gulf	137	54	39.4	17	37	29	25
Hamilton	162	75	46.3	28	47	28	47
Hardee	445	193	43.4	81	111	171	22
Hendry	615	300	48.8	83	217	205	94
Hernando	1,065	383	36.0	120	263	325	58
Highlands	838	357	42.6	102	255	243	114
Hillsborough	14,444	5,564	38.5	1,731	3,832	3,375	2,184
Holmes	199	61	30.7	26	35	56	5
Indian River	1,017	351	34.5	106	245	239	112
Jackson	577	228	39.5	62	166	100	128
Jefferson	171	73	42.7	21	52	18	55
Lafayette	71	27	38.0	13	14	24	3
Lake	2,236	835	37.3	280	555	580	255
Lee	4,758	1,917	40.3	593	1,324	1,400	516

See footnotes at end of table.   Continued . . .

Table 3.11. BIRTHS TO UNWED MOTHERS: RESIDENT LIVE BIRTHS AND BIRTHS TO UNWED
MOTHERS BY AGE AND RACE OF THE MOTHER IN THE STATE
AND COUNTIES OF FLORIDA, 1999 (Continued)

County	Total resi-dent live births	Num-ber 1/	Percent-age of total	Age of mother Under 20	Age of mother 20 and over	Race of mother White 2/	Race of mother Non-white
Leon	2,934	1,124	38.3	274	850	324	797
Levy	374	150	40.1	53	97	100	50
Liberty	82	36	43.9	12	24	27	9
Madison	201	106	52.7	39	67	22	84
Manatee	3,044	1,189	39.1	352	836	836	352
Marion	2,767	1,153	41.7	412	741	759	394
Martin	1,197	403	33.7	105	298	262	141
Miami-Dade	31,484	12,932	41.1	3,008	9,922	6,640	6,271
Monroe	802	253	31.5	49	204	197	56
Nassau	763	225	29.5	84	141	169	56
Okaloosa	2,274	646	28.4	234	412	452	194
Okeechobee	483	196	40.6	67	129	170	26
Orange	13,176	4,939	37.5	1,365	3,573	2,676	2,260
Osceola	2,355	813	34.5	223	590	685	128
Palm Beach	13,059	4,509	34.5	1,110	3,399	2,313	2,195
Pasco	3,501	1,193	34.1	358	835	1,092	100
Pinellas	9,257	3,549	38.3	1,003	2,544	2,337	1,210
Polk	6,594	2,861	43.4	989	1,872	1,865	996
Putnam	956	430	45.0	153	277	260	169
St. Johns	1,210	315	26.0	101	214	231	84
St. Lucie	2,151	934	43.4	278	655	502	432
Santa Rosa	1,551	391	25.2	137	254	343	48
Sarasota	2,638	793	30.1	239	554	600	193
Seminole	4,445	1,282	28.8	335	947	847	435
Sumter	423	205	48.5	60	145	133	72
Suwannee	472	169	35.8	66	103	121	48
Taylor	241	104	43.2	32	72	62	42
Union	157	57	36.3	21	36	40	17
Volusia	4,449	1,721	38.7	494	1,227	1,213	508
Wakulla	272	105	38.6	43	62	76	29
Walton	445	155	34.8	48	107	122	33
Washington	235	79	33.6	30	49	52	27

1/ Includes data for mothers whose age was not stated.
2/ Persons designating "Hispanic" as a race were counted as white.

Source: State of Florida, Department of Health, Office of Vital Statistics, Public Health Statistics Section,
Florida Vital Statistics Annual Report, 1999, preliminary final.

University of Florida   **Bureau of Economic and Business Research**

Table 3.15. DEATHS: RESIDENT DEATH RATES BY RACE IN THE STATE AND COUNTIES
OF FLORIDA, 1998

County	Number of deaths			Death rates 1/		
	Total 2/	White 3/	Nonwhite	Total 2/	White 3/	Nonwhite
Florida	157,160	139,940	17,009	10.4	11.0	7.2
Alachua	1,495	1,152	343	7.0	7.0	7.3
Baker	175	156	19	8.3	8.6	6.3
Bay	1,315	1,168	147	8.9	9.1	7.5
Bradford	255	215	40	10.0	10.7	7.5
Brevard	4,728	4,405	316	10.1	10.4	7.0
Broward	15,633	13,943	1,641	10.6	11.9	5.5
Calhoun	133	119	14	9.7	10.6	5.6
Charlotte	2,030	1,979	50	15.1	15.5	7.2
Citrus	1,939	1,910	27	17.2	17.4	8.0
Clay	996	926	69	7.3	7.4	6.5
Collier	2,077	2,014	61	9.8	10.0	5.7
Columbia	539	455	84	9.7	10.2	7.4
De Soto	251	221	30	8.9	9.8	5.5
Dixie	143	137	6	10.8	11.6	4.3
Duval	6,403	4,724	1,672	8.5	8.6	8.2
Escambia	2,733	2,124	608	9.2	9.4	8.6
Flagler	583	528	53	13.3	13.2	13.4
Franklin	101	93	8	9.4	9.8	6.0
Gadsden	436	213	223	8.6	10.2	7.4
Gilchrist	129	124	5	9.7	10.2	4.2
Glades	84	72	12	8.4	9.0	6.0
Gulf	160	137	23	11.2	12.7	6.5
Hamilton	105	64	41	7.4	7.6	7.0
Hardee	240	222	18	10.5	10.8	7.8
Hendry	240	201	39	7.9	8.0	7.2
Hernando	1,967	1,914	52	15.6	15.9	9.9
Highlands	1,212	1,130	80	15.0	15.5	10.3
Hillsborough	8,178	7,075	1,094	8.6	8.8	7.5
Holmes	225	216	9	12.5	13.2	5.3
Indian River	1,475	1,378	95	13.8	13.9	11.7
Jackson	526	418	108	10.6	11.9	7.4
Jefferson	129	78	51	9.0	9.4	8.5
Lafayette	58	53	5	8.2	9.1	4.1
Lake	2,719	2,541	176	13.7	14.0	10.4
Lee	4,673	4,460	207	11.4	11.8	7.0
Leon	1,388	1,022	366	5.9	5.9	5.8

See footnotes at end of table.   Continued . . .

University of Florida   **Bureau of Economic and Business Research**

Table 3.15. DEATHS: RESIDENT DEATH RATES BY RACE IN THE STATE AND COUNTIES
OF FLORIDA, 1998 (Continued)

County	Number of deaths Total 2/	White 3/	Nonwhite	Death rates 1/ Total 2/	White 3/	Nonwhite
Levy	386	347	39	11.8	12.1	10.2
Liberty	53	50	3	6.8	8.0	2.0
Madison	217	140	77	11.2	12.3	9.7
Manatee	3,254	3,068	184	13.1	13.5	8.8
Marion	3,018	2,730	286	12.4	12.8	9.3
Martin	1,508	1,453	51	12.6	13.0	6.4
Miami-Dade	18,583	15,223	3,336	8.9	9.6	6.5
Monroe	707	662	42	8.2	8.2	7.7
Nassau	428	378	49	7.8	7.6	9.7
Okaloosa	1,229	1,140	87	7.0	7.4	3.7
Okeechobee	408	389	19	11.6	12.1	6.1
Orange	5,708	4,732	970	6.9	7.0	6.3
Osceola	1,263	1,184	77	8.4	8.6	6.6
Palm Beach	12,487	11,380	1,063	12.2	12.9	7.6
Pasco	5,013	4,940	67	15.6	15.8	7.1
Pinellas	12,607	11,841	761	14.1	14.7	8.8
Polk	5,112	4,558	552	10.9	11.3	8.6
Putnam	830	692	138	11.6	11.8	10.4
St. Johns	1,073	966	105	9.7	9.4	12.5
St. Lucie	2,149	1,869	276	11.7	12.1	9.2
Santa Rosa	837	808	29	7.7	8.0	3.9
Sarasota	4,855	4,714	139	15.3	15.6	9.0
Seminole	2,401	2,123	277	6.9	6.8	7.7
Sumter	519	478	41	10.7	12.1	4.5
Suwannee	433	388	45	12.8	13.2	9.9
Taylor	189	156	32	9.6	10.0	8.0
Union	186	140	46	13.7	13.6	14.0
Volusia	5,450	5,107	339	12.9	13.4	8.3
Wakulla	173	154	19	8.6	8.9	6.7
Walton	402	362	40	10.4	10.3	11.1
Washington	209	181	28	9.7	10.4	6.8

1/ Rates per 1,000 population, July 1, 1998.
2/ Unknown race included in total only.
3/ Persons designating "Hispanic" as a race were counted as white.
Note: Data are for deaths occurring to residents of the specified area regardless of place of occurrence.

Source: State of Florida, Department of Health, Office of Vital Statistics, Public Health Statistics Section, *Florida Vital Statistics Annual Report, 1998*, preliminary final.

Table 3.17. CAUSE OF DEATH: NUMBER OF RESIDENT DEATHS BY CAUSE IN FLORIDA
1996, 1997, AND 1998

Cause of death and international list number	1996	1997	1998
All causes	152,697	153,830	157,160
Intestinal infectious diseases, 001-009	44	42	55
Tuberculosis, 010-018	90	77	72
Meningococcal infection, 036	12	19	11
Septicemia, 038	793	857	946
Human immunodeficiency virus (HIV), 042-044	3,093	1,879	1,547
Herpes zoster and simplex, 053-054	14	19	20
Viral hepatitis, 070	300	313	363
Syphilis, 090-097	6	6	4
Mycoses, 110-118	146	154	156
Late effects--tuberculosis, 137	10	14	9
Other infectious and parasitic diseases, 020-139	226	235	238
Malignant neoplasm (cancer), 140-208	37,476	37,813	37,783
Neoplasm not specified malignant, 210-239	422	449	418
Diabetes mellitus, 250	3,797	3,828	4,018
Nutritional deficiencies, 260-269	197	208	221
Anemias, 280-285	304	300	301
Alcohol psychosis, dependence, abuse, 291, 303, 305.0	409	434	466
Meningitis, 320-322	44	38	42
Parkinson's disease, 332	911	879	952
Motor neurone disease, 335.2	271	249	287
Major cardiovascular diseases, 390-448	63,276	63,536	64,961
Phlebitis and thrombophlebitis, 451	92	70	74
Venous embolism and thrombosis, 452-453	31	28	33
Other circulatory diseases, 454-459	137	145	170
Pneumonia and influenza, 480-487	3,785	3,869	4,080
Chronic obstructive pulmonary disease, 490-496	7,679	8,067	8,151
Pulmonary fibrosis and other alveular pneumopathy, 515-516	634	667	693
Ulcer of stomach and duodenum, 531-533	359	379	301
Hernia and intestinal obstruction, 550-553, 560	363	393	396
Diverticula of intestine, 562	225	250	217
Chronic liver disease and cirrhosis, 571	1,821	1,937	1,872
Cholelithiasis, other gallbladder diseases, 574-575	163	172	151
Diseases of pancreas, 577	188	209	234
Nephritis, nephrosis, renal failure, 580-589	1,008	991	1,142
Infections of kidney, 590	52	29	29
Maternal causes, 630-676	21	21	18
Congenital anomalies, 740-759	643	622	618
Perinatal conditions, 760-779	647	661	693
Symptoms, signs, ill-defined condition, 780-799	2,574	2,826	3,039
All other diseases, 240-739	11,631	A/ 12,310	A/ 13,203
Unintentional injury (accident), E800-E949	5,373	5,509	5,823
Suicide, E950-E959	2,144	2,097	2,156
Homicide and legal intervention, E960-E978	1,189	1,120	1,081
All other external causes, E980-E999	97	109	116

A/ Beginning in 1997, data are categorized as all other natural causes, 001-799.

Source: State of Florida, Department of Health, Office of Vital Statistics, Public Health Statistics Section, *Florida Vital Statistics Annual Report, 1998*, and previous editions.

Table 3.18. DEATHS: NUMBER OF RESIDENT DEATHS AND DEATH RATES BY LEADING CAUSE AND BY RACE IN FLORIDA, 1998

Cause	Number of deaths			Death rate 1/		
	Total 2/	White 3/	Non-white	Total 2/	White 3/	Non-white
Heart disease	50,734	46,230	4,473	336.7	364.2	188.4
Malignant neoplasm (cancer)	37,783	34,165	3,614	250.7	269.1	152.2
Cerebrovascular disease (stroke)	10,035	8,851	1,181	66.6	69.7	49.7
Chronic obstructive pulmonary disease (COPD)	8,151	7,671	480	54.1	60.4	20.2
Unintentional injury (accident)	5,823	4,979	836	38.6	39.2	35.2
Pneumonia and influenza	4,080	3,714	365	27.1	29.3	15.4
Diabetes mellitus	4,018	3,253	764	26.7	25.6	32.2
Suicide	2,156	2,015	139	14.3	15.9	5.9
Chronic liver disease and cirrhosis	1,872	1,726	146	12.4	13.6	6.1
Human Immunodeficiency Virus (HIV)	1,547	560	986	10.3	4.4	41.5
Aortic aneurysm	1,212	1,146	66	8.0	9.0	2.8
Homicide and legal intervention	1,081	611	467	7.2	4.8	19.7

1/ Rate per 100,000 population, July 1, 1998.
2/ Unknown race included in total only.
3/ Persons designating "Hispanic" as a race were counted as white.
Note: Data are for deaths occurring to residents of Florida regardless of the state of occurrence.

Table 3.19. DEATHS: RESIDENT ACCIDENT AND SUICIDE DEATHS AND DEATH RATES BY RACE AND SEX IN FLORIDA, 1994 THROUGH 1998

Year	Number of deaths					Death rate 1/				
	Total 3/	White 2/		Nonwhite		Total 3/	White 2/		Nonwhite	
		Male	Fe-male	Male	Fe-male		Male	Fe-male	Male	Fe-male
				Unintentional injury (accident)						
1994	4,971	2,763	1,408	577	204	35.6	48.4	23.3	55.0	17.9
1995	5,259	2,942	1,520	566	228	37.0	51.1	24.9	50.1	18.0
1996	5,373	2,963	1,615	552	240	37.1	50.5	26.1	47.4	19.3
1997	5,509	3,085	1,592	567	252	37.3	51.0	24.9	50.0	21.0
1998	5,823	3226	1,752	577	259	38.6	52.3	26.9	50.0	21.2
				Suicide						
1994	2,062	1,528	392	109	27	14.8	26.8	6.5	10.4	2.4
1995	2,139	1,589	408	114	27	15.1	27.6	6.7	10.1	2.1
1996	2,144	1,588	404	128	24	14.8	27.0	6.5	11.0	1.9
1997	2,097	1,522	432	113	26	14.2	25.2	6.8	10.0	2.2
1998	2,156	1,533	482	107	32	14.3	24.8	7.4	9.3	2.6

1/ Rate per 100,000 population, July 1, 1998.
2/ Persons designating "Hispanic" as a race were counted as white.
3/ Unknown race included in total only.

Source for Tables 3.18 and 3.19: State of Florida, Department of Health, Office of Vital Statistics, Public Health Statistics Section, *Florida Vital Statistics Annual Report, 1998*.

Table 3.20. CHILD WELL-BEING: INDICATORS OF CHILD WELL-BEING
IN THE STATE AND COUNTIES OF FLORIDA, 1997

County	Child deaths 3/	Teen violent deaths 2/ Number	Teen violent deaths 2/ Rate 4/	Dissolutions of marriage with children affected Number	Dissolutions of marriage with children affected Minimum number of children affected	Closure status of initial reports of maltreatments 1/ Total	Closure status of initial reports of maltreatments 1/ Some indication	Closure status of initial reports of maltreatments 1/ Verified
Florida	743	491	5.5	34,522	56,832	111,576	38,816	15,321
Alachua	9	9	4.4	388	652	1,447	435	175
Baker	4	0	0.0	69	113	211	54	35
Bay	8	2	2.1	477	752	1,756	456	297
Bradford	1	0	0.0	59	87	275	122	30
Brevard	18	11	4.0	1,026	1,644	4,277	1,798	810
Broward	76	39	5.2	3,525	5,746	7,824	2,467	939
Calhoun	0	2	22.3	30	50	111	55	9
Charlotte	7	3	4.9	224	384	761	189	52
Citrus	2	0	0.0	162	289	672	209	139
Clay	4	3	3.0	469	770	1,088	409	83
Collier	11	8	8.2	491	822	1,467	335	219
Columbia	7	6	14.2	148	272	525	154	52
De Soto	0	2	12.0	68	130	315	38	12
Dixie	1	0	0.0	37	68	139	62	24
Duval	49	19	3.9	2,138	3,466	6,928	2,223	852
Escambia	14	7	3.2	717	1,131	2,721	805	274
Flagler	0	2	9.8	63	102	241	73	32
Franklin	0	2	34.0	24	39	93	31	12
Gadsden	2	1	2.7	68	112	400	183	84
Gilchrist	1	2	16.9	34	59	117	45	30
Glades	0	2	32.5	2	3	62	18	2
Gulf	0	1	11.2	3	4	101	42	15
Hamilton	0	1	8.9	34	554	128	18	14
Hardee	2	0	0.0	50	84	302	83	39
Hendry	2	3	13.0	63	107	336	77	15
Hernando	5	3	4.9	236	403	857	308	157
Highlands	5	4	10.9	148	273	708	247	143
Hillsborough	51	32	5.4	2,282	3,703	7,641	3,221	1,084
Holmes	2	2	16.6	43	64	223	98	45
Indian River	4	1	1.9	212	347	611	183	93
Jackson	1	2	5.6	98	155	392	163	46
Jefferson	0	0	0.0	103	156	80	25	7
Lafayette	0	0	0.0	17	34	55	11	3
Lake	7	2	2.2	432	750	1,639	565	261
Lee	17	11	5.6	938	1,545	2,946	734	293
Leon	7	6	2.5	475	765	1,314	483	216
Levy	1	2	10.3	72	128	275	121	49
Liberty	0	1	20.6	8	13	86	42	13

See footnotes at end of table.   Continued . . .

University of Florida   **Bureau of Economic and Business Research**

Table 3.20. CHILD WELL-BEING: INDICATORS OF CHILD WELL-BEING
IN THE STATE AND COUNTIES OF FLORIDA, 1997 (Continued)

County	Child deaths 3/	Teen violent deaths 2/ Number	Rate 4/	Dissolutions of marriage with children affected Number	Minimum number of children affected	Closure status of initial reports of maltreatments 1/ Total	Some indication	Verified
Madison	0	0	0.0	30	53	148	41	17
Manatee	11	13	11.0	390	645	2,235	906	369
Marion	18	14	10.3	679	1,161	2,340	821	332
Martin	5	2	3.6	237	397	643	193	83
Miami-Dade	113	75	5.5	4,978	8,134	9,736	3,603	1,208
Monroe	3	1	2.7	134	209	680	274	126
Nassau	3	4	10.6	179	284	547	162	39
Okaloosa	5	5	4.4	559	892	1,522	508	321
Okeechobee	1	0	0.0	90	148	511	149	65
Orange	48	27	4.8	1,807	3,058	7,546	2,404	1,805
Osceola	10	10	10.6	466	746	1,377	488	209
Palm Beach	48	41	8.1	1,971	3,334	6,240	1,981	897
Pasco	15	13	8.7	690	1,128	2,611	982	142
Pinellas	35	19	4.3	1,858	2,990	7,147	2,739	702
Polk	33	19	6.7	1,247	2,095	5,511	2,183	743
Putnam	6	8	17.2	181	317	863	370	70
St. Johns	4	4	6.1	206	348	835	291	140
St. Lucie	6	4	3.9	468	792	1,313	437	161
Santa Rosa	7	5	7.3	188	323	1,190	437	159
Sarasota	5	4	3.1	649	1,090	1,772	668	207
Seminole	15	13	5.8	735	1,202	2,001	605	188
Sumter	3	1	3.4	81	129	467	193	86
Suwannee	1	6	24.3	100	167	312	68	22
Taylor	2	1	7.7	30	49	184	87	18
Union	0	0	0.0	18	33	137	50	24
Volusia	21	11	4.6	957	1,566	3,702	1,279	409
Wakulla	1	0	0.0	49	86	247	85	46
Walton	3	0	0.0	85	140	397	143	37
Washington	3	0	0.0	27	40	238	87	41

1/ Data are for fiscal year 1996-97.
2/ Deaths from homicides, suicides, and accidents to teens aged 15-19 years.
3/ Deaths from all causes to children aged 1-14 years.
4/ Per 10,000 population aged 15-19 years.

Source: University of South Florida, Louis de la Parte Florida Mental Health Institute, Department of Child and Family Studies, Center for the Study of Children's Futures, *Florida's Children At a Glance: The 1999 Statewide and County Update* (copyright).

University of Florida   **Bureau of Economic and Business Research**

Table 3.22. ELDER ABUSE: NUMBER OF REPORTED CASES IN THE STATE, DEPARTMENT OF CHILDREN AND FAMILIES DISTRICTS, AND COUNTIES OF FLORIDA, FISCAL YEAR 1998-1999

County and district	Popu- lation 65 and over	Cases re- ported	Abuse rate 1/	County and district	Popu- lation 65 and over	Cases re- ported	Abuse rate 1/
Florida 2/	2,815,398	31,993	1.1	District 6	195,987	2,534	1.3
				Hillsborough	127,636	2,034	1.6
District 1	77,973	1,421	1.8	Manatee	68,351	500	0.7
Escambia	38,378	799	2.1	District 7	237,093	3,130	1.3
Okaloosa	19,262	313	1.6	Brevard	86,949	776	0.9
Santa Rosa	12,400	207	1.7	Orange	91,957	1,564	1.7
Walton	7,933	102	1.3	Osceola	21,394	290	1.4
District 2	75,183	1,664	2.2	Seminole	36,793	500	1.4
Bay	19,927	334	1.7	District 8	315,608	2,474	0.8
Calhoun	2,058	32	1.6	Charlotte	44,416	293	0.7
Franklin	2,258	28	1.2	Collier	53,216	264	0.5
Gadsden	5,788	512	8.8	De Soto	5,567	327	5.9
Gulf	2,127	29	1.4	Glades	1,927	12	0.6
Holmes	3,003	40	1.3	Hendry	3,272	52	1.6
Jackson	6,649	159	2.4	Lee	102,906	792	0.8
Jefferson	2,063	24	1.2	Sarasota	104,304	734	0.7
Leon	18,840	333	1.8	District 9	244,214	1,900	0.8
Liberty	854	12	1.4	Palm Beach	244,214	1,900	0.8
Madison	2,565	28	1.1	District 10	281,036	2,942	1.0
Taylor	2,827	44	1.6	Broward	281,036	2,942	1.0
Wakulla	2,429	29	1.2	District 11	302,630	3,612	1.2
Washington	3,795	60	1.6	Miami-Dade	289,309	3,383	1.2
District 3	66,972	1,391	2.1	Monroe	13,321	229	1.7
Alachua	19,875	676	3.4	District 12	109,286	1,129	1.0
Bradford	3,431	67	2.0	Flagler	13,580	46	0.3
Columbia	7,562	143	1.9	Volusia	95,706	1,083	1.1
Dixie	2,574	44	1.7	District 13	212,625	1,729	0.8
Gilchrist	1,807	22	1.2	Citrus	38,011	266	0.7
Hamilton	1,543	14	0.9	Hernando	40,397	315	0.8
Lafayette	836	7	0.8	Lake	59,636	461	0.8
Levy	7,454	71	1.0	Marion	63,156	593	0.9
Putnam	14,371	258	1.8	Sumter	11,425	94	0.8
Suwannee	6,321	80	1.3	District 14	131,462	1,415	1.1
Union	1,198	9	0.8	Hardee	3,497	78	2.2
District 4	126,707	1,926	1.5	Highlands	30,065	235	0.8
Baker	1,967	207	10.5	Polk	97,900	1,102	1.1
Clay	13,823	156	1.1	District 15	113,428	861	0.8
Duval	84,807	1,358	1.6	Indian River	31,613	210	0.7
Nassau	6,269	74	1.2	Martin	33,830	211	0.6
St. Johns	19,841	131	0.7	Okeechobee	6,763	84	1.2
District 5	325,194	3,865	1.2	St. Lucie	41,222	356	0.9
Pasco	104,382	873	0.8				
Pinellas	220,812	2,992	1.4				

1/ Cases per 1,000 of the population aged 65 and over based on April 1, 2000 population estimates.
2/ Unduplicated total.

Source: University of Florida, Bureau of Economic and Business Research, Population Program, unpublished data, and State of Florida, Department of Children and Families, "Adult Abuse Reports by County, Fiscal Year 1998-99," Internet site <http://www.state.fl.us/cf_web/fs/doc/fahia989.xls> (accessed 18 August 2000).

Table 3.28. HIV AND AIDS: CASES, 1999, AND CUMULATIVE CASES OF AIDS JANUARY 1, 1980 THROUGH DECEMBER 31, 1999, IN THE STATE AND COUNTIES OF FLORIDA

County	Number of cases reported 1/ HIV 2/	AIDS	Cumulative cases 1980-1999 Number 3/	Rate per 100,000 popula- tion 4/	County	Number of cases reported 1/ HIV 2/	AIDS	Cumulative cases 1980-1999 Number 3/	Rate per 100,000 popula- tion 4/
Florida	6,258	5,444	75,694	494.0	Lee	110	102	1,319	316.2
					Leon	67	34	511	215.0
Alachua	39	64	567	262.2	Levy	2	4	36	107.8
Baker	5	7	49	224.0	Liberty	1	0	24	298.2
Bay	20	13	250	166.5	Madison	4	3	78	397.3
Bradford	2	3	121	474.5	Manatee	30	44	662	261.4
Brevard	59	79	1,169	246.2	Marion	25	52	509	204.1
Broward	959	914	12,130	813.9	Martin	27	16	341	280.6
Calhoun	1	0	38	269.2	Miami-Dade	1,784	1,331	22,889	1,076.3
Charlotte	12	14	206	150.6	Monroe	38	77	1,113	1,278.9
Citrus	3	13	92	80.1	Nassau	7	7	65	113.3
Clay	6	8	141	101.0	Okaloosa	13	14	204	113.6
Collier	39	45	681	310.0	Okeechobee	3	13	90	253.4
Columbia	13	11	123	217.6	Orange	426	314	4,359	515.0
De Soto	5	12	127	446.6	Osceola	36	36	392	249.1
Dixie	2	1	39	289.4	Palm Beach	576	471	7,189	689.8
Duval	268	272	3,777	495.1	Pasco	28	31	482	147.6
Escambia	65	66	926	307.0	Pinellas	238	217	3,002	334.0
Flagler	7	11	66	144.0	Polk	82	95	1,184	249.4
Franklin	2	0	11	101.2	Putnam	19	21	147	201.7
Gadsden	10	11	124	240.9	St. Johns	18	24	236	207.1
Gilchrist	0	2	8	59.7	St. Lucie	113	116	1,214	649.5
Glades	3	2	26	263.5	Santa Rosa	9	8	85	75.5
Gulf	0	1	57	395.8	Sarasota	44	53	687	214.0
Hamilton	2	1	40	278.2	Seminole	56	36	669	188.9
Hardee	2	1	62	274.4	Sumter	12	3	98	192.8
Hendry	13	9	160	523.7	Suwannee	5	8	62	180.3
Hernando	8	12	162	127.2	Taylor	3	0	42	211.7
Highlands	17	9	143	176.2	Union	2	1	477	3,448.3
Hillsborough	374	263	4,337	448.3	Volusia	111	148	1,001	234.5
Holmes	2	0	45	238.1	Wakulla	3	2	27	130.8
Indian River	19	23	218	198.9	Walton	0	3	57	140.9
Jackson	5	2	166	335.6	Washington	2	0	27	121.9
Jefferson	2	2	70	485.3					
Lafayette	0	0	15	215.5	Unknown	0	0	5	(X)
Lake	20	30	265	130.0	DC	380	259	A/	(X)

HIV Human Immunodeficiency Virus. AIDS Acquired Immunodeficiency Syndrome.
DC Department of Corrections.
(X) Not applicable.
A/ Department of Corrections AIDS cases diagnosed or reported have been included in the counties where the facilities are located.
1/ Includes diagnosed cases from earlier years not previously reported. See Appendix for further discussion.
2/ Includes only persons reported with HIV infection who have not developed AIDS.
3/ Includes 1,368 diagnosed and reported pediatric (under age 13) cases of AIDS.
4/ Based on April 1, 1999 Bureau of Economic and Business Research population estimates.

Source: State of Florida, Department of Health, Division of Disease Control, *The Florida HIV/AIDS, STD, and TB Surveillance Report,* January 2000, Number 185, Internet site <http://www.doh.state.fl.us/disease_ctrl/hsd/mrs0100.pdf> (accessed 3 May 2000).

Table 3.32. MARRIAGES AND DISSOLUTIONS OF MARRIAGE: NUMBER PERFORMED OR GRANTED IN THE STATE AND COUNTIES OF FLORIDA, 1998 AND 1999

County	Marriages 1/ 1998	Marriages 1/ 1999	Dissolutions of marriage 2/ 1998	Dissolutions of marriage 2/ 1999	County	Marriages 1/ 1998	Marriages 1/ 1999	Dissolutions of marriage 2/ 1998	Dissolutions of marriage 2/ 1999
Florida	141,344	136,403	80,466	80,983	Lake	1,688	1,512	1,039	1,022
					Lee	3,447	3,559	2,116	2,127
Alachua	1,866	1,708	1,005	926	Leon	2,192	2,012	1,100	921
Baker	309	261	151	118	Levy	255	222	191	150
Bay	2,069	2,013	1,069	1,058	Liberty	72	49	44	41
Bradford	299	252	170	155	Madison	187	144	87	80
Brevard	3,728	3,792	2,364	2,577	Manatee	1,716	1,797·	1,002	929
Broward	11,625	10,803	7,882	8,280	Marion	2,109	1,961	1,547	1,445
Calhoun	149	108	58	76	Martin	935	865	529	533
Charlotte	973	964	471	479	Miami-Dade	21,351	21,409	11,852	12,108
Citrus	814	815	571	643	Monroe	2,349	2,531	302	465
Clay	1,455	1,277	860	751	Nassau	774	609	327	305
Collier	2,050	2,182	1,009	1,089	Okaloosa	2,067	2,034	1,378	1,305
Columbia	712	585	411	467	Okeechobee	354	257	210	160
De Soto	250	252	140	154	Orange	9,195	9,497	4,553	4,774
Dixie	155	136	75	71	Osceola	3,866	3,547	1,041	953
Duval	7,314	6,266	4,796	4,521	Palm Beach	8,088	8,359	4,797	5,102
Escambia	3,310	3,019	1,540	1,659	Pasco	2,299	2,262	1,441	1,366
Flagler	286	317	239	247	Pinellas	7,925	7,441	4,506	4,231
Franklin	140	144	58	64	Polk	4,047	3,858	2,678	2,776
Gadsden	338	317	160	212	Putnam	620	523	334	372
Gilchrist	175	135	101	90	St. Johns	1,280	1,164	533	536
Glades	50	32	29	35	St. Lucie	1,289	1,239	936	887
Gulf	149	132	74	75	Santa Rosa	826	824	568	552
Hamilton	164	142	53	67	Sarasota	2,766	2,750	1,799	1,580
Hardee	179	157	125	87	Seminole	3,006	3,052	1,675	1,683
Hendry	359	307	182	130	Sumter	270	278	196	212
Hernando	914	804	467	494	Suwannee	326	290	227	170
Highlands	597	559	328	368	Taylor	199	144	104	129
Hillsborough	9,051	8,758	5,059	5,212	Union	83	108	68	62
Holmes	211	189	134	125	Volusia	3,552	3,386	2,247	2,272
Indian River	883	863	556	546	Wakulla	230	198	105	121
Jackson	477	354	247	282	Walton	443	450	180	204
Jefferson	234	180	210	185	Washington	171	186	107	125
Lafayette	82	63	53	42					

1/ State total may include a few marriages performed out of state but recorded in Florida.
2/ Includes divorces and annulments.

Source: State of Florida, Department of Health, Office of Vital Statistics, Public Health Statistics Section, *Florida Vital Statistics Annual Report, 1999*, preliminary final, and previous edition.

EDUCATION

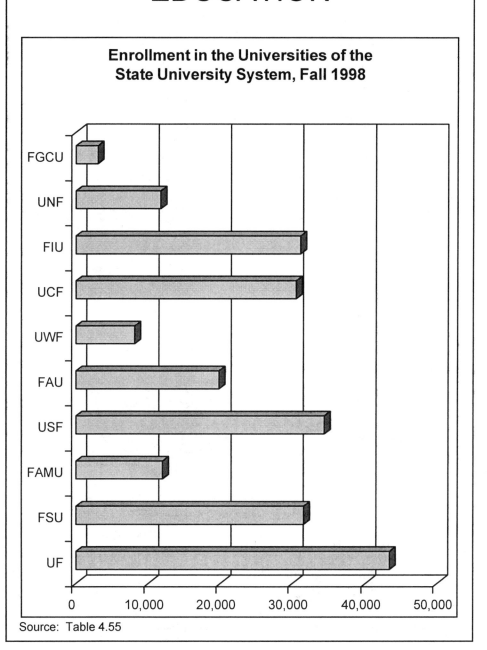

Enrollment in the Universities of the State University System, Fall 1998

Source: Table 4.55

SECTION 4.00
EDUCATION

TABLES LISTED BY MAJOR HEADINGS

University of Florida   **Bureau of Economic and Business Research**

SECTION 4.00
EDUCATION
(Continued)

TABLES LISTED BY MAJOR HEADINGS

University of Florida   **Bureau of Economic and Business Research**

Table 4.01. SCHOOL-AGE POPULATION: ESTIMATES OF THE POPULATION AGED 5 TO 17
YEARS BY SEX AND RACE IN THE STATE AND COUNTIES OF FLORIDA, APRIL 1, 1999

County	Total school-age population	Percentage-- Female	White	Black	County	Total school-age population	Percentage-- Female	White	Black
Florida	2,475,372	48.89	76.67	20.96	Lake	28,261	48.87	84.88	13.91
					Lee	60,307	48.77	86.84	11.81
Alachua	33,352	49.36	67.50	29.73	Leon	37,605	48.95	65.58	31.99
Baker	4,418	48.82	88.82	10.80	Levy	5,450	49.28	83.43	15.10
Bay	27,534	49.09	81.58	14.80	Liberty	1,237	48.91	89.17	10.51
Bradford	4,003	48.29	81.49	17.69	Madison	3,742	47.94	52.41	46.79
Brevard	77,488	49.11	85.80	11.88	Manatee	34,994	48.83	84.81	13.64
Broward	234,159	48.84	67.53	29.36	Marion	38,585	48.73	80.71	17.96
Calhoun	2,178	49.08	81.68	16.12	Martin	15,782	48.99	88.99	9.45
Charlotte	16,314	49.04	91.77	6.64	Miami-Dade	389,943	48.87	67.25	30.50
Citrus	14,391	48.81	94.40	4.34	Monroe	11,250	48.84	89.59	8.84
Clay	29,282	49.04	89.54	7.25	Nassau	11,085	48.75	88.71	10.61
Collier	31,711	49.13	91.61	7.27	Okaloosa	34,398	49.09	82.37	13.14
Columbia	11,213	48.44	77.32	21.49	Okeechobee	6,508	47.37	89.97	8.65
De Soto	4,629	48.33	78.48	20.11	Orange	144,388	49.54	73.80	22.73
Dixie	2,149	49.28	92.14	7.45	Osceola	28,495	48.77	89.39	8.31
Duval	138,956	49.19	64.65	31.82	Palm Beach	153,384	48.83	77.11	20.91
Escambia	53,030	48.53	65.92	29.17	Pasco	42,320	48.69	94.95	3.65
Flagler	6,138	49.45	89.49	9.16	Pinellas	121,322	48.87	82.79	14.45
Franklin	1,502	48.93	80.36	18.91	Polk	78,738	48.53	78.91	19.50
Gadsden	10,139	48.43	31.99	67.10	Putnam	13,085	49.07	74.13	24.58
Gilchrist	2,308	46.71	89.95	9.10	St. Johns	17,242	48.72	88.84	10.18
Glades	1,533	47.88	73.45	17.74	St. Lucie	30,340	49.01	74.23	24.21
Gulf	2,340	47.99	79.19	19.87	Santa Rosa	21,061	48.45	92.44	5.26
Hamilton	2,472	47.86	53.36	45.47	Sarasota	36,984	48.84	89.92	8.77
Hardee	4,312	47.52	92.32	6.56	Seminole	64,321	48.71	86.52	10.94
Hendry	6,801	48.88	82.46	15.04	Sumter	7,274	47.14	74.37	24.36
Hernando	17,782	49.07	93.10	5.92	Suwannee	6,102	48.74	82.51	16.67
Highlands	10,219	49.27	80.14	18.04	Taylor	3,583	48.73	77.25	21.07
Hillsborough	169,179	48.72	78.25	19.38	Union	1,910	47.28	82.98	16.44
Holmes	3,191	48.20	93.26	4.04	Volusia	62,053	49.03	86.45	12.06
Indian River	15,554	49.34	86.84	12.00	Wakulla	3,825	48.73	85.70	13.28
Jackson	7,682	48.26	68.06	30.86	Walton	6,259	48.38	90.17	7.64
Jefferson	2,534	50.51	51.34	47.75	Washington	3,959	48.98	78.43	18.72
Lafayette	1,087	48.85	88.78	11.04					

Source: University of Florida, Bureau of Economic and Business Research, Population Program, unpublished data.

University of Florida   **Bureau of Economic and Business Research**

Table 4.02. ELEMENTARY AND SECONDARY SCHOOLS: SPECIFIED STUDENT DATA
IN FLORIDA, 1995-96 THROUGH 1998-99

Item	1995-96	1996-97	1997-98	1998-99	Percentage change since 1995-96
Student membership 1/	2,176,930	2,239,411	2,294,160	2,336,793	7.3
Prekindergarten	51,629	53,989	54,083	54,068	4.7
Kindergarten	176,775	176,275	174,857	174,371	-1.4
Grade 1	180,172	185,351	185,593	184,704	2.5
Grade 2	175,887	181,537	186,219	186,308	5.9
Grade 3	172,036	178,059	184,143	188,343	9.5
Grade 4	173,189	174,914	180,871	186,115	7.5
Grade 5	175,354	175,323	177,254	182,677	4.2
Grade 6	174,078	179,578	181,707	183,844	5.6
Grade 7	171,383	176,053	181,647	183,908	7.3
Grade 8	163,522	169,264	173,917	179,003	9.5
Grade 9	183,053	193,129	203,557	214,427	17.1
Grade 10	154,067	161,624	168,083	171,360	11.2
Grade 11	126,206	128,820	133,782	134,968	6.9
Grade 12	99,579	105,495	108,447	112,697	13.2
Graduates (standard diplomas)	(NA)	92,430	95,716	98,933	(X)
Exceptional student membership	369,788	385,641	418,376	440,846	19.2
Educable mentally handicapped	24,628	26,326	27,523	28,305	14.9
Trainable mentally handicapped	7,714	7,800	8,043	8,195	6.2
Orthopedically impaired	(NA)	(NA)	5,559	5,314	(X)
Speech impaired	A/ 85,699	A/ 89,077	54,489	54,073	(X)
Language impaired	(NA)	(NA)	29,038	31,640	(X)
Deaf/hard of hearing	(NA)	(NA)	2,670	3,282	(X)
Visually impaired	(NA)	1,122	1,104	1,272	(X)
Emotionally handicapped	24,740	25,276	27,659	28,951	17.0
Specific learning disability	122,606	129,655	144,860	153,088	24.9
Gifted	83,576	85,163	93,395	99,697	19.3
Hospital/homebound	(NA)	2,240	2,052	2,415	(X)
Profoundly handicapped	11,267	12,005	B/ 2,846	B/ 2,825	(X)
Autistic	(NA)	(NA)	2,729	3,243	(X)
Severely emotionally disturbed	(NA)	(NA)	7,685	7,697	(X)
Developmentally delayed	(NA)	(NA)	6,282	7,525	(X)
Other exceptionalities	(NA)	(NA)	2,442	3,324	(X)
Disciplinary actions					
Out-of-school suspensions	(NA)	215,685	216,018	224,452	(X)
In-school suspensions	(NA)	224,431	230,616	235,101	(X)
Referrals to dropout prevention for disciplinary reasons	(NA)	50,972	69,656	71,424	(X)
Corporal punishment	(NA)	13,817	12,813	13,166	(X)
Expulsions	(NA)	1,259	1,061	1,031	(X)
Referrals to court/juvenile authorities	(NA)	38,681	3,778	4,264	(X)
Nonpromotions	(NA)	112,948	139,816	161,753	(X)
Dropouts	(NA)	31,926	29,558	65,060	(X)

(NA) Not available. (X) Not applicable.
A/ Includes speech-, language-, and hearing-impaired students. B/ Includes only profoundly mentally handicapped students. 1/ Based on fall membership survey. Note: Data are for public schools only.
Source: State of Florida, Department of Education, Division of Administration, Education Information and Accountability Services, *Profiles of Florida School Districts, 1998-99, Student and Staff Data*, Series 2000-06, February 2000. Internet site <http://www.firn.edu/doe/bin00050/eiaspubs/profiles.htm> (accessed 1 May 2000).

Table 4.03. ELEMENTARY AND SECONDARY SCHOOLS: MEMBERSHIP IN EXCEPTIONAL STUDENT PROGRAMS IN THE STATE AND COUNTIES OF FLORIDA, FALL 1999

County	Total	Students in specified programs (percentage)				
		Specific learning disabil- ities	Speech language and hearing	Gifted	Educable mentally handi- capped	Emotion- ally handi- capped
Florida	454,522	34.86	19.90	22.68	6.39	6.46
Alachua	7,465	32.73	10.41	34.68	4.58	8.75
Baker	668	28.74	37.57	10.18	12.13	3.74
Bay	5,196	40.38	22.07	13.16	5.45	8.41
Bradford	926	41.58	13.93	6.48	13.50	15.77
Brevard	15,519	36.27	17.29	30.07	4.41	4.76
Broward	34,785	22.04	35.49	21.36	5.28	3.20
Calhoun	437	37.30	28.83	9.61	11.21	10.30
Charlotte	3,661	49.63	13.22	18.30	3.39	5.95
Citrus	3,850	35.35	22.57	21.04	5.53	6.05
Clay	6,123	36.57	26.18	14.80	3.63	9.96
Collier	6,017	41.38	25.51	12.40	4.80	4.39
Columbia	1,680	31.19	22.02	5.71	14.05	11.25
De Soto	1,026	42.20	23.00	11.21	7.31	9.45
Dixie	593	29.85	31.87	0.51	12.98	12.98
Duval	23,516	37.13	20.04	14.20	8.20	7.47
Escambia	9,370	37.75	17.39	22.86	6.26	6.83
Flagler	1,377	47.42	20.77	16.27	2.83	5.37
Franklin	240	30.83	31.67	1.67	15.00	10.42
Gadsden	1,436	32.45	30.15	5.29	15.46	3.62
Gilchrist	521	46.64	11.32	5.95	9.02	10.75
Glades	208	50.48	19.23	11.06	8.17	7.21
Gulf	415	40.72	15.18	22.17	9.88	6.75
Hamilton	403	27.79	23.82	2.23	17.87	7.44
Hardee	1,102	47.46	20.60	8.53	11.89	5.17
Hendry	1,358	55.60	14.87	6.63	11.34	4.79
Hernando	3,073	38.53	26.16	16.14	4.07	7.48
Highlands	2,537	42.29	13.01	19.71	8.12	9.74
Hillsborough	29,970	29.28	21.36	25.42	7.21	7.06
Holmes	556	44.96	23.38	0.00	19.24	6.12
Indian River	3,061	37.67	17.02	26.33	6.31	4.57
Jackson	1,552	21.65	19.39	8.63	16.75	23.07
Jefferson	453	19.43	13.25	8.39	22.08	23.18
Lafayette	148	28.38	21.62	14.86	17.57	7.43
Lake	5,692	31.29	29.13	13.84	10.93	6.45
Lee	13,291	35.16	13.54	31.75	3.58	6.53
Leon	8,326	21.87	34.58	27.12	6.08	2.51

See footnotes at end of table.   Continued . . .

University of Florida   **Bureau of Economic and Business Research**

Table 4.03. ELEMENTARY AND SECONDARY SCHOOLS: MEMBERSHIP IN EXCEPTIONAL STUDENT
PROGRAMS IN THE STATE AND COUNTIES OF FLORIDA, FALL 1999 (Continued)

County	Total	Students in specified programs (percentage)				
		Specific learning disabil- ities	Speech language and hearing	Gifted	Educable mentally handi- capped	Emotion- ally handi- capped
Levy	1,310	38.24	22.60	9.62	9.62	11.76
Liberty	256	37.50	39.45	0.00	9.38	9.77
Madison	941	33.79	17.00	13.92	15.52	6.16
Manatee	7,886	40.40	23.46	14.70	5.74	7.68
Marion	7,118	37.58	20.95	12.60	9.12	8.43
Martin	3,172	40.83	19.01	16.42	5.14	8.07
Miami-Dade	61,448	34.80	8.57	35.99	4.82	5.79
Monroe	1,728	43.23	12.79	15.16	5.09	12.44
Nassau	1,784	47.37	12.39	10.03	7.62	11.83
Okaloosa	5,763	39.06	19.94	23.25	5.57	4.04
Okeechobee	1,336	44.69	17.14	7.26	9.51	7.11
Orange	27,809	38.39	18.63	18.84	9.56	5.18
Osceola	4,996	39.63	26.16	8.19	8.53	6.43
Palm Beach	27,945	33.35	24.22	25.83	5.44	4.66
Pasco	10,778	38.67	23.29	15.31	5.38	8.29
Pinellas	25,568	40.09	15.46	19.57	4.94	9.05
Polk	14,398	39.12	16.49	19.41	10.87	5.21
Putnam	2,154	45.64	19.45	10.72	8.31	4.04
St. Johns	3,381	44.81	21.27	17.27	6.15	3.31
St. Lucie	5,586	23.76	26.96	26.01	8.65	6.75
Santa Rosa	4,416	37.32	26.63	18.43	4.82	4.87
Sarasota	8,882	37.02	11.51	32.14	2.63	9.61
Seminole	10,253	26.63	25.49	30.05	4.55	5.20
Sumter	1,237	26.11	25.38	14.31	12.45	12.13
Suwannee	811	34.16	25.65	3.21	19.24	9.37
Taylor	774	44.44	22.09	13.31	6.98	5.56
Union	425	41.18	21.88	10.82	6.82	11.29
Volusia	11,938	38.69	14.53	18.83	5.98	10.37
Wakulla	1,027	34.27	25.02	16.16	7.30	6.43
Walton	978	41.62	26.38	6.03	11.04	5.52
Washington	544	32.17	39.15	4.60	8.27	10.48
Other schools 1/	1,329	15.35	43.87	12.79	2.33	6.92

1/ Includes Florida School for the Deaf, Dozier School, and University Developmental Research schools.
Note: Data were obtained from the Fall 1999 Florida DOE Student Information Data Base, Survey 2, as
of December 23, 1999, and are for public schools only.

Source: State of Florida, Department of Education, Division of Administration, Education Information
and Accountability Services, *Statistical Brief: Membership in Programs for Exceptional Students, Fall
1999,* Series 2000-05B. Internet site <http:/www.firn.edu.doe/bin00050/eiaspubs/ese.htm> (accessed
2 May 2000).

University of Florida   **Bureau of Economic and Business Research**

Table 4.05. PUBLIC ELEMENTARY AND SECONDARY SCHOOLS: SPECIFIED CHARACTERISTICS
IN FLORIDA, 1984-85 THROUGH 1998-99

School year	Resident population 1/ Total	Aged 5-17	Fall member- ship 2/	High school gradu- ates 3/	Instruc- tional personnel
1984-85	10,930,389	1,752,422	1,520,975	81,140	94,048
1985-86	11,287,932	1,675,790	1,559,507	81,508	97,139
1986-87	11,549,831	1,667,636	1,603,033	83,692	100,498
1987-88	12,043,618	1,688,627	1,664,563	90,792	104,848
1988-89	12,417,608	1,695,383	1,720,927	92,449	109,865
1989-90	13,152,691	1,700,468	1,789,925	90,790	114,501
1990-91	12,937,926	2,016,641	1,861,671	89,494	119,123
1991-92	13,195,952	2,057,688	1,930,719	93,368	121,185
1992-93	13,424,416	2,100,608	1,981,731	91,423	118,713
1993-94	13,608,627	2,135,410	2,041,714	90,034	124,027
1994-95	14,149,317	2,207,525	2,109,052	91,899	129,223
1995-96	14,411,563	2,297,513	2,176,930	91,495	132,079
1996-97	14,712,922	2,356,578	2,239,411	95,082	135,527
1997-98	15,000,475	2,412,497	2,294,160	98,435	140,163
1998-99	15,322,040	2,475,372	2,336,793	102,382	144,324

	Average teacher salary 4/ (dollars)	Number of schools	Assessed valuation of property ($1,000)	Total expenditure all purposes ($1,000)	Current expense per pupil 5/ (dollars)
1984-85	20,836	2,304	266,774,135	5,461,194	2,964
1985-86	22,250	2,296	323,579,927	6,103,747	3,205
1986-87	23,734	2,400	353,683,447	6,909,814	3,423
1987-88	25,198	2,438	378,703,589	7,643,660	3,679
1988-89	26,974	2,485	411,786,114	8,793,842	3,964
1989-90	28,803	2,591	414,018,411	10,125,835	4,248
1990-91	30,555	2,694	449,979,199	11,308,952	4,475
1991-92	31,067	2,730	475,960,538	11,745,293	4,439
1992-93	31,174	2,784	479,892,429	11,750,331	4,525
1993-94	31,948	2,867	488,458,004	12,780,952	4,724
1994-95	32,600	2,946	511,789,104	13,801,787	4,879
1995-96	33,330	3,003	535,588,385	14,455,035	5,026
1996-97	33,887	3,156	559,519,989	12,144,938	5,120
1997-98	34,473	3,178	592,847,936	12,846,999	5,317
1998-99	35,915	3,179	630,165,205	13,686,201	5,860

1/ Population figures for noncensus years are mid-year estimates as of April 1; 1985-86 through 1989-90 population breakdowns are for aged 15-24. Population figures as of 1992-93 are from the University of Florida, Bureau of Economic and Business Research, Population Program.
2/ Based on fall membership survey.
3/ Regular day school only; excludes state/university schools and adult programs. Includes standard and special diplomas.
4/ A professional paid on the instructional salary schedule negotiated by a Florida school district.
5/ Based on full-time equivalent student count.
Note: Data are for public schools only.

Source: State of Florida, Department of Education, Division of Administration, Education Information and Accountability Services, *Profiles of Florida School Districts, 1998-99, Student and Staff Data,* Internet site <http://www.firn.edu/doe/bin00050/eiaspubs/profile.htm> (accessed 1 May 200), and *Profiles of Florida School Districts, 1998-99, Financial Data Statistical Report,* prepublication release.

Table 4.06. ELEMENTARY AND SECONDARY SCHOOLS: ENROLLMENT IN KINDERGARTEN
THROUGH GRADE TWELVE IN THE STATE OF FLORIDA
1990-91 THROUGH 1999-2000

School year	Total enrollment	Public schools Enrollment	Percentage of total	Nonpublic schools 1/ Enrollment	Percentage of total
1990-91	2,035,145	1,841,206	90.47	193,939	9.53
1991-92	2,097,761	1,902,563	90.69	195,198	9.31
1992-93	2,150,377	1,950,114	90.59	200,263	9.31
1993-94	2,227,240	2,005,970	90.07	221,270	9.93
1994-95	2,298,752	2,064,884	89.83	233,868	10.17
1995-96	2,370,328	2,125,099	89.65	245,229	10.35
1996-97	2,446,044	2,188,239	89.47	257,805	10.54
1997-98	2,563,647	2,293,093	89.45	270,554	10.55
1998-99	2,610,392	2,335,681	89.48	274,711	10.52
1999-2000	2,670,108	2,381,860	89.20	288,248	10.80

1/ Private (nonpublic) elementary and secondary schools in Florida are not licensed, approved, accredited, or regulated by the state but they are required to make their existence known to the Department of Education and respond to an annual survey. See Glossary under Private school for definition.
Note: Based on DOE survey taken during the school year. Data may differ slightly from data based on fall surveys as shown in other *Abstract* tables.
Source: State of Florida, Department of Education, Division of Public Schools, *Statistical Brief: Florida's Nonpublic Schools, 1999-2000,* Series 2000-13B.

Table 4.07. ELEMENTARY AND SECONDARY SCHOOLS: CHANGE IN MEMBERSHIP
IN PREKINDERGARTEN THROUGH GRADE TWELVE IN THE STATE AND
COUNTIES OF FLORIDA, FALL 1995 TO FALL 1999

County	Number	Per- cent- age	County	Number	Per- cent- age	County	Number	Per- cent- age
Florida	200,895	9.24	Gulf	44	1.93	Nassau	635	6.63
			Hamilton	-132	-5.59	Okaloosa	794	2.70
Alachua	708	2.43	Hardee	-258	-4.87	Okeechobee	302	4.68
Baker	-37	-0.80	Hendry	475	6.72	Orange	20,993	17.06
Bay	199	0.79	Hernando	1,261	8.19	Osceola	6,214	24.21
Bradford	-14	-0.34	Highlands	249	2.31	Palm Beach	17,449	13.20
Brevard	4,040	6.16	Hillsborough	16,287	11.37	Pasco	5,642	13.50
Broward	32,682	15.69	Holmes	-109	-2.90	Pinellas	7,455	7.15
Calhoun	-66	-2.90	Indian River	1,093	8.00	Polk	5,935	8.15
Charlotte	1,160	7.44	Jackson	-411	-5.14	Putnam	-288	-2.23
Citrus	954	6.85	Jefferson	-188	-8.84	St. Johns	3,605	23.42
Clay	2,732	10.98	Lafayette	0	0.00	St. Lucie	2,312	8.55
Collier	5,930	22.48	Lake	3,676	14.81	Santa Rosa	2,447	12.37
Columbia	307	3.36	Lee	5,159	10.13	Sarasota	3,541	11.41
De Soto	158	3.50	Leon	-209	-0.67	Seminole	4,810	8.81
Dixie	45	1.98	Levy	531	9.26	Sumter	101	1.75
Duval	2,449	1.98	Liberty	-32	-2.58	Suwannee	67	1.18
Escambia	81	0.18	Madison	73	2.13	Taylor	-84	-2.16
Flagler	904	16.86	Manatee	3,647	11.47	Union	146	6.67
Franklin	-194	-11.37	Marion	2,922	8.22	Volusia	3,877	6.83
Gadsden	-726	-8.37	Martin	1,881	13.09	Wakulla	350	8.20
Gilchrist	208	8.23	Miami-Dade	26,311	7.88	Walton	682	13.03
Glades	70	6.35	Monroe	-139	-1.46	Washington	189	5.95

Source: State of Florida, Department of Education, Division of Administration, Education Information and Accountability Services, *Statistical Brief: Membership in Florida Public Schools, Fall 1999,* January 2000, Series 2000-04B, Internet site <http://www.firn.edu.doe/bin00050/eiaspubs/rankchng.htm> (accessed 1 May 2000).

University of Florida   **Bureau of Economic and Business Research**

Table 4.20. ELEMENTARY AND SECONDARY SCHOOLS: PUPIL MEMBERSHIP IN PREKINDERGARTEN THROUGH GRADE TWELVE BY RACE OR HISPANIC ORIGIN IN THE STATE AND COUNTIES OF FLORIDA, FALL 1999

County	Total member- ship	Total minority	White	Black	Asian/ Pacific Islander	American Indian/ Alaskan native	Multi- racial	His- panic ori- gin 1/
Florida	2,380,451	1,101,865	53.71	25.09	1.84	0.26	1.11	17.99
Alachua	29,874	13,580	54.54	37.80	2.29	0.20	1.25	3.92
Baker	4,598	776	83.12	15.85	0.35	0.07	0.15	0.46
Bay	25,427	5,166	79.68	15.40	2.02	0.28	1.18	1.44
Bradford	4,099	1,047	74.46	23.30	0.73	0.15	0.17	1.20
Brevard	69,659	15,321	78.01	14.17	1.66	0.27	1.68	4.22
Broward	241,036	139,144	42.27	35.99	2.70	0.30	1.19	17.55
Calhoun	2,213	390	82.38	14.10	0.86	0.23	0.45	1.99
Charlotte	16,753	2,459	85.32	7.94	1.35	0.23	1.40	3.75
Citrus	14,888	1,429	90.40	4.79	1.07	0.45	0.61	2.68
Clay	27,607	4,293	84.45	9.31	1.97	0.21	0.69	3.38
Collier	32,306	13,389	58.56	11.47	0.67	0.54	0.71	28.06
Columbia	9,444	2,728	71.11	24.27	0.76	0.39	1.20	2.27
De Soto	4,666	1,954	58.12	20.38	0.43	0.15	0.11	20.81
Dixie	2,319	255	89.00	9.57	0.00	0.00	0.69	0.73
Duval	126,354	63,152	50.02	42.41	2.70	0.15	1.28	3.44
Escambia	45,296	19,054	57.93	36.28	2.71	0.66	0.85	1.57
Flagler	6,265	1,385	77.89	13.28	1.55	0.24	1.92	5.12
Franklin	1,512	287	81.02	17.39	0.46	0.00	0.66	0.46
Gadsden	7,948	7,441	6.38	85.18	0.13	0.01	0.38	7.93
Gilchrist	2,736	186	93.20	5.19	0.15	0.04	0.22	1.21
Glades	1,172	630	46.25	26.02	0.43	0.94	0.77	25.60
Gulf	2,323	493	78.78	19.72	0.39	0.22	0.30	0.60
Hamilton	2,228	1,234	44.61	48.97	0.18	0.18	0.27	5.79
Hardee	5,040	2,783	44.78	8.91	0.24	0.06	0.04	45.97
Hendry	7,539	4,532	39.89	19.43	0.56	0.45	0.92	38.76
Hernando	16,654	2,447	85.31	7.44	0.80	0.15	0.94	5.36
Highlands	11,007	4,263	61.27	21.23	0.74	0.49	0.54	15.73
Hillsborough	159,479	77,010	51.71	23.68	2.16	0.34	2.15	19.97
Holmes	3,650	175	95.21	2.88	0.47	0.14	0.16	1.15
Indian River	14,762	4,181	71.68	17.48	1.12	0.24	0.91	8.58
Jackson	7,580	2,732	63.96	32.60	0.29	0.41	1.06	1.69
Jefferson	1,938	1,319	31.94	67.13	0.15	0.21	0.10	0.46
Lafayette	1,052	215	79.56	12.17	0.19	0.00	0.29	7.79
Lake	28,503	7,299	74.39	16.61	0.94	0.19	0.56	7.30
Lee	56,104	18,391	67.22	15.77	1.06	0.29	1.27	14.39
Leon	31,123	13,493	56.65	38.64	1.66	0.13	1.01	1.91

See footnotes at end of table.

Continued . . .

University of Florida   **Bureau of Economic and Business Research**

Table 4.20. ELEMENTARY AND SECONDARY SCHOOLS: PUPIL MEMBERSHIP IN PREKINDERGARTEN THROUGH GRADE TWELVE BY RACE OR HISPANIC ORIGIN IN THE STATE AND COUNTIES OF FLORIDA, FALL 1999 (Continued)

County	Total member- ship	Total minority	White	Black	Asian/ Pacific Islander	American Indian/ Alaskan native	Multi- racial	His- panic ori- gin 1/
Levy	6,267	1,348	78.49	16.83	0.48	0.21	0.40	3.59
Liberty	1,210	211	82.56	13.80	0.08	0.33	0.66	2.56
Madison	3,507	2,044	41.72	56.57	0.03	0.26	0.20	1.23
Manatee	35,450	11,746	66.87	17.48	0.98	0.10	0.83	13.74
Marion	38,449	11,931	68.97	21.82	0.72	0.25	1.11	7.12
Martin	16,250	4,133	74.57	11.54	0.87	0.26	0.95	11.80
Miami-Dade	360,142	317,723	11.78	32.15	1.25	0.08	0.57	54.17
Monroe	9,369	2,907	68.97	9.13	1.10	0.26	1.75	18.80
Nassau	10,214	1,270	87.57	10.66	0.40	0.24	0.14	0.99
Okaloosa	30,248	6,438	78.72	12.24	2.82	0.45	2.49	3.29
Okeechobee	6,758	2,091	69.06	9.22	0.64	1.79	0.25	19.04
Orange	144,057	78,042	45.83	29.05	3.49	0.33	0.46	20.85
Osceola	31,884	15,252	52.16	9.48	2.64	0.20	1.60	33.91
Palm Beach	149,664	75,137	49.80	29.49	2.05	0.47	1.85	16.34
Pasco	47,433	6,018	87.31	3.58	1.11	0.25	1.06	6.69
Pinellas	111,786	30,883	72.37	18.97	2.95	0.21	1.22	4.28
Polk	78,742	28,322	64.03	23.44	0.92	0.16	0.52	10.93
Putnam	12,647	4,593	63.68	26.88	0.52	0.14	0.78	7.99
St. Johns	19,001	2,780	85.37	10.69	0.94	0.15	0.95	1.91
St. Lucie	29,357	12,360	57.90	30.18	1.01	0.22	1.05	9.63
Santa Rosa	22,226	2,068	90.70	5.26	1.42	0.56	0.46	1.61
Sarasota	34,576	6,532	81.11	9.75	1.29	0.18	1.61	6.06
Seminole	59,409	18,477	68.90	14.16	2.81	0.26	2.13	11.74
Sumter	5,868	1,867	68.18	25.89	0.31	0.32	0.34	4.96
Suwannee	5,757	1,322	77.04	19.19	0.49	0.26	0.30	2.73
Taylor	3,805	998	73.77	24.42	0.37	0.58	0.21	0.66
Union	2,335	460	80.30	17.73	0.26	0.04	0.30	1.37
Volusia	60,665	16,052	73.54	15.82	1.02	0.23	1.19	8.20
Wakulla	4,620	611	86.77	11.84	0.24	0.28	0.54	0.32
Walton	5,915	752	87.29	9.52	0.51	0.61	0.57	1.50
Washington	3,363	723	78.50	18.38	0.54	0.71	0.77	1.10

1/ Persons of Hispanic origin may be of any race. However, these data are not distributed by race. Note: Data were obtained from the Florida DOE Student Information Data Base, Survey 2, as of December 23, 1999, and are for public schools that responded to the survey only.

Source: State of Florida, Department of Education, Division of Administration, Education Information and Accountability Services, *Statistical Brief: Membership in Florida Public Schools, Fall 1999,* January 2000, Series 2000-04B. Internet site <http://www.firn.edu.doe/bin00050/eiaspubs/racethnc.htm> (accessed 1 May 2000).

Table 4.25. HOME EDUCATION: NUMBER OF CHILDREN AND FAMILIES REGISTERED IN HOME EDUCATION PROGRAMS IN THE STATE AND COUNTIES OF FLORIDA, 1999-2000

County	Children	Families	County	Children	Families
Florida	37,196	26,656	Lake	598	423
			Lee	890	573
Alachua	700	423	Leon	885	583
Baker	59	40	Levy	211	150
Bay	685	411	Liberty	5	4
Bradford	69	45	Madison	56	37
Brevard	1,568	1,042	Manatee	496	351
Broward	2,321	1,813	Marion	741	530
Calhoun	71	51	Martin	315	203
Charlotte	310	226	Miami-Dade	1,821	1,592
Citrus	511	356	Monroe	200	144
Clay	441	289	Nassau	231	168
Collier	629	434	Okaloosa	660	468
Columbia	466	352	Okeechobee	118	80
De Soto	46	31	Orange	1,840	1,277
Dixie	44	29	Osceola	320	219
Duval	2,335	1,952	Palm Beach	2,708	2,069
Escambia	1,211	753	Pasco	846	806
Flagler	108	71	Pinellas	1,711	1,075
Franklin	52	35	Polk	1,953	1,462
Gadsden	226	124	Putnam	188	127
Gilchrist	66	40	St. Johns	407	271
Glades	28	18	St. Lucie	229	151
Gulf	13	10	Santa Rosa	688	576
Hamilton	32	17	Sarasota	656	465
Hardee	25	19	Seminole	1,198	798
Hendry	133	90	Sumter	73	49
Hernando	420	276	Suwannee	170	109
Highlands	309	194	Taylor	43	33
Hillsborough	1,915	1,236	Union	27	22
Holmes	96	58	Volusia	967	664
Indian River	352	296	Wakulla	68	48
Jackson	165	100	Walton	252	162
Jefferson	72	36	Washington	134	91
Lafayette	13	9			

Note: Home education is defined by Florida Statutes as the "sequentially progressive instruction of a student in his or her home by his or her parent or guardian." No curriculum is prescribed.

Source: State of Florida, Department of Education, Division of Public Schools, *Statistical Brief: Florida Home Education Programs, 1999-2000, June 2000,* Series 2000-14B.

Table 4.26. NONPUBLIC ELEMENTARY AND SECONDARY SCHOOLS: PUPIL MEMBERSHIP
IN THE STATE AND COUNTIES OF FLORIDA, 1999-2000

County	Member-ship K-12	Per-centage change 1998-99 to 1999-2000	As a percent-age of total K-12 member-ship	County	Member-ship K-12	Per-centage change 1998-99 to 1999-2000	As a percent-age of total K-12 member-ship
Florida	288,248	4.93	10.80	Lake	2,769	12.79	8.85
				Lee	6,206	11.22	9.93
Alachua	2,485	4.63	7.68	Leon	4,726	0.08	13.04
Baker	70	677.78	1.50	Levy	37	-2.63	0.59
Bay	3,833	158.46	12.93	Liberty	37	-17.78	2.97
Bradford	94	10.59	2.24	Madison	299	0.00	7.86
Brevard	8,567	-0.57	10.94	Manatee	3,241	7.50	8.38
Broward	34,043	8.01	12.38	Marion	5,347	-4.64	12.21
Calhoun	19	0.00	0.85	Martin	1,743	-1.47	9.70
Charlotte	879	20.08	4.99	Miami-Dade	52,432	4.49	12.71
Citrus	677	3.99	4.35	Monroe	537	-4.62	5.42
Clay	3,447	11.30	11.11	Nassau	515	47.56	4.80
Collier	2,537	15.69	7.29	Okaloosa	1,700	4.10	5.33
Columbia	345	-11.08	3.53	Okeechobee	175	-3.85	2.52
De Soto	40	0.00	0.85	Orange	19,367	2.95	11.84
Dixie	0	(X)	0.00	Osceola	2,407	5.99	7.02
Duval	21,740	4.44	14.69	Palm Beach	23,863	4.52	13.74
Escambia	6,422	0.28	12.43	Pasco	2,104	5.84	4.23
Flagler	195	44.44	3.01	Pinellas	17,346	2.25	13.44
Franklin	58	-34.09	3.69	Polk	6,990	19.20	8.15
Gadsden	663	-0.75	7.64	Putnam	484	-4.91	3.69
Gilchrist	101	-54.30	3.56	St. Johns	1,791	-31.95	8.60
Glades	22	-43.59	1.85	St. Lucie	2,742	4.82	8.54
Gulf	53	-22.06	2.23	Santa Rosa	536	-12.56	2.36
Hamilton	43	230.77	1.89	Sarasota	4,819	7.35	12.21
Hardee	25	-39.02	0.49	Seminole	8,141	5.05	12.04
Hendry	325	5.86	4.13	Sumter	77	-11.49	1.30
Hernando	1,675	-14.37	9.06	Suwannee	421	12.27	6.73
Highlands	613	6.61	5.28	Taylor	13	30.00	0.34
Hillsborough	20,324	1.27	11.31	Union	0	(X)	0.00
Holmes	23	15.00	0.63	Volusia	5,633	2.62	8.50
Indian River	1,662	1.78	10.12	Wakulla	72	24.14	1.54
Jackson	284	24.56	3.62	Walton	142	2.90	2.35
Jefferson	272	-6.85	12.31	Washington	0	(X)	0.00
Lafayette	0	(X)	0.00				

K-12 Kindergarten through grade 12; no prekindergarten.
(X) Not applicable.
Note: See Glossary under Private school for definition of nonpublic schools.

Source: State of Florida, Department of Education, Division of Public Schools, *Statistical Brief: Florida's Nonpublic Schools, 1999-2000,* Series 2000-13B.

University of Florida   **Bureau of Economic and Business Research**

Table 4.27. ELEMENTARY AND SECONDARY SCHOOLS: NUMBER AND PUPIL MEMBERSHIP
IN THE STATE AND COUNTIES OF FLORIDA, SCHOOL YEAR 1998-99

County	Number of schools	Membership 1/ Total	Membership 1/ Percentage change from 1997-98	County	Number of schools	Membership 1/ Total	Membership 1/ Percentage change from 1997-98
Florida 2/	3,179	2,282,725	1.9	Lake	49	27,355	2.6
				Lee	76	53,172	1.7
Alachua	51	28,599	-0.9	Leon	50	30,544	0.6
Baker	9	4,588	0.2	Levy	13	6,073	1.8
Bay	36	25,304	-0.3	Liberty	5	1,146	-5.8
Bradford	10	4,028	0.4	Madison	11	3,320	-1.1
Brevard	104	67,329	1.1	Manatee	69	33,278	1.4
Broward	215	225,984	2.9	Marion	56	37,052	1.7
Calhoun	7	2,172	-0.5	Martin	33	15,584	3.2
Charlotte	23	16,176	1.7	Miami-Dade	375	343,653	1.9
Citrus	20	14,333	0.4	Monroe	18	9,128	-1.2
Clay	31	26,959	2.2	Nassau	17	10,150	0.1
Collier	47	29,846	5.5	Okaloosa	44	29,889	0.1
Columbia	14	9,245	0.6	Okeechobee	14	6,497	2.8
De Soto	11	4,500	1.8	Orange	171	136,276	3.8
Dixie	6	2,281	1.3	Osceola	34	29,665	5.0
Duval	161	124,693	0.5	Palm Beach	197	143,479	2.8
Escambia	78	44,353	-0.7	Pasco	57	44,799	2.9
Flagler	10	6,020	4.3	Pinellas	151	108,631	1.2
Franklin	6	1,453	2.9	Polk	125	75,892	1.3
Gadsden	24	7,777	-1.3	Putnam	25	12,500	-1.6
Gilchrist	7	2,580	3.4	St. Johns	28	18,009	4.2
Glades	6	1,107	2.6	St. Lucie	40	28,357	2.3
Gulf	8	2,214	-2.5	Santa Rosa	34	21,460	2.1
Hamilton	9	2,152	-3.6	Sarasota	38	33,242	2.5
Hardee	9	4,948	-2.7	Seminole	65	57,234	2.3
Hendry	18	7,279	1.1	Sumter	12	5,714	0.8
Hernando	25	16,067	1.5	Suwannee	9	5,652	-1.5
Highlands	18	10,832	0.0	Taylor	10	3,668	1.2
Hillsborough	213	152,448	2.1	Union	5	2,275	1.0
Holmes	9	3,635	-3.5	Volusia	78	58,919	1.0
Indian River	22	14,307	2.1	Wakulla	9	4,445	-0.2
Jackson	20	7,444	-2.6	Walton	13	5,701	1.8
Jefferson	7	1,829	-3.1	Washington	9	3,304	1.2
Lafayette	5	1,023	-0.4				

1/ Based on kindergarten through grade 12 fall membership survey.
2/ Detail may not add to total due to receipt of reports not distributed by county.
Note: Data are for public schools only.

Source: State of Florida, Department of Education, Division of Administration, Education Information
and Accountability Services, *Profiles of Florida School Districts, 1998-99, Student and Staff Data*.
Series 2000-06, February 2000. Internet site <http://www.firn.edu/doe/bin00050/eiaspubs/profiles.htm>
(accessed 1 May 2000).

University of Florida   **Bureau of Economic and Business Research**

Table 4.50. HIGHER EDUCATION: ENROLLMENT IN SELECTED COLLEGES AND UNIVERSITIES IN SPECIFIED CITIES AND COUNTIES OF FLORIDA, ACADEMIC YEAR 1996-97

School 1/	City	County	Enroll-ment 2/
Art Institute of Ft. Lauderdale	Ft. Lauderdale	Broward	1,698
ATI Health Education Center	Miami	Miami-Dade	217
Barry University	Miami	Miami-Dade	7,048
Bethune Cookman College	Daytona Beach	Volusia	2,402
Brevard Community College	Cocoa	Brevard	14,188
Broward Community College	Ft. Lauderdale	Broward	25,738
Caribbean Center for Advanced Studies/ Miami Institute of Psychology	Miami	Miami-Dade	516
Central Florida Community College	Ocala	Marion	6,330
Chipola Junior College	Marianna	Jackson	2,385
Clearwater Christian College	Clearwater	Pinellas	528
Daytona Beach Community College	Daytona Beach	Volusia	11,227
Eckerd College	St. Petersburg	Pinellas	1,335
Edison Community College	Ft. Myers	Lee	9,810
Education America-Tampa Technical Institute	Tampa	Hillsborough	1,129
Edward Waters College	Jacksonville	Duval	524
Embry-Riddle Aeronautical University	Daytona Beach	Volusia	11,714
Flagler Career Institute	Jacksonville	Duval	205
Flagler College	St. Augustine	St. Johns	1,426
Florida Agricultural and Mechanical University	Tallahassee	Leon	10,306
Florida Atlantic University	Boca Raton	Palm Beach	17,704
Florida Baptist Theological College	Graceville	Jackson	535
Florida Christian College Inc.	Kissimmee	Osceola	153
Florida College	Temple Terrace	Hillsborough	378
Florida Community College at Jacksonville	Jacksonville	Duval	21,237
Florida Institute of Technology	Melbourne	Brevard	4,232
Florida International University	Miami	Miami-Dade	28,171
Florida Keys Community College	Key West	Monroe	1,861
Florida Memorial College	Miami	Miami-Dade	1,457
Florida Southern College	Lakeland	Polk	2,571
Florida State University	Tallahassee	Leon	30,155
Ft. Lauderdale College	Ft. Lauderdale	Broward	427
Gulf Coast Community	Panama City	Bay	5,988
Hillsborough Community College	Tampa	Hillsborough	20,311
Hobe Sound Bible College	Hobe Sound	Martin	144
Indian River Community College	Ft. Pierce	St. Lucie	13,763
International Academy of Merchandising and Design	Tampa	Hillsborough	411
International College	Naples	Collier	230
International College	Ft. Myers	Lee	257
International Fine Arts College	Miami	Miami-Dade	665
ITT Technical Institute	Tampa	Hillsborough	613

See footnotes at end of table.

Continued . . .

University of Florida   **Bureau of Economic and Business Research**

Table 4.50. HIGHER EDUCATION: ENROLLMENT IN SELECTED COLLEGES AND UNIVERSITIES
IN SPECIFIED CITIES AND COUNTIES OF FLORIDA, ACADEMIC YEAR 1996-97 (Continued)

School 1/	City	County	Enroll-ment 2/
ITT Technical Institute	Maitland	Orange	464
Jacksonville University	Jacksonville	Duval	2,415
Johnson and Wales University/			
Florida campus	North Miami	Miami-Dade	716
Jones College Jacksonville	Jacksonville	Duval	672
Jones College/Miami campus	Miami	Miami-Dade	220
Keiser College of Technology	Ft. Lauderdale	Broward	1,316
Keiser College/Melbourne	Melbourne	Brevard	0
Keiser College/Sarasota	Sarasota	Sarasota	(NA)
Keiser College/Tallahassee	Tallahassee	Leon	0
Lake City Community College	Lake City	Columbia	2,481
Lake-Sumter Community College	Leesburg	Lake	2,562
Lynn University	Boca Raton	Palm Beach	1,566
Manatee Community College	Bradenton	Manatee	7,524
Miami-Miami-Dade Community College	Miami	Miami-Dade	47,060
National School of Technology	Miami	Miami-Dade	419
New England Institute of Technology/			
Palm Beach	West Palm Beach	Palm Beach	702
New York Institute of Technology/			
Florida campus	Boca Raton	Palm Beach	0
North Florida Junior College	Madison	Madison	1,223
Northwood University-Florida			
Education Center	West Palm Beach	Palm Beach	566
Nova Southeastern University	Ft. Lauderdale	Broward	13,941
Okaloosa-Walton Community College	Niceville	Okaloosa	6,607
Orlando College	Orlando	Orange	599
Orlando College South	Orlando	Orange	721
Orlando College-Melbourne	Melbourne	Brevard	(NA)
Palm Beach Atlantic College	West Palm Beach	Palm Beach	1,953
Palm Beach Community College	Lake Worth	Palm Beach	18,310
Pasco-Hernando Community College	Miami-Dade City	Pasco	5,327
Pensacola Junior College	Pensacola	Escambia	11,250
Polk Community College	Winter Haven	Polk	5,461
Prospect Hall School of Business	Hollywood	Broward	155
Reformed Theological Seminary	Maitland	Orange	297
Ringling School of Art and Design	Sarasota	Sarasota	823
Rollins College	Winter Park	Orange	3,237
Rollins College/Brevard campus	West Melbourne	Brevard	0
St. John Vianney College Seminary	Miami	Miami-Dade	41
St. Johns River Community College	Palatka	Putnam	3,189
St. Leo College	St. Leo	Pasco	7,176
St. Petersburg Junior College	St. Petersburg	Pinellas	21,176
St. Thomas University	Miami	Miami-Dade	2,125

See footnotes at end of table.   Continued . . .

University of Florida   **Bureau of Economic and Business Research**

Table 4.50. HIGHER EDUCATION: ENROLLMENT IN SELECTED COLLEGES AND UNIVERSITIES IN SPECIFIED CITIES AND COUNTIES OF FLORIDA, ACADEMIC YEAR 1996-97 (Continued)

School 1/	City	County	Enroll-ment 2/
St. Vincent of De Paul Regional Seminary	Boynton Beach	Palm Beach	84
Santa Fe Community College	Gainesville	Alachua	12,463
Seminole Community College	Sanford	Seminole	7,742
South College	West Palm Beach	Palm Beach	312
South Florida Community College	Avon Park	Highlands	2,717
Southeastern College Assemblies of God	Lakeland	Polk	1,065
Spurgeon Baptist Bible College	Mulberry	Polk	40
Stetson University	DeLand	Volusia	2,897
Tallahassee Community	Tallahassee	Leon	10,067
Talmudic College of Florida	Tampa	Hillsborough	45
Tampa College	Tampa	Hillsborough	868
Tampa College/Brandon	Tampa	Hillsborough	704
Tampa College/Lakeland	Lakeland	Polk	469
Tampa College/Pinellas	Clearwater	Pinellas	706
The Union Institute	North Miami Beach	Miami-Dade	(NA)
The University of West Florida	Pensacola	Escambia	8,052
Trinity College of Florida	New Port Richey	Pasco	154
Trinity International University	Miami	Miami-Dade	356
University of Central Florida	Orlando	Orange	26,556
University of Florida	Gainesville	Alachua	39,412
University of Miami	Coral Gables	Miami-Dade	13,541
University of North Florida	Jacksonville	Duval	10,463
University of Sarasota	Sarasota	Sarasota	539
University of South Florida	Tampa	Hillsborough	36,142
University of Tampa	Tampa	Hillsborough	2,521
Valencia Community College	Orlando	Orange	23,569
Warner Southern College	Lake Wales	Polk	581
Webber College	Babson Park	Polk	453

(NA) Not available.
1/ Includes institutions accredited at the college level by an agency recognized by the U.S. Secretary of Education.
2/ Includes undergraduate, graduate, first-professional, and unclassified students, both full- and part-time.
Note: Only accredited schools are listed.

Source: U.S., Department of Education, National Center for Education Statistics, Office of Educational Research and Improvement, *1997 Directory of Postsecondary Institutions: Volume I, Degree-granting Institutions.*

University of Florida   **Bureau of Economic and Business Research**

Table 4.53. HIGHER EDUCATION: ENROLLMENT IN THE UNIVERSITIES OF THE STATE UNIVERSITY SYSTEM OF FLORIDA BY LEVEL, SEX, RACE OR HISPANIC ORIGIN AND STATUS, FALL 1998

Sex and race	Educational and general				Health or medical center 1/			
			1998				1998	
	1996	1997	Total	Under-graduates (percent-age)	1996	1997	Total	Under-graduates (percent-age)
				Part-time 2/				
Total	73,204	72,326	73,343	78.6	1,438	1,533	986	19.8
Sex								
Female	41,613	41,133	41,687	78.2	943	983	605	27.1
Male	31,582	30,775	31,297	78.9	495	550	381	8.1
Not reported	9	418	359	100.0	0	0	0	(NA)
Race								
Asian	2,639	2,683	2,738	81.6	93	99	74	9.5
Black	7,731	7,733	8,209	86.0	66	96	68	25.0
American Indian or Alaskan native	219	255	254	85.8	10	11	7	28.6
White	48,511	47,133	47,196	75.9	1,147	1,187	755	2,314.3
Other	1,649	1,691	1,727	52.1	25	29	11	0.0
Not reported	567	547	603	96.0	3	5	3	33.3
Hispanic origin 3/	11,888	12,284	12,616	85.8	94	106	68	8.8
				Full-time 4/				
Total	126,134	131,393	142,878	87.1	3,744	3,833	1,563	10.1
Sex								
Female	67,973	71,297	78,864	87.9	2,465	2,558	916	15.4
Male	58,186	60,073	63,990	86.2	1,279	1,275	647	2.6
Not reported	5	23	24	100.0	0	0	0	(NA)
Race								
Asian	5,141	5,359	6,118	89.2	312	315	147	6.8
Black	18,809	19,959	21,768	91.5	228	246	100	17.0
American Indian or Alaskan native	440	462	509	86.1	17	19	10	20.0
White	81,122	83,433	89,937	87.2	2,807	2,837	1,108	9.7
Other	5,246	5,704	6,688	57.3	130	124	47	6.4
Not reported	144	205	350	89.4	4	6	4	50.0
Hispanic origin 3/	15,232	16,271	17,508	91.7	246	286	147	11.6

(NA) Not available.
1/ Includes veterinary medicine.
2/ Includes undergraduates enrolled for fewer than 12 hours and graduate students enrolled for fewer than 9 hours.
3/ Persons of Hispanic origin may be of any race. However, these data are not distributed by race.
4/ Includes undergraduates enrolled for 12 or more hours and graduate students enrolled for 9 or more hours.
Note: Unclassified students are counted as undergraduates. Data are from the student data course file enrollment report, Fall 1998. Staff and senior citizen waivers are excluded.

Source: State of Florida, State University System, Board of Regents, *Fact Book, 1998-99.*

University of Florida
Bureau of Economic and Business Research

Table 4.54. HIGHER EDUCATION: ENROLLMENT IN THE UNIVERSITIES OF THE STATE
UNIVERSITY SYSTEM OF FLORIDA, FALL 1991 THROUGH 1998

University	1991	1992	1993	1994
Total	181,889	182,896	188,928	197,931
Educational and general, total	176,077	176,762	182,579	191,148
University of Florida	32,159	31,922	32,578	32,827
Florida State University	28,093	27,810	27,951	28,794
Florida A & M University	8,801	9,049	9,378	9,650
University of South Florida	31,771	32,467	32,773	33,614
Florida Atlantic University	14,264	14,822	15,760	17,367
University of West Florida	7,943	7,386	7,564	7,716
University of Central Florida	21,267	21,682	23,531	25,363
Florida International University	23,275	22,597	23,832	26,040
University of North Florida	8,504	9,027	9,212	9,777
Florida Gulf Coast University	(X)	(X)	(X)	(X)
Special units, total 1/	5,812	6,134	6,349	6,783
University of Florida				
Institute of Food and Agriculture				
Science (IFAS)	1,748	1,971	2,141	2,403
Health and Medical Center	2,932	2,961	2,965	3,087
University of South Florida				
Medical Center	1,132	1,202	1,243	1,293

	1995	1996	1997	1998
Total	203,478	208,033	213,066	218,770
Educational and general, total	196,246	199,338	203,719	216,221
University of Florida	33,394	32,314	33,524	41,652
Florida State University	29,390	29,345	29,629	30,389
Florida A & M University	9,784	10,206	10,477	11,324
University of South Florida	33,829	34,024	31,906	31,555
Florida Atlantic University	17,671	18,350	19,107	19,153
University of West Florida	8,087	7,882	7,855	7,790
University of Central Florida	26,325	27,411	28,302	30,009
Florida International University	27,542	29,098	29,357	30,096
University of North Florida	10,224	10,708	11,116	11,360
Florida Gulf Coast University	(X)	(X)	2,446	2,893
Special units, total 1/	7,232	8,695	9,347	2,549
University of Florida				
Institute of Food and Agriculture				
Science (IFAS)	2,772	3,513	3,981	A/
Health and Medical Center	3,174	3,845	3,924	1,072
University of South Florida				
Medical Center	1,286	1,337	1,442	1,477

A/ Beginning in 1998, the headcount enrollment for IFAS and nonmedical professional students at
the University of Florida is included in the University of Florida educational and general headcount total.
1/ Includes medical professionals.
Note: Data are from the student data course file enrollment reports. Staff and senior citizen waivers
are excluded.

Source: State of Florida, State University System, Board of Regents, *Fact Book, 1998-99.*

University of Florida   **Bureau of Economic and Business Research**

Table 4.55. HIGHER EDUCATION: ENROLLMENT IN THE UNIVERSITIES OF THE STATE UNIVERSITY SYSTEM BY RESIDENCE AT TIME OF ADMISSION OR READMISSION IN THE STATE AND COUNTIES OF FLORIDA, FALL 1998

County	Total	UF	FSU	FAMU	USF	FAU	UWF	UCF	FIU	UNF	FGCU
Florida	225,216	43,327	31,496	11,948	34,316	19,783	8,084	30,472	31,066	11,696	3,028
Alachua	6,062	4,857	316	159	262	51	26	195	64	121	11
Baker	133	29	19	14	1	0	0	7	0	63	0
Bay	1,664	265	1,019	75	37	11	171	68	1	14	3
Bradford	127	64	4	6	3	0	3	6	0	40	1
Brevard	5,874	1,115	585	131	329	70	17	3,357	64	201	5
Broward	21,382	3,709	2,074	757	792	8,525	54	1,683	3,622	149	17
Calhoun	98	9	50	28	3	0	3	3	0	1	1
Charlotte	941	161	104	12	272	13	16	135	17	22	189
Citrus	687	211	124	13	146	11	16	138	3	24	1
Clay	1,981	561	269	27	37	3	17	93	5	965	4
Collier	1,915	347	243	11	155	50	23	263	40	19	764
Columbia	382	153	88	50	7	0	5	21	0	57	1
De Soto	126	27	15	5	33	1	1	16	2	3	23
Dixie	33	16	10	4	1	0	0	0	0	1	1
Duval	10,752	1,733	1,223	642	193	49	38	316	31	6,522	5
Escambia	4,433	487	417	190	63	4	3,180	66	8	18	0
Flagler	393	102	49	6	11	3	1	135	1	85	0
Franklin	55	5	26	13	2	0	7	1	0	1	0
Gadsden	644	27	276	321	3	2	4	5	3	3	0
Gilchrist	88	62	12	6	3	0	0	0	0	4	1
Glades	42	12	1	2	4	4	1	1	0	1	16
Gulf	119	18	56	21	0	0	21	2	0	1	0
Hamilton	61	16	5	31	0	0	2	2	0	4	1
Hardee	101	18	21	4	49	1	0	7	1	0	0
Hendry	225	49	15	11	23	16	1	35	9	9	57
Hernando	925	170	116	12	475	2	11	111	0	27	1
Highlands	412	108	57	28	114	9	5	68	2	17	4
Hillsborough	16,596	2,143	1,137	370	12,145	53	58	530	68	79	13
Holmes	93	16	39	7	0	1	29	0	0	0	1
Indian River	795	188	117	32	55	158	3	218	5	19	0
Jackson	421	54	184	97	11	1	58	14	1	0	1
Jefferson	205	19	101	76	0	0	3	4	0	2	0
Lafayette	31	7	7	14	1	0	0	1	0	1	0
Lake	1,206	310	174	55	93	10	9	521	3	28	3
Lee	4,046	697	466	49	486	74	20	444	47	38	1,725
Leon	7,653	712	4,598	1,821	166	39	68	158	24	60	7
Levy	133	79	18	5	9	1	5	8	1	6	1
Liberty	54	2	35	16	0	0	1	0	0	0	0
Madison	152	16	51	67	4	2	2	5	1	4	0

See footnotes at end of table.

Continued . . .

University of Florida

Bureau of Economic and Business Research

Table 4.55. HIGHER EDUCATION: ENROLLMENT IN THE UNIVERSITIES OF THE STATE
UNIVERSITY SYSTEM BY RESIDENCE AT TIME OF ADMISSION OR READMISSION
IN THE STATE AND COUNTIES OF FLORIDA, FALL 1998 (Continued)

County	Total	UF	FSU	FAMU	USF	FAU	UWF	UCF	FIU	UNF	FGCU
Manatee	1,969	311	220	50	1,075	14	18	219	10	41	11
Marion	1,478	662	236	56	137	17	23	257	2	83	5
Martin	1,055	258	163	17	62	309	5	200	17	21	3
Miami-Dade	32,957	3,060	2,249	1,229	638	846	49	629	24,175	71	11
Monroe	470	111	83	6	46	26	13	64	103	13	5
Nassau	455	81	59	16	19	1	12	14	3	250	0
Okaloosa	2,683	480	480	60	42	5	1,500	101	3	12	0
Okeechobee	196	38	7	7	7	75	3	54	1	2	2
Orange	11,773	1,802	971	408	516	55	45	7,769	97	105	5
Osceola	1,170	190	98	10	113	6	9	711	14	19	0
Palm Beach	13,534	2,406	1,454	358	514	7,007	45	1,311	362	70	7
Pasco	2,534	417	192	20	1,632	14	36	184	11	28	0
Pinellas	11,553	2,240	1,148	239	6,835	55	60	809	52	103	12
Polk	3,518	657	438	195	1,643	26	20	460	15	59	5
Putnam	367	128	80	24	11	0	3	35	1	85	0
St. Johns	6,339	1,404	630	126	219	46	27	3,753	30	103	1
St. Lucie	1,373	347	199	33	27	14	3	74	6	670	0
Santa Rosa	1,625	156	192	24	15	2	1,188	38	0	10	0
Sarasota	3,168	745	403	33	1,372	45	41	432	23	42	32
Seminole	6,339	1,404	630	126	219	46	27	3,753	30	103	1
Sumter	174	47	35	20	43	1	0	22	0	2	4
Suwannee	249	81	75	60	9	0	8	3	0	12	1
Taylor	181	24	82	62	1	0	2	6	0	4	0
Union	78	40	12	8	1	0	0	4	0	11	2
Volusia	3,910	826	467	149	158	27	22	2,026	36	198	1
Wakulla	201	10	141	37	2	1	7	1	1	1	0
Walton	209	21	58	9	1	0	117	0	0	3	0
Washington	134	17	72	21	1	0	20	3	0	0	0
County not reported 1/	29,425	7,879	6,995	3,391	3,097	1,582	918	2,378	2,064	1,057	64

1/ Includes two previously reported categories, "NonFlorida" and "NonUSA."
Note: County of residence shown as self-reported by students. Headcounts include nonfee-paying students. See Table 4.54 for a complete list of university names.

Source: State of Florida, State University System, Board of Regents, *Fact Book, 1998-99.*

University of Florida   **Bureau of Economic and Business Research**

Table 4.60. PUBLIC COMMUNITY COLLEGES: COLLEGE LEVEL HEADCOUNT ENROLLMENT
BY PROGRAM AND INSTITUTION IN FLORIDA, 1998-99

Community college	Total Undupli-cated	Total Dupli-cated	Advanced and profes-sional	Voca-tional (credit)	Adult general	Other objectives Community instruc-tional serv-ices 1/	Lifelong learning
Total	737,864	979,096	199,076	278,911	160,319	334,053	6,737
Brevard	27,552	35,771	9,595	11,444	3,276	10,982	474
Broward	47,915	62,816	14,466	12,663	10,203	24,887	597
Central Florida	16,976	19,663	4,198	8,698	2,326	2,617	1,824
Chipola	5,410	6,784	1,644	3,509	575	1,056	0
Daytona Beach	32,603	40,437	7,415	13,905	11,461	7,656	0
Edison	21,229	22,047	5,412	9,982	2,345	4,151	157
Florida Community College at Jacksonville	69,416	81,190	7,375	31,804	25,299	16,712	0
Florida Keys	4,068	4,509	628	1,248	258	2,253	122
Gulf Coast	21,723	21,880	4,354	14,094	1,906	1,526	0
Hillsborough	37,413	42,049	15,646	13,136	5,616	7,651	0
Indian River	41,213	55,800	4,804	13,067	12,135	25,794	0
Lake City	6,451	7,704	1,443	3,838	1,571	849	3
Lake-Sumter	6,254	8,120	852	2,732	753	3,547	236
Manatee	17,024	20,422	3,897	7,182	1,974	7,108	261
Miami-Dade	98,924	142,988	20,727	27,298	20,318	74,645	0
North Florida	3,741	4,242	489	1,644	770	1,339	0
Okaloosa-Walton	13,633	19,985	3,878	1,870	3,569	10,668	0
Palm Beach	42,944	51,632	7,554	14,253	5,313	24,512	0
Pasco-Hernando	10,879	12,952	4,281	4,859	1,312	1,513	987
Pensacola	22,393	30,713	6,446	4,364	7,199	11,283	1,421
Polk	18,451	30,244	3,137	11,951	2,128	13,024	4
St. Johns River	8,259	8,837	1,793	2,322	1,455	3,267	0
St. Petersburg	44,209	75,981	18,128	20,866	6,682	30,305	0
Santa Fe	20,731	33,608	11,668	3,903	4,171	13,866	0
Seminole	22,343	31,558	5,840	10,046	7,468	7,926	278
South Florida	8,195	13,439	1,571	3,258	3,514	5,096	0
Tallahassee	19,047	24,205	6,484	4,680	3,307	9,734	0
Valencia	48,868	69,520	25,351	20,295	13,415	10,086	373

1/ Includes students awaiting enrollment in limited access programs, students enrolled in apprenticeship courses, students who are enrolled in courses related to employment, as general freshmen or for other personal objectives.
Note: There may be some duplication between major program areas.

Source: State of Florida, Department of Education, Florida Community College System, *The Fact Book: Report for the Florida Community College System,* February 2000, Internet site <http://www.dcc.firn.edu/dccrepts/factbook/fb1999/table08.pdf> (accessed 5 April 2000).

University of Florida   **Bureau of Economic and Business Research**

Table 4.61. PUBLIC COMMUNITY COLLEGES: TRANSFER STUDENTS FROM FLORIDA
COMMUNITY COLLEGES TO FLORIDA UNIVERSITIES BY SEX AND UNIVERSITY
FALL 1996 AND 1997

	1996			1997		
Institution	Total	Male	Female	Total	Male	Female
State University System, total	66,547	29,018	37,529	66,299	28,745	37,554
Florida Agricultural and Mechanical University	1,140	533	607	1,017	456	561
Florida Atlantic University	6,947	2,628	4,319	7,147	2,654	4,493
Florida Gulf Coast University	(X)	(X)	(X)	480	139	341
Florida International University	10,081	4,278	5,803	9,920	4,274	5,646
Florida State University	9,898	4,449	5,449	9,733	4,319	5,414
University of Central Florida	13,270	5,899	7,371	13,460	5,890	7,570
University of Florida	6,535	3,666	2,869	6,834	3,837	2,997
University of North Florida	4,300	1,747	2,553	4,472	1,799	2,673
University of South Florida	11,333	4,586	6,747	10,377	4,218	6,159
University of West Florida	3,043	1,232	1,811	2,859	1,159	1,700

(X) Not applicable.

Table 4.62. PUBLIC COMMUNITY COLLEGES: TRANSFER STUDENTS FROM FLORIDA COMMUNITY
COLLEGES TO FLORIDA UNIVERSITIES BY RACE OR HISPANIC ORIGIN
AND UNIVERSITY, FALL 1997

				Race		Other 1/	His- panic origin 2/
Institution	Total	White	Black	Amer- ican Indian	Asian		
State University System, total	66,299	45,286	6,802	331	2,517	1,230	10,133
Florida Agricultural and Mechanical University	1,017	216	734	0	21	7	39
Florida Atlantic University	7,147	4,782	991	46	228	210	890
Florida Gulf Coast University	480	407	15	3	12	7	36
Florida International University	9,920	2,131	1,589	6	302	363	5,529
Florida State University	9,733	7,972	850	52	224	47	588
University of Central Florida	13,460	10,111	976	80	653	224	1,416
University of Florida	6,834	5,520	263	36	286	166	563
University of North Florida	4,472	3,663	397	21	200	18	173
University of South Florida	10,377	8,092	770	53	471	181	810
University of West Florida	2,859	2,392	217	34	120	7	89

1/ Includes students classified as nonresident aliens and unclassified students.
2/ Persons of Hispanic origin may be of any race. However, these data are not distributed by race.

Source for Tables 4.61 and 4.62: State of Florida, Department of Education, Division of Community
Colleges, *Articulation Report*, March 2000, Internet site <http://www.dcc.firn.edu/dccrepts/artic/
artic2000/table1.pdf> (accessed 1 May 2000).

University of Florida   **Bureau of Economic and Business Research**

Table 4.76. PUBLIC HIGH SCHOOL TESTING: PERCENTAGE OF STUDENTS PASSING
THE HIGH SCHOOL COMPETENCY TEST (HSCT) IN THE STATE AND COUNTIES
OF FLORIDA, OCTOBER 1998 AND 1999

County	Communi-cations 1998	1999	Mathe-matics 1998	1999	County	Communi-cations 1998	1999	Mathe-matics 1998	1999
Florida	81	71	77	54	Lake	82	72	80	56
					Lee	79	70	75	54
Alachua	85	71	79	52	Leon	86	73	80	56
Baker	85	81	73	53	Levy	77	75	71	56
Bay	82	72	76	55	Liberty	82	73	77	35
Bradford	84	71	78	57	Madison	75	61	70	43
Brevard	87	78	83	57	Manatee	79	73	78	58
Broward	76	68	73	55	Marion	83	77	77	57
Calhoun	90	82	85	66	Martin	83	77	76	58
Charlotte	87	76	84	51	Miami-Dade	70	61	66	46
Citrus	91	79	90	68	Monroe	89	82	85	65
Clay	88	78	83	60	Nassau	84	74	81	67
Collier	81	69	85	59	Okaloosa	85	76	80	56
Columbia	79	67	74	46	Okeechobee	80	72	74	54
De Soto	80	75	76	55	Orange	82	72	78	53
Dixie	75	67	78	61	Osceola	82	74	72	55
Duval	82	73	73	51	Palm Beach	83	68	80	54
Escambia	83	75	76	59	Pasco	84	77	82	61
Flagler	83	74	81	65	Pinellas	83	76	78	58
Franklin	80	75	79	59	Polk	84	75	82	62
Gadsden	54	45	48	39	Putnam	76	69	72	53
Gilchrist	79	59	81	35	St. Johns	84	83	81	55
Glades	71	57	67	64	St. Lucie	79	68	70	52
Gulf	79	73	80	61	Santa Rosa	87	76	83	55
Hamilton	73	53	64	32	Sarasota	88	80	86	60
Hardee	82	70	84	73	Seminole	88	79	87	62
Hendry	74	66	68	56	Sumter	88	69	83	62
Hernando	88	83	78	64	Suwannee	77	67	66	47
Highlands	86	80	80	60	Taylor	85	71	80	54
Hillsborough	89	78	89	66	Union	83	80	90	52
Holmes	85	75	86	69	Volusia	83	75	78	54
Indian River	84	75	78	55	Wakulla	88	80	87	70
Jackson	80	69	78	54	Walton	81	69	81	48
Jefferson	69	67	61	42	Washington	83	75	81	61
Lafayette	84	62	78	29	Developmental 1/	88	69	76	56

1/ Developmental research schools funded through and administered by the State University System.
Note: Data are for public school students in grade 11. The High School Competency Test (HSCT)
measures the application of basic skills to everyday life situations. Minimum student performance skills
were established in the basic areas of reading and writing (communications) and mathematics. Passing
both the communications section and the mathematics section of the HSCT is a requirement for high
school graduation in Florida.

Caution: Beginning in 1999, students passing the Florida Comprehensive Assessment Test (FCAT) in
the spring of their 10th grade year were exempt from the HSCT. Therefore caution should be used
when comparing 1999 data to previous years. See Table 4.77 for a breakdown of students taking and
exempt from the 1999 HSCT.

Source: State of Florida, Department of Education, Division of Public Schools, *Florida Statewide Assessment Program, High School Competency Test (HSCT), October 1999,* Internet site <http://www.firn.edu.
doe/sas/hsct99.pdf> (accessed 19 June 2000).

Table 4.77. PUBLIC HIGH SCHOOL TESTING: PERCENTAGE OF STUDENTS MEETING
MINIMUM SKILLS GRADUATION REQUIREMENTS IN THE STATE AND COUNTIES
OF FLORIDA, FALL 1999

County	Meeting minimum skills graduation requirement Communications	Mathematics	Exempt from HSCT Communications	Mathematics	County	Meeting minimum skills graduation requirement Communications	Mathematics	Exempt from HSCT Communications	Mathematics
Florida	81	77	32	50	Lake	80	78	30	49
					Lee	79	76	33	56
Alachua	84	79	45	57	Leon	85	81	42	57
Baker	87	75	24	41	Levy	82	78	23	44
Bay	82	78	35	51	Liberty	83	69	41	56
Bradford	79	77	26	47	Madison	72	66	28	42
Brevard	88	85	41	63	Manatee	83	80	37	58
Broward	76	73	27	43	Marion	85	78	33	49
Calhoun	87	84	26	54	Martin	87	83	45	62
Charlotte	85	82	37	64	Miami-Dade	70	65	22	34
Citrus	87	90	31	58	Monroe	90	89	41	65
Clay	86	85	33	61	Nassau	83	83	34	49
Collier	81	82	37	58	Okaloosa	85	81	39	61
Columbia	78	71	27	41	Okeechobee	80	73	25	41
De Soto	82	71	26	34	Orange	81	76	35	52
Dixie	74	73	20	30	Osceola	80	74	25	44
Duval	82	73	31	46	Palm Beach	79	79	35	55
Escambia	83	80	30	49	Pasco	85	83	27	50
Flagler	83	83	35	53	Pinellas	87	85	39	58
Franklin	81	73	20	33	Polk	84	83	27	48
Gadsden	50	47	8	12	Putnam	78	74	26	43
Gilchrist	67	59	24	44	St. Johns	89	82	36	59
Glades	64	75	16	31	St. Lucie	79	72	32	44
Gulf	81	78	30	48	Santa Rosa	86	81	39	58
Hamilton	60	46	14	20	Sarasota	90	87	45	65
Hardee	81	86	25	35	Seminole	88	85	45	65
Hendry	74	73	20	35	Sumter	78	83	28	52
Hernando	89	83	35	55	Suwannee	78	71	31	43
Highlands	86	83	26	53	Taylor	81	77	29	44
Hillsborough	87	87	36	60	Union	86	76	31	50
Holmes	85	86	37	55	Volusia	84	78	35	50
Indian River	84	78	33	49	Wakulla	88	88	35	52
Jackson	79	76	32	48	Walton	77	70	27	43
Jefferson	74	60	21	31	Washington	84	80	33	44
Lafayette	73	64	32	56					

HSCT High School Competency Test.
Note: Students passing the Florida Competency Assessment Test (FCAT) in the spring of their sophomore year are exempt from taking the High Schoool Competency Test (HSCT) in the fall of their junior year.

Source: State of Florida, Department of Education, Division of Public Schools, *Florida Statewide Assessment Program, High School Competency Test (HSCT), October 1999,* Internet site <http://www.firn.edu. doe/sas/hsct99.pdf> (accessed 19 June 2000).

Table 4.78. ELEMENTARY AND SECONDARY SCHOOLS: AVERAGE SCORES FOR STUDENTS
TAKING THE FLORIDA WRITING ASSESSMENT TEST IN THE STATE
AND COUNTIES OF FLORIDA, SPRING 1999

County	Grade 4	Grade 8	Grade 10	County	Grade 4	Grade 8	Grade 10
Florida	3.1	3.4	3.6	Leon	3.1	3.5	3.6
				Levy	3.1	3.3	3.6
Alachua	3.2	3.5	3.7	Liberty	2.6	3.2	3.9
Baker	2.9	3.2	3.3	Madison	2.8	3.2	3.3
Bay	3.0	3.4	3.5	Manatee	3.2	3.4	3.5
Bradford	2.9	3.2	3.2	Marion	2.9	3.2	3.4
Brevard	3.2	3.5	3.7	Martin	3.1	3.7	3.7
Broward	3.1	3.3	3.4	Miami-Dade	3.1	3.3	3.5
Calhoun	3.3	3.6	3.8	Monroe	3.3	3.6	3.5
Charlotte	3.4	3.8	3.7	Nassau	3.1	3.4	3.8
Citrus	2.9	3.3	3.6	Okaloosa	3.1	3.6	3.8
Clay	3.1	3.5	3.7	Okeechobee	2.9	3.2	3.4
Collier	3.1	3.5	3.4	Orange	3.0	3.3	3.5
Columbia	2.9	3.2	3.4	Osceola	2.9	3.2	3.3
De Soto	2.8	3.2	3.5	Palm Beach	3.0	3.4	3.5
Dixie	2.7	3.5	3.2	Pasco	2.9	3.4	3.5
Duval	3.0	3.4	3.6	Pinellas	3.4	3.6	3.7
Escambia	2.8	3.3	3.6	Polk	3.1	3.4	3.7
Flagler	3.1	3.7	3.7	Putnam	2.9	3.4	3.5
Franklin	2.9	3.3	3.3	St. Johns	3.2	3.7	3.8
Gadsden	2.7	3.1	3.3	St. Lucie	3.1	3.3	3.6
Gilchrist	3.1	3.3	3.6	Santa Rosa	2.9	3.4	3.5
Glades	2.3	2.9	3.1	Sarasota	3.3	3.6	3.7
Gulf	3.1	3.3	3.3	Seminole	3.2	3.6	3.8
Hamilton	2.9	3.1	3.2	Sumter	3.0	3.6	3.5
Hardee	3.2	3.4	3.5	Suwannee	3.0	3.4	3.5
Hendry	2.7	3.2	3.5	Taylor	2.6	3.2	3.6
Hernando	3.0	3.3	3.4	Union	3.5	3.5	3.5
Highlands	3.1	3.5	3.5	Volusia	3.0	3.4	3.6
Hillsborough	3.3	3.7	3.7	Wakulla	3.0	3.6	3.7
Holmes	2.6	3.2	3.5	Walton	3.0	3.2	3.1
Indian River	3.1	3.3	3.3	Washington	2.7	3.7	3.6
Jackson	2.8	3.3	3.6	FAU Henderson	3.2	3.9	(NA)
Jefferson	2.9	3.2	3.5	FSU Developmental	3.4	3.5	3.6
Lafayette	3.1	3.1	3.5	FAMU High	2.8	3.3	3.6
Lake	3.1	3.3	3.4	UF P.K. Yonge			
Lee	3.1	3.3	3.5	Developmental	3.1	3.3	3.7

(NA) Not available.

Note: The Florida Writing Assessment Test is given to public elementary and secondary students in
grades 4, 8, and 10 and is designed to assess higher-order skills and to measure students' proficiency in
writing responses to assigned topics within a designated tested period. It was established in response to
changes in the law made by the 1990 legislature. Student writings are scored by trained readers consider-
ing four elements: focus, organization, support, and conventions. Scores range from U (unscorable) to 6.

Source: State of Florida, Department of Education, Division of Public Schools, Student Assessment Services Sections, Internet site <http://www.firn.edu/doe/sas/fwdtrpt.htm>.

Table 4.79. PUBLIC HIGH SCHOOL TESTING: RESULTS OF THE FLORIDA COMPREHENSIVE ASSESSMENT TEST (FCAT) ACROSS ALL CURRICULUM GROUPS IN THE STATE AND COUNTIES OF FLORIDA, 2000

| | Reading | | | | | | | Mathematics | | | | | | |
| | Number of students | Mean scale score | Percentage in each achievement level | | | | | Number of students | Mean scale score | Percentage in each achievement level | | | | |
County			1	2	3	4	5			1	2	3	4	5
Florida	144,789	298	35	36	19	6	4	144,830	311	26	23	23	22	6
Alachua	1,958	311	28	31	22	10	8	1,967	318	24	19	21	26	10
Baker	256	300	35	37	21	4	3	256	306	26	30	25	16	2
Bay	1,540	303	31	40	21	6	3	1,545	317	20	25	26	23	6
Bradford	278	287	43	34	15	5	3	280	295	34	26	23	16	2
Brevard	4,426	309	25	40	23	8	4	4,427	326	15	22	25	29	10
Broward	14,288	297	37	36	19	5	3	14,355	309	28	24	22	21	6
Calhoun	141	296	36	40	13	8	3	141	314	20	21	30	27	2
Charlotte	1,199	306	28	40	21	7	3	1,203	325	16	18	27	31	8
Citrus	959	303	28	43	21	5	3	954	320	16	22	30	26	6
Clay	1,853	307	27	42	21	7	3	1,848	324	14	23	26	30	7
Collier	1,906	301	33	38	20	5	3	1,909	321	17	22	27	26	7
Columbia	595	301	33	41	17	4	4	602	310	25	28	25	18	4
De Soto	260	291	39	39	14	5	3	253	298	28	32	28	11	3
Dixie	172	278	56	33	8	2	1	170	295	35	27	26	8	1
Duval	6,187	297	35	38	19	6	3	6,196	307	27	24	25	21	3
Escambia	2,802	301	35	36	20	5	4	2,815	311	24	26	25	20	4
Flagler	427	305	26	44	21	6	2	427	318	18	22	28	29	2
Franklin	67	279	60	31	7	0	1	67	297	34	39	18	9	1
Gadsden	436	265	66	26	6	2	1	434	267	59	25	12	4	1
Gilchrist	191	294	35	43	16	4	2	194	308	29	23	23	24	2
Glades	63	301	33	37	24	3	3	64	313	25	23	25	20	3
Gulf	147	303	27	43	23	4	3	146	314	18	24	28	29	3
Hamilton	129	288	50	33	14	3	1	126	288	43	33	18	9	1
Hardee	277	287	47	33	16	3	1	274	300	28	29	24	16	2
Hendry	268	294	41	37	17	4	1	269	312	21	29	27	20	3

See footnote at end of table.

Continued . . .

Table 4.79. PUBLIC HIGH SCHOOL TESTING: RESULTS OF THE FLORIDA COMPREHENSIVE ASSESSMENT TEST (FCAT) ACROSS ALL CURRICULUM GROUPS IN THE STATE AND COUNTIES OF FLORIDA, 2000 (Continued)

County	Reading							Mathematics						
	Number of students	Mean scale score	Percentage in each achievement level					Number of students	Mean scale score	Percentage in each achievement level				
			1	2	3	4	5			1	2	3	4	5
Hernando	1,016	308	25	43	23	6	3	1,007	318	17	27	29	23	4
Highlands	610	297	34	43	17	3	3	608	312	21	24	25	25	4
Hillsborough	8,347	306	29	38	21	7	5	8,343	321	19	23	25	26	8
Holmes	247	296	40	36	18	3	3	247	312	21	30	22	23	4
Indian River	1,037	304	30	38	21	6	5	1,055	314	23	22	25	24	6
Jackson	509	296	38	35	21	5	2	511	309	24	26	26	22	3
Jefferson	109	283	52	25	15	5	4	111	280	51	23	15	9	1
Lafayette	82	303	33	29	23	10	5	82	309	27	22	22	27	2
Lake	1,814	297	36	38	18	5	3	1,812	308	27	24	24	22	4
Lee	3,337	298	35	38	19	5	3	3,341	312	25	23	23	23	6
Leon	1,957	309	25	37	26	8	4	1,964	321	19	21	24	26	10
Levy	407	290	42	39	15	2	2	411	305	28	26	22	20	3
Liberty	65	296	37	45	14	2	3	64	319	27	19	20	23	11
Madison	179	303	30	44	21	3	2	179	306	29	21	28	19	3
Manatee	1,807	299	33	38	20	6	3	1,799	315	22	22	26	24	6
Marion	2,370	301	32	39	20	6	3	2,379	313	24	23	24	23	6
Martin	1,026	308	24	43	22	8	3	1,037	322	17	20	26	27	10
Miami-Dade	23,073	282	49	31	14	4	3	22,983	291	40	24	19	14	4
Monroe	554	302	29	43	21	6	2	551	318	19	21	28	24	7
Nassau	682	301	32	40	21	4	4	669	314	21	23	27	25	4
Okaloosa	2,097	310	25	38	23	8	5	2,092	323	17	21	25	28	8
Okeechobee	402	286	45	34	14	5	2	407	303	27	34	23	14	2
Orange	7,701	301	33	38	19	6	4	7,678	315	23	24	23	23	8
Osceola	2,286	293	40	38	16	4	2	2,301	306	28	25	24	19	4
Palm Beach	10,290	294	38	34	18	6	4	10,296	309	28	21	22	22	7
Pasco	3,139	294	39	40	16	4	2	3,114	310	25	27	24	21	4
Pinellas	6,953	307	29	37	22	8	5	7,001	320	19	22	26	25	8

See footnote at end of table.

Continued . . .

Table 4.79. PUBLIC HIGH SCHOOL TESTING: RESULTS OF THE FLORIDA COMPREHENSIVE ASSESSMENT TEST (FCAT) ACROSS ALL CURRICULUM GROUPS IN THE STATE AND COUNTIES OF FLORIDA, 2000 (Continued)

County	Reading								Mathematics							
	Number of students	Mean scale score	Percentage in each achievement level						Number of students	Mean scale score	Percentage in each achievement level					
			1	2	3	4	5				1	2	3	4	5	
Polk	4,446	296	38	37	17	5	3		4,444	310	26	25	24	20	5	
Putnam	642	291	41	36	16	6	2		637	296	34	24	20	18	3	
St. Johns	1,268	307	29	36	21	8	6		1,264	316	22	23	23	24	8	
St. Lucie	1,481	298	34	38	20	5	3		1,486	308	26	26	23	20	4	
Santa Rosa	1,638	307	26	42	22	6	4		1,633	324	15	21	27	29	7	
Sarasota	2,180	311	24	37	25	8	5		2,175	325	16	20	26	28	10	
Seminole	4,184	312	24	36	25	8	6		4,171	327	16	18	22	33	12	
Sumter	298	298	37	38	16	5	4		298	305	28	28	24	18	3	
Suwannee	386	289	44	32	18	5	2		388	299	32	24	26	14	4	
Taylor	202	302	32	38	16	8	6		204	308	22	25	27	22	4	
Union	144	299	32	42	17	6	2		144	301	29	35	19	15	2	
Volusia	3,936	303	30	39	21	6	3		3,943	314	23	22	25	24	6	
Wakulla	268	306	29	43	19	6	3		274	318	19	24	26	27	4	
Walton	324	299	35	32	24	7	3		336	308	24	24	26	23	3	
Washington	215	300	33	42	17	7	0		215	314	27	19	25	26	4	
Deaf/Blind	78	218	83	6	6	4	0		73	232	84	5	5	5	0	
FSU Developmental	107	317	18	36	31	13	3		105	331	12	21	29	27	11	
FAMU Developmental	41	294	29	59	10	2	0		41	298	27	34	29	7	2	
UF P.K.Yonge Developmental	108	319	13	48	25	10	4		108	334	9	21	19	40	10	

Note: The Florida Comprehensive Assessment Test (FCAT) measures student performance on selected benchmarks in reading and mathematics that are defined by Sunshine State Standards articulating challenging content that Florida students are expected to know and be able to do. Achievement levels range from 1, indicating little success with the challenging content, to 5, indicating success with the most challenging content of the Sunshine State Standards.

Source: State of Florida, Department of Education, Student Assessment Services Section, Internet site <http://www.firn.edu/doe/sas/fcds9900.xls> (accessed 14 August 2000).

Table 4.80. HIGH SCHOOL GRADUATES AND DROPOUTS: GRADUATION AND DROPOUT RATES IN THE STATE AND COUNTIES OF FLORIDA, 1998-99

County	Gradu-ation rates	Drop-out rates	County	Gradu-ation rates	Drop-out rates
Florida	60.23	5.40	Lake	65.02	3.60
			Lee	69.35	4.90
Alachua	63.34	5.70	Leon	64.65	4.00
Baker	55.73	9.70	Levy	61.24	3.60
Bay	55.93	2.50	Liberty	71.71	5.90
Bradford	60.41	3.20	Madison	67.46	5.20
Brevard	63.98	3.50	Manatee	56.23	7.40
Broward	53.45	2.80	Marion	57.91	5.70
Calhoun	83.53	1.80	Martin	60.64	3.60
Charlotte	68.42	3.20	Miami-Dade	53.23	10.60
Citrus	70.81	7.90	Monroe	70.98	4.70
Clay	65.30	2.80	Nassau	73.71	3.20
Collier	63.02	5.80	Okaloosa	77.08	4.40
Columbia	63.60	4.90	Okeechobee	62.71	6.60
De Soto	62.71	5.40	Orange	51.33	5.70
Dixie	60.54	3.50	Osceola	55.67	6.10
Duval	58.65	8.60	Palm Beach	58.19	3.80
Escambia	62.59	2.60	Pasco	63.50	5.50
Flagler	63.52	1.80	Pinellas	65.26	3.70
Franklin	71.17	3.90	Polk	53.26	8.70
Gadsden	46.02	7.10	Putnam	65.80	3.70
Gilchrist	64.08	3.10	St. Johns	72.03	2.50
Glades	66.66	9.30	St. Lucie	63.45	4.70
Gulf	80.00	1.60	Santa Rosa	75.38	2.10
Hamilton	54.32	4.00	Sarasota	62.96	7.60
Hardee	65.02	8.80	Seminole	63.26	2.10
Hendry	66.73	7.40	Sumter	71.42	3.60
Hernando	68.72	6.10	Suwannee	60.60	3.40
Highlands	70.01	4.20	Taylor	61.40	3.60
Hillsborough	69.47	4.20	Union	61.03	1.70
Holmes	76.64	4.00	Volusia	70.07	1.80
Indian River	65.20	4.90	Wakulla	76.23	4.40
Jackson	58.06	0.90	Walton	68.88	5.30
Jefferson	62.58	2.70	Washington	65.93	2.90
Lafayette	80.61	6.00			

Note: Data are for public schools only. Beginning in 1998-99, graduation rates track individuals by student I.D. numbers, beginning with their first-time enrollment in ninth grade, and account for incoming transfer students. The reported dropout rate is for all dropouts in grades 9-12. Prior years' statistics showed a rate only for dropouts aged 16 and over. Due to changes in methodology, these data are not comparable to earlier years.

Source: State of Florida, Department of Education, Division of Administration, Education Information and Accountability Services, *Graduation and Dropout Rates by District, 1998-99*, Internet site <http://www.firn.edu/doe/bin00050/eiaspubs/graddrop.htm> (accessed 3 May 2000).

Table 4.81. HIGH SCHOOL GRADUATES: NONPUBLIC HIGH SCHOOL GRADUATES, 2000
AND GRADUATES CONTINUING EDUCATION BY TYPE OF POST-SECONDARY
INSTITUTION ENTERED, 2000-2001, IN THE STATE
AND COUNTIES OF FLORIDA

		Graduates continuing education							
		Graduates entering--							
County	Total graduates 2000 A/	Total	Florida community colleges		Florida colleges and universities		Out-of-state colleges and universities	Technical trade and other	
			Pub-lic	Pri-vate	Pub-lic	Pri-vate		In-state	Out-of-state
Florida	13,318	11,533	2,821	165	3,926	1,255	3,162	126	78
Alachua	99	86	27	0	23	5	31	0	0
Baker	0	0	0	0	0	0	0	0	0
Bay	40	36	21	0	7	3	5	0	0
Bradford	2	0	0	0	0	0	0	0	0
Brevard	381	346	85	4	143	52	59	3	0
Broward	1,774	1,680	278	11	698	165	514	12	2
Calhoun	0	0	0	0	0	0	0	0	0
Charlotte	13	12	4	0	2	2	4	0	0
Citrus	0	0	0	0	0	0	0	0	0
Clay	217	137	19	2	26	12	61	5	12
Collier	86	81	6	0	23	13	39	0	0
Columbia	1	6	5	0	1	0	0	0	0
De Soto	1	1	0	0	0	1	0	0	0
Dixie	(NA)	(NA)	(NA)	(NA)	(NA)	(NA)	(NA)	(NA)	(NA)
Duval	1,051	973	299	18	339	71	234	10	2
Escambia	255	243	84	1	44	40	74	0	0
Flagler	5	5	4	0	0	0	1	0	0
Franklin	0	1	1	0	0	0	0	0	0
Gadsden	59	54	31	0	17	0	2	4	0
Gilchrist	20	35	24	2	1	3	3	0	2
Glades	0	0	0	0	0	0	0	0	0
Gulf	6	3	3	0	0	0	0	0	0
Hamilton	1	0	0	0	0	0	0	0	0
Hardee	3	2	0	0	0	1	1	0	0
Hendry	2	0	0	0	0	0	0	0	0
Hernando	47	32	12	0	7	5	5	1	2
Highlands	17	22	11	5	0	1	3	2	0
Hillsborough	843	774	94	3	322	91	258	2	4
Holmes	3	3	3	0	0	0	0	0	0
Indian River	85	86	6	0	7	12	61	0	0
Jackson	11	10	3	3	0	2	1	1	0
Jefferson	24	23	18	0	4	0	1	0	0
Lafayette	(NA)	(NA)	(NA)	(NA)	(NA)	(NA)	(NA)	(NA)	(NA)
Lake	65	65	21	2	14	5	20	2	1
Lee	351	303	85	0	87	36	90	4	1

See footnotes at end of table.   Continued . . .

University of Florida   **Bureau of Economic and Business Research**

Table 4.81. HIGH SCHOOL GRADUATES: NONPUBLIC HIGH SCHOOL GRADUATES, 2000
AND GRADUATES CONTINUING EDUCATION BY TYPE OF POST-SECONDARY
INSTITUTION ENTERED, 2000-2001, IN THE STATE
AND COUNTIES OF FLORIDA (Continued)

County	Total graduates 2000 A/	Total	Graduates continuing education						
			Graduates entering--						
			Florida community colleges		Florida colleges and universities		Out-of-state colleges and universities	Technical trade and other	
			Pub-lic	Pri-vate	Pub-lic	Pri-vate		In-state	Out-of-state
Leon	166	162	58	1	50	7	44	1	1
Levy	1	0	0	0	0	0	0	0	0
Liberty	0	0	0	0	0	0	0	0	0
Madison	0	0	0	0	0	0	0	0	0
Manatee	236	180	49	2	36	24	66	3	0
Marion	183	93	43	0	31	9	10	0	0
Martin	26	16	4	0	0	9	2	1	0
Miami-Dade	3,097	2,795	617	50	1,048	355	658	24	43
Monroe	9	9	2	0	1	2	3	1	0
Nassau	21	12	9	0	1	1	1	0	0
Okaloosa	44	43	29	2	3	4	5	0	0
Okeechobee	7	0	0	0	0	0	0	0	0
Orange	755	683	158	6	217	63	228	10	1
Osceola	63	23	15	0	1	1	4	2	0
Palm Beach	866	806	183	5	284	81	238	12	3
Pasco	40	34	5	0	4	4	21	0	0
Pinellas	1,062	611	223	4	172	46	155	10	1
Polk	270	181	28	3	52	33	60	3	2
Putnam	23	15	11	1	0	2	1	0	0
St. Johns	92	85	20	3	39	10	11	1	1
St. Lucie	154	138	62	0	49	15	12	0	0
Santa Rosa	29	31	5	7	1	10	8	0	0
Sarasota	222	180	37	3	71	20	45	4	0
Seminole	298	263	68	22	54	22	96	1	0
Sumter	0	1	0	0	0	1	0	0	0
Suwannee	16	10	3	0	1	3	1	2	0
Taylor	1	0	0	0	0	0	0	0	0
Union	(NA)	(NA)	(NA)	(NA)	(NA)	(NA)	(NA)	(NA)	(NA)
Volusia	174	142	48	5	46	13	25	5	0
Wakulla	1	1	0	0	0	0	1	0	0
Walton	0	0	0	0	0	0	0	0	0
Washington	(NA)	(NA)	(NA)	(NA)	(NA)	(NA)	(NA)	(NA)	(NA)

(NA) Not available.
A/ Includes standard and special diploma graduates.
Note: See Glossary under Private school for definition of nonpublic schools. Data are based on a sur-
vey and are unaudited.

Source: State of Florida, Department of Education, Division of Public Schools, *Statistical Brief: Florida's
Nonpublic Schools, 1999-2000,* Series 2000-13B.

University of Florida   **Bureau of Economic and Business Research**

Table 4.82. HIGH SCHOOL GRADUATES: GRADUATES, 1999, AND GRADUATES CONTINUING EDUCATION BY TYPE OF POST-SECONDARY INSTITUTION ENTERED, 1999-2000 IN THE STATE AND COUNTIES OF FLORIDA

County	Total diploma grad- uates 1999 A/	Total		Florida junior college		Florida university		Non- Florida college or uni- versity	Technical trade and other	
		Num- ber	Per- cent- age	Pub- lic	Pri- vate	Pub- lic	Pri- vate		In- state	Out- of- state
Florida	102,382	65,845	64.3	28,545	375	22,408	3,900	6,636	3,422	559
Alachua	1,483	1,118	75.4	591	4	349	41	121	9	3
Baker	204	126	61.8	80	0	26	4	10	6	0
Bay	1,149	545	47.4	336	5	89	21	41	44	9
Bradford	210	85	40.5	65	10	3	2	5	0	0
Brevard	3,278	2,155	65.7	1,183	23	568	108	199	36	38
Broward	9,541	6,353	66.6	2,225	62	2,704	433	578	304	47
Calhoun	120	94	78.3	66	0	2	1	5	20	0
Charlotte	877	452	51.5	178	16	139	29	45	41	4
Citrus	711	523	73.6	282	7	146	16	44	17	11
Clay	1,312	960	73.2	488	2	264	37	72	91	6
Collier	1,346	935	69.5	325	1	302	97	122	82	6
Columbia	403	277	68.7	186	3	44	10	15	13	6
De Soto	177	141	79.7	67	1	32	4	10	20	7
Dixie	116	70	60.3	65	0	3	0	1	1	0
Duval	4,684	2,937	62.7	1,274	0	1,086	235	288	54	0
Escambia	2,076	1,127	54.3	530	12	337	17	162	51	18
Flagler	310	247	79.7	126	2	66	13	28	7	5
Franklin	81	49	60.5	33	0	10	0	0	6	0
Gadsden	365	242	66.3	88	2	116	1	12	21	2
Gilchrist	138	91	65.9	66	1	16	2	4	0	2
Glades	59	51	86.4	23	0	10	1	6	10	1
Gulf	119	85	71.4	64	0	6	2	8	5	0
Hamilton	93	81	87.1	33	0	19	2	16	6	5
Hardee	247	142	57.5	92	1	29	10	5	5	0
Hendry	327	189	57.8	128	0	34	2	11	13	1
Hernando	814	637	78.3	317	2	183	27	56	44	8
Highlands	541	406	75.1	249	3	64	29	37	19	5
Hillsborough	6,770	4,435	65.5	1,424	23	2,073	208	452	221	34
Holmes	221	134	60.6	55	0	40	0	15	24	0
Indian River	709	528	74.5	302	1	96	39	87	2	1
Jackson	521	195	37.4	137	1	21	2	12	17	5
Jefferson	77	64	83.1	34	2	14	3	1	9	1
Lafayette	77	60	77.9	21	0	33	0	4	1	1
Lake	1,300	493	37.9	244	1	121	31	26	67	3
Lee	2,535	1,647	65.0	679	4	599	97	167	89	12
Leon	1,535	1,115	72.6	465	6	417	29	135	42	21
Levy	269	142	52.8	77	1	34	8	14	7	1
Liberty	68	33	48.5	25	0	2	0	0	6	0
Madison	182	116	63.7	87	1	16	0	12	0	0

See footnotes at end of table.					Continued . . .

University of Florida					**Bureau of Economic and Business Research**

147

Table 4.82. HIGH SCHOOL GRADUATES: GRADUATES, 1999, AND GRADUATES CONTINUING EDUCATION BY TYPE OF POST-SECONDARY INSTITUTION ENTERED, 1999-2000 IN THE STATE AND COUNTIES OF FLORIDA (Continued)

| | | | | Graduates continuing education | | | | | |
| | | | | Graduates entering-- | | | | | |
County	Total diploma graduates 1999 A/	Total Number	Per-centage	Florida junior college Public	Florida junior college Private	Florida university Public	Florida university Private	Non-Florida college or university	Technical trade and other In-state	Technical trade and other Out-of-state
Manatee	1,236	862	69.7	278	8	351	46	109	67	3
Marion	1,672	1,111	66.5	716	4	247	31	56	45	12
Martin	705	473	67.1	210	0	159	42	59	2	1
Miami-Dade	14,179	10,147	71.6	3,841	55	3,952	810	958	460	71
Monroe	446	341	76.5	164	6	82	26	48	14	1
Nassau	476	179	37.6	81	0	63	17	12	5	1
Okaloosa	1,765	1,181	66.9	634	10	274	25	187	27	24
Okeechobee	279	210	75.3	150	0	34	6	7	10	3
Orange	5,792	3,471	59.9	1,398	0	996	178	422	477	0
Osceola	1,377	943	68.5	507	2	189	57	60	110	18
Palm Beach	6,343	2,351	37.1	857	6	981	128	272	98	9
Pasco	1,956	1,022	52.3	517	9	273	66	79	76	2
Pinellas	4,939	3,378	68.4	1,460	8	1,213	167	334	189	7
Polk	3,364	2,164	64.3	1,107	6	479	210	170	135	57
Putnam	543	405	74.6	239	4	65	14	23	50	10
St. Johns	888	469	52.8	143	5	221	30	61	4	5
St. Lucie	1,022	767	75.1	379	1	249	38	77	18	5
Santa Rosa	1,104	926	83.9	428	10	279	22	145	18	24
Sarasota	1,574	1,138	72.3	395	4	403	91	188	46	11
Seminole	2,993	2,131	71.2	736	23	936	123	253	48	12
Sumter	264	193	73.1	106	0	51	5	15	14	2
Suwannee	294	54	18.4	32	0	9	0	6	4	3
Taylor	181	132	72.9	92	0	16	0	7	17	0
Union	131	95	72.5	73	2	5	5	10	0	0
Volusia	2,780	1,993	71.7	974	11	585	187	183	47	6
Wakulla	226	134	59.3	86	0	34	3	0	11	0
Walton	267	166	62.2	81	2	42	8	21	3	9
Washington	177	29	16.4	25	0	3	0	1	0	0
Deaf/Blind	81	47	58.0	19	0	2	2	14	10	0
Dozier	16	0	0.0	0	0	0	0	0	0	0
FSU Developmental	109	103	94.5	42	2	39	0	15	5	0
FAMU Developmental	61	59	96.7	22	0	26	1	8	2	0
UF P.K. Yonge Developmental	97	91	93.8	43	0	37	1	10	0	0

A/ Includes standard and special diploma graduates.
Note: Data were obtained from the Florida DOE Student Information Data Base, Survey 5, as of November 10, 1999, and are for public schools only. Because some high schools do not have a formal follow-up program for graduates, it was necessary for the principal or guidance counselor to prepare estimates for some of the items included. Figures include twelfth grade graduates from adult centers and exceptional and gifted schools.

Source: State of Florida, Department of Education, Education Information and Accountability Services, *Statistical Brief: Florida Public High School Graduates, 1998-99 School Year.* Series 99-04B. Internet site <http://www.firn.edu/doe/bin00050/eiaspubs/graduate.htm> (accessed 7 March 2000).

Table 4.83. HIGH SCHOOL GRADUATES: GRADUATES RECEIVING STANDARD DIPLOMAS BY SEX AND BY RACE OR HISPANIC ORIGIN IN THE STATE AND COUNTIES OF FLORIDA, 1998-99

County	Total 1/		White		Black		Asian or Pacific Islander		American Indian, Eskimo, or Aleut		Hispanic origin 2/	
	Male	Female	Male	Female	Male	Female	Male	Female	Male	Female	Male	Female
Florida	46,401	52,532	29,142	31,582	8,894	11,417	1,365	1,463	112	122	6,763	7,774
Alachua	696	740	515	488	149	198	10	28	0	2	21	22
Baker	87	109	76	97	9	12	1	0	0	0	1	0
Bay	527	611	426	497	71	75	14	22	2	2	12	13
Bradford	96	90	80	75	15	14	0	1	0	0	1	0
Brevard	1,540	1,674	1,239	1,341	167	202	43	32	6	3	80	79
Broward	4,304	5,021	2,093	2,267	1,323	1,721	181	216	7	9	686	776
Calhoun	59	57	51	43	7	13	0	1	0	0	1	0
Charlotte	449	415	382	361	37	36	10	3	1	0	16	12
Citrus	315	369	284	332	16	20	6	3	0	2	8	12
Clay	650	632	551	547	60	45	19	21	2	1	18	18
Collier	618	678	412	489	84	79	5	7	3	1	110	102
Columbia	176	200	137	139	35	52	1	3	2	1	1	5
De Soto	83	86	55	58	13	14	0	1	0	0	15	13
Dixie	52	61	48	55	4	5	0	0	0	0	0	1
Duval	1,914	2,521	1,089	1,361	665	950	94	121	4	4	56	83
Escambia	949	1,069	667	692	225	291	34	60	6	5	16	20
Flagler	153	149	126	115	15	17	6	6	0	1	6	8
Franklin	33	47	27	39	5	5	0	1	1	1	0	1
Gadsden	171	182	9	9	153	167	0	0	0	0	9	5
Gilchrist	65	68	64	64	0	4	0	0	0	0	1	0
Glades	21	36	12	26	6	7	0	0	0	0	3	3
Gulf	57	56	49	45	8	11	0	0	0	0	0	0
Hamilton	44	39	27	19	17	20	0	0	0	0	0	0
Hardee	106	136	72	82	10	14	0	2	0	0	24	38
Hendry	161	144	92	60	32	37	0	1	0	3	37	43

Continued . . .

See footnotes at end of table.

Table 4.83. HIGH SCHOOL GRADUATES: GRADUATES RECEIVING STANDARD DIPLOMAS BY SEX AND BY RACE OR HISPANIC ORIGIN IN THE STATE AND COUNTIES OF FLORIDA, 1998-99 (Continued)

County	Total 1/		Race									
			White		Black		Asian or Pacific Islander		American Indian, Eskimo, or Aleut		Hispanic origin 2/	
	Male	Female	Male	Female	Male	Female	Male	Female	Male	Female	Male	Female
Hernando	341	437	304	376	17	32	4	0	1	0	15	28
Highlands	234	250	161	173	50	40	3	2	0	0	20	35
Hillsborough	3,165	3,498	1,972	2,062	544	719	119	114	10	12	496	557
Holmes	94	119	92	112	2	1	0	3	0	0	0	3
Indian River	329	370	267	282	34	59	4	9	0	1	24	18
Jackson	207	210	144	130	59	73	1	5	0	0	3	2
Jefferson	27	46	12	16	15	30	0	0	0	0	0	0
Lafayette	40	33	35	27	5	5	0	0	0	0	0	1
Lake	575	653	459	511	80	90	9	12	1	0	26	40
Lee	1,113	1,336	861	1,024	123	161	22	16	3	2	101	132
Leon	676	803	464	532	182	241	16	18	1	2	12	8
Levy	120	131	92	106	18	19	3	0	1	0	6	6
Liberty	30	32	29	31	0	1	1	0	0	0	0	0
Madison	81	93	44	38	34	54	0	0	0	1	3	0
Manatee	553	630	441	508	67	77	8	8	0	0	35	34
Marion	737	816	576	586	100	152	11	8	2	1	48	67
Martin	339	342	296	292	24	28	3	9	0	0	15	13
Miami–Dade	6,392	7,462	1,146	1,175	1,821	2,365	145	127	4	6	3,266	3,786
Monroe	203	219	166	172	15	22	1	7	0	1	21	16
Nassau	215	246	187	203	25	33	2	1	5	2	1	6
Okaloosa	872	877	697	708	86	105	40	28	5	3	38	30
Okeechobee	113	152	96	115	5	17	0	1	1	4	10	15
Orange	2,501	3,009	1,413	1,556	474	736	162	167	16	9	432	534
Osceola	642	686	366	417	52	66	32	24	0	1	188	176
Palm Beach	3,010	3,169	1,843	1,886	696	795	92	94	1	12	357	364
Pasco	860	1,023	771	929	27	29	10	21	1	3	47	36
Pinellas	2,288	2,477	1,869	1,964	249	315	99	91	4	8	65	88

See footnotes at end of table.

Continued . . .

Table 4.83. HIGH SCHOOL GRADUATES: GRADUATES RECEIVING STANDARD DIPLOMAS BY SEX AND BY RACE OR HISPANIC ORIGIN IN THE STATE AND COUNTIES OF FLORIDA, 1998-99 (Continued)

| County | Total 1/ | | Race | | | | | | | | | |
| | | | White | | Black | | Asian or Pacific Islander | | American Indian, Eskimo, or Aleut | | Hispanic origin 2/ | |
	Male	Female	Male	Female	Male	Female	Male	Female	Male	Female	Male	Female
Polk	1,448	1,681	1,062	1,217	265	331	26	23	5	2	89	108
Putnam	240	279	180	192	47	64	5	2	1	2	7	19
St. Johns	416	451	365	386	38	51	4	3	2	1	5	10
St. Lucie	457	545	292	343	130	142	10	14	3	2	22	43
Santa Rosa	524	568	487	517	17	24	6	14	0	2	11	11
Sarasota	689	819	622	746	35	29	9	18	1	2	22	22
Seminole	1,375	1,550	1,029	1,130	128	159	56	60	1	2	156	192
Sumter	115	135	91	102	23	26	1	0	0	0	0	6
Suwannee	126	155	105	132	18	21	0	1	0	0	3	1
Taylor	91	86	73	64	15	21	2	1	0	0	1	0
Union	73	56	54	49	17	7	0	0	1	3	2	0
Volusia	1,299	1,419	1,041	1,118	141	170	28	24	0	0	85	101
Wakulla	95	114	89	101	6	12	0	0	2	1	0	1
Walton	121	135	111	119	5	9	3	3	0	0	0	3
Washington	82	89	62	66	17	19	3	3	0	0	0	1
Deaf/Blind	14	11	9	10	4	0	0	0	0	0	1	1
Dozier	16	0	9	0	4	0	1	2	1	0	3	0
FSU Developmental	59	50	37	30	16	13	0	0	0	0	4	3
FAMU Developmental	25	36	0	0	25	36	0	0	0	0	0	0
UF P.K.Yonge Developmental	53	44	38	28	13	9	0	1	0	2	1	3

1/ Includes multiracial not shown separately.
2/ Persons of Hispanic origin may be of any race. However, these data are not distributed by race.
Note: Data were obtained from the Florida DOE Student Information Data Base, Survey 5, as of November 10, 1999, and are for public schools only. Standard diplomas are awarded to students who have mastered eleventh grade minimum student performance standards, passed both sections of the High School Competency Test (HSCT or SSAT II), successfully completed the minimum number of academic credits, and successfully completed any other requirements prescribed by state or the local school board. Also includes differentiated diplomas awarded in lieu of the standard diplomas to those students exceeding the prescribed minimums.

Source: State of Florida, Department of Education, Education Information and Accountability Services, *Statistical Brief: Florida Public High School Graduates, 1998-99 School Year*, Series 99-04B. Internet site <http://www.firn.edu/doe/bin00050/eiaspubs/graduate.htm> (accessed 7 March 2000).

Table 4.84. HIGH SCHOOL COMPLETERS: STUDENTS COMPLETING HIGH SCHOOL BY SEX
AND BY RACE OR HISPANIC ORIGIN IN THE STATE AND COUNTIES OF FLORIDA,
SCHOOL YEAR 1998-99

County	Total 1/	Sex Male	Female	White	Black	Asian or Pacific Islander	American Indian Eskimo or Aleut	Hispanic origin 2/
Florida	105,773	49,990	55,783	63,304	23,278	2,929	250	15,705
Alachua	1,514	744	770	1,036	389	39	2	45
Baker	223	101	122	187	34	1	0	1
Bay	1,173	541	632	945	157	36	4	27
Bradford	210	114	96	172	36	1	0	1
Brevard	3,345	1,613	1,732	2,651	418	78	9	167
Broward	9,925	4,608	5,317	4,515	3,365	411	16	1,571
Calhoun	122	60	62	97	23	1	0	1
Charlotte	883	464	419	757	78	13	1	28
Citrus	715	332	383	640	41	9	2	22
Clay	1,363	688	675	1,157	120	44	3	39
Collier	1,360	647	713	926	183	14	4	229
Columbia	424	195	229	303	107	4	3	7
De Soto	183	91	92	119	32	1	0	31
Dixie	116	54	62	106	9	0	0	1
Duval	4,709	2,092	2,617	2,580	1,746	215	9	151
Escambia	2,123	1,009	1,114	1,400	578	95	11	37
Flagler	324	162	162	249	40	12	1	20
Franklin	81	33	48	67	10	1	2	1
Gadsden	376	184	192	19	342	0	0	14
Gilchrist	149	74	75	140	8	0	0	1
Glades	61	24	37	39	15	0	0	7
Gulf	123	61	62	99	24	0	0	0
Hamilton	102	56	46	49	52	0	0	1
Hardee	262	114	148	160	30	3	0	69
Hendry	328	176	152	162	78	1	3	84
Hernando	841	369	472	731	55	4	2	48
Highlands	554	279	275	367	121	5	1	60
Hillsborough	6,867	3,261	3,606	4,118	1,346	236	22	1,087
Holmes	222	99	123	213	3	3	0	3
Indian River	719	341	378	565	95	13	1	44
Jackson	538	281	257	331	194	6	0	6
Jefferson	87	33	54	29	57	0	0	1
Lafayette	77	42	35	63	13	0	0	1
Lake	1,369	656	713	1,063	205	22	1	78
Lee	2,680	1,214	1,466	1,980	387	39	5	265
Leon	1,551	724	827	1,020	467	35	4	22
Levy	275	131	144	215	44	3	1	12
Liberty	75	38	37	70	4	1	0	0

See footnotes at end of table.   Continued . . .

University of Florida   **Bureau of Economic and Business Research**

Florida Statistical Abstract 2000

Table 4.84. HIGH SCHOOL COMPLETERS: STUDENTS COMPLETING HIGH SCHOOL BY SEX
AND BY RACE OR HISPANIC ORIGIN IN THE STATE AND COUNTIES OF FLORIDA,
SCHOOL YEAR 1998-99 (Continued)

County	Total 1/	Sex Male	Sex Female	White	Black	Race Asian or Pacific Islander	Race American Indian Eskimo or Aleut	Hispanic origin 2/
Madison	194	94	100	85	105	0	1	3
Manatee	1,257	605	652	987	171	17	0	77
Marion	1,735	849	886	1,265	310	22	3	132
Martin	725	362	363	613	68	12	0	31
Miami-Dade	14,951	6,898	8,053	2,407	4,686	279	10	7,556
Monroe	461	229	232	355	48	10	2	45
Nassau	478	225	253	404	61	3	2	7
Okaloosa	1,776	890	886	1,421	200	68	8	70
Okeechobee	288	129	159	224	28	1	6	28
Orange	6,001	2,746	3,255	3,095	1,468	343	27	1,057
Osceola	1,453	702	751	828	137	57	4	420
Palm Beach	6,713	3,286	3,427	3,842	1,812	200	25	805
Pasco	1,989	919	1,070	1,780	71	32	3	92
Pinellas	5,052	2,427	2,625	4,003	657	203	12	164
Polk	3,519	1,683	1,836	2,444	782	52	10	230
Putnam	583	269	314	395	146	8	3	30
St. Johns	895	429	466	774	93	7	3	16
St. Lucie	1,080	492	588	665	313	25	5	71
Santa Rosa	1,105	528	577	1,013	45	20	5	22
Sarasota	1,619	749	870	1,438	94	30	2	51
Seminole	2,993	1,419	1,574	2,199	303	117	3	359
Sumter	275	127	148	206	61	1	0	6
Suwannee	307	140	167	251	50	2	0	4
Taylor	198	100	98	147	47	3	0	1
Union	133	75	58	105	26	0	0	2
Volusia	2,894	1,391	1,503	2,245	369	53	4	216
Wakulla	230	111	119	209	20	0	0	1
Walton	270	127	143	240	18	6	3	3
Washington	183	86	97	136	40	6	0	1
Deaf/Blind	82	44	38	44	27	2	0	9
Dozier School	16	16	0	9	4	0	0	3
FSU Developmental	110	60	50	68	29	3	0	7
FAMU Developmental	61	25	36	0	61	0	0	1
UF P.K. Yonge Developmental	98	53	45	67	22	1	2	4

1/ Includes multiracial not shown separately.
2/ Persons of Hispanic origin may be of any race. However, these data are not distributed by race.
Note: Data were obtained from the Florida DOE Student Information Data Base, Survey 5, as of November 10, 1999, and are for public schools only.

Source: State of Florida, Department of Education, Education Information and Accountability Services, *Statistical Brief: Florida Public High School Graduates, 1998-99 School Year,* Series 99-04B. Internet site <http://www.firn.edu/doe/bin00050/eiaspubs/graduate.htm> (accessed 7 March 2000).

University of Florida   **Bureau of Economic and Business Research**

Table 4.85. READINESS FOR COLLEGE: PERCENTAGE OF STUDENTS ENTERING COLLEGE WHO TESTED COMPETENT IN READING, WRITING, AND MATHEMATICS SKILLS IN THE STATE AND COUNTIES OF FLORIDA, 1998-99

County	Students taking college entry test 1/	Ready in all areas		Per-cent-age	Percentage ready in--		
		Number	Per-centage change from 1997-98 A/		Reading	Writing	Mathe-matics
Florida	47,578	28,280	11.4	61.5	74.3	80.9	69.7
Alachua	877	579	9.7	37.5	77.0	75.0	75.9
Baker	73	48	33.3	66.7	76.7	87.5	73.6
Bay	670	368	29.6	57.6	72.6	83.0	68.2
Bradford	70	36	-10.0	52.9	61.8	75.0	57.4
Brevard	1,730	1,129	2.8	66.5	77.5	85.9	73.0
Broward	4,633	2,808	2.9	63.4	75.8	81.6	71.6
Calhoun	60	41	5.1	68.3	81.7	78.3	73.3
Charlotte	396	247	9.8	65.7	79.5	81.5	72.3
Citrus	295	218	14.1	74.9	83.9	86.6	81.5
Clay	573	380	21.8	68.5	77.6	84.2	72.2
Collier	519	376	5.9	75.0	80.6	83.0	83.5
Columbia	189	114	16.3	60.6	76.2	84.1	68.1
De Soto	57	34	13.3	59.6	87.7	87.7	63.2
Dixie	34	15	-31.8	44.1	73.5	85.3	47.1
Duval	2,321	1,425	28.0	64.0	70.8	80.7	70.7
Escambia	918	563	6.4	62.3	77.0	82.3	70.5
Flagler	158	90	16.9	60.4	77.5	86.1	65.8
Franklin	28	9	-40.0	33.3	67.9	78.6	37.0
Gadsden	130	42	10.5	41.2	50.0	65.4	48.2
Gilchrist	60	33	-5.7	55.9	74.6	74.6	55.9
Glades	22	11	83.3	50.0	59.1	72.7	54.5
Gulf	66	28	-15.2	43.8	66.7	78.8	50.0
Hamilton	38	18	28.6	47.4	73.7	76.3	65.8
Hardee	79	54	31.7	71.1	83.1	83.1	80.5
Hendry	110	56	-9.7	50.9	67.3	64.5	62.7
Hernando	367	226	-8.5	62.6	79.8	83.7	68.7
Highlands	231	158	8.2	69.9	83.7	83.3	80.1
Hillsborough	3,183	2,153	7.5	70.3	80.2	84.0	76.8
Holmes	60	28	-22.2	49.1	63.8	86.2	63.2
Indian River	280	193	12.9	70.2	79.3	86.5	77.8
Jackson	220	128	1.6	58.4	73.1	74.9	75.9
Jefferson	29	15	15.4	55.6	70.4	77.8	64.3
Lafayette	24	18	63.6	75.0	83.3	95.8	79.2
Lake	532	276	15.0	53.8	73.8	83.6	60.8
Lee	1,057	695	4.7	67.0	81.5	85.1	73.4
Leon	850	491	11.6	67.9	78.7	83.8	75.8

See footnotes at end of table.   Continued . . .

University of Florida   **Bureau of Economic and Business Research**

Table 4.85. READINESS FOR COLLEGE: PERCENTAGE OF STUDENTS ENTERING COLLEGE WHO TESTED COMPETENT IN READING, WRITING, AND MATHEMATICS SKILLS IN THE STATE AND COUNTIES OF FLORIDA, 1998-99 (Continued)

County	Students taking college entry test 1/	Number	Ready in all areas Percentage change from 1997-98 A/	Percentage	Percentage ready in-- Reading	Writing	Mathematics
Levy	87	51	-21.5	59.3	69.8	75.6	66.3
Liberty	37	19	72.7	52.8	63.9	66.7	64.9
Madison	69	30	57.9	45.5	63.2	82.1	52.2
Manatee	547	351	26.3	66.7	74.6	78.7	75.2
Marion	746	463	27.2	62.9	76.4	80.5	70.7
Martin	317	215	13.2	69.8	79.9	84.1	75.6
Miami-Dade	6,551	2,883	6.8	45.4	59.9	72.2	58.0
Monroe	150	102	75.9	72.9	82.6	88.3	79.0
Nassau	208	122	76.8	60.7	69.5	77.3	63.4
Okaloosa	859	574	9.8	70.3	81.0	84.3	78.7
Okeechobee	74	48	-4.0	66.7	76.4	88.9	79.2
Orange	2,638	1,507	19.3	57.7	72.2	80.3	67.5
Osceola	527	228	34.1	43.7	65.3	76.0	51.0
Palm Beach	2,969	1,985	8.4	68.0	79.2	82.0	75.9
Pasco	797	543	15.5	69.1	83.1	85.7	76.8
Pinellas	2,655	1,577	11.4	62.9	78.1	83.6	66.5
Polk	1,364	700	27.5	51.7	69.9	80.3	60.9
Putnam	200	106	34.2	55.2	70.6	79.3	64.1
St. Johns	390	267	42.0	69.9	78.9	84.6	74.7
St. Lucie	478	259	11.2	55.8	68.1	76.5	67.9
Santa Rosa	514	350	-1.1	71.1	83.2	82.8	77.7
Sarasota	736	502	13.3	70.4	81.4	85.8	76.5
Seminole	1,762	1,189	3.9	68.6	80.2	83.4	76.4
Sumter	82	48	65.5	60.0	68.8	78.8	72.5
Suwannee	138	78	8.3	57.4	67.2	82.4	73.0
Taylor	75	42	27.3	59.2	68.5	69.4	70.8
Union	55	27	22.7	49.1	65.5	74.5	54.5
Volusia	1,255	702	37.9	59.5	77.0	83.7	67.5
Wakulla	71	35	12.9	68.6	85.5	92.6	67.9
Walton	102	66	15.8	66.7	81.8	88.9	72.7
Washington	73	43	-10.4	61.4	78.6	80.0	65.7

A/ Change in overall readiness.
1/ High school graduates, 1997-98, who enrolled as degree-seeking students in Florida public community colleges and state universities during the 1998-99 academic year.

Source: State of Florida, Department of Education, *Readiness for Postsecondary Education,* February 2000, Internet site <http://www.firn.edu/doe/postsecondary/college.pdf> (accessed 22 June 2000).

University of Florida   **Bureau of Economic and Business Research**

INCOME
AND WEALTH

Transfer Payments as a Percentage of Total Personal Income, 1998

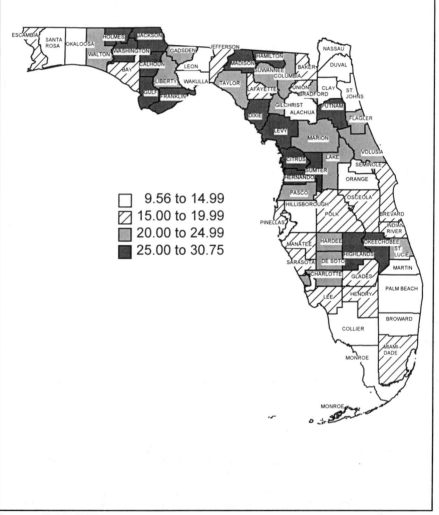

☐ 9.56 to 14.99
▨ 15.00 to 19.99
▦ 20.00 to 24.99
■ 25.00 to 30.75

Source: Table 5.39

SECTION 5.00
INCOME AND WEALTH

TABLES LISTED BY MAJOR HEADINGS

HEADING   PAGE

University of Florida   **Bureau of Economic and Business Research**

SECTION 5.00
INCOME AND WEALTH
(Continued)

TABLES LISTED BY MAJOR HEADINGS

Table 5.01. INDIVIDUAL INCOME TAXES: RETURNS, SPECIFIED INCOME, DEDUCTION, AND
TAX ITEMS IN FLORIDA AND THE UNITED STATES, 1998

(numbers in thousands; amounts in millions of dollars)

Item	Florida Number	Florida Amount	United States Number	United States Amount
All returns	7,076	(X)	125,394	(X)
Number of exemptions 1/	13,661	(X)	251,220	(X)
Adjusted gross income (AGI)	(X)	298,976	(X)	5,381,508
Salaries and wages in AGI	5,734	185,761	106,692	3,872,173
Taxable interest	3,509	13,688	67,379	176,575
Tax-exempt interest 2/	333	5,844	4,853	53,383
Dividends	1,772	10,053	30,517	117,401
Business or profession net income (less loss)	995	9,920	17,313	199,871
Number of farm returns	40	(X)	2,116	(X)
Net capital gain (less loss) in AGI	1,529	36,434	25,680	426,922
Taxable Individual Retirement				
Arrangements (IRA) distributions	530	6,228	7,973	76,305
Pensions and annuities in AGI	1,325	20,169	20,368	278,998
Social Security benefits in AGI	703	5,776	8,809	68,778
Total statutory adjustments	1,249	2,636	22,047	51,467
Self-employment retirement plans	42	358	1,218	11,090
Total itemized deductions 3/	1,766	(X)	38,407	(X)
Average (whole dollars)	(X)	16,705	(X)	17,829
Medical and dental expense	411	2,454	5,788	34,732
Taxes paid	1,674	5,687	38,056	245,623
Interest paid	1,537	13,861	32,267	274,618
Contributions	1,529	5,807	33,895	107,435
Taxable income	5,586	216,648	100,728	3,770,080
Total tax credits	1,631	1,255	32,108	27,750
Child care credit	347	150	5,864	2,550
Earned income credit	1,283	2,048	19,442	30,812
Excess earned income credit (refundable) 4/	1,053	1,734	16,035	26,333
Income tax	5,342	46,836	96,632	792,296
Total tax liability	5,632	48,526	100,852	828,274
Tax due at time of filing	1,648	6,870	28,241	101,021
Overpayments	4,992	7,975	90,465	145,078

(X) Not applicable.
1/ Includes exemptions for age and blindness.
2/ Not included in adjusted gross income.
3/ Includes any amounts reported by the taxpayer, even if they could not be used in computing "taxable income," the base on which tax was computed.
4/ Represents the refundable portion of the credit and equals the amount in excess of total tax liability, including any advance earned income credit payments for those returns which had such an excess.
Note: Data are estimates based on samples and are preliminary.

Source: U.S., Department of the Treasury, Internal Revenue Service, *Statistics of Income: SOI Bulletin*, Spring 2000.

Table 5.02. INDIVIDUAL INCOME TAXES: RETURNS, ADJUSTED GROSS INCOME
EXEMPTIONS, AND INCOME TAX IN FLORIDA AND THE UNITED STATES
1989 THROUGH 1998

| | Number (1,000) | | | | Amount ($1,000,000) | | | |
| | Returns | | Exemptions 1/ | | Adjusted gross income 2/ | | Total income tax | |
Year	Florida	United States	Florida	United States	Florida	United States	Florida	United States
1989	5,971	112,136	12,973	223,756	169,688	3,256,358	25,035	432,940
1990	6,141	113,717	13,390	227,549	176,297	3,405,427	25,643	447,127
1991	6,250	114,730	13,721	231,297	177,889	3,464,534	25,504	448,430
1992	6,239	113,605	13,702	230,547	187,754	3,629,130	27,732	476,239
1993	6,282	115,061	13,840	253,489	193,995	3,720,611	29,539	532,213
1994	6,381	116,466	13,945	253,599	203,882	3,898,340	31,427	564,526
1995	6,553	118,784	14,281	257,737	221,515	4,182,770	34,968	620,972
1996	6,749	120,787	12,979	239,908	245,122	4,520,289	40,152	693,529
1997	6,898	123,057	14,993	267,906	273,066	4,950,214	45,054	770,465
1998	7,076	125,394	13,661	251,220	298,976	5,381,508	46,836	792,296

1/ Includes exemptions for age and blindness.
2/ Less deficit.
Note: Includes taxable and nontaxable returns. All figures are estimates based on samples. Some data are revised. 1997 data are preliminary.

Source: U.S., Department of the Treasury, Internal Revenue Service, *Statistics of Income: SOI Bulletin*, Spring 2000, and previous editions.

Table 5.03. HOUSEHOLD INCOME: PERCENTAGE DISTRIBUTION OF ANNUAL INCOME BY INCOME
CATEGORY AND HOUSEHOLD SIZE IN FLORIDA, 1999

| Income category | Total house-holds | Household size | | | | | |
		1	2	3	4	5	6 or more
Total	100.00	18.78	36.46	19.12	15.87	6.82	2.94
Less than $10,000	5.83	31.69	39.80	6.92	7.30	14.29	0.00
$10,000 to $19,999	11.65	24.40	41.52	20.69	7.38	0.00	6.00
$20,000 to $29,999	14.06	31.71	32.57	17.61	9.10	5.44	3.57
$30,000 to $39,999	15.06	19.44	39.84	23.04	9.40	5.12	3.15
$40,000 to $49,999	16.15	13.08	33.69	22.44	20.14	8.23	2.42
$50,000 to $59,999	7.88	16.54	27.67	21.06	25.65	9.08	0.00
$60,000 to $79,000	12.79	19.32	30.12	12.44	28.60	5.76	3.76
$80,000 to $99,000	7.63	7.48	47.46	22.19	13.69	9.19	0.00
$100,000 or more	8.96	2.80	40.58	19.96	21.40	10.83	4.43

Note: Distribution of household income is based on telephone surveys with sample size of approximately 1,000 Florida households. The surveys are conducted throughout the year and the monthly results have been pooled to develop the annual frequency distributions.

Source: University of Florida, Bureau of Economic and Business Research, Survey Program, unpublished data.

University of Florida   **Bureau of Economic and Business Research**

Table 5.05. PERSONAL INCOME: TOTAL AND PER CAPITA AMOUNTS IN FLORIDA, OTHER SUNBELT STATES, OTHER POPULOUS STATES, AND THE UNITED STATES 1997 THROUGH 1999

State	Total personal income ($1,000,000) 1997	1998	1999	Per-cent-age change 1998-1999	Per capita personal income (amounts in dollars) 1997	1998	1999 Amount	Rank among states
			Sunbelt states					
Florida	376,559	400,209	423,460	5.8	25,645	26,845	28,023	18
Alabama	91,848	95,956	100,269	4.5	21,260	22,054	22,946	43
Arizona	103,968	112,974	120,923	7.0	22,839	24,206	25,307	35
Arkansas	51,344	53,725	56,421	5.0	20,342	21,167	22,114	47
California	862,756	920,452	988,339	7.4	26,779	28,163	29,819	13
Georgia	184,113	197,319	211,823	7.4	24,594	25,839	27,198	23
Louisiana	92,486	96,878	99,646	2.9	21,254	22,206	22,792	45
Mississippi	51,557	54,410	56,773	4.3	18,873	19,776	20,506	50
New Mexico	34,955	36,688	38,386	4.6	20,288	21,164	22,063	48
North Carolina	179,845	190,009	200,601	5.6	24,210	25,181	26,220	28
Oklahoma	69,865	73,350	76,566	4.4	21,080	21,964	22,801	44
South Carolina	81,169	85,898	91,300	6.3	21,416	22,372	23,496	39
Tennessee	126,096	132,756	140,275	5.7	23,445	24,437	25,581	34
Texas	464,500	500,087	531,675	6.3	23,998	25,369	26,525	27
Virginia	180,510	190,528	202,642	6.4	26,810	28,063	29,484	15
			Other populous states					
Illinois	341,938	360,317	379,351	5.3	28,468	29,853	31,278	7
Indiana	140,405	148,651	155,061	4.3	23,909	25,163	26,092	30
Massachusetts	193,199	205,814	220,658	7.2	31,592	33,496	35,733	3
Michigan	252,266	264,016	274,643	4.0	25,780	26,885	27,844	19
New Jersey	262,423	278,349	294,024	5.6	32,582	34,383	36,106	2
New York	554,061	583,061	617,709	5.9	30,538	32,108	33,946	4
Ohio	280,289	292,999	304,847	4.0	24,998	26,073	27,081	25
Pennsylvania	314,944	329,687	343,946	4.3	26,211	27,469	28,676	16
United States	6,942,114	7,351,547	7,776,493	5.8	25,924	27,203	28,518	(X)

(X) Not applicable.
Note: Data for 1997 and 1998 are revised; 1999 are preliminary.

Source: U.S., Department of Commerce, Bureau of Economic Analysis, Internet site <http://www.bea.doc/gov/bea/regional/articles/spi/summary.htm> (accessed 17 July 2000).

University of Florida   **Bureau of Economic and Business Research**

Table 5.08. DISPOSABLE PERSONAL INCOME: TOTAL AND PER CAPITA AMOUNTS IN FLORIDA OTHER SUNBELT STATES, OTHER POPULOUS STATES, AND THE UNITED STATES 1997 THROUGH 1999

State	Total personal income ($1,000,000)			Per-cent-age change 1998-1999	Per capita personal income (amounts in dollars)			1999
	1997	1998	1999		1997	1998	Amount	Rank among states
			Sunbelt states					
Florida	328,706	346,602	365,711	5.5	22,386	23,249	24,201	19
Alabama	80,911	84,046	87,693	4.3	18,728	19,316	20,068	41
Arizona	90,496	97,740	104,430	6.8	19,880	20,942	21,855	36
Arkansas	45,361	47,174	49,527	5.0	17,972	18,586	19,412	47
California	736,458	778,309	831,948	6.9	22,859	23,814	25,100	14
Georgia	158,735	168,896	180,881	7.1	21,204	22,117	23,225	22
Louisiana	81,667	85,095	87,510	2.8	18,768	19,505	20,016	42
Mississippi	46,205	48,525	50,504	4.1	16,914	17,637	18,241	50
New Mexico	30,857	32,233	33,746	4.7	17,910	18,594	19,396	48
North Carolina	155,509	163,045	171,564	5.2	20,934	21,607	22,424	31
Oklahoma	61,161	63,775	66,491	4.3	18,454	19,097	19,800	45
South Carolina	71,015	74,814	79,622	6.4	18,737	19,485	20,491	39
Tennessee	112,276	117,550	124,068	5.5	20,875	21,638	22,626	28
Texas	409,803	438,293	465,480	6.2	21,172	22,234	23,223	23
Virginia	155,254	162,496	171,894	5.8	23,059	23,934	25,010	15
			Other populous states					
Illinois	292,889	306,256	321,633	5.0	24,384	25,374	26,519	8
Indiana	120,783	127,061	132,069	3.9	20,568	21,508	22,223	35
Massachusetts	161,316	170,771	182,716	7.0	26,378	27,793	29,589	3
Michigan	216,124	224,926	233,614	3.9	22,086	22,904	23,684	21
New Jersey	222,746	234,042	246,349	5.3	27,656	28,910	30,251	2
New York	465,130	484,178	510,808	5.5	25,637	26,663	28,072	4
Ohio	240,700	249,868	259,108	3.7	21,467	22,235	23,018	25
Pennsylvania	271,855	282,658	293,835	4.0	22,625	23,550	24,498	17
United States	5,974,812	6,280,017	6,625,556	5.5	22,312	23,238	24,297	(X)

(X) Not applicable.
Note: Data for 1997 and 1998 are revised; 1999 are preliminary.

Source: U.S., Department of Commerce, Bureau of Economic Analysis, Internet site <http://www.bea. doc/gov/bea/regional/articles/spi/summary.htm> (accessed 17 July 2000).

Table 5.09. PERSONAL INCOME: TOTAL AMOUNT ON A PLACE-OF-RESIDENCE BASIS IN THE UNITED STATES AND IN THE STATE AND COUNTIES OF FLORIDA, 1989 THROUGH 1998

(in millions, rounded to hundred thousands of dollars)

County	1989	1990	1991	1992	1993	1994	1995	1996	1997	1998
United States 1/	4,582,429	4,885,525	5,065,416	5,376,622	5,598,446	5,878,362	6,192,235	6,538,103	6,942,114	7,351,547
Florida	240,686.7	258,479.0	268,304.2	279,028.3	296,927.4	311,908.9	333,525.4	355,135.9	376,559.1	400,208.5
Alachua	2,907.3	3,131.3	3,288.2	3,473.4	3,660.1	3,844.4	4,097.3	4,312.3	4,566.9	4,887.3
Baker	227.1	246.0	258.2	273.5	287.5	298.3	315.0	335.9	357.2	382.9
Bay	1,855.3	2,024.4	2,178.4	2,322.8	2,476.3	2,564.9	2,655.4	2,944.7	3,119.2	3,252.0
Bradford	253.1	267.5	280.4	301.6	314.1	327.6	345.6	373.2	403.4	419.6
Brevard	6,992.6	7,484.7	7,858.6	8,346.7	8,641.5	8,974.8	9,412.6	9,830.2	10,529.6	11,043.3
Broward	27,921.2	29,692.9	30,206.2	31,341.2	33,160.7	34,614.3	36,997.1	39,012.9	40,657.3	43,040.5
Calhoun	108.3	122.8	127.8	134.6	139.6	148.7	158.4	169.8	182.3	190.9
Charlotte	1,881.5	2,046.4	2,112.8	2,227.0	2,319.7	2,487.4	2,654.5	2,832.0	3,043.8	3,200.9
Citrus	1,337.8	1,468.3	1,528.0	1,613.9	1,679.2	1,799.9	1,873.3	1,992.9	2,158.4	2,259.0
Clay	1,755.1	1,961.7	2,037.0	2,137.4	2,253.0	2,371.2	2,547.8	2,790.4	3,002.0	3,235.7
Collier	3,962.7	4,308.0	4,604.3	5,194.2	5,675.6	6,259.6	6,627.6	7,217.8	8,081.8	8,552.9
Columbia	545.3	581.7	609.9	657.7	705.1	750.8	819.4	886.8	951.0	1,005.6
De Soto	340.0	353.8	406.8	407.8	427.1	449.0	457.5	468.2	497.0	532.7
Dixie	111.8	120.4	120.0	127.8	127.7	148.5	159.1	169.3	177.7	189.5
Duval	12,064.8	12,984.8	13,399.1	14,099.3	14,786.0	15,474.9	16,455.8	17,548.5	18,567.9	19,569.2
Escambia	4,009.0	4,298.4	4,474.5	4,727.2	4,825.1	4,972.4	5,183.4	5,592.6	5,951.4	6,159.7
Flagler	409.5	464.0	496.6	565.4	629.9	701.9	772.1	847.5	939.3	1,007.3
Franklin	108.1	118.6	125.6	137.4	147.1	159.1	176.0	176.7	183.7	191.8
Gadsden	485.1	512.4	541.5	581.1	604.0	628.6	670.1	702.1	738.0	782.0
Gilchrist	105.9	117.1	126.0	138.3	148.3	157.9	167.3	184.8	200.5	213.5
Glades	92.1	99.1	108.0	109.4	115.2	117.9	124.4	128.6	137.1	147.2

Continued . . .

See footnotes at end of table.

University of Florida   **Bureau of Economic and Business Research**

Table 5.09. PERSONAL INCOME: TOTAL AMOUNT ON A PLACE-OF-RESIDENCE BASIS IN THE UNITED STATES AND IN THE STATE AND COUNTIES OF FLORIDA, 1989 THROUGH 1998 (Continued)

(in millions, rounded to hundred thousands of dollars)

County	1989	1990	1991	1992	1993	1994	1995	1996	1997	1998
Gulf	138.4	148.0	155.4	167.3	181.1	193.7	203.6	216.5	225.7	226.0
Hamilton	120.4	129.6	130.0	137.7	136.7	142.2	154.6	165.7	171.3	177.1
Hardee	296.3	298.6	317.7	316.6	325.6	344.6	364.2	373.2	398.4	422.5
Hendry	413.2	429.4	488.6	494.9	528.5	538.9	570.2	557.9	598.5	652.3
Hernando	1,479.6	1,626.0	1,704.2	1,807.2	1,900.1	2,052.8	2,203.2	2,390.2	2,595.6	2,732.7
Highlands	1,079.9	1,140.0	1,198.1	1,238.8	1,297.7	1,372.0	1,452.9	1,512.1	1,593.1	1,661.3
Hillsborough	13,970.6	15,049.1	15,697.0	16,601.0	17,424.9	18,489.7	19,965.6	21,365.6	22,991.5	24,389.3
Holmes	166.9	175.6	186.2	200.6	209.3	223.1	239.6	256.4	272.2	282.1
Indian River	2,114.8	2,341.6	2,478.3	2,588.9	2,653.9	2,822.8	3,094.1	3,309.6	3,441.9	3,617.7
Jackson	504.8	544.4	584.9	618.2	634.9	657.8	686.4	722.8	747.4	775.4
Jefferson	141.9	158.0	169.6	178.7	188.0	198.1	212.9	227.3	239.2	253.7
Lafayette	60.1	66.2	68.5	73.6	75.8	80.8	82.8	91.3	98.8	105.4
Lake	2,472.8	2,662.1	2,793.6	2,990.1	3,129.7	3,322.8	3,591.9	3,888.6	4,221.0	4,498.3
Lee	6,471.7	6,963.3	7,174.1	7,574.3	7,909.3	8,406.2	9,113.4	9,533.0	10,244.9	10,860.1
Leon	3,185.5	3,505.7	3,705.5	3,917.8	4,176.1	4,441.6	4,791.9	5,059.9	5,332.6	5,690.4
Levy	303.3	330.2	350.7	378.9	402.8	426.9	450.2	488.0	531.3	559.8
Liberty	62.1	68.4	71.1	75.1	78.5	83.0	88.2	94.0	100.4	101.9
Madison	176.7	191.1	199.0	208.8	214.2	226.0	244.7	261.0	274.2	283.1
Manatee	4,008.6	4,332.3	4,480.8	4,810.3	5,047.0	5,419.2	6,027.9	6,353.5	6,900.8	7,294.2
Marion	2,821.6	3,071.5	3,224.6	3,424.2	3,632.1	3,894.6	4,194.9	4,531.4	4,852.6	5,195.2
Martin	2,734.0	3,081.1	3,159.1	3,273.5	3,404.9	3,520.2	3,871.7	4,139.0	4,408.5	4,653.4
Miami-Dade	34,200.8	36,163.0	37,038.4	35,336.6	40,541.5	42,018.6	44,565.6	46,930.0	48,682.5	51,447.9
Monroe	1,657.3	1,801.7	1,836.6	1,882.7	2,095.4	2,094.9	2,251.3	2,351.6	2,483.8	2,627.8
Nassau	765.2	813.5	862.5	926.2	996.6	1,039.6	1,124.4	1,234.3	1,348.0	1,450.3

See footnotes at end of table.

Continued . . . .

Table 5.09. PERSONAL INCOME: TOTAL AMOUNT ON A PLACE-OF-RESIDENCE BASIS IN THE UNITED STATES AND IN THE STATE AND COUNTIES OF FLORIDA, 1989 THROUGH 1998 (Continued)

(in millions, rounded to hundred thousands of dollars)

County	1989	1990	1991	1992	1993	1994	1995	1996	1997	1998
Okaloosa	2,278.1	2,451.0	2,638.8	2,853.3	3,057.1	3,153.0	3,297.6	3,650.4	3,934.5	4,155.1
Okeechobee	374.7	402.0	418.7	435.7	455.5	471.8	488.3	525.2	568.4	598.7
Orange	11,899.3	12,934.2	13,460.3	14,204.6	15,045.2	15,707.0	16,777.2	17,958.7	19,397.5	21,066.2
Osceola	1,515.7	1,662.1	1,774.2	1,882.9	1,990.1	2,100.8	2,238.4	2,388.7	2,591.7	2,800.6
Palm Beach	23,636.0	26,274.2	28,313.0	29,728.0	31,081.8	32,626.0	35,172.1	37,819.2	38,835.7	41,360.6
Pasco	4,201.9	4,435.9	4,553.8	4,767.6	4,966.0	5,339.0	5,820.8	6,271.4	6,846.2	7,377.5
Pinellas	17,727.8	18,306.5	18,575.1	19,317.1	20,540.1	21,021.2	22,386.9	23,553.9	25,108.4	26,873.6
Polk	6,206.0	6,514.3	6,682.4	7,054.1	7,358.4	7,909.6	8,470.2	8,990.4	9,461.2	10,234.1
Putnam	742.7	795.2	839.4	915.6	974.9	1,005.8	1,089.8	1,118.9	1,168.0	1,222.8
St. Johns	1,769.6	1,949.4	2,048.6	2,237.3	2,398.3	2,608.1	2,901.0	3,235.0	3,703.7	4,179.9
St. Lucie	2,234.4	2,401.8	2,497.4	2,616.1	2,752.6	2,940.0	3,194.4	3,400.4	3,630.6	3,831.5
Santa Rosa	1,198.2	1,301.6	1,407.2	1,534.5	1,646.7	1,778.0	1,910.9	2,150.4	2,377.3	2,566.3
Sarasota	7,364.7	7,857.2	7,991.7	8,335.8	8,543.5	9,151.4	9,513.4	10,051.0	10,752.5	11,263.3
Seminole	5,209.8	5,640.0	5,795.8	6,235.8	6,657.5	7,149.6	7,688.3	8,354.8	9,156.1	10,040.6
Sumter	364.5	383.8	404.4	439.7	460.5	493.0	534.7	593.1	648.7	687.2
Suwannee	351.4	385.7	404.2	434.9	454.9	472.9	506.9	549.3	580.1	616.5
Taylor	218.2	230.0	234.2	249.9	243.8	275.3	290.2	306.5	319.2	333.5
Union	94.1	99.7	104.9	111.9	117.9	123.4	131.1	136.3	147.3	153.0
Volusia	5,805.7	6,219.2	6,400.1	6,674.1	6,952.3	7,330.6	7,827.7	8,319.4	8,822.8	9,221.3
Wakulla	185.9	206.5	219.5	235.2	254.1	275.3	319.7	361.1	408.5	449.9
Walton	303.4	333.2	362.9	394.3	429.9	464.5	477.7	540.2	586.9	623.6
Washington	184.5	200.8	215.0	230.1	238.6	250.5	272.1	291.8	314.1	331.5

1/ United States numbers are rounded to millions of dollars.
Note: Some data are revised.

Source: U.S., Department of Commerce, Bureau of Economic Analysis, Regional Economic Information System, CD-ROM, June 2000.

Table 5.10. PERSONAL INCOME: PER CAPITA AMOUNTS ON A PLACE-OF-RESIDENCE BASIS IN THE UNITED STATES AND IN THE STATE AND COUNTIES OF FLORIDA, 1988 THROUGH 1998

(rounded to dollars)

County	1988	1989	1990	1991	1992	1993	1994	1995	1996	1997	1998
United States	17,403	18,566	19,584	20,089	21,082	21,718	22,581	23,562	24,651	25,924	27,203
Florida	17,593	19,045	19,855	20,189	20,661	21,652	22,340	23,512	24,616	25,645	26,845
Alachua	14,960	16,192	17,180	17,696	18,375	19,181	19,879	20,954	21,948	23,114	24,656
Baker	12,064	12,492	13,238	13,456	14,074	14,573	15,083	15,627	16,333	17,156	18,191
Bay	13,886	14,759	15,901	16,764	17,420	18,075	18,389	18,713	20,366	21,314	22,163
Bradford	10,648	11,249	11,849	12,144	12,935	13,464	13,655	14,489	15,412	16,397	16,893
Brevard	16,839	18,100	18,567	18,934	19,651	19,862	20,273	20,944	21,680	22,934	23,758
Broward	20,772	22,644	23,530	23,429	23,880	24,500	24,952	26,143	27,042	27,530	28,546
Calhoun	9,951	9,896	11,132	11,325	11,895	12,279	12,683	13,374	13,612	14,725	15,380
Charlotte	16,322	18,083	18,153	18,001	18,550	18,864	19,763	20,620	21,758	23,002	23,752
Citrus	13,757	14,930	15,518	15,679	16,140	16,511	17,295	17,487	18,217	19,386	19,878
Clay	16,219	17,014	18,369	18,524	18,793	19,305	19,733	20,554	21,646	22,452	23,519
Collier	25,900	27,369	27,934	28,689	31,448	33,250	35,452	36,632	38,806	41,913	42,813
Columbia	12,353	13,017	13,585	14,018	14,850	15,406	15,688	16,576	17,540	18,411	19,004
De Soto	13,737	14,460	14,781	16,626	16,755	17,350	18,056	18,288	18,936	20,086	21,560
Dixie	10,169	10,916	11,298	10,889	11,364	11,192	12,673	13,139	13,750	14,018	14,726
Duval	16,777	18,294	19,184	19,451	20,157	21,130	22,055	23,370	24,334	25,429	26,637
Escambia	14,411	15,268	16,346	16,825	17,543	17,965	18,332	19,086	20,372	21,252	21,682
Flagler	15,990	15,884	15,737	15,749	16,836	17,574	18,542	19,179	19,996	20,910	21,413
Franklin	11,078	12,088	13,238	13,538	14,690	15,145	16,079	17,373	17,443	18,185	18,988
Gadsden	10,706	11,825	12,424	12,825	13,795	14,173	14,658	15,497	15,950	16,727	17,771
Gilchrist	10,968	11,541	12,009	12,219	13,239	13,243	13,244	13,616	14,299	15,002	15,450
Glades	11,778	12,348	13,031	14,362	14,688	15,456	15,531	16,276	15,188	16,228	17,139
Gulf	11,382	11,998	12,863	13,495	14,461	14,646	14,878	15,362	16,154	16,720	16,754

Continued . . . .

See footnote at end of table.

Table 5.10. PERSONAL INCOME: PER CAPITA AMOUNTS ON A PLACE-OF-RESIDENCE BASIS IN THE UNITED STATES AND IN THE STATE AND COUNTIES OF FLORIDA, 1988 THROUGH 1998 (Continued)

(rounded to dollars)

County	1988	1989	1990	1991	1992	1993	1994	1995	1996	1997	1998
Hamilton	10,601	11,201	11,805	11,571	12,146	12,078	12,346	12,930	13,306	13,718	13,967
Hardee	14,675	15,179	15,278	15,901	15,133	15,393	16,206	17,022	17,786	18,915	20,081
Hendry	16,204	16,008	16,639	18,162	18,051	19,033	18,975	19,919	19,435	20,457	22,193
Hernando	14,570	15,525	15,832	15,952	16,477	16,785	17,582	18,554	19,736	20,934	21,587
Highlands	15,277	16,279	16,532	17,073	17,413	17,930	18,667	19,573	20,225	21,233	22,175
Hillsborough	15,612	16,885	18,003	18,581	19,418	20,156	21,193	22,624	23,914	25,277	26,355
Holmes	9,845	10,579	11,101	11,686	12,337	12,712	13,177	13,427	14,248	14,805	15,149
Indian River	22,593	24,158	25,769	26,857	27,659	28,229	29,671	32,227	34,311	35,156	36,501
Jackson	11,415	12,235	13,143	13,947	14,344	14,584	15,009	15,442	16,288	16,777	17,425
Jefferson	11,926	12,735	13,907	14,247	14,619	15,249	15,724	16,560	17,572	18,306	19,228
Lafayette	9,786	11,069	11,785	12,152	13,041	13,605	13,926	13,227	14,490	15,846	16,675
Lake	15,355	16,854	17,336	17,694	18,456	18,717	19,189	19,974	20,801	21,689	22,256
Lee	18,181	20,083	20,585	20,661	21,477	22,052	22,895	24,342	25,114	26,557	27,640
Leon	15,820	16,947	18,101	18,563	19,491	20,313	21,133	22,595	23,814	24,891	26,453
Levy	11,421	12,000	12,654	13,207	13,971	14,343	14,807	15,168	16,129	17,086	17,668
Liberty	10,566	11,432	12,245	12,420	13,230	13,646	13,276	13,665	14,333	14,880	15,139
Madison	10,435	10,748	11,522	11,900	12,422	12,639	13,149	14,114	14,894	15,618	15,959
Manatee	17,622	19,558	20,322	20,660	21,987	22,693	23,998	26,338	27,387	29,365	30,440
Marion	14,012	15,044	15,600	15,913	16,519	17,155	17,756	18,623	19,691	20,585	21,533
Martin	24,734	28,075	30,252	30,389	31,234	31,884	32,414	35,269	36,979	38,744	40,133
Miami-Dade	16,780	17,916	18,614	18,738	17,648	20,287	20,713	21,565	22,270	22,833	23,919
Monroe	18,917	21,507	23,032	23,253	23,633	25,497	25,671	27,635	28,906	30,699	32,501
Nassau	16,589	17,803	18,386	18,972	19,766	20,635	21,011	22,195	23,654	24,977	26,175
Okaloosa	14,987	16,022	16,966	17,804	18,663	19,421	19,616	20,194	22,040	23,471	24,655
Okeechobee	12,284	12,807	13,508	13,782	14,318	14,814	15,474	16,175	17,132	18,396	18,725

See footnote at end of table.

Continued . . .

Table 5.10. PERSONAL INCOME: PER CAPITA AMOUNTS ON A PLACE-OF-RESIDENCE BASIS IN THE UNITED STATES AND IN THE STATE AND COUNTIES OF FLORIDA, 1988 THROUGH 1998 (Continued)

(rounded to dollars)

County	1988	1989	1990	1991	1992	1993	1994	1995	1996	1997	1998
Orange	17,262	18,292	18,897	19,238	19,924	20,684	21,215	22,378	23,504	24,707	26,186
Osceola	14,637	15,285	15,108	15,314	15,817	16,166	16,626	17,123	17,581	18,393	19,216
Palm Beach	25,690	28,068	30,201	31,798	32,631	33,266	34,072	36,065	38,070	38,272	40,044
Pasco	14,251	15,238	15,742	15,983	16,636	17,023	17,879	19,086	20,118	21,499	22,691
Pinellas	19,029	21,082	21,407	21,546	22,399	23,790	24,268	25,762	27,105	28,761	30,633
Polk	14,569	15,584	15,997	16,203	16,868	17,437	18,440	19,462	20,428	21,179	22,609
Putnam	11,373	11,601	12,171	12,666	13,691	14,395	14,674	15,778	16,044	16,677	17,393
St. Johns	20,292	21,995	22,982	23,387	24,830	25,390	26,527	28,448	30,302	33,199	36,014
St. Lucie	15,080	15,752	15,755	15,901	16,248	16,711	17,420	18,658	19,499	20,460	21,362
Santa Rosa	14,467	15,151	15,772	16,406	16,986	17,347	17,893	18,357	19,797	20,895	21,808
Sarasota	23,578	27,148	28,130	28,135	29,261	29,714	31,359	32,294	33,850	35,809	37,131
Seminole	17,748	18,943	19,377	19,235	20,166	21,041	22,075	23,319	24,892	26,650	28,647
Sumter	11,013	11,761	12,097	12,606	13,579	14,097	14,791	15,376	15,586	16,029	16,549
Suwannee	12,242	13,305	14,340	14,610	15,413	15,731	16,059	16,969	17,739	18,219	18,972
Taylor	12,217	12,766	13,404	13,494	14,464	14,162	15,893	16,202	16,444	17,097	17,669
Union	8,902	9,259	9,700	9,312	9,875	10,026	10,038	10,764	11,031	11,839	12,194
Volusia	15,279	16,190	16,633	16,729	17,140	17,571	18,225	19,251	20,275	21,216	21,920
Wakulla	12,617	13,673	14,364	14,771	15,254	15,770	16,505	18,438	20,107	22,178	24,169
Walton	10,254	10,975	11,984	12,289	13,028	13,801	14,211	14,106	15,370	16,040	16,664
Washington	10,540	11,070	11,835	12,489	13,272	13,422	13,966	14,385	14,790	15,515	16,381

Note: These data were derived by dividing each type of income by the total population of the area, not just the segment of the population receiving that particular type of income. All per capita figures are prepared by the Bureau of Economic Analysis using Bureau of the Census population data.

Source: U.S., Department of Commerce, Bureau of Economic Analysis, Regional Economic Information System, CD-ROM, June 2000.

Table 5.11. PERSONAL INCOME: TOTAL AND PER CAPITA AMOUNTS ON A PLACE-OF
RESIDENCE BASIS IN THE STATE AND METROPOLITAN AREAS OF FLORIDA
1996, 1997, AND 1998

Metropolitan area	Total personal income ($1,000,000)			Per capita personal income (dollars)		
	1996	1997	1998	1996	1997	1998
Florida	355,136	376,559	400,209	24,616	25,645	26,845
Daytona Beach	9,167	9,762	10,229	20,249	21,186	21,869
Flagler County	848	939	1,007	19,996	20,910	21,413
Volusia County	8,319	8,823	9,221	20,275	21,216	21,920
Ft. Lauderdale	39,013	40,657	43,041	27,042	27,530	28,546
Ft. Myers-Cape Coral	9,533	10,245	10,860	25,114	26,557	27,640
Ft. Pierce-Port St. Lucie	7,539	8,039	8,485	26,332	27,604	28,732
Martin County	4,139	4,408	4,653	36,979	38,744	40,133
St. Lucie County	3,400	3,631	3,831	19,499	20,460	21,362
Ft. Walton Beach	3,650	3,935	4,155	22,040	23,471	24,655
Gainesville	4,312	4,567	4,887	21,948	23,114	24,656
Jacksonville	24,808	26,622	28,435	24,587	25,861	27,244
Clay County	2,790	3,002	3,236	21,646	22,452	23,519
Duval County	17,548	18,568	19,569	24,334	25,429	26,637
Nassau County	1,234	1,348	1,450	23,654	24,977	26,175
St. Johns County	3,235	3,704	4,180	30,302	33,199	36,014
Lakeland-Winter Haven	8,990	9,461	10,234	20,428	21,179	22,609
Melbourne-Titusville-Palm Bay	9,830	10,530	11,043	21,680	22,934	23,758
Miami	46,930	48,682	51,448	22,270	22,833	23,919
Naples	7,218	8,082	8,553	38,806	41,913	42,813
Ocala	4,531	4,853	5,195	19,691	20,585	21,533
Orlando	32,591	35,366	38,406	22,911	24,154	25,555
Lake County	3,889	4,221	4,498	20,801	21,689	22,256
Orange County	17,959	19,397	21,066	23,504	24,707	26,186
Osceola County	2,389	2,592	2,801	17,581	18,393	19,216
Seminole County	8,355	9,156	10,041	24,892	26,650	28,647
Panama City	2,945	3,119	3,252	20,366	21,314	22,163
Pensacola	7,743	8,329	8,726	20,209	21,149	21,719
Escambia County	5,593	5,951	6,160	20,372	21,252	21,682
Santa Rosa County	2,150	2,377	2,566	19,797	20,895	21,808
Punta Gorda	2,832	3,044	3,201	21,758	23,002	23,752
Sarasota-Bradenton	16,405	17,653	18,558	31,015	32,980	34,178
Manatee County	6,354	6,901	7,294	27,387	29,365	30,440
Sarasota County	10,051	10,753	11,263	33,850	35,809	37,131
Tallahassee	5,762	6,071	6,472	22,464	23,497	24,978
Gadsden County	702	738	782	15,950	16,727	17,771
Leon County	5,060	5,333	5,690	23,814	24,891	26,453
Tampa-St. Petersburg-Clearwater	53,581	57,542	61,373	24,408	25,861	27,224
Hernando County	2,390	2,596	2,733	19,736	20,934	21,587
Hillsborough County	21,366	22,992	24,389	23,914	25,277	26,535
Pasco County	6,271	6,846	7,378	20,118	21,499	22,691
Pinellas County	23,554	25,108	26,874	27,105	28,761	30,633
West Palm Beach-Boca Raton	37,819	38,836	41,361	38,070	38,272	40,044

Note: Data for Metropolitan Statistical Areas (MSAs) and Primary Metropolitan Statistical Areas (PMSAs) based on 1999 MSA designations. See Glossary for definitions and map at the front of the book for area boundaries. Data for 1996 and 1997 are revised. See footnote about per capita data on Table 5.10.

Source: U.S., Department of Commerce, Bureau of Economic Analysis, Regional Economic Information System, CD-ROM, June 2000.

University of Florida   **Bureau of Economic and Business Research**

Table 5.12. PERSONAL INCOME: PER CAPITA AMOUNTS BY TYPE IN THE UNITED STATES AND IN THE STATE AND COUNTIES OF FLORIDA, 1997 AND 1998

(rounded to dollars)

County	1997 Total personal income	1997 Non-farm personal income	1997 Income main-te-nance 1/	1997 Unem-ploy-ment insur-ance	1997 Re-tire-ment and other	1997 Divi-dends inter-est and rent 2/	1998 Total personal income	1998 Non-farm personal income	1998 Income main-te-nance 1/	1998 Unem-ploy-ment insur-ance	1998 Re-tire-ment and other	1998 Divi-dends inter-est and rent 2/
United States	25,924	25,754	4,920	374	76	3,144	27,203	27,044	5,115	373	75	3,191
Florida	25,645	25,498	6,778	326	48	3,778	26,845	26,678	6,971	322	49	3,823
Alachua	23,114	23,019	4,583	389	29	2,935	24,656	24,558	4,785	404	39	3,051
Baker	17,156	16,712	2,079	383	34	2,694	18,191	17,717	2,172	358	30	2,922
Bay	21,314	21,304	4,291	350	55	3,193	22,163	22,152	4,439	343	65	3,324
Bradford	16,397	16,204	2,195	512	31	2,889	16,893	16,685	2,291	520	51	2,936
Brevard	22,934	22,911	5,632	229	47	3,809	23,758	23,732	5,825	219	48	3,899
Broward	27,530	27,514	7,418	230	64	3,701	28,546	28,530	7,579	220	66	3,650
Calhoun	14,725	14,337	2,038	563	44	3,387	15,380	15,109	2,140	574	49	3,581
Charlotte	23,002	22,922	9,380	148	21	5,621	23,752	23,659	9,607	146	20	5,704
Citrus	19,386	19,372	6,380	245	46	5,496	19,878	19,866	6,553	235	51	5,545
Clay	22,452	22,396	3,677	154	28	2,240	23,519	23,451	3,744	152	31	2,319
Collier	41,913	41,273	20,430	183	37	4,158	42,813	42,083	20,460	173	34	4,208
Columbia	18,411	18,318	3,104	512	38	3,431	19,004	18,933	3,193	523	45	3,533
De Soto	20,086	17,861	3,996	489	55	4,302	21,560	18,838	4,191	476	57	4,469
Dixie	14,018	13,892	2,628	595	42	3,610	14,726	14,593	2,727	617	40	3,820
Duval	25,429	25,412	4,141	383	40	2,872	26,637	26,620	4,319	361	37	2,920
Escambia	21,252	21,230	4,120	450	28	3,135	21,682	21,669	4,247	448	28	3,207
Flagler	20,910	20,706	7,005	173	23	4,546	21,413	21,219	6,997	158	24	4,614
Franklin	18,185	18,185	3,980	539	57	4,325	18,988	18,988	4,160	560	49	4,338
Gadsden	16,727	15,701	2,153	824	37	3,146	17,771	16,712	2,272	860	46	3,231
Gilchrist	15,002	13,894	2,098	330	19	3,039	15,450	14,275	2,139	323	19	3,120
Glades	16,228	15,011	4,233	366	70	2,778	17,139	15,601	4,355	364	74	2,833
Gulf	16,720	16,720	3,109	484	90	4,021	16,754	16,754	3,272	474	90	4,176

See footnotes at end of table.

Continued . . .

Table 5.12. PERSONAL INCOME: PER CAPITA AMOUNTS BY TYPE IN THE UNITED STATES AND IN THE STATE AND COUNTIES OF FLORIDA, 1997 AND 1998 (Continued)

(rounded to dollars)

County	1997 Total personal income	1997 Non-farm personal income	1997 Transfer payments Income maintenance 1/	1997 Transfer payments Unemployment insurance	1997 Transfer payments Retirement and other	1997 Dividends interest and rent 2/	1998 Total personal income	1998 Non-farm personal income	1998 Transfer payments Income maintenance 1/	1998 Transfer payments Unemployment insurance	1998 Transfer payments Retirement and other	1998 Dividends interest and rent 2/
Hamilton	13,718	13,290	1,948	610	23	2,967	13,967	13,703	2,029	647	27	3,074
Hardee	18,915	16,427	2,840	673	95	3,348	20,081	17,118	2,979	660	86	3,416
Hendry	20,457	16,848	2,850	467	123	2,947	22,193	17,674	2,989	456	119	2,977
Hernando	20,934	20,874	6,172	227	28	5,857	21,587	21,524	6,339	213	30	5,872
Highlands	21,233	20,458	6,863	356	50	5,841	22,175	21,214	7,195	361	53	5,994
Hillsborough	25,277	25,087	4,818	376	45	3,056	26,355	26,145	4,969	372	42	3,108
Holmes	14,805	14,054	2,202	629	27	3,976	15,149	14,401	2,283	620	30	4,008
Indian River	35,156	34,874	17,159	210	66	5,472	36,501	36,155	17,609	214	70	5,550
Jackson	16,777	16,448	2,713	536	31	3,902	17,425	17,245	2,850	555	37	4,122
Jefferson	18,306	17,629	3,220	669	24	3,082	19,228	18,614	3,334	707	23	3,087
Lafayette	15,846	12,832	1,973	362	19	2,679	16,675	13,434	2,045	418	20	2,650
Lake	21,689	21,383	6,616	274	32	4,798	22,256	21,940	6,668	255	29	4,825
Lee	26,557	26,449	9,766	206	29	4,601	27,640	27,528	9,998	202	28	4,653
Leon	24,891	24,879	4,160	302	26	2,201	26,453	26,442	4,332	310	28	2,309
Levy	17,086	16,120	3,470	450	32	3,952	17,668	16,632	3,579	456	32	4,073
Liberty	14,880	14,826	1,728	431	17	3,162	15,139	15,081	1,828	443	21	2,665
Madison	15,618	14,886	2,317	764	27	3,478	15,959	15,380	2,417	793	44	3,557
Manatee	29,365	28,860	9,391	236	29	4,313	30,440	29,875	9,597	229	28	4,346
Marion	20,585	20,320	5,226	357	34	4,501	21,533	21,238	5,358	351	34	4,594
Martin	38,744	38,398	19,764	191	57	5,098	40,133	39,701	20,135	197	52	5,192
Miami-Dade	22,833	22,764	4,248	558	68	3,465	23,919	23,842	4,411	569	76	3,534
Monroe	30,699	30,699	12,289	248	24	2,978	32,501	32,501	12,798	253	30	3,015
Nassau	24,977	24,705	5,215	213	33	2,748	26,175	25,894	5,310	207	32	2,816
Okaloosa	23,471	23,457	5,697	209	31	2,769	24,655	24,649	5,931	207	31	2,876
Okeechobee	18,396	16,591	3,294	365	69	4,385	18,725	16,732	3,360	360	67	4,373

See footnotes at end of table.

Continued . . .

Table 5.12. PERSONAL INCOME: PER CAPITA AMOUNTS BY TYPE IN THE UNITED STATES AND IN THE STATE AND COUNTIES OF FLORIDA, 1997 AND 1998 (Continued)

(rounded to dollars)

County	1997		Transfer payments				1998		Transfer payments			
	Total personal income	Non-farm personal income	Income maintenance 1/	Unemployment insurance	Retirement and other	Dividends interest and rent 2/	Total personal income	Non-farm personal income	Income maintenance 1/	Unemployment insurance	Retirement and other	Dividends interest and rent 2/
Orange	24,707	24,583	4,107	309	34	2,771	26,186	26,056	4,219	296	34	2,791
Osceola	18,393	18,229	2,934	246	36	2,966	19,216	19,022	2,990	229	33	2,990
Palm Beach	38,272	38,030	15,571	197	70	4,609	40,044	39,719	5,892	196	69	4,657
Pasco	21,499	21,418	5,176	255	32	5,253	22,691	22,602	5,321	256	33	5,213
Pinellas	28,761	28,756	7,979	251	41	4,682	30,633	30,628	8,296	249	42	4,678
Polk	21,179	20,940	4,426	378	51	3,630	22,609	22,333	4,586	377	47	3,691
Putnam	16,677	16,461	3,075	571	45	3,918	17,393	17,167	3,232	583	48	3,985
St. Johns	33,199	33,087	9,021	204	26	3,447	36,014	35,905	9,027	194	24	3,436
St. Lucie	20,460	20,313	5,783	335	95	4,627	21,362	21,146	5,980	344	99	4,664
Santa Rosa	20,895	20,804	3,703	241	26	2,477	21,808	21,747	3,749	242	31	2,551
Sarasota	35,809	35,767	15,500	162	27	5,591	37,131	37,086	15,965	159	28	5,641
Seminole	26,650	26,623	4,427	183	37	2,470	28,647	28,619	4,545	176	37	2,526
Sumter	16,029	15,753	3,628	441	26	4,240	16,549	16,279	3,724	424	21	4,287
Suwannee	18,219	16,764	3,082	504	25	4,088	18,972	17,481	3,182	505	28	4,185
Taylor	17,097	16,999	2,658	607	61	3,580	17,669	17,560	2,774	648	54	3,699
Union	11,839	11,617	1,655	310	13	1,893	12,194	11,974	1,729	324	11	1,988
Volusia	21,216	21,080	6,222	282	37	4,322	21,920	21,783	6,431	283	34	4,403
Wakulla	22,178	22,053	2,950	361	21	2,809	24,169	24,039	3,073	382	22	2,892
Walton	16,040	15,856	3,496	392	31	3,160	16,664	16,503	3,586	384	40	3,272
Washington	15,515	15,387	2,420	552	50	3,864	16,381	16,287	2,546	556	49	4,026

1/ Includes supplemental security income payments, payments to families with dependent children (AFDC), general assistance payments, food stamp payments, and other assistance payments, including emergency assistance.

2/ Includes the capital consumption adjustment for rental income of persons.

Note: These data were derived by dividing each type of income by the total population of the area, not just the segment of the population receiving that particular type of income. All per capita figures are prepared by the Bureau of Economic Analysis using Bureau of the Census population data.

Source: U.S., Department of Commerce, Bureau of Economic Analysis, Regional Economic Information System, CD-ROM, June 2000.

Table 5.13. DERIVATION OF PERSONAL INCOME: DERIVATION ON A PLACE-OF-RESIDENCE BASIS IN THE STATE AND METROPOLITAN AREAS OF FLORIDA, 1998

(in millions of dollars)

Metropolitan Statistical Area (MSA) 1/	Total earn- ings by place of work	Less per- sonal contribu- tions for social insurance	Plus resi- dence ad- just- ment	Plus divi- dends inter- est and rent	Plus trans- fer pay- ments	Person- al in- come by place of res- idence
Florida	248,372	15,506	897	103,922	62,523	400,209
Daytona Beach	4,584	314	713	3,034	2,211	10,229
Flagler County	331	25	147	329	226	1,007
Volusia County	4,253	289	567	2,705	1,986	9,221
Ft. Lauderdale	24,225	1,544	2,998	11,427	5,935	43,041
Ft. Myers-Cape Coral	5,463	354	-96	3,928	1,919	10,860
Ft. Pierce-Port St. Lucie	3,384	227	374	3,407	1,547	8,485
Martin County	1,747	121	61	2,335	631	4,653
St. Lucie County	1,637	106	313	1,073	916	3,831
Ft. Walton Beach	3,059	155	-273	525	2,631	4,155
Gainesville	3,701	168	-286	949	693	4,887
Jacksonville	21,399	1,297	-73	5,030	3,376	28,435
Clay County	1,076	68	1,368	515	344	3,236
Duval County	18,460	1,113	-3,388	3,173	2,438	19,569
Nassau County	8,503	590	632	7,142	2,871	1,450
St. Johns County	1,280	83	1,511	1,048	424	4,180
Lakeland-Winter Haven	6,398	411	308	2,076	1,862	10,234
Melbourne-Titusville-Palm Bay	6,790	434	43	2,707	1,937	11,043
Miami	39,463	2,399	-4,092	9,488	8,987	51,448
Naples	3,743	251	92	4,087	882	8,553
Ocala	2,644	177	234	1,293	1,201	5,195
Orlando	29,768	1,898	-1,212	6,771	4,978	38,406
Lake County	1,910	136	344	1,348	1,033	4,498
Orange County	21,763	1,373	-5,229	3,394	2,511	21,066
Osceola County	1,419	88	560	436	474	2,801
Seminole County	4,676	301	3,112	1,593	960	10,041
Panama City	2,214	127	-34	651	548	3,252
Pensacola	5,744	321	277	1,648	1,379	8,726
Escambia County	4,809	266	-636	1,207	1,046	6,160
Santa Rosa County	935	55	913	441	332	2,566
Punta Gorda	1,110	83	88	1,295	791	3,201
Sarasota-Bradenton	8,503	590	632	7,142	2,871	18,558
Manatee County	3,812	250	330	2,300	1,103	7,294
Sarasota County	4,691	340	302	4,843	1,768	11,263
Tallahassee	5,286	220	-376	1,032	751	6,472
Gadsden County	433	18	84	100	182	782
Leon County	4,853	203	-461	932	569	5,690
Tampa-St. Petersburg-Clearwater	39,962	2,601	-578	14,408	10,181	61,373
Hernando County	3,059	155	-273	1,000	525	2,733
Hillsborough County	21,492	1,325	-3,635	4,598	3,260	24,389
Pasco County	2,261	170	1,768	1,730	1,789	7,378
Pinellas County	15,359	1,039	917	7,278	4,359	26,874
West Palm Beach-Boca Raton	20,348	1,326	841	16,414	5,083	41,361

1/ Based on 1999 MSA designations.
Note: See Table 5.14 for derivation of personal income notes. See Glossary for MSA definitions and map at the front of the book for area boundaries.
Source: U.S., Department of Commerce, Bureau of Economic Analysis, Regional Economic Information System, CD-ROM, June 2000.

University of Florida   **Bureau of Economic and Business Research**

Table 5.14. DERIVATION OF PERSONAL INCOME: DERIVATION ON A PLACE-OF-RESIDENCE BASIS IN THE UNITED STATES AND IN THE STATE AND COUNTIES OF FLORIDA 1997 AND 1998

(rounded to millions of dollars)

County	Total earn- ings by place of work 1/	Less personal contri- butions for social insurance	Plus resi- dence adjust- ment 2/	Plus dividends interest and rent 3/	Plus transfer payments	Personal income by place of residence
			1997 A/			
United States	4,960,879	297,564	-979	4,662,336	1,317,431	962,347
Florida	229,760	14,520	848	216,088	99,522	60,948
Alachua	3,424	158	-267	2,999	906	662
Baker	154	6	101	249	43	65
Bay	2,108	116	-28	1,965	628	527
Bradford	193	9	81	265	54	84
Brevard	6,456	417	29	6,068	2,586	1,876
Broward	22,489	1,455	2,768	23,802	10,955	5,900
Calhoun	98	5	15	108	25	49
Charlotte	1,033	78	81	1,036	1,241	766
Citrus	812	66	58	804	710	644
Clay	980	63	1,270	2,187	492	324
Collier	3,437	233	95	3,298	3,939	844
Columbia	565	31	51	585	160	206
De Soto	287	12	4	278	99	120
Dixie	80	4	15	91	33	54
Duval	17,108	1,034	-2,936	13,138	3,024	2,406
Escambia	4,602	254	-563	3,786	1,154	1,012
Flagler	310	24	125	412	315	213
Franklin	80	5	18	94	40	50
Gadsden	404	17	79	466	95	177
Gilchrist	84	4	46	127	28	45
Glades	43	2	33	74	36	27
Gulf	131	8	-1	122	42	62
Hamilton	147	7	-38	102	24	45
Hardee	239	11	24	252	60	87
Hendry	413	18	17	412	83	103
Hernando	799	64	338	1,072	765	758
Highlands	666	48	-9	609	515	469
Hillsborough	19,444	1,210	-2,786	15,448	4,382	3,162
Holmes	108	5	44	147	40	85
Indian River	1,316	93	-23	1,199	1,680	563
Jackson	405	18	41	427	121	199
Jefferson	86	4	66	148	42	49

See footnotes at end of table.   Continued . . .

University of Florida   **Bureau of Economic and Business Research**

Table 5.14. DERIVATION OF PERSONAL INCOME: DERIVATION ON A PLACE-OF-RESIDENCE
BASIS IN THE UNITED STATES AND IN THE STATE AND COUNTIES OF FLORIDA
1997 AND 1998 (Continued)

(rounded to millions of dollars)

County	Total earnings by place of work 1/	Less personal contributions for social insurance	Plus residence adjustment 2/	Plus dividends interest and rent 3/	Plus transfer payments	Personal income by place of residence
			1997 A/ (Continued)			
Lafayette	59	2	10	67	12	19
Lake	1,746	126	320	1,940	1,288	993
Lee	5,042	332	-98	4,612	3,768	1,865
Leon	4,509	188	-422	3,900	891	542
Levy	225	13	73	286	108	138
Liberty	53	3	14	64	12	24
Madison	147	8	20	159	41	75
Manatee	3,521	235	333	3,618	2,207	1,076
Marion	2,438	166	195	2,467	1,232	1,153
Martin	1,573	111	89	1,551	2,249	608
Miami-Dade	37,042	2,283	-3,856	30,903	9,058	8,721
Monroe	1,220	72	78	1,227	994	263
Nassau	556	31	381	905	281	162
Okaloosa	2,893	146	-272	2,475	955	504
Okeechobee	306	17	29	318	102	149
Orange	19,547	1,244	-4,574	13,728	3,224	2,445
Osceola	1,309	83	495	1,721	413	458
Palm Beach	18,450	1,220	858	18,088	15,801	4,948
Pasco	2,136	165	1,463	3,434	1,648	1,764
Pinellas	14,240	980	540	13,800	6,966	4,343
Polk	5,925	387	132	5,670	1,977	1,813
Putnam	545	34	124	635	215	318
St. Johns	1,141	75	1,221	2,287	1,006	410
St. Lucie	1,563	104	248	1,707	1,026	897
Santa Rosa	857	50	837	1,644	421	312
Sarasota	4,373	323	312	4,363	4,654	1,735
Seminole	4,288	279	2,703	6,711	1,521	924
Sumter	267	15	59	311	147	191
Suwannee	304	17	48	335	98	147
Taylor	214	13	-11	190	50	79
Union	129	4	-26	99	21	28
Volusia	4,066	281	521	4,306	2,587	1,930
Wakulla	124	7	179	295	54	59
Walton	286	17	59	328	128	131
Washington	169	8	14	175	49	90

See footnotes at end of table.   Continued . . .

University of Florida   **Bureau of Economic and Business Research**

Table 5.14. DERIVATION OF PERSONAL INCOME: DERIVATION ON A PLACE-OF-RESIDENCE BASIS IN THE UNITED STATES AND IN THE STATE AND COUNTIES OF FLORIDA 1997 AND 1998 (Continued)

(rounded to millions of dollars)

County	Total earn- ings by place of work 1/	Less personal contri- butions for social insurance	Plus resi- dence adjust- ment 2/	Plus dividends interest and rent 3/	Plus transfer payments	Personal income by place of residence
			1998			
United States	5,302,066	315,446	-1,019	4,985,601	1,382,416	983,530
Florida	248,372	15,506	897	233,763	103,922	62,523
Alachua	3,701	168	-286	3,246	949	693
Baker	166	6	107	268	46	70
Bay	2,214	127	-34	2,053	651	548
Bradford	203	10	82	276	57	87
Brevard	6,790	434	43	6,399	2,707	1,937
Broward	24,225	1,544	2,998	25,679	11,427	5,935
Calhoun	103	6	15	112	27	52
Charlotte	1,110	83	88	1,115	1,295	791
Citrus	853	67	66	852	745	663
Clay	1,076	68	1,368	2,376	515	344
Collier	3,743	251	92	3,584	4,087	882
Columbia	598	32	53	620	169	217
De Soto	314	13	5	306	104	124
Dixie	86	5	15	97	35	58
Duval	18,460	1,113	-3,388	13,958	3,173	2,438
Escambia	4,809	266	-636	3,907	1,207	1,046
Flagler	331	25	147	453	329	226
Franklin	86	5	19	100	42	50
Gadsden	433	18	84	500	100	182
Gilchrist	88	4	51	136	30	48
Glades	49	2	35	82	37	28
Gulf	121	7	4	118	44	64
Hamilton	150	8	-39	104	26	48
Hardee	258	12	26	272	63	88
Hendry	460	18	18	460	88	104
Hernando	851	67	373	1,156	802	774
Highlands	699	49	-8	642	539	480
Hillsborough	21,492	1,325	-3,635	16,532	4,598	3,260
Holmes	113	6	45	153	43	87
Indian River	1,420	98	-27	1,294	1,745	578
Jackson	413	19	45	439	127	210
Jefferson	88	4	76	159	44	50
Lafayette	63	2	12	73	13	20
Lake	1,910	136	344	2,118	1,348	1,033
Lee	5,463	354	-96	5,013	3,928	1,919
Leon	4,853	203	-461	4,189	932	569
Levy	235	13	80	302	113	145

See footnotes at end of table.   Continued . . .

University of Florida   **Bureau of Economic and Business Research**

Table 5.14. DERIVATION OF PERSONAL INCOME: DERIVATION ON A PLACE-OF-RESIDENCE
BASIS IN THE UNITED STATES AND IN THE STATE AND COUNTIES OF FLORIDA
1997 AND 1998 (Continued)

(rounded to millions of dollars)

County	Total earnings by place of work 1/	Less personal contributions for social insurance	Plus residence adjustment 2/	Plus dividends interest and rent 3/	Plus transfer payments	Personal income by place of residence
			1998 (Continued)			
Liberty	54	2	17	69	12	21
Madison	148	8	22	162	43	78
Manatee	3,812	250	330	3,892	2,300	1,103
Marion	2,644	177	234	2,701	1,293	1,201
Martin	1,747	121	61	1,688	2,335	631
Miami-Dade	39,463	2,399	-4,092	32,972	9,488	8,987
Monroe	1,320	77	83	1,326	1,035	267
Nassau	583	32	436	987	294	169
Okaloosa	3,059	155	-273	2,631	1,000	525
Okeechobee	323	17	31	338	107	153
Orange	21,763	1,373	-5,229	15,161	3,394	2,511
Osceola	1,419	88	560	1,891	436	474
Palm Beach	20,348	1,326	841	19,863	16,414	5,083
Pasco	2,261	170	1,768	3,859	1,730	1,789
Pinellas	15,359	1,039	917	15,237	7,278	4,359
Polk	6,398	411	308	6,296	2,076	1,862
Putnam	572	35	134	671	227	325
St. Johns	1,280	83	1,511	2,708	1,048	424
St. Lucie	1,637	106	313	1,843	1,073	916
Santa Rosa	935	55	913	1,793	441	332
Sarasota	4,691	340	302	4,653	4,843	1,768
Seminole	4,676	301	3,112	7,487	1,593	960
Sumter	286	15	66	336	155	196
Suwannee	329	18	49	360	103	153
Taylor	223	13	-11	198	52	83
Union	128	3	-22	102	22	29
Volusia	4,253	289	567	4,530	2,705	1,986
Wakulla	148	8	192	331	57	61
Walton	306	18	63	351	134	138
Washington	182	9	13	186	52	94

A/ Revised.
1/ Consists of wage and salary disbursements, other labor income, and proprietors' income.
2/ An estimate of the net gain or loss to an area because of commuting from place of residence to place of work. Some persons earn income in the area in which they live; others earn income outside that area. United States includes adjustments for border workers, U.S. residents commuting outside U.S. borders less income of foreign residents commuting inside U.S. borders, plus certain Caribbean seasonal workers.
3/ Includes the capital consumption adjustment for rental income of persons.

Source: U.S., Department of Commerce, Bureau of Economic Analysis, Regional Economic Information System, CD-ROM, June 2000.

University of Florida   **Bureau of Economic and Business Research**

Table 5.20. EARNED INCOME: TOTAL EARNINGS ON A PLACE-OF-WORK BASIS AND PERCENTAGE DISTRIBUTION BY TYPE AND MAJOR INDUSTRIAL SOURCE IN FLORIDA, OTHER SUNBELT STATES, OTHER POPULOUS STATES AND THE UNITED STATES, 1998

Item	Florida	Other sunbelt states											
		Ala-bama	Ari-zona	Ar-kansas	Cali-fornia	Georgia	Loui-siana	Mis-sis-sippi	New Mexico	North Caro-lina	Okla-homa	South Caro-lina
Earnings by place of work ($1,000,000)	248,372	66,930	79,155	37,067	677,217	151,756	67,725	36,726	25,320	138,538	51,096	60,400
Percentage distribution by type of income												
Wage and salary disbursements	79.7	79.4	80.8	76.4	76.5	79.2	77.9	77.8	77.8	80.4	73.9	80.9
Other labor income	10.5	10.7	9.0	9.8	9.1	10.0	10.8	10.9	11.2	10.0	11.0	10.4
Proprietors' income	9.8	10.0	10.1	13.7	14.5	10.8	11.3	11.2	11.0	9.5	15.1	8.7
Percentage distribution by industrial source of income												
Farm	1.0	1.6	1.0	4.1	1.2	1.2	0.6	2.3	2.4	1.6	1.3	0.5
Agricultural services 1/	1.0	0.6	0.9	0.7	1.0	0.6	0.5	0.7	0.6	0.7	0.5	0.6
Mining	0.2	1.0	0.9	0.5	0.4	0.3	5.1	0.9	3.2	0.2	5.1	0.1
Construction	5.9	6.2	7.4	5.6	5.3	5.7	7.7	6.3	6.5	6.7	4.9	7.1
Manufacturing	8.2	20.5	13.5	21.9	15.2	15.6	13.6	20.7	7.3	22.5	16.0	22.9
Transportation, communications, and public utilities	6.2	6.3	5.7	8.3	6.1	9.5	7.6	6.2	5.8	5.9	8.1	5.2
Wholesale trade	6.5	5.7	6.3	5.1	6.0	8.5	5.5	4.7	4.0	6.0	4.9	5.0
Retail trade	11.0	9.4	10.4	10.9	8.8	8.8	9.0	9.7	10.6	9.2	9.4	10.6
Finance, insurance, and real estate	9.9	5.6	9.5	4.9	8.9	7.8	5.4	4.5	5.2	7.0	5.3	6.2
Services	33.0	23.1	28.6	21.5	31.6	26.0	26.3	22.8	27.2	22.6	24.0	22.1
Government	17.0	20.0	15.9	16.5	15.6	16.2	18.7	21.1	27.2	17.7	20.5	19.5

See footnote at end of table.

Continued . . .

Table 5.20. EARNED INCOME: TOTAL EARNINGS ON A PLACE-OF-WORK BASIS AND PERCENTAGE DISTRIBUTION BY TYPE AND MAJOR INDUSTRIAL SOURCE IN FLORIDA, OTHER SUNBELT STATES, OTHER POPULOUS STATES AND THE UNITED STATES, 1998 (Continued)

Item	Other sunbelt states (Continued)			Other populous states								United States
	Tennessee	Texas	Virginia	Illinois	Indiana	Massachusetts	Michigan	New Jersey	New York	Ohio	Pennsylvania	
Earnings by place of work ($1,000,000)	98,605	388,314	138,258	263,398	106,049	154,006	192,096	190,546	432,572	208,360	226,718	5,302,066
Percentage distribution by type of income												
Wage and salary disbursements	77.9	75.5	80.9	79.8	81.5	80.1	81.9	79.8	79.0	81.7	78.3	78.9
Other labor income	9.3	8.8	11.8	9.3	10.1	9.2	10.5	8.5	8.1	10.0	9.6	9.6
Proprietors' income	12.8	15.7	7.4	10.9	8.4	10.6	7.6	11.8	12.9	8.4	12.1	11.4
Percentage distribution by industrial source of income												
Farm	0.1	0.6	0.3	0.4	0.5	0.1	0.2	0.1	0.1	0.5	0.3	0.8
Agricultural services 1/	0.5	0.6	0.5	0.5	0.4	0.5	0.5	0.4	0.4	0.5	0.5	0.6
Mining	0.3	4.9	0.5	0.3	0.4	0.1	0.3	0.1	0.1	0.4	0.7	0.9
Construction	6.3	6.3	5.7	5.3	6.6	4.8	5.4	4.4	3.6	5.6	5.5	5.7
Manufacturing	20.4	14.1	11.9	18.6	30.1	16.0	31.2	15.2	11.6	25.5	20.6	16.8
Transportation, communications, and public utilities	7.4	8.9	6.8	7.5	6.1	4.9	5.0	8.6	6.0	5.7	6.8	6.7
Wholesale trade	6.4	7.0	5.1	7.1	5.7	6.7	6.2	8.8	5.6	6.5	5.6	6.2
Retail trade	10.4	8.9	8.1	7.7	9.1	8.3	8.1	7.5	6.4	9.2	8.7	8.8
Finance, insurance, and real estate	6.8	7.4	7.2	10.3	6.2	10.6	5.7	9.5	20.7	6.8	8.0	9.0
Services	27.7	26.5	29.6	29.3	21.8	35.6	24.2	31.3	31.0	24.8	29.9	28.4
Government	13.5	14.8	24.3	13.2	13.1	12.3	13.2	14.1	14.5	14.6	13.3	16.0

1/ Includes forestry, fisheries, and other.

Source: U.S., Department of Commerce, Bureau of Economic Analysis, Regional Economic Information System, CD-ROM, June 2000.

University of Florida   **Bureau of Economic and Business Research**

Table 5.21. PERSONAL INCOME: AMOUNTS BY MAJOR SOURCE IN THE METROPOLITAN AND NONMETROPOLITAN AREAS OF FLORIDA, THE SOUTHEAST, AND THE UNITED STATES, 1997 AND 1998

(rounded to millions of dollars)

Item	Florida			Southeast			United States		
	Total	Metro-politan areas	Non-metro-politan areas	Total	Metro-politan areas	Non-metro-politan areas	Total	Metro-politan areas	Non-metro-politan areas
	Income by place of residence, 1997 A/								
Total personal income	376,559	355,393	21,166	1,533,940	1,184,271	349,669	6,942,114	5,888,223	1,053,891
Derivation of personal income									
Total earnings by place of work	229,760	219,808	9,953	1,056,680	846,507	210,173	4,960,879	4,327,136	633,743
Less: Personal contributions for social insurance	14,520	13,933	586	64,662	51,728	12,934	297,564	259,768	37,796
Plus: Adjustment for resi-dence	848	-367	1,215	8,202	-7,362	15,564	-979	-47,845	46,866
Equals: Net earnings by place of residence	216,088	205,507	10,581	1,000,220	787,417	212,803	4,662,336	4,019,523	642,813
Plus: Dividends, interest, and rent	99,522	93,655	5,868	299,131	238,095	61,036	1,317,431	1,112,059	205,372
Plus: Transfer payments	60,948	56,231	4,717	234,589	158,759	75,830	962,347	756,641	205,706
	Earnings by place of work, 1997 A/								
Components of earnings									
Wages and salaries	181,755	174,496	7,259	832,702	673,260	159,442	3,885,737	3,410,708	475,029
Other labor income	25,244	24,094	1,151	114,681	92,271	22,411	496,450	430,593	65,857
Proprietors' income 1/	22,761	21,218	1,543	109,297	80,976	28,321	578,692	485,836	92,856
Farm	1,274	849	425	10,263	3,190	7,073	29,570	10,255	19,315
Nonfarm	21,487	20,369	1,118	99,034	77,787	21,247	549,122	475,581	73,541

Continued ....

See footnotes at end of table.

University of Florida   **Bureau of Economic and Business Research**

Table 5.21. PERSONAL INCOME: AMOUNTS BY MAJOR SOURCE IN THE METROPOLITAN AND NONMETROPOLITAN AREAS OF FLORIDA, THE SOUTHEAST, AND THE UNITED STATES, 1997 AND 1998 (Continued)

(rounded to millions of dollars)

Earnings by place of work, 1997 A/ (Continued)

Item	Florida Total	Florida Metropolitan areas	Florida Non-metropolitan areas	Southeast Total	Southeast Metropolitan areas	Southeast Non-metropolitan areas	United States Total	United States Metropolitan areas	United States Non-metropolitan areas
Earnings by industry									
Farm	2,169	1,569	600	13,145	4,519	8,626	45,698	19,204	26,494
Nonfarm	227,591	218,238	9,353	1,043,535	841,988	201,547	4,915,181	4,307,933	607,248
Private	187,295	180,481	6,814	846,154	686,197	159,957	4,094,756	3,617,045	477,711
Agricultural services 2/	2,304	1,861	(D)	6,892	4,426	(D)	31,401	25,094	6,307
Mining	357	302	(D)	9,228	4,773	3,858	45,988	31,601	14,387
Construction	13,508	12,864	627	64,290	51,869	11,922	276,965	237,725	39,240
Manufacturing	19,432	18,466	965	173,546	117,772	55,766	847,972	705,864	142,108
Durable goods	12,243	11,799	(D)	91,529	60,540	(D)	523,667	440,254	83,413
Nondurable goods	7,189	6,667	(D)	82,017	51,791	(D)	324,305	265,610	58,695
Transportation 3/	14,552	14,009	(D)	73,821	61,579	10,905	336,749	297,009	39,740
Wholesale trade	14,862	14,534	290	63,880	56,080	7,537	304,106	279,400	24,706
Retail trade	25,718	24,507	1,211	103,332	81,668	20,795	438,125	373,679	64,446
Finance, insurance, and real estate	21,856	21,406	449	72,900	65,811	6,955	430,953	407,308	23,645
Services	74,707	72,431	2,221	278,266	239,037	36,490	1,382,497	1,259,365	123,132
Government 4/	40,296	37,758	2,538	197,381	155,791	41,590	820,425	690,888	129,537
Federal, civilian	6,929	6,630	299	41,600	36,045	5,555	169,753	150,940	18,813
Federal, military	4,566	4,467	99	28,056	24,027	4,029	70,622	60,911	9,711
State and local	28,801	26,661	2,140	127,725	95,720	32,005	580,050	479,038	101,012

See footnotes at end of table.

Continued . . . .

Table 5.21. PERSONAL INCOME: AMOUNTS BY MAJOR SOURCE IN THE METROPOLITAN AND NONMETROPOLITAN AREAS OF FLORIDA, THE SOUTHEAST, AND THE UNITED STATES, 1997 AND 1998 (Continued)

(rounded to millions of dollars)

Item	Florida Total	Florida Metro-politan areas	Florida Non-metro-politan areas	Southeast Total	Southeast Metro-politan areas	Southeast Non-metro-politan areas	United States Total	United States Metro-politan areas	United States Non-metro-politan areas
				Income by place of residence, 1998					
Total personal income	400,209	377,913	22,295	1,621,530	1,257,117	364,413	7,351,547	6,251,031	1,100,516
Derivation of personal income									
Total earnings by place of work	248,372	237,787	10,585	1,128,310	909,260	219,050	5,302,066	4,639,410	662,656
Less: Personal contributions for social insurance	15,506	14,896	610	68,486	55,108	13,377	315,446	276,148	39,298
Plus: Adjustment for residence	897	-421	1,318	8,282	-8,667	16,949	-1,019	-52,019	51,000
Equals: Net earnings by place of residence	233,763	222,470	11,294	1,068,106	845,485	222,621	4,985,601	4,311,243	674,358
Plus: Dividends, interest, and rent	103,922	97,788	6,134	312,943	248,942	64,001	1,382,416	1,166,771	215,645
Plus: Transfer payments	62,523	57,656	4,867	240,481	162,690	77,791	983,530	773,017	210,513
				Earnings by place of work, 1998					
Components of earnings									
Wages and salaries	197,864	190,140	7,724	896,249	728,475	167,774	4,184,088	3,682,912	501,176
Other labor income	26,142	24,962	1,180	118,304	95,418	22,885	511,221	443,940	67,281
Proprietors' income 1/	24,366	22,685	1,681	113,757	85,367	28,391	606,757	512,558	94,199
Farm	1,565	1,071	494	8,967	3,129	5,838	25,724	9,560	16,164
Nonfarm	22,801	21,613	1,187	104,790	82,238	22,552	581,033	502,998	78,035

See footnotes at end of table.

Continued . . .

Table 5.21. PERSONAL INCOME: AMOUNTS BY MAJOR SOURCE IN THE METROPOLITAN AND NONMETROPOLITAN AREAS OF FLORIDA, THE SOUTHEAST, AND THE UNITED STATES, 1997 AND 1998 (Continued)

(rounded to millions of dollars)

Earnings by place of work, 1998 (Continued)

Item	Florida			Southeast			United States		
	Total	Metro-politan areas	Non-metro-politan areas	Total	Metro-politan areas	Non-metro-politan areas	Total	Metro-politan areas	Non-metro-politan areas
Earnings by industry									
Farm	2,493	1,817	675	12,074	4,545	7,528	43,016	19,091	23,925
Nonfarm	245,880	235,970	9,910	1,116,236	904,714	211,521	5,259,050	4,620,319	638,731
Private	203,745	196,519	7,226	910,337	742,308	168,029	4,408,261	3,904,404	503,857
Agricultural services 2/	2,507	(D)	363	7,619	(D)	(D)	34,445	27,614	6,831
Mining	386	(D)	(D)	9,577	4,841	(D)	47,984	33,470	14,514
Construction	14,766	14,073	654	69,761	55,985	12,595	302,174	259,751	42,423
Manufacturing	20,490	19,485	(D)	180,667	122,897	56,703	891,190	743,591	147,599
Durable goods	12,937	12,468	(D)	96,979	64,910	(D)	554,820	467,182	87,638
Nondurable goods	7,553	7,016	(D)	83,688	54,040	(D)	336,370	276,409	59,961
Transportation 3/	15,502	14,945	(D)	79,042	65,715	11,593	357,379	315,542	41,837
Wholesale trade	16,029	15,678	(D)	69,151	60,899	7,841	329,422	303,297	26,125
Retail trade	27,399	26,125	1,273	109,593	87,589	21,846	464,753	397,183	67,570
Finance, insurance, and real estate	24,671	24,196	474	81,618	73,747	7,314	477,189	451,750	25,439
Services	81,994	79,540	2,388	303,310	262,194	39,788	1,503,725	1,372,205	131,520
Government 4/	42,135	39,450	2,684	205,899	162,407	43,492	850,789	715,915	134,874
Federal, civilian	7,160	6,845	315	42,535	36,837	5,698	173,093	153,686	19,407
Federal, military	4,436	4,336	96	27,909	23,828	4,081	70,159	60,441	9,718
State and local	30,539	28,266	2,273	135,455	101,742	33,713	607,537	501,788	105,749

(D) Data withheld to avoid disclosure of information about individual firms.
A/ Revised. B/ This estimate constitutes the major portion of the true estimate.
1/ Includes the inventory valuation and capital consumption adjustments.
2/ Includes forestry, fisheries, and other. "Other" includes wages and salaries of U.S. residents employed by foreign embassies, consulates, and international organizations in the United States.
3/ Includes communications and public utilities.
4/ Includes government enterprises.
Note: See Table 5.14 for derivation of personal income notes.

Source: U.S., Department of Commerce, Bureau of Economic Analysis, Regional Economic Information System, CD-ROM, June 2000.

Table 5.23. PERSONAL INCOME: AMOUNTS BY MAJOR SOURCE IN FLORIDA
FOURTH QUARTER 1998 THROUGH FOURTH QUARTER 1999

(in millions of dollars)

Item	Fourth quarter 1998	1999 First quarter	Second quarter	Third quarter	Fourth quarter
Total personal income 1/	409,456	413,483	420,507	425,494	434,354
Derivation of total personal income					
Total earnings by place of work	255,890	258,343	263,859	266,883	273,465
Less personal contributions for					
social insurance	15,829	16,008	16,338	16,494	16,861
Plus adjustment for residence	915	941	946	966	966
Equals net earnings by place of residence	240,976	243,276	248,467	251,354	257,570
Plus dividends, interest, and rent 2/	105,436	105,921	107,311	108,859	110,825
Plus transfer payments	63,044	64,287	64,729	65,280	65,959
State unemployment benefits	684	708	700	659	671
Other transfer payments	62,360	63,578	64,030	64,621	65,288
Components of earnings 1/					
Wages and salaries	203,810	205,179	210,151	213,056	218,624
Other labor income	26,535	26,475	26,989	27,206	27,711
Proprietors' income 3/	25,546	26,689	26,719	26,622	27,130
Farm	2,188	2,911	2,297	1,677	1,630
Nonfarm	23,357	23,778	24,422	24,945	25,500
Earnings by industry 1/					
Farm	3,125	3,862	3,266	2,668	2,639
Nonfarm	252,765	254,481	260,592	264,216	270,826
Private	210,015	212,354	217,486	220,564	226,724
Agricultural services, forestry,					
and fisheries, and other 4/	2,629	2,657	2,654	2,723	2,853
Mining	385	339	350	353	346
Construction	15,160	15,200	15,626	15,702	15,978
Manufacturing	20,599	20,315	20,669	20,497	20,932
Nondurable goods	7,659	7,608	7,783	7,653	7,636
Durable goods	12,941	12,707	12,886	12,844	13,296
Transportation, communications, and					
public utilities	16,067	16,243	16,220	16,536	16,890
Wholesale trade	16,599	17,058	17,430	17,631	18,159
Retail trade	28,038	28,337	29,015	29,076	29,443
Finance, insurance, and real estate	25,273	25,581	26,221	26,949	27,574
Services	85,265	86,624	89,302	91,097	94,549
Government and government enterprises	42,750	42,127	43,106	43,651	44,101
Federal, civilian	7,282	7,666	7,555	7,534	7,517
Federal, military	4,292	4,307	4,168	4,087	4,062
State and local	31,176	30,154	31,383	32,029	32,522

1/ Income by place of residence; earnings by place of work.
2/ Includes capital consumption adjustment for rental income of persons.
3/ Includes the inventory valuation and capital consumption adjustments.
4/ Includes wages and salaries of U.S. residents employed by foreign embassies, consulates, and international organizations in the United States.
Note: Seasonally adjusted at annual rates. Data reported in April 2000. See Table 5.14 for derivation of personal income notes.

Source: U.S., Department of Commerce, Bureau of Economic Analysis, Regional Economic Information System, CD-ROM, June 2000.

University of Florida   **Bureau of Economic and Business Research**

Table 5.26. EARNED INCOME: TOTAL EARNINGS ON A PLACE-OF-WORK BASIS BY MAJOR TYPE OF INCOME IN THE UNITED STATES AND IN THE STATE AND COUNTIES OF FLORIDA, 1997 AND 1998

(in thousands of dollars)

County	Total earnings	Wage and salary dis- bursements	Other labor income	Proprietors' income Total 1/	Farm	Nonfarm
			1997 A/			
United States 2/	4,960,879	3,885,737	496,450	578,692	29,570	549,122
Florida	229,760,229	181,755,239	25,244,457	22,760,533	1,273,778	21,486,755
Alachua	3,424,009	2,736,811	488,521	198,677	13,018	185,659
Baker	153,770	108,534	22,700	22,536	5,893	16,643
Bay	2,108,454	1,585,992	307,215	215,247	1,186	214,061
Bradford	193,241	148,116	26,404	18,721	4,714	14,007
Brevard	6,455,988	5,306,164	769,330	380,494	6,030	374,464
Broward	22,489,099	18,431,934	2,320,590	1,736,575	10,580	1,725,995
Calhoun	97,961	70,617	12,202	15,142	3,008	12,134
Charlotte	1,033,199	783,154	107,977	142,068	6,059	136,009
Citrus	811,672	624,224	87,326	100,122	1,475	98,647
Clay	979,656	748,605	102,115	128,936	5,004	123,932
Collier	3,436,545	2,453,967	295,953	686,625	72,462	614,163
Columbia	564,713	445,077	77,453	42,183	4,322	37,861
De Soto	286,584	190,418	31,401	64,765	40,803	23,962
Dixie	80,036	54,869	10,479	14,688	1,550	13,138
Duval	17,107,616	13,696,085	2,183,549	1,227,982	5,244	1,222,738
Escambia	4,602,218	3,602,880	729,313	270,025	5,241	264,784
Flagler	310,137	253,299	36,560	20,278	7,532	12,746
Franklin	80,395	51,708	8,243	20,444	0	20,444
Gadsden	403,611	295,670	55,273	52,668	23,987	28,681
Gilchrist	84,332	50,093	9,905	24,334	11,595	12,739
Glades	43,177	26,787	4,259	12,131	4,678	7,453
Gulf	130,783	102,086	16,506	12,191	0	12,191
Hamilton	147,178	114,081	21,284	11,813	4,740	7,073
Hardee	238,830	156,243	23,735	58,852	39,823	19,029
Hendry	412,661	283,334	40,283	89,044	60,484	28,560
Hernando	799,001	615,279	90,329	93,393	6,916	86,477
Highlands	666,065	476,170	67,972	121,923	40,106	81,817
Hillsborough	19,443,782	15,884,572	2,104,289	1,454,921	103,254	1,351,667
Holmes	108,482	66,198	12,941	29,343	13,745	15,598
Indian River	1,315,512	1,003,740	127,374	184,398	9,503	174,895
Jackson	404,629	297,663	59,223	47,743	13,364	34,379
Jefferson	85,654	57,293	10,171	18,190	6,471	11,719

See footnotes at end of table.   Continued . . .

University of Florida   **Bureau of Economic and Business Research**

Table 5.26. EARNED INCOME: TOTAL EARNINGS ON A PLACE-OF-WORK BASIS BY MAJOR
TYPE OF INCOME IN THE UNITED STATES AND IN THE STATE AND COUNTIES
OF FLORIDA, 1997 AND 1998 (Continued)

(in thousands of dollars)

County	Total earnings	Wage and salary dis- bursements	Other labor income	Proprietors' income Total 1/	Farm	Nonfarm
			1997 A/ (Continued)			
Lafayette	58,946	29,512	5,914	23,520	16,801	6,719
Lake	1,746,438	1,312,289	181,708	252,441	31,774	220,667
Lee	5,042,100	3,822,717	522,602	696,781	24,516	672,265
Leon	4,509,439	3,629,720	623,362	256,357	777	255,580
Levy	225,159	148,472	23,737	52,950	23,472	29,478
Liberty	52,770	39,595	7,983	5,192	366	4,826
Madison	146,511	105,195	17,933	23,383	11,553	11,830
Manatee	3,520,833	2,661,509	326,565	532,759	76,625	456,134
Marion	2,437,930	1,838,535	268,151	331,244	44,770	286,474
Martin	1,572,602	1,220,962	151,627	200,013	22,451	177,562
Miami-Dade	37,042,490	29,631,902	3,943,313	3,467,275	68,105	3,399,170
Monroe	1,220,490	907,308	142,066	171,116	0	171,116
Nassau	555,617	417,466	66,800	71,351	8,335	63,016
Okaloosa	2,893,212	2,149,961	523,563	219,688	2,171	217,517
Okeechobee	305,520	210,643	30,364	64,513	29,593	34,920
Orange	19,546,748	15,934,310	2,010,583	1,601,855	26,204	1,575,651
Osceola	1,309,034	1,041,748	140,383	126,903	16,214	110,689
Palm Beach	18,449,615	13,863,459	1,723,297	2,862,859	102,360	2,760,499
Pasco	2,135,631	1,665,712	237,859	232,060	16,420	215,640
Pinellas	14,239,926	11,565,612	1,451,945	1,222,369	1,432	1,220,937
Polk	5,924,823	4,544,810	621,891	758,122	69,440	688,682
Putnam	544,821	440,536	69,076	35,209	10,341	24,868
St. Johns	1,141,461	879,832	121,089	140,540	7,425	133,115
St. Lucie	1,562,731	1,222,876	176,153	163,702	15,639	148,063
Santa Rosa	857,029	602,206	115,302	139,521	9,393	130,128
Sarasota	4,373,462	3,405,092	415,595	552,775	7,335	545,440
Seminole	4,287,555	3,455,791	435,033	396,731	4,196	392,535
Sumter	267,403	188,691	38,752	39,960	8,622	31,338
Suwannee	303,644	179,304	27,645	96,695	42,432	54,263
Taylor	214,305	170,423	25,800	18,082	1,809	16,273
Union	128,986	98,347	20,974	9,665	2,416	7,249
Volusia	4,065,603	3,235,178	446,070	384,355	26,946	357,409
Wakulla	123,760	81,316	14,803	27,641	2,301	25,340
Walton	285,691	205,150	32,379	48,162	6,543	41,619
Washington	168,954	127,397	23,265	18,292	2,214	16,078

See footnotes at end of table.   Continued . . .

University of Florida   **Bureau of Economic and Business Research**

Table 5.26. EARNED INCOME: TOTAL EARNINGS ON A PLACE-OF-WORK BASIS BY MAJOR TYPE OF INCOME IN THE UNITED STATES AND IN THE STATE AND COUNTIES OF FLORIDA, 1997 AND 1998 (Continued)

(in thousands of dollars)

County	Total earnings	Wage and salary dis- bursements	Other labor income	Proprietors' income Total 1/	Farm	Nonfarm
			1998			
United States 2/	5,302,066	4,184,088	511,221	606,757	25,724	581,033
Florida	248,372,175	197,864,425	26,142,173	24,365,577	1,564,987	22,800,590
Alachua	3,700,716	2,979,274	513,977	207,465	13,342	194,123
Baker	166,373	118,176	23,901	24,296	6,530	17,766
Bay	2,213,735	1,687,897	297,574	228,264	1,182	227,082
Bradford	202,736	155,754	26,930	20,052	5,122	14,930
Brevard	6,790,272	5,606,900	778,421	404,951	7,499	397,452
Broward	24,224,915	19,982,165	2,396,814	1,845,936	12,166	1,833,770
Calhoun	102,982	75,976	12,496	14,510	1,513	12,997
Charlotte	1,109,569	846,573	111,127	151,869	7,931	143,938
Citrus	852,691	657,846	88,643	106,202	1,313	104,889
Clay	1,075,667	830,532	107,605	137,530	6,667	130,863
Collier	3,742,666	2,684,908	306,416	751,342	93,145	658,197
Columbia	598,002	474,647	80,076	43,279	3,270	40,009
De Soto	313,911	203,978	31,880	78,053	52,483	25,570
Dixie	86,146	59,430	10,912	15,804	1,677	14,127
Duval	18,459,653	14,929,602	2,231,899	1,298,152	5,246	1,292,906
Escambia	4,808,873	3,799,555	724,439	284,879	2,690	282,189
Flagler	330,985	272,289	37,678	21,018	7,439	13,579
Franklin	86,105	55,791	8,522	21,792	0	21,792
Gadsden	433,351	320,694	57,580	55,077	24,546	30,531
Gilchrist	88,405	51,761	10,058	26,586	12,922	13,664
Glades	48,508	28,938	4,414	15,156	7,387	7,769
Gulf	121,387	93,460	15,209	12,718	0	12,718
Hamilton	150,094	118,402	21,551	10,141	2,722	7,419
Hardee	258,075	164,683	23,875	69,517	49,339	20,178
Hendry	459,918	302,487	41,138	116,293	85,968	30,325
Hernando	850,691	658,152	93,021	99,518	7,452	92,066
Highlands	698,749	491,583	67,675	139,491	53,275	86,216
Hillsborough	21,492,269	17,722,530	2,225,741	1,543,998	121,922	1,422,076
Holmes	113,458	69,829	13,171	30,458	13,860	16,598
Indian River	1,419,559	1,086,093	131,361	202,105	15,580	186,525
Jackson	413,017	309,890	60,094	43,033	6,665	36,368
Jefferson	88,059	5ᶜ,690	10,276	18,093	5,647	12,446
Lafayette	63,297	31,684	6,030	25,583	18,420	7,163
Lake	1,909,905	1,449,383	191,206	269,316	35,133	234,183

See footnotes at end of table.   Continued . . .

University of Florida   **Bureau of Economic and Business Research**

Table 5.26. EARNED INCOME: TOTAL EARNINGS ON A PLACE-OF-WORK BASIS BY MAJOR
TYPE OF INCOME IN THE UNITED STATES AND IN THE STATE AND COUNTIES
OF FLORIDA, 1997 AND 1998 (Continued)

(in thousands of dollars)

County	Total earnings	Wage and salary dis- bursements	Other labor income	Proprietors' income Total 1/	Farm	Nonfarm
			1998 (Continued)			
Lee	5,463,090	4,174,797	544,117	744,176	26,724	717,452
Leon	4,852,635	3,935,790	646,165	270,680	599	270,081
Levy	235,293	154,121	23,922	57,250	26,000	31,250
Liberty	53,696	40,221	7,983	5,492	394	5,098
Madison	148,465	108,539	18,261	21,665	8,927	12,738
Manatee	3,811,944	2,897,347	338,603	575,994	91,887	484,107
Marion	2,644,353	2,007,423	280,654	356,276	52,770	303,506
Martin	1,747,432	1,366,170	160,336	220,926	32,633	188,293
Miami-Dade	39,462,970	31,714,170	4,067,415	3,681,385	84,089	3,597,296
Monroe	1,320,150	990,178	148,275	181,697	0	181,697
Nassau	583,151	439,440	68,092	75,619	8,948	66,671
Okaloosa	3,059,090	2,292,709	533,183	233,198	842	232,356
Okeechobee	323,208	219,102	30,557	73,549	36,556	36,993
Orange	21,762,715	17,939,497	2,141,034	1,682,184	30,330	1,651,854
Osceola	1,418,717	1,132,867	146,105	139,745	21,197	118,548
Palm Beach	20,348,336	15,389,032	1,816,839	3,142,465	187,186	2,955,279
Pasco	2,260,764	1,771,745	241,693	247,326	19,193	228,133
Pinellas	15,358,612	12,554,345	1,498,643	1,305,624	1,293	1,304,331
Polk	6,398,494	4,939,181	647,004	812,309	86,278	726,031
Putnam	571,887	464,215	70,526	37,146	10,906	26,240
St. Johns	1,280,132	1,000,191	131,418	148,523	7,305	141,218
St. Lucie	1,636,603	1,274,931	177,091	184,581	27,789	156,792
Santa Rosa	934,836	669,188	121,476	144,172	6,285	137,887
Sarasota	4,690,950	3,674,532	426,960	589,458	7,965	581,493
Seminole	4,676,201	3,801,967	452,073	422,161	4,349	417,812
Sumter	285,929	203,573	40,438	41,918	8,579	33,339
Suwannee	328,817	197,525	29,297	101,995	44,436	57,559
Taylor	222,731	177,448	26,081	19,202	2,032	17,170
Union	127,869	96,944	20,725	10,200	2,409	7,791
Volusia	4,252,530	3,394,328	449,733	408,469	27,275	381,194
Wakulla	147,556	100,636	17,643	29,277	2,415	26,862
Walton	306,075	222,579	33,703	49,793	5,848	43,945
Washington	182,205	139,142	24,418	18,645	1,495	17,150

A/ Revised.
B/ Less than $50,000, but greater than 0.
1/ Includes the inventory valuation and capital consumption adjustments.
2/ United States numbers are rounded to millions of dollars.

Source: U.S., Department of Commerce, Bureau of Economic Analysis, Regional Economic Information
System, CD-ROM, June 2000.

University of Florida   **Bureau of Economic and Business Research**

Table 5.30. EARNED INCOME: TOTAL, FARM, AND NONFARM EARNINGS ON A PLACE-OF-WORK BASIS IN THE UNITED STATES AND IN THE STATE AND COUNTIES OF FLORIDA, 1997 AND 1998

(in thousands of dollars)

1997 A/

County	Total earnings	Farm income	Nonfarm Total	Nonfarm Private 1/	Government and government enterprises Total	Federal Civilian	Federal Military	State and local
United States 2/	4,960,879	45,698	4,915,181	4,094,756	820,425	169,753	70,622	580,050
Florida	229,760,229	2,169,340	227,590,889	187,295,045	40,295,844	6,928,655	4,565,835	28,801,354
Alachua	3,424,009	18,941	3,405,068	2,102,472	1,302,596	166,155	12,328	1,124,113
Baker	153,770	9,238	144,532	66,612	77,920	2,987	590	74,343
Bay	2,108,454	1,564	2,106,890	1,396,618	710,272	186,799	248,173	275,300
Bradford	193,241	4,765	188,476	109,909	78,567	1,645	695	76,227
Brevard	6,455,988	10,576	6,445,412	5,253,874	1,191,538	363,670	175,496	652,372
Broward	22,489,099	22,341	22,466,758	19,041,030	3,425,728	424,273	54,966	2,946,489
Calhoun	97,961	4,801	93,160	63,568	29,592	1,596	350	27,646
Charlotte	1,033,199	10,527	1,022,672	845,302	177,370	12,706	3,813	160,851
Citrus	811,672	1,558	810,114	686,877	123,237	10,102	3,151	109,984
Clay	979,656	7,521	972,135	802,255	169,880	16,698	3,917	149,265
Collier	3,436,545	123,525	3,313,020	2,976,884	336,136	31,146	5,487	299,503
Columbia	564,713	4,787	559,926	382,572	177,354	53,763	1,506	122,085
De Soto	286,584	55,052	231,532	140,663	90,869	2,525	701	87,643
Dixie	80,036	1,589	78,447	47,650	30,797	967	358	29,472
Duval	17,107,616	12,530	17,095,086	13,484,396	3,610,690	954,611	1,385,872	1,270,207
Escambia	4,602,218	6,162	4,596,056	2,979,357	1,616,699	362,806	743,235	510,658
Flagler	310,137	9,161	300,976	245,506	55,470	5,045	1,273	49,152
Franklin	80,395	0	80,395	60,429	19,966	1,300	287	18,379
Gadsden	403,611	45,277	358,334	191,126	167,208	6,394	1,249	159,565
Gilchrist	84,332	14,800	69,532	37,627	31,905	1,129	377	30,399
Glades	43,177	10,279	32,898	22,584	10,314	595	238	9,481

See footnotes at end of table.

Continued . . .

Table 5.30. EARNED INCOME: TOTAL, FARM, AND NONFARM EARNINGS ON A PLACE-OF-WORK BASIS IN THE UNITED STATES AND IN THE STATE AND COUNTIES OF FLORIDA, 1997 AND 1998 (Continued)

(in thousands of dollars)

County	Total earnings	Farm income	Nonfarm Total	Private 1/	Government and government enterprises Total	Federal Civilian	Military	State and local
				1997 A/ (Continued)				
Gulf	130,783	0	130,783	96,609	34,174	894	382	32,898
Hamilton	147,178	5,354	141,824	97,309	44,515	1,326	353	42,836
Hardee	238,830	52,407	186,423	128,992	57,431	2,531	595	54,305
Hendry	412,661	105,605	307,056	228,649	78,407	6,115	826	71,466
Hernando	799,001	7,430	791,571	622,429	169,142	13,242	3,576	152,324
Highlands	666,065	58,124	607,941	486,907	121,034	14,294	2,122	104,618
Hillsborough	19,443,782	173,198	19,270,584	16,301,667	2,968,917	638,311	349,897	1,980,709
Holmes	108,482	13,807	94,675	54,610	40,065	2,658	520	36,887
Indian River	1,315,512	27,589	1,287,923	1,106,797	181,126	19,239	2,766	159,121
Jackson	404,629	14,686	389,943	204,757	185,186	28,395	1,895	154,896
Jefferson	85,654	8,850	76,804	47,704	29,100	1,398	364	27,338
Lafayette	58,946	18,792	40,154	20,566	19,588	811	177	18,600
Lake	1,746,438	59,479	1,686,959	1,408,841	278,118	25,359	8,907	243,852
Lee	5,042,100	41,467	5,000,633	4,090,233	910,400	101,122	12,753	796,525
Leon	4,509,439	2,504	4,506,935	2,547,550	1,959,385	102,488	15,632	1,841,265
Levy	225,159	30,037	195,122	141,538	53,584	3,327	1,751	48,506
Liberty	52,770	367	52,403	29,019	23,384	2,191	190	21,003
Madison	146,511	12,859	133,652	89,661	43,991	2,276	496	41,219
Manatee	3,520,833	118,653	3,402,180	2,996,645	405,535	61,775	7,575	336,185
Marion	2,437,930	62,381	2,375,549	1,932,785	442,764	31,969	6,858	403,937
Martin	1,572,602	39,300	1,533,302	1,350,850	182,452	15,443	3,401	163,608
Miami-Dade	37,042,490	148,070	36,894,420	30,846,585	6,047,835	1,162,677	153,972	4,731,186
Monroe	1,220,490	0	1,220,490	933,210	287,280	58,725	68,715	159,840

Continued . . .

See footnotes at end of table.

Table 5.30. EARNED INCOME: TOTAL, FARM, AND NONFARM EARNINGS ON A PLACE-OF-WORK BASIS IN THE UNITED STATES AND IN THE STATE AND COUNTIES OF FLORIDA, 1997 AND 1998 (Continued)

(in thousands of dollars)

County	Total earnings	Farm income	Nonfarm Total	Private 1/	Government and government enterprises Total	Federal Civilian	Federal Military	State and local
				1997 A/ (Continued)				
Nassau	555,617	14,715	540,902	400,861	140,041	60,053	1,527	78,461
Okaloosa	2,893,212	2,313	2,890,899	1,555,598	1,335,301	324,125	779,069	232,107
Okeechobee	305,520	55,773	249,747	188,808	60,939	3,659	875	56,405
Orange	19,546,748	97,388	19,449,360	17,162,034	2,287,326	463,294	224,340	1,599,692
Osceola	1,309,034	23,047	1,285,987	1,048,953	237,034	13,765	3,986	219,283
Palm Beach	18,449,615	246,026	18,203,589	15,985,029	2,218,560	349,647	32,276	1,836,637
Pasco	2,135,631	25,824	2,109,807	1,717,518	392,289	33,855	9,023	349,411
Pinellas	14,239,926	4,589	14,235,337	12,536,406	1,698,931	343,203	70,209	1,285,519
Polk	5,924,823	106,807	5,818,016	4,970,594	847,422	75,031	13,304	759,087
Putnam	544,821	15,173	529,648	381,584	148,064	7,526	1,981	138,557
St. Johns	1,141,461	12,550	1,128,911	938,954	189,957	21,840	4,011	164,106
St. Lucie	1,562,731	26,163	1,536,568	1,199,956	336,612	29,048	7,140	300,424
Santa Rosa	857,029	10,265	846,764	589,178	257,586	34,230	91,334	132,022
Sarasota	4,373,462	12,642	4,360,820	3,895,157	465,663	48,427	8,913	408,323
Seminole	4,287,555	9,597	4,277,958	3,759,654	518,304	76,761	9,805	431,738
Sumter	267,403	11,175	256,228	149,771	106,457	43,316	1,112	62,029
Suwannee	303,644	46,325	257,319	204,178	53,141	5,610	901	46,630
Taylor	214,305	1,843	212,462	167,757	44,705	1,677	527	42,501
Union	128,986	2,765	126,221	47,775	78,446	837	349	77,260
Volusia	4,065,603	56,753	4,008,850	3,304,467	704,383	73,911	13,461	617,011
Wakulla	123,760	2,309	121,451	85,248	36,203	3,191	521	32,491
Walton	285,691	6,736	278,955	210,166	68,789	9,989	2,814	55,986
Washington	168,954	2,609	166,345	94,175	72,170	2,182	572	69,416

See footnotes at end of table.

Continued . . . .

Table 5.30. EARNED INCOME: TOTAL, FARM, AND NONFARM EARNINGS ON A PLACE-OF-WORK BASIS IN THE UNITED STATES AND IN THE STATE AND COUNTIES OF FLORIDA, 1997 AND 1998 (Continued)

(in thousands of dollars)

1998

County	Total earnings	Farm income	Nonfarm Total	Nonfarm Private 1/	Government and government enterprises Total	Federal Civilian	Federal Military	State and local
United States 2/	5,302,066	43,016	5,259,050	4,408,261	850,789	173,093	70,159	607,537
Florida	248,372,175	2,492,670	245,879,505	203,744,929	42,134,576	7,159,920	4,435,617	30,539,039
Alachua	3,700,716	19,470	3,681,246	2,275,873	1,405,373	177,258	15,234	1,212,881
Baker	166,373	9,983	156,390	70,923	85,467	3,450	601	81,416
Bay	2,213,735	1,574	2,212,161	1,585,745	626,416	179,965	217,579	228,872
Bradford	202,736	5,175	197,561	116,011	81,550	1,819	706	79,025
Brevard	6,790,272	12,213	6,778,059	5,564,640	1,213,419	368,784	161,473	683,162
Broward	24,224,915	24,364	24,200,551	20,582,321	3,618,230	442,944	56,239	3,119,047
Calhoun	102,982	3,372	99,610	68,791	30,819	1,235	355	29,229
Charlotte	1,109,569	12,573	1,096,996	911,304	185,692	13,563	3,904	168,225
Citrus	852,691	1,398	851,293	719,277	132,016	10,682	3,248	118,086
Clay	1,075,667	9,276	1,066,391	880,527	185,864	17,140	4,049	164,675
Collier	3,742,666	145,812	3,596,854	3,239,584	357,270	34,025	5,725	317,520
Columbia	598,002	3,749	594,253	403,213	191,040	59,311	1,517	130,212
De Soto	313,911	67,261	246,650	152,324	94,326	2,699	706	90,921
Dixie	86,146	1,716	84,430	52,247	32,183	999	369	30,815
Duval	18,459,653	12,804	18,446,849	14,817,030	3,629,819	961,527	1,320,748	1,347,544
Escambia	4,808,873	3,640	4,805,233	3,214,455	1,590,778	360,380	701,014	529,384
Flagler	330,985	9,124	321,861	262,680	59,181	5,246	1,352	52,583
Franklin	86,105	0	86,105	65,155	20,950	1,295	288	19,367
Gadsden	433,351	46,584	386,767	210,332	176,435	6,787	1,254	168,394
Gilchrist	88,405	16,244	72,161	38,686	33,475	1,391	393	31,691
Glades	48,508	13,205	35,303	24,154	11,149	601	242	10,306

See footnotes at end of table.

Continued . . . .

Table 5.30. EARNED INCOME: TOTAL, FARM, AND NONFARM EARNINGS ON A PLACE-OF-WORK BASIS IN THE UNITED STATES AND IN THE STATE AND COUNTIES OF FLORIDA, 1997 AND 1998 (Continued)

(in thousands of dollars)

County	Total earnings	Farm income	Nonfarm Total	Private 1/	Government and government enterprises Total	Federal Civilian	Military	State and local
				1998 (Continued)				
Gulf	121,387	0	121,387	85,715	35,672	948	383	34,341
Hamilton	150,094	3,351	146,743	100,851	45,892	1,420	360	44,112
Hardee	258,075	62,359	195,716	136,858	58,858	2,577	600	55,681
Hendry	459,918	132,823	327,095	242,669	84,426	6,214	836	77,376
Hernando	850,691	7,985	842,706	663,396	179,310	14,399	3,662	161,249
Highlands	698,749	71,967	626,782	500,929	125,853	15,036	2,142	108,675
Hillsborough	21,492,269	194,123	21,298,146	18,148,846	3,149,300	661,621	365,658	2,122,021
Holmes	113,458	13,923	99,535	58,516	41,019	2,889	530	37,600
Indian River	1,419,559	34,367	1,385,192	1,197,256	187,936	20,282	2,824	164,830
Jackson	413,017	8,025	404,992	212,636	192,356	29,093	1,581	161,682
Jefferson	88,059	8,107	79,952	49,819	30,133	1,370	369	28,394
Lafayette	63,297	20,473	42,824	22,570	20,254	699	180	19,375
Lake	1,909,905	63,847	1,846,058	1,550,701	295,357	26,957	7,331	261,069
Lee	5,463,090	44,288	5,418,802	4,439,911	978,891	106,767	13,278	858,846
Leon	4,852,635	2,386	4,850,249	2,793,616	2,056,633	106,153	15,386	1,935,094
Levy	235,293	32,819	202,474	145,228	57,246	3,631	1,767	51,848
Liberty	53,696	395	53,301	28,698	24,603	2,509	192	21,902
Madison	148,465	10,271	138,194	90,585	47,609	2,415	504	44,690
Manatee	3,811,944	135,230	3,676,714	3,248,724	427,990	63,940	7,844	356,206
Marion	2,644,353	71,009	2,573,344	2,099,403	473,941	33,834	7,075	433,032
Martin	1,747,432	50,104	1,697,328	1,507,777	189,551	16,058	3,495	169,998
Miami-Dade	39,462,970	166,897	39,296,073	32,865,922	6,430,151	1,211,833	186,019	5,032,299
Monroe	1,320,150	0	1,320,150	1,010,956	309,194	61,746	65,745	181,703
Nassau	583,151	15,595	567,556	421,639	145,917	61,139	1,578	83,200

See footnotes at end of table.

Continued . . . .

Table 5.30. EARNED INCOME: TOTAL, FARM, AND NONFARM EARNINGS ON A PLACE-OF-WORK BASIS IN THE UNITED STATES AND IN THE STATE AND COUNTIES OF FLORIDA, 1997 AND 1998 (Continued)

(in thousands of dollars)

1998 (Continued)

County	Total earnings	Farm income	Nonfarm Total	Nonfarm Private 1/	Government and government enterprises Total	Federal Civilian	Federal Military	State and local
Okaloosa	3,059,090	988	3,058,102	1,688,668	1,369,434	336,834	782,922	249,678
Okeechobee	323,208	63,730	259,478	194,932	64,546	3,805	888	59,853
Orange	21,762,715	104,239	21,658,476	19,242,358	2,416,118	479,059	186,271	1,750,788
Osceola	1,418,717	28,286	1,390,431	1,130,402	260,029	14,969	4,149	240,911
Palm Beach	20,348,336	336,284	20,012,052	17,704,188	2,307,864	370,886	33,036	1,903,942
Pasco	2,260,764	28,929	2,231,835	1,810,959	420,876	37,206	9,334	374,336
Pinellas	15,358,612	4,569	15,354,043	13,562,201	1,791,842	359,841	72,131	1,359,870
Polk	6,398,494	125,029	6,273,465	5,377,229	896,236	77,062	13,559	805,615
Putnam	571,887	15,880	556,007	399,425	156,582	8,126	2,006	146,450
St. Johns	1,280,132	12,616	1,267,516	1,061,495	206,021	23,669	4,052	178,300
St. Lucie	1,636,603	38,713	1,597,890	1,248,799	349,091	31,309	7,335	310,447
Santa Rosa	934,836	7,186	927,650	653,340	274,310	35,774	94,001	144,535
Sarasota	4,690,950	13,460	4,677,490	4,184,162	493,328	50,769	9,074	433,485
Seminole	4,676,201	9,959	4,666,242	4,119,217	547,025	79,662	10,039	457,324
Sumter	285,929	11,222	274,707	161,448	113,259	45,588	1,151	66,520
Suwannee	328,817	48,453	280,364	223,039	57,325	5,840	931	50,554
Taylor	222,731	2,068	220,663	174,516	46,147	1,740	538	43,869
Union	127,869	2,771	125,098	43,486	81,612	888	355	80,369
Volusia	4,252,530	58,033	4,194,497	3,451,800	742,697	77,233	13,597	651,867
Wakulla	147,556	2,422	145,134	104,850	40,284	3,454	530	36,300
Walton	306,075	6,048	300,027	226,616	73,411	9,394	2,804	61,213
Washington	182,205	1,904	180,301	103,306	76,995	2,181	579	74,235

A/ Revised.
1/ See Table 5.34 for private nonfarm income by industrial source.
2/ In millions of dollars.

Source: U.S., Department of Commerce, Bureau of Economic Analysis, Regional Economic Information System, CD-ROM, June 2000.

Table 5.33. EARNED INCOME: PRIVATE NONFARM EARNINGS ON A PLACE-OF-WORK BASIS BY INDUSTRIAL SOURCE IN FLORIDA 1993 THROUGH 1998

(in thousands of dollars)

Item	1993	1994	1995	1996	1997	1998	Change 1/
Agricultural services, forestry, fisheries, and other 2/	1,980,466	1,975,226	2,001,957	2,134,297	2,303,640	2,507,378	26.6
Agricultural services	1,857,044	1,841,922	1,895,780	2,040,277	2,194,145	2,392,841	28.9
Forestry	26,651	31,325	24,116	24,760	36,362	35,501	33.2
Fisheries	90,857	95,596	74,751	61,980	65,613	71,264	-21.6
Other 2/	5,914	6,383	7,310	7,280	7,520	7,772	31.4
Mining	332,978	332,606	353,907	392,754	356,777	386,247	16.0
Coal mining	(D)	15,541	24,113	17,722	17,913	(D)	(X)
Oil and gas extraction	-69,321	67,172	56,429	89,849	68,575	71,431	3.0
Metal mining	(D)	8,495	7,379	8,383	11,046	(D)	(X)
Nonmetallic minerals, except fuels	242,792	241,398	265,986	276,800	259,243	285,375	17.5
Construction	10,427,945	11,027,101	11,761,127	12,811,839	13,507,946	14,766,457	41.6
General building contractors	2,556,955	2,617,997	2,737,606	2,868,442	3,051,609	3,373,377	31.9
Heavy construction contractors	1,210,152	1,374,801	1,439,646	1,523,175	1,577,761	1,727,666	42.8
Special trade contractors	6,660,838	7,034,303	7,583,875	8,420,222	8,878,576	9,665,414	45.1
Manufacturing	17,371,878	17,933,804	18,048,653	18,637,071	19,431,632	20,489,647	17.9
Nondurable goods	6,588,418	6,805,838	6,848,582	6,949,908	7,188,839	7,553,022	14.6
Food and kindred products	1,466,685	1,483,909	1,429,903	1,465,049	1,495,115	1,553,712	5.9
Textile mill products	31,597	32,456	50,299	59,451	68,312	86,235	172.9
Apparel and other textile products	102,768	102,543	110,934	119,734	126,037	127,764	24.3
Paper and allied products	595,897	590,206	544,395	534,888	521,470	522,170	-12.4
Printing and publishing	603,081	620,322	626,746	631,200	656,801	643,932	6.8
Chemicals and allied products	2,031,684	2,137,917	2,179,801	2,244,802	2,324,918	2,476,687	21.9
Petroleum and coal products	1,063,108	1,108,688	1,164,096	1,096,344	1,160,872	1,295,357	21.8
Tobacco products	79,719	78,532	67,015	69,246	95,314	98,017	23.0
Rubber and miscellaneous plastics products	568,355	603,882	622,769	661,188	673,776	692,176	21.8
Leather and leather products	45,524	47,383	52,624	68,006	66,224	56,972	25.1
Durable goods	10,783,460	11,127,966	11,200,071	11,687,163	12,242,793	12,936,625	20.0
Lumber and wood products	557,430	607,201	640,735	700,706	722,152	775,834	39.2

See footnotes at end of table.

Continued . . .

Table 5.33. EARNED INCOME: PRIVATE NONFARM EARNINGS ON A PLACE-OF-WORK BASIS BY INDUSTRIAL SOURCE IN FLORIDA 1993 THROUGH 1998 (Continued)

(in thousands of dollars)

Item	1993	1994	1995	1996	1997	1998	Change 1/
Manufacturing (Continued)							
Durable goods (Continued)							
Furniture and fixtures	330,395	339,112	333,407	353,740	374,959	375,446	13.6
Primary metal industries	665,591	723,691	760,065	833,033	863,571	927,628	39.4
Fabricated metal products	188,346	205,878	218,748	238,460	256,096	279,491	48.4
Industrial machinery and equipment	946,906	997,031	1,009,712	1,057,972	1,102,965	1,165,361	23.1
Electronic and other electric equipment	1,631,195	1,713,462	1,582,664	1,563,410	1,529,072	1,619,606	-0.7
Transportation equipment, excluding motor vehicles	2,595,873	2,697,232	2,733,094	2,780,446	2,988,152	3,089,954	19.0
Motor vehicles and equipment	238,495	239,128	271,595	268,266	288,279	298,316	25.1
Stone, clay, and glass products	2,079,256	1,988,718	2,011,708	2,061,243	2,184,305	2,287,497	10.0
Instruments and related products	1,297,416	1,338,520	1,351,418	1,511,699	1,606,735	1,768,467	36.3
Miscellaneous manufacturing industries	252,557	277,993	286,925	318,188	326,507	349,025	38.2
Transportation, communications, and public utilities	11,973,040	12,595,958	13,170,052	13,736,333	14,552,141	15,501,751	29.5
Railroad transportation	407,602	423,740	450,156	455,066	449,332	470,007	15.3
Trucking and warehousing	2,138,605	2,326,298	2,262,568	2,389,148	2,585,612	2,796,201	30.7
Water transportation	625,982	663,449	675,271	714,604	807,605	870,377	39.0
Other transportation	3,103,233	3,351,548	3,733,125	4,060,821	4,308,502	4,622,552	49.0
Local and interurban passenger transit	393,802	378,140	397,611	438,479	469,834	507,561	28.9
Transportation by air	1,896,335	2,060,696	2,356,252	2,577,062	2,733,730	2,956,402	55.9
Pipelines, except natural gas	4,026	5,661	5,584	5,204	4,685	3,693	-8.3
Transportation services	809,070	907,051	973,678	1,040,076	1,100,253	1,154,896	42.7
Communications	3,643,855	3,867,974	3,987,171	3,923,009	4,131,321	4,435,718	21.7
Electric, gas, and sanitary services	2,053,763	1,962,949	2,061,761	2,193,685	2,269,769	2,306,896	12.3
Wholesale trade	11,020,906	11,809,230	12,717,021	13,944,290	14,862,006	16,029,247	45.4
Retail trade	20,524,854	21,718,880	22,829,371	24,483,351	25,717,809	27,398,904	33.5
Building materials and garden equipment	1,021,613	1,062,840	1,108,089	1,224,532	1,307,624	1,430,784	40.1

See footnotes at end of table.

Continued . . .

Table 5.33. EARNED INCOME: PRIVATE NONFARM EARNINGS ON A PLACE-OF-WORK BASIS BY INDUSTRIAL SOURCE IN FLORIDA 1993 THROUGH 1998 (Continued)

(in thousands of dollars)

Item	1993	1994	1995	1996	1997	1998	Change 1/
Retail trade (Continued)							
General merchandise stores	2,169,469	2,270,562	2,375,771	2,474,851	2,557,995	2,678,466	23.5
Food stores	3,339,341	3,500,618	3,683,971	3,969,033	4,099,183	4,430,659	32.7
Automotive dealers and service stations	3,525,450	3,843,134	4,080,111	4,317,640	4,409,346	4,714,972	33.7
Apparel and accessory stores	982,800	1,008,197	1,051,845	1,088,739	1,165,613	1,252,581	27.5
Home furniture and furnishings stores	1,261,821	1,365,016	1,456,605	1,576,792	1,713,753	1,910,084	51.4
Eating and drinking places	5,186,055	5,553,771	5,760,016	6,260,627	6,606,202	6,876,037	32.6
Miscellaneous retail	3,038,305	3,114,742	3,312,963	3,571,137	3,858,093	4,105,321	35.1
Finance, insurance, and real estate	15,620,108	15,983,014	17,604,359	19,461,459	21,856,182	24,671,071	57.9
Depository and nondepository credit institutions	4,266,691	4,451,673	4,596,122	4,989,078	5,703,246	6,525,467	52.9
Other finance, insurance, and real estate	11,353,417	11,531,341	13,008,237	14,472,381	16,152,936	18,145,604	59.8
Security and commodity brokers and services	1,884,120	1,814,101	2,100,821	2,603,222	2,889,502	3,299,891	75.1
Insurance carriers	2,665,439	2,859,446	2,968,712	3,144,128	3,317,541	3,673,392	37.8
Insurance agents, brokers, and services	1,829,032	1,949,382	2,106,073	2,237,988	2,305,595	2,508,838	37.2
Real estate	4,234,773	4,065,186	4,903,207	5,411,405	6,417,961	7,184,999	69.7
Holding and other investment companies	740,053	843,226	929,424	1,075,638	1,222,337	1,478,484	99.8
Services	55,820,468	59,734,074	65,211,167	69,078,275	74,706,912	81,994,227	46.9
Hotels and other lodging places	2,723,353	2,738,923	2,934,096	3,124,142	3,312,606	3,645,342	33.9
Personal services	1,841,229	1,865,924	1,964,689	2,031,787	2,144,192	2,254,182	22.4
Private households	682,738	712,228	768,726	783,052	791,989	926,199	35.7
Business services	9,716,373	10,830,499	12,610,981	13,139,863	15,461,686	18,506,096	90.5
Auto repair, services, and parking	1,678,914	1,767,272	1,851,473	1,947,051	2,091,653	2,220,996	32.3
Miscellaneous repair services	819,922	828,892	908,401	935,526	931,786	997,313	21.6
Amusement and recreation services	2,879,690	3,100,133	3,421,427	3,708,955	4,036,911	4,414,494	53.3
Motion pictures	372,545	400,574	455,754	450,273	480,345	530,222	42.3
Health services	19,123,834	20,337,180	21,756,006	23,114,096	23,922,794	24,731,173	29.3

See footnotes at end of table.

Continued ...

Table 5.33. EARNED INCOME: PRIVATE NONFARM EARNINGS ON A PLACE-OF-WORK BASIS BY INDUSTRIAL SOURCE IN FLORIDA 1993 THROUGH 1998 (Continued)

(in thousands of dollars)

Item	1993	1994	1995	1996	1997	1998	Change 1/
Services (Continued)							
Legal services	4,224,070	4,362,435	4,570,511	4,851,120	5,106,986	5,661,376	34.0
Educational services	1,403,478	1,565,119	1,657,606	1,762,116	1,876,779	2,035,358	45.0
Social services	1,697,038	1,858,686	1,963,180	2,064,544	2,172,595	2,356,207	38.8
Museums, botanical, zoological gardens	50,488	56,227	63,111	68,345	73,118	77,603	53.7
Membership organizations	2,158,757	2,285,515	2,367,197	2,467,155	2,549,301	2,664,107	23.4
Engineering and management services	5,976,635	6,408,728	7,272,934	7,801,710	8,770,947	9,966,834	66.8
Miscellaneous services	471,404	615,739	645,075	828,540	983,224	1,006,725	113.6
Government and government enterprises	34,369,245	35,535,597	36,772,148	38,508,885	40,295,844	42,134,576	22.6
Federal, civilian	6,234,216	6,277,746	6,462,010	6,769,214	6,928,655	7,159,920	14.8
Military	4,273,077	4,017,217	3,865,926	4,307,412	4,565,835	4,435,617	3.8
State and local	23,861,952	25,240,634	26,444,212	27,432,259	28,801,354	30,539,039	28.0

(D) Data withheld to avoid disclosure of information about individual industries.
(X) Not applicable.
1/ Percentage change 1993 to 1998.
2/ Includes wages and salaries of U.S. residents employed by foreign embassies, consulates and international organizations in the United States.
Note: Some data are revised.

Source: U.S., Department of Commerce, Bureau of Economic Analysis, Regional Economic Information System, CD-ROM, June 2000.

Table 5.34. EARNED INCOME: PRIVATE NONFARM EARNINGS ON A PLACE-OF-WORK BASIS BY MAJOR INDUSTRIAL SOURCE IN THE UNITED STATES AND IN THE STATE AND COUNTIES OF FLORIDA, 1997 AND 1998

(in thousands of dollars)

1997 A/

County	Total private nonfarm earnings	Agriculture services 1/	Manufacturing	Mining	Construction	Wholesale trade	Retail trade	Finance insurance and real estate	Transportation 2/	Services
United States 3/	4,094,756	31,401	847,972	45,988	276,965	304,106	438,125	430,953	336,749	1,382,497
Florida 3/	187,295	2,304	19,432	357	13,508	14,862	25,718	21,856	14,552	74,707
Alachua	2,102,472	(D)	191,129	(D)	154,448	87,425	320,947	206,097	93,870	1,021,964
Baker	66,612	362	8,657	0	(D)	2,222	14,308	3,678	9,794	(D)
Bay	1,396,618	10,560	130,029	109	176,012	87,906	267,226	113,707	111,712	499,357
Bradford	109,909	875	18,496	0	7,248	(D)	19,411	3,143	9,201	(D)
Brevard	5,253,874	40,903	1,293,864	2,725	351,996	193,928	618,104	251,339	199,950	2,301,065
Broward	19,041,030	141,807	1,714,971	11,171	1,426,595	1,795,211	2,872,294	2,354,245	1,345,057	7,379,679
Calhoun	63,568	(D)	8,712	0	8,633	3,027	9,828	2,390	(D)	20,935
Charlotte	845,302	17,760	29,675	1,920	99,554	21,795	171,368	66,561	38,843	397,826
Citrus	686,877	8,009	31,036	(D)	65,133	12,958	109,458	49,879	(D)	273,709
Clay	802,255	(D)	62,442	(D)	91,829	32,513	192,142	40,092	55,218	303,195
Collier	2,976,884	93,267	97,366	6,501	387,751	105,543	432,126	498,316	90,165	1,265,849
Columbia	382,572	3,982	65,518	80	44,291	32,440	76,712	17,476	26,675	115,398
De Soto	140,663	49,093	8,505	163	8,660	4,980	22,524	5,628	4,609	36,501
Dixie	47,650	1,482	17,824	(D)	4,016	(D)	8,057	1,294	3,610	8,632
Duval	13,484,396	79,623	1,255,572	14,653	937,422	1,163,646	1,466,588	2,649,859	1,430,488	4,486,545
Escambia	2,979,357	19,208	413,250	7,395	302,303	191,787	477,845	188,412	241,169	1,137,988
Flagler	245,506	(D)	53,361	(D)	16,647	4,936	37,943	20,910	8,877	97,032
Franklin	60,429	(D)	4,485	(D)	5,149	5,644	12,120	4,986	6,245	17,818
Gadsden	191,126	8,311	48,179	(D)	20,273	(D)	29,758	7,734	11,538	44,464
Gilchrist	37,627	2,797	6,532	0	3,597	2,499	4,664	1,734	3,972	11,832

See footnotes at end of table.

Continued . . .

Table 5.34. EARNED INCOME: PRIVATE NONFARM EARNINGS ON A PLACE-OF-WORK BASIS BY MAJOR INDUSTRIAL SOURCE IN THE UNITED STATES AND IN THE STATE AND COUNTIES OF FLORIDA, 1997 AND 1998 (Continued)

(in thousands of dollars)

County	Total private nonfarm earnings	Agriculture services 1/	Manufacturing	Mining	Construction	Wholesale trade	Retail trade	Finance insurance and real estate	Transportation 2/	Services
					1997 A/ (Continued)					
Glades	22,584	3,485	1,857	(D)	2,028	1,438	3,644	(D)	3,947	4,719
Gulf	96,609	751	46,017	0	9,396	1,392	8,557	3,356	11,733	15,407
Hamilton	97,309	987	68,057	0	2,808	931	5,643	846	7,390	10,647
Hardee	128,992	28,426	8,283	(D)	(D)	8,620	16,971	7,644	5,778	35,707
Hendry	228,649	59,125	50,375	(D)	13,853	12,736	31,684	8,246	(D)	40,264
Hernando	622,429	9,675	47,277	10,952	60,074	28,524	126,210	46,476	39,863	253,378
Highlands	486,907	54,356	45,106	1,175	39,130	18,033	89,751	29,309	26,088	183,959
Hillsborough	16,301,667	120,932	1,329,906	1,381	1,049,213	1,732,943	1,896,994	2,002,232	1,470,505	6,697,561
Holmes	54,610	376	9,010	53	5,895	1,738	9,882	2,480	4,579	20,597
Indian River	1,106,797	79,033	89,187	2,188	110,174	58,010	182,638	122,168	28,908	434,491
Jackson	204,757	(D)	38,376	(D)	11,956	20,223	47,604	13,718	17,774	51,227
Jefferson	47,704	2,174	5,514	0	6,402	1,864	7,579	4,447	4,906	14,818
Lafayette	20,566	5,013	4,176	0	1,548	2,012	1,797	650	1,768	3,602
Lake	1,408,841	28,669	136,670	10,991	200,878	58,134	237,472	118,291	93,154	524,582
Lee	4,090,233	63,696	232,510	7,413	489,430	203,675	752,913	456,627	277,998	1,605,971
Leon	2,547,550	(D)	126,479	(D)	201,531	147,140	384,321	243,081	141,003	1,281,288
Levy	141,538	9,180	12,025	(D)	24,667	(D)	29,484	8,798	13,402	37,087
Liberty	29,019	(D)	8,057	0	6,977	243	2,655	(D)	3,237	6,899
Madison	89,661	2,273	31,968	0	2,306	3,483	12,340	2,411	6,328	28,552
Manatee	2,996,645	75,680	476,010	1,385	180,423	133,381	372,797	156,339	74,550	1,526,080
Marion	1,932,785	41,742	364,677	3,805	203,739	126,599	334,359	131,053	123,680	603,131
Martin	1,350,850	46,692	125,601	1,325	131,876	55,358	223,272	139,157	78,929	548,640
Miami-Dade	30,846,585	159,151	2,539,348	22,777	1,323,080	3,543,606	3,707,775	3,792,702	3,845,027	11,913,119
Monroe	933,210	18,192	16,317	3,712	79,962	33,519	226,116	83,148	54,982	417,262

See footnotes at end of table.

Continued . . .

Table 5.34. EARNED INCOME: PRIVATE NONFARM EARNINGS ON A PLACE-OF-WORK BASIS BY MAJOR INDUSTRIAL SOURCE IN THE UNITED STATES AND IN THE STATE AND COUNTIES OF FLORIDA, 1997 AND 1998 (Continued)

(in thousands of dollars)

County	Total private nonfarm earnings	Agriculture services 1/	Manufacturing	Mining	Construction	Wholesale trade	Retail trade	Finance insurance and real estate	Transportation 2/	Services
					1997 A/ (Continued)					
Nassau	400,861	16,325	105,891	B/	35,805	13,322	60,160	25,133	27,038	117,156
Okaloosa	1,555,598	14,518	124,565	1,616	155,382	42,665	301,060	176,203	77,192	662,397
Okeechobee	188,808	8,189	6,754	0	14,612	13,944	41,193	9,285	13,016	81,815
Orange	17,162,034	130,525	1,660,116	5,907	1,128,645	1,400,788	1,975,058	1,649,268	1,342,840	7,868,887
Osceola	1,048,953	16,726	80,498	B/	85,764	61,914	239,062	82,343	24,793	457,821
Palm Beach	15,985,029	258,399	1,695,558	26,979	1,049,991	1,062,707	1,903,652	2,827,241	809,090	6,351,412
Pasco	1,717,518	30,479	121,931	1,268	170,558	59,048	315,324	117,041	96,526	805,343
Pinellas	12,536,406	83,469	1,713,629	1,101	743,270	1,042,178	1,647,978	1,406,838	611,310	5,286,633
Polk	4,970,594	125,904	855,885	144,343	357,477	316,065	836,405	324,199	439,061	1,571,255
Putnam	381,584	7,358	133,779	2,974	27,639	12,209	60,832	15,089	20,660	101,044
St. Johns	938,954	12,131	134,453	552	68,510	57,595	154,493	77,243	38,934	395,043
St. Lucie	1,199,956	79,736	76,911	1,584	105,792	62,366	193,788	96,763	142,451	440,565
Santa Rosa	589,178	9,518	77,441	8,142	104,425	16,540	80,309	35,632	41,391	215,780
Sarasota	3,895,157	46,554	294,166	5,118	339,231	184,841	640,127	508,088	139,694	1,737,338
Seminole	3,759,654	43,245	419,034	424	446,525	338,629	637,125	347,819	303,212	1,223,641
Sumter	149,771	2,248	25,548	2,850	14,071	12,821	28,583	6,489	26,553	30,608
Suwannee	204,178	(D)	39,432	(D)	29,862	10,775	35,530	10,609	20,271	52,562
Taylor	167,757	5,195	76,067	2,057	19,048	3,815	20,064	6,586	4,507	30,418
Union	47,775	2,115	9,424	(D)	2,270	(D)	4,175	763	12,765	14,858
Volusia	3,304,467	36,228	437,801	583	267,167	160,823	599,832	248,882	143,851	1,409,300
Wakulla	85,248	2,056	24,665	0	15,501	2,406	10,849	4,951	4,949	19,871
Walton	210,166	4,317	24,226	552	27,665	4,702	39,913	14,974	16,533	77,284
Washington	94,175	(D)	21,452	(D)	12,710	1,671	16,416	3,095	14,541	22,880

See footnotes at end of table.

Continued . . .

Table 5.34. EARNED INCOME: PRIVATE NONFARM EARNINGS ON A PLACE-OF-WORK BASIS BY MAJOR INDUSTRIAL SOURCE IN THE UNITED STATES AND IN THE STATE AND COUNTIES OF FLORIDA, 1997 AND 1998 (Continued)

(in thousands of dollars)

1998

County	Total private nonfarm earnings	Agriculture services 1/	Manufacturing	Mining	Construction	Wholesale trade	Retail trade	Finance insurance and real estate	Transportation 2/	Services
United States 3/	4,408,261	34,445	891,190	47,984	302,174	329,422	464,753	477,189	357,379	1,503,725
Florida 3/	203,745	2,507	20,490	386	14,766	16,029	27,399	24,671	15,502	81,994
Alachua	2,275,873	(D)	193,603	(D)	162,922	83,711	342,931	239,253	98,849	1,125,571
Baker	70,923	394	9,391	0	8,519	2,542	15,647	4,647	10,466	19,317
Bay	1,585,745	11,764	153,159	116	204,868	89,680	280,353	126,507	123,350	595,948
Bradford	116,011	(D)	20,571	0	7,704	(D)	21,544	5,853	9,525	(D)
Brevard	5,564,640	(D)	1,347,983	(D)	380,529	214,979	654,338	278,127	198,437	2,440,522
Broward	20,582,321	161,641	1,758,256	12,179	1,521,672	1,934,958	3,092,161	2,651,140	1,398,086	8,052,228
Calhoun	68,791	2,514	8,261	0	9,525	3,812	10,147	2,308	5,534	26,690
Charlotte	911,304	(D)	30,399	(D)	107,834	23,506	187,633	74,357	40,878	426,314
Citrus	719,277	8,833	35,558	(D)	71,263	13,701	114,957	53,721	(D)	286,885
Clay	880,527	(D)	72,764	(D)	97,735	30,106	207,326	43,794	62,466	341,824
Collier	3,239,584	106,745	106,585	6,887	439,144	116,525	474,049	548,527	98,962	1,342,160
Columbia	403,213	4,593	66,700	85	44,662	36,281	83,071	17,598	28,159	122,064
De Soto	152,247	54,099	8,327	(D)	8,824	6,377	23,568	6,032	(D)	39,164
Dixie	52,247	1,716	(D)	(D)	4,819	(D)	8,239	1,314	4,793	9,597
Duval	14,817,030	85,016	1,346,490	15,283	1,020,686	1,289,702	1,537,639	3,098,275	1,515,287	4,908,652
Escambia	3,214,455	(D)	418,228	(D)	322,191	194,677	484,088	203,616	268,144	1,296,046
Flagler	262,680	(D)	54,925	(D)	17,783	6,300	41,365	20,659	9,808	106,346
Franklin	65,155	(D)	4,598	(D)	5,693	7,053	13,265	5,606	6,337	18,147
Gadsden	210,332	8,336	53,003	(D)	21,474	(D)	31,950	8,353	11,976	43,761
Gilchrist	38,686	2,923	6,195	0	3,657	2,935	5,201	1,366	4,187	12,222
Glades	24,154	3,903	(D)	(D)	2,368	1,546	3,530	(D)	(D)	5,580
Gulf	85,715	794	31,108	0	6,356	2,466	8,534	3,701	11,594	21,162

See footnotes at end of table.

Continued . . .

Table 5.34. EARNED INCOME: PRIVATE NONFARM EARNINGS ON A PLACE-OF-WORK BASIS BY MAJOR INDUSTRIAL SOURCE IN THE UNITED STATES AND IN THE STATE AND COUNTIES OF FLORIDA, 1997 AND 1998 (Continued)

(in thousands of dollars)

1998 (Continued)

County	Total private nonfarm earnings	Agriculture services 1/	Manufacturing	Mining	Construction	Wholesale trade	Retail trade	Finance insurance and real estate	Transportation 2/	Services
Hamilton	100,851	1,109	(D)	0	3,616	(D)	5,720	868	6,134	10,408
Hardee	136,858	30,414	8,736	(D)	(D)	8,669	17,579	8,122	5,777	38,285
Hendry	242,669	64,595	51,398	(D)	14,363	13,224	33,449	7,746	(D)	44,684
Hernando	663,396	11,589	47,615	12,417	66,771	31,874	131,697	51,309	41,310	268,814
Highlands	500,929	58,020	43,941	(D)	40,826		90,992	26,071	25,112	196,407
Hillsborough	18,148,846	137,570	1,442,112	1,643	1,169,817	1,771,171	2,107,800	2,282,292	1,581,578	7,654,863
Holmes	58,516	(D)	8,842	59	6,808	(D)	11,002	2,528	4,839	22,145
Indian River	1,197,256	82,557	104,365	(D)	115,690	54,178	201,712	140,972	(D)	465,131
Jackson	212,636	(D)	36,151	(D)	15,421	19,646	50,676	12,413	19,626	55,010
Jefferson	49,819	2,472	5,697	0	6,651	2,259	7,988	4,908	4,586	15,258
Lafayette	22,570	5,452	3,800	(D)	1,778	2,175	2,566	878	(D)	4,000
Lake	1,550,701	29,348	139,884	12,660	240,334	66,901	256,303	140,335	98,969	565,967
Lee	4,439,911	69,077	243,244	8,631	544,185	227,246	819,906	502,658	305,462	1,719,502
Leon	2,793,616	(D)	117,058	(D)	216,990	160,070	405,142	276,500	153,707	1,439,090
Levy	145,228	9,334	11,496	(D)	25,602	(D)	31,179	8,201	13,878	37,415
Liberty	28,698	379	7,930	0	(D)	277	2,491	(D)	3,598	6,085
Madison	90,585	2,272	32,160	0	2,137	2,869	13,033	2,592	6,997	28,525
Manatee	3,248,724	(D)	519,087	(D)	192,132	148,439	388,409	173,376	78,854	1,678,474
Marion	2,099,403	48,561	385,128	4,209	224,398	127,183	362,924	160,957	132,206	653,837
Martin	1,507,777	(D)	149,631	(D)	141,605	59,270	220,777	181,393	82,674	621,077
Miami-Dade	32,865,922	169,650	2,658,549	22,347	1,406,837	3,818,473	3,846,523	4,089,272	4,127,582	12,726,689
Monroe	1,010,956	(D)	18,507	B/	83,933	34,187	230,048	84,702	60,847	475,075
Nassau	421,639	17,158	108,414	1,726	34,382	13,384	64,707	28,940	27,999	126,621
Okaloosa	1,688,668	17,750	127,371		155,811	44,857	318,843	186,912	100,657	734,741
Okeechobee	194,932	9,010	6,115	0	15,815	14,109	40,386	8,252	15,656	85,589
Orange	19,242,358	152,356	1,848,324	7,080	1,246,440	1,523,290	2,184,686	1,882,377	1,472,022	8,925,783

See footnotes at end of table.

Continued . . .

Table 5.34. EARNED INCOME: PRIVATE NONFARM EARNINGS ON A PLACE-OF-WORK BASIS BY MAJOR INDUSTRIAL SOURCE IN THE UNITED STATES AND IN THE STATE AND COUNTIES OF FLORIDA, 1997 AND 1998 (Continued)

(in thousands of dollars)

County	Total private nonfarm earnings	Agriculture services 1/	Manufacturing	Mining	Construction	Wholesale trade	Retail trade	Finance insurance and real estate	Transportation 2/	Services
					1998 (Continued)					
Osceola	1,130,402	18,150	76,647	B/	94,626	66,395	251,357	96,445	26,741	500,007
Palm Beach	17,704,188	280,881	1,849,290	27,631	1,158,959	1,213,903	2,036,232	3,256,263	845,885	7,035,144
Pasco	1,810,959	33,934	115,485	1,447	187,260	70,403	340,773	122,670	100,530	838,457
Pinellas	13,562,201	(D)	1,798,886	(D)	810,907	1,110,172	1,682,888	1,676,330	631,783	5,758,843
Polk	5,377,229	129,393	897,916	161,617	415,122	336,852	930,574	368,652	469,541	1,667,562
Putnam	399,425	7,474	136,693	3,007	32,382	14,799	62,753	14,692	20,257	107,368
St. Johns	1,061,495	(D)	163,494	(D)	75,902	61,074	163,335	87,895	43,232	451,568
St. Lucie	1,248,799	85,529	79,369	965	111,334	68,195	206,114	92,580	135,148	469,565
Santa Rosa	653,340	10,276	80,223	8,527	117,167	17,183	91,717	40,017	46,030	242,200
Sarasota	4,184,162	56,726	313,724	5,491	376,250	194,166	679,164	560,195	142,101	1,856,345
Seminole	4,119,217	(D)	399,298	(D)	499,041	393,411	685,567	374,134	307,809	1,413,326
Sumter	161,448	2,432	24,860	3,512	17,518	13,723	29,280	6,580	26,542	37,001
Suwannee	223,039	(D)	(D)	(D)	33,957	10,924	39,633	11,215	20,878	57,126
Taylor	174,516	3,956	80,047	1,966	(D)	5,043	18,478	4,565	3,596	(D)
Union	43,486	1,106	9,808	(D)	2,060	(D)	4,376	795	11,110	13,548
Volusia	3,451,800	(D)	388,370	(D)	290,118	169,628	616,210	271,449	167,330	1,511,724
Wakulla	104,850	(D)	38,509	0	16,898	2,772	11,456	5,734	4,644	22,499
Walton	226,616	2,338	26,341	(D)	27,202	5,112	44,005	16,921	19,274	81,971
Washington	103,306	(D)	22,831	(D)	18,253	1,877	16,918	3,318	15,445	23,194

(D) Data withheld to avoid disclosure of information about individual industries.
A/ Revised.
B/ Less than $50,000. Estimates are included in totals.
1/ Includes forestry, fisheries, and other.
2/ Includes communications and public utilities.
3/ United States and Florida numbers are rounded to millions of dollars.

Source: U.S., Department of Commerce, Bureau of Economic Analysis, Regional Economic Information System, CD-ROM, June 2000.

Table 5.38. TRANSFER PAYMENTS: AMOUNTS BY TYPE IN FLORIDA, 1997 AND 1998

(in thousands of dollars)

Type of transfer payment	1997 A/	1998
Total personal income by place of residence	376,559,054	400,208,545
Total transfer payments	60,948,356	62,522,927
Percentage of personal income	16.19	15.62
Government payments to individuals	58,450,844	59,884,986
Retirement and disability insurance benefit payments	26,286,143	27,309,617
Old age, survivors, and disability insurance	25,479,062	26,497,831
Railroad retirement and disability	422,612	428,556
Workers' compensation (federal and state)	327,036	332,519
Other government disability insurance and retirement 1/	57,433	50,711
Medical payments	24,376,102	24,673,632
Medicare payments	17,825,020	17,778,765
Public assistance medical care	6,333,763	6,680,420
Military medical insurance payments	217,319	214,447
Income maintenance benefit payments	4,780,585	4,805,609
Supplemental Security Income (SSI)	1,472,576	1,533,878
Family assistance	626,821	530,431
Food stamps	989,844	829,295
Other income maintenance 2/	1,691,344	1,912,005
Unemployment insurance benefit payments	700,558	729,917
State unemployment insurance compensation	676,778	672,397
Unemployment Compensation for Federal Civilian Employees (UCFE)	6,436	6,024
Unemployment Compensation for Railroad Employees	1,280	1,084
Unemployment Compensation for Veterans (UCX)	13,906	13,376
Other unemployment compensation 3/	2,158	37,036
Veterans' benefit payments	1,709,822	1,766,947
Veterans' pensions and compensation	1,458,427	1,516,961
Veterans' readjustment payments	80,450	80,048
Veterans' life insurance benefit	170,680	169,673
Other assistance to veterans 4/	265	265
Federal education and training assistance payments (excluding veterans) 5	545,635	545,914
Other payments to individuals 6/	51,999	53,350
Payments to nonprofit institutions	1,429,804	1,558,407
Federal government payments	343,179	380,341
State and local government payments 7/	625,476	671,938
Business payments	461,149	506,128
Business payments to individuals 8/	1,067,708	1,079,534

A/ Revised.   1/ Includes temporary disability and black lung payments.
2/ Includes general, emergency, refugee, and energy assistance, foster home care payments and earned-income tax credits.
3/ Includes trade readjustment, public service employment benefit, and transitional benefit payments.
4/ Includes payments to paraplegics, transportation payments for disabled veterans, and veterans' aid and bonuses.
5/ Includes federal fellowship and Job Corps payments, basic educational opportunity grants, and loan interest subsidies.
6/ Includes Bureau of Indian Affairs and education exchange payments, compensation of survivors of public safety officers, crime victims, Japanese interment, natural disasters, and other special payments.
7/ Foster home care supervised by private agency, educational assistance to nonprofit institutions and other payments to nonprofit institutions.
8/ Personal injury payments to individuals other than employees and other business transfer payments.
Note: The reclassification of government employee retirement plans covering federal civilian, military, and state and local government employees as "other labor income" has resulted in an increase in personal income. See the Appendix for discussion.

Source: U.S., Department of Commerce, Bureau of Economic Analysis, Regional Economic Information System, CD-ROM, June 2000.

Table 5.39. TRANSFER PAYMENTS: TOTAL AMOUNTS IN THE UNITED STATES AND IN THE STATE AND COUNTIES OF FLORIDA, 1996, 1997, AND 1998

(amounts in thousands of dollars, except where indicated)

County	1996 A/ Amount	1996 A/ As a percentage of total personal income	1997 A/ Amount	1997 A/ As a percentage of total personal income	1998 Amount	1998 As a percentage of total personal income
United States 1/	928,697	14.2	962,347	13.9	983,530	13.4
Florida	57,975,818	16.3	60,948,356	16.2	62,522,927	15.6
Alachua	632,928	14.7	662,475	14.5	692,551	14.2
Baker	61,392	18.3	64,774	18.1	69,672	18.2
Bay	493,664	16.8	526,558	16.9	547,519	16.8
Bradford	80,694	21.6	84,408	20.9	87,094	20.8
Brevard	1,754,709	17.9	1,875,629	17.8	1,936,554	17.5
Broward	5,685,225	14.6	5,900,093	14.5	5,934,664	13.8
Calhoun	46,660	27.5	49,460	27.1	52,170	27.3
Charlotte	726,022	25.6	766,262	25.2	791,138	24.7
Citrus	608,502	30.5	644,274	29.9	662,600	29.3
Clay	300,799	10.8	323,829	10.8	344,235	10.6
Collier	784,841	10.9	844,198	10.4	881,892	10.3
Columbia	194,242	21.9	205,654	21.6	217,005	21.6
De Soto	116,582	24.9	119,889	24.1	123,573	23.2
Dixie	52,312	30.9	53,849	30.3	57,610	30.4
Duval	2,288,656	13.0	2,405,804	13.0	2,438,413	12.5
Escambia	961,134	17.2	1,011,929	17.0	1,046,213	17.0
Flagler	194,092	22.9	213,016	22.7	225,600	22.4
Franklin	52,604	29.8	49,723	27.1	49,959	26.0
Gadsden	170,485	24.3	176,817	24.0	182,060	23.3
Gilchrist	43,057	23.3	45,275	22.6	47,837	22.4
Glades	25,655	20.0	27,146	19.8	28,084	19.1
Gulf	59,225	27.4	62,036	27.5	63,938	28.3
Hamilton	41,486	25.0	44,961	26.2	47,535	26.8
Hardee	80,903	21.7	86,711	21.8	87,551	20.7
Hendry	98,366	17.6	103,486	17.3	104,399	16.0
Hernando	713,469	29.9	757,788	29.2	774,049	28.3
Highlands	446,115	29.5	468,754	29.4	480,083	28.9
Hillsborough	3,006,342	14.1	3,161,933	13.8	3,259,595	13.4
Holmes	79,443	31.0	85,189	31.3	86,744	30.7
Indian River	529,088	16.0	562,730	16.3	578,276	16.0
Jackson	190,593	26.4	199,120	26.6	209,786	27.1
Jefferson	47,144	20.7	49,316	20.6	50,363	19.8
Lafayette	17,170	18.8	19,079	19.3	19,512	18.5
Lake	923,649	23.8	993,486	23.5	1,032,739	23.0
Lee	1,764,426	18.5	1,865,389	18.2	1,918,782	17.7

See footnote at end of table.   Continued . . .

University of Florida   **Bureau of Economic and Business Research**

Table 5.39. TRANSFER PAYMENTS: TOTAL AMOUNTS IN THE UNITED STATES AND IN THE STATE AND COUNTIES OF FLORIDA, 1996, 1997, AND 1998 (Continued)

(amounts in thousands of dollars, except where indicated)

County	1996 A/ Amount	1996 A/ As a percentage of total personal income	1997 A/ Amount	1997 A/ As a percentage of total personal income	1998 Amount	1998 As a percentage of total personal income
Leon	509,985	10.1	541,809	10.2	569,319	10.0
Levy	129,860	26.6	137,901	26.0	144,511	25.8
Liberty	23,269	24.8	24,340	24.3	21,065	20.7
Madison	70,016	26.8	74,945	27.3	77,953	27.5
Manatee	1,029,971	16.2	1,075,929	15.6	1,102,844	15.1
Marion	1,076,966	23.8	1,153,191	23.8	1,201,201	23.1
Martin	582,643	14.1	608,263	13.8	630,848	13.6
Miami-Dade	8,420,910	17.9	8,721,296	17.9	8,987,182	17.5
Monroe	250,699	10.7	262,964	10.6	266,677	10.1
Nassau	152,427	12.3	161,594	12.0	169,301	11.7
Okaloosa	466,754	12.8	504,445	12.8	524,833	12.6
Okeechobee	141,276	26.9	148,889	26.2	153,494	25.6
Orange	2,318,406	12.9	2,444,873	12.6	2,510,837	11.9
Osceola	428,320	17.9	457,593	17.7	473,841	16.9
Palm Beach	4,690,522	12.4	4,947,633	12.7	5,083,486	12.3
Pasco	1,683,588	26.8	1,764,254	25.8	1,788,763	24.2
Pinellas	4,198,112	17.8	4,342,577	17.3	4,358,873	16.2
Polk	1,719,271	19.1	1,813,381	19.2	1,862,358	18.2
Putnam	302,482	27.0	317,555	27.2	324,534	26.5
St. Johns	382,330	11.8	410,341	11.1	424,038	10.1
St. Lucie	822,147	24.2	897,195	24.7	915,860	23.9
Santa Rosa	286,600	13.3	312,157	13.1	332,419	13.0
Sarasota	1,649,185	16.4	1,735,369	16.1	1,767,702	15.7
Seminole	859,311	10.3	924,288	10.1	960,207	9.6
Sumter	181,419	30.6	190,529	29.4	196,493	28.6
Suwannee	136,786	24.9	147,039	25.3	153,301	24.9
Taylor	76,591	25.0	79,318	24.8	83,073	24.9
Union	26,182	19.2	27,570	18.7	29,148	19.0
Volusia	1,827,530	22.0	1,929,784	21.9	1,985,607	21.5
Wakulla	54,857	15.2	58,781	14.4	61,357	13.6
Walton	121,577	22.5	131,090	22.3	138,286	22.2
Washington	84,152	28.8	90,423	28.8	93,721	28.3

A/ Revised.
1/ In millions of dollars.
Note: The reclassification of government employee retirement plans covering federal civilian, military, and state and local government employees as "other labor income" has resulted in an increase in personal income. See the Appendix for discussion.

Source: U.S., Department of Commerce, Bureau of Economic Analysis, Regional Economic Information System, CD-ROM, June 2000.

University of Florida   **Bureau of Economic and Business Research**

Table 5.41. MILITARY RETIREES: PERSONS RECEIVING MILITARY RETIREMENT INCOME AND AMOUNT OF MONTHLY PAYMENT IN FLORIDA, SEPTEMBER 30, 1998 AND 1999

Branch and type of service	Total 1/		Paid by Department of Defense		Monthly payment 2/($1,000)	
	1998	1999	1998	1999	1998	1999
Total	179,506	178,570	162,436	164,308	257,656	263,126
Army	44,677	44,392	39,212	39,623	60,562	61,726
Navy	59,213	58,862	53,855	54,795	83,053	85,265
Marine Corps	7,874	7,851	6,660	6,784	11,297	11,687
Air Force	67,742	67,465	62,709	63,106	102,745	104,448
Coast Guard	3,945	(NA)	A/ 3,746	(NA)	6,354	(NA)
Officers	54,892	54,128	52,870	52,960	127,671	129,591
Nondisabled and						
reserve	50,640	50,225	49,166	49,417	119,918	122,133
Disabled	4,252	3,903	3,704	3,543	7,753	7,458
Enlisted	124,614	124,442	109,566	111,348	129,985	133,535
Nondisabled and						
reserve	110,550	111,110	102,778	104,843	125,033	128,737
Disabled	14,064	13,332	6,788	6,505	4,952	4,798

(NA) Not available.

A/ Paid by the Department of Transportation.

1/ Includes retirees whose monthly payment is zero or less after survivor benefit deductions and/or other offsets such as Veterans Administration payments, dual compensation, pay cap limitations from civil service employment, and refusal of retired pay.

2/ Monthly payment prior to deductions for withholding taxes and allotments, but after deductions for survivor benefits, waivers to obtain benefits from the Veterans Administration, dual compensation, and other adjustments.

Table 5.42. MILITARY RETIREES: SURVIVING FAMILIES RECEIVING RETIREMENT PAYMENTS AND AMOUNT OF MONTHLY PAYMENT IN FLORIDA, SEPTEMBER 30, 1997, 1998, AND 1999

Branch of service	Total			Monthly payment received (dollars)		
	1997	1998	1999	1997	1998	1999
Total	22,627	23,668	24,463	15,160,105	16,065,028	16,571,482
Army	7,927	8,189	8,411	5,413,257	5,656,975	5,793,501
Navy	6,656	6,985	7,252	4,130,160	4,397,552	4,570,898
Marine Corps	741	781	809	528,855	558,067	576,329
Air Force	7,303	7,713	7,991	5,087,833	5,452,434	5,630,754

Note: Data are for families receiving payments under the Retired Servicemen's Family Protection Plan or the Survivor Benefit Plan.

Source for Tables 5.41 and 5.42: U.S., Department of Defense, Office of the Actuary, *DoD Statistical Report on the Military Retirement System, Fiscal 1999,* and previous editions.

University of Florida   **Bureau of Economic and Business Research**

Table 5.46. POVERTY THRESHOLDS: AVERAGE POVERTY THRESHOLDS FOR A FAMILY
OF FOUR AND THE ANNUAL CONSUMER PRICE INDEX IN THE UNITED STATES
1986 THROUGH 1999

Year	Average threshold (dollars)	Consumer Price Index (1982-84=100)	Year	Average threshold (dollars)	Consumer Price Index (1982-84=100)
1986	11,203	109.6	1993	14,763	144.5
1987	11,611	113.6	1994	15,141	148.2
1988	12,092	118.3	1995	15,569	152.4
1989	12,674	124.0	1996	16,036	156.9
1990	13,359	130.7	1997	16,400	160.5
1991	13,924	136.2	1998	16,813	163.0
1992	14,335	140.3	1999 A/	17,028	166.6

A/ Preliminary.
Note: See Glossary under Poverty status for definition of poverty thresholds.

Source: U.S., Department of Commerce, Bureau of the Census, *Statistical Abstract of the United States,*
1995, previous editions, and Internet site <http://www.census.gov/hhes/poverty/threshld/> (accessed
12 June 2000), and U.S., Department of Commerce, Bureau of Labor Statistics, Internet site <http://
stats.bls.gov/top20.html> (accessed 12 June 2000).

Table 5.47. POVERTY THRESHOLDS: POVERTY LEVEL BASED ON MONEY INCOME BY SIZE
OF FAMILY IN THE UNITED STATES, 1996 THROUGH 1999

(in dollars)

Size of family unit	1996	1997	1998	1999 A/
1 person (unrelated individual)	7,995	8,183	8,316	8,500
Under 65 years	8,163	8,350	8,480	8,667
65 years and over	7,525	7,698	7,818	7,991
2 persons	10,233	10,473	10,634	10,869
Householder under 65 years	10,564	10,805	10,972	11,214
Householder 65 years and over	9,491	9,712	9,862	10,080
3 persons	12,516	12,802	13,003	13,290
4 persons	16,036	16,400	16,660	17,028
5 persons	18,952	19,380	19,680	20,115
6 persons	21,389	21,886	22,228	22,719
7 persons	24,268	24,802	25,257	25,815
8 persons	27,091	27,593	28,166	28,788
9 persons or more	31,971	32,566	33,339	34,075

A/ Preliminary.
Note: See Glossary under Poverty status for definition of poverty thresholds. Some data may be
revised.

Source: U.S., Department of Commerce, Bureau of the Census, Internet site <http://www.census.gov/
hhes/poverty/threshld/> (accessed 12 June 2000).

Table 5.48. INCOME AND POVERTY ESTIMATES: MEDIAN HOUSEHOLD INCOME
POOR PERSONS AND CHILDREN LIVING IN POVERTY IN THE STATE
AND COUNTIES OF FLORIDA, 1995

County	Median household income (dollars)	Poor persons		Persons under age 18 in poverty		Related children living in poverty 1/	
		Total	Per-centage	Total	Per-centage	Total	Per-centage
Florida	29,998	2,183,686	15.2	837,705	24.1	522,558	21.3
Alachua	27,860	36,242	19.2	11,930	24.9	7,554	22.4
Baker	31,198	3,415	18.1	1,602	23.4	1,055	20.7
Bay	29,600	22,048	15.3	9,532	23.4	6,477	22.2
Bradford	28,225	4,578	22.2	1,790	29.1	1,294	28.3
Brevard	34,729	51,979	11.4	19,351	17.7	12,305	16.0
Broward	33,895	177,365	12.2	64,110	19.8	38,789	17.3
Calhoun	24,013	2,564	22.9	962	27.6	691	27.0
Charlotte	30,650	12,678	9.7	3,926	17.4	2,591	15.9
Citrus	25,402	16,934	15.3	5,686	26.8	3,708	23.9
Clay	41,161	10,168	7.8	4,576	11.1	2,833	9.2
Collier	38,303	22,759	12.0	9,058	21.4	5,533	18.9
Columbia	28,359	10,203	20.4	4,591	30.1	3,116	28.0
De Soto	23,364	6,143	24.8	2,404	35.0	1,551	31.6
Dixie	20,367	3,060	25.7	1,186	35.9	834	35.2
Duval	33,810	105,120	14.5	46,897	22.6	28,813	20.0
Escambia	29,527	51,684	19.0	23,193	30.1	14,853	27.0
Flagler	34,891	4,595	10.4	1,657	17.9	1,086	16.0
Franklin	23,586	2,064	20.8	785	30.5	539	28.5
Gadsden	23,482	12,142	28.2	5,492	38.5	3,718	34.9
Gilchrist	26,825	2,153	18.1	829	24.3	558	22.5
Glades	25,830	1,543	17.2	626	26.4	441	25.4
Gulf	28,458	2,295	18.5	885	26.0	633	24.7
Hamilton	22,719	2,845	25.8	1,276	33.7	871	30.7
Hardee	23,008	5,991	29.1	2,414	36.3	1,510	31.6
Hendry	26,940	7,337	23.9	3,172	30.4	1,961	26.6
Hernando	27,532	17,597	14.3	6,058	24.4	4,076	22.5
Highlands	24,403	12,794	16.8	4,510	28.7	2,820	24.7
Hillsborough	32,650	147,856	16.5	60,164	25.3	36,894	22.1
Holmes	22,470	4,389	25.9	1,747	36.3	1,154	31.8
Indian River	33,667	10,701	11.0	3,669	17.9	2,246	15.3
Jackson	24,661	8,521	21.0	3,215	28.1	2,152	24.7
Jefferson	26,515	2,777	22.3	1,222	31.2	821	27.7
Lafayette	24,505	1,301	24.7	500	30.9	368	30.3
Lake	28,327	25,539	13.5	9,257	22.5	5,861	19.8
Lee	31,904	44,205	11.6	16,266	19.8	9,982	17.4
Leon	35,111	29,722	14.3	10,185	18.9	6,435	16.6

See footnotes at end of table.

Continued . . .

University of Florida   **Bureau of Economic and Business Research**

Table 5.48. INCOME AND POVERTY ESTIMATES: MEDIAN HOUSEHOLD INCOME POOR PERSONS AND CHILDREN LIVING IN POVERTY IN THE STATE AND COUNTIES OF FLORIDA, 1995 (Continued)

County	Median household income (dollars)	Poor persons Total	Poor persons Per-centage	Persons under age 18 in poverty Total	Persons under age 18 in poverty Per-centage	Related children living in poverty 1/ Total	Related children living in poverty 1/ Per-centage
Levy	23,779	6,455	20.7	2,546	30.6	1,731	28.0
Liberty	26,780	983	19.0	354	21.8	249	20.3
Madison	23,323	3,726	23.2	1,624	32.0	1,109	30.2
Manatee	31,416	28,393	12.1	9,881	20.0	6,248	18.3
Marion	26,950	39,957	17.3	16,069	28.4	10,308	25.5
Martin	36,470	11,228	10.0	3,827	17.3	2,350	15.1
Miami-Dade	33,375	480,990	23.6	185,949	36.0	114,998	32.2
Monroe	28,915	9,871	12.0	3,051	19.5	1,997	19.2
Nassau	37,813	5,726	10.9	2,458	16.0	1,555	13.9
Okaloosa	33,467	17,465	10.7	7,776	16.3	4,882	14.4
Okeechobee	24,231	6,861	21.5	2,906	30.9	1,904	29.2
Orange	34,558	99,568	13.2	40,216	20.0	24,235	17.5
Osceola	30,946	18,236	13.3	7,271	19.2	4,500	16.8
Palm Beach	35,833	118,676	11.9	42,082	19.5	24,742	16.7
Pasco	26,232	44,456	14.2	14,415	23.5	9,028	20.7
Pinellas	30,088	111,178	12.9	37,835	22.3	22,953	19.1
Polk	29,393	73,866	16.8	30,260	25.8	18,547	22.2
Putnam	24,590	16,846	24.2	7,212	37.2	4,830	34.2
St. Johns	39,519	11,411	10.6	4,317	16.6	2,855	15.3
St. Lucie	30,392	27,174	15.4	11,187	24.9	7,181	22.9
Santa Rosa	36,537	13,410	12.2	5,989	18.3	3,991	17.0
Sarasota	34,448	27,289	9.2	8,326	16.1	5,111	13.9
Seminole	41,428	33,444	9.9	13,175	14.1	8,364	12.3
Sumter	24,024	7,790	22.4	3,131	35.7	2,192	33.9
Suwannee	25,175	6,127	19.1	2,605	28.4	1,832	25.8
Taylor	25,912	3,773	21.2	1,707	31.4	1,196	30.4
Union	27,882	1,670	19.4	668	21.5	481	20.8
Volusia	28,253	60,255	14.8	20,537	23.3	13,087	20.8
Wakulla	33,085	2,513	13.9	1,124	20.4	755	17.9
Walton	26,599	6,903	19.4	2,784	30.1	2,029	29.7
Washington	24,177	4,138	22.4	1,702	33.0	1,195	31.3

1/ Related children aged 5 to 17 living in families in poverty.
Note: Released in February 1999, these estimates are based on a model which combines population, federal income tax returns, food stamp participation, and the 1990 decennial census.

Source: U.S., Department of Commerce, Bureau of the Census, Internet site <http://www.census.gov/hhes/www/saipe/estimatetoc.html> (accessed 13 June 2000).

University of Florida   **Bureau of Economic and Business Research**

LABOR FORCE, EMPLOYMENT, AND EARNINGS

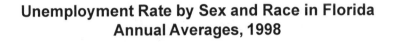

Unemployment Rate by Sex and Race in Florida
Annual Averages, 1998

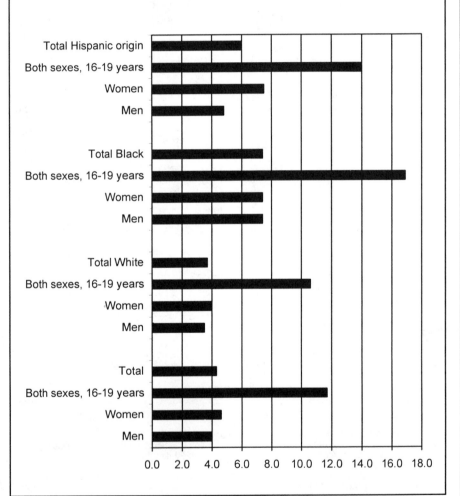

Source: Table 6.09

SECTION 6.00
LABOR FORCE, EMPLOYMENT, AND EARNINGS

TABLES LISTED BY MAJOR HEADINGS

University of Florida   **Bureau of Economic and Business Research**

Table 6.01. NONAGRICULTURAL EMPLOYMENT: EMPLOYMENT BY INDUSTRIAL CLASSIFICATION IN FLORIDA, 1961 THROUGH 1999

(in thousands)

Year	Total	Min-ing	Con-struc-tion	Manu-factur-ing	Trans-porta-tion and public utili-ties 1/	Whole-sale and retail trade	Fi-nance insur-ance and real estate	Serv-ices	Gov-ern-ment
1961	1,333.9	8.3	112.4	211.8	99.8	350.9	84.6	233.8	232.3
1962	1,387.8	8.2	112.7	223.1	99.4	365.0	87.4	244.6	247.4
1963	1,447.4	8.5	120.2	229.3	100.7	375.1	90.8	260.3	262.5
1964	1,526.5	9.2	130.1	237.9	106.0	395.0	93.7	275.9	278.7
1965	1,619.1	9.6	138.8	252.6	109.9	417.7	97.4	291.9	301.2
1966	1,726.8	9.7	137.1	276.1	116.8	443.1	101.7	316.1	326.2
1967	1,816.4	8.9	131.7	293.8	127.1	466.3	106.2	340.1	342.3
1968	1,932.3	8.4	143.6	311.4	135.1	491.5	112.6	367.9	361.8
1969	2,069.9	7.8	169.2	329.2	145.4	521.3	123.0	396.1	377.9
1970	2,152.1	8.3	175.7	322.5	154.5	545.8	131.3	416.2	397.8
1971	2,276.4	8.9	186.8	322.7	161.7	583.5	143.8	449.9	419.1
1972	2,513.1	8.8	230.1	351.3	173.5	643.5	162.4	505.6	437.9
1973	2,778.6	9.2	290.2	380.6	186.7	703.2	182.6	556.2	469.9
1974	2,863.8	9.9	276.1	375.9	189.8	727.6	192.5	581.5	510.5
1975	2,746.4	9.4	182.5	339.4	182.9	713.6	188.3	584.3	546.0
1976	2,784.3	8.8	166.7	354.0	181.4	730.8	191.3	608.5	542.8
1977	2,933.2	9.1	178.9	380.9	185.1	771.0	202.5	640.0	565.7
1978	3,180.6	9.5	209.5	415.5	194.2	836.9	219.3	693.9	601.8
1979	3,381.2	10.1	241.4	443.6	208.5	889.5	235.0	752.6	600.5
1980	3,576.2	11.0	263.9	456.4	220.8	939.8	254.2	814.6	618.8
1981	3,736.0	11.3	283.1	472.2	229.8	984.2	274.3	861.0	620.1
1982	3,761.9	9.6	256.6	456.7	229.9	995.0	276.6	905.0	632.5
1983	3,905.4	9.6	268.8	464.3	231.4	1,034.5	283.2	974.3	639.3
1984	4,204.2	10.2	318.3	501.9	241.1	1,118.0	299.5	1,065.7	649.5
1985	4,410.0	10.1	334.3	514.4	243.0	1,184.8	319.2	1,129.8	674.4
1986	4,599.4	9.3	339.5	517.2	247.4	1,238.8	339.7	1,205.6	701.9
1987	4,848.1	8.7	341.5	531.0	254.8	1,316.7	359.3	1,304.4	731.8
1988	5,066.6	9.1	346.3	539.6	260.8	1,378.8	365.1	1,393.9	773.0
1989	5,260.9	9.2	340.2	537.9	266.4	1,432.6	370.3	1,504.3	800.1
1990	5,387.4	8.9	323.2	522.1	278.4	1,444.4	370.7	1,593.0	846.7
1991	5,294.3	8.2	276.9	492.8	274.9	1,402.6	358.2	1,621.5	859.3
1992	5,358.7	7.1	266.5	482.9	275.8	1,411.7	351.9	1,692.7	870.1
1993	5,571.4	6.3	285.3	485.2	287.1	1,456.3	360.3	1,809.2	881.6
1994	5,799.4	6.8	296.0	484.0	296.3	1,507.2	375.6	1,922.9	910.6
1995	5,996.1	6.8	308.3	486.5	305.5	1,553.8	378.7	2,038.2	918.4
1996	6,183.3	6.8	325.4	489.7	314.5	1,607.4	394.0	2,117.2	928.4
1997	6,414.4	6.6	334.3	492.0	326.8	1,649.2	408.4	2,254.9	942.2
1998	6,636.5	6.7	348.8	493.5	337.4	1,684.0	430.7	2,380.6	954.8
1999	6,876.9	6.1	364.9	487.8	349.9	1,721.0	449.1	2,531.1	967.0

1/ Includes communications except U.S. Postal Service.
Note: Benchmark 1999, not seasonally adjusted. Data for some years have been revised.

Source: U.S., Department of Labor, Bureau of Labor Statistics, *Employment and Earnings,* May issues.

University of Florida   **Bureau of Economic and Business Research**

Table 6.02. EMPLOYMENT AND EARNINGS: NUMBER OF JOBS AND PROPRIETORS AND AVERAGE EARNINGS PER JOB IN THE UNITED STATES AND IN THE STATE AND COUNTIES OF FLORIDA, 1997 AND 1998

County	Total employment 1/			Average earnings per job (dollars)		
	Wage and salary jobs	Number of proprietors			Wage and salary	Per non-farm pro-prietor
		Non-farm 2/	Farm	Total		
			1997 A/			
United States	130,373,000	23,648,200	2,210,000	31,753	29,805	23,220
Florida	6,865,792	1,176,917	41,021	28,423	26,473	18,257
Alachua	116,784	15,348	1,350	25,651	23,435	12,097
Baker	5,547	1,130	197	22,370	19,566	14,728
Bay	68,539	13,273	80	25,747	23,140	16,128
Bradford	7,103	1,176	315	22,486	20,853	11,911
Brevard	188,225	36,315	602	28,675	28,191	10,312
Broward	653,933	114,741	268	29,247	28,186	15,043
Calhoun	3,635	801	156	21,333	19,427	15,149
Charlotte	36,192	11,991	269	21,324	21,639	11,343
Citrus	27,091	9,262	337	22,122	23,042	10,651
Clay	35,943	9,010	243	21,676	20,828	13,755
Collier	95,322	24,313	298	28,654	25,744	25,261
Columbia	20,089	1,931	700	24,855	22,155	19,607
De Soto	11,777	1,631	1,047	19,826	16,169	14,692
Dixie	2,767	953	203	20,402	19,830	13,786
Duval	464,812	67,997	340	32,088	29,466	17,982
Escambia	143,370	20,080	550	28,062	25,130	13,186
Flagler	12,169	894	119	23,527	20,815	14,257
Franklin	2,861	1,615	0	17,961	18,073	12,659
Gadsden	14,730	2,104	347	23,492	20,073	13,632
Gilchrist	2,576	859	458	21,662	19,446	14,830
Glades	1,472	431	252	20,036	18,198	17,292
Gulf	3,916	940	0	26,932	26,069	12,969
Hamilton	4,102	616	313	29,254	27,811	11,482
Hardee	8,895	1,631	1,424	19,986	17,565	11,667
Hendry	16,193	2,132	573	21,836	17,497	13,396
Hernando	28,642	7,928	492	21,558	21,482	10,908
Highlands	26,545	5,804	921	20,020	17,938	14,097
Hillsborough	578,651	66,327	3,084	30,003	27,451	20,379
Holmes	3,602	1,110	672	20,149	18,378	14,052
Indian River	43,313	8,985	535	24,899	23,174	19,465
Jackson	15,038	2,473	1,086	21,758	19,794	13,902
Jefferson	3,180	800	460	19,291	18,017	14,649
Lafayette	1,655	370	258	25,820	17,832	18,159

See footnotes at end of table.   Continued . . .

Table 6.02. EMPLOYMENT AND EARNINGS: NUMBER OF JOBS AND PROPRIETORS AND
AVERAGE EARNINGS PER JOB IN THE UNITED STATES AND IN THE STATE
AND COUNTIES OF FLORIDA, 1997 AND 1998 (Continued)

County	Total employment 1/ Wage and salary jobs	Number of proprietors Non-farm 2/	Farm	Average earnings per job (dollars) Total	Wage and salary	Per non-farm pro-prietor
			1997 A/ (Continued)			
Lake	63,001	13,707	1,571	22,310	20,830	16,099
Lee	159,198	37,949	623	25,495	24,012	17,715
Leon	144,195	18,815	292	27,614	25,172	13,584
Levy	8,007	2,426	673	20,274	18,543	12,151
Liberty	1,830	340	58	23,685	21,637	14,194
Madison	5,634	970	591	20,363	18,671	12,196
Manatee	126,320	21,023	808	23,765	21,070	21,697
Marion	82,909	18,304	1,895	23,644	22,175	15,651
Miami-Dade	1,021,127	158,480	1,427	31,364	29,019	21,449
Martin	49,777	11,243	313	25,640	24,529	15,793
Monroe	40,110	11,003	0	23,878	22,620	15,552
Nassau	16,445	3,964	273	26,865	25,386	15,897
Okaloosa	89,937	15,234	429	27,398	23,905	14,278
Okeechobee	10,712	2,304	542	22,534	19,664	15,156
Orange	581,713	64,095	884	30,226	27,392	24,583
Osceola	50,524	5,974	595	22,928	20,619	18,528
Palm Beach	472,243	93,734	727	32,556	29,357	29,450
Pasco	77,814	16,792	1,095	22,316	21,406	12,842
Pinellas	428,768	81,744	162	27,885	26,974	14,936
Polk	182,523	31,974	3,188	27,217	24,900	21,539
Putnam	19,566	2,009	446	24,741	22,515	12,378
St. Johns	38,383	8,423	201	24,283	22,922	15,804
St. Lucie	53,028	12,376	672	23,651	23,061	11,964
Santa Rosa	27,490	8,501	514	23,477	21,906	15,307
Sarasota	135,737	35,589	373	25,472	25,086	15,326
Seminole	132,754	30,639	344	26,186	26,032	12,812
Sumter	8,430	2,253	824	23,238	22,383	13,909
Suwannee	9,493	3,388	1,025	21,835	18,888	16,016
Taylor	7,123	1,195	154	25,296	23,926	13,618
Union	4,322	418	260	25,797	22,755	17,342
Volusia	147,493	21,140	1,047	23,960	21,934	16,907
Wakulla	3,854	1,705	105	21,850	21,099	14,862
Walton	10,454	2,895	564	20,534	19,624	14,376
Washington	6,209	1,340	397	21,263	20,518	11,999

See footnotes at end of table.   Continued . . .

University of Florida   **Bureau of Economic and Business Research**

Table 6.02. EMPLOYMENT AND EARNINGS: NUMBER OF JOBS AND PROPRIETORS AND
AVERAGE EARNINGS PER JOB IN THE UNITED STATES AND IN THE STATE
AND COUNTIES OF FLORIDA, 1997 AND 1998 (Continued)

County	Total employment 1/			Average earnings per job (dollars)		
	Wage and salary jobs	Number of proprietors			Wage and salary	Per non-farm pro-prietor
		Non-farm 2/	Farm	Total		
			1998			
United States	133,681,000	24,270,700	2,247,000	33,097	31,299	23,940
Florida	7,101,414	1,205,583	41,691	29,750	27,863	18,913
Alachua	120,524	15,716	1,372	26,892	24,719	12,352
Baker	5,707	1,160	200	23,542	20,707	15,316
Bay	69,212	13,604	81	26,705	24,387	16,692
Bradford	6,820	1,207	320	24,288	22,838	12,370
Brevard	191,574	37,206	612	29,601	29,268	10,682
Broward	675,558	117,490	272	30,536	29,579	15,608
Calhoun	3,862	819	159	21,277	19,673	15,869
Charlotte	37,619	12,294	273	22,109	22,504	11,708
Citrus	28,067	9,492	343	22,497	23,438	11,050
Clay	38,368	9,231	247	22,482	21,646	14,176
Collier	102,240	24,912	303	29,365	26,261	26,421
Columbia	20,317	1,978	711	25,993	23,362	20,227
De Soto	11,642	1,671	1,064	21,834	17,521	15,302
Dixie	2,828	979	207	21,461	21,015	14,430
Duval	477,069	69,650	346	33,743	31,294	18,563
Escambia	145,543	20,570	559	28,852	26,106	13,718
Flagler	12,618	918	121	24,236	21,579	14,792
Franklin	2,916	1,656	0	18,833	19,133	13,159
Gadsden	14,616	2,157	352	25,305	21,941	14,154
Gilchrist	2,592	879	466	22,455	19,970	15,545
Glades	1,537	441	256	21,714	18,828	17,617
Gulf	3,725	963	0	25,893	25,090	13,207
Hamilton	4,079	631	318	29,852	29,027	11,758
Hardee	8,734	1,672	1,447	21,773	18,855	12,068
Hendry	16,177	2,185	583	24,276	18,699	13,879
Hernando	29,677	8,124	500	22,211	22,177	11,333
Highlands	26,082	5,949	936	21,195	18,848	14,493
Hillsborough	610,402	67,930	3,134	31,538	29,034	20,934
Holmes	3,592	1,136	683	20,968	19,440	14,611
Indian River	45,655	9,205	544	25,622	23,789	20,263
Jackson	15,062	2,534	1,103	22,088	20,574	14,352
Jefferson	3,103	818	467	20,068	19,236	15,215
Lafayette	1,662	378	262	27,497	19,064	18,950
Lake	66,247	14,048	1,597	23,322	21,878	16,670

See footnotes at end of table. Continued . . .

Table 6.02. EMPLOYMENT AND EARNINGS: NUMBER OF JOBS AND PROPRIETORS AND
AVERAGE EARNINGS PER JOB IN THE UNITED STATES AND IN THE STATE
AND COUNTIES OF FLORIDA, 1997 AND 1998 (Continued)

| County | Total employment 1/ | | | Average earnings per job (dollars) | | |
| | Wage and salary jobs | Number of proprietors | | | Wage and salary | Per non-farm pro-prietor |
		Non-farm 2/	Farm	Total		
			1998 (Continued)			
Lee	166,290	38,887	633	26,544	25,106	18,450
Leon	146,126	19,273	297	29,286	26,934	14,013
Levy	7,983	2,488	684	21,093	19,306	12,560
Liberty	1,727	348	59	25,162	23,290	14,649
Madison	5,641	993	601	20,520	19,241	12,828
Manatee	124,872	21,533	822	25,892	23,203	22,482
Marion	86,242	18,764	1,926	24,729	23,277	16,175
Martin	52,152	11,514	318	27,310	26,196	16,353
Miami-Dade	1,041,256	162,290	1,450	32,749	30,458	22,166
Monroe	41,190	11,272	0	25,164	24,039	16,119
Nassau	16,926	4,063	277	27,422	25,962	16,409
Okaloosa	91,094	15,614	436	28,551	25,169	14,881
Okeechobee	10,570	2,363	551	23,970	20,729	15,655
Orange	619,590	65,659	899	31,717	28,954	25,158
Osceola	52,355	6,125	605	24,011	21,638	19,355
Palm Beach	492,855	96,012	739	34,512	31,224	30,780
Pasco	79,450	17,211	1,113	23,122	22,300	13,255
Pinellas	446,194	83,711	165	28,975	28,137	15,581
Polk	189,793	32,756	3,237	28,339	26,024	22,165
Putnam	20,086	2,059	453	25,307	23,111	12,744
St. Johns	40,448	8,629	205	25,976	24,728	16,366
St. Lucie	54,335	12,684	683	24,174	23,464	12,361
Santa Rosa	29,206	8,707	523	24,322	22,913	15,836
Sarasota	139,814	36,461	379	26,554	26,282	15,948
Seminole	138,973	31,373	349	27,395	27,358	13,318
Sumter	8,652	2,310	838	24,231	23,529	14,432
Suwannee	10,032	3,469	1,042	22,610	19,689	16,592
Taylor	7,083	1,225	156	26,315	25,053	14,016
Union	4,036	428	265	27,039	24,020	18,203
Volusia	149,768	21,669	1,064	24,652	22,664	17,592
Wakulla	4,167	1,748	107	24,503	24,151	15,367
Walton	10,906	2,968	573	21,186	20,409	14,806
Washington	6,176	1,374	404	22,907	22,529	12,482

A/ Revised.
1/ Full- and part-time jobs.
2/ Includes limited partners.

Source: U.S., Department of Commerce, Bureau of Economic Analysis, Regional Economic Information System, CD-ROM, June 2000.

Table 6.03. EMPLOYMENT: AVERAGE MONTHLY PRIVATE EMPLOYMENT COVERED BY UNEMPLOYMENT COMPENSATION LAW BY INDUSTRY IN FLORIDA, 1998 AND 1999

SIC code	Industry	1998	1999
01-99	All industries	5,668,631	5,883,883
01-09	Agriculture, forestry, and fishing	155,269	154,803
01	Agricultural production--crops	58,561	59,464
02	Agricultural production--livestock and animal specialties	6,483	6,463
07	Agricultural services	88,140	86,488
08	Forestry	1,317	1,573
09	Fishing, hunting, and trapping	768	815
10-14	Mining	6,728	6,168
12	Coal mining	13	22
13	Oil and gas extraction	363	336
14	Nonmetallic minerals, except fuels	6,181	5,647
15-17	Construction	347,899	365,128
15	Building--general contractors and builders	75,610	80,017
16	Heavy construction other than building construction--contractors	44,878	47,773
17	Special trade contractors	227,412	237,337
20-39	Manufacturing	492,153	488,042
20	Food and kindred products	40,977	40,578
21	Tobacco products	1,929	1,938
22	Textile mill products	4,292	3,750
23	Apparel and other finished products made from fabrics and similar materials	22,298	20,052
24	Lumber and wood products, except furniture	22,139	23,006
25	Furniture and fixtures	11,940	11,850
26	Paper and allied products	14,090	13,377
27	Printing, publishing, and allied industries	65,316	64,962
28	Chemicals and allied products	21,003	22,030
29	Petroleum refining and related industries	2,293	2,305
30	Rubber and miscellaneous plastics products	20,589	20,355
31	Leather and leather products	2,606	2,166
32	Stone, clay, glass, and concrete products	23,568	24,186
33	Primary metal industries	6,860	6,520
34	Fabricated metal products, except machinery and transportation equipment	32,998	34,377
35	Industrial and commercial machinery and computer equipment	36,796	36,459
36	Electronic and other electrical equipment and components, except computer equipment	61,647	59,542
37	Transportation equipment	53,236	53,840
38	Measuring, analyzing, and controlling instruments; photographic, medical, and optical goods; watches and clocks	37,622	36,478
39	Miscellaneous manufacturing industries	9,955	10,270
40-49	Transportation, communications, and public utilities	329,013	342,178
40	Railroad transportation	20	93
41	Passenger transportation	16,029	16,035
42	Motor freight transportation and warehousing	63,672	66,203
44	Water transportation	22,783	22,069
45	Transportation by air	75,161	76,627
46	Pipelines, except natural gas	81	57
47	Transportation services	34,044	34,634
48	Telecommunications	82,836	92,008
49	Electric, gas, and sanitary services	34,389	34,452

See footnotes at end of table.   Continued . . .

Table 6.03. EMPLOYMENT: AVERAGE MONTHLY PRIVATE EMPLOYMENT COVERED BY UNEMPLOYMENT COMPENSATION LAW BY INDUSTRY IN FLORIDA, 1998 AND 1999 (Continued)

SIC code	Industry	1998	1999
50-51	Wholesale trade	357,051	364,383
50	Wholesale trade--durable goods	213,535	217,003
51	Wholesale trade--nondurable goods	143,516	147,380
52-59	Retail trade	1,322,476	1,348,272
52	Building materials, hardware, garden supply, and mobile home dealers	53,043	55,994
53	General merchandise stores	151,659	155,547
54	Food stores	251,371	252,974
55	Automotive dealers and gasoline service stations	128,443	130,463
56	Apparel and accessory stores	71,841	73,867
57	Furniture and home furnishings stores	65,320	66,771
58	Eating and drinking places	443,972	450,993
59	Miscellaneous retail	156,826	161,663
60-67	Finance, insurance, and real estate	422,317	439,312
60	Depository institutions	99,590	100,863
61	Nondeposit credit institutions	50,871	55,306
62	Security and commodity brokers, dealers, exchanges, and services	30,536	30,582
63	Insurance carriers	70,566	74,676
64	Insurance agents, brokers, and service	48,371	48,547
65	Real estate	112,526	119,544
67	Holding and other investment offices	9,856	9,796
70-89	Services	2,207,353	2,348,188
70	Hotels, rooming houses, camps, and other lodging places	150,171	152,559
72	Personal services	70,263	71,620
73	Business services	643,480	753,355
75	Automotive repair services, and parking	69,941	71,016
76	Miscellaneous repair services	25,199	25,306
78	Motion pictures	23,385	25,260
79	Amusement and recreation services	144,331	147,322
80	Health services	576,228	576,613
81	Legal services	66,310	67,538
82	Educational services	58,593	62,655
83	Social services	119,292	121,302
84	Museums, art galleries, botanical and zoological gardens	3,673	3,859
86	Membership organizations	52,850	53,962
87	Engineering, accounting, research, management and related services	184,267	197,508
88	Private households	17,028	15,866
89	Services, NEC	2,344	2,447
99	Nonclassifiable establishments	28,372	27,406

NEC Not elsewhere classified.
Note: Private employment. Data for 1998 are revised and data for 1999 are preliminary. Detail may not add to totals due to disclosure editing and/or rounding. See Tables 23.70, 23.71, 23.72, 23.73, and 23.74 for public employment data.

Source: State of Florida, Department of Labor and Employment Security, Bureau of Labor Market Information, "Employment and Wages" (ES-202), unpublished data.

University of Florida   **Bureau of Economic and Business Research**

Table 6.04. EMPLOYMENT AND PAYROLL: AVERAGE MONTHLY PRIVATE REPORTING UNITS
EMPLOYMENT, AND PAYROLL COVERED BY UNEMPLOYMENT COMPENSATION LAW
FOR ALL INDUSTRIES IN THE STATE AND COUNTIES OF FLORIDA
1998 AND 1999

County	Number of reporting units	Number of employees	Payroll ($1,000)	County	Number of reporting units	Number of employees	Payroll ($1,000)
			All industries, 1998 A/ (SIC codes 01-99)				
Florida	420,405	5,668,631	13,057,352	Lee	11,197	128,327	260,036
				Leon	6,884	83,236	174,764
Alachua	5,117	73,349	144,370	Levy	556	5,424	8,403
Baker	222	2,771	3,866	Liberty	85	821	1,577
Bay	3,799	50,221	93,933	Madison	323	3,898	5,606
Bradford	346	3,806	6,733	Manatee	5,621	101,083	194,544
Brevard	10,224	149,229	361,353	Marion	5,292	65,583	126,224
Broward	46,903	534,609	1,301,154	Martin	4,079	42,038	93,601
Calhoun	217	2,480	3,823	Miami-Dade	68,309	810,597	2,027,678
Charlotte	2,684	28,551	52,885	Monroe	3,517	30,915	57,423
Citrus	2,143	21,877	42,381	Nassau	1,088	12,572	25,248
Clay	2,426	29,873	51,426	Okaloosa	4,359	56,540	101,356
Collier	8,153	83,491	183,814	Okeechobee	726	8,381	13,159
Columbia	1,106	13,868	25,032	Orange	24,063	512,363	1,222,761
De Soto	521	6,093	9,508	Osceola	2,888	40,445	69,387
Dixie	181	1,524	2,577	Palm Beach	34,662	394,920	1,039,304
Duval	19,079	360,510	923,783	Pasco	5,690	60,812	109,938
Escambia	6,703	98,313	201,497	Pinellas	24,990	366,876	855,375
Flagler	876	9,403	17,031	Polk	9,258	150,816	329,981
Franklin	287	2,009	2,972	Putnam	1,121	14,085	26,679
Gadsden	599	8,061	14,767	St. Johns	2,974	31,353	63,031
Gilchrist	163	1,312	1,888	St. Lucie	3,543	39,916	77,384
Glades	101	788	1,375	Santa Rosa	1,919	19,729	34,742
Gulf	237	2,278	4,927	Sarasota	11,046	115,689	250,272
Hamilton	168	2,392	6,321	Seminole	9,230	113,456	259,129
Hardee	488	5,484	8,755	Sumter	501	5,089	8,540
Hendry	579	10,729	18,128	Suwannee	551	7,600	11,715
Hernando	2,139	22,064	39,436	Taylor	365	5,023	11,013
Highlands	1,688	21,310	30,961	Union	130	1,389	2,397
Hillsborough	25,343	485,051	1,162,413	Volusia	9,781	116,605	214,290
Holmes	232	1,969	2,797	Wakulla	276	2,530	5,262
Indian River	3,386	36,576	71,952	Walton	682	7,835	12,519
Jackson	735	7,986	12,375	Washington	308	3,533	5,668
Jefferson	228	1,835	2,733				
Lafayette	94	954	1,221	Multicounty 1/	13,224	176,455	456,569
Lake	4,008	51,934	93,594				

See footnotes at end of table.

Continued . . .

University of Florida   **Bureau of Economic and Business Research**

Table 6.04. EMPLOYMENT AND PAYROLL: AVERAGE MONTHLY PRIVATE REPORTING UNITS EMPLOYMENT, AND PAYROLL COVERED BY UNEMPLOYMENT COMPENSATION LAW FOR ALL INDUSTRIES IN THE STATE AND COUNTIES OF FLORIDA 1998 AND 1999 (Continued)

County	Number of reporting units	Number of employees	Payroll ($1,000)	County	Number of reporting units	Number of employees	Payroll ($1,000)
			All industries, 1999 B/ (SIC codes 01-99)				
Florida	432,090	5,883,883	13,922,969	Lee	11,654	132,076	279,462
				Leon	7,066	85,464	186,428
Alachua	5,103	75,414	150,702	Levy	585	5,536	8,810
Baker	238	2,898	4,000	Liberty	86	810	1,550
Bay	3,809	50,504	96,225	Madison	323	4,174	5,844
Bradford	359	3,963	7,051	Manatee	5,753	99,800	200,254
Brevard	10,414	150,784	371,412	Marion	5,383	67,123	131,716
Broward	48,369	542,397	1,374,135	Martin	4,166	43,744	96,252
Calhoun	220	2,118	4,027	Miami-Dade	70,070	819,904	2,127,805
Charlotte	2,810	30,163	56,750	Monroe	3,615	30,923	59,340
Citrus	2,223	22,784	45,307	Nassau	1,120	12,871	26,515
Clay	2,496	32,595	54,763	Okaloosa	4,309	56,962	103,741
Collier	8,509	86,862	199,148	Okeechobee	739	7,978	13,592
Columbia	1,100	13,561	25,375	Orange	24,667	533,439	1,318,527
De Soto	528	6,042	9,292	Osceola	2,992	41,296	74,267
Dixie	186	1,557	2,546	Palm Beach	35,706	406,688	1,101,771
Duval	19,358	366,939	942,253	Pasco	5,889	60,131	112,384
Escambia	6,544	100,615	207,877	Pinellas	25,165	375,977	919,573
Flagler	903	9,187	16,781	Polk	9,283	151,654	339,740
Franklin	291	2,075	3,103	Putnam	1,125	14,242	27,737
Gadsden	598	8,833	15,440	St. Johns	3,083	32,334	68,220
Gilchrist	172	1,238	1,817	St. Lucie	3,608	39,666	79,197
Glades	101	776	1,330	Santa Rosa	1,916	18,732	34,361
Gulf	227	1,951	3,684	Sarasota	11,329	135,492	288,674
Hamilton	171	2,394	6,256	Seminole	9,524	118,346	282,609
Hardee	499	5,422	9,062	Sumter	507	5,231	9,402
Hendry	575	10,474	18,196	Suwannee	556	7,423	11,532
Hernando	2,238	23,330	42,648	Taylor	378	5,118	11,142
Highlands	1,704	22,535	32,372	Union	135	1,237	2,216
Hillsborough	25,844	504,377	1,256,628	Volusia	9,927	118,389	225,540
Holmes	238	1,946	2,839	Wakulla	284	2,541	5,638
Indian River	3,420	36,595	76,873	Walton	742	8,465	13,776
Jackson	736	7,470	11,611	Washington	317	3,982	6,297
Jefferson	234	1,728	2,694				
Lafayette	106	1,090	1,433	Multicounty 1/	15,553	221,028	547,661
Lake	4,104	52,109	98,007	Out-of-state 2/	72	313	538

A/ Revised.
B/ Preliminary.
1/ Reporting units without a fixed location within the state or of unknown county location.
2/ Employment based in Florida, but working out of the state or country.
Note: Private employment. Detail may not add to totals due to disclosure editing and/or rounding.
See Tables 23.70, 23.71, 23.72, 23.73, and 23.74 for public employment data.

Source: State of Florida, Department of Labor and Employment Security, Bureau of Labor Market Information, "Employment and Wages" (ES-202), unpublished data.

Table 6.05. EMPLOYMENT: AVERAGE MONTHLY PRIVATE EMPLOYMENT COVERED BY UNEMPLOYMENT COMPENSATION LAW BY MAJOR INDUSTRY GROUP IN THE STATE AND COUNTIES OF FLORIDA, 1998 AND 1999

1998 A/

County	All industries (01-99)	Agriculture forestry and fishing (01-09)	Mining (10-14)	Construction (15-17)	Manufacturing (20-39)	Transportation communications and public utilities (40-49)	Wholesale trade (50-51)	Retail trade (52-59)	Finance insurance and real estate (60-67)	Services (70-89)	Other (99)
Florida	5,668,630	155,268	6,728	347,899	492,152	329,013	357,050	1,322,476	422,316	2,207,353	28,372
Alachua	73,348	1,321	39	4,480	5,377	2,286	2,216	20,976	5,006	31,458	185
Baker	2,770	306	(NA)	220	255	155	65	1,018	132	615	0
Bay	50,220	298	(NA)	4,434	3,952	2,535	2,341	15,761	3,455	17,329	111
Bradford	3,805	24	(NA)	198	651	168	300	1,243	117	1,090	11
Brevard	149,229	2,039	29	9,268	26,527	4,901	5,215	36,540	6,034	58,071	600
Broward	534,609	6,061	137	34,649	39,717	29,900	38,561	138,185	46,255	197,691	3,448
Calhoun	2,479	208	(NA)	235	233	144	163	582	81	830	0
Charlotte	28,550	596	36	2,394	1,004	926	658	9,486	1,596	11,764	87
Citrus	21,876	270	35	1,904	1,327	2,013	475	6,419	1,151	8,201	78
Clay	29,873	672	167	2,234	1,856	1,124	859	11,369	908	10,571	110
Collier	83,490	7,768	36	9,957	2,658	2,376	2,748	21,223	5,511	30,730	479
Columbia	13,867	173	(NA)	1,081	2,091	622	1,023	4,374	509	3,958	32
De Soto	6,093	2,973	13	210	192	93	237	1,130	172	1,048	20
Dixie	1,523	17	29	84	550	112	63	417	46	198	3
Duval	360,509	3,151	218	23,137	31,062	30,332	25,772	72,780	50,709	122,336	1,008
Escambia	98,313	815	52	8,152	8,255	6,208	5,409	26,414	5,066	37,602	335
Flagler	9,402	267	8	566	1,507	218	188	2,652	427	3,532	32
Franklin	2,009	25	13	100	144	114	155	702	181	559	12
Gadsden	8,061	1,837	186	458	1,718	221	328	1,784	210	1,312	3
Gilchrist	1,311	252	(NA)	38	172	24	69	281	31	440	1
Glades	788	259	28	50	1	72	29	147	22	177	0
Gulf	2,277	21	(NA)	85	579	228	57	459	133	709	2

See footnotes at end of table.

Continued . . .

Table 6.05. EMPLOYMENT: AVERAGE MONTHLY PRIVATE EMPLOYMENT COVERED BY UNEMPLOYMENT COMPENSATION LAW BY MAJOR INDUSTRY GROUP IN THE STATE AND COUNTIES OF FLORIDA, 1998 AND 1999 (Continued)

1998 A/ (Continued)

County	All industries (01-99)	Agriculture forestry and fishing (01-09)	Mining (10-14)	Construction (15-17)	Manufacturing (20-39)	Transportation communications and public utilities (40-49)	Wholesale trade (50-51)	Retail trade (52-59)	Finance insurance and real estate (60-67)	Services (70-89)	Other (99)
Hamilton	2,392	91	(NA)	89	1,379	115	29	351	29	294	11
Hardee	5,483	2,470	175	162	250	109	236	847	242	978	10
Hendry	10,729	5,423	25	266	1,048	310	350	1,797	244	1,247	14
Hernando	22,063	387	359	1,705	1,374	859	924	7,653	1,178	7,490	130
Highlands	21,310	6,276	35	960	1,223	624	565	4,752	674	6,104	93
Hillsborough	485,051	11,680	25	26,648	37,377	30,219	35,273	89,633	45,131	207,451	1,610
Holmes	1,968	14	(NA)	132	357	75	66	518	63	736	5
Indian River	36,576	3,884	8	2,724	2,629	807	1,314	10,186	2,017	12,809	194
Jackson	7,986	200	33	486	1,253	394	656	2,857	321	1,729	54
Jefferson	1,834	240	(NA)	121	167	84	72	512	130	501	2
Lafayette	953	336	8	38	199	20	72	125	35	112	12
Lake	51,934	2,888	374	4,751	4,628	2,074	1,752	13,285	4,103	17,860	213
Lee	128,326	3,534	155	13,229	6,961	7,341	5,329	38,432	8,658	44,247	438
Leon	83,236	1,004	47	5,499	3,098	3,715	3,569	24,242	5,811	36,047	200
Levy	5,424	508	106	730	392	296	190	1,835	222	1,125	17
Liberty	820	4	(NA)	164	247	70	(NA)	132	22	177	1
Madison	3,897	270	(NA)	60	1,181	132	110	939	67	1,128	6
Manatee	101,082	6,030	57	4,377	12,869	1,679	3,415	18,362	3,115	50,948	228
Marion	65,582	2,684	119	5,256	11,524	2,978	3,484	18,833	3,724	16,724	252
Martin	42,037	2,471	6	3,334	3,338	1,719	1,224	10,905	2,480	16,282	274
Miami-Dade	810,597	11,431	319	33,064	72,591	84,375	76,790	169,803	65,680	290,587	5,953
Monroe	30,914	425	8	2,109	601	1,747	756	10,923	1,508	12,594	239
Nassau	12,572	706	(NA)	838	2,140	493	291	3,690	405	3,972	34
Okaloosa	56,540	622	6	3,977	3,836	2,481	1,242	17,466	3,919	22,781	205

See footnotes at end of table.

Continued . . .

Table 6.05. EMPLOYMENT: AVERAGE MONTHLY PRIVATE EMPLOYMENT COVERED BY UNEMPLOYMENT COMPENSATION LAW BY MAJOR INDUSTRY GROUP IN THE STATE AND COUNTIES OF FLORIDA, 1998 AND 1999 (Continued)

1998 A/ (Continued)

County	All industries (01-99)	Agriculture forestry and fishing (01-09)	Mining (10-14)	Construction (15-17)	Manufacturing (20-39)	Transportation communications and public utilities (40-49)	Wholesale trade (50-51)	Retail trade (52-59)	Finance insurance and real estate (60-67)	Services (70-89)	Other (99)
Okeechobee	8,381	2,183	(NA)	432	171	294	476	2,239	252	2,304	25
Orange	512,363	8,659	79	26,753	36,840	32,912	31,710	96,234	32,796	244,919	1,457
Osceola	40,444	764	(NA)	2,252	1,687	733	1,862	14,681	2,446	15,842	172
Palm Beach	394,919	18,619	13	26,136	30,638	15,680	21,786	91,326	31,714	156,630	2,373
Pasco	60,812	2,457	41	4,959	3,726	2,274	1,966	19,054	2,838	23,244	250
Pinellas	366,876	3,119	7	19,792	46,171	14,020	20,665	78,989	29,057	153,424	1,628
Polk	150,815	9,034	3,138	9,680	20,576	8,438	8,343	40,072	8,061	43,102	366
Putnam	14,084	665	77	999	3,369	430	472	3,679	533	3,784	74
St. Johns	31,353	918	15	1,755	4,101	700	1,321	9,281	1,344	11,741	173
St. Lucie	39,916	5,225	27	2,751	2,602	2,581	1,900	10,104	2,256	12,286	179
Santa Rosa	19,728	377	117	2,488	2,163	1,014	480	5,522	768	6,686	108
Sarasota	115,689	2,060	32	8,576	7,994	3,396	4,597	31,480	8,396	48,667	486
Seminole	113,455	1,804	6	11,666	10,457	6,107	7,610	32,756	6,457	35,985	604
Sumter	5,088	278	107	341	852	369	360	1,582	169	1,008	18
Suwannee	7,599	434	9	496	2,000	395	335	1,933	270	1,717	5
Taylor	5,023	71	51	524	1,894	59	184	1,138	147	941	11
Union	1,388	69	8	52	251	302	15	208	23	455	1
Volusia	116,604	3,660	5	7,208	11,338	4,232	4,681	34,258	6,101	44,687	430
Wakulla	2,530	49	(NA)	267	629	95	76	696	150	554	11
Walton	7,835	135	22	448	1,048	478	168	2,343	488	2,664	36
Washington	3,532	51	1	298	887	337	69	1,009	73	788	15
Multicounty 1/	176,454	1,677	66	5,341	2,238	6,650	23,307	21,841	10,417	101,747	3,167

See footnotes at end of table.

Continued . . .

Table 6.05. EMPLOYMENT: AVERAGE MONTHLY PRIVATE EMPLOYMENT COVERED BY UNEMPLOYMENT COMPENSATION LAW BY MAJOR INDUSTRY GROUP IN THE STATE AND COUNTIES OF FLORIDA, 1998 AND 1999 (Continued)

1999 B/

County	All industries (01-99)	Agriculture forestry and fishing (01-09)	Mining (10-14)	Construction (15-17)	Manufacturing (20-39)	Transportation communications and public utilities (40-49)	Wholesale trade (50-51)	Retail trade (52-59)	Finance insurance and real estate (60-67)	Services (70-89)	Other (99)
Florida	5,883,883	154,802	6,168	365,127	488,041	342,177	364,382	1,348,272	439,312	2,348,188	27,405
Alachua	75,414	1,413	40	4,472	5,561	2,247	2,360	21,312	5,113	32,753	139
Baker	2,898	294	(NA)	232	271	148	54	1,092	139	663	1
Bay	50,503	322	3	4,447	3,665	2,445	2,413	16,100	3,377	17,621	106
Bradford	3,962	36	0	205	692	174	292	1,292	127	1,136	5
Brevard	150,783	2,085	22	9,865	25,651	5,240	5,882	37,600	6,120	57,883	431
Broward	542,397	6,018	146	36,077	37,875	30,968	39,968	137,252	47,621	203,015	3,453
Calhoun	2,117	217	(NA)	227	222	58	196	521	70	600	4
Charlotte	30,162	611	10	2,571	1,149	899	709	9,833	1,734	12,554	88
Citrus	22,783	298	39	2,094	1,480	2,021	418	6,572	1,197	8,571	89
Clay	32,595	642	168	2,231	1,833	1,129	777	11,505	920	13,275	112
Collier	86,861	7,861	35	10,652	2,847	2,278	2,723	21,993	5,801	32,286	383
Columbia	13,561	168	(NA)	1,121	2,026	568	727	4,583	405	3,935	24
De Soto	6,041	2,874	9	262	190	110	243	1,172	172	995	15
Dixie	1,556	20	21	79	554	112	51	425	46	243	1
Duval	366,938	3,239	225	23,626	30,620	30,782	25,895	75,371	51,726	124,552	897
Escambia	100,614	843	62	8,389	7,987	6,346	5,495	26,346	4,897	39,994	252
Flagler	9,187	256	9	623	1,337	176	128	2,696	428	3,507	23
Franklin	2,075	26	17	108	155	111	180	715	188	556	16
Gadsden	8,832	1,992	195	555	1,760	236	483	1,755	201	1,643	7
Gilchrist	1,237	238	(NA)	42	142	25	70	253	40	423	0
Glades	775	247	24	43	0	71	30	132	19	206	0
Gulf	1,950	13	(NA)	60	147	216	165	484	134	719	9
Hamilton	2,394	78	(NA)	137	1,289	120	61	366	35	305	1

See footnotes at end of table.

Continued . . .

Table 6.05. EMPLOYMENT: AVERAGE MONTHLY PRIVATE EMPLOYMENT COVERED BY UNEMPLOYMENT COMPENSATION LAW BY MAJOR INDUSTRY GROUP IN THE STATE AND COUNTIES OF FLORIDA, 1998 AND 1999 (Continued)

1999 B/ (Continued)

County	All industries (01-99)	Agriculture forestry and fishing (01-09)	Mining (10-14)	Construction (15-17)	Manufacturing (20-39)	Transportation communications and public utilities (40-49)	Wholesale trade (50-51)	Retail trade (52-59)	Finance insurance and real estate (60-67)	Services (70-89)	Other (99)
Hardee	5,421	2,250	197	180	241	118	254	882	243	1,027	26
Hendry	10,474	5,100	17	271	1,091	330	380	1,788	240	1,234	19
Hernando	23,329	440	331	1,818	1,342	903	904	8,811	1,210	7,458	107
Highlands	22,534	7,465	35	974	1,120	606	594	4,745	653	6,257	82
Hillsborough	504,376	11,984	28	27,338	37,154	31,881	34,791	91,051	46,524	222,169	1,451
Holmes	1,945	18	(NA)	178	334	61	68	507	50	724	2
Indian River	36,595	3,415	9	2,678	2,968	755	1,170	10,275	1,973	13,241	108
Jackson	7,469	212	35	544	819	399	507	2,800	328	1,786	34
Jefferson	1,728	224	(NA)	138	177	85	70	376	128	524	3
Lafayette	1,089	332	7	59	208	28	76	122	43	197	13
Lake	52,109	2,764	389	5,049	4,266	2,395	1,925	13,727	4,303	17,131	155
Lee	132,075	3,431	161	15,089	6,894	7,507	5,627	39,396	9,155	44,337	472
Leon	85,464	1,034	57	5,593	2,989	3,666	3,728	24,347	6,105	37,563	376
Levy	5,536	561	99	751	372	294	201	1,824	245	1,175	10
Liberty	809	4	(NA)	198	238	70	8	144	24	120	4
Madison	4,174	293	(NA)	67	1,141	159	91	985	75	1,352	5
Manatee	99,800	6,264	142	5,121	13,675	1,812	3,697	19,041	3,090	46,745	208
Marion	67,123	2,759	120	5,462	11,493	3,001	3,531	18,772	3,894	17,903	185
Martin	43,743	2,328	6	4,023	3,140	1,946	1,287	11,403	2,321	17,151	135
Miami-Dade	819,904	12,152	294	34,322	69,757	86,873	76,281	173,666	65,300	295,155	6,099
Monroe	30,922	373	1	2,355	574	1,628	774	10,726	1,595	12,725	169
Nassau	12,870	875	(NA)	855	2,015	547	316	3,521	399	4,291	48
Okaloosa	56,962	702	17	4,152	3,361	2,564	1,404	16,900	4,212	23,509	136
Okeechobee	7,978	1,714	(NA)	461	161	475	232	2,311	243	2,352	25
Orange	533,438	8,484	107	27,047	36,904	34,204	33,299	100,787	38,669	252,473	1,398
Osceola	41,296	824	(NA)	2,724	1,711	702	1,950	14,864	2,705	15,627	185

Continued . . .

See footnotes at end of table.

Table 6.05. EMPLOYMENT: AVERAGE MONTHLY PRIVATE EMPLOYMENT COVERED BY UNEMPLOYMENT COMPENSATION LAW BY MAJOR INDUSTRY GROUP IN THE STATE AND COUNTIES OF FLORIDA, 1998 AND 1999 (Continued)

1999 B/ (Continued)

County	All industries (01-99)	Agriculture forestry and fishing (01-09)	Mining (10-14)	Construction (15-17)	Manufacturing (20-39)	Transportation communications and public utilities (40-49)	Wholesale trade (50-51)	Retail trade (52-59)	Finance insurance and real estate (60-67)	Services (70-89)	Other (99)
Palm Beach	406,687	18,167	13	26,854	32,501	15,796	21,883	92,046	32,265	164,848	2,309
Pasco	60,131	2,354	43	5,321	3,442	2,278	1,847	19,032	3,155	22,383	274
Pinellas	375,977	3,324	7	20,235	47,260	15,879	20,944	79,308	30,386	157,266	1,363
Polk	151,654	7,914	2,505	9,804	20,324	8,777	8,335	40,848	8,078	44,693	373
Putnam	14,242	627	75	1,263	3,187	418	350	4,038	540	3,703	38
St. Johns	32,334	882	16	2,004	3,985	658	1,437	9,528	1,262	12,380	177
St. Lucie	39,665	4,741	22	2,938	2,684	2,454	2,009	10,149	2,352	12,153	160
Santa Rosa	18,731	396	115	2,402	1,649	1,060	447	5,332	832	6,420	75
Sarasota	135,492	2,057	13	9,331	8,139	3,543	4,067	31,560	8,581	67,625	573
Seminole	118,346	1,830	7	12,511	10,565	5,943	8,064	33,921	6,963	37,929	608
Sumter	5,230	294	104	440	849	343	393	1,540	196	1,053	13
Suwannee	7,422	394	9	336	2,035	339	288	1,982	290	1,734	12
Taylor	5,118	104	51	425	2,009	87	203	1,112	152	962	9
Union	1,236	74	6	72	232	350	13	188	23	265	11
Volusia	118,388	3,488	7	7,230	10,871	5,346	5,045	34,120	6,257	45,646	374
Wakulla	2,541	48	(NA)	263	586	159	70	712	172	504	23
Walton	8,465	155	22	500	903	383	192	2,850	552	2,881	22
Washington	3,981	51	1	436	988	391	63	1,112	90	830	14
Multicounty 1/	285,482	2,905	57	7,184	4,277	8,545	26,881	25,889	13,374	192,921	3,444
Out-of-state 2/	312	(NA)	(NA)	0	0	1	47	174	1	87	(NA)

(NA) Not available.
A/ Revised. B/ Preliminary. 1/ Reporting units without a fixed or known location within the state. 2/ Employment based in Florida, but working out of the state or country.

Note: Private employment. Detail may not add to totals due to disclosure editing and/or rounding. See Tables 23.70, 23.71, 23.72, 23.73, and 23.74 for public employment data.

Source: State of Florida, Department of Labor and Employment Security, Bureau of Labor Market Information, "Employment and Wages" (ES-202), unpublished data.

Table 6.06. EMPLOYMENT: AVERAGE MONTHLY EMPLOYMENT COVERED BY UNEMPLOYMENT COMPENSATION LAW IN THE STATE AND METROPOLITAN STATISTICAL AREAS (MSAS) OF FLORIDA, 1999

Metropolitan area	Total 1/	Private	Government Federal	Government State	Government Local
Florida	6,837,372	5,883,883	120,290	208,343	624,856
MSA, total	6,259,280	5,384,197	113,693	181,841	579,552
Daytona Beach	150,350	127,576	1,394	3,661	17,719
Flagler County	11,165	9,187	96	161	1,721
Volusia County	139,185	118,389	1,299	3,500	15,997
Ft. Lauderdale	623,864	542,397	7,255	7,220	66,992
Ft. Myers-Cape Coral	157,757	132,076	1,918	3,784	19,979
Ft. Pierce-Port St. Lucie	98,088	83,410	820	2,227	11,632
Martin County	48,848	43,744	291	853	3,961
St. Lucie County	49,241	39,666	529	1,375	7,671
Ft. Walton Beach	70,827	56,962	6,513	996	6,356
Gainesville	115,014	75,414	2,891	26,676	10,032
Jacksonville	509,007	444,739	17,926	9,246	37,096
Clay County	37,670	32,595	323	423	4,329
Duval County	417,007	366,939	16,583	7,184	26,301
Nassau County	16,062	12,871	599	266	2,327
St. Johns County	38,268	32,334	420	1,373	4,140
Lakeland-Winter Haven	178,043	151,654	1,430	4,523	20,436
Melbourne-Titusville-Palm Bay	175,909	150,784	5,467	2,275	17,384
Miami	956,752	819,904	18,379	18,229	100,240
Naples	96,370	86,862	629	843	8,036
Ocala	81,564	67,123	691	2,117	11,633
Orlando	833,772	745,191	9,624	14,444	64,513
Lake County	61,223	52,109	520	1,171	7,423
Orange County	590,847	533,439	7,343	11,759	38,307
Osceola County	48,835	41,296	272	630	6,638
Seminole County	132,866	118,346	1,489	884	12,146
Panama City	60,436	50,504	3,048	1,182	5,702
Pensacola	148,206	119,347	7,642	5,731	15,487
Escambia County	124,036	100,615	6,815	4,848	11,758
Santa Rosa County	24,170	18,732	827	883	3,728
Punta Gorda	35,405	30,163	281	700	4,262
Sarasota-Bradenton	258,472	235,293	2,051	2,641	18,487
Manatee County	110,994	99,800	1,160	983	9,051
Sarasota County	147,478	135,492	891	1,658	9,436
Tallahassee	153,493	94,297	1,813	44,678	12,705
Gadsden County	14,096	8,833	122	3,366	1,775
Leon County	139,396	85,464	1,691	41,312	10,929
Tampa-St. Petersburg-Clearwater	1,092,118	963,815	18,336	22,259	87,708
Hernando County	28,476	23,330	293	605	4,249
Hillsborough County	571,882	504,377	11,218	15,697	40,590
Pasco County	72,557	60,131	681	1,352	10,393
Pinellas County	419,203	375,977	6,144	4,605	32,476
West Palm Beach-Boca Raton	463,834	406,688	5,585	8,408	43,154

1/ Total private and public employment. Private industry data appear in various tables throughout the *Abstract*. See Section 23.00 for additional public employment tables.

Note: Data are preliminary. Detail may not add to totals due to disclosure editing and/or rounding.

Source: State of Florida, Department of Labor and Employment Security, Bureau of Labor Market Information, "Employment and Wages" (ES-202), unpublished data.

Table 6.09. LABOR FORCE PARTICIPATION: LABOR FORCE STATUS OF THE POPULATION 16 YEARS OLD AND OVER BY SEX AND RACE, AND HISPANIC ORIGIN IN FLORIDA AND THE UNITED STATES, ANNUAL AVERAGES 1998

Area and population group	Civilian noninstitutional population (1,000)	Civilian labor force Number (1,000)	Percentage of population	Employment Number (1,000)	Percentage of population	Unemployment Number (1,000)	Rate	Error range of rate 1/
Florida								
Total	11,610	7,228	62.3	6,918	59.6	310	4.3	4-4.6
Men	5,496	3,858	70.2	3,703	67.4	155	4.0	3.6-4.4
Women	6,114	3,370	55.1	3,215	52.6	155	4.6	4.2-5
Both sexes, 16-19 years	745	387	51.9	342	45.9	45	11.7	10-13.4
White	9,834	5,985	60.9	5,763	58.6	222	3.7	3.4-4
Men	4,688	3,254	69.4	3,140	67.0	114	3.5	3.1-3.9
Women	5,146	2,730	53.1	2,622	51.0	108	4.0	3.6-4.4
Both sexes, 16-19 years	580	324	55.9	290	50.0	34	10.6	8.8-12.4
Black	1,519	1,064	70.0	986	64.9	79	7.4	6.5-8.3
Men	676	497	73.5	460	68.0	37	7.4	6.1-8.7
Women	843	567	67.3	525	62.3	42	7.4	6.2-8.6
Both sexes, 16-19 years	147	57	38.8	47	32.0	10	16.9	12.2-21.6
Hispanic origin 2/	1,855	1,232	66.4	1,158	62.4	74	6.0	5.2-6.8
Men	908	709	78.1	675	74.3	34	4.8	3.9-5.7
Women	947	523	55.2	484	51.1	39	7.5	6.2-8.8
Both sexes, 16-19 years	123	62	50.4	54	43.9	9	14.0	9.4-18.6
United States								
Total	205,220	137,673	67.1	131,463	64.1	6,210	4.5	4.4-4.6
Men	98,758	73,959	74.9	70,693	71.6	3,266	4.4	4.3-4.5
Women	106,462	63,714	59.8	60,771	57.1	2,944	4.6	4.5-4.7
Both sexes, 16-19 years	15,644	8,256	52.8	7,051	45.1	1,205	14.6	14.1-15.1
White	171,478	115,415	67.3	110,931	64.7	4,484	3.9	3.8-4
Men	83,352	63,034	75.6	60,604	72.7	2,431	3.9	3.8-4
Women	88,126	52,380	59.4	50,327	57.1	2,053	3.9	3.8-4
Both sexes, 16-19 years	12,439	6,965	56.0	6,089	49.0	876	12.6	12.1-13.1
Black	24,373	15,982	65.6	14,556	59.7	1,426	8.9	8.6-9.2
Men	10,927	7,542	69.0	6,871	62.9	671	8.9	8.5-9.3
Women	13,446	8,441	62.8	7,685	57.2	756	9.0	8.6-9.4
Both sexes, 16-19 years	2,443	1,017	41.6	736	30.1	281	27.6	26.1-29.1
Hispanic origin 2/	21,070	14,317	67.9	13,291	63.1	1,026	7.2	6.9-7.5
Men	10,734	8,571	79.8	8,018	74.7	552	6.4	6.1-6.7
Women	10,335	5,746	55.6	5,273	51.0	473	8.2	7.8-8.6
Both sexes, 16-19 years	2,204	1,007	45.7	793	36.0	214	21.3	19.8-22.8

1/ If repeated samples were drawn from the same population and an error range constructed around each sample estimate, in 9 out of 10 cases the true value based on a complete census of the population would be contained within these error ranges.
2/ Persons of Hispanic origin may be of any race.

Source: U.S., Department of Labor, Bureau of Labor Statistics, *Geographic Profile of Employment and Unemployment, 1998,* Bulletin 2524, Internet site <http://stats.bls.gov/opub/gp/pdf/gp98_12.pdf> (accessed 18 May 2000).

Table 6.10. LABOR FORCE PARTICIPATION: FULL- AND PART-TIME STATUS AND UNEMPLOYED PERSONS SEEKING WORK BY SEX, AGE, AND RACE AND HISPANIC ORIGIN IN FLORIDA, ANNUAL AVERAGES 1997 AND 1998

(in thousands)

Population group	Employed 1/										Unemployed	
	Full-time workers					Part-time workers 2/						
			1 to 34 hours				At work					
	Total	35 hours or more	Economic reasons	Non-economic reasons	Not at work	Total	Part-time for economic reasons	Part-time for non-economic reasons	Not at work	Seeking full-time work	Seeking part-time work
1997												
Total	5,687	5,030	80	390	188	1,081	136	879	66	272	66
Men	3,242	2,913	52	181	95	390	54	313	23	144	34
Women	2,445	2,117	27	208	92	691	82	566	43	128	32
Both sexes, 16-19 years	112	94	5	9	4	190	14	168	8	21	28
White	4,789	4,243	66	326	155	934	101	773	60	191	47
Black	764	666	12	56	29	130	31	93	6	76	17
Hispanic origin 3/	991	873	18	72	27	155	37	112	7	62	10
1998												
Total	5,863	5,092	68	495	207	1,055	125	854	76	257	53
Men	3,319	2,957	41	224	97	384	53	301	30	130	25
Women	2,543	2,135	28	271	110	672	72	553	46	127	28
Both sexes, 16-19 years	135	113	3	13	5	208	17	180	10	(NA)	(NA)
White	4,873	4,223	57	415	178	890	89	733	67	182	40
Black	842	734	10	69	28	144	31	105	7	68	11
Hispanic origin 3/	1,011	884	14	81	32	147	26	113	8	66	7

1/ Employed persons are classified as full- or part-time workers based on their usual weekly hours at all jobs regardless of the number of hours they are at work during the reference week. Persons absent from work are classified according to their usual status.

2/ Includes some persons at work 35 hours or more classified by their reason for working part time.

3/ Persons of Hispanic origin may be of any race.

Source: U.S. Department of Labor, Bureau of Labor Statistics, *Geographic Profile of Employment and Unemployment, 1998*, Bulletin 2524, Internet site <http://stats.bls.gov/opub/gp/pdf/gp98_13.pdf> (accessed 18 May 2000).

Table 6.11. LABOR FORCE: ESTIMATES BY EMPLOYMENT STATUS IN THE UNITED STATES AND IN THE STATE AND COUNTIES OF FLORIDA, 1997, 1998, AND 1999

County	1997 A/ Labor force	1997 A/ Employment	1997 A/ Unemployment Number	1997 A/ Rate	1998 B/ Labor force	1998 B/ Employment	1998 B/ Unemployment Number	1998 B/ Rate	1999 B/ Labor force	1999 B/ Employment	1999 B/ Unemployment Number	1999 B/ Rate
United States 1/	136,297	129,558	6,739	4.9	137,673	131,463	6,210	4.5	139,368	133,488	5,880	4.2
Florida	7,119,000	6,780,000	339,000	4.8	7,230,000	6,920,000	310,000	4.3	7,366,000	7,082,000	284,000	3.9
Alachua	101,937	99,060	2,877	2.8	103,494	100,877	2,617	2.5	105,303	103,055	2,248	2.1
Baker	8,360	7,979	381	4.6	8,584	8,260	324	3.8	8,618	8,331	287	3.3
Bay	65,183	60,879	4,304	6.6	65,762	61,390	4,372	6.6	65,935	61,898	4,037	6.1
Bradford	9,773	9,413	360	3.7	9,538	9,120	418	4.4	9,613	9,293	320	3.3
Brevard	202,865	193,632	9,233	4.6	204,294	195,551	8,743	4.3	206,340	198,321	8,019	3.9
Broward	751,021	714,447	36,574	4.9	758,767	724,443	34,324	4.5	770,374	739,217	31,157	4.0
Calhoun	5,217	4,936	281	5.4	5,101	4,819	282	5.5	4,884	4,568	316	6.5
Charlotte	45,246	43,438	1,808	4.0	45,908	44,305	1,603	3.5	46,899	45,390	1,509	3.2
Citrus	34,848	32,856	1,992	5.7	35,358	33,288	2,070	5.9	35,214	33,547	1,667	4.7
Clay	66,458	64,441	2,017	3.0	68,601	66,743	1,858	2.7	69,673	67,849	1,824	2.6
Collier	87,526	83,115	4,411	5.0	92,044	88,224	3,820	4.2	93,644	90,114	3,530	3.8
Columbia	24,413	23,296	1,117	4.6	24,559	23,447	1,112	4.5	24,443	23,383	1,060	4.3
De Soto	9,752	9,075	677	6.9	8,967	8,328	639	7.1	8,590	8,025	565	6.6
Dixie	3,852	3,572	280	7.3	3,760	3,515	245	6.5	3,729	3,537	192	5.1
Duval	372,609	358,453	14,156	3.8	376,221	364,000	12,221	3.2	381,867	370,030	11,837	3.1
Escambia	119,473	114,448	5,025	4.2	120,032	115,377	4,655	3.9	120,859	116,589	4,270	3.5
Flagler	16,126	15,613	513	3.2	16,926	16,414	512	3.0	17,144	16,582	562	3.3
Franklin	4,452	4,155	297	6.7	4,544	4,311	233	5.1	4,776	4,566	210	4.4
Gadsden	19,124	18,249	875	4.6	19,348	18,480	868	4.5	19,615	18,912	703	3.6
Gilchrist	4,547	4,363	184	4.0	4,565	4,384	181	4.0	4,446	4,273	173	3.9
Glades	4,012	3,678	334	8.3	3,764	3,436	328	8.7	3,728	3,453	275	7.4
Gulf	5,668	4,992	676	11.9	5,226	4,612	614	11.7	5,467	4,746	721	13.2

See footnotes at end of table.

Continued . . .

Table 6.11. LABOR FORCE: ESTIMATES BY EMPLOYMENT STATUS IN THE UNITED STATES AND IN THE STATE AND COUNTIES OF FLORIDA, 1997, 1998, AND 1999 (Continued)

County	1997 A/				1998 B/				1999 B/			
	Labor force	Employ-ment	Unemployment Number	Rate	Labor force	Employ-ment	Unemployment Number	Rate	Labor force	Employ-ment	Unemployment Number	Rate
Hamilton	3,419	3,179	240	7.0	3,414	3,145	269	7.9	3,365	3,145	220	6.5
Hardee	10,647	9,294	1,353	12.7	9,405	8,296	1,109	11.8	9,148	8,205	943	10.3
Hendry	16,759	14,566	2,193	13.1	15,561	13,596	1,965	12.6	15,558	13,663	1,895	12.2
Hernando	44,855	43,089	1,766	3.9	46,632	44,834	1,798	3.9	47,777	46,189	1,588	3.3
Highlands	27,108	24,860	2,248	8.3	27,141	24,950	2,191	8.1	25,869	24,116	1,753	6.8
Hillsborough	516,089	498,897	17,192	3.3	531,124	516,406	14,718	2.8	546,338	532,012	14,326	2.6
Holmes	6,598	6,184	414	6.3	6,571	6,145	426	6.5	6,627	6,269	358	5.4
Indian River	44,015	40,438	3,577	8.1	45,454	41,887	3,567	7.8	45,043	41,668	3,375	7.5
Jackson	18,070	17,209	861	4.8	18,151	17,195	956	5.3	17,677	16,544	1,133	6.4
Jefferson	5,151	4,920	231	4.5	4,969	4,763	206	4.1	4,904	4,700	204	4.2
Lafayette	2,795	2,720	75	2.7	2,775	2,700	75	2.7	3,030	2,964	66	2.2
Lake	83,394	80,116	3,278	3.9	87,177	84,386	2,791	3.2	90,483	88,154	2,329	2.6
Lee	171,334	165,545	5,789	3.4	175,238	170,032	5,206	3.0	179,970	175,372	4,598	2.6
Leon	124,723	121,175	3,548	2.8	127,197	123,640	3,557	2.8	129,722	126,535	3,187	2.5
Levy	12,876	12,322	554	4.3	12,810	12,281	529	4.1	12,530	12,125	405	3.2
Liberty	2,471	2,362	109	4.4	2,337	2,211	126	5.4	2,254	2,145	109	4.8
Madison	7,191	6,830	361	5.0	7,189	6,850	339	4.7	7,168	6,902	266	3.7
Manatee	113,989	110,614	3,375	3.0	114,520	111,526	2,994	2.6	121,309	118,646	2,663	2.2
Marion	94,581	90,270	4,311	4.6	96,340	92,311	4,029	4.2	98,169	94,603	3,566	3.6
Martin	46,246	43,071	3,175	6.9	46,889	44,165	2,724	5.8	48,074	45,682	2,392	5.0
Miami-Dade	1,045,835	971,609	74,226	7.1	1,042,922	975,918	67,004	6.4	1,045,018	984,468	60,550	5.8
Monroe	45,505	44,446	1,059	2.3	45,979	44,769	1,210	2.6	46,109	45,085	1,024	2.2
Nassau	27,007	26,022	985	3.6	27,777	26,859	918	3.3	28,253	27,304	954	3.4
Okaloosa	78,881	76,092	2,789	3.5	79,387	76,784	2,603	3.3	80,527	77,891	2,636	3.3
Okeechobee	16,750	15,328	1,422	8.5	16,045	14,717	1,328	8.3	15,819	14,634	1,185	7.5

See footnotes at end of table.

Continued . . .

Table 6.11. LABOR FORCE: ESTIMATES BY EMPLOYMENT STATUS IN THE UNITED STATES AND IN THE STATE AND COUNTIES OF FLORIDA, 1997, 1998, AND 1999 (Continued)

County	1997 A/ Labor force	1997 A/ Employment	1997 A/ Unemployment Number	1997 A/ Rate	1998 B/ Labor force	1998 B/ Employment	1998 B/ Unemployment Number	1998 B/ Rate	1999 B/ Labor force	1999 B/ Employment	1999 B/ Unemployment Number	1999 B/ Rate
Orange	453,499	438,360	15,139	3.3	471,227	457,130	14,097	3.0	490,919	477,542	13,377	2.7
Osceola	76,875	74,061	2,814	3.7	80,159	77,672	2,487	3.1	83,411	81,140	2,271	2.7
Palm Beach	484,716	454,424	30,292	6.2	496,678	468,782	27,896	5.6	506,543	481,071	25,472	5.0
Pasco	128,012	122,910	5,102	4.0	132,832	127,852	4,980	3.7	135,965	131,716	4,249	3.1
Pinellas	450,804	435,276	15,528	3.4	459,361	445,129	14,232	3.1	471,280	458,582	12,698	2.7
Polk	196,579	184,019	12,560	6.4	198,169	187,348	10,821	5.5	200,286	190,575	9,711	4.8
Putnam	27,562	25,973	1,589	5.8	27,889	26,446	1,443	5.2	27,928	26,533	1,395	5.0
St. Johns	56,606	54,920	1,686	3.0	59,036	57,586	1,450	2.5	60,016	58,540	1,476	2.5
St. Lucie	74,963	66,981	7,982	10.6	75,947	68,168	7,779	10.2	77,502	70,509	6,993	9.0
Santa Rosa	49,463	47,705	1,758	3.6	51,721	49,638	2,083	4.0	52,227	50,160	2,067	4.0
Sarasota	144,229	140,456	3,773	2.6	143,892	140,319	3,573	2.5	152,524	149,277	3,247	2.1
Seminole	201,778	195,208	6,570	3.3	208,018	202,288	5,730	2.8	217,115	211,321	5,794	2.7
Sumter	14,076	13,467	609	4.3	13,907	13,453	454	3.3	14,360	13,968	392	2.7
Suwannee	12,899	12,343	556	4.3	13,350	12,779	571	4.3	13,462	12,942	520	3.9
Taylor	7,359	6,693	666	9.1	7,479	6,929	550	7.4	7,326	6,801	525	7.2
Union	3,922	3,778	144	3.7	3,628	3,526	102	2.8	3,481	3,391	90	2.6
Volusia	172,456	165,680	6,776	3.9	173,236	167,273	5,963	3.4	174,365	168,983	5,382	3.1
Wakulla	10,042	9,678	364	3.6	10,789	10,427	362	3.4	10,953	10,622	331	3.0
Walton	14,978	14,338	640	4.3	15,235	14,619	616	4.0	15,315	14,736	579	3.8
Washington	9,048	8,569	479	5.3	8,917	8,484	433	4.9	9,617	9,224	393	4.1

A/ Benchmark 1996 = 1997.
B/ Benchmark 1997 and 1998 = 1998.
1/ United States numbers are rounded to thousands. Data are from U.S., Department of Labor, Bureau of Labor Statistics.
Note: Civilian labor force. Data are generated for federal fund allocations. Caution is urged when using these data for short-term economic analysis. Detail may not add to totals because of rounding.

Source: State of Florida, Department of Labor and Employment Security, Bureau of Labor Market Information, *Labor Force Summary: 1999 Annual Averages*, and previous editions, Internet site <ftp://207.156.40.162/laus/laus.htm> (accessed 4 May 2000).

Table 6.12. LABOR FORCE: ESTIMATES BY EMPLOYMENT STATUS IN THE STATE, METROPOLITAN STATISTICAL AREAS (MSAS) AND SELECTED CITIES OF FLORIDA, 1998 AND 1999

MSA or city 1/	1998 Labor force	1998 Employment	1998 Unemployment Number	1998 Rate	1999 Labor force	1999 Employment	1999 Unemployment Number	1999 Rate
Florida	7,230,000	6,920,000	310,000	4.3	7,366,000	7,082,000	284,000	3.9
Daytona Beach MSA	190,162	183,687	6,475	3.4	191,508	185,565	5,943	3.1
Ft. Lauderdale MSA	758,767	724,443	34,324	4.5	770,374	739,217	31,157	4.0
Ft. Myers-Cape Coral MSA	175,238	170,032	5,206	3.0	179,970	175,372	4,598	2.6
Ft. Pierce-Port St. Lucie MSA	122,836	112,334	10,502	8.5	125,577	116,192	9,385	7.5
Ft. Walton Beach MSA	79,387	76,784	2,603	3.3	80,527	77,891	2,636	3.3
Gainesville MSA	103,494	100,877	2,617	2.5	105,303	103,055	2,248	2.1
Jacksonville MSA	531,635	515,188	16,447	3.1	539,813	523,722	16,091	3.0
Lakeland-Winter Haven MSA	198,169	187,348	10,821	5.5	200,286	190,575	9,711	4.8
Melbourne-Titusville-Palm Bay MSA	204,294	195,551	8,743	4.3	206,340	198,321	8,019	3.9
Miami MSA	1,042,922	975,918	67,004	6.4	1,045,018	984,468	60,550	5.8
Naples MSA	92,044	88,224	3,820	4.2	93,644	90,114	3,530	3.8
Ocala MSA	96,340	92,311	4,029	4.2	98,169	94,603	3,566	3.6
Orlando MSA	846,581	821,476	25,105	3.0	881,929	858,158	23,771	2.7
Panama City MSA	65,762	61,390	4,372	6.6	65,935	61,898	4,037	6.1
Pensacola MSA	171,753	165,015	6,738	3.9	173,085	166,749	6,336	3.7
Punta Gorda MSA	45,908	44,305	1,603	3.5	46,899	45,390	1,509	3.2
Sarasota-Bradenton MSA	258,412	251,845	6,567	2.5	273,832	267,922	5,910	2.2
Tallahassee MSA	146,545	142,120	4,425	3.0	149,337	145,447	3,890	2.6
Tampa-St. Petersburg-Clearwater MSA	1,169,948	1,134,221	35,727	3.1	1,201,359	1,168,498	32,861	2.7
West Palm Beach-Boca Raton MSA	496,678	468,782	27,896	5.6	506,543	481,071	25,472	5.0
Altamonte Springs	29,136	28,362	774	2.7	30,411	29,629	782	2.6
Boca Raton	38,139	36,767	1,372	3.6	38,984	37,731	1,253	3.2
Boynton Beach	25,149	23,705	1,444	5.7	25,644	24,326	1,318	5.1
Bradenton	23,716	23,000	716	3.0	25,105	24,468	637	2.5
Cape Coral	39,993	38,830	1,163	2.9	41,076	40,049	1,027	2.5
Clearwater	54,397	52,609	1,788	3.3	55,794	54,199	1,595	2.9
Coconut Creek	14,730	13,953	777	5.3	14,943	14,237	706	4.7
Cooper City	13,998	13,656	342	2.4	14,246	13,935	311	2.2
Coral Gables	23,279	22,498	781	3.4	23,400	22,695	705	3.0
Coral Springs	52,011	50,319	1,692	3.3	52,881	51,345	1,536	2.9

Continued . . .

See footnotes at end of table.

Table 6.12. LABOR FORCE: ESTIMATES BY EMPLOYMENT STATUS IN THE STATE, METROPOLITAN STATISTICAL AREAS (MSAS) AND SELECTED CITIES OF FLORIDA, 1998 AND 1999 (Continued)

MSA or city 1/	1998				1999			
	Labor force	Employment	Unemployment Number	Rate	Labor force	Employment	Unemployment Number	Rate
Davie	32,610	31,324	1,286	3.9	33,130	31,963	1,167	3.5
Daytona Beach	30,124	28,742	1,382	4.6	30,284	29,036	1,248	4.1
Deerfield Beach	24,755	23,753	1,002	4.0	25,148	24,238	910	3.6
Delray Beach	25,704	23,692	2,012	7.8	26,151	24,313	1,838	7.0
Deltona	23,355	22,452	903	3.9	23,497	22,682	815	3.5
Dunedin	17,438	16,975	463	2.7	17,901	17,488	413	2.3
Ft. Lauderdale	93,110	87,838	5,272	5.7	94,416	89,630	4,786	5.1
Ft. Myers	25,319	24,260	1,059	4.2	25,957	25,022	935	3.6
Ft. Pierce	18,053	14,999	3,054	16.9	18,259	15,514	2,745	15.0
Gainesville	46,958	45,544	1,414	3.0	47,742	46,527	1,215	2.5
Greenacres	11,963	11,339	624	5.2	12,206	11,636	570	4.7
Hallandale	12,886	12,087	799	6.2	13,058	12,333	725	5.6
Hialeah	104,121	97,132	6,989	6.7	104,300	97,983	6,317	6.1
Hollywood	71,853	68,164	3,689	5.1	72,903	69,554	3,349	4.6
Homestead	12,971	12,182	789	6.1	13,002	12,289	713	5.5
Jacksonville	352,774	341,088	11,686	3.3	358,058	346,739	11,319	3.2
Jupiter	16,474	15,826	648	3.9	16,832	16,240	592	3.5
Key West	14,804	14,414	390	2.6	14,845	14,515	330	2.2
Kissimmee	25,430	24,509	921	3.6	26,445	25,604	841	3.2
Lake Worth	16,834	15,800	1,034	6.1	17,158	16,214	944	5.5
Lakeland	34,605	32,876	1,729	5.0	34,993	33,442	1,551	4.4
Largo	34,496	33,575	921	2.7	35,412	34,590	822	2.3
Lauderdale Lakes	14,094	13,198	896	6.4	14,280	13,467	813	5.7
Lauderhill	29,239	27,865	1,374	4.7	29,681	28,434	1,247	4.2
Margate	24,156	23,075	1,081	4.5	24,527	23,546	981	4.0
Melbourne	30,988	29,466	1,522	4.9	31,279	29,883	1,396	4.5
Miami	180,684	163,888	16,796	9.3	180,502	165,324	15,178	8.4
Miami Beach	44,298	40,978	3,320	7.5	44,337	41,337	3,000	6.8
Miramar	26,893	25,802	1,091	4.1	27,319	26,328	991	3.6
North Lauderdale	18,508	17,720	788	4.3	18,797	18,082	715	3.8
North Miami	28,655	26,674	1,981	6.9	28,698	26,908	1,790	6.2
North Miami Beach	18,721	17,735	986	5.3	18,781	17,890	891	4.7
Oakland Park	19,215	18,468	747	3.9	19,522	18,844	678	3.5

Continued . . .

See footnotes at end of table.

Table 6.12. LABOR FORCE: ESTIMATES BY EMPLOYMENT STATUS IN THE STATE, METROPOLITAN STATISTICAL AREAS (MSAS) AND SELECTED CITIES OF FLORIDA, 1998 AND 1999 (Continued)

MSA or city 1/	1998				1999			
	Labor force	Employ- ment	Unemployment Number	Rate	Labor force	Employ- ment	Unemployment Number	Rate
Ocala	22,247	21,259	988	4.4	22,661	21,787	874	3.9
Orlando	110,583	107,038	3,545	3.2	115,180	111,817	3,363	2.9
Ormond Beach	14,090	13,752	338	2.4	14,197	13,892	305	2.1
Palm Bay	33,298	31,820	1,478	4.4	33,626	32,270	1,356	4.0
Palm Beach Gardens	15,320	14,889	431	2.8	15,672	15,279	393	2.5
Panama City	17,696	16,288	1,408	8.0	17,724	16,423	1,301	7.3
Pembroke Pines	40,223	39,029	1,194	3.0	40,908	39,825	1,083	2.6
Pensacola	26,773	25,637	1,136	4.2	26,948	25,906	1,042	3.9
Pinellas Park	24,104	23,415	689	2.9	24,737	24,122	615	2.5
Plant City	13,054	12,696	358	2.7	13,428	13,080	348	2.6
Plantation	45,327	43,832	1,495	3.3	46,082	44,725	1,357	2.9
Pompano Beach	40,705	38,520	2,185	5.4	41,288	39,305	1,983	4.8
Port Orange	17,729	17,268	461	2.6	17,861	17,445	416	2.3
Port St. Lucie	30,163	27,765	2,398	8.0	30,874	28,718	2,156	7.0
Riviera Beach	15,855	14,293	1,562	9.9	16,094	14,668	1,426	8.9
St. Petersburg	132,359	127,619	4,740	3.6	135,705	131,476	4,229	3.1
Sanford	20,546	19,832	714	3.5	21,440	20,718	722	3.4
Sarasota	29,856	28,937	919	3.1	31,620	30,784	836	2.6
Sunrise	37,629	36,080	1,549	4.1	38,221	36,815	1,406	3.7
Tallahassee	81,227	78,402	2,825	3.5	82,768	80,237	2,531	3.1
Tamarac	20,745	19,724	1,021	4.9	21,053	20,126	927	4.4
Tampa	168,478	162,656	5,822	3.5	173,239	167,572	5,667	3.3
Titusville	20,295	19,437	858	4.2	20,499	19,712	787	3.8
Wellington	12,744	12,350	394	3.1	13,033	12,674	359	2.8
West Palm Beach	43,607	40,517	3,090	7.1	44,401	41,579	2,822	6.4
Winter Haven	11,523	10,948	575	5.0	11,652	11,136	516	4.4
Winter Springs	15,978	15,603	375	2.3	16,679	16,300	379	2.3

Note: Civilian labor force.

1/ Metropolitan Statistical Areas (MSAs) and Primary Metropolitan Statistical Areas (PMSAs) based on 1999 MSA designations and cities with a population of 25,000 or more in 1999.

Source: State of Florida, Department of Labor and Employment Security, Bureau of Labor Market Information, *Labor Force Summary: 1999 Annual Averages*, and previous editions, Internet site <ftp://207.156.40.162/laus/laus.htm> (accessed 4 May 2000).

Table 6.20. OCCUPATIONS: PRIVATE INDUSTRY EMPLOYMENT, PARTICIPATION RATE
AND OCCUPATIONAL DISTRIBUTION OF WHITE AND MINORITY EMPLOYEES
BY SEX AND BY OCCUPATION IN FLORIDA, 1996

Occupation	All		White		Minority 1/	
	Male	Female	Male	Female	Male	Female
			Number employed			
Total	917,524	921,625	626,922	619,993	290,602	301,632
Officials and managers	116,909	65,273	98,920	53,309	17,989	11,964
Professionals	104,268	142,520	85,426	112,275	18,842	30,245
Technicians	57,201	55,824	42,369	39,197	14,832	16,627
Sales workers	139,154	174,948	99,432	123,247	39,722	51,701
Office and clerical workers	56,197	236,592	36,390	162,248	19,807	74,344
Craft workers	106,148	16,592	79,983	10,905	26,165	5,687
Operatives	125,630	48,225	74,429	23,942	51,201	24,283
Laborers	80,877	29,308	37,730	13,812	43,147	15,496
Service workers	131,140	152,343	72,243	81,058	58,897	71,285
			Participation rate (percentage)			
Total	49.9	50.1	34.1	33.7	15.8	16.4
Officials and managers	64.2	35.8	54.3	29.3	9.9	6.6
Professionals	42.3	57.7	34.6	45.5	7.6	12.3
Technicians	50.6	49.4	37.5	34.7	13.1	14.7
Sales workers	44.3	55.7	31.7	39.2	12.6	16.5
Office and clerical workers	19.2	80.8	12.4	55.4	6.8	25.4
Craft workers	86.5	13.5	65.2	8.9	21.3	4.6
Operatives	72.3	27.7	42.8	13.8	29.5	14.0
Laborers	73.4	26.6	34.2	12.5	39.2	14.1
Service workers	46.3	53.7	25.5	28.6	20.8	25.1
			Occupational distribution (percentage)			
Total	100.0	100.0	100.0	100.0	100.0	100.0
Officials and managers	12.7	7.1	15.8	8.6	6.2	4.0
Professionals	11.4	15.5	13.6	18.1	6.5	10.0
Technicians	6.2	6.1	6.8	6.3	5.1	5.5
Sales workers	15.2	19.0	15.9	19.9	13.7	17.1
Office and clerical workers	6.1	25.7	5.8	26.2	6.8	24.6
Craft workers	11.6	1.8	12.8	1.8	9.0	1.9
Operatives	13.7	5.2	11.9	3.9	17.6	8.1
Laborers	8.8	3.2	6.0	2.2	14.8	5.1
Service workers	14.3	16.5	11.5	13.1	20.3	23.6

1/ Includes Black, Asian or Pacific Islander, American Indian, Eskimo, or Aleut, and persons of Hispanic origin.

Note: Private industry data, based on 1987 standard industrial classification (SIC) codes, from the 1996 Equal Employment Opportunity employer information report (EEO-1). Includes private employers with 100 or more employees, or 50 or more employees and: 1) have a federal contract or first-tier subcontract worth $50,000 or more, or 2) act as depositories of federal funds in any amount, or 3) act as issuing and paying agents for U.S. Savings Bonds and Notes. EEO-1 businesses account for 48.4 percent of all private U.S. employment.

Source: U.S., Equal Employment Opportunity Commission, *Job Patterns for Minorities and Women in Private Industry, 1996.*

University of Florida   **Bureau of Economic and Business Research**

Table 6.21. MINORITY EMPLOYMENT: PRIVATE INDUSTRY EMPLOYMENT OF FEMALE AND MINORITY EMPLOYEES BY INDUSTRY AND BY OCCUPATION IN FLORIDA, 1996

Occupation and minority group 1/	Agriculture forestry and fishing SIC 01-09 (63 units)	Mining SIC 10-14 (20 units)	Construction SIC 15-17 (207 units)	Manufacturing SIC 20-39 (1,062 units)	Transportation communications and public utilities SIC 40-49 (864 units)	Wholesale trade SIC 50-51 (426 units)	Retail trade SIC 52-59 (3,703 units)	Finance insurance and real estate SIC 60-67 (768 units)	Services SIC 70-89 (2,409 units)
Total employment	16,791	3,208	35,279	274,653	192,476	65,904	472,189	131,965	646,684
Female	4,414	379	4,298	94,503	66,966	21,362	244,871	89,088	395,744
Minority	8,275	1,045	9,658	84,386	61,957	20,213	142,071	40,326	224,303
Officials and managers	1,585	463	3,301	31,910	21,549	8,353	42,932	20,395	51,694
Female	213	27	276	6,083	5,772	1,787	15,208	10,627	25,280
Minority	196	78	288	4,183	4,068	1,448	7,367	3,787	8,538
Professionals	379	236	1,255	43,005	18,393	4,007	5,851	26,537	147,125
Female	109	57	198	11,288	5,783	1,379	2,605	16,732	104,369
Minority	41	52	153	6,787	3,307	949	1,129	5,945	30,724
Technicians	385	118	938	17,843	9,735	3,006	5,672	7,172	68,156
Female	143	15	71	3,886	1,882	608	1,805	4,729	42,685
Minority	86	13	123	4,110	2,333	842	1,691	2,045	20,216
Sales workers	102	31	886	13,416	14,028	13,794	241,885	8,448	21,512
Female	42	6	303	5,257	8,314	3,940	141,011	3,935	12,140
Minority	4	5	93	2,427	4,866	2,770	72,723	1,875	6,660
Office and clerical workers	999	263	3,009	28,680	43,201	11,922	33,447	59,141	112,127
Female	838	208	2,408	22,776	32,176	9,149	26,739	49,690	92,608
Minority	170	72	489	6,947	15,464	3,554	9,317	22,033	36,105

See footnotes at end of table.

Continued . . . .

Table 6.21. MINORITY EMPLOYMENT: PRIVATE INDUSTRY EMPLOYMENT OF FEMALE AND MINORITY EMPLOYEES BY INDUSTRY AND BY OCCUPATION IN FLORIDA, 1996 (Continued)

Occupation and minority group 1/	Agriculture forestry and fishing SIC 01-09 (63 units)	Mining SIC 10-14 (20 units)	Construction SIC 15-17 (207 units)	Manufacturing SIC 20-39 (1,062 units)	Transportation communications and public utilities SIC 40-49 (864 units)	Wholesale trade SIC 50-51 (426 units)	Retail trade SIC 52-59 (3,703 units)	Finance insurance and real estate SIC 60-67 (768 units)	Services SIC 70-89 (2,409 units)
Craft workers	2,592	955	13,005	40,482	28,305	3,545	14,721	1,157	17,978
Female	152	7	297	5,590	2,479	376	4,889	143	2,659
Minority	738	295	2,804	10,972	7,131	1,057	3,472	360	5,023
Operatives	5,035	908	6,818	72,065	31,854	13,007	16,832	1,428	25,908
Female	1,041	38	352	29,561	2,780	2,298	3,146	236	8,773
Minority	2,773	411	2,370	32,720	12,695	5,322	5,446	661	13,086
Laborers	5,394	218	5,789	24,256	16,647	7,384	29,056	1,815	19,626
Female	1,723	20	264	9,235	2,624	1,636	8,856	225	4,725
Minority	4,125	114	3,245	14,761	8,694	3,912	11,930	1,210	10,652
Service workers	320	16	278	2,996	8,764	886	81,793	5,872	182,558
Female	153	1	129	827	5,156	189	40,612	2,771	102,505
Minority	142	5	93	1,479	3,399	359	28,996	2,410	93,299

1/ Includes Black, Asian or Pacific Islander, American Indian, Eskimo, or Aleut, and persons of Hispanic origin.
Note: Private industry data, based on 1987 standard industrial classification (SIC) codes, from the 1995 Equal Employment Opportunity Employer Information Report (EEO-1). Includes private employers with 100 or more employees, or 50 or more employees and: 1) have a federal contract or first-tier subcontract worth $50,000 or more, or 2) act as depositories of federal funds in any amount, or 3) act as issuing and paying agents for U.S. Savings Bonds and Notes. EEO-1 businesses account for 48.4 percent of all private U.S. employment.

Source: U.S., Equal Employment Opportunity Commission, *Job Patterns for Minorities and Women in Private Industry, 1996.*

Table 6.25. OCCUPATIONS: EMPLOYMENT ESTIMATES, 1998, PROJECTIONS, 2008, AND AVERAGE ANNUAL JOB OPENINGS FOR MAJOR OCCUPATIONAL CATEGORIES IN THE STATE OF FLORIDA

Occupation	Estimates 1998	Projections 2008	Change Number	Change Percentage	Average annual openings Total	Due to growth	Due to separations
All occupations, total	7,351,873	9,034,714	1,682,841	23	344,194	168,300	175,894
Executive, administrative, and managerial	549,298	669,063	119,765	22	21,583	11,976	9,607
Professional, paraprofessional, and technical	1,474,789	1,927,004	452,215	31	73,646	45,226	28,420
Management support	237,416	292,353	54,937	23	10,045	5,495	4,550
Engineers and related occupations	134,378	169,653	35,275	26	6,313	3,528	2,785
Natural scientist and related occupations	25,132	30,765	5,633	22	1,144	563	581
Computer and mathematical	96,432	165,068	68,636	71	8,339	6,864	1,475
Social scientists, recreation, and religion	91,643	124,636	32,993	36	5,020	3,300	1,720
Law and related occupations	62,200	78,638	16,438	26	2,300	1,644	656
Teachers, librarians, and counselors	323,879	414,756	90,877	28	15,871	9,087	6,784
Health practitioners, and technicians	355,878	460,846	104,968	29	17,100	10,499	6,601
Writers, Artists, Entertainers, Athletes	102,872	132,301	29,429	29	5,122	2,944	2,178
All Other Prof., Paraprof. Technicians	44,959	57,988	13,029	29	2,392	1,302	1,090
Marketing and sales	1,014,607	1,246,203	231,596	23	51,391	23,161	28,230
Administrative support and clerical	1,278,622	1,511,455	232,833	18	49,430	23,285	26,145
Service	1,247,702	1,533,413	285,711	23	68,835	28,574	40,261
First line supervisor	63,145	79,510	16,365	26	3,147	1,637	1,510
Protective	163,661	218,131	54,470	33	9,873	5,448	4,425
Food and beverage	528,870	614,010	85,140	16	33,399	8,514	24,885
Health	141,673	198,672	56,999	40	8,091	5,701	2,390
Cleaning and building (excluding private)	183,850	213,863	30,013	16	6,780	3,001	3,779
Personal service	147,119	185,011	37,892	26	6,516	3,790	2,726
Agriculture, forestry, and fishing	280,509	305,514	25,005	9	9,610	2,500	7,110
Production, construction, operators, maintenance, and related workers	1,506,346	1,842,062	335,716	22	69,699	33,578	36,121
Mechanics, installers, and repairers	266,890	315,623	48,733	18	11,190	4,878	6,312
Construction trades and extraction	213,487	248,410	34,923	16	8,424	3,494	4,930
Operators, fabricators, and laborers	831,566	1,046,107	214,541	26	41,625	21,456	20,169

Source: State of Florida, Department of Labor and Employment Security, Office of Labor Market Statistics, *Florida Industry and Occupational Employment Projections, 1998-2008,* prepublication release.

Table 6.26. OCCUPATIONS: EMPLOYMENT ESTIMATES, 1998, AND PROJECTIONS, 2008
OF THE FASTEST-GROWING OCCUPATIONS IN THE STATE OF FLORIDA

Occupation	Estimates 1998	Projections 2008	Percentage change
Computer Support Specialist	21,044	43,328	105.89
Systems Analyst	29,018	56,184	93.62
Computer Engineer	11,742	20,355	73.35
Surgical Technician	3,610	6,028	66.98
Paralegal	9,445	15,736	66.61
Instructional Coordinator	5,362	8,730	62.81
Database Administrator	3,724	6,047	62.38
Medical Assistant	17,978	28,926	60.90
Packaging and Filling Machine Operator	11,951	19,143	60.18
Medical Records Technician	6,223	9,871	58.62
Physician Assistant	4,029	6,264	55.47
Respiratory Therapist	5,087	7,858	54.47
Human Services Worker	10,430	15,851	51.98
Correction Officer and Jailer	28,112	42,369	50.71
Telemarketer, Door-To-Door Sales, Street Vendor	42,995	64,742	50.58
Home Health Aide	24,463	36,605	49.63
Adjustment Clerk	29,307	43,778	49.38
Securities, Financial Service Sales	20,877	30,744	47.26
Producer, Director, Actor, Entertainer	5,395	7,874	45.95
Engineering, Science, Comp. Systems Manager	12,683	18,362	44.78
Dental Assistant	12,825	18,501	44.26
Director, Religious Activities/Education	7,439	10,692	43.73
Social Worker, Medical and Psychiatric	13,258	19,038	43.60
Instructor, Nonvocational Education	9,059	13,003	43.54
Sheriff and Deputy Sheriff	12,976	18,588	43.25
Physical, Corrective Therapy Assistant	4,745	6,796	43.22
Teacher, Special Education	17,616	25,100	42.48
Dental Hygienist	7,459	10,619	42.36
Personal Home Care Aide	6,961	9,900	42.22
Sales Agent, Business Services	19,010	27,004	42.05
Teacher's Aide, Paraprofessional	23,158	32,838	41.80
Social Worker, Exc. Medical and Psychiatric	18,643	26,205	40.56
Police Patrol Officer	21,971	30,879	40.54
Amusement and Recreation Attendant	26,016	36,285	39.47
Bill and Account Collector	17,396	24,256	39.43
Insurance Adjuster, Investigator	9,350	12,885	37.81
Medicine and Health Service Manager	12,823	17,651	37.65
Production Inspector, Grader	17,422	23,934	37.38
Instructor and Coach, Sports	16,449	22,591	37.34
Designer, Exc. Interior Designer	16,365	22,364	36.66
Teacher's Aide and Educational Assistant	27,942	38,036	36.12
Tax Preparer	5,837	7,919	35.67
Food Server, Outside	5,896	7,980	35.35
Hand Packer and Packager	48,597	65,712	35.22
Personnel, Training, Labor Rel. Specialist	21,113	28,439	34.70
Nursing Aide and Orderly	62,332	83,466	33.91
Receptionist, Information Clerk	90,352	120,089	32.91
Artist and Commercial Artist	17,712	23,535	32.88
Human Resources Assistant, Except Payroll	15,540	20,614	32.65
Music Director, Singer, and Related	7,220	9,559	32.40
Human Resources Manager	11,534	15,218	31.94
Interviewing Clerk, Exc. Personnel	11,003	14,484	31.64
Physical Therapist	7,133	9,353	31.12

See footnote at end of table.   Continued . . .

University of Florida   **Bureau of Economic and Business Research**

Table 6.26. OCCUPATIONS: EMPLOYMENT ESTIMATES, 1998, AND PROJECTIONS, 2008
OF THE FASTEST-GROWING OCCUPATIONS IN THE STATE OF FLORIDA (Continued)

Occupation	Estimates 1998	Projections 2008	Percentage change
Truck Driver, Light	83,881	109,848	31.0
Insurance Claims Clerk	8,689	11,362	30.8
Telephone and Cable TV Installer/Repairer	8,751	11,431	30.6
Counselor	8,551	11,144	30.3
Lawn Service Manager	7,780	10,129	30.2
Public Relations Specialist	8,462	11,003	30.0
Teacher, Secondary School	60,365	78,461	30.0
Laborer, Landscaper, Groundskeeper	83,927	108,887	29.7
Administrative Service Manager	19,195	24,859	29.5
Guard	63,661	82,429	29.5
Clergy	7,598	9,824	29.3
Vehicle, Equipment Cleaner	15,238	19,686	29.2
Emergency Medical Technician	7,043	9,095	29.1
Recreation Worker	13,492	17,386	28.9
Baker, Bread and Pastry	8,164	10,520	28.9
Order Filler, Sales	9,288	11,964	28.8
Loan Officer and Counselor	14,917	19,173	28.5
Licensed Practical Nurse	44,628	57,248	28.3
Communication, Transport., Utility Manager	9,266	11,845	27.8
Bus Driver	9,250	11,824	27.8
Cashier	173,492	221,667	27.8
Radiologic Technician	9,429	12,046	27.8
Marketing, Adv., Public Relations Manager	24,560	31,356	27.7
Registered Nurse	118,634	151,205	27.5
Customer Service Representative, Utilities	12,203	15,542	27.4
Physician	35,624	45,367	27.3
Electrical and Electronic Engineer	18,083	22,983	27.1
Writer and Editor	8,812	11,183	26.9
Computer Programmer	25,223	31,928	26.6
Pest Controller and Assistant	7,932	10,033	26.5
Civil Engineer, Including Traffic	8,850	11,147	26.0
Heating, A/C, Refrigeration Mechanic	19,615	24,590	25.4
Child Care Worker	49,466	61,973	25.3
Billing, Cost and Rate Clerk	17,365	21,689	24.9
Teacher, Preschool and Kindergarten	28,159	35,063	24.5
Machinist	11,348	14,121	24.4
General Office Clerk	186,127	230,240	23.7
Welder and Cutter	11,563	14,254	23.3
Sales Rep., Scientific Prod., Exc. Retail	19,371	23,866	23.2
Industrial Truck and Tractor Operator	14,101	17,336	22.9
Teacher, Vocational Education	18,278	22,465	22.9
Management Analyst	19,706	24,178	22.7
Salesperson, Retail	243,823	298,791	22.5
General Manager and Top Executive	188,938	231,497	22.5
Financial Manager	37,650	45,887	21.9
Stock Clerk, Stockroom or Warehouse	41,571	50,612	21.7
Accountant and Auditor	54,273	65,883	21.4

Note: Occupations are ranked based on the anticipated rate of growth between 1998 and 2008. Only occupations with a minimum total change of 2,000 jobs are included.

Source: State of Florida, Department of Labor and Employment Security, Office of Labor Market Statistics, *Florida Industry and Occupational Employment Projections, 1998-2008,* prepublication release.

Table 6.40. INDUSTRY GROWTH TRENDS: EMPLOYMENT ESTIMATES, 1998, AND PROJECTIONS 2008, OF THE FASTEST-GROWING INDUSTRIES AND INDUSTRIES GAINING THE MOST NEW GROWTH IN THE STATE OF FLORIDA

SIC code	Industry	Estimates 1998	Projections 2008	Change Number	Change Percentage
		Fastest-growing industries			
73	Business Services	644,030	1,017,730	373,700	58.03
84	Museums and Botanical and Zoological Gardens	3,684	5,514	1,830	49.67
89	Miscellaneous Business Services	2,353	3,401	1,048	44.54
62	Security and Commodity Brokers	30,557	43,424	12,867	42.11
61	Nondepository Institutions	50,975	71,560	20,585	40.38
83	Social Services	128,085	175,681	47,596	37.16
79	Amusement and Recreation Services	144,480	196,246	51,766	35.83
87	Engineering and Management Services	184,089	249,687	65,598	35.63
41	Local and Interurban Transit	16,077	21,651	5,574	34.67
45	Transportation by Air	75,192	100,054	24,862	33.06
75	Auto Repair Services and Parking	70,059	91,400	21,341	30.46
80	Health Services	577,320	750,580	173,260	30.01
52	Building Materials and Garden Supplies	53,057	68,074	15,017	28.30
47	Transportation Services	34,086	43,662	9,576	28.09
48	Communications	82,937	104,949	22,012	26.54
81	Legal Services	66,384	83,330	16,946	25.53
63	Insurance Carriers	77,700	96,578	18,878	24.30
86	Membership Organizations	119,995	148,811	28,816	24.01
57	Furniture and Homefurnishings Stores	65,422	81,066	15,644	23.91
54	Food Stores	251,579	310,708	59,129	23.50
		Industries gaining the most new jobs			
73	Business Services	644,030	1,017,730	373,700	58.03
80	Health Services	577,320	750,580	173,260	30.01
93	Local Government	629,429	771,196	141,767	22.52
58	Eating and Drinking Places	444,517	524,541	80,024	18.00
87	Engineering and Management Services	184,089	249,687	65,598	35.63
54	Food Stores	251,579	310,708	59,129	23.50
79	Amusement and Recreation Services	144,480	196,246	51,766	35.83
50	Wholesale Trade, Durable Goods	213,737	263,522	49,785	23.29
83	Social Services	128,085	175,681	47,596	37.16
92	State Government	204,972	241,805	36,833	17.97
59	Miscellaneous Retail Stores	157,019	192,849	35,830	22.82
17	Special Trade Contractors	227,731	263,542	35,811	15.73
86	Membership Organizations	119,995	148,811	28,816	24.01
70	Hotels and Other Lodging Places	150,329	178,655	28,326	18.84
45	Transportation by Air	75,192	100,054	24,862	33.06
51	Wholesale Trade, Nondurable Goods	143,734	167,139	23,405	16.28
48	Communications	82,937	104,949	22,012	26.54
75	Auto Repair Services and Parking	70,059	91,400	21,341	30.46
55	Auto Dealers and Service Stations	128,548	149,643	21,095	16.41
53	General Merchandise Stores	151,671	172,743	21,072	13.89

Source: State of Florida, Department of Labor and Employment Security, Office of Labor Market Statistics, *Florida Industry and Occupational Employment Projections, 1998-2008,* prepublication release.

University of Florida   **Bureau of Economic and Business Research**

Table 6.41. OCCUPATION GROWTH TRENDS: EMPLOYMENT ESTIMATES, 1998, AND PROJECTIONS 2008, OF THE FASTEST-GROWING OCCUPATIONS AND OCCUPATIONS GAINING THE MOST NEW GROWTH IN THE STATE OF FLORIDA

SIC code	Industry	Estimates 1998	Projec- tions 2008	Change Number	Per- centage
		Occupations gaining the most new jobs			
49011	Salesperson, Retail	243,823	298,791	54,968	22.54
49023	Cashier	173,492	221,667	48,175	27.77
55347	General Office Clerk	186,127	230,240	44,113	23.70
19005	General Manager and Top Executive	188,938	231,497	42,559	22.53
32502	Registered Nurse	118,634	151,205	32,571	27.46
55305	Receptionist, Information Clerk	90,352	120,089	29,737	32.91
25102	Systems Analyst	29,018	56,184	27,166	93.62
97105	Truck Driver, Light	83,881	109,848	25,967	30.96
79041	Laborer, Landscaper, Groundskeeper	83,927	108,887	24,960	29.74
25104	Computer Support Specialist	21,044	43,328	22,284	105.89
49026	Telemarketer, Door-To-Door Sales, Street Vendor	42,995	64,742	21,747	50.58
66008	Nursing Aide and Orderly	62,332	83,466	21,134	33.91
65008	Waiter and Waitress	127,541	147,920	20,379	15.98
63047	Guard	63,661	82,429	18,768	29.48
31308	Teacher, Secondary School	60,365	78,461	18,096	29.98
65041	Food Preparation Server, Fast Food	116,384	134,244	17,860	15.35
98902	Hand Packer and Packager	48,597	65,712	17,115	35.22
53123	Adjustment Clerk	29,307	43,778	14,471	49.38
63017	Correction Officer and Jailer	28,112	42,369	14,257	50.71
31305	Teacher, Elementary	73,501	87,066	13,565	18.46
		Declining or slow-growth occupations			
92541	Typesetting Machine Operator/Tender	595	253	-342	-57.48
89706	Paste-Up Worker	306	168	-138	-45.10
97317	Railroad Brake, Signal, Switch	205	126	-79	-38.54
56014	Peripheral EDP Equipment Operator	1,050	670	-380	-36.19
85726	Station Installer and Repairer, Telephone	910	630	-280	-30.77
89713	Camera Operator	307	213	-94	-30.62
92717	Sewing Machine Operator, Garment	8,035	5,630	-2,405	-29.93
89717	Photolithographic Stripper	960	704	-256	-26.67
53108	Transit Clerk	341	259	-82	-24.05
92545	Photoengraving and Lithographer Operator	214	166	-48	-22.43
56021	Data Entry Keyer, Composing	966	783	-183	-18.94
89126	Hand Worker, Jewelry, Precision	375	304	-71	-18.93
56011	Computer Operator, Exc. Peripheral Equip.	12,026	9,760	-2,266	-18.84
92515	Letterpress Setter/Operator	573	466	-107	-18.67
57108	Central Office Operator	2,128	1,773	-355	-16.68
85714	Electric Motor Repairer	587	491	-96	-16.35
93935	Cannery Worker	2,545	2,138	-407	-15.99
22102	Aeronautical and Astronautical Engineer	2,686	2,286	-400	-14.89
34053	Dancer and Choreographer	4,199	3,591	-608	-14.48
32926	EKG Technician	1,033	884	-149	-14.42

Source: State of Florida, Department of Labor and Employment Security, Office of Labor Market Statistics, *Florida Industry and Occupational Employment Projections, 1998-2008,* prepublication release.

University of Florida   **Bureau of Economic and Business Research**

Table 6.57. AVERAGE ANNUAL PAY: PAY OF EMPLOYEES COVERED BY STATE AND FEDERAL
UNEMPLOYMENT INSURANCE PROGRAMS IN THE UNITED STATES AND IN THE STATE
AND METROPOLITAN AREAS OF FLORIDA, 1997 AND 1998

Industry or metropolitan area	1997 (dollars)	1998 (dollars)	Per-centage change 1997-98	1998 MSA ranking
United States	30,064	31,722	5.5	(X)
Florida				
Private industry 1/	26,092	27,585	5.7	(X)
Mining	38,947	41,093	5.5	(X)
Construction	27,254	28,939	6.2	(X)
Manufacturing	33,491	35,331	5.5	(X)
Transportation, communications, and public utilities	33,910	35,245	3.9	(X)
Wholesale trade	36,792	38,690	5.2	(X)
Retail trade	16,294	17,143	5.2	(X)
Finance, insurance, and real estate	37,867	40,680	7.4	(X)
Services	25,697	27,148	5.6	(X)
Government	30,106	31,534	4.7	(X)
MSA				
Daytona Beach	21,932	22,730	3.6	289
Ft. Lauderdale	28,502	29,939	5.0	82
Ft. Myers-Cape Coral	24,197	25,267	4.4	225
Ft. Pierce-Port St. Lucie	24,810	25,507	2.8	215
Ft. Walton Beach	22,108	23,352	5.6	277
Gainesville	23,612	24,956	5.7	236
Jacksonville	27,959	29,937	7.1	83
Lakeland-Winter Haven	25,036	26,189	4.6	188
Melbourne-Titusville-Palm Bay	28,366	29,462	3.9	95
Miami	29,385	30,828	4.9	64
Naples	(NA)	26,739	(NA)	171
Ocala	22,420	23,570	5.1	273
Orlando	(NA)	27,759	(NA)	134
Panama City	22,569	23,873	5.8	264
Pensacola	23,830	24,854	4.3	241
Punta Gorda	22,199	23,102	4.1	281
Sarasota-Bradenton	23,588	25,208	6.9	227
Tallahassee	25,064	26,803	6.9	166
Tampa-St. Petersburg-Clearwater	26,831	28,220	5.2	127
West Palm Beach-Boca Raton	29,808	31,735	6.5	48

(NA) Not available.
(X) Not applicable.
1/ Includes industries not listed separately.
Note: Some 1997 data are revised. 1998 data are preliminary. Data are for Metropolitan Statistical Areas (MSAs) and Primary Metropolitan Statistical Areas (PMSAs) defined as of June 30, 1996, and are not comparable to data in previous *Abstracts.*

Source: U.S., Department of Labor, Bureau of Labor Statistics, *News: Average Annual Pay by State and Industry, 1998,* release of December 15, 1999, and *News: Average Annual Pay Levels in Metropolitan Areas, 1998*, release of December 30, 1999, Internet site <http://stats.bls.gov/news.release/> (accessed 11 April 2000).

University of Florida   **Bureau of Economic and Business Research**

SOCIAL INSURANCE AND WELFARE

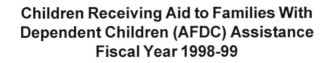

Children Receiving Aid to Families With Dependent Children (AFDC) Assistance Fiscal Year 1998-99

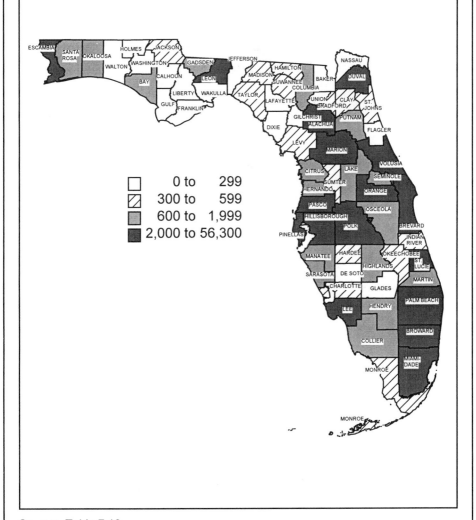

	0 to	299
	300 to	599
	600 to	1,999
	2,000 to	56,300

Source: Table 7.18

SECTION 7.00
SOCIAL INSURANCE AND WELFARE

TABLES LISTED BY MAJOR HEADINGS

University of Florida   **Bureau of Economic and Business Research**

Table 7.03. MEDICARE: ENROLLMENT IN HOSPITAL AND/OR MEDICAL INSURANCE BY METROPOLITAN/NONMETROPOLITAN RESIDENCE IN FLORIDA, 1997 AND 1998

Item	Total enrollment		Persons aged 65 and over		Disability beneficiaries 1/	
	1997	1998	1997	1998	1997	1998
Florida, total	2,727,545	2,761,156	2,460,069	2,476,804	267,476	284,352
Metropolitan counties 2/	2,407,410	2,434,677	2,173,563	2,186,266	233,847	248,411
With central city	2,128,701	2,150,820	1,925,274	1,934,841	203,427	215,979
Without central city	278,709	283,857	248,289	251,425	30,420	32,432
Nonmetropolitan counties	318,721	324,785	285,205	288,994	33,516	35,791

1/ Persons under age 65 entitled to cash disability benefits for at least 24 consecutive months and also those eligible solely on the basis of end-stage renal disease.
2/ Counties included in Metropolitan Statistical Areas (MSAs).
Note: Geographic classification is based on the address to which the enrollee's cash benefit check is mailed or the mailing address recorded in the health insurance master file.

Table 7.04. MEDICARE: ENROLLMENT, JULY 1, AND BENEFIT PAYMENTS OR REIMBURSEMENTS CALENDAR YEARS, OF PERSONS AGED 65 AND OVER IN FLORIDA, 1985 THROUGH 1998

Year	Hospital and/or medical insurance		Hospital insurance		Supplementary medical insurance	
	Enroll-ment (1,000)	Payments 1/ ($1,000)	Enroll-ment (1,000)	Payments 1/ ($1,000)	Enroll-ment (1,000)	Payments 1/ ($1,000)
1985	1,856	5,040,418	1,820	3,267,584	1,829	1,772,834
1986	1,921	5,394,033	1,881	3,347,974	1,893	2,046,059
1987	2,135	5,720,000	2,092	3,275,000	2,095	2,445,000
1988	2,114	5,517,000	2,070	2,869,000	2,072	2,648,000
1989	2,174	6,470,000	2,165	3,340,000	2,129	3,130,000
1990	2,174	6,960,000	2,165	3,565,000	2,129	3,394,000
1991	2,230	7,440,000	2,221	3,742,000	2,183	3,698,000
1992	2,273	8,247,006	2,265	4,789,953	2,228	3,457,053
1993	2,322	8,812,192	2,313	5,087,368	2,275	3,724,823
1994	2,367	(NA)	2,359	(NA)	2,318	(NA)
1995	2,396	(NA)	2,385	(NA)	2,344	(NA)
1996	2,434	(NA)	2,421	(NA)	2,381	(NA)
1997	2,460	(NA)	2,447	(NA)	2,405	(NA)
1998	2,477	(NA)	2,464	(NA)	2,420	(NA)

(NA) Not available.
1/ Benefit payments were reported prior to 1993. In 1993, reimbursement payments derived from reimbursed bills or claims for services were reported. Reimbursement data for the aged are inflated for a 5 percent sample of Medicare beneficiaries. Data prior to 1993 are not comparable to data reported for 1993.
Note: Data from 1985 are estimated.

Source for Tables 7.03 and 7.04: U.S., Department of Health and Human Services, Health Care Financing Administration, unpublished data.

University of Florida   **Bureau of Economic and Business Research**

Table 7.05. MEDICARE: PERSONS AGED 65 AND OVER AND DISABLED BENEFICIARIES ENROLLED
IN HOSPITAL INSURANCE IN THE STATE AND COUNTIES OF FLORIDA, JULY 1, 1998

County	Persons aged 65 and over	Disabled benefi- ciaries 1/	County	Persons aged 65 and over	Disabled benefi- ciaries 1/
Florida	2,464,219	284,352	Lake	53,231	4,607
			Lee	90,985	7,892
Alachua	20,828	3,890	Leon	18,518	2,498
Baker	1,772	637	Levy	5,352	1,096
Bay	18,649	3,279	Liberty	663	198
Bradford	2,618	632	Madison	2,521	531
Brevard	82,279	9,686	Manatee	50,143	4,289
Broward	230,337	22,040	Marion	58,880	6,917
Calhoun	1,554	357	Martin	31,495	2,011
Charlotte	35,592	2,703	Miami-Dade	265,238	29,052
Citrus	31,757	3,079	Monroe	9,770	1,152
Clay	12,238	1,977	Nassau	6,287	1,193
Collier	44,308	2,633	Okaloosa	19,707	2,731
Columbia	6,962	1,658	Okeechobee	5,716	980
De Soto	4,338	738	Orange	85,741	15,315
Dixie	1,937	518	Osceola	17,187	3,478
Duval	78,055	13,475	Palm Beach	225,643	14,625
Escambia	35,848	6,042	Pasco	76,938	8,615
Flagler	11,969	1,174	Pinellas	188,634	19,736
Franklin	1,554	254	Polk	77,422	10,769
Gadsden	5,200	1,478	Putnam	11,425	2,240
Gilchrist	1,685	356	St. Johns	18,052	2,098
Glades	770	132	St. Lucie	34,933	4,583
Gulf	2,057	334	Santa Rosa	11,617	2,139
Hamilton	1,405	386	Sarasota	97,488	5,996
Hardee	2,815	535	Seminole	32,438	4,673
Hendry	3,050	508	Sumter	7,145	1,165
Hernando	36,641	4,138	Suwannee	5,572	1,121
Highlands	23,532	1,980	Taylor	2,561	517
Hillsborough	111,042	19,741	Union	871	261
Holmes	2,684	622	Volusia	89,168	10,790
Indian River	29,659	1,944	Wakulla	2,073	402
Jackson	6,572	1,576	Walton	4,272	899
Jefferson	1,704	330	Washington	3,012	700
Lafayette	566	101	Unknown	1,544	150

1/ Persons under age 65 entitled to cash disability benefits for at least 24 consecutive months and
also those eligible solely on the basis of end-stage renal disease.
Note: Geographic classification is based on the address to which the enrollee's cash benefit check is
mailed or the mailing address recorded in the health insurance master file.

Source: U.S., Department of Health and Human Services, Health Care Financing Administration,
unpublished data.

University of Florida   **Bureau of Economic and Business Research**

Table 7.12. SOCIAL SECURITY: NUMBER OF BENEFICIARIES AND AMOUNT OF BENEFITS IN CURRENT-PAYMENT STATUS BY TYPE OF BENEFICIARY IN THE STATE AND COUNTIES OF FLORIDA, DECEMBER 1998

Residence of beneficiary	Total	Retired workers 1/	Disabled workers	Wives and husbands	Children	Widows and widowers 2/
			Number of beneficiaries			
Florida	3,109,035	2,102,502	281,198	203,025	208,451	313,859
Alachua	27,353	16,365	3,110	1,670	3,180	3,030
Baker	3,082	1,470	565	170	515	360
Bay	26,367	15,630	3,245	1,980	2,320	3,190
Bradford	3,194	1,790	435	180	370	420
Brevard	108,141	73,095	9,870	7,900	6,350	10,925
Broward	279,948	194,210	22,340	15,070	17,025	31,300
Calhoun	2,327	1,225	320	165	280	340
Charlotte	49,396	37,115	3,100	3,420	1,770	3,990
Citrus	42,361	30,930	3,230	2,885	1,845	3,470
Clay	18,693	11,220	2,285	1,265	1,865	2,055
Collier	52,833	38,280	2,685	5,030	2,030	4,810
Columbia	10,494	5,925	1,630	635	1,150	1,150
De Soto	6,043	3,850	725	390	525	555
Dixie	3,128	1,775	510	190	330	320
Duval	105,051	62,255	12,975	5,985	10,930	12,905
Escambia	49,532	28,960	5,675	4,105	4,535	6,255
Flagler	15,802	11,790	1,190	1,025	755	1,040
Franklin	2,216	1,410	275	145	130	260
Gadsden	8,360	4,520	1,320	375	1,315	830
Gilchrist	2,547	1,450	340	175	280	300
Glades	1,767	1,200	190	115	115	150
Gulf	2,863	1,620	330	260	230	425
Hamilton	2,179	1,110	355	140	300	275
Hardee	4,065	2,400	500	255	475	435
Hendry	4,765	2,775	530	315	640	505
Hernando	47,171	34,070	3,935	3,200	2,380	3,585
Highlands	28,716	21,000	1,955	2,010	1,380	2,370
Hillsborough	152,215	92,780	19,405	9,030	14,480	16,520
Holmes	4,326	2,245	685	340	465	595
Indian River	33,400	24,195	1,915	2,735	1,385	3,170
Jackson	9,542	5,175	1,280	565	1,265	1,260
Jefferson	2,428	1,415	315	150	245	305
Lafayette	1,068	600	145	90	105	125
Lake	60,890	44,440	4,475	4,070	2,640	5,265
Lee	110,604	79,780	7,735	7,805	5,550	9,735
Leon	24,314	15,395	2,370	1,425	2,415	2,710
Levy	8,344	5,000	1,155	555	765	870
Liberty	1,070	535	195	65	135	140
Madison	3,599	1,985	500	225	400	490
Manatee	66,077	47,505	4,585	4,405	3,000	6,585
Marion	74,980	52,495	6,600	4,975	4,665	6,245
Martin	36,239	26,525	2,030	2,890	1,315	3,480
Miami-Dade	307,785	204,655	28,115	20,710	25,235	29,070
Monroe	13,045	9,120	1,200	930	605	1,190
Nassau	9,255	5,320	1,160	750	915	1,110
Okaloosa	26,049	16,085	2,555	2,335	1,960	3,115
Okeechobee	7,181	4,315	920	465	695	785

See footnotes at end of table.   Continued . . .

University of Florida   **Bureau of Economic and Business Research**

Table 7.12. SOCIAL SECURITY: NUMBER OF BENEFICIARIES AND AMOUNT OF BENEFITS IN CURRENT-PAYMENT STATUS BY TYPE OF BENEFICIARY IN THE STATE AND COUNTIES OF FLORIDA, DECEMBER 1998 (Continued)

Residence of beneficiary	Total	Retired workers 1/	Disabled workers	Wives and husbands	Children	Widows and widowers 2/
			Number of beneficiaries (Continued)			
Orange	115,415	69,900	14,655	6,980	11,895	11,985
Osceola	25,374	15,295	3,390	1,520	2,830	2,340
Palm Beach	259,559	190,620	14,655	17,130	11,730	25,425
Pasco	103,141	72,630	9,505	6,270	5,325	9,410
Pinellas	225,889	157,675	19,455	12,870	10,865	25,025
Polk	104,308	68,440	11,165	6,435	8,050	10,215
Putnam	16,943	10,050	2,240	1,180	1,640	1,830
St. Johns	23,027	15,355	2,000	1,750	1,565	2,355
St. Lucie	49,250	33,875	4,800	3,025	3,520	4,030
Santa Rosa	17,465	10,300	2,170	1,450	1,645	1,900
Sarasota	102,046	75,545	5,440	7,705	3,215	10,145
Seminole	49,923	31,600	5,180	3,285	4,470	5,390
Sumter	14,448	10,230	1,310	870	810	1,225
Suwannee	7,902	4,630	1,055	540	750	925
Taylor	3,964	2,225	530	260	425	525
Union	1,433	745	215	85	230	155
Volusia	113,077	77,720	10,435	7,070	6,620	11,235
Wakulla	3,092	1,810	415	175	390	305
Walton	7,581	4,500	1,005	560	705	810
Washington	4,355	2,345	620	310	475	605
			Amount of monthly cash benefits ($1,000)			
Florida	2,235,695	1,635,929	206,575	80,093	76,613	236,484
Alachua	18,820	12,580	2,182	674	1,223	2,161
Baker	1,924	1,054	400	56	181	232
Bay	17,264	11,242	2,285	708	824	2,202
Bradford	2,019	1,243	309	61	129	275
Brevard	78,216	56,811	7,651	3,079	2,434	8,241
Broward	213,881	159,050	16,924	6,072	6,637	25,198
Calhoun	1,372	809	215	51	96	200
Charlotte	36,785	29,147	2,505	1,355	659	3,121
Citrus	30,732	23,740	2,599	1,114	681	2,599
Clay	12,686	8,305	1,714	481	739	1,450
Collier	42,084	32,668	2,142	2,317	797	4,161
Columbia	6,635	4,133	1,159	218	378	746
De Soto	4,048	2,839	503	140	171	394
Dixie	1,967	1,247	352	61	104	204
Duval	71,855	46,991	9,243	2,350	4,113	9,158
Escambia	31,875	20,608	3,978	1,485	1,596	4,208
Flagler	11,996	9,466	1,013	419	295	802
Franklin	1,437	991	189	52	44	164
Gadsden	4,809	2,968	827	125	398	492
Gilchrist	1,637	1,022	258	56	100	197
Glades	1,225	888	146	43	48	104
Gulf	1,984	1,251	243	102	85	305
Hamilton	1,292	746	251	42	90	164
Hardee	2,515	1,673	318	86	161	278

See footnotes at end of table.   Continued . . .

University of Florida   **Bureau of Economic and Business Research**

Table 7.12. SOCIAL SECURITY: NUMBER OF BENEFICIARIES AND AMOUNT OF BENEFITS IN CURRENT-PAYMENT STATUS BY TYPE OF BENEFICIARY IN THE STATE AND COUNTIES OF FLORIDA, DECEMBER 1998 (Continued)

Residence of beneficiary	Total	Retired workers 1/	Disabled workers	Wives and husbands	Children	Widows and widowers 2/
			Amount of monthly cash benefits ($1,000) (Continued)			
Hendry	3,101	2,073	358	111	208	349
Hernando	34,471	26,410	3,247	1,237	864	2,712
Highlands	20,255	15,833	1,445	762	454	1,761
Hillsborough	105,123	70,653	13,803	3,509	5,201	11,955
Holmes	2,463	1,429	473	98	138	327
Indian River	25,508	19,707	1,472	1,196	536	2,600
Jackson	5,674	3,441	878	175	434	746
Jefferson	1,484	961	207	51	88	177
Lafayette	668	421	103	29	31	80
Lake	43,977	34,140	3,342	1,607	958	3,930
Lee	82,923	63,871	5,988	3,218	2,136	7,714
Leon	17,260	12,079	1,632	599	923	2,026
Levy	5,483	3,592	861	192	250	589
Liberty	648	372	130	22	47	79
Madison	2,112	1,315	330	73	118	278
Manatee	49,164	37,631	3,462	1,811	1,142	5,122
Marion	53,005	39,971	4,972	1,896	1,602	4,566
Martin	28,372	22,125	1,619	1,283	501	2,844
Miami-Dade	199,152	144,078	18,514	7,217	8,947	20,396
Monroe	9,489	7,032	949	375	236	899
Nassau	6,633	4,227	916	309	374	808
Okaloosa	16,928	11,424	1,800	844	744	2,116
Okeechobee	4,813	3,217	662	163	231	537
Orange	79,462	53,451	10,400	2,679	4,234	8,698
Osceola	17,091	11,437	2,498	520	991	1,646
Palm Beach	210,583	165,100	11,400	7,768	4,572	21,743
Pasco	73,867	55,240	7,340	2,343	1,912	7,030
Pinellas	164,948	122,282	14,295	5,181	4,197	18,995
Polk	72,884	52,109	7,942	2,498	2,817	7,513
Putnam	11,202	7,372	1,603	415	546	1,266
St. Johns	16,975	12,275	1,494	745	600	1,862
St. Lucie	35,759	26,665	3,629	1,190	1,170	3,106
Santa Rosa	11,644	7,574	1,643	525	624	1,278
Sarasota	78,674	61,534	4,252	3,294	1,312	8,282
Seminole	35,630	24,637	3,927	1,287	1,718	4,061
Sumter	10,247	7,808	965	331	274	869
Suwannee	5,016	3,231	757	179	250	598
Taylor	2,599	1,633	389	95	141	341
Union	866	504	152	28	83	98
Volusia	81,069	59,573	7,901	2,742	2,503	8,349
Wakulla	1,958	1,276	288	61	135	199
Walton	4,808	3,158	715	197	225	514
Washington	2,627	1,592	420	99	154	361

1/ Includes "special age 72" beneficiaries.
2/ Includes nondisabled and disabled widows and widowers, widowed mothers and fathers, and parents.
Note: Detail may not add to totals because of rounding.

Source: U.S., Department of Health and Human Services, Social Security Administration, *OASDI Beneficiaries by State and County, December 1998,* Internet site <http://www.ssa.gov/statistics/oasdi_sc/1998/index.html> (accessed 1 May 2000).

University of Florida **Bureau of Economic and Business Research**

Table 7.14. SOCIAL SECURITY: AVERAGE MONTHLY BENEFITS OF BENEFICIARIES
AGED 65 AND OVER AND RETIRED WORKERS IN THE STATE
AND COUNTIES OF FLORIDA, DECEMBER 1998

(in dollars)

County	All beneficiaries aged 65 and over	Retired workers	County	All beneficiaries aged 65 and over	Retired workers
Florida	759.33	526.19	Lake	748.47	560.68
			Lee	779.12	577.47
Alachua	746.87	459.91	Leon	765.73	496.79
Baker	695.15	341.99	Levy	697.47	430.49
Bay	695.16	426.37	Liberty	651.97	347.66
Bradford	675.96	389.17	Madison	626.87	365.38
Brevard	752.44	525.34	Manatee	771.84	569.50
Broward	804.94	568.14	Marion	741.58	533.09
Calhoun	627.52	347.66	Martin	809.21	610.53
Charlotte	765.16	590.07	Miami-Dade	693.78	468.11
Citrus	746.65	560.42	Monroe	749.70	539.06
Clay	719.55	444.28	Nassau	762.52	456.73
Collier	827.42	618.33	Okaloosa	680.39	438.56
Columbia	675.86	393.84	Okeechobee	723.09	447.99
De Soto	719.53	469.80	Orange	745.76	463.12
Dixie	683.03	398.66	Osceola	728.36	450.74
Duval	736.18	447.32	Palm Beach	848.00	636.08
Escambia	680.32	416.05	Pasco	742.62	535.58
Flagler	784.55	599.04	Pinellas	757.65	541.34
Franklin	672.78	447.20	Polk	743.64	499.57
Gadsden	640.36	355.02	Putnam	709.23	435.11
Gilchrist	684.11	401.26	St. Johns	778.10	533.07
Glades	725.10	502.55	St. Lucie	770.39	541.42
Gulf	737.91	436.95	Santa Rosa	703.17	433.67
Hamilton	640.30	342.36	Sarasota	792.83	603.00
Hardee	681.33	411.56	Seminole	759.20	493.50
Hendry	728.18	435.05	Sumter	742.13	540.42
Hernando	754.43	559.88	Suwannee	669.89	408.88
Highlands	734.36	551.37	Taylor	703.70	411.96
Hillsborough	742.40	464.17	Union	651.50	351.71
Holmes	597.07	330.33	Volusia	747.78	526.84
Indian River	791.22	590.03	Wakulla	680.92	412.68
Jackson	635.04	360.62	Walton	672.89	416.57
Jefferson	641.89	395.80	Washington	643.03	365.56
Lafayette	668.57	394.19			

Source: U.S., Department of Health and Human Services, Social Security Administration, *OASDI Beneficiaries by State and County, December 1998,* Internet site <http://www.ssa.gov/statistics/oasdi_sc/1998/index.html> (accessed 1 May 2000).

University of Florida   **Bureau of Economic and Business Research**

Table 7.15. PUBLIC ASSISTANCE: DIRECT ASSISTANCE PAYMENTS, CALENDAR YEARS, 1996 THROUGH 1999, AND MEDICAL ASSISTANCE PAYMENTS, FISCAL YEARS 1995-96 THROUGH 1998-99, BY PROGRAM IN FLORIDA

(rounded to thousands of dollars)

Type of assistance	1996	1997	1998	1999
Direct assistance, total	2,114,379	2,164,642	(NA)	(NA)
Basic Supplemental Security Income (SSI)	1,408,440	1,448,658	1,515,121	1,564,230
Old-Age Assistance (OAA)	299,359	303,614	307,165	305,900
Aid to the Blind (AB)	12,753	12,664	12,875	13,084
Aid to the Disabled (AD)	1,096,329	1,132,380	1,195,081	1,245,246
SSI State Supplementation 1/	18,384	18,384	18,384	24,271
Aid to Families with Dependent Children (AFDC)	687,555	697,600	(NA)	(NA)

	1995-96	1996-97	1997-98	1998-99
Medical assistance, total 2/	4,743,272	4,929,041	(NA)	5,032,532
Aid to the Blind	15,266	15,867	(NA)	(NA)
Aid to the Disabled	2,067,941	2,223,067	(NA)	2,655,894
Aid to Families with Dependent Children (AFDC)	1,351,103	1,282,788	(NA)	71,819
Old-Age Assistance	1,249,245	1,346,236	(NA)	1,482,380

1/ Payments to persons eligible for state benefits but not eligible under federal requirements.
2/ Federal fiscal year ending September 30. The total for 1996-97 and 1998-99 includes other Title XIX recipients and is not comparable to earlier years.

Source: U.S., Department of Health and Human Services, Social Security Administration, *Social Security Bulletin: Annual Statistical Supplement, 2000,* Internet site <http://www.ssa.gov/statistics/Supplement/2000> (accessed 25 August 2000), and previous editions, and State of Florida, Agency for Health Care Administration, unpublished data.

Table 7.16. MEDICAL ASSISTANCE: NUMBER OF RECIPIENTS BY AGE OF RECIPIENT AND BY TYPE OF SERVICE, IN FLORIDA, FEDERAL FISCAL YEAR 1998-99

Type of service	Total	Aged 5 and under	Aged 6 to 20	Aged 21 to 64	Aged 65 to 84	Aged 85 and over
Unduplicated total	1,634,804	395,858	503,166	494,875	178,078	62,827
Inpatient hospital	229,699	32,779	32,168	109,444	39,656	15,652
Mental hospital--aged	225	0	1	75	128	21
Intermediate care facilities	39,434	5	198	6,362	15,843	17,026
Skilled nursing facilities	73,580	55	96	8,089	33,161	32,179
Physician	1,241,752	338,088	379,260	383,808	109,205	31,391
Dental	339,256	74,483	210,426	29,871	17,426	7,050
Other practitioners	246,606	25,217	64,474	99,657	43,283	13,975
Outpatient hospital	625,517	150,437	142,690	235,971	76,464	19,955
Clinic	131,328	7,115	49,278	55,046	17,213	2,676
Home health	89,350	23,195	12,815	35,178	12,360	5,802
Family planning	104,569	416	34,509	69,153	393	98
Lab and X-ray	680,903	171,371	180,370	270,036	44,385	14,741
Prescribed drugs	982,886	229,156	228,535	322,569	150,770	51,856
Early and periodic screening	268,621	189,953	78,479	188	0	1
Rural health clinic	105,345	33,524	30,106	33,971	6,473	1,271
Other care	345,929	34,401	65,727	127,744	83,533	34,524

Note: Data are for fiscal year ending September 30.
Source: State of Florida, Agency for Health Care Administration, unpublished data.

Table 7.18. PUBLIC ASSISTANCE: AVERAGE MONTHLY AID TO FAMILIES WITH DEPENDENT CHILDREN (AFDC) CASES BY TYPE OF RECIPIENT AND AVERAGE MONTHLY PAYMENTS FOR ALL CASES IN THE STATE, DEPARTMENT OF HEALTH DISTRICTS, AND COUNTIES OF FLORIDA, FISCAL YEAR 1998-99

District and county	Assistance groups (families)	Average monthly cases			Average monthly expenditure (dollars)
		Adults	Children	Persons	
Florida	89,889	55,953	169,401	225,353	20,768,154
District 1	3,309	1,756	6,210	7,966	751,721
Escambia	2,325	1,231	4,543	5,774	539,494
Okaloosa	451	230	776	1,006	96,719
Santa Rosa	428	265	716	981	93,450
Walton	105	30	175	205	22,058
District 2	4,433	2,753	7,877	10,631	981,420
Bay	579	325	1,023	1,348	126,841
Calhoun	139	99	240	339	30,579
Franklin	39	14	68	82	8,473
Gadsden	730	413	1,340	1,753	163,162
Gulf	77	39	124	163	15,157
Holmes	135	69	250	319	28,514
Jackson	285	155	497	653	61,155
Jefferson	164	108	298	406	36,350
Leon	1,514	1,081	2,732	3,813	340,478
Liberty	43	21	66	86	9,192
Madison	198	87	320	407	42,131
Taylor	255	179	457	637	59,864
Wakulla	151	106	242	348	32,759
Washington	124	57	220	277	26,765
District 3	4,379	2,741	8,061	10,802	1,000,887
Alachua	1,753	1,135	3,244	4,379	400,418
Bradford	200	124	357	481	45,270
Columbia	554	339	1,018	1,358	126,057
Dixie	158	112	293	406	37,109
Gilchrist	75	45	131	176	16,860
Hamilton	186	129	363	492	42,412
Lafayette	41	28	72	99	9,310
Levy	264	152	465	617	57,607
Putnam	773	446	1,439	1,885	180,579
Suwannee	288	167	509	675	64,013
Union	87	64	170	234	21,252
District 4	4,595	1,988	8,211	10,197	1,018,351
Baker	135	73	236	308	30,287
Clay	340	152	576	728	77,297
Duval	3,626	1,578	6,643	8,221	805,159
Nassau	196	78	293	370	40,752
St. Johns	298	107	463	570	64,856
District 5	5,549	3,289	9,873	13,162	1,259,496
Pasco	1,426	927	2,473	3,400	319,766
Pinellas	4,123	2,362	7,400	9,762	939,730
District 6	7,825	4,288	14,902	19,189	1,836,794
Hillsborough	6,809	3,799	12,989	16,788	1,598,066
Manatee	1,016	489	1,913	2,401	238,728

See footnotes at end of table.   Continued . . .

University of Florida   **Bureau of Economic and Business Research**

Health Districts
Effective July 1, 1993

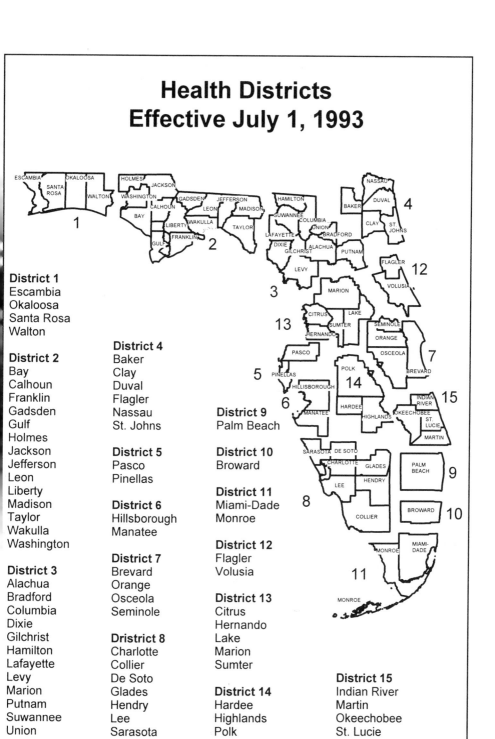

District 1
Escambia
Okaloosa
Santa Rosa
Walton

District 2
Bay
Calhoun
Franklin
Gadsden
Gulf
Holmes
Jackson
Jefferson
Leon
Liberty
Madison
Taylor
Wakulla
Washington

District 3
Alachua
Bradford
Columbia
Dixie
Gilchrist
Hamilton
Lafayette
Levy
Marion
Putnam
Suwannee
Union

District 4
Baker
Clay
Duval
Flagler
Nassau
St. Johns

District 5
Pasco
Pinellas

District 6
Hillsborough
Manatee

District 7
Brevard
Orange
Osceola
Seminole

Dristrict 8
Charlotte
Collier
De Soto
Glades
Hendry
Lee
Sarasota

District 9
Palm Beach

District 10
Broward

District 11
Miami-Dade
Monroe

District 12
Flagler
Volusia

District 13
Citrus
Hernando
Lake
Marion
Sumter

District 14
Hardee
Highlands
Polk

District 15
Indian River
Martin
Okeechobee
St. Lucie

Table 7.18. PUBLIC ASSISTANCE: AVERAGE MONTHLY AID TO FAMILIES WITH DEPENDENT CHILDREN (AFDC) CASES BY TYPE OF RECIPIENT AND AVERAGE MONTHLY PAYMENTS FOR ALL CASES IN THE STATE, DEPARTMENT OF HEALTH DISTRICTS, AND COUNTIES OF FLORIDA, FISCAL YEAR 1998-99 (Continued)

| District and county | Assistance groups (families) | Average monthly cases | | | Average monthly expenditure (dollars) |
		Adults	Children	Persons	
District 7	7,620	3,940	13,734	17,674	1,734,337
Brevard	1,549	699	2,637	3,336	336,556
Orange	4,221	2,128	7,791	9,919	972,225
Osceola	763	486	1,338	1,825	172,090
Seminole	1,087	627	1,968	2,594	253,466
District 8	2,935	1,420	5,409	6,832	656,337
Charlotte	235	112	398	511	51,161
Collier	481	215	909	1,125	108,566
De Soto	156	76	265	341	34,848
Glades 1/	0	0	0	0	0
Hendry	379	225	746	971	89,356
Lee	1,120	531	2,124	2,655	248,837
Sarasota	564	261	967	1,229	123,569
District 9	4,096	2,524	8,153	10,677	951,980
Palm Beach	4,096	2,524	8,153	10,677	951,980
District 10	4,940	2,472	9,463	11,935	1,122,143
Broward	4,940	2,472	9,463	11,935	1,122,143
District 11	28,798	22,646	56,653	79,299	6,838,761
Miami-Dade	28,565	22,503	56,271	78,774	6,787,534
Monroe	233	143	382	525	51,227
District 12	2,233	1,375	3,997	5,372	511,053
Flagler	131	61	224	285	28,985
Volusia	2,102	1,314	3,773	5,087	482,068
District 13	3,247	1,737	5,780	7,517	730,011
Citrus	385	234	641	875	87,690
Hernando	487	306	841	1,147	112,763
Lake	890	453	1,588	2,041	197,850
Marion	1,219	611	2,226	2,837	272,221
Sumter	266	133	484	617	59,487
District 14	3,746	1,855	6,990	8,844	864,900
Hardee	197	75	396	471	47,349
Highlands	427	209	814	1,023	100,963
Polk	3,122	1,571	5,780	7,350	716,588
District 15	2,184	1,169	4,088	5,256	509,963
Indian River	337	172	588	760	76,477
Martin	436	245	784	1,028	103,527
Okeechobee	171	78	310	388	37,641
St. Lucie	1,240	674	2,406	3,080	292,318

1/ Payments issued by Hendry County.

Note: Detail may not add to total because of rounding.

Source: State of Florida, Department of Health, unpublished data.

Table 7.19. PUBLIC ASSISTANCE: RECIPIENTS OF SUPPLEMENTAL SECURITY INCOME
AND AMOUNT OF PAYMENTS IN THE STATE AND COUNTIES
OF FLORIDA, DECEMBER 1999

County	Total	Reason for eligibility Aged	Reason for eligibility Blind and disabled	Age Under 18	Age 18 to 64	Age 65 and over	SSI re- cipients with OASDI	Payments ($1,000)
Florida	366,966	94,272	272,694	60,843	173,985	132,138	129,355	134,978
Alachua	4,777	536	4,241	975	2,850	952	1,656	1,767
Baker	458	53	405	79	291	88	147	174
Bay	3,413	447	2,966	546	2,076	791	1,347	1,219
Bradford	710	92	618	125	416	169	268	279
Brevard	7,552	1,006	6,546	1,818	4,283	1,451	2,578	2,802
Broward	26,211	6,830	19,381	4,444	12,752	9,015	8,642	9,857
Calhoun	501	85	416	52	270	179	224	175
Charlotte	1,433	265	1,168	230	845	358	576	482
Citrus	1,656	238	1,418	235	1,056	365	677	595
Clay	1,207	133	1,074	270	715	222	397	473
Collier	1,923	487	1,436	283	962	678	734	669
Columbia	2,219	297	1,922	382	1,313	524	875	819
De Soto	721	108	613	152	418	151	295	250
Dixie	549	60	489	86	342	121	222	200
Duval	17,911	2,743	15,168	3,931	9,681	4,299	6,128	6,658
Escambia	8,331	1,020	7,311	1,566	5,001	1,764	2,965	3,031
Flagler	515	95	420	109	287	119	186	204
Franklin	436	105	331	50	221	165	215	156
Gadsden	2,612	428	2,184	537	1,323	752	1,218	916
Gilchrist	376	51	325	54	237	85	168	130
Glades	108	26	82	14	53	41	40	41
Gulf	382	58	324	35	235	112	160	130
Hamilton	578	102	476	93	301	184	275	200
Hardee	850	167	683	130	459	261	407	274
Hendry	695	135	560	142	347	206	259	253
Hernando	1,975	241	1,734	370	1,223	382	766	707
Highlands	1,971	331	1,640	428	1,056	487	826	713
Hillsborough	25,476	4,349	21,127	5,181	13,671	6,624	8,806	9,520
Holmes	728	163	565	66	399	263	356	238
Indian River	1,280	185	1,095	243	735	302	545	447
Jackson	2,101	449	1,652	271	1,072	758	983	715
Jefferson	675	133	542	119	333	223	286	230
Lafayette	132	21	111	20	76	36	57	42
Lake	3,675	549	3,126	826	2,015	834	1,513	1,249

Continued . . .

Table 7.19. PUBLIC ASSISTANCE: RECIPIENTS OF SUPPLEMENTAL SECURITY INCOME
AND AMOUNT OF PAYMENTS IN THE STATE AND COUNTIES
OF FLORIDA, DECEMBER 1999 (CONTINUED)

| County | Total | Reason for eligibility | | Beneficiaries Age | | | SSI recipients with | Payments |
		Aged	Blind and disabled	Under 18	18 to 64	65 and over	OASDI	($1,000)
Lee	5,812	746	5,066	1,228	3,401	1,183	2,104	2,057
Leon	3,886	592	3,294	845	2,104	937	1,416	1,399
Levy	976	151	825	173	574	229	407	383
Liberty	230	31	199	27	150	53	98	86
Madison	1,091	181	910	242	526	323	436	393
Manatee	3,415	446	2,969	802	1,911	702	1,317	1,228
Marion	5,888	861	5,027	1,167	3,371	1,350	2,312	2,129
Martin	1,284	208	1,076	314	681	289	512	462
Miami-Dade	113,801	51,825	61,976	10,109	35,386	68,306	36,854	42,606
Monroe	1,161	306	855	111	618	432	442	433
Nassau	810	96	714	138	501	171	308	289
Okaloosa	2,383	286	2,097	410	1,473	500	939	889
Okeechobee	884	119	765	173	511	200	368	326
Orange	19,526	3,313	16,213	4,873	9,773	4,880	6,196	7,286
Osceola	2,395	466	1,929	529	1,202	664	793	878
Palm Beach	13,416	3,311	10,105	2,454	6,518	4,444	4,553	5,046
Pasco	6,144	720	5,424	1,100	3,921	1,123	2,405	2,258
Pinellas	15,090	2,341	12,749	2,886	8,714	3,490	5,692	5,315
Polk	12,109	1,559	10,550	3,008	6,627	2,474	4,717	4,417
Putnam	2,604	315	2,289	447	1,594	563	1,060	918
St. Johns	1,735	262	1,473	359	977	399	728	568
St. Lucie	4,505	499	4,006	1,197	2,522	786	1,648	1,703
Santa Rosa	1,543	192	1,351	265	949	329	561	550
Sarasota	3,216	613	2,603	464	1,929	823	1,322	1,037
Seminole	4,472	783	3,689	1,058	2,250	1,164	1,480	1,578
Sumter	1,267	156	1,111	298	708	261	520	446
Suwannee	1,100	191	909	160	625	315	467	367
Taylor	743	111	632	148	406	189	300	261
Union	300	44	256	56	174	70	113	118
Volusia	8,491	1,159	7,332	1,639	5,071	1,781	3,340	3,067
Wakulla	472	70	402	72	277	123	205	173
Walton	905	139	766	95	559	251	405	306
Washington	839	132	707	78	486	275	425	266
Unknown	336	60	276	56	182	98	115	121

Source: U.S., Department of Health and Human Services, Social Security Administration, *SSI Recipients
by State and County*, December 1999, Internet site <http:/www.ssa.gov/statistics/ssi_st_cty/1999/pdf/
florida.pdf> (accessed 3 May 2000).

University of Florida   **Bureau of Economic and Business Research**

Table 7.20. MEDICAID: RECIPIENTS AND EXPENDITURE IN THE STATE AND COUNTIES OF FLORIDA, FISCAL YEAR 1998-99

County	Recipients	Expenditure (dollars)	County	Recipients	Expenditure (dollars)
Florida	1,890,663	6,195,388,053	Lake	22,858	62,328,145
			Lee	39,314	140,077,262
Alachua	28,832	127,442,693	Leon	24,539	74,715,454
Baker	3,247	11,607,792	Levy	5,614	16,030,685
Bay	23,330	69,224,973	Liberty	1,115	2,819,692
Bradford	4,650	15,664,883	Madison	3,898	13,513,568
Brevard	44,373	137,068,219	Manatee	25,325	70,405,049
Broward	131,536	428,969,918	Marion	36,371	92,232,853
Calhoun	2,967	11,758,468	Martin	9,862	31,934,993
Charlotte	9,899	39,813,628	Miami-Dade	411,229	1,508,304,230
Citrus	13,169	42,280,214	Monroe	6,512	23,912,711
Clay	8,060	15,713,664	Nassau	4,270	11,612,095
Collier	18,661	46,555,812	Okaloosa	15,282	49,590,737
Columbia	10,936	33,547,191	Okeechobee	5,615	15,497,776
De Soto	4,889	17,922,435	Orange	104,574	318,941,385
Dixie	2,902	6,727,628	Osceola	20,741	54,103,321
Duval	92,201	309,204,970	Palm Beach	92,071	314,398,987
Escambia	46,455	131,425,245	Pasco	37,253	119,697,449
Flagler	3,452	6,303,342	Pinellas	87,783	369,103,271
Franklin	1,868	7,636,524	Polk	73,517	186,529,179
Gadsden	11,342	29,944,328	Putnam	15,598	42,037,761
Gilchrist	2,451	8,016,538	St. Johns	8,776	35,907,683
Glades	152	629,250	St. Lucie	26,680	78,034,838
Gulf	2,532	8,315,914	Santa Rosa	11,705	29,719,289
Hamilton	2,823	7,928,981	Sarasota	19,097	87,755,702
Hardee	6,511	16,074,968	Seminole	24,812	74,123,190
Hendry	7,286	17,289,808	Sumter	8,852	22,746,787
Hernando	13,719	34,928,596	Suwannee	5,786	23,330,646
Highlands	11,930	34,669,910	Taylor	4,128	12,039,992
Hillsborough	135,229	370,005,413	Union	1,818	3,678,357
Holmes	4,531	13,429,055	Volusia	51,344	177,795,519
Indian River	9,349	28,535,993	Wakulla	2,698	7,606,950
Jackson	8,753	53,728,625	Walton	5,486	16,446,941
Jefferson	2,763	8,822,281	Washington	4,416	15,071,391
Lafayette	923	2,096,050	Unknown county	3	60,856

Source: State of Florida, Agency for Health Care Administration, Medicaid Program Analysis, unpublished data.

University of Florida   **Bureau of Economic and Business Research**

Table 7.22. FOOD STAMPS: RECIPIENTS AND BENEFITS IN THE STATE AND COUNTIES
OF FLORIDA, DECEMBER 1999

County	Recipients Total	Receiving public assistance	Benefits in food stamps ($1,000)	County	Recipients Total	Receiving public assistance	Benefits in food stamps ($1,000)
Florida	912,351	424,804	68,275	Lake	9,777	4,218	648
				Lee	12,790	5,561	906
Alachua	15,714	6,756	1,153	Leon	12,731	5,480	977
Baker	1,708	691	120	Levy	3,145	1,364	206
Bay	11,957	5,142	877	Liberty	681	321	46
Bradford	2,430	1,005	172	Madison	1,845	871	117
Brevard	20,299	9,059	1,459	Manatee	10,399	4,410	805
Broward	55,281	26,335	4,377	Marion	17,103	7,428	1,161
Calhoun	1,641	731	112	Martin	4,304	1,919	330
Charlotte	3,561	1,758	256	Miami-Dade	260,566	139,428	20,094
Citrus	6,276	2,791	437	Monroe	2,981	1,711	219
Clay	3,338	1,416	239	Nassau	1,933	929	138
Collier	6,445	2,917	474	Okaloosa	7,053	2,836	492
Columbia	5,521	2,267	385	Okeechobee	2,102	878	149
De Soto	1,991	826	137	Orange	36,348	15,420	2,788
Dixie	1,693	723	111	Osceola	8,791	3,736	656
Duval	36,291	15,013	2,737	Palm Beach	38,651	17,324	2,983
Escambia	23,038	9,057	1,647	Pasco	17,370	7,578	1,234
Flagler	1,766	731	124	Pinellas	38,118	18,663	2,816
Franklin	595	263	40	Polk	36,177	15,401	2,635
Gadsden	6,259	2,575	415	Putnam	8,045	3,309	547
Gilchrist	1,067	418	71	St. Johns	3,594	1,689	258
Glades 1/	(X)	(X)	(X)	St. Lucie	13,720	5,881	1,010
Gulf	1,355	638	97	Santa Rosa	5,416	2,161	404
Hamilton	1,573	609	106	Sarasota	6,582	3,315	464
Hardee	3,055	1,190	225	Seminole	9,842	4,190	729
Hendry 1/	3,755	1,440	300	Sumter	3,312	1,450	215
Hernando	6,064	2,631	432	Suwannee	2,761	1,197	182
Highlands	5,760	2,422	403	Taylor	2,406	1,067	169
Hillsborough	62,676	26,745	4,975	Union	1,029	394	72
Holmes	2,809	1,196	175	Volusia	22,886	10,201	1,696
Indian River	4,157	1,995	302	Wakulla	1,157	492	84
Jackson	3,862	1,677	246	Walton	2,246	1,020	147
Jefferson	1,637	707	109	Washington	2,335	998	151
Lafayette	581	240	37				

(X) Not applicable.
1/ No food stamp issuance office located in Glades County. Food stamp activities are handled in Hendry County.
Note: Figures represent regular participation. Issuance includes duplicate mail issuance.

Source: State of Florida, Department of Health, Office of Economic Services, *Florida Food Stamp Program Participation Statistics for Federal Fiscal Year 1999-2000.*

University of Florida   **Bureau of Economic and Business Research**

Table 7.56. AVERAGE WEEKLY WAGES: AMOUNT RECEIVED BY PERSONS COVERED BY
UNEMPLOYMENT COMPENSATION LAW IN FLORIDA, 1961 THROUGH 1999

(in dollars)

Year	Average weekly wages 1/	Year	Average weekly wages 1/	Year	Average weekly wages 1/
1961	82.64	1974	155.82	1987	344.32
1962	85.50	1975	167.02	1988	362.41
1963	88.23	1976	175.27	1989	382.00
1964	92.54	1977	185.69	1990	392.18
1965	96.34	1978	195.01	1991	408.82
1966	100.25	1979	210.73	1992	424.66
1967	104.80	1980	227.97	1993	443.95
1968	111.71	1981	252.92	1994	453.38
1969	122.57	1982	271.25	1995	465.23
1970	129.33	1983	288.34	1996	479.30
1971	131.97	1984	306.55	1997	493.80
1972	138.02	1985	314.88	1998	522.28
1973	143.30	1986	329.60	1999	541.19

1/ Data prior to 1972 do not include state, local, or federal government figures. Beginning in 1972
state data were included, and beginning in 1974 local data were included. Does not include federal data
after 1974. Data are for fiscal years from 1971 to date; data are for calendar years prior to 1971.
Note: In 1972 and 1978 changes were made extending coverage of workers.

Table 7.57. UNEMPLOYMENT INSURANCE: CONTRIBUTIONS AND DISBURSEMENTS
FOR UNEMPLOYMENT INSURANCE IN FLORIDA, 1961 THROUGH 1999

(rounded to thousands of dollars)

Year	Contributions deposits 1/	Total disbursements 2/	Year	Contributions deposits 1/	Total disbursements 2/	Year	Contributions deposits 1/	Total disbursements 2/
1961	41,970	43,830	1974	99,304	117,453	1987	469,296	285,736
1962	52,392	33,201	1975	263,243	496,688	1988	468,348	304,930
1963	45,079	29,652	1976	342,166	407,060	1989	480,211	355,749
1964	45,956	24,492	1977	360,650	271,917	1990	461,103	488,961
1965	45,160	20,273	1978	424,988	136,723	1991	560,898	897,263
1966	40,720	17,410	1979	389,370	135,457	1992	1,275,490	1,512,423
1967	37,029	20,639	1980	321,578	197,981	1993	1,259,207	1,199,657
1968	34,094	22,343	1981	305,028	206,012	1994	927,283	801,120
1969	42,145	20,875	1982	326,706	379,067	1995	694,134	632,215
1970	48,594	37,306	1983	451,459	406,075	1996	647,922	635,512
1971	57,425	49,704	1984	526,691	279,457	1997	607,804	610,951
1972	71,799	45,441	1985	514,281	277,463	1998	463,692	628,370
1973	85,861	44,962	1986	478,859	315,337	1999	549,539	633,496

1/ Includes interest, reimbursable interstate and state and local government benefits.
2/ Includes payable interstate benefits.

Source for Tables 7.56 and 7.57: State of Florida, Department of Labor and Employment Security,
Division of Employment Security, *Historical Series of Unemployment Insurance Statistical Data, 1937-
1979*, and State of Florida, Department of Labor and Employment Security, Division of Unemployment
Compensation, unpublished data, and Internet site <http://lmi.floridajobs.org/>.

University of Florida   **Bureau of Economic and Business Research**

Table 7.61. OCCUPATIONAL INJURIES: INCIDENCE RATES OF NONFATAL OCCUPATIONAL INJURIES AND ILLNESSES BY INDUSTRY IN FLORIDA 1995 THROUGH 1997

Industry	Total cases			Lost workday cases						Cases without lost workdays		
				Total 1/			With days away from work 2/					
	1995	1996	1997	1995	1996	1997	1995	1996	1997	1995	1996	1997
Private industry 3/	8.1	6.9	6.6	3.4	3.2	3.0	2.2	2.0	1.8	4.6	3.7	3.6
Agriculture, forestry, and fishing 3/	10.5	8.0	8.5	4.2	3.5	3.8	3.2	2.7	2.8	6.4	4.5	4.7
Mining	3.2	3.0	2.8	1.7	1.8	1.5	1.1	1.1	1.0	1.5	1.2	1.3
Construction	9.5	8.7	9.8	4.1	4.6	4.3	3.3	3.5	3.2	5.4	4.1	5.4
Manufacturing	8.9	8.7	8.5	4.1	4.2	4.1	2.4	2.1	2.0	4.7	4.5	4.4
Durable goods	9.2	8.9	8.8	4.0	4.1	3.9	2.2	2.0	1.9	5.1	4.7	4.8
Nondurable goods	8.4	8.5	8.1	4.3	4.2	4.3	2.5	2.4	2.1	4.1	4.3	3.8
Transportation, communications, and public utilities	9.3	8.5	7.1	4.7	5.1	4.2	3.2	3.8	2.8	4.6	3.5	3.0
Wholesale and retail trade	7.7	5.6	6.6	3.1	2.7	2.7	2.1	1.9	1.8	4.6	2.9	3.9
Wholesale trade	6.6	5.8	5.7	2.8	3.0	2.6	1.8	1.8	1.7	3.8	2.8	3.1
Retail trade	8.1	5.6	6.9	3.2	2.6	2.8	2.2	1.9	1.9	4.9	3.0	4.1
Finance, insurance, and real estate	4.2	3.0	2.4	1.5	1.1	0.8	1.0	0.7	0.6	2.7	1.9	1.6
Services	8.4	7.8	6.1	3.5	3.3	2.8	2.1	1.8	1.6	4.8	4.5	3.3

1/ Total lost workday cases involve days away from work, or days of restricted activity, or both.
2/ Days-away-from-work cases include those which result in days away from work with or without restricted work activity.
3/ Excludes farms with fewer than 11 employees.
Note: Incidence rates represent the number of injuries and illnesses per 100 full-time workers.

Source: State of Florida, Department of Labor and Employment Security, Division of Safety, *Occupational Injuries and Illnesses in Florida, 1997*, Internet site <http://www.fdles/state.fl.us/safety/stats/pr975fl.pdf> (accessed 18 August 2000).

PHYSICAL GEOGRAPHY AND ENVIRONMENT

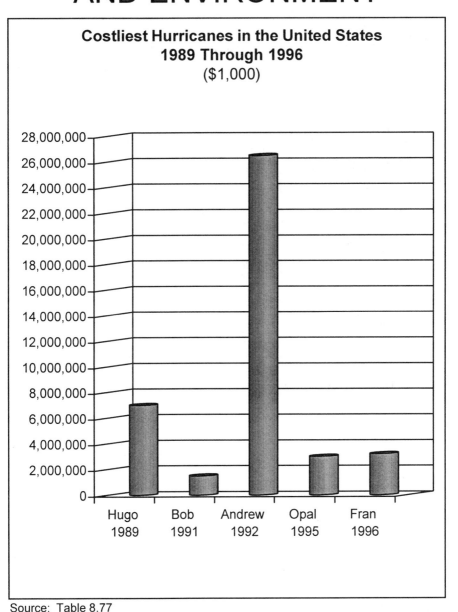

**Costliest Hurricanes in the United States
1989 Through 1996**
($1,000)

Source: Table 8.77

Table 8.01. GEOGRAPHY: LAND AND WATER AREAS, COASTLINE, AND ELEVATIONS
OF FLORIDA OTHER SUNBELT STATES, OTHER POPULOUS STATES
AND THE UNITED STATES, 1990

State	Area (square miles)			Coastline (statute miles)		Elevation (feet)		
	Total	Land 1/	Water 2/	General coast-line 3/	Tidal shore-line 4/	High-est	Low-est	Ap-prox-imate mean
Sunbelt states								
Florida	59,928	53,937	5,991	1,350	8,426	345	A/	100
Alabama	52,237	50,750	1,486	53	607	2,405	A/	500
Arizona	114,006	113,642	364	0	0	12,633	70	4,100
Arkansas	53,182	52,075	1,107	0	0	2,753	55	650
California	158,869	155,973	2,895	840	3,427	14,494	-282	2,900
Georgia	58,977	57,919	1,058	100	2,344	4,784	A/	600
Louisiana	49,651	43,566	6,085	397	7,721	535	-8	100
Mississippi	48,286	46,914	1,372	44	359	806	A/	300
New Mexico	121,598	121,364	234	0	0	13,161	2,842	5,700
North Carolina	52,672	48,718	3,954	301	3,375	6,684	A/	700
Oklahoma	69,903	68,679	1,224	0	0	4,973	289	1,300
South Carolina	31,189	30,111	1,078	187	2,876	3,560	A/	350
Tennessee	42,146	41,219	926	0	0	6,643	178	900
Texas	267,277	261,914	5,363	367	3,359	8,749	A/	1,700
Virginia	42,326	39,598	2,729	112	3,315	5,729	A/	950
Other populous states								
Illinois	57,918	55,593	2,325	0	0	1,235	279	600
Indiana	36,420	35,870	550	0	0	1,257	320	700
Massachusetts	9,241	7,838	1,403	192	1,519	3,487	A/	500
Michigan	96,705	56,809	39,895	0	0	1,979	571	900
New Jersey	8,215	7,419	796	130	1,792	1,803	A/	250
New York	53,989	47,224	6,766	127	1,850	5,344	A/	1,000
Ohio	44,828	40,953	3,875	0	0	1,549	455	850
Pennsylvania	46,058	44,820	1,239	0	89	3,213	A/	1,100
United States	3,717,796	3,536,278	181,518	12,383	88,633	20,320	-282	2,500

A/ Sea level.
1/ Dry land and land temporarily or partially covered by water, as marshland and swamps.
2/ Includes inland and coastal waters. In 1990, inland water was defined as lakes, reservoirs, ponds and rivers, canals, estuaries, and bays from the point downstream at which they are narrower than one nautical mile to the point upstream where they appear as a single line feature on the Census Bureau's TIGER File. Coastal water is within embayments separated from territorial waters by 1 to 24 nautical miles Excludes territorial waters (waters between the 3-mile limit and the shoreline).
3/ Figures are lengths of general outline of seacoast. Unit of measure is 30 minutes of latitude on charts at approximate scale of 1:1,200,000.
4/ Figures are lengths of shoreline of outer coast, offshore islands, sounds, bays, rivers, and creeks to the head of tidewater, and were obtained in 1961.
Note: Some data are revised.

Source: U.S., Department of Commerce, Bureau of the Census, *Statistical Abstract of the United States, 2000,* U.S., Department of Commerce, Geography Division, unpublished data, and U.S., Department of Commerce, National Oceanic and Atmospheric Administration, unpublished data.

Table 8.03. LAND AND WATER AREA: AREA OF THE STATE AND COUNTIES
OF FLORIDA, APRIL 1, 1990

(square miles)

County	Total 1/	Land area	Water area 1/ Total	Inland	Coastal	Terri- torial
Florida	65,758.1	53,937.0	11,821.1	4,682.9	1,308.1	5,830.0
Alachua	969.2	874.3	94.9	94.9	0.0	0.0
Baker	588.9	585.3	3.7	3.7	0.0	0.0
Bay	1,033.4	763.7	269.6	118.9	0.0	150.7
Bradford	300.1	293.2	6.9	6.9	0.0	0.0
Brevard	1,557.3	1,018.5	538.8	276.0	0.0	262.8
Broward	1,319.7	1,208.9	110.9	12.7	0.0	98.2
Calhoun	574.4	567.4	7.0	7.0	0.0	0.0
Charlotte	859.3	693.7	165.6	122.4	0.0	43.2
Citrus	773.2	583.6	189.6	79.8	0.0	109.8
Clay	643.7	601.1	42.6	42.6	0.0	0.0
Collier	2,305.1	2,025.5	279.6	91.0	0.0	188.7
Columbia	801.1	797.2	4.0	4.0	0.0	0.0
De Soto	639.6	637.3	2.2	2.2	0.0	0.0
Dixie	863.7	704.1	159.7	20.4	0.0	139.2
Duval	918.3	773.9	144.4	75.7	0.0	68.8
Escambia	893.9	663.6	230.3	88.1	0.0	142.2
Flagler	570.8	485.0	85.8	22.6	0.0	63.1
Franklin	1,026.5	534.0	492.5	32.1	198.9	261.5
Gadsden	528.5	516.2	12.4	12.4	0.0	0.0
Gilchrist	355.5	348.9	6.6	6.6	0.0	0.0
Glades	986.2	773.5	212.7	212.7	0.0	0.0
Gulf	755.8	565.1	190.7	17.9	65.3	107.6
Hamilton	519.4	514.9	4.5	4.5	0.0	0.0
Hardee	638.4	637.4	1.0	1.0	0.0	0.0
Hendry	1,189.9	1,152.7	37.2	37.2	0.0	0.0
Hernando	589.1	478.3	110.8	23.7	0.0	87.1
Highlands	1,106.4	1,028.5	77.9	77.9	0.0	0.0
Hillsborough	1,266.4	1,051.0	215.3	39.7	155.9	19.8
Holmes	488.8	482.6	6.2	6.2	0.0	0.0
Indian River	617.0	503.3	113.7	36.8	0.0	76.9
Jackson	954.7	915.8	38.9	38.9	0.0	0.0
Jefferson	636.7	597.8	38.9	15.4	0.0	23.5
Lafayette	548.0	542.8	5.1	5.1	0.0	0.0
Lake	1,156.5	953.1	203.4	203.4	0.0	0.0
Lee	1,212.0	803.6	408.4	236.5	6.1	165.9
Leon	701.8	666.8	35.0	35.0	0.0	0.0

See footnote at end of table.   Continued . . .

University of Florida   **Bureau of Economic and Business Research**

Table 8.03. LAND AND WATER AREA: AREA OF THE STATE AND COUNTIES
OF FLORIDA, APRIL 1, 1990 (Continued)

(square miles)

County	Total 1/	Land area	Water area 1/			
			Total	Inland	Coastal	Terri-torial
Levy	1,412.4	1,118.4	294.0	46.9	0.0	247.1
Liberty	843.2	835.9	7.3	7.3	0.0	0.0
Madison	715.9	692.0	23.9	23.9	0.0	0.0
Manatee	892.8	741.2	151.6	55.2	46.7	49.8
Marion	1,663.1	1,579.0	84.1	84.1	0.0	0.0
Martin	752.9	555.7	197.2	121.4	0.0	75.8
Miami-Dade	2,429.6	1,944.5	485.1	76.8	199.8	208.5
Monroe	3,737.4	997.3	2,740.2	406.8	540.6	1,792.8
Nassau	725.9	651.6	74.3	18.5	0.0	55.7
Okaloosa	1,082.1	935.8	146.3	59.8	0.0	86.5
Okeechobee	892.0	774.3	117.7	117.7	0.0	0.0
Orange	1,004.3	907.6	96.7	96.7	0.0	0.0
Osceola	1,506.5	1,322.0	184.5	184.5	0.0	0.0
Palm Beach	2,386.5	1,974.2	412.3	256.3	0.0	156.0
Pasco	868.0	745.0	123.0	23.1	0.0	99.9
Pinellas	607.8	280.2	327.6	65.4	94.9	167.3
Polk	2,010.2	1,874.9	135.3	135.3	0.0	0.0
Putnam	827.2	722.2	105.1	105.1	0.0	0.0
St. Johns	821.5	609.0	212.4	64.0	0.0	148.4
St. Lucie	688.1	572.5	115.6	43.3	0.0	72.3
Santa Rosa	1,155.3	1,015.8	139.5	128.7	0.0	10.8
Sarasota	725.3	571.8	153.5	34.2	0.0	119.3
Seminole	344.9	308.2	36.7	36.7	0.0	0.0
Sumter	580.4	545.7	34.7	34.7	0.0	0.0
Suwannee	691.9	687.7	4.3	4.3	0.0	0.0
Taylor	1,232.1	1,042.0	190.1	13.5	0.0	176.6
Union	249.7	240.3	9.4	9.4	0.0	0.0
Volusia	1,432.5	1,105.9	326.6	159.0	0.0	167.7
Wakulla	735.8	606.7	129.1	32.9	0.0	96.2
Walton	1,238.1	1,057.7	180.5	90.1	0.0	90.3
Washington	615.8	579.9	36.0	36.0	0.0	0.0

1/ Water area measurement figures in the 1990 census data reflect all water, including inland, coastal, territorial, new reservoirs, and other man-made lakes. Measurement figures reported in previous censuses were only for inland water; the total water area of the state has increased substantially. See note on Table 8.01 for definitions of inland, coastal, and territorial waters.

Source: U.S., Department of Commerce, Bureau of the Census, Geography Division, unpublished data.

University of Florida   **Bureau of Economic and Business Research**

Table 8.15. SOLID WASTE: TONNAGE BY DISPOSAL PROCESS AND PER CAPITA AMOUNT
IN THE STATE AND COUNTIES OF FLORIDA, 1997 AND 1998

| County | Disposal process 1/ | | | | | | Per capita tons 2/ | |
| | Recycled | | Landfilled | | Combusted | | | |
	1997	1998	1997	1998	1997	1998	1997	1998
Florida	9,046.1	6,877.3	10,845.6	14,108.1	5,575.8	5,618.2	1.73	1.77
Alachua	111.1	83.5	137.2	152.1	0.0	0.0	1.19	1.11
Baker	6.1	1.4	12.8	15.1	0.0	0.0	0.89	0.78
Bay	58.0	23.6	154.1	89.1	138.9	150.3	2.43	1.78
Bradford	5.5	4.0	14.4	15.5	0.0	0.0	0.79	0.77
Brevard	363.0	286.4	377.1	378.4	0.0	0.0	1.62	1.43
Broward	675.0	558.8	833.2	868.2	1,021.6	1,058.8	1.78	1.70
Calhoun	1.8	1.6	1.8	1.8	6.0	4.8	0.75	0.60
Charlotte	88.4	33.1	91.0	93.4	0.0	0.0	1.37	0.95
Citrus	38.9	69.4	68.1	157.0	0.0	0.0	0.97	2.01
Clay	23.0	17.4	92.8	100.6	0.0	0.0	0.91	0.88
Collier	161.4	104.8	182.7	362.3	0.0	0.0	1.72	2.22
Columbia	17.3	17.8	49.6	53.1	0.0	0.0	1.25	1.28
De Soto	1.9	1.7	20.2	16.9	0.0	0.0	0.81	0.67
Dixie	1.5	1.1	8.5	7.5	0.0	0.0	0.76	0.65
Duval	663.6	470.2	716.0	808.0	0.0	0.0	1.86	1.70
Escambia	104.5	88.0	371.1	408.7	0.0	0.0	1.63	1.68
Flagler	17.3	6.2	41.1	66.3	0.0	0.0	1.42	1.67
Franklin	1.5	1.9	6.1	5.3	9.1	9.0	1.59	1.51
Gadsden	5.4	3.4	29.4	28.7	0.0	0.0	0.70	0.63
Gilchrist	1.6	1.4	5.2	5.7	0.0	0.0	0.54	0.55
Glades	0.9	1.2	6.1	6.4	0.0	0.0	0.72	0.77
Gulf	4.6	4.9	9.6	9.1	7.2	7.0	1.52	1.48
Hamilton	0.6	0.7	5.7	5.9	0.0	0.0	0.46	0.46
Hardee	5.3	2.1	13.7	15.4	0.0	0.0	0.85	0.76
Hendry	2.2	1.1	7.2	15.0	27.7	29.0	1.22	1.49
Hernando	35.1	42.5	55.6	91.0	36.7	37.1	1.04	1.36
Highlands	26.0	19.6	69.1	69.6	0.0	0.0	1.20	1.11
Hillsborough	630.0	588.0	360.1	977.1	758.7	735.5	1.88	2.44
Holmes	0.6	1.1	5.5	6.1	0.0	0.0	0.34	0.40
Indian River	90.7	78.1	124.8	117.9	0.0	0.0	2.06	1.84
Jackson	3.4	1.5	37.4	32.3	0.0	0.1	0.83	0.68
Jefferson	1.0	1.1	8.8	9.2	0.0	0.0	0.70	0.73
Lafayette	0.2	0.3	1.9	2.0	0.0	0.0	0.30	0.34
Lake	71.1	85.4	57.4	135.8	133.9	137.3	1.39	1.83
Lee	212.2	255.2	128.3	170.3	320.6	349.9	1.68	1.91
Leon	153.5	133.0	236.4	207.9	0.0	0.0	1.71	1.46

See footnotes at end of table.   Continued . . .

University of Florida   **Bureau of Economic and Business Research**

Table 8.15. SOLID WASTE: TONNAGE BY DISPOSAL PROCESS AND PER CAPITA AMOUNT
IN THE STATE AND COUNTIES OF FLORIDA, 1997 AND 1998 (Continued)

County	Disposal process 1/						Per capita tons 2/	
	Recycled		Landfilled		Combusted			
	1997	1998	1997	1998	1997	1998	1997	1998
Levy	3.7	2.9	20.4	21.4	0.0	0.0	0.76	0.75
Liberty	0.9	0.3	3.7	3.6	0.0	0.0	0.59	0.50
Madison	2.7	3.0	12.9	13.0	0.0	0.0	0.82	0.83
Manatee	115.0	152.8	341.0	324.6	0.0	0.0	1.89	1.93
Marion	76.0	101.7	197.2	215.9	0.0	0.0	1.15	1.31
Martin	89.2	72.6	123.5	122.0	0.0	0.0	1.83	1.63
Miami-Dade	1,171.6	793.7	1,566.9	1,706.8	1,102.3	1,159.6	1.85	1.75
Monroe	49.5	35.6	77.8	76.9	36.5	52.5	1.93	1.93
Nassau	12.5	7.3	39.6	50.0	0.0	0.0	0.99	1.05
Okaloosa	51.6	43.9	143.7	261.1	0.0	0.0	1.14	1.74
Okeechobee	31.1	20.9	37.6	85.5	0.0	0.0	1.98	3.04
Orange	852.3	519.5	893.6	1,370.6	0.0	0.0	2.17	2.29
Osceola	54.8	41.5	188.1	224.5	0.0	0.0	1.69	1.79
Palm Beach	974.5	544.6	555.2	623.1	815.0	803.6	2.34	1.93
Pasco	115.6	68.4	100.2	293.2	259.5	265.8	1.51	1.95
Pinellas	688.8	332.1	229.5	520.0	759.1	766.5	1.89	1.81
Polk	241.4	401.4	556.9	667.8	112.5	28.3	1.98	2.36
Putnam	29.3	25.6	59.8	58.2	0.0	0.0	1.27	1.17
St. Johns	41.0	37.8	99.8	212.1	0.0	0.0	1.33	2.32
St. Lucie	83.1	83.7	178.9	125.3	0.0	0.0	1.46	0.66
Santa Rosa	49.3	51.3	62.6	135.2	1.2	1.0	1.11	0.54
Sarasota	283.5	191.7	237.8	367.6	0.0	0.0	1.68	5.09
Seminole	159.0	90.7	307.4	421.2	0.0	0.0	1.38	2.79
Sumter	6.9	11.8	16.9	24.8	17.3	12.0	0.93	1.01
Suwannee	13.6	10.3	21.1	35.7	0.0	0.0	1.04	1.36
Taylor	3.9	3.6	5.8	6.4	1.5	0.0	0.58	0.51
Union	3.0	1.7	8.3	8.5	0.0	0.0	0.87	0.76
Volusia	249.0	227.9	383.9	523.1	0.0	0.0	1.53	1.79
Wakulla	1.4	1.7	5.4	4.9	6.2	6.6	0.69	0.66
Walton	6.0	4.6	21.9	91.3	0.0	0.0	0.77	2.50
Washington	1.6	0.9	8.5	8.9	4.4	3.6	0.72	0.63

1/ In thousand tons, rounded to hundreds.
2/ Based on April 1, 1997 and 1998 population estimates prepared by the Bureau of Economic and Business Research, University of Florida.

Source: State of Florida, Department of Environmental Protection, Division of Waste Management, Bureau of Solid and Hazardous Waste, *2000 Solid Waste Management in Florida Annual Report,* prepublication release.

University of Florida   **Bureau of Economic and Business Research**

Table 8.16. SOLID WASTE: MUNICIPAL TONNAGE COLLECTED AND RECYCLED BY TYPE OF GENERATOR IN THE STATE AND COUNTIES OF FLORIDA, 1998

County	Tons	Per capita per year (pounds)	Per capita per day (pounds)	Percentage recycled	Amount collected (tons)	Percentage recycled	Amount collected (tons)	Percentage recycled
	Total municipal solid waste				Residential		Commercial	
Florida	24,857,981	3,314	9.1	27.67	12,073,987	24.5	12,783,994	30.7
Alachua	235,662	2,230	6.1	35.45	92,622	41.8	143,040	31.3
Baker	16,526	1,564	4.3	8.56	7,473	5.7	9,053	10.9
Bay	203,020	2,753	7.5	11.63	40,376	11.8	162,644	11.6
Bradford	19,513	1,539	4.2	20.62	13,750	12.3	5,763	40.5
Brevard	664,859	2,855	7.8	43.08	365,875	9.7	298,984	83.9
Broward	2,159,989	2,957	8.1	25.87	1,237,450	18.5	922,539	35.8
Calhoun	6,241	920	2.5	24.98	4,965	12.9	1,276	72.1
Charlotte	126,449	1,701	4.7	26.16	95,729	34.6	30,720	0.0
Citrus	226,477	4,029	11.0	30.66	106,101	36.7	120,376	25.4
Clay	118,033	1,755	4.8	14.76	47,633	27.3	70,400	6.3
Collier	467,118	4,447	12.2	22.43	196,418	9.4	270,700	31.9
Columbia	70,833	2,559	7.0	25.06	42,512	19.8	28,321	33.0
De Soto	18,630	1,334	3.7	9.23	6,754	9.2	11,876	9.3
Dixie	8,541	1,294	3.5	12.68	8,541	12.7	0	0.0
Duval	1,278,217	3,391	9.3	36.79	575,198	46.2	703,019	29.1
Escambia	496,738	3,354	9.2	17.72	334,180	16.8	162,558	19.6
Flagler	72,710	3,348	9.2	8.50	41,999	10.4	30,711	5.8
Franklin	12,659	2,358	6.5	15.22	9,326	14.9	3,333	16.2
Gadsden	32,075	1,262	3.5	10.50	18,640	11.5	13,435	9.1
Gilchrist	7,166	1,091	3.0	20.03	6,420	20.1	746	19.3
Glades	7,582	1,536	4.2	15.97	5,535	14.6	2,047	19.7
Gulf	18,230	2,557	7.0	27.13	12,983	38.1	5,247	0.0
Hamilton	6,534	925	2.5	9.99	3,989	14.8	2,545	2.5
Hardee	17,403	1,527	4.2	11.78	11,788	4.7	5,615	26.7
Hendry	36,644	2,414	6.6	2.96	29,442	3.0	7,202	3.0
Hernando	159,478	2,551	7.0	26.63	87,011	35.0	72,467	16.6
Highlands	89,266	2,219	6.1	21.99	68,432	21.5	20,834	23.5
Hillsborough	2,097,233	4,451	12.2	28.04	792,806	33.7	1,304,427	24.6
Holmes	7,231	806	2.2	15.64	4,956	15.5	2,275	15.9
Indian River	196,026	3,675	10.1	39.86	109,855	39.1	86,171	40.8
Jackson	33,897	1,365	3.7	4.47	19,431	4.4	14,466	4.5
Jefferson	10,306	1,451	4.0	10.45	7,214	3.5	3,092	26.7
Lafayette	2,376	679	1.9	14.52	1,901	16.0	475	8.7
Lake	317,956	3,243	8.9	26.86	131,533	36.4	186,423	20.1
Lee	677,994	3,343	9.2	37.64	272,903	32.6	405,091	41.0
Leon	340,962	2,924	8.0	39.02	148,033	23.3	192,929	51.1

Continued . . .

Table 8.16. SOLID WASTE: MUNICIPAL TONNAGE COLLECTED AND RECYCLED BY TYPE OF GENERATOR IN THE STATE AND COUNTIES OF FLORIDA, 1998 (Continued)

	Total municipal solid waste				Residential		Commercial	
	Amount collected			Per-		Per-		Per-
		Per	Per	cent-		cent-		cent-
		capita	capita	age	Amount	age	Amount	age
		per year	per day	re-	collected	re-	collected	re-
County	Tons	(pounds)	(pounds)	cycled	(tons)	cycled	(tons)	cycled
Levy	24,304	1,500	4.1	11.76	21,607	11.6	2,697	13.4
Liberty	3,897	1,011	2.8	6.95	2,180	4.1	1,717	10.6
Madison	16,045	1,665	4.6	18.87	9,892	8.1	6,153	36.2
Manatee	477,430	3,865	10.6	32.01	193,446	31.8	283,984	32.1
Marion	317,694	2,622	7.2	32.03	178,371	18.5	139,323	49.4
Martin	194,666	3,262	8.9	37.31	85,726	51.9	108,940	25.9
Miami-Dade	3,419,768	3,272	9.0	23.21	1,784,566	15.3	1,635,202	31.8
Monroe	150,062	3,504	9.6	23.75	79,125	38.4	70,937	7.4
Nassau	57,276	2,100	5.8	12.76	28,905	12.7	28,371	12.8
Okaloosa	304,989	3,474	9.5	14.41	89,169	39.0	215,820	4.2
Okeechobee	106,419	6,071	16.6	19.63	71,301	8.8	35,118	41.6
Orange	1,890,112	4,587	12.6	27.49	756,045	27.5	1,134,067	27.5
Osceola	265,971	3,980	10.9	15.59	142,500	18.6	123,471	12.2
Palm Beach	1,556,620	3,051	8.4	34.99	719,951	36.4	836,669	33.8
Pasco	543,958	3,388	9.3	12.57	250,221	26.5	293,738	0.7
Pinellas	1,409,845	3,160	8.7	23.56	800,196	23.2	609,649	24.0
Polk	1,075,954	4,619	12.7	37.30	464,139	39.7	611,815	35.4
Putnam	83,764	2,345	6.4	30.56	56,722	13.5	27,042	66.3
St. Johns	249,935	4,549	12.5	15.14	84,427	24.9	165,508	10.2
St. Lucie	208,976	2,281	6.2	40.06	106,188	32.5	102,788	47.9
Santa Rosa	187,375	3,476	9.5	27.38	127,387	34.2	59,988	12.9
Sarasota	559,260	3,539	9.7	34.27	250,615	25.3	308,645	41.6
Seminole	511,870	2,966	8.1	17.72	246,255	7.2	265,615	27.5
Sumter	45,416	1,896	5.2	25.91	18,661	40.1	26,755	16.0
Suwannee	46,039	2,729	7.5	22.44	43,126	20.4	2,913	53.2
Taylor	10,015	1,026	2.8	35.62	7,067	35.3	2,948	36.3
Union	10,197	1,515	4.2	16.65	5,445	10.0	4,752	24.3
Volusia	750,960	3,572	9.8	30.35	451,894	5.9	299,066	67.3
Wakulla	10,487	1,058	2.9	16.14	6,502	16.8	3,985	15.0
Walton	95,942	5,010	13.7	4.80	25,845	11.3	70,097	2.4
Washington	12,160	1,141	3.1	7.69	6,739	3.2	5,421	13.3

Source: State of Florida, Department of Environmental Protection, Division of Waste Management, Bureau of Solid and Hazardous Waste, *2000 Solid Waste Management in Florida Annual Report,* prepublication release.

University of Florida   **Bureau of Economic and Business Research**

Table 8.35. WATER USE: WATER WITHDRAWALS BY WATER TYPE, SOURCE
AND CATEGORY IN FLORIDA, OTHER SUNBELT STATES
AND THE UNITED STATES, 1995

(in millions of gallons per day)

State	Total	Water type Fresh	Water type Saline	Water source Ground	Water source Sur-face	Ir-riga-tion 1/	Pub-lic sup-ply 2/	In-dus-tri-al 3/	Pow-er 4/
Florida	18,180	7,215	10,965	4,340	13,840	3,526	2,363	692	636
Alabama	7,099	7,090	9	445	6,650	268	875	749	5,196
Arizona	6,834	6,820	14	2,840	3,990	5,702	746	204	62
Arkansas	8,770	8,770	0	5,460	3,310	6,294	419	287	1,775
California	45,940	36,300	9,640	14,700	21,800	29,359	5,740	999	206
Georgia	5,814	5,750	64	1,190	4,630	770	1,249	691	3,045
Louisiana	9,850	9,850	0	1,350	8,500	1,094	677	2,593	5,481
Mississippi	3,202	3,090	112	2,590	614	2,196	377	312	262
New Mexico	3,510	3,510	0	1,700	1,800	3,020	337	89	55
North Carolina	9,290	7,730	1,560	535	8,750	536	941	393	5,860
Oklahoma	2039	1,780	259	1,220	822	1,011	597	49	125
South Carolina	6200	6,200	0	322	5,880	77	614	705	4,809
Tennessee	10,100	10,100	0	435	9,640	61	831	889	8,300
Texas	29,580	24,300	5,280	8,780	20,800	9,765	3,420	1,555	9,589
Virginia	8,270	5,470	2,800	358	7,900	66	911	596	3,890
United States	401,800	341,000	60,800	77,500	324,000	139,490	43,500	26,150	131,565

1/ Includes water withdrawn for crop irrigation, livestock, and fish farming purposes and recreational irrigation including turf grass for golf courses and landscape irrigation.
2/ Includes water withdrawn by water supply systems or domestic self-supplied users.
3/ Includes water withdrawn for commercial, industrial, and mining purposes.
4/ Includes water withdrawn for all uses at fossil fuel or nuclear power plants.

Source: U.S., Department of the Interior, Geological Survey, Water Resource Division, Information Circular 1200, *Estimated Use of Water in the United States, 1995.*

Table 8.36. WATER USE: WITHDRAWALS BY CATEGORY OF USE AND BY SOURCE
IN FLORIDA, 1995

(in millions of gallons per day)

Category	Freshwater Total	Freshwater Ground	Freshwater Surface	Saline Total	Saline Ground	Saline Saline
Total	7,216	4,336	2,880	10,966	5	10,961
Public supply	2,066	1,856	210	0	0	0
Domestic self-supplied	297	297	0	0	0	0
Commercial/industrial	692	438	254	6	0	6
Agricultural irrigation	3,245	1,528	1,717	0	0	0
Recreational irrigation	280	196	84	0	0	0
Power generation	636	21	615	10,960	5	10,955

Note: Detail may not add to totals due to rounding.

Source: U.S., Department of Interior, Geological Survey, Water Resource Division, Water-resources Investigations Report 99-4002, *Water Withdrawals, Use, Discharge, and Trends in Florida, 1995.*

University of Florida   **Bureau of Economic and Business Research**

Table 8.39. WATER USE: FRESHWATER WITHDRAWALS BY CATEGORY OF USE
AND BY WATER MANAGEMENT DISTRICT IN FLORIDA, 1995

(in millions of gallons per day)

Category	North-west Florida	St. Johns River	South Florida	South-west Florida	Su-wannee River
Total	660	1,298	3,571	1,351	334
Public supply	168	462	973	449	14
Domestic self-supplied	33	93	75	72	23
Commercial/industrial	106	132	121	235	98
Agricultural irrigation 1/	52	492	2,193	424	83
Recreational irrigation 2/	16	27	187	50	1
Power generation	285	92	22	121	115

1/ Withdrawals for crops, livestock, and fish farming.
2/ Withdrawals for turf grass and landscaping. Included under agricultural irrigation prior to 1985.

Note: Values may not be identical to the data reported by the water management districts due to differences in data collection or revisions. Detail may not add to totals because of rounding.

Table 8.40. WATER USE: FRESHWATER WITHDRAWALS BY CATEGORY OF USE IN FLORIDA
1970, 1975, 1980, 1985, 1990 AND 1995

(in millions of gallons per day)

Disposition	1970	1975	1980	1985	1990	1995
Total	5,612	6,773	6,701	6,313	7,583	7,215
Public supply	883	1,124	1,406	1,685	1,925	2,065
Domestic self-supplied	209	228	243	259	299	297
Commercial/industrial	900	883	700	709	770	692
Agricultural irrigation 1/	2,100	2,930	3,026	2,798	3,495	3,244
Recreational irrigation 2/	(NA)	(NA)	(NA)	182	310	280
Power generation	1,520	1,608	1,326	680	784	637

(NA) Not available.
1/ Withdrawals for crops, livestock, and fish farming.
2/ Withdrawals for turf grass and landscaping. Included under agricultural irrigation prior to 1985.

Note: Detail may not add to totals due to rounding.

Source for Tables 8:39 and 8:40: U.S., Department of Interior, Geological Survey, Water Resource Division, Water-resources Investigations Report 99-4002, *Water Withdrawals, Use, Discharge, and Trends in Florida, 1995.*

University of Florida   **Bureau of Economic and Business Research**

Water Management Districts

Northwest Florida

St. Johns River

Suwannee River

Southwest Florida

South Florida

HEADQUARTERS

District	City	County
Northwest Florida	Havana	Gadsden
Suwannee River	Live Oak	Suwannee
St. Johns River	Palatka	Putnam
Southwest Florida	Brooksville	Hernando
South Florida	West Palm Beach	Palm Beach

Table 8.41. WATER USE: WATER WITHDRAWALS BY SOURCE IN THE STATE AND COUNTIES
OF FLORIDA, 1995

(in millions of gallons per day)

County	Total	Ground Total	Ground Fresh	Ground Saline	Surface Total	Surface Fresh	Surface Saline
Florida	18,180.63	4,340.21	4,335.58	4.63	13,840.42	2,879.36	10,961.06
Alachua	48.31	47.56	47.56	0.00	0.75	0.75	0.00
Baker	5.37	4.74	4.74	0.00	0.63	0.63	0.00
Bay	318.51	14.26	14.26	0.00	304.25	44.60	259.65
Bradford	7.51	7.46	7.46	0.00	0.05	0.05	0.00
Brevard	1,332.84	113.03	113.03	0.00	1,219.81	22.50	1,197.31
Broward	1,515.60	267.58	267.58	0.00	1,248.02	19.75	1,228.27
Calhoun	4.19	3.38	3.38	0.00	0.81	0.81	0.00
Charlotte	49.88	36.17	36.17	0.00	13.71	13.71	0.00
Citrus	1,685.32	28.28	28.28	0.00	1,657.04	1.73	1,655.31
Clay	21.52	21.28	21.28	0.00	0.24	0.24	0.00
Collier	208.20	186.98	186.98	0.00	21.22	21.22	0.00
Columbia	16.74	16.15	16.15	0.00	0.59	0.59	0.00
De Soto	70.94	58.59	58.59	0.00	12.35	12.35	0.00
Dixie	3.41	3.41	3.41	0.00	0.00	0.00	0.00
Duval	720.18	144.61	144.61	0.00	575.57	0.48	575.09
Escambia	269.55	86.83	86.83	0.00	182.72	182.72	0.00
Flagler	14.15	13.30	13.30	0.00	0.85	0.85	0.00
Franklin	2.89	2.89	2.89	0.00	0.00	0.00	0.00
Gadsden	16.38	7.71	7.71	0.00	8.67	8.67	0.00
Gilchrist	9.36	9.26	9.26	0.00	0.10	0.10	0.00
Glades	99.59	20.95	20.95	0.00	78.64	78.64	0.00
Gulf	36.85	3.11	3.11	0.00	33.74	27.98	5.76
Hamilton	46.18	46.18	46.18	0.00	0.00	0.00	0.00
Hardee	51.00	50.49	50.49	0.00	0.51	0.51	0.00
Hendry	557.01	156.35	156.35	0.00	400.66	400.66	0.00
Hernando	41.62	39.58	39.58	0.00	2.04	2.04	0.00
Highlands	119.47	112.83	112.83	0.00	6.64	6.64	0.00
Hillsborough	2,628.16	169.22	169.22	0.00	2,458.94	77.12	2,381.82
Holmes	7.24	6.53	6.53	0.00	0.71	0.71	0.00
Indian River	266.46	76.58	76.58	0.00	189.88	136.29	53.59
Jackson	81.05	28.22	28.22	0.00	52.83	52.83	0.00
Jefferson	11.61	11.09	11.09	0.00	0.52	0.52	0.00
Lafayette	7.45	7.11	7.11	0.00	0.34	0.34	0.00
Lake	83.11	75.43	75.43	0.00	7.68	7.68	0.00
Lee	499.26	112.56	112.56	0.00	386.70	21.45	365.25
Leon	39.30	38.55	38.55	0.00	0.75	0.75	0.00

See footnote at end of table.   Continued . . .

University of Florida   **Bureau of Economic and Business Research**

Table 8.41. WATER USE: WATER WITHDRAWALS BY SOURCE IN THE STATE AND COUNTIES
OF FLORIDA, 1995 (Continued)

(in millions of gallons per day)

| County | Total | Ground | | | Surface | | |
		Total	Fresh	Saline	Total	Fresh	Saline
Levy	23.42	20.93	20.93	0.00	2.49	2.49	0.00
Liberty	1.63	1.56	1.56	0.00	0.07	0.07	0.00
Madison	9.33	8.78	8.78	0.00	0.55	0.55	0.00
Manatee	122.72	90.70	90.70	0.00	32.02	32.02	0.00
Marion	52.07	51.03	51.03	0.00	1.04	1.04	0.00
Martin	170.03	49.80	49.80	0.00	120.23	120.23	0.00
Miami-Dade	651.75	554.73	550.42	4.31	97.02	18.83	78.19
Monroe	2.10	2.10	1.78	0.32	0.00	0.00	0.00
Nassau	44.65	44.54	44.54	0.00	0.11	0.11	0.00
Okaloosa	29.94	29.71	29.71	0.00	0.23	0.23	0.00
Okeechobee	41.22	35.75	35.75	0.00	5.47	5.47	0.00
Orange	259.56	228.56	228.56	0.00	31.00	31.00	0.00
Osceola	81.48	68.27	68.27	0.00	13.21	13.21	0.00
Palm Beach	1,432.60	219.80	219.80	0.00	1,212.80	740.04	472.76
Pasco	1,169.25	129.63	129.63	0.00	1,039.62	12.19	1,027.43
Pinellas	529.91	42.73	42.73	0.00	487.18	2.02	485.16
Polk	391.85	242.98	242.98	0.00	148.87	148.87	0.00
Putnam	88.43	38.11	38.11	0.00	50.32	50.32	0.00
St. Johns	46.37	45.73	45.73	0.00	0.64	0.64	0.00
St. Lucie	1,485.34	80.76	80.76	0.00	1,404.58	229.11	1,175.47
Santa Rosa	23.25	23.03	23.03	0.00	0.22	0.22	0.00
Sarasota	47.86	38.84	38.84	0.00	9.02	9.02	0.00
Seminole	69.78	68.90	68.90	0.00	0.88	0.88	0.00
Sumter	66.14	12.55	12.55	0.00	53.59	53.59	0.00
Suwannee	142.48	29.10	29.10	0.00	113.38	113.38	0.00
Taylor	53.08	51.10	51.10	0.00	1.98	1.98	0.00
Union	2.70	2.57	2.57	0.00	0.13	0.13	0.00
Volusia	156.60	81.16	81.16	0.00	75.44	75.44	0.00
Wakulla	72.52	3.60	3.60	0.00	68.92	68.92	0.00
Walton	11.77	10.59	10.59	0.00	1.18	1.18	0.00
Washington	4.59	4.32	4.32	0.00	0.27	0.27	0.00

Note: Values may not be identical to the data reported or published by the water management districts due to differences in data collection procedures and categories used or revisions in reported values.

Source: U.S., Department of Interior, Geological Survey, Water Resource Division, Water-resources Investigations Report 99-4002, *Water Withdrawals, Use, Discharge, and Trends in Florida, 1995.*

Table 8.42. WATER USE: PUBLIC SUPPLY WATER DELIVERIES AND WATER USE BY TYPE
OF USE IN THE STATE AND COUNTIES OF FLORIDA, 1995

(in millions of gallons per day)

County	Population served	Total	Resi-dential/ domestic	Commer-cial/ insti-tutional	Indus-trial	Public uses and losses 1/	Other 2/
Florida	12,213,389	2,065.27	1,260.29	385.83	103.34	284.75	31.06
Alachua	153,809	24.09	13.32	6.51	0.67	3.23	0.36
Baker	4,130	0.68	0.29	0.26	0.04	0.09	0.00
Bay	109,645	49.32	12.37	4.23	25.37	6.61	0.74
Bradford	8,502	1.33	0.69	0.39	0.06	0.18	0.01
Brevard	403,819	51.09	30.32	10.34	2.81	6.85	0.77
Broward	1,351,085	222.30	144.08	38.56	6.54	29.79	3.33
Calhoun	4,170	0.68	0.38	0.16	0.05	0.09	0.00
Charlotte	102,919	14.05	9.65	2.11	0.21	1.88	0.20
Citrus	56,740	10.08	6.71	1.63	0.24	1.35	0.15
Clay	93,055	12.04	8.13	1.78	0.34	1.61	0.18
Collier	163,396	39.30	27.22	5.62	0.60	5.27	0.59
Columbia	19,570	2.87	1.26	1.04	0.15	0.38	0.04
De Soto	7,762	4.79	0.83	0.27	0.02	3.65	0.02
Dixie	4,212	0.64	0.42	0.09	0.04	0.09	0.00
Duval	641,774	99.62	54.54	22.22	8.02	13.35	1.49
Escambia	259,387	37.73	23.77	6.67	1.66	5.06	0.57
Flagler	26,213	4.51	3.12	0.54	0.18	0.60	0.07
Franklin	8,352	1.75	1.29	0.19	0.02	0.23	0.02
Gadsden	27,673	3.86	2.34	0.79	0.15	0.52	0.06
Gilchrist	1,765	0.22	0.10	0.08	0.01	0.03	0.00
Glades	3,456	0.38	0.29	0.04	0.00	0.05	0.00
Gulf	10,108	1.28	0.92	0.17	0.01	0.17	0.01
Hamilton	6,342	0.87	0.46	0.25	0.04	0.12	0.00
Hardee	8,565	1.61	1.06	0.30	0.01	0.22	0.02
Hendry	20,826	4.02	1.61	0.37	1.44	0.54	0.06
Hernando	102,490	17.07	12.79	1.48	0.25	2.29	0.26
Highlands	55,760	8.33	5.52	1.40	0.17	1.12	0.12
Hillsborough	760,450	118.77	64.08	29.95	7.04	15.92	1.78
Holmes	5,360	1.18	0.67	0.26	0.07	0.16	0.02
Indian River	61,886	11.16	6.98	2.19	0.32	1.50	0.17
Jackson	16,270	2.31	1.02	0.69	0.26	0.31	0.03
Jefferson	4,852	0.71	0.46	0.12	0.03	0.10	0.00
Lafayette	1,225	0.18	0.10	0.04	0.02	0.02	0.00
Lake	160,089	26.46	18.90	3.08	0.53	3.55	0.40
Lee	317,708	40.73	21.67	9.78	1.18	7.49	0.61
Leon	186,440	28.74	15.66	8.17	0.63	3.85	0.43

See footnotes at end of table.   Continued . . .

University of Florida   **Bureau of Economic and Business Research**

Table 8.42. WATER USE: PUBLIC SUPPLY WATER WITHDRAWALS AND WATER USE BY TYPE OF USE IN THE STATE AND COUNTIES OF FLORIDA, 1995 (Continued)

(in millions of gallons per day)

County	Population served	Total	Resi-dential/ domestic	Commer-cial/ insti-tutional	Indus-trial	Public uses and losses 1/	Other 2/
Levy	9,700	1.85	1.16	0.33	0.08	0.25	0.03
Liberty	2,679	0.32	0.22	0.05	0.01	0.04	0.00
Madison	7,341	1.58	0.64	0.28	0.43	0.21	0.02
Manatee	205,300	33.10	22.19	5.00	0.97	4.44	0.50
Marion	107,610	20.27	12.00	4.00	1.25	2.72	0.30
Martin	72,577	14.00	8.65	2.82	0.44	1.88	0.21
Miami-Dade	1,947,265	372.53	244.41	60.68	11.93	49.92	5.59
Monroe	80,500	14.07	7.92	3.20	0.15	2.59	0.21
Nassau	26,499	4.96	2.92	1.16	0.15	0.66	0.07
Okaloosa	149,665	21.20	13.41	4.01	0.62	2.84	0.32
Okeechobee	21,200	1.95	1.20	0.44	0.05	0.26	0.00
Orange	695,162	141.05	78.36	35.82	5.85	18.90	2.12
Osceola	100,855	19.15	11.93	4.05	0.31	2.57	0.29
Palm Beach	881,737	186.88	124.85	28.88	5.12	25.04	2.99
Pasco	223,605	26.14	17.33	4.45	0.47	3.50	0.39
Pinellas	867,440	113.35	65.60	24.28	6.58	15.19	1.70
Polk	386,054	58.42	37.29	9.35	3.07	7.83	0.88
Putnam	21,118	3.59	2.06	0.83	0.17	0.48	0.05
St. Johns	76,651	10.30	5.84	2.59	0.34	1.38	0.15
St. Lucie	107,162	15.31	9.27	2.82	0.40	2.05	0.77
Santa Rosa	91,030	12.08	8.84	1.19	0.25	1.62	0.18
Sarasota	247,250	36.18	19.06	8.34	1.54	7.06	0.18
Seminole	277,249	50.73	34.51	6.84	1.82	6.80	0.76
Sumter	16,609	2.45	1.56	0.41	0.13	0.33	0.02
Suwannee	9,276	1.42	0.79	0.36	0.07	0.19	0.01
Taylor	10,127	1.93	1.03	0.37	0.25	0.26	0.02
Union	4,000	0.38	0.20	0.09	0.04	0.05	0.00
Volusia	352,682	48.78	29.80	10.23	1.47	6.55	0.73
Wakulla	8,563	1.06	0.71	0.17	0.03	0.14	0.01
Walton	29,138	4.35	2.89	0.79	0.05	0.58	0.04
Washington	7,540	1.14	0.63	0.23	0.12	0.15	0.01

1/ Water used for fire fighting system flushing or maintenance and water lost to leakage or processing.
2/ Includes water used for power generation, heating and cooling systems, and urban irrigation.
Note: Public supply refers to municipal or other private water utilities which serve the public.

Source: U.S., Department of the Interior, Geological Survey, Water Resource Division, Water-resources Investigations Report 99-4002, *Water Withdrawals, Use, Discharge, and Trends in Florida, 1995.*

University of Florida   **Bureau of Economic and Business Research**

Table 8.43. WATER USE: WATER DISCHARGED FROM WASTEWATER TREATMENT FACILITIES
BY TYPE OF FACILITY IN THE STATE AND COUNTIES OF FLORIDA, 1995

(in millions of gallons per day)

County	Total	Domes-tic	Indus-trial	County	Total	Domes-tic	Indus-trial
Florida	1,836.74	1,544.39	292.35	Lake	10.01	8.93	1.08
				Lee	34.76	34.76	0.00
Alachua	17.24	16.53	0.71	Leon	17.46	17.46	0.00
Baker	0.96	0.96	0.00	Levy	0.65	0.65	0.00
Bay	37.76	37.76	0.00	Liberty	0.11	0.11	0.00
Bradford	9.89	2.28	7.61	Madison	0.92	0.92	0.00
Brevard	40.21	40.21	0.00	Manatee	28.93	25.81	3.12
Broward	191.19	191.19	0.00	Marion	7.41	7.41	0.00
Calhoun	0.69	0.69	0.00	Martin	5.63	5.28	0.35
Charlotte	7.15	7.15	0.00	Miami-Dade	323.91	323.91	0.00
Citrus	2.57	2.57	0.00	Monroe	9.05	9.05	0.00
Clay	16.58	8.78	7.80	Nassau	39.21	3.36	35.85
Collier	20.77	20.77	0.00	Okaloosa	17.41	17.41	0.00
Columbia	1.90	1.90	0.00	Okeechobee	0.57	0.57	0.00
De Soto	1.31	1.31	0.00	Orange	94.67	94.67	0.00
Dixie	0.30	0.30	0.00	Osceola	14.36	14.36	0.00
Duval	100.76	81.41	19.35	Palm Beach	107.80	107.70	0.10
Escambia	69.56	20.29	49.27	Pasco	26.37	16.27	10.10
Flagler	3.15	3.15	0.00	Pinellas	121.73	121.73	0.00
Franklin	1.10	1.10	0.00	Polk	41.30	28.47	12.83
Gadsden	2.07	2.07	0.00	Putnam	31.80	3.22	28.58
Gilchrist	0.16	0.16	0.00	St. Johns	7.82	7.82	0.00
Glades	0.00	0.00	0.00	St. Lucie	10.55	10.55	0.00
Gulf	36.99	28.65	8.34	Santa Rosa	5.39	2.91	2.48
Hamilton	18.74	0.81	17.93	Sarasota	27.93	22.79	5.14
Hardee	1.59	1.59	0.00	Seminole	35.73	35.73	0.00
Hendry	4.23	1.77	2.46	Sumter	0.79	0.79	0.00
Hernando	3.98	3.98	0.00	Suwannee	2.30	0.96	1.34
Highlands	2.15	2.15	0.00	Taylor	50.02	1.00	49.02
Hillsborough	112.06	86.33	25.73	Union	0.40	0.40	0.00
Holmes	0.70	0.70	0.00	Volusia	40.02	40.02	0.00
Indian River	6.46	5.63	0.83	Wakulla	1.53	0.13	1.40
Jackson	2.87	2.87	0.00	Walton	3.35	2.42	0.93
Jefferson	0.54	0.54	0.00	Washington	0.98	0.98	0.00
Lafayette	0.24	0.24	0.00				

Note: Discharge is to both surface and ground. Domestic facilities include those operated by public or private utilities. Industrial facilities exclude discharge from power plants or mining operations.

Source: U.S., Department of Interior, Geological Survey, Water Resource Division, Water-resources Investigations Report 99-4002, *Water Withdrawals, Use, Discharge, and Trends in Florida, 1995*.

University of Florida   **Bureau of Economic and Business Research**

National Weather Station Offices

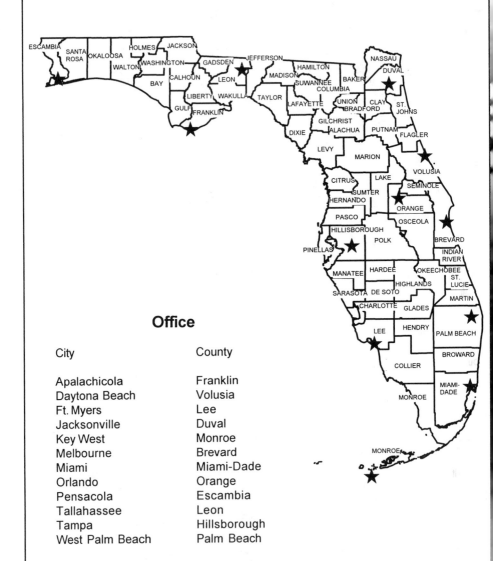

Office

City	County
Apalachicola	Franklin
Daytona Beach	Volusia
Ft. Myers	Lee
Jacksonville	Duval
Key West	Monroe
Melbourne	Brevard
Miami	Miami-Dade
Orlando	Orange
Pensacola	Escambia
Tallahassee	Leon
Tampa	Hillsborough
West Palm Beach	Palm Beach

Table 8.70. CLIMATE: TEMPERATURE CHARACTERISTICS AND TOTAL PRECIPITATION AT NATIONAL WEATHER STATION OFFICES IN FLORIDA BY MONTH, 1999

(temperature in degrees Fahrenheit)

Station and characteristics	January	February	March	April	May	June	July	August	September	October	November	December
Apalachicola												
Temperature												
Average maximum	68.8	71.0	72.2	82.7	87.1	90.3	93.4	94.5	90.9	84.2	76.5	69.5
Average minimum	43.5	49.0	47.8	58.3	64.6	72.1	74.7	76.4	69.4	60.5	50.0	40.0
Heating degree days	275	162	153	13	0	0	0	0	0	21	90	313
Cooling degree days	11	29	5	186	344	496	599	641	464	258	46	0
Days with maximum 90 degrees or more	0	0	0	2	10	22	28	27	20	3	0	0
Days with minimum 32 degrees or less	6	0	0	0	0	0	0	0	0	0	0	4
Precipitation (inches)	4.5	1.7	3.6	2.2	3.8	5.9	2.3	5.3	4.3	3.7	2.8	2.7
Pensacola												
Temperature												
Average maximum	64.7	68.1	70.0	79.5	82.9	87.2	89.2	91.8	87.3	79.4	72.8	63.2
Average minimum	46.5	48.3	49.7	62.5	64.8	72.8	74.3	76.6	68.4	60.4	50.0	42.9
Heating degree days	305	208	163	24	1	0	0	0	0	39	124	362
Cooling degree days	21	21	11	210	283	457	527	601	393	200	23	2
Days with maximum 90 degrees or more	0	0	0	0	0	5	11	26	13	0	0	0
Days with minimum 32 degrees or less	7	1	0	0	0	0	0	0	0	0	0	3
Precipitation (inches)	5.9	0.8	4.9	0.7	5.4	5.9	9.5	5.0	1.3	2.8	1.5	3.9
Tallahassee												
Temperature												
Average maximum	67.6	70.6	73.3	83.9	86.4	88.8	92.0	94.1	88.8	81.5	73.9	66.0
Average minimum	39.9	42.6	43.0	57.1	61.5	71.0	73.1	74.3	67.4	59.9	45.5	38.0
Heating degree days	347	247	210	38	1	0	0	0	0	49	165	396
Cooling degree days	3	19	5	211	287	456	552	604	401	234	14	1
Days with maximum 90 degrees or more	0	0	0	6	5	10	26	28	18	0	0	0
Days with minimum 32 degrees or less	8	6	2	1	0	0	0	0	0	1	2	11
Precipitation (inches)	4.3	1.6	3.2	0.9	6.9	7.5	7.4	6.1	5.8	1.6	2.2	2.6

See footnote at end of table.

Continued . . .

Table 8.70. CLIMATE: TEMPERATURE CHARACTERISTICS AND TOTAL PRECIPITATION AT NATIONAL WEATHER STATION OFFICES IN FLORIDA BY MONTH, 1999 (Continued)

(temperature in degrees Fahrenheit)

Station and characteristics	January	February	March	April	May	June	July	August	September	October	November	December
Jacksonville												
Temperature												
Average maximum	69.5	70.3	72.5	81.7	83.6	86.3	92.4	92.2	85.3	79.5	73.4	66.1
Average minimum	43.4	46.5	44.3	59.9	60.5	69.4	72.7	73.2	67.9	61.7	50.7	42.4
Heating degree days	272	199	204	40	11	0	0	0	0	34	115	331
Cooling degree days	16	23	6	221	236	392	552	556	356	213	36	4
Days with maximum 90 degrees or more	0	0	0	4	4	7	22	24	9	0	0	0
Days with minimum 32 degrees or less	6	4	1	0	0	0	0	0	0	0	0	6
Precipitation (inches)	4.5	1.7	0.4	1.9	1.0	7.8	3.6	3.5	13.0	3.2	0.8	0.9
Daytona Beach												
Temperature												
Average maximum	72.8	73.3	74.2	83.9	84.5	87.2	90.8	91.7	86.4	81.3	75.8	70.1
Average minimum	51.1	50.8	50.2	60.9	64.4	72.0	74.0	74.0	71.6	67.5	58.7	49.9
Heating degree days	141	126	105	17	6	0	0	0	0	1	30	174
Cooling degree days	54	47	26	249	307	442	548	561	429	291	106	29
Days with maximum 90 degrees or more	0	0	0	8	8	5	18	24	8	0	0	0
Days with minimum 32 degrees or less	1	0	0	0	0	0	0	0	0	0	0	0
Precipitation (inches)	4.9	1.8	1.0	1.5	1.5	8.5	4.0	3.6	7.1	7.8	3.1	1.6
Orlando												
Temperature												
Average maximum	75.3	76.1	78.4	86.9	86.6	88.3	91.9	92.6	88.9	82.9	77.9	71.7
Average minimum	52.5	51.8	50.7	61.5	64.3	71.9	73.6	74.1	72.0	67.3	58.9	51.3
Heating degree days	109	92	61	12	5	0	0	0	0	3	20	140
Cooling degree days	82	69	54	297	336	460	573	578	471	321	130	38
Days with maximum 90 degrees or more	0	0	0	11	8	11	27	26	16	0	0	0
Days with minimum 32 degrees or less	1	0	0	0	0	0	0	0	0	0	0	0
Precipitation (inches)	3.0	0.4	0.6	2.4	5.4	13.8	5.1	4.5	6.4	8.4	2.1	2.7

See footnote at end of table.

Continued . . . .

Table 8.70. CLIMATE: TEMPERATURE CHARACTERISTICS AND TOTAL PRECIPITATION AT NATIONAL WEATHER STATION OFFICES IN FLORIDA BY MONTH, 1999 (Continued)

(temperature in degrees Fahrenheit)

Station and characteristics	January	February	March	April	May	June	July	August	September	October	November	December
Melbourne												
Temperature												
Average maximum	74.9	75.6	77.2	85.0	85.1	87.4	92.1	92.9	89.1	83.7	78.8	73.0
Average minimum	54.2	52.0	51.9	60.8	64.1	71.5	72.5	73.3	71.9	69.1	61.6	53.1
Heating degree days	91	90	63	10	6	0	0	0	0	0	10	110
Cooling degree days	86	65	54	256	311	440	544	568	473	364	175	56
Days with maximum 90 degrees or more	0	0	0	8	7	5	25	28	13	0	0	0
Days with minimum 32 degrees or less	1	0	0	0	0	0	0	0	0	0	0	0
Precipitation (inches)	3.6	0.5	0.6	1.3	6.5	5.7	1.2	6.8	17.1	13.4	2.5	2.4
Tampa												
Temperature												
Average maximum	73.5	73.2	75.9	83.5	86.8	88.6	90.8	90.4	87.9	84.0	78.2	71.7
Average minimum	54.0	55.2	54.2	65.0	68.7	73.7	76.3	77.0	73.9	68.5	59.5	54.6
Heating degree days	118	97	44	6	5	0	0	0	0	5	20	110
Cooling degree days	85	84	52	294	409	492	583	589	481	363	144	62
Days with maximum 90 degrees or more	0	0	0	3	4	11	20	22	11	4	0	0
Days with minimum 32 degrees or less	1	0	0	0	0	0	0	0	0	0	0	0
Precipitation (inches)	3.0	0.3	0.7	0.4	1.5	4.7	3.7	11.2	6.1	2.9	1.8	1.0
Naples												
Temperature												
Average maximum	78.6	77.5	79.3	84.7	90.4	89.0	90.9	91.2	89.9	86.6	81.0	76.6
Average minimum	57.4	55.8	55.6	65.1	62.6	72.7	74.0	75.4	73.7	70.9	61.0	57.2
Heating degree days	47	54	16	1	0	0	0	0	0	0	0	0
Cooling degree days	150	105	102	306	365	486	547	576	512	441	184	118
Days with maximum 90 degrees or more	0	0	0	0	22	11	27	24	21	9	0	0
Days with minimum 32 degrees or less	0	0	0	0	0	0	0	0	0	0	0	0
Precipitation (inches)	1.5	1.2	0.7	0.4	5.1	9.8	10.4	6.0	13.6	1.9	2.2	0.4

See footnote at end of table.

Continued . . .

Table 8.70. CLIMATE: TEMPERATURE CHARACTERISTICS AND TOTAL PRECIPITATION AT NATIONAL WEATHER STATION OFFICES IN FLORIDA BY MONTH, 1999 (Continued)

(temperature in degrees Fahrenheit)

Station and characteristics	January	February	March	April	May	June	July	August	September	October	November	December
Miami												
Temperature												
Average maximum	77.3	77.9	79.2	85.8	86.7	87.1	90.2	91.0	88.1	84.6	80.5	76.8
Average minimum	62.7	61.2	61.8	69.7	70.5	74.6	77.7	76.1	75.7	73.7	68.0	63.2
Heating degree days	35	19	5	0	0	0	0	0	0	0	0	26
Cooling degree days	195	152	184	390	429	482	594	583	513	447	285	190
Days with maximum 90 degrees or more	0	0	0	0	6	2	22	22	10	0	0	0
Days with minimum 32 degrees or less	0	0	0	0	0	0	0	0	0	0	0	0
Precipitation (inches)	3.0	0.3	0.3	1.5	4.9	11.1	3.6	13.9	7.0	14.6	1.5	2.7
West Palm Beach												
Temperature												
Average maximum	76.5	76.7	78.5	85.7	86.3	86.1	89.9	90.6	88.7	84.4	79.9	75.9
Average minimum	60.2	56.6	58.2	66.8	68.3	73.9	76.3	75.9	74.9	72.8	66.6	60.5
Heating degree days	44	42	19	0	1	0	0	0	0	0	0	56
Cooling degree days	154	95	131	343	390	458	569	574	512	429	256	160
Days with maximum 90 degrees or more	0	0	0	7	6	0	16	22	10	0	0	0
Days with minimum 32 degrees or less	0	0	0	0	0	0	0	0	0	0	0	0
Precipitation (inches)	6.7	1.9	0.6	0.7	2.0	13.6	1.7	12.1	5.0	15.6	1.4	1.5
Key West												
Temperature												
Average maximum	77.0	76.7	77.9	83.2	85.9	87.6	88.6	89.1	88.7	84.0	78.7	77.0
Average minimum	67.3	66.1	65.9	73.6	74.8	78.0	79.5	78.9	78.0	75.5	70.8	67.2
Heating degree days	16	8	2	0	0	0	0	0	0	0	0	4
Cooling degree days	244	195	223	410	484	500	599	595	556	466	300	232
Days with maximum 90 degrees or more	0	0	0	0	0	0	12	16	12	0	0	0
Days with minimum 32 degrees or less	0	0	0	0	0	0	0	0	0	0	0	0
Precipitation (inches)	2.2	1.9	0.7	1.2	3.0	6.0	2.0	9.6	7.7	12.6	0.4	0.7

Note: Degree day totals are the sums of the negative (heating) or positive (cooling) departures of average daily temperatures from 65 degrees Fahrenheit.

Source: U.S., Department of Commerce, National Oceanic and Atmospheric Administration, National Environmental Satellite, Data and Information Service, *Climatological Data: Florida*, 1999 monthly reports, Internet site <http://www5.ncdc.noaa.gov/pdfs/cd/florida/1999> (accessed 5 June 2000).

Table 8.74. CLIMATE: CHARACTERISTICS FOR JACKSONVILLE, MIAMI, LOS ANGELES, ATLANTA CHICAGO, AND NEW YORK, SPECIFIED DATES THROUGH 1998

Characteristic	Jackson-ville Florida	Miami Florida	Los Angeles Cali-fornia	Atlanta Georgia	Chicago Illinois	New York New York 1/
Normal temperature 2/						
January average	52.4	67.2	56.8	41.0	21.0	31.5
July average	81.6	82.6	69.1	78.9	73.2	76.8
Annual average	68.0	75.9	63.0	61.3	49.0	54.7
January normal high	64.2	75.2	65.7	50.4	29.0	37.6
July normal high	91.4	89.0	75.3	88.0	83.7	85.2
Annual average high	78.9	82.8	70.4	71.2	58.6	62.3
January normal low	40.5	59.2	47.8	31.5	12.9	25.3
July normal low	71.9	76.2	62.8	69.5	62.6	68.4
Annual average low	57.1	69.0	55.5	51.3	39.5	47.1
Extreme temperatures 3/						
Highest temperature of record	105	98	110	105	104	106
Lowest temperature of record	7	30	23	-8	-27	-15
Length of record (years)	57	58	63	50	40	130
Normal annual precipitation 2/						
(inches)	51.32	55.91	12.01	50.77	35.82	47.25
Average number of days precipi-tation 0.01 or more 3/	116	131	35	116	125	121
Length of record (years)	57	56	63	64	40	129
Average total snow and ice pellets 3/ (inches)	T	T	T	2.0	37.6	28.4
Length of record (years)	57	56	62	62	39	130
Average annual percentage of possible sunshine 3/ 4/	61	68	72	59	52	64
Length of record (years)	47	46	60	61	37	42
Average annual wind speed 3/ (MPH)	7.9	9.2	7.5	9.1	10.4	9.3
Length of record (years)	49	49	50	59	40	61
Heating and cooling degree days 2/ 5/						
Heating degree days	1,434	200	1,458	2,991	6,536	4,805
Cooling degree days	2,551	4,198	727	1,667	752	1,096
Average relative humidity 3/						
Length of record	62	34	39	38	40	64
Annual (percentage)						
Morning	89	83	79	82	80	72
Afternoon	56	61	65	56	61	56

T Trace.
MPH Miles per hour.
1/ City office data.
2/ Based on 1961-90 period of record.
3/ Record through 1998.
4/ Percentage of days that are either clear or partly cloudy.
5/ Degree day normals are used to determine relative estimates of heating requirements for buildings. Each day that the average temperature for a day is below 65 degrees F. produces one heating degree day and each day it is above 65 degrees F. produces one cooling degree day.
Note: All temperatures are in degrees Fahrenheit.

Source: U.S., Department of Commerce, Bureau of the Census, *Statistical Abstract of the United States, 2000* Data from U.S. National Oceanic and Atmospheric Administration.

University of Florida   **Bureau of Economic and Business Research**

Table 8.76. HURRICANES: AREA OF LANDFALL, NAME, YEAR, FORCE CATEGORY, AND RANK OF THE FIFTEEN DEADLIEST HURRICANES IN THE UNITED STATES, 1900 THROUGH 1996

Area of landfall/name	Year	Force cate- gory 1/	Deaths Number	Rank
Galveston, Texas/(NA)	1900	4	A/ 8,000	1
Lake Okeechobee, Florida/(NA)	1928	4	1,836	2
Florida Keys; S. Texas/(NA)	1919	4	B/ 600	3
New England/(NA)	1938	3	600	4
Florida Keys/(NA)	1935	5	408	5
S.W. Louisiana; N. Texas/Audrey	1957	4	390	6
N.E. United States/(NA)	1944	3	C/ 390	7
Grand Isle, Louisiana/(NA)	1909	4	350	8
New Orleans, Louisiana/(NA)	1915	4	275	9
Galveston, Texas/(NA)	1915	4	275	10
Mississippi; Louisiana/Camille	1969	5	256	11
Miami, Florida/(NA)	1926	4	243	12
N.E. United States/Diane	1955	1	184	13
S.E. Florida/(NA)	1906	2	164	14
Mississippi; Alabama; Pensacola, Florida/(NA)	1906	3	134	15

(NA) Not available.
A/ May actually have been as high as 10,000 to 12,000. B/ Over 500 lost at sea; 600-900 estimated deaths. C/ Approximately 344 lost on ships at sea.
1/ Assigned based on the Saffir/Simpson scale. Ratings are 1-5 and a "5" indicates central pressure less than 920 millibars or winds greater than 155 mph or storm surge higher than 18 feet and damage classified as catastrophic.

Table 8.77. HURRICANES: AREA OF LANDFALL, NAME, YEAR, FORCE CATEGORY, AND RANK OF THE TEN COSTLIEST HURRICANES IN THE UNITED STATES, 1900 THROUGH 1996

Area of landfall/name	Year	Force cate- gory 1/	Value of damage 2/ Amount ($1,000)	Rank
Florida; Louisiana/Andrew	1992	4	26,500,000	1
South Carolina/Hugo	1989	4	7,000,000	2
North Carolina/Fran	1996	3	3,200,000	3
Florida/Opal	1995	3	3,000,000	4
Alabama; Mississippi/Frederic	1979	3	2,300,000	5
N.E. United States/Agnes	1972	1	2,100,000	6
Texas/Alicia	1983	3	2,000,000	7
North Carolina and N.E. United States /Bob	1991	2	1,500,000	8
Louisiana/Juan	1985	1	1,500,000	9
Mississippi; Alabama/Camille	1969	5	1,420,700	10

1/ Assigned based on the Saffir/Simpson scale. Ratings are 1-5 and a "5" indicates central pressure less than 920 millibars or winds greater than 155 mph or storm surge higher than 18 feet and damage classified as catastrophic.
2/ Adjusted to 1996 dollars on basis of U.S. Department of Commerce Implicit Price Deflator for construction.

Source for Tables 8.76 and 8.77: U.S., Department of Commerce, National Oceanic and Atmospheric Administration, *The Deadliest Hurricanes in the United States, 1990-1996* and *The Costliest Hurricanes in the United States, 1900-1996*, Internet site <http://www.nhc.noaa.gov/> (accessed 21 August 2000).

Table 8.80. AIR POLLUTION: PARTICULATE MATTER (PM) CONCENTRATIONS IN SPECIFIED CITIES OF FLORIDA, 1999

County and area 1/	Site Address	PM10 concentration (UG/M³) 2nd highest 24-hour value 2/	Annual arith- metic mean 3/
Alachua			
Gainesville	721 N.W. Sixth Street	38	21
Bay			
Panama City	Cherry Street & Henderson Avenue S.T.P.	50	25
Brevard			
Titusville	611 Singleton Avenue	52	19
Broward			
Hollywood	1000 E. Sunrise Boulevard	28	18
Ft. Lauderdale	Lincoln Park Elementary	31	19
Davie	3205 S.W. 70th Avenue	26	16
Pembroke Pines	11251 Taft Street	27	15
County	4010 Winston Park Boulevard	31	17
Plantation	1200 N.W. 72 Avenue	25	15
Pompano Beach	301 N.E. 12th Street	33	17
Collier			
Naples	East Naples Fire Dept, SR 858	30	17
Duval			
Jacksonville	2221 Buckman Street	53	28
Escambia			
Pensacola	Ellyson Industrial Park	56	23
Gulf			
Port St. Joe	City Water Plant	64	26
Hamilton			
County	County Road 137	39	25
Hillsborough			
Brandon	2929 S. Kingsway Avenue	81	35
Ruskin	Hwy 41, Gibsonton	51	28
Tampa	900 Harbour Island Boulevard	37	22
Lake			
County	Highway 19, Ocala National Forest	49	19
Lee			
Ft. Myers	Princeton Street	32	19
Leon			
County	Route 16, 3000 Tallahassee	55	19
Manatee			
County	Holland House 100 yards east of US 41	42	24
Miami-Dade			
Miami	7100 Northwest 36th Street	44	24
Monroe			
Stock Island	Stock Island Gerald A.	30	15
Marathon	2796 Overseas Highway	25	15
Nassau			
Fernandina Beach	5th Street North of Lime Avenue	59	27
Orange			
Orlando	2401 West 33rd Street	44	26
Winter Park	Morris Boulevard	35	21
Palm Beach			
Belle Glade	38745 SR 80	31	19
Delray Beach	345 South Congress Avenue	33	20

See footnotes at end of table.   Continued . . .

University of Florida   **Bureau of Economic and Business Research**

Table 8.80. AIR POLLUTION: PARTICULATE MATTER (PM) CONCENTRATIONS
IN SPECIFIED CITIES OF FLORIDA, 1999 (Continued)

County and area 1/	Site Address	PM10 concentration (UG/M³) 2nd highest 24-hour value 2/	Annual arith-metic mean 3/
Pinellas			
Largo	1301 Ulmerton Road	49	25
St. Petersburg	NE Corner of 13th Avenue	43	26
Tarpon Springs	County Road 77 Booker	34	20
Polk			
Mulberry	NW 4th Circle	50	22
Putnam			
Palatka	Comfort and Port Road	44	24
St. Lucie			
Ft. Pierce	6120 S.W. Glades Cutoff Road	39	20
Sarasota			
Sarasota	1642 12th Street	42	24
Venice	200 Warfield Avenue	34	20
Seminole			
Sanford	300 North Park Avenue	28	19
Volusia			
Daytona Beach	1185-A Dunn Avenue	54	21

UG/M³ Micrograms per cubic meter.
1/ Source includes more sites than could be reported here. Major cities in each county are reported. If more than one site was available, the one with the highest annual arithmetic mean is reported.
2/ Florida standard is 150 UG/M³, not to be exceeded more than once per year.
3/ Florida standard is 50 UG/M³.
Note: Particulate describes airborne solid or liquid particles of about 0.1 to 50 microns in diameter (1 micron = 0.0001 centimeter). PM consists of sulfate, nitrate, and acidic particles formed by oxidation of the pollutant gases sulfur dioxide and nitrogen dioxide; of soot and organic particles released in forest fires and other low-temperature combustion processes; of lead-containing particles emitted from motor vehicles; of products of industrial processes and high temperature fuel combustion; of local soil; and of airborne sea salt. PM10 is a subset of particulate matter and refers to airborne particles that are 10 microns or less in size.

Source: State of Florida, Department of Environmental Protection, Division of Air Resources Management, *Comparison of Air Quality Data with the National Ambient Air Quality Standards, 1999,* Internet site <http://www2.dep.state.fl.us/air/info/allsum/all99.htm> (accessed 1 August 2000).

AGRICULTURE

Farm Production Expense, 1998
($1,000)

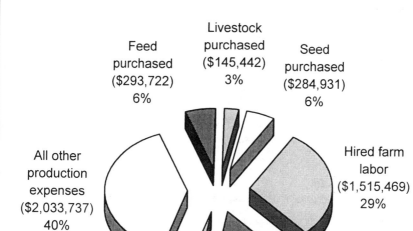

Feed purchased ($293,722) 6%

Livestock purchased ($145,442) 3%

Seed purchased ($284,931) 6%

All other production expenses ($2,033,737) 40%

Hired farm labor ($1,515,469) 29%

Petroleum products purchased ($119,768) 2%

Fertilizer and lime purchased ($744,206) 14%

Source: Table 9.21

TABLES LISTED BY MAJOR HEADINGS

SECTION 9.00
AGRICULTURE
(Continued)

TABLES LISTED BY MAJOR HEADINGS

Table 9.04. VETERINARIANS: LICENSED DOCTORS OF VETERINARY MEDICINE
IN THE STATE AND COUNTIES OF FLORIDA, JULY 24, 2000

County	Active	Inactive Voluntary	Inactive In-voluntary		Active	Inactive Voluntary	Inactive In-voluntary
Total	4,692	345	364	Lafayette	2	0	0
Out-of-state	1,247	315	186	Lake	42	0	0
Foreign	37	10	8	Lee	99	0	4
Alachua	188	1	9	Leon	59	1	2
Baker	1	0	0	Levy	15	0	2
Bay	28	0	3	Liberty	0	0	0
Bradford	6	0	0	Madison	2	0	0
Brevard	96	2	1	Manatee	40	1	0
Broward	331	2	26	Marion	130	0	12
Calhoun	1	0	0	Martin	44	0	2
Charlotte	28	0	0	Miami-Dade	294	1	13
Citrus	21	0	1	Monroe	31	0	2
Clay	47	0	6	Nassau	12	0	0
Collier	49	0	1	Okaloosa	45	1	3
Columbia	10	0	1	Okeechobee	7	0	1
De Soto	9	0	0	Orange	163	0	11
Dixie	2	0	0	Osceola	23	1	2
Duval	138	1	9	Palm Beach	287	1	14
Escambia	64	1	3	Pasco	54	0	1
Flagler	9	0	0	Pinellas	194	4	10
Franklin	2	0	0	Polk	77	0	1
Gadsden	8	0	0	Putnam	18	0	2
Gilchrist	3	0	1	St. Johns	33	1	0
Glades	0	0	0	St. Lucie	31	0	0
Gulf	1	0	0	Santa Rosa	22	0	0
Hamilton	1	0	0	Sarasota	102	0	5
Hardee	4	0	0	Seminole	98	1	4
Hendry	5	0	1	Sumter	8	0	0
Hernando	22	0	0	Suwannee	14	0	0
Highlands	14	0	0	Taylor	2	0	0
Hillsborough	240	1	9	Union	0	0	0
Holmes	0	0	0	Volusia	81	0	5
Indian River	28	0	2	Wakulla	4	0	0
Jackson	4	0	0	Walton	5	0	0
Jefferson	6	0	1	Washington	4	0	0

Source: State of Florida, Department of Business and Professional Regulation, unpublished data.

University of Florida   **Bureau of Economic and Business Research**

Table 9.10. EMPLOYMENT: ESTIMATES OF AVERAGE MONTHLY EMPLOYMENT OF FARM PROPRIETORS AND WAGE AND SALARY WORKERS IN THE UNITED STATES AND IN THE STATE AND COUNTIES OF FLORIDA, 1997 AND 1998

County	1997 A/ Farm proprie-tors	Farm wage and salary employees Number	As a per-centage of all wage and salary employees	1998 Farm proprie-tors	Farm wage and salary employees Number	As a per-centage of all wage and salary employees
United States	2,210,000	876,000	0.67	2,247,000	880,000	0.66
Florida	41,021	52,698	0.77	41,691	50,028	0.70
Alachua	1,350	388	0.33	1,372	368	0.31
Baker	197	259	4.67	200	246	4.31
Bay	80	21	0.03	81	20	0.03
Bradford	315	3	0.04	320	3	0.04
Brevard	602	242	0.13	612	229	0.12
Broward	268	616	0.09	272	585	0.09
Calhoun	156	106	2.92	159	101	2.62
Charlotte	269	199	0.55	273	189	0.50
Citrus	337	8	0.03	343	8	0.03
Clay	243	141	0.39	247	134	0.35
Collier	298	4,093	4.29	303	3,885	3.80
Columbia	700	35	0.17	711	33	0.16
De Soto	1,047	748	6.35	1,064	710	6.10
Dixie	203	3	0.11	207	2	0.07
Duval	340	380	0.08	346	361	0.08
Escambia	550	68	0.05	559	64	0.04
Flagler	119	101	0.83	121	95	0.75
Franklin	0	0	0.00	0	0	0.00
Gadsden	347	1,318	8.95	352	1,251	8.56
Gilchrist	458	173	6.72	466	164	6.33
Glades	252	242	16.44	256	230	14.96
Gulf	0	0	0.00	0	0	0.00
Hamilton	313	73	1.78	318	69	1.69
Hardee	1,424	812	9.13	1,447	771	8.83
Hendry	573	2,101	12.97	583	1,994	12.33
Hernando	492	32	0.11	500	30	0.10
Highlands	921	924	3.48	936	877	3.36
Hillsborough	3,084	5,329	0.92	3,134	5,059	0.83
Holmes	672	6	0.17	683	6	0.17
Indian River	535	819	1.89	544	778	1.70
Jackson	1,086	118	0.78	1,103	112	0.74
Jefferson	460	172	5.41	467	164	5.29
Lafayette	258	155	9.37	262	147	8.84
Lake	1,571	1,562	2.48	1,597	1,483	2.24

See footnote at end of table.   Continued . . .

University of Florida   **Bureau of Economic and Business Research**

Table 9.10. EMPLOYMENT: ESTIMATES OF AVERAGE MONTHLY EMPLOYMENT OF FARM PROPRIETORS AND WAGE AND SALARY WORKERS IN THE UNITED STATES AND IN THE STATE AND COUNTIES OF FLORIDA, 1997 AND 1998 (Continued)

	1997 A/	Farm wage and salary employees		1998	Farm wage and salary employees	
County	Farm proprie- tors	Number	As a per- centage of all wage and salary employees	Farm proprie- tors	Number	As a per- centage of all wage and salary employees
Lee	623	982	0.62	633	933	0.56
Leon	292	111	0.08	297	106	0.07
Levy	673	305	3.81	684	289	3.62
Liberty	58	0	0.00	59	0	0.00
Madison	591	121	2.15	601	115	2.04
Manatee	808	3,396	2.69	822	3,224	2.58
Marion	1,895	1,056	1.27	1,926	1,002	1.16
Martin	313	901	1.81	318	856	1.64
Miami-Dade	1,427	4,837	0.47	1,450	4,592	0.44
Monroe	0	0	0.00	0	0	0.00
Nassau	273	194	1.18	277	184	1.09
Okaloosa	429	7	0.01	436	6	0.01
Okeechobee	542	1,273	11.88	551	1,208	11.43
Orange	884	3,353	0.58	899	3,183	0.51
Osceola	595	351	0.69	605	334	0.64
Palm Beach	727	7,143	1.51	739	6,785	1.38
Pasco	1,095	572	0.74	1,113	543	0.68
Pinellas	162	160	0.04	165	152	0.03
Polk	3,188	1,987	1.09	3,237	1,886	0.99
Putnam	446	431	2.20	453	409	2.04
St. Johns	201	289	0.75	205	274	0.68
St. Lucie	672	502	0.95	683	476	0.88
Santa Rosa	514	63	0.23	523	59	0.20
Sarasota	373	315	0.23	379	299	0.21
Seminole	344	242	0.18	349	229	0.16
Sumter	824	167	1.98	838	159	1.84
Suwannee	1,025	301	3.17	1,042	285	2.84
Taylor	154	4	0.06	156	4	0.06
Union	260	25	0.58	265	24	0.59
Volusia	1,047	2,327	1.58	1,064	2,209	1.47
Wakulla	105	0	0.00	107	0	0.00
Walton	564	10	0.10	573	10	0.09
Washington	397	26	0.42	404	25	0.40

A/ Revised.

Source: U.S., Department of Commerce, Bureau of Economic Analysis, Regional Economic Information System, CD-ROM, June 2000.

University of Florida   **Bureau of Economic and Business Research**

Table 9.15. PRODUCTION AND SERVICES: AVERAGE MONTHLY PRIVATE REPORTING UNITS EMPLOYMENT, AND PAYROLL COVERED BY UNEMPLOYMENT COMPENSATION LAW IN THE STATE AND COUNTIES OF FLORIDA, 1999

County	Number of reporting units	Number of employees	Payroll ($1,000)	County	Number of reporting units	Number of employees	Payroll ($1,000)
				Agriculture production--crops (SIC code 01)			
Florida	2,285	59,464	85,184	Levy	11	61	102
				Madison	8	101	64
Alachua	20	358	442	Manatee	59	4,247	4,692
Baker	4	275	316	Marion	26	224	276
Brevard	16	157	244	Martin	34	971	1,629
Broward	54	612	1,004	Miami-Dade	284	5,853	9,104
Charlotte	15	192	361	Okeechobee	23	380	843
Collier	66	4,418	5,222	Orange	170	3,486	5,657
De Soto	53	946	1,310	Osceola	27	285	586
Duval	13	381	712	Palm Beach	244	8,013	15,410
Flagler	8	79	141	Pasco	32	317	356
Gadsden	17	1,680	2,345	Pinellas	15	163	273
Glades	9	142	291	Polk	148	1,740	2,996
Hardee	57	687	876	Putnam	25	384	417
Hendry	46	2,633	4,396	St. Johns	42	338	583
Hernando	4	7	10	St. Lucie	34	568	1,008
Highlands	76	5,341	4,437	Santa Rosa	9	54	66
Hillsborough	227	6,769	7,459	Sarasota	19	198	302
Indian River	40	833	1,592	Seminole	21	345	578
Jackson	8	121	117	Sumter	8	167	231
Jefferson	11	148	209	Suwannee	15	159	188
Lake	84	1,371	2,371	Volusia	119	2,227	2,569
Lee	31	1,078	1,661				
Leon	9	121	172	Multicounty 1/	11	69	116
				Agriculture production--livestock (SIC code 02)			
Florida	609	6,463	10,353	Jackson	7	27	36
				Lafayette	22	182	215
Alachua	14	90	161	Lake	14	145	237
Brevard	8	116	250	Leon	5	16	19
Broward	11	68	132	Levy	12	320	632
Clay	5	113	183	Madison	4	68	76
Collier	7	29	47	Manatee	13	108	131
Columbia	4	19	26	Marion	101	1,070	1,664
De Soto	12	117	211	Martin	8	56	93
Duval	6	63	113	Miami-Dade	21	120	229
Glades	6	76	134	Nassau	5	19	28
Hardee	26	204	375	Okeechobee	39	1,178	1,629
Hendry	4	22	30	Orange	6	33	44
Hernando	6	38	57	Osceola	13	102	188
Highlands	19	153	227	Palm Beach	18	76	114
Hillsborough	34	497	885	Pasco	26	386	635
Indian River	8	59	122	Polk	26	165	259

See footnote at end of table.   Continued . . .

University of Florida   **Bureau of Economic and Business Research**

Table 9.15. PRODUCTION AND SERVICES: AVERAGE MONTHLY PRIVATE REPORTING UNITS
EMPLOYMENT, AND PAYROLL COVERED BY UNEMPLOYMENT COMPENSATION LAW
IN THE STATE AND COUNTIES OF FLORIDA, 1999 (Continued)

County	Number of re- porting units	Number of em- ployees	Payroll ($1,000)	County	Number of re- porting units	Number of em- ployees	Payroll ($1,000)
			Agriculture production--livestock (SIC code 02) (Continued)				
St. Lucie	5	31	73	Suwannee	13	122	183
Sarasota	8	39	54	Volusia	11	82	132
Sumter	9	53	69	Multicounty 1/	8	16	28
			Agriculture services (SIC code 07)				
Florida	9,848	86,488	133,156	Levy	21	130	175
				Manatee	215	1,904	2,526
Alachua	118	918	1,184	Marion	194	1,456	2,255
Bay	51	284	440	Martin	154	1,298	2,050
Bradford	9	29	38	Miami-Dade	724	6,057	8,989
Brevard	260	1,703	2,605	Monroe	67	264	432
Broward	911	5,293	9,036	Nassau	29	178	256
Charlotte	72	377	592	Okaloosa	100	671	973
Citrus	65	259	362	Okeechobee	28	149	228
Clay	76	453	666	Orange	528	4,923	9,610
Collier	321	3,389	5,240	Osceola	73	437	720
Columbia	18	130	185	Palm Beach	1,029	9,984	15,697
De Soto	77	1,805	2,210	Pasco	202	1,587	2,210
Duval	429	2,688	4,199	Pinellas	514	3,085	5,036
Escambia	107	742	1,097	Polk	407	5,967	8,643
Flagler	30	177	233	Putnam	30	149	179
Gadsden	17	294	341	St. Johns	69	530	777
Gilchrist	4	39	54	St. Lucie	188	4,132	6,714
Glades	7	27	53	Santa Rosa	63	330	493
Hardee	75	1,359	1,471	Sarasota	314	1,812	3,005
Hendry	61	2,446	2,979	Seminole	235	1,474	2,390
Hernando	74	377	573	Sumter	14	75	75
Highlands	140	1,958	2,387	Suwannee	21	90	125
Hillsborough	517	4,585	6,971	Taylor	9	63	64
Indian River	178	2,521	4,189	Union	5	38	43
Jackson	15	56	78	Volusia	251	1,154	1,646
Jefferson	9	33	35	Wakulla	4	36	48
Lake	139	1,248	1,581	Walton	23	151	271
Lee	333	2,099	3,354	Washington	5	21	28
Leon	129	857	1,294	Multicounty 1/	66	1,147	2,122

1/ Reporting units without a fixed location within the state or of unknown county location.

Note: Private employment. Three-digit classifications of these two-digit groups are listed in Table 9.27.
Data are preliminary. Only counties for which data are disclosed are shown. Detail may not add to
totals due to disclosure editing and/or rounding. See Tables in 23.70, 23.71, 23.72, 23.73, and 23.74
for public employment data.

Source: State of Florida, Department of Labor and Employment Security, Bureau of Labor Market
Information, "Employment and Wages" (ES-202), unpublished data.

University of Florida   **Bureau of Economic and Business Research**

Table 9.21. LABOR AND PROPRIETORS' INCOME: FARM LABOR AND EXPENSE IN FLORIDA
1995 THROUGH 1998

(in thousands of dollars)

Item	1995	1996	1997	1998
Cash receipts from marketing	6,072,797	6,455,116	6,623,015	6,855,313
Total livestock and products	1,222,002	1,375,910	1,507,183	1,503,549
Total crops	4,850,795	5,079,206	5,115,832	5,351,764
Other income	272,861	241,224	271,492	273,212
Government payments	55,045	22,842	19,044	24,918
Imputed income and rent received 1/	217,816	218,382	252,448	248,294
Production expenses	4,685,449	4,902,374	5,019,760	5,137,275
Feed purchased	313,297	323,247	306,517	293,722
Livestock purchased	139,097	116,288	145,770	145,442
Seed purchased	221,251	262,603	280,589	284,931
Fertilizer and lime purchased	666,843	709,565	746,688	744,206
Petroleum products purchased	112,691	126,719	131,740	119,768
Hired farm labor 2/	1,355,597	1,427,767	1,449,605	1,515,469
All other production expenses 3/	1,876,673	1,936,185	1,958,851	2,033,737
Value of inventory change	-24,370	411	-30,962	-48,011
Livestock	-19,002	-19,204	-35,185	-36,483
Crops	-5,368	19,615	4,223	-11,528
Derivation of farm labor and proprietors' income:				
Total cash receipts and other income	6,345,658	6,696,340	6,894,507	7,128,525
Less: Total production expenses	4,685,449	4,902,374	5,019,760	5,137,275
Realized net income	1,660,209	1,793,966	1,874,747	1,991,250
Plus: Value of inventory change	-24,370	411	-30,962	-48,011
Total net income including corporate farms	1,635,839	1,794,377	1,843,785	1,943,239
Less: Corporate farms	236,448	650,107	570,019	378,244
Plus: Statistical adjustment	A/	A/	A/	A/
Total net farm proprietors' income	1,399,388	1,144,260	1,273,778	1,564,987
Plus: Farm wages and perquisites	772,855	750,117	805,048	842,356
Plus: Farm other labor income	83,874	84,299	90,514	85,327
Total farm labor and proprietors' income	2,256,117	1,978,676	2,169,340	2,492,670

A/ Less than $50,000. Estimates are included in totals.
1/ Includes imputed income such as gross rental value of dwellings and value of home consumption and other farm-related income components such as machine hire and custom work income, rental income, and income from forest products.
2/ Consists of hired workers' cash wages, social security, perquisites, and contract labor, machine hire and custom work expenses.
3/ Includes repair and operation of machinery; depreciation, interest, rent and taxes; and other miscellaneous expenses, including agricultural chemicals.
Note: Data for 1995 through 1997 may be revised.

Source: U.S., Department of Commerce, Bureau of Economic Analysis, Regional Economic Information System, CD-ROM, June 2000.

University of Florida   **Bureau of Economic and Business Research**

Table 9.22. LABOR AND PROPRIETORS' INCOME: DERIVATION OF FARM LABOR AND PROPRIETORS' INCOME IN THE UNITED STATES AND IN THE STATE AND COUNTIES OF FLORIDA, 1997 AND 1998

(in thousands of dollars)

1997 A/

County	Cash receipts from marketings	Plus other income 1/	Less production expenses	Plus value of inventory change	Total net farm income	Less corporate farm income	Total net farm proprietors' income 2/	Plus farm wages	Plus farm other labor income	Total farm labor and proprietors' income
United States 3/	213,739	26,057	207,813	2,769	239,796	5,181	29,570	15,048	1,080	45,698
Florida	6,623,015	271,492	5,019,760	-30,962	6,894,507	570,019	1,273,778	805,048	90,514	2,169,340
Alachua	59,466	2,896	45,748	-1,218	62,362	2,378	13,018	5,305	618	18,941
Baker	25,203	530	18,917	B/	25,733	942	5,893	2,977	368	9,238
Bay	2,632	75	1,469	B/	2,707	B/	1,186	341	B/	1,564
Bradford	19,031	910	14,799	-54	19,941	374	4,714	B/	B/	4,765
Brevard	41,212	3,245	34,908	-602	44,457	2,917	6,030	4,099	447	10,576
Broward	48,806	2,014	35,196	-320	50,820	4,724	10,580	10,610	1,151	22,341
Calhoun	15,619	1,425	13,437	-163	17,044	436	3,008	1,612	181	4,801
Charlotte	55,835	2,188	49,095	-537	58,023	2,332	6,059	4,049	419	10,527
Citrus	7,473	558	6,244	-186	8,031	126	1,475	72	B/	1,558
Clay	31,900	1,127	23,758	-275	33,027	3,990	5,004	2,266	251	7,521
Collier	329,251	3,860	216,365	302	333,111	44,587	72,462	45,360	5,703	123,525
Columbia	25,244	3,601	23,708	-611	28,845	204	4,322	414	51	4,787
De Soto	208,733	6,436	162,499	-1,631	215,169	10,236	40,803	12,854	1,395	55,052
Dixie	5,727	321	4,237	-86	6,048	175	1,550	B/	B/	1,589
Duval	27,382	1,754	23,290	-276	29,136	326	5,244	6,574	712	12,530
Escambia	17,331	5,864	17,369	-448	23,195	137	5,241	821	100	6,162
Flagler	28,906	1,967	23,327	459	30,873	473	7,532	1,462	167	9,161
Franklin	0									0
Gadsden	95,488	2,848	70,266	-133	98,336	3,950	23,987	19,105	2,185	45,277
Gilchrist	56,597	2,509	44,733	-697	59,106	2,081	11,595	2,888	317	14,800
Glades	64,324	2,306	56,329	-1,441	66,630	4,182	4,678	5,078	523	10,279

See footnotes at end of table.

Continued . . .

University of Florida

Bureau of Economic and Business Research

Table 9.22. LABOR AND PROPRIETORS' INCOME: DERIVATION OF FARM LABOR AND PROPRIETORS' INCOME IN THE UNITED STATES AND IN THE STATE AND COUNTIES OF FLORIDA, 1997 AND 1998 (Continued)

(in thousands of dollars)

1997 A/ (Continued)

County	Cash receipts from marketings	Plus other income 1/	Less production expenses	Plus value of inventory change	Total net farm income	Less corporate farm income	Total net farm proprietors' income 2/	Plus farm wages	Plus farm other labor income	Total farm labor and proprietors' income
Gulf	0	0	0	0	0	0	0	0	0	0
Hamilton	15,444	2,694	12,340	-680	18,138	378	4,740	534	80	5,354
Hardee	176,673	12,887	137,172	-1,775	189,560	10,790	39,823	11,276	1,308	52,407
Hendry	361,333	8,096	268,900	-2,007	369,429	38,039	60,484	40,838	4,283	105,605
Hernando	26,263	1,481	19,379	-304	27,744	1,145	6,916	462	52	7,430
Highlands	230,373	11,087	180,758	-2,336	241,460	18,260	40,106	16,265	1,753	58,124
Hillsborough	392,004	11,258	271,076	-1,039	403,262	27,894	103,254	62,271	7,673	173,198
Holmes	33,259	4,781	23,664	-377	38,040	254	13,745	54	B/	13,807
Indian River	109,744	5,097	99,668	-441	114,841	5,229	9,503	16,380	1,706	27,589
Jackson	56,417	6,919	47,276	-1,707	63,336	989	13,364	1,168	154	14,686
Jefferson	20,459	2,829	16,028	-439	23,288	350	6,471	2,123	256	8,850
Lafayette	58,412	3,100	42,741	-371	61,512	1,599	16,801	1,770	221	18,792
Lake	167,214	5,613	131,753	-569	172,827	8,731	31,774	24,939	2,766	59,479
Lee	130,755	2,863	104,571	81	133,618	4,612	24,516	15,246	1,705	41,467
Leon	4,146	3,329	6,251	-196	7,475	251	777	1,547	180	2,504
Levy	62,997	5,904	40,325	-915	68,901	4,189	23,472	5,943	622	30,037
Liberty	966	194	699	B/	1,160	65	366	0	B/	367
Madison	35,714	4,078	27,081	-800	39,792	358	11,553	1,152	154	12,859
Manatee	277,100	4,213	173,777	-448	281,313	30,464	76,625	37,320	4,708	118,653
Marion	168,171	14,840	122,179	-1,051	183,011	15,011	44,770	15,822	1,789	62,381
Martin	165,319	2,306	129,549	-589	167,625	15,036	22,451	15,191	1,658	39,300
Miami-Dade	435,565	8,950	334,123	838	444,515	43,126	68,105	71,818	8,147	148,070
Monroe	0	0	0	0	0	0	0	0	0	0

See footnotes at end of table.

Continued . . .

Table 9.22. LABOR AND PROPRIETORS' INCOME: DERIVATION OF FARM LABOR AND PROPRIETORS' INCOME IN THE UNITED STATES AND IN THE STATE AND COUNTIES OF FLORIDA, 1997 AND 1998 (Continued)

(in thousands of dollars)

1997 A/ (Continued)

County	Cash receipts from marketings	Plus other income 1/	Less production expenses	Plus value of inventory change	Total net farm income	Less corporate farm income	Total net farm proprietors' income 2/	Plus farm wages	Plus farm other labor income	Total farm labor and proprietors' income
Nassau	28,471	973	21,218	203	29,444	94	8,335	5,826	554	14,715
Okaloosa	9,236	1,789	8,529	-171	11,025	154	2,171	129	B/	2,313
Okeechobee	156,978	6,095	116,859	-3,062	163,073	13,559	29,593	23,668	2,512	55,773
Orange	249,982	5,728	213,441	-312	255,710	15,753	26,204	64,406	6,778	97,388
Osceola	100,162	13,369	81,928	-1,886	113,531	13,503	16,214	6,168	665	23,047
Palm Beach	899,319	12,945	651,800	-139	912,264	157,971	102,360	129,800	13,866	246,026
Pasco	91,738	4,436	73,532	-296	96,174	5,926	16,420	8,444	960	25,824
Pinellas	10,909	179	9,501	B/	11,088	154	1,432	2,852	305	4,589
Polk	288,412	14,905	215,013	-1,627	303,317	17,238	69,440	33,696	3,671	106,807
Putnam	33,284	6,673	27,200	560	39,957	2,976	10,341	4,270	562	15,173
St. Johns	45,111	1,603	39,883	3,627	46,714	3,033	7,425	4,614	511	12,550
St. Lucie	197,684	3,751	170,584	-698	201,435	14,514	15,639	9,518	1,006	26,163
Santa Rosa	30,061	6,245	26,268	-220	36,306	425	9,393	778	94	10,265
Sarasota	28,518	1,687	19,857	-505	30,205	2,508	7,335	4,769	538	12,642
Seminole	19,513	1,225	15,204	-138	20,738	1,200	4,196	4,893	508	9,597
Sumter	40,100	2,129	31,351	-845	42,229	1,411	8,622	2,287	266	11,175
Suwannee	130,511	7,295	91,645	-1,189	137,806	2,540	42,432	3,464	429	46,325
Taylor	5,269	577	3,886	-105	5,846	B/	1,809	B/	B/	1,843
Union	12,009	1,130	10,328	-231	13,139	164	2,416	312	B/	2,765
Volusia	112,807	4,888	85,565	-272	117,695	4,912	26,946	26,509	3,298	56,753
Wakulla	5,466	375	3,410	B/	5,841	91	2,301	0	B/	2,309
Walton	21,479	2,556	16,925	-180	24,035	387	6,543	174	B/	6,736
Washington	11,508	1,986	10,829	-343	13,494	108	2,214	354	B/	2,609

See footnotes at end of table.

Continued . . .

Table 9.22. LABOR AND PROPRIETORS' INCOME: DERIVATION OF FARM LABOR AND PROPRIETORS' INCOME IN THE UNITED STATES AND IN THE STATE AND COUNTIES OF FLORIDA, 1997 AND 1998 (Continued)

(in thousands of dollars)

1998

County	Cash receipts from marketings	Plus other income 1/	Less production expenses	Plus value of inventory change	Total net farm income	Less corporate farm income	Total net farm proprietors' income 2/	Plus farm wages	Plus farm other labor income	Total farm labor and proprietors' income
United States 3/	202,437	32,455	206,740	260	234,892	2,688	25,724	16,223	1,069	43,016
Florida	6,855,313	273,212	5,137,275	-48,011	7,128,525	378,244	1,564,987	842,356	85,327	2,492,670
Alachua	59,569	3,039	46,635	-1,238	62,608	1,393	13,342	5,545	583	19,470
Baker	25,813	513	19,067	-128	26,326	601	6,530	3,104	349	9,983
Bay	2,666	70	1,503	B/	2,736	B/	1,182	357	B/	1,574
Bradford	19,456	960	14,770	-283	20,416	241	5,122	B/	B/	5,175
Brevard	42,365	3,304	35,728	-572	45,669	1,870	7,499	4,293	421	12,213
Broward	49,615	1,982	36,273	-324	51,597	2,834	12,166	11,114	1,084	24,364
Calhoun	14,414	1,638	13,802	-610	16,052	127	1,513	1,687	172	3,372
Charlotte	58,378	2,127	50,410	-538	60,505	1,626	7,931	4,248	394	12,573
Citrus	7,451	538	6,380	-230	7,989	66	1,313	75	B/	1,398
Clay	32,357	1,097	24,033	-268	33,454	2,486	6,667	2,373	236	9,276
Collier	340,613	3,779	222,702	-222	344,392	28,323	93,145	47,279	5,388	145,812
Columbia	24,124	3,626	23,821	-566	27,750	93	3,270	431	B/	3,749
De Soto	221,100	6,295	165,879	-1,689	227,395	7,344	52,483	13,464	1,314	67,261
Dixie	5,879	315	4,296	-110	6,194	111	1,677	B/	B/	1,716
Duval	27,595	1,742	23,608	-288	29,337	195	5,246	6,887	671	12,804
Escambia	14,372	7,193	17,645	-1,187	21,565	B/	2,690	856	94	3,640
Flagler	29,811	1,928	23,852	-169	31,739	279	7,439	1,529	156	9,124
Franklin	0	0	0	0	0	0	0	0	0	0
Gadsden	96,997	2,840	72,674	-292	99,837	2,325	24,546	19,979	2,059	46,584
Gilchrist	57,912	2,504	45,296	-870	60,416	1,328	12,922	3,024	298	16,244
Glades	67,088	2,252	57,548	-1,403	69,340	3,002	7,387	5,327	491	13,205
Gulf	0	0	0	0	0	0	0	0	0	0

See footnotes at end of table.

Continued . . .

Table 9.22. LABOR AND PROPRIETORS' INCOME: DERIVATION OF FARM LABOR AND PROPRIETORS' INCOME IN THE UNITED STATES AND IN THE STATE AND COUNTIES OF FLORIDA, 1997 AND 1998 (Continued)

(in thousands of dollars)

1998 (Continued)

County	Cash receipts from marketings	Plus other income 1/	Less production expenses	Plus value of inventory change	Total net farm income	Less corporate farm income	Total net farm proprietors' income 2/	Plus farm wages	Plus farm other labor income	Total farm labor and proprietors' income
Hamilton	12,948	2,898	12,441	-554	2,851	129	2,722	553	76	3,351
Hardee	185,601	12,839	139,872	-1,824	56,744	7,405	49,339	11,786	1,234	62,359
Hendry	384,532	7,702	277,718	-1,943	112,573	26,605	85,968	42,823	4,032	132,823
Hernando	26,732	1,502	19,622	-450	8,162	710	7,452	483	50	7,985
Highlands	242,063	11,115	184,976	-2,308	65,894	12,619	53,275	17,042	1,650	71,967
Hillsborough	408,602	11,207	278,197	-1,441	140,171	18,249	121,922	64,953	7,248	194,123
Holmes	33,708	4,643	23,699	-636	14,016	156	13,860	56	B/	13,923
Indian River	117,188	5,231	102,108	-407	19,904	4,324	15,580	17,181	1,606	34,367
Jackson	49,618	7,940	47,904	-2,695	6,959	294	6,665	1,215	145	8,025
Jefferson	19,656	3,040	16,369	-497	5,830	183	5,647	2,217	243	8,107
Lafayette	59,694	3,142	42,787	-595	19,454	1,034	18,420	1,846	207	20,473
Lake	171,339	5,480	135,577	-768	40,474	5,341	35,133	26,107	2,607	63,847
Lee	135,275	2,873	108,260	-296	29,592	2,868	26,724	15,956	1,608	44,288
Leon	3,983	3,276	6,374	-181	704	105	599	1,618	169	2,386
Levy	64,510	6,082	40,875	-1,060	28,657	2,657	26,000	6,232	587	32,819
Liberty	988	191	712	B/	467	B/	394	B/	B/	395
Madison	33,220	3,973	27,233	-866	9,094	167	8,927	1,198	146	10,271
Manatee	286,487	4,145	177,926	-1,445	111,261	19,374	91,887	38,894	4,449	135,230
Marion	172,430	14,733	123,587	-1,222	62,354	9,584	52,770	16,552	1,687	71,009
Martin	173,825	2,215	132,132	-589	43,319	10,620	32,633	15,910	1,561	50,104
Miami-Dade	447,216	7,851	344,627	-183	110,257	26,167	84,089	75,125	7,683	166,897
Monroe	0	0	0	0	0	0	0	0	0	0
Nassau	29,412	931	21,076	-257	9,010	62	8,948	6,127	520	15,595
Okaloosa	7,960	1,926	8,666	-342	878	B/	842	134	B/	988
Okeechobee	161,021	6,078	118,552	-3,285	45,262	8,706	36,556	24,809	2,365	63,730
Orange	255,073	5,365	220,746	-312	39,380	9,050	30,330	67,530	6,379	104,239

See footnotes at end of table.

Continued . . .

Table 9.22. LABOR AND PROPRIETORS' INCOME: DERIVATION OF FARM LABOR AND PROPRIETORS' INCOME IN THE UNITED STATES AND IN THE STATE AND COUNTIES OF FLORIDA, 1997 AND 1998 (Continued)

(in thousands of dollars)

1998 (Continued)

County	Cash receipts from marketings	Plus other income 1/	Less production expenses	Plus value of inventory change	Total net farm income	Less corporate farm income	Total net farm proprietors' income 2/	Plus farm wages	Plus farm other labor income	Total farm labor and proprietors' income
Osceola	101,701	13,240	83,622	-1,954	114,941	8,168	21,197	6,463	626	28,286
Palm Beach	953,500	12,509	668,097	-101	966,009	110,618	187,186	136,039	13,059	336,284
Pasco	93,704	4,385	74,204	-973	98,089	3,719	19,193	8,832	904	28,929
Pinellas	11,046	173	9,844	0	11,219	82	1,293	2,988	288	4,569
Polk	304,841	14,888	219,521	-1,971	319,729	11,959	86,278	35,293	3,458	125,029
Putnam	34,136	6,668	27,903	-267	40,804	1,728	10,906	4,443	531	15,880
St. Johns	48,463	1,581	40,751	-412	50,044	1,576	7,305	4,829	482	12,616
St. Lucie	210,778	3,652	174,354	-679	214,430	11,608	27,789	9,978	946	38,713
Santa Rosa	26,862	8,076	26,808	-1,674	34,938	171	6,285	812	89	7,186
Sarasota	28,629	1,641	20,345	-488	30,270	1,472	7,965	4,989	506	13,460
Seminole	19,655	1,212	15,695	-137	20,867	686	4,349	5,132	478	9,959
Sumter	40,010	2,135	31,659	-1,099	42,145	808	8,579	2,391	252	11,222
Suwannee	131,989	7,597	92,326	-1,233	139,586	1,591	44,436	3,612	405	48,453
Taylor	5,536	554	3,889	-137	6,090		2,032		B/	2,068
Union	12,071	1,114	10,357	-322	13,185	97	2,409	326	B/	2,771
Volusia	113,936	4,845	88,372	-292	118,781	2,842	27,275	27,642	3,116	58,033
Wakulla	5,633	366	3,485	B/	5,999	58	2,415	0	B/	2,422
Walton	21,152	2,538	17,040	-595	23,690	207	5,848	181	B/	6,048
Washington	11,015	1,918	10,979	-416	12,933	B/	1,495	371	B/	1,904

A/ Revised.
B/ Less than $50,000. Estimates are included in totals.
1/ Includes government payments, imputed income, and rent received.
2/ Includes statistical adjustment.
3/ United States numbers are rounded to millions of dollars.
Note: See also tables in Section 5.00.

Source: U.S., Department of Commerce, Bureau of Economic Analysis, Regional Economic Information System, CD-ROM, June 2000.

Table 9.25. INCOME: ESTIMATED CASH RECEIPTS FROM FARM MARKETINGS BY SPECIFIED COMMODITY IN THE UNITED STATES AND LEADING STATES IN RANK ORDER, 1998

(in millions of dollars)

Commodity and state	Cash receipts	Commodity and state	Cash receipts	Commodity and state	Cash receipts
All commodities		All livestock 1/		All crops	
United States	196,761	United States	94,539	United States	102,222
California	24,616	Texas	8,220	California	17,771
Texas	13,206	California	6,845	Iowa	6,217
Iowa	10,994	Nebraska	5,124	Illinois	6,167
Nebraska	8,848	Iowa	4,778	Florida	5,355
Kansas	7,784	Kansas	4,537	Texas	4,986
Illinois	7,742	Wisconsin	4,492	Minnesota	3,925
Minnesota	7,680	North Carolina	3,917	Nebraska	3,724
North Carolina	7,164	Minnesota	3,755	Washington	3,424
Florida	6,762	Georgia	3,408	Kansas	3,247
Wisconsin	6,193	Arkansas	3,250	North Carolina	3,247
Greenhouse 2/ (6)		Tobacco (12)		Potatoes (15)	
United States	12,115	United States	2,989	United States	2,455
California	2,469	Kentucky	1,051	Idaho	574
Florida	1,279	North Carolina	998	Washington	432
Texas	1,120	Tennessee	225	Wisconsin	155
North Carolina	958	Virginia	178	California	152
Oregon	579	South Carolina	175	North Dakota	132
Ohio	543	Georgia	159	Oregon	129
Michigan	475	Indiana	55	Florida	123
Pennsylvania	347	Ohio	46	Colorado	110
New Jersey	299	Florida	30	Maine	109
Washington	269	Maryland	17	Michigan	102
Horses/mules (17)		Tomatoes (19)		Lettuce (20)	
United States	1,895	United States	1,640	United States	1,577
Kentucky	790	California	783	California	1,114
Florida	112	Florida	507	Arizona	410
Texas	90	Ohio	42	New Jersey	13
Virginia	60	Virginia	40	Florida	11
California	60	Tennessee	30	Colorado	9
New Jersey	59	New Jersey	29	New Mexico	7
Tennessee	49	Georgia	29	Ohio	6
New York	45	Michigan	28	New York	3
Pennsylvania	44	Indiana	26	Washington	3
Maryland	40	South Carolina	24		
Oranges (16)		Strawberries (23)		Strawberries (Cont.)	
United States	1,955	United States	1,029	New York	7
Florida	1,358	California	783	Wisconsin	7
California	587	Florida	161	Washington	6
Arizona	5	Oregon	26	Pennsylvania	5
Texas	5	North Carolina	15	Ohio	5
		Michigan	7		

1/ Includes poultry and products.   2/ Includes nursery.
Note: Commodities listed are among 25 leading commodities ranked by value of farm marketings. The number after the commodity name indicates rank order in cash receipts in the United States. Receipts include commodity credit corporation loans.
Source: U.S., Department of Agriculture, Economic Research Service, "Ranking of 10 Leading States in Cash Receipts for Top 25 Commodities, 1998," Internet site <http://www.ers.usda.gov/briefing/farmincome/firkdmu.htm> (accessed 31 May 2000).

University of Florida   **Bureau of Economic and Business Research**

Table 9.26. INCOME: CASH RECEIPTS BY COMMODITY AND COMMODITY GROUP IN FLORIDA, 1996 THROUGH 1998

Commodity	1996 Cash ($1,000)	Per-cent-total	1997 Cash ($1,000)	Per-cent-total	1998 A/ Cash ($1,000)	Per-cent-total
Cash receipts 1/	6,308,580	100.00	6,441,016	100.00	6,686,356	100.00
Crops	5,079,841	80.52	5,116,136	79.43	5,354,616	80.08
Citrus	1,582,372	25.08	1,491,140	23.15	1,607,610	24.04
Grapefruit	216,209	3.43	186,190	2.89	145,698	2.18
K-early citrus fruit	669	0.01	40	0.00	40	0.00
Lemons	2,879	0.05	1,341	0.02	2,631	0.04
Limes	1,860	0.03	5,159	0.08	4,826	0.07
Oranges	1,258,710	19.95	1,213,596	18.84	1,346,562	20.14
Tangelos	16,281	0.26	17,391	0.27	20,337	0.30
Tangerines	71,671	1.14	54,882	0.85	76,512	1.14
Temples	14,093	0.22	12,541	0.19	11,004	0.16
Other fruits and nuts	166,700	2.64	206,545	3.21	228,553	3.42
Avocados	12,408	0.20	14,016	0.22	16,468	0.25
Mangos	1,500	0.02	1,450	0.02	(NA)	(NA)
Pecans	1,095	0.02	1,320	0.02	1,045	0.02
Blueberries	4,965	0.08	5,040	0.08	6,240	0.09
Strawberries	112,632	1.79	146,119	2.27	161,200	2.41
Other	34,100	0.54	38,600	0.60	43,600	0.65
Vegetables and melons	1,354,966	21.48	1,459,558	22.66	1,536,371	22.98
Cabbage	26,768	0.42	39,701	0.62	26,325	0.39
Carrots	12,516	0.20	16,538	0.26	11,340	0.17
Celery	4,745	0.08	(NA)	(NA)	(NA)	(NA)
Cucumbers	79,761	1.26	98,867	1.53	69,492	1.04
Eggplant	14,784	0.23	15,548	0.24	15,523	0.23
Escarole	5,776	0.09	7,000	0.11	11,550	0.17
Green peppers	222,768	3.53	251,766	3.91	245,686	3.67
Lettuce	6,691	0.11	3,360	0.05	11,024	0.16
Potatoes	98,944	1.57	89,195	1.38	123,491	1.85
Radishes	20,021	0.32	19,018	0.30	18,816	0.28
Snap beans	75,842	1.20	65,838	1.02	130,153	1.95
Squash	34,121	0.54	36,228	0.56	54,515	0.82
Sweet corn	100,526	1.59	127,331	1.98	103,249	1.54
Tomatoes	447,556	7.09	487,060	7.56	506,607	7.58
Watermelons	49,980	0.79	54,750	0.85	60,120	0.90
Other	154,167	2.44	147,358	2.29	148,480	2.22
Field crops	667,443	10.58	636,494	9.88	644,953	9.65
Corn	20,919	0.33	16,298	0.25	8,022	0.12
Cotton	44,171	0.70	43,987	0.68	34,359	0.51
Hay	11,906	0.19	13,179	0.20	13,886	0.21
Peanuts	66,361	1.05	63,857	0.99	57,343	0.86
Soybeans	6,214	0.10	7,733	0.12	4,961	0.07
Sugarcane	455,434	7.22	434,187	6.74	472,303	7.06
Tobacco	31,021	0.49	32,293	0.50	29,942	0.45
Wheat	1,534	0.02	2,072	0.03	1,509	0.02
Other	29,883	0.47	22,888	0.36	22,628	0.34
Foliage and floriculture	676,727	10.73	656,234	10.19	653,700	9.78
Aquatic Plants	10,900	0.17	13,200	0.20	12,300	0.18
Other crops and products	620,733	9.84	652,965	10.14	671,129	10.04
Livestock and products	1,228,739	19.48	1,324,880	20.57	1,331,740	19.92
Milk	431,280	6.84	407,715	6.33	423,878	6.34
Cattle and calves	218,919	3.47	320,424	4.97	293,327	4.39
Poultry and eggs	362,760	5.75	353,838	5.49	367,313	5.49
Broilers	230,607	3.66	229,383	3.56	252,840	3.78

See footnotes at end of table.   Continued . . .

Table 9.26. INCOME: CASH RECEIPTS BY COMMODITY AND COMMODITY GROUP IN FLORIDA 1996 THROUGH 1998 (Continued)

Commodity	1996 Cash receipts ($1,000)	1996 Per-cent-age of total	1997 Cash receipts ($1,000)	1997 Per-cent-age of total	1998 A/ Cash receipts ($1,000)	1998 A/ Per-cent-age of total
Livestock and products (Cont.)						
Eggs	131,355	2.08	123,701	1.92	112,707	1.69
Other	798	0.01	754	0.01	1,766	0.03
Aquaculture	80,250	1.27	88,016	1.37	92,674	1.39
Catfish	350	0.01	352	0.01	674	0.01
Tropical fish	55,000	0.87	57,200	0.89	55,100	0.82
Alligators farmed	3,900	0.06	3,190	0.05	2,300	0.03
Clams and oysters	9,000	0.14	13,100	0.20	11,200	0.17
Other	12,000	0.19	14,174	0.22	23,400	0.35
Hogs	15,409	0.24	12,335	0.19	5,772	0.09
Horses and mules	B/	(X)	108,000	1.68	111,600	1.67
Honey	21,672	0.34	11,738	0.18	14,426	0.22
Sheep and lamb's wool	135	0.00	138	0.00	135	0.00
Other	98,314	1.56	22,676	0.35	22,615	0.34

(NA) Not available. A/ Preliminary. B/ Included in "other."
1/ Farm marketings. Includes additional receipts not published.
Source: State of Florida, Department of Agriculture and Consumer Services, Florida Agricultural Statistics Service, *Florida Agriculture: Farm Cash Receipts and Expenditures, 1998,* released August 1999, Internet site <http://www.nass.usda.gov/fl/rtoc0.htm> (accessed 23 May 2000).

Table 9.27. PRODUCTION AND SERVICES: AVERAGE MONTHLY PRIVATE REPORTING UNITS EMPLOYMENT, AND PAYROLL COVERED BY UNEMPLOYMENT COMPENSATION LAW BY INDUSTRY IN FLORIDA, 1999

SIC code	Industry	Number of reporting units	Number of employees	Payroll ($1,000)
01	Agricultural production--crops	2,285	59,464	85,184
011	Cash grains	22	214	334
013	Field crops, except cash grains	183	3,936	10,031
016	Vegetables and melons	325	15,763	17,804
017	Fruits and tree nuts	634	15,832	19,950
018	Horticultural specialties	1,078	22,931	35,821
019	General farms, primarily crop	44	789	1,244
02	Agricultural production--livestock	609	6,463	10,353
021	Livestock, except dairy, and poultry	215	1,570	2,199
024	Dairy farms	142	2,501	4,219
025	Poultry and eggs	29	645	1,092
027	Animal specialties	207	1,673	2,752
029	General farms, primarily animal	16	74	90
07	Agricultural services	9,848	86,488	133,156
071	Soil preparation services	41	224	387
072	Crop services	347	9,977	15,788
074	Veterinary services	1,511	13,243	23,538
075	Animal services, except veterinary	624	2,409	3,244
076	Farm labor and management services	734	20,133	24,017
078	Landscape and horticultural services	6,592	40,503	66,182

Note: Private employment. Detail may not add to totals due to disclosure editing and/or rounding. See Tables 23.70, 23.71, 23.72, 23.73, and 23.74 for public employment data.
Source: State of Florida, Department of Labor and Employment Security, Bureau of Labor Market Information, "Employment and Wages" (ES-202), unpublished data.

Florida Statistical Abstract 2000

Table 9.34. FARMS: SPECIFIED CHARACTERISTICS OF FARMS IN FLORIDA
1992 AND 1997

	All farms			Farms with sales of $10,000 or more		
Item	1992	1997	Per-centage change	1992	1997	Per-centage change
Number of farms	35,204	34,799	-1.2	14,945	14,742	-1.4
By size						
1 to 9 acres	7,664	7,394	-3.5	2,185	2,302	5.4
10 to 49 acres	12,692	12,750	0.5	4,074	4,081	0.2
50 to 179 acres	7,738	7,932	2.5	3,309	3,356	1.4
180 to 499 acres	4,011	3,687	-8.1	2,683	2,416	-10.0
500 to 999 acres	1,451	1,390	-4.2	1,195	1,111	-7.0
1,000 to 1,999 acres	776	802	3.4	689	689	0.0
2,000 acres or more	872	844	-3.2	810	787	-2.8
With irrigated land	13,500	12,673	-6.1	8,265	8,331	0.8
By NAICS code						
Oilseed and grain (1111)	(NA)	1,118	(X)	(NA)	208	(X)
Vegetable and melon (1112)	(NA)	1,250	(X)	(NA)	991	(X)
Fruit and tree nut (1113)	(NA)	8,245	(X)	(NA)	4,157	(X)
Greenhouse, nursery, and floriculture (1114)	(NA)	4,902	(X)	(NA)	3,598	(X)
Other crop farming (1119)	(NA)	2,137	(X)	(NA)	1,241	(X)
Beef cattle ranching and farming (112111)	(NA)	12,040	(X)	(NA)	121	(X)
Cattle feedlots (112112)	(NA)	309	(X)	(NA)	2,631	(X)
Dairy cattle and milk pro-duction (11212)	(NA)	296	(X)	(NA)	67	(X)
Hog and pig farming (1122)	(NA)	468	(X)	(NA)	291	(X)
Poultry and egg pro-duction (1123)	(NA)	560	(X)	(NA)	407	(X)
Sheep and goat farming (1124)	(NA)	272	(X)	(NA)	23	(X)
Animal aquaculture and other animal produc-tion (1125, 1129)	(NA)	3,202	(X)	(NA)	1,026	(X)
Selected farm production expenses 1/ ($1,000)						
Livestock and poultry purchased	131,497	145,770	10.9	123,668	139,289	(X)
Feed for livestock and poultry	382,945	446,861	16.7	369,869	434,789	17.6
Commercial fertilizer	283,424	347,559	22.6	268,075	335,365	25.1
Petroleum products	128,168	131,636	2.7	120,122	123,610	2.9
Hired farm labor	937,571	925,607	-1.3	932,283	921,203	-1.2
Interest expense	219,234	237,536	8.3	207,581	226,378	(X)
Agricultural chemicals 2/	320,675	350,556	9.3	311,910	343,995	10.3
Livestock and poultry inventory						
Cattle and calves						
Farms	15,522	15,849	2.1	5,474	5,153	-5.9
Number	1,783,968	1,808,900	1.4	1,553,165	1,555,678	0.2
Beef cows						
Farms	13,423	13,600	1.3	4,785	4,564	-4.6
Number	962,527	1,003,072	4.2	827,655	854,990	3.3

See footnotes at end of table.

Continued . . .

University of Florida

Bureau of Economic and Business Research

Table 9.34. FARMS: SPECIFIED CHARACTERISTICS OF FARMS IN FLORIDA
1992 AND 1997 (Continued)

Item	All farms			Farms with sales of $10,000 or more		
	1992	1997	Per-centage change	1992	1997	Per-centage change
Livestock/poultry inventory (Continued)						
Cattle and calves (Continued)						
Milk cows						
Farms	877	666	-24.1	487	354	-27.3
Number	171,675	159,614	-7.0	170,852	158,804	-7.1
Chickens 3/						
Farms	1,454	1,203	-17.3	(NA)	225	(X)
Number	10,802,573	12,605,047	16.7	(NA)	11,589,123	(X)
Crops harvested 4/						
Corn						
Farms	1,548	1,268	-18.1	905	748	-17.3
Acres	86,407	69,623	-19.4	76,488	(D)	(X)
Bushels	6,377,801	5,440,956	-14.7	5,920,036	(D)	(X)
Soybeans						
Farms	415	404	-2.7	351	348	-0.9
Acres	49,072	41,021	-16.4	47,215	39,740	-15.8
Bushels	1,523,227	1,025,521	-32.7	1,477,006	1,003,636	-32.0
Sugarcane						
Farms	139	152	9.4	(NA)	(NA)	(X)
Acres	431,677	421,421	-2.4	(NA)	(NA)	(X)
Tons	16,151,380	15,718,897	-2.7	(NA)	(NA)	(X)
Hay						
Farms	(NA)	(NA)	(X)	2,527	2,383	-5.7
Acres	(NA)	(NA)	(X)	218,675	215,665	-1.4
Tons	(NA)	(NA)	(X)	572,878	600,407	4.8
Vegetables						
Farms	1,988	1,500	-24.5	1,532	1,214	-20.8
Acres	299,867	250,562	-16.4	297,934	249,719	-16.2
Orchards						
Farms	10,258	9,379	-8.6	4,539	4,689	3.3
Acres	914,642	981,910	7.4	834,170	933,231	11.9

NAICS North American Industry Classification System. See Glossary.
(NA) Not available.
(X) Not applicable.
(D) Data witheld to avoid disclosure of information about individual farms.
1/ Data are based on a sample of farms. In current dollars and unadjusted.
2/ Excludes the cost of lime.
3/ Layers and pullets 13 weeks old and older.
4/ Corn for grain or seed; soybeans for beans; sugarcane for sugar; hay includes alfalfa, and other
tame, small grain, wild, grass silage, green chop, etc.; vegetables harvested for sale; vegetable acreage is
counted only once even when it is replanted.
Note: Livestock and poultry inventories are as of December 31. Crop and livestock production, sales,
and expense data are for the calendar year, except for a few crops for which the production and calendar
years overlap. The agriculture census is on a 5-year cycle collecting data for years ending in 2 or 7.

Source: U.S., Department of Commerce, Bureau of the Census, *1997 Census of Agriculture: State
and County Data, Florida,* AC92-A-9, issued March 1999. Internet site <http://www.census.gov/prod/
ac97/ac97a-9.pdf> (accessed 7 September 1999).

Table 9.35. FARMS: NUMBER, LAND IN FARMS, AND VALUE OF LAND AND BUILDINGS
IN THE STATE AND COUNTIES OF FLORIDA, 1992 AND 1997

County	Number of farms		Land in farms (acres)					
			Total		Average size of farm		Average market value 1/ (dollars)	
	1992	1997	1992	1997	1992	1997	1992	1997
Florida	35,204	34,799	10,766,077	10,454,217	306	300	619,265	662,538
Alachua	1,089	1,086	191,140	198,193	176	182	275,767	360,956
Baker	193	157	24,489	13,035	127	83	227,722	247,169
Bay	63	70	9,135	6,732	145	96	220,367	178,733
Bradford	315	274	36,230	43,579	115	159	202,625	262,500
Brevard	496	470	199,724	276,573	403	588	562,655	909,187
Broward	393	347	23,735	30,897	60	89	315,376	414,044
Calhoun	132	130	43,314	43,799	328	337	355,378	395,452
Charlotte	214	209	227,202	290,340	1,062	1,389	1,310,837	1,877,627
Citrus	288	294	70,672	49,192	245	167	449,229	339,900
Clay	210	211	86,026	70,834	410	336	884,620	623,247
Collier	254	235	301,977	277,279	1,189	1,180	2,305,229	2,152,046
Columbia	523	600	96,968	97,100	185	162	234,203	348,563
De Soto	804	715	334,623	322,402	416	451	848,575	1,133,735
Dixie	106	155	31,693	33,508	299	216	227,346	211,203
Duval	378	320	40,039	35,531	106	111	307,468	390,172
Escambia	454	466	57,179	54,617	126	117	166,769	248,484
Flagler	93	91	52,259	87,737	562	964	797,013	1,235,927
Franklin	6	19	(D)	5,125	(D)	270	49,979	358,268
Gadsden	333	290	57,853	57,933	174	200	322,888	545,860
Gilchrist	329	365	70,987	78,090	216	214	317,870	428,540
Glades	206	188	369,965	380,377	1,796	2,023	1,243,443	1,663,359
Gulf	27	33	14,203	3,823	526	116	733,567	131,637
Hamilton	224	256	69,405	66,379	310	259	251,658	302,842
Hardee	1,169	1,045	327,611	345,643	280	331	569,627	859,608
Hendry	389	403	529,835	604,677	1,362	1,500	2,539,049	4,288,707
Hernando	411	432	61,019	52,999	148	123	339,864	415,946
Highlands	652	779	483,835	489,579	742	628	1,532,899	1,190,743
Hillsborough	2,760	2,639	265,443	247,502	96	94	364,794	391,045
Holmes	523	578	86,706	87,582	166	152	141,788	217,569
Indian River	447	437	174,673	168,399	391	385	1,400,034	1,243,117
Jackson	808	844	244,185	244,552	302	290	247,068	300,497
Jefferson	297	342	118,352	126,590	398	370	575,501	498,805
Lafayette	252	221	95,833	93,434	380	423	373,438	547,086
Lake	1,320	1,389	199,098	185,311	151	133	480,005	406,637

See footnotes at end of table.   Continued . . .

University of Florida   **Bureau of Economic and Business Research**

Table 9.35. FARMS: NUMBER, LAND IN FARMS, AND VALUE OF LAND AND BUILDINGS
IN THE STATE AND COUNTIES OF FLORIDA, 1992 AND 1997 (Continued)

County	Number of farms		Land in farms (acres)				Average market value 1/ (dollars)	
			Total		Average size of farm			
	1992	1997	1992	1997	1992	1997	1992	1997
Lee	517	509	106,721	129,001	206	253	606,292	723,893
Leon	263	243	100,764	67,539	383	278	666,946	456,258
Levy	473	549	190,553	157,376	403	287	374,647	364,963
Liberty	71	47	11,738	7,238	165	154	186,451	227,102
Madison	481	486	132,208	131,577	275	271	212,290	380,680
Manatee	728	697	299,699	267,993	412	384	796,187	921,872
Marion	1,654	1,669	296,242	265,572	179	159	448,675	491,266
Martin	305	305	190,788	183,724	626	602	1,863,414	1,617,780
Miami-Dade	1,891	1,576	83,681	85,093	44	54	389,694	408,330
Monroe	15	13	32	1,241	2	95	173,818	296,297
Nassau	277	238	44,962	35,165	162	148	250,847	275,889
Okaloosa	315	342	56,704	50,822	180	149	232,732	249,245
Okeechobee	418	459	351,885	391,871	842	854	1,264,286	1,227,122
Orange	990	862	138,418	175,017	140	203	541,725	603,726
Osceola	499	485	716,542	610,825	1,436	1,259	1,492,793	1,646,904
Palm Beach	924	855	637,934	604,703	690	707	2,417,525	2,397,652
Pasco	922	951	221,232	161,939	240	170	506,609	500,412
Pinellas	124	129	4,123	1,895	33	15	227,337	283,991
Polk	2,294	2,464	611,336	621,489	266	252	676,596	531,715
Putnam	400	391	105,621	85,794	264	219	352,198	467,078
St. Johns	166	149	48,839	49,631	294	333	558,362	748,864
St. Lucie	539	500	300,622	227,414	558	455	1,667,942	1,182,701
Santa Rosa	430	438	79,270	87,971	184	201	202,461	297,052
Sarasota	328	315	151,242	128,655	461	408	878,490	899,896
Seminole	352	344	59,642	37,222	169	108	476,796	331,507
Sumter	720	718	253,330	183,374	352	255	489,501	467,695
Suwannee	932	840	161,936	158,406	174	189	232,428	289,572
Taylor	125	126	(D)	56,784	(D)	451	353,773	396,058
Union	175	213	48,280	62,503	276	293	355,457	408,651
Volusia	978	910	138,208	111,502	141	123	382,517	447,093
Wakulla	83	88	8,679	11,426	105	130	149,612	223,264
Walton	383	476	96,730	78,844	253	166	228,124	202,967
Washington	274	322	45,214	55,268	165	172	143,811	229,495

(D) Data withheld to avoid disclosure of information about individual farms.
1/ Average estimated market value of land and buildings per farm. Data are based on a sample of farms.
Note: The agriculture census is on a 5-year cycle collecting data for years ending in 2 and 7.

Source: U.S., Department of Commerce, Bureau of the Census, *1997 Census of Agriculture: State and County Data, Florida,* AC92-A-9, issued March 1999. Internet site <http://www.census.gov/prod/ac97/ac97a-9.pdf> (accessed 7 September 1999).

Table 9.36. FARMS: LAND IN FARMS BY USE IN THE STATE AND COUNTIES
OF FLORIDA, 1997

(acres)

County	Total land in farms	Cropland Total	Harvested	Woodland 1/	Pastureland 2/	Other 3/	Irrigated land
Florida	10,454,217	3,639,850	2,435,702	2,132,308	4,069,927	612,132	1,862,404
Alachua	198,193	75,368	31,132	48,600	65,125	9,100	7,942
Baker	13,035	4,911	1,723	5,308	1,760	1,056	803
Bay	6,732	3,087	1,111	2,475	644	526	437
Bradford	43,579	10,268	4,143	10,170	21,263	1,878	264
Brevard	276,573	26,729	21,691	40,055	200,214	9,575	30,636
Broward	30,897	6,569	3,737	1,179	20,964	2,185	2,133
Calhoun	43,799	27,223	19,928	14,321	1,023	1,232	1,107
Charlotte	290,340	44,577	28,755	95,813	132,020	17,930	26,496
Citrus	49,192	20,661	6,950	10,351	15,834	2,346	508
Clay	70,834	7,863	3,582	49,043	10,429	3,499	1,443
Collier	277,279	69,212	55,213	52,707	121,921	33,439	53,188
Columbia	97,100	46,268	16,002	31,220	13,956	5,656	2,916
De Soto	322,402	126,633	89,405	15,244	155,345	25,180	72,939
Dixie	33,508	6,371	1,771	14,956	10,467	1,714	636
Duval	35,531	11,127	6,617	11,098	10,174	3,132	624
Escambia	54,617	34,942	28,235	12,909	2,038	4,728	1,111
Flagler	87,737	12,656	8,871	57,881	15,659	1,541	7,924
Franklin	5,125	(D)	(D)	3,475	(D)	551	19
Gadsden	57,933	23,827	14,088	24,692	3,824	5,590	5,253
Gilchrist	78,090	43,552	20,403	23,494	8,477	2,567	6,336
Glades	380,377	41,361	29,099	5,984	304,328	28,704	26,334
Gulf	3,823	968	241	944	768	1,143	6
Hamilton	66,379	25,398	11,445	29,142	7,860	3,979	4,336
Hardee	345,643	105,878	67,465	52,306	177,011	10,448	54,026
Hendry	604,677	204,996	183,206	104,758	262,555	32,368	184,109
Hernando	52,999	21,024	7,460	10,025	19,336	2,614	1,142
Highlands	489,579	121,762	93,135	44,673	303,736	19,408	88,103
Hillsborough	247,502	103,266	60,333	44,551	81,644	18,041	46,298
Holmes	87,582	41,243	18,969	33,751	6,019	6,569	276
Indian River	168,399	85,820	76,135	41,296	32,085	9,198	77,411
Jackson	244,552	136,123	89,386	72,627	20,594	15,208	18,314
Jefferson	126,590	33,477	17,860	71,136	14,081	7,896	1,432
Lafayette	93,434	22,221	8,454	53,933	14,193	3,087	3,865
Lake	185,311	80,063	41,475	34,429	54,341	16,478	26,206
Lee	129,001	34,155	25,025	12,738	74,827	7,281	26,106
Leon	67,539	16,467	4,613	38,192	4,522	8,358	2,531

See footnotes at end of table.   Continued . . .

University of Florida   **Bureau of Economic and Business Research**

Table 9.36. FARMS: LAND IN FARMS BY USE IN THE STATE AND COUNTIES
OF FLORIDA, 1997 (Continued)

(acres)

County	Total land in farms	Cropland Total	Cropland Har-vested	Wood-land 1/	Pasture-land 2/	Other 3/	Irri-gated land
Levy	157,376	68,488	31,715	48,388	31,502	8,998	13,022
Liberty	7,238	1,179	343	5,328	313	418	6
Madison	131,577	54,254	26,437	54,271	13,282	9,770	4,312
Manatee	267,993	105,743	64,302	32,305	116,749	13,196	57,790
Marion	265,572	100,264	34,020	66,181	88,288	10,839	6,115
Martin	183,724	75,180	64,205	14,154	74,170	20,220	61,615
Miami-Dade	85,093	67,550	62,693	5,714	6,289	5,540	57,585
Monroe	1,241	(D)	(D)	392	(D)	10	33
Nassau	35,165	6,131	2,874	21,064	6,683	1,287	54
Okaloosa	50,822	21,161	10,027	24,082	3,215	2,364	156
Okeechobee	391,871	72,659	36,466	28,606	269,390	21,216	35,210
Orange	175,017	44,266	30,286	53,996	67,205	9,550	25,489
Osceola	610,825	50,505	30,345	58,575	487,869	13,876	58,024
Palm Beach	604,703	529,138	462,690	18,460	15,503	41,602	417,368
Pasco	161,939	58,038	24,949	28,742	61,610	13,549	12,940
Pinellas	1,895	902	530	132	531	330	249
Polk	621,489	186,878	129,262	114,480	289,985	30,146	118,085
Putnam	85,794	17,218	9,556	43,659	16,323	8,594	6,630
St. Johns	49,631	24,597	20,319	11,742	9,799	3,493	19,861
St. Lucie	227,414	136,131	122,287	5,028	71,615	14,640	139,412
Santa Rosa	87,971	59,263	47,476	19,947	4,693	4,068	5,487
Sarasota	128,655	18,781	5,323	21,704	85,501	2,669	5,008
Seminole	37,222	6,599	4,020	14,949	14,130	1,544	3,658
Sumter	183,374	54,694	17,562	31,217	85,743	11,720	2,106
Suwannee	158,406	86,524	47,269	47,431	13,314	11,137	15,244
Taylor	56,784	6,027	1,299	38,910	4,836	7,011	488
Union	62,503	15,504	6,763	38,535	7,402	1,062	1,651
Volusia	111,502	30,134	14,292	52,754	20,440	8,174	10,419
Wakulla	11,426	3,640	1,412	5,897	971	918	221
Walton	78,844	35,304	15,014	27,795	9,918	5,827	634
Washington	55,268	25,583	13,404	22,394	3,132	4,159	322

(D) Data withheld to avoid disclosure of information about individual farms.
1/ Includes woodland pasture.
2/ Pastureland and rangeland other than cropland and woodland pasture.
3/ Land in house lots, ponds, roads, wasteland, etc.
Note: Because data for selected items are collected from a sample of operators, the results are subject to sampling variability. The agriculture census is on a 5-year cycle collecting data for years ending in 2 or 7.
Correction: Data for some counties were incorrect in the previous *Abstract*. Those counties have been corrected in this edition.

Source: U.S., Department of Commerce, Bureau of the Census, *1997 Census of Agriculture: State and County Data, Florida,* AC92-A-9, issued March 1999. Internet site <http://www.census.gov/prod/ac97/ac97a-9.pdf> (accessed 7 September 1999).

Table 9.37. INCOME: CASH RECEIPTS BY COMMODITY GROUP AND SPECIFIED
COMMODITY IN FLORIDA, 1994 THROUGH 1998

(in thousands of dollars)

Commodity 1/	1994	1995	1996	1997	1998
All commodities	6,049,056	5,984,677	6,383,145	6,515,687	6,761,965
Livestock and products	1,194,603	1,134,378	1,303,304	1,399,551	1,407,349
Meat animals	348,328	299,558	234,455	332,885	299,226
Cattle and calves	335,837	287,352	218,919	320,424	293,327
Hogs	12,399	12,098	15,409	12,335	5,772
Dairy products,	408,408	363,528	431,280	407,715	423,878
wholesale milk	408,408	363,528	431,280	407,715	423,878
Poultry and eggs	291,605	315,277	362,760	353,838	367,313
Broilers	191,151	218,361	230,607	229,383	252,840
Farm chickens	(NA)	(NA)	(NA)	(NA)	(NA)
Chicken eggs	98,348	95,320	131,355	123,701	112,707
Crops	4,854,453	4,850,299	5,079,841	5,116,136	5,354,616
Food grains, wheat	1,717	1,255	1,534	2,072	1,509
Feed crops, corn	11,045	12,793	20,919	16,298	8,022
Hay	14,025	11,849	11,906	13,179	13,886
Cotton	37,916	38,598	44,171	43,987	34,359
Tobacco	27,248	30,907	31,021	32,293	29,942
Oil crops, peanuts	58,302	52,463	66,361	63,857	57,343
Soybeans	7,490	5,165	6,214	7,733	4,961
Vegetables	1,448,816	1,325,702	1,354,966	1,459,558	1,536,371
Potatoes	118,655	84,010	98,944	89,195	123,491
Beans, snap	59,076	63,206	75,182	65,020	129,505
Cabbage, fresh	29,568	18,135	26,768	39,701	26,325
Carrots	11,252	16,971	12,516	16,538	11,340
Corn, sweet	105,232	108,423	100,526	127,331	103,249
Cucumbers	58,200	51,081	79,761	98,867	69,492
Eggplant, all	15,606	14,005	14,784	15,548	15,523
Escarole	8,969	9,440	5,776	7,000	11,550
Lettuce	16,884	10,118	6,691	3,360	11,024
Peppers, green	197,465	177,188	222,768	251,766	245,686
Tomatoes, fresh	465,663	414,966	447,556	487,060	506,607
Radishes	25,888	23,873	20,021	19,018	18,816
Squash	43,216	46,591	34,121	36,228	54,515
Watermelons	57,868	62,700	49,980	54,750	60,120
Fruits and nuts	1,619,356	1,716,441	1,749,072	1,697,685	1,836,163
Grapefruit	251,406	225,204	216,209	186,190	145,698
Lemons	2,675	2,079	2,879	1,341	2,631
Limes	3,687	3,479	1,860	5,159	4,826
Oranges	1,168,788	1,201,720	1,272,803	1,226,137	1,357,566
Tangelos	13,508	16,942	16,281	17,391	20,337
Tangerines	37,154	98,560	71,671	54,882	76,512
Avocados	12,320	11,324	12,408	14,016	16,468
Mangos	1,500	1,725	1,500	1,450	(NA)
Strawberries	101,425	118,608	112,632	146,119	161,200
Blueberries	5,690	5,050	4,965	5,040	6,240
Pecans	1,600	945	1,095	1,320	1,045

1/ Totals include data for "other" categories not shown.
Note: Data are estimates. Value of sales for some individual commodities may be understated;
balance is included in totals.
Source: U.S., Department of Agriculture, Economic Research Service, "Cash Receipts by Commodity
Groups and Selected Commodities, United States and States, 1992-98," Internet site <http://www.ers.
usda.gov/briefing/farmincome/finfidmu.htm> (accessed 31 May 2000).

Table 9.38. INCOME: MARKET VALUE OF AGRICULTURAL PRODUCTS SOLD
IN THE STATE AND COUNTIES OF FLORIDA, 1997

(in thousands of dollars, except where indicated)

County	All products Total	Average per farm (dollars)	Crops 1/	Livestock poultry and their products
Florida	6,004,554	172,550	4,817,261	1,187,292
Alachua	50,256	46,276	31,112	19,144
Baker	25,204	160,535	9,728	15,476
Bay	2,672	38,176	2,453	219
Bradford	17,402	63,509	1,160	16,242
Brevard	37,956	80,758	32,485	5,471
Broward	49,024	141,280	42,078	6,946
Calhoun	16,197	124,592	14,495	1,702
Charlotte	50,162	240,010	44,862	5,300
Citrus	6,172	20,992	3,692	2,480
Clay	30,118	142,739	3,284	26,834
Collier	276,924	1,178,401	267,865	9,059
Columbia	22,060	36,767	10,227	11,833
De Soto	180,983	253,123	158,512	22,471
Dixie	4,626	29,844	1,581	3,045
Duval	26,463	82,697	9,777	16,686
Escambia	16,183	34,727	9,436	6,747
Flagler	27,837	305,906	26,612	1,226
Franklin	(D)	(D)	139	(D)
Gadsden	92,632	319,421	85,452	7,181
Gilchrist	52,043	142,583	7,821	44,222
Glades	58,589	311,642	37,899	20,690
Gulf	359	10,876	47	312
Hamilton	13,080	51,094	6,879	6,201
Hardee	154,837	148,170	117,577	37,261
Hendry	323,438	802,575	308,649	14,788
Hernando	23,011	53,267	6,349	16,662
Highlands	202,863	260,414	167,155	35,708
Hillsborough	332,736	126,084	263,704	69,032
Holmes	31,534	54,557	5,210	26,324
Indian River	95,144	217,722	90,076	5,069
Jackson	51,455	60,965	38,411	13,044
Jefferson	18,050	52,779	13,970	4,080
Lafayette	54,322	245,800	5,883	48,439
Lake	168,137	121,049	144,075	24,062

See footnotes at end of table.   Continued . . .

University of Florida   **Bureau of Economic and Business Research**

Table 9.38. INCOME: MARKET VALUE OF AGRICULTURAL PRODUCTS SOLD
IN THE STATE AND COUNTIES OF FLORIDA, 1997 (Continued)

(in thousands of dollars, except where indicated)

County	All products Total	Average per farm (dollars)	Crops 1/	Livestock poultry and their products
Lee	116,397	228,678	114,048	2,349
Leon	3,463	14,252	1,345	2,118
Levy	51,822	94,393	16,562	35,260
Liberty	551	11,733	42	510
Madison	31,992	65,827	11,678	20,314
Manatee	239,624	343,793	219,428	20,196
Marion	101,530	60,833	22,934	78,596
Martin	145,023	475,486	116,737	28,286
Miami-Dade	416,502	264,278	408,854	7,648
Monroe	(D)	(D)	10	(D)
Nassau	27,572	115,849	552	27,020
Okaloosa	8,711	25,470	5,307	3,404
Okeechobee	138,006	300,666	33,243	104,762
Orange	247,759	287,423	244,298	3,461
Osceola	88,784	183,061	60,473	28,312
Palm Beach	872,877	1,020,908	868,894	3,983
Pasco	84,301	88,644	30,208	54,093
Pinellas	11,867	91,994	11,707	160
Polk	253,459	102,865	204,062	49,396
Putnam	34,023	87,017	30,538	3,486
St. Johns	46,047	309,042	44,030	2,017
St. Lucie	173,137	346,274	163,017	10,120
Santa Rosa	29,971	68,426	27,891	2,080
Sarasota	24,147	76,657	17,053	7,094
Seminole	19,966	58,040	18,232	1,733
Sumter	34,442	47,970	9,488	24,954
Suwannee	121,153	144,230	40,493	80,660
Taylor	4,312	34,226	846	3,467
Union	11,009	51,687	3,764	7,245
Volusia	120,358	132,261	114,011	6,346
Wakulla	3,062	34,798	498	2,564
Walton	19,768	41,529	4,737	15,031
Washington	9,352	29,042	3,629	5,722

(D) Data withheld to avoid disclosure of information about individual farms.
1/ Includes nursery and greenhouse products.
Note: The agriculture census is on a 5-year cycle collecting data for years ending in 2 and 7.

Source: U.S., Department of Commerce, Bureau of the Census, *1997 Census of Agriculture: State and County Data, Florida,* AC92-A-9, issued March 1999. Internet site <http://www.census.gov/prod/ac97/ac97a-9.pdf> (accessed 7 September 1999).

Table 9.39. FARM OPERATORS: NUMBER OF OPERATORS BY PRINCIPAL OCCUPATION
AGE, AND RACE AND HISPANIC ORIGIN AND NUMBER OF FARMS AND ACRES
OPERATED BY FEMALES IN THE STATE AND COUNTIES
OF FLORIDA, 1997

County	Total	Principal occupation Farming	Principal occupation Other	Average age (years)	Non-white	His-panic ori-gin 1/	Female operators Number of farms	Female operators Land in farms (acres)
Florida	34,799	15,782	19,017	56.5	1,318	1,060	5,384	793,485
Alachua	1,086	443	643	56.3	75	24	202	13,909
Baker	157	71	86	56.1	7	3	12	819
Bay	70	28	42	60.1	3	A/	16	466
Bradford	274	111	163	55.1	4	3	30	2,359
Brevard	470	170	300	57.2	10	9	76	10,865
Broward	347	193	154	53.2	13	40	71	1,403
Calhoun	130	69	61	57.0	4	A/	9	6,446
Charlotte	209	99	110	57.1	3	5	24	14,161
Citrus	294	117	177	57.1	4	5	50	3,407
Clay	211	93	118	56.6	A/	A/	27	1,436
Collier	235	110	125	53.8	6	7	22	2,083
Columbia	600	241	359	57.0	46	9	90	12,677
De Soto	715	330	385	57.9	13	16	133	30,456
Dixie	155	54	101	57.2	A/	A/	11	887
Duval	320	147	173	58.5	3	A/	53	2,564
Escambia	466	196	270	56.9	25	A/	55	5,909
Flagler	91	49	42	53.7	A/	A/	11	(D)
Franklin	19	9	10	49.1	A/	A/	1	(D)
Gadsden	290	115	175	58.8	19	3	33	5,184
Gilchrist	365	166	199	56.3	A/	4	46	6,628
Glades	188	118	70	57.3	9	5	21	15,073
Gulf	33	9	24	53.7	A/	A/	2	(D)
Hamilton	256	100	156	57.1	34	6	22	5,238
Hardee	1,045	486	559	59.0	18	24	166	32,880
Hendry	403	209	194	55.5	15	20	46	10,841
Hernando	432	170	262	56.7	10	11	86	8,218
Highlands	779	346	433	56.0	22	12	132	75,468
Hillsborough	2,639	1,208	1,431	57.7	111	132	452	24,894
Holmes	578	259	319	56.5	8	3	59	7,697
Indian River	437	256	181	58.8	7	8	57	3,691
Jackson	844	444	400	56.5	75	5	83	16,915
Jefferson	342	126	216	57.1	33	6	36	6,018
Lafayette	221	112	109	54.4	A/	A/	25	3,461
Lake	1,389	553	836	56.3	43	27	202	21,823
Lee	509	205	304	54.2	6	6	79	3,598
Leon	243	70	173	57.3	32	A/	36	21,812

See footnotes at end of table.

Continued . . .

University of Florida   **Bureau of Economic and Business Research**

Table 9.39. FARM OPERATORS: NUMBER OF OPERATORS BY PRINCIPAL OCCUPATION
AGE, AND RACE AND HISPANIC ORIGIN AND NUMBER OF FARMS AND ACRES
OPERATED BY FEMALES IN THE STATE AND COUNTIES
OF FLORIDA, 1997 (Continued)

County	Total	Principal occupation		Average age (years)	Non-white	His-panic ori-gin 1/	Female operators	
		Farming	Other				Number of farms	Land in farms (acres)
Levy	549	232	317	55.4	15	9	66	10,643
Liberty	47	17	30	60.7	A/	A/	7	726
Madison	486	227	259	57.6	30	5	83	17,826
Manatee	697	361	336	57.3	15	9	124	19,001
Marion	1,669	784	885	56.4	107	51	363	33,406
Martin	305	143	162	55.5	12	11	38	25,183
Miami-Dade	1,576	831	745	54.3	172	357	218	3,407
Monroe	13	5	8	58.5	A/	A/	4	4
Nassau	238	95	143	56.4	A/	4	25	935
Okaloosa	342	125	217	57.4	A/	A/	49	7,367
Okeechobee	459	190	269	55.4	3	15	65	38,179
Orange	862	477	385	55.6	51	25	147	12,209
Osceola	485	239	246	57.3	12	A/	82	29,974
Palm Beach	855	487	368	51.7	36	50	157	5,649
Pasco	951	411	540	56.9	16	23	169	12,867
Pinellas	129	53	76	57.5	A/	A/	33	244
Polk	2,464	969	1,495	58.5	33	19	405	60,499
Putnam	391	181	210	57.1	11	5	74	13,194
St. Johns	149	91	58	53.2	4	A/	30	1,153
St. Lucie	500	248	252	56.8	10	6	65	5,769
Santa Rosa	438	217	221	55.2	5	A/	36	3,039
Sarasota	315	117	198	54.6	3	A/	57	21,240
Seminole	344	152	192	58.1	20	10	66	1,865
Sumter	718	298	420	56.6	30	11	128	22,507
Suwannee	840	420	420	56.1	23	17	121	18,615
Taylor	126	48	78	57.3	3	A/	7	374
Union	213	78	135	55.6	4	A/	23	3,229
Volusia	910	452	458	54.6	16	15	151	11,523
Wakulla	88	34	54	52.7	5	A/	20	765
Walton	476	188	288	58.1	9	A/	62	7,507
Washington	322	130	192	57.8	3	A/	33	4,141
All other counties	0	0	0	0.0	12	25	0	0

(D) Data withheld to avoid disclosure of information about individual farms.
A/ Included with "all other counties."
1/ Persons of Hispanic origin may be of any race.
Note: The agriculture census is on a 5-year cycle collecting data for years ending in 2 and 7.

Source: U.S., Department of Commerce, Bureau of the Census, *1997 Census of Agriculture: State and County Data, Florida,* AC92-A-9, issued March 1999. Internet site <http://www.census.gov/prod/ac97/ac97a-9.pdf> (accessed 7 September 1999).

Table 9.42. INCOME: CASH RECEIPTS FROM FARMING IN FLORIDA, OTHER AGRICULTURAL
STATES, AND THE UNITED STATES, 1998

(amounts in thousands of dollars)

State	Total	Rank among states	Per- centage change from previous year	Crops	Livestock and products	Govern- ment payments
Florida	6,761,965	9	8.3	5,354,616	1,407,349	24,918
California	24,616,242	1	-2.7	17,771,171	6,845,071	352,710
Texas	13,206,203	2	-1.9	4,986,047	8,220,156	998,457
Iowa	10,994,252	3	-14.4	6,216,645	4,777,607	1,146,046
Nebraska	8,848,014	4	-12.3	3,724,514	5,123,500	797,382
Kansas	7,784,013	5	-13.5	3,246,911	4,537,102	872,524
Illinois	7,742,280	6	-16.5	6,167,021	1,575,259	934,043
Minnesota	7,679,914	7	-5.8	3,925,101	3,754,813	762,449
North Carolina	7,163,967	8	-13.7	3,246,807	3,917,160	129,375
Wisconsin	6,193,000	10	7.6	1,700,577	4,492,423	252,787
Georgia	5,454,249	11	-7.4	2,046,648	3,407,601	178,283
Arkansas	5,421,870	12	-7.5	2,171,726	3,250,144	466,712
Washington	5,154,635	13	-4.2	3,424,474	1,730,161	257,165
Ohio	4,972,519	14	-7.0	3,124,412	1,848,107	313,123
Indiana	4,884,568	15	-11.3	3,245,248	1,639,320	463,999
United States	196,761,410	(X)	-5.7	102,222,386	94,539,024	12,219,559

(X) Not applicable.

Table 9.43. TAXES: AMOUNT LEVIED ON FARM REAL ESTATE IN FLORIDA AND THE
UNITED STATES, 1993, 1994, AND 1995

Item	Florida			United States 1/		
	1993	1994	1995	1993	1994	1995
Total taxes levied ($1,000,000)	140.7	130.8	170.2	5,023.3	4,908.6	5,090.7
Taxes per acre Amount (dollars)	14.71	13.68	17.90	5.98	5.86	5.94
Taxes per $100 of full value (dollars)	0.71	0.62	0.80	0.85	0.75	0.73

1/ Excludes Alaska.

Source for Tables 9.42 and 9.43: U.S., Department of Agriculture, *Agricultural Statistics, 2000*, Internet
site <http://www.usda.gov/nass/pubs/agr00/acro00.htm> (accessed 10 August 2000).

University of Florida   **Bureau of Economic and Business Research**

Table 9.45. LAND: TOTAL FARM ACREAGE, 1990, AND ACREAGE OWNED BY NONRESIDENT ALIENS, 1997 IN THE STATE AND COUNTIES OF FLORIDA

County	Estimated total farmland acreage 2/	Foreign-owned acreage 1/			Type of land (percentage)			
		Amount	Reported value 3/ ($1,000)	As a percentage of total farmland	Crop-land	Pasture	Forest	Other
Florida	24,300,104	682,402	1,273,723	2.81	32.63	24.21	22.19	14.79
Alachua	519,000	8,123	5,322	1.57	15.47	41.94	38.80	3.51
Baker	301,528	0	0	(X)	(X)	(X)	(X)	(X)
Bay	410,490	0	0	(X)	(X)	(X)	(X)	(X)
Bradford	173,000	0	0	(X)	(X)	(X)	(X)	(X)
Brevard	478,050	5,900	12,621	1.23	3.92	89.78	0.00	5.24
Broward	28,670	1,932	20,423	6.74	9.94	36.65	0.00	27.85
Calhoun	343,710	2,397	2,239	0.70	78.72	0.00	20.03	1.25
Charlotte	268,170	7,250	15,860	2.70	32.19	37.21	0.00	27.61
Citrus	178,310	973	1,010	0.55	0.00	98.97	0.72	0.00
Clay	368,000	7,088	10,500	1.93	0.00	7.76	0.00	0.00
Collier	576,400	11,504	23,708	2.00	0.17	18.49	75.17	5.22
Columbia	534,065	4,705	2,186	0.88	0.00	66.61	100.00	0.00
De Soto	354,000	5,005	10,801	1.41	9.85	66.61	3.26	20.24
Dixie	278,725	157	157	0.06	0.00	66.88	0.00	29.94
Duval	301,900	0	0	(X)	(X)	(X)	(X)	(X)
Escambia	308,207	249	401	0.08	0.00	0.00	0.00	100.00
Flagler	310,100	0	0	(X)	(X)	(X)	(X)	(X)
Franklin	310,000	37,026	17,107	11.94	0.00	0.00	100.00	0.00
Gadsden	261,800	12,352	8,377	4.72	12.31	2.12	75.04	2.48
Gilchrist	216,560	32,563	14,804	15.04	0.09	1.62	71.22	27.05
Glades	443,500	7,869	10,183	1.77	0.00	96.59	0.00	3.41
Gulf	363,000	311	256	0.09	0.00	0.00	0.00	100.00
Hamilton	333,219	18,726	7,515	5.62	1.50	0.14	74.36	0.00
Hardee	326,302	4,957	12,063	1.52	12.83	36.64	0.00	49.73
Hendry	734,000	12,621	26,321	1.72	42.20	25.43	0.00	32.37

See footnotes at end of table.

Continued . . .

Table 9.45. LAND: TOTAL FARM ACREAGE, 1990, AND ACREAGE OWNED BY NONRESIDENT ALIENS, 1997 IN THE STATE AND COUNTIES OF FLORIDA (Continued)

County	Estimated total farmland acreage 2/	Foreign-owned acreage 1/			Type of land (percentage)			
		Amount	Reported value 3/ ($1,000)	As a percentage of total farmland	Crop-land	Pasture	Forest	Other
Hernando	216,299	0	0	(X)	(X)	(X)	(X)	(X)
Highlands	600,549	5,636	14,147	0.94	15.83	51.54	7.10	25.00
Hillsborough	530,000	12,057	20,047	2.27	9.94	25.69	31.41	32.88
Holmes	343,300	0	0	(X)	(X)	(X)	(X)	(X)
Indian River	210,161	26,632	61,528	12.67	60.96	31.57	3.99	2.52
Jackson	576,000	5,324	4,262	0.92	61.93	0.71	36.59	0.77
Jefferson	346,072	3,408	1,293	0.98	27.29	0.00	71.24	1.17
Lafayette	337,868	0	0	(X)	(X)	(X)	(X)	(X)
Lake	515,245	14,813	39,039	2.87	8.53	39.70	23.54	17.74
Lee	244,484	8,119	38,847	3.32	12.19	83.69	0.95	1.54
Leon	304,350	0	0	(X)	(X)	(X)	(X)	(X)
Levy	646,185	9,976	2,560	1.54	9.75	6.29	76.78	5.18
Liberty	268,375	850	393	0.32	0.00	0.00	100.00	0.00
Madison	417,961	277	266	0.07	52.35	3.61	32.49	2.53
Manatee	329,388	9,005	30,356	2.73	32.95	1.95	0.31	61.84
Marion	575,000	18,354	53,334	3.19	4.35	45.42	21.41	27.97
Martin	278,000	33,762	72,017	12.14	2.40	32.18	2.69	61.59
Miami-Dade	85,306	17,918	197,220	21.00	60.35	4.34	1.57	31.13
Monroe	0	0	0	(X)	(X)	(X)	(X)	(X)
Nassau	351,800	315	1,009	0.09	0.00	0.00	100.00	0.00
Okaloosa	208,069	21,818	24,075	10.49	0.92	97.52	1.15	0.39
Okeechobee	465,500	17,822	20,935	3.83	0.12	99.46	0.00	0.42
Orange	323,984	32,060	185,297	9.90	0.89	48.99	20.97	9.57
Osceola	802,100	20,601	69,793	2.57	35.34	10.30	0.00	13.10
Palm Beach	569,135	139,755	110,683	24.56	93.52	0.50	0.00	5.51
Pasco	324,755	2,213	6,991	0.68	0.90	49.21	29.82	20.06
Pinellas	47,000	55	900	0.12	100.00	0.00	0.00	0.00

See footnotes at end of table.

Continued . . .

Table 9.45. LAND: TOTAL FARM ACREAGE, 1990, AND ACREAGE OWNED BY NONRESIDENT ALIENS, 1997 IN THE STATE AND COUNTIES OF FLORIDA (Continued)

County	Estimated total farmland acreage 2/	Foreign-owned acreage 1/			Type of land (percentage)			
		Amount	Reported value 3/ ($1,000)	As a percentage of total farmland	Crop-land	Pasture	Forest	Other
Polk	851,600	27,598	45,016	3.24	0.46	28.47	0.93	39.24
Putnam	330,670	1,829	849	0.55	2.19	0.00	63.91	14.76
St. Johns	340,000	1,156	1,488	0.34	56.06	0.00	43.94	0.00
St. Lucie	294,158	20,371	26,041	6.93	33.16	45.31	5.29	15.76
Santa Rosa	550,080	1,263	1,089	0.23	0.00	0.00	100.00	0.00
Sarasota	166,766	513	1,077	0.31	0.00	100.00	0.00	0.00
Seminole	116,200	2,087	16,965	1.80	0.00	20.41	1.96	68.23
Sumter	595,000	4,252	5,862	0.71	2.82	65.50	15.50	16.18
Suwannee	441,600	4,733	4,669	1.07	62.56	2.56	29.03	5.85
Taylor	296,800	20	3	0.01	0.00	0.00	100.00	0.00
Union	149,932	0	0	(X)	(X)	(X)	(X)	(X)
Volusia	529,360	8,321	11,942	1.57	10.05	18.62	29.78	28.72
Wakulla	160,472	61	56	0.04	0.00	0.00	100.00	0.00
Walton	505,222	27,720	1,820	5.49	61.61	12.85	25.53	0.00
Washington	334,652	0	0	(X)	(X)	(X)	(X)	(X)

(X) Not applicable.
1/ A foreign investor is defined as any nonresident alien, any corporation incorporated outside the U.S., or any U.S. corporation with 5 percent or more foreign interest. A foreign investor holding more than 5 percent interest in any agricultural lands must disclose such holdings.
2/ Land currently used for agricultural, forestry, or timber production or, if idle, land used for such purposes within the last five years.
3/ Reported value is purchase price or nonpurchase price (estimated value) at time of acquisition.

Note: Data were compiled by the U.S. Department of Agriculture, Agricultural Stabilization and Conservation Service from disclosure forms filed under the Agriculture Foreign Investment Disclosure Act of 1978. Detail may not add to total because of rounding.

Source: U.S., Department of Agriculture, Agricultural Stabilization and Conservation Service, *Foreign Ownership of U.S. Agricultural Land Through December 31, 1997,* Internet site <http://www.ers.usda.gov/epubs/htmlsum/> (accessed 15 August 2000).

Florida Statistical Abstract 2000

Table 9.50. IRRIGATION: ESTIMATED AGRICULTURAL ACREAGE IRRIGATED AND WATER USE BY CROP AND TYPE IN FLORIDA, 1995

| Product | Acreage irrigated | Irrigated water use (millions of gallons per day) | | | |
		Total 1/	Ground	Surface	Reclaimed
Total 2/					
Agricultural irrigation	1,972,257	3,259.16	1,477.26	1,710.67	71.23
Vegetable crops	277,313	393.55	302.79	90.76	0.00
Cabbage	8,683	14.00	13.84	0.16	0.00
Carrots	7,425	8.61	1.15	7.46	0.00
Cucumbers	16,975	32.73	24.66	8.07	0.00
Peppers	22,725	47.19	36.08	11.11	0.00
Potatoes	37,510	53.15	52.32	0.83	0.00
Tomatoes	51,286	98.92	87.39	11.53	0.00
Sweet corn	32,265	29.73	9.27	20.46	0.00
Other	100,444	109.22	78.08	31.14	0.00
Fruit crops	894,445	1,495.07	793.76	665.41	35.90
Blueberries	2,037	1.97	1.90	0.07	0.00
Citrus 3/	830,072	1,419.45	721.59	661.96	35.90
Grapes	513	0.44	0.39	0.05	0.00
Peaches	138	0.17	0.17	0.00	0.00
Pecans	3,355	3.90	3.85	0.05	0.00
Strawberries	6,204	6.35	6.05	0.30	0.00
Watermelons/lopes	39,332	36.42	34.36	2.06	0.00
Other	12,794	26.37	25.45	0.92	0.00
Field crops	539,118	942.78	96.08	832.57	14.13
Cotton	14,081	11.10	10.04	1.06	0.00
Field corn	26,315	27.67	24.38	3.29	0.00
Peanuts	29,193	23.04	21.50	1.54	0.00
Rice	18,414	10.97	0.16	10.81	0.00
Sorghum	6,818	3.46	3.38	0.08	0.00
Soybeans	3,388	2.85	2.75	0.10	0.00
Sugarcane	417,000	832.80	17.80	815.00	0.00
Tobacco	6,382	6.67	6.33	0.34	0.00
Wheat	2,000	1.27	1.18	0.09	0.00
Other	15,527	22.95	8.56	0.26	14.13
Ornamentals/grasses	261,381	427.76	284.63	121.93	21.20
Ferns	6,393	31.59	26.25	5.34	0.00
Ornamentals (field grown)	9,518	18.75	15.00	3.75	0.00
Ornamentals (container grown)	32,997	116.38	81.39	33.48	1.51
Improved Pasture	164,322	166.10	118.65	28.15	19.30
Sod	48,151	94.94	43.34	51.21	0.39
Nonagricultural irrigation 4/	0	64.40	50.26	5.91	8.23
Recreation/lawn/aesthetic	130,974	434.86	196.38	84.50	153.98
Turf grass recreation (golf)	98,498	284.97	132.39	55.03	97.55
Turf grass lawn	32,476	131.05	56.51	18.11	56.43
Other	0	18.84	7.48	11.36	0.00

1/ Reclaimed water use values are not included in the totals.
2/ Includes crops not shown separately.
3/ Includes oranges, grapefruit, limes, lemons, and all other citrus.
4/ Includes ferns, ornamentals (field and container grown), improved pasture, and sod.

Source: U.S., Department of the Interior, Geological Survey; University of Florida, County Extension Service; Florida Crop Reporting Service; and the five Water Management Districts.

University of Florida   **Bureau of Economic and Business Research**

Table 9.51. CITRUS: ESTIMATED PRODUCTION AND VALUE OF CITRUS BY TYPE IN FLORIDA CROP YEARS 1994-95 THROUGH 1998-99

Type of citrus	1994-95	1995-96	1996-97	1997-98	1998-99 A/
		Production (1,000 boxes)			
All citrus	271,020	265,375	295,315	304,450	242,865
Oranges	205,500	203,300	226,200	244,000	185,700
Early and midseason	113,900	116,000	127,800	133,700	107,000
Late (Valencia)	85,800	82,100	92,000	104,000	73,700
Navel	5,800	5,200	6,400	6,300	5,000
Grapefruit	55,700	B/ 52,350	B/ 55,800	B/ 49,550	47,050
Seedy	1,300	1,050	900	650	550
White seedless	25,700	23,200	B/ 23,500	C/ 18,300	17,800
Colored seedless	28,700	B/ 28,100	B/ 31,400	D/ 30,600	28,700
Other citrus	9,820	9,725	13,315	10,900	10,115
Temples	2,550	2,150	2,400	2,250	1,800
Tangelos	3,150	2,450	3,950	2,850	2,550
Tangerines 1/	2,350	2,900	4,500	3,200	3,050
Honey tangerines	1,200	1,600	1,800	2,000	1,900
K-early citrus	120	160	150	40	80
Limes	230	300	320	440	500
Lemons 2/	220	165	195	120	235
		Value of production ($1,000)			
All citrus	948,173	1,075,817	960,496	1,023,383	1,149,166
Oranges	767,924	895,465	801,344	900,815	953,450
Early and midseason	367,615	414,299	403,478	373,405	495,325
Late (Valencia)	378,409	457,115	374,000	507,238	420,735
Navel	21,900	24,051	23,866	20,172	37,390
Grapefruit	116,602	101,140	86,583	63,000	106,127
Seedy	2,639	1,817	117	65	561
White seedless	66,382	49,726	26,413	16,995	35,710
Colored seedless	47,581	49,597	60,053	45,940	69,856
Other citrus	63,647	79,212	71,143	59,568	89,589
Temples	8,848	9,543	7,723	6,898	9,371
Tangelos	8,318	8,883	8,645	4,723	11,714
Tangerines 1/	18,823	32,384	28,414	21,447	31,103
Honey tangerines	23,716	24,262	21,929	22,679	29,805
K-early citrus	276	365	210	-53	171
Limes	1,989	2,414	2,216	3,035	5,716
Lemons 2/	1,677	1,361	2,006	839	1,709

A/ Preliminary.
B/ Excludes 3 million boxes of economic abandonment in 1995-96 and 6 million in both 1996-97 and 1997-98.
C/ Excludes 5 million boxes of economic abandonment.
D/ Excludes 1 million boxes of economic abandonment.
1/ Excludes honey tangerines.
2/ Florida lemons bloom and harvest during the calendar year; data are for the years 1994 through 1998.
Note: Some data may be revised.

Source: State of Florida, Department of Agriculture and Consumer Services, Florida Agricultural Statistics Service, *Florida Agricultural Statistics: Citrus Summary, 1998-99,* Internet site <http://www.nass.usda.gov/fl/rtoc0.html> (accessed 5 April 2000).

University of Florida   **Bureau of Economic and Business Research**

Table 9.52. ORANGES AND GRAPEFRUIT: BEARING ACREAGE, PRODUCTION, AND YIELD PER ACRE IN FLORIDA, OTHER CITRUS STATES, AND THE UNITED STATES, CROP YEARS 1992-93 THROUGH 1998-99

State and year	Oranges			Grapefruit		
	Bearing acreage (1,000 acres)	Produc- tion (1,000 tons)	Yield per acre (tons)	Bearing acreage (1,000 acres)	Produc- tion (1,000 tons)	Yield per acre (tons)
Florida						
1992-93	489.2	8,397	17.2	111.9	2,344	20.9
1993-94	510.8	7,849	15.4	118.3	2,171	18.4
1994-95	562.8	9,248	16.4	127.3	2,367	18.6
1995-96	594.8	9,149	15.4	132.8	B/ 2,225	16.8
1996-97	624.9	10,179	16.3	139.2	B/ 2,371	17.0
1997-98	609.2	10,980	18.0	127.8	B/ 2,106	16.5
1998-99 A/	612.6	8,357	13.6	116.6	2,000	17.2
Arizona						
1992-93	10.6	69	6.5	5.9	69	11.7
1993-94	10.6	71	6.7	5.9	B/ 59	10.0
1994-95	10.4	39	3.8	5.7	47	8.2
1995-96	9.4	62	6.6	5.1	40	7.8
1996-97	10.0	53	5.3	4.4	27	6.1
1997-98	9.1	38	4.2	4.0	27	6.8
1998-99 A/	8.2	43	5.2	3.6	25	6.9
California						
1992-93	184.0	2,505	13.6	17.8	303	17.0
1993-94	185.0	2,385	12.9	18.0	C/ 311	17.3
1994-95	191.0	2,101	11.0	18.4	312	17.0
1995-96	196.0	2,175	11.1	18.8	271	14.4
1996-97	200.0	2,400	12.0	18.0	275	15.3
1997-98	200.2	2,587	12.9	16.8	268	16.0
1998-99 A/	201.5	1,425	7.1	16.6	251	15.1
Texas						
1992-93	4.4	21	4.8	10.1	75	7.4
1993-94	5.5	24	4.4	12.8	120	9.4
1994-95	7.0	44	6.3	15.0	186	12.4
1995-96	7.9	40	5.1	17.7	182	10.3
1996-97	8.7	60	6.9	20.4	212	10.4
1997-98	9.5	65	6.8	23.1	192	8.3
1998-99 A/	9.1	61	6.7	20.0	244	12.2
United States						
1992-93	688.2	10,992	16.0	145.7	2,791	19.2
1993-94	711.9	10,329	14.5	155.0	2,661	17.2
1994-95	771.2	11,432	14.8	166.4	2,912	17.5
1995-96	808.1	11,426	14.1	174.4	2,718	15.6
1996-97	843.6	12,692	15.0	182.0	2,885	15.9
1997-98	828.0	13,670	16.5	171.7	2,593	15.1
1998-99 A/	831.4	9,886	11.9	156.8	2,520	16.1

A/ Preliminary.
B/ Excludes economic abandonment of colored seedless and white seedless grapefruit.
C/ Box weight for California Desert and Arizona grapefruit changed in 1993-94.
Note: Some data may be revised.
Source: State of Florida, Department of Agriculture and Consumer Services, Florida Agricultural Statistics Service, *Florida Agricultural Statistics: Citrus Summary, 1998-99,* Internet site <http://www.nass.usda. gov/fl/rtoc0.html> (accessed 5 April 2000).

University of Florida   **Bureau of Economic and Business Research**

Table 9.53. ORANGES AND GRAPEFRUIT: SEASON AVERAGE ON-TREE PRICES PER BOX AND VALUE OF PRODUCTION IN FLORIDA AND THE UNITED STATES, CROP YEARS 1991-1992 THROUGH 1998-99

Crop year	Season average price (in dollars per box)			Value of production (in thousands of dollars)		
	Total	Fresh use	Process-ing	Total	Fresh use	Process-ing

Oranges 1/

Crop year	Total	Fresh use	Process-ing	Total	Fresh use	Process-ing
Florida						
1991-92	5.93	8.52	5.69	828,749	98,404	730,345
1992-93	3.48	3.81	3.46	649,713	40,877	608,836
1993-94	4.09	5.98	3.98	713,312	59,162	654,150
1994-95	3.74	4.07	3.72	767,924	42,516	725,408
1995-96	4.40	5.46	4.35	895,465	54,404	841,061
1996-97	3.54	4.57	3.49	801,344	48,836	752,508
1997-98	3.69	3.85	3.68	900,815	42,425	858,390
1998-99 A/	5.13	8.77	4.91	953,450	94,899	858,551
United States						
1991-92	5.52	8.06	4.72	1,146,430	439,856	706,574
1992-93	3.88	6.92	3.03	1,005,498	433,663	571,835
1993-94	4.40	7.67	3.48	1,067,256	448,199	619,057
1994-95	4.23	7.63	3.42	1,134,352	436,807	697,545
1995-96	4.79	8.27	3.96	1,279,601	472,879	806,722
1996-97	4.22	7.96	3.31	1,268,660	520,649	748,011
1997-98	4.29	7.64	3.48	1,383,516	532,735	850,781
1998-99 A/	5.94	14.86	4.50	1,374,252	524,645	849,607

Grapefruit

Crop year	Total	Fresh use	Process-ing	Total	Fresh use	Process-ing
Florida						
1991-92	6.62	8.69	4.20	280,629	198,391	82,238
1992-93	2.66	4.86	1.06	146,432	112,476	33,956
1993-94	3.28	5.52	1.51	167,211	124,167	43,044
1994-95	2.09	4.00	0.83	116,602	88,993	27,609
1995-96	1.93	3.71	0.56	101,140	84,733	16,407
1996-97	1.55	3.74	-0.01	86,583	86,911	-328
1997-98	1.27	3.42	-0.33	63,000	72,428	-9,428
1998-99 A/	2.26	5.04	0.21	106,127	100,530	5,597
United States						
1991-92	6.20	8.34	3.44	336,939	258,803	78,136
1992-93	2.75	5.10	0.77	188,014	162,415	25,599
1993-94	3.33	5.61	1.21	217,055	179,341	37,714
1994-95	2.30	4.40	0.59	167,011	146,852	20,159
1995-96	2.32	4.36	0.39	157,596	145,730	11,866
1996-97	1.93	4.25	-0.11	140,250	145,400	-5,150
1997-98	2.00	4.64	-0.43	134,115	149,102	-14,987
1998-99 A/	3.22	6.41	0.13	208,048	204,670	3,378

A/ Preliminary.
1/ Includes early, midseason, and late type (Valencia) oranges.
Note: Charges for picking, hauling, and packing are deducted from the weighted average of prices obtained from all segments of the citrus industry to arrive at the final on-tree price received by producers. United States data include Arizona, California, Florida, and Texas. Some data may be revised.

Source: State of Florida, Department of Agriculture and Consumer Services, Florida Agricultural Statistics Service, *Florida Agricultural Statistics: Citrus Summary, 1998-99,* Internet site <http://www.nass.usda.gov/fl/rtoc0.html> (accessed 5 April 2000).

University of Florida   **Bureau of Economic and Business Research**

Table 9.54. CITRUS: ESTIMATED PRODUCTION OF PRINCIPAL TYPES OF CITRUS IN THE STATE AND COUNTIES OF FLORIDA, CROP YEAR 1998-99

(in 1,000 boxes)

Area and county	Total 1/	All oranges	Oranges Early and mid-season	Valen-cias	All grape-fruit	Spe-cialty fruit 2/
Florida	242,130	185,700	112,000	73,700	47,050	9,380
District						
Indian River	50,209	17,100	9,500	7,600	31,550	1,559
Northern	10,872	9,041	7,734	1,307	510	1,321
Central	57,758	49,359	27,266	22,093	4,763	3,636
Western	57,875	55,000	37,400	17,600	1,807	1,068
Southern	65,416	55,200	30,100	25,100	8,420	1,796
County						
Brevard	2,062	1,418	971	447	552	92
Charlotte	5,446	4,082	1,906	2,176	1,193	171
Collier	10,218	8,668	4,868	3,800	1,340	210
De Soto	22,736	21,893	12,125	9,768	526	317
Glades	2,818	2,548	1,711	837	210	60
Hardee	17,772	17,122	13,378	3,744	346	304
Hendry	28,209	23,950	12,728	11,222	3,563	696
Hernando	263	244	241	3	4	15
Highlands	23,625	21,151	9,585	11,566	1,181	1,293
Hillsborough	8,761	8,242	6,715	1,527	287	232
Indian River	17,870	5,255	3,196	2,059	12,188	427
Lake	4,866	3,682	3,213	469	355	829
Lee	3,253	2,765	1,425	1,340	429	59
Manatee	7,838	7,219	4,897	2,322	432	187
Marion	232	192	181	11	9	31
Martin	11,656	9,873	4,531	5,342	1,554	229
Okeechobee	3,096	2,563	1,774	789	469	64
Orange	2,067	1,730	1,324	406	67	270
Osceola	4,971	4,014	2,910	1,104	702	255
Palm Beach	3,108	1,852	1,273	579	901	355
Pasco	2,946	2,798	2,422	376	48	100
Polk	29,649	24,594	15,122	9,472	2,943	2,112
St. Lucie	27,226	8,822	4,797	4,025	17,441	963
Sarasota	733	496	269	227	215	22
Seminole	279	219	185	34	11	49
Volusia	288	209	180	29	68	11
Other 3/	142	99	73	26	16	27

1/ Does not include lemon and lime production.
2/ Includes tangelos, temples, tangerines, and K-early citrus.
3/ Includes Broward, Citrus, Flagler, Pinellas, Putnam, and Sumter counties.
Note: Citrus districts are based on citrus marketings/production areas. Several counties are in more than one district.

Source: State of Florida, Department of Agriculture and Consumer Services, Florida Agricultural Statistic Service, *Florida Agricultural Statistics: Citrus Summary, 1998-99,* Internet site <http://www.nass.usda. gov/fl/rtoc0.html> (accessed 5 April 2000).

Table 9.55. CITRUS: ACREAGE BY TYPE OF FRUIT IN THE STATE AND SPECIFIED
COUNTIES OF FLORIDA, JANUARY 1, 1998

County	Total	All oranges 1/	Early and mid-season	Valencias	All grape-fruit 1/	Specialty fruit 2/
			Oranges			
Florida	833,701	658,390	332,878	314,310	121,258	54,053
Brevard	10,528	8,172	4,923	3,154	1,599	757
Broward	97	85	30	34	10	2
Charlotte	21,478	16,936	6,430	10,114	3,090	1,452
Citrus	258	203	179	24	27	28
Collier	35,453	31,054	13,681	17,117	2,976	1,423
De Soto	67,032	63,458	29,282	32,901	1,530	2,044
Glades	10,765	9,952	5,635	4,256	366	447
Hardee	52,228	49,341	34,536	14,305	773	2,114
Hendry	98,949	86,519	35,791	49,671	7,787	4,643
Hernando	1,099	987	964	15	13	99
Highlands	75,039	67,492	24,710	42,347	2,861	4,686
Hillsborough	27,328	25,113	18,845	5,781	731	1,484
Indian River	62,133	27,611	14,153	12,807	32,249	2,273
Lake	20,807	15,359	12,386	2,534	1,120	4,328
Lee	11,782	10,095	4,389	5,624	1,093	594
Manatee	23,641	21,424	12,876	8,490	1,348	869
Marion	1,181	946	820	115	36	199
Martin	45,552	39,776	13,869	24,276	4,326	1,450
Miami-Dade 3/	2,792	0	0	0	0	2,792
Okeechobee	12,075	10,227	5,868	4,359	1,306	542
Orange	9,155	7,653	5,063	2,374	216	1,286
Osceola	15,480	13,140	8,890	4,158	1,434	906
Palm Beach	10,485	6,213	3,843	2,285	2,019	2,253
Pasco	11,340	10,507	8,453	1,832	229	604
Pinellas	133	104	57	47	5	24
Polk	101,482	84,974	44,599	38,579	6,742	9,766
Putnam	191	112	89	22	5	74
St. Lucie	99,858	46,911	19,847	25,778	46,753	6,194
Sarasota	2,303	1,699	851	845	410	194
Seminole	1,411	1,111	874	209	30	270
Volusia	1,471	1,181	910	257	174	116
Other 4/	175	35	35	0	0	140

1/ Includes unidentified variety acreage. Grapefruit updated 1999.
2/ Includes limes and lemons.
3/ Surveyed as of October 1996. Reflected in the state total.
4/ Includes Flagler and Sumter counties.

Source: State of Florida, Department of Agriculture and Consumer Services, Florida Agricultural Statistics Service, *Florida Agricultural Statistics: Citrus Summary, 1998-99,* Internet site <http://www.nass.usda.gov/fl/rtoc0.html> (accessed 5 April 2000).

Table 9.56. ORANGE JUICE SALES: GALLONS SOLD AND CONSUMER RETAIL DOLLARS SPENT
IN UNITED STATES FOOD STORES SEASONS 1988-89 THROUGH 1998-99

Season 1/	Total			Frozen		
	Volume (million gallons)	Value (million gallons)	Price (dollars/ gallon)	Volume (million gallons)	Value (million gallons)	Price (dollars/ gallon)
1988-89	755.2	2,811.8	3.7	321.9	1,046.3	3.3
1989-90	701.9	2,944.6	4.2	286.9	1,044.3	3.6
1990-91	754.2	2,848.0	3.8	305.4	944.6	3.1
1991-92	749.9	2,874.4	3.8	290.1	897.9	3:1
1992-93	807.9	2,742.1	3.4	287.3	777.7	2.7
1993-94	803.8	2,732.6	3.4	263.6	720.3	2.7
1994-95	806.7	2,768.6	3.4	243.3	660.8	2.7
1995-96	789.9	2,877.1	3.6	218.8	635.9	2.9
1996-97	796.4	3,030.3	3.8	197.1	594.2	3.0
1997-98	818.9	3,082.6	3.8	179.4	518.8	2.9
1998-99	794.4	3,344.1	4.2	154.7	487.8	3.2

	Refrigerated 2/					
	Not from concentrate			Reconstituted		
	Volume (million gallons)	Value (million gallons)	Price (dollars/ gallon)	Volume (million gallons)	Value (million gallons)	Price (dollars/ gallon)
1988-89	105.4	524.8	5.0	313.4	1,164.3	3.7
1989-90	112.6	618.7	5.5	288.1	1,201.6	4.2
1990-91	125.7	652.9	5.2	309.7	1,177.8	3.8
1991-92	140.6	735.5	5.2	305.7	1,170.1	3.8
1992-93	175.4	833.7	4.8	332.6	1,067.4	3.2
1993-94	191.6	882.3	4.6	336.2	1,071.3	3.2
1994-95	207.5	965.5	4.7	345.0	1,090.3	3.2
1995-96	216.4	1,031.2	4.8	344.3	1,159.6	3.4
1996-97	223.8	1,098.4	4.9	365.8	1,289.2	3.5
1997-98	260.9	1,240.7	4.8	369.6	1,277.0	3.5
1998-99	286.4	1,488.7	5.2	344.5	1,320.4	3.8

1/ October of the previous year through September of the present year.
2/ Includes glass and plastic containers and cartons.
Note: Data are Nielsen retail orange juice sales from scanner supermarkets doing over $2 million in
annual retail sales. Canned and aseptic shelf-stable orange juice included in totals only.

Source: State of Florida, Department of Citrus, unpublished data.

University of Florida   **Bureau of Economic and Business Research**

Table 9.61. FIELD CROPS: ACREAGE HARVESTED, PRODUCTION, YIELD, AND VALUE OF PRODUCTION IN FLORIDA, CROP YEARS 1997 AND 1998

Crop	Harvested acres (1,000) 1997	Harvested acres (1,000) 1998	Unit	Production Total (1,000) 1997	Production Total (1,000) 1998	Production Yield per acre (1,000) 1997	Production Yield per acre (1,000) 1998	Production Value ($1,000) 1997	Production Value ($1,000) 1998
Corn 1/	75	55	Bu.	6,000	3,410	80	62	17,400	7,843
Cotton	99	80	2/	119	82	577	489	37,388	21,203
Cottonseed	(X)	(X)	Tons	45	26	(X)	(X)	5,400	2,860
Hay, all	250	230	Tons	650	575	3	3	55,900	58,650
Peanuts 3/	84	90	Lbs.	228,060	233,100	2,715	2,590	63,857	57,343
Potatoes	42	43	Cwt.	9,030	8,798	214	207	110,359	129,051
Soybeans 4/	45	30	Bu.	1,125	690	25	23	7,875	3,726
Sugarcane 5/	440	447	Tons	16,236	17,925	37	40	465,973	528,788
Tobacco, flue- cured, Type 14	7	7	Lbs.	19,053	17,102	2,610	2,515	32,790	29,022
Wheat	17	13	Bu.	663	559	39	43	2,254	1,398

(X) Not applicable.
1/ Harvested for grain.   2/ Production in 1,000 bales. Yield in pounds.   3/ Harvested for dry nuts.
4/ Harvested for beans.   5/ For sugar and seed.
Note: Data for 1997 may be revised. All 1998 estimates are preliminary.

Table 9.62. CORN: ACREAGE HARVESTED FOR GRAIN AND BUSHELS PRODUCED IN THE STATE CROP-REPORTING DISTRICTS AND SPECIFIED COUNTIES OF FLORIDA, 1998

District and county	Acres harvested (1,000)	Production (1,000 bushels)	District and county	Acres harvested (1,000)	Production (1,000 bushels)
Florida	55.0	3,410	District 3--North (Continued)		
			Hamilton	4.8	327
District 1--West	24.4	1,607	Lafayette	0.4	25
Calhoun	0.9	50	Madison	4.9	284
Escambia	2.9	197	Suwannee	4.3	267
Gadsden	0.8	51	Other counties	1.0	61
Holmes	1.1	59			
Jackson	11.9	876	District 5--Central	10.8	563
Jefferson	2.2	115	Alachua	3.0	152
Leon	0.7	37	Gilchrist	2.8	142
Okaloosa	0.6	33	Levy	0.6	30
Santa Rosa	0.6	31	Marion	0.7	45
Walton	0.7	38	St. Johns	0.8	39
Washington	1.9	114	Union	1.0	50
Other counties	0.1	6	Other counties	1.9	105
District 3--North	17.3	1,069	District 8--South	2.5	171
Columbia	1.9	105	Manatee	0.7	63
			Other counties	1.8	108

Note: See accompanying map for counties in crop-reporting districts. Data are preliminary.

Source for Tables 9.61 and 9.62: State of Florida, Department of Agriculture and Consumer Services, Florida Agricultural Statistics Service, *Florida Agricultural Statistics: Field Crops Summary, 1998,* Internet site <http://www.nass.usda.gov/fl/rtoc0.html> (accessed 5 April 2000).

University of Florida   **Bureau of Economic and Business Research**

Crop-reporting Districts

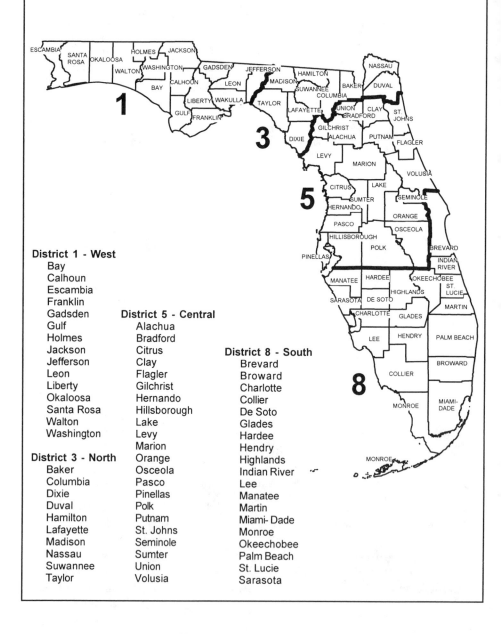

District 1 - West
Bay
Calhoun
Escambia
Franklin
Gadsden
Gulf
Holmes
Jackson
Jefferson
Leon
Liberty
Okaloosa
Santa Rosa
Walton
Washington

District 3 - North
Baker
Columbia
Dixie
Duval
Hamilton
Lafayette
Madison
Nassau
Suwannee
Taylor

District 5 - Central
Alachua
Bradford
Citrus
Clay
Flagler
Gilchrist
Hernando
Hillsborough
Lake
Levy
Marion
Orange
Osceola
Pasco
Pinellas
Polk
Putnam
St. Johns
Seminole
Sumter
Union
Volusia

District 8 - South
Brevard
Broward
Charlotte
Collier
De Soto
Glades
Hardee
Hendry
Highlands
Indian River
Lee
Manatee
Martin
Miami- Dade
Monroe
Okeechobee
Palm Beach
St. Lucie
Sarasota

Table 9.63. POTATOES: ACREAGE HARVESTED IN THE STATE AND SPECIFIED COUNTIES OF FLORIDA, 1993 THROUGH 1998

(in acres)

County or season	1993	1994	1995	1996	1997	1998 A/
Florida	41,900	46,400	42,900	44,300	42,100	42,500
Winter	8,400	7,800	6,900	8,800	9,400	8,000
Spring	33,500	38,600	36,000	35,500	37,700	34,500
Flagler	2,500	2,600	2,000	2,500	2,800	2,600
Miami-Dade	4,700	4,300	3,100	4,600	5,600	5,000
Putnam	4,900	5,400	5,000	4,000	3,700	3,700
St. Johns	18,600	21,000	20,000	21,000	17,400	18,200
Other counties	11,200	13,100	12,800	12,200	12,600	13,000

A/ Preliminary.

Table 9.64. PEANUTS: ACREAGE HARVESTED AND PRODUCTION IN THE STATE CROP-REPORTING DISTRICTS, AND SPECIFIED COUNTIES OF FLORIDA, 1998

District and county	Acres har- vested	Production (1,000 pounds)	District and county	Acres har- vested	Production (1,000 pounds)
Florida	90,000	233,100	District 3--North	10,500	23,474
			Columbia	3,900	4,703
District 1--West	61,900	163,686	Madison	700	2,383
Calhoun	3,900	11,481	Suwannee	5,300	14,440
Gadsden	700	1,200	Other counties	600	1,948
Holmes	4,500	8,999			
Jackson	30,100	78,701	District 5--Central	17,600	45,940
Jefferson	800	2,420	Alachua	2,600	6,569
Okaloosa	1,600	3,974	Gilchrist	900	1,964
Santa Rosa	13,500	39,902	Levy	9,400	27,342
Walton	3,800	8,257	Marion	4,600	9,813
Washington	1,600	4,617	Other counties	100	252
Other counties	1,400	4,135			

Note: See accompanying map for counties in crop-reporting districts.

Table 9.65. SOYBEANS: ACREAGE HARVESTED FOR GRAIN AND BUSHELS PRODUCED IN THE STATE AND SPECIFIED COUNTIES OF FLORIDA, 1998

County	Acres har- vested	Production (1,000 bushels)	County	Acres har- vested	Production (1,000 bushels)
Florida	30,000	690	Jefferson	1,400	21
Calhoun	3,800	98	Okaloosa	500	12
Escambia	4,200	91	Santa Rosa	1,500	24
Gadsden	800	18	Walton	1,200	26
Holmes	1,400	23	Washington	1,600	41
Jackson	8,300	205	Other counties	5,300	131

Source for Tables 9.63, 9.64, and 9.65: State of Florida, Department of Agriculture and Consumer Services, Florida Agricultural Statistics Service, *Florida Agricultural Statistics: Field Crops Summary, 1998,* Internet site <http://www.nass.usda.gov/fl/rtoc0.html> (accessed 5 April 2000).

University of Florida   **Bureau of Economic and Business Research**

Table 9.66. COTTON: ACREAGE HARVESTED AND PRODUCTION IN THE STATE, CROP-REPORTING DISTRICTS, AND SPECIFIED COUNTIES OF FLORIDA, 1998

District and county	Acres harvested	Production (bales)	District and county	Acres harvested	Production (bales)
Florida	80,000	81,500	District 1 (Continued)		
			Walton	4,100	4,000
District 1	72,200	74,100	Washington	700	700
Calhoun	5,800	5,800	District 3	4,000	3,800
Escambia	13,700	12,600	Columbia	300	300
Holmes	2,800	2,800	Hamilton	1,900	1,900
Jackson	15,100	17,500	Madison	1,800	1,600
Jefferson	2,200	1,900	District 5	(D)	(D)
Okaloosa	2,900	2,700	Other counties,		
Santa Rosa	24,900	26,100	all districts 1/	3,800	3,600

(D) Data withheld to avoid disclosure of individual operations.
1/ Includes Gadsden and Alachua counties to avoid disclosure of individual operations.
Note: See accompanying map for counties in crop-reporting districts.

Table 9.67. SUGARCANE FOR SUGAR: ACREAGE HARVESTED AND PRODUCTION IN THE STATE AND SPECIFIED COUNTIES OF FLORIDA, 1998

County	Acres harvested	Production (tons)	County	Acres harvested	Production (tons)
Florida	426,000	17,083,000	Hendry	55,000	2,208,000
Glades	15,000	542,000	Martin and Palm Beach	356,000	14,333,000

Note: Data are preliminary.

Table 9.68. TOBACCO: ACREAGE HARVESTED AND PRODUCTION OF FLUE-CURED TOBACCO IN THE STATE, CROP-REPORTING DISTRICTS, AND SPECIFIED COUNTIES OF FLORIDA, 1998

District and county	Acres harvested	Production (pounds)	District and county	Acres harvested	Production (pounds)
Florida	6,800	17,102,000	District 3 (Continued)		
			Madison	690	1,580,100
District 1--West	500	1,109,000	Suwannee	1,590	4,023,000
Gadsden	100	189,000	Other counties	140	320,600
Jefferson	300	708,000	District 5--Central	1,600	4,008,000
Other counties	100	212,000	Alachua	950	2,441,500
District 3--North	4,700	11,985,000	Bradford	100	197,500
Baker	130	296,400	Gilchrist	150	309,000
Columbia	630	1,801,800	Union	200	512,000
Hamilton	990	2,267,100	Other counties	200	548,000
Lafayette	530	1,696,000			

Note: See accompanying map for counties in crop-reporting districts.
Source for Tables 9.66, 9.67, and 9.68: State of Florida, Department of Agriculture and Consumer Services, Florida Agricultural Statistics Service, *Florida Agricultural Statistics: Field Crops Summary, 1998,* Internet site <http://www.nass.usda.gov/fl/rtoc0.html> (accessed 5 April 2000).

University of Florida   **Bureau of Economic and Business Research**

Table 9.69. CROPS: ACREAGE PLANTED AND HARVESTED, PRODUCTION, AND VALUE OF CROPS IN FLORIDA, CROP YEAR 1998-99

Crop	Acreage planted	Acreage harvested	Production (1,000 CWT)	Total value ($1,000)
All crops, total	316,000	300,900	67,579	1,582,713
Vegetables, total	175,400	172,200	36,739	1,082,896
Snap beans	32,000	31,300	2,606	114,650
Cabbage	8,500	8,400	2,049	20,495
Sweet corn	39,900	39,600	5,478	100,325
Cucumbers	8,900	8,800	2,800	53,565
Eggplant	2,000	2,000	535	16,788
Bell peppers	19,200	19,000	6,056	243,024
Radishes	8,500	7,100	398	19,647
Squash	13,000	12,600	1,482	53,802
Tomatoes	43,400	43,400	15,335	460,600
Other 1/	51,000	49,000	7,840	143,472
Watermelons	45,000	35,000	10,500	72,450
Potatoes	38,400	37,300	A/ 10,625	126,220
Strawberries	6,200	6,200	1,860	150,660
Blueberries	0	1,200	15	7,015

CWT Hundred weight.
A/ Production sold.
1/ Fresh and processing vegetables and cantaloupes.

Source: State of Florida, Department of Agriculture and Consumer Services, Florida Agricultural Statistics Service, *Florida Agricultural Statistics: Vegetable Summary, 1998-99.*

Table 9.70. LIVESTOCK: CASH RECEIPTS FROM MARKETINGS IN FLORIDA 1992 THROUGH 1998

(in thousands of dollars, except where indicated)

Year	Total livestock and products Amount	Percentage of total farm cash receipts	Cattle and calves	Hogs	Milk	Chickens and eggs	Honey
1992	1,165,874	19	349,447	13,126	401,700	258,988	12,126
1993	1,211,131	20	362,495	15,106	385,503	298,121	11,300
1994	1,194,603	20	335,837	12,399	408,408	290,905	9,080
1995	1,134,378	19	287,352	12,098	363,528	314,577	12,659
1996	1,303,304	19	218,919	15,409	431,280	362,050	21,672
1997	1,399,551	20	320,424	12,335	407,715	353,128	11,738
1998	1,407,349	21	293,327	5,772	423,878	366,603	14,426

Note: Data are for calendar year, except for hogs, chickens and eggs, and honey, which report for a marketing year of December through November. Value of eggs is for total production including consumption on farms where produced. Data do not include government payments. Some data are revised.

Source: State of Florida, Department of Agriculture and Consumer Services, Florida Agricultural Statistics Service, *Florida Agricultural Statistics: Livestock, Dairy, and Poultry Summary, 1998,* Internet site <http://www.nass.usda.gov/fl/rtoc0.html> (accessed 10 April 2000).

Table 9.71. CATTLE AND CALVES: NUMBER AND RANK OF CATTLE AND CALVES AND BEEF COWS IN THE STATE AND COUNTIES OF FLORIDA, JANUARY 1, 1999

(number in thousands, rounded to hundreds)

County	Cattle and calves 1/ Number	Rank	Beef cows 2/ Number	Rank	County	Cattle and calves 1/ Number	Rank	Beef cows 2/ Number	Rank
Florida	1,800.0	(X)	973.0	(X)	Lee	13.0	33	8.0	30
					Leon	6.5	49	2.5	56
Alachua	46.0	13	26.0	12	Levy	44.0	14	21.0	16
Baker	5.0	55	2.0	59	Liberty	1.5	61	1.0	60
Bradford	10.0	40	5.5	38	Madison	18.0	29	10.0	26
Brevard	28.0	21	15.0	20	Manatee	64.0	10	34.0	9
Broward	16.0	33	5.5	38	Marion	49.0	11	26.0	12
Calhoun	4.5	59	2.5	56	Martin	28.0	21	15.0	20
Charlotte	26.0	23	17.0	17	Miami-Dade	5.0	55	3.0	52
Citrus	9.5	41	6.5	34	Nassau	9.0	42	3.5	49
Clay	12.0	35	2.5	56	Okaloosa	5.5	54	3.0	52
Collier	9.0	42	6.5	34	Okeechobee	154.0	1	63.0	3
Columbia	20.0	26	12.0	24	Orange	15.0	32	10.0	26
De Soto	80.0	7	47.0	7	Osceola	96.0	4	69.0	1
Dixie	5.0	55	2.0	59	Palm Beach	5.0	55	3.0	52
Duval	12.0	35	4.0	45	Pasco	40.0	15	22.0	14
Escambia	8.0	47	3.0	52	Polk	93.0	5	56.0	4
Flagler	6.0	50	4.5	43	Putnam	9.0	42	5.5	38
Gadsden	6.0	50	4.5	43	St. Johns	4.5	59	3.5	49
Gilchrist	32.0	20	9.0	29	St. Lucie	33.0	18	22.0	14
Glades	69.0	8	39.0	8	Santa Rosa	7.5	48	4.0	45
Hamilton	9.0	42	6.0	37	Sarasota	24.0	24	15.0	20
Hardee	87.0	6	48.0	6	Seminole	6.0	50	5.0	41
Hendry	97.0	3	54.0	5	Sumter	48.0	12	28.0	11
Hernando	19.0	28	9.5	28	Suwannee	36.0	16	16.0	19
Highlands	112.0	2	68.0	2	Taylor	6.0	50	3.5	49
Hillsborough	65.0	9	33.0	10	Union	11.0	39	7.5	32
Holmes	16.0	30	8.0	30	Volusia	13.0	33	7.0	33
Indian River	20.0	26	12.0	24	Wakulla	1.5	61	1.0	60
Jackson	34.0	17	15.0	20	Walton	12.0	35	5.0	41
Jefferson	12.0	35	6.5	34	Washington	9.0	42	4.0	45
Lafayette	23.0	25	4.0	45					
Lake	33.0	18	17.0	17	Other 3/	2.0	(X)	1.0	(X)

(X) Not applicable.
1/ All classes, beef and dairy.
2/ Beef production brood cows only, which have calved at least once.
3/ Includes Bay, Franklin, Gulf, Monroe, and Pinellas counties.

Source: State of Florida, Department of Agriculture and Consumer Services, Florida Agricultural Statistics Service, *Florida Agricultural Statistics: Livestock, Dairy, and Poultry Summary, 1998,* Internet site <http://www.nass.usda.gov/fl/rtoc0.html> (accessed 10 April 2000).

Table 9.72. CATTLE AND CALVES: MARKETINGS, PRICE, AND CASH RECEIPTS IN FLORIDA AND THE UNITED STATES, 1994 THROUGH 1998

	Florida			United States			
Year	Market-ings 1/ (1,000 lbs.)	Price per 100 lbs. (dollars) Cattle	Calves	Cash re-ceipts 2/ ($1,000)	Market-ings 1/ (1,000 lbs.)	Price per 100 lbs. (dollars) Cattle	Calves	Cash re-ceipts 2/ ($1,000)
1994	468,900	53.20	84.60	335,836	53,865,297	66.70	87.20	36,253,055
1995	485,400	44.30	70.00	287,352	56,349,075	61.80	73.10	34,044,038
1996	479,500	33.40	54.60	218,919	55,873,153	58.70	58.40	30,976,861
1997	507,000	42.20	81.20	320,424	56,968,131	63.10	78.90	35,999,620
1998	480,250	39.00	78.60	293,327	55,831,066	59.60	78.80	33,723,926

1/ Excludes custom slaughter for use on farms where produced and interfarm sales within states.
2/ Receipts from marketings and sales of farm slaughter.

Table 9.73. LIVESTOCK INVENTORY: NUMBER ON FARMS IN FLORIDA, LEADING STATE AND THE UNITED STATES, 1998 OR 1999

(numbers in thousands)

Type of livestock	Florida Rank among states	Number	Leading state Name	Number	United States
Cattle and calves 1/	18	1,800	Texas	14,000	98,522
Beef cows 1/	12	973	Texas	5,530	33,472
Hogs 2/	33	55	Iowa	15,300	62,156

1/ January 1, 1999.
2/ December 1, 1998.

Table 9.74. HONEY: PRODUCTION AND VALUE IN FLORIDA AND THE UNITED STATES 1995 THROUGH 1998

	Florida			United States		
Year	Number of colonies (1,000)	Production (1,000 pounds)	Value ($1,000)	Number of colonies (1,000)	Production (1,000 pounds)	Value ($1,000)
1995	230	19,780	12,659	2,655	211,073	144,585
1996	240	25,200	21,672	2,581	199,511	177,166
1997	240	16,080	11,738	2,631	196,536	147,795
1998	230	22,540	14,426	2,633	220,311	144,304

Note: Some data may be revised.

Source: State of Florida, Department of Agriculture and Consumer Services, Florida Agricultural Statistics Service, *Florida Agricultural Statistics: Livestock, Dairy, and Poultry Summary, 1998,* Internet site <http://www.nass.usda.gov/fl/rtoc0.html> (accessed 10 April 2000).

University of Florida   **Bureau of Economic and Business Research**

Table 9.86. DAIRY PRODUCTION: NUMBER OF MILK COWS AND ANNUAL MILK PRODUCTION
IN FLORIDA, OTHER LEADING PRODUCTION STATES, AND THE UNITED STATES, 1998

State	Milk cows 2/ (1,000)	Total milk (1,000,000 pounds)	Rank among states	Per milk cow (pounds)	Milkfat in milk (per-centage)
			Production 1/		
Florida	160	2,334	15	14,588	3.58
California	1,420	27,607	1	19,442	3.67
Wisconsin	1,369	22,842	2	16,685	3.73
New York	701	11,740	3	16,748	3.66
Pennsylvania	623	10,847	4	17,411	3.70
Minnesota	551	9,275	5	16,833	3.70
Texas	352	5,605	6	15,923	3.57
Michigan	300	5,391	7	17,970	3.63
Idaho	292	5,765	8	19,743	3.57
Ohio	264	4,390	9	16,629	3.69
Washington	248	5,326	10	21,476	3.66
Iowa	223	3,833	11	17,188	3.73
New Mexico	217	4,534	12	20,065	3.51
Missouri	170	2,367	13	13,924	3.64
Vermont	161	2,705	14	16,801	3.70
United States	9,158	157,441	(X)	17,192	3.66

1/ Average number on farms during year, excluding heifers not yet fresh.
2/ Excludes milk sucked by calves.

Table 9.87. CHICKEN AND EGGS: CASH RECEIPTS IN FLORIDA, MARKETING YEARS
1991 THROUGH 1998

(in thousands of dollars)

Year	Total	Broilers	Eggs 1/	Other chickens 2/
1991	276,371	151,704	120,903	3,764
1992	258,988	164,856	91,104	3,028
1993	298,121	187,714	106,838	3,569
1994	290,905	191,151	98,348	1,406
1995	314,577	218,361	95,320	896
1996	362,050	230,607	131,355	88
1997	353,128	229,383	123,701	44
1998	366,603	252,840	112,707	1,056

1/ Total production, including consumption on farms where produced.
2/ Value of sales.
Note: Data are for marketing years beginning December 1 and ending November 30. Some data may
be revised.

Source: State of Florida, Department of Agriculture and Consumer Services, Florida Agricultural Statistics
Service, *Florida Agricultural Statistics: Livestock, Dairy, and Poultry Summary, 1998,* Internet site <http://
www.nass.usda.gov/fl/rtoc0.html> (accessed 10 April 2000).

University of Florida   **Bureau of Economic and Business Research**

FORESTRY, FISHERIES, AND MINERALS

Private Forestry and Fishing Industry Employment, 1999

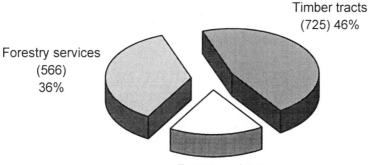

Timber tracts
(725) 46%

Forestry services
(566)
36%

Forest products
(282) 18%

Forestry Industry

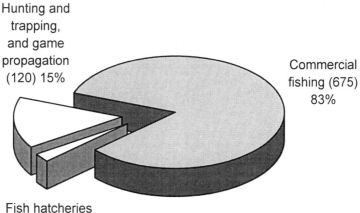

Hunting and
trapping,
and game
propagation
(120) 15%

Commercial
fishing (675)
83%

Fish hatcheries
and preserves
(20) 2%

Fishing Industry

Source: Table 10.35

SECTION 10.00
FORESTRY, FISHERIES, AND MINERALS

TABLES LISTED BY MAJOR HEADINGS

Table 10.07. FOREST PRODUCTS: HARVEST BY PRODUCT AND BY SPECIES GROUP
IN THE STATE AND COUNTIES OF FLORIDA, 1995

	Softwood				Hardwood			
County	Saw logs (MBF)	Veneer logs (MBF)	Pulp- wood 1/ (Cords)	Other pro- ducts 2/ (MCF)	Saw logs (MBF)	Veneer logs (MBF)	Pulp- wood 3/ (Cords)	Other pro- ducts 2/ (MCF)
Florida	769,017	141,626	3,957,034	23,697	36,260	11,274	534,851	3,243
Alachua	23,714	11,352	124,934	1,280	355	0	10,816	56
Baker	28,170	5,676	76,792	477	0	120	3,494	0
Bay	17,687	0	171,620	120	1,484	0	1,625	0
Bradford	39,409	5,676	79,309	267	5	0	25,989	0
Brevard	877	0	7,810	0	0	0	594	0
Broward	0	0	2,491	0	0	0	0	0
Calhoun	19,295	5,441	164,201	208	9,110	105	19,255	0
Charlotte	124	0	4,876	132	165	0	0	0
Citrus	1,585	0	19,311	0	0	150	5,081	0
Clay	20,850	5,676	45,174	396	0	0	5,869	0
Collier	26	0	436	0	0	0	47	0
Columbia	38,282	5,676	131,526	131	5	777	12,606	512
De Soto	324	0	1,546	0	0	0	0	0
Dixie	30,457	5,676	136,020	1,089	2,265	777	60,270	0
Duval	18,095	5,676	73,269	282	28	0	778	0
Escambia	25,366	2,908	86,243	250	1	191	8,799	0
Flagler	24,552	5,676	61,823	401	0	0	9,492	0
Franklin	7,661	0	70,307	56	0	0	28	0
Gadsden	5,361	6,801	118,838	133	2,937	1,036	21,233	18
Gilchrist	12,063	5,676	51,424	163	0	518	4,495	56
Glades	198	0	30,939	63	261	0	0	0
Gulf	6,588	0	66,534	123	1,939	105	1,338	0
Hamilton	14,120	0	57,464	860	0	0	10,486	0
Hardee	173	0	2,456	0	228	0	0	0
Hendry	0	0	10,189	0	0	0	0	0
Hernando	1,884	0	17,669	89	350	0	2,826	0
Highlands	0	0	0	547	0	0	0	0
Hillsborough	710	0	5,779	25	0	930	64	0
Holmes	17,051	0	53,022	154	1,216	396	16,721	0
Indian River	0	0	801	0	0	0	0	0
Jackson	26,768	4,761	132,698	272	4,094	396	17,308	0
Jefferson	12,775	5,441	44,512	3	875	0	28,992	994
Lafayette	13,897	5,676	33,589	278	0	260	10,343	0
Lake	3,954	0	12,829	614	0	300	1,142	0
Lee	0	0	2,276	132	0	0	0	0
Leon	10,902	0	39,262	95	830	210	14,929	73

See footnotes at end of table.   Continued . . .

University of Florida   **Bureau of Economic and Business Research**

Table 10.07. FOREST PRODUCTS: HARVEST BY PRODUCT AND BY SPECIES GROUP
IN THE STATE AND COUNTIES OF FLORIDA, 1995 (Continued)

	Softwood				Hardwood			
County	Saw logs (MBF)	Veneer logs (MBF)	Pulp-wood 1/ (Cords)	Other pro-ducts 2/ (MCF)	Saw logs (MBF)	Veneer logs (MBF)	Pulp-wood 3/ (Cords)	Other pro-ducts 2/ (MCF)
Levy	30,092	5,676	78,564	3,053	2,224	1,036	21,011	28
Liberty	6,273	3,400	95,546	140	2,157	0	6,904	0
Madison	17,688	0	62,596	704	0	571	31,648	994
Manatee	85	0	1,811	0	0	0	0	0
Marion	23,029	5,676	83,280	771	2,566	150	17,649	0
Martin	0	0	63	0	0	0	0	0
Miami-Dade	0	0	22	0	0	0	0	0
Monroe	0	0	10	0	0	0	0	0
Nassau	58,813	0	128,891	1,882	19	0	14,972	0
Okaloosa	7,883	4,017	116,446	190	0	205	5,552	0
Okeechobee	0	0	847	0	0	0	0	0
Orange	1,023	0	8,423	289	0	0	0	0
Osceola	7,838	0	8,626	2,364	0	180	12	0
Palm Beach	0	0	71	0	0	0	0	0
Pasco	5,727	0	13,122	515	0	630	2,610	0
Pinellas	0	0	62	0	0	0	0	0
Polk	13,350	0	9,246	692	0	0	0	0
Putnam	18,371	5,676	76,703	305	166	150	10,231	0
St. Johns	7,337	5,676	110,578	168	18	0	11,525	0
St. Lucie	0	0	2,487	0	0	0	0	0
Santa Rosa	11,349	4,017	136,432	1,400	0	0	4,616	0
Sarasota	399	0	6,067	0	0	0	0	0
Seminole	565	0	15,079	275	0	0	0	0
Sumter	4,065	0	19,575	194	0	90	4,711	0
Suwannee	12,088	5,676	73,078	52	0	518	9,388	0
Taylor	37,612	0	564,241	804	1,340	777	39,000	512
Union	20,743	5,676	66,919	238	5	0	5,588	0
Volusia	19,713	0	97,757	536	0	300	6,282	0
Wakulla	12,473	3,400	25,505	165	0	0	4,993	0
Walton	13,313	2,908	133,062	158	0	0	13,145	0
Washington	16,270	2,040	83,956	162	1,617	396	30,394	0

MBF Thousand board feet.
MCF Thousand cubic feet.
1/ Includes 82,548 roundwood that was delivered to nonpulp mills, chipped and then sold to pulp mills
as residues.
2/ Includes composite board, poles/piling, post and other industrial.
3/ Includes 2,213 roundwood that was delivered to nonpulp mills, chipped and then sold to pulp mills as
residues.

Source: State of Florida, Department of Agriculture and Consumer Services, Division of Forestry,
unpublished data.

Table 10.25. NATIONAL FOREST LAND: GROSS AND NET AREA OF NATIONAL FOREST AND OTHER LAND ADMINISTERED BY THE NATIONAL FOREST SYSTEM IN FLORIDA AND THE UNITED STATES AS OF SEPTEMBER 30, 1999

(in acres)

Unit name and area	Gross area within unit boundaries	National forest sy-stem lands	Other lands within unit boundaries
Florida	1,434,134	1,152,824	281,310
Apalachicola National Forest	632,890	565,543	67,347
National wilderness areas			
Bradwell Bay 1/	24,602	24,602	0
Mud Swamp/New River	8,090	8,090	0
Choctawhatchee National Forest	1,152	1,152	0
Ocala National Forest	430,441	383,573	46,868
National wilderness areas			
Alexander Springs	7,941	7,941	0
Billies Bay	3,092	3,092	0
Juniper Prairie	14,281	14,277	4
Little Lake George	2,833	2,833	0
National game refuge, Ocala	79,735	79,735	0
Osceola National Forest	190,932	158,255	32,677
National wilderness area, Big Gum Swamp	13,660	13,660	0
United States	232,169,908	192,046,672	40,123,236

1/ Protected under the Clean Air Act, without visibility protection.

Table 10.26. NATIONAL FOREST LAND: NET AREA OF LAND ADMINISTERED BY THE NATIONAL FOREST SYSTEM IN THE STATE AND COUNTIES OF FLORIDA AND THE UNITED STATES AS OF SEPTEMBER 30, 1999

County	National forest area	Acres
Florida	(X)	1,152,824
Baker	Nekoosa Purchase Units	32
	Osceola National Forest	79,428
	Pinhook Purchase Units	23,233
Columbia	Nekoosa Purchase Units	191
	Osceola National Forest	78,827
	Pinhook Purchase Units	16,792
Franklin	Apalachicola National Forest	21,816
	Tates Hell-New River Purchase Units	976
Lake	Ocala National Forest	84,361
Leon	Apalachicola National Forest	104,568
Liberty	Apalachicola National Forest	267,298
	Tates Hell-New River Purchase Units	3,077
Marion	Ocala National Forest	275,590
Okaloosa	Choctawhatchee National Forest	523
Putnam	Ocala National Forest	23,622
Santa Rosa	Choctawhatchee National Forest	108
Wakulla	Apalachicola National Forest	171,861
Walton	Choctawhatchee National Forest	521
United States	(X)	192,046,672

(X) Not applicable.

Source for Tables 10.25 and 10.26: U.S., Department of Agriculture, Forest Service, *Land Areas of the National Forest System as of September 30, 1999,* Internet site <http://www.fs.fed.us/land/staff/lar/LAR99> (accessed 8 May 2000) .

Table 10.34. FORESTRY: AVERAGE MONTHLY PRIVATE REPORTING UNITS, EMPLOYMENT
AND PAYROLL COVERED BY UNEMPLOYMENT COMPENSATION LAW IN THE STATE
AND COUNTIES OF FLORIDA, 1999

County	Number of reporting units	Number of employees	Payroll ($1,000)	County	Number of reporting units	Number of employees	Payroll ($1,000)
				Forestry (SIC code 08)			
Florida	**166**	**1,573**	**3,775**	Miami-Dade	13	122	200
				Nassau	7	342	1,199
Broward	6	32	58	Orange	3	41	93
Columbia	4	12	29	Palm Beach	4	71	162
Duval	7	50	133	Pasco	5	50	82
Hamilton	4	8	8	Putnam	5	90	273
Hillsborough	8	72	102	Taylor	5	31	69
Leon	9	40	66	Volusia	4	17	83
Levy	8	28	83	Multicounty 1/	5	29	74

1/ Reporting units without a fixed location within the state or of unknown county location.
Note: Private employment. For a list of three-digit code industries included see Table 10.35. Data are preliminary. Only counties for which data are disclosed are shown. Detail may not add to totals due to disclosure editing and/or rounding. See Tables 23.70, 23.71, 23.72, 23.73, and 23.74 for public employment data.

Table 10.35. FORESTRY AND FISHING INDUSTRIES: AVERAGE MONTHLY PRIVATE REPORTING
UNITS, EMPLOYMENT, AND PAYROLL COVERED BY UNEMPLOYMENT COMPENSATION
LAW BY INDUSTRY IN FLORIDA, 1999

SIC code	Industry	Number of reporting units	Number of employees	Payroll ($1,000)
08	Forestry	166	1,573	3,775
081	Timber tracts	79	725	1,554
083	Forest products	24	282	421
085	Forestry services	64	566	1,800
09	Fishing, hunting, and trapping	225	815	1,457
091	Commercial fishing	199	675	1,247
092	Fish hatcheries and preserves	8	20	29
097	Hunting and trapping, and game propagation	18	120	181

Note: Private employment. Data are preliminary. Detail may not add to totals due to disclosure editing and/or rounding. See Tables 23.70, 23.71, 23.72, 23.73, and 23.74 for public employment data.

Source for Tables 10.34 and 10.35: State of Florida, Department of Labor and Employment Security, Bureau of Labor Market Information, "Employment and Wages" (ES-202), unpublished data.

University of Florida   **Bureau of Economic and Business Research**

Table 10.36. FISHERIES: NUMBER OF PROCESSING AND WHOLESALING PLANTS AND AVERAGE ANNUAL EMPLOYMENT IN FLORIDA, GEOGRAPHIC AREAS, OTHER MAJOR PRODUCTION STATES AND THE UNITED STATES, 1997

Area	Number of plants Total	Number of plants Pro-cessing	Number of plants Whole-sale	Average annual employment Total	Average annual employment Pro-cessing	Average annual employment Whole-sale
Area						
South Atlantic	285	102	183	5,240	3,607	1,633
New England	809	159	650	9,990	5,168	4,822
Mid-Atlantic	834	113	721	10,821	5,348	5,473
Gulf	1,119	379	740	15,579	8,852	6,727
Pacific	1,305	478	827	27,177	20,017	7,160
Inland States	381	38	343	5,372	1,730	3,642
State						
Florida	488	119	364	6,153	3,008	3,140
Maine	277	54	223	3,284	1,768	1,516
Massachusetts	376	73	303	5,120	2,647	2,473
North Carolina	152	52	100	2,344	1,451	893
Washington	294	96	198	5,638	3,927	1,711
California	534	141	393	11,765	6,974	4,791
Alaska	414	201	213	7,988	7,652	336
United States 1/	4,817	1,297	3,520	83,155	53,698	29,457

1/ Includes American Samoa, Hawaii, and Puerto Rico.

Source: U.S., Department of Commerce, National Oceanic and Atmospheric Administration, National Marine Fisheries Service, *Fisheries of the United States, 1998.*

Table 10.37. FISHING, HUNTING, AND TRAPPING: AVERAGE MONTHLY PRIVATE REPORTING UNITS, EMPLOYMENT, AND PAYROLL COVERED BY UNEMPLOYMENT COMPENSATION LAW IN THE STATE AND COUNTIES OF FLORIDA, 1999

County	Number of re-porting units	Number of em-ployees	Payroll ($1,000)	County	Number of re-porting units	Number of em-ployees	Payroll ($1,000)
			Fishing, hunting, and trapping (SIC code 09)				
Florida	230	771	1,492	Okaloosa	6	17	41
				Palm Beach	4	24	37
Charlotte	3	8	8	Pasco	8	15	31
Citrus	5	9	17	Pinellas	17	63	151
Escambia	5	13	11	Volusia	4	9	14
Monroe	30	88	152				

Note: Private employment. For a list of three-digit code industries included see Table 10.35. Data are preliminary. Only counties for which data are disclosed are shown. Detail may not add to totals due to disclosure editing and/or rounding. See Tables 23.70, 23.71, 23.72, 23.73, and 23.74 for public employment data.

Source: State of Florida, Department of Labor and Employment Security, Bureau of Labor Market Information, "Employment and Wages" (ES-202), unpublished data.

University of Florida   **Bureau of Economic and Business Research**

Table 10.40. FISH AND SHELLFISH: QUANTITY OF LANDINGS BY TYPE OF SPECIES AND TRIPS IN THE STATE AND SPECIFIED COUNTIES OF FLORIDA, 1999

Area and county	Landings 1/ (pounds) Total	Fish	Shellfish 2/	Trips 3/
Florida	120,870,401	57,741,890	63,128,511	305,166
East coast	30,002,111	14,600,249	15,401,862	91,555
West coast	90,664,236	42,957,381	47,706,855	213,444
Inland/out of state 4/	204,054	184,260	19,794	167
Bay	4,225,002	3,816,245	408,757	4,717
Brevard	9,293,655	2,613,964	6,679,691	23,683
Broward	1,314,118	918,829	395,289	3,266
Charlotte	2,387,320	882,955	1,504,365	10,396
Citrus	3,797,802	1,087,986	2,709,816	13,023
Clay	194,033	0	194,033	644
Collier	3,204,679	1,418,893	1,785,786	6,746
Dixie	1,313,554	148,842	1,164,712	6,028
Duval	4,628,594	1,553,338	3,075,256	9,107
Escambia	1,881,437	1,073,180	808,257	4,142
Flagler	13,670	8,571	5,099	34
Franklin	6,779,385	1,223,427	5,555,958	30,669
Gulf	7,223,424	5,048,172	2,175,252	1,436
Hernando	714,973	25,762	689,211	5,057
Hillsborough	2,745,957	475,674	2,270,283	3,298
Indian River	1,243,835	1,227,274	16,561	5,785
Lee	9,886,058	3,321,278	6,564,780	25,617
Levy	2,531,747	324,490	2,207,257	10,417
Manatee	3,874,902	3,656,219	218,683	3,250
Martin	1,791,099	1,766,885	24,214	2,653
Miami-Dade	2,047,468	705,391	1,342,077	11,817
Monroe	20,824,481	6,336,342	14,488,139	54,315
Nassau	1,521,987	113,156	1,408,831	1,673
Okaloosa	2,336,079	2,144,938	191,141	3,625
Palm Beach	1,231,195	1,100,394	130,801	7,783
Pasco	605,572	259,633	345,939	1,673
Pinellas	12,491,462	10,191,381	2,300,081	17,417
Putnam	176,027	8,999	167,028	919
St. Johns	1,232,967	173,282	1,059,685	3,439
St. Lucie	3,033,469	2,978,822	54,647	8,255
Santa Rosa	432,498	143,756	288,742	1,907
Sarasota	129,947	71,097	58,850	660
Taylor	1,036,213	638,679	397,534	3,093
Volusia	2,279,994	1,431,344	848,650	12,497
Wakulla	2,183,850	649,398	1,534,452	5,317
Walton	57,894	19,034	38,860	641

1/ Based on whole weight of species with some exceptions, e.g. stone crabs, sponges.
2/ Includes clams, conch, crabs, lobster, octopus, oysters, scallops, shrimp, sponges, and squid.
3/ Only successful trips of fishermen.
4/ Landings from seafood dealers residing in inland counties or out-of-state who bought Florida produced seafood.
Note: Landings are recorded in county where products first crossed the shore. Data are preliminary.

Source: State of Florida, Department of Natural Resources, Marine Fisheries Information System, unpublished data.

Table 10.60. MINERAL INDUSTRIES: ESTABLISHMENTS, EMPLOYMENT, PAYROLL, VALUE ADDED BY MINING, AND CAPITAL EXPENDITURE BY INDUSTRY IN FLORIDA, CENSUS YEARS 1997

NAICS Code	Industry	Number of establishments Total	Number of establishments With 20 employees or more	All employees Number (1,000)	All employees Payroll 1/ (million dollars)	Value added by mining (thousand dollars)	Capital expenditure (million dollars)
21	Mining	225	55	6,688	248,626	1,008,554	202.2
211	Oil and gas extraction	27	1	138	5,411	135,739	39.3
212	Mining (except oil and gas)	148	51	6,296	236,209	857,874	160.8
21231	Some mining and quarrying	54	25	1,635	52,583	169,026	21.7
213	Support activities for mining	50	3	254	7,006	14,941	2.1

1/ For pay period including March 12. Industries with 100 employees or more are shown.
Note: The mining industries census is on a 5-year cycle collecting data for years ending in 2 and 7. Data are for the North American Industry Classification System (NAICS) and are not comparable to previous Standard Industrial Classification System (SIC) data. See Glossary for definitions.

Table 10.61. MINERAL INDUSTRIES: CHARACTERISTICS OF MINERAL INDUSTRIES IN FLORIDA, 1997

(in thousands of dollars, except where indicated)

Item	1997
Companies 1/	188
Establishments during year (number)	225
0-19 employees	170
20-99 employees	39
100 employees or more	16
Employees for pay periods including March 12 (number)	6,688
Annual payroll	248,626
Annual fringe benefits included in payroll	65,738
Production, development, and exploration workers (number)	5,424
Annual wages	185,773
Cost of supplies	631,487
Quantity of electricity purchased (1,000 kWh)	2,971,537
Cost of purchased communication services	3,528
Value of shipments and receipts	1,437,805
Value added by mining	1,008,554
Inventories, end of 1996	184,139
Inventories, end of 1997	205,971
Capital expenditure (except land an mineral rights)	202,236
For land and mineral rights 2/	7,420
Rental payments during year	35,754

kWh Kilowatt hour.
1/ A business organization consisting of one or more establishments under common ownership or control.
2/ Excludes mining service industries and natural gas liquids industries where data were not collected.
Note: The mining industries census is on a 5-year cycle collecting data for years ending in 2 and 7. Data are for the North American Industry Classification System (NAICS) and are not comparable to previous Standard Industrial Classification System (SIC) data. See Glossary for definitions.

Source for Tables 10.60 and 10.61: U.S., Department of Commerce, Bureau of the Census, *1997 Economic Census: Mining,* Geographic Area Series EC97N21A-FL, Issued April 2000, Internet site <http://www.census.gov/prod/ec97/97n21-fl.pdf> (accessed 26 June 2000).

University of Florida   **Bureau of Economic and Business Research**

Table 10.71. NONFUEL MINERAL PRODUCTION: QUANTITY AND VALUE IN FLORIDA
1996 THROUGH 1998

(quantity in thousand metric tons; value in millions of dollars)

	1996		1997		1998	
Mineral	Quan- tity	Value	Quan- tity	Value	Quan- tity	Value
Total	(X)	1,760.0	(X)	1,830.0	(X)	1,960.0
Cement: Masonry	422	35.0	406	36.2	413	38.1
Portland	3,450	245.0	3,750	274.0	3,880	190.0
Clays 1/	412	62.6	(D)	(D)	(D)	(D)
Gemstones	(NA)	A/	(NA)	A/	(NA)	A/
Peat	298	6.0	361	5.7	263	7.2
Sand and gravel: Construction	18,500	68.8	19,200	75.5	20,100	81.2
Industrial	515	6.3	507	5.8	536	6.2
Stone (crushed) 2/	73,600	394.0	73,800	396.0	81,700	449.0
Combined value 3/	(X)	947.0	(X)	1,040.0	(X)	1,090.0

(X) Not applicable.   (NA) Not available.
(D) Data withheld to avoid disclosure of information about individual companies.
A/ Less than $500,000.   1/ Includes Fuller's earth and Kaolin clays.
2/ Excludes certain stones; included with "Combined value."
3/ Includes minerals not listed separately and values indicated by symbol (D).
Note: Production as measured by mine shipments, sales, or marketable production (including con-
sumption by producers). Some data are estimated. 1998 data are preliminary.
Source: U.S., Department of the Interior, U.S. Geological Survey, *The Minerals Yearbook, Volume II:
Area Reports, Domestic, 1998*, Internet site <http://minerals.usgs.gov/minerals/pubs/state/981299.pdf>
(accessed 23 June 2000).

Table 10.72. MINING: AVERAGE MONTHLY PRIVATE REPORTING UNITS, EMPLOYMENT
AND PAYROLL COVERED BY UNEMPLOYMENT COMPENSATION LAW
BY INDUSTRY IN FLORIDA, 1999

SIC code	Industry	Number of re- porting units	Number of em- ployees	Payroll ($1,000)
	Mining	213	5,983	20,716
13	Oil and gas extraction	69	336	1,379
131	Crude petroleum and natural gas	16	135	643
138	Oil and gas fields services	53	201	736
14	Nonmetallic minerals, except fuels	144	5,647	19,337
141	Dimension stone	5	71	154
142	Crushed and broken stone, including riprap	37	1,598	5,267
144	Sand and gravel	47	699	1,936
145	Clay, ceramic, and refractory minerals	4	215	706
147	Chemical and fertilizer mineral mining	16	2,631	10,041
148	Nonmetallic minerals services, except fuels	4	16	29
149	Miscellaneous nonmetallic minerals, except fuels	33	417	1,206

Note: Private employment. Data are preliminary. Detail may not add to totals due to disclosure
editing and/or rounding. See Tables 23.70, 23.71, 23.72, 23.73, and 23.74 for public employment data.
Source: State of Florida, Department of Labor and Employment Security, Bureau of Labor Market
Information, "Employment and Wages" (ES-202), unpublished data.

University of Florida   **Bureau of Economic and Business Research**

CONSTRUCTION

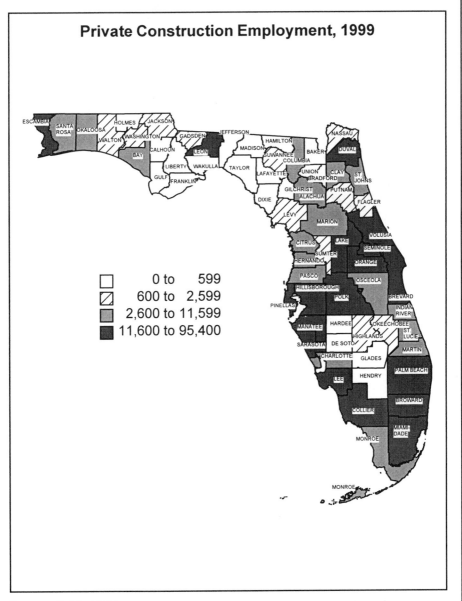

Private Construction Employment, 1999

Legend:
- 0 to 599
- 600 to 2,599
- 2,600 to 11,599
- 11,600 to 95,400

Source: Table 11.21

SECTION 11.00
CONSTRUCTION

TABLES LISTED BY MAJOR HEADINGS

Table 11.01. CONSTRUCTION: ESTABLISHMENTS, EMPLOYMENT, AND PAYROLL
IN FLORIDA, 1997

NAICS code	Industry	Number of estab-lishments	Number of employees 1/ All	Construc-tion workers (percent-age)	Payroll ($1,000) All	Construc-tion workers (percent-age)
23	Construction	36,608	324,844	72.3	8,802,536	62.2
233	Building, developing, and general contracting	10130	77238	54.0	2389503	41.6
2331	Land subdivision and land development	698	4,733	22.9	156,657	A/
2332	Residential building construction	7,223	43,009	51.1	1,254,514	39.1
2333	Nonresidential building construction	2,209	29,496	63.3	978,332	49.1
234	Heavy construction	2,028	45,084	80.4	1,319,444	71.9
2341	Highway, street, bridge, and tunnel construction	406	17,167	80.4	512,337	71.5
2349	Other heavy construction	1,622	27,917	80.3	807,107	72.2
235	Special trade contractors	24,450	202,522	77.5	5,093,589	69.3
2351	Plumbing, heating, and air-conditioning contractors	4,803	44,510	74.1	1,210,184	66.8
2352	Painting and wall covering contractors	2,283	11,697	77.7	234,117	67.8
2353	Electrical contractors	3,775	40,728	79.3	1,072,319	72.6
2354	Masonry, drywall, insulation, and tile contractors	3,389	29,330	84.6	693,693	76.4
2355	Carpentry and floor contractors	2,796	12,625	74.0	279,960	64.9
2356	Roofing, siding, and sheet metal contractors	1,944	16,766	74.3	392,397	62.3
2357	Concrete contractors	1,773	15,250	84.3	354,810	74.3
2358	Water well drilling contractors	251	1,820	70.6	52,411	62.7
2359	Other special trade contractors	3,436	29,797	73.1	803,697	66.1

A/ Sampling error exceeds 40 percent.
1/ Paid employment for the pay period including March 12.
Note: The economic censuses are conducted on a 5-year cycle collecting data for years ending in 2 and 7. Data are for North American Classification System (NAICS) code 23 and may not be comparable to earlier years. See Glossary for definition.

Source: U.S., Department of Commerce, Bureau of the Census, *1997 Economic Census: Construction,* Geographic Area Series EC97C23A-FL, Issued March 2000, Internet site <http://www.census.gov/prod/ec97/97c23-fl.pdf> (accessed 26 June 2000).

Table 11.03. HOUSING STARTS: NEW PRIVATELY-OWNED HOUSING UNITS STARTED IN
FLORIDA AND THE UNITED STATES, 1992 THROUGH 1999

(in thousands)

Year	Florida	United States	Year	Florida	United States
1992	106.1	1,201.0	1997	135.0	1,476.0
1993	115.1	1,199.0	1998	149.8	1,623.0
1994	131.0	1,457.0	1999 A/		
1995	123.4	1,354.0	Total units	152.6	1,631.0
1996	129.1	1,469.0	Single-family units	110.0	1,286.0

A/ Estimates.
Source: U.S., Department of Commerce, Bureau of the Census, *Statistical Abstract of the United States,*
1999, and previous editions.

Table 11.04. BUILDING PERMIT ACTIVITY: PRIVATE RESIDENTIAL HOUSING UNITS AUTHORIZED
BY BUILDING PERMITS IN FLORIDA, OTHER SUNBELT STATES, OTHER POPULOUS
STATES, AND THE UNITED STATES, 1996 THROUGH 1999

State	1996	1997	1998	1999
Florida	124,318	133,990	148,603	164,722
Other sunbelt states				
Alabama 1/	20,475	17,732	20,533	19,029
Arizona	53,977	57,762	63,930	65,109
Arkansas 1/	11,818	11,026	10,021	11,502
California	91,909	109,589	124,035	138,039
Georgia	79,703	75,123	85,401	89,581
Louisiana	16,177	15,144	16,483	17,836
Mississippi 1/	10,409	10,079	12,879	12,871
New Mexico	10,565	10,265	10,312	9,716
North Carolina	66,713	73,015	80,514	84,754
Oklahoma 1/	10,201	11,201	14,389	14,182
South Carolina	29,016	30,072	33,576	36,161
Tennessee 1/	45,852	34,054	34,126	37,034
Texas 1/	116,541	125,974	156,729	146,564
Virginia	45,976	45,523	50,204	53,151
Other populous states				
Illinois	50,000	46,323	47,984	53,974
Indiana	39,145	35,241	40,709	41,469
Massachusetts	17,163	17,186	19,254	18,967
Michigan	51,523	49,237	54,474	54,257
New Jersey	24,564	28,018	31,345	31,976
New York	35,988	32,881	38,420	42,593
Ohio 1/	49,223	46,487	48,034	55,880
Pennsylvania	37,211	39,877	41,616	42,662
United States	1,433,670	1,441,136	1,612,260	1,663,533

1/ Percentage of population in permit-issuing places is less than 90.
Note: Data are from a national sample of 19,000 permit-issuing places, a universe which accounts for
approximately 92 percent of new residential construction. Some data may be revised. See also Table
24.20.

Source: U.S., Department of Commerce, Bureau of the Census, *Housing Units Authorized by Building
Permits*, Series C-40, Internet site <http://www.census.gov/const/www.C40/table2.html> (accessed
8 May 2000).

University of Florida   **Bureau of Economic and Business Research**

Table 11.05. CONSTRUCTION ACTIVITY: SINGLE- AND MULTIFAMILY HOUSING UNITS PERMITTED AND CONSTRUCTION STARTS IN THE STATE AND COUNTIES OF FLORIDA, 1997, 1998, AND 1999

| County | Single-family housing units | | | | | | Multifamily housing units | | | | | |
| | Permitted | | | Construction starts | | | Permitted | | | Construction starts | | |
	1997	1998 A/	1999 A/	1997	1998 A/	1999 A/	1997	1998 A/	1999 A/	1997	1998 A/	1999 A/
Florida	90,390	97,584	104,666	90,627	97,426	102,753	43,482	48,172	56,831	40,177	37,922	45,283
Alachua	1,059	1,091	1,182	1,046	1,087	1,166	606	1,013	1,963	654	772	1,326
Baker	81	84	95	72	80	91	4	8	2	2	5	1
Bay	932	1,101	856	931	1,069	891	630	476	186	529	294	255
Bradford	61	56	62	56	52	56	2	0	0	1	0	0
Brevard	2,984	3,320	3,352	2,974	3,335	3,305	380	691	1,028	385	522	823
Broward	7,492	8,904	8,470	7,634	8,872	8,348	5,487	3,678	3,692	5,585	2,951	3,318
Calhoun	29	16	23	28	15	20	0	0	0	0	0	0
Charlotte	1,096	1,244	1,257	1,077	1,239	1,242	59	299	258	72	209	164
Citrus	1,039	1,084	1,135	1,046	1,078	1,122	16	9	18	12	5	6
Clay	1,208	1,293	1,493	1,224	1,289	1,470	2	16	6	1	11	4
Collier	2,811	2,807	3,692	2,795	2,857	3,526	3,353	4,024	3,748	2,954	3,077	3,107
Columbia	279	244	278	271	241	264	10	8	0	6	8	0
De Soto	103	95	78	99	88	72	90	74	170	75	59	64
Dixie	30	40	34	26	37	31	0	0	0	0	0	0
Duval	3,668	4,025	3,898	3,675	4,020	3,839	1,298	1,274	2,062	1,676	941	1,558
Escambia	1,635	1,614	1,587	1,682	1,599	1,591	453	518	313	605	476	260
Flagler	1,054	1,173	1,233	1,051	1,176	1,223	11	30	64	10	20	46
Franklin	75	83	89	72	77	82	0	2	0	0	1	0
Gadsden	118	122	101	115	112	93	0	0	0	0	0	0
Gilchrist	62	66	63	57	60	58	0	0	0	0	0	0
Glades	33	25	29	29	23	27	0	0	0	0	0	0

See footnotes at end of table.

Continued . . .

Table 11.05. CONSTRUCTION ACTIVITY: SINGLE- AND MULTIFAMILY HOUSING UNITS PERMITTED AND CONSTRUCTION STARTS IN THE STATE AND COUNTIES OF FLORIDA, 1997, 1998, AND 1999 (Continued)

County	Single-family housing units						Multifamily housing units					
	Permitted			Construction starts			Permitted			Construction starts		
	1997	1998 A/	1999 A/	1997	1998 A/	1999 A/	1997	1998 A/	1999 A/	1997	1998 A/	1999 A/
Gulf	95	114	127	89	109	121	0	0	0	0	0	0
Hamilton	27	30	33	27	27	31	0	0	0	0	0	0
Hardee	35	34	40	33	35	36	0	0	0	0	0	0
Hendry	61	50	44	59	43	40	2	4	0	2	1	1
Hernando	1,210	973	1,244	1,235	973	1,212	46	53	37	35	37	24
Highlands	521	509	639	515	507	622	82	66	26	68	42	20
Hillsborough	5,410	5,908	7,028	5,350	5,930	6,880	3,659	5,144	7,504	3,019	3,607	6,676
Holmes	45	49	62	43	42	60	0	0	0	0	0	0
Indian River	909	981	1,060	903	980	1,038	163	78	468	174	63	283
Jackson	110	118	117	105	108	110	0	6	4	12	6	1
Jefferson	38	82	72	39	76	69	0	0	0	0	0	0
Lafayette	22	29	25	21	26	24	0	0	0	0	0	0
Lake	2,770	2,934	3,333	2,761	2,935	3,257	91	77	385	87	56	256
Lee	3,534	3,982	4,690	3,541	3,975	4,607	2,359	4,050	4,265	2,181	3,269	3,183
Leon	1,161	942	1,168	1,198	938	1,130	723	519	685	579	611	477
Levy	151	150	153	139	143	143	6	18	0	3	11	2
Liberty	10	9	12	9	10	10	0	0	0	0	0	0
Madison	101	87	68	95	79	66	0	0	0	0	0	0
Manatee	2,074	2,388	2,614	2,058	2,383	2,567	589	450	231	417	485	204
Marion	2,395	2,629	2,618	2,358	2,671	2,575	803	53	163	715	83	95
Martin	905	987	1,045	921	993	1,038	620	433	59	577	390	48
Miami-Dade	5,150	5,052	6,166	5,323	5,089	6,041	4,592	5,126	6,672	4,465	4,042	5,683
Monroe	364	419	465	386	416	445	156	83	51	114	52	60
Nassau	471	542	554	467	534	543	22	106	106	28	71	82

See footnotes at end of table.

Continued . . .

Table 11.05. CONSTRUCTION ACTIVITY: SINGLE- AND MULTIFAMILY HOUSING UNITS PERMITTED AND CONSTRUCTION STARTS IN THE STATE AND COUNTIES OF FLORIDA, 1997, 1998, AND 1999 (Continued)

County	Single-family housing units						Multifamily housing units					
	Permitted			Construction starts			Permitted			Construction starts		
	1997	1998 A/	1999 A/	1997	1998 A/	1999 A/	1997	1998 A/	1999 A/	1997	1998 A/	1999 A/
Okaloosa	1,496	1,560	1,411	1,541	1,537	1,410	575	939	754	525	769	529
Okeechobee	129	127	134	121	120	124	0	2	0	1	0	2
Orange	5,787	6,727	6,868	5,803	6,647	6,815	5,645	7,078	7,942	5,106	5,371	6,457
Osceola	2,995	2,635	2,998	2,892	2,724	2,914	1,184	948	1,540	801	916	909
Palm Beach	6,192	6,152	6,436	6,315	6,145	6,320	2,793	3,351	3,548	2,513	2,530	2,816
Pasco	2,273	2,584	3,117	2,262	2,582	3,061	302	620	709	266	456	512
Pinellas	1,856	1,981	1,830	1,886	1,977	1,795	2,234	1,244	1,400	1,883	1,122	982
Polk	2,645	2,871	2,940	2,620	2,884	2,877	717	426	1,053	535	304	945
Putnam	132	145	160	126	138	154	2	0	60	0	0	52
St. Johns	1,614	1,780	1,925	1,615	1,773	1,894	273	205	369	226	181	272
St. Lucie	1,380	1,456	1,672	1,399	1,461	1,622	171	657	639	226	548	300
Santa Rosa	1,205	1,116	965	1,223	1,115	969	20	80	23	28	63	16
Sarasota	2,383	2,727	2,814	2,375	2,711	2,788	1,233	1,865	1,187	1,219	1,519	930
Seminole	2,142	2,725	2,808	2,146	2,692	2,799	765	1,803	2,104	592	1,499	1,635
Sumter	1,301	1,233	1,573	1,272	1,226	1,534	4	0	2	4	1	1
Suwannee	119	119	111	108	111	100	0	0	0	0	0	0
Taylor	55	53	69	53	49	63	0	0	0	0	0	0
Union	36	34	41	32	31	35	0	0	0	0	0	0
Volusia	2,297	3,102	3,262	2,290	3,108	3,190	189	149	599	267	114	351
Wakulla	208	227	220	198	217	208	2	24	10	2	15	5
Walton	632	649	833	621	658	815	1,059	369	721	940	318	536
Washington	95	96	95	94	92	84	0	26	5	0	19	7

A/ Preliminary.
Note: Permit data compiled by BEBR based on data from the U.S. Bureau of the Census.

Source: University of Florida, Bureau of Economic and Business Research (BEBR), unpublished data.

Table 11.15. BUILDING PERMIT ACTIVITY: VALUE REPORTED ON BUILDING PERMITS AND NEW HOUSING UNITS AUTHORIZED BY BUILDING PERMITS IN THE STATE, COUNTIES, MUNICIPALITIES, AND UNINCORPORATED AREAS OF FLORIDA, 1999

Area 1/	Number of months reported	Total residential value ($1,000)	Number of housekeeping units 2/ Single-family	Number of housekeeping units 2/ Multi-family
Florida	(X)	16,114,166	106,253	58,126
Alachua	(X)	181,649	1,179	1,549
Alachua	12	7,546	95	0
Archer	12	0	0	0
Gainesville	12	19,306	190	62
Hawthorne	12	532	8	0
High Springs	12	2,598	43	0
Micanopy	12	432	6	0
Newberry	12	2,799	35	0
Waldo	12	0	0	0
County office	12	148,436	802	1,487
Baker	(X)	6,196	95	2
MacClenny	12	1,493	29	0
County office	12	4,703	66	2
Bay	(X)	98,589	858	186
Lynn Haven	12	18,871	168	0
Panama City Beach	12	18,493	122	68
County office	12	61,225	568	118
Bradford	(X)	3,974	62	0
County office	(X)	3,974	62	0
Brevard	(X)	496,716	3,381	1,278
Cape Canaveral	12	17,816	15	104
Cocoa	12	3,292	7	50
Cocoa Beach	12	7,434	11	56
Indialantic	12	1,963	7	15
Indian Harbour Beach	12	21,227	47	116
Malabar	12	2,443	18	0
Melbourne	12	60,096	415	309
Brevard (Continued)				
Melbourne Beach	12	1,418	7	0
Melbourne Village	12	0	0	0
Palm Bay	12	74,328	559	304
Palm Shores	12	1,115	9	0
Rockledge	12	32,683	260	0
Satellite Beach	12	4,915	27	13
Titusville	12	9,199	73	5
West Melbourne	12	18,965	110	0
County office	12	239,822	1,816	306
Broward	(X)	1,409,810	8,574	3,439
Coconut Creek	12	48,095	361	272
Cooper City	12	9,820	64	0
Coral Springs	12	145,881	1,070	132
Dania	12	778	8	0
Davie	12	81,303	735	0
Deerfield Beach	12	29,517	331	0
Ft. Lauderdale	12	203,760	117	1,174
Hallandale	12	2,384	16	18
Hillsboro Beach	12	3,108	1	0
Hollywood	12	24,122	175	96
Lauderdale Lakes	12	0	0	0
Lauderhill	12	3,242	30	0
Lighthouse Point	12	12,513	36	23
Margate	12	7,754	48	44
Miramar	12	214,187	1,851	228
North Lauderdale	12	0	0	0
Oakland Park	12	24,587	49	312
Parkland	12	82,258	319	0

Continued . . . .

See footnotes at end of table.

Table 11.15. BUILDING PERMIT ACTIVITY: VALUE REPORTED ON BUILDING PERMITS AND NEW HOUSING UNITS AUTHORIZED BY BUILDING PERMITS IN THE STATE, COUNTIES, MUNICIPALITIES, AND UNINCORPORATED AREAS OF FLORIDA, 1999 (Continued)

Area 1/	Number of months reported	Total residential value ($1,000)	Number of housekeeping units 2/ Single-family	Number of housekeeping units 2/ Multi-family
Broward (Continued)				
Pembroke Park	12	0	0	0
Pembroke Pines	12	177,003	1,181	743
Plantation	12	29,611	136	0
Pompano Beach	12	3,921	45	4
Sea Ranch Lakes Village	12	350	1	0
Sunrise	12	29,904	397	0
Tamarac	12	16,953	9	266
Weston	12	239,197	1,482	74
Wilton Manors	12	0	0	0
County office	(X)	19,562	112	53
Calhoun	12	1,350	22	0
Blountstown	12	0	0	0
County office	12	1,350	22	0
Charlotte	(X)	149,417	1,197	221
Punta Gorda	12	42,114	325	51
County office	12	107,303	872	170
Citrus	(X)	70,737	1,136	36
Crystal River	12	1,332	6	0
Inverness	12	2,579	30	36
County office	12	66,826	1,100	0
Clay	(X)	154,885	1,518	4
Green Cove Springs	12	9,289	77	0
Orange Park	12	6,796	83	0
Penney Farms	12	193	3	0
County office	12	138,607	1,355	4
Collier	(X)	931,570	3,765	3,777
Everglades	12	250	4	0
Marco Island	12	71,506	338	51
Collier (Continued)				
Naples	12	129,598	117	196
County office	12	730,216	3,306	3,530
Columbia	(X)	17,083	279	0
Lake City	12	1,827	28	0
County office	12	15,256	251	0
De Soto	(X)	15,186	85	153
County office	12	15,186	85	153
Dixie	(X)	2,197	33	0
Horseshoe Beach	12	204	2	0
County office	12	1,993	31	0
Duval	(X)	581,096	4,067	2,344
Atlantic Beach	12	7,996	42	46
Baldwin	12	225	3	0
Jacksonville 3/	12	549,435	3,878	2,278
Jacksonville Beach	12	22,685	139	18
Neptune Beach	12	755	5	2
Escambia	(X)	191,849	1,587	313
Pensacola	12	12,775	102	14
County office	12	179,074	1,485	299
Flagler	(X)	97,919	1,341	65
Beverly Beach	12	NA	NA	NA
Bunnell	12	88	1	0
Flagler Beach	12	8,023	58	54
Marineland	12	0	0	0
County office	12	89,808	1,282	11
Franklin	(X)	18,061	103	0
Apalachicola	12	534	8	0
County office	12	17,527	95	0

See footnotes at end of table.

Continued . . .

Table 11.15. BUILDING PERMIT ACTIVITY: VALUE REPORTED ON BUILDING PERMITS AND NEW HOUSING UNITS AUTHORIZED BY BUILDING PERMITS IN THE STATE, COUNTIES, MUNICIPALITIES, AND UNINCORPORATED AREAS OF FLORIDA, 1999 (Continued)

Area 1/	Number of months reported	Total residential value ($1,000)	Number of housekeeping units 2/ Single-family	Multi-family
Gadsden	(X)	11,824	100	0
Quincy	12	1,114	17	0
County office	12	10,710	83	0
Gilchrist	(X)	5,612	66	0
County office	12	5,612	66	0
Glades	(X)	2,444	29	0
Moore Haven	12	NA	NA	NA
County office	12	2,444	29	0
Gulf	(X)	13,398	127	0
County office	12	13,398	127	0
Hamilton	(X)	2,353	29	0
County office	12	2,353	29	0
Hardee	(X)	3,700	38	0
Wauchula	12	261	5	0
County office	12	3,439	33	0
Hendry	(X)	4,042	43	2
Clewiston	12	620	6	2
La Belle	12	311	4	0
County office	12	3,111	33	0
Hernando	(X)	111,943	1,217	37
Brooksville	12	8,461	101	0
Weeki Wachee	12	0	0	0
County office	12	103,482	1,116	37
Highlands	(X)	55,379	641	26
Avon Park	4	826	11	0
Sebring	12	7,939	159	0
County office	12	46,614	471	26
Hillsborough	(X)	1,094,231	7,152	7,513
Plant City	12	38,892	231	568
Hillsborough (Continued)				
Tampa	12	247,109	1,247	1,911
Temple Terrace	12	7,467	12	180
County office	12	800,763	5,662	4,854
Holmes	(X)	5,215	62	0
County office	12	5,215	62	0
Indian River	(X)	253,202	1,103	215
Fellsmere	12	953	15	0
Indian River Shores	12	47,941	51	18
Orchid	12	26,122	47	0
Sebastian	12	24,778	259	10
Vero Beach	12	12,019	26	26
County office	12	141,389	705	161
Jackson	(X)	9,259	136	0
County office	12	9,259	136	0
Jefferson	(X)	6,986	72	0
County office	12	6,986	72	0
Lafayette	(X)	2,230	25	0
Mayo 4/	9	139	1	0
County office	(X)	2,091	24	0
Lake	(X)	326,041	3,485	661
Eustis	12	9,114	96	0
Fruitland Park	12	1,292	14	0
Groveland	4	2,588	29	0
Lady Lake	12	11,730	77	12
Leesburg	12	3,673	27	25
Mascotte	12	2,242	38	0
Mount Dora	12	30,816	107	460
Tavares	12	10,249	103	24

See footnotes at end of table.

Continued . . .

Table 11.15. BUILDING PERMIT ACTIVITY: VALUE REPORTED ON BUILDING PERMITS AND NEW HOUSING UNITS AUTHORIZED BY BUILDING PERMITS IN THE STATE, COUNTIES, MUNICIPALITIES, AND UNINCORPORATED AREAS OF FLORIDA, 1999 (Continued)

Area 1/	Number of months reported	Total residential value ($1,000)	Number of housekeeping units 2/ Single-family	Number of housekeeping units 2/ Multi-family
Lake (Continued)				
Umatilla	12	823	9	0
County office	12	253,514	2,985	140
Lee	(X)	1,021,860	4,722	4,094
Cape Coral	12	147,969	1,719	288
Ft. Myers	12	58,880	120	772
Sanibel	12	24,819	74	12
County office	12	790,192	2,809	3,022
Leon	(X)	172,939	1,184	685
Tallahassee	12	118,868	773	685
County office	12	54,071	411	0
Levy	(X)	15,743	155	0
Cedar Key	12	1,115	6	0
Chiefland	12	140	1	0
Fanning Springs	12	427	6	0
Williston	12	305	6	0
County office	12	13,756	136	0
Liberty	(X)	1,207	12	0
County office	12	1,207	12	0
Madison	(X)	4,640	63	0
Madison	12	420	12	0
County office	12	4,220	51	0
Manatee	(X)	330,520	2,625	238
Anna Maria	12	2,323	12	0
Bradenton	12	3,587	50	24
Bradenton Beach	12	3,402	27	8
Holmes Beach	12	1,426	9	2
Palmetto	12	3,289	70	0
County office	12	316,493	2,457	204

Area 1/	Number of months reported	Total residential value ($1,000)	Number of housekeeping units 2/ Single-family	Number of housekeeping units 2/ Multi-family
Marion	(X)	273,829	2,593	166
Belleview	12	725	12	0
Dunellon	6	586	6	0
McIntosh	12	0	0	0
Ocala	12	23,692	153	133
County office	12	248,826	2,422	33
Martin	(X)	228,252	1,055	59
Jupiter Island	12	2,933	5	0
Ocean Breeze Park	12	0	0	0
Sewall's Point	12	9,366	32	0
Stuart	12	7,058	44	0
County office	12	208,895	974	59
Miami-Dade	(X)	1,078,640	6,671	7,090
Aventura	12	48,621	44	885
Bal Harbour	12	0	0	0
Bay Harbor Islands	12	2,372	1	9
Biscayne Park	12	0	0	0
Coral Gables	12	18,271	37	0
El Portal	12	137	1	0
Florida City	12	1,052	14	0
Golden Beach	12	766	2	0
Hialeah	12	17,840	57	225
Hialeah Gardens	12	18,947	74	184
Homestead	12	3,781	62	0
Indian Creek Village	12	0	0	0
Islandia	12	0	0	0
Key Biscayne	(NA)	(NA)	(NA)	(NA)
Medley	12	0	0	0
Miami	12	164,595	50	1,522

Continued . . .

See footnotes at end of table.

Table 11.15. BUILDING PERMIT ACTIVITY: VALUE REPORTED ON BUILDING PERMITS AND NEW HOUSING UNITS AUTHORIZED BY BUILDING PERMITS IN THE STATE, COUNTIES, MUNICIPALITIES, AND UNINCORPORATED AREAS OF FLORIDA, 1999 (Continued)

Area 1/	Number of months reported	Total residential value ($1,000)	Number of housekeeping units 2/ Single-family	Multi-family
Miami-Dade (Continued)				
Miami Beach	12	27,348	8	469
Miami Shores	12	0	0	0
Miami Springs	12	0	0	0
North Bay Village	12	130	1	0
North Miami	12	0	0	0
North Miami Beach	12	1,934	5	4
Opa-Locka	12	0	0	0
Pine Crest	12	6,413	29	0
South Miami	12	3,189	15	0
Surfside	12	182	2	0
Sweetwater	12	1,827	20	2
Virginia Gardens	12	298	2	2
County office	12	760,937	6,247	3,790
Monroe	(X)	47,642	391	16
Islamorada	12	5,015	23	4
Key Colony Beach	12	4,816	25	0
Key West	12	12,456	114	12
Layton	12	494	3	0
County office	12	24,861	226	0
Nassau	12	69,137	549	102
Callahan	12	0	0	0
Fernandina Beach	12	19,820	131	16
Hilliard	12	1,329	20	0
County office	12	47,988	398	86
Okaloosa	12	187,694	1,392	415
Crestview	12	14,003	191	0
Destin	12	72,878	188	188
Ft. Walton Beach	12	2,456	22	2
Mary Esther	12	285	1	0
Niceville	12	9,866	68	42
Okaloosa (Continued)				
Valparaiso	12	1,549	8	2
County office	12	86,657	914	181
Okeechobee	(X)	11,944	143	0
Okeechobee	12	1,667	16	0
County office	12	10,277	127	0
Orange	(X)	1,164,948	6,965	8,535
Apopka	12	35,679	453	73
Bay Lake	12	0	0	0
Eatonville	12	70	0	0
Edgewood	12	2,665	10	2
Lake Buena Vista	12	0	0	0
Maitland	12	4,040	14	10
Ocoee	12	44,482	272	282
Orlando	12	176,988	430	2,459
Winter Garden	12	41,175	257	0
Winter Park	12	14,636	50	11
County office	12	845,213	5,479	5,698
Osceola	(X)	441,144	3,042	1,675
Kissimmee	12	57,302	536	72
St. Cloud	12	21,304	234	79
County office	12	362,538	2,272	1,524
Palm Beach	(X)	1,123,178	6,417	3,587
Atlantis	12	2,800	29	0
Belle Glade	12	850	7	13
Boca Raton	12	84,204	151	82
Boynton Beach	12	40,990	175	388
Briny Breezes	12	0	0	0
Cloud Lake	12	0	0	0
Delray Beach	12	39,312	307	128
Glen Ridge	12	160	1	0

See footnotes at end of table.

Continued . . .

Table 11.15. BUILDING PERMIT ACTIVITY: VALUE REPORTED ON BUILDING PERMITS AND NEW HOUSING UNITS AUTHORIZED BY BUILDING PERMITS IN THE STATE, COUNTIES, MUNICIPALITIES, AND UNINCORPORATED AREAS OF FLORIDA, 1999 (Continued)

Area 1/	Number of months reported	Total residential value ($1,000)	Number of housekeeping units 2/ Single-family	Multi-family
Palm Beach (Continued)				
Golf Village	12	0	0	0
Golfview	(NA)	(NA)	(NA)	(NA)
Greenacres	12	18,871	197	164
Haverhill	12	2,936	28	0
Highland Beach	12	8,125	17	4
Hypoluxo	12	0	0	0
Jupiter	12	1,666	3	0
Jupiter Inlet Colony	12	123,834	653	0
Lake Clarke Shores	12	442	4	0
Lake Park	12	0	0	0
Lake Worth	12	1,037	10	0
Lantana	12	2,950	6	0
Manalapan	12	3,585	3	0
Mangonia Park	12	0	0	0
North Palm Beach	12	6,841	36	4
Pahokee	12	1,565	28	0
Palm Beach	12	56,245	192	43
Palm Beach Gardens	12	11,188	2	70
Palm Beach Shores	12	38,788	26	7
Palm Springs	12	2,922	9	36
Riviera Beach	12	22,658	75	408
Royal Palm Beach	12	36,449	217	290
South Bay	12	140	2	0
South Palm Beach	12	0	0	0
Tequesta	12	10,146	8	84
Wellington	7	56,909	362	16
West Palm Beach	12	58,834	516	34
County office	12	488,731	3,353	1,816
Pasco	(X)	331,256	3,115	709
Dade City	12	723	9	0

Area 1/	Number of months reported	Total residential value ($1,000)	Number of housekeeping units 2/ Single-family	Multi-family
Pasco (Continued)				
New Port Richey	12	0	0	0
Port Richey	12	1,695	3	11
San Antonio	12	1,148	13	0
Zephyrhills	12	3,399	57	0
County office	(X)	324,291	3,033	698
Pinellas	(NA)	425,880	1,825	1,412
Belleair	12	10,595	19	0
Belleair Beach	(NA)	(NA)	(NA)	(NA)
Clearwater	12	14,695	43	204
Dunedin	12	12,494	102	3
Gulfport	12	5,257	16	0
Indian Rocks Beach	12	6,708	9	40
Indian Shores	12	155	0	3
Kenneth City	12	0	0	0
Largo	12	15,672	138	3
Madeira Beach 5/	5	160	1	0
North Redington Beach	12	8,027	21	36
Oldsmar	12	21,666	235	5
Pinellas Park	12	5,865	63	0
Redington Shores	12	240	2	0
Safety Harbor	12	9,144	53	41
Seminole	12	4,799	3	0
South Pasadena	12	0	0	0
St. Petersburg	12	7,171	9	61
St. Pete Beach	12	80,195	179	521
Tarpon Springs	12	26,462	198	0
Treasure Island	12	1,980	9	2
County office	12	194,595	725	493

See footnotes at end of table.

Continued . . .

Table 11.15. BUILDING PERMIT ACTIVITY: VALUE REPORTED ON BUILDING PERMITS AND NEW HOUSING UNITS AUTHORIZED BY BUILDING PERMITS IN THE STATE, COUNTIES, MUNICIPALITIES, AND UNINCORPORATED AREAS OF FLORIDA, 1999 (Continued)

Area 1/	Number of months reported	Total residential value ($1,000)	Number of housekeeping units 2/ Single-family	Multi-family
Polk	(X)	284,806	2,967	912
Auburndale	12	7,656	89	0
Bartow	12	4,379	48	0
Davenport	12	303	5	0
Dundee	12	792	15	0
Eagle Lake	12	196	4	0
Ft. Meade	12	743	11	0
Frostproof	12	60	1	0
Haines City	12	12,903	140	0
Lake Alfred	12	750	9	0
Lake Hamilton	12	2,183	15	0
Lake Wales	12	7,269	54	4
Lakeland	12	62,958	231	774
Mulberry	12	67	1	0
Polk City	12	78	1	0
Winter Haven	12	5,382	29	57
County office	12	179,087	2,314	77
Putnam	(X)	15,269	151	60
Palatka	12	3,620	14	60
Welaka	12	213	7	0
County office	12	11,436	130	0
St. Johns	(X)	411,309	1,918	1,102
St. Augustine	12	38,206	16	818
St. Augustine Beach	12	13,681	79	78
County office	12	359,422	1,823	206
St. Lucie	(X)	217,473	1,648	589
Ft. Pierce	12	26,461	70	337

Area 1/	Number of months reported	Total residential value ($1,000)	Number of housekeeping units 2/ Single-family	Multi-family
St. Lucie (Continued)				
Port St. Lucie	12	122,893	1,121	0
St. Lucie Village	12	436	4	0
County office	12	67,683	453	252
Santa Rosa	(X)	107,115	965	23
County office 6/	12	107,115	965	23
Sarasota	(X)	420,757	2,816	1,186
Longboat Key	12	15,203	40	0
North Port Charlotte	12	55,484	478	0
Sarasota	12	13,453	74	148
Venice	12	22,491	117	64
County office	12	314,126	2,107	974
Seminole	(X)	680,138	2,876	2,354
Altamonte Springs	12	16,899	23	392
Casselberry	12	9,397	58	0
Lake Mary	12	31,312	250	0
Longwood	12	4,533	35	0
Oviedo	12	88,481	414	0
Sanford	12	42,341	231	486
Winter Springs	12	108,149	408	602
County office	12	379,026	1,457	874
Sumter	(X)	77,299	1,574	2
Wildwood	12	786	12	0
County office	12	76,513	1,562	2
Suwannee	(X)	10,089	111	0
Live Oak	12	749	14	0
County office	12	9,340	97	0

Continued . . .

See footnotes at end of table.

Table 11.15. BUILDING PERMIT ACTIVITY: VALUE REPORTED ON BUILDING PERMITS AND NEW HOUSING UNITS AUTHORIZED BY BUILDING PERMITS IN THE STATE, COUNTIES, MUNICIPALITIES, AND UNINCORPORATED AREAS OF FLORIDA, 1999 (Continued)

Area 1/	Number of months reported	Total residential value ($1,000)	Number of housekeeping units 2/ Single-family	Number of housekeeping units 2/ Multi-family
Taylor	(X)	4,950	69	0
Perry	12	2,060	22	0
County office	12	2,890	47	0
Union	(X)	3,360	41	0
County office	12	3,360	41	0
Volusia	(X)	385,020	3,285	573
Daytona Beach	12	31,285	115	216
Daytona Beach Shores	12	1,458	15	0
DeLand	12	25,598	73	323
Deltona	12	57,838	691	2
Edgewater	12	17,895	175	2
Holly Hill	12	660	9	0
Lake Helen	12	825	11	0
New Smyrna Beach	12	17,666	120	24
Oak Hill	12	223	4	0
Volusia (Continued)				
Orange City	12	3,134	28	0
Ormond Beach	12	40,183	286	0
Pierson	12	114	2	0
Ponce Inlet	12	2,890	14	0
Port Orange	12	62,981	467	2
South Daytona	12	3,172	43	0
County office	12	119,098	1,232	4
Wakulla	(X)	25,825	379	0
County office	12	25,825	379	0
Walton	(X)	197,864	833	721
DeFuniak Springs	12	2,071	23	0
County office	12	195,793	810	721
Washington	(X)	6,296	94	0
County office	12	6,296	94	0

(X) Not applicable.
(NA) Not available.
1/ County office data includes permitting for unincorporated areas and occasionally may include incorporated areas in the same county not shown separately. The definition is more service-based than geographical.
2/ Excludes mobile homes.
3/ Includes unincorporated Duval County.
4/ Included in unincorporated area beginning October 1999.
5/ Included in unincorporated area beginning June 1999.
6/ Includes unincorporated Navarre Beach located entirely in Escambia County.
Note: Data are based on voluntary reports from local building officials processed by the Bureau of the Census by the 12th working day of the month. Data may also include estimates for nonreports. Value figures are estimated on a cost-per-foot basis by each jurisdiction and may not be comparable to other locations.

Source: University of Florida, Bureau of Economic and Business Research, *Building Permit Activity in Florida, Revised Annual 1999.*

Table 11.20. EMPLOYMENT AND PAYROLL: AVERAGE MONTHLY PRIVATE REPORTING UNITS EMPLOYMENT AND PAYROLL COVERED BY UNEMPLOYMENT COMPENSATION LAW BY CONSTRUCTION INDUSTRY IN FLORIDA, 1999

SIC code	Industry	Number of reporting units	Number of employees	Payroll ($1,000)
	Construction	40,325	365,128	910,987
15	Building--general contractors and operative builders	10,614	80,017	234,224
152	General building contractors--residential	8,981	53,125	144,779
153	Operative builders	118	1,617	5,572
154	General building contractors--nonresidential	1,516	25,276	83,873
16	Heavy construction other than building--contractors	2,111	47,773	129,930
161	Highway and street, except elevated highways	390	13,909	36,631
162	Heavy construction, except highway and street	1,722	33,864	93,299
17	Special trade contractors	27,600	237,337	546,834
171	Plumbing, heating, and air-conditioning	4,974	52,868	128,399
172	Painting and paper hanging	2,481	12,066	23,547
173	Electrical work	4,449	51,707	127,761
174	Masonry, stonework, tile setting, and plastering	3,750	31,403	68,209
175	Carpentry and floor work	3,135	14,841	30,028
176	Roofing, siding, and sheet metal work	2,051	17,644	36,008
177	Concrete work	2,043	20,481	44,010
178	Water well drilling	235	1,406	3,491
179	Miscellaneous special trade contractors	4,483	34,923	85,381

Note: Private employment. Detail may not add to totals due to disclosure editing and/or rounding. See Tables 23.70, 23.71, 23.72, 23.73, and 23.74 for public employment data.

Source: State of Florida, Department of Labor and Employment Security, Bureau of Labor Market Information, "Employment and Wages" (ES-202), unpublished data.

University of Florida   **Bureau of Economic and Business Research**

Table 11.21. EMPLOYMENT AND PAYROLL: AVERAGE MONTHLY PRIVATE REPORTING UNITS
EMPLOYMENT, AND PAYROLL COVERED BY UNEMPLOYMENT COMPENSATION LAW
IN THE STATE AND COUNTIES OF FLORIDA, 1999

County	Number of re-porting units	Number of em-ployees	Payroll ($1,000)	County	Number of re-porting units	Number of em-ployees	Payroll ($1,000)
			Construction (SIC codes 15-17)				
Florida	40,325	365,128	910,987	Lafayette	9	59	96
				Lake	501	5,050	11,767
Alachua	494	4,472	9,017	Lee	1,706	15,089	36,093
Baker	33	233	371	Leon	706	5,593	12,886
Bay	463	4,448	9,091	Levy	67	751	1,581
Bradford	37	206	355	Madison	22	68	80
Brevard	1,156	9,865	23,092	Manatee	692	5,122	12,832
Broward	3,897	36,077	95,360	Marion	638	5,462	11,139
Calhoun	25	228	491	Martin	493	4,024	10,103
Charlotte	419	2,572	5,702	Miami-Dade	3,808	34,322	89,886
Citrus	315	2,095	3,879	Monroe	385	2,355	5,376
Clay	361	2,231	4,852	Nassau	159	855	1,747
Collier	1,133	10,652	28,302	Okaloosa	555	4,153	8,089
Columbia	142	1,122	2,619	Okeechobee	88	462	767
De Soto	52	262	457	Orange	2,130	27,048	72,959
Dixie	15	80	137	Osceola	284	2,724	6,355
Duval	1,923	23,627	63,124	Palm Beach	3,194	26,855	73,200
Escambia	756	8,389	19,115	Pasco	805	5,321	10,394
Flagler	135	624	1,144	Pinellas	2,165	20,235	50,542
Franklin	23	108	169	Polk	1,007	9,805	24,173
Gadsden	64	555	997	Putnam	152	1,264	2,379
Gilchrist	24	43	62	St. Johns	302	2,005	4,357
Glades	12	43	88	St. Lucie	491	2,938	5,868
Gulf	23	60	83	Santa Rosa	350	2,402	4,594
Hamilton	21	137	197	Sarasota	1,411	9,331	21,737
Hardee	33	180	416	Seminole	1,021	12,512	33,543
Hendry	47	272	571	Sumter	70	441	961
Hernando	373	1,818	3,450	Suwannee	72	336	602
Highlands	190	974	1,719	Union	15	72	107
Hillsborough	2,212	27,338	75,528	Volusia	1,105	7,231	15,626
Holmes	33	178	318	Wakulla	51	264	458
Indian River	390	2,678	5,781	Walton	107	501	890
Jackson	60	545	828	Washington	40	436	892
Jefferson	25	138	223	Multicounty 1/	806	7,186	19,751

1/ Reporting units without a fixed location within the state or of unknown county location.
   Note: Construction includes general contractors and operative builders (SIC code 15), heavy construction contractors (SIC code 16), and special trade contractors (SIC code 17). Private employment.
Data are preliminary. Only counties for which data are disclosed are shown. Detail may not add to
totals due to disclosure editing and/or rounding. See Tables 23.70, 23.71, 23.72, 23.73, and 23.74
for public employment data.

   Source: State of Florida, Department of Labor and Employment Security, Bureau of Labor Market
Information, "Employment and Wages" (ES-202), unpublished data.

University of Florida   **Bureau of Economic and Business Research**

Table 11.22. BUILDING MATERIALS, HARDWARE, GARDEN SUPPLY, AND MOBILE HOME DEALERS
AVERAGE MONTHLY PRIVATE REPORTING UNITS, EMPLOYMENT AND PAYROLL COVERED
BY UNEMPLOYMENT COMPENSATION LAW IN THE STATE AND COUNTIES
OF FLORIDA, 1999

County	Number of re-porting units	Number of em-ployees	Payroll ($1,000)	County	Number of re-porting units	Number of em-ployees	Payroll ($1,000)
Building materials, hardware, garden supply, and mobile home dealers (SIC code 52)							
Florida	3,675	55,994	110,498	Levy	14	90	126
				Madison	7	82	86
Alachua	49	764	1,338	Manatee	59	714	1,320
Baker	7	46	45	Marion	89	1,189	2,217
Bay	55	794	1,406	Martin	41	803	1,623
Bradford	6	37	70	Miami-Dade	383	5,440	10,960
Brevard	119	1,839	3,031	Monroe	39	515	981
Broward	295	5,025	10,607	Nassau	12	138	230
Calhoun	7	34	62	Okaloosa	58	762	1,251
Charlotte	35	469	902	Orange	185	2,826	5,888
Citrus	36	350	488	Osceola	23	449	876
Clay	34	624	1,164	Palm Beach	216	3,499	7,381
Collier	73	1,343	2,834	Pasco	74	1,047	1,815
Columbia	29	339	646	Pinellas	184	3,029	5,515
De Soto	6	44	76	Polk	107	1,777	3,522
Duval	159	3,102	6,003	Putnam	27	218	381
Escambia	96	1,411	2,498	St. Johns	34	340	686
Flagler	12	64	141	St. Lucie	35	413	820
Gadsden	8	75	93	Santa Rosa	35	169	255
Gilchrist	4	26	39	Sarasota	97	1,533	3,203
Gulf	6	38	52	Seminole	86	2,235	4,904
Hendry	13	119	247	Sumter	9	64	113
Hernando	26	399	641	Suwannee	10	131	200
Highlands	24	272	372	Taylor	7	57	86
Hillsborough	191	3,763	8,031	Union	3	10	20
Holmes	4	22	33	Volusia	109	1,578	2,876
Indian River	40	531	1,022	Wakulla	7	47	42
Jackson	14	134	190	Walton	16	114	202
Jefferson	6	22	36	Washington	4	35	62
Lake	60	894	1,643				
Lee	119	2,238	4,553	Multicounty 1/	72	542	2,022
Leon	79	1,105	2,217				

1/ Reporting units without a fixed location within the state or of unknown county location.
Note: Private employment. For a list of three-digit code industries included see Table 16.43. Data are preliminary. Only counties for which data are disclosed are shown. Detail may not add to totals due to disclosure editing and/or rounding. See Tables in 23.70, 23.71, 23.72, 23.73, and 23.74 for public employment data.

Source: State of Florida, Department of Labor and Employment Security, Bureau of Labor Market Information, "Employment and Wages" (ES-202), unpublished data.

University of Florida   **Bureau of Economic and Business Research**

Table 11.25. MOBILE HOMES: PLACEMENTS OF NEW MOBILE HOMES AND AVERAGE SALES PRICES IN FLORIDA, SELECTED STATES AND THE UNITED STATES, 1998

| State 1/ | Placements (1,000) | | | Average sales price (dollars) | | |
	Total 2/	Single-wide	Double-wide	Total	Single-wide	Double-wide
Florida	20.3	4.3	15.3	46,700	30,100	50,400
Alabama	19.8	11.1	8.5	38,400	29,500	49,400
Arizona	8.3	2.0	6.1	46,800	26,000	52,900
Arkansas	7.9	4.1	3.7	39,300	29,200	48,900
California	7.2	0.7	6.2	55,700	30,700	56,900
Colorado	4.6	1.3	3.3	52,300	34,900	59,000
Delaware	2.1	0.7	1.4	48,900	33,000	55,800
Georgia	23.2	7.7	15.1	42,000	28,800	48,000
Idaho	3.0	0.4	2.4	56,000	32,700	57,800
Illinois	4.2	1.8	2.5	43,000	30,000	51,100
Indiana	8.3	2.7	5.6	44,300	30,100	51,100
Kansas	3.4	1.9	1.5	44,100	33,800	58,000
Kentucky	11.2	6.3	4.8	36,100	26,400	48,600
Louisiana	9.8	7.1	2.6	37,100	30,700	54,300
Michigan	12.8	2.7	10.0	46,500	33,700	49,800
Minnesota	3.3	1.1	2.2	48,600	37,300	54,200
Mississippi	11.9	6.6	5.3	39,200	29,600	50,900
Missouri	8.0	4.1	3.8	39,700	29,400	50,700
Montana	2.0	0.7	1.2	50,300	34,600	57,900
Nevada	2.6	0.3	2.2	53,000	33,800	54,100
New Mexico	6.4	2.5	3.8	44,800	32,200	52,900
New York	4.7	1.7	3.0	42,700	30,700	49,700
North Carolina	34.7	13.0	21.2	45,400	30,000	54,400
Ohio	8.4	3.7	4.7	40,800	28,200	50,200
Oklahoma	7.4	3.8	3.6	41,800	29,900	53,700
Oregon	5.3	0.3	4.3	59,200	33,800	58,700
Pennsylvania	5.4	1.9	3.4	45,700	32,300	53,000
South Carolina	19.4	7.3	11.7	43,700	30,900	51,100
South Dakota	2.3	1.0	1.3	47,300	35,300	55,400
Tennessee	23.2	10.7	12.3	38,400	26,800	47,800
Texas	42.1	21.9	19.9	42,800	32,000	54,400
Virginia	6.0	2.4	3.6	41,800	27,700	51,100
Washington	7.7	0.6	6.4	59,200	32,400	59,600
West Virginia	6.1	3.0	3.1	38,200	27,500	48,300
Wisconsin	4.2	1.9	2.3	44,300	34,800	52,500
United States	369.0	147.6	215.5	43,800	30,300	52,300

1/ States with 1998 placements of 2,000 or more are listed.
2/ Includes mobile homes with more than two sections.

Source: U.S., Department of Commerce, Bureau of the Census, Internet site <http://www.census.gov/pub/const/mhs/> (accessed 17 August 2000).

University of Florida   **Bureau of Economic and Business Research**

MANUFACTURING

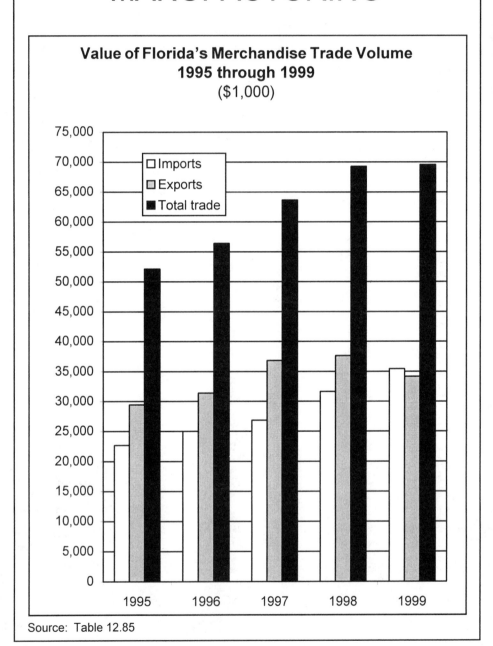

Value of Florida's Merchandise Trade Volume
1995 through 1999
($1,000)

Legend:
- □ Imports
- ▨ Exports
- ■ Total trade

Source: Table 12.85

TABLES LISTED BY MAJOR HEADINGS

University of Florida   **Bureau of Economic and Business Research**

TABLES LISTED BY MAJOR HEADINGS

Table 12.01. MANUFACTURING: CHARACTERISTICS IN THE STATE AND SELECTED METROPOLITAN AREAS OF FLORIDA, SPECIFIED YEARS 1992 THROUGH 1997

Year and source 2/	Number of establishments 1/ Total	Number of establishments 1/ With 20 employees or more	All employees Number (1,000)	All employees Payroll (million dollars)	All employees Per-centage of U.S. total	Value added by manu-facture (million dollars)	New capital expendi-ture (million dollars)
Florida							
1992--census	16,382	3,758	472.4	12,991.0	2.59	32,641.4	2,111.5
1993--ASM	(NA)	(NA)	479.9	13,257.9	2.63	33,615.2	1,772.3
1994--ASM	(NA)	(NA)	472.0	13,257.5	2.58	35,100.6	2,040.9
1995--ASM	(NA)	(NA)	480.5	13,941.0	2.57	37,460.0	2,345.9
1996--ASM	(NA)	(NA)	486.1	14,852.5	2.60	38,621.3	2,643.9
1997--census	15,992	3,628	433.1	13,185.1	2.56	40,213.4	2,979.5
Miami-Ft. Lauderdale CMSA 3/							
1992--census	5,215	1,185	122.1	3,047.6	0.67	7,132.2	337.2
1997--census	4,998	1,034	103.5	2,779.2	0.61	8,144.9	391.1
Miami PMSA							
1992--census	3,336	815	80.3	1,811.3	0.44	4,244.0	203.3
1997--census	3,031	663	66.4	1,663.8	0.39	4,856.0	228.2
Orlando MSA							
1992--census	1,574	390	53.3	1,661.5	0.29	3,754.2	195.2
1997--census	1,564	390	47.1	1,627.7	0.28	4,679.8	527.3
Tampa-St. Petersburg-Clearwater MSA							
1992--census	2,583	639	83.6	2,330.5	0.46	5,164.9	315.5
1997--census	2,580	642	77.1	2,246.2	0.46	6,317.4	516.7

(NA) Not available.

1/ Includes establishments with payroll at any time during the year.

2/ Data for 1992 are from the Census of Manufactures and are based on SIC classifications for industries. Data for 1997 are from the Economic Census based on the NAICS industry classification system and may not be comparable to earlier years. See Glossary for definitions. Data for Annual Survey of Manufactures (ASM) years are estimates based on a representative sample of establishments canvassed annually and may differ from results of a complete canvas of all establishments.

3/ Consists of Dade and Broward counties.

Note: Data are reported for metropolitan areas with 40,000 manufacturing employees or more in 1992. The manufactures census is on a 5-year cycle collecting data for years ending in 2 and 7. See Glossary for definitions of metropolitan areas and maps at the front of the book for area boundaries.

Source: U.S., Department of Commerce, Bureau of the Census, *1997 Economic Census: Manufacturing*, Geographic Area Series EC97M31A-FL, Issued May 2000, previous manufacturing censuses, and *1996 Annual Survey of Manufactures*, Geographic Area Series, and previous editions, Internet site <http://www.census.gov/>.

Table 12.05. MANUFACTURING: ESTABLISHMENTS, EMPLOYMENT, AND PAYROLL
IN FLORIDA, 1997

NAICS code	Industry	Number of establishments	Number of employees 1/	Annual payroll ($1,000)
31-33	Manufacturing	15,992	433,149	13,185,078
311	Food	946	36,948	994,858
3111	Animal food	34	852	23,027
3112	Grain and oilseed milling	14	188	6,482
3113	Sugar and confectionery	52	3,191	108,330
3114	Fruit and vegetable	79	9,737	304,900
3115	Dairy product	41	2,074	62,965
3116	Meat product	86	7,127	120,530
3117	Seafood product	43	2,368	52,830
3118	Bakeries and tortilla	501	8,301	219,367
3119	Other food	96	3,110	96,427
312	Beverage and tobacco product	110	8,382	261,410
3121	Beverage	89	6,273	211,518
3122	Tobacco	21	2,109	49,892
313	Textile mills	160	2,995	71,201
3132	Fabric mills	78	1,789	39,715
3133	Textile and fabric and fishing fabric coating mills	76	1,119	28,785
314	Textile products	543	7,111	127,416
3141	Textile furnishing mills	210	2,521	43,556
3149	Other textile product mills	333	4,590	83,860
315	Apparel	661	18,771	302,688
3151	Apparel knitting mills	24	778	14,670
3152	Cut and saw apparel	520	16,984	270,703
3159	Apparel accessories and other apparel	117	1,009	17,315
316	Leather and allied product	76	3,720	62,368
3162	Footwear	17	1,537	25,394
3169	Other leather and allied product	49	2,100	35,542
321	Wood product	524	15,379	360,731
3211	Sawmills and wood preservation	71	2,457	59,487
3212	Veneer, plywood, and engineered wood product	120	5,055	119,666
3219	Other wood product	333	7,867	181,578
322	Paper	166	12,602	521,620
3221	Pulp, paper, and paperboard mills	10	5,824	310,248
3222	Converted paper products	156	6,778	211,372
323	Printing and related support activities	2,365	27,641	743,902
3231	Printing and related support activities	2,365	27,641	743,902
324	Petroleum and coal products	48	857	28,878
3241	Petroleum and coal products	48	857	28,878
325	Chemical	576	20,163	776,048
3251	Basic chemical	60	2,113	95,423

See footnotes at end of table.   Continued . . .

University of Florida   **Bureau of Economic and Business Research**

Table 12.05. MANUFACTURING: ESTABLISHMENTS, EMPLOYMENT, AND PAYROLL
IN FLORIDA, 1997 (Continued)

NAICS code	Industry	Number of estab- lishments	Number of em- ployees 1/	Annual payroll ($1,000)
325	Chemical (Continued)			
3252	Resin, synthetic, fibers, and artificial and synthetic fibers and filaments	28	2,420	112,147
3253	Pesticide, fertilizer, and other agriculture chemical	73	5,575	229,293
3254	Pharmaceutical and medicine	69	3,860	151,390
3255	Paint, coating, and adhesive	109	1,874	60,281
3256	Soap, cleaning compound, and toilet preparation	132	2,275	59,029
3259	Other chemical product	105	2,046	68,485
326	Plastics and rubber products	703	20,044	487,226
3261	Plastics product	592	17,276	416,247
3262	Rubber product	111	2,768	70,979
327	Nonmetallic mineral product	894	20,862	614,147
3271	Clay product and refractory	82	(D)	(D)
3272	Glass and glass product	138	3,309	98,535
3273	Cement and concrete product	554	13,944	397,618
3274	Lime and gypsum product	15	(D)	(D)
3279	Other nonmetallic mineral	105	1,725	57,690
331	Primary metal	104	5,250	161,401
3311	Ion and steel mills and ferroalloy	3	(D)	(D)
3312	Steel product from purchased steel	19	1,748	61,887
3313	Alumina and aluminum	10	1,911	47,523
3314	Nonferrous metal (except aluminum) production and processing	18	(D)	(D)
3315	Foundries	54	974	26,209
332	Fabricated metal product	1,998	41,656	1,134,259
3321	Forging and stamping	74	3,029	89,400
3322	Cutlery and handtool	46	739	23,720
3323	Architectural and structural metals	640	17,257	432,682
3324	Boiler, tank, and shipping container	56	2,088	84,858
3325	Hardware	47	1,576	40,078
3326	Spring and wire product	50	1,511	31,975
3327	Machine shops, turned product, and screw, nut, and bolt	704	7,556	205,983
3328	Coating, engraving, heat treating, and allied activities	170	1,867	51,039
3329	Other fabricated metal	211	6,033	174,524
333	Machinery	957	26,743	909,449
3331	Agriculture, construction, and mining machinery	81	1,505	39,181
3332	Industrial machinery	112	2,761	104,164
3333	Commercial and service industry machinery	145	8,305	300,549
3334	Ventilation, heating, AC, and commercial refrigeration equipment	73	2,468	63,929
3335	Metalworking machinery	236	3,022	100,805
3336	Engine, turbine, and power transmission equipment	39	811	37,432
3339	Other general-purpose machinery	271	7,871	263,389
334	Computer and electronic product	783	68,225	2,744,822
3341	Computer and peripheral equipment	79	3,474	144,919
3342	Communications equipment	145	15,973	775,668

See footnotes at end of table. Continued . . .

Table 12.05. MANUFACTURING: ESTABLISHMENTS, EMPLOYMENT, AND PAYROLL
IN FLORIDA, 1997 (Continued)

NAICS code	Industry	Number of estab-lishments	Number of em-ployees 1/	Annual payroll ($1,000)
334	Computer and electronic product (Continued)			
3343	Audio and video equipment	27	363	11,663
3344	Semiconductor and other electronic component	251	20,018	555,096
3345	Navigational, measuring, medical, and control instruments	249	27,792	1,239,363
3346	Magnetic and optical media	32	605	18,113
335	Electrical equipment. Appliance, and component	279	11,228	320,339
3351	Electric lighting equipment	68	1,593	35,170
3353	Electrical equipment	110	4,286	134,778
3359	Other electrical equipment and component	94	5,337	150,199
336	Transportation equipment	762	38,023	1,322,321
3362	Motor vehicle body and trailer	98	4,914	123,611
3363	Motor vehicle parts	196	7,062	171,247
3364	Aerospace product and parts	133	14,285	714,653
3365	Railroad rolling stock	5	103	3,536
3366	Ship and boat building	282	11,214	298,317
3369	Other transportation equipment	35	(D)	(D)
337	Furniture and related product	1,422	18,698	412,674
3371	Household and institutional furniture and kitchen cabinet	1,094	10,539	225,773
3372	Office furniture (including fixtures)	197	4,296	104,560
3379	Other furniture related product	131	3,863	82,341
339	Miscellaneous	1,915	27,851	827,320
3399	Other miscellaneous	1,022	10,482	246,186

(D) Data withheld to avoid disclosure of information about individual firms.
1/ Industries with 100 employees or more are shown.
Note: The economic censuses are conducted on a 5-year cycle collecting data for years ending in 2 and 7. Data are for North American Classification System (NAICS) codes 31-33 and may not be comparable to earlier years. See Glossary for definition.

Source: U.S., Department of Commerce, Bureau of the Census, *1997 Economic Census: Manufacturing*, Geographic Area Series EC97M31A-FL, Issued May 2000, Internet site <http://www.census.gov/prod/ec97/97m31-fl.pdf> (accessed 26 June 2000).

University of Florida   **Bureau of Economic and Business Research**

Table 12.06. MANUFACTURING: ESTABLISHMENTS, EMPLOYMENT, VALUE ADDED
BY MANUFACTURE, VALUE OF SHIPMENTS, AND NEW CAPITAL
EXPENDITURE IN THE STATE AND COUNTIES
OF FLORIDA, 1997

(in millions of dollars, except where indicated)

County	Estab-lish-ments (number)	All employees Num-ber 1/ (1,000)	Payroll	Value added by manu-facture	Value of ship-ments	Capital expen-diture
Florida	15,992	433.1	13,185.1	40,213.4	77,477.5	2,979.5
Alachua	151	5.3	157.1	458.3	1,010.3	73.2
Baker	0	0.0	0.0	0.0	0.0	0.0
Bay	136	3.5	108.7	330.5	719.0	38.5
Bradford	15	0.7	10.7	22.0	44.1	0.5
Brevard	494	20.8	753.9	1,855.7	3,450.7	105.6
Broward	1,967	37.1	1,115.4	3,288.9	5,788.3	162.8
Calhoun	0	0.0	0.0	0.0	0.0	0.0
Charlotte	74	0.6	13.8	39.0	77.7	1.8
Citrus	58	1.0	18.2	43.8	92.4	2.4
Clay	74	1.6	43.7	120.9	247.2	9.5
Collier	205	2.3	62.4	141.7	259.0	12.3
Columbia	35	1.8	46.3	106.6	244.5	4.1
De Soto	0	0.0	0.0	0.0	0.0	0.0
Dixie	0	0.0	0.0	0.0	0.0	0.0
Duval	754	28.2	944.1	3,893.9	7,231.0	254.6
Escambia	236	7.5	294.6	977.6	2,214.1	(D)
Flagler	42	1.6	45.9	109.7	260.7	6.0
Franklin	0	0.0	0.0	0.0	0.0	0.0
Gadsden	32	1.4	32.3	78.8	187.8	4.4
Gilchrist	0	0.0	0.0	0.0	0.0	0.0
Glades	0	0.0	0.0	0.0	0.0	0.0
Gulf	12	(D)	(D)	(D)	(D)	10.0
Hamilton	4	(D)	(D)	(D)	(D)	(D)
Hardee	0	0.0	0.0	0.0	0.0	0.0
Hendry	22	0.7	26.8	141.9	437.7	(D)
Hernando	72	1.2	29.4	150.6	235.2	13.9
Highlands	54	1.2	27.0	71.4	191.6	22.8
Hillsborough	960	30.9	859.3	2,707.2	6,019.8	216.5
Holmes	0	0.0	0.0	0.0	0.0	0.0
Indian River	116	1.8	55.4	103.7	219.8	9.1
Jackson	26	1.3	27.3	61.3	182.1	5.8
Jefferson	0	0.0	0.0	0.0	0.0	0.0
Lafayette	0	0.0	0.0	0.0	0.0	0.0
Lake	164	3.7	90.2	234.6	578.5	17.9
Lee	357	5.4	141.1	388.9	741.8	22.2
Leon	127	2.7	68.0	253.0	557.6	8.7

See footnotes at end of table.   Continued . . .

University of Florida   **Bureau of Economic and Business Research**

Table 12.06. MANUFACTURING: ESTABLISHMENTS, EMPLOYMENT, VALUE ADDED
BY MANUFACTURE, VALUE OF SHIPMENTS, AND NEW CAPITAL
EXPENDITURE IN THE STATE AND COUNTIES
OF FLORIDA, 1997 (Continued)

(in millions of dollars, except where indicated)

County	Estab- lish- ments (number)	All employees Num- ber 1/ (1,000)	Payroll	Value added by manu- facture	Value of ship- ments	Capital expen- diture
Levy	0	0.0	0.0	0.0	0.0	0.0
Liberty	0	0.0	0.0	0.0	0.0	0.0
Madison	11	1.1	25.8	73.4	270.3	(D)
Manatee	284	11.2	348.4	685.7	2,115.7	122.1
Marion	215	9.6	238.0	640.4	1,287.8	37.5
Martin	172	3.3	101.7	295.6	555.2	18.4
Miami-Dade	3,031	66.4	1,663.8	4,856.0	8,523.9	228.2
Monroe	0	0.0	0.0	0.0	0.0	0.0
Nassau	34	1.8	77.3	298.5	630.6	32.9
Okaloosa	133	3.4	81.5	167.7	296.5	11.7
Okeechobee	0	0.0	0.0	0.0	0.0	0.0
Orange	889	32.4	1,213.4	3,402.7	5,786.6	427.3
Osceola	77	1.3	37.1	190.7	379.9	14.2
Palm Beach	1,051	26.3	1,138.1	4,116.1	6,344.5	160.0
Pasco	213	4.1	100.7	264.4	713.3	16.1
Pinellas	1,335	41.0	1,256.8	3,195.1	5,732.8	270.1
Polk	480	20.6	633.5	2,587.4	5,999.9	190.7
Putnam	48	2.6	88.9	283.5	730.2	35.1
St. Johns	88	2.3	53.8	163.7	299.6	20.1
St. Lucie	124	2.2	60.1	228.4	542.7	43.1
Santa Rosa	59	1.9	41.6	229.2	427.7	(D)
Sarasota	379	7.8	222.9	473.8	872.6	37.7
Seminole	434	9.6	287.1	851.8	1,582.2	67.9
Sumter	30	0.9	19.6	51.8	200.9	2.4
Suwannee	19	(D)	(D)	(D)	(D)	(D)
Taylor	20	1.6	58.0	270.8	496.1	33.7
Union	0	0.0	0.0	0.0	0.0	0.0
Volusia	392	10.2	263.2	683.2	1,212.6	47.3
Wakulla	0	0.0	0.0	0.0	0.0	0.0
Walton	35	0.9	12.5	47.4	108.7	1.1
Washington	14	0.8	15.7	40.3	85.8	(D)

(D) Data withheld to avoid disclosure of information about individual companies.
1/ Industries with 100 employees or more are shown for the state and those with 500 employees or more are shown for counties.
Note: The economic censuses are conducted are conducted on a 5-year cycle collecting data for years ending in 2 and 7. Data are for North American Classification System (NAICS) codes 31-33 and may not be comparable to earlier years. See Glossary for definition.

Source: U.S., Department of Commerce, Bureau of the Census, *1997 Economic Census: Manufactur-ing*, Geographic Area Series EC97M31A-FL, Issued May 2000, Internet site <http://www.census.gov/prod/ec97/97m31-fl.pdf> (accessed 26 June 2000).

University of Florida   **Bureau of Economic and Business Research**

Table 12.50. EMPLOYMENT AND PAYROLL: AVERAGE MONTHLY PRIVATE REPORTING UNITS
EMPLOYMENT, AND PAYROLL COVERED BY UNEMPLOYMENT COMPENSATION LAW
BY MANUFACTURING INDUSTRY IN FLORIDA, 1998 and 1999

SIC code	Industry	Number of reporting units	Number of employees	Payroll ($1,000)
		1998 A/		
	Manufacturing	16,357	492,153	1,452,216
20	Food and kindred products	718	40,977	112,631
201	Meat products	82	5,985	10,775
202	Dairy products	49	1,976	5,565
203	Canned, frozen, and preserved fruits, vegetables, and food specialties	107	10,470	30,500
204	Grain mill products	57	802	2,169
205	Bakery products	111	5,415	13,859
206	Sugar and confectionery products	31	3,405	12,333
207	Fats and oils	8	203	536
208	Beverages	67	7,012	23,938
209	Miscellaneous food preparations and kindred products	207	5,709	12,955
21	Tobacco products	36	1,929	5,723
212	Cigars	31	1,892	5,637
22	Textile mill products	225	4,292	9,280
221	Broadwoven fabric mills, cotton	21	197	386
222	Broadwoven fabric mills, manmade fiber and silk	12	193	441
224	Narrow fabrics and other smallwares mills-- cotton, wool, silk, and manmade fiber	16	382	1,174
225	Knitting Mills	40	1,057	2,491
226	Dyeing and finishing textiles, except wool fabrics and knit goods	70	1,372	2,313
227	Carpets and rugs	23	107	244
229	Miscellaneous textile goods	38	929	2,159
23	Apparel and other fabricated textile products	989	22,298	37,247
231	Men's and boys' suits, coats, and overcoats	13	294	502
232	Men's and boys' furnishings, work clothing, and allied garments	70	4,654	8,439
233	Women's, misses', and juniors' outerwear	232	4,977	7,093
234	Women's, misses', children's, and infants' undergarments	16	934	1,160
235	Hats, caps, and millinery	19	463	800
236	Girls', children's, and infants' outerwear	29	777	1,338
238	Miscellaneous apparel and accessories	48	1,623	2,314
239	Miscellaneous fabricated textile products	562	8,574	15,600
24	Lumber and wood products, except furniture	1,184	22,139	48,364
241	Logging	338	2,602	5,672
242	Sawmills and planing mills	81	2,351	5,442
243	Millwork, veneer, plywood, and structural wood members	527	11,066	23,270

See footnotes at end of table.   Continued . . .

University of Florida   **Bureau of Economic and Business Research**

Table 12.50. EMPLOYMENT AND PAYROLL: AVERAGE MONTHLY PRIVATE REPORTING UNITS EMPLOYMENT, AND PAYROLL COVERED BY UNEMPLOYMENT COMPENSATION LAW BY MANUFACTURING INDUSTRY IN FLORIDA, 1998 and 1999 (Continued)

SIC code	Industry	Number of re- porting units	Number of em- ployees	Payroll ($1,000)
	1998 A/ (Continued)			
24	Lumber and wood products, except furniture (Continued)			
244	Wood containers	73	1,122	2,018
245	Wood buildings and mobile homes	31	3,441	8,729
249	Miscellaneous wood products	135	1,559	3,233
25	Furniture and fixtures	534	11,940	24,458
251	Household furniture	262	5,948	11,422
252	Office furniture	42	679	1,338
253	Public building and related furniture	12	660	1,519
254	Partitions, shelving, lockers, and office and store fixtures	83	1,989	4,581
259	Miscellaneous furniture and fixtures	134	2,664	5,599
26	Paper and allied products	231	14,090	47,328
262	Paper mills	17	1,864	8,199
263	Paperboard mills	16	1,618	7,109
265	Paperboard containers and boxes	90	4,623	13,274
267	Converted paper and paperboard products, except containers and boxes	102	5,192	15,071
27	Printing, publishing, and allied industries	3,411	65,316	174,865
271	Newspapers: publishing, or publishing and printing	302	25,305	65,784
272	Periodicals: publishing, or publishing and printing	397	7,007	20,651
273	Books	166	2,934	10,239
274	Miscellaneous publishing	336	5,715	18,673
275	Commercial printing	2,013	20,430	49,188
276	Manifold business forms	25	872	2,399
277	Greeting cards	6	16	64
278	Blankbooks, loose-leaf binders, and bookbinding and related work	46	1,066	2,408
279	Service industries for the printing trade	122	1,971	5,459
28	Chemicals and allied products	604	21,003	85,336
281	Industrial inorganic chemicals	43	522	2,104
282	Plastics materials and synthetic resins, synthetic rubber, cellulosic and other manmade fibers, except glass	54	3,214	14,152
283	Drugs	99	2,769	15,096
284	Soap, detergents, and cleaning preparations; perfumes, cosmetics, and other toilet preparations	137	2,892	7,991
285	Paints, varnishes, lacquers, enamels, and allied products	71	1,492	4,602
286	Industrial organic chemicals	33	1,839	8,613
287	Agricultural chemicals	87	6,497	25,386
289	Miscellaneous chemical products	81	1,778	7,393

See footnotes at end of table.

Continued . . .

University of Florida

Bureau of Economic and Business Research

Table 12.50. EMPLOYMENT AND PAYROLL: AVERAGE MONTHLY PRIVATE REPORTING UNITS EMPLOYMENT, AND PAYROLL COVERED BY UNEMPLOYMENT COMPENSATION LAW BY MANUFACTURING INDUSTRY IN FLORIDA, 1998 and 1999 (Continued)

SIC code	Industry	Number of re- porting units	Number of em- ployees	Payroll ($1,000)
	1998 A/ (Continued)			
29	Petroleum refining and related industries	74	2,293	7,044
295	Asphalt paving and roofing materials	54	1,849	5,476
299	Miscellaneous products of petroleum and coal	9	265	699
30	Rubber and miscellaneous plastics products	687	20,589	49,731
305	Gaskets, packing, and sealing devices and rubber and plastics hose and belting	19	1,178	3,031
306	Fabricated rubber products, NEC	63	1,946	4,931
308	Miscellaneous plastics products	601	16,659	40,524
31	Leather and leather products	77	2,606	4,133
311	Leather tanning and finishing	8	32	70
313	Boot and shoe cut stock and findings	5	17	58
314	Footwear, except rubber	17	232	474
316	Luggage	13	307	496
317	Handbags and other personal leather goods	24	768	1,112
319	Leather goods, NEC	11	1,250	1,924
32	Stone, clay, glass, and concrete products	820	23,568	65,717
321	Flat glass	16	239	512
322	Glass and glassware, pressed or blown	36	1,399	4,953
323	Glass products, made of purchased glass	94	1,994	3,886
324	Cement, hydraulic	16	809	2,639
325	Structural clay products	27	735	1,965
326	Pottery and related products	42	212	342
327	Concrete, gypsum, and plaster products	470	16,083	43,315
328	Cut stone and stone products	50	626	1,509
329	Abrasive, asbestos, and miscellaneous nonmetallic mineral products	70	1,469	6,596
33	Primary metal industries	209	6,860	19,432
331	Steel works, blast furnaces and rolling and finishing mills	51	1,926	7,273
332	Iron and steel foundries	17	975	2,501
333	Primary smelting and refining of nonferrous metals	5	16	21
334	Secondary smelting and refining of nonferrous metals	12	139	420
335	Rolling, drawing, and extruding of nonferrous metals	72	3,065	7,506
336	Nonferrous foundries (castings)	37	572	1,191
339	Miscellaneous primary metal products	15	167	519
34	Fabricated metal products, except machinery and transportation equipment	1,335	32,998	81,774
341	Metal cans and shipping containers	16	854	3,415
342	Cutlery, handtools, and general hardware	83	2,021	4,658
343	Heating equipment, except electric and warm air; and plumbing fixtures	52	680	1,405

See footnotes at end of table.   Continued . . .

Table 12.50. EMPLOYMENT AND PAYROLL: AVERAGE MONTHLY PRIVATE REPORTING UNITS EMPLOYMENT, AND PAYROLL COVERED BY UNEMPLOYMENT COMPENSATION LAW BY MANUFACTURING INDUSTRY IN FLORIDA, 1998 and 1999 (Continued)

SIC code	Industry	Number of re-porting units	Number of em-ployees	Payroll ($1,000)
	1998 A/ (Continued)			
34	Fabricated metal products, except machinery and transportation equipment (Continued)			
344	Fabricated structural metal products	659	16,766	39,036
345	Screw machine products, and bolts, nuts, screws, rivets, and washers	49	1,269	3,478
346	Metal forgings and stampings	87	2,892	7,380
347	Coating, engraving, and allied services	156	1,937	4,757
348	Ordnance and accessories, except vehicles and guided missiles	25	631	1,722
349	Miscellaneous fabricated metal products	208	5,948	15,922
35	Industrial and commercial machinery and computer equipment	1,784	36,796	117,991
351	Engines and turbines	29	2,358	12,745
352	Farm and garden machinery and equipment	66	1,229	3,081
353	Construction, mining, and materials handling machinery and equipment	144	3,215	9,436
354	Metalworking machinery and equipment	325	4,876	13,464
355	Special industry machinery, except metal-working machinery	142	2,648	8,743
356	General industrial machinery and equipment	186	5,073	15,541
357	Computer and office equipment	132	6,019	25,293
358	Refrigeration and service industry machinery	188	5,885	16,007
359	Miscellaneous industrial and commercial machinery and equipment	573	5,492	13,681
36	Electronic and other electrical equipment and components, except computer equipment	843	61,647	222,272
361	Electric transmission and distribution equipment	39	2,206	5,862
362	Electrical industrial apparatus	72	2,315	7,374
363	Household appliances	28	828	7,240
364	Electric lighting and wiring equipment	120	3,809	7,973
365	Household audio and video equipment, and audio recordings	44	2,615	6,702
366	Communications equipment	194	20,977	88,608
367	Electronic components and accessories	253	22,597	76,975
369	Miscellaneous electrical machinery, equip-ment, and supplies	93	6,299	21,538
37	Transportation equipment	1,110	53,236	184,766
371	Motor vehicles and motor vehicle equipment	200	8,102	19,952
372	Aircraft and parts	183	17,342	70,874
373	Ship and boat building and repairing	613	16,239	40,984
374	Railroad equipment	8	221	479
375	Motorcycles, bicycles, and parts	14	90	164
376	Guided missiles and space vehicles and parts	22	10,014	49,677
379	Miscellaneous transportation equipment	71	1,227	2,638

See footnotes at end of table.   Continued . . .

Table 12.50. EMPLOYMENT AND PAYROLL: AVERAGE MONTHLY PRIVATE REPORTING UNITS EMPLOYMENT, AND PAYROLL COVERED BY UNEMPLOYMENT COMPENSATION LAW BY MANUFACTURING INDUSTRY IN FLORIDA, 1998 and 1999 (Continued)

SIC code	Industry	Number of re-porting units	Number of em-ployees	Payroll ($1,000)
	1998 A/ (Continued)			
38	Measuring, analyzing, and controlling instru-ments; photographic, medical, and optical goods; watches and clocks	661	37,622	131,583
381	Search, detection, navigation, guidance, aero-nautical, and nautical systems, instruments, and equipment	55	9,543	38,356
382	Laboratory apparatus and analytical, optical, measuring, and controlling instruments	235	6,484	20,235
384	Surgical, medical, and dental instruments and supplies	268	15,353	53,430
385	Ophthalmic goods	64	5,739	18,278
386	Photographic equipment and supplies	32	385	1,119
387	Watches, clocks, clockwork operated devices, and parts	7	119	166
39	Miscellaneous manufacturing industries	827	9,955	22,540
391	Jewelry, silverware, and plated ware	118	884	1,898
393	Musical instruments	18	205	458
394	Dolls, toys, games, and sporting and athletic goods	209	2,288	4,399
395	Pens, pencils, and other artists' materials	47	1,385	3,959
396	Costume jewelry, costume novelties, buttons, and miscellaneous notions, except precious metal	18	457	1,100
399	Miscellaneous manufacturing industries	418	4,736	10,726

See footnotes at end of table.   Continued . . .

University of Florida   **Bureau of Economic and Business Research**

Table 12.50. EMPLOYMENT AND PAYROLL: AVERAGE MONTHLY PRIVATE REPORTING UNITS
EMPLOYMENT, AND PAYROLL COVERED BY UNEMPLOYMENT COMPENSATION LAW
BY MANUFACTURING INDUSTRY IN FLORIDA, 1998 and 1999 (Continued)

SIC code	Industry	Number of reporting units	Number of employees	Payroll ($1,000)
		1999 B/		
	Manufacturing	16,454	488,042	1,472,794
20	Food and kindred products	721	40,578	116,416
201	Meat products	83	5,952	10,848
202	Dairy products	42	2,024	5,844
203	Canned, frozen, and preserved fruits, vegetables, and food specialties	104	9,991	33,040
204	Grain mill products	60	749	2,061
205	Bakery products	117	5,429	13,914
206	Sugar and confectionery products	29	3,391	12,710
207	Fats and oils	8	212	536
208	Beverages	72	7,144	24,126
209	Miscellaneous food preparations and kindred products	208	5,685	13,337
21	Tobacco products	39	1,938	5,869
212	Cigars	35	1,884	5,756
22	Textile mill products	233	3,750	7,859
221	Broadwoven fabric mills, cotton	20	120	250
222	Broadwoven fabric mills, manmade fiber and silk	16	199	419
224	Narrow fabrics and other smallwares mills-- cotton, wool, silk, and manmade fiber	19	359	1,093
225	Knitting Mills	36	723	1,556
226	Dyeing and finishing textiles, except wool fabrics and knit goods	75	1,372	2,360
227	Carpets and rugs	22	116	250
228	Yarn and thread mills	6	101	153
229	Miscellaneous textile goods	40	759	1,776
23	Apparel and other fabricated textile products	935	20,052	35,621
231	Men's and boys' suits, coats and overcoats	9	286	511
232	Men's and boys' furnishings, work clothing, and allied garments	64	4,015	8,154
233	Women's, misses', and juniors' outerwear	207	4,389	6,310
234	Women's, misses', children's, and infants' undergarments	13	535	660
235	Hats, caps, and millinery	17	473	896
236	Girls', children's, and infants' outerwear	24	591	1,001
238	Miscellaneous apparel and accessories	50	1,540	2,336
239	Miscellaneous fabricated textile products	548	8,220	15,751
24	Lumber and wood products, except furniture	1,172	23,006	49,982
241	Logging	331	2,405	5,205
242	Sawmills and planing mills	82	2,292	5,358
243	Millwork, veneer, plywood, and structural wood members	534	12,481	25,421

See footnotes at end of table.   Continued . . .

Table 12.50. EMPLOYMENT AND PAYROLL: AVERAGE MONTHLY PRIVATE REPORTING UNITS EMPLOYMENT, AND PAYROLL COVERED BY UNEMPLOYMENT COMPENSATION LAW BY MANUFACTURING INDUSTRY IN FLORIDA, 1998 and 1999 (Continued)

SIC code	Industry	Number of re- porting units	Number of em- ployees	Payroll ($1,000)
	1999 B/ (Continued)			
24	Lumber and wood products, except furniture (Continued)			
244	Wood containers	77	1,128	2,097
245	Wood buildings and mobile homes	30	3,242	8,122
249	Miscellaneous wood products	119	1,458	3,779
25	Furniture and fixtures	542	11,850	25,512
251	Household furniture	275	5,772	11,547
252	Office furniture	39	606	1,205
253	Public building and related furniture	13	681	1,802
254	Partitions, shelving, lockers, and office and store fixtures	81	2,015	4,946
259	Miscellaneous furniture and fixtures	135	2,777	6,012
26	Paper and allied products	242	13,377	46,859
262	Paper mills	16	1,866	8,644
263	Paperboard mills	15	1,073	5,237
265	Paperboard containers and boxes	93	4,293	13,053
267	Converted paper and paperboard products, except containers and boxes	113	5,363	16,402
27	Printing, publishing, and allied industries	3,436	64,962	180,122
271	Newspapers: publishing, or publishing and printing	338	24,882	67,298
272	Periodicals: publishing, or publishing and printing	405	7,157	20,438
273	Books	187	2,680	10,183
274	Miscellaneous publishing	326	5,935	20,314
275	Commercial printing	1,982	20,255	50,339
276	Manifold business forms	30	924	2,772
277	Greeting cards	7	28	66
278	Blankbooks, loose-leaf binders, and bookbinding and related work	45	953	2,106
279	Service industries for the printing trade	116	2,150	6,605
28	Chemicals and allied products	593	22,030	86,158
281	Industrial inorganic chemicals	44	526	2,328
282	Plastics materials and synthetic resins, synthetic rubber, cellulosic and other manmade fibers, except glass	54	3,230	12,225
283	Drugs	95	3,936	18,761
284	Soap, detergents, and cleaning preparations; perfumes, cosmetics, and other toilet preparations	137	2,847	8,453
285	Paints, varnishes, lacquers, enamels, and allied products	66	1,573	4,752
286	Industrial organic chemicals	27	1,596	6,580
287	Agricultural chemicals	84	6,550	24,878
289	Miscellaneous chemical products	86	1,771	8,182

See footnotes at end of table.

Continued . . .

Table 12.50. EMPLOYMENT AND PAYROLL: AVERAGE MONTHLY PRIVATE REPORTING UNITS
EMPLOYMENT, AND PAYROLL COVERED BY UNEMPLOYMENT COMPENSATION LAW
BY MANUFACTURING INDUSTRY IN FLORIDA, 1998 and 1999 (Continued)

SIC code	Industry	Number of re- porting units	Number of em- ployees	Payroll ($1,000)
	1999 B/ (Continued)			
29	Petroleum refining and related industries	80	2,305	7,365
295	Asphalt paving and roofing materials	58	1,829	5,772
299	Miscellaneous products of petroleum and coal	10	283	730
30	Rubber and miscellaneous plastics products	667	20,355	50,568
305	Gaskets, packing, and sealing devices and rubber and plastics hose and belting	22	1,391	3,326
306	Fabricated rubber products, NEC	60	1,917	4,846
308	Miscellaneous plastics products	579	16,269	41,227
31	Leather and leather products	75	2,166	3,631
311	Leather tanning and finishing	8	41	84
313	Boot and shoe cut stock and findings	6	16	49
314	Footwear, except rubber	16	201	396
316	Luggage	13	294	488
317	Handbags and other personal leather goods	22	558	843
319	Leather goods, NEC	10	1,041	1,764
32	Stone, clay, glass, and concrete products	824	24,186	70,353
321	Flat glass	16	245	515
322	Glass and glassware, pressed or blown	39	1,281	4,898
323	Glass products, made of purchased glass	93	1,764	3,545
324	Cement, hydraulic	13	723	2,686
325	Structural clay products	31	726	2,393
326	Pottery and related products	37	187	333
327	Concrete, gypsum, and plaster products	471	17,606	50,456
328	Cut stone and stone products	50	743	1,804
329	Abrasive, asbestos, and miscellaneous nonmetallic mineral products	74	910	3,724
33	Primary metal industries	228	6,520	19,025
331	Steel works, blast furnaces and rolling and finishing mills	57	1,719	6,532
332	Iron and steel foundries	19	969	2,635
334	Secondary smelting and refining of nonferrous metals	12	166	489
335	Rolling, drawing, and extruding of nonferrous metals	81	2,878	7,607
336	Nonferrous foundries (castings)	39	570	1,159
339	Miscellaneous primary metal products	13	156	494
34	Fabricated metal products, except machinery and transportation equipment	1,356	34,377	86,305
341	Metal cans and shipping containers	17	927	3,811
342	Cutlery, handtools, and general hardware	89	2,042	4,933
343	Heating equipment, except electric and warm air; and plumbing fixtures	56	749	1,560

See footnotes at end of table.   Continued . . .

University of Florida   **Bureau of Economic and Business Research**

Table 12.50. EMPLOYMENT AND PAYROLL: AVERAGE MONTHLY PRIVATE REPORTING UNITS EMPLOYMENT, AND PAYROLL COVERED BY UNEMPLOYMENT COMPENSATION LAW BY MANUFACTURING INDUSTRY IN FLORIDA, 1998 and 1999 (Continued)

SIC code	Industry	Number of re-porting units	Number of em-ployees	Payroll ($1,000)
	1999 B/ (Continued)			
34	<u>Fabricated metal products, except machinery and transportation equipment</u> (Continued)			
344	Fabricated structural metal products	665	17,427	41,221
345	Screw machine products, and bolts, nuts, screws, rivets, and washers	46	1,163	3,263
346	Metal forgings and stampings	86	2,969	7,940
347	Coating, engraving, and allied services	160	1,916	4,676
348	Ordnance and accessories, except vehicles and guided missiles	23	734	1,731
349	Miscellaneous fabricated metal products	215	6,449	17,171
35	<u>Industrial and commercial machinery and computer equipment</u>	1,808	36,459	118,927
352	Farm and garden machinery and equipment	68	1,187	2,833
353	Construction, mining, and materials handling machinery and equipment	156	3,574	10,838
354	Metalworking machinery and equipment	322	4,779	12,930
355	Special industry machinery, except metal-working machinery	142	2,402	8,051
356	General industrial machinery and equipment	196	4,968	15,476
357	Computer and office equipment	136	5,907	23,293
358	Refrigeration and service industry machinery	189	5,687	15,719
359	Miscellaneous industrial and commercial machinery and equipment	576	5,526	14,471
36	<u>Electronic and other electrical equipment and components, except computer equipment</u>	849	59,542	225,501
361	Electric transmission and distribution equipment	38	2,221	6,301
362	Electrical industrial apparatus	84	2,527	8,373
363	Household appliances	34	1,066	5,106
364	Electric lighting and wiring equipment	117	4,381	9,776
365	Household audio and video equipment, and audio recordings	50	2,533	6,818
366	Communications equipment	190	19,483	93,183
367	Electronic components and accessories	248	21,247	74,791
369	Miscellaneous electrical machinery, equip-ment, and supplies	90	6,085	21,154
37	<u>Transportation equipment</u>	1,121	53,840	185,755
371	Motor vehicles and motor vehicle equipment	186	7,829	19,798
372	Aircraft and parts	174	16,985	68,961
373	Ship and boat building and repairing	651	17,649	44,813
374	Railroad equipment	7	510	1,286
375	Motorcycles, bicycles, and parts	17	104	205
376	Guided missiles and space vehicles and parts	22	9,456	47,912
379	Miscellaneous transportation equipment	65	1,309	2,779

See footnotes at end of table.   Continued . . .

University of Florida   **Bureau of Economic and Business Research**

Table 12.50. EMPLOYMENT AND PAYROLL: AVERAGE MONTHLY PRIVATE REPORTING UNITS EMPLOYMENT, AND PAYROLL COVERED BY UNEMPLOYMENT COMPENSATION LAW BY MANUFACTURING INDUSTRY IN FLORIDA, 1998 and 1999 (Continued)

SIC code	Industry	Number of re-porting units	Number of em-ployees	Payroll ($1,000)
	1999 B/ (Continued)			
38	Measuring, analyzing, and controlling instruments; photographic, medical, and optical goods; watches and clocks	686	36,478	127,383
381	Search, detection, navigation, guidance, aero-nautical, and nautical systems, instruments, and equipment	54	9,444	38,467
382	Laboratory apparatus and analytical, optical, measuring, and controlling instruments	243	5,887	18,864
384	Surgical, medical, and dental instruments and supplies	282	15,198	50,075
385	Ophthalmic goods	63	5,524	18,800
386	Photographic equipment and supplies	34	318	1,003
387	Watches, clocks, clockwork operated devices, and parts	9	108	173
39	Miscellaneous manufacturing industries	847	10,270	23,582
391	Jewelry, silverware, and plated ware	120	832	1,893
393	Musical instruments	18	156	383
394	Dolls, toys, games, and sporting and athletic goods	217	2,344	4,511
395	Pens, pencils, and other artists' materials	52	1,512	4,224
396	Costume jewelry, costume novelties, buttons, and miscellaneous notions, except precious metal	17	466	1,143
399	Miscellaneous manufacturing industries	424	4,961	11,428

NEC Not elsewhere classified.
A/ Revised.
B/ Preliminary.

Note: Private employment. Detail may not add to totals due to disclosure editing and/or rounding. See Tables 23.70, 23.71, 23.72, 23.73, and 23.74 for public employment data.

Source: State of Florida, Department of Labor and Employment Security, Bureau of Labor Market Information, "Employment and Wages" (ES-202), unpublished data.

University of Florida   **Bureau of Economic and Business Research**

Table 12.51. EMPLOYMENT: AVERAGE MONTHLY PRIVATE REPORTING UNITS, EMPLOYMENT AND PAYROLL COVERED BY UNEMPLOYMENT COMPENSATION LAW IN THE STATE AND COUNTIES OF FLORIDA, 1998 AND 1999

County	Number of reporting units	Number of employees	Payroll ($1,000)	County	Number of reporting units	Number of employees	Payroll ($1,000)
			Manufacturing industry, 1998 A/ (SIC codes 20-39)				
Florida	16,357	492,153	1,452,216	Lee	410	6,961	17,308
				Leon	171	3,099	7,632
Alachua	170	5,377	13,833	Levy	46	392	697
Baker	9	256	473	Liberty	18	247	543
Bay	139	3,952	10,862	Madison	21	1,182	2,175
Bradford	27	652	1,344	Manatee	298	12,869	37,538
Brevard	493	26,527	95,768	Marion	245	11,525	27,430
Broward	1,787	39,718	125,655	Martin	171	3,338	10,712
Calhoun	28	233	434	Miami-Dade	2,827	72,591	187,881
Charlotte	81	1,005	2,098	Monroe	80	602	1,248
Citrus	59	1,327	2,501	Nassau	60	2,140	7,580
Clay	86	1,856	4,886	Okaloosa	137	3,837	9,047
Collier	210	2,659	7,107	Okeechobee	20	172	389
Columbia	60	2,092	4,632	Orange	873	36,840	131,783
De Soto	15	193	474	Osceola	85	1,688	5,484
Dixie	22	550	1,124	Palm Beach	988	30,639	129,444
Duval	761	31,063	94,011	Pasco	176	3,726	7,983
Escambia	236	8,255	28,806	Pinellas	1,268	46,171	129,248
Flagler	45	1,508	3,936	Polk	473	20,577	59,531
Franklin	13	144	262	Putnam	63	3,369	9,959
Gadsden	48	1,718	3,678	St. Johns	90	4,102	11,584
Gilchrist	12	173	286	St. Lucie	128	2,603	5,687
Gulf	13	580	2,128	Santa Rosa	67	2,164	5,491
Hardee	16	251	492	Sarasota	418	7,995	21,387
Hendry	18	1,049	3,695	Seminole	417	10,457	28,852
Hernando	75	1,375	3,424	Sumter	30	852	1,656
Highlands	57	1,224	2,850	Taylor	37	1,894	5,763
Hillsborough	1,007	37,377	99,777	Union	11	252	560
Holmes	24	358	503	Volusia	417	11,339	27,454
Indian River	112	2,629	7,400	Wakulla	18	630	2,541
Jackson	28	1,253	2,477	Walton	27	1,049	1,753
Jefferson	17	168	359	Washington	27	887	1,530
Lafayette	5	199	240				
Lake	167	4,629	9,535	Multicounty 1/	372	2,239	11,396

See footnotes at end of table.   Continued . . .

University of Florida   **Bureau of Economic and Business Research**

Table 12.51. EMPLOYMENT: AVERAGE MONTHLY PRIVATE REPORTING UNITS, EMPLOYMENT AND PAYROLL COVERED BY UNEMPLOYMENT COMPENSATION LAW IN THE STATE AND COUNTIES OF FLORIDA, 1998 AND 1999 (Continued)

County	Number of reporting units	Number of employees	Payroll ($1,000)	County	Number of reporting units	Number of employees	Payroll ($1,000)
			Manufacturing industry, 1999 B/ (SIC codes 20-39)				
Florida	16,454	488,042	1,472,794	Lee	417	6,895	17,747
				Leon	172	2,990	7,451
Alachua	174	5,562	14,698	Levy	47	373	697
Baker	9	272	519	Liberty	17	239	500
Bay	133	3,666	10,658	Madison	20	1,142	2,069
Bradford	30	692	1,427	Manatee	302	13,675	41,923
Brevard	495	25,652	95,348	Marion	237	11,493	27,395
Broward	1,794	37,875	121,907	Martin	170	3,141	10,268
Calhoun	27	222	1,178	Miami-Dade	2,776	69,758	178,983
Charlotte	85	1,149	2,567	Monroe	82	575	1,297
Citrus	64	1,480	2,940	Nassau	59	2,016	7,464
Clay	90	1,833	4,870	Okaloosa	137	3,362	8,443
Collier	217	2,847	7,873	Okeechobee	20	161	390
Columbia	55	2,026	4,910	Orange	880	36,968	138,271
De Soto	14	191	453	Osceola	78	1,712	5,577
Dixie	21	555	1,127	Palm Beach	1,031	32,502	133,587
Duval	773	30,621	95,631	Pasco	185	3,442	7,633
Escambia	242	7,988	27,013	Pinellas	1,277	47,260	140,885
Flagler	46	1,337	3,377	Polk	474	20,325	59,562
Franklin	13	156	309	Putnam	67	3,187	9,993
Gadsden	47	1,761	3,646	St. Johns	93	3,986	11,195
Gilchrist	11	143	219	St. Lucie	129	2,684	6,521
Gulf	12	148	399	Santa Rosa	61	1,649	4,532
Hardee	15	241	485	Sarasota	420	8,139	22,905
Hendry	16	1,092	3,909	Seminole	417	10,565	30,339
Hernando	74	1,342	3,308	Sumter	29	849	1,809
Highlands	55	1,121	2,780	Taylor	37	2,009	5,943
Hillsborough	990	37,155	102,343	Union	9	232	486
Holmes	22	335	499	Volusia	416	10,871	27,592
Indian River	115	2,968	8,497	Wakulla	20	586	2,760
Jackson	24	820	1,659	Walton	24	904	1,695
Jefferson	17	177	321	Washington	25	989	1,732
Lafayette	5	208	264				
Lake	168	4,266	9,400	Multicounty 1/	453	4,278	12,798

A/ Revised.
B/ Preliminary.
1/ Reporting units without a fixed location within the state or of unknown county location.
Note: See Table 12.50 for a list of industries. Private employment. Only counties for which data are disclosed are shown. Detail may not add to totals due to disclosure editing and/or rounding. See Tables 23.70, 23.71, 23.72, 23.73, and 23.74 for public employment data.

Source: State of Florida, Department of Labor and Employment Security, Bureau of Labor Market Information, "Employment and Wages" (ES-202), unpublished data.

University of Florida   **Bureau of Economic and Business Research**

Table 12.52. FOOD PRODUCTS: AVERAGE MONTHLY PRIVATE REPORTING UNITS, EMPLOYMENT AND PAYROLL COVERED BY UNEMPLOYMENT COMPENSATION LAW IN THE STATE AND COUNTIES OF FLORIDA, 1999

County	Number of reporting units	Number of employees	Payroll ($1,000)	County	Number of reporting units	Number of employees	Payroll ($1,000)
			Food and kindred products (SIC code 20)				
Florida	721	40,578	116,416	Manatee	14	2,873	11,578
				Marion	8	308	703
Alachua	4	51	42	Martin	3	189	490
Bay	5	35	31	Miami-Dade	162	5,020	13,656
Brevard	8	98	140	Monroe	6	35	84
Broward	46	1,460	3,936	Okaloosa	5	21	34
Clay	6	261	637	Okeechobee	5	84	215
Collier	7	44	83	Orange	34	3,020	10,329
Columbia	3	61	115	Osceola	6	223	741
Duval	33	4,267	13,891	Palm Beach	42	2,884	11,091
Escambia	9	84	166	Pinellas	32	1,439	4,577
Franklin	6	86	133	Polk	35	4,357	12,262
Hendry	6	1,028	3,757	St. Johns	7	133	69
Hernando	3	24	32	St. Lucie	8	463	1,224
Hillsborough	63	3,981	10,043	Sarasota	4	27	32
Jackson	3	17	30	Seminole	14	376	984
Lake	11	1,103	2,637	Volusia	18	356	877
Lee	14	498	986	Wakulla	5	127	92
Leon	8	147	131				
			Meat products (SIC code 201)				
Florida	83	5,952	10,848	Palm Beach	7	103	240
Broward	5	54	102	Seminole	3	87	205
Miami-Dade	25	715	1,484	Multicounty 1/	3	2	11
			Canned, frozen, and preserved fruits, vegetables, and food specialties (SIC code 203)				
Florida	104	9,991	33,040	Orange	7	355	1,743
				Pinellas	4	505	2,259
Broward	5	45	95	Polk	13	2,161	6,856
Hillsborough	6	227	740	St. Lucie	6	438	1,190
Lake	6	981	2,400	Seminole	4	153	631
Manatee	7	2,630	10,944				
Miami-Dade	17	632	1,419	Multicounty 1/	5	10	79
			Bakery products (SIC code 205)				
Florida	117	5,429	13,914	Miami-Dade	42	1,434	3,925
				Orange	6	638	1,796
Broward	7	150	315	Palm Beach	7	253	751
Duval	5	509	1,593	Polk	3	1,014	2,776
Hillsborough	14	501	981	Multicounty 1/	3	8	26

1/ Reporting units without a fixed location within the state or of unknown county location.
Note: Private employment. For a list of three-digit code industries included see Table 12.50. Data are preliminary. Only counties for which data are disclosed are shown. Detail may not add to totals due to disclosure editing and/or rounding. See Tables 23.70, 23.71, 23.72, 23.73, and 23.74 for public employment data.
Source: State of Florida, Department of Labor and Employment Security, Bureau of Labor Market Information, "Employment and Wages" (ES-202), unpublished data.

University of Florida   **Bureau of Economic and Business Research**

Table 12.53. TOBACCO, TEXTILE, AND APPAREL PRODUCTS: AVERAGE MONTHLY PRIVATE
REPORTING UNITS, EMPLOYMENT, AND PAYROLL COVERED BY UNEMPLOYMENT
COMPENSATION LAW IN THE STATE AND COUNTIES OF FLORIDA, 1999

County	Number of re- porting units	Number of em- ployees	Payroll ($1,000)	County	Number of re- porting units	Number of em- ployees	Payroll ($1,000)
			Tobacco products (SIC code 21)				
Florida	39	1,938	5,869	Miami-Dade	24	173	397
Hillsborough	9	712	2,007				
			Textile mill products (SIC code 22)				
Florida	233	3,750	7,859	Miami-Dade	78	2,097	4,138
				Orange	7	54	123
Bay	5	10	14	Palm Beach	15	95	190
Broward	29	527	1,295	Pinellas	8	75	122
Duval	5	23	31	Sarasota	10	58	103
Escambia	4	229	593	Seminole	3	8	13
Hillsborough	5	6	14	Volusia	7	173	476
Lee	5	14	19				
Martin	3	3	4	Multicounty 1/	8	11	36
			Apparel and other textile products (SIC code 23)				
Florida	935	20,052	35,621	Leon	5	306	563
				Manatee	12	560	1,327
Alachua	4	35	45	Marion	6	61	85
Bay	4	87	165	Martin	15	109	245
Brevard	26	145	284	Miami-Dade	369	9,545	15,899
Broward	118	1,245	2,465	Monroe	6	28	53
Charlotte	6	16	34	Okaloosa	11	150	196
Collier	9	42	69	Orange	30	259	464
Duval	20	274	524	Palm Beach	44	545	1,455
Escambia	5	21	35	Pasco	10	96	152
Gadsden	6	55	61	Pinellas	58	864	1,760
Hillsborough	32	2,367	4,736	Polk	12	389	601
Indian River	6	97	126	Sarasota	19	92	157
Lake	7	36	58	Seminole	14	228	431
Lee	29	144	201	Volusia	15	175	308

1/ Reporting units without a fixed location within the state or of unknown county location.
Note: Private employment. For a list of three-digit code industries included see Table 12.50. Data are
preliminary. Only counties for which data are disclosed are shown. Detail may not add to totals due to
disclosure editing and/or rounding. See Tables 23.70, 23.71, 23.72, 23.73, and 23.74 for public
employment data.

Source: State of Florida, Department of Labor and Employment Security, Bureau of Labor Market Information, "Employment and Wages" (ES-202), unpublished data.

Table 12.57. LUMBER AND WOOD PRODUCTS, EXCEPT FURNITURE: AVERAGE MONTHLY PRIVATE REPORTING UNITS, EMPLOYMENT, AND PAYROLL COVERED BY UNEMPLOYMENT COMPENSATION LAW IN THE STATE AND COUNTIES OF FLORIDA, 1999

County	Number of reporting units	Number of employees	Payroll ($1,000)	County	Number of reporting units	Number of employees	Payroll ($1,000)
			Lumber and wood products, except furniture (SIC code 24)				
Florida	1,172	23,006	49,982	Lee	23	231	520
				Levy	24	196	349
Alachua	15	384	876	Liberty	16	228	493
Baker	4	21	37	Madison	14	206	416
Bay	24	366	718	Manatee	17	162	357
Bradford	13	125	266	Marion	39	1,481	3,427
Brevard	15	507	984	Martin	5	26	58
Broward	67	782	1,834	Miami-Dade	102	2,254	4,471
Calhoun	21	158	1,083	Monroe	5	16	27
Charlotte	11	186	372	Nassau	26	140	394
Citrus	4	47	111	Okaloosa	15	140	254
Clay	18	76	172	Orange	42	935	2,231
Collier	12	83	141	Osceola	7	124	229
Columbia	23	926	1,827	Palm Beach	48	856	2,202
De Soto	3	42	95	Pasco	16	177	314
Dixie	17	542	1,112	Pinellas	51	1,211	3,053
Duval	46	875	2,488	Polk	36	2,117	5,219
Escambia	27	227	423	Putnam	28	591	1,783
Flagler	7	184	341	St. Lucie	9	186	433
Gadsden	10	443	1,029	Santa Rosa	10	107	224
Gilchrist	6	102	126	Sarasota	18	228	451
Hardee	6	72	143	Seminole	15	319	771
Hernando	9	136	263	Sumter	6	97	171
Hillsborough	63	1,177	2,505	Suwannee	8	84	212
Holmes	14	82	135	Taylor	18	359	800
Indian River	7	81	136	Union	7	214	457
Jackson	9	253	536	Volusia	38	363	668
Jefferson	6	108	229	Washington	14	119	189
Lake	23	580	1,141				

1/ Reporting units without a fixed location within the state or of unknown county location.
Note: Private employment. For a list of three-digit code industries included see Table 12.50. Data are preliminary. Only counties for which data are disclosed are shown. Detail may not add to totals due to disclosure editing and/or rounding. See Tables 23.70, 23.71, 23.72, 23.73, and 23.74 for public employment data.

Source: State of Florida, Department of Labor and Employment Security, Bureau of Labor Market Information, "Employment and Wages" (ES-202), unpublished data.

University of Florida   **Bureau of Economic and Business Research**

Table 12.63. FURNITURE AND FIXTURES AND PAPER AND ALLIED PRODUCTS: AVERAGE MONTHLY PRIVATE REPORTING UNITS, EMPLOYMENT, AND PAYROLL COVERED BY UNEMPLOYMENT COMPENSATION LAW IN THE STATE AND COUNTIES OF FLORIDA, 1999

County	Number of reporting units	Number of employees	Payroll ($1,000)	County	Number of reporting units	Number of employees	Payroll ($1,000)
			Furniture and fixtures (SIC code 25)				
Florida	542	11,850	25,512	Marion	13	439	726
				Martin	7	22	61
Alachua	4	7	6	Miami-Dade	160	3,264	6,625
Bay	5	51	83	Orange	24	750	1,847
Brevard	12	100	183	Palm Beach	38	500	1,309
Broward	72	1,598	4,396	Pasco	8	96	136
Charlotte	3	14	13	Pinellas	33	820	1,516
Duval	22	611	1,327	Polk	8	218	413
Escambia	5	59	102	St. Lucie	4	55	73
Hillsborough	25	839	2,047	Sarasota	11	231	477
Jackson	3	13	34	Seminole	17	446	1,030
Lake	4	28	45	Volusia	8	66	90
Lee	10	91	172	Multicounty 1/	7	5	25
			Household furniture (SIC code 251)				
Florida	275	5,772	11,547	Jackson	3	13	34
				Miami-Dade	94	1,531	2,532
Brevard	4	33	55	Orange	12	411	920
Broward	35	409	1,073	Palm Beach	22	367	1,040
Collier	6	31	48	Pinellas	11	227	401
Duval	12	248	726	Seminole	8	100	181
Escambia	4	53	96				
Hillsborough	9	285	807	Multicounty 1/	3	2	11
			Paper and allied products (SIC code 26)				
Florida	242	13,377	46,859	Miami-Dade	45	1,845	4,496
				Nassau	4	1,105	4,502
Broward	18	514	1,513	Orange	18	482	1,635
Duval	31	2,308	7,586	Palm Beach	8	59	153
Escambia	4	1,386	6,500	Pinellas	13	554	1,259
Hillsborough	26	1,085	3,117	Polk	12	433	1,636
Lee	3	14	259	Sarasota	5	39	97
Marion	6	146	317	Multicounty 1/	10	16	64

1/ Reporting units without a fixed location within the state or of unknown county location.
Note: Private employment. For a list of three-digit code industries included see Table 12.50. Data are preliminary. Only counties for which data are disclosed are shown. Detail may not add to totals due to disclosure editing and/or rounding. See Tables 23.70, 23.71, 23.72, 23.73, and 23.74 for public employment data.

Source: State of Florida, Department of Labor and Employment Security, Bureau of Labor Market Information, "Employment and Wages" (ES-202), unpublished data.

University of Florida   **Bureau of Economic and Business Research**

Table 12.64. PRINTING, PUBLISHING, AND ALLIED INDUSTRIES: AVERAGE MONTHLY PRIVATE REPORTING UNITS, EMPLOYMENT, AND PAYROLL COVERED BY UNEMPLOYMENT COMPENSATION LAW IN THE STATE AND COUNTIES OF FLORIDA, 1999

County	Number of reporting units	Number of employees	Payroll ($1,000)	County	Number of reporting units	Number of employees	Payroll ($1,000)
			Printing, publishing, and allied industries (SIC code 27)				
Florida	3,436	64,962	180,122	Manatee	41	603	1,789
				Marion	25	865	1,430
Alachua	46	886	2,010	Martin	30	608	1,497
Bay	13	341	727	Miami-Dade	607	10,375	32,194
Brevard	74	1,252	3,715	Monroe	20	222	515
Broward	414	6,198	20,300	Nassau	9	46	100
Citrus	14	237	347	Okaloosa	24	428	769
Clay	13	165	373	Orange	229	5,953	19,688
Collier	47	737	2,016	Osceola	16	171	369
Columbia	5	36	77	Palm Beach	241	3,650	11,555
Duval	181	3,143	8,803	Pasco	32	332	627
Escambia	58	1,128	2,693	Pinellas	231	7,823	18,929
Flagler	5	32	69	Polk	68	1,118	2,571
Hernando	17	285	788	St. Johns	24	399	774
Hillsborough	233	8,366	20,516	St. Lucie	28	327	633
Indian River	22	385	1,083	Santa Rosa	14	90	162
Jackson	3	7	7	Sarasota	104	1,466	4,576
Lake	27	367	714	Seminole	98	1,002	2,644
Lee	93	1,305	3,852	Suwannee	3	55	69
Leon	71	1,152	2,939	Volusia	82	1,636	3,993
Levy	5	38	62	Multicounty 1/	98	495	1,738

1/ Reporting units without a fixed location within the state or of unknown county location.
Note: Private employment. For a list of three-digit code industries included see Table 12.50. Data are preliminary. Only counties for which data are disclosed are shown. Detail may not add to totals due to disclosure editing and/or rounding. See Tables 23.70, 23.71, 23.72, 23.73, and 23.74 for public employment data.

Source: State of Florida, Department of Labor and Employment Security, Bureau of Labor Market Information, "Employment and Wages" (ES-202), unpublished data.

University of Florida   **Bureau of Economic and Business Research**

Table 12.67. CHEMICALS AND ALLIED PRODUCTS: AVERAGE MONTHLY PRIVATE REPORTING UNITS, EMPLOYMENT, AND PAYROLL COVERED BY UNEMPLOYMENT COMPENSATION LAW IN THE STATE AND COUNTIES OF FLORIDA, 1999

County	Number of re-porting units	Number of em-ployees	Payroll ($1,000)	County	Number of re-porting units	Number of em-ployees	Payroll ($1,000)
\multicolumn{8}{c}{Chemicals and allied products (SIC code 28)}
Florida	593	22,030	86,158	Marion	6	114	324
				Martin	5	30	71
Alachua	9	332	1,000	Miami-Dade	98	2,507	11,109
Brevard	20	332	1,146	Orange	32	767	2,524
Broward	47	644	2,213	Osceola	3	8	47
Collier	5	14	44	Pasco	5	79	195
Duval	38	1,483	7,122	Pinellas	40	1,437	5,083
Escambia	12	2,066	8,575	Polk	44	3,821	14,926
Flagler	6	21	39	St. Johns	5	42	71
Gadsden	4	22	57	Santa Rosa	4	535	2,526
Hillsborough	54	1,877	7,566	Sarasota	7	54	212
Lake	7	114	285	Seminole	16	152	415
Lee	11	180	495	Volusia	15	642	1,667
Manatee	6	275	851	Multicounty 1/	29	411	2,638
\multicolumn{8}{c}{Drugs (SIC code 283)}
Florida	95	3,936	18,761	Hillsborough	6	24	265
Brevard	5	40	115	Miami-Dade	27	1,139	7,148
Broward	9	87	585	Pinellas	9	918	3,661
Duval	6	87	163	Volusia	4	13	39
\multicolumn{8}{c}{Soap, detergents, and cleaning preparations; perfumes, cosmetics, and other toilet preparations (SIC code 284)}
Florida	137	2,847	8,453	Miami-Dade	36	694	1,759
				Orange	6	43	118
Brevard	5	74	124	Palm Beach	10	65	108
Broward	14	205	536	Pinellas	11	143	491
Duval	6	649	2,578	Polk	6	148	692
Hillsborough	13	305	785	Seminole	5	25	61
\multicolumn{8}{c}{Agricultural chemicals (SIC code 287)}
Florida	84	6,550	24,878	Palm Beach	3	14	27
Orange	6	203	775	Polk	23	3,114	11,991

1/ Reporting units without a fixed location within the state or of unknown county location.

Note: Private employment. For a list of three-digit code industries included see Table 12.50. Data are preliminary. Only counties for which data are disclosed are shown. Detail may not add to totals due to disclosure editing and/or rounding. See Tables 23.70, 23.71, 23.72, 23.73, and 23.74 for public employment data.

Source: State of Florida, Department of Labor and Employment Security, Bureau of Labor Market Information, "Employment and Wages" (ES-202), unpublished data.

University of Florida   **Bureau of Economic and Business Research**

Table 12.70. PETROLEUM, RUBBER, PLASTICS, AND LEATHER PRODUCTS: AVERAGE MONTHLY PRIVATE REPORTING UNITS, EMPLOYMENT, AND PAYROLL COVERED BY UNEMPLOYMENT COMPENSATION LAW IN THE STATE AND COUNTIES OF FLORIDA, 1999

County	Number of reporting units	Number of employees	Payroll ($1,000)	County	Number of reporting units	Number of employees	Payroll ($1,000)
			Petroleum refining and related industries (SIC code 29)				
Florida	80	2,305	7,365	Hillsborough	12	1,002	3,186
Duval	9	341	1,416	Marion	5	64	129
			Rubber and miscellaneous plastics products (SIC code 30)				
Florida	667	20,355	50,568	Miami-Dade	93	3,323	6,848
				Okaloosa	4	109	232
Brevard	30	440	863	Orange	44	1,665	5,121
Broward	73	1,780	4,316	Osceola	9	506	2,394
Charlotte	3	37	78	Palm Beach	34	804	1,752
Collier	10	178	429	Pasco	7	59	112
Duval	32	1,085	2,734	Pinellas	64	2,283	5,830
Escambia	11	170	363	Polk	36	1,201	2,814
Hillsborough	41	1,258	2,947	St. Johns	4	26	54
Indian River	6	136	302	St. Lucie	8	303	653
Lake	5	87	252	Sarasota	21	1,375	4,196
Lee	10	211	528	Seminole	13	278	704
Manatee	14	338	701	Volusia	24	430	1,029
Marion	19	1,250	3,060				
Martin	5	35	109	Multicounty 1/	13	18	118
			Leather and leather products (SIC code 31)				
Florida	75	2,166	3,631	Palm Beach	7	21	76
				Pinellas	9	409	601
Miami-Dade	25	909	1,490	Multicounty 1/	4	6	36

1/ Reporting units without a fixed location within the state or of unknown county location.
Note: Private employment. For a list of three-digit code industries included see Table 12.50. Data are preliminary. Only counties for which data are disclosed are shown. Detail may not add to totals due to disclosure editing and/or rounding. See Tables 23.70, 23.71, 23.72, 23.73, and 23.74 for public employment data.

Source: State of Florida, Department of Labor and Employment Security, Bureau of Labor Market Information, "Employment and Wages" (ES-202), unpublished data.

University of Florida   **Bureau of Economic and Business Research**

Table 12.71. STONE, CLAY, GLASS, AND CONCRETE PRODUCTS: AVERAGE MONTHLY PRIVATE REPORTING UNITS, EMPLOYMENT, AND PAYROLL COVERED BY UNEMPLOYMENT COMPENSATION LAW IN THE STATE AND COUNTIES OF FLORIDA, 1999

County	Number of reporting units	Number of employees	Payroll ($1,000)	County	Number of reporting units	Number of employees	Payroll ($1,000)
			Stone, clay, glass, and concrete products (SIC code 32)				
Florida	824	24,186	70,353	Lee	35	832	2,275
				Manatee	17	679	2,209
Alachua	10	501	1,434	Marion	17	281	694
Brevard	24	432	1,034	Martin	9	371	1,051
Broward	83	2,410	6,760	Miami-Dade	99	2,977	8,181
Charlotte	6	188	460	Okaloosa	7	103	212
Citrus	7	119	276	Orange	46	1,687	4,545
Clay	7	255	739	Osceola	9	155	377
Collier	28	569	1,732	Palm Beach	67	1,701	6,328
Columbia	4	30	75	Pasco	15	316	784
Duval	30	2,375	6,466	Pinellas	33	481	1,375
Escambia	16	769	2,239	Polk	28	1,139	3,848
Gadsden	6	59	139	St. Lucie	11	186	447
Hernando	7	270	1,016	Sarasota	32	713	1,661
Highlands	3	84	188	Seminole	21	481	1,114
Hillsborough	43	2,059	7,776	Sumter	4	35	69
Indian River	10	104	279	Volusia	15	293	648
Lake	14	779	1,824				
			Concrete, gypsum, and plaster products (SIC code 327)				
Florida	471	17,606	50,456	Marion	12	153	364
				Miami-Dade	54	1,792	4,902
Alachua	7	478	1,404	Okaloosa	6	96	189
Brevard	14	332	843	Orange	32	1,564	4,304
Broward	40	1,796	5,168	Osceola	6	130	330
Charlotte	5	187	460	Palm Beach	35	1,198	3,508
Clay	5	246	720	Pasco	11	279	735
Collier	10	378	1,204	Pinellas	16	397	1,212
Duval	18	1,311	3,912	Polk	15	458	1,317
Escambia	12	760	2,227	St. Lucie	8	124	319
Hillsborough	23	1,614	5,856	Sarasota	18	613	1,524
Lake	12	756	1,778	Seminole	9	249	607
Lee	18	759	2,127	Sumter	3	29	65
Manatee	10	167	484	Volusia	11	289	634

Note: Private employment. For a list of three-digit code industries included see Table 12.50. Data are preliminary. Only counties for which data are disclosed are shown. Detail may not add to totals due to disclosure editing and/or rounding. See Tables 23.70, 23.71, 23.72, 23.73, and 23.74 for public employment data.

Source: State of Florida, Department of Labor and Employment Security, Bureau of Labor Market Information, "Employment and Wages" (ES-202), unpublished data.

Table 12.72. FABRICATED METAL PRODUCTS, EXCEPT MACHINERY AND TRANSPORTATION
EQUIPMENT: AVERAGE MONTHLY PRIVATE REPORTING UNITS, EMPLOYMENT
AND PAYROLL COVERED BY UNEMPLOYMENT COMPENSATION LAW
IN THE STATE AND COUNTIES OF FLORIDA, 1999

County	Number of re- porting units	Number of em- ployees	Payroll ($1,000)	County	Number of re- porting units	Number of em- ployees	Payroll ($1,000)
Fabricated metal products, except machinery and transportation equipment (SIC code 34)							
Florida	1,356	34,377	86,305	Marion	19	1,446	2,935
				Martin	11	81	204
Alachua	9	366	1,354	Miami-Dade	181	4,437	9,874
Bay	13	402	1,241	Monroe	4	25	86
Brevard	57	1,109	2,720	Okaloosa	11	88	152
Broward	148	2,919	8,524	Orange	85	2,040	5,220
Charlotte	7	35	56	Osceola	7	79	162
Clay	10	285	819	Palm Beach	80	1,133	3,019
Collier	22	408	1,372	Pasco	11	225	429
Duval	75	3,187	7,959	Pinellas	117	3,220	7,834
Escambia	30	1,051	2,109	Polk	46	1,123	2,746
Hernando	6	120	186	St. Johns	6	204	456
Highlands	6	31	68	St. Lucie	10	99	251
Hillsborough	92	2,973	8,087	Sarasota	37	1,222	3,391
Indian River	14	173	405	Seminole	44	828	2,271
Lake	11	225	557	Taylor	4	260	558
Lee	40	651	1,612	Volusia	30	715	1,905
Leon	18	385	981				
Manatee	35	1,240	3,230	Multicounty 1/	32	65	392
Fabricated structural metal products (SIC code 344)							
Florida	665	17,427	41,221	Leon	7	69	140
				Manatee	19	418	1,023
Alachua	6	32	67	Marion	12	343	667
Bay	6	64	138	Miami-Dade	91	2,750	5,873
Brevard	18	336	845	Monroe	3	23	84
Broward	60	1,323	3,653	Okaloosa	5	25	52
Charlotte	4	17	42	Orange	42	931	2,469
Clay	3	74	204	Osceola	3	13	25
Collier	13	116	268	Palm Beach	41	689	1,673
Duval	44	2,144	4,915	Pasco	3	76	174
Escambia	18	500	1,182	Pinellas	55	1,480	3,533
Hernando	4	85	119	Polk	25	899	2,202
Hillsborough	55	1,532	3,833	Sarasota	13	263	568
Indian River	8	91	197	Seminole	24	511	1,387
Lake	6	156	373	Volusia	9	243	568
Lee	21	389	1,033	Multicounty 1/	10	32	134

1/ Reporting units without a fixed location within the state or of unknown county location.
Note: Private employment. For a list of three-digit code industries included see Table 12.50. Data
are preliminary. Only counties for which data are disclosed are shown. Detail may not add to totals
due to disclosure editing and/or rounding. See Tables 23.70, 23.71, 23.72, 23.73, and 23.74 for public
employment data.

Source: State of Florida, Department of Labor and Employment Security, Bureau of Labor Market
Information, "Employment and Wages" (ES-202), unpublished data.

University of Florida   **Bureau of Economic and Business Research**

Table 12.74. INDUSTRIAL AND COMMERCIAL MACHINERY AND COMPUTER EQUIPMENT
AND REFRIGERATION AND SERVICE INDUSTRY MACHINERY: AVERAGE MONTHLY
PRIVATE REPORTING UNITS EMPLOYMENT, AND PAYROLL COVERED
BY UNEMPLOYMENT COMPENSATION LAW IN THE STATE
AND COUNTIES OF FLORIDA, 1999

County	Number of reporting units	Number of employees	Payroll ($1,000)	County	Number of reporting units	Number of employees	Payroll ($1,000)
Industrial and commercial machinery and computer equipment (SIC code 35)							
Florida	1,808	36,459	118,927	Levy	5	13	20
				Manatee	46	1,211	4,655
Alachua	14	359	1,019	Marion	30	615	1,787
Bay	11	217	586	Martin	18	270	1,332
Brevard	56	1,884	4,553	Miami-Dade	202	3,457	8,477
Broward	211	4,494	16,146	Nassau	4	33	76
Charlotte	10	174	512	Okaloosa	19	169	477
Citrus	3	9	16	Orange	88	4,396	21,026
Clay	13	58	123	Osceola	6	32	91
Collier	25	209	699	Palm Beach	108	2,704	10,020
Columbia	8	94	232	Pasco	29	317	823
Duval	82	1,988	5,736	Pinellas	239	4,029	12,832
Escambia	22	254	636	Polk	69	1,760	5,031
Flagler	9	136	504	St. Johns	12	97	298
Hendry	6	47	130	St. Lucie	20	318	1,130
Hernando	8	103	185	Sarasota	55	656	1,857
Hillsborough	107	1,305	3,877	Seminole	39	1,133	3,640
Indian River	12	331	1,019	Sumter	4	11	24
Lake	16	296	675	Suwannee	3	20	46
Lee	43	768	2,266	Volusia	51	1,189	3,217
Leon	11	56	133	Multicounty 1/	54	228	744
Computer and office equipment (SIC code 357)							
Florida	136	5,907	23,293	Miami-Dade	12	232	806
				Palm Beach	16	1,111	4,438
Brevard	9	1,387	3,196	Pinellas	19	875	3,506
Broward	26	1,026	6,281	Volusia	3	20	39
Hillsborough	7	25	81	Multicounty 1/	9	61	177
Refrigeration and service industry machinery (SIC code 358)							
Florida	189	5687	15,719	Orange	10	314	990
Broward	25	760	2,312	Palm Beach	13	447	1,902
Duval	11	328	1,045	Pasco	4	5	5
Hillsborough	16	344	868	Pinellas	15	279	653
Lee	7	143	514	Seminole	7	471	1,402
Miami-Dade	28	1251	2,927	Volusia	6	191	375

1/ Reporting units without a fixed location within the state or of unknown county location.
Note: Private employment. For a list of three-digit code industries included see Table 12.50. Data
are preliminary. Only counties for which data are disclosed are shown. Detail may not add to totals
due to disclosure editing and/or rounding. See Tables 23.70, 23.71, 23.72, 23.73, and 23.74 for public
employment data.

Source: State of Florida, Department of Labor and Employment Security, Bureau of Labor Market
Information, "Employment and Wages" (ES-202), unpublished data.

Table 12.77. ELECTRONIC AND OTHER ELECTRICAL EQUIPMENT AND COMPONENTS, EXCEPT COMPUTER EQUIPMENT: AVERAGE MONTHLY PRIVATE REPORTING UNITS, EMPLOYMENT AND PAYROLL COVERED BY UNEMPLOYMENT COMPENSATION LAW IN THE STATE AND COUNTIES OF FLORIDA, 1999

County	Number of reporting units	Number of employees	Payroll ($1,000)	County	Number of reporting units	Number of employees	Payroll ($1,000)
\multicolumn{8}{c}{Electronic and other electrical equipment and components, except computer equipment (SIC code 36)}
Florida	849	59,542	225,501	Leon	11	524	1,797
				Manatee	21	2,272	6,833
Alachua	15	890	2,631	Marion	9	338	788
Bay	4	26	50	Martin	7	194	693
Brevard	52	8,022	35,614	Miami-Dade	98	2,790	6,521
Broward	117	6,534	27,258	Orange	60	6,867	27,850
Charlotte	3	41	80	Palm Beach	68	8,994	45,210
Collier	8	73	157	Pasco	6	61	112
Duval	31	632	1,922	Pinellas	88	9,166	30,516
Escambia	4	67	1,247	Polk	12	466	1,380
Hernando	4	205	536	St. Lucie	3	37	53
Hillsborough	49	3,609	11,033	Sarasota	16	733	2,376
Indian River	3	19	120	Seminole	46	3,439	12,031
Lake	9	142	187	Volusia	17	1,118	2,640
Lee	24	678	1,629	Multicounty 1/	35	215	984
\multicolumn{8}{c}{Communications equipment (SIC code 366)}
Florida	190	19,483	93,183	Leon	6	512	1,773
				Miami-Dade	21	340	796
Brevard	16	681	4,705	Orange	14	498	1,967
Duval	8	92	263	Palm Beach	16	7,037	36,162
Hillsborough	12	1,002	2,980	Pinellas	14	2,642	13,127
Lee	8	30	65	Multicounty 1/	10	52	210
\multicolumn{8}{c}{Electronic components and accessories (SIC code 367)}
Florida	248	21,247	74,791	Palm Beach	24	1,349	4,724
				Pinellas	36	3,502	10,065
Broward	47	1,360	3,976	Sarasota	5	338	927
Hillsborough	14	1,125	2,954	Seminole	15	559	1,420
Lee	6	492	1,079	Volusia	7	457	1,376
Miami-Dade	10	437	1,014				
Orange	15	2,879	12,918	Multicounty 1/	10	67	422

1/ Reporting units without a fixed location within the state or of unknown county location.
Note: Private employment. For a list of three-digit code industries included see Table 12.50. Data are preliminary. Only counties for which data are disclosed are shown. Detail may not add to totals due to disclosure editing and/or rounding. See Tables 23.70, 23.71, 23.72, 23.73, and 23.74 for public employment data.

Source: State of Florida, Department of Labor and Employment Security, Bureau of Labor Market Information, "Employment and Wages" (ES-202), unpublished data.

University of Florida   **Bureau of Economic and Business Research**

Table 12.83. SHIP AND BOAT BUILDING: AVERAGE MONTHLY PRIVATE REPORTING UNITS EMPLOYMENT, AND PAYROLL COVERED BY UNEMPLOYMENT COMPENSATION LAW IN THE STATE AND COUNTIES OF FLORIDA, 1999

County	Number of reporting units	Number of em- ployees	Payroll ($1,000)	County	Number of reporting units	Number of em- ployees	Payroll ($1,000)
			Ship and boat building and repairing (SIC code 373)				
Florida	651	17,649	44,813	Martin	26	335	868
				Miami-Dade	85	1,346	3,295
Alachua	7	768	1,834	Monroe	20	104	211
Bay	20	866	2,087	Orange	12	1,010	2,515
Brevard	26	1,422	4,219	Palm Beach	45	502	1,580
Broward	95	1,649	4,637	Pinellas	58	934	2,240
Charlotte	5	20	61	Polk	9	22	27
Collier	12	61	135	Putnam	5	52	84
Duval	25	1,552	4,626	St. Lucie	9	373	920
Escambia	11	104	283	Santa Rosa	4	97	143
Hillsborough	19	1,063	2,772	Sarasota	18	74	171
Lee	29	419	946	Seminole	7	47	95
Manatee	20	1,475	3,384	Multicounty 1/	4	6	25

1/ Reporting units without a fixed location within the state or of unknown county location.
Note: See Note on Table 12.84.

Table 12.84. INSTRUMENTS AND RELATED PRODUCTS: AVERAGE MONTHLY PRIVATE REPORTING UNITS, EMPLOYMENT, AND PAYROLL COVERED BY UNEMPLOYMENT COMPENSATION LAW IN THE STATE AND COUNTIES OF FLORIDA, 1999

County	Number of reporting units	Number of em- ployees	Payroll ($1,000)	County	Number of reporting units	Number of em- ployees	Payroll ($1,000)
			Instruments and related products (SIC code 38)				
Florida	686	36,478	127,383	Martin	10	107	429
				Miami-Dade	99	7,618	25,568
Alachua	15	344	967	Okaloosa	8	471	1,542
Brevard	29	4,474	16,566	Orange	44	1,101	4,268
Broward	69	1,541	5,892	Palm Beach	46	836	3,181
Citrus	4	17	31	Pinellas	80	9,233	34,100
Duval	25	2,825	12,161	Polk	13	519	1,424
Hernando	5	117	173	St. Lucie	4	102	225
Hillsborough	29	727	2,779	Santa Rosa	6	42	105
Lake	7	182	456	Sarasota	21	399	1,077
Leon	11	29	137	Seminole	24	532	1,266
Manatee	9	678	1,828	Volusia	22	1,791	5,096
Marion	11	1,143	3,560	Multicounty 1/	47	236	865

1/ Reporting units without a fixed location within the state or of unknown county location.
Note: Private employment. For a list of three-digit code industries included see Table 12.50. Data are preliminary. Only counties for which data are disclosed are shown. Detail may not add to totals due to disclosure editing and/or rounding. See Tables 23.70, 23.71, 23.72, 23.73, and 23.74 for public employment data.

Source for Tables 12.83 and 12.84: State of Florida, Department of Labor and Employment Security, Bureau of Labor Market Information, "Employment and Wages" (ES-202), unpublished data.

University of Florida   **Bureau of Economic and Business Research**

Table 12.85. TRADE: VALUE OF FLORIDA'S MERCHANDISE TRADE VOLUME, 1995 THROUGH 1999

Year	Value ($1,000,000)			Percentage change from previous year		
	Total trade	Exports	Imports	Total trade	Exports	Imports
1995	52,113.43	29,432.70	22,680.73	13.4	17.4	8.7
1996	56,429.91	31,408.70	25,021.21	8.3	6.7	10.3
1997	63,669.09	36,824.67	26,844.42	12.8	17.2	7.3
1998	69,282.76	37,639.56	31,643.20	8.8	2.2	17.9
1999	69,592.48	34,155.95	35,436.53	0.4	-9.3	12.0

Note: Data are from the Foreign Trade Division of the U.S. Bureau of the Census.

Table 12.86. TRADE: VALUE OF FLORIDA PRODUCTS EXPORTED BY INDUSTRY IN FLORIDA 1997, 1998, AND 1999

Industry	Value ($1,000,000)			Percentage change	
	1997	1998	1999	1997 to 1998	1998 to 1999
Total	36,824.67	37,639.56	34,155.95	2.2	-9.3
Machinery	9,220.16	9,491.16	8,304.23	2.9	-12.5
Electrical machinery	5,869.77	5,860.09	6,032.58	-0.2	2.9
Optical and medical instruments	1,945.94	2,071.15	1,877.26	6.4	-9.4
Fertilizers	1,739.87	1,809.49	1,737.50	4.0	-4.0
Knit apparel	1,382.36	1,396.04	1,686.22	1.0	20.8
Vehicles, not railway	2,526.45	2,512.74	1,658.69	-0.5	-34.0
Aircraft, spacecraft	1,489.77	1,638.02	1,598.63	10.0	-2.4
Woven apparel	1,859.65	1,868.52	1,461.60	0.5	-21.8
Pharmaceutical products	501.93	732.18	706.82	45.9	-3.5
Plastic	743.46	776.90	628.58	4.5	-19.1
Special other	373.11	429.11	576.56	15.0	34.4
Paper, paperboard	601.18	581.47	530.36	-3.3	-8.8
Organic chemicals	589.45	535.84	405.21	-9.1	-24.4
Perfumery, cosmetic, etc.	364.20	402.98	346.64	10.6	-14.0
Miscellaneous chemical products	393.73	393.59	335.80	0.0	-14.7
Meat	379.02	419.32	319.68	10.6	-23.8
Precious stones, metals	87.93	222.52	301.12	153.1	35.3
Furniture and bedding	326.20	368.13	300.86	12.9	-18.3
Preserved food	265.41	279.44	265.16	5.3	-5.1
Tanning, dye, paint, putty	205.04	246.63	225.02	20.3	-8.8
Rubber	357.43	311.12	219.22	-13.0	-29.5
Toys and sports equipment	277.54	249.55	217.80	-10.1	-12.7
Wood	157.34	176.85	211.81	12.4	19.8
Iron and steel products	327.65	303.09	207.17	-7.5	-31.6
Aluminum	265.73	270.64	178.81	1.8	-33.9
Miscellaneous food	176.81	188.35	175.41	6.5	-6.9
Woodpulp, etc.	175.82	147.94	171.07	-15.9	15.6
Tool, cutlery, of base metals	157.80	182.45	158.19	15.6	-13.3
Cotton, yarn, fabric	212.31	215.72	144.81	1.6	-32.9
Ships and boats	156.69	136.39	136.91	-13.0	0.4
All other commodities	3,694.93	3,422.11	3,036.22	-7.4	-11.3

Note: Data are from the Foreign Trade Division of the U.S. Bureau of the Census.

Source for Tables 12.85 and 12.86: Enterprise Florida, Inc., Department of Research, Internet site <http://www.floridabusiness.com/infocenter/IntlTradeInvest/TradeWeb/tradeweb.htm> (accessed 11 August 2000).

University of Florida   **Bureau of Economic and Business Research**

Table 12.87. TRADE: VALUE OF FLORIDA PRODUCTS EXPORTED BY SELECTED DESTINATIONS, 1997, 1998, AND 1999

Location 1/	Value ($1,000,000)			Percentage change	
	1997	1998	1999	1997 to 1998	1998 to 1999
Total	36,824.67	37,639.56	34,155.95	2.2	-9.3
Brazil	6,034.84	6,266.84	5,839.93	3.8	-6.8
Venezuela	3,577.87	3,389.75	2,605.78	-5.3	-23.1
Dominican Republic	2,085.83	2,187.88	2,248.18	4.9	2.8
Argentina	2,499.85	2,498.03	1,996.22	-0.1	-20.1
Colombia	2,745.08	2,606.40	1,813.94	-5.1	-30.4
Costa Rica	1,169.91	1,377.30	1,503.99	17.7	9.2
Honduras	1,191.49	1,404.13	1,463.05	17.9	4.2
Chile	1,136.60	1,068.85	1,036.76	-6.0	-3.0
Guatemala	873.53	1,001.00	946.79	14.6	-5.4
El Salvador	758.29	833.09	927.80	9.9	11.4
Mexico	629.62	826.10	864.13	31.2	4.6
United Kingdom	881.35	809.25	768.67	-8.2	-5.0
Panama	667.68	816.09	724.08	22.2	-11.3
Jamaica	817.20	741.46	713.06	-9.3	-3.8
Bahamas	657.74	646.19	657.95	-1.8	1.8
China	684.03	681.07	644.58	-0.4	-5.4
Peru	887.44	858.87	628.08	-3.2	-26.9
France	425.51	411.15	600.99	-3.4	46.2
Paraguay	754.35	659.33	435.41	-12.6	-34.0
Haiti	320.13	372.88	422.01	16.5	13.2
Ecuador	639.66	694.64	421.02	8.6	-39.4
Netherlands	513.40	466.10	394.94	-9.2	-15.3
India	225.25	261.81	390.75	16.2	49.3
Germany	342.78	376.51	388.24	9.8	3.1
Trinidad and Tobago	355.40	413.01	363.36	16.2	-12.0
Italy	348.13	429.29	295.19	23.3	-31.2
Spain	312.63	300.88	289.74	-3.8	-3.7
Uruguay	293.24	305.26	285.91	4.1	-6.3
Netherlands Antilles	236.92	222.10	263.41	-6.3	18.6
Cayman Islands	184.13	219.37	231.19	19.1	5.4
All Other Countries	4,574.80	4,494.93	3,990.81	-1.8	-11.2

1/ Florida's top merchandise export destinations.
Note: Data are unpublished trade data from the Foreign Trade Division of the U.S. Bureau of the Census.

Source: Enterprise Florida, Inc., Department of Research, Internet site <http://www.floridabusiness. com/infocenter/IntlTradeInvest/TradeWeb/tradeweb.htm> (accessed 11 August 2000).

University of Florida   **Bureau of Economic and Business Research**

TRANSPORTATION

Transportation Industry Employment, 1999

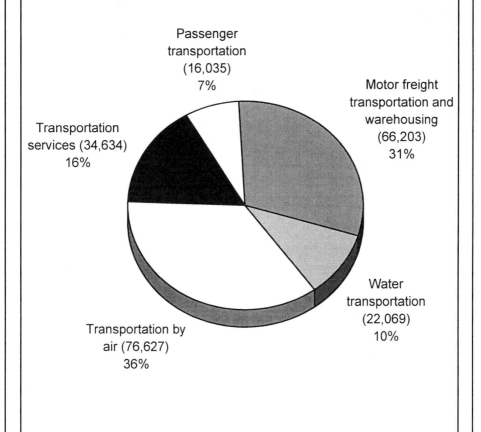

Passenger transportation (16,035) 7%

Motor freight transportation and warehousing (66,203) 31%

Transportation services (34,634) 16%

Water transportation (22,069) 10%

Transportation by air (76,627) 36%

Source: Table 13.35

University of Florida   **Bureau of Economic and Business Research**

TABLES LISTED BY MAJOR HEADINGS

Table 13.01. TRANSPORTATION AND WAREHOUSING: ESTABLISHMENTS, EMPLOYMENT REVENUE, AND ANNUAL PAYROLL BY KIND OF BUSINESS IN FLORIDA, 1997

NAICS code	Kind of business	Number of establishments	Number of employees 1/	Revenue ($1,000)	Annual payroll ($1,000)
48-49	Transportation and warehousing 2/	9,768	157,343	19,852,130	4,429,793
481	Air transportation 2/	334	8,228	1,770,277	236,340
4811	Scheduled air transportation 2/	186	7,178	1,533,797	202,823
4812	Nonscheduled air transportation	148	1,050	236,480	33,517
483	Water transportation	198	12,215	5,008,538	448,117
4831	Deep sea, coastal, and Great Lakes water transportation	154	11,608	4,960,359	432,878
4832	Inland water transportation	44	607	48,179	15,239
484	Truck transportation	3,922	52,124	6,149,233	1,652,082
4841	General freight trucking	2,568	31,622	4,121,698	1,139,249
4842	Specialized freight trucking	3,354	20,502	2,027,535	512,833
485	Transit and ground passenger transportation	784	9,761	489,276	155,003
4851	Urban transit systems	37	835	35,260	17,979
4852	Interurban and rural bus transportation	21	583	43,352	11,094
4853	Taxi and limousine service	303	1,811	115,287	27,928
4854	School and employee bus transportation	127	1,467	41,804	15,195
4855	Charter bus industry	83	1,903	93,930	29,224
4859	Other transit and ground passenger transportation	213	3,162	159,643	53,583
486	Pipeline transportation	30	290	224,051	13,949
4862	Pipeline transportation of natural gas	18	A/	(D)	(D)
4869	Other pipeline transportation	9	B/	(D)	(D)
487	Scenic and sightseeing transportation	406	3,359	232,073	54,095
4871	Scenic and sightseeing transportation, land	33	330	29,826	6,553
4872	Scenic and sightseeing transportation, water	360	2,966	195,478	46,409
4879	Scenic and sightseeing transportation, other	13	63	6,769	1,133
488	Support activities for transportation	2,986	43,400	3,589,969	1,110,320
4881	Support activities for air transportation	476	15,321	1,182,358	387,132
4882	Support activities for rail transportation	44	1,139	136,865	25,323
4883	Support activities for water transportation	373	8,508	482,054	175,962
4884	Support activities for road transportation	409	3,182	164,834	56,234
4885	Freight transportation arrangement	1,595	9,893	1,080,646	304,417
4889	Other support activities for transportation	89	5,357	543,212	161,252
492	Couriers and messengers	790	23,696	2,008,899	659,136
4921	Couriers	418	21,565	1,840,892	617,572
4922	Local messengers and local delivery	372	2,131	168,007	41,564
493	Warehousing and storage	318	4,270	379,814	100,751

(D) Data withheld to avoid disclosure of information about individual firms.
Employment ranges: A/ 100-249. B/ 20-99.
1/ Paid employment for the pay period including March 12.
2/ Excludes large, certificated passenger carriers that report to the Office of Airline Statistics, U. S. Department of Transportation.
Note: The economic censuses are conducted on a 5-year cycle collecting data for years ending in 2 and 7. Railroad transportation and U.S. Postal Service are out of scope for the 1997 Economic Census. Data are for North American Classification System (NAICS) codes 48-49 and may not be comparable to earlier years. See Glossary for definition.

Source: U.S., Department of Commerce, Bureau of the Census, *1997 Economic Census: Transportation and Warehousing*, Geographic Area Series EC97T48-FL, Issued January 2000, Internet site <http://www. census.gov/prod/ec97/97t48-fl.pdf> (accessed 27 June 2000).

Table 13.16. ROADS AND HIGHWAYS: EXISTING MILEAGE OF PUBLIC ROADS AND HIGHWAYS BY JURISDICTION IN FLORIDA, DECEMBER 1995 THROUGH 1998

Jurisdiction	1995	1996	1997	1998
Total	113,778	114,422	114,572	115,416
Rural mileage	65,440	66,083	66,251	67,079
State highway agency	6,976	7,018	7,007	6,999
County roads	57,155	57,579	57,758	58,240
Other jurisdictions 1/	186	200	198	193
Under federal control 2/	1,309	1,486	1,486	1,647
Urban mileage	48,338	48,339	48,321	48,337
Under state control	4,945	4,907	4,920	4,943
County roads	2,992	3,199	3,221	3,232
Other jurisdictions 1/	40,401	40,233	40,180	40,162

1/ Includes state park, state toll, and other state agency roadways. Includes mileage not identified by ownership. Contains mainly municipal mileage for urban summaries.
2/ Includes mileage in federal parks, forests, and reservations that are not part of the state and local highway system.

Table 13.17. ROADS AND HIGHWAYS: EXISTING MILEAGE OF PUBLIC ROADS AND HIGHWAYS BY FUNCTIONAL SYSTEM OF HIGHWAY AND BY PAVEMENT CONDITION IN FLORIDA, DECEMBER 31, 1998

Function	Total existing mileage	Pavement conditions				
		Poor	Medi-ocre	Fair	Good	Very good
Total	115,415	(NA)	(NA)	(NA)	(NA)	(NA)
Rural	67,079	(NA)	(NA)	(NA)	(NA)	(NA)
Interstate	954	0	0	136	70	703
Other principal arterial	3,718	24	39	551	1,403	1,615
Minor arterial	2,582	0	30	412	1,323	575
Major collector	4,368	44	602	1,535	947	1,240
Minor collector	4,198	(NA)	(NA)	(NA)	(NA)	(NA)
Local	51,259	(NA)	(NA)	(NA)	(NA)	(NA)
Urban	48,336	(NA)	(NA)	(NA)	(NA)	(NA)
Interstate	518	0	0	92	114	271
Other freeways and expressways	420	0	0	42	170	188
Other principal arterial	2,687	27	83	681	1,096	511
Minor arterial	3,062	48	116	1,281	935	675
Collector	5,829	331	420	2,218	1,539	1,315
Local	35,820	(NA)	(NA)	(NA)	(NA)	(NA)

(NA) Not available.

Source for Tables 13.16 and 13.17: U.S., Department of Transportation, Federal Highway Administration, *Highway Statistics, 1998,* Internet site <http://www.fhwa.dot.gov/ohim/hs98/roads.htm> (accessed 21 April 2000), and previous editions.

University of Florida   **Bureau of Economic and Business Research**

Table 13.20. ROADS AND HIGHWAYS: RECEIPTS AND DISBURSEMENTS FOR ROADS
AND HIGHWAYS BY ALL UNITS OF GOVERNMENT IN FLORIDA
FISCAL YEARS 1994-95 THROUGH 1996-97

(in thousands of dollars)

Item	1994-95	1995-96	1996-97
Total receipts	4,895,041	4,967,097	5,239,792
Bond proceeds, par value 1/	673,657	604,900	413,162
Total current income	4,221,384	4,362,197	4,826,630
Highway-user tax revenue 2/	2,775,610	2,881,393	2,906,254
Federal agencies	842,430	784,673	701,038
State agencies	1,500,310	1,629,830	1,657,626
Local	432,870	466,890	547,590
Road and crossing tolls	363,642	412,374	482,835
Appropriations from general fund	173,539	173,718	346,145
Property taxes	144,866	147,768	194,143
Other imposts	415,314	414,827	588,989
Miscellaneous receipts 3/	348,413	332,117	308,264
Total disbursements 4/	4,824,183	4,995,976	5,069,113
Bond retirement, par value 1/	127,012	124,577	141,381
Total direct expenditure	4,697,171	4,871,399	4,927,732
Capital outlay	2,869,157	2,901,869	2,876,361
State-administered highways	2,088,012	2,140,695	2,110,615
Locally administered roads	780,938	760,934	762,617
Federal roads and unclassified	207	240	3,129
Maintenance	920,650	985,816	977,733
State-administered highways	425,667	463,498	413,780
Locally administered roads	494,980	522,248	563,950
Federal roads and unclassified	3	73	3
Administration and miscellaneous	331,724	368,099	386,157
Highway law enforcement and safety	346,173	348,419	414,676
Interest	229,467	267,196	272,805

1/ Excludes short-term notes and refunding bond issues.
2/ Excludes amounts allocated for collection expenses and nonhighway purposes.
3/ Includes interest earned on Highway Trust Fund reserves.
4/ Disbursements are classified by system on which expended, rather than by expending agencies; capital outlay on county and other local rural roads includes expenditures from federal, state, and local funds.
Note: This table presents combined summaries of the highway finances of all government agencies in net amounts; duplications that would otherwise have resulted from interfund or intergovernmental transfers have been removed. Data may include estimates.

Source: U.S., Department of Transportation, Federal Highway Administration, *Highway Statistics, 1998,* Internet site <http://www.fhwa.dot.gov/ohim/hs98/hfpage.htm> (accessed 21 April 2000), and previous editions.

University of Florida   **Bureau of Economic and Business Research**

Table 13.21. ROAD AND HIGHWAY BRIDGES: NUMBER BY FUNCTIONAL SYSTEM OF HIGHWAY IN FLORIDA AND THE UNITED STATES, 1996 AND 1997

Functional system	Florida 1996	Florida 1997	United States 1996	United States 1997
Total	10,902	11,009	577,070	580,793
Rural	5,761	5,859	452,820	454,127
Interstate	820	825	28,500	27,899
Other principal arterial	1,247	1,258	34,400	34,787
Minor arterial	736	736	38,424	38,297
Major collector	627	612	96,584	95,512
Minor collector	615	607	46,979	47,233
Local	1,716	1,821	207,933	210,399
Urban	5,141	5,150	124,250	126,666
Interstate	950	943	26,402	26,926
Other freeways and expressways	860	868	14,757	15,044
Other principal arterial	948	940	23,080	23,142
Minor arterial	746	759	20,888	22,148
Collector	460	442	14,764	14,785
Local	1,177	1,198	24,359	24,621

Note: Highway bridges, tunnels, and other structures that are greater than or equal to 20 feet. Because functional system has been estimated or assigned in some cases, data may not be precise.

Source: U.S., Department of Transportation, Federal Highway Administration, *Highway Statistics, 1997,* Internet site <http://www.fhwa.dod.gov/>, and previous edition.

Table 13.22. ROADS AND HIGHWAYS: PERCENTAGE DISTRIBUTION OF ANNUAL VEHICLE DISTANCE TRAVELED BY FUNCTIONAL SYSTEM OF HIGHWAY AND BY VEHICLE TYPE IN FLORIDA, 1998

Type of vehicle	Rural Interstate	Rural Other principal arterial	Rural Minor arterial	Urban Interstate	Urban Other freeways and expressways	Urban Other principal arterial	Urban Minor arterial
All motor vehicles	100.0	100.0	100.0	100.0	100.0	100.0	100.0
Passenger cars and other 2-axle, 4-tire vehicles	83.1	88.3	91.3	89.3	94.9	95.3	95.5
Passenger cars	68.7	71.0	73.3	76.9	82.3	82.0	82.5
Motorcycles	0.2	0.3	0.2	0.3	0.3	0.4	0.3
Buses	0.8	0.6	0.5	0.5	0.6	0.4	0.4
Other 2-axle, 4-tire vehicles 1/	13.4	16.4	17.3	11.6	11.7	12.5	12.3
Single unit 2-axle, 6-tire or more and combination trucks	16.9	11.7	8.7	10.7	5.1	4.7	4.5
Single unit 2-axle, 6-tire or more trucks	3.5	3.7	3.6	2.4	2.9	2.4	2.3
Combination trucks Single trailer	12.8	7.7	5.0	7.9	1.9	2.1	2.0
Multiple trailer	0.6	0.3	0.1	0.4	0.3	0.2	0.2

1/ Excludes passenger cars. Includes vans, pickup trucks, and sport/utility vehicles.

Source: U.S., Department of Transportation, Federal Highway Administration, *Highway Statistics, 1998,* Internet site <http://www.fhwa.dot.gov/ohim/hs98/roads.htm> (accessed 21 April 2000), and previous editions.

University of Florida   **Bureau of Economic and Business Research**

Table 13.29. ROADS AND HIGHWAYS: ESTIMATED ANNUAL VEHICLE MILES OF TRAVEL
BY FUNCTIONAL SYSTEM OF HIGHWAY IN FLORIDA, 1997 AND 1998

(in millions of miles)

Functional system of highway	Total 1997 A/	1998	Rural 1997 A/	1998	Urban 1997 A/	1998
Total	134,007	137,495	34,507	35,644	99,500	101,851
Interstate	27,089	27,687	10,686	11,159	16,403	16,528
Other freeways and expressways	6,837	7,305	0	0	6,837	7,305
Other principal arterial	40,764	41,947	12,154	12,581	28,610	29,366
Minor arterial	20,314	21,165	4,025	4,163	16,289	17,002
Collector	15,944	16,281	3,962	3,999	11,982	12,282
Local	23,059	23,110	3,680	3,742	19,379	19,368

A/ Revised.
Note: Data are estimated highway travel based on traffic counts taken at selected highway locations.

Table 13.30. MOTOR VEHICLE REGISTRATIONS: NUMBER BY TYPE OF VEHICLE IN FLORIDA
1981 THROUGH 1998

(in thousands, rounded to hundreds, except where indicated)

Year	All motor vehicles 1/	Percentage change from previous year	Automobiles 2/	Buses	Trucks 2/	Motorcycles
1981	8,194.1	4.6	6,484.6	30.4	1,459.1	220.0
1982	8,561.0	4.5	6,753.6	32.2	1,548.8	226.4
1983	9,041.0	5.6	7,113.9	33.3	1,661.3	232.5
1984	9,635.1	6.6	7,552.4	34.4	1,807.4	240.9
1985	10,096.8	4.8	7,849.1	35.8	1,979.9	232.0
1986	10,591.2	4.9	8,263.3	34.2	2,064.0	229.7
1987	10,903.1	2.9	8,521.6	34.8	2,127.1	219.5
1988	11,183.1	2.6	8,713.2	35.5	2,234.9	199.5
1989	11,410.8	2.0	8,972.7	36.2	2,197.9	203.9
1990	11,155.6	-2.2	8,694.9	36.8	2,218.1	205.8
1991	10,176.1	-8.8	7,910.3	37.5	2,032.3	196.0
1992	10,426.1	2.5	8,131.4	38.1	2,062.8	193.7
1993	10,358.4	-0.6	8,072.5	38.8	2,058.3	188.8
1994	10,429.2	0.7	7,519.2	39.6	2,693.0	177.4
1995	10,559.5	1.2	7,594.9	40.3	2,734.3	190.1
1996	11,091.9	5.0	7,285.6	41.2	3,561.9	203.3
1997	11,083.5	-0.1	7,374.8	42.1	3,457.1	209.5
1998	11,498.4	3.7	7,437.6	43.1	3,795.7	222.0

1/ Includes motorcycles.
2/ Beginning in 1994, personal passenger vans, passenger minivans, and utility-type vehicles were
classified by the source as trucks rather than automobiles. Therefore, caution should be used when
making comparisons to earlier years.
Note: Excludes vehicles owned by the military service.

Source for Tables 13.29 and 13.30: U.S., Department of Transportation, Federal Highway Administration, *Highway Statistics, 1998*, Internet site <http://www.fhwa.dot.gov/ohim/hs98/> (accessed 21
April 2000), and previous editions.

University of Florida   **Bureau of Economic and Business Research**

Table 13.32. MOTOR VEHICLE TAGS: TOTAL TAGS AND PASSENGER CAR TAGS SOLD
AND REVENUE COLLECTED IN THE STATE AND COUNTIES OF FLORIDA
FISCAL YEAR 1998-99

County	Total tags Number	Percentage change from 1997-98	Passenger car tags Number	Percentage change from 1997-98	Total revenue ($1,000)
Florida 1/	18,507,126	1.1	9,018,164	16.0	460,626
Alachua	234,620	0.8	116,205	1.2	4,713
Baker	26,891	-0.7	10,532	-1.2	596
Bay	177,767	1.5	86,574	1.4	3,898
Bradford	32,676	0.4	11,679	-0.6	681
Brevard	592,450	1.5	286,876	2.6	11,881
Broward	1,457,780	4.9	794,929	6.2	33,126
Calhoun	12,467	1.3	4,663	-1.1	296
Charlotte	174,112	-1.5	87,211	0.9	3,795
Citrus	148,181	1.2	65,021	3.0	3,056
Clay	164,069	1.3	76,986	2.6	3,555
Collier	282,363	3.2	154,073	4.8	7,256
Columbia	70,558	0.0	25,896	2.3	1,437
De Soto	37,982	-0.1	12,280	2.5	867
Dixie	15,162	2.6	5,114	3.8	366
Duval	904,047	0.8	416,457	0.4	19,216
Escambia	301,772	-0.2	159,435	-0.8	6,828
Flagler	55,878	-0.5	31,408	3.6	1,336
Franklin	11,658	7.8	4,791	5.4	260
Gadsden	37,826	-2.2	17,366	-0.6	811
Gilchrist	15,523	-2.3	5,212	-1.8	365
Glades	7,738	11.3	2,484	8.0	188
Gulf	14,646	0.4	6,516	1.4	338
Hamilton	11,175	0.5	4,588	-0.2	265
Hardee	31,156	0.5	10,020	2.9	727
Hendry	53,028	7.1	18,964	9.9	1,372
Hernando	136,278	-0.4	70,594	1.8	3,021
Highlands	113,397	-1.3	45,849	1.3	2,397
Hillsborough	1,152,006	1.7	508,048	2.6	27,527
Holmes	18,749	1.7	7,294	-0.6	418
Indian River	143,533	-2.2	71,576	1.0	3,126
Jackson	54,706	-0.1	21,619	0.3	1,101
Jefferson	22,446	6.0	10,917	25.4	622
Lafayette	6,861	5.8	2,313	5.6	164
Lake	263,152	0.2	110,447	2.0	5,577
Lee	539,288	0.6	256,947	3.3	11,889
Leon	254,387	0.0	124,171	-1.2	5,139
Levy	42,245	1.1	14,930	1.1	1,082
Liberty	6,972	1.8	2,256	-1.8	174

See footnotes at end of table.   Continued . . .

University of Florida   **Bureau of Economic and Business Research**

Table 13.32. MOTOR VEHICLE TAGS: TOTAL TAGS AND PASSENGER CAR TAGS SOLD
AND REVENUE COLLECTED IN THE STATE AND COUNTIES OF FLORIDA
FISCAL YEAR 1998-99 (Continued)

	Total tags		Passenger car tags		
County	Number	Per-centage change from 1997-98	Number	Per-centage change from 1997-98	Total revenue ($1,000)
Madison	18,304	1.6	7,462	4.1	411
Manatee	695,293	7.1	387,274	19.6	18,703
Marion	340,991	1.8	139,319	2.3	7,282
Martin	168,024	-0.8	89,067	2.2	3,925
Miami-Dade	2,392,339	-0.4	1,290,001	1.6	60,480
Monroe	109,179	-0.2	47,545	-1.6	2,408
Nassau	64,339	4.7	28,807	5.4	1,448
Okaloosa	222,055	1.8	109,587	2.4	4,494
Okeechobee	48,156	2.5	16,128	5.7	1,127
Orange	1,075,941	2.2	516,639	1.9	25,678
Osceola	194,899	4.8	91,746	6.0	3,917
Palm Beach	997,812	0.3	617,477	1.5	27,644
Pasco	439,219	-1.7	195,838	1.0	9,242
Pinellas	1,036,700	-1.7	522,724	-0.2	21,209
Polk	597,465	0.4	247,085	2.1	14,361
Putnam	82,636	1.2	31,543	1.3	1,731
St. Johns	148,455	4.0	74,451	1.7	3,458
St. Lucie	214,925	-0.3	103,912	1.7	4,650
Santa Rosa	134,612	3.0	61,200	2.3	2,838
Sarasota	421,775	-1.2	222,833	1.3	9,200
Seminole	424,137	-5.6	217,299	-1.8	9,253
Sumter	52,675	3.0	21,327	9.3	1,331
Suwannee	45,323	3.5	14,458	3.9	952
Taylor	23,806	4.0	8,166	3.9	494
Union	11,599	4.3	4,123	1.7	334
Volusia	537,079	0.5	246,512	2.0	10,832
Wakulla	21,950	1.9	8,232	1.1	501
Walton	36,333	6.2	15,716	7.1	821
Washington	19,638	4.2	7,773	4.1	443
Office agency	49,794	-2.2	11,403	-0.1	1,414
DHSMV 2/	157,452	0.3	(NA)	(X)	170
Motor carrier service	97,936	44.9	(NA)	(X)	40,588

(NA) Not applicable.
1/ Details may not add to totals due to reporting practices involving tags outside the computer system and refunds.
2/ Sales made by the Department of Highway Safety and Motor Vehicles district offices.
Note: See Table 2.36 for mobile home and recreational vehicle tag sales.

Source: State of Florida, Department of Highway Safety and Motor Vehicles, *Revenue Report, July 1, 1998 through June 30, 1999.*

University of Florida   **Bureau of Economic and Business Research**

Table 13.33. DRIVER LICENSES: NUMBER ISSUED BY TYPE AND BY AGE OF DRIVER
IN FLORIDA, JANUARY 1, 2000

Age	Re-strict-ed	Oper-ator	Chauf-feur	Com-mer-cial	Age	Re-strict-ed	Oper-ator	Chauf-feur	Com-mer-cial
Total	50,247	11,782,440	1,038,230	527,978	45	663	207,231	28,881	15,456
					46	624	199,767	27,741	14,529
15	0	57,615	0	0	47	545	195,068	26,756	13,954
16	0	119,820	16	1	48	512	187,946	25,908	13,485
17	1	151,093	88	0	49	549	181,191	24,219	12,575
18	1,254	168,483	601	62	50	524	180,344	23,871	12,223
19	2,968	182,364	1,609	312	51	503	181,398	23,626	11,908
20	3,616	189,351	2,806	637	52	428	189,952	24,150	12,190
21	3,475	195,690	3,951	1,399	53	438	172,470	21,765	10,983
22	3,527	207,218	5,460	2,448	54	374	145,848	18,681	9,377
23	2,504	202,760	6,414	3,575	55	364	147,280	18,419	9,435
24	2,031	206,706	7,626	4,870	56	374	154,394	19,039	9,653
25	1,791	217,630	8,817	6,500	57	382	150,589	18,302	8,829
26	1,484	221,350	10,077	7,741	58	328	134,022	16,205	8,036
27	1,367	230,770	11,799	9,567	59	323	129,069	15,732	7,298
28	1,249	248,469	14,292	11,590	60	305	124,869	15,153	6,782
29	1,235	250,377	16,653	12,490	61	303	125,616	14,726	6,571
30	1,149	238,636	17,392	12,739	62	263	122,354	14,176	5,831
31	1,082	230,276	18,476	13,499	63	244	120,248	13,706	5,410
32	998	225,828	19,745	13,766	64	236	119,990	13,100	4,725
33	977	230,114	22,008	15,030	65	227	117,860	12,740	4,248
34	1,038	236,722	23,911	15,975	66	181	115,426	11,993	3,472
35	949	249,555	26,932	17,241	67	181	121,047	12,018	3,198
36	926	249,161	28,096	17,627	68	157	120,081	11,346	2,715
37	934	248,790	29,224	17,586	69	181	125,013	11,560	2,417
38	823	245,514	29,649	17,994	70	148	121,640	10,430	1,826
39	785	242,094	30,313	17,970	71	140	123,770	10,210	1,480
40	816	234,867	30,258	17,414	72	147	122,836	9,828	1,187
41	761	229,986	29,906	16,898	73	101	118,331	8,709	893
42	705	228,560	30,229	17,056	74	110	116,021	7,911	693
43	651	219,949	29,607	16,892	75	100	114,448	7,107	459
44	656	213,126	28,856	15,931	76+	540	923,447	35,411	1,330

Note: Data are essentially an inventory of current licenses as of January 1, 2000, according to the records of the Florida Department of Highway Safety and Motor Vehicles. Figures do not include temporary permits.

Source: State of Florida, Department of Highway Safety and Motor Vehicles, Division of Driver Licenses, unpublished data.

University of Florida   **Bureau of Economic and Business Research**

Table 13.34. DRIVER LICENSES: NUMBER ISSUED BY COUNTY OF DRIVER'S MAILING
ADDRESS AND BY SEX OF LICENSE HOLDER IN THE STATE AND COUNTIES
OF FLORIDA, JANUARY 1, 2000

County of driver's mailing address	Male	Female	County of driver's mailing address	Male	Female
Florida	6,851,471	6,547,424	Lee	187,298	180,563
			Leon	86,688	89,363
Alachua	82,545	82,344	Levy	14,059	13,660
Baker	7,998	7,798	Liberty	2,200	2,120
Bay	68,443	66,069	Madison	6,420	6,299
Bradford	6,839	6,725	Manatee	106,174	105,062
Brevard	211,914	205,565	Marion	110,200	111,045
Broward	680,966	642,502	Martin	58,501	56,707
Calhoun	4,417	4,212	Miami-Dade	851,310	738,012
Charlotte	61,284	61,956	Monroe	50,599	37,546
Citrus	52,646	52,414	Nassau	26,270	25,105
Clay	60,106	59,009	Okaloosa	78,750	75,547
Collier	108,777	98,510	Okeechobee	15,409	13,318
Columbia	20,335	20,308	Orange	353,245	331,190
De Soto	11,033	9,431	Osceola	77,186	69,867
Dixie	5,176	4,880	Palm Beach	441,584	431,094
Duval	275,460	283,156	Pasco	147,284	145,742
Escambia	110,763	111,167	Pinellas	363,101	370,489
Flagler	21,995	21,820	Polk	179,618	176,638
Franklin	4,100	3,980	Putnam	27,480	26,818
Gadsden	16,004	15,608	St. Johns	53,561	53,427
Gilchrist	5,063	4,930	St. Lucie	81,317	77,861
Glades	3,158	2,740	Santa Rosa	50,221	49,157
Gulf	5,389	5,294	Sarasota	145,558	148,836
Hamilton	4,742	4,428	Seminole	152,894	151,220
Hardee	10,577	8,343	Sumter	17,092	17,026
Hendry	15,330	11,460	Suwannee	14,154	13,716
Hernando	56,894	57,533	Taylor	7,057	7,210
Highlands	36,280	34,936	Union	3,441	3,461
Hillsborough	378,695	367,944	Volusia	179,218	176,037
Holmes	7,279	6,925	Wakulla	8,319	8,119
Indian River	50,015	49,579	Walton	15,158	14,776
Jackson	17,344	17,302	Washington	8,291	8,153
Jefferson	4,916	4,746			
Lafayette	1,866	1,738	Unknown county 1/	254,730	210,720
Lake	90,683	90,878	Out-of-state 2/	178,052	175,290

1/ Licenses mailed to addresses which do not permit specification of county. Also includes licenses
with incorrect or unknown zip codes.

2/ Licenses mailed to out-of-state addresses.

Note: Data are essentially an inventory of current licenses as of January 1, 2000, according to the
records of the Florida Department of Highway Safety and Motor Vehicles. Figures include restricted, operator, chauffeur, and commercial licenses. Figures do not include temporary permits.

Source: State of Florida, Department of Highway Safety and Motor Vehicles, Division of Driver Licenses,
unpublished data.

University of Florida   **Bureau of Economic and Business Research**

Table 13.35. EMPLOYMENT AND PAYROLL: AVERAGE MONTHLY PRIVATE REPORTING UNITS EMPLOYMENT AND PAYROLL COVERED BY UNEMPLOYMENT COMPENSATION LAW BY TRANSPORTATION INDUSTRY IN FLORIDA, 1999

SIC code	Industry	Number of reporting units	Number of employees	Payroll ($1,000)
41	Passenger transportation	953	16,035	28,473
411	Local and suburban passenger transportation	589	10,036	19,052
412	Taxicabs	125	1,197	2,201
413	Intercity and rural bus transportation	25	957	1,785
414	Bus charter service	93	2,358	3,973
415	School buses	110	1,365	1,215
417	Terminal and service facilities for motor vehicle passenger transportation	12	122	248
42	Motor freight transportation and warehousing	5,646	66,203	169,141
421	Trucking and courier services, except air	4,837	59,068	153,682
422	Public warehousing and storage	793	6,997	15,158
423	Terminal and joint terminal maintenance facilities for motor freight transportation	17	138	301
44	Water transportation	1,293	22,069	64,714
441	Deep sea foreign transportation of freight	31	1,130	3,983
442	Deep sea domestic transportation of freight	18	1,336	5,699
444	Water transportation of freight, NEC	19	887	2,949
448	Water transportation of passengers	112	6,720	23,481
449	Services incidental to water transportation	1,114	11,996	28,602
45	Transportation by air	1,315	76,627	224,304
451	Air transportation, scheduled, and air courier services	523	58,180	182,319
452	Air transportation, nonscheduled	216	3,883	11,169
458	Airports, flying fields, and airport terminal services	576	14,565	30,816
47	Transportation services	4,597	34,634	81,731
472	Arrangement of passenger transportation	2,530	17,648	38,158
473	Arrangement of transportation of freight and cargo	1,819	13,163	36,992
478	Miscellaneous services incidental to transportation	241	3,750	6,353

NEC Not elsewhere classified.
Note: Private employment. Data are preliminary. Detail may not add to totals due to disclosure editing and/or rounding. See Tables 23.70, 23.71, 23.72, 23.73, and 23.74 for public employment data.

Source: State of Florida, Department of Labor and Employment Security, Bureau of Labor Market Information, "Employment and Wages" (ES-202), unpublished data.

University of Florida | **Bureau of Economic and Business Research**

Table 13.36. TRANSPORTATION AND PUBLIC UTILITIES: AVERAGE MONTHLY PRIVATE REPORTING UNITS, EMPLOYMENT, AND PAYROLL COVERED BY UNEMPLOYMENT COMPENSATION LAW IN THE STATE AND COUNTIES OF FLORIDA, 1999

County	Number of reporting units	Number of employees	Payroll ($1,000)	County	Number of reporting units	Number of employees	Payroll ($1,000)
			Transportation and public utilities (SIC codes 40-49)				
Florida	17,311	342,178	1,055,284	Lee	445	7,508	19,628
				Leon	215	3,667	9,600
Alachua	133	2,248	6,582	Levy	19	294	650
Baker	24	148	384	Liberty	11	70	137
Bay	177	2,445	6,113	Madison	24	160	357
Bradford	23	174	504	Manatee	179	1,812	4,876
Brevard	374	5,241	14,438	Marion	228	3,002	7,910
Broward	1,738	30,969	96,999	Martin	153	1,946	5,858
Calhoun	12	58	123	Miami-Dade	3,821	86,873	283,411
Charlotte	89	900	2,422	Monroe	173	1,628	4,018
Citrus	100	2,022	9,285	Nassau	76	547	1,285
Clay	104	1,129	3,380	Okaloosa	148	2,565	6,417
Collier	259	2,278	6,701	Okeechobee	36	476	1,250
Columbia	46	569	1,485	Orange	1,097	34,205	101,755
De Soto	21	111	223	Osceola	94	702	1,468
Dixie	28	112	187	Palm Beach	1,034	15,797	53,915
Duval	977	30,783	86,190	Pasco	231	2,278	5,823
Escambia	301	6,346	15,704	Pinellas	709	15,880	51,744
Flagler	33	177	487	Polk	453	8,777	24,725
Franklin	17	111	229	Putnam	55	419	1,178
Gadsden	26	237	652	St. Johns	98	659	1,818
Gilchrist	11	26	80	St. Lucie	155	2,454	8,401
Gulf	14	216	652	Santa Rosa	95	1,060	2,781
Hamilton	15	120	278	Sarasota	305	3,543	10,243
Hardee	17	118	301	Seminole	282	5,944	23,145
Hendry	29	330	754	Sumter	27	344	1,052
Hernando	88	903	2,239	Suwannee	39	339	899
Highlands	62	606	1,472	Taylor	20	88	249
Hillsborough	970	31,881	106,627	Union	16	350	724
Holmes	14	62	167	Volusia	326	5,346	12,814
Indian River	106	755	1,756	Wakulla	19	160	329
Jackson	39	399	977	Walton	37	384	1,014
Jefferson	7	85	272	Washington	25	391	1,075
Lafayette	5	28	67	Multicounty 1/	668	8,546	30,497
Lake	148	2,396	6,275	Out-of-state 2/	3	1	1

1/ Reporting units without a fixed location within the state or of unknown county location.
2/ Employment based in Florida, but working out of the state or country.
Note: See Table 13.35 for a list of industries. Private employment. Only counties for which data are disclosed are shown. Detail may not add to totals due to disclosure editing and/or rounding. See Tables 23.70, 23.71, 23.72, 23.73, and 23.74 for public employment data.

Source: State of Florida, Department of Labor and Employment Security, Bureau of Labor Market Information, "Employment and Wages" (ES-202), unpublished data.

University of Florida   **Bureau of Economic and Business Research**

Table 13.37. PASSENGER TRANSPORTATION AND MOTOR FREIGHT TRANSPORTATION AND WAREHOUSING: AVERAGE MONTHLY PRIVATE REPORTING UNITS, EMPLOYMENT AND PAYROLL COVERED BY UNEMPLOYMENT COMPENSATION LAW IN THE STATE AND COUNTIES OF FLORIDA, 1999

County	Number of re- porting units	Number of em- ployees	Payroll ($1,000)	County	Number of re- porting units	Number of em- ployees	Payroll ($1,000)
			Passenger transportation (SIC code 41)				
Florida	953	16,035	28,473	Miami-Dade	156	2,215	4,340
Alachua	10	53	69	Monroe	14	196	363
Brevard	21	279	493	Nassau	3	19	14
Broward	114	1,805	3,361	Orange	90	3,168	6,073
Citrus	6	22	22	Palm Beach	67	869	2,033
Collier	16	150	221	Pasco	11	68	84
Duval	129	2,574	4,094	Pinellas	39	1,184	2,108
Escambia	15	312	457	Polk	14	198	335
Hernando	9	21	19	St. Johns	7	51	53
Hillsborough	26	348	577	St. Lucie	12	127	155
Indian River	5	18	18	Sarasota	17	47	61
Lee	28	261	342	Seminole	18	192	242
Manatee	9	21	27	Volusia	20	668	1,146
Marion	7	24	28	Multicounty 1/	16	50	90
			Motor freight transportation and warehousing (SIC code 42)				
Florida	5,646	66,203	169,141	Jackson	18	60	93
				Lafayette	4	24	52
Alachua	53	679	2,148	Lake	64	982	2,222
Baker	12	43	87	Lee	155	2,130	3,920
Bay	64	493	988	Leon	75	700	1,445
Brevard	129	1,482	3,182	Levy	8	145	210
Broward	461	3,980	10,353	Liberty	8	30	49
Calhoun	8	36	68	Madison	9	52	74
Charlotte	30	101	145	Manatee	75	511	1,045
Citrus	40	186	330	Marion	119	1,694	4,285
Clay	55	199	438	Martin	42	768	2,154
Collier	78	322	733	Miami-Dade	857	8,811	23,869
Columbia	31	187	339	Monroe	27	191	398
De Soto	12	37	74	Nassau	39	160	303
Dixie	12	31	69	Okaloosa	39	556	1,032
Duval	402	9,764	29,425	Okeechobee	21	313	768
Escambia	126	1,064	2,269	Orange	391	6,664	17,010
Flagler	11	40	70	Osceola	30	82	115
Franklin	3	17	17	Palm Beach	316	2,273	5,550
Gadsden	14	85	152	Pasco	105	828	1,814
Gilchrist	6	9	13	Pinellas	198	1,823	4,211
Gulf	4	15	21	Polk	262	6,044	16,082
Hamilton	9	65	145	Putnam	29	149	253
Hardee	8	19	35	St. Johns	27	114	176
Hendry	15	129	177	St. Lucie	69	429	926
Hernando	37	293	633	Santa Rosa	40	125	231
Highlands	27	206	405	Sarasota	88	468	843
Hillsborough	360	5,829	15,895	Seminole	85	403	765
Holmes	7	16	21	Sumter	18	105	153
Indian River	36	177	369	Suwannee	18	98	170

See footnotes at end of table.   Continued . . .

Table 13.37. PASSENGER TRANSPORTATION AND MOTOR FREIGHT TRANSPORTATION AND
WAREHOUSING: AVERAGE MONTHLY PRIVATE REPORTING UNITS, EMPLOYMENT
AND PAYROLL COVERED BY UNEMPLOYMENT COMPENSATION LAW
IN THE STATE AND COUNTIES OF FLORIDA, 1999 (Continued)

County	Number of reporting units	Number of employees	Payroll ($1,000)	County	Number of reporting units	Number of employees	Payroll ($1,000)
			Motor freight transportation and warehousing (SIC code 42) (Continued)				
Taylor	9	24	40	Walton	13	86	193
Union	13	303	654	Washington	14	78	216
Volusia	121	1,336	3,220	Multicounty 1/	173	1,923	5,467
Wakulla	7	64	114	Out-of-state 2/	3	1	1

1/ Reporting units without a fixed location within the state or of unknown county location.
2/ Employment based in Florida, but working out of the state or country.
Note: Private employment. For a list of three-digit code industries included see Table 13.35. Data are
preliminary. Only counties for which data are disclosed are shown. Detail may not add to totals due to
disclosure editing and/or rounding. See Tables 23.70, 23.71, 23.72, 23.73, and 23.74 for public
employment data.

Table 13.38. WATER AND AIR TRANSPORTATION AND TRANSPORTATION SERVICES: AVERAGE
MONTHLY PRIVATE REPORTING UNITS, EMPLOYMENT, AND PAYROLL COVERED
BY UNEMPLOYMENT COMPENSATION LAW IN THE STATE AND COUNTIES
OF FLORIDA, 1999

County	Number of reporting units	Number of employees	Payroll ($1,000)	County	Number of reporting units	Number of employees	Payroll ($1,000)
			Water transportation (SIC code 44)				
Florida	1,293	22,069	64,714	Martin	38	185	365
				Miami-Dade	200	8,864	29,864
Bay	29	305	672	Monroe	66	411	873
Brevard	39	561	880	Nassau	10	129	294
Broward	207	2,996	9,403	Okaloosa	27	144	259
Charlotte	8	60	116	Orange	8	17	26
Citrus	7	71	84	Palm Beach	99	510	1,326
Collier	38	244	553	Pasco	8	14	27
Dixie	5	25	18	Pinellas	77	494	890
Duval	90	3,997	11,287	Putnam	7	21	54
Escambia	26	108	208	St. Johns	12	51	138
Flagler	5	13	14	St. Lucie	9	55	97
Franklin	7	37	54	Santa Rosa	5	8	14
Hillsborough	54	1,315	4,576	Sarasota	23	82	122
Indian River	12	109	172	Seminole	9	82	136
Lake	4	18	27	Volusia	25	219	310
Lee	47	386	706	Wakulla	5	32	44
Leon	5	9	24				
Manatee	22	180	383	Multicounty 1/	34	56	165

See footnotes at end of table.   Continued . . .

University of Florida   **Bureau of Economic and Business Research**

Table 13.38. WATER AND AIR TRANSPORTATION AND TRANSPORTATION SERVICES: AVERAGE MONTHLY PRIVATE REPORTING UNITS, EMPLOYMENT, AND PAYROLL COVERED BY UNEMPLOYMENT COMPENSATION LAW IN THE STATE AND COUNTIES OF FLORIDA, 1999 (Continued)

County	Number of reporting units	Number of employees	Payroll ($1,000)	County	Number of reporting units	Number of employees	Payroll ($1,000)
			Air transportation (SIC code 45)				
Florida	1,315	76,627	224,304	Miami-Dade	413	32,170	102,757
Alachua	9	353	1,022	Monroe	12	224	519
Bay	14	251	640	Okaloosa	11	577	1,646
Brevard	30	744	1,821	Orange	99	10,445	32,952
Broward	163	7,231	19,841	Osceola	6	61	93
Collier	19	430	1,165	Palm Beach	73	1,902	5,580
Duval	50	5,135	10,459	Pasco	8	166	326
Escambia	23	706	2,190	Pinellas	35	1,530	3,901
Highlands	7	27	64	Polk	22	466	1,392
Hillsborough	53	7,508	21,323	St. Johns	6	104	309
Indian River	9	87	201	Santa Rosa	9	365	1,072
Lee	17	783	2,004	Sarasota	13	617	1,434
Leon	19	540	1,289	Seminole	15	957	2,222
Manatee	10	155	386	Volusia	31	537	1,234
Martin	16	209	505	Multicounty 1/	66	946	2,347
			Transportation services (SIC code 47)				
Florida	4,597	34,634	81,731	Marion	28	108	211
				Martin	27	129	253
Alachua	23	159	280	Miami-Dade	1,707	13,810	35,540
Bay	25	100	192	Monroe	28	133	219
Brevard	77	377	731	Nassau	10	42	91
Broward	487	3,923	9,827	Okaloosa	26	119	125
Charlotte	16	123	206	Okeechobee	4	16	18
Citrus	17	53	81	Orange	307	3,498	6,600
Clay	14	82	207	Osceola	36	257	453
Collier	59	205	428	Palm Beach	285	2,105	5,700
Duval	143	1,765	5,569	Pasco	48	200	358
Escambia	33	308	583	Pinellas	190	1,123	2,153
Flagler	7	22	29	Polk	70	414	901
Hernando	22	90	133	Putnam	7	23	46
Highlands	8	42	74	St. Johns	23	55	113
Hillsborough	213	1,920	4,533	St. Lucie	26	131	210
Indian River	23	82	161	Santa Rosa	13	58	73
Jackson	3	7	7	Sarasota	86	405	675
Lake	29	127	248	Seminole	77	488	842
Lee	90	255	430	Suwannee	5	6	8
Leon	39	179	344	Volusia	72	807	762
Manatee	30	120	142	Multicounty 1/	136	683	2,002

1/ Reporting units without a fixed location within the state or of unknown county location.
Note: Private employment. For a list of three-digit code industries included see Table 13.35. Data are preliminary. Only counties for which data are disclosed are shown. Detail may not add to totals due to disclosure editing and/or rounding. See Tables 23.70, 23.71, 23.72, 23.73, and 23.74 for public employment data.

Source for Tables 13.37 and 13.38: State of Florida, Department of Labor and Employment Security, Bureau of Labor Market Information, "Employment and Wages" (ES-202), unpublished data.

Table 13.40. MOTOR VEHICLE REGISTRATIONS: NUMBER OF OUT-OF-STATE VEHICLES REGISTERED IN FLORIDA BY STATE OF PREVIOUS REGISTRATION 1995 THROUGH 1999

State in 1999 rank order	1995	1996	1997	1998	1999 Number	1999 Per-centage of total
Total	479,275	478,842	511,925	530,021	449,377	100.00
Georgia	45,040	46,924	51,490	57,281	48,862	10.87
New York	51,013	49,153	51,327	51,622	39,628	8.82
Alabama	25,948	26,687	26,989	28,279	23,739	5.28
New Jersey	27,896	27,332	28,562	28,290	23,659	5.26
Ohio	24,341	24,811	26,008	27,426	22,751	5.06
Michigan	21,945	22,547	23,496	23,780	22,521	5.01
North Carolina	20,837	20,563	23,233	25,819	21,622	4.81
Pennsylvania	23,032	23,049	24,366	25,469	21,313	4.74
Virginia	19,998	19,906	20,790	21,209	16,968	3.78
Texas	17,505	16,779	17,170	18,333	16,664	3.71
Illinois	18,475	17,891	19,165	19,491	16,359	3.64
South Carolina	12,677	12,518	13,340	15,616	15,365	3.42
Tennessee	14,221	16,047	19,277	16,954	14,244	3.17
Massachusetts	15,232	13,745	16,084	15,181	13,103	2.92
California	17,816	16,202	15,547	14,726	12,895	2.87
Indiana	11,211	10,879	12,385	14,274	11,266	2.51
Maryland	11,740	11,519	12,409	12,590	10,332	2.30
Connecticut	10,995	10,397	10,841	10,710	8,317	1.85
Louisiana	6,217	6,894	7,596	7,667	7,368	1.64
Kentucky	6,358	6,324	6,811	7,237	6,267	1.39
Missouri	5,608	5,623	6,156	6,803	5,786	1.29
Wisconsin	5,379	5,571	6,244	6,466	5,404	1.20
Mississippi	4,562	5,005	5,736	5,517	5,223	1.16
Colorado	4,941	4,818	5,386	5,090	4,459	0.99
New Hampshire	4,684	4,490	4,739	4,972	4,155	0.92
Arizona	3,494	3,826	4,001	4,040	3,657	0.81
Minnesota	3,667	3,842	4,193	4,285	3,591	0.80
Oklahoma	3,090	3,097	3,301	3,817	3,421	0.76
Maine	3,837	3,461	4,018	3,978	3,246	0.72
Arkansas	2,315	2,636	2,746	3,485	2,928	0.65
Washington	2,523	2,859	2,785	2,915	2,614	0.58
West Virginia	2,872	2,976	2,988	3,148	2,597	0.58
Iowa	2,573	2,393	2,479	2,712	2,264	0.50
Kansas	2,192	2,290	2,451	2,575	2,214	0.49
Rhode Island	2,971	2,718	2,956	2,794	2,208	0.49
Other states	14,559	16,051	17,684	16,981	14,687	3.27
Other areas 1/	7,225	6,762	6,978	8,296	7,628	1.70
Special affidavit	286	257	198	193	52	0.01

1/ Includes Washington D.C., Canada, Puerto Rico, other Caribbean islands, Armed Forces, and other foreign countries.

Source: State of Florida, Department of Highway Safety and Motor Vehicles, Division of Motor Vehicles, unpublished data.

University of Florida   **Bureau of Economic and Business Research**

Table 13.41. MOTOR VEHICLE REGISTRATIONS: NUMBER OF OUT-OF-STATE VEHICLES
REGISTERED BY COUNTY OF REGISTRATION IN THE STATE AND COUNTIES
OF FLORIDA, 1998 AND 1999

County	1998	1999 Number	1999 Per-centage of total		1998	1999 Number	1999 Per-centage of total
Florida	530,021	449,377	100.0	Lake	7,533	5,511	1.2
				Lee	17,054	13,104	2.9
Alachua	6,513	5,341	1.2	Leon	8,345	8,660	1.9
Baker	529	366	0.1	Levy	770	576	0.1
Bay	9,681	7,571	1.7	Liberty	146	116	A/
Bradford	604	507	0.1	Madison	707	442	0.1
Brevard	17,930	14,464	3.2	Manatee	16,917	10,134	2.3
Broward	28,027	26,148	5.8	Marion	10,673	8,111	1.8
Calhoun	275	282	0.1	Martin	4,563	3,764	0.8
Charlotte	6,788	5,107	1.1	Miami-Dade	49,169	50,288	11.2
Citrus	4,850	3,921	0.9	Monroe	4,192	3,325	0.7
Clay	4,997	4,018	0.9	Nassau	2,448	2,089	0.5
Collier	11,075	10,621	2.4	Okaloosa	11,468	9,703	2.2
Columbia	1,725	1,736	0.4	Okeechobee	1,240	902	0.2
De Soto	1,229	1,155	0.3	Orange	32,155	25,736	5.7
Dixie	377	231	0.1	Osceola	6,705	5,917	1.3
Duval	28,359	23,075	5.1	Palm Beach	28,543	26,665	5.9
Escambia	19,210	16,147	3.6	Pasco	12,238	9,473	2.1
Flagler	2,679	2,536	0.6	Pinellas	27,033	18,932	4.2
Franklin	419	372	0.1	Polk	14,067	11,977	2.7
Gadsden	1,009	904	0.2	Putnam	1,778	1,301	0.3
Gilchrist	290	183	A/	St. Johns	5,413	4,605	1.0
Glades	192	163	A/	St. Lucie	5,950	5,327	1.2
Gulf	588	486	0.1	Santa Rosa	7,539	7,610	1.7
Hamilton	508	312	0.1	Sarasota	14,121	11,523	2.6
Hardee	735	606	0.1	Seminole	12,831	10,597	2.4
Hendry	1,345	1,272	0.3	Sumter	2,106	1,814	0.4
Hernando	3,947	2,982	0.7	Suwannee	1,285	1,035	0.2
Highlands	3,034	1,930	0.4	Taylor	479	345	0.1
Hillsborough	29,065	22,641	5.0	Union	221	183	A/
Holmes	1,131	770	0.2	Volusia	16,959	13,964	3.1
Indian River	4,380	3,746	0.8	Wakulla	499	377	0.1
Jackson	2,665	2,286	0.5	Walton	1,904	1,612	0.4
Jefferson	7,908	11,091	2.5	Washington	747	576	0.1
Lafayette	159	113	A/				

A/ Less than 0.05 percent.

Source: State of Florida, Department of Highway Safety and Motor Vehicles, Division of Motor Vehicles, unpublished data.

University of Florida   **Bureau of Economic and Business Research**

Table 13.45. TRAFFIC STATISTICS: DRIVERS, VEHICLES, MILEAGE, CRASHES, INJURIES AND DEATHS IN FLORIDA, 1987 THROUGH 1999

Year	Licensed drivers	Registered vehicles	Vehicle miles (millions)	Crashes 1/	Nonfatal injuries	Deaths	Mileage death rate 2/
1987	10,241,063	11,738,273	92,865	240,429	215,886	2,891	3.1
1988	10,648,019	11,997,948	105,030	256,543	230,738	3,152	3.0
1989	11,109,288	12,276,272	108,876	252,439	230,060	3,033	2.8
1990	11,612,402	12,465,790	109,997	216,245	214,208	2,951	2.7
1991	12,170,821	A/ 11,184,146	113,484	195,312	195,122	2,523	2.2
1992	A/ 11,550,126	11,205,298	114,000	196,176	205,432	2,480	2.2
1993	11,767,409	11,159,938	119,768	199,039	212,454	2,719	2.3
1994	11,992,578	11,393,982	120,929	206,183	223,458	2,722	2.3
1995	12,019,156	11,557,811	127,800	228,589	233,900	2,847	2.2
1996	12,343,598	12,003,929	129,637	241,377	243,320	2,806	2.2
1997	12,691,835	12,170,375	133,276	240,639	240,001	2,811	2.1
1998	13,012,132	B/ 11,277,808	136,680	245,440	241,863	2,889	2.1
1999	13,398,895	B/ 11,611,993	139,329	243,409	232,225	2,920	2.1

A/ Decrease reflects changes in accounting method.
B/ Excludes count of trailers with tags.
1/ Statutory revisions in 1989 reduced the number of non-injury accidents required to be reported.
2/ The number of deaths per 100 million vehicle miles traveled.
Note: Some data may be revised. See Note on Table 13.47.

Table 13.46. MOTOR VEHICLE CRASHES: NUMBER OF DRIVERS ASSIGNED A CONTRIBUTING CAUSE BY TYPE OF CIRCUMSTANCE IN FLORIDA, 1999

Cause of crash	All crashes		Fatal crashes		Injury crashes	
	Number	Percentage of total	Number	Percentage of total	Number	Percentage of total
Total	196,653	100.0	3,627	100.0	148,039	100.0
Speed too fast	7,140	3.6	472	13.0	5,255	3.5
Failed to yield right of way	41,045	20.9	632	17.4	32,345	21.8
Disregarded stop sign	3,491	1.8	78	2.2	2,724	1.8
Disregarded other traffic control	8,900	4.5	119	3.3	7,209	4.9
Drove left of center	1,642	0.8	130	3.6	1,171	0.8
Improper overtaking	6,678	3.4	108	3.0	4,814	3.3
Followed too closely	7,173	3.6	7	0.2	5,475	3.7
Alcohol, under influence	7,797	4.0	320	8.8	4,031	2.7
Careless driving	71,468	36.3	858	23.7	54,540	36.8
Mechanical defect	1,970	1.0	28	0.8	1,397	0.9
Other	39,349	20.0	875	24.1	29,078	19.6

Source for Tables 13.45 and 13.46: State of Florida, Department of Highway Safety and Motor Vehicles, Office of Management and Planning Services, *1999 Florida Traffic Crash Facts,* Internet site <http://www.hsmv.state.fl.us/hsmvdocs/cf99.pdf> (accessed 14 June 2000).

University of Florida   **Bureau of Economic and Business Research**

Table 13.47. MOTOR VEHICLE CRASHES: COMPARATIVE SAFETY EQUIPMENT USAGE BY TYPE
OF INJURY IN FLORIDA, 1999

Safety equipment usage	Total	No injury	Possible	Noninca-pacitating	Incapac-itating	Fatal
			Type of injury (percentage)			
Drivers	360,326	60.41	21.92	12.56	4.72	0.39
Safety belt	264,962	64.68	21.41	10.32	3.45	0.13
Safety belt and air bag	53,772	50.13	24.96	18.77	5.83	0.31
Air bag only	2,004	29.19	33.88	21.76	13.07	2.10
Not using safety equipment	39,588	47.37	20.55	18.64	11.28	2.16
Other vehicle occupants	174,596	60.41	22.39	12.18	4.64	0.39
Safety belt	118,911	62.82	23.38	10.36	3.31	0.14
Safety belt and air bag	13,640	49.33	25.72	18.06	6.43	0.45
Air bag only	557	30.16	28.55	25.49	14.72	1.08
Not using safety equipment	41,488	57.55	18.37	15.29	7.71	1.08
Motorcyclist	5,127	10.22	17.73	41.12	27.72	3.22
With safety helmet	3,745	7.50	16.58	42.24	29.85	3.82
Driver	3,322	6.80	16.62	42.72	29.86	4.00
Passenger	423	13.00	16.31	38.53	29.79	2.36
Without safety helmet	1,382	17.58	20.84	38.06	21.92	1.59
Driver	1,201	15.90	20.40	39.05	22.81	1.83
Passenger	181	28.73	23.76	31.49	16.02	0.00
Bicyclist	5,511	10.16	27.89	43.68	16.11	2.16
With safety helmet	591	4.74	25.72	53.47	15.06	1.02
Driver	579	4.32	25.91	53.89	14.85	1.04
Passenger	12	25.00	16.67	33.33	25.00	0.00
Without safety helmet	4,920	10.81	28.15	42.50	16.24	2.30
Driver	4,732	9.19	28.49	43.32	16.67	2.32
Passenger	188	51.60	19.68	21.81	5.32	1.60
Children 1/	17,406	73.68	26.18	(NA)	(NA)	0.14
With restraint	15,603	75.92	24.02	(NA)	(NA)	0.06
Less than 4 years	9,400	77.64	22.30	(NA)	(NA)	0.06
4 to 5 years	6,203	73.32	26.63	(NA)	(NA)	0.05
Without restraint	1,803	54.30	44.87	(NA)	(NA)	0.83
Less than 4 years	1,040	55.10	44.04	(NA)	(NA)	0.87
4 to 5 years	763	53.21	46.00	(NA)	(NA)	0.79

(NA) Not available.
1/ Injury breakdowns are unavailable for children and are listed together under "possible" injury.
    Note: Legally reportable accidents are those involving death, bodily injury, or one or more of the following circumstances: (1) driver leaves the accident scene where death, injury, or property damage has occurred; (2) driver is under the influence of alcohol or drugs; and, (3) a wrecker is required to remove an inoperative vehicle.

Source: State of Florida, Department of Highway Safety and Motor Vehicles, Office of Management and Planning Services, *Florida Traffic Crash Facts, 1999,* Internet site <http://www.hsmv.state.fl.us/hsmvdocs/cf99.pdf> (accessed 14 June 2000).

University of Florida   **Bureau of Economic and Business Research**

Table 13.48. MOTOR VEHICLE CRASHES: DRIVERS AND MOTOR VEHICLES INVOLVED
IN CRASHES BY AGE, SEX, AND RESIDENCE OF DRIVER AND BY TYPE
OF MOTOR VEHICLE IN FLORIDA, 1999

Item	All crashes	Fatal crashes	Injury crashes
Drivers involved in crashes, total 1/	350,372	3,827	(NA)
Age and sex			
Under 15	456	3	(NA)
15	642	8	(NA)
16	7,426	57	(NA)
17	9,972	88	(NA)
18	11,815	120	(NA)
19	11,116	128	(NA)
20-24	44,914	402	(NA)
25-29	40,804	439	(NA)
30-39	78,073	800	(NA)
40-49	60,829	628	(NA)
50-59	36,839	437	(NA)
60-69	21,558	235	(NA)
70-79	16,028	260	(NA)
80-84	4,527	119	(NA)
85 and over	2,975	85	(NA)
Not stated	2,398	18	(NA)
Male	(NA)	1,290	81,310
Female	(NA)	414	70,475
Residence			
County of crash	307,772	1,278	126,155
Resident elsewhere in state	48,553	333	19,697
Nonresident of state	13,727	80	4,942
Foreign	2,366	6	654
Not stated	1,275	10	385
Vehicles involved in crashes, total	373,693	4,260	268,537
Automobile	259,942	2,481	186,144
Passenger van	28,542	327	20,719
Light truck (2 rear tires)	56,894	759	40,471
Medium truck (4 rear tires)	5,428	88	3,696
Heavy truck	3,264	70	2,092
Truck-tractor (cab)	3,785	114	2,379
Motor home (RV)	354	10	245
Bus	2,428	33	1,495
Bicycle	5,351	128	4,847
Motorcycle	4,544	172	4,128
Moped	425	9	386
All terrain vehicle	383	8	322
Train	70	15	29
Other	2,283	46	1,584

(NA) Not available.
1/ Excludes bicycles, mopeds, all terrain vehicles (ATVs), and trains.
Note: Legally reportable accidents are those involving death, bodily injury, or one or more of the following circumstances: (1) driver leaves the accident scene where death, injury, or property damage has occurred; (2) driver is under the influence of alcohol or drugs; and, (3) a wrecker is required to remove an inoperative vehicle.

Source: State of Florida, Department of Highway Safety and Motor Vehicles, Office of Management and Planning Services, *Florida Traffic Crash Facts, 1999,* Internet site <http://www.hsmv.state.fl.us/hsmvdocs/cf99.pdf> (accessed 14 June 2000).

University of Florida   **Bureau of Economic and Business Research**

Table 13.49. MOTOR VEHICLE CRASHES: PERSONS KILLED OR INJURED IN CRASHES AND ALCOHOL-RELATED CRASHES IN THE STATE AND COUNTIES OF FLORIDA, 1999

County	Total crashes			Fatalities			Injuries		
	Number	Alcohol-related	Per-centage	Number	Alcohol-related	Per-centage	Number	Alcohol-related	Per-centage
Florida 1/	243,409	22,252	9.1	2,920	936	32.1	232,225	19,073	8.2
Alachua	3,874	385	9.9	48	12	25.0	3,355	297	8.9
Baker	248	47	19.0	10	6	60.0	259	48	18.5
Bay	1,979	368	18.6	28	12	42.9	2,045	310	15.2
Bradford	223	42	18.8	3	0	0.0	237	52	21.9
Brevard	4,713	735	15.6	81	34	42.0	4,986	586	11.8
Broward	27,435	1,984	7.2	214	62	29.0	25,936	1,640	6.3
Calhoun	110	30	27.3	1	0	0.0	141	36	25.5
Charlotte	1,580	166	10.5	31	11	35.5	1,516	145	9.6
Citrus	976	120	12.3	26	5	19.2	1,124	109	9.7
Clay	1,303	156	12.0	16	6	37.5	1,239	116	9.4
Collier	2,771	395	14.3	60	13	21.7	2,638	290	11.0
Columbia	654	91	13.9	18	5	27.8	797	94	11.8
De Soto	304	34	11.2	14	3	21.4	417	31	7.4
Dixie	126	32	25.4	3	1	33.3	139	25	18.0
Duval	13,664	1,101	8.1	116	37	31.9	11,020	825	7.5
Escambia	3,820	527	13.8	38	18	47.4	4,227	429	10.1
Flagler	382	46	12.0	16	4	25.0	426	46	10.8
Franklin	98	18	18.4	1	1	100.0	98	21	21.4
Gadsden	631	100	15.8	21	12	57.1	716	113	15.8
Gilchrist	127	22	17.3	6	2	33.3	142	20	14.1
Glades	90	13	14.4	8	5	62.5	98	7	7.1
Gulf	143	23	16.1	1	1	100.0	157	27	17.2
Hamilton	114	19	16.7	2	2	100.0	175	22	12.6
Hardee	256	26	10.2	14	2	14.3	307	20	6.5
Hendry	364	56	15.4	14	9	64.3	427	69	16.2
Hernando	1,231	168	13.6	25	8	32.0	1,526	159	10.4
Highlands	583	59	10.1	30	8	26.7	725	51	7.0
Hillsborough	18,091	1,705	9.4	197	78	39.6	17,864	1,533	8.6
Holmes	133	24	18.0	7	0	0.0	161	20	12.4
Indian River	1,233	138	11.2	22	3	13.6	1,211	112	9.2
Jackson	492	58	11.8	25	6	24.0	649	70	10.8
Jefferson	163	14	8.6	12	5	41.7	198	16	8.1
Lafayette	84	17	20.2	2	2	100.0	75	9	12.0
Lake	2,239	245	10.9	47	12	25.5	2,230	208	9.3
Lee	4,919	685	13.9	99	29	29.3	4,974	572	11.5
Leon	5,886	518	8.8	16	5	31.3	4,302	369	8.6

See footnotes at end of table.

Continued . . .

University of Florida   **Bureau of Economic and Business Research**

Table 13.49. MOTOR VEHICLE CRASHES: PERSONS KILLED OR INJURED IN CRASHES AND ALCOHOL-RELATED CRASHES IN THE STATE AND COUNTIES OF FLORIDA, 1998 (Continued)

County	Total crashes Number	Alcohol-related	Per-centage	Fatalities Number	Alcohol-related	Per-centage	Injuries Number	Alcohol-related	Per-centage
Levy	402	77	19.2	16	10	62.5	475	77	16.2
Liberty	79	17	21.5	1	0	0.0	99	13	13.1
Madison	251	32	12.7	10	3	30.0	301	33	11.0
Manatee	3,368	490	14.5	58	23	39.7	3,465	446	12.9
Marion	2,939	304	10.3	74	28	37.8	3,543	291	8.2
Martin	1,436	238	16.6	26	6	23.1	1,510	190	12.6
Miami-Dade	49,804	2,036	4.1	316	59	18.7	40,641	1,727	4.2
Monroe	1,363	211	15.5	25	12	48.0	1,220	170	13.9
Nassau	542	66	12.2	18	8	44.4	601	56	9.3
Okaloosa	1,747	298	17.1	16	9	56.3	1,760	206	11.7
Okeechobee	414	59	14.3	7	4	57.1	452	66	14.6
Orange	16,604	1,366	8.2	153	49	32.0	16,974	1,183	7.0
Osceola	2,272	222	9.8	50	10	20.0	2,693	245	9.1
Palm Beach	14,387	1,298	9.0	189	54	28.6	14,741	1,117	7.6
Pasco	4,104	446	10.9	79	36	45.6	4,736	407	8.6
Pinellas	13,196	1,486	11.3	116	40	34.5	13,243	1,302	9.8
Polk	7,220	707	9.8	123	28	22.8	7,379	684	9.3
Putnam	1,039	149	14.3	19	8	42.1	936	142	15.2
St. Johns	1,607	217	13.5	45	13	28.9	1,624	215	13.2
St. Lucie	2,086	242	11.6	31	6	19.4	2,176	219	10.1
Santa Rosa	1,114	138	12.4	15	11	73.3	1,468	141	9.6
Sarasota	4,229	511	12.1	35	12	34.3	4,180	428	10.2
Seminole	3,284	348	10.6	40	13	32.5	2,874	238	8.3
Sumter	561	78	13.9	33	11	33.3	698	82	11.7
Suwannee	470	56	11.9	14	7	50.0	445	67	15.1
Taylor	242	37	15.3	15	8	53.3	244	33	13.5
Union	88	12	13.6	3	0	0.0	108	13	12.0
Volusia	6,468	743	11.5	86	34	39.5	5,784	592	10.2
Wakulla	231	57	24.7	6	3	50.0	294	61	20.7
Walton	500	98	19.6	16	8	50.0	671	92	13.7
Washington	196	39	19.9	12	4	33.3	254	39	15.4

1/ Includes data not distributed by county.

Note: Legally reportable accidents are those involving death, bodily injury, or one or more of the following circumstances: (1) driver leaves the accident scene where death, injury, or property damage has occurred; (2) driver is under the influence of alcohol or drugs; and, (3) a wrecker is required to remove an inoperable vehicle.

Source: State of Florida, Department of Highway Safety and Motor Vehicles, Office of Management and Planning Services, *Florida Traffic Crash Facts, 1999,* Internet site <http://www.hsmv.state.fl.us/hsmvdocs/cf99.pdf> (accessed 14 June 2000).

University of Florida   **Bureau of Economic and Business Research**

Table 13.60. RAILROADS: MILES OF RAILROAD TRACK OPERATED AND PERCENTAGE OF STATE SYSTEM BY RAILROAD COMPANY IN FLORIDA, 1998

Company	Tracks (in miles)	Percent-age of state system	Company	Tracks (in miles)	Percent-age of state system
Total	2,887	100.0	Florida Northern	27	0.9
			Florida West Coast	14	0.5
Alabama and Gulf Coast	44	1.5	Georgia and Florida	48	1.7
Apalachicola Northern	96	3.3	Norfolk Southern 2/	96	3.3
Bay Line	63	2.2	Seminole Gulf	119	4.1
CSX Transportation 1/	1,619	56.1	South Central Florida	158	5.5
Florida Central	66	2.3	South Florida Rail		
Florida East Coast	386	13.4	Corridor 3/	81	2.8
Florida Midland	40	1.4	Terminal Companies	30	1.0

1/ Amtrak operates in Florida but owns no trackage in the state other than yard and terminal tracks. It operates mainly over CSXT main tracks. It also operates over trackage owned by the State of Florida between West Palm Beach and Miami (81 miles).
2/ Previously two companies - Georgia Southern and Florida and Live Oak Perry and South Georgia.
3/ Not an operating carrier.

Source: State of Florida, Department of Transportation, Rail Office, *1998 Florida Rail System Plan.*

Table 13.61. PORT ACTIVITY: TONNAGE HANDLED IN SPECIFIED PORTS IN FLORIDA FISCAL YEAR 1998-99 OR CALENDAR YEAR 1999

Port and type of cargo	Short tons	Port and type of cargo	Short tons
Canaveral (fiscal year 1998-99),		Miami (fiscal year	
total	4,139,573	1998-99), total	6,930,372
Exports	1,035,344	Exports	3,190,769
Imports	3,104,229	Imports	3,739,603
Everglades (fiscal year 1998-99),		Palm Beach (fiscal year	
total	23,681,273	1998-99), total	4,283,424
Ft. Pierce (calendar year 1999),		Panama City (calendar	
total	20,105	year 1999), total	591,011
Exports	3,038	Exports	285,002
Imports	17,067	Imports	212,424
Jacksonville 1/ (fiscal year 1998-99),		Domestic	93,586
total JPA terminals	7,524,271	Pensacola (fiscal year	
General cargo exports	3,551,066	1998-99), total	581,542
General cargo imports	3,973,205	Exports	351,269
Containerized cargo	4,163,829	Imports	230,273
Bulk cargo and other	2,838,141	Tampa (fiscal year	
Manatee (fiscal year 1998-99),		1998-99), total	52,300,000
total	5,567,810	Exports	10,700,000
Exports	1,621,978	Imports	7,300,000
Imports	3,945,762	Domestic	34,300,000

1/ Tonnage passing through facilities owned by the Jacksonville Port Authority only; therefore they differ from movements into and out of the Port of Jacksonville.

Source: Data are reported in annual or cumulative monthly reports of each port authority.

University of Florida   **Bureau of Economic and Business Research**

Table 13.73. EXPORTS AND IMPORTS: VALUE OF SHIPMENTS HANDLED BY CUSTOMS DISTRICTS IN FLORIDA, 1999

Customs district and commodity	Exports Value (million dollars)	Exports Percentage change from prior year	Customs district and commodity	Imports Value (million dollars)	Imports Percentage change from prior year
Miami	28,538	-5.5	Miami	23,409	8.8
Machinery	7,777	-11.7	Knit apparel	4,085	16.9
Electrical machinery	5,866	3.9	Woven apparel	3,632	-1.9
Optical and medical			Machinery	2,524	65.3
instruments	1,683	-8.5	Aircraft, spacecraft	1,278	39.1
Knit apparel	1,630	18.3	Electrical machinery	1,236	-15.6
Woven apparel	1,429	-19.3	Fish and seafood	1,148	5.2
Aircraft, spacecraft	1,248	1.1	Special other	996	26.5
Vehicles, not railway	1,039	-18.5	Optical and medical		
Pharmaceutical products	663	-7.6	instruments	595	9.3
Special other	525	35.6	Precious stones, metals	571	-27.2
Plastic	501	-0.1	Live trees and plants	502	-2.6
Perfumery, cosmetic, etc.	319	-13.2	Beverages	427	36.3
Paper, paperboard	308	-1.9	Mineral fuel, oil etc.	416	12.5
Organic chemicals	300	-20.2	Organic chemicals	397	-42.3
Precious atones, metals	299	35.2	Furniture and bedding	382	23.2
Miscellaneous chemical			Footwear	345	-13.8
products	278	-6.1	Ships and boats	338	1.4
Furniture and bedding	268	-17.3	Perfumery, cosmetic, etc.	281	3.6
Toys and sports equipment	204	-9.8	Tobacco	272	-10.8
Tanning, dye, paint, putty	200	-7.3	Vehicles, not railway	228	19.9
Rubber	195	-14.9	Spices, coffee and tea	215	-26.8
Iron and steel products	182	-17.4			
Tampa	5,618	-24.4	Tampa	12,027	18.7
Fertilizers	1,730	-3.8	Vehicles, not railway	6,549	10.7
Vehicles, not railway	620	-50.0	Aircraft, spacecraft	1,886	193.3
Machinery	527	-22.9	Mineral fuel, oil etc.	583	26.7
Aircraft, spacecraft	351	-13.2	Machinery	387	9.0
Paper, paperboard	222	-16.9	Inorganic chemical; rare		
Optical and medical			earth materials	225	-20.4
instruments	194	-16.4	Iron and steel	178	-20.4
Meat	169	-37.1	Paper, paperboard	153	22.4
Electrical machinery	167	-21.7	Preserved food	147	7.4
Preserved food	164	-8.9	Salt; sulfur; earth, stone	147	11.3
Woodpulp, etc.	151	15.5	Electrical machinery	146	20.7
Plastic	127	-53.7	Special other	141	-21.4
Organic chemicals	106	-34.2	Edible fruit and nuts	112	16.7
Food waste; animal feed	91	-0.7	Spices, coffee and tea	104	-48.1
Aluminum	83	-45.3	Woodpulp, etc.	94	-17.7
Miscellaneous chemical			Aluminum	93	218.3
products	58	-40.9	Optical and medical		
Knit apparel	56	198.5	instruments	90	-7.4
Special other	51	22.8	Footwear	68	77.1
Ships and boats	48	17.3	Rubber	66	-23.1
Wood	46	44.7	Woven apparel	63	10.9
Edible fruit and nuts	45	-15.1	Fish and seafood	58	-13.1

Note: Data from the Foreign Trade Division of the U.S. Bureau of the Census.

Source: Enterprise Florida, Department of Research, unpublished data.

University of Florida   **Bureau of Economic and Business Research**

Table 13.90. AIRPORT ACTIVITY: OPERATIONS AT AIRPORTS WITH FEDERAL AVIATION
ADMINISTRATION (FAA)-OPERATED AND -CONTRACTED TRAFFIC CONTROL TOWERS
IN FLORIDA, FISCAL YEAR ENDING SEPTEMBER 30, 1999

Location and type of operation	Total operations 1/	Air carrier 2/	Air taxi 3/	General aviation 4/	Military
Florida	6,306,735	1,039,270	626,246	4,452,656	188,563
Itinerant	4,475,737	1,039,270	626,246	2,696,454	113,767
Local	1,830,998	0	0	1,756,202	74,796
Daytona Beach	376,057	5,408	892	368,858	899
Itinerant	318,207	5,408	892	311,012	895
Local	57,850	0	0	57,846	4
Ft. Lauderdale	279,823	131,577	50,818	96,604	824
Itinerant	277,037	131,577	50,818	93,959	683
Local	2,786	0	0	2,645	141
Ft. Lauderdale Executive	247,228	0	8,159	239,038	31
Itinerant	186,240	0	8,159	178,052	29
Local	60,988	0	0	60,986	2
Ft. Myers Page Field	97,566	0	3,296	94,063	207
Itinerant	55,630	0	3,296	52,149	185
Local	41,936	0	0	41,914	22
Ft. Myers Regional	74,174	38,330	16,366	17,623	1,855
Itinerant	70,314	38,330	16,366	14,773	845
Local	3,860	0	0	2,850	1,010
Ft. Pierce	155,461	0	1,477	153,822	162
Itinerant	81,776	0	1,477	80,166	133
Local	73,685	0	0	73,656	29
Gainesville	81,638	1,608	11,498	63,408	5,124
Itinerant	57,530	1,608	11,498	42,632	1,792
Local	24,108	0	0	20,776	3,332
Hollywood	168,260	9	16	167,467	768
Itinerant	60,631	9	16	60,382	224
Local	107,629	0	0	107,085	544
Jacksonville/Craig Field	146,102	0	9,956	118,588	17,558
Itinerant	93,886	0	9,956	70,066	13,864
Local	52,216	0	0	48,522	3,694
Jacksonville International	162,628	59,953	27,458	49,274	25,943
Itinerant	125,238	59,953	27,458	29,092	8,735
Local	37,390	0	0	20,182	17,208
Key West	128,521	1,031	38,921	67,066	21,503
Itinerant	100,467	1,031	38,921	43,963	16,552
Local	28,054	0	0	23,103	4,951
Kissimmee	141,215	2	239	140,845	129
Itinerant	60,720	2	239	60,380	99
Local	80,495	0	0	80,465	30

See footnotes at end of table.

Continued . . .

University of Florida   **Bureau of Economic and Business Research**

Table 13.90. AIRPORT ACTIVITY: OPERATIONS AT AIRPORTS WITH FEDERAL AVIATION ADMINISTRATION (FAA)-OPERATED AND -CONTRACTED TRAFFIC CONTROL TOWERS IN FLORIDA, FISCAL YEAR ENDING SEPTEMBER 30, 1999 (Continued)

Location and type of operation	Total operations 1/	Air carrier 2/	Air taxi 3/	General aviation 4/	Military
Lakeland	221,059	0	930	216,566	3,563
Itinerant	110,015	0	930	107,580	1,505
Local	111,044	0	0	108,986	2,058
Melbourne	145,484	5,676	1,170	138,179	459
Itinerant	83,568	5,676	1,170	76,263	459
Local	61,916	0	0	61,916	0
Miami International	523,277	315,256	128,039	74,509	5,473
Itinerant	523,277	315,256	128,039	74,509	5,473
Local	0	0	0	0	0
Naples	123,379	0	13,783	109,540	56
Itinerant	94,555	0	13,783	80,720	52
Local	28,824	0	0	28,820	4
Opa-Locka	113,153	29	6,332	95,274	11,518
Itinerant	70,615	29	6,332	57,924	6,330
Local	42,538	0	0	37,350	5,188
Orlando Executive	221,282	0	13,228	207,256	798
Itinerant	154,233	0	13,228	140,326	679
Local	67,049	0	0	66,930	119
Orlando International	363,261	249,632	71,780	37,441	4,408
Itinerant	363,261	249,632	71,780	37,441	4,408
Local	0	0	0	0	0
Panama City-Bay County	93,859	3,494	17,224	67,062	6,079
Itinerant	55,724	3,494	17,224	32,964	2,042
Local	38,135	0	0	34,098	4,037
Pensacola	128,074	13,283	19,484	63,459	31,848
Itinerant	97,058	13,283	19,484	38,830	25,461
Local	31,016	0	0	24,629	6,387
Pompano Beach Airpark	181,454	0	14	181,440	0
Itinerant	55,851	0	14	55,837	0
Local	125,603	0	0	125,603	0
Sanford	372,057	4,017	498	367,481	61
Itinerant	155,562	4,017	498	151,010	37
Local	216,495	0	0	216,471	24
Sarasota-Bradenton	194,151	12,257	9,974	169,244	2,676
Itinerant	151,007	12,257	9,974	126,780	1,996
Local	43,144	0	0	42,464	680
St. Petersburg-Clearwater	224,558	7,566	7,678	179,167	30,147
Itinerant	126,395	7,566	7,678	99,181	11,970
Local	98,163	0	0	79,986	18,177

See footnotes at end of table. Continued . . .

University of Florida **Bureau of Economic and Business Research**

Table 13.90. AIRPORT ACTIVITY: OPERATIONS AT AIRPORTS WITH FEDERAL AVIATION ADMINISTRATION (FAA)-OPERATED AND -CONTRACTED TRAFFIC CONTROL TOWERS IN FLORIDA, FISCAL YEAR ENDING SEPTEMBER 30, 1999 (Continued)

Location and type of operation	Total oper- ations 1/	Air car- rier 2/	Air taxi 3/	General aviation 4/	Mili- tary
St. Petersburg Whitt	91,648	0	3,250	87,636	762
Itinerant	41,331	0	3,250	37,937	144
Local	50,317	0	0	49,699	618
Stuart/Witham Field	115,299	0	2,808	111,937	554
Itinerant	61,499	0	2,808	58,203	488
Local	53,800	0	0	53,734	66
Tallahassee	118,099	4,972	38,888	61,748	12,491
Itinerant	93,661	4,972	38,888	43,516	6,285
Local	24,438	0	0	18,232	6,206
Tamiami	204,118	2	926	203,067	123
Itinerant	93,516	2	926	92,506	82
Local	110,602	0	0	110,561	41
Tampa International	272,330	134,339	86,938	50,229	824
Itinerant	272,150	134,339	86,938	50,049	824
Local	180	0	0	180	0
Titusville-Cocoa	121,384	0	1,942	118,788	654
Itinerant	56,984	0	1,942	54,437	605
Local	64,400	0	0	64,351	49
Vero Beach	223,270	0	1,754	221,417	99
Itinerant	140,748	0	1,754	138,897	97
Local	82,522	0	0	82,520	2
West Palm Beach	196,866	50,829	30,510	114,560	967
Itinerant	187,051	50,829	30,510	104,918	794
Local	9,815	0	0	9,642	173

1/ An aircraft arrival at or departure from an airport with FAA traffic control.
2/ Air carrier authorized by the Department of Transportation to provide scheduled service over specified routes with limited nonscheduled operations.
3/ Performs at least five round trips per week between two or more points and publishes flight schedules or transports mail.
4/ All operations not classified as an air carrier, air taxi, or military.
Note: Itinerant includes all aircraft arrivals and departures other than local. Local includes aircraft operations which operate in the local traffic pattern or within sight of the tower.

Source: U.S., Department of Transportation, Federal Aviation Administration, Internet site <http://www. apo.data.faa.gov/faaatadsall.HTM> (accessed 4 August 2000).

Table 13.93. AIRCRAFT PILOTS: ACTIVE AIRCRAFT PILOTS BY TYPE OF CERTIFICATE AND FLIGHT INSTRUCTORS IN THE STATE AND COUNTIES OF FLORIDA DECEMBER 31, 1998

County	Pilots						Flight instructors
			Airplane pilots 1/				
	Total 2/	Student 3/	Private	Commercial	Airline transport 4/	Miscellaneous 5/	
Florida	45,993	6,841	15,819	9,830	12,695	808	6,460
Alachua	475	111	194	82	75	13	52
Baker	18	5	10	2	1	0	0
Bay	556	84	176	135	146	15	82
Bradford	21	6	10	1	4	0	2
Brevard	2,038	282	757	435	532	32	305
Broward	5,096	619	1,406	1,020	1,968	83	844
Calhoun	15	0	8	3	3	1	1
Charlotte	441	51	162	96	126	6	67
Citrus	276	45	135	51	42	3	33
Clay	573	58	145	119	245	6	56
Collier	1,054	103	411	191	340	9	139
Columbia	85	12	41	17	15	0	6
De Soto	46	4	21	19	2	0	8
Dixie	11	1	6	3	1	0	2
Duval	1,575	256	530	334	421	34	194
Escambia	1,183	151	261	273	457	41	108
Flagler	139	17	48	36	34	4	26
Franklin	32	4	14	5	9	0	1
Gadsden	42	5	25	6	5	1	6
Gilchrist	14	2	6	4	2	0	3
Glades	13	1	7	4	1	0	0
Gulf	25	5	12	5	3	0	0
Hamilton	6	2	2	1	1	0	0
Hardee	32	4	18	7	3	0	1
Hendry	71	11	28	21	11	0	10
Hernando	217	33	111	37	35	1	21
Highlands	206	30	107	34	30	5	30
Hillsborough	2,121	392	850	365	466	48	231
Holmes	15	3	4	4	4	0	4
Indian River	953	157	300	327	163	6	196
Jackson	62	8	25	16	10	3	8
Jefferson	17	4	8	2	3	0	1
Lafayette	1	0	1	0	0	0	0
Lake	517	78	221	115	94	9	78
Lee	1,241	188	535	233	272	13	114
Leon	458	98	196	78	74	12	40

See footnotes at end of table.

Continued . . .

Table 13.93. AIRCRAFT PILOTS: ACTIVE AIRCRAFT PILOTS BY TYPE OF CERTIFICATE AND FLIGHT INSTRUCTORS IN THE STATE AND COUNTIES OF FLORIDA DECEMBER 31, 1998 (Continued)

	Pilots						
			Airplane pilots 1/				
County	Total 2/	Student 3/	Private	Commercial	Airline transport 4/	Miscellaneous 5/	Flight instructors
Levy	59	11	24	17	7	0	9
Liberty	5	0	1	2	1	1	0
Madison	17	3	10	2	2	0	4
Manatee	592	93	232	110	150	7	70
Marion	642	90	285	139	120	8	89
Martin	690	97	249	113	223	8	98
Miami-Dade	4,494	653	1,177	1,017	1,569	78	597
Monroe	706	77	235	121	265	8	90
Nassau	260	34	89	63	73	1	34
Okaloosa	965	117	239	232	361	16	118
Okeechobee	84	9	47	18	9	1	6
Orange	2,295	356	823	450	615	51	334
Osceola	333	69	115	62	77	10	57
Palm Beach	3,678	483	1,331	664	1,125	75	504
Pasco	597	112	259	118	90	18	75
Pinellas	2,557	397	972	491	659	38	292
Polk	1,031	191	452	204	165	19	159
Putnam	98	15	44	21	13	5	13
St. Johns	471	64	161	106	134	6	58
St. Lucie	480	79	203	119	79	0	65
Santa Rosa	684	61	127	179	282	35	72
Sarasota	1,037	133	461	224	206	13	139
Seminole	1,470	261	461	441	283	24	294
Sumter	67	11	35	11	7	3	3
Suwannee	81	15	36	16	13	1	12
Taylor	20	2	10	4	3	1	0
Union	9	3	3	1	2	0	0
Volusia	2,751	546	875	778	522	30	589
Wakulla	40	6	19	8	7	0	5
Walton	102	19	38	14	28	3	4
Washington	25	2	13	4	4	2	1
Unknown	8	2	2	0	3	1	0

1/ Includes pilots with airplane only certificates and with airplane and helicopter and/or glider certificates.
2/ Includes recreational pilots not shown separately.
3/ Category of certificate unknown.
4/ Includes airline transport airplane only and airline transport airplane and helicopter certificates.
5/ Includes helicopter, gyroplane, glider and recreational certificates.

Source: U.S., Department of Transportation, Federal Aviation Administration, Office of Aviation Policy and Plans, *U.S. Civil Airmen Statistics, Calendar Year 1998,* Internet site <http://www.api.faa.gov/airmen/98AirmenCnty.pdf> (accessed 6 June 2000).

COMMUNICATIONS

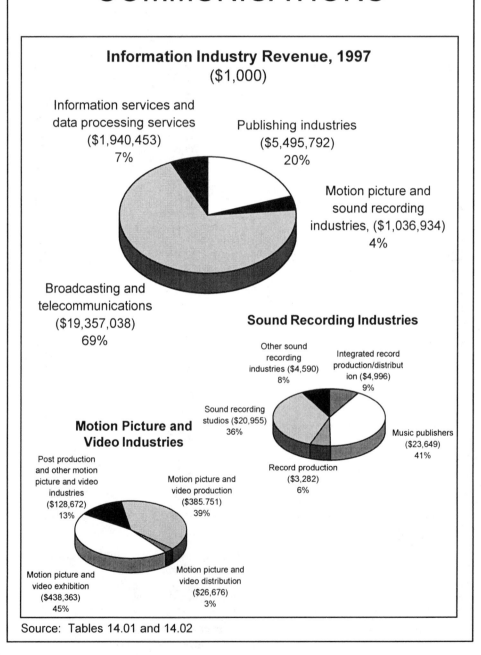

Information Industry Revenue, 1997
($1,000)

Information services and
data processing services
($1,940,453)
7%

Publishing industries
($5,495,792)
20%

Motion picture and
sound recording
industries, ($1,036,934)
4%

Broadcasting and
telecommunications
($19,357,038)
69%

Sound Recording Industries

Other sound
recording
industries ($4,590)
8%

Integrated record
production/distribut
ion ($4,996)
9%

Sound recording
studios ($20,955)
36%

Music publishers
($23,649)
41%

Record production
($3,282)
6%

Motion Picture and
Video Industries

Post production
and other motion
picture and video
industries
($128,672)
13%

Motion picture and
video production
($385.751)
39%

Motion picture and
video exhibition
($438,363)
45%

Motion picture and
video distribution
($26,676)
3%

Source: Tables 14.01 and 14.02

TABLES LISTED BY MAJOR HEADINGS

Table 14.01. INFORMATION: ESTABLISHMENTS, EMPLOYMENT, REVENUE, AND ANNUAL PAYROLL BY KIND OF BUSINESS IN FLORIDA, 1997

NAICS code	Industry	Number of estab- lishments	Number of em- ployees 1/	Revenue ($1,000)	Annual payroll ($1,000)
51	Information	5,883	145,025	27,830,217	5,522,364
511	Publishing industries	1,628	40,014	5,495,792	1,436,410
5111	Newspaper, periodical, book, and database publishers	1,099	32,470	4,288,228	1,017,050
5112	Software publishers	529	7,544	1,207,564	419,360
512	Motion picture and sound recording industries	1,040	10,952	1,036,934	204,094
5121	Motion picture and video industries	905	10,116	979,462	182,473
5122	Sound recording industries	135	836	57,472	21,621
513	Broadcasting and telecommunications	2,506	78,187	19,357,038	3,231,660
5131	Radio and television broadcasting	487	14,198	2,075,831	517,914
5132	Cable networks and program distribution	249	9,628	1,925,176	317,400
5133	Telecommunications	1,770	54,361	15,356,031	2,396,346
514	Information services and data processing services	709	15,872	1,940,453	650,200
5141	Information services	328	2,662	270,305	77,910
5142	Data processing services	381	13,210	1,670,148	572,290

1/ Paid employment for the pay period including March 12.
Note: The economic censuses are conducted on a 5-year cycle collecting data for years ending in 2 and 7. Data are for North American Classification System (NAICS) code 51 and may not be comparable to earlier years. See Glossary for definition.

Table 14.02. MOTION PICTURE AND SOUND RECORDING INDUSTRIES: ESTABLISHMENTS EMPLOYMENT, REVENUE, AND ANNUAL PAYROLL BY KIND OF BUSINESS IN FLORIDA, 1997

NAICS code	Industry	Number of estab- lishments	Number of em- ployees 1/	Revenue ($1,000)	Annual payroll ($1,000)
512	Motion picture and sound recording industries	1,040	10,952	1,036,934	204,094
5121	Motion picture and video industries	905	10,116	979,462	182,473
51211	Motion picture and video production	405	2,428	385,751	91,049
51212	Motion picture and video distribution	28	152	26,676	6,945
51213	Motion picture and video exhibition	292	6,432	438,363	46,073
51219	Post production and other motion picture and video industries	180	1,104	128,672	38,406
5122	Sound recording industries	135	836	57,472	21,621
51221	Record production	12	10	3,282	392
51222	Integrated record production/distribution	12	40	4,996	1,307
51223	Music publishers	29	331	23,649	11,112
51224	Sound recording studios	63	373	20,955	6,825
51229	Other sound recording industries	19	82	4,590	1,985

1/ Paid employment for the pay period including March 12.
Note: The economic censuses are conducted on a 5-year cycle collecting data for years ending in 2 and 7. Data are for North American Classification System (NAICS) code 512 and may not be comparable to earlier years. See Glossary for definition.

Source for Tables 14.01 and 14.02: U.S., Department of Commerce, Bureau of the Census, *1997 Economic Census: Information*, Geographic Area Series EC97S51-FL, Issued October 1999, Internet site <http://www.census.gov/prod/ec97/97s51-fl.pdf> (accessed 26 June 2000).

University of Florida   **Bureau of Economic and Business Research**

Table 14.03. TELECOMMUNICATIONS: ESTABLISHMENTS, EMPLOYMENT, REVENUE, AND ANNUAL PAYROLL BY KIND OF BUSINESS IN FLORIDA, 1997

NAICS code	Industry	Establish-ments	Employ-ment 1/	Revenue ($1,000)	Payroll ($1,000)
5133	Telecommunications	1,770	54,361	15,356,031	2,396,346
51331	Wired telecommunications carriers	1,076	42,925	12,202,676	1,966,715
51332	Wireless telecommunications carriers (except satellite)	418	8,757	2,295,443	334,167
51333	Telecommunications resellers	174	1,695	545,136	61,013
51334	Satellite telecommunications	44	750	255,623	27,452
51339	Other telecommunications	58	234	57,153	6,999

1/ Paid employment for the pay period including March 12.
Note: Data are for (NAICS) code 5133 and may not be comparable to earlier years. See Note on table 14.04

Table 14.04. BROADCASTING AND TELECOMMUNICATIONS: ESTABLISHMENTS, EMPLOYMENT REVENUE, AND ANNUAL PAYROLL IN THE STATE AND SPECIFIED COUNTIES OF FLORIDA, 1997

County	Number of establish-ments	Number of em-ployees 1/	Annual payroll ($1,000)	County	Number of establish-ments	Number of em-ployees 1/	Annual payroll ($1,000)
Florida	2,506	78,187	3,231,660	Marion	29	566	21,691
Alachua	41	2,389	94,442	Martin	15	351	12,548
Baker	2	A/	(D)	Miami-Dade	426	11,862	522,436
Bay	41	719	21,776	Monroe	28	282	8,295
Brevard	71	1,390	51,133	Nassau	6	55	1,498
Broward	279	7,909	328,876	Okaloosa	23	C/	(D)
Charlotte	13	B/	(D)	Okeechobee	7	84	2,839
Citrus	12	169	5,350	Orange	176	9,673	395,460
Clay	12	A/	(D)	Osceola	9	B/	(D)
Collier	24	596	23,215	Palm Beach	203	5,076	215,239
Columbia	8	173	5,951	Pasco	19	E/	(D)
Duval	144	7,318	291,168	Pinellas	141	3,470	125,555
Escambia	45	1,113	43,198	Polk	58	971	41,618
Gadsden	7	A/	(D)	Putnam	8	58	2,420
Gulf	2	A/	(D)	St. Johns	14	B/	(D)
Hernando	13	B/	(D)	St. Lucie	22	529	20,774
Highlands	10	B/	(D)	Santa Rosa	9	184	5,284
Hillsborough	187	8,738	382,548	Sarasota	51	1,250	47,653
Indian River	19	243	8,199	Seminole	62	F/	(D)
Jackson	6	A/	(D)	Sumter	7	68	2,317
Lake	25	C/	(D)	Suwannee	5	B/	(D)
Lee	63	2,418	96,514	Volusia	57	1,050	42,645
Leon	40	D/	(D)	Walton	5	A/	(D)
Manatee	16	706	20,355	Washington	6	B/	(D)

(D) Data withheld to avoid disclosure of information about individual firms.
Employment ranges: A/ 20-99. B/ 100-249. C/ 500-999. D/ 1,000-2,499. E/ 250-499.
F/ 2,500-4,999. 1/ Paid employment for the pay period including March 12.
Note: The economic censuses are conducted on a 5-year cycle collecting data for years ending in 2 and 7. Data are for North American Classification System (NAICS) code 513 and may not be comparable to earlier years. See Glossary for definition.

Source for Tables 14.03 and 14.04: U.S., Department of Commerce, Bureau of the Census, *1997 Economic Census: Information*, Geographic Area Series EC97S51-FL, Issued October 1999, Internet site <http://www.census.gov/prod/ec97/97s51-fl.pdf> (accessed 26 June 2000).

Table 14.33. POST OFFICES: ZIP CODES AND NET POSTAL REVENUE IN THE STATE AND SPECIFIED CITIES OF FLORIDA, FISCAL YEAR 1998-99

First class post office	ZIP code	Net revenue (dollars)	Percentage change from prior year	First class post office	ZIP code	Net revenue (dollars)	Percentage change from prior year
Florida	(X)	2,773,956,307	2.0	Crestview	32536	1,840,527	3.3
				Cross City	32628	367,624	11.4
Alachua	32615	731,644	11.1	Crystal River	34429	1,915,949	-1.9
Altamonte				Dade City	33525	2,484,385	-0.6
Springs	32714	8,402,427	-0.9	Dania	33004	2,398,007	7.3
Anna Maria	34216	319,610	6.6	Davenport	33837	612,237	-0.5
Anthony	32617	306,409	(X)	Daytona Beach	32114	50,241,754	5.1
Apalachicola	32320	407,851	1.9	De Leon Springs	32130	430,674	6.4
Apopka	32703	17,125,530	0.7	DeBary	32713	897,599	4.9
Arcadia	33821	1,369,144	2.3	Deerfield Beach	33441	11,693,639	4.3
Auburndale	33823	1,814,995	2.9	DeFuniak			
Avon Park	33825	1,535,095	1.7	Springs	32433	1,153,706	1.6
Bartow	33830	3,202,839	-1.1	DeLand	32720	10,270,027	15.5
Bay Pines	33504	667,877	19.6	Delray Beach	33444	12,167,243	8.5
Belle Glade	33430	1,046,054	0.7	Deltona	32738	3,077,983	363.8
Belleview	34420	1,488,912	8.3	Destin	32541	4,274,634	33.7
Blountstown	32424	731,168	23.1	Dover	33527	333,890	3.4
Boca Grande	33921	413,791	0.7	Dundee	33838	487,491	5.8
Boca Raton	33431	54,522,582	11.1	Dunedin	34698	3,830,212	-3.4
Bonifay	32425	705,242	4.1	Dunnellon	34432	1,304,888	5.8
Bonita Springs	33923	4,212,675	6.6	Eagle Lake	33839	391,317	-0.5
Boynton Beach	33436	9,062,050	6.5	Eaton Park	33840	875,236	-3.5
Bradenton	34205	15,508,524	6.2	Edgewater	32132	1,291,311	1.3
Bradenton Beach	34217	440,947	4.4	Eglin Air Force Base	32542	833,366	-1.5
Brandon	33511	7,761,821	0.1	Elfers	34259	1,638,005	5.7
Bronson	32621	340,684	11.1	Ellenton	34222	1,072,209	10.6
Brooksville	34601	10,775,292	5.8	Englewood	34223	3,379,737	1.9
Bunnell	32110	876,588	14.3	Estero	33928	1,135,158	5.6
Bushnell	33513	748,227	9.8	Eustis	32726	1,668,820	-2.1
Callahan	32011	608,417	15.5	Fernandina Beach	32834	2,544,546	3.8
Cantonment	32533	695,683	-0.1	Flagler Beach	32136	24,930,762	0.6
Cape Canaveral	32920	1,739,196	-6.2	Floral City	34436	472,757	0.7
Casselberry	32707	6,524,638	-0.5	Ft. Lauderdale	33310	236,004,370	0.8
Chattahoochee	32324	355,480	2.5	Ft. Meade	33841	321,448	-2.7
Chiefland	32626	865,124	6.8	Ft. Myers	33906	45,031,111	6.6
Chipley	32428	904,727	14.0	Ft. Myers Beach	33931	1,890,963	5.0
Clarcona	32709	425,492	30.2	Ft. Pierce	34981	14,451,713	5.7
Clearwater	34625	54,090,045	0.2	Ft. Walton Beach	32548	6,106,589	0.6
Clermont	34711	2,090,781	12.6	Frostproof	33843	517,405	0.4
Clewiston	33440	1,004,643	-1.1	Fruitland Park	34731	809,986	6.4
Cocoa	32922	4,468,903	2.6	Gainesville	32601	25,854,009	4.3
Cocoa Beach	32931	1,713,250	6.2	Goldenrod	32733	1,677,441	13.8
Crawfordville	32327	622,076	2.3	Gonzalez	32560	790,009	18.0
Crescent City	32112	619,635	-22.9	Gotha	34734	652,224	7.0

See footnotes at end of table.

Continued . . .

University of Florida   **Bureau of Economic and Business Research**

Florida Statistical Abstract 2000

Table 14.33. POST OFFICES: ZIP CODES AND NET POSTAL REVENUE IN THE STATE AND SPECIFIED CITIES OF FLORIDA, FISCAL YEAR 1998-99 (Continued)

First class post office	ZIP code	Net revenue (dollars)	Percentage change from prior year	First class post office	ZIP code	Net revenue (dollars)	Percentage change from prior year
Graceville	32440	426,946	-3.7	Lake Worth	33461	12,665,984	0.6
Grand Island	32735	355,322	22.5	Land O' Lakes	34639	1,291,182	5.6
Green Cove				Largo	34640	17,328,313	-4.8
Springs	32043	1,217,034	1.8	Lecanto	34465	1,770,817	10.4
Groveland	34736	469,840	12.6	Leesburg	34748	4,969,119	2.6
Gulf Breeze	32561	3,287,720	8.4	Lehigh Acres	33936	1,805,385	4.3
Haines City	33844	1,612,189	-15.7	Live Oak	32060	1,920,555	3.2
Hallandale	33009	5,807,118	8.5	Longboat Key	34228	1,447,610	-0.8
Havana	32333	500,617	5.0	Longwood	32779	10,818,040	-9.5
Hawthorne	32640	295,509	-0.5	Loxahatchee	33470	1,049,186	7.1
Hernando	34442	992,198	-2.7	Lutz	33549	1,935,099	10.2
Hialeah	33010	19,432,457	-14.7	Lynn Haven	32444	1,744,487	10.7
Highland City	33846	452,390	5.3	Macclenny	32063	664,865	1.2
High Springs	32643	567,889	2.2	Madison	32348	782,105	4.5
Hobe Sound	33455	1,653,891	4.6	Maitland	32751	9,256,773	6.7
Hollywood	33022	37,055,853	6.8	Malabar	32950	509,027	19.8
Homestead	33030	3,869,654	3.5	Mango	34262	2,957,887	-51.2
Homosassa				Marathon	33050	1,818,884	-0.2
Springs	34447	1,244,471	A/	Marco	33937	2,897,764	5.2
Immokalee	33934	896,280	3.2	Marianna	32446	1,692,202	1.3
Indian Rocks				Mary Esther	32569	1,567,058	3.6
Beach	34635	1,039,831	-4.8	Melbourne	32901	28,970,529	12.2
Indiantown	34956	507,557	-0.4	Melrose	32666	295,508	11.8
Interlachen	32148	364,031	6.1	Merritt Island	32952	3,475,388	1.0
Inverness	32650	3,027,821	6.7	Miami	33152	287,078,660	-1.5
Islamorada	33036	692,931	2.1	Middleburg	32068	1,095,504	6.0
Jacksonville	32203	214,191,695	-4.2	Milton	32570	3,348,285	9.9
Jasper	32052	378,567	4.5	Mims	32754	545,592	10.9
Jensen Beach	34957	2,459,404	9.3	Minneola	34755	545,928	-43.7
Jupiter	33458	7,969,859	7.5	Monticello	32344	684,253	2.5
Kathleen	33849	544,629	8.4	Moore Haven	33471	314,931	5.6
Key Largo	33037	1,881,671	3.6	Mount Dora	32757	2,032,332	4.5
Keystone Heights	32656	1,140,841	-4.3	Mulberry	33860	2,304,520	4.7
Key West	33040	5,609,297	0.7	Naples	33940	27,147,212	4.2
Kissimmee	34744	11,125,385	1.2	New Port Richey	34652	5,396,972	8.1
La Belle	33935	965,839	2.8	New Smyrna Beach	32169	4,410,661	34.2
Lady Lake	32159	2,619,245	14.0	Newberry	32669	348,434	5.5
Lake Alfred	33858	482,921	-9.4	Niceville	32578	2,717,344	32.9
Lake Butler	32054	372,573	9.0	Nokomis	34275	2,277,672	11.4
Lake City	32055	3,473,816	-10.9	Ocala	34478	18,359,739	4.9
Lakeland	33802	21,850,463	2.5	Ocoee	34761	1,810,209	165.1
Lake Mary	32746	8,492,449	14.4	Odessa	33556	1,070,593	266.5
Lake Monroe	32747	634,790	22.1	Okahumpka	34762	372,998	27.7
Lake Placid	33852	1,411,916	0.5	Okeechobee	34972	2,156,297	5.9
Lake Wales	33853	2,483,995	0.9	Oldsmar	34677	2,273,618	-71.3

See footnotes at end of table. Continued . . .

University of Florida **Bureau of Economic and Business Research**

Table 14.33. POST OFFICES: ZIP CODES AND NET POSTAL REVENUE IN THE STATE AND SPECIFIED CITIES OF FLORIDA, FISCAL YEAR 1998-99 (Continued)

First class post office	ZIP code	Net revenue (dollars)	Percentage change from prior year	First class post office	ZIP code	Net revenue (dollars)	Percentage change from prior year
Oneco	34264	1,272,453	8.5	Sanibel	33957	1,711,552	0.9
Opa-locka	33054	3,210,826	-0.5	Santa Rosa Beach	32459	992,823	9.5
Orange City	32763	2,340,384	-42.0	Sarasota	34230	32,291,556	2.8
Orange Park	32073	5,524,775	2.1	Sebastian	32958	1,543,660	4.3
Orlando	32862	189,969,480	0.5	Sebring	33870	3,693,904	6.4
Ormond Beach	32174	6,372,063	2.8	Seffner	33584	1,163,148	2.3
Osprey	34229	1,883,983	25.1	Shalimar	32579	1,429,602	8.9
Oviedo	32765	3,381,621	15.4	Sharpes	32959	605,489	7.4
Palatka	32177	2,202,114	0.9	Silver Springs	34488	1,477,465	8.0
Palm Beach	33480	3,225,517	3.0	Sorento	32776	358,479	13.6
Palm City	34990	3,460,114	26.8	Starke	32091	897,155	5.6
Palmetto	34221	1,944,088	-0.4	Stuart	34994	10,473,167	21.6
Palm Harbor	34683	7,011,207	6.3	Summerfield	34491	538,529	18.2
Panama City	32401	12,723,493	2.9	Summerland Key	33042	1,165,715	4.9
Parrish	34219	328,054	14.0	Sumterville	34267	479,930	6.0
Pembroke Pines	33082	50,762,113	0.3	Tallahassee	32301	65,246,509	7.5
Pensacola	32501	30,995,975	-0.2	Tallevast	34270	2,134,555	-9.8
Perry	32347	1,127,420	2.1	Tampa	33630	361,871,161	2.1
Pinellas Park	34665	5,690,815	4.8	Tarpon Springs	34689	5,751,486	9.7
Placida	33946	555,116	5.4	Tavares	32778	2,082,153	8.2
Plant City	33566	3,603,722	2.7	Tavernier	33070	909,220	-0.3
Plymouth	32768	373,040	8.3	Thonotosassa	33592	595,378	12.0
Polk City	33868	373,277	11.2	Titusville	32780	5,382,034	4.3
Pompano Beach	33060	41,529,172	7.0	Trenton	32693	438,260	7.1
Ponte Vedra				Umatilla	32784	644,362	1.9
Beach	32082	3,337,033	8.8	Valpariso	32580	753,104	8.6
Port Richey	34668	6,466,221	2.2	Valrico	33594	2,070,648	17.0
Port St. Joe	32456	786,940	4.0	Venice	34285	8,573,651	2.0
Port Salerno	34992	1,071,682	8.4	Vero Beach	32960	13,401,469	6.1
Punta Gorda	33950	10,611,447	2.8	Wabasso	32970	2,544,490	11.5
Quincy	32351	3,178,484	9.7	Wauchula	33873	1,031,576	3.7
Riverview	33569	1,830,447	22.0	Weirsdale	32195	1,348,986	24.9
Rockledge	32955	2,298,712	8.4	West Palm Beach	33406	69,686,713	8.4
Roseland	32957	595,896	6.0	Wildwood	34785	666,509	7.1
Ruskin	33570	2,836,046	2.8	Williston	32696	682,809	0.1
Safety Harbor	34695	1,284,048	-8.2	Windermere	34786	1,798,606	11.5
St. Augustine	32084	7,255,160	4.7	Winter Garden	32787	1,542,667	6.8
St. Cloud	34769	2,013,857	2.9	Winter Haven	33880	8,681,779	10.5
St. James City	33956	379,487	3.8	Winter Park	32789	12,696,184	0.4
St. Petersburg	33730	115,380,238	6.6	Yulee	32097	412,155	5.2
San Antonio	33576	350,481	12.2	Zephyrhills	33540	3,700,586	6.7
Sanford	32771	4,468,578	-24.9				

A/ Less than 0.05 percent.
(X) Not applicable.
Note: Data are for first class post offices. Florida totals include revenue from all post offices.

Source: U.S., Postal Service Headquarters, unpublished data.

University of Florida   **Bureau of Economic and Business Research**

Table 14.35. EMPLOYMENT AND PAYROLL: AVERAGE MONTHLY PRIVATE REPORTING UNITS EMPLOYMENT AND PAYROLL COVERED BY UNEMPLOYMENT COMPENSATION LAW BY INDUSTRY IN FLORIDA, 1999

SIC code	Industry	Number of reporting units	Number of em- ployees	Payroll ($1,000)
27	Printing, publishing, and allied industries	3,436	64,961	180,121
48	Telecommunications	2,566	92,008	340,031
481	Telephone communications	1,738	63,679	236,103
482	Telegraph and other message communications	33	292	1,837
483	Radio and television broadcasting stations	389	13,431	54,895
484	Cable and other pay television services	321	13,103	41,562
489	Communication services, NEC	84	1,500	5,632

NEC Not elsewhere classified.

Note: Private employment. Data are preliminary. Detail may not add to totals due to disclosure editing and/or rounding. See Tables in Section 23.00 for public employment data. See Appendix for an explanation of selection of industries included.

Table 14.36. NEWSPAPER PRINTING AND PUBLISHING: AVERAGE MONTHLY PRIVATE REPORTING UNITS, EMPLOYMENT, AND PAYROLL COVERED BY UNEMPLOYMENT COMPENSATION LAW IN THE STATE AND COUNTIES OF FLORIDA, 1999

Industry	Number of reporting units	Number of em- ployees	Payroll ($1,000)	Industry	Number of reporting units	Number of em- ployees	Payroll ($1,000)
Newspaper printing and publishing (SIC code 271)							
Florida	338	24,882	67,298	Monroe	5	191	468
				Okaloosa	4	279	489
Alachua	7	430	955	Orange	20	1,629	6,213
Broward	27	2,114	7,483	Osceola	4	101	232
Escambia	4	380	828	Palm Beach	23	1,721	5,763
Hillsborough	30	2,881	5,601	Polk	9	647	1,580
Lake	11	290	570	Santa Rosa	6	51	94
Lee	7	826	1,884	Sarasota	6	720	2,577
Manatee	5	370	1,055	Seminole	8	71	169
Miami-Dade	40	2,863	10,082	Volusia	12	916	2,345

Note: Private employment. Data are preliminary. Detail may not add to totals due to disclosure editing and/or rounding. See Tables in Section 23.00 for public employment data. See Appendix for an explanation of selection of industries included.

Source for Tables 14.35 and 14.36: State of Florida, Department of Labor and Employment Security, Bureau of Labor Market Information, "Employment and Wages" (ES-202), unpublished data.

Table 14.37. TELECOMMUNICATIONS: AVERAGE MONTHLY PRIVATE REPORTING UNITS EMPLOYMENT, AND PAYROLL COVERED BY UNEMPLOYMENT COMPENSATION LAW IN THE STATE AND COUNTIES OF FLORIDA, 1999

County	Number of reporting units	Number of em- ployees	Payroll ($1,000)	County	Number of reporting units	Number of em- ployees	Payroll ($1,000)
				Telecommunications (SIC code 48)			
Florida	2,566	92,008	340,032	Manatee	21	410	1,385
				Marion	36	566	1,625
Alachua	27	873	2,616	Martin	10	287	911
Baker	5	78	215	Miami-Dade	432	16,064	63,613
Bay	24	676	1,741	Monroe	15	310	1,051
Bradford	4	12	42	Nassau	6	46	177
Brevard	66	1,323	5,363	Okaloosa	26	790	2,395
Broward	238	8,496	32,740	Okeechobee	5	56	157
Charlotte	10	113	398	Orange	172	9,312	34,828
Citrus	16	216	528	Osceola	11	139	465
Clay	13	183	628	Palm Beach	162	5,269	18,448
Collier	27	498	1,972	Pasco	22	325	969
Dixie	3	33	69	Pinellas	135	6,942	26,729
Duval	123	6,966	23,640	Polk	51	985	3,533
Escambia	50	2,788	5,973	Putnam	8	71	212
Flagler	5	43	111	St. Johns	15	211	741
Hardee	3	26	62	St. Lucie	18	553	1,466
Hendry	3	46	113	Santa Rosa	9	280	754
Highlands	7	133	421	Sarasota	52	1,294	4,517
Hillsborough	204	10,701	41,120	Seminole	57	3,069	16,219
Indian River	17	259	794	Suwannee	5	88	284
Jackson	7	100	267	Volusia	42	1,077	3,265
Lake	23	722	2,237	Walton	8	69	232
Lee	79	2,869	9,365	Washington	5	174	512
Leon	54	1,822	5,492	Multicounty 1/	192	3,946	17,475
				Telephone communications (SIC code 481)			
Florida	1,738	63,679	236,104	Marion	25	454	1,359
				Martin	8	199	650
Alachua	19	661	2,158	Miami-Dade	300	9,957	36,170
Bay	12	402	1,105	Okaloosa	16	329	1,158
Brevard	38	656	3,267	Orange	120	6,682	25,148
Broward	169	6,003	23,689	Osceola	8	119	430
Charlotte	8	110	394	Palm Beach	104	3,281	10,768
Citrus	7	139	340	Pasco	14	147	546
Collier	17	179	772	Pinellas	103	5,035	19,209
Duval	82	4,836	16,666	Polk	35	598	2,539
Escambia	40	2,546	5,324	St. Johns	9	106	436
Highlands	4	103	378	Santa Rosa	4	77	271
Hillsborough	167	8,683	32,987	Sarasota	36	681	2,613
Indian River	10	109	377	Seminole	47	3,005	15,978
Lake	15	615	1,990	Volusia	16	555	1,893
Lee	47	1,818	6,209	Walton	4	37	169
Leon	38	1,305	4,225	Washington	4	171	507
Manatee	12	201	818	Multicounty 1/	125	2,394	10,585

1/ Reporting units without a fixed location within the state or of unknown county location.
Note: Private employment. Data are preliminary. Only counties for which data are disclosed are shown. Detail may not add to totals due to disclosure editing and/or rounding. See Tables in Section 23.00 for public employment data.
Source: State of Florida, Department of Labor and Employment Security, Bureau of Labor Market Information, "Employment and Wages" (ES-202), unpublished data.

University of Florida   **Bureau of Economic and Business Research**

Table 14.38. RADIO AND TELEVISION BROADCASTING STATIONS AND CABLE AND OTHER PAY
TELEVISION SERVICES: AVERAGE MONTHLY PRIVATE REPORTING UNITS, EMPLOYMENT
AND PAYROLL COVERED BY UNEMPLOYMENT COMPENSATION LAW
IN THE STATE AND COUNTIES OF FLORIDA, 1999

County	Number of reporting units	Number of employees	Payroll ($1,000)	County	Number of reporting units	Number of employees	Payroll ($1,000)
Radio and television broadcasting stations (SIC code 483)							
Florida	389	13,432	54,896	Miami-Dade	58	3,871	19,192
				Monroe	5	75	182
Alachua	6	187	413	Okaloosa	7	88	286
Bay	10	202	438	Orange	21	1,161	4,886
Brevard	12	258	833	Palm Beach	32	1,040	4,624
Broward	21	619	2,811	Pinellas	16	906	4,337
Collier	5	88	513	Polk	8	91	233
Duval	18	954	2,926	St. Johns	4	32	47
Escambia	6	221	618	St. Lucie	5	66	84
Hillsborough	14	1,154	4,897	Sarasota	8	143	389
Lee	19	687	2,007	Seminole	4	21	39
Leon	12	319	753	Volusia	15	189	515
Manatee	4	13	18				
Marion	7	98	250	Multicounty 1/	26	536	2,808
Cable and other pay television services (SIC code 484)							
Florida	321	13,103	41,562	Manatee	4	189	542
				Miami-Dade	46	1,941	7,249
Brevard	7	301	703	Monroe	4	81	243
Broward	32	1,672	5,357	Orange	25	1,320	4,530
Citrus	4	56	145	Palm Beach	20	913	2,870
Clay	3	37	138	Pasco	5	152	377
Collier	5	214	657	Pinellas	14	993	3,148
Duval	19	1,122	3,972	Sarasota	5	346	965
Escambia	3	16	24	Seminole	4	41	192
Hillsborough	18	790	2,325	Volusia	10	333	843
Lee	14	364	1,149				
Leon	3	197	510	Multicounty 1/	28	683	2,137

1/ Reporting units without a fixed location within the state or of unknown county location.

Note: Private employment. Data are preliminary. Only counties for which data are disclosed are shown. Detail may not add to totals due to disclosure editing and/or rounding. See Tables in Section 23.00 for public employment data.

Source: State of Florida, Department of Labor and Employment Security, Bureau of Labor Market Information, "Employment and Wages" (ES-202), unpublished data.

University of Florida   **Bureau of Economic and Business Research**

Table 14.60. TELEPHONE COMPANIES: SPECIFIED CHARACTERISTICS OF COMPANIES
IN FLORIDA, DECEMBER 1999

| Companies and headquarters | Number of exchanges | Florida access lines 1/ | | |
		Total number	Percentage of state total	Annual growth rate (percentage)
Florida	284	11,410,995	100.00	3.05
ALLTEL Florida, Inc. Live Oak	27	87,373	0.77	5.63
BellSouth Telecommunications Miami	102	6,617,173	57.99	2.09
Frontier Communications of the South Atmore, Alabama	2	4,537	0.04	6.35
GT COM 2/ Florala, Alabama	2	2,525	0.02	3.48
GT COM 3/ Port St. Joe	13	35,532	0.31	5.43
GT COM 4/ Perry	2	10,963	0.10	6.72
GTE Florida, Inc. Tampa	24	2,443,575	21.41	3.15
ITS 5/ Indiantown	1	3,705	0.03	4.75
Northeast Florida Telephone Company Macclenny	2	9,280	0.08	8.01
Quincy Telephone Company Quincy	3	13,623	0.12	2.66
Sprint Florida (Centel) Tallahassee	35	449,340	3.94	4.79
Sprint Florida (United) Altamonte Springs	69	1,714,663	15.03	5.89
Vista-United Telecommunications Lake Buena Vista	2	18,706	0.16	22.78

1/ An access line is the line going to a home or building for the main telephone located there.
2/ Formerly Florala Telephone Company.
3/ Formerly St. Joseph Telephone.
4/ Formerly Gulf Telephone Company.
5/ Formerly Indiantown Telephone System, Inc.
Note: Telephone companies listed above have headquarters in Florida, except as specified. Detail may not add to totals due to rounding.

Source: State of Florida, Public Service Commission, *1999 Annual Report.*

Table 14.62. TELEPHONE COMPANIES: INCUMBENT LOCAL EXCHANGE COMPANIES (ILEC) ACCESS LINES IN SERVICE BY TYPE IN FLORIDA, DECEMBER 31, 1999

Company	Total	Residential access lines		Business access lines		Inter-exchange access lines	LEC pay-phones	CPE coin access lines
		Number	Percentage of total	Number	Percentage of total			
Florida	11,429,425	7,942,087	69.5	3,352,402	29.3	21,441	13,616	99,879
ALLTEL	89,546	69,338	77.4	17,072	19.1	2,173	334	629
BellSouth	6,632,408	4,626,344	69.8	1,919,477	28.9	15,235	0	71,352
Frontier	4,537	4,102	90.4	411	9.1	0	14	10
GTCOM	49,020	36,433	74.3	12,038	24.6	0	178	371
GTEFL	2,444,656	1,681,938	68.8	739,446	30.2	1,081	11,250	10,941
ITS	3,705	2,621	70.7	1,019	27.5	0	34	31
Northeast	9,280	7,211	77.7	1,956	21.1	0	0	113
Sprint-Florida	2,163,944	1,501,290	69.4	645,762	29.8	400	1,805	14,687
TDS (Quincy)	13,623	10,132	74.4	3,338	24.5	0	0	153
Vista	18,706	2,678	14.3	11,883	63.5	2,552	1	1,592

LEC Local Exchange Company.
CPE Customer Premises Exchange.
Note: See Table 14.60 for a complete list of company names and headquarters.

Source: State of Florida, Public Service Commission, Division of Research and Regulatory Review, *Statistics of Florida Telecommunications Companies, 1999.*

Table 14.63. TELEPHONE COMPANIES: LEADING INCUMBENT LOCAL EXCHANGE COMPANIES (ILEC) AND LEADING INTEREXCHANGE COMPANIES (IXC) BY REVENUE REPORTED IN FLORIDA, 1999

Company	Incumbent Local Exchange Companies		Company	Interexchange Companies	
	Intrastate operating revenues ($1,000)	Per-cent-age of total		Intrastate operating revenues ($1,000)	Per-cent-age of total
Total	5,579,768	100.0	Total	1,191,639	100.0
BellSouth Telecommunica-tions, Inc.	3,442,884	61.7	MCI WorldCom	351,674	29.5
GTE, Florida Incorporated	1,186,425	21.3	AT&T	336,368	28.2
Sprint, Florida Incorporated	882,292	15.8	Sprint	113,095	9.5
ALLTEL Florida, Inc.	36,923	0.7	MCI	112,504	9.4
Vista-United Telecommuni-cations	14,303	0.3	WorldCom	77,587	6.5
TDS Telecom	6,528	0.1	Excel	29,643	2.5
Northeast Florida Telephone Company, Inc.	4,759	0.1	GTE	25,810	2.2
GTCOM	2,493	A/	Cable & Wireless, Inc.	25,233	2.1
Indiantown Telephone System, Inc.	2,001	A/	Intermedia Communica-tions, Inc.	21,144	1.8
Frontier Communications of the South, Inc.	1,161	A/	LCI International Telecom Corp.	16,097	1.4
			All other IXCS reporting	82,485	6.9

A/ Less than 0.05 percent.

Table 14.64. TELEPHONE COMPANIES: LEADING PAY TELEPHONE COMPANIES (PAT) AND LEADING ALTERNATIVE LOCAL EXCHANGE COMPANIES (ALEC) BY REVENUE REPORTED IN FLORIDA, 1999

Company	Pay telephone service providers		Company	Alternative Local Exchange Companies	
	Intrastate operating revenues ($1,000)	Per-cent-age of total		Intrastate operating revenues ($1,000)	Per-cent-age of total
Total	118,630	100.0	Total	186,904	100.0
BellSouth Public Communica-tions, Inc.	64,842	54.7	Intermedia Communications, Inc.	49,868	26.7
GTE Florida Incorporated	14,573	12.3	GTE	29,040	15.5
Sprint Payphone Services	7,496	6.3	TCG South Florida	27,216	14.6
Sprint	6,226	5.2	MCI Metro Access Trans-mission Services, Inc.	22,138	11.8
Global Tel*Link Corporation	4,659	3.9	The Other Phone Company	12,271	6.6
ETS Payphone of Florida, Inc.	3,512	3.0	Sprint	9,087	4.9
Peoples Telephone Company	3,025	2.6	ACSI Local Switched Services, Inc.	4,624	2.5
PhoneTel Technologies, Inc.	2,277	1.9	MCI WorldCom	3,995	2.1
Telaleasing Enterprises	2,102	1.8	Time Warner Telecom	3,815	2.0
Goran Dragoslavic	1,936	1.6	Adelphia Business Solutions	3,558	1.9
All other PATS reporting	7,980	6.7	All other ALECS	21,291	11.4

Source for Tables 14.63 and 14.64: State of Florida, Public Service Commission, Division of Research and Regulatory Review, *Statistics of Florida Telecommunications Companies, 1999.*

POWER
AND ENERGY

**Electric, Gas, and Sanitary Services
Employment, 1999**

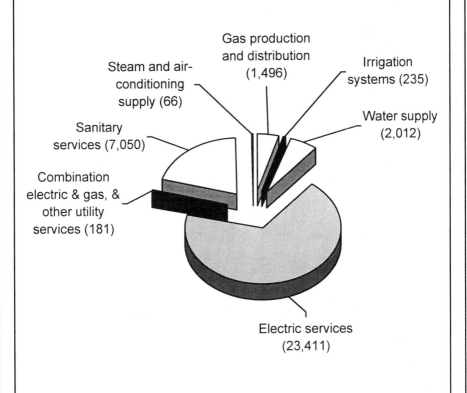

Gas production
and distribution
(1,496)

Steam and air-
conditioning
supply (66)

Irrigation
systems (235)

Sanitary
services (7,050)

Water supply
(2,012)

Combination
electric & gas, &
other utility
services (181)

Electric services
(23,411)

Source: Table 15.15

SECTION 15.00
POWER AND ENERGY

TABLES LISTED BY MAJOR HEADINGS

University of Florida   **Bureau of Economic and Business Research**

Table 15.01. UTILITIES: ESTABLISHMENTS, EMPLOYMENT, AND ANNUAL PAYROLL
BY KIND OF BUSINESS IN FLORIDA, 1997

NAICS code	Industry	Number of reestablishments	Number of employees 1/	Payroll ($1,000)
22	Utilities	524	27,652	1,385,824
2211	Electric power generation, transmission, and distribution	249	23,557	1,268,932
22111	Electric power generation	125	9,479	566,914
22112	Electric power transmission, control, and distribution	124	14,078	702,018
2212	Natural gas distribution	40	1,905	60,890
2213	Water, sewage, and other systems	235	2,190	56,002
22131	Water supply and irrigation systems	146	1,478	36,129
22132	Sewage treatment facilities	88	A/	(D)

(D) Data withheld to avoid disclosure of information about individual firms.
Employment range: A/ 500-999.
1/ Paid employment for the pay period including March 12.
Note: The economic censuses are conducted on a 5-year cycle collecting data for years ending in 2 and 7. Data are for North American Classification System (NAICS) code 22 and may not be comparable to earlier years. See Glossary for definition.

Table 15.02. UTILITIES: REVENUE IN THE STATE, METROPOLITAN STATISTICAL AREAS (MSAS)
AND NONMETROPOLITAN AREAS OF FLORIDA, 1997

(in thousands of dollars)

Area	Amount	Area	Amount
Florida	12,879,426	Metropolitan areas (Continued)	
		Ocala	119,201
Metropolitan area		Orlando	681,816
Daytona Beach	301,129	Panama City	121,974
Ft. Myers-Cape Coral	321,441	Pensacola	(D)
Ft. Pierce-Port St. Lucie	(D)	Punta Gorda	(D)
Ft. Walton Beach	(D)	Sarasota-Bradenton	346,409
Gainesville	68,618	Tallahassee	(D)
Jacksonville	393,993	Tampa-St. Petersburg-Clearwater	2,545,108
Lakeland-Winter Haven	151,917	West Palm Beach-Boca Raton	(D)
Melbourne-Titusville-Palm Bay	(D)		
Miami-Ft. Lauderdale	(D)	Nonmetropolitan areas	1,624,568
Naples	(D)		

(D) Data withheld to avoid disclosure of information about individual firms.
Note: The economic censuses are conducted on a 5-year cycle collecting data for years ending in 2 and 7. Data are for North American Classification System (NAICS) code 22 and may not be comparable to earlier years. See Glossary for definition.

Source for Tables 15.01 and 15.02: U.S., Department of Commerce, Bureau of the Census, *1997 Economic Census: Utilities*, Geographic Area Series EC97T22A-FL, Issued December 1999, Internet site <http://www.census.gov/prod/ec97/97t22-fl.pdf> (accessed 27 June 2000).

University of Florida   **Bureau of Economic and Business Research**

Table 15.06. ENERGY CONSUMPTION ESTIMATES: AMOUNT CONSUMED BY TYPE OF FUEL
IN FLORIDA 1987 THROUGH 1997

(in trillions of British thermal units)

Year	Total	Petro-leum 1/	Coal	Natural gas	Nuclear	Electric inter-state 2/	Hydro-elec-tric
1987	2,892.2	1,470.8	586.6	313.6	202.3	219.2	2.3
1988	3,054.6	1,582.7	611.5	305.8	281.4	169.8	2.2
1989	3,183.1	1,586.3	630.2	337.2	224.3	248.0	2.4
1990	3,162.5	1,578.1	624.3	342.0	232.6	286.7	1.8
1991	3,099.8	1,548.8	642.8	361.0	220.3	241.1	2.7
1992	3,150.9	1,573.0	652.7	370.3	268.2	196.8	2.4
1993	3,215.0	1,632.4	652.2	353.4	276.5	207.4	2.2
1994	3,373.7	1,685.9	641.7	392.5	284.9	266.5	2.8
1995	3,508.9	1,620.2	653.0	532.6	306.3	291.7	2.4
1996	3,572.0	1,629.6	694.5	510.7	270.6	352.3	2.2
1997	3,614.7	1,691.4	697.3	509.0	244.0	352.0	10.6

1/ Includes asphalt, aviation gasoline, jet fuel, distillates, kerosene, lubricants, motor gasoline, residual fuel, and liquefied petroleum gas.
2/ Combines electric sales and energy losses associated with interstate sales. Losses estimated to be 7,088 of the 10,400 British thermal units per kilowatt-hour purchased.
Note: Totals from 1990 include expanded coverage of nonelectric utility use of renewable energy and are not comparable to previous years.

Table 15.07. ENERGY CONSUMPTION ESTIMATES: PER CAPITA ENERGY CONSUMPTION
BY TYPE OF FUEL IN FLORIDA, 1987 THROUGH 1997

(in millions of British thermal units)

Year	Total	Petro-leum 1/	Natural gas	Coal	Nuclear	Electric inter-state 2/	Hydro-elec-tric
1987	242.9	123.5	49.3	26.3	17.0	18.4	0.2
1988	248.9	129.0	49.8	24.9	22.9	13.8	0.2
1989	252.3	125.7	49.9	26.7	17.8	19.7	0.2
1990	244.4	122.0	48.3	26.4	18.0	22.2	0.1
1991	234.9	117.4	48.7	27.4	16.7	18.3	0.2
1992	234.7	117.2	48.6	27.6	20.0	14.7	0.2
1993	236.2	120.0	47.9	26.0	20.3	15.2	0.2
1994	243.1	121.5	46.2	28.3	20.5	19.2	0.2
1995	248.0	114.5	46.2	37.6	21.6	20.6	0.2
1996	247.9	113.1	48.2	35.4	18.8	24.4	0.2
1997	245.7	115.0	47.4	34.6	16.6	23.9	0.7

1/ Includes asphalt, aviation gasoline, jet fuel, distillates, kerosene, lubricants, motor gasoline, residual fuel, and liquefied petroleum gas.
2/ Combines electric sales and energy losses associated with interstate sales. Losses estimated to be 7,088 of the 10,400 British thermal units per kilowatt-hour purchased.
Note: Totals from 1990 include expanded coverage of nonelectric utility use of renewable energy and are not comparable to previous years. Per capita is computed using Bureau of the Census data for 1990 and *Florida Estimates of Population* for all other years.

Source for Tables 15.06 and 15.07: U.S., Department of Energy, Energy Information Administration, *State Energy Data Report*, 1997, Internet site <http://www.eia.doe.gov/emeu/states/main_fl.html> (accessed 22 September 1999).

University of Florida   **Bureau of Economic and Business Research**

Table 15.08. ENERGY CONSUMPTION: AMOUNT CONSUMED BY SECTOR IN FLORIDA, OTHER LEADING CONSUMPTION STATES, AND THE UNITED STATES, 1997

State	Total consumption Amount (trillion BTU)	Rank	Residential Per-cent-age	Rank	Commercial Per-cent-age	Rank	Industrial Per-cent-age	Rank	Trans-portation Per-cent-age	Rank
Florida	3,614.7	8	27.4	4	21.5	4	15.6	20	35.4	3
Texas	11,396.1	1	11.6	2	9.9	3	57.5	1	21.0	2
California	7,727.5	2	17.3	1	16.2	1	30.1	3	36.5	1
Ohio	4,144.3	3	21.5	7	15.7	6	40.4	4	22.4	6
New York	4,093.2	4	25.8	3	28.6	2	22.1	10	23.5	4
Louisiana	4,093.0	5	8.0	22	5.6	22	67.4	2	19.0	11
Pennsylvania	3,900.7	6	23.0	6	15.2	7	37.5	5	24.3	5
Illinois	3,900.2	7	24.0	5	18.4	5	35.9	6	21.7	8
Michigan	3,259.1	9	23.6	8	17.6	8	34.5	8	24.3	10
Indiana	2,683.6	10	18.1	13	11.2	18	47.6	7	23.1	15
United States	94,063.6	(X)	19.6	(X)	15.9	(X)	38.1	(X)	26.5	(X)

BTU British thermal units.
(X) Not applicable.

Source: U.S., Department of Energy, Energy Information Administration, *State Energy Data Report, 1997*, Internet site <http://www.eia.doe.gov/emeu/states/main_fl.html> (accessed 22 September 1999).

Table 15.09. CRUDE OIL AND NATURAL GAS: AMOUNT PRODUCED BY FIELD IN FLORIDA 1997 THROUGH 1999

Field	Crude oil (barrels) 1997	1998	1999	Natural gas (1,000 cubic feet) 1997	1998	1999
Total	6,380,771	5,970,820	4,888,581	6,944,296	6,582,936	6,738,397
South Florida	2,345,399	2,099,578	1,127,828	218,920	204,162	126,899
Bear Island	207,417	119,536	30,120	17,716	12,758	3,458
Corkscrew	49,142	19,843	22,565	0	0	0
Lake Trafford	1,022	822	1,082	0	0	0
Lehigh Park	53,177	49,151	44,537	5,691	6,354	5,980
Mid-Felda	8,815	6,069	50	0	0	0
Raccoon Point	1,506,177	1,439,689	745,835	139,649	137,417	89,632
Sunniland	2,044	2,461	0	0	88	0
Sunoco Felda	0	0	0	0	0	0
Townsend Canal	4,273	0	0	0	0	0
West Felda	513,332	462,007	283,639	55,864	47,545	27,829
Northwest Florida	4,035,372	3,871,242	3,760,753	6,725,376	6,378,774	6,611,498
Blackjack Creek	260,560	264,604	208,334	628,123	695,709	583,023
Jay	3,759,700	3,592,132	3,540,332	6,093,128	5,680,900	6,026,604
McLellan	15,112	14,506	12,087	4,125	2,165	1,871

Source: State of Florida, Department of Environmental Protection, Florida Geological Survey, Oil and Gas Section, unpublished data.

University of Florida   **Bureau of Economic and Business Research**

Table 15.14. ELECTRIC UTILITY INDUSTRY: SALES, CUSTOMERS, AND COUNTIES SERVED
BY PRIVATELY AND PUBLICLY OWNED UTILITIES AND BY RURAL
ELECTRIC COOPERATIVES IN FLORIDA, 1998

Utility	Electricity sales to ultimate customers (MWH)	Number of ultimate customers December 1/	Counties served
Investor-owned systems			
Florida Power and Light	85,130,914	3,680,461	Alachua, Baker, Bradford, Brevard, Broward, Charlotte, Clay, Collier, Columbia, De Soto, Duval, Flagler, Glades, Hardee, Hendry, Highlands, Indian River, Lee, Manatee, Martin, Miami-Dade, Monroe, Nassau, Okeechobee, Palm Beach, Putnam, St. Johns, St. Lucie, Sarasota, Seminole, Suwannee, Union, Volusia
Florida Power 2/	33,386,610	1,340,834	Alachua, Bay, Brevard, Citrus, Columbia, Dixie, Flagler, Franklin, Gadsden, Gilchrist, Gulf, Hamilton, Hardee, Hernando, Highlands, Jefferson, Lafayette, Lake, Leon, Levy, Liberty, Madison, Marion, Orange, Osceola, Pasco, Pinellas, Polk, Seminole, Sumter, Suwannee, Taylor, Volusia, Wakulla
Florida Public Utilities	711,205	24,114	Calhoun, Jackson, Liberty, Nassau
Gulf Power	9,402,018	350,445	Bay, Escambia, Holmes, Jackson, Okaloosa, Santa Rosa, Walton, Washington
Tampa Electric	16,027,356	530,252	Hillsborough, Pasco, Pinellas, Polk
Generating municipal systems			
Ft. Pierce	541,111	24,179	St. Lucie
Gainesville	1,595,283	77,197	Alachua
Homestead	299,156	15,132	Miami-Dade
Jacksonville	11,028,073	336,294	Clay, Duval, St. Johns
Key West	631,405	26,765	Monroe
Kissimmee	1,005,833	45,090	Osceola
Lake Worth	383,129	25,081	Palm Beach
Lakeland	2,432,126	106,191	Polk
New Smyrna Beach	340,930	20,793	Volusia
Orlando 3/	4,424,495	182,479	Orange
Reedy Creek	1,068,271	1,293	Orange
Starke	65,841	2,560	Bradford
Tallahassee	2,348,928	91,507	Leon
Vero Beach	658,811	28,097	Indian River
Florida Keys 4/	624,734	29,370	Monroe

See footnotes at end of table.   Continued . . .

Table 15.14. ELECTRIC UTILITY INDUSTRY: SALES, CUSTOMERS, AND COUNTIES SERVED BY PRIVATELY AND PUBLICLY OWNED UTILITIES AND BY RURAL ELECTRIC COOPERATIVES IN FLORIDA, 1998 (Continued)

Utility	Electricity sales to ultimate customers (MWH)	Number of ultimate customers December 1/	Counties served
Nongenerating municipal systems			
Alachua	64,313	2,749	Alachua
Bartow	275,895	9,896	Polk
Blountstown	34,924	1,442	Calhoun
Bushnell	28,769	942	Sumter
Chattahoochee	48,894	1,304	Gadsden
Clewiston	116,134	4,043	Hendry
Ft. Meade	40,296	2,524	Polk
Green Cove Springs	123,344	2,863	Clay
Havana	22,000	1,281	Gadsden
Jacksonville Beach	(NA)	(NA)	Duval, St. Johns
Leesburg	433,473	18,000	Lake
Moore Haven	16,983	1,055	Glades
Mount Dora	86,613	4,765	Lake
Newberry	31,707	984	Alachua
Ocala	1,148,524	43,836	Marion
Quincy	162,359	4,484	Gadsden
Wauchula	61,648	2,570	Hardee
Williston	29,840	1,255	Levy
Nongenerating rural electric cooperatives			
Central Florida	358,020	26,231	Alachua, Dixie, Gilchrist, Levy, Marion
Choctawhatchee	487,441	29,636	Holmes, Okaloosa, Santa Rosa, Walton
Clay	2,246,527	126,314	Alachua, Baker, Bradford, Clay, Columbia, Duval, Flagler, Lake, Levy, Marion, Putnam, Suwannee Union, Volusia
Escambia River	145,027	8,827	Escambia, Santa Rosa
Glades	279,393	14,091	Glades, Hendry, Highlands, Okeechobee
Gulf Coast	247,472	15,977	Bay, Calhoun, Gulf, Jackson, Walton, Washington
Lee County	2,479,850	139,169	Charlotte, Collier, Hendry, Lee
Okefenokee 5/	128,528	7,483	Baker, Nassau
Peace River	343,477	22,511	Brevard, De Soto, Hardee, Highlands, Hillsborough, Indian River, Manatee, Osceola, Polk, Sarasota
Sumter	1,456,527	94,488	Citrus, Hernando, Lake, Levy, Marion, Pasco, Sumter
Suwannee Valley	288,279	19,234	Columbia, Hamilton, Lafayette, Suwannee
Talquin	818,747	45,320	Franklin, Gadsden, Leon, Liberty, Wakulla
Tri-county	190,298	14,377	Dixie, Jefferson, Madison, Taylor

See footnotes at end of table.

Continued . . .

University of Florida   **Bureau of Economic and Business Research**

Table 15.14. ELECTRIC UTILITY INDUSTRY: SALES, CUSTOMERS, AND COUNTIES SERVED
BY PRIVATELY AND PUBLICLY OWNED UTILITIES AND BY RURAL
ELECTRIC COOPERATIVES IN FLORIDA, 1998 (Continued)

Utility	Electricity sales to ultimate customers (MWH)	Number of ultimate customers December 1/	Counties served
Nongenerating rural elec- tric cooperatives (Continued)			
West Florida	328,119	23,956	Calhoun, Holmes, Jackson, Washington
Withlacoochee	2,560,502	147,808	Citrus, Hernando, Pasco, Polk, Sumter

(NA) Not available.
MWH Megawatt-hours (1,000 kilowatt-hours).
1/ Year-end monthly average.
2/ Includes the Sebring municipal system.
3/ Includes St. Cloud.
4/ Generating rural system.
5/ Florida customers only.

Source: State of Florida, Public Service Commission, Division of Research and Regulatory Review, *Statistics of the Florida Electric Utility Industry, 1998.*

Table 15.15. ELECTRIC, GAS, AND SANITARY SERVICES: AVERAGE MONTHLY PRIVATE REPORTING
UNITS, EMPLOYMENT, AND PAYROLL COVERED BY UNEMPLOYMENT COMPENSATION
LAW BY INDUSTRY IN FLORIDA, 1999

SIC code	Industry	Number of re- porting units	Number of em- ployees	Payroll ($1,000)
49	Electric, gas, and sanitary services	920	34,452	146,437
491	Electric services	198	23,411	112,116
492	Gas production and distribution	63	1,496	4,965
493	Combination electric and gas, and other utility services	57	181	370
494	Water supply	140	2,012	5,200
495	Sanitary services	382	7,050	23,139
496	Steam and air-conditioning supply	21	66	206
497	Irrigation systems	60	235	441

Note: Private employment. Data are preliminary. Detail may not add to totals due to disclosure editing and/or rounding. See Tables 23.70, 23.71, 23.72, 23.73, and 23.74 for public employment data.

Source: State of Florida, Department of Labor and Employment Security, Bureau of Labor Market Information, "Employment and Wages" (ES-202), unpublished data.

Table 15.16. ELECTRIC, GAS, AND SANITARY SERVICES: AVERAGE MONTHLY PRIVATE REPORTING UNITS, EMPLOYMENT, AND PAYROLL COVERED BY UNEMPLOYMENT COMPENSATION LAW IN THE STATE AND COUNTIES OF FLORIDA, 1999

County	Number of reporting units	Number of employees	Payroll ($1,000)	County	Number of reporting units	Number of employees	Payroll ($1,000)
			Electric, gas, and sanitary services (SIC code 49)				
Florida	920	34,452	146,437	Lee	29	824	2,860
				Leon	14	251	808
Alachua	10	129	442	Manatee	13	415	1,508
Baker	3	24	73	Marion	32	399	1,338
Bay	17	411	1,414	Monroe	10	162	590
Bradford	3	26	131	Nassau	6	132	375
Brevard	12	476	1,968	Okaloosa	16	332	914
Broward	65	2,487	11,314	Okeechobee	3	84	299
Charlotte	14	295	1,067	Orange	29	1,091	4,221
Clay	13	399	1,403	Osceola	5	19	88
Collier	23	429	1,629	Pasco	30	678	2,245
Columbia	6	116	423	Pinellas	36	2,785	11,752
Dixie	4	11	20	Polk	31	648	2,419
Duval	39	568	1,680	St. Johns	11	73	288
Escambia	29	1,060	4,024	Santa Rosa	17	223	636
Flagler	5	58	262	Sarasota	25	631	2,590
Hendry	4	91	395	Seminole	21	753	2,719
Highlands	9	94	346	Taylor	6	36	140
Hillsborough	56	4,232	18,505	Volusia	17	702	2,877
Indian River	5	22	40	Wakulla	4	47	121
Jackson	6	165	507	Walton	11	226	585
Lake	13	256	817	Multicounty 1/	40	757	2,620
			Sanitary services (SIC code 495)				
Florida	382	7,050	23,139	Martin	6	28	57
				Miami-Dade	29	359	1,264
Alachua	5	58	174	Monroe	7	37	111
Bay	7	135	380	Okaloosa	6	145	315
Brevard	7	81	115	Orange	14	184	368
Broward	39	1,404	6,542	Pasco	9	42	88
Citrus	5	26	46	Pinellas	19	146	524
Clay	9	97	262	Polk	12	154	340
Duval	25	449	1,328	St. Johns	6	33	86
Escambia	8	72	117	Sarasota	10	243	888
Flagler	3	33	114	Seminole	8	277	749
Hillsborough	19	799	2,740	Volusia	6	241	661
Lake	6	161	481	Walton	6	113	213
Lee	11	203	561				
Marion	11	150	430	Multicounty 1/	22	146	413

1/ Reporting units without a fixed location within the state or of unknown county location.

Note: Private employment. For a list of three-digit industries included see Table 15.15. Data are preliminary. Only counties for which data are disclosed are shown. Detail may not add to totals due to disclosure editing and/or rounding. See Tables 23.70, 23.71, 23.72, 23.73, and 23.74 for public employment data.

Source: State of Florida, Department of Labor and Employment Security, Bureau of Labor Market Information, "Employment and Wages" (ES-202), unpublished data.

University of Florida   **Bureau of Economic and Business Research**

Table 15.25. ELECTRIC RATES: RESIDENTIAL ELECTRIC RATES CHARGED BY MUNICIPAL COOPERATIVE, AND INVESTOR-OWNED UTILITIES IN FLORIDA
DECEMBER 31, 1998

(in dollars)

Utility	Minimum bill or customer charge	500 KWH	750 KWH	1,000 KWH	1,500 KWH
Municipal					
Alachua	8.00	49.90	70.85	91.80	133.70
Bartow	6.60	48.69	69.74	90.78	132.87
Blountstown	3.50	40.02	58.28	76.54	113.06
Bushnell	6.75	43.95	62.55	81.15	118.35
Chattahoochee	4.50	40.94	59.15	77.37	113.81
Clewiston	6.50	40.40	57.35	74.30	108.20
Ft. Meade	12.96	51.42	70.65	89.88	128.34
Ft. Pierce	5.35	44.48	64.04	83.60	122.73
Gainesville	4.90	38.38	55.11	73.00	108.78
Green Cove Springs	6.00	43.46	62.19	80.92	118.38
Havana	6.00	49.99	71.99	93.98	137.97
Homestead	5.50	44.30	63.69	83.09	121.89
Jacksonville	5.50	36.83	52.49	68.15	99.48
Jacksonville Beach	4.50	41.90	60.60	79.30	116.70
Key West	4.76	47.51	68.89	90.26	133.01
Kissimmee	3.90	36.81	53.26	69.71	102.62
Lake Worth	2.78	40.96	60.05	79.14	117.32
Lakeland	3.94	40.02	58.06	76.10	112.18
Leesburg	5.00	40.98	58.96	76.95	112.93
Moore Haven	8.50	45.55	64.08	82.60	119.65
Mount Dora	4.94	45.14	65.24	85.34	125.54
New Smyrna Beach	5.65	40.24	57.53	74.82	109.41
Newberry	7.50	47.20	67.04	86.89	126.59
Ocala	7.00	42.47	60.21	77.94	113.41
Orlando	6.00	41.74	59.60	77.47	113.21
Quincy	2.40	40.23	59.15	78.06	115.89
Reedy Creek	2.85	40.61	59.48	78.36	116.12
St. Cloud	6.48	45.07	64.37	83.66	122.25
Starke	6.45	43.70	62.33	80.95	129.20
Tallahassee	4.94	45.84	66.29	86.74	127.64
Vero Beach	7.00	44.10	62.65	81.20	118.30
Wauchula	8.62	44.48	62.40	80.33	116.19
Williston	6.00	49.42	71.13	92.84	136.26

See footnotes at end of table.

Continued . . .

University of Florida

Bureau of Economic and Business Research

Table 15.25. ELECTRIC RATES: RESIDENTIAL ELECTRIC RATES CHARGED BY MUNICIPAL
COOPERATIVE, AND INVESTOR-OWNED UTILITIES IN FLORIDA
DECEMBER 31, 1998 (Continued)

(in dollars)

Utility	Minimum bill or customer charge	500 KWH	750 KWH	1,000 KWH	1,500 KWH
Cooperative					
Central Florida	8.50	44.25	62.13	80.00	115.75
Choctawhatchee	12.32	42.46	57.53	72.60	102.75
Clay	9.00	38.65	53.48	68.30	104.20
Escambia River	7.00	41.40	58.60	75.80	110.20
Florida Keys	7.00	41.23	58.35	75.46	109.69
Glades	10.50	49.50	69.00	88.50	127.50
Gulf Coast	10.00	42.40	58.60	74.80	107.20
Lee County	5.00	42.30	60.95	79.60	116.90
Okefenokee	10.00	45.50	63.25	81.00	116.49
Peace River	10.50	50.75	70.88	91.00	131.25
Sumter	8.25	44.00	61.88	79.75	115.50
Suwannee Valley	8.73	47.73	67.23	86.73	125.73
Talquin	8.00	43.50	61.25	79.00	114.50
Tri-county	10.00	51.46	72.19	92.93	134.39
West Florida	8.00	42.46	59.69	76.92	111.38
Withlacoochee River	9.75	44.87	62.42	79.98	115.10
Investor-owned					
Florida Power and Light	5.65	38.76	55.31	74.36	112.47
Florida Power	8.85	46.22	64.90	83.58	120.95
Gulf Power	8.07	34.95	48.39	61.83	88.71
Tampa Electric	8.50	43.26	60.64	78.02	112.78
Florida Public Utilities Fernandina Beach Division	7.00	31.20	43.29	55.39	79.59
Marianna Division	8.30	35.26	48.73	62.21	89.17

KWH Kilowatt-hour.
Note: Cost excludes local taxes. December 1998 fuel costs are included for municipal and cooperative utilities.

Source: State of Florida, Public Service Commission, Division of Research and Regulatory Review, *Statistics of the Florida Electric Utility Industry, 1998*.

University of Florida   **Bureau of Economic and Business Research**

Table 15.26. ELECTRIC RATES: COMMERCIAL AND INDUSTRIAL ELECTRIC RATES
CHARGED BY MUNICIPAL, COOPERATIVE, AND INVESTOR-OWNED UTILITIES
IN FLORIDA, DECEMBER 31, 1998

(in dollars)

Utility	15,000 KWH	45,000 KWH	150,000 KWH	400,000 KWH	800,000 KWH
Municipal					
Alachua	1,393	3,687	12,238	30,613	61,203
Bartow	1,643	4,260	14,158	34,923	69,827
Blountstown	1,234	3,688	12,277	32,727	65,447
Bushnell	1,390	3,618	12,011	29,729	59,437
Chattahoochee	1,211	3,722	12,406	31,408	62,816
Clewiston	1,247	3,401	11,255	28,755	57,475
Ft. Meade	1,267	3,871	12,693	30,558	61,026
Ft. Pierce	1,277	3,311	10,957	27,159	54,283
Gainesville	1,133	3,017	10,018	21,761	43,461
Green Cove Springs	1,359	3,501	11,613	22,693	31,261
Havana	1,326	3,965	13,203	35,198	70,390
Homestead	1,377	3,733	12,524	31,371	62,777
Jacksonville	1,016	2,551	8,385	20,450	40,700
Jacksonville Beach	1,611	4,162	13,836	34,036	68,056
Key West	1,705	4,589	15,285	38,455	76,905
Kissimmee	1,147	2,746	9,583	21,621	43,201
Lake Worth	1,454	3,835	12,753	31,754	63,496
Lakeland	1,115	2,948	10,208	24,178	47,980
Leesburg	1,347	3,406	11,315	27,477	54,937
Moore Haven	1,490	3,807	12,620	30,920	61,810
Mount Dora	1,128	2,983	9,910	24,755	49,495
New Smyrna Beach	1255	3285	10873	27106	54178
Newberry	1,507	3,742	12,439	29,811	59,607
Ocala	1,110	2,841	9,421	23,103	46,185
Orlando	1,122	2,811	9,337	22,539	45,063
Quincy	1,044	2,734	8,971	22,588	44,068
Reedy Creek	1,197	3,252	10,805	27,415	54,815
St. Cloud	1,347	3,374	11,204	27,046	54,074
Starke	1,457	4,352	14,484	38,609	77,209
Tallahassee	1,270	3,187	10,486	25,478	50,916
Vero Beach	1,197	3,242	10,704	27,229	54,389
Wauchula	1,117	3,626	11,937	29,879	59,693
Williston	1,457	3,961	12,950	32,450	66,793

See footnotes at end of table.   Continued . . .

University of Florida   **Bureau of Economic and Business Research**

Table 15.26. ELECTRIC RATES: COMMERCIAL AND INDUSTRIAL ELECTRIC RATES
CHARGED BY MUNICIPAL, COOPERATIVE, AND INVESTOR-OWNED UTILITIES
IN FLORIDA, DECEMBER 31, 1998 (Continued)

(in dollars)

Utility	15,000 KWH	45,000 KWH	150,000 KWH	400,000 KWH	800,000 KWH
Cooperative					
Central Florida	1,288	3,215	10,600	25,350	50,650
Choctawhatchee	1,014	2,647	9,137	20,366	40,231
Clay	1,031	2,694	8,850	22,225	40,770
Escambia River	1,203	3,115	10,290	25,540	51,040
Florida Keys	1,112	3,234	10,902	28,242	56,536
Glades	1,511	4,193	13,375	32,375	64,575
Gulf Coast	992	2,651	8,807	22,132	44,252
Lee County	1,119	2,952	10,380	25,055	50,095
Okefenokee	1,202	2,935	9,549	23,198	46,297
Peace River	1,138	2,870	9,450	23,150	46,250
Sumter	1,213	3,043	10,025	23,650	47,250
Suwannee Valley	1,433	3,755	12,421	31,001	61,961
Talquin	1,081	2,878	9,780	21,480	42,660
Tri-county	1,374	3,367	10,989	26,670	53,241
West Florida	1,019	2,507	8,240	19,890	39,730
Withlacoochee River	1,140	2,909	9,639	23,609	47,193
Investor-owned					
Florida Power and Light	1,053	2,950	9,570	22,857	45,614
Florida Power	990	2,663	8,848	22,308	44,604
Gulf Power 1/	851	2,129	7,950	17,965	35,703
Tampa Electric	1,169	2,879	9,498	22,945	45,635
Florida Public Utilities					
Fernandina Beach Division	731	1,985	6,527	16,752	33,466
Marianna Division	778	2,066	6,785	17,220	34,396

KWH Kilowatt-hour.
1/ Summer/winter rates in effect. Winter rates are shown.
Note: Cost excludes local taxes. December 1998 fuel costs are included for municipal and cooperative utilities.

Source: State of Florida, Public Service Commission, Division of Research and Regulatory Review, *Statistics of the Florida Electric Utility Industry, 1998.*

University of Florida   **Bureau of Economic and Business Research**

Table 15.27. ELECTRIC UTILITY INDUSTRY: CAPACITY, NET GENERATION, FUEL
CONSUMPTION, SALES, PER CAPITA CONSUMPTION, AND REVENUE
IN FLORIDA, 1994 THROUGH 1998

Item	1994	1995	1996	1997	1998
Nameplate capacity, total (MW)	39,084	38,954	40,334	42,610	42,363
Conventional steam	27,263	27,107	25,950	28,848	28,885
Internal combustion and gas turbine	6,234	6,261	6,343	6,450	6,493
Combined cycle	1,442	1,442	3,910	3,181	2,854
Hydroelectric	21	20	21	21	21
Steam-nuclear	4,124	4,124	4,110	4,110	4,110
Net generation, total (GWH)	152,779	159,156	157,946	161,961	181,147
By prime mover					
Conventional steam	115,196	117,474	114,725	117,801	131,756
Internal combustion and					
gas turbine	8,537	10,348	15,268	18,759	20,981
Combined cycle	0	0	0	0	0
Hydroelectric	295	250	235	264	295
Steam-nuclear	28,750	31,084	27,718	25,137	28,115
By fuel type					
Natural gas	20,420	33,483	30,496	33,123	31,319
Coal	62,511	65,714	70,008	74,219	73,184
Residual	33,286	22,521	22,537	23,874	37,191
Distillate	10,267	9,665	10,523	8,687	9,239
Hydroelectric	80	47	49	58	46
Steam-nuclear	26,216	27,726	24,333	22,000	30,168
By type of ownership					
Investor-owned	117,134	121,496	120,267	122,264	139,909
Municipal	35,645	37,660	37,679	39,697	41,238
Fuel consumed for generation					
Natural gas (billion cubic feet)	181	322	285	300	284
Coal (1,000 short tons)	30,239	30,912	32,083	34,992	34,936
Residual (1,000 barrels)	52,233	33,662	35,328	28,635	58,810
Distillate (1,000 barrels)	1,195	1,283	2,811	1,592	2,860
U-235 (trillion BTU)	286	301	266	242	326
Sales to ultimate consumers,					
total (GWH)	159,570	167,311	172,106	175,129	187,190
Residential	80,405	85,536	88,240	87,675	95,419
Commercial	51,519	51,446	53,667	56,133	59,368
Industrial	22,057	24,973	24,701	25,513	26,458
Other public utilities	5,589	5,356	5,498	5,808	5,944
Per capita consumption 1/ (KWH)					
Sales per capita, total	11,725	12,055	12,164	12,152	12,724
Residential sales per capita	5,908	6,163	6,236	6,084	6,486
Kilowatt-hours per capita 2/	11,226	11,467	11,163	11,239	12,313

See footnotes at end of table.   Continued . . .

University of Florida   **Bureau of Economic and Business Research**

Table 15.27. ELECTRIC UTILITY INDUSTRY: CAPACITY, NET GENERATION, FUEL
CONSUMPTION, SALES, PER CAPITA CONSUMPTION, AND REVENUE
IN FLORIDA, 1994 THROUGH 1998 (Continued)

Item	1994	1995	1996	1997	1998
Revenues per GWH by class of service ($1,000)					
Total	69.5	70.4	71.9	71.8	69.9
Residential	77.8	77.6	80.0	80.7	78.9
Commercial	63.3	64.2	66.5	66.3	62.1
Industrial	55.6	54.2	55.2	54.2	56.1
Other	64.3	90.6	68.5	67.3	64.6

MW Megawatt (1,000 kilowatts).
GWH Gigawatt-hours (million kilowatt-hours).
BTU British thermal units.
KWH Kilowatt-hours.
1/ Total sales divided by population.
2/ Net generation divided by population.
Note: Detail may not add to totals because of rounding. Some data may be revised.

Source: State of Florida, Public Service Commission, Division of Research and Regulatory Review,
Statistics of the Florida Electric Utility Industry, 1998.

Table 15.28. ELECTRIC UTILITY INDUSTRY: OPERATIONS AND GROWTH AND USE COMPARISONS
OF INVESTOR-OWNED ELECTRIC UTILITY COMPANIES IN FLORIDA, 1999

ITEM	Florida Power Corporation	Florida Power and Light Company	Florida Public Utilities Company	Gulf Power Company	Tampa Electric Company
Operating Statistics, 1999					
Gross electric plant in service ($1,000,000)	6,779.8	17,556.3	50.7	1,845.0	3,892.1
Operating revenue ($1,000,000)	2,632.6	6,057.5	37.6	674.0	1,207.6
Operating expenditure ($1,000,000)	2,257.4	5,311.4	35.0	587.0	1,008.0
Net operating income ($1,000,000)	375.2	746.1	2.6	87.0	199.6
Number of customers at year end (1,000)	1,377.0	3,799.8	24.9	364.0	552.1
Growth and Use, December 31, 1999					
Average residential consumption (KWH)	13,439	13,260	(NA)	14,318	14,590
Percentage increase	-3.81	-4.70	(NA)	-1.78	-3.50
Number of residential customers	1,208,739	3,332,422	21,155	315,240	477,533
Percentage increase	2.19	2.00	(NA)	2.66	2.40
Annual residential revenue ($1,000,000)	1,366	3,357	18	277	557
Percentage increase	-1.82	-6.20	(NA)	0.40	-1.00
Average revenue per KWH sold (cents)	8.41	7.60	(NA)	6.20	8.00
Annual retail operating revenue ($1,000,000)	2,281	5,886	37	513	1,100
Percentage increase	-1.30	-3.50	(NA)	0.72	0.20

KWH Kilowatt-hours.
(NA) Not available.

Source: State of Florida, Public Service Commission, *1999 Annual Report.*

University of Florida   **Bureau of Economic and Business Research**

Table 15.40. NATURAL GAS: TYPICAL NATURAL GAS BILLS FOR COMMERCIAL SERVICE OF INVESTOR-OWNED NATURAL GAS COMPANIES IN FLORIDA, DECEMBER 31, 1999

(amounts in dollars)

Company	Mini-mum bill	70 therms	90 therms	150 therms	200 therms	300 therms
Chesapeake Utilities Corporation	15.00	59.65	72.40	110.67	142.57	206.35
City Gas Company of Florida	17.00	55.80	66.89	100.15	127.87	183.31
Florida Public Utilities Company	15.00	51.06	61.36	92.27	118.03	169.54
Indiantown Gas Company	10.00	45.61	55.79	86.31	111.75	162.63
Peoples Gas System, Inc.	17.00	64.53	78.10	118.84	152.79	220.68
Peoples Gas System (Western Division) 1/	10.00	51.93	63.91	99.85	129.79	189.69
Sebring Gas System, Inc.	17.00	64.08	77.53	117.88	151.50	218.75
St. Joe Natural Gas Company	12.00	32.91	38.89	56.81	71.75	101.63
South Florida Natural Gas Company	12.00	47.38	57.49	87.81	113.08	163.63

1 Therm = 100,000 British thermal units.
1/ Formerly West Florida Natural Gas Company.

Table 15.41. NATURAL GAS: TYPICAL NATURAL GAS BILLS FOR RESIDENTIAL SERVICE OF INVESTOR-OWNED NATURAL GAS COMPANIES IN FLORIDA, DECEMBER 31, 1999

(amounts in dollars)

Company	Mini-mum bill	20 therms	30 therms	40 therms	50 therms	100 therms
Chesapeake Utilities Corporation	7.00	24.71	33.57	42.43	51.29	95.57
City Gas Company of Florida	7.00	23.31	31.46	39.61	47.76	88.53
Florida Public Utilities Company	8.00	20.70	27.05	33.40	39.76	71.51
Indiantown Gas Company	5.00	15.27	20.41	25.55	30.69	56.37
Peoples Gas System, Inc.	7.00	23.93	32.39	40.85	49.32	91.64
Peoples Gas System (Western Division) 1/	7.00	22.21	29.81	37.42	45.02	83.04
Sebring Gas System, Inc.	7.00	22.25	29.88	37.50	45.13	83.25
St. Joe Natural Gas Company	6.00	10.83	13.24	15.66	18.07	30.15
South Florida Natural Gas Company	7.00	23.74	32.10	40.47	48.84	90.68

1 Therm = 100,000 British thermal units.
1/ Formerly West Florida Natural Gas Company.

Source for Tables 15.40 and 15.41: State of Florida, Public Service Commission, *1999 Annual Report.*

University of Florida   **Bureau of Economic and Business Research**

Table 15.42. NATURAL GAS: PRODUCTION, MOVEMENT, AND CONSUMPTION IN FLORIDA
AND THE UNITED STATES, 1997 AND 1998

(quantity in millions of cubic feet)

Item	Florida 1997	Florida 1998	United States 1997	United States 1998
Marketed production 1/	6,114	5,796	19,865,182	19,645,554
Net interstate movements	503,126	472,632	0	0
Net movements across U.S. borders	0	0	2,868,547	3,015,170
Net storage changes 2/	0	0	-23,603	529,763
Extraction loss	1,563	1,523	963,759	937,798
Supplemental gas supplies	0	0	103,153	102,189
Balancing item 3/	-21,960	-10,664	76,044	-33,330
Consumption, total	485,679	466,241	21,958,660	21,262,023
Delivered to consumers	477,601	460,082	20,004,012	19,469,047
Lease fuel	2,321	2,200	776,306	756,184
Plant fuel	5,644	3,830	751,470	635,477
Pipeline fuel	113	129	426,873	401,314

1/ Gross withdrawals from gas and oil wells less gas used for repressuring, nonhydrocarbon gases removed, and quantities vented and flared.
2/ Positive numbers indicate an increase in storage, thus a decrease in supply.
3/ Represents an imbalance between available supplies and consumption.
Note: Some data may be revised.

Table 15.43. NATURAL GAS: VOLUME CONSUMED, CONSUMERS, AND PRICE OF NATURAL GAS DELIVERED TO CONSUMERS IN FLORIDA AND THE UNITED STATES, 1998

Item	Resi-dential	Com-mercial	Indus-trial	Vehi-cle fuel	Electric util-ities
Florida					
Volume consumed (MCF)	14,102	37,659	126,891	84	281,346
Consumers	542,770	46,778	579	(NA)	(NA)
Average price (dollars per thousand cubic feet)	11.29	6.41	3.98	4.72	2.27
United States					
Volume consumed (MCF)	4,520,276	2,999,491	8,686,147	5,079	3,258,054
Consumers	57,321,746	5,044,497	231,438	(NA)	(NA)
Average price (dollars per thousand cubic feet)	6.82	5.48	3.14	4.59	2.40

MCF Million cubic feet.
(NA) Not available.

Source for Tables 15.42 and 15.43: U.S., Department of Energy, Energy Information Administration, *Natural Gas Annual, 1998,* Internet site <http://www.eia.doe.gov/pub/oil_gas/natural_gas/data_ publications/natural_gas_annual/current/pdf/nga98.pdf> (accessed 18 May 2000).

University of Florida   **Bureau of Economic and Business Research**

Table 15.50. NUCLEAR POWER PLANTS: NUMBER OF UNITS, NET GENERATION, AND NET SUMMER CAPABILITY IN FLORIDA, OTHER LEADING GENERATING STATES, AND THE UNITED STATES, 1997

Leading State	Number of units	Net generation Total (million kWh)	Net generation Percent-age of total	Net summer capability Total (million kWh)	Net summer capability Percent-age of total
Florida	5	22,968	15.5	3.88	10.4
Illinois	13	51,069	38.9	12.61	37.6
Pennsylvania	9	67,655	38.2	8.96	26.4
South Carolina	7	44,916	57.3	6.42	36.9
New York	6	29,570	27.4	4.85	16.0
Alabama	5	29,573	26.0	4.84	23.4
California	5	30,512	27.2	4.75	10.8
North Carolina	5	32,453	30.2	4.64	22.2
Georgia	4	30,414	29.9	3.95	17.3
Texas	4	37,358	13.5	4.93	7.6
United States	110	628,644	20.1	100.76	14.2

kWh Kilo-watt hour.
Source: U.S., Department of Commerce, Bureau of the Census, *Statistical Abstract of the United States, 1999.*

Table 15.51. ENERGY CONSUMPTION ESTIMATES: AMOUNT CONSUMED BY SECTOR IN FLORIDA 1983 THROUGH 1997

(in trillions of British thermal units)

Year	Total	Resi-dential	Commer-cial 1/	Indus-trial 2/	Transpor-tation 3/
1983	2,461.9	620.6	461.5	441.6	938.2
1984	2,552.4	664.7	489.0	471.5	927.2
1985	2,701.1	716.4	559.5	473.8	951.4
1986	2,798.7	745.2	589.3	458.1	1,006.1
1987	2,892.2	765.0	612.5	452.5	1,062.2
1988	3,054.6	797.7	640.7	490.8	1,125.4
1989	3,183.0	861.5	667.9	511.5	1,142.1
1990	3,162.5	840.1	691.5	491.0	1,139.9
1991	3,099.8	858.1	700.4	466.5	1,074.8
1992	3,151.0	856.5	695.8	486.4	1,112.3
1993	3,215.1	889.8	702.1	516.7	1,106.5
1994	3,373.7	921.3	720.9	543.1	1,188.4
1995	3,508.9	974.5	751.3	557.7	1,225.4
1996	3,571.9	1,004.1	760.9	573.2	1,233.7
1997	3,614.7	991.0	778.5	565.1	1,280.1

1/ Includes establishments under SIC codes 15-17, 48-49 (except 491 and part of 493), 50-59, 70-89, and 91-93.
2/ Includes establishments under SIC codes 1-14 and 20-39.
3/ Includes establishments under SIC codes 40-47.
Note: Some data may be revised.

Source: U.S., Department of Energy, Energy Information Administration, *State Energy Data Report, 1997*, Internet site <http://www.eia.doe.gov/emeu/states/main_fl.html> (accessed 22 September 1999).

University of Florida   **Bureau of Economic and Business Research**

Florida Statistical Abstract 2000

Table 15.60. MOTOR FUELS: CONSUMPTION BY USE IN FLORIDA, 1962 THROUGH 1998

(in thousands of gallons)

Year	Total quantity consumed 1/	Nonhighway use 2/	Highway use
1962	2,071,490	133,801	1,917,987
1963	2,169,084	124,988	2,022,714
1964	2,286,002	112,073	2,160,479
1965	2,409,617	104,646	2,291,031
1966	2,562,586	120,505	2,428,962
1967	2,711,163	135,851	2,561,698
1968	2,959,259	138,496	2,803,754
1969	3,215,457	129,949	3,069,173
1970	3,484,439	153,969	3,312,830
1971	3,771,337	146,210	3,585,727
1972	4,215,995	124,098	4,045,322
1973	4,695,983	126,054	4,494,951
1974	4,510,456	123,058	4,342,185
1975	4,639,217	135,547	4,456,610
1976	4,827,840	136,774	4,650,302
1977	5,023,007	131,635	4,846,201
1978	5,337,604	139,114	5,152,263
1979	5,374,535	142,358	5,171,693
1980	5,293,548	164,430	5,116,312
1981	5,390,545	137,165	5,240,229
1982	5,469,775	139,779	5,317,892
1983	5,723,316	163,810	5,548,590
1984	5,934,391	181,767	5,740,587
1985	6,110,435	254,402	5,843,396
1986	6,394,295	263,337	6,116,961
1987	6,700,629	275,337	6,387,472
1988	6,863,376	281,739	6,530,151
1989	7,034,489	292,036	6,680,708
1990	7,043,054	306,520	6,674,542
1991	6,930,325	319,863	6,549,254
1992	7,163,374	264,516	6,827,210
1993	7,431,207	169,860	7,187,669
1994	7,487,188	178,304	7,308,884
1995	7,680,638	206,176	7,474,462
1996	7,800,062	201,216	7,598,846
1997	8,019,637	206,247	7,813,390
1998	8,371,333	241,386	8,129,947

1/ Includes losses allowed for evaporation and handling.
2/ Gasoline. Includes gasohol.
Note: Includes gasoline and all other fuels (except under nonhighway use) under state motor fuel laws.
Data for earlier years may not be comparable due to revised estimation procedures.

Source: U.S., Department of Transportation, Federal Highway Administration, *Highway Statistics, 1998,* Internet site <http://www.fhwa.dot.gov/ohim/hs98/mfpage.htm> (accessed 21 April 2000), and previous editions.

University of Florida **Bureau of Economic and Business Research**

Table 15.66. GASOLINE: AVERAGE PUMP PRICES IN SELECTED CITIES IN FLORIDA, DECEMBER 1997 THROUGH 1999, AND ANNUALLY IN THE UNITED STATES, 1996 THROUGH 1998

(prices in dollars per gallon)

City	Regular 1997	Regular 1998	Regular 1999	Mid-grade 1997	Mid-grade 1998	Mid-grade 1999	Premium 1997	Premium 1998	Premium 1999
State average	1.166	1.010	1.333	1.285	1.133	1.440	1.363	1.213	1.523
Bradenton	1.153	1.012	1.320	1.267	1.127	1.427	1.361	1.225	1.519
Brandon	1.121	0.969	1.289	1.230	1.089	1.398	1.308	1.156	1.478
Cocoa/Melbourne	1.132	0.970	1.307	1.237	1.099	1.403	1.331	1.184	1.500
Daytona Beach	1.154	0.994	1.314	1.269	1.101	1.417	1.363	1.191	1.514
Delray Beach	1.220	1.114	1.420	1.365	1.252	1.551	1.421	1.314	1.619
Ft. Lauderdale	1.189	1.042	1.297	1.317	1.177	1.404	1.381	1.246	1.491
Ft. Myers	1.293	1.034	1.372	1.377	1.146	1.500	1.470	1.238	1.562
Ft. Pierce	1.132	0.965	1.349	1.247	1.089	1.457	1.304	1.159	1.542
Gainesville	1.232	1.072	1.333	1.335	1.176	1.447	1.434	1.264	1.526
Jacksonville	1.221	1.044	1.354	1.320	1.158	1.464	1.423	1.256	1.554
Lakeland	1.116	0.951	1.354	1.249	1.067	1.458	1.338	1.137	1.558
Leesburg	1.147	0.949	1.310	1.385	1.066	1.400	1.359	1.163	1.485
Miami	1.214	1.095	1.387	1.333	1.226	1.525	1.377	1.275	1.577
Naples	1.263	1.109	1.389	1.344	1.216	1.499	1.429	1.305	1.571
Ocala	1.105	0.970	1.314	1.209	1.068	1.407	1.297	1.164	1.476
Orlando	1.141	0.993	1.329	1.286	1.135	1.442	1.364	1.207	1.522
Palm Beach	1.228	1.096	1.419	1.362	1.235	1.547	1.443	1.312	1.615
Pensacola	1.133	0.987	1.316	1.239	1.082	1.417	1.339	1.172	1.517
Pompano Beach	1.239	1.041	1.363	1.337	1.161	1.483	1.417	1.234	1.549
Port Charlotte	1.117	0.974	1.291	1.254	1.113	1.398	1.371	1.210	1.499
Port Richey	1.089	0.946	1.258	1.195	1.035	1.341	1.265	1.100	1.423
St. Petersburg	1.084	0.972	1.325	1.226	1.129	1.437	1.284	1.179	1.523
Sarasota	1.148	0.988	1.285	1.256	1.144	1.399	1.360	1.244	1.482
Stuart	1.183	0.999	1.355	1.277	1.130	1.432	1.366	1.187	1.520
Tallahassee	1.185	1.019	1.320	1.289	1.136	1.421	1.379	1.240	1.502
Tampa	1.113	0.991	1.313	1.244	1.142	1.414	1.299	1.187	1.496
Venice	1.132	0.975	1.301	1.243	1.100	1.402	1.331	1.195	1.489

	Average sales price to end users 1/		Real price (1996 dollars)	
	Nominal price	Implicit price deflator 2/ (1996 = 1.000)	Amount	Per- centage change
United States				
1996	115.0	1.0000	115.0	4.64
1997	113.4	1.0198	111.2	-3.31
1998	95.2	1.0293	92.5	-16.82

1/ Prices are in cents per gallon and exclude all federal, state, and county taxes.
2/ For personal consumption expenditures. Data from U.S. Department of Commerce, Bureau of Economic Analysis.
Note: City data are from AAA Clubs of Florida Survey and are for self-service pumps. Some data may be revised.

Source: State of Florida, Department of Community Affairs, *1999 Florida Motor Gasoline and Diesel Fuel Report,* April 2000, Internet site <http://www.dca.state.fl.us/fhcd/gas_report/> (accessed 15 June 2000).

University of Florida   **Bureau of Economic and Business Research**

Table 15.67. GASOLINE: TOTAL AND PER CAPITA GALLONS SOLD IN THE STATE AND
COUNTIES OF FLORIDA, 1997, 1998, AND 1999

County	Total sales (1,000 gallons)			Per-centage change from 1997 to 1999	Per capita sales (gallons)			Per-centage change from 1997 to 1999
	1997	1998	1999	1999	1997	1998	1999	1999
Florida	6,951,400	7,179,638	7,400,055	6.5	472.5	478.6	483.0	2.2
Alachua	102,513	104,117	101,950	-0.5	492.6	492.5	471.4	-4.3
Baker	12,157	13,224	14,703	20.9	575.1	625.8	672.0	16.8
Bay	81,658	83,911	84,819	3.9	564.8	568.9	565.0	0.0
Bradford	14,997	14,776	14,433	-3.8	594.4	582.8	566.0	-4.8
Brevard	213,542	219,673	227,147	6.4	466.2	471.6	478.4	2.6
Broward	685,558	717,429	734,192	7.1	481.5	491.1	492.7	2.3
Calhoun	5,520	5,343	6,166	11.7	428.7	393.7	436.8	1.9
Charlotte	72,716	75,204	75,515	3.8	553.8	562.7	552.1	-0.3
Citrus	47,190	49,190	50,150	6.3	429.1	437.5	436.5	1.7
Clay	58,061	61,023	62,671	7.9	453.9	453.6	448.8	-1.1
Collier	101,644	104,485	112,047	10.2	508.2	497.3	510.0	0.4
Columbia	41,431	43,118	44,228	6.8	771.8	778.8	782.6	1.4
De Soto	9,768	8,893	9,376	-4.0	358.8	318.4	329.7	-8.1
Dixie	6,033	5,585	6,795	12.6	462.7	423.2	504.2	9.0
Duval	354,179	363,722	373,253	5.4	477.6	482.5	489.3	2.4
Escambia	133,824	136,702	136,316	1.9	459.7	461.6	452.0	-1.7
Flagler	20,245	20,199	21,766	7.5	491.5	465.0	475.1	-3.3
Franklin	6,088	6,217	6,463	6.2	580.0	578.9	594.5	2.5
Gadsden	23,627	23,898	26,201	10.9	475.0	470.2	509.0	7.2
Gilchrist	4,268	5,016	4,772	11.8	340.6	381.7	356.0	4.5
Glades	3,574	3,755	3,715	3.9	370.4	380.3	376.5	1.6
Gulf	5,294	5,210	4,673	-11.7	375.4	365.4	324.4	-13.6
Hamilton	10,870	10,784	10,622	-2.3	793.0	763.7	738.9	-6.8
Hardee	10,431	10,440	10,575	1.4	464.7	457.9	468.0	0.7
Hendry	19,419	19,716	20,607	6.1	640.7	649.3	674.5	5.3
Hernando	57,145	56,412	56,637	-0.9	468.0	451.3	444.6	-5.0
Highlands	35,872	36,425	36,725	2.4	451.0	452.7	452.6	0.4
Hillsborough	444,730	466,850	487,298	9.6	478.9	495.4	503.7	5.2
Holmes	7,939	8,802	9,753	22.8	450.8	490.4	516.1	14.5
Indian River	50,483	54,797	56,706	12.3	482.6	513.6	517.5	7.2
Jackson	32,256	30,316	29,678	-8.0	653.1	610.3	599.9	-8.1
Jefferson	9,380	8,995	9,885	5.4	670.6	633.1	685.3	2.2
Lafayette	2,313	2,229	2,445	5.7	330.3	318.5	351.2	6.3
Lake	88,746	96,139	97,194	9.5	471.2	490.3	476.8	1.2
Lee	194,030	203,373	216,652	11.7	492.2	501.4	519.4	5.5
Leon	103,395	107,250	108,327	4.8	454.1	459.8	455.9	0.4

See footnote at end of table.   Continued . . .

University of Florida   **Bureau of Economic and Business Research**

Table 15.67. GASOLINE: TOTAL AND PER CAPITA GALLONS SOLD IN THE STATE AND COUNTIES OF FLORIDA, 1997, 1998, AND 1999 (Continued)

County	Total sales (1,000 gallons)			Per-centage change from 1997 to 1999	Per capita sales (gallons)			Per-centage change from 1997 to 1999
	1997	1998	1999	1999	1997	1998	1999	1999
Levy	20,025	20,172	19,938	-0.4	633.9	622.3	596.8	-5.8
Liberty	3,499	3,077	3,063	-12.5	454.8	399.2	380.6	-16.3
Madison	9,416	10,324	10,907	15.8	494.7	535.6	555.6	12.3
Manatee	103,036	104,686	107,505	4.3	426.8	423.8	424.6	-0.5
Marion	135,393	140,315	143,329	5.9	570.8	579.0	574.6	0.7
Martin	59,524	62,899	66,493	11.7	511.6	526.9	547.2	7.0
Miami-Dade	844,024	851,895	879,346	4.2	407.6	407.5	413.5	1.4
Monroe	54,209	55,095	55,559	2.5	639.7	643.3	638.4	-0.2
Nassau	28,728	26,489	26,468	-7.9	544.7	485.7	461.3	-15.3
Okaloosa	90,990	89,666	93,771	3.1	532.0	510.7	522.1	-1.9
Okeechobee	26,097	25,558	24,765	-5.1	751.1	729.0	697.4	-7.1
Orange	445,872	468,663	482,847	8.3	554.8	568.7	570.5	2.8
Osceola	91,059	94,870	101,186	11.1	633.1	637.9	643.0	1.6
Palm Beach	431,879	448,245	461,048	6.8	430.2	439.2	442.4	2.8
Pasco	129,196	136,477	144,679	12.0	409.1	425.1	443.1	8.3
Pinellas	355,188	364,309	368,437	3.7	399.9	408.3	409.9	2.5
Polk	220,899	227,365	234,014	5.9	481.3	488.1	493.0	2.4
Putnam	31,940	33,953	33,554	5.1	454.7	475.2	460.4	1.2
St. Johns	60,601	64,448	68,807	13.5	571.9	586.5	603.9	5.6
St. Lucie	88,820	92,869	94,117	6.0	495.8	506.9	503.6	1.6
Santa Rosa	54,221	54,058	54,967	1.4	529.8	501.4	488.0	-7.9
Sarasota	135,123	141,919	148,175	9.7	434.4	449.1	461.5	6.2
Seminole	141,013	155,380	160,168	13.6	417.8	450.2	452.3	8.2
Sumter	37,434	35,769	36,290	-3.1	843.8	746.6	714.0	-15.4
Suwannee	20,353	21,742	22,728	11.7	612.6	644.3	661.0	7.9
Taylor	13,012	11,993	12,709	-2.3	678.3	614.2	640.7	-5.5
Union	4,109	4,186	4,301	4.7	313.6	311.0	310.9	-0.9
Volusia	195,451	207,968	216,366	10.7	472.5	494.7	506.9	7.3
Wakulla	10,329	11,232	10,534	2.0	553.5	566.5	510.2	-7.8
Walton	27,931	28,000	28,459	1.9	773.8	731.0	703.3	-9.1
Washington	11,160	10,399	11,069	-0.8	554.8	487.8	499.6	-9.9

Note: Includes gasohol. Per capita is computed using Bureau of Economic and Business Research *Florida Estimates of Population.* Some data are revised.

Source: State of Florida, Department of Community Affairs, *1999 Florida Motor Gasoline and Diesel Fuel Report,* April 2000, Internet site <http://www.dca.state.fl.us/fhcd/gas_report/> (accessed 15 June 2000).

University of Florida   **Bureau of Economic and Business Research**

WHOLESALE AND RETAIL TRADE

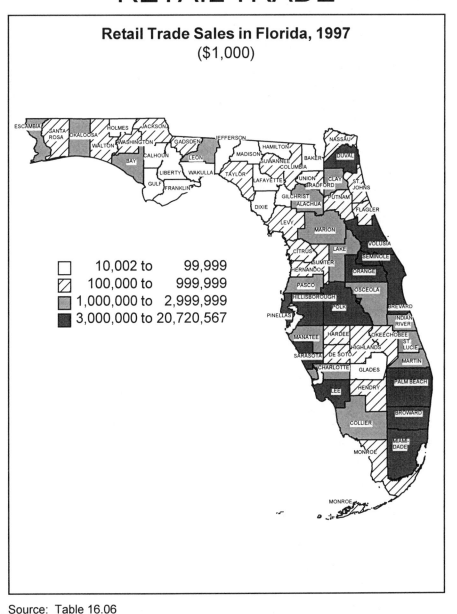

Retail Trade Sales in Florida, 1997
($1,000)

☐	10,002 to 99,999
▨	100,000 to 999,999
▦	1,000,000 to 2,999,999
■	3,000,000 to 20,720,567

Source: Table 16.06

SECTION 16.00
WHOLESALE AND RETAIL TRADE

TABLES LISTED BY MAJOR HEADINGS

University of Florida   **Bureau of Economic and Business Research**

Table 16.01. WHOLESALE TRADE: ESTABLISHMENTS, EMPLOYMENT, SALES, ANNUAL PAYROLL AND OPERATING EXPENSES IN THE WHOLESALE TRADE INDUSTRY IN FLORIDA, 1997

Industry	Estab-lishments	Employ-ment	Sales ($1,000)	Payroll ($1,000)	Expenses ($1,000)
Wholesale trade	31,214	296,139	187,079,940	9,678,165	20,378,702
Wholesaler distributors and jobbers	22,825	209,878	92,720,415	6,467,591	13,356,694
Importers	861	8,909	5,621,417	313,369	804,390
Exporters	2,724	16,861	14,793,764	556,195	1,445,887
Own brand importer - marketers	163	3,619	6,407,864	137,203	362,100
Terminal grain elevators	1	(D)	(D)	(D)	A/
Country grain elevators	3	15	8,714	291	679
Assemblers of farm products 1/	173	(D)	(D)	(D)	B/
Sales branches (with stock)	820	21,184	16,431,933	798,809	1,806,982
Sales offices (without stock)	533	13,346	27,002,431	763,970	1,325,691
Auction companies	37	4,434	6,462,052	53,223	115,429
Brokers	672	3,656	5,425,680	112,614	206,302
Commission merchants	417	1,329	1,716,108	59,280	111,230
Import agents	45	251	226,709	9,932	22,214
Export agents	300	826	759,820	26,968	57,685
Manufacturers' agents	1,640	5,919	7,795,156	262,481	497,203

Employment ranges: A/ 20-99. B/ 5,000-9,999.   1/ Except country grain elevators.
Note: See footnotes on Table 16.02.

Table 16.02. WHOLESALE TRADE: ESTABLISHMENTS, SALES, AND SALES PER ESTABLISHMENT BY KIND OF BUSINESS IN FLORIDA, 1997

NAICS code	Kind of business	Es-tablish-ments	Sales Amount ($1,000)	Sales Establish-ment (dollars)
421	Wholesale trade, durable goods	20,492	109,900,920	5,363,113
4211	Motor vehicle and motor vehicle parts and supplies	2,190	33,218,922	15,168,458
4212	Furniture and home furnishings	1,226	3,622,826	2,954,997
4213	Lumber and other construction materials	1,069	4,681,898	4,379,699
4214	Professional and commercial equipment and supplies	3,664	21,387,001	5,837,064
4215	Metal and mineral (except petroleum)	581	(D)	(X)
4216	Electrical goods	2,953	17,558,286	5,945,915
4217	Hardware, plumbing, heating equipment and supplies	1,438	4,241,895	2,949,857
4218	Machinery, equipment, and supplies	4,407	13,240,301	3,004,380
4219	Miscellaneous durable goods	2,964	(D)	(X)
422	Wholesale trade, nondurable goods	10,722	77,179,020	7,198,193
4221	Paper and paper product	935	3,909,435	4,181,214
4222	Drugs, and druggists' sundries	824	9,379,965	11,383,453
4223	Apparel, piece goods, and notions	1,399	3,504,673	2,505,127
4224	Grocery and related products	3,002	29,630,238	9,870,166
4225	Farm product raw material	136	1,268,830	9,329,632
4226	Chemical and allied products	964	3,127,849	3,244,657
4227	Petroleum and petroleum products	430	12,305,018	28,616,321
4228	Beer, wine, and distilled alcoholic beverage	199	4,632,773	23,280,266
4229	Miscellaneous nondurable goods	2,833	9,420,239	3,325,181

(D) Data withheld to avoid disclosure of information about individual firms. (X) Not applicable.
Note: The economic censuses are conducted on a 5-year cycle collecting data for years ending in 2 and 7. Data are for NAICS code 42 and may not be comparable to earlier years. See Glossary.

Source for Tables 16.01 and 16.02: U.S., Department of Commerce, Bureau of the Census, *1997 Economic Census: Wholesale Trade,* Geographic Area Series EC97W42A-FL(RV), Issued March 2000, Internet site <http://www.census.gov/prod/ec97/97w42-fl.pdf> (accessed 27 June 2000).

Table 16.06. WHOLESALE AND RETAIL TRADE: SALES IN THE STATE AND COUNTIES
OF FLORIDA, 1997

(in thousands of dollars)

County	Wholesale trade	Retail trade	County	Wholesale trade	Retail trade
Florida	187,079,940	151,191,241	Lake	680,221	1,514,280
			Lee	1,450,292	4,367,000
Alachua	738,040	1,934,539	Leon	(D)	2,244,368
Baker	(D)	95,726	Levy	37,720	234,515
Bay	422,076	1,496,794	Liberty	(D)	11,908
Bradford	31,102	151,665	Madison	60,916	64,143
Brevard	1,362,388	3,900,522	Manatee	1,087,635	2,140,956
Broward	26,122,200	17,979,812	Marion	999,606	2,221,375
Calhoun	(D)	81,037	Martin	423,775	1,454,037
Charlotte	117,208	1,063,313	Miami-Dade	43,604,363	20,720,567
Citrus	90,411	800,641	Monroe	217,493	914,215
Clay	220,577	1,100,525	Nassau	158,350	332,224
Collier	813,802	2,627,103	Okaloosa	248,294	1,754,851
Columbia	286,735	555,998	Okeechobee	(D)	270,099
De Soto	(D)	196,983	Orange	24,089,127	10,450,934
Dixie	(D)	39,174	Osceola	1,070,100	1,349,700
Duval	16,590,011	8,034,132	Palm Beach	11,544,458	11,731,186
Escambia	1,615,989	2,874,679	Pasco	351,585	2,247,139
Flagler	94,555	244,118	Pinellas	11,558,651	10,183,888
Franklin	64,067	57,007	Polk	4,176,162	3,844,279
Gadsden	(D)	179,825	Putnam	(D)	397,730
Gilchrist	(D)	29,879	St. Johns	427,955	862,484
Glades	(D)	35,172	St. Lucie	581,483	1,387,215
Gulf	28,232	48,906	Santa Rosa	103,050	561,093
Hamilton	(D)	53,618	Sarasota	1,035,855	3,606,588
Hardee	92,410	116,762	Seminole	3,669,710	3,550,143
Hendry	(D)	202,616	Sumter	84,377	185,283
Hernando	142,272	821,522	Suwannee	(D)	204,992
Highlands	184,058	618,176	Taylor	(D)	144,206
Hillsborough	23,668,468	10,931,594	Union	(D)	27,187
Holmes	(D)	46,291	Volusia	1,629,722	3,887,639
Indian River	(D)	1,143,861	Wakulla	(D)	57,596
Jackson	86,036	376,889	Walton	98,237	262,614
Jefferson	(D)	51,505	Washington	(D)	104,421
Lafayette	(D)	10,002			

(D) Data withheld to avoid disclosure of information about individual industries.
Note: The economic censuses are conducted on a 5-year cycle collecting data for years ending in 2 and 7. Data are for North American Classification System (NAICS) code 42 and 44-45 and may not be comparable to earlier years. See Glossary for definition.

Source: U.S., Department of Commerce, Bureau of the Census, *1997 Economic Census: Wholesale Trade*, Geographic Area Series EC97W42A-FL(RV), Issued March 2000, and *1997 Economic Census: Retail Trade*, Geographic Area Series EC97R44A-FL, Issued December 1999, Internet site <http://www.census. gov/prod/ec97/> (accessed 27 June 2000).

Table 16.11. RETAIL TRADE: ESTABLISHMENTS, EMPLOYMENT, SALES, AND ANNUAL PAYROLL BY KIND OF BUSINESS IN FLORIDA, 1997

NAICS code	Kind of business	Number of estab-lishments	Number of em-ployees 1/	Sales ($1,000)	Annual payroll ($1,000)
44-45	Retail trade	66,643	841,814	151,191,241	14,169,511
441	Motor vehicle and parts dealers	7,340	107,767	44,398,982	3,197,890
4411	Automobile dealers	2,679	71,358	37,922,106	2,408,373
4412	Other motor vehicle dealers	1,258	9,865	3,202,160	252,754
4413	Automotive parts, accessories, and tire stores	3,403	26,544	3,274,716	536,763
442	Furniture and home furnishings stores	4,569	29,706	4,891,648	632,683
4421	Furniture stores	2,068	15,584	2,930,414	378,060
4422	Home furnishings stores	2,501	14,122	1,961,234	254,623
443	Electronics and appliance stores	2,624	21,309	4,437,446	429,252
444	Building material, garden equipment and supplies dealers	4,723	59,226	11,694,267	1,324,411
4441	Building material and supplies dealers	3,838	53,512	10,788,946	1,225,245
4442	Lawn and garden equipment and supplies	885	5,714	905,321	99,166
445	Food and beverage stores	7,563	196,921	23,898,453	2,426,547
4451	Grocery stores	5,221	185,001	22,487,722	2,277,848
4452	Specialty food stores	1,227	6,495	622,179	83,166
4453	Beer, wine, and liquor stores	1,115	5,425	788,552	65,533
446	Health and personal care stores	5,471	60,979	8,033,682	1,017,584
447	Gasoline stations	6,853	43,133	10,643,605	575,071
448	Clothing and clothing accessories stores	10,875	80,667	9,289,463	1,070,043
4481	Clothing stores	6,604	57,005	6,416,075	714,310
4482	Shoe stores	2,015	12,827	1,427,753	159,452
4483	Jewelry, luggage, and leather goods stores	2,256	10,835	1,445,635	196,281
451	Sporting goods, hobby, book, and music stores	3,984	28,201	3,396,919	390,965
4511	Sporting goods, hobby, and musical instrument stores	2,795	18,250	2,334,799	271,324
4512	Book, periodical, and music stores	1,189	9,951	1,062,120	119,641
452	General merchandise stores	1,914	143,248	19,703,433	1,872,649
4521	Department stores (includes leased departments) 2/	614	(NA)	13,769,050	(NA)
4521	Department stores (excludes leased departments)	614	106,980	13,566,905	1,413,527
4529	Other general merchandise stores	1,300	36,268	6,136,528	459,122
453	Miscellaneous store retailers	8,211	44,873	4,736,498	603,120
4531	Florists	1,413	6,138	341,418	73,758
4532	Office supplies, stationery, and gift stores	2,708	19,411	2,067,829	227,243
4533	Used merchandise stores	1,307	5,802	375,222	70,830
4539	Other miscellaneous store retailers	2,783	13,522	1,952,029	231,289
454	Nonstore retailers	2,516	25,784	6,066,845	629,296
4541	Electronic shopping and mail-order houses	682	14,023	4,552,063	382,898
4542	Vending machine operators	394	1,856	237,413	36,646
4543	Direct selling establishments	1,440	9,905	1,277,369	209,752

(NA) Not available.
1/ Paid employment for pay period including March 12.
2/ Data for this line not included in broader kind-of-business totals.
Note: The economic censuses are conducted on a 5-year cycle collecting data for years ending in 2 and 7. Data are for North American Classification System (NAICS) codes 44-45 and may not be comparable to earlier years. See Glossary for definition.

Source: U.S., Department of Commerce, Bureau of the Census, *1997 Economic Census: Retail Trade,* Geographic Area Series EC97R44A-FL, Issued December 1999, Internet site <http://www.census. gov/prod/ec97/97r44-fl.pdf> (accessed 27 June 2000).

University of Florida   **Bureau of Economic and Business Research**

Table 16.43. EMPLOYMENT AND PAYROLL: AVERAGE MONTHLY PRIVATE REPORTING UNITS EMPLOYMENT, AND PAYROLL COVERED BY UNEMPLOYMENT COMPENSATION LAW BY WHOLESALE AND RETAIL TRADE INDUSTRY IN FLORIDA, 1998 AND 1999

SIC code	Industry	Number of re- porting units	Number of em- ployees	Payroll ($1,000)
		1998 A/		
	Wholesale trade	39,915	357,051	1,154,604
50	Wholesale trade--durable goods	25,846	213,535	718,277
501	Motor vehicles and motor vehicle parts and supplies	2,661	27,557	72,131
502	Furniture and home furnishings	1,171	8,500	25,320
503	Lumber and other construction materials	1,795	14,439	41,496
504	Professional and commercial equipment and supplies	5,258	52,079	212,827
505	Metals and minerals, except petroleum	548	4,623	14,627
506	Electrical goods	3,642	33,281	125,651
507	Hardware, plumbing and heating equipment and supplies	1,764	15,603	49,675
508	Machinery, equipment, and supplies	4,683	36,951	120,794
509	Miscellaneous durable goods	4,325	20,502	55,757
51	Wholesale trade--nondurable goods	14,070	143,516	436,327
511	Paper and paper products	1,311	18,137	52,797
512	Drugs, drug proprietaries, and druggists' sundries	1,112	13,980	60,810
513	Apparel, piece goods, and notions	1,542	9,377	24,167
514	Groceries and related products	3,414	48,566	140,104
515	Farm-product raw materials	114	935	1,711
516	Chemicals and allied products	1,074	7,307	27,281
517	Petroleum and petroleum products	468	6,469	17,299
518	Beer, wine, and distilled alcoholic beverages	273	10,477	38,735
519	Miscellaneous nondurable goods	4,762	28,268	73,422
	Retail trade	81,186	1,322,476	1,895,145
52	Building materials, hardware, garden supply, and mobile home dealers	3,708	53,043	102,679
521	Lumber and other building materials dealers	1,194	36,434	72,384
523	Paint, glass, and wallpaper stores	727	4,052	9,155
525	Hardware stores	745	5,844	8,993
526	Retail nurseries, lawn and garden supply stores	700	4,414	6,839
527	Mobile home dealers	342	2,299	5,307
53	General merchandise stores	1,786	151,659	199,044
531	Department stores	941	136,775	182,253
533	Variety stores	435	5,191	4,294
539	Miscellaneous general merchandise stores	410	9,694	12,497
54	Food stores	9,459	251,371	312,778
541	Grocery stores	6,582	229,092	284,539
542	Meat and fish markets and freezer provisioners	483	3,403	5,385
543	Fruit and vegetable markets	349	2,522	3,551
544	Candy, nut, and confectionery stores	168	1,119	1,126
545	Dairy products stores	69	408	330

See footnotes at end of table.   Continued . . .

University of Florida   **Bureau of Economic and Business Research**

Table 16.43. EMPLOYMENT AND PAYROLL: AVERAGE MONTHLY PRIVATE REPORTING UNITS EMPLOYMENT, AND PAYROLL COVERED BY UNEMPLOYMENT COMPENSATION LAW BY WHOLESALE AND RETAIL TRADE INDUSTRY IN FLORIDA, 1998 AND 1999 (Continued)

SIC code	Industry	Number of reporting units	Number of employees	Payroll ($1,000)
	1998 A/ (Continued)			
	Retail trade (Continued)			
54	Food stores (Continued)			
546	Retail bakeries	954	9,250	10,416
549	Miscellaneous food stores	855	5,576	7,430
55	Automotive dealers and gasoline service stations	9,565	128,443	335,912
551	Motor vehicle dealers (new and used)	1,349	65,445	215,274
552	Motor vehicle dealers (used only)	1,282	7,061	19,666
553	Auto and home supply stores	2,495	21,594	42,891
554	Gasoline service stations	3,343	25,044	34,514
555	Boat dealers	665	4,836	10,981
556	Recreational vehicle dealers	161	2,300	7,320
557	Motorcycle dealers	183	1,752	4,138
559	Automotive dealers, NEC	89	411	1,129
56	Apparel and accessory stores	7,143	71,841	90,143
561	Men's and boys' clothing and accessory stores	435	3,405	5,517
562	Women's clothing stores	2,113	18,771	21,519
563	Women's accessory and specialty stores	491	3,345	4,429
564	Children's and infants' wear stores	221	1,584	1,715
565	Family clothing stores	902	21,931	26,374
566	Shoe stores	1,727	12,637	15,810
569	Miscellaneous apparel and accessory stores	1,255	10,168	14,780
57	Furniture and home furnishings stores	8,098	65,320	138,639
571	Home furniture and furnishings store	4,640	37,103	76,015
572	Household appliance stores	536	2,627	5,398
573	Radio, television, and computer stores	2,922	25,590	57,226
58	Eating and drinking places	22,823	443,972	446,677
59	Miscellaneous retail	18,604	156,826	269,273
591	Drug stores and proprietary stores	1,915	41,470	77,281
592	Liquor stores	689	4,072	4,996
593	Used merchandise stores	1,490	6,553	9,348
594	Miscellaneous shopping goods stores	6,988	49,783	70,556
596	Nonstore retailers	1,017	17,766	45,874
598	Fuel dealers	337	2,705	5,751
599	Retail stores, NEC	6,169	34,477	55,466

See footnotes at end of table.

Continued . . .

University of Florida   **Bureau of Economic and Business Research**

Table 16.43. EMPLOYMENT AND PAYROLL: AVERAGE MONTHLY PRIVATE REPORTING UNITS EMPLOYMENT, AND PAYROLL COVERED BY UNEMPLOYMENT COMPENSATION LAW BY WHOLESALE AND RETAIL TRADE INDUSTRY IN FLORIDA, 1998 AND 1999 (Continued)

SIC code	Industry	Number of reporting units	Number of employees	Payroll ($1,000)
		1999 B/		
	Wholesale trade	40,106	364,383	1,246,908
50	Wholesale trade--durable goods	25,976	217,003	775,525
501	Motor vehicles and motor vehicle parts and supplies	2,588	27,701	77,353
502	Furniture and home furnishings	1,152	9,211	27,137
503	Lumber and other construction materials	1,807	15,480	45,559
504	Professional and commercial equipment and supplies	5,310	51,777	231,089
505	Metals and minerals, except petroleum	584	5,138	16,826
506	Electrical goods	3,652	34,384	141,423
507	Hardware, plumbing and heating equipment and supplies	1,790	16,563	54,452
508	Machinery, equipment, and supplies	4,726	36,935	124,182
509	Miscellaneous durable goods	4,369	19,813	57,504
51	Wholesale trade--nondurable goods	14,130	147,380	471,384
511	Paper and paper products	1,326	18,991	57,840
512	Drugs, drug proprietaries, and druggists' sundries	1,175	14,950	69,086
513	Apparel, piece goods, and notions	1,552	9,307	25,406
514	Groceries and related products	3,413	49,203	150,031
515	Farm-product raw materials	114	905	1,875
516	Chemicals and allied products	1,082	7,964	31,094
517	Petroleum and petroleum products	479	6,285	18,976
518	Beer, wine, and distilled alcoholic beverages	290	10,752	39,764
519	Miscellaneous nondurable goods	4,700	29,023	77,313
	Retail trade	81,519	1,348,272	2,001,211
52	Building materials, hardware, garden supply, and mobile home dealers	3,675	55,994	110,498
521	Lumber and other building materials dealers	1,191	39,415	79,795
523	Paint, glass, and wallpaper stores	709	3,795	8,989
525	Hardware stores	725	5,828	9,119
526	Retail nurseries, lawn and garden supply stores	701	4,828	7,916
527	Mobile home dealers	349	2,127	4,679
53	General merchandise stores	1,752	155,547	211,618
531	Department stores	901	141,081	195,122
533	Variety stores	441	5,054	4,254
539	Miscellaneous general merchandise stores	411	9,412	12,242
54	Food stores	9,701	252,974	322,265
541	Grocery stores	6,797	229,851	293,174
542	Meat and fish markets and freezer provisioners	474	3,488	5,515
543	Fruit and vegetable markets	340	2,648	3,556
544	Candy, nut, and confectionery stores	162	1,052	1,057
545	Dairy products stores	67	375	341

See footnotes at end of table.

Continued . . .

University of Florida

Bureau of Economic and Business Research

Table 16.43. EMPLOYMENT AND PAYROLL: AVERAGE MONTHLY PRIVATE REPORTING UNITS EMPLOYMENT, AND PAYROLL COVERED BY UNEMPLOYMENT COMPENSATION LAW BY WHOLESALE AND RETAIL TRADE INDUSTRY IN FLORIDA, 1998 AND 1999 (Continued)

SIC code	Industry	Number of re- porting units	Number of em- ployees	Payroll ($1,000)
	1999 B/ (Continued)			
	Retail trade (Continued)			
54	Food stores (Continued)			
546	Retail bakeries	951	9,325	10,427
549	Miscellaneous food stores	911	6,235	8,195
55	Automotive dealers and gasoline service stations	9,446	130,463	358,542
551	Motor vehicle dealers (new and used)	1,428	67,384	232,633
552	Motor vehicle dealers (used only)	1,295	6,798	20,134
553	Auto and home supply stores	2,380	22,115	44,529
554	Gasoline service stations	3,191	24,426	35,620
555	Boat dealers	699	5,041	11,918
556	Recreational vehicle dealers	163	2,440	7,973
557	Motorcycle dealers	190	1,805	4,473
559	Automotive dealers, NEC	102	455	1,262
56	Apparel and accessory stores	6,979	73,867	94,178
561	Men's and boys' clothing and accessory stores	431	3,926	6,087
562	Women's clothing stores	2,006	18,672	21,946
563	Women's accessory and specialty stores	484	3,347	4,356
564	Children's and infants' wear stores	225	1,887	2,100
565	Family clothing stores	919	25,165	30,566
566	Shoe stores	1,773	12,791	16,486
569	Miscellaneous apparel and accessory stores	1,143	8,078	12,636
57	Furniture and home furnishings stores	8,131	66,771	149,820
571	Home furniture and furnishings store	4,650	37,456	79,973
572	Household appliance stores	529	2,626	5,662
573	Radio, television, and computer stores	2,952	26,689	64,185
58	Eating and drinking places	22,960	450,993	464,054
59	Miscellaneous retail	18,875	161,663	290,237
591	Drug stores and proprietary stores	1,972	42,812	84,243
592	Liquor stores	709	4,191	5,295
593	Used merchandise stores	1,546	7,044	10,235
594	Miscellaneous shopping goods stores	7,169	53,169	74,914
596	Nonstore retailers	1,081	17,738	52,803
598	Fuel dealers	306	2,620	5,536
599	Retail stores, NEC	6,094	34,091	57,209

NEC Not elsewhere classified.
A/ Revised.
B/ Preliminary.
Note: Private employment. Detail may not add to totals due to disclosure editing and/or rounding.
See Tables 23.70, 23.71, 23.72, 23.73, and 23.74 for public employment data.

Source: State of Florida, Department of Labor and Employment Security, Bureau of Labor Market Information, "Employment and Wages" (ES-202), unpublished data.

University of Florida   **Bureau of Economic and Business Research**

Table 16.44. WHOLESALE TRADE: AVERAGE MONTHLY PRIVATE REPORTING UNITS, EMPLOYMENT AND PAYROLL COVERED BY UNEMPLOYMENT COMPENSATION LAW IN THE STATE AND COUNTIES OF FLORIDA, 1999

County	Number of reporting units	Number of employees	Payroll ($1,000)	County	Number of reporting units	Number of employees	Payroll ($1,000)
			Wholesale trade (SIC codes 50-51)				
Florida	40,106	364,383	1,246,908	Lee	756	5,628	15,199
				Leon	431	3,729	11,443
Alachua	276	2,360	6,184	Levy	33	201	331
Baker	10	54	113	Madison	18	92	157
Bay	237	2,414	6,274	Manatee	365	3,698	11,230
Brevard	688	5,883	15,648	Marion	357	3,531	8,749
Broward	4,740	39,969	139,584	Martin	251	1,287	3,981
Calhoun	17	196	280	Miami-Dade	9,464	76,282	255,447
Charlotte	144	710	1,740	Monroe	183	774	2,204
Citrus	103	418	841	Nassau	57	317	894
Clay	155	778	2,151	Okaloosa	197	1,405	3,498
Collier	460	2,723	7,953	Okeechobee	42	232	401
Columbia	82	727	1,671	Orange	2,434	33,299	116,880
De Soto	23	244	441	Osceola	163	1,950	4,806
Dixie	7	52	72	Palm Beach	2,598	21,884	82,234
Duval	1,602	25,896	90,499	Pasco	305	1,847	4,462
Escambia	505	5,496	15,396	Pinellas	2,052	20,945	72,531
Flagler	56	129	319	Polk	761	8,335	22,653
Franklin	26	180	301	Putnam	65	350	648
Gadsden	24	484	1,494	St. Johns	213	1,438	5,076
Gilchrist	17	71	134	St. Lucie	248	2,009	4,636
Glades	4	30	79	Santa Rosa	110	448	1,149
Gulf	12	165	572	Sarasota	698	4,067	11,245
Hamilton	8	61	111	Seminole	1,034	8,064	27,757
Hardee	33	254	563	Sumter	32	393	956
Hendry	42	380	1,010	Suwannee	40	288	609
Hernando	141	905	2,117	Taylor	27	204	333
Highlands	90	594	1,375	Union	4	14	17
Hillsborough	2,656	34,792	123,889	Volusia	590	5,046	11,204
Holmes	12	68	107	Wakulla	16	70	136
Indian River	175	1,170	4,500	Walton	34	193	398
Jackson	49	507	991	Washington	13	64	93
Jefferson	17	70	142				
Lafayette	7	77	138	Multicounty 1/	3,840	26,883	133,080
Lake	261	1,926	4,543	Out-of-state 2/	10	47	68

1/ Reporting units without a fixed location within the state or of unknown county location.
2/ Employment based in Florida, but working out of the state or country.
Note: Private employment. For a list of three-digit code industries included see Table 16.43. Data are preliminary. Only counties for which data are disclosed are shown. Detail may not add to totals due to disclosure editing and/or rounding. See Tables 23.70, 23.71, 23.72, 23.73, and 23.74 for public employment data.

Source: State of Florida, Department of Labor and Employment Security, Bureau of Labor Market Information, "Employment and Wages" (ES-202), unpublished data.

University of Florida   **Bureau of Economic and Business Research**

Table 16.45. RETAIL TRADE: AVERAGE MONTHLY PRIVATE REPORTING UNITS, EMPLOYMENT AND PAYROLL COVERED BY UNEMPLOYMENT COMPENSATION LAW IN THE STATE AND COUNTIES OF FLORIDA, 1998 AND 1999

County	Number of re-porting units	Number of em-ployees	Payroll ($1,000)	County	Number of re-porting units	Number of em-ployees	Payroll ($1,000)
			Retail trade, 1998 A/	(SIC codes 52-59)			
Florida	81,186	1,322,476	1,895,145	Lake	887	13,285	16,795
				Lee	2,333	38,432	55,552
Alachua	1,152	20,977	23,202	Leon	1,312	24,243	28,019
Baker	71	1,018	1,000	Levy	142	1,835	1,947
Bay	974	15,761	18,740	Liberty	21	132	148
Bradford	88	1,244	1,360	Madison	86	940	948
Brevard	2,292	36,541	45,353	Manatee	1,195	18,362	25,604
Broward	8,525	138,186	217,827	Marion	1,162	18,833	24,572
Calhoun	64	583	616	Martin	800	10,906	14,968
Charlotte	615	9,487	12,522	Miami-Dade	12,054	169,804	259,414
Citrus	515	6,419	7,602	Monroe	953	10,923	14,954
Clay	613	11,369	13,700	Nassau	272	3,690	4,147
Collier	1,566	21,224	32,519	Okaloosa	1,126	17,467	22,283
Columbia	283	4,375	5,642	Okeechobee	175	2,240	2,594
De Soto	99	1,130	1,569	Orange	4,635	96,234	146,438
Dixie	48	418	429	Osceola	768	14,682	17,547
Duval	3,785	72,781	102,975	Palm Beach	5,972	91,327	140,084
Escambia	1,584	26,415	32,455	Pasco	1,240	19,054	23,228
Flagler	185	2,653	2,930	Pinellas	4,777	78,989	114,968
Franklin	97	702	747	Polk	1,938	40,073	65,243
Gadsden	163	1,785	2,018	Putnam	253	3,679	4,375
Gilchrist	39	281	265	St. Johns	696	9,282	10,715
Glades	20	147	148	St. Lucie	703	10,104	13,223
Gulf	75	459	478	Santa Rosa	434	5,522	5,938
Hamilton	54	351	348	Sarasota	2,142	31,481	46,023
Hardee	80	848	1,059	Seminole	1,740	32,756	46,742
Hendry	128	1,797	2,119	Sumter	126	1,583	1,780
Hernando	456	7,653	8,939	Suwannee	145	1,934	2,393
Highlands	365	4,752	5,778	Taylor	105	1,138	1,130
Hillsborough	4,396	89,633	136,995	Union	31	209	236
Holmes	63	519	568	Volusia	2,201	34,259	42,767
Indian River	711	10,186	13,715	Wakulla	70	696	632
Jackson	233	2,857	3,189	Walton	217	2,344	2,742
Jefferson	49	513	463	Washington	83	1,009	1,047
Lafayette	17	125	137	Multicounty 1/	989	21,842	38,542

See footnotes at end of table.   Continued . . .

University of Florida   **Bureau of Economic and Business Research**

Table 16.45. RETAIL TRADE: AVERAGE MONTHLY PRIVATE REPORTING UNITS, EMPLOYMENT AND PAYROLL COVERED BY UNEMPLOYMENT COMPENSATION LAW IN THE STATE AND COUNTIES OF FLORIDA, 1998 AND 1999 (Continued)

County	Number of reporting units	Number of employees	Payroll ($1,000)	County	Number of reporting units	Number of employees	Payroll ($1,000)
			Retail trade, 1999 B/ (SIC codes 52-59)				
Florida	81,519	1,348,272	2,001,211	Lee	2,375	39,396	59,938
				Leon	1,314	24,348	29,279
Alachua	1,134	21,313	24,241	Levy	150	1,825	1,954
Baker	74	1,092	1,022	Liberty	20	145	160
Bay	962	16,101	19,962	Madison	89	985	978
Bradford	92	1,293	1,452	Manatee	1,207	19,041	27,233
Brevard	2,309	37,600	48,010	Marion	1,198	18,773	25,585
Broward	8,582	137,252	223,292	Martin	802	11,403	16,235
Calhoun	65	522	573	Miami-Dade	12,050	173,666	270,837
Charlotte	620	9,833	13,201	Monroe	967	10,726	15,521
Citrus	516	6,572	7,971	Nassau	263	3,521	4,152
Clay	597	11,506	14,094	Okaloosa	1,066	16,900	21,764
Collier	1,634	21,994	35,462	Okeechobee	178	2,312	2,734
Columbia	277	4,584	6,303	Orange	4,702	100,787	156,870
DeSoto	98	1,172	1,714	Osceola	764	14,864	18,824
Dixie	51	426	438	Palm Beach	6,029	92,047	147,127
Duval	3,787	75,371	109,450	Pasco	1,255	19,032	24,214
Escambia	1,517	26,347	33,258	Pinellas	4,736	79,308	127,269
Flagler	178	2,697	3,053	Polk	1,921	40,848	68,056
Franklin	96	715	769	Putnam	256	4,038	5,079
Gadsden	160	1,755	2,116	Saint Johns	699	9,529	11,832
Gilchrist	40	253	253	Saint Lucie	698	10,150	13,526
Glades	19	133	127	Santa Rosa	415	5,333	6,076
Gulf	74	485	496	Sarasota	2,094	31,561	47,744
Hamilton	51	366	363	Seminole	1,771	33,922	49,814
Hardee	84	883	1,109	Sumter	129	1,540	1,737
Hendry	131	1,788	2,165	Suwannee	139	1,983	2,414
Hernando	466	8,812	12,091	Taylor	107	1,113	1,115
Highlands	363	4,745	5,865	Union	32	188	206
Hillsborough	4,408	91,052	142,681	Volusia	2,188	34,120	44,176
Holmes	65	507	511	Wakulla	73	713	625
Indian River	713	10,276	14,072	Walton	225	2,851	3,499
Jackson	227	2,801	3,240	Washington	86	1,112	1,135
Jefferson	52	377	376				
Lafayette	18	122	136	Multicounty 1/	1,188	25,890	45,605
Lake	884	13,727	17,824	Out-of-state 2/	23	175	210

A/ Revised.
B/ Preliminary.
1/ Reporting units without a fixed location within the state or of unknown county location.
2/ Employment based in Florida, but working out of the state or country.
Note: For a list of three-digit code industries included see Table 16.43. Private employment. Only counties for which data are disclosed are shown. Detail may not add to totals due to disclosure editing and/or rounding. See Tables 23.70, 23.71, 23.72, 23.73, and 23.74 for public employment data.

Source: State of Florida, Department of Labor and Employment Security, Bureau of Labor Market Information, "Employment and Wages" (ES-202), unpublished data.

University of Florida   **Bureau of Economic and Business Research**

Table 16.46. GENERAL MERCHANDISE STORES: AVERAGE MONTHLY PRIVATE REPORTING
UNITS, EMPLOYMENT, AND PAYROLL COVERED BY UNEMPLOYMENT COMPENSATION
LAW IN THE STATE AND COUNTIES OF FLORIDA, 1999

County	Number of re- porting units	Number of em- ployees	Payroll ($1,000)	County	Number of re- porting units	Number of em- ployees	Payroll ($1,000)
			General merchandise stores (SIC code 53)				
Florida	1,752	155,547	211,618	Leon	28	2,956	3,805
				Manatee	32	2,334	3,201
Alachua	30	2,230	2,992	Marion	29	3,160	4,650
Baker	4	166	177	Martin	19	1,290	1,667
Bay	19	2,186	2,727	Miami-Dade	219	16,595	24,129
Brevard	49	5,163	6,240	Monroe	19	588	761
Broward	142	13,406	18,850	Okaloosa	18	2,030	2,428
Calhoun	4	17	15	Orange	109	9,441	13,464
Charlotte	21	1,977	2,533	Osceola	18	1,664	2,074
Citrus	11	824	905	Palm Beach	107	9,568	14,442
Clay	15	1,484	1,890	Pasco	35	2,571	3,140
Collier	25	2,165	3,123	Pinellas	103	9,149	13,008
Duval	83	9,925	12,565	Polk	55	5,602	7,438
Escambia	35	3,800	4,823	Putnam	8	447	526
Gadsden	9	167	169	St. Johns	9	759	862
Gulf	4	29	30	St. Lucie	16	1,278	1,574
Hernando	13	2,380	4,457	Santa Rosa	11	886	1,032
Highlands	8	753	859	Sarasota	37	3,438	4,545
Hillsborough	91	9,537	12,996	Seminole	44	4,444	6,084
Indian River	15	1,698	2,175	Sumter	5	146	160
Jefferson	3	17	12	Volusia	44	3,934	5,088
Lake	21	2,180	2,573				
Lee	50	4,534	6,134	Multicounty 1/	35	3,097	4,949

1/ Reporting units without a fixed location within the state or of unknown county location.

Note: Private employment. For a list of three-digit code industries included see Table 16.43. Data are
preliminary. Only counties for which data are disclosed are shown. Detail may not add to totals due to
disclosure editing and/or rounding. See Tables 23.70, 23.71, 23.72, 23.73, and 23.74 for public
employment data.

Source: State of Florida, Department of Labor and Employment Security, Bureau of Labor Market Information, "Employment and Wages" (ES-202), unpublished data.

Table 16.47. FOOD STORES: AVERAGE MONTHLY PRIVATE REPORTING UNITS, EMPLOYMENT AND PAYROLL COVERED BY UNEMPLOYMENT COMPENSATION LAW IN THE STATE AND COUNTIES OF FLORIDA, 1999

County	Number of reporting units	Number of employees	Payroll ($1,000)	County	Number of reporting units	Number of employees	Payroll ($1,000)
				Food stores (SIC code 54)			
Florida	9,701	252,974	322,265	Lee	245	6,778	8,505
				Leon	136	4,280	4,535
Alachua	129	3,950	4,073	Levy	20	395	384
Baker	14	250	249	Liberty	8	35	36
Bay	141	2,213	2,814	Madison	9	199	187
Bradford	11	281	273	Manatee	140	3,104	3,562
Brevard	279	6,738	7,286	Marion	190	3,735	4,217
Broward	873	26,315	33,236	Martin	77	2,233	2,829
Calhoun	11	192	180	Miami-Dade	1,390	32,564	41,907
Charlotte	58	1,865	2,025	Monroe	82	1,883	2,626
Citrus	73	1,709	1,762	Nassau	38	883	899
Clay	83	2,329	2,735	Okaloosa	151	2,397	2,938
Collier	149	4,317	5,682	Okeechobee	29	491	556
Columbia	48	1,011	1,621	Orange	582	17,843	24,355
De Soto	15	270	295	Osceola	99	2,683	3,050
Duval	558	16,438	24,054	Palm Beach	625	16,923	21,617
Escambia	201	3,216	3,682	Pasco	168	4,742	5,133
Flagler	24	662	679	Pinellas	511	12,820	15,173
Franklin	18	205	264	Polk	272	11,219	20,978
Gadsden	38	487	547	Putnam	32	1,261	1,950
Gilchrist	8	99	80	St. Johns	83	2,005	2,235
Glades	6	50	62	St. Lucie	95	2,419	2,746
Gulf	20	206	198	Santa Rosa	81	1,238	1,271
Hamilton	10	98	93	Sarasota	179	6,166	7,794
Hardee	18	280	304	Seminole	183	5,934	6,980
Hendry	24	435	473	Sumter	27	414	393
Hernando	65	1,956	2,094	Suwannee	28	411	463
Highlands	50	1,123	1,288	Taylor	16	256	256
Hillsborough	587	15,398	20,212	Union	6	47	44
Holmes	15	144	120	Volusia	259	7,429	8,132
Indian River	72	1,957	2,454	Walton	31	362	423
Jackson	39	493	520	Washington	19	238	244
Jefferson	12	155	129				
Lafayette	3	32	33	Multicounty 1/	100	916	2,445
Lake	127	3,460	3,558				

1/ Reporting units without a fixed location within the state or of unknown county location.
Note: Private employment. For a list of three-digit code industries included see Table 16.43. Data are preliminary. Only counties for which data are disclosed are shown. Detail may not add to totals due to disclosure editing and/or rounding. See Tables 23.70, 23.71, 23.72, 23.73, and 23.74 for public employment data.

Source: State of Florida, Department of Labor and Employment Security, Bureau of Labor Market Information, "Employment and Wages" (ES-202), unpublished data.

University of Florida — **Bureau of Economic and Business Research**

Table 16.48. AUTOMOTIVE DEALERS AND GASOLINE SERVICE STATIONS: AVERAGE MONTHLY PRIVATE REPORTING UNITS, EMPLOYMENT, AND PAYROLL COVERED BY UNEMPLOYMENT COMPENSATION LAW IN THE STATE AND COUNTIES OF FLORIDA, 1999

County	Number of re-porting units	Number of em-ployees	Payroll ($1,000)	County	Number of re-porting units	Number of em-ployees	Payroll ($1,000)
				Automotive dealers and gasoline service stations (SIC code 55)			
Florida	9,446	130,463	358,542	Lee	267	3,956	11,288
				Leon	159	2,088	5,130
Alachua	107	1,841	4,479	Levy	26	192	349
Baker	14	170	186	Madison	26	328	390
Bay	111	1,492	3,351	Manatee	147	1,641	4,395
Bradford	20	205	403	Marion	171	2,201	5,484
Brevard	300	3,522	8,911	Martin	104	1,231	3,117
Broward	959	14,774	49,225	Miami-Dade	1,321	15,369	41,738
Calhoun	16	83	133	Monroe	61	533	1,233
Charlotte	79	1,048	2,688	Nassau	33	382	701
Citrus	74	882	2,013	Okaloosa	108	1,423	3,666
Clay	66	969	2,262	Okeechobee	28	239	447
Collier	123	1,893	5,721	Orange	567	7,836	22,412
Columbia	46	689	1,448	Osceola	80	1,055	2,686
De Soto	18	253	703	Palm Beach	568	8,532	24,778
Dixie	12	62	84	Pasco	185	2,034	4,977
Duval	463	8,663	24,117	Pinellas	497	7,644	22,039
Escambia	189	2,657	6,651	Polk	291	4,544	12,629
Flagler	22	189	434	Putnam	43	421	850
Franklin	10	43	57	St. Johns	75	803	1,785
Gadsden	27	203	408	St. Lucie	102	1,309	3,407
Gilchrist	6	22	28	Santa Rosa	47	581	1,225
Gulf	12	49	67	Sarasota	222	3,054	8,921
Hamilton	12	58	64	Seminole	188	2,681	8,118
Hardee	18	146	314	Sumter	23	325	490
Hendry	17	184	417	Suwannee	33	296	541
Hernando	54	636	1,590	Taylor	21	178	250
Highlands	75	727	1,519	Union	7	27	36
Hillsborough	516	8,745	26,798	Volusia	295	3,483	8,924
Holmes	11	47	74	Wakulla	10	67	75
Indian River	56	862	2,054	Walton	19	183	260
Jackson	45	532	947	Washington	16	60	70
Jefferson	9	71	101				
Lafayette	3	6	8	Multicounty 1/	88	2,631	5,212
Lake	123	1,354	3,556	Out-of-state 2/	5	7	9

1/ Reporting units without a fixed location within the state or of unknown county location.
2/ Employment based in Florida, but working out of the state or country.
Note: Private employment. For a list of three-digit code industries included see Table 16.43. Data are preliminary. Only counties for which data are disclosed are shown. Detail may not add to totals due to disclosure editing and/or rounding. See Tables 23.70, 23.71, 23.72, 23.73, and 23.74 for public employment data.

Source: State of Florida, Department of Labor and Employment Security, Bureau of Labor Market Information, "Employment and Wages" (ES-202), unpublished data.

Table 16.49. AUTO AND HOME SUPPLY STORES: AVERAGE MONTHLY PRIVATE REPORTING
UNITS, EMPLOYMENT, AND PAYROLL COVERED BY UNEMPLOYMENT COMPENSATION
LAW IN THE STATE AND COUNTIES OF FLORIDA, 1999

County	Number of reporting units	Number of employees	Payroll ($1,000)	County	Number of reporting units	Number of employees	Payroll ($1,000)
			Auto and home supply stores (SIC code 553)				
Florida	2,380	22,115	44,529	Leon	50	387	745
				Levy	9	57	82
Alachua	32	376	726	Madison	5	32	52
Baker	5	35	53	Manatee	33	267	498
Bay	36	271	510	Marion	51	459	899
Bradford	6	38	49	Martin	22	144	270
Brevard	77	673	1,225	Miami-Dade	346	2,597	4,750
Broward	186	1,612	3,336	Monroe	6	69	125
Calhoun	8	31	44	Nassau	8	42	49
Charlotte	24	212	384	Okaloosa	41	332	585
Citrus	20	158	238	Okeechobee	9	72	137
Clay	20	229	439	Orange	144	1,527	3,429
Collier	27	207	444	Osceola	17	241	436
Columbia	10	117	208	Palm Beach	135	1,484	3,500
De Soto	7	48	70	Pasco	46	348	599
Duval	131	1,442	3,010	Pinellas	110	1,030	2,680
Escambia	58	653	1,137	Polk	79	1,606	3,575
Flagler	7	38	72	Putnam	9	90	143
Gadsden	10	47	74	St. Johns	14	84	144
Gilchrist	4	17	20	St. Lucie	21	222	373
Gulf	6	20	35	Santa Rosa	20	137	245
Hardee	4	26	54	Sarasota	45	450	856
Hernando	16	155	280	Seminole	47	473	1,008
Highlands	18	102	187	Sumter	5	44	59
Hillsborough	133	1,287	2,528	Suwannee	9	56	78
Holmes	6	27	36	Taylor	4	38	58
Indian River	13	116	196	Volusia	69	705	1,376
Jackson	16	88	152	Walton	7	53	90
Lake	28	215	414	Washington	8	31	38
Lee	64	582	1,076	Multicounty 1/	29	132	514

1/ Reporting units without a fixed location within the state or of unknown county location.
Note: Private employment. Data are preliminary. Only counties for which data are disclosed are
shown. Detail may not add to totals due to disclosure editing and/or rounding. See Tables 23.70, 23.71,
23.72, 23.73, and 23.74 for public employment data.

Source: State of Florida, Department of Labor and Employment Security, Bureau of Labor Market Information, "Employment and Wages" (ES-202), unpublished data.

University of Florida   **Bureau of Economic and Business Research**

Table 16.50. GASOLINE SERVICE STATIONS: AVERAGE MONTHLY PRIVATE REPORTING UNITS EMPLOYMENT, AND PAYROLL COVERED BY UNEMPLOYMENT COMPENSATION LAW IN THE STATE AND COUNTIES OF FLORIDA, 1999

County	Number of re-porting units	Number of em-ployees	Payroll ($1,000)	County	Number of re-porting units	Number of em-ployees	Payroll ($1,000)
			Gasoline service stations (SIC code 554)				
Florida	3,191	24,426	35,620	Levy	11	51	51
				Madison	19	288	329
Alachua	39	322	391	Manatee	42	214	280
Baker	6	109	74	Marion	38	455	562
Bay	27	397	552	Martin	26	176	217
Bradford	8	43	43	Miami-Dade	530	3,499	6,576
Brevard	99	505	609	Monroe	23	143	230
Broward	352	2,080	2,830	Nassau	15	192	223
Calhoun	4	12	14	Okaloosa	21	103	128
Charlotte	22	183	213	Okeechobee	9	61	67
Citrus	16	73	74	Orange	180	1,038	1,408
Clay	20	157	152	Osceola	22	165	208
Collier	40	309	446	Palm Beach	228	1,559	2,202
Columbia	16	208	252	Pasco	51	341	423
De Soto	7	32	48	Pinellas	183	1,172	1,703
Dixie	7	22	19	Polk	87	496	655
Duval	134	1,784	2,995	Putnam	11	49	58
Escambia	39	267	320	St. Johns	33	226	275
Flagler	7	62	66	St. Lucie	33	230	311
Gadsden	7	45	45	Santa Rosa	12	112	101
Gulf	4	26	26	Sarasota	78	476	671
Hamilton	8	44	37	Seminole	53	395	711
Hardee	8	33	42	Sumter	15	215	247
Hendry	8	35	48	Suwannee	12	79	101
Hernando	14	67	71	Taylor	11	90	86
Highlands	19	113	145	Union	4	10	8
Hillsborough	193	1,378	2,266	Volusia	86	437	553
Indian River	24	244	322	Wakulla	4	42	30
Jackson	17	207	253	Walton	6	89	99
Jefferson	7	68	94	Washington	5	19	19
Lake	37	209	252				
Lee	66	511	738	Multicounty 1/	28	1,951	3,054
Leon	48	429	477	Out-of-state 2/	5	7	9

1/ Reporting units without a fixed location within the state or of unknown county location.
2/ Employment based in Florida, but working out of the state or country.
Note: Private employment. Data are preliminary. Only counties for which data are disclosed are shown. Detail may not add to totals due to disclosure editing and/or rounding. See Tables 23.70, 23.71, 23.72, 23.73, and 23.74 for public employment data.

Source: State of Florida, Department of Labor and Employment Security, Bureau of Labor Market Information, "Employment and Wages" (ES-202), unpublished data.

University of Florida   **Bureau of Economic and Business Research**

Table 16.51. APPAREL AND ACCESSORY STORES: AVERAGE MONTHLY PRIVATE REPORTING UNITS, EMPLOYMENT, AND PAYROLL COVERED BY UNEMPLOYMENT COMPENSATION LAW IN THE STATE AND COUNTIES OF FLORIDA, 1999

County	Number of reporting units	Number of employees	Payroll ($1,000)	County	Number of reporting units	Number of employees	Payroll ($1,000)
			Apparel and accessory stores (SIC code 56)				
Florida	6,979	73,867	94,178	Madison	6	32	24
				Manatee	116	2,042	3,498
Alachua	100	871	797	Marion	60	561	588
Bay	90	890	927	Martin	52	382	380
Bradford	5	29	32	Miami-Dade	1,406	14,180	19,632
Brevard	140	1,264	1,435	Monroe	97	414	559
Broward	787	8,069	11,553	Nassau	23	132	106
Charlotte	47	426	390	Okaloosa	105	1,155	1,413
Citrus	21	184	176	Okeechobee	8	67	79
Clay	51	517	479	Orange	437	6,125	7,158
Collier	192	1,570	2,364	Osceola	57	743	818
Columbia	12	77	64	Palm Beach	561	6,479	9,542
De Soto	5	23	20	Pasco	58	527	488
Duval	280	3,331	4,335	Pinellas	355	3,283	3,407
Escambia	111	1,249	1,237	Polk	122	1,064	1,089
Gadsden	8	23	16	Putnam	10	51	42
Hendry	6	32	30	St. Johns	72	484	519
Hernando	22	163	159	St. Lucie	44	363	335
Highlands	22	158	124	Santa Rosa	14	65	68
Hillsborough	317	4,318	4,270	Sarasota	182	1,416	1,850
Holmes	4	38	35	Seminole	158	1,898	1,827
Indian River	81	749	818	Suwannee	4	18	13
Jackson	19	134	137	Taylor	8	35	27
Lake	37	262	264	Volusia	138	1,321	1,239
Lee	232	2,214	3,351	Walton	14	109	164
Leon	123	1,695	1,589	Washington	4	7	7
Levy	5	18	12	Multicounty 1/	136	2,590	4,575

1/ Reporting units without a fixed location within the state or of unknown county location.

Note: Private employment. For a list of three-digit code industries included see Table 16.43. Data are preliminary. Only counties for which data are disclosed are shown. Detail may not add to totals due to disclosure editing and/or rounding. See Tables 23.70, 23.71, 23.72, 23.73, and 23.74 for public employment data.

Source: State of Florida, Department of Labor and Employment Security, Bureau of Labor Market Information, "Employment and Wages" (ES-202), unpublished data.

University of Florida   **Bureau of Economic and Business Research**

Table 16.52. HOME FURNITURE, FURNISHINGS, AND EQUIPMENT STORES: AVERAGE MONTHLY PRIVATE REPORTING UNITS, EMPLOYMENT, AND PAYROLL COVERED BY UNEMPLOYMENT COMPENSATION LAW IN THE STATE AND COUNTIES OF FLORIDA, 1999

County	Number of reporting units	Number of employees	Payroll ($1,000)	County	Number of reporting units	Number of employees	Payroll ($1,000)
			Home furniture, furnishings, and equipment stores (SIC code 57)				
Florida	**8,131**	**66,771**	**149,820**	Levy	6	16	22
				Madison	6	29	38
Alachua	104	955	1,457	Manatee	112	711	1,397
Baker	3	17	30	Marion	115	830	1,529
Bay	72	510	887	Martin	105	648	1,223
Bradford	8	28	47	Miami-Dade	1,169	9,151	20,355
Brevard	232	1,528	3,122	Monroe	56	223	484
Broward	929	8,840	22,205	Nassau	16	54	120
Charlotte	73	450	867	Okaloosa	97	733	1,336
Citrus	46	226	360	Okeechobee	9	39	65
Clay	44	339	630	Orange	385	3,831	8,414
Collier	235	1,309	2,991	Osceola	50	244	492
Columbia	20	158	291	Palm Beach	682	5,083	12,375
De Soto	10	25	38	Pasco	116	811	1,541
Dixie	5	28	49	Pinellas	479	4,085	9,342
Duval	342	2,803	5,965	Polk	177	3,748	9,892
Escambia	140	1,231	2,237	Putnam	15	97	177
Flagler	17	77	128	St. Johns	55	332	600
Franklin	3	3	6	St. Lucie	77	336	588
Gadsden	11	173	311	Santa Rosa	29	123	211
Gulf	5	17	26	Sarasota	257	1,944	4,596
Hardee	6	20	31	Seminole	229	2,371	4,585
Hendry	8	25	42	Sumter	7	38	52
Hernando	53	208	376	Suwannee	7	73	188
Highlands	41	174	249	Taylor	7	44	85
Hillsborough	426	4,497	10,691	Volusia	205	1,439	2,753
Indian River	100	591	1,117	Wakulla	5	7	18
Jackson	14	53	61	Walton	17	56	94
Lake	92	529	1,094	Washington	8	30	35
Lee	259	2,624	6,759				
Leon	133	1,166	2,280	Multicounty 1/	192	986	2,787

1/ Reporting units without a fixed location within the state or of unknown county location.
Note: Private employment. For a list of three-digit code industries included see Table 16.43. Data are preliminary. Only counties for which data are disclosed are shown. Detail may not add to totals due to disclosure editing and/or rounding. See Tables 23.70, 23.71, 23.72, 23.73, and 23.74 for public employment data.

Source: State of Florida, Department of Labor and Employment Security, Bureau of Labor Market Information, "Employment and Wages" (ES-202), unpublished data.

Table 16.81. GROSS AND TAXABLE SALES: SALES REPORTED TO THE DEPARTMENT OF REVENUE BY KIND OF BUSINESS IN FLORIDA 1998 AND 1999

(amounts rounded to thousands of dollars)

Code	Kind of business Description	Gross sales 1998	1999	Percentage change	Taxable sales 1998	1999	Percentage change
	Total	495,076,575	538,986,640	8.9	208,234,873	226,636,112	8.8
	Food and beverage group	52,888,856	57,372,257	8.5	28,904,403	30,652,278	6.0
01	Grocery stores	30,190,070	32,774,956	8.6	9,374,790	10,234,528	9.2
02	Meat markets, poultry	263,776	281,469	6.7	12,776	12,811	0.3
03	Seafood dealers	127,629	112,733	-11.7	16,145	14,619	-9.5
04	Vegetable and fruit markets	373,938	198,049	-47.0	50,637	38,884	-23.2
05	Bakeries	315,436	326,260	3.4	111,148	121,277	9.1
06	Delicatessens	331,940	389,765	17.4	172,395	239,597	39.0
07	Candy and confectionery	1,142,208	962,805	-15.7	421,643	447,648	6.2
08	Restaurants and lunchrooms	17,971,132	19,895,623	10.7	16,703,341	17,363,077	3.9
09	Taverns, nightclubs, liquor stores	2,172,730	2,430,598	11.9	2,041,528	2,179,836	6.8
	Apparel group	7,953,376	8,384,642	5.4	6,805,643	7,068,373	3.9
10	Clothing stores, alterations	6,638,563	6,920,172	4.2	5,613,127	5,745,191	2.4
11	Shoe stores	1,164,250	1,215,150	4.4	1,073,076	1,109,890	3.4
12	Hat shops	150,563	249,320	65.6	119,440	213,292	78.6
	General merchandise group	52,015,642	56,767,487	9.1	30,851,190	32,375,280	4.9
13	Department stores	16,043,122	16,335,222	1.8	13,161,112	12,978,458	-1.4
14	Variety stores	9,932,312	9,873,378	-0.6	7,010,130	7,033,174	0.3
15	Drug stores	7,960,026	8,479,501	6.5	2,085,353	2,035,037	-2.4
16	Jewelry, leather, sporting goods	4,093,322	4,061,782	-0.8	2,592,664	2,534,827	-2.2
17	Feed, seed, and fertilizer stores	425,051	455,815	7.2	100,317	112,194	11.8
18	Hardware, paints, machinery	4,162,666	4,244,658	2.0	2,097,274	2,103,537	0.3
19	Farm implements and supplies	1,283,914	1,520,638	18.4	444,209	721,245	62.4
20	General merchandise stores	6,753,301	10,359,369	53.4	2,593,397	4,062,309	56.6
21	Second-hand stores	712,020	783,926	10.1	430,737	446,860	3.7
22	Dry good stores	649,909	653,199	0.5	335,997	347,639	3.5

See footnotes at end of table.

Continued . . .

Table 16.81. GROSS AND TAXABLE SALES: SALES REPORTED TO THE DEPARTMENT OF REVENUE BY KIND OF BUSINESS IN FLORIDA 1998 AND 1999 (Continued)

(amounts rounded to thousands of dollars)

Code	Kind of business — Description	Gross sales 1998	Gross sales 1999	Percentage change	Taxable sales 1998	Taxable sales 1999	Percentage change
	Automotive group	85,057,243	94,902,716	11.6	39,395,410	44,223,272	12.3
23	Motor vehicle dealers	58,191,704	65,132,529	11.9	30,879,873	34,893,142	13.0
24	Auto accessories, tires, parts	8,597,554	9,973,554	16.0	2,625,906	2,782,167	6.0
25	Filling and service stations	5,538,113	5,714,913	3.2	1,035,475	1,167,183	12.7
26	Garages, auto paint and body shops	4,080,463	4,467,855	9.5	2,732,497	2,956,926	8.2
27	Aircraft dealers	4,593,217	5,086,052	10.7	239,576	256,967	7.3
28	Motorboat and yacht dealers	4,056,192	4,527,813	11.6	1,882,084	2,166,887	15.1
	Furniture and appliances group	33,289,607	38,157,571	14.6	15,356,788	17,476,045	13.8
29	Furniture stores, new and used	6,676,057	7,335,074	9.9	4,626,368	5,107,096	10.4
30	Household appliances, dinnerware, etc.	2,924,492	3,179,846	8.7	1,572,306	1,823,212	16.0
31	Store and office equipment	5,377,856	5,528,317	2.8	2,617,150	2,802,101	7.1
32	Music stores, radios, televisions	18,311,201	22,114,335	20.8	6,540,965	7,743,637	18.4
	Lumber, builders, contractors group	21,048,744	23,243,321	10.4	12,016,627	13,299,880	10.7
33	Building contractors	2,431,762	2,929,249	20.5	465,552	636,293	36.7
34	Heating and air conditioning	1,761,529	1,979,850	12.4	527,500	550,538	4.4
35	Electrical and plumbing	2,809,126	3,296,349	17.3	1,331,516	1,441,804	8.3
36	Decorating, painting, papering	1,261,342	1,412,460	12.0	742,836	829,989	11.7
37	Roofing and sheet metal	395,428	423,773	7.2	179,748	192,141	6.9
38	Lumber and building materials	12,389,557	13,201,639	6.6	8,769,475	9,649,115	10.0
	General classification group	242,827,102	258,157,826	6.3	74,908,807	81,234,799	8.4
39	Hotels, apartment houses, etc. 1/	11,573,688	10,873,498	-6.0	9,882,466	10,859,790	9.9
40	Auctioneers and commission dealers	3,978,809	3,942,088	-0.9	580,194	581,431	0.2
41	Barber and beauty shops	1,658,546	1,750,144	5.5	671,921	688,861	2.5
42	Book stores	1,168,817	1,301,140	11.3	804,400	887,749	10.4
43	Cigar stands and tobacco shops	258,562	274,009	6.0	79,324	87,838	10.7
44	Florists	451,244	529,775	17.4	310,453	328,828	5.9

See footnotes at end of table.

Continued . . .

Table 16.81. GROSS AND TAXABLE SALES: SALES REPORTED TO THE DEPARTMENT OF REVENUE BY KIND OF BUSINESS IN FLORIDA 1998 AND 1999 (Continued)

(amounts rounded to thousands of dollars)

Code	Kind of business — Description	Gross sales 1998	Gross sales 1999	Percentage change	Taxable sales 1998	Taxable sales 1999	Percentage change
	General classification group (Continued)						
45	Fuel and L.P. gas dealers	3,095,084	4,060,212	31.2	426,556	370,418	-13.2
46	Funeral directors and monuments	576,481	355,442	-38.3	54,746	48,746	-11.0
47	Scrap metal, junk yards	428,706	300,135	-30.0	30,870	24,292	-21.3
48	Itinerant vendors	753,402	879,714	16.8	316,512	346,928	9.6
49	Laundry and cleaning services	768,408	776,014	1.0	203,588	208,399	2.4
50	Machine shops and foundries	851,151	907,796	6.7	221,301	233,190	5.4
51	Horse, cattle, pet dealers	3,132,738	3,166,749	1.1	1,380,845	1,013,634	-26.6
52	Photographers, photo and art supplies	1,682,450	2,250,905	33.8	911,004	923,219	1.3
53	Shoe repair shops	47,581	53,643	12.7	40,464	45,016	11.2
54	Storage and warehousing	268,590	306,564	14.1	164,605	186,558	13.3
55	Gift, card, novelty shops	2,599,370	2,838,893	9.2	1,972,774	2,077,185	5.3
56	Newsstands	148,133	136,997	-7.5	52,374	55,160	5.3
57	Social clubs and associations	524,315	540,213	3.0	469,548	487,416	3.8
58	Industrial machinery equipment	8,994,520	8,524,770	-5.2	3,098,967	3,114,335	0.5
59	Admissions	4,587,143	5,474,808	19.4	4,157,394	4,855,127	16.8
60	Holiday season vendors	13,723	15,096	10.0	10,330	9,236	-10.6
61	Rental of tangible property	6,944,057	7,822,647	12.7	4,014,898	4,629,483	15.3
62	Fabrication, sales of cabinets, etc.	2,186,632	2,415,159	10.5	871,502	946,164	8.6
63	Manufacturing and mining	35,874,573	37,301,223	4.0	4,443,519	4,767,750	7.3
64	Bottlers, soft drinks, etc.	1,324,347	1,065,812	-19.5	111,430	90,906	-18.4
65	Pawn shops	138,373	148,711	7.5	110,744	118,964	7.4
66	Communications	14,690,363	16,214,882	10.4	8,385,563	9,734,555	16.1
67	Transportation	438,031	462,788	5.7	109,703	109,965	0.2
68	Graphic arts and printing	5,404,189	5,671,044	4.9	1,674,874	1,722,156	2.8
69	Insurance, banking, etc.	1,123,456	1,001,522	-10.9	157,624	151,369	-4.0
70	Sanitary and industrial supplies	3,027,950	2,590,932	-14.4	471,920	472,984	0.2
71	Packaging materials and paper boxes	1,010,685	947,312	-6.3	139,061	136,728	-1.7
72	Repair of tangible personal property	3,098,939	3,759,137	21.3	1,106,407	1,197,315	8.2

See footnotes at end of table.

Continued . . .

Table 16.81. GROSS AND TAXABLE SALES: SALES REPORTED TO THE DEPARTMENT OF REVENUE BY KIND OF BUSINESS IN FLORIDA 1998 AND 1999 (Continued)

(amounts rounded to thousands of dollars)

Code	Kind of business — Description	Gross sales 1998	Gross sales 1999	Percentage change	Taxable sales 1998	Taxable sales 1999	Percentage change
	General classification group (Continued)						
73	Advertising	1,871,418	2,000,820	6.9	337,180	306,185	-9.2
74	Top soil, clay, sand, fill dirt	1,212,012	1,411,166	16.4	295,201	345,448	17.0
75	Trade stamp redemption centers	581	26	-95.6	285	19	-93.4
76	Nurseries and landscaping	1,471,168	1,637,477	11.3	483,110	533,739	10.5
77	Vending machines	745,696	809,395	8.5	378,691	432,460	14.2
78	Importing and exporting	10,733,086	10,874,048	1.3	217,620	246,167	13.1
79	Medical, dental, surgical, optical	6,773,884	7,434,692	9.8	657,665	670,837	2.0
80	Wholesale dealers	53,643,171	60,505,810	12.8	5,091,159	5,573,528	9.5
81	Schools and colleges	114,471	114,436	0.0	60,423	58,826	-2.6
82	Office space and commercial rentals	16,248,692	17,396,544	7.1	12,084,678	13,109,117	8.5
83	Parking lots, boat docking, storage	425,577	477,363	12.2	333,301	372,399	11.7
84	Utilities, electricity or gas	13,867,262	13,585,133	-2.0	3,629,298	3,547,357	-2.3
86	Dual uses of special fuels	71,815	58,046	-19.2	8,006	3,569	-55.4
87	Motion picture industry	113,226	137,010	21.0	108,050	125,409	16.1
88	Public works, governmental contractor	116,567	56,209	-51.8	34,262	24,076	-29.7
90	Flea markets	185,305	213,658	15.3	130,343	129,830	-0.4
91	Fairs, concessions, carnivals	13,418	16,429	22.4	6,505	8,212	26.3
92	Other professional services	1,087,288	921,333	-15.3	78,912	120,618	52.9
93	Other personal services	2,906,338	3,136,079	7.9	1,550,360	1,633,717	5.4
94	Other industrial services	742,204	803,890	8.3	122,048	123,390	1.1
98	Commercial fisherman	7,141	3,279	-54.1	973	524	-46.2
99	Miscellaneous	7,762,957	9,906,031	27.6	1,966,908	2,663,860	35.4

1/ Includes sales reported under categories 85 and 89 which are for hotels, rooming houses and apartments.

Note: Data are audited sales reported to the Florida Department of Revenue for the 6 percent regular sales tax, 6 percent use tax, and 3 percent vehicle and farm equipment sales tax. Sales occurred, for the most part, from December 1, 1997, through November 30, 1999. Data are not comparable with retail sales reported by the U.S. Bureau of the Census. Some data may be revised.

Source: State of Florida, Department of Revenue, unpublished data prepared by the University of Florida, Bureau of Economic and Business Research.

Table 16.82. GROSS AND TAXABLE SALES: SALES REPORTED TO THE DEPARTMENT OF REVENUE IN THE STATE AND COUNTIES OF FLORIDA, 1998 AND 1999

(rounded to thousands of dollars)

	Gross sales			Taxable sales		
County	1998	1999	Percent-age change	1998	1999	Percent-age change
Florida	495,076,575	538,986,640	8.9	208,234,873	226,636,112	8.8
Alachua	4,356,983	4,375,137	0.4	2,621,630	2,415,525	-7.9
Baker	198,181	251,668	27.0	89,910	99,373	10.5
Bay	3,621,578	3,802,114	5.0	2,000,396	2,158,998	7.9
Bradford	338,073	313,261	-7.3	158,149	160,131	1.3
Brevard	9,843,998	10,430,909	6.0	4,478,102	4,829,041	7.8
Broward	50,515,796	56,645,237	12.1	20,623,189	22,251,805	7.9
Calhoun	125,781	122,334	-2.7	57,751	53,907	-6.7
Charlotte	2,197,471	2,352,019	7.0	1,341,564	1,440,452	7.4
Citrus	1,457,507	1,625,693	11.5	851,560	912,968	7.2
Clay	2,202,456	2,450,368	11.3	1,191,366	1,268,291	6.5
Collier	6,281,589	6,975,459	11.0	3,940,172	4,378,454	11.1
Columbia	1,165,673	1,201,194	3.0	554,964	584,807	5.4
De Soto	336,590	361,680	7.5	181,293	191,935	5.9
Dixie	118,089	126,973	7.5	41,648	47,124	13.1
Duval	25,414,504	26,928,621	6.0	10,514,929	11,450,973	8.9
Escambia	6,557,229	6,946,107	5.9	3,209,557	3,418,727	6.5
Flagler	676,711	784,207	15.9	293,787	326,391	11.1
Franklin	128,977	142,677	10.6	77,026	87,329	13.4
Gadsden	735,366	873,753	18.8	189,599	205,811	8.6
Gilchrist	93,418	101,414	8.6	34,330	37,146	8.2
Glades	85,892	74,509	-13.3	19,572	18,943	-3.2
Gulf	138,784	139,119	0.2	52,465	56,944	8.5
Hamilton	131,406	122,406	-6.8	49,009	46,824	-4.5
Hardee	266,156	271,114	1.9	118,786	122,492	3.1
Hendry	880,015	989,301	12.4	235,919	250,510	6.2
Hernando	3,587,363	3,888,086	8.4	832,823	888,940	6.7
Highlands	1,227,205	1,325,876	8.0	630,966	685,604	8.7
Hillsborough	37,324,587	39,868,866	6.8	14,507,845	15,907,555	9.6
Holmes	115,376	122,764	6.4	56,709	62,819	10.8
Indian River	2,321,119	2,556,658	10.1	1,327,036	1,439,656	8.5
Jackson	609,875	631,863	3.6	311,194	315,686	1.4
Jefferson	94,229	95,223	1.1	42,427	43,301	2.1
Lafayette	52,726	57,153	8.4	14,988	16,076	7.3
Lake	3,327,183	3,731,783	12.2	1,723,532	1,905,212	10.5
Lee	9,646,414	10,787,030	11.8	5,894,740	6,686,466	13.4
Leon	4,767,710	5,075,955	6.5	2,718,129	2,921,223	7.5
Levy	396,768	426,067	7.4	215,410	240,195	11.5
Liberty	59,344	61,937	4.4	11,814	11,029	-6.7

See footnotes at end of table.   Continued . . .

University of Florida   **Bureau of Economic and Business Research**

Table 16.82. GROSS AND TAXABLE SALES: SALES REPORTED TO THE DEPARTMENT OF REVENUE IN THE STATE AND COUNTIES OF FLORIDA, 1998 AND 1999 (Continued)

(rounded to thousands of dollars)

County	Gross sales 1998	Gross sales 1999	Percent-age change	Taxable sales 1998	Taxable sales 1999	Percent-age change
Madison	130,597	148,715	13.9	62,912	67,645	7.5
Manatee	5,716,459	6,126,048	7.2	2,634,524	2,809,072	6.6
Marion	5,455,312	6,572,631	20.5	2,594,533	2,837,191	9.4
Martin	3,052,555	3,309,082	8.4	1,737,930	1,876,935	8.0
Miami-Dade	69,979,658	73,414,199	4.9	25,063,830	26,943,647	7.5
Monroe	2,589,225	2,842,216	9.8	1,794,208	1,955,269	9.0
Nassau	1,192,401	1,360,290	14.1	472,763	515,749	9.1
Okaloosa	3,650,558	3,974,948	8.9	2,052,303	2,231,074	8.7
Okeechobee	515,205	572,806	11.2	275,120	297,635	8.2
Orange	41,779,123	43,967,480	5.2	20,770,417	22,355,439	7.6
Osceola	5,102,932	5,598,920	9.7	2,252,278	2,421,761	7.5
Palm Beach	27,828,417	30,213,935	8.6	15,064,801	16,215,155	7.6
Pasco	4,558,918	6,008,454	31.8	2,439,968	2,637,547	8.1
Pinellas	24,482,100	25,939,257	6.0	10,589,770	11,134,607	5.1
Polk	12,724,235	13,783,796	8.3	4,751,864	5,076,707	6.8
Putnam	1,470,173	1,502,074	2.2	414,434	441,456	6.5
St. Johns	2,039,218	2,262,811	11.0	1,236,985	1,380,283	11.6
St. Lucie	2,833,854	3,091,751	9.1	1,449,619	1,556,455	7.4
Santa Rosa	1,295,950	1,229,235	-5.1	576,785	608,073	5.4
Sarasota	7,839,928	8,496,915	8.4	4,379,114	4,724,114	7.9
Seminole	9,299,645	10,069,507	8.3	4,708,614	5,136,807	9.1
Sumter	515,989	589,117	14.2	200,839	223,004	11.0
Suwannee	424,442	473,492	11.6	208,451	231,674	11.1
Taylor	372,126	402,893	8.3	137,335	143,122	4.2
Union	152,477	206,198	35.2	31,265	34,711	11.0
Volusia	8,222,428	9,382,983	14.1	4,335,129	4,701,944	8.5
Wakulla	171,913	189,598	10.3	73,219	80,756	10.3
Walton	777,802	895,401	15.1	519,781	604,243	16.2
Washington	182,716	200,605	9.8	85,602	95,497	11.6
Out-of-state	67,923,982	77,303,397	13.8	15,975,908	19,165,976	20.0
In/out state 1/	1,398,113	1,821,347	30.3	130,281	193,906	48.8

1/ Reports that have not yet been allocated to counties.
Note: Data are audited sales reported to the Florida Department of Revenue. Taxable sales are sales subject to the 6 percent regular sales tax and 3 percent vehicle and farm equipment sales tax. Sales occurred, for the most part, December 1, 1997, through November 30, 1999. Kind of business data for counties are available from the Bureau of Economic and Business Research, University of Florida. Data are not comparable with retail sales reported by the U.S. Bureau of the Census.

Source: State of Florida, Department of Revenue, unpublished data prepared by the University of Florida, Bureau of Economic and Business Research.

University of Florida   **Bureau of Economic and Business Research**

FINANCE, INSURANCE, AND REAL ESTATE

Insurance and Annuity Benefit Payments in Florida and the United States, 1998 ($1,000)

Annuity payments ($3,191,000) 25.1%

Death payments ($2,318,131) 18.2%

Disability payments ($56.062) 0.4% and Matured endowments ($26,613) 0.2%

Policy and contract dividends ($834,963) 6.6%

Surrender values ($6,292,385) 49.5%

Florida

Annuity payments ($62,614,060) 27.0%

Death payments ($39,622,123) 17.1%

Disability payments ($927,146) 0.4% and Matured endowments ($475,097) 0.2%

Policy and contract dividends ($18,240,290) 7.9%

Surrender values ($110,207,989) 47.5%

United States

Source: Table 17.60

SECTION 17.00
FINANCE, INSURANCE, AND REAL ESTATE

TABLES LISTED BY MAJOR HEADINGS

University of Florida					**Bureau of Economic and Business Research**

495

TABLES LISTED BY MAJOR HEADINGS

Table 17.01. FINANCE AND INSURANCE: ESTABLISHMENTS, EMPLOYMENT, REVENUE, AND PAYROLL BY KIND OF BUSINESS IN FLORIDA, 1997

NAICS code	Industry	Number of establishments	Number of employees 1/	Revenue ($1,000)	Annual payroll ($1,000)
52	Finance and insurance	24,785	317,250	(NA)	11,928,267
521	Monetary authorities - central bank	2	575	63,070	20,091
522	Credit intermediation and related activities	10,055	153,005	36,343,241	4,854,288
5221	Depository credit intermediation	5,343	104,114	23,696,319	3,136,816
52211	Commercial banking	4,005	84,356	19,728,258	2,586,814
52212	Savings institutions	747	10,706	2,442,725	330,852
52213	Credit unions	591	9,052	1,525,336	219,150
5222	Nondepository credit intermediation	3,415	34,423	9,665,524	1,242,457
52221	Credit card issuing	15	A/	193,213	27,002
52222	Sales financing	642	7,777	3,484,811	284,858
52229	Other nondepository credit intermediation	2,758	25,946	5,987,500	930,597
5223	Activities related to credit intermediation	1,297	14,468	2,981,398	475,015
52231	Mortgage and nonmortgage loan brokers	826	3,135	312,965	102,170
52232	Financial transactions processing, reserve, and clearinghouse act	98	7,927	2,256,236	275,238
52239	Other activities related to credit intermediation	373	3,406	412,197	97,607
523	Securities intermediation and related activities	3,401	33,293	7,707,631	2,301,507
5231	Securities and commodity contracts intermediation and brokerage	1,672	23,053	5,055,652	1,713,810
52311	Investment banking and securities dealing	273	4,552	1,099,805	312,323
52312	Securities brokerage	1,314	17,786	3,822,812	1,353,661
52313	Commodity contracts dealing	27	153	37,956	12,920
52314	Commodity contracts brokerage	58	562	95,079	34,906
5239	Other financial investment activities	1,729	10,240	2,651,979	587,697
52391	Miscellaneous intermediation	454	1,773	859,503	64,926
52392	Portfolio management	581	4,707	1,166,899	344,853
52393	Investment advice	550	1,719	263,884	99,851
52399	All other financial investment activities	144	2,041	361,693	78,067
524	Insurance carriers and related activities	11,190	128,814	(NA)	4,723,322
5241	Insurance carriers	2,739	80,269	(NA)	3,033,920
52411	Direct life, health, and medical insurance carriers	1,024	49,125	(NA)	1,810,639
52412	Other direct insurance carriers	1,677	30,895	(NA)	1,208,970
52413	Reinsurance carriers	38	249	(NA)	14,311
5242	Agencies, brokerages, and other insurance related activities	8,451	48,545	5,345,706	1,689,402
52421	Insurance agencies and brokerages	7,515	34,994	3,800,162	1,166,726
52429	Other insurance related activities	936	13,551	1,545,544	522,676
525	Funds, trusts, and other financial vehicles (part)	137	1,563	341,305	29,059

(NA) Not available.
Employment range: A/ 500-999.
1/ Paid employment for the pay period including March 12.
Note: The economic censuses are conducted on a 5-year cycle collecting data for years ending in 2 and 7. Data are for North American Classification System (NAICS) code 52 and may not be comparable to earlier years. See Glossary for definition.

Source: U.S., Department of Commerce, Bureau of the Census, *1997 Economic Census: Finance and Insurance*, Geographic Area Series EC97F52A-FL, Issued January 2000, Internet site <http://www.census.gov/prod/ec97/97f52-fl.pdf> (accessed 26 June 2000).

Table 17.07. BANKING OFFICES: NUMBER OF FDIC-INSURED COMMERCIAL BANKS AND TRUST COMPANIES BY CHARTER CLASS AND OFFICE TYPE IN FLORIDA DECEMBER 31, 1998 AND 1999

Charter class	All offices	Banks Total	Banks Unit banks	Banks operating branches	Branches
Total by charter class	4,047	272	71	201	3,775
National	2,624	89	20	69	2,535
State	1,423	183	51	132	1,240
Member of Federal Reserve System	631	37	10	27	594
Nonmember of Federal Reserve System	792	146	41	105	646
Total in operation					
December 31, 1998	4,632	292	(NA)	(NA)	4,340
December 31, 1999	4,650	318	(NA)	(NA)	4,332
Net change	18	26	(NA)	(NA)	-8
Beginning operation	(NA)	43	(NA)	(NA)	(NA)
Ceasing operation	(NA)	16	(NA)	(NA)	(NA)
Failed banks	(NA)	2	(NA)	(NA)	(NA)
Mergers, absorptions, and consolidations	(NA)	14	(NA)	(NA)	(NA)

(NA) Not available.

Table 17.08. BANKING ACTIVITY: NUMBER OF FDIC-INSURED COMMERCIAL BANKS AND TRUST COMPANIES AND AMOUNT OF ASSETS AND DEPOSITS BY ASSET SIZE IN FLORIDA, DECEMBER 31, 1999

(amounts in millions of dollars)

Size of assets	Number of banks	Assets	Deposits
All banks	272	86,271	64,931
Less than $25 million	29	456	285
$25 to $50 million	44	1,611	1,307
$50 to $100 million	71	5,224	4,448
$100 to $300 million	82	14,506	11,867
$300 to $500 million	21	8,107	6,453
$500 million to $1 billion	2	1,378	1,031
$1 to $3 billion	18	29,326	22,957
$3 to $10 billion	5	25,662	16,583
$10 billion or more	0	0	0

Note: Asset size of bank determined from domestic and foreign consolidated assets.

Source for Tables 17.07 and 17.08: Federal Deposit Insurance Corporation, Division of Research and Statistics, *Statistics on Banking, 1999.*

University of Florida   **Bureau of Economic and Business Research**

Table 17.09. BANKING ACTIVITY: NUMBER OF FDIC-INSURED COMMERCIAL AND SAVINGS BANKS AND BANKING OFFICES AND AMOUNT OF DEPOSITS IN THE STATE AND COUNTIES OF FLORIDA, JUNE 30, 1999

County	Number of banks 1/	Number of banking offices 2/	Deposits ($1,000)	County	Number of banks 1/	Number of banking offices 2/	Deposits ($1,000)
Florida	333	4,509	200,783,393	Lake	17	82	2,563,111
				Lee	27	146	5,628,240
Alachua	11	56	1,567,101	Leon	14	70	2,473,797
Baker	3	4	117,992	Levy	4	15	280,136
Bay	11	46	1,330,488	Liberty	1	1	43,017
Bradford	3	5	119,734	Madison	5	6	122,945
Brevard	20	124	4,182,299	Manatee	22	92	2,962,068
Broward	44	404	22,770,631	Marion	19	71	2,542,145
Calhoun	3	4	90,631	Martin	15	63	2,002,055
Charlotte	15	47	1,884,586	Miami-Dade	69	535	39,633,149
Citrus	12	39	1,523,957	Monroe	11	48	1,286,023
Clay	8	26	509,431	Nassau	6	14	374,799
Collier	28	98	4,102,784	Okaloosa	18	68	1,803,280
Columbia	7	14	375,995	Okeechobee	5	8	289,395
De Soto	5	6	207,474	Orange	29	197	9,098,398
Dixie	3	4	58,368	Osceola	14	40	1,106,753
Duval	20	168	8,417,853	Palm Beach	52	426	20,527,821
Escambia	18	79	2,492,956	Pasco	21	95	3,976,735
Flagler	7	12	538,191	Pinellas	34	315	13,415,480
Franklin	3	9	110,252	Polk	16	111	3,932,004
Gadsden	4	9	186,493	Putnam	6	15	479,696
Gilchrist	2	4	84,382	St. Johns	12	36	1,040,926
Glades	2	2	17,057	St. Lucie	14	53	1,784,668
Gulf	3	5	101,401	Santa Rosa	13	30	686,499
Hamilton	2	2	41,606	Sarasota	32	148	6,673,553
Hardee	3	5	249,701	Seminole	23	85	2,883,016
Hendry	5	13	282,656	Sumter	5	10	154,226
Hernando	13	37	1,737,403	Suwannee	5	7	288,658
Highlands	7	27	1,036,536	Taylor	3	4	112,225
Hillsborough	37	227	9,995,799	Union	1	1	30,000
Holmes	3	3	112,371	Volusia	19	132	5,215,987
Indian River	18	60	2,126,341	Wakulla	2	6	115,063
Jackson	7	16	345,991	Walton	8	15	286,458
Jefferson	2	2	84,592	Washington	3	4	96,572
Lafayette	2	2	40,056				

1/ Number of banks in each county includes each bank operating at least one office within the county, regardless of the location of its main office; therefore, a bank operating a branch in a second county would be counted as a bank in each county, but only once in the state total.

2/ Includes each location at which deposit business is transacted.

Source: Federal Deposit Insurance Corporation, Division of Supervision, *1999 Bank and Thrift Branch Office Data Book: Summary of Deposits, Southeast Region.*

University of Florida   **Bureau of Economic and Business Research**

Table 17.20. STATE-CHARTERED BANKS AND TRUST COMPANIES: NUMBER, ASSETS
CAPITAL ACCOUNTS, LOANS, AND DEPOSITS IN FLORIDA
SPECIFIED YEARS 1895 THROUGH 1999

(amounts in thousands of dollars)

Year	Number	Assets	Capital accounts	Loans	Deposits
1895	21	1,692	666	943	974
1900	22	4,510	1,006	2,637	3,408
1905	41	14,338	3,222	9,332	10,291
1910	113	27,599	5,607	17,711	20,884
1915	192	42,656	9,811	26,280	30,527
1920	212	114,374	13,272	71,347	95,349
1925	271	539,101	33,427	309,492	501,553
1930	151	92,928	16,422	38,534	70,235
1935	102	64,276	9,768	13,662	53,552
1940	114	116,169	14,233	31,285	101,545
1945	112	450,838	20,135	36,851	430,256
1950	130	619,824	37,603	128,517	580,607
1955	146	1,138,114	67,726	329,340	1,064,763
1960	181	1,781,837	139,368	711,387	1,620,185
1965	243	2,571,685	216,444	1,139,398	2,541,195
1970	282	5,603,445	425,945	2,668,971	4,996,082
1975	449	11,757,147	989,185	5,860,781	10,346,695
1980	358	22,416,088	1,679,111	10,380,658	17,942,643
1981	321	21,303,799	1,609,024	10,423,906	17,991,930
1982	297	20,912,278	1,570,467	9,978,160	18,175,117
1983	274	22,940,431	1,678,551	11,152,310	20,212,039
1984	256	23,186,313	1,636,747	12,568,673	20,319,366
1985	251	24,160,155	1,627,920	13,372,532	21,321,726
1986	241	28,055,385	1,896,402	16,174,559	24,948,817
1987	246	30,362,358	2,136,083	18,647,857	26,683,250
1988	251	31,658,397	2,264,319	19,950,857	27,831,065
1989	258	32,801,720	2,402,253	21,338,510	29,128,762
1990	261	37,247,099	2,587,920	23,793,358	33,324,544
1991	260	39,051,128	2,852,114	24,076,458	35,021,312
1992	256	41,551,323	3,196,327	25,095,945	37,137,219
1993	248	51,271,342	4,265,301	32,194,235	44,490,477
1994	238	58,803,093	4,783,598	38,780,991	50,081,893
1995	224	58,344,123	5,143,296	38,320,163	49,393,436
1996	194	40,904,042	3,693,747	26,214,925	33,128,637
1997	180	35,464,125	3,266,522	23,194,221	28,937,982
1998	166	37,565,723	3,194,845	24,301,914	30,948,982
1999	182	41,547,418	3,527,556	27,790,873	33,141,500

Note: Data for 1986 through 1999 excludes nondeposit trust companies and industrial savings banks.

Source: State of Florida, Office of the Comptroller, *Annual Report of the Division of Banking, 1995,* and unpublished data.

University of Florida   **Bureau of Economic and Business Research**

Table 17.21. STATE-CHARTERED BANKS AND TRUST COMPANIES: NUMBER
ASSETS, AND DEPOSITS IN THE STATE AND COUNTIES
OF FLORIDA, DECEMBER 31, 1999

(amounts in thousands of dollars)

County	Num-ber	Assets	Deposits	County	Num-ber	Assets	Deposits
Florida	182	41,547,418	33,141,500	Lake	5	609,424	519,679
				Lee	4	1,833,639	1,221,496
Alachua	2	138,550	113,520	Leon	5	2,885,216	2,312,423
Baker	0	0	0	Levy	2	216,891	189,340
Bay	1	168,232	146,251	Liberty	1	117,001	106,340
Bradford	1	46,055	36,333	Madison	1	16,907	12,162
Brevard	3	195,591	141,915	Manatee	3	520,244	395,220
Broward	8	767,645	633,023	Marion	5	1,274,400	990,373
Calhoun	0	0	0	Martin	2	73,791	56,243
Charlotte	3	359,427	314,537	Miami-Dade	18	6,265,607	5,289,265
Citrus	3	342,260	317,244	Monroe	3	826,464	703,163
Clay	1	31,338	27,274	Nassau	1	98,579	68,152
Collier	5	784,855	663,718	Okaloosa	4	659,925	551,329
Columbia	2	80,198	68,252	Okeechobee	0	0	0
De Soto	1	102,106	86,109	Orange	6	918,621	718,070
Dixie	0	0	0	Osceola	1	71,444	60,563
Duval	4	295,116	244,458	Palm Beach	10	3,879,677	2,682,254
Escambia	4	378,422	325,911	Pasco	0	0	0
Flagler	1	24,276	17,184	Pinellas	13	4,107,394	3,616,439
Franklin	2	107,574	95,659	Polk	3	531,400	461,026
Gadsden	1	105,537	80,913	Putnam	1	71,505	63,984
Gilchrist	1	45,927	41,259	St. Johns	1	228,749	195,284
Glades	0	0	0	St. Lucie	1	16,676	12,309
Gulf	1	38,686	35,577	Santa Rosa	0	0	0
Hamilton	0	0	0	Sarasota	7	2,602,226	1,931,807
Hardee	1	260,722	224,147	Seminole	1	101,419	87,592
Hendry	1	110,023	99,469	Sumter	0	0	0
Hernando	2	1,762,350	1,435,753	Suwannee	0	0	0
Highlands	1	85,380	76,419	Taylor	1	51,337	45,087
Hillsborough	16	4,934,304	3,628,051	Union	0	0	0
Holmes	1	72,718	62,947	Volusia	8	1,699,334	1,393,332
Indian River	1	47,095	39,900	Wakulla	2	207,753	180,418
Jackson	3	96,527	81,373	Walton	1	85,967	70,890
Jefferson	1	162,932	142,235	Washington	0	0	0
Lafayette	1	31,982	27,829				

Source: State of Florida, Office of the Comptroller, unpublished data.

University of Florida   **Bureau of Economic and Business Research**

Table 17.23. STATE-CHARTERED BANKS AND TRUST COMPANIES: ASSETS, DEPOSITS
CAPITAL, NET INCOME, AND NUMBER OF BANKS BY ASSET SIZE
IN FLORIDA, DECEMBER 31, 1999

(in thousands of dollars, except where indicated)

Item	All banks	Less than 50 million	50-500 million	Over 500 million
Assets	41,547,418	1,583,222	17,883,881	22,080,315
Deposits	33,141,500	1,257,892	15,080,264	16,803,344
Capital	3,527,556	287,878	1,523,702	1,715,976
Net income 1/	417,298	-9,474	168,216	258,556
Number of institutions	182	56	115	11

1/ After taxes and extraordinary items.
Note: Nondeposit trust companies and industrial savings banks are excluded.

Table 17.24. INTERNATIONAL BANKS: NUMBER AND ASSETS OF AGENCIES BY NATION
OF ORIGIN IN FLORIDA, DECEMBER 31, 1997, 1998, AND 1999

Nation of origin	1997 Number	1997 Assets ($1,000)	1998 Number	1998 Assets ($1,000)	1999 Number	1999 Assets ($1,000)
Total	43	18,508,047	42	20,036,075	38	19,631,567
Argentina	1	70,093	1	82,456	1	86,678
Bolivia	2	99,884	2	166,469	1	118,812
Brazil	3	276,035	3	198,046	2	194,696
Canada	1	554,209	1	612,262	1	643,444
Cayman Islands	1	32,740	1	27,996	1	26,415
Chile	1	254,540	1	217,174	2	245,053
Colombia	2	236,437	2	231,647	2	17,162
Ecuador	2	230,002	2	156,913	1	78,082
England	4	8,483,689	4	8,567,601	4	9,268,746
France	3	785,708	3	914,836	3	952,116
Germany	1	1,792,150	1	3,597,137	1	2,177,568
Israel	3	788,692	3	779,687	3	827,691
Jamaica	1	27,985	1	25,599	1	244
Japan	1	316,220	1	277,611	1	258,946
Korea	1	138,902	0	0	0	0
Netherlands	1	878,262	1	748,986	1	940,471
Panama	1	310,957	1	325,176	1	284,979
Peru	0	0	0	0	0	0
Portugal	1	62,602	1	79,479	1	91,937
Spain	7	1,811,948	7	1,967,157	6	2,274,914
Switzerland	2	796,837	2	396,466	1	490,907
United States	1	86,524	1	125,799	1	104,660
Venezuela	3	473,631	3	537,578	3	548,046

Source for Tables 17.23 and 17.24: State of Florida, Office of the Comptroller, unpublished data.

Table 17.30. CREDIT UNIONS: FINANCIAL CONDITION OF STATE-CHARTERED CREDIT UNIONS IN FLORIDA, DECEMBER 31, 1999

(in thousands of dollars, except where indicated)

Item	Amount	Item	Amount
Number of institutions 1/	113	Gross income, total	542,813
Net loans	4,085,948	Operating expense, total	282,444
Assets, total	6,474,673	Net income	67,471
Shares and deposits, total	5,691,037	Ratio of expense to $100	
Liabilities and equity, total	(NA)	gross income (dollars)	52.0

1/ Does not include credit unions in liquidation.

Table 17.31. CREDIT UNIONS: ASSETS AND DEPOSITS OF STATE-CHARTERED CREDIT UNIONS IN THE STATE AND COUNTIES OF FLORIDA, DECEMBER 31, 1999

(amounts in thousands of dollars)

County	Number of institutions	Assets	Deposits	County	Number of institutions	Assets	Deposits
Florida	113	6,474,673	5,691,037	Leon	8	426,628	380,533
				Madison	1	2,049	1,588
Alachua	5	480,627	421,143	Marion	2	40,803	35,974
Bay	1	39,838	35,228	Martin	1	9,336	8,036
Bradford	1	3,563	3,088	Miami-Dade	13	292,776	253,126
Brevard	2	799,148	723,606	Nassau	1	8,662	6,770
Broward	7	399,203	354,376	Orange	5	672,060	596,491
Calhoun	1	18,463	16,186	Palm Beach	7	170,665	134,638
Clay	1	7,072	6,160	Pinellas	5	354,398	307,176
Columbia	1	13,896	11,973	Polk	5	116,118	99,647
Duval	12	1,275,897	1,124,225	Putnam	1	16,842	14,727
Escambia	5	356,370	307,223	St. Johns	1	9,075	7,909
Gadsden	1	60,579	53,257	St. Lucie	1	4,953	4,655
Hillsborough	7	437,246	383,611	Santa Rosa	2	20,722	17,688
Holmes	1	8,855	7,318	Sarasota	3	144,333	128,632
Jackson	2	17,309	13,830	Taylor	1	10,810	9,816
Jefferson	1	4,119	3,605	Volusia	2	10,382	8,826
Lake	3	214,198	186,414	Washington	1	23,457	19,954
Lee	2	4,222	3,609				

Source for Tables 17.30 and 17.31: State of Florida, Office of the Comptroller, unpublished data.

Table 17.38. EMPLOYMENT AND PAYROLL: AVERAGE MONTHLY PRIVATE REPORTING UNITS EMPLOYMENT, AND PAYROLL COVERED BY UNEMPLOYMENT COMPENSATION LAW BY FINANCE INSURANCE, AND REAL ESTATE INDUSTRY IN FLORIDA, 1998 AND 1999

SIC code	Industry	Number of re- porting units	Number of em- ployees	Payroll ($1,000)
		1998 A/		
	Finance, insurance, and real estate	39,000	422,317	1,433,186
60	Depository institutions	3,742	99,590	304,279
601	Central reserve depository institutions	13	708	1,907
602	Commercial banks	2,493	70,642	211,283
603	Savings institutions	516	10,859	36,120
606	Credit unions	383	9,778	20,360
608	Foreign banking and branches and agencies of foreign banks	70	2,780	16,584
609	Functions related to depository banking	266	4,823	18,025
61	Nondepository credit institutions	3,865	50,871	177,646
611	Federal and federally-sponsored credit agencies	86	1,381	3,230
614	Personal credit institutions	1,242	13,125	45,380
615	Business credit institutions	245	12,433	39,017
616	Mortgage bankers and brokers	2,292	23,933	90,019
62	Security and commodity brokers, dealers, exchanges, and services	2,594	30,536	214,936
621	Security brokers, dealers, flotation companies	1,328	25,256	181,741
622	Commodity contracts brokers and dealers	75	454	4,741
623	Security and commodity exchanges	15	38	134
628	Services allied with the exchange of securities or commodities	1,176	4,788	28,320
63	Insurance carriers	2,262	70,566	246,906
631	Life insurance	504	20,035	70,511
632	Accident and health insurance and medical service plans	284	17,091	58,088
633	Fire, marine, and casualty insurance	709	25,072	92,044
635	Surety insurance	85	781	3,562
636	Title insurance	600	6,809	19,407
637	Pension, health, and welfare funds	61	565	2,453
639	Insurance carriers, NEC	20	213	839
64	Insurance agents, brokers, and service	7,615	48,371	152,197
65	Real estate	17,575	112,526	263,673
651	Real estate operators (except developers) and lessors	5,092	31,540	59,407
653	Real estate agents and managers	10,840	61,722	151,230
654	Title abstract offices	338	2,117	5,254
655	Land subdividers and developers	1,306	17,147	47,781
67	Holding and other investment offices	1,348	9,856	73,550
671	Holding offices	481	5,096	52,321
672	Investment offices	103	833	3,927
673	Trusts	185	1,249	4,780
679	Miscellaneous investing	580	2,679	12,522

See footnotes at end of table.   Continued . . .

Table 17.38. EMPLOYMENT AND PAYROLL: AVERAGE MONTHLY PRIVATE REPORTING UNITS EMPLOYMENT, AND PAYROLL COVERED BY UNEMPLOYMENT COMPENSATION LAW BY FINANCE INSURANCE, AND REAL ESTATE INDUSTRY IN FLORIDA, 1998 AND 1999 (Continued)

SIC code	Industry	Number of re- porting units	Number of em- ployees	Payroll ($1,000)
		1999 B/		
	Finance, insurance, and real estate	39,675	439,312	1,485,545
60	Depository institutions	3,401	100,863	309,315
601	Central reserve depository institutions	15	770	2,233
602	Commercial banks	2,143	71,577	214,938
603	Savings institutions	514	10,950	34,540
606	Credit unions	380	10,236	22,426
608	Foreign banking and branches and agencies of foreign banks	67	2,830	18,077
609	Functions related to depository banking	282	4,500	17,101
61	Nondepository credit institutions	4,155	55,306	188,030
611	Federal and federally-sponsored credit agencies	79	1,239	3,019
614	Personal credit institutions	1,267	14,165	50,334
615	Business credit institutions	263	14,461	46,902
616	Mortgage bankers and brokers	2,547	25,441	87,776
62	Security and commodity brokers, dealers, exchanges, and services	2,729	30,582	227,612
621	Security brokers, dealers, flotation companies	1,417	25,522	196,693
622	Commodity contracts brokers and dealers	88	426	3,162
623	Security and commodity exchanges	17	46	195
628	Services allied with the exchange of securities or commodities	1,208	4,588	27,562
63	Insurance carriers	2,290	74,676	262,109
631	Life insurance	483	19,501	68,875
632	Accident and health insurance and medical service plans	294	17,385	58,718
633	Fire, marine, and casualty insurance	723	27,727	102,152
635	Surety insurance	83	781	4,105
636	Title insurance	616	7,289	21,582
637	Pension, health, and welfare funds	66	1,601	5,416
639	Insurance carriers, NEC	26	392	1,262
64	Insurance agents, brokers, and service	7,759	48,547	160,295
65	Real estate	17,985	119,544	285,669
651	Real estate operators (except developers) and lessors	4,913	31,073	63,776
653	Real estate agents and managers	11,391	65,843	160,566
654	Title abstract offices	367	2,241	5,593
655	Land subdividers and developers	1,314	20,387	55,734
67	Holding and other investment offices	1,357	9,796	52,514
671	Holding offices	493	4,934	31,605
672	Investment offices	111	825	4,524
673	Trusts	195	1,323	4,507
679	Miscellaneous investing	558	2,714	11,878

NEC Not elsewhere classified.　A/ Revised.　B/ Preliminary.
Note: Private employment. Detail may not add to totals due to disclosure editing and/or rounding. See Tables 23.70, 23.71, 23.72, 23.73, and 23.74 for public employment data.

Source: State of Florida, Department of Labor and Employment Security, Bureau of Labor Market Information, "Employment and Wages" (ES-202), unpublished data.

University of Florida　　　　　　　　　**Bureau of Economic and Business Research**

Table 17.39. EMPLOYMENT AND PAYROLL: AVERAGE MONTHLY PRIVATE REPORTING UNITS EMPLOYMENT, AND PAYROLL COVERED BY UNEMPLOYMENT COMPENSATION LAW IN THE STATE AND COUNTIES OF FLORIDA, 1998 AND 1999

County	Number of reporting units	Number of employees	Payroll ($1,000)	County	Number of reporting units	Number of employees	Payroll ($1,000)
			Finance, insurance, and real estate, 1998 A/ (SIC codes 60-67)				
Florida	39,000	422,317	1,433,186	Lake	336	4,104	8,188
				Lee	1,163	8,658	24,449
Alachua	488	5,007	15,264	Leon	662	5,812	16,900
Baker	13	133	278	Levy	38	222	455
Bay	322	3,456	7,217	Madison	20	68	114
Bradford	28	117	190	Manatee	514	3,115	8,361
Brevard	829	6,035	16,714	Marion	490	3,724	9,506
Broward	4,396	46,255	161,668	Martin	375	2,481	10,321
Calhoun	12	81	150	Miami-Dade	6,341	65,680	234,153
Charlotte	246	1,596	3,847	Monroe	279	1,509	3,942
Citrus	192	1,151	2,495	Nassau	73	405	1,135
Clay	181	908	2,301	Okaloosa	414	3,920	8,649
Collier	909	5,512	20,415	Okeechobee	46	252	472
Columbia	76	510	1,050	Orange	2,267	32,797	110,670
De Soto	29	173	351	Osceola	307	2,447	5,627
Dixie	12	47	64	Palm Beach	3,480	31,715	141,092
Duval	1,889	50,709	193,609	Pasco	492	2,838	6,559
Escambia	550	5,067	12,288	Pinellas	2,461	29,058	100,494
Flagler	89	427	1,189	Polk	753	8,061	22,153
Franklin	24	181	322	Putnam	92	533	983
Gadsden	35	211	489	St. Johns	259	1,345	4,292
Gilchrist	7	32	61	St. Lucie	296	2,256	5,466
Glades	5	22	38	Santa Rosa	144	768	1,470
Gulf	18	133	239	Sarasota	1,071	8,396	29,604
Hamilton	8	29	54	Seminole	875	6,458	20,636
Hardee	26	242	485	Sumter	28	170	364
Hendry	40	245	427	Suwannee	40	270	567
Hernando	173	1,178	3,065	Taylor	21	147	258
Highlands	117	675	1,389	Union	8	24	39
Hillsborough	2,590	45,132	147,928	Volusia	852	6,101	14,994
Holmes	13	64	126	Wakulla	22	150	306
Indian River	322	2,018	6,421	Walton	65	489	922
Jackson	53	321	766	Washington	18	73	155
Jefferson	17	131	266				
Lafayette	3	35	50	Multicounty 1/	988	10,417	38,636

See footnotes at end of table.

Continued . . .

University of Florida

Bureau of Economic and Business Research

Table 17.39. EMPLOYMENT AND PAYROLL: AVERAGE MONTHLY PRIVATE REPORTING UNITS EMPLOYMENT, AND PAYROLL COVERED BY UNEMPLOYMENT COMPENSATION LAW IN THE STATE AND COUNTIES OF FLORIDA, 1998 AND 1999 (Continued)

County	Number of reporting units	Number of employees	Payroll ($1,000)	County	Number of reporting units	Number of employees	Payroll ($1,000)
			Finance, insurance, and real estate, 1999 B/ (SIC codes 60-67)				
Florida	39,675	439,312	1,485,545	Lake	349	4,304	8,472
				Lee	1,215	9,155	27,473
Alachua	469	5,114	16,276	Leon	665	6,106	18,101
Baker	14	139	305	Levy	41	246	518
Bay	335	3,377	7,441	Madison	20	76	156
Bradford	29	127	211	Manatee	514	3,091	8,151
Brevard	840	6,120	17,028	Marion	488	3,894	10,376
Broward	4,458	47,621	168,969	Martin	379	2,321	8,426
Calhoun	12	70	134	Miami-Dade	6,391	65,301	248,120
Charlotte	249	1,734	4,142	Monroe	284	1,595	4,111
Citrus	195	1,197	2,669	Nassau	75	399	990
Clay	188	920	2,359	Okaloosa	422	4,213	9,180
Collier	973	5,801	21,956	Okeechobee	46	243	477
Columbia	73	406	915	Orange	2,308	38,670	125,017
De Soto	30	173	392	Osceola	311	2,705	6,108
Dixie	13	46	69	Palm Beach	3,540	32,266	140,722
Duval	1,888	51,726	175,954	Pasco	513	3,155	7,261
Escambia	547	4,897	12,928	Pinellas	2,467	30,386	103,724
Flagler	97	428	1,174	Polk	744	8,079	22,410
Franklin	25	189	389	Putnam	92	540	1,017
Gadsden	37	201	468	St. Johns	266	1,262	4,264
Gilchrist	9	41	84	St. Lucie	300	2,352	5,736
Glades	5	20	29	Santa Rosa	150	832	1,678
Gulf	19	134	265	Sarasota	1,076	8,582	32,671
Hamilton	8	36	72	Seminole	899	6,964	22,692
Hardee	26	243	510	Sumter	35	197	439
Hendry	40	240	434	Suwannee	38	290	699
Hernando	185	1,211	3,112	Taylor	25	152	291
Highlands	118	654	1,404	Union	8	23	41
Hillsborough	2,614	46,525	156,038	Volusia	861	6,258	14,571
Holmes	10	51	115	Wakulla	22	172	342
Indian River	322	1,973	6,756	Walton	74	552	1,149
Jackson	57	329	742	Washington	23	91	227
Jefferson	19	128	280	Multicounty 1/	1,139	13,375	46,193
Lafayette	4	43	70	Out-of-state 2/	7	2	3

A/ Revised.
B/ Preliminary.
1/ Reporting units without a fixed location within the state or of unknown county location.
2/ Employment based in Florida, but working out of the state or country.
Note: Private employment. Only counties for which data are disclosed are shown. Detail may not add to totals due to disclosure editing and/or rounding. See Tables 23.70, 23.71, 23.72, 23.73, and 23.74 for public employment data.
Source: State of Florida, Department of Labor and Employment Security, Bureau of Labor Market Information, "Employment and Wages" (ES-202), unpublished data.

University of Florida   **Bureau of Economic and Business Research**

Table 17.40. DEPOSITORY INSTITUTIONS: AVERAGE MONTHLY PRIVATE REPORTING UNITS EMPLOYMENT, AND PAYROLL COVERED BY UNEMPLOYMENT COMPENSATION LAW IN THE STATE AND COUNTIES OF FLORIDA, 1999

County	Number of reporting units	Number of employees	Payroll ($1,000)	County	Number of reporting units	Number of employees	Payroll ($1,000)
			Depository institutions (SIC code 60)				
Florida	3,401	100,863	309,315	Leon	66	1,620	4,551
				Levy	8	144	333
Alachua	36	966	5,358	Madison	4	35	81
Baker	3	115	264	Manatee	62	894	2,197
Bay	26	1,259	2,937	Marion	54	1,260	3,755
Bradford	6	61	114	Martin	36	581	1,976
Brevard	68	1,361	3,246	Miami-Dade	498	19,994	71,905
Broward	301	8,451	28,391	Monroe	28	660	1,732
Calhoun	5	52	105	Nassau	13	183	465
Charlotte	18	397	1,140	Okaloosa	43	1,214	2,851
Citrus	39	472	1,064	Okeechobee	6	104	227
Clay	16	224	477	Orange	171	8,065	22,076
Collier	73	1,346	4,421	Osceola	24	456	1,240
Columbia	12	215	500	Palm Beach	269	6,938	24,833
De Soto	5	79	189	Pasco	67	850	2,025
Duval	184	11,068	33,696	Pinellas	223	5,498	14,697
Escambia	50	1,586	4,111	Polk	60	1,580	4,009
Flagler	12	85	174	Putnam	15	304	629
Franklin	7	80	164	St. Johns	19	301	780
Gadsden	8	116	283	St. Lucie	28	1,185	2,906
Gilchrist	3	21	55	Santa Rosa	18	321	729
Gulf	5	101	207	Sarasota	95	2,069	5,984
Hardee	5	171	377	Seminole	46	1,270	3,476
Hendry	6	143	297	Suwannee	8	171	446
Hernando	35	463	1,258	Taylor	5	101	194
Highlands	10	201	468	Volusia	68	1,771	4,122
Hillsborough	234	9,852	28,943	Wakulla	3	133	262
Indian River	33	542	1,794	Walton	9	78	143
Jackson	10	143	322	Washington	4	36	70
Lake	40	937	2,084	Multicounty 1/	56	309	1,844
Lee	121	1,934	5,566	Out-of-State 2/	5	2	2

1/ Reporting units without a fixed location within the state or of unknown county location.
2/ Employment based in Florida, but working out of the state or country.
Note: Private employment. For a list of three-digit code industries included see Table 17.38. Data are preliminary. Only counties for which data are disclosed are shown. Detail may not add to totals due to disclosure editing and/or rounding. See Tables 23.70, 23.71, 23.72, 23.73, and 23.74 for public employment data.

Source: State of Florida, Department of Labor and Employment Security, Bureau of Labor Market Information, "Employment and Wages" (ES-202), unpublished data.

University of Florida   **Bureau of Economic and Business Research**

Table 17.41. NONDEPOSITORY CREDIT INSTITUTIONS, MORTGAGE BANKERS AND BROKERS AND SECURITY AND COMMODITY BROKERS: AVERAGE MONTHLY PRIVATE REPORTING UNITS EMPLOYMENT, AND PAYROLL COVERED BY UNEMPLOYMENT COMPENSATION LAW IN THE STATE AND COUNTIES OF FLORIDA, 1999

County	Number of reporting units	Number of employees	Payroll ($1,000)	County	Number of reporting units	Number of employees	Payroll ($1,000)
Nondepository credit institutions (SIC code 61)							
Florida	4,155	55,306	188,030	Manatee	36	171	557
				Marion	53	239	612
Alachua	43	241	670	Martin	22	145	297
Bay	24	136	343	Miami-Dade	709	4,592	17,625
Brevard	72	432	1,431	Monroe	18	59	134
Broward	522	10,929	36,215	Nassau	3	11	76
Charlotte	27	127	350	Okaloosa	33	206	597
Citrus	13	35	90	Orange	247	2,949	11,865
Clay	17	52	141	Osceola	25	94	297
Collier	67	284	867	Palm Beach	330	3,298	12,539
Columbia	7	19	54	Pasco	34	149	295
Duval	212	12,105	39,116	Pinellas	258	4,639	15,159
Escambia	63	551	1,642	Polk	70	334	1,001
Flagler	8	39	112	Putnam	9	28	62
Hernando	16	44	204	St. Johns	23	67	274
Highlands	8	16	27	St. Lucie	25	93	233
Hillsborough	371	8,317	27,950	Santa Rosa	10	46	148
Indian River	20	56	160	Sarasota	77	452	1,825
Jackson	8	60	188	Seminole	141	971	3,151
Lake	22	70	159	Suwannee	3	15	68
Lee	111	634	2,072	Taylor	3	6	14
Leon	55	514	1,535	Volusia	65	536	1,166
Levy	4	4	14	Multicounty 1/	248	1,422	6,365
Mortgage bankers and brokers (SIC code 616)							
Florida	547	25,441	87,776	Flagler	5	35	108
				Hernando	11	31	161
Alachua	22	129	379	Highlands	4	7	8
Bay	8	16	25	Hillsborough	218	3,550	12,999
Brevard	40	185	566	Indian River	14	35	104
Broward	348	2,597	9,199	Lake	11	36	85
Charlotte	16	102	290	Lee	68	430	1,407
Citrus	9	27	67	Leon	25	250	790
Clay	7	15	33	Manatee	19	112	362
Collier	52	228	685	Marion	29	92	194
Duval	138	6,029	20,558	Martin	16	126	243
Escambia	33	261	771	Miami-Dade	457	2,654	8,726

See footnotes at end of table.

Continued . . .

University of Florida

Bureau of Economic and Business Research

Table 17.41. NONDEPOSITORY CREDIT INSTITUTIONS, MORTGAGE BANKERS AND BROKERS AND SECURITY AND COMMODITY BROKERS: AVERAGE MONTHLY PRIVATE REPORTING UNITS EMPLOYMENT, AND PAYROLL COVERED BY UNEMPLOYMENT COMPENSATION LAW IN THE STATE AND COUNTIES OF FLORIDA, 1999 (Continued)

County	Number of re-porting units	Number of em-ployees	Payroll ($1,000)	County	Number of re-porting units	Number of em-ployees	Payroll ($1,000)
			Mortgage bankers and brokers (SIC code 616) (Continued)				
Monroe	14	40	90	St. Johns	16	50	201
Okaloosa	17	105	363	St. Lucie	13	61	140
Orange	154	1,862	7,674	Santa Rosa	4	11	27
Osceola	20	78	257	Sarasota	54	283	1,050
Palm Beach	212	1,451	5,537	Seminole	96	775	2,370
Pasco	18	104	169	Volusia	37	185	501
Pinellas	168	2,611	8,561				
Polk	28	113	312	Multicounty 1/	135	721	2,609
			Security and commodity brokers, dealers, exchanges, and services (SIC code 62)				
Florida	2,729	30,582	227,612	Marion	19	175	1,029
				Martin	37	286	2,995
Alachua	14	85	523	Miami-Dade	478	3,958	39,583
Bay	16	85	503	Monroe	10	32	242
Brevard	53	433	2,665	Nassau	9	14	32
Broward	302	4,240	26,978	Okaloosa	15	70	547
Charlotte	17	119	658	Orange	139	1,373	10,548
Citrus	12	38	209	Osceola	8	26	60
Clay	5	15	41	Palm Beach	416	4,943	43,421
Collier	75	597	5,832	Pasco	32	210	1,170
Duval	86	1,793	12,143	Pinellas	185	5,633	29,507
Escambia	24	242	1,728	Polk	38	236	1,728
Flagler	8	16	59	St. Johns	17	111	1,348
Hernando	9	59	362	St. Lucie	13	38	172
Hillsborough	177	1,749	13,104	Santa Rosa	5	5	20
Indian River	30	202	1,766	Sarasota	97	1,164	9,527
Lake	11	81	517	Seminole	48	285	2,248
Lee	60	462	3,450	Volusia	38	365	1,718
Leon	41	188	1,316				
Manatee	21	149	1,090	Multicounty 1/	155	1,076	8,488

1/ Reporting units without a fixed location within the state or of unknown county location.
Note: Private employment. For a list of three-digit code industries included see Table 17.38. Data are preliminary. Only counties for which data are disclosed are shown. Detail may not add to totals due to disclosure editing and/or rounding. See Tables 23.70, 23.71, 23.72, 23.73, and 23.74 for public employment data.

Source: State of Florida, Department of Labor and Employment Security, Bureau of Labor Market Information, "Employment and Wages" (ES-202), unpublished data.

University of Florida   **Bureau of Economic and Business Research**

Table 17.43. INSURANCE CARRIERS: AVERAGE MONTHLY PRIVATE REPORTING UNITS EMPLOYMENT, AND PAYROLL COVERED BY UNEMPLOYMENT COMPENSATION LAW IN THE STATE AND COUNTIES OF FLORIDA, 1999

County	Number of reporting units	Number of employees	Payroll ($1,000)	County	Number of reporting units	Number of employees	Payroll ($1,000)
			Insurance carriers (SIC code 63)				
Florida	2,290	74,676	262,109	Levy	5	14	25
				Manatee	22	157	643
Alachua	43	1,983	5,699	Marion	27	308	951
Bay	31	316	872	Martin	14	97	330
Bradford	4	9	16	Miami-Dade	299	9,509	39,724
Brevard	55	551	2,015	Monroe	7	33	101
Broward	238	5,725	21,474	Okaloosa	24	251	782
Charlotte	12	93	380	Orange	174	6,113	24,829
Citrus	13	91	198	Osceola	8	53	150
Clay	14	98	391	Palm Beach	174	2,888	10,676
Collier	28	209	675	Pasco	29	214	685
Columbia	8	56	164	Pinellas	135	5,021	17,018
Duval	161	17,453	55,728	Polk	46	3,247	10,067
Escambia	36	381	1,472	Putnam	6	38	68
Flagler	6	36	108	St. Johns	16	69	177
Hernando	10	85	234	St. Lucie	18	224	820
Highlands	10	61	147	Santa Rosa	3	11	51
Hillsborough	232	14,114	46,544	Sarasota	49	968	3,961
Indian River	10	49	205	Seminole	45	787	2,836
Jackson	6	44	127	Volusia	47	504	1,642
Lake	11	97	323	Walton	3	10	19
Lee	66	847	2,986				
Leon	55	810	2,813	Multicounty 1/	68	918	3,651

1/ Reporting units without a fixed location within the state or of unknown county location.
Note: Private employment. For a list of three-digit code industries included see Table 17.38. Data are preliminary. Only counties for which data are disclosed are shown. Detail may not add to totals due to disclosure editing and/or rounding. See Tables 23.70, 23.71, 23.72, 23.73, and 23.74 for public employment data.

Source: State of Florida, Department of Labor and Employment Security, Bureau of Labor Market Information, "Employment and Wages" (ES-202), unpublished data.

Table 17.44. INSURANCE AGENTS, BROKERS, AND SERVICE: AVERAGE MONTHLY PRIVATE REPORTING UNITS, EMPLOYMENT, AND PAYROLL COVERED BY UNEMPLOYMENT COMPENSATION LAW IN THE STATE AND COUNTIES OF FLORIDA, 1999

County	Number of reporting units	Number of employees	Payroll ($1,000)	County	Number of reporting units	Number of employees	Payroll ($1,000)
				Insurance agents, brokers, and service (SIC code 64)			
Florida	7,759	48,547	160,295	Leon	152	1,238	4,003
				Levy	8	44	89
Alachua	90	376	1,208	Madison	5	15	24
Bay	67	264	719	Manatee	84	434	1,162
Bradford	6	19	26	Marion	104	500	1,202
Brevard	173	1,090	3,209	Martin	74	372	1,020
Broward	999	6,152	20,536	Miami-Dade	1,138	7,085	24,617
Calhoun	5	11	20	Monroe	27	169	506
Charlotte	42	152	310	Nassau	13	60	124
Citrus	27	131	342	Okaloosa	91	336	855
Clay	40	98	155	Okeechobee	8	38	88
Collier	124	655	2,245	Orange	478	3,357	10,878
Columbia	14	41	76	Osceola	35	174	422
De Soto	7	30	57	Palm Beach	647	3,852	15,759
Duval	411	2,952	11,774	Pasco	114	875	1,487
Escambia	137	522	1,371	Pinellas	471	3,363	11,074
Flagler	14	49	92	Polk	169	1,045	2,638
Gadsden	10	41	103	Putnam	25	87	169
Gulf	5	12	28	St. Johns	38	104	326
Hardee	7	18	38	St. Lucie	70	175	359
Hendry	10	35	63	Santa Rosa	19	74	146
Hernando	43	258	612	Sarasota	199	1,635	5,453
Highlands	25	117	246	Seminole	224	1,441	5,551
Hillsborough	523	4,709	15,305	Sumter	6	18	42
Holmes	4	9	15	Suwannee	13	57	93
Indian River	63	282	867	Taylor	6	14	23
Jackson	14	39	45	Volusia	169	806	2,096
Jefferson	7	15	23	Walton	6	23	59
Lake	73	291	710	Washington	8	24	80
Lee	207	897	2,814	Multicounty 1/	197	1,806	6,826

1/ Reporting units without a fixed location within the state or of unknown county location
Note: Private employment. For a list of three-digit code industries included see Table 17.38. Data are preliminary. Only counties for which data are disclosed are shown. Detail may not add to totals due to disclosure editing and/or rounding. See Tables 23.70, 23.71, 23.72, 23.73, and 23.74 for public employment data.

Source: State of Florida, Department of Labor and Employment Security, Bureau of Labor Market Information, "Employment and Wages" (ES-202), unpublished data.

University of Florida   **Bureau of Economic and Business Research**

Table 17.45. REAL ESTATE: AVERAGE MONTHLY PRIVATE REPORTING UNITS, EMPLOYMENT
AND PAYROLL COVERED BY UNEMPLOYMENT COMPENSATION LAW IN THE STATE
AND COUNTIES OF FLORIDA, 1999

County	Number of reporting units	Number of employees	Payroll ($1,000)	County	Number of reporting units	Number of employees	Payroll ($1,000)
				Real estate (SIC code 65)			
Florida	17,985	119,544	285,669	Leon	276	1,510	2,939
				Levy	16	41	58
Alachua	230	1,312	2,439	Madison	6	14	18
Baker	5	13	15	Manatee	276	1,173	2,167
Bay	168	1,298	2,037	Marion	226	1,374	2,615
Bradford	10	32	39	Martin	181	820	1,676
Brevard	405	2,182	4,131	Miami-Dade	2,971	18,943	48,554
Broward	1,936	10,779	29,063	Monroe	182	611	1,292
Charlotte	132	845	1,301	Nassau	34	102	219
Citrus	89	425	734	Okaloosa	210	2,064	3,438
Clay	95	432	1,146	Okeechobee	25	61	88
Collier	569	2,525	7,378	Orange	1,020	16,022	40,548
Columbia	29	70	110	Osceola	210	1,892	3,894
De Soto	13	29	32	Palm Beach	1,539	9,554	26,509
Dixie	6	21	23	Pasco	233	852	1,591
Duval	769	5,031	14,295	Pinellas	1,116	5,341	11,944
Escambia	232	1,600	2,570	Polk	347	1,613	2,920
Flagler	51	204	629	Putnam	37	79	86
Franklin	12	85	171	St. Johns	149	594	1,289
Gadsden	14	31	50	St. Lucie	143	608	1,061
Gulf	7	19	27	Santa Rosa	90	358	535
Hamilton	3	5	9	Sarasota	513	1,985	5,156
Hardee	13	46	72	Seminole	372	2,112	4,762
Hendry	20	53	60	Sumter	20	100	83
Hernando	72	300	441	Suwannee	10	17	34
Highlands	62	238	389	Taylor	8	31	51
Hillsborough	1,000	6,500	17,655	Volusia	457	2,211	3,567
Indian River	158	832	1,949	Wakulla	11	18	29
Jackson	20	42	51	Walton	50	418	857
Jefferson	6	9	12	Washington	10	26	62
Lake	185	2,813	4,662				
Lee	623	4,323	10,392	Multicounty 1/	308	6,475	15,067

1/ Reporting units without a fixed location within the state or of unknown county location.
Note: Private employment. For a list of three-digit code industries included see Table 17.38. Data are
preliminary. Only counties for which data are disclosed are shown. Detail may not add to totals due to
disclosure editing and/or rounding. See Tables 23.70, 23.71, 23.72, 23.73, and 23.74 for public
employment data.

Source: State of Florida, Department of Labor and Employment Security, Bureau of Labor Market Information, "Employment and Wages" (ES-202), unpublished data.

University of Florida   **Bureau of Economic and Business Research**

Table 17.47. REAL ESTATE: HOMEOWNER AND RENTAL VACANCY RATES IN FLORIDA OTHER SUNBELT STATES, OTHER POPULOUS STATES, AND THE UNITED STATES, SPECIFIED YEARS 1990 THROUGH 1999

State	Homeowner vacancy rates					Rental vacancy rates				
	1990	1996	1997	1998	1999	1990	1996	1997	1998	1999
Sunbelt states										
Florida	2.7	2.4	2.5	2.3	2.3	9.0	9.0	9.5	8.8	10.3
Alabama	1.5	1.8	1.7	2.7	2.3	8.1	8.7	7.3	9.7	13.5
Arizona	2.5	1.7	2.8	2.8	1.9	10.7	10.2	9.1	9.3	10.6
Arkansas	2.5	1.4	1.4	2.0	2.4	7.9	7.2	8.1	13.1	11.4
California	1.8	2.0	1.8	1.7	1.5	6.0	7.2	6.5	6.0	5.0
Georgia	1.8	2.0	1.5	1.6	1.8	9.4	11.6	11.2	12.0	10.3
Louisiana	1.7	1.1	1.3	1.5	1.4	13.1	7.8	8.4	9.7	12.8
Mississippi	1.6	1.0	1.1	1.2	1.8	8.7	13.2	11.5	9.9	11.2
New Mexico	2.4	1.3	2.2	1.8	2.4	13.7	7.1	9.5	10.2	12.5
North Carolina	1.6	1.4	1.8	2.1	1.9	7.2	8.0	9.7	11.5	10.8
Oklahoma	3.1	1.6	2.3	2.5	2.8	14.6	11.0	11.4	12.9	14.0
South Carolina	1.0	1.7	1.5	1.2	1.5	8.4	14.1	15.1	16.7	16.4
Tennessee	2.4	1.6	1.3	1.2	1.7	9.5	5.4	7.2	7.4	8.2
Texas	2.5	1.4	1.8	2.0	1.6	9.7	8.0	8.4	8.6	9.3
Virginia	1.7	2.2	2.4	2.8	3.0	5.8	7.4	6.3	8.4	9.0
Other populous states										
Illinois	1.3	1.4	1.6	1.7	1.5	6.1	7.9	8.5	7.4	6.9
Indiana	1.5	1.1	1.4	1.7	1.4	5.3	6.9	7.2	8.1	11.5
Massachusetts	1.4	1.1	0.8	0.9	0.9	6.9	5.8	5.2	5.7	4.7
Michigan	1.1	1.4	1.2	1.2	1.0	7.3	10.2	8.9	8.3	10.2
New Jersey	1.8	1.6	2.0	1.4	1.2	5.9	7.7	5.5	4.5	3.9
New York	1.8	1.7	2.0	1.9	1.6	4.9	6.9	6.2	6.6	6.1
Ohio	1.2	1.1	1.0	1.5	1.1	5.5	8.1	8.9	8.7	9.8
Pennsylvania	1.1	1.6	1.4	1.7	1.6	7.2	8.7	10.1	9.1	10.3
United States	1.7	1.6	1.6	1.7	1.7	7.2	7.8	7.7	7.9	8.1

Note: Data are based on a monthly sample survey conducted by the Bureau of the Census. See Glossary for definitions.

Source: U.S., Department of Commerce, Bureau of the Census, *Housing Vacancies and Homeownership Annual Statistics: 1999,* Internet site <http://www.census.gov/hhes/www/housing/hvs/annual99/ann99ind.html> (accessed 9 June 2000).

University of Florida   **Bureau of Economic and Business Research**

Table 17.48. REAL ESTATE: LICENSED BROKERS AND SALESPERSONS IN THE STATE AND COUNTIES OF FLORIDA, JULY 24, 2000

Location of licensee	Brokers	Sales-persons	Location of licensee	Brokers	Sales-persons
Total 1/	64,952	182,900	Lafayette	4	7
Out-of-state	3,301	8,298	Lake	842	2,430
Unknown	16	173	Lee	2,483	6,689
Foreign	76	206	Leon	869	1,898
Alachua	715	1,441	Levy	114	242
Baker	17	52	Liberty	4	5
Bay	530	1,398	Madison	26	48
Bradford	40	86	Manatee	885	2,422
Brevard	1,748	4,838	Marion	923	2,247
Broward	6,232	21,664	Martin	824	1,930
Calhoun	14	31	Miami-Dade	7,346	22,448
Charlotte	570	1,745	Monroe	570	1,442
Citrus	472	1,185	Nassau	169	461
Clay	412	1,193	Okaloosa	811	1,918
Collier	1,791	5,181	Okeechobee	82	179
Columbia	123	307	Orange	3,689	12,294
De Soto	79	160	Osceola	522	2,239
Dixie	20	44	Palm Beach	5,983	17,133
Duval	2,232	5,446	Pasco	869	2,621
Escambia	724	1,972	Pinellas	4,348	10,677
Flagler	255	876	Polk	1,196	2,654
Franklin	43	145	Putnam	160	327
Gadsden	61	120	St. Johns	682	1,590
Gilchrist	29	57	St. Lucie	671	1,578
Glades	10	30	Santa Rosa	393	1,195
Gulf	42	110	Sarasota	2,245	5,825
Hamilton	13	11	Seminole	1,705	5,004
Hardee	44	95	Sumter	75	233
Hendry	68	132	Suwannee	67	154
Hernando	365	1,305	Taylor	29	55
Highlands	248	594	Union	11	29
Hillsborough	3,198	8,645	Volusia	1,770	4,981
Holmes	29	51	Wakulla	70	187
Indian River	678	1,467	Walton	174	394
Jackson	72	148	Washington	44	92
Jefferson	30	66			

1/ Total includes all active, involuntary inactive, and voluntary inactive licensed persons.

Source: State of Florida, Department of Business and Professional Regulation, unpublished data.

University of Florida   **Bureau of Economic and Business Research**

Table 17.60. LIFE INSURANCE: NUMBER OF COMPANIES, POLICIES IN FORCE, PURCHASES AND AMOUNT OF LIFE INSURANCE, BENEFIT PAYMENTS, PREMIUM RECEIPTS MORTGAGES, AND REAL ESTATE OWNED BY U.S. LIFE INSURANCE COMPANIES IN FLORIDA AND THE UNITED STATES, 1998

Item	Florida	United States
Purchases of ordinary life insurance ($1,000,000)	85,865	1,324,565
Insurance in force		
Total		
Policies (1,000)	10,505	206,707
Amount ($1,000,000)	727,545	14,471,448
Ordinary		
Policies (1,000)	6,907	136,266
Amount ($1,000,000)	458,772	8,505,894
Group		
Amount ($1,000,000)	256,184	5,735,273
Industrial		
Policies (1,000)	1,214	24,065
Amount ($1,000,000)	858	17,365
Credit		
Policies 1/ (1,000)	2,384	46,376
Amount ($1,000,000)	11,730	212,917
Insurance and annuity benefit payments ($1,000)	12,719,144	232,086,705
Death payments	2,318,131	39,622,123
Matured endowments	26,613	475,097
Annuity payments	3,191,000	62,614,060
Disability payments	56,052	927,146
Surrender values	6,292,385	110,207,989
Policy and contract dividends	834,963	18,240,290
Payments to beneficiaries ($1,000), total	2,317,827	39,622,272
Ordinary	1,586,536	23,807,570
Group	638,368	14,416,399
Industrial	21,711	437,572
Credit	71,212	960,731
Premium receipts of companies ($1,000,000)	22,647	422,488
Life	5,764	106,230
Annuity	2,544	43,858
Health	5,888	89,574
Deposit-type funds	8,452	182,826
Mortgages owned by companies ($1,000), total	13,875,675	A/ 213,479,795
Farm	1,323,327	11,242,769
Nonfarm	12,552,349	A/ 202,237,026
Real estate owned by companies (1,000)	13,875,675	A/ 213,479,795

A/ Mortgages owned includes Puerto Rico and U.S. territories and possessions. Real estate owned includes Puerto Rico.
1/ Includes group credit certificates.

Source: American Council of Life Insurance, *Life Insurance Fact Book, 1999.*

University of Florida   **Bureau of Economic and Business Research**

Table 17.61. LIFE INSURANCE: DIRECT WRITINGS, DIRECT LOSSES, AND LIFE INSURANCE
IN FORCE IN FLORIDA, 1991 THROUGH 1998

(amounts rounded to thousands of dollars)

Year	Life insurance in force at end of year	Direct writings	Direct losses paid	Losses as a per-centage of writings
	All life insurance companies			
1991	378,564,234	5,561,421	4,939,376	88.8
1992	409,360,123	6,130,141	5,321,483	86.8
1993	445,360,646	6,108,608	3,202,293	52.4
1994	498,573,171	6,744,535	3,726,052	55.2
1995	(NA)	7,421,766	4,073,619	54.9
1996	(NA)	7,608,996	8,965,220	117.8
1997	(NA)	8,528,907	10,029,715	117.6
1998	(NA)	8,274,259	12,103,659	146.3
	Florida life insurance companies only			
1991	15,232,004	241,948	116,200	48.0
1992	15,839,284	214,372	159,425	74.4
1993	17,893,604	208,847	91,460	43.8
1994	20,478,864	239,026	92,493	38.7
1995	(NA)	248,262	105,880	42.6
1996	(NA)	255,081	159,880	62.7
1997	(NA)	193,997	103,280	53.2
1998	(NA)	192,405	106,889	55.6

(NA) Not available.
Note: Includes ordinary, group, industrial, and credit insurance and annuities.

Table 17.62. FRATERNAL INSURANCE SOCIETIES: DIRECT PREMIUMS WRITTEN, BENEFITS
PAID, AND INSURANCE IN FORCE IN FLORIDA, 1991 THROUGH 1998

(rounded to thousands of dollars)

Year	Life insurance in force at end of year	Direct premiums written		Direct losses paid	
		Life and annuities	Accident and health	Life	Accident and health
1991	4,580,593	112,686	6,650	30,978	5,546
1992	4,951,219	148,764	7,842	29,627	6,559
1993	5,315,106	141,262	7,536	45,781	5,885
1994	5,638,132	135,716	7,215	59,808	7,189
1995	(NA)	129,801	9,460	129,801	5,111
1996	(NA)	141,480	13,392	141,480	8,389
1997	(NA)	140,065	16,369	132,478	10,463
1998	(NA)	143,068	17,027	139,418	12,022

(NA) Not available.

Source for Tables 17.61 and 17.62: State of Florida, Department of Insurance, *Florida Department of Insurance 1999 Annual Report,* and previous editions.

University of Florida   **Bureau of Economic and Business Research**

Table 17.72. PROPERTY AND CASUALTY INSURANCE: PREMIUMS WRITTEN AND LOSSES
PAID BY PROPERTY AND CASUALTY, TITLE, AND LIFE INSURANCE
COMPANIES IN FLORIDA, 1998

(rounded to thousands of dollars)

	All companies		Florida companies	
Line of business	Direct premiums written	Direct losses paid	Direct premiums written	Direct losses paid
Total	18,015,683	9,967,829	3,483,576	2,023,964
Fire	191,315	52,919	32,706	12,988
Allied lines	191,653	55,030	27,151	3,982
Multiple peril crop	37,032	22,920	0	0
Federal Flood	397,588	62,829	123,097	22,455
Farmowners' multiple peril	12,645	6,411	757	246
Homeowners' multiple peril	2,322,668	743,291	413,354	106,164
Commercial multiple peril	1,191,702	526,862	116,681	44,907
Mortgage guaranty	186,972	62,406	629	65
Ocean marine	152,329	80,924	8,879	2,049
Inland marine	380,932	172,472	44,950	18,583
Financial guaranty	71,305	-22,473	0	1
Medical malpractice	406,445	289,916	89,747	44,965
Earthquake	2,894	2,174	17	0
Accident and health, total 1/	6,261,256	5,055,716	2,170,672	1,760,252
Group	219,061	152,103	23,154	15,620
Credit	17,756	2,786	164	61
Collectively renewable	391	56	0	0
Noncancellable	-12	7	0	0
Guaranteed renewable	68,607	33,838	0	0
Nonrenewable for stated reasons only	22,661	17,281	0	0
Other accident only	9,036	2,385	0	0
All other	38,439	6,370	32,181	1,281
Federal Employees Health Benefits	0	21	0	0
Workers' compensation	2,216,505	1,572,567	742,532	712,143
Other liability	888,132	506,051	46,778	22,631
Products liability	46,984	41,920	1,045	216
Private passenger automobile no-fault, PIP	1,164,291	855,735	311,872	233,863
Other private passenger automobile liability	3,748,747	2,265,379	721,941	372,098
Commercial automobile no-fault, PIP	31,059	22,230	6,823	7,644
Other commercial automobile liability	805,595	537,697	95,590	61,889
Private passenger automobile physical damage	2,390,348	1,470,565	503,427	303,523
Commercial automobile physical damage	230,342	138,218	26,276	13,449
Aircraft (all perils)	66,567	48,005	0	0
Fidelity	24,774	21,421	1,378	511
Surety	197,569	69,441	46,357	4,083
Burglary and theft	5,273	1,078	184	5
Boiler and machinery	24,359	12,512	29	20
Credit	38,666	9,482	7,090	1,736
All other lines	215,055	124,999	58,786	16,788

PIP Personal injury protection.
1/ Includes policies written by life insurance companies.

Source: State of Florida, Department of Insurance, *Florida Department of Insurance 1999 Annual Report.*

University of Florida   **Bureau of Economic and Business Research**

PERSONAL AND BUSINESS SERVICES

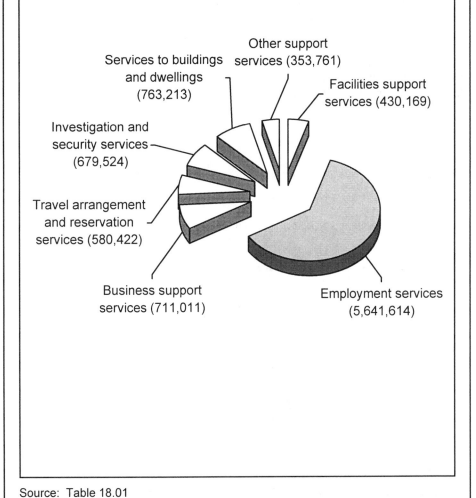

Administrative and Support Services Employment, 1997

Other support services (353,761)

Services to buildings and dwellings (763,213)

Facilities support services (430,169)

Investigation and security services (679,524)

Travel arrangement and reservation services (580,422)

Business support services (711,011)

Employment services (5,641,614)

Source: Table 18.01

SECTION 18.00
PERSONAL AND BUSINESS SERVICES

TABLES LISTED BY MAJOR HEADINGS

Table 18.01. ADMINISTRATIVE AND SUPPORT AND WASTE MANAGEMENT AND REMEDIATION
SERVICES AND OTHER SERVICES: ESTABLISHMENT, EMPLOYMENT, AND PAYROLL
IN FLORIDA, 1997

NAICS code	Industry	Number of estab- lishments	Number of em- ployees 1/	Payroll ($1,000)
56	Administrative and support and waste management and remediation services	21,046	574,246	10,225,346
561	Administrative and support services	20400	560775	9844689
5612	Facilities support services	136	13,793	430,169
5613	Employment services	2,265	345,942	5,641,614
5614	Business support services	2,634	33,979	711,011
5615	Travel arrangement and reservation services	3,061	24,882	580,422
5616	Investigation and security services	1,789	43,752	679,524
5617	Services to buildings and dwellings	6,675	57,882	763,213
5619	Other support services	1,812	18,616	353,761
562	Waste management and remediation services	646	13,471	380,657
5621	Waste collection	248	7,541	212,032
5622	Waste treatment and disposal	100	2,126	66,830
5629	Remediation and other waste management services	298	3,804	101,795
81	Other services (except public administration)	26,121	146,360	2,665,728
811	Repair and maintenance	14,726	72,673	1,618,300
8111	Automotive repair and maintenance	9,370	42,277	828,168
8112	Electronic and precision equipment repair and maintenance	1,380	8,145	249,429
8113	Commercial and industrial machinery and equipment (except auto and electronic) repair and maintenance	1,238	8,756	241,251
8114	Personal and household goods repair and maintenance	2,738	13,495	299,452
812	Personal and laundry services	11,395	73,687	1,047,428
8121	Personal care services	6,477	31,438	402,841
8122	Death care services	876	9,983	184,168
8123	Drycleaning and laundry services	2,708	21,370	306,295
8129	Other personal services	1,334	10,896	154,124

1/ Paid employment for the pay period including March 12.
Note: The economic censuses are conducted on a 5-year cycle collecting data for years ending in 2 and 7. Data are for North American Classification System (NAICS) codes 56 and 81 and may not be comparable to earlier years. See Glossary for definition.

Source: U.S., Department of Commerce, Bureau of the Census, *1997 Economic Census: Administrative and Support and Waste Management and Remediation Services,* Geographic Area Series EC97S56A-FL, Issued January 2000, Internet site <http://www.census.gov/prod/ec97/97s56-fl.pdf>, and *1997 Economic Census: Other Services (Except Public Administration),* Geographic Area Series EC97M31A-FL, Issued May 2000, Internet site <http://www.census.gov/prod/ec97/97s81-fl.pdf> (accessed 26 June 2000).

Table 18.02. PROFESSIONAL, SCIENTIFIC, AND TECHNICAL SERVICES: ESTABLISHMENTS
EMPLOYMENT, AND PAYROLL IN FLORIDA, 1997

NAICS code	Industry	Number of establishments	Number of employees 1/	Payroll ($1,000)
54	Professional, scientific, and technical services	42,403	276,263	10,803,522
5411	Legal services	13,241	67,822	3,456,158
54111	Offices of lawyers	12,628	64,507	3,358,702
54119	Other legal services	613	3,315	97,456
5412	Accounting, tax return preparations, bookkeeping, and payroll services	6,871	54,881	1,394,911
5413	Architectural, engineering, and related services	6,125	52,415	2,031,394
54131	Architectural services	1,472	7,826	307,179
54133	Engineering services	3,270	34,323	1,446,230
54134	Drafting services	177	393	11,330
54135	Building inspection services	243	617	12,708
54136	Geophysical surveying and mapping services	13	18	530
54137	Surveying and mapping (except geophysical) services	674	5,543	142,421
54138	Testing laboratories	276	3,695	110,996
5414	Specialized design services	2,051	6,499	174,718
54141	Interior design services	1,096	3,363	88,792
54142	Industrial design services	54	178	4,144
54143	Graphic design services	848	2,479	65,538
54149	Other specialized design services	53	479	16,244
5415	Computer systems design and related services	3,720	31,272	1,533,501
5416	Management, scientific, and technical consulting services	5,908	28,231	1,264,445
54161	Management consulting services	4,570	22,531	1,044,343
54162	Environmental consulting services	414	2,355	77,016
54169	Other scientific and technical consulting services	924	3,345	143,086
5417	Scientific research and development services	366	3,739	146,481
54171	Research and development in the physical, engineering, and life sciences	324	3,131	129,682
54172	Research and development in the social sciences and humanities	42	608	16,799
5418	Advertising and related services	2,695	19,034	565,023
54181	Advertising agencies	955	5,273	218,469
54182	Public relations agencies	385	1,441	47,984
54183	Media buying services	69	272	9,205
54184	Media representatives	214	1,469	47,996
54185	Display advertising	166	3,425	48,669
54186	Direct mail advertising	208	3,914	109,658
54187	Advertising material distribution services	32	132	3,259
54189	Other services related to advertising	666	3,108	79,783
5419	Other professional, scientific, and technical services	1,426	12,370	236,891
54191	Marketing research and public opinion polling	208	7,023	132,457
54192	Photographic services	921	4,248	75,158
54193	Translation and interpretation services	80	221	6,953
54199	All other professional, scientific, and technical services	217	878	22,323

1/ Paid employment for pay period including March 12.
Note: The economic censuses are conducted on a 5-year cycle collecting data for years ending in 2 and 7. Data are for North American Classification System (NAICS) code 54 and may not be comparable to earlier years. See Glossary for definition.

Source: U.S., Department of Commerce, Bureau of the Census, *1997 Economic Census: Professional; Scientific, and Technical Services,* Geographic Area Series EC97S54A-FL, Issued December 1999, Internet site <http://www.census.gov/prod/ec97/97s54-fl.pdf> (accessed 27 June 2000).

Table 18.05. ADMINISTRATIVE AND SUPPORT AND WASTE MANAGEMENT AND REMEDIATION SERVICES: ESTABLISHMENTS, EMPLOYMENT, AND PAYROLL IN THE STATE AND COUNTIES OF FLORIDA, 1997

County	Number of estab- lishments	Number of em- ployees 1/	Annual payroll ($1,000)	County	Number of estab- lishments	Number of em- ployees 1/	Annual payroll ($1,000)
Florida	21,046	574,246	10,225,346	Lake	147	1,475	34,970
				Lee	571	12,676	197,513
Alachua	204	3,180	53,374	Leon	314	4,767	74,423
Baker	9	26	763	Levy	14	27	389
Bay	159	4,425	87,794	Liberty	1	(D)	(D)
Bradford	9	28	666	Madison	6	17	203
Brevard	527	11,076	291,684	Manatee	258	29,384	491,993
Broward	3,002	58,720	1,237,310	Marion	203	2,858	39,277
Calhoun	2	(D)	(D)	Martin	186	1,543	38,674
Charlotte	113	1,640	22,669	Miami-Dade	3,336	71,916	1,319,742
Citrus	102	923	17,815	Monroe	149	890	19,308
Clay	120	974	19,519	Nassau	43	219	4,725
Collier	384	8,457	132,081	Okaloosa	219	9,167	125,948
Columbia	31	1,018	29,263	Okeechobee	18	266	7,279
De Soto	8	19	397	Orange	1,471	50,044	841,151
Dixie	2	(D)	(D)	Osceola	168	2,329	36,161
Duval	1,013	32,888	562,005	Palm Beach	1,972	44,306	859,675
Escambia	274	10,722	179,168	Pasco	281	3,664	50,514
Flagler	51	738	12,903	Pinellas	1,377	52,710	911,700
Franklin	6	(D)	(D)	Polk	378	9,541	125,311
Gadsden	14	390	8,523	Putnam	39	169	3,278
Gilchrist	4	14	133	St. Johns	140	3,779	62,497
Glades	6	(D)	(D)	St. Lucie	172	2,267	28,301
Gulf	3	6	286	Santa Rosa	86	1,564	22,684
Hamilton	0	0	0	Sarasota	564	22,705	367,708
Hardee	6	19	449	Seminole	557	8,248	185,332
Hendry	12	230	899	Sumter	14	42	373
Hernando	113	3,407	54,222	Suwannee	13	84	1,235
Highlands	56	2,414	24,359	Taylor	17	94	1,551
Hillsborough	1,395	85,558	1,449,086	Union	2	(D)	(D)
Holmes	5	24	517	Volusia	473	8,451	144,718
Indian River	142	1,642	27,251	Wakulla	12	29	399
Jackson	27	120	2,163	Walton	36	141	2,083
Jefferson	3	4	19	Washington	7	65	663
Lafayette	0	0	0				

(D) Data withheld to avoid disclosure of information about individual firms.
1/ Paid employment for the pay period including March 12.
Note: The economic censuses are conducted on a 5-year cycle collecting data for years ending in 2 and 7. Data are for North American Classification System (NAICS) code 81 and may not be comparable to earlier years. See Glossary for definition.

Source: U.S., Department of Commerce, Bureau of the Census, *1997 Economic Census: Administrative and Support and Waste Management and Remediation Services,* Geographic Area Series EC97S56A-FL, Issued January 2000, Internet site <http://www.census.gov/prod/ec97/97s56-fl.pdf> (accessed 26 June 2000).

University of Florida   **Bureau of Economic and Business Research**

Table 18.06. PROFESSIONAL, SCIENTIFIC, AND TECHNICAL SERVICES: ESTABLISHMENTS EMPLOYMENT, AND PAYROLL IN THE STATE AND COUNTIES OF FLORIDA, 1997

County	Number of estab- lishments	Number of em- ployees 1/	Annual payroll ($1,000)	County	Number of estab- lishments	Number of em- ployees 1/	Annual payroll ($1,000)
Florida	42,403	276,263	10,803,522	Lake	313	1,397	37,215
				Lee	997	6,053	197,398
Alachua	570	3,788	126,389	Leon	838	6,865	292,939
Baker	8	32	361	Levy	30	104	2,099
Bay	268	1,730	56,057	Liberty	1	A/	(D)
Bradford	22	72	1,913	Madison	13	64	1,153
Brevard	1,073	11,192	455,048	Manatee	445	1,884	56,106
Broward	5,625	27,496	1,103,659	Marion	361	1,882	52,788
Calhoun	11	34	514	Martin	409	1,598	55,452
Charlotte	194	1,083	37,337	Miami-Dade	7,821	42,781	1,855,966
Citrus	136	602	16,000	Monroe	262	835	26,580
Clay	188	685	19,759	Nassau	65	256	11,656
Collier	743	3,074	196,520	Okaloosa	417	3,181	113,508
Columbia	67	287	7,782	Okeechobee	28	142	2,159
De Soto	21	83	2,020	Orange	2,878	25,810	1,077,692
Dixie	8	14	246	Osceola	172	758	18,791
Duval	1,959	17,491	690,047	Palm Beach	4,211	21,787	985,480
Escambia	547	3,956	132,323	Pasco	417	1,931	41,566
Flagler	70	242	7,463	Pinellas	2,799	26,125	861,641
Franklin	14	48	838	Polk	712	4,006	135,354
Gadsden	39	133	2,415	Putnam	67	171	3,534
Gilchrist	10	38	671	St. Johns	294	961	34,671
Glades	9	34	742	St. Lucie	257	1,442	38,621
Gulf	15	147	2,808	Santa Rosa	122	490	11,412
Hamilton	7	A/	(D)	Sarasota	1,070	5,780	206,982
Hardee	22	69	1,363	Seminole	1,102	6,182	210,719
Hendry	23	71	1,763	Sumter	21	60	1,053
Hernando	132	523	11,386	Suwannee	35	94	1,725
Highlands	106	410	9,757	Taylor	18	61	1,427
Hillsborough	3,050	34,249	1,403,863	Union	3	12	159
Holmes	14	53	946	Volusia	844	4,048	120,708
Indian River	281	1,296	43,295	Wakulla	19	72	1,431
Jackson	35	177	4,625	Walton	54	162	4,609
Jefferson	16	36	608	Washington	19	80	1,213
Lafayette	6	B/	(D)				

(D) Data withheld to avoid disclosure of information about individual firms.
Employment ranges: A/ 0-19. B/ 50-99.
1/ Paid employment for pay period including March 12.
Note: The economic censuses are conducted on a 5-year cycle collecting data for years ending in 2 and 7. Data are for North American Classification System (NAICS) code 54 and may not be comparable to earlier years. See Glossary for definition.

Source: U.S., Department of Commerce, Bureau of the Census, *1997 Economic Census: Professional, Scientific, and Technical Services,* Geographic Area Series EC97S54A-FL, Issued December 1999, Internet site <http://www.census.gov/prod/ec97/97s54-fl.pdf> (accessed 27 June 2000).

Table 18.20. PERSONAL AND HOUSEHOLD SERVICES: AVERAGE MONTHLY PRIVATE REPORTING UNITS, EMPLOYMENT, AND PAYROLL COVERED BY UNEMPLOYMENT COMPENSATION LAW BY INDUSTRY IN FLORIDA, 1999

SIC code	Industry	Number of reporting units	Number of em-ployees	Payroll ($1,000)
72	Personal services	11,430	71,620	100,126
721	Laundry, cleaning, and garment services	3,227	23,242	33,310
722	Photographic studios, portrait	611	2,889	4,396
723	Beauty shops	5,265	27,858	35,809
724	Barber shops	152	442	534
725	Shoe repair shops and shoeshine parlors	117	230	296
726	Funeral service and crematories	444	5,062	10,295
729	Miscellaneous personal services	1,611	11,893	15,484
88	Private households 1/	11,639	15,866	22,842

1/ Private households which employ workers in domestic services such as cooks, maids, sitters, butlers, personal secretaries, gardeners and caretakers, and managers of personal affairs.
Note: Private employment. Data are preliminary. Detail may not add to totals due to disclosure editing and/or rounding. See Tables 23.70, 23.71, 23.72, 23.73, and 23.74 for public employment data.

Table 18.21. BUSINESS AND MISCELLANEOUS SERVICES: AVERAGE MONTHLY PRIVATE REPORTING UNITS, EMPLOYMENT, AND PAYROLL COVERED BY UNEMPLOYMENT COMPENSATION LAW BY INDUSTRY IN FLORIDA, 1998 AND 1999

SIC code	Industry	Number of reporting units	Number of em-ployees	Payroll ($1,000)
	1998 A/			
73	Business services	31,157	643,480	1,208,745
731	Advertising	1,645	11,742	37,312
732	Credit reporting and collection	447	6,661	15,114
733	Mailing, reproduction, and stenographic	2,371	18,484	37,777
734	Services to dwellings and other buildings	5,019	53,998	67,674
735	Miscellaneous equipment rental and leasing	1,862	16,884	45,662
736	Personnel supply services	3,519	348,360	501,783
737	Computer and data processing services	5,731	66,052	280,306
738	Miscellaneous business services	10,564	121,301	223,118
	1999 B/			
73	Business services	32,944	753,355	1,463,221
731	Advertising	1,763	12,622	41,747
732	Credit reporting and collection	461	6,866	17,773
733	Mailing, reproduction, and stenographic	2,544	19,587	42,555
734	Services to dwellings and other buildings	5,236	54,455	70,783
735	Miscellaneous equipment rental and leasing	1,932	18,026	48,716
736	Personnel supply services	3,382	441,847	638,644
737	Computer and data processing services	6,939	71,084	357,230
738	Miscellaneous business services	10,690	128,866	245,773

A/ Revised.
B/ Preliminary.
Note: Private employment. Detail may not add to totals due to disclosure editing and/or rounding. See Tables 23.70, 23.71, 23.72, 23.73, and 23.74 for public employment data.

Source for Tables 18.20 and 18.21: State of Florida, Department of Labor and Employment Security, Bureau of Labor Market Information, "Employment and Wages" (ES-202), unpublished data.

University of Florida   **Bureau of Economic and Business Research**

Table 18.22. AUTOMOTIVE AND MISCELLANEOUS REPAIR SERVICES: AVERAGE MONTHLY PRIVATE REPORTING UNITS, EMPLOYMENT, AND PAYROLL COVERED BY UNEMPLOYMENT COMPENSATION LAW BY INDUSTRY IN FLORIDA, 1999

SIC code	Industry	Number of reporting units	Number of employees	Payroll ($1,000)
75	Automotive repair, services, and parking	10,531	71,016	138,203
751	Automotive rental, no driver	811	19,067	43,073
752	Automobile parking	63	2,667	2,682
753	Automotive repair shops	8,000	36,774	74,810
754	Automotive services, except repair	1,656	12,507	17,639
76	Miscellaneous repair services	4,849	25,306	59,255
762	Electrical repair shops	1,643	9,598	23,375
763	Watch, clock, and jewelry repair	142	404	610
764	Reupholstery and furniture repair	445	1,371	2,121
769	Miscellaneous repair shops and related services	2,619	13,933	33,150

Note: Private employment. Data are preliminary. Detail may not add to totals due to disclosure editing and/or rounding. See Tables 23.70, 23.71, 23.72, 23.73, and 23.74 for public employment data.

Table 18.23. ENGINEERING AND MANAGEMENT SERVICES: AVERAGE MONTHLY PRIVATE REPORTING UNITS, EMPLOYMENT, AND PAYROLL COVERED BY UNEMPLOYMENT COMPENSATION LAW BY INDUSTRY IN FLORIDA, 1999

SIC code	Industry	Number of reporting units	Number of employees	Payroll ($1,000)
87	Engineering, accounting, research, management, and related services	26,369	197,508	695,631
871	Engineering, architectural, and surveying services	4,735	51,496	188,024
872	Accounting, auditing, and bookkeeping services	6,974	40,042	127,390
873	Research, development, and testing services	1,257	18,937	54,804
874	Management and public relations services	13,403	87,033	325,413

Note: Private employment. Data are preliminary. Detail may not add to totals due to disclosure editing and/or rounding. See Tables 23.70, 23.71, 23.72, 23.73, and 23.74 for public employment data.

Source for Tables 18.22 and 18.23: State of Florida, Department of Labor and Employment Security, Bureau of Labor Market Information, "Employment and Wages" (ES-202), unpublished data.

University of Florida   **Bureau of Economic and Business Research**

Table 18.28. SERVICES: AVERAGE MONTHLY PRIVATE REPORTING UNITS, EMPLOYMENT AND PAYROLL COVERED BY UNEMPLOYMENT COMPENSATION LAW IN THE STATE AND COUNTIES OF FLORIDA, 1998 AND 1999

County	Number of reporting units	Number of employees	Payroll ($1,000)	County	Number of reporting units	Number of employees	Payroll ($1,000)
			Services, 1998 A/ (SIC codes 70-89)				
Florida	163,661	2,207,353	5,006,481	Lake	1,414	17,861	32,483
				Lee	3,881	44,247	93,658
Alachua	2,183	31,459	68,666	Leon	3,145	36,047	87,684
Baker	57	615	850	Levy	154	1,125	1,665
Bay	1,379	17,329	34,697	Liberty	21	178	232
Bradford	116	1,090	1,854	Madison	107	1,129	1,578
Brevard	3,974	58,072	152,017	Manatee	2,047	50,948	91,423
Broward	19,392	197,692	472,758	Marion	1,785	16,725	33,454
Calhoun	48	830	1,253	Martin	1,589	16,283	36,129
Charlotte	976	11,764	24,465	Miami-Dade	26,869	290,587	732,635
Citrus	780	8,202	16,293	Monroe	1,314	12,594	25,404
Clay	822	10,572	18,960	Nassau	349	3,973	6,599
Collier	3,076	30,731	72,916	Okaloosa	1,613	22,781	43,106
Columbia	368	3,958	6,919	Okeechobee	221	2,305	4,378
De Soto	138	1,048	1,975	Orange	9,435	244,919	551,831
Dixie	44	199	385	Osceola	1,038	15,842	28,070
Duval	7,426	122,336	297,677	Palm Beach	15,255	156,630	396,803
Escambia	2,473	37,603	78,872	Pasco	2,132	23,244	48,599
Flagler	293	3,533	6,603	Pinellas	10,435	153,425	344,594
Franklin	70	559	774	Polk	3,126	43,103	89,658
Gadsden	194	1,313	1,976	Putnam	366	3,785	6,318
Gilchrist	42	440	623	St. Johns	1,156	11,742	25,638
Glades	28	178	194	St. Lucie	1,240	12,286	26,235
Gulf	72	710	1,094	Santa Rosa	605	6,687	11,919
Hamilton	44	295	459	Sarasota	4,512	48,668	107,441
Hardee	123	979	2,045	Seminole	3,400	35,986	82,319
Hendry	153	1,247	1,931	Sumter	150	1,008	1,492
Hernando	742	7,491	14,869	Suwannee	134	1,718	2,584
Highlands	534	6,104	10,297	Taylor	106	941	1,751
Hillsborough	10,194	207,451	472,140	Union	35	456	744
Holmes	73	737	1,103	Volusia	3,761	44,688	87,963
Indian River	1,290	12,810	26,694	Wakulla	67	554	893
Jackson	228	1,729	2,683	Walton	172	2,664	4,440
Jefferson	69	502	737	Washington	86	789	997
Lafayette	19	113	148	Multicounty 1/	4,531	101,747	200,833

See footnotes at end of table.   Continued . . .

University of Florida   **Bureau of Economic and Business Research**

Table 18.28. SERVICES: AVERAGE MONTHLY PRIVATE REPORTING UNITS, EMPLOYMENT AND PAYROLL COVERED BY UNEMPLOYMENT COMPENSATION LAW IN THE STATE AND COUNTIES OF FLORIDA, 1998 AND 1999 (Continued)

County	Number of reporting units	Number of employees	Payroll ($1,000)	County	Number of reporting units	Number of employees	Payroll ($1,000)
				Services, 1999 B/ (SIC codes 70-89)			
Florida	168,452	2,348,188	5,426,670	Lee	4,058	44,337	96,321
				Leon	3,176	37,564	94,964
Alachua	2,195	32,753	71,319	Levy	169	1,175	1,795
Baker	63	664	949	Liberty	20	121	184
Bay	1,395	17,622	36,023	Madison	105	1,353	1,800
Bradford	118	1,137	1,871	Manatee	2,074	46,746	85,826
Brevard	4,041	57,884	153,496	Marion	1,823	17,903	35,729
Broward	20,007	203,015	509,976	Martin	1,623	17,152	37,026
Calhoun	51	601	876	Miami-Dade	27,496	295,156	768,801
Charlotte	1,051	12,554	25,717	Monroe	1,348	12,725	25,850
Citrus	813	8,572	17,054	Nassau	365	4,292	7,578
Clay	866	13,276	21,130	Okaloosa	1,615	23,510	45,074
Collier	3,208	32,286	79,264	Okeechobee	224	2,353	4,832
Columbia	382	3,936	7,197	Orange	9,697	252,473	588,140
DeSoto	138	995	1,828	Osceola	1,081	15,627	29,333
Dixie	45	243	429	Palm Beach	15,670	164,848	432,708
Duval	7,521	124,552	312,754	Pasco	2,176	22,383	48,696
Escambia	2,456	39,994	82,663	Pinellas	10,540	157,267	364,700
Flagler	304	3,507	6,798	Polk	3,132	44,693	96,044
Franklin	73	556	840	Putnam	360	3,703	6,304
Gadsden	193	1,643	2,699	Saint Johns	1,218	12,381	27,896
Gilchrist	46	424	602	Saint Lucie	1,269	12,153	26,364
Glades	30	206	232	Santa Rosa	612	6,421	12,379
Gulf	67	720	1,190	Sarasota	4,682	67,625	137,459
Hamilton	49	305	444	Seminole	3,519	37,930	90,910
Hardee	122	1,028	2,150	Sumter	144	1,054	1,803
Hendry	150	1,235	1,870	Suwannee	147	1,734	2,638
Hernando	777	7,459	14,588	Taylor	108	963	1,786
Highlands	555	6,257	10,497	Union	36	266	485
Hillsborough	10,490	222,170	530,620	Volusia	3,846	45,647	94,410
Holmes	75	725	1,100	Wakulla	71	505	915
Indian River	1,316	13,241	29,400	Walton	199	2,882	4,760
Jackson	228	1,786	2,833	Washington	90	831	1,047
Jefferson	71	525	762				
Lafayette	24	198	242	Multicounty 1/	5,404	192,923	288,447
Lake	1,457	17,132	34,000	Out-of-state 2/	28	88	256

A/ Revised.
B/ Preliminary.
1/ Reporting units without a fixed location within the state or of unknown county location.
2/ Employment based in Florida, but working out of the state or country.
Note: Private employment. Only counties for which data are disclosed are shown. Detail may not add to totals due to disclosure editing and/or rounding. See Tables 23.70, 23.71, 23.72, 23.73, and 23.74 for public employment data.

Source: State of Florida, Department of Labor and Employment Security, Bureau of Labor Market Information, "Employment and Wages" (ES-202), unpublished data.

University of Florida   **Bureau of Economic and Business Research**

Table 18.30. PERSONAL SERVICES: AVERAGE MONTHLY PRIVATE REPORTING UNITS EMPLOYMENT AND PAYROLL COVERED BY UNEMPLOYMENT COMPENSATION LAW IN THE STATE AND COUNTIES OF FLORIDA, 1999

County	Number of reporting units	Number of employees	Payroll ($1,000)	County	Number of reporting units	Number of employees	Payroll ($1,000)
			Personal services (SIC code 72)				
Florida	11,430	71,620	100,127	Lake	123	591	834
				Lee	285	1,627	2,430
Alachua	135	999	1,196	Leon	161	1,907	3,295
Baker	8	28	29	Levy	10	49	62
Bay	93	509	671	Madison	6	40	52
Bradford	10	95	125	Manatee	170	1,355	1,903
Brevard	296	1,938	2,590	Marion	146	922	1,150
Broward	1,386	8,627	12,022	Martin	126	594	841
Calhoun	10	65	51	Miami-Dade	1,741	10,584	14,072
Charlotte	87	421	539	Monroe	72	216	314
Citrus	88	334	418	Nassau	33	121	149
Clay	83	444	448	Okaloosa	119	554	615
Collier	244	1,256	1,959	Okeechobee	17	67	74
Columbia	23	136	122	Orange	638	4,974	7,274
De Soto	14	34	34	Osceola	90	425	496
Duval	595	3,786	5,352	Palm Beach	967	5,862	8,841
Escambia	176	1,400	1,745	Pasco	201	991	1,117
Flagler	31	114	117	Pinellas	748	4,642	6,888
Franklin	3	8	12	Polk	224	1,342	1,833
Gadsden	17	69	71	Putnam	29	131	139
Gilchrist	3	13	16	St. Johns	73	411	535
Gulf	9	11	9	St. Lucie	106	570	691
Hamilton	5	25	20	Santa Rosa	48	238	245
Hendry	9	27	39	Sarasota	331	1,749	2,684
Hernando	70	311	297	Seminole	279	1,825	2,526
Highlands	51	234	221	Sumter	6	22	19
Hillsborough	631	5,463	7,611	Suwannee	7	47	61
Holmes	3	20	40	Taylor	11	32	38
Indian River	106	440	640	Volusia	313	1,673	2,035
Jackson	16	87	94	Walton	8	24	24
Jefferson	6	23	41	Washington	5	13	10
Lafayette	4	12	11	Multicounty 1/	119	1,046	2,271

1/ Reporting units without a fixed location within the state or of unknown county location.
Note: Private employment. For a list of three-digit code industries included see Table 18.20. Data are preliminary. Only counties for which data are disclosed are shown. Detail may not add to totals due to disclosure editing and/or rounding. See Tables 23.70, 23.71, 23.72, 23.73, and 23.74 for public employment data.

Source: State of Florida, Department of Labor and Employment Security, Bureau of Labor Market Information, "Employment and Wages" (ES-202), unpublished data.

University of Florida   **Bureau of Economic and Business Research**

Table 18.35. BUSINESS SERVICES: AVERAGE MONTHLY PRIVATE REPORTING UNITS, EMPLOYMENT AND PAYROLL COVERED BY UNEMPLOYMENT COMPENSATION LAW IN THE STATE AND COUNTIES OF FLORIDA, 1998 AND 1999

County	Number of re-porting units	Number of em-ployees	Payroll ($1,000)	County	Number of re-porting units	Number of em-ployees	Payroll ($1,000)
			Business services, 1998 A/ (SIC code 73)				
Florida	31,157	643,480	1,208,745	Lee	725	9,238	14,153
				Leon	558	7,080	13,785
Alachua	278	4,523	6,933	Levy	15	76	154
Baker	6	16	18	Madison	14	90	131
Bay	204	2,289	3,597	Manatee	384	33,988	54,246
Bradford	16	64	101	Marion	283	3,182	4,356
Brevard	753	11,336	24,747	Martin	251	2,367	3,924
Broward	3,940	53,745	119,416	Miami-Dade	4,706	68,416	130,867
Calhoun	4	9	11	Monroe	174	600	1,121
Charlotte	150	2,097	2,560	Nassau	51	237	537
Citrus	117	1,176	2,202	Okaloosa	260	8,041	11,571
Clay	139	2,406	3,495	Okeechobee	21	116	196
Collier	597	5,402	10,331	Orange	1,998	55,077	110,696
Columbia	47	527	570	Osceola	163	1,869	3,180
De Soto	15	87	192	Palm Beach	2,659	36,282	77,127
Dixie	4	13	21	Pasco	343	3,558	5,423
Duval	1,483	41,202	84,378	Pinellas	2,152	52,945	110,944
Escambia	413	8,562	11,057	Polk	476	9,273	15,447
Flagler	46	1,056	1,445	Putnam	48	754	1,009
Franklin	9	104	108	St. Johns	199	1,340	2,800
Gadsden	18	80	128	St. Lucie	198	1,402	1,982
Gilchrist	6	27	58	Santa Rosa	117	1,330	1,531
Gulf	6	31	31	Sarasota	814	8,111	13,937
Hardee	8	27	168	Seminole	837	11,056	24,510
Hendry	12	72	114	Sumter	21	182	298
Hernando	140	1,127	1,807	Suwannee	21	163	195
Highlands	69	914	922	Taylor	21	61	103
Hillsborough	2,371	103,852	195,832	Volusia	581	7,276	10,578
Holmes	7	28	51	Wakulla	11	46	73
Indian River	174	1,379	2,161	Walton	34	168	217
Jackson	28	129	226	Washington	8	36	71
Lake	202	3,948	4,181	Multicounty 1/	1,744	72,709	116,452

See footnotes at end of table.

Continued . . .

University of Florida

Table 18.35. BUSINESS SERVICES: AVERAGE MONTHLY PRIVATE REPORTING UNITS, EMPLOYMENT AND PAYROLL COVERED BY UNEMPLOYMENT COMPENSATION LAW IN THE STATE AND COUNTIES OF FLORIDA, 1998 AND 1999 (Continued)

County	Number of reporting units	Number of employees	Payroll ($1,000)	County	Number of reporting units	Number of employees	Payroll ($1,000)
				Business services, 1999 B/ (SIC code 73)			
Florida	32,944	753,355	1,463,221	Levy	18	100	239
				Madison	12	75	120
Alachua	296	5,439	8,489	Manatee	388	29,128	46,930
Baker	8	53	74	Marion	303	3,417	4,761
Bay	202	2,252	3,788	Martin	266	2,917	4,395
Bradford	15	89	107	Miami-Dade	4,821	69,734	148,484
Brevard	770	11,562	26,774	Monroe	188	651	1,502
Broward	4,200	58,475	142,562	Nassau	54	245	628
Calhoun	4	10	14	Okaloosa	258	9,130	13,638
Charlotte	174	2,705	3,458	Okeechobee	23	124	197
Citrus	127	1,481	2,854	Orange	2,116	58,836	125,196
Collier	613	5,901	12,120	Osceola	175	1,817	3,184
Columbia	49	533	682	Palm Beach	2,828	42,697	101,348
De Soto	16	75	161	Pasco	360	3,548	6,495
Duval	1,564	42,220	96,815	Pinellas	2,245	58,368	126,884
Escambia	414	10,512	14,608	Polk	495	9,996	17,738
Flagler	46	924	1,643	Putnam	44	790	996
Franklin	7	41	40	St. Johns	214	1,543	3,669
Gadsden	18	75	116	St. Lucie	204	1,593	2,341
Gilchrist	9	34	57	Santa Rosa	112	1,246	1,894
Gulf	3	10	10	Sarasota	876	27,176	41,718
Hardee	9	32	148	Seminole	881	12,413	29,480
Hendry	12	97	150	Sumter	19	237	379
Hernando	145	1,295	1,942	Suwannee	23	159	232
Highlands	78	1,352	1,305	Taylor	20	62	110
Hillsborough	2,456	111,290	222,385	Union	4	5	15
Holmes	8	36	64	Volusia	614	7,279	11,141
Indian River	180	1,502	2,849	Wakulla	11	42	72
Jackson	28	113	187	Walton	34	149	250
Lake	219	2,789	3,625	Washington	7	25	27
Lee	813	10,389	16,827	Multicounty 1/	2,108	153,046	182,854
Leon	587	8,004	17,148	Out-of-state 2/	20	80	242

A/ Revised.
B/ Preliminary.
1/ Reporting units without a fixed location within the state or of unknown county location.
2/ Employment based in Florida, but working out of the state or country.
Note: Private employment. For a list of three-digit code industries included see Table 18.21. Data are preliminary. Only counties for which data are disclosed are shown. Detail may not add due to disclosure editing and/or rounding. See Tables 23.70, 23.71, 23.72, 23.73, and 23.74 for public employment data.

Source: State of Florida, Department of Labor and Employment Security, Bureau of Labor Market Information, "Employment and Wages" (ES-202), unpublished data.

Table 18.40. AUTOMOTIVE REPAIR, SERVICES, AND PARKING: AVERAGE MONTHLY PRIVATE REPORTING UNITS, EMPLOYMENT, AND PAYROLL COVERED BY UNEMPLOYMENT COMPENSATION LAW IN THE STATE AND COUNTIES OF FLORIDA, 1999

County	Number of reporting units	Number of employees	Payroll ($1,000)	County	Number of reporting units	Number of employees	Payroll ($1,000)
			Automotive repair, services, and parking (SIC code 75)				
Florida	10,531	71,016	138,203	Leon	195	1,545	2,664
				Levy	10	50	65
Alachua	140	969	1,699	Madison	11	36	52
Baker	8	18	30	Manatee	147	751	1,329
Bay	91	543	884	Marion	169	863	1,602
Bradford	8	21	36	Martin	89	324	636
Brevard	312	1,609	2,757	Miami-Dade	1,536	11,311	21,281
Broward	1,212	9,420	19,925	Monroe	63	319	566
Charlotte	82	287	499	Nassau	32	131	251
Citrus	71	257	420	Okaloosa	141	760	1,289
Clay	72	835	1,191	Okeechobee	29	102	156
Collier	165	729	1,479	Orange	571	8,677	18,087
Columbia	44	141	212	Osceola	90	436	716
De Soto	13	37	48	Palm Beach	758	4,106	8,084
Duval	548	4,156	8,751	Pasco	211	1,010	1,870
Escambia	223	1,443	2,407	Pinellas	664	3,384	6,346
Flagler	18	69	124	Polk	265	1,710	3,619
Gadsden	13	55	77	Putnam	34	135	240
Gulf	5	13	24	St. Johns	58	223	414
Hamilton	4	10	13	St. Lucie	123	421	786
Hardee	14	40	51	Santa Rosa	54	360	619
Hendry	18	38	68	Sarasota	255	1,277	2,275
Hernando	74	359	608	Seminole	202	1,068	2,283
Highlands	39	124	210	Sumter	15	73	113
Hillsborough	678	5,509	11,347	Suwannee	14	44	69
Holmes	9	41	56	Taylor	9	28	46
Indian River	74	344	602	Volusia	286	1,455	2,373
Jackson	18	80	132	Wakulla	10	28	45
Jefferson	3	10	18	Walton	14	41	62
Lake	119	504	879	Washington	4	9	20
Lee	306	2,184	4,222	Multicounty 1/	89	458	1,415

1/ Reporting units without a fixed location within the state or of unknown county location.

Note: Private employment. For a list of three-digit code industries included see Table 18.22. Data are preliminary. Only counties for which data are disclosed are shown. Detail may not add to totals due to disclosure editing and/or rounding. See Tables 23.70, 23.71, 23.72, 23.73, and 23.74 for public employment data.

Source: State of Florida, Department of Labor and Employment Security, Bureau of Labor Market Information, "Employment and Wages" (ES-202), unpublished data.

Table 18.51. ENGINEERING, ACCOUNTING, RESEARCH, MANAGEMENT, AND RELATED SERVICES
AVERAGE MONTHLY PRIVATE REPORTING UNITS, EMPLOYMENT, AND PAYROLL COVERED
BY UNEMPLOYMENT COMPENSATION LAW IN THE STATE AND COUNTIES
OF FLORIDA, 1999

County	Number of re-porting units	Number of em-ployees	Payroll ($1,000)	County	Number of re-porting units	Number of em-ployees	Payroll ($1,000)
			Engineering, accounting, research, management, and related services (SIC code 87)				
Florida	26,369	197,508	695,631	Leon	559	3,647	13,830
				Levy	20	58	118
Alachua	357	2,943	7,843	Madison	12	77	190
Bay	172	1,787	4,935	Manatee	288	1,165	4,043
Bradford	16	113	268	Marion	187	1,166	2,622
Brevard	639	13,951	53,869	Martin	250	1,044	3,416
Broward	3,216	18,954	70,915	Miami-Dade	4,151	25,258	95,054
Calhoun	6	12	17	Monroe	168	850	2,510
Charlotte	127	670	2,057	Nassau	56	146	436
Citrus	76	352	864	Okaloosa	246	3,264	11,364
Clay	126	751	2,504	Okeechobee	17	128	379
Collier	559	2,048	8,237	Orange	1,687	19,530	66,748
Columbia	37	217	628	Osceola	135	522	1,513
De Soto	10	19	26	Palm Beach	2,563	13,543	57,692
Dixie	5	19	82	Pasco	221	982	2,064
Duval	1,063	11,112	37,996	Pinellas	1,630	12,627	40,240
Escambia	284	2,782	8,199	Polk	408	2,506	8,375
Flagler	50	168	560	Putnam	43	77	135
Franklin	11	24	64	St. Johns	208	549	1,969
Gilchrist	4	8	8	St. Lucie	161	899	2,794
Glades	4	27	57	Santa Rosa	90	1,132	3,128
Gulf	9	60	119	Sarasota	722	4,794	14,832
Hardee	18	123	569	Seminole	663	4,829	14,572
Hendry	19	64	151	Sumter	19	34	105
Hernando	77	356	794	Suwannee	18	44	101
Highlands	47	206	513	Taylor	7	24	69
Hillsborough	1,725	18,724	68,283	Volusia	462	2,068	5,579
Holmes	10	49	63	Wakulla	11	91	204
Indian River	188	887	2,864	Walton	26	90	313
Jackson	18	90	258	Washington	13	53	101
Jefferson	11	32	91				
Lake	160	1,224	3,344	Multicounty 1/	1,655	13,836	51,135
Lee	609	4,320	12,725	Out-of-state 2/	6	6	11

1/ Reporting units without a fixed location within the state or of unknown county location.
2/ Employment based in Florida, but working out of the state or country.
Note: Private employment. For a list of three-digit code industries included see Table 18.23. Data
are preliminary. Only counties for which data are disclosed are shown. Detail may not add to totals
due to disclosure editing and/or rounding. See Tables 23.70, 23.71, 23.72, 23.73, and 23.74 for public
employment data.

Source: State of Florida, Department of Labor and Employment Security, Bureau of Labor Market Information, "Employment and Wages" (ES-202), unpublished data.

Table 18.56. ARCHITECTS AND ACCOUNTANTS: NUMBER LICENSED IN THE STATE
AND COUNTIES OF FLORIDA, JULY 24, 2000

Location of licensee	Archi-tects	Account-ants	Location of licensee	Archi-tects	Account-ants
Total 1/	9,457	27,703	Lafayette	0	3
Out-of-state	4,645	4,780	Lake	34	175
Foreign	31	142	Lee	113	443
Unknown	0	1	Leon	147	831
Alachua	109	342	Levy	2	16
Baker	0	8	Liberty	0	5
Bay	21	121	Madison	0	7
Bradford	1	14	Manatee	44	256
Brevard	61	438	Marion	24	140
Broward	410	3,120	Martin	41	155
Calhoun	0	7	Miami-Dade	1,175	3,619
Charlotte	16	69	Monroe	30	91
Citrus	11	47	Nassau	20	28
Clay	18	150	Okaloosa	36	128
Collier	99	299	Okeechobee	0	8
Columbia	1	41	Orange	418	1,702
De Soto	0	8	Osceola	19	73
Dixie	0	1	Palm Beach	406	2,140
Duval	250	1,412	Pasco	14	164
Escambia	99	306	Pinellas	250	1,577
Flagler	5	17	Polk	51	409
Franklin	5	8	Putnam	10	29
Gadsden	6	35	St. Johns	34	170
Gilchrist	0	2	St. Lucie	15	97
Glades	0	2	Santa Rosa	14	96
Gulf	2	6	Sarasota	158	490
Hamilton	0	3	Seminole	141	615
Hardee	1	9	Sumter	0	6
Hendry	3	20	Suwannee	2	16
Hernando	6	60	Taylor	2	12
Highlands	5	45	Union	0	2
Hillsborough	320	2,067	Volusia	60	406
Holmes	1	5	Wakulla	4	35
Indian River	45	129	Walton	14	6
Jackson	2	20	Washington	2	8
Jefferson	4	11			

1/ Total includes all active, involuntary inactive, and voluntary inactive licensed persons.

Source: State of Florida, Department of Business and Professional Regulation, unpublished data.

University of Florida **Bureau of Economic and Business Research**

TOURISM AND RECREATION

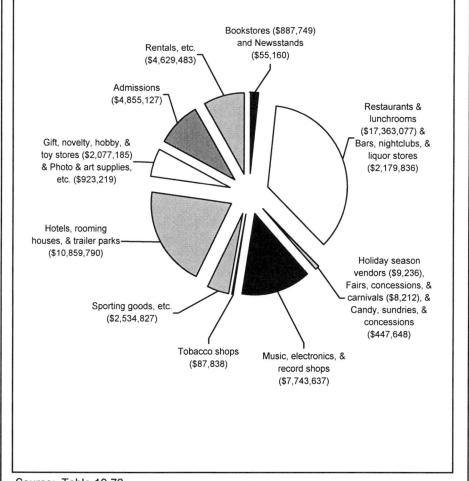

Taxable Sales of Tourist- and Recreation-related Businesses, 1999
($1,000)

Bookstores ($887,749) and Newsstands ($55,160)

Rentals, etc. ($4,629,483)

Admissions ($4,855,127)

Gift, novelty, hobby, & toy stores ($2,077,185) & Photo & art supplies, etc. ($923,219)

Restaurants & lunchrooms ($17,363,077) & Bars, nightclubs, & liquor stores ($2,179,836)

Hotels, rooming houses, & trailer parks ($10,859,790)

Holiday season vendors ($9,236), Fairs, concessions, & carnivals ($8,212), & Candy, sundries, & concessions ($447,648)

Sporting goods, etc. ($2,534,827)

Tobacco shops ($87,838)

Music, electronics, & record shops ($7,743,637)

Source: Table 19.70

SECTION 19.00
TOURISM AND RECREATION

TABLES LISTED BY MAJOR HEADINGS

University of Florida   **Bureau of Economic and Business Research**

Table 19.01. ARTS, ENTERTAINMENT, AND RECREATION: ESTABLISHMENTS, EMPLOYMENT RECEIPTS, AND ANNUAL PAYROLL BY KIND OF BUSINESS IN FLORIDA, 1997

NAICS code	Industry	Number of estab- lishments	Number of em- ployees 1/	Receipts ($1,000)	Annual payroll ($1,000)
72	Accommodation and foodservices	28,999	608,834	24,165,336	6,239,469
721	Accommodation	3,843	146,568	8,810,470	2,102,864
7211	Traveler accommodation	3,210	142,368	8,522,534	2,043,418
72111	Hotels (except casino hotels) and motels	3,089	141,746	8,479,059	2,034,609
72112	Casino hotels	2	A/	(D)	(D)
72119	Other traveler accommodation	119	B/	(D)	(D)
7212	Recreational vehicle parks and recreational camps	493	3,397	253,395	52,067
7213	Rooming and boarding houses	140	803	34,541	7,379
722	Foodservices and drinking places	25,156	462,266	15,354,866	4,136,605
7221	Full-service restaurants	11,989	253,417	8,228,070	2,371,461
7222	Limited-service eating places	10,245	173,621	5,604,318	1,397,145
7223	Special foodservices	1,113	21,310	914,101	243,213
72231	Foodservice contractors	644	16,990	738,269	204,953
72232	Caterers	299	3,673	119,942	30,863
72233	Mobile foodservices	170	647	55,890	7,397
7224	Drinking places (alcoholic beverages)	1,809	13,918	608,377	124,786

Note: See footnotes on Table 19.02

Table 19.02. ACCOMMODATION AND FOODSERVICES: ESTABLISHMENTS, EMPLOYMENT SALES, AND ANNUAL PAYROLL BY KIND OF BUSINESS IN FLORIDA, 1997

NAICS code	Industry	Number of estab- lishments	Number of em- ployees 1/	Sales ($1,000)	Annual payroll ($1,000)
71	Arts, entertainment, and recreation	4,763	103,980	7,871,475	1,972,914
711	Performing arts, spectator sports, and related industries	1,474	18,287	2,012,802	701,826
7111	Performing arts companies	284	2,294	168,494	49,378
7112	Spectator sports	387	11,202	1,166,745	533,889
7113	Promoters	189	2,980	414,764	58,325
7114	Agents/managers	152	656	132,176	22,748
7115	Independent artists, writers, and performers	462	1,155	130,623	37,486
712	Museums, historical sites, similar institutions	62	1,448	107,527	23,751
713	Amusement, gambling, and recreation	3,227	84,245	5,751,146	1,247,337
7131	Amusement parks and arcades	228	35,113	3,276,730	571,478
7132	Gambling industries	65	4,037	390,125	71,236
7139	Other amusement and recreation services	2,934	45,095	2,084,291	604,623

(D) Data withheld to avoid disclosure of information about individual firms.
Employment range: A/ 0-19. B/ 500-999.
1/ Paid employment for the pay period including March 12.
Note: The economic censuses are conducted on a 5-year cycle collecting data for years ending in 2 and 7. Data are for North American Classification System (NAICS) codes 71 and 72 and may not be comparable to earlier years. See Glossary for definition.

Source for Tables 19.01 and 19.02: U.S., Department of Commerce, Bureau of the Census, *1997 Economic Census: Arts, Entertainment, and Recreation,* Geographic Area Series EC97S71A-FL, Issued November 1999, and *1997 Economic Census: Accommodation and Foodservices,* Geographic Area Series EC97R72A-FL, Issued December 1999, Internet site <http://www.census.gov/prod/ec97/>, (accessed 26 June 2000).

University of Florida   **Bureau of Economic and Business Research**

Table 19.05. ARTS, ENTERTAINMENT, AND RECREATION AND ACCOMMODATION
AND FOODSERVICES: SALES OR RECEIPTS IN THE STATE AND COUNTIES
OF FLORIDA, 1997

(in thousands of dollars)

County	Arts, enter-tainment and recreation receipts	Accom-modation and food-services sales	County	Arts, enter-tainment and recreation receipts	Accom-modation and food-services sales
Florida	7,871,475	24,165,336	Lake	20,837	154,595
			Lee	123,089	699,097
Alachua	26,539	263,040	Leon	(D)	296,768
Baker	(D)	9,780	Levy	3,218	19,497
Bay	59,801	336,289	Liberty	0	(D)
Bradford	(D)	17,261	Madison	(D)	9,941
Brevard	125,397	495,297	Manatee	34,146	241,506
Broward	762,541	2,474,496	Marion	37,865	200,914
Calhoun	(D)	4,118	Martin	73,301	167,804
Charlotte	21,619	123,457	Miami-Dade	765,145	3,199,453
Citrus	19,475	66,323	Monroe	72,571	569,086
Clay	24,927	114,573	Nassau	7,366	143,312
Collier	85,429	536,740	Okaloosa	29,964	261,745
Columbia	5,547	54,117	Okeechobee	3,753	34,804
De Soto	2,124	12,413	Orange	3,314,175	4,058,657
Dixie	866	3,543	Osceola	87,756	762,955
Duval	187,580	917,173	Palm Beach	416,275	1,659,834
Escambia	47,159	350,884	Pasco	40,652	246,305
Flagler	10,975	42,350	Pinellas	202,904	1,383,434
Franklin	(D)	14,942	Polk	61,401	419,264
Gadsden	(D)	10,731	Putnam	948	37,485
Gilchrist	0	(D)	St. Johns	94,094	263,564
Glades	(D)	4,698	St. Lucie	21,838	147,643
Gulf	799	4,631	Santa Rosa	12,859	53,759
Hamilton	(D)	3,708	Sarasota	134,853	481,774
Hardee	1,280	7,351	Seminole	87,049	423,115
Hendry	7,208	18,414	Sumter	2,778	23,597
Hernando	17,061	74,047	Suwannee	876	15,512
Highlands	10,330	52,337	Taylor	1,665	11,881
Hillsborough	564,092	1,248,260	Union	(D)	(D)
Holmes	(D)	4,530	Volusia	156,483	635,582
Indian River	24,828	112,351	Wakulla	6,060	9,751
Jackson	1,803	25,991	Walton	3,831	107,172
Jefferson	(D)	3,351	Washington	(D)	8,771
Lafayette	0	3,120			

(D) Data withheld to avoid disclosure of information about individual firms.
Note: The economic censuses are conducted on a 5-year cycle collecting data for years ending in 2
and 7. Data are for North American Classification System (NAICS) codes 71 and 72 and may not be
comparable to earlier years. See Glossary for definition.

Source: U.S., Department of Commerce, Bureau of the Census, *1997 Economic Census: Arts, Enter-
tainment, and Recreation,* Geographic Area Series EC97S71A-FL, Issued November 1999, and *1997
Economic Census: Accommodation and Foodservices,* Geographic Area Series EC97R72A-FL, Issued
December 1999, Internet site <http://www.census.gov/prod/ec97/>, (accessed 26 June 2000).

Table 19.20. TOURISTS: CHARACTERISTICS OF AIR AND AUTOMOBILE VISITORS TO FLORIDA, 1998

Characteristic	Total	Air	Auto-mobile
Visitors (number)	48,698,736	27,082,875	21,615,861
Percentage	100.0	55.6	44.4
Purpose of trip (percentage)			
Leisure	80.1	70.0	87.6
General vacation	36.5	30.2	41.8
Visit friends/relatives	27.2	25.8	28.4
Special event	6.3	6.7	5.8
Getaway weekend	5.0	3.9	6.0
Other personal	5.0	3.5	5.6
Business	19.9	30.0	12.4
Convention	3.7	6.7	2.0
Seminar/training	4.4	6.2	3.2
Other group meetings	2.6	4.5	1.6
Sales/consulting	2.1	3.4	1.3
Other	7.1	9.2	4.3
Average expenditure per person per day (dollars)	117.80	157.30	87.20
Transportation	32.50	56.10	11.90
Food	23.10	26.90	20.50
Room	24.80	32.00	20.10
Shopping	15.30	17.80	13.80
Entertainment	16.50	18.30	15.70
Miscellaneous	5.60	6.40	5.00
Length of trip (average nights)	8.2	7.4	9.1
1-3 nights	26.3	22.9	25.0
4-7 nights	39.5	47.5	33.9
8 nights or over	34.3	29.7	41.1
Travel party size (average persons)	2.6	2.2	2.9
One adult	30.0	44.3	16.1
Couples (male/female)	27.0	21.6	32.3
Two males or two females	6.9	7.4	6.6
Families	10.0	10.0	9.8
Accommodations (percentage)	26.0	16.7	35.2
Paid lodging	65.1	65.8	65.3
Hotel/motel	50.9	56.0	48.0
Condominium/timeshare	5.4	4.0	7.1
Bed and breakfast	0.4	0.3	0.4
Ship	1.5	2.5	0.4
Other	6.9	3.1	9.4
Unpaid lodging	31.3	31.2	31.0
Private home	21.4	21.8	21.5
Other	9.9	9.4	9.5
One-way distance traveled (average miles)	748	955	589
Miles traveled (percentage)			
100 miles or less	0.9	0.0	1.7
101-150	1.5	0.0	2.7
151-250	5.9	0.2	9.9
251-500	19.1	5.8	27.9
501-750	20.7	17.3	23.3
750-1,000	37.5	50.7	29.2
Over 1,000 miles	14.5	25.9	5.3
Rental car use (percentage)	20.1	52.4	4.7
Rented car and flew	17.7	52.4	(X)
Rented car, did not fly	2.4	(X)	4.7

(X) Not applicable.

Source: State of Florida, Visit Florida, *1998 Florida Visitor Study*, prepublication release.

Table 19.24. TOURISTS: PERCENTAGE DISTRIBUTION OF VISITORS TRAVELING BY AIR AND AUTOMOBILE TO FLORIDA BY ORIGIN AND COUNTY DESTINATION, 1998

Origin	Total	Air	Auto	County of destination	Total	Air	Auto
Georgia	9.8	3.4	14.0	Orange	24.1	31.6	20.2
New York	8.6	13.3	5.6	Hillsborough	7.2	9.1	5.2
Alabama	5.4	0.9	8.5	Miami-Dade	5.7	10.0	1.9
Ohio	5.2	4.8	5.6	Broward	5.4	8.0	3.0
Illinois	4.5	6.0	4.2	Duval	4.7	2.8	5.9
North Carolina	4.5	2.2	5.6	Palm Beach	4.4	6.6	2.5
Texas	4.5	5.2	4.1	Volusia	4.3	2.1	5.6
Michigan	4.3	4.5	4.3	Pinellas	4.2	4.3	3.8
Pennsylvania	4.3	5.2	3.6	Bay	4.0	0.6	6.8
Tennessee	4.3	1.7	6.5	Okaloosa	3.9	1.1	6.4
New Jersey	4.3	7.2	2.2	Lee	3.5	4.3	3.0
Virginia	3.8	3.3	4.2	Escambia	3.2	0.8	5.2
South Carolina	3.2	0.9	5.2	Sarasota	2.7	2.9	2.9
Indiana	3.1	2.8	3.7	Monroe	2.6	2.9	2.0
California	3.0	6.2	0.3	Brevard	2.4	1.9	2.8

Note: Data based on approximately 9,500 person-to-person interviews conducted annually with non-resident visitors to Florida staying longer than one night and less than 180 as they are leaving the state.

Table 19.25. TOURISTS: INTERNATIONAL TRAVELERS TO FLORIDA BY SPECIFIED COUNTRY OF ORIGIN, 1994 THROUGH 1998

(in thousands)

Country or region	1994	1995	1996	1997	1998 Number	1998 Percentage change
Total	6,765	7,074	7,838	8,401	7,787	-4.7
Canada (air & auto)	1,855	1,729	1,913	2,098	1,720	-18.0
Overseas	4,910	5,345	5,710	6,073	6,067	-0.1
Argentina	255	283	278	312	322	3.2
Australia	53	45	52	66	57	-13.6
Brazil	401	490	468	499	444	-11.0
France	177	179	170	159	127	-20.1
Germany	411	471	487	81	470	-2.3
Italy	136	160	146	157	134	-14.6
Japan	148	212	187	193	166	-14.0
Netherlands	(NA)	(NA)	71	80	88	10.0
Switzerland	86	105	104	91	122	34.1
United Kingdom	987	1,077	1,214	1,347	1,431	6.2
Venezuela	315	425	362	383	391	2.1

(NA) Not available.

Source for Tables 19.24 and 19.25: State of Florida, Visit Florida, *1998 Florida Visitor Study,* prepublication release.

University of Florida   **Bureau of Economic and Business Research**

Table 19.26. TRAFFIC COUNTS: AVERAGE DAILY TRAFFIC ENTERING AND LEAVING
FLORIDA AND PASSING OTHER SPECIFIC POINTS, MONTHS OF 1999

Location and direction		January	February	March	April	May	June
I-95 Georgia	N	20,814	22,701	27,486	30,542	25,046	25,382
	S	22,968	23,658	24,627	23,357	23,065	24,264
U.S. 1 Georgia	N	(NA)	4,705	4,882	5,226	4,922	(NA)
	S	(NA)	4,731	4,754	5,037	4,847	(NA)
I-75 Georgia	N	14,103	15,052	19,660	21,509	16,599	18,205
	S	14,774	15,627	18,074	16,851	14,898	18,857
U.S. 27 Georgia	N	3,498	3,816	3,886	4,080	3,926	4,209
	S	3,559	3,834	3,890	3,976	3,976	4,138
U.S. 231 Alabama	N	(NA)	(NA)	(NA)	(NA)	(NA)	(NA)
	S	5,000	5,200	6,832	7,013	7,260	7,800
I-275 Tampa	N	30,446	32,304	32,400	32,472	30,550	31,474
	S	29,245	32,042	31,900	31,766	31,300	30,767
I-4 Orlando	E	66,507	71,230	73,135	72,394	69,821	71,704
	W	67,209	71,899	73,760	72,000	71,511	73,642

		July	August	September	October	November	December
I-95 Georgia	N	27,263	23,314	20,385	22,433	24,020	24,013
	S	27,223	25,034	18,174	25,252	26,495	28,008
U.S. 1 Georgia	N	5,077	(NA)	(NA)	(NA)	(NA)	(NA)
	S	5,078	(NA)	(NA)	(NA)	(NA)	(NA)
I-75 Georgia	N	21,482	18,745	14,400	15,044	17,612	16,601
	S	21,314	18,500	15,000	17,347	19,233	20,080
U.S. 27 Georgia	N	4,085	3,944	3,580	3,793	4,123	3,837
	S	4,114	3,977	3,708	3,867	4,183	3,946
U.S. 231 Alabama	N	(NA)	(NA)	(NA)	(NA)	(NA)	(NA)
	S	8,442	6,608	6,955	5,946	6,061	6,107
I-275 Tampa	N	30,822	30,871	29,601	30,671	31,280	30,859
	S	30,462	30,849	27,305	29,834	30,824	30,627
I-4 Orlando	E	74,775	71,731	63,805	68,743	68,575	66,407
	W	79,029	73,961	60,646	72,121	70,574	68,927

(NA) Not available.

Source: State of Florida, Department of Transportation, Transportation Statistics Office, unpublished data.

University of Florida   **Bureau of Economic and Business Research**

Table 19.45. BOATS: NUMBER REGISTERED BY TYPE IN THE STATE AND COUNTIES
OF FLORIDA, FISCAL YEAR 1998-99

County	Total	Pleasure boats	Commercial boats	County	Total	Pleasure boats	Commercial boats
Florida	829,971	791,410	32,554	Lake	18,033	17,706	226
				Lee	37,328	35,465	1,632
Alachua	8,925	8,689	177	Leon	11,990	11,824	139
Baker	1,697	1,693	4	Levy	3,390	2,976	409
Bay	17,633	16,106	1,452	Liberty	964	960	1
Bradford	1,986	1,960	20	Madison	880	877	3
Brevard	31,842	30,105	1,239	Manatee	17,506	16,564	695
Broward	45,041	42,455	1,867	Marion	17,165	16,785	331
Calhoun	1,232	1,220	9	Martin	15,338	14,469	559
Charlotte	18,015	17,068	785	Miami-Dade	53,290	50,811	2,046
Citrus	13,380	12,483	819	Monroe	25,862	21,336	4,414
Clay	9,465	9,232	202	Nassau	4,096	3,892	197
Collier	19,232	17,886	1,234	Okaloosa	16,872	15,932	846
Columbia	4,602	4,580	8	Okeechobee	4,928	4,680	235
De Soto	2,170	2,123	44	Orange	31,186	30,680	251
Dixie	2,127	1,822	300	Osceola	7,122	6,868	227
Duval	30,563	29,765	645	Palm Beach	35,024	33,855	904
Escambia	17,146	16,607	415	Pasco	19,189	18,560	532
Flagler	3,380	3,278	78	Pinellas	52,568	50,030	1,993
Franklin	2,743	1,836	902	Polk	26,436	25,921	377
Gadsden	2,191	2,126	58	Putnam	7,441	7,050	359
Gilchrist	1,337	1,312	24	St. Johns	8,489	8,102	333
Glades	1,259	1,106	149	St. Lucie	10,701	10,165	466
Gulf	2,578	2,320	252	Santa Rosa	10,288	9,953	305
Hamilton	669	664	4	Sarasota	19,435	18,756	516
Hardee	1,531	1,517	13	Seminole	18,405	18,022	263
Hendry	3,444	3,188	240	Sumter	3,168	3,052	109
Hernando	6,657	6,427	220	Suwannee	2,326	2,295	27
Highlands	8,715	8,582	111	Taylor	3,154	3,001	135
Hillsborough	38,234	37,031	1,015	Union	594	593	1
Holmes	1,702	1,690	9	Volusia	23,118	22,175	787
Indian River	9,510	9,002	459	Wakulla	3,996	3,650	339
Jackson	4,020	3,991	26	Walton	3,422	3,350	68
Jefferson	775	753	22	Washington	1,740	1,719	21
Lafayette	647	640	6				

Source: State of Florida, Department of Highway Safety and Motor Vehicles, Bureau of Vessel Titles
and Registrations, *Vessels Registered in Florida, Fiscal Year 1998-99.*

University of Florida   **Bureau of Economic and Business Research**

Table 19.46. RECREATIONAL BOATING ACCIDENTS: BOATING AND PERSONAL WATERCRAFT ACCIDENTS BY LOCATION, TYPE, OPERATION, AND OPERATOR IN FLORIDA, 1999

Item	Boats 1/ Number	Fatal	Personal water-craft 2/	Item	Boats 1/ Number	Fatal	Personal water-craft 2/
Location				Operation at time			
Bay/sound	266	8	114	of accident			
Canal/cut	143	4	19	(Continued)			
Inlet	102	1	24	Cruising	769	30	249
Lake/pond	159	18	80	Changing direction	358	9	200
Ocean/gulf	240	4	82	Changing speed	55	1	20
Port/harbor	72	0	11	Docked	207	0	5
River/creek	260	12	54	Docking/undocking	86	0	5
Other 3/	50	4	13	Drifting	74	10	13
				Launching/loading	6	0	1
Accidents, total	1,292	51	397	Rowing/paddling	3	2	0
Type 4/				Sailing	6	0	0
Capsizing	43	7	1	Towing	4	0	0
Collision				Wake/surf jumping	34	0	32
Fixed object	227	9	64	Other	0	0	25
Floating object/person	25	0	10				
Skier hit object	5	0	2	Operators, total	1,769	58	545
Struck by boat	7	0	2	Age (years)			
Struck by prop	4	1	0	0-16	72	4	44
Struck underwater				17-21	151	3	121
object	24	0	2	22-35	465	15	225
Vessel	398	10	193	36-50	491	17	106
Fallen skier	25	1	6	51 and over	369	19	22
Fall on PWC	72	0	73	No entry	221	0	27
Fall in boat	32	0	0	Experience (hours)			
Fall overboard	58	15	18	Less than 10	243	9	193
Fire or explosion, fuel	28	0	3	10-100	351	12	181
Flooding	94	7	2	100+	903	30	132
Grounding	96	0	7	No entry	272	7	39
Sinking	16	0	6				
Starting engine	9	0	2	With no instruction			
Vessel wake damage	59	0	2	by age (years)			
Other	41	1	7	All ages	1,303	54	467
				1-16	50	4	34
Operation at time				17-21	127	3	105
of accident 5/				22-35	383	14	198
At anchor	88	3	0	36-50	335	14	88
Being towed	4	0	1	51 and over	193	19	15

1/ Registered recreational vessels.
2/ Accidents involving a small vessel designed to be operated by a person sitting, standing, or kneeling on, or being towed behind the vessel, rather than in the conventional manner of sitting or standing inside the vessel.
3/ May include no entry.
4/ Based on first harmful event.
5/ Each accident may contain multiple entries.
Note: A reportable boat accident is any boating accident that results in death, disappearance of any person, injury requiring medical treatment beyond first aid, and/or property damage totaling more than $500.

Source: State of Florida, Fish and Wildlife Conservation Commission, *1999 Boating Accident Statistics,* Internet site <http://fcn.state.fl.us/fwc/law/boating/99stats/> (accessed 13 July 2000).

University of Florida   **Bureau of Economic and Business Research**

Table 19.48. RECREATIONAL BOATING ACCIDENTS: VESSELS , ACCIDENTS, AND PROPERTY DAMAGES RESULTING FROM RECREATIONAL BOATING AND PERSONAL WATERCRAFT ACCIDENTS IN THE STATE AND COUNTIES OF FLORIDA, 1999

County	Registered vessels — Boats	Registered vessels — Personal water-craft	Reported accidents 1/ Boating — Num-ber	Boating — Fatal-ities	Boating — Inju-ries	Personal watercraft — Num-ber	Personal watercraft — Inju-ries	Damages (dollars) — Boating	Damages (dollars) — Personal water-craft
Florida	829,971	81,693	1,292	58	589	397	308	8,007,231	550,167
Alachua	8,925	607	2	1	1	0	0	0	0
Baker	1,697	92	1	0	2	1	2	500	500
Bay	17,633	2,088	31	0	17	14	11	126,325	32,825
Bradford	1,986	112	0	0	0	0	0	0	0
Brevard	31,842	3,031	39	1	19	15	11	105,847	8,236
Broward	45,041	6,931	149	3	26	15	13	1,440,632	17,500
Calhoun	1,232	37	1	1	0	0	0	0	0
Charlotte	18,015	1,017	20	0	12	7	6	350,040	5,600
Citrus	13,380	497	10	0	5	1	2	22,800	1,000
Clay	9,465	1,049	10	0	9	3	3	58,700	1,500
Collier	19,232	1,666	36	0	28	10	14	204,550	14,750
Columbia	4,602	277	0	0	0	0	0	0	0
De Soto	2,170	100	3	0	2	3	2	3,550	3,550
Dixie	2,127	60	2	0	2	0	0	2,500	0
Duval	30,563	3,088	28	1	9	5	4	192,550	4,000
Escambia	17,146	1,395	40	4	25	16	13	110,200	18,100
Flagler	3,380	174	2	0	1	1	1	5,000	0
Franklin	2,743	40	5	1	2	0	0	10,000	0
Gadsden	2,191	75	1	1	0	0	0	0	0
Gilchrist	1,337	33	4	0	3	2	2	1,000	400
Glades	1,259	14	8	4	3	0	0	17,320	0
Gulf	2,578	57	6	0	3	1	0	5,175	2,000
Hamilton	669	3	1	1	0	0	0	0	0
Hardee	1,531	131	0	0	0	0	0	0	0
Hendry	3,444	421	2	0	5	3	1	2,000	2,400
Hernando	6,657	0	5	0	4	0	0	5,400	0
Highlands	8,715	917	14	1	9	8	8	7,900	4,800
Hillsborough	38,234	3,998	35	0	23	14	18	70,300	15,150
Holmes	1,702	28	0	0	0	0	0	0	0
Indian River	9,510	0	9	0	6	0	0	60,100	0
Jackson	4,020	168	4	1	1	1	1	2,300	0
Jefferson	775	15	1	0	0	1	0	400	400
Lafayette	647	21	0	0	0	0	0	0	0
Lake	18,033	1,405	14	1	5	4	4	46,105	1,600
Lee	37,328	3,137	45	0	17	15	8	205,750	21,000
Leon	11,990	837	2	1	3	0	0	1,200	0

See footnote at end of table.   Continued . . .

University of Florida   **Bureau of Economic and Business Research**

Table 19.48. RECREATIONAL BOATING ACCIDENTS: VESSELS , ACCIDENTS, AND PROPERTY DAMAGES RESULTING FROM RECREATIONAL BOATING AND PERSONAL WATERCRAFT ACCIDENTS IN THE STATE AND COUNTIES OF FLORIDA, 1999 (Continued)

| County | Registered vessels | | Reported accidents 1/ | | | | | Damages (dollars) | |
	Boats	Personal water-craft	Boating Num-ber	Fatal-ities	Inju-ries	Personal watercraft Num-ber	Inju-ries	Boating	Personal water-craft
Levy	3,390	61	2	0	0	0	0	2,011	0
Liberty	964	53	1	0	0	0	0	1,100	0
Madison	880	30	0	0	0	0	0	0	0
Manatee	17,506	1,713	19	0	9	7	5	226,051	11,551
Marion	17,165	1,216	11	1	14	6	7	8,000	2,050
Martin	15,338	941	30	4	13	5	4	59,400	2,800
Miami-Dade	53,290	8,111	88	9	39	14	16	661,122	16,901
Monroe	25,862	1,545	199	1	67	61	38	884,981	64,944
Nassau	4,096	194	4	0	0	0	0	6,000	0
Okaloosa	16,872	2,295	42	0	19	30	17	100,275	53,975
Okeechobee	4,928	222	4	0	4	1	1	8,450	450
Orange	31,186	4,844	25	2	17	13	5	47,463	19,863
Osceola	7,122	877	10	1	7	0	0	25,650	0
Palm Beach	35,024	4,848	100	2	33	27	15	1,716,750	36,550
Pasco	19,189	1,377	8	1	4	4	2	10,000	7,000
Pinellas	52,568	6,862	81	4	45	44	24	351,199	74,010
Polk	26,436	2,271	18	3	16	8	4	17,700	8,500
Putnam	7,441	431	5	0	4	1	3	10,750	3,000
St. Johns	8,489	690	19	1	5	1	2	305,150	5,000
St. Lucie	10,701	669	5	0	0	0	0	20,450	0
Santa Rosa	10,288	738	16	1	11	6	5	25,750	3,750
Sarasota	19,435	1,967	13	0	5	7	3	223,250	11,600
Seminole	18,405	2,787	10	2	9	1	1	5,750	0
Sumter	3,168	60	1	0	2	1	2	700	700
Suwannee	2,326	91	0	0	0	0	0	0	0
Taylor	3,154	108	3	0	3	0	0	10,500	0
Union	594	20	0	0	0	0	0	0	0
Volusia	23,118	2,016	36	4	17	13	11	136,325	69,112
Wakulla	3,996	118	2	0	0	0	0	4,800	0
Walton	3,422	90	3	0	1	0	0	5,600	0
Washington	1,740	31	2	0	1	1	0	600	600

1/ A reportable boat accident is any boating accident that results in death, disappearance of any person, injury requiring medical treatment beyond first aid, and/or property damage totaling more than $500.00

Source: State of Florida, Fish and Wildlife Conservation Commission, *1999 Boating Accident Statistics*, Internet site <http://fcn.state.fl.us/fwc/law/boating/99stats/> (accessed 13 July 2000).

University of Florida   **Bureau of Economic and Business Research**

Table 19.52. STATE PARKS AND AREAS: ATTENDANCE AT PARKS BY DEPARTMENT OF ENVIRONMENTAL PROTECTION DISTRICTS IN THE STATE AND SPECIFIED COUNTIES OF FLORIDA, FISCAL YEARS 1998-99 AND 1999-2000

Property designation	County	1998-99	1999-2000	Per-centage change
Total	(X)	14,646,288	16,451,587	12.3
District 1	(X)	2,290,024	2,579,168	12.6
Alfred B. Maclay Gardens	Leon	57,876	61,634	6.5
Big Lagoon	Escambia	114,190	145,453	27.4
Blackwater River	Santa Rosa	31,557	44,478	40.9
Camp Helen	Bay	(X)	6,572	(X)
Constitution Convention	Gulf	1,399	1,951	39.5
Dead Lakes	Gulf	12,398	8,855	-28.6
Deer Lake	Walton	(X)	25,277	(X)
Econfina River	Taylor	8,108	11,093	36.8
Eden	Walton	50,695	51,665	1.9
Falling Waters	Washington	28,063	28,370	1.1
Florida Caverns	Jackson	109,005	112,722	3.4
Grayton Beach	Walton	59,543	62,061	4.2
Henderson Beach	Okaloosa	115,146	145,554	26.4
John Gorrie	Franklin	5,308	5,824	9.7
Lake Jackson Mounds	Leon	53,099	57,931	9.1
Lake Talquin	Gadsden, Leon, Liberty	16,336	19,085	16.8
Natural Bridge Battlefield	Leon	17,004	19,696	15.8
Ochlockonee River	Wakulla	32,167	38,107	18.5
Perdido Key	Escambia	29,375	33,914	15.5
Ponce De Leon Springs	Holmes, Walton	25,766	34,428	33.6
Rocky Bayou	Okaloosa	37,543	46,905	24.9
St. Andrews	Bay	540,580	578,922	7.1
St. George Island	Franklin	186,923	209,350	12.0
St. Joseph Peninsula	Gulf	127,112	145,627	14.6
San Marcos de Apalache	Wakulla	18,871	21,089	11.8
Shell Island	Bay	134,594	73,793	-45.2
Tallahassee/St. Marks R/R	Leon	205,681	285,848	39.0
Three Rivers	Jackson	20,557	19,498	-5.2
Topsail Hill	Walton	42,794	52,139	21.8
Torreya	Liberty	20,469	21,703	6.0
Wakulla Springs	Wakulla	187,865	209,624	11.6
District 2	(X)	2,226,052	2,366,346	6.3
Amelia Island	Nassau	55,573	165,854	198.4
Big Talbot Island	Duval	54,662	61,699	12.9
Cedar Key	Levy	20,554	20,408	-0.7
Cedar Key Scrub	Levy	9,627	11,572	20.2
Crystal River	Citrus	24,457	23,321	-4.6
Devil's Millhopper	Alachua	44,934	42,373	-5.7
Dudley Farm	Alachua	2,277	2,782	22.2
Fanning Springs	Levy	277,363	261,010	-5.9
Forest Capital	Taylor	22,953	25,702	12.0
Ft. Clinch	Nassau	167,335	168,004	0.4
Ft. George Island	Duval	31,116	28,687	-7.8
Gold Head Branch	Clay	54,971	56,992	3.7
Homosassa Springs	Citrus	247,313	263,575	6.6
Ichetucknee Springs	Columbia, Suwannee	184,607	219,447	18.9
Little Talbot Island	Leon	100,693	106,109	5.4

See footnotes at end of table.   Continued . . .

Table 19.52. STATE PARKS AND AREAS: ATTENDANCE AT PARKS BY DEPARTMENT OF ENVIRONMENTAL PROTECTION DISTRICTS IN THE STATE AND SPECIFIED COUNTIES OF FLORIDA, FISCAL YEARS 1998-99 AND 1999-2000 (Continued)

Property designation	County	1998-99	1999-2000	Per-centage change
District 2 (Continued)				
Manatee Springs	Dixie	119,879	117,917	-1.6
Marjorie Kinnan Rawlings	Alachua	21,300	20,609	-3.2
O'Leno	Alachua, Columbia	58,683	60,766	3.5
Olustee Battlefield	Baker	36,303	38,101	5.0
Paynes Prairie	Alachua	126,564	125,674	-0.7
Peacock Springs	Suwannee	10,995	10,117	-8.0
Rainbow Springs	Marion	143,918	164,589	14.4
River Rise	Columbia	2,900	1,938	-33.2
San Felasco Hammock	Alachua	27,709	27,372	-1.2
Stephen Foster	Hamilton	67,021	61,203	-8.7
Suwannee River	Hamilton, Madison, Suwannee	55,389	30,858	-44.3
Troy Springs	Suwannee	748	487	-34.9
Van Fleet	Lake, Polk, Sumter	23,737	28,183	18.7
Waccasassa Bay	Levy	27,321	27,127	-0.7
Withlacoochee	Citrus, Pasco, Hernando	165,939	155,925	-6.0
Yulee Sugar Mill Ruins	Citrus	39,211	37,945	-3.2
District 3	(X)	2,580,281	3,121,877	21.0
Anastasia	St. Johns	450,227	927,295	106.0
Blue Spring	Volusia	278,548	298,539	7.2
Bulow Creek	Flagler, Volusia	0	437	(X)
Bulow Plantation Ruins	Flagler	22,802	22,889	0.4
De Leon Springs	Volusia	227,280	255,775	12.5
Faver-Dykes	St. Johns	28,514	27,553	-3.4
Flagler Beach	Flagler	73,000	85,058	16.5
Guana River	St. Johns	125,413	147,442	17.6
Hontoon Island	Volusia, Lake	22,682	23,274	2.6
Kissimmee Prairie	Okeechobee	1,250	1,250	0.0
Lake Griffin	Lake	36,747	34,400	-6.4
Lake Kissimmee	Polk	48,156	49,029	1.8
Lake Louisa	Lake	17,408	28,573	64.1
Lower Wekiva River	Lake, Seminole	3,081	4,054	31.6
North Peninsula	Volusia	24,865	29,786	19.8
Ravine	Putnam	99,712	108,194	8.5
Rock Springs Run	Orange	6,174	6,464	4.7
Sebastian Inlet	Brevard, Indian River	748,130	693,739	-7.3
Silver River	Marion	31,839	41,326	29.8
Tomoka	Volusia	57,055	54,104	-5.2
Tosohatchee	Orange	11,769	10,378	-11.8
Washington Oaks	Flagler	60,676	60,035	-1.1
Wekiwa Springs	Orange, Seminole	204,953	212,283	3.6
District 4	(X)	3,546,440	3,813,261	7.5
Alafia River	Hillsborough	2,260	3,469	53.5
Anclote Key	Pasco, Pinellas	189,505	279,821	47.7
Beker	Manatee	2	2	0.0
Caladesi Island	Pinellas	143,187	147,105	2.7
Cayo Costa	Lee	56,459	55,803	-1.2
Collier-Seminole	Collier	53,284	61,365	15.2
Dade Battlefield	Sumter	26,749	23,204	-13.3
Delnor-Wiggins Pass	Collier	502,941	532,757	5.9

See footnotes at end of table.   Continued . . .

Table 19.52. STATE PARKS AND AREAS: ATTENDANCE AT PARKS BY DEPARTMENT
OF ENVIRONMENTAL PROTECTION DISTRICTS IN THE STATE AND SPECIFIED
COUNTIES OF FLORIDA, FISCAL YEARS 1998-99 AND 1999-2000 (Continued)

Property designation	County	1998-99	1999-2000	Per-centage change
District 4 (Continued)				
Don Pedro Island	Charlotte	34,766	33,824	-2.7
Egmont Key	Hillsborough	100,870	109,829	8.9
Fakahatchee Strand	Collier	100,931	57,480	-43.1
Ft. Cooper	Citrus	23,122	18,320	-20.8
Gamble Plantation	Manatee	34,156	37,723	10.4
Gasparilla Island	Hillsborough	463,423	454,621	-1.9
Highlands Hammock	Hardee	177,535	183,918	3.6
Hillsborough River	Hillsborough	114,722	150,747	31.4
Honeymoon Island	Pinellas	646,460	728,393	12.7
Koreshan	Lee	47,465	49,859	5.0
Lake Manatee	Manatee	45,618	44,395	-2.7
Little Manatee River	Manatee	21,589	26,349	22.0
Lovers Key	Lee	121,893	144,854	18.8
Madira Bickel Mound	Manatee	2,983	2,721	-8.8
Mound Key	Lee	3,103	2,923	-5.8
Myakka River	Manatee, Sarasota	239,298	243,638	1.8
Oscar Scherer	Sarasota	93,923	96,505	2.7
Paynes Creek	Hardee	31,646	32,102	1.4
Port Charlotte Beach	Charlotte	42,004	61,786	47.1
Skyway State Fishing Piers	Hillsborough, Pinellas	213,710	212,807	-0.4
Ybor City	Hillsborough	12,836	16,941	32.0
District 5	(X)	4,003,491	4,570,935	14.2
Avalon	St. Lucie	138,749	88,093	-36.5
Bahia Honda	Monroe	284,331	483,892	70.2
Barnacle, The	Miami-Dade	17,649	22,303	26.4
Cape Florida	Miami-Dade	593,283	867,512	46.2
Coral Reef	Monroe	1,039,762	972,480	-6.5
Curry Hammock	Monroe	43,106	103,385	139.8
Ft. Pierce Inlet	St. Lucie	162,399	158,842	-2.2
Ft. Zachary Taylor	Monroe	246,093	260,098	5.7
Hugh Taylor Birch	Broward	225,157	262,282	16.5
Indian Key	Monroe	3,286	4,426	34.7
Jack Island	Martin, Palm Beach	61,590	45,699	-25.8
Jonathan Dickinson	Martin	167,819	169,768	1.2
Key Largo Hammock	Monroe	13,973	14,900	6.6
Lignumvitae Key	Monroe	4,667	5,359	14.8
Lloyd Beach	Broward	541,545	615,222	13.6
Long Key	Monroe	53,301	61,439	15.3
MacArthur Beach	Palm Beach	94,907	83,856	-11.6
Oleta River	Miami-Dade	271,339	314,054	15.7
St. Lucie Inlet	St. Lucie	24,717	16,522	-33.2
San Pedro	Monroe	1,357	816	-39.9
Seabranch	Martin	10,198	10,496	2.9
Windley Key Fossil Reef	Monroe	4,263	9,491	122.6

(X) Not applicable.
Note: Data include areas reporting actual visitor counts from full-time entrance stations and areas
reporting estimates of attendance from sample counts. Some parks may have been closed for repairs.
Totals may include data from parks that are closed or no longer under the state system.

Source: State of Florida, Department of Environmental Protection, Recreation and Parks Management
Information System, unpublished data.

Table 19.53. NATIONAL PARK SYSTEMS: RECREATIONAL VISITS TO NATIONAL PARK SERVICE AREAS IN FLORIDA, 1998 AND 1999

Park, monument, or memorial	County	1998	1999
Florida	(X)	8,053.5	8,749.1
Big Cypress Preserve	Broward, Hendry	A/ 474.9	503.1
Biscayne Park	Miami-Dade	403.2	442.6
Canaveral Seashore	Brevard, Volusia	703.3	846.5
Castillo de San Marcos Monument	St. Johns	562.7	A/ 692.7
De Soto Memorial	Miami-Dade	242.2	275.5
Everglades Park	Miami-Dade	1,118.2	1,074.0
Ft. Caroline Memorial	Duval	129.3	A/ 176.2
Ft. Matanzas Monument	St. Johns	506.2	A/ 579.4
Gulf Islands Seashore 1/	Escambia, Okaloosa, Santa Rosa	A/ 4,293.3	4,597.3
Jefferson National Expansion Memorial	Monroe	A/ 3,420.4	3,481.0

A/ Due to changes in counting procedures, closings, or special events, data may not be comparable to earlier years.
1/ Part located in Mississippi; excluded from total.
Note: Data are in thousands, rounded to hundreds.

Source: U.S., Department of the Interior, National Park Service, *National Park Service Statistical Abstract, 1999,* and previous editions, Internet site <http://www2.nature.nps.gov/stats/abstract99.pdf> (accessed 15 June 2000).

Table 19.54. TOURIST DEVELOPMENT TAXES: LOCAL OPTION TAX COLLECTIONS IN THE STATE AND COUNTIES OF FLORIDA, FISCAL YEAR 1998-99

County	Amount ($1,000)	Per-centage change	County	Amount ($1,000)	Per-centage change	County	Amount $1,000)	Per-centage change
Florida	796,557	10.3	Hamilton	644	-0.5	Miami-Dade	113,953	4.4
			Hardee	1,184	13.0	Monroe	27,149	8.8
Baker	836	-4.3	Hendry	1,865	8.0	Nassau	4,833	9.5
Bay	18,709	90.0	Hernando	1,649	(X)	Okaloosa	19,564	7.5
Bradford	1,271	5.4	Highlands	5,815	6.4	Okeechobee	2,547	8.9
Calhoun	485	15.0	Hillsborough	97,728	0.0	Osceola	21,032	4.5
Charlotte	12,328	6.6	Holmes	517	6.6	Pinellas	94,459	4.8
Clay	10,480	6.3	Indian River	12,546	7.7	St. Lucie	6,564	6.3
Columbia	4,563	7.2	Jackson	3,817	3.7	Santa Rosa	3,286	-29.2
De Soto	1,386	2.3	Jefferson	396	8.4	Sarasota	39,797	5.6
Dixie	401	4.3	Lafayette	152	25.5	Seminole	39,730	11.3
Duval	47,922	7.7	Lake	15,071	10.0	Sumter	1,905	9.3
Escambia	43,820	31.5	Leon	25,563	5.4	Suwannee	1,847	15.6
Flagler	2,690	13.7	Levy	1,865	8.8	Taylor	1,456	7.8
Gadsden	1,703	9.2	Liberty	127	2.6	Union	287	14.4
Gilchrist	320	13.8	Madison	620	4.9	Wakulla	725	12.8
Glades	183	17.3	Manatee	24,215	7.2	Walton	5,467	12.9
Gulf	301	-0.4	Martin	6,405	A/	Washington	919	9.2

A/ Martin County local option tax collections increased from approximately $96,000 to $6.4 million dollars within one fiscal year, a change of 6,604.3 percent.
Note: Data reflect both state- and locally-administered tourist development tax collections.

Source: State of Florida, Department of Revenue, Internet site http://sun6.dms.state.fl.us/dor/.

Table 19.60. TOURIST FACILITIES: HOTELS AND MOTELS BY NUMBER OF UNITS AND FOOD SERVICE ESTABLISHMENTS BY SEATING CAPACITY IN THE STATE AND COUNTIES OF FLORIDA, FISCAL YEAR 1999-2000

| County | Licensed hotels | | Licensed motels | | Food service establishments | |
	Number	Units	Number	Units	Number of licenses	Seating capacity
Florida	1,063	172,171	3,642	198,790	37,076	3,187,167
Alachua	9	1,423	43	2,730	427	35,378
Baker	0	0	3	148	27	1,362
Bay	6	856	190	8,638	521	47,203
Bradford	1	29	12	352	35	2,242
Brevard	16	2,213	98	6,342	1,084	91,237
Broward	112	16,839	385	11,706	3,636	295,564
Calhoun	0	0	2	24	18	1,270
Charlotte	4	424	23	933	293	26,837
Citrus	2	111	23	882	238	17,175
Clay	4	362	8	839	225	19,225
Collier	21	3,740	61	2,828	740	72,797
Columbia	2	117	33	1,863	110	8,586
De Soto	0	0	5	128	37	2,820
Dixie	0	0	9	142	22	1,519
Duval	51	7,159	83	6,850	1,859	142,224
Escambia	13	1,304	66	4,899	558	47,709
Flagler	2	232	14	354	109	8,676
Franklin	3	58	16	411	42	3,588
Gadsden	0	0	10	233	50	3,519
Gilchrist	0	0	1	28	10	829
Glades	0	0	9	174	17	1,039
Gulf	2	16	6	64	29	1,484
Hamilton	0	0	8	292	17	896
Hardee	0	0	3	45	36	1,626
Hendry	2	107	14	299	59	4,199
Hernando	0	0	14	646	238	18,159
Highlands	6	575	20	681	157	13,800
Hillsborough	63	12,079	113	6,829	2,219	182,729
Holmes	0	0	5	193	18	1,352
Indian River	1	208	33	1,531	292	24,036
Jackson	0	0	14	712	66	5,033
Jefferson	0	0	5	181	20	1,309
Lafayette	0	0	2	33	7	426
Lake	5	299	42	1,533	413	34,030
Lee	31	3,572	136	5,104	1,204	109,602

See footnote at end of table.

Continued . . .

Table 19.60. TOURIST FACILITIES: HOTELS AND MOTELS BY NUMBER OF UNITS AND FOOD SERVICE ESTABLISHMENTS BY SEATING CAPACITY IN THE STATE AND COUNTIES OF FLORIDA, FISCAL YEAR 1999-2000 (Continued)

County	Licensed hotels		Licensed motels		Food service establishments	
	Number	Units	Number	Units	Number of licenses	Seating capacity
Leon	18	2,052	39	2,904	509	45,302
Levy	1	13	24	401	78	5,009
Liberty	0	0	1	13	5	423
Madison	1	60	3	138	30	2,043
Manatee	2	145	67	2,884	582	45,315
Marion	7	869	67	2,836	488	35,369
Martin	5	351	20	874	365	29,707
Miami-Dade	277	35,196	189	11,937	5,087	340,057
Monroe	28	2,409	173	5,880	527	43,478
Nassau	6	924	23	669	141	11,008
Okaloosa	8	551	55	4,422	438	39,149
Okeechobee	0	0	10	347	73	5,055
Orange	130	42,959	114	25,613	2,903	384,173
Osceola	22	8,214	109	17,001	565	74,018
Palm Beach	68	10,243	151	5,935	2,649	247,524
Pasco	3	311	40	1,856	540	46,193
Pinellas	38	5,180	362	13,965	2,336	202,501
Polk	15	1,315	98	5,440	846	66,124
Putnam	0	0	24	512	117	7,980
St. Johns	14	1,882	70	3,169	369	27,023
St. Lucie	9	1,368	30	1,163	363	27,010
Santa Rosa	2	72	10	773	158	10,023
Sarasota	14	1,535	67	2,868	844	74,430
Seminole	12	1,530	25	2,391	683	58,071
Sumter	0	0	8	547	98	5,048
Suwannee	0	0	11	309	43	2,793
Taylor	1	60	24	491	33	2,903
Union	0	0	0	0	4	384
Volusia	23	2,572	291	13,825	1,147	102,999
Wakulla	1	27	5	113	36	2,803
Walton	2	610	16	620	153	11,448
Washington	0	0	7	247	33	2,324

Note: Apartment buildings, rooming houses, rental condominiums, transient apartments, and total public lodgings are shown in Table 2.30. Excludes 226 bed and breakfast establishments.

Source: State of Florida, Department of Business and Professional Regulation, Division of Hotels and Restaurants, *Master File Statistics: Public Lodging and Food Service Establishments,* Fiscal Year 1999-2000.

University of Florida   **Bureau of Economic and Business Research**

Table 19.70. TOURIST- AND RECREATION-RELATED BUSINESSES: GROSS AND TAXABLE SALES AND SALES AND USE TAX COLLECTIONS BY KIND OF BUSINESS IN FLORIDA, 1998 AND 1999

(rounded to thousands of dollars)

Kind of business	Gross sales	Taxable sales	Sales and use tax collections
1998			
Candy, sundries, and concessions	1,142,208	421,643	26,398
Restaurants and lunchrooms	17,971,132	16,703,341	1,017,046
Bars, nightclubs, and liquor stores	2,172,730	2,041,528	124,881
Sporting goods, pro shops, jewelry, and leather	4,093,322	2,592,664	157,028
Motorboats, yachts, and marine parts	4,056,192	1,882,084	112,607
Music, electronics, and record shops	18,311,201	6,540,965	406,059
Hotels, rooming houses, and trailer parks	11,573,688	9,882,466	603,680
Bookstores	1,168,817	804,400	49,310
Tobacco shops	258,562	79,324	4,821
Photo and art supplies, photographers, and art galleries	1,682,450	911,004	55,437
Gift, novelty, hobby, and toy stores	2,599,370	1,972,774	119,534
Newsstands	148,133	52,374	3,274
Admissions	4,587,143	4,157,394	272,337
Holiday season vendors	13,723	10,330	626
Rental of amusement machines, houseboats, and horses	6,944,057	4,014,898	247,080
Fairs, concessions, and carnivals	13,418	6,505	394
1999			
Candy, sundries, and concessions	962,805	447,648	27,713
Restaurants and lunchrooms	19,895,623	17,363,077	1,057,128
Bars, nightclubs, and liquor stores	2,430,598	2,179,836	133,398
Sporting goods, pro shops, jewelry, and leather	4,061,782	2,534,827	153,330
Motorboats, yachts, and marine parts	4,527,813	2,166,887	130,711
Music, electronics, and record shops	22,114,335	7,743,637	480,918
Hotels, rooming houses, and trailer parks	10,873,498	10,859,790	662,272
Bookstores	1,301,140	887,749	54,287
Tobacco shops	274,009	87,838	5,339
Photo and art supplies, photographers, and art galleries	2,250,905	923,219	56,281
Gift, novelty, hobby, and toy stores	2,838,893	2,077,185	126,157
Newsstands	136,997	55,160	3,413
Admissions	5,474,808	4,855,127	334,889
Holiday season vendors	15,096	9,236	554
Rental of amusement machines, houseboats, and horses	7,822,647	4,629,483	291,545
Fairs, concessions, and carnivals	16,429	8,212	499

Note: Audited sales reported for the 6 percent regular sales tax, 6 percent use tax, and 3 percent ve- hicle and farm equipment sales tax. Sales occurred, for the most part, from December 1, 1997, through November 30, 1999. Kind of business data for counties are available from the Bureau of Economic and Business Research, University of Florida. Data includes all sales in the category. See Table 16.81 for taxable sales for all businesses; see Table 23.43 for tax collections.

Source: State of Florida, Department of Revenue, unpublished data prepared by the University of Florida, Bureau of Economic and Business Research.

University of Florida   **Bureau of Economic and Business Research**

Table 19.73. EATING AND DRINKING PLACES: AVERAGE MONTHLY PRIVATE REPORTING UNITS
EMPLOYMENT, AND PAYROLL COVERED BY UNEMPLOYMENT COMPENSATION LAW
IN THE STATE AND COUNTIES OF FLORIDA, 1998 AND 1999

County	Number of reporting units	Number of employees	Payroll ($1,000)	County	Number of reporting units	Number of employees	Payroll ($1,000)
			Eating and drinking places, 1998 A/ (SIC code 58)				
Florida	22,823	443,972	446,677	Lake	242	3,745	3,386
				Lee	659	12,445	11,661
Alachua	334	8,011	5,971	Leon	392	8,717	6,656
Baker	19	322	249	Levy	44	532	372
Bay	288	6,539	5,562	Liberty	4	38	35
Bradford	18	438	320	Madison	17	213	147
Brevard	702	12,904	11,157	Manatee	357	5,609	5,492
Broward	2,513	43,673	44,328	Marion	297	5,248	4,172
Calhoun	12	156	98	Martin	213	3,391	3,074
Charlotte	168	2,484	2,131	Miami-Dade	3,127	53,496	64,994
Citrus	142	1,786	1,389	Monroe	326	4,995	5,940
Clay	171	4,097	3,251	Nassau	80	1,424	1,406
Collier	424	6,574	7,367	Okaloosa	315	6,720	5,951
Columbia	65	1,387	1,119	Okeechobee	51	650	563
De Soto	26	291	247	Orange	1,319	39,378	49,820
Dixie	18	163	123	Osceola	262	6,697	6,429
Duval	1,150	22,920	20,222	Palm Beach	1,702	30,340	33,040
Escambia	426	10,064	8,329	Pasco	362	5,805	4,759
Flagler	63	941	705	Pinellas	1,497	26,030	24,585
Franklin	37	301	245	Polk	492	9,590	8,016
Gadsden	29	434	297	Putnam	73	1,264	863
Gilchrist	13	72	40	St. Johns	208	3,888	3,460
Glades	9	73	60	St. Lucie	189	2,929	2,411
Gulf	12	82	69	Santa Rosa	111	1,814	1,249
Hamilton	7	76	60	Sarasota	580	10,206	10,469
Hardee	17	192	145	Seminole	445	9,863	9,643
Hendry	39	492	368	Sumter	33	467	371
Hernando	140	2,386	1,769	Suwannee	27	462	330
Highlands	73	1,174	879	Taylor	24	333	216
Hillsborough	1,259	31,375	31,130	Volusia	671	11,944	10,260
Holmes	14	198	175	Wakulla	20	257	173
Indian River	161	2,906	2,701	Walton	63	909	945
Jackson	47	790	521	Washington	18	309	225
Jefferson	7	85	41				
Lafayette	5	35	15	Multicounty 1/	204	10,807	14,456

See footnotes at end of table.   Continued . . .

Table 19.73. EATING AND DRINKING PLACES: AVERAGE MONTHLY PRIVATE REPORTING UNITS EMPLOYMENT, AND PAYROLL COVERED BY UNEMPLOYMENT COMPENSATION LAW IN THE STATE AND COUNTIES OF FLORIDA, 1998 AND 1999 (Continued)

County	Number of re- porting units	Number of em- ployees	Payroll ($1,000)	County	Number of re- porting units	Number of em- ployees	Payroll ($1,000)
			Eating and drinking places, 1999 B/ (SIC code 58)				
Florida	22,960	450,993	464,054	Lake	237	3,933	3,497
				Lee	682	12,833	12,770
Alachua	323	8,321	6,158	Leon	371	8,550	6,388
Baker	20	373	237	Levy	52	567	383
Bay	291	6,680	6,129	Madison	17	239	161
Bradford	22	509	370	Manatee	362	5,579	5,404
Brevard	688	13,236	11,605	Marion	296	5,254	4,284
Broward	2,532	43,468	45,522	Martin	216	3,494	3,275
Calhoun	12	141	100	Miami-Dade	3,208	54,669	64,995
Charlotte	167	2,688	2,452	Monroe	344	4,983	6,229
Citrus	149	1,794	1,362	Nassau	78	1,358	1,327
Clay	164	4,120	3,420	Okaloosa	298	6,621	5,994
Collier	454	6,937	8,328	Okeechobee	53	680	605
Columbia	66	1,342	989	Orange	1,351	40,046	52,728
De Soto	26	326	298	Osceola	262	6,713	6,904
Dixie	18	153	116	Palm Beach	1,761	30,011	34,095
Duval	1,141	23,806	21,040	Pasco	348	5,461	4,445
Escambia	400	10,110	8,496	Pinellas	1,431	25,917	24,614
Flagler	60	979	772	Polk	478	9,748	8,098
Franklin	36	347	278	Putnam	71	1,300	816
Gadsden	27	416	279	St. Johns	197	3,871	3,763
Gilchrist	13	60	32	St. Lucie	194	3,124	2,563
Glades	9	66	48	Santa Rosa	107	1,728	1,322
Gulf	15	117	91	Sarasota	567	10,367	10,835
Hamilton	11	126	86	Seminole	470	10,237	9,622
Hardee	19	220	167	Sumter	35	431	354
Hendry	41	500	391	Suwannee	28	467	319
Hernando	140	2,433	1,884	Taylor	22	300	192
Highlands	73	1,153	922	Union	5	49	31
Hillsborough	1,272	32,130	32,975	Volusia	643	11,526	10,172
Holmes	14	190	174	Wakulla	20	269	168
Indian River	168	2,718	2,626	Walton	68	1,004	1,069
Jackson	42	736	498	Washington	17	337	228
Jefferson	6	57	26	Multicounty 1/	250	13,056	18,365
Lafayette	6	33	18	Out-of-state 2/	11	75	121

A/ Revised.
B/ Preliminary.
1/ Reporting units without a fixed location within the state or of unknown county location.
2/ Employment based in Florida, but working out of the state or country.
Note: Private employment. Only counties for which data are disclosed are shown. Detail may not add to totals due to disclosure editing and/or rounding. See Tables 23.70, 23.71, 23.72, 23.73, and 23.74 for public employment data.

Source: State of Florida, Department of Labor and Employment Security, Bureau of Labor Market Information, "Employment and Wages" (ES-202), unpublished data.

University of Florida   **Bureau of Economic and Business Research**

Table 19.75. TOURIST- AND RECREATION-RELATED INDUSTRIES: AVERAGE MONTHLY PRIVATE REPORTING UNITS, EMPLOYMENT, AND PAYROLL COVERED BY UNEMPLOYMENT COMPENSATION LAW BY INDUSTRY IN FLORIDA, 1999

SIC code	Industry	Number of reporting units	Number of employees	Payroll ($1,000)
413	Intercity and rural bus transportation	24	956	1,785
414	Bus charter service	92	2,358	3,972
448	Water transportation of passengers	111	6,719	23,481
451	Air transportation, scheduled, and air courier services	523	58,179	182,318
452	Air transportation, nonscheduled	216	3,882	11,168
472	Arrangement of passenger transportation	2,530	17,647	38,157
544	Candy, nut, and confectionery stores	161	1,052	1,057
555	Boat dealers	698	5,040	11,918
556	Recreational vehicle dealers	163	2,439	7,972
573	Radio, television, consumer electronics, and music stores	2,952	26,689	64,185
581	Eating and drinking places	22,960	450,992	464,054
592	Liquor stores	708	4,190	5,295
594	Miscellaneous shopping goods stores	7,168	53,168	74,914
701	Hotels and motels	3,082	147,843	231,963
703	Camps and recreational vehicle parks	418	2,837	3,595
751	Automotive rental and leasing, without drivers	811	19,067	43,072
783	Motion picture theaters	273	8,553	5,930
784	Video tape rental	581	8,168	7,504
79	Amusement and recreation services	6,168	147,322	301,873
791	Dance studios, schools, and halls	324	1,432	1,462
792	Theatrical producers, orchestras, entertainers	791	7,311	18,764
793	Bowling centers	147	2,931	2,765
794	Commercial sports	615	14,893	72,018
841	Museums and art galleries	151	2,335	4,153
842	Arboreta, botanical and zoological gardens	50	1,523	2,448

Note: Private employment. Data are preliminary. Detail may not add to totals due to disclosure editing and/or rounding. See Tables 23.70, 23.71, 23.72, 23.73, and 23.74 for public employment data.

Source: State of Florida, Department of Labor and Employment Security, Bureau of Labor Market Information, "Employment and Wages" (ES-202), unpublished data.

University of Florida   **Bureau of Economic and Business Research**

Table 19.76. HOTELS, ROOMING HOUSES, CAMPS, AND LODGING PLACES: AVERAGE MONTHLY PRIVATE REPORTING UNITS, EMPLOYMENT, AND PAYROLL COVERED BY UNEMPLOYMENT COMPENSATION LAW IN THE STATE AND COUNTIES OF FLORIDA, 1999

County	Number of reporting units	Number of employees	Payroll ($1,000)	County	Number of reporting units	Number of employees	Payroll ($1,000)
			Hotels, rooming houses, camps, and lodging places (SIC code 70)				
Florida	3,658	152,559	238,813	Leon	65	1,246	1,230
				Levy	14	104	65
Alachua	64	1,303	1,624	Madison	7	325	200
Bay	103	2,292	3,067	Manatee	48	643	729
Bradford	6	18	13	Marion	54	744	763
Brevard	88	2,516	2,923	Martin	18	665	1,065
Broward	305	9,134	15,248	Miami-Dade	412	20,111	33,601
Charlotte	25	399	423	Monroe	188	5,761	9,911
Citrus	30	479	507	Nassau	23	2,041	3,174
Clay	12	545	620	Okaloosa	46	987	1,044
Collier	69	4,220	8,358	Okeechobee	12	95	101
Columbia	27	381	310	Orange	226	41,513	67,305
De Soto	6	52	37	Osceola	125	5,483	8,565
Dixie	5	23	10	Palm Beach	159	9,407	17,223
Duval	95	2,919	3,983	Pasco	37	1,127	1,671
Escambia	50	959	927	Pinellas	253	6,672	9,920
Flagler	15	429	538	Polk	95	1,840	2,323
Franklin	11	132	116	Putnam	14	157	131
Gadsden	10	38	26	St. Johns	88	2,417	3,681
Glades	9	31	32	St. Lucie	22	798	803
Hamilton	4	20	12	Santa Rosa	13	196	201
Hardee	4	16	15	Sarasota	79	2,021	3,012
Hendry	11	111	125	Seminole	28	781	951
Hernando	12	132	119	Sumter	17	108	82
Highlands	22	144	136	Suwannee	6	34	31
Hillsborough	122	6,323	9,480	Taylor	9	60	47
Holmes	4	22	17	Volusia	208	3,788	4,390
Indian River	22	543	672	Wakulla	4	16	16
Jackson	10	117	91	Walton	14	1,444	2,565
Lake	47	875	960	Washington	6	30	14
Lee	127	2,847	4,237	Multicounty 1/	46	4,773	9,211

1/ Reporting units without a fixed location within the state or of unknown county location.

Note: Private employment. Data are preliminary. Only counties for which data are disclosed are shown. Detail may not add to totals due to disclosure editing and/or rounding. See Tables 23.70, 23.71, 23.72, 23.73, and 23.74 for public employment data.

Source: State of Florida, Department of Labor and Employment Security, Bureau of Labor Market Information, "Employment and Wages" (ES-202), unpublished data.

Table 19.78. AMUSEMENT AND RECREATION SERVICES: AVERAGE MONTHLY PRIVATE REPORTING UNITS, EMPLOYMENT, AND PAYROLL COVERED BY UNEMPLOYMENT COMPENSATION LAW IN THE STATE AND COUNTIES OF FLORIDA, 1999

County	Number of reporting units	Number of employees	Payroll ($1,000)	County	Number of reporting units	Number of employees	Payroll ($1,000)
			Amusement and recreation services (SIC code 79)				
Florida	6,168	147,322	301,874	Levy	13	51	62
				Madison	8	48	89
Alachua	75	1,597	2,097	Manatee	66	1,162	1,984
Bay	103	1,282	1,348	Marion	85	1,194	1,568
Brevard	135	1,672	2,095	Martin	79	1,694	2,747
Broward	743	10,713	19,074	Miami-Dade	780	11,990	33,134
Charlotte	46	707	767	Monroe	165	1,000	2,070
Citrus	37	314	258	Nassau	17	109	112
Clay	34	961	1,114	Okaloosa	105	1,030	1,328
Collier	142	3,921	7,005	Okeechobee	6	76	94
Columbia	15	125	108	Orange	385	52,623	113,320
De Soto	9	97	97	Osceola	66	885	1,302
Duval	185	3,243	11,384	Palm Beach	586	11,861	22,713
Escambia	93	1,148	1,180	Pasco	78	644	786
Flagler	9	137	181	Pinellas	326	5,033	7,098
Franklin	5	4	3	Polk	130	2,528	3,402
Gadsden	4	17	19	Putnam	8	38	30
Hendry	3	11	11	St. Johns	53	1,453	5,031
Hernando	33	497	491	St. Lucie	35	435	553
Highlands	21	386	654	Santa Rosa	29	260	245
Hillsborough	319	9,045	24,498	Sarasota	183	4,159	5,864
Indian River	59	1,669	2,885	Seminole	139	1,875	2,764
Jackson	8	71	79	Suwannee	5	18	12
Lake	58	590	631	Volusia	188	2,953	8,039
Lee	178	2,750	4,026	Walton	13	105	141
Leon	75	958	1,180	Multicounty 1/	208	1,665	5,680

1/ Reporting units without a fixed location within the state or of unknown county location.
Note: Private employment. For a list of three-digit code industries included see Table 19.75. Data are preliminary. Only counties for which data are disclosed are shown. Detail may not add to totals due to disclosure editing and/or rounding. See Tables 23.70, 23.71, 23.72, 23.73, and 23.74 for public employment data.

Source: State of Florida, Department of Labor and Employment Security, Bureau of Labor Market Information, "Employment and Wages" (ES-202), unpublished data.

University of Florida   **Bureau of Economic and Business Research**

HEALTH, EDUCATION, AND CULTURAL SERVICES

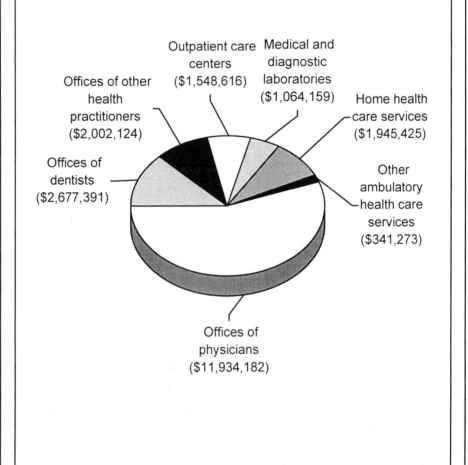

Ambulatory Health Care Services
Revenue, 1997
($1,000)

Outpatient care centers ($1,548,616)

Medical and diagnostic laboratories ($1,064,159)

Offices of other health practitioners ($2,002,124)

Home health care services ($1,945,425)

Offices of dentists ($2,677,391)

Other ambulatory health care services ($341,273)

Offices of physicians ($11,934,182)

Source: Table 20.01

University of Florida   **Bureau of Economic and Business Research**

TABLES LISTED BY MAJOR HEADINGS

Table 20.01.   HEALTH AND SOCIAL ASSISTANCE: ESTABLISHMENTS, EMPLOYMENT, RECEIPTS AND PAYROLL BY KIND OF BUSINESS IN FLORIDA, 1997

NAICS code	Industry	Number of establishments	Number of employees 1/	Revenue ($1,000)	Annual payroll ($1,000)
62	Health care and social assistance	35,568	447,117	32,559,076	13,610,691
621	Ambulatory health care services	30,366	254,419	21,513,170	9,616,351
6211	Offices of physicians	14,577	111,593	11,934,182	5,918,735
6212	Offices of dentists	6,182	34,667	2,677,391	1,064,916
6213	Offices of other health practitioners	6,164	28,488	2,002,124	806,330
6214	Outpatient care centers	1,102	15,584	1,548,616	459,714
6215	Medical and diagnostic laboratories	809	9,680	1,064,159	332,052
6216	Home health care services	1,293	49,415	1,945,425	923,178
6219	Other ambulatory health care services	239	4,992	341,273	111,426
622	Hospitals	145	81,958	6,478,501	2,133,625
6221	General medical and surgical hospitals	102	74,709	5,941,244	1,953,035
6222	Psychiatric and substance abuse hospitals	30	3,372	207,587	74,632
6223	Specialty (except psychiatric and substance abuse) hospitals	13	3,877	329,670	105,958
623	Nursing and residential care facilities	1,790	82,736	3,803,629	1,526,388
6231	Nursing care facilities	625	62,657	2,970,314	1,236,803
6232	Residential mental retardation/health and substance abuse facility	294	3,842	152,812	61,675
6233	Community care facilities for the elderly	797	15,269	639,321	212,037
6239	Other residential care facilities	74	968	41,182	15,873
624	Social assistance	3,267	28,004	763,776	334,327
6241	Individual and family services	670	2,835	142,717	53,982
6242	Community food and housing/emergency and other relief services	16	43	2,793	753
6243	Vocational rehabilitation services	121	1,209	70,148	29,410
6244	Child day care services	2,460	23,917	548,118	250,182

1/ Paid employment for the pay period including March 12.
Note: The economic censuses are conducted on a 5-year cycle collecting data for years ending in 2 and 7. Data are for North American Classification System (NAICS) code 62 and may not be comparable to earlier years. See Glossary for definition.

Table 20.02.   HEALTH AND SOCIAL ASSISTANCE: REVENUE AND EXPENDITURE FOR FIRMS EXEMPT FROM FEDERAL INCOME TAX BY KIND OF BUSINESS IN FLORIDA, 1997

NAICS code	Industry	Revenue ($1,000)	Expenditure ($1,000)
62	Health care and social assistance	19,415,124	18,414,308
621	Ambulatory health care services	1,483,926	1,423,297
622	Hospitals	14,638,636	13,845,155
623	Nursing and residential care facilities	1,595,676	1,525,163
624	Social assistance	1,696,886	1,620,693

Note: The economic censuses are conducted on a 5-year cycle collecting data for years ending in 2 and 7. Data are for North American Classification System (NAICS) code 62 and may not be comparable to earlier years. See Glossary for definition.

Source Tables 20.01 and 20.02: U.S., Department of Commerce, Bureau of the Census, *1997 Economic Census: Health Care and Social Assistance*, Geographic Area Series EC97S62A-FL, Issued October 1999, Internet site <http://www.census.gov/prod/ec97/97s62-fl.pdf> (accessed 26 June 2000).

University of Florida   **Bureau of Economic and Business Research**

Table 20.03. HEALTH AND SOCIAL ASSISTANCE: ESTABLISHMENTS, EMPLOYMENT, AND PAYROLL IN THE STATE AND COUNTIES OF FLORIDA, 1997

County	Number of establishments	Number of employees 1/	Annual payroll ($1,000)	County	Number of establishments	Number of employees 1/	Annual payroll ($1,000)
Florida	35,568	447,117	13,610,691	Lake	376	3,834	107,467
				Lee	825	12,968	408,448
Alachua	502	6,499	201,159	Leon	441	6,479	210,216
Baker	21	299	4,921	Levy	33	534	7,780
Bay	317	4,398	131,153	Liberty	8	156	2,154
Bradford	27	609	9,567	Madison	16	179	3,193
Brevard	1,017	10,631	357,959	Manatee	472	9,114	243,656
Broward	4,226	51,708	1,602,978	Marion	466	6,512	185,851
Calhoun	13	49	1,040	Martin	317	3,142	101,132
Charlotte	305	4,286	134,674	Miami-Dade	6,157	60,718	1,877,500
Citrus	228	3,228	84,981	Monroe	162	1,416	39,953
Clay	250	3,913	97,560	Nassau	56	683	16,438
Collier	492	5,124	174,952	Okaloosa	356	5,134	142,695
Columbia	108	1,406	35,313	Okeechobee	68	1,153	27,105
De Soto	37	253	5,242	Orange	1,792	22,044	774,021
Dixie	6	60	978	Osceola	252	4,024	103,751
Duval	1,579	23,107	810,500	Palm Beach	3,280	39,623	1,257,508
Escambia	535	9,282	301,329	Pasco	676	12,112	342,502
Flagler	62	305	9,772	Pinellas	2,633	36,006	1,051,977
Franklin	15	279	4,033	Polk	643	9,886	279,358
Gadsden	26	156	3,800	Putnam	93	1,961	47,678
Gilchrist	7	21	355	St. Johns	249	2,057	66,939
Glades	2	A/	(D)	St. Lucie	360	7,250	193,743
Gulf	16	370	8,276	Santa Rosa	127	1,881	42,818
Hamilton	14	188	4,261	Sarasota	1,032	12,069	369,461
Hardee	27	554	10,664	Seminole	716	8,306	254,896
Hendry	28	311	5,520	Sumter	23	332	6,518
Hernando	252	2,630	84,154	Suwannee	27	382	7,355
Highlands	184	1,759	47,248	Taylor	24	325	7,782
Hillsborough	2,233	29,728	905,656	Union	6	46	881
Holmes	16	367	7,226	Volusia	906	10,079	253,345
Indian River	287	3,388	96,368	Wakulla	8	171	2,861
Jackson	62	701	13,999	Walton	31	505	11,051
Jefferson	12	77	1,207	Washington	27	289	5,074
Lafayette	4	A/	(D)				

(D) Data withheld to avoid disclosure of information about individual firms.
Employment range: A/ 20-99.
1/ Paid employment for the pay period including March 12.
Note: The economic censuses are conducted on a 5-year cycle collecting data for years ending in 2 and 7. Data are for North American Classification System (NAICS) code 62 and may not be comparable to earlier years. See Glossary for definition.

Source: U.S., Department of Commerce, Bureau of the Census, *1997 Economic Census: Health and Social Assistance,* Geographic Area Series EC97S62A-FL, Issued October 1999, Internet site <http://www.census.gov/prod/ec97/97s62-fl.pdf> (accessed 26 June 2000).

Table 20.05. EMPLOYMENT AND PAYROLL: AVERAGE MONTHLY PRIVATE REPORTING UNITS, EMPLOYMENT AND PAYROLL COVERED BY UNEMPLOYMENT COMPENSATION LAW BY INDUSTRY IN FLORIDA, 1998 AND 1999

SIC code	Industry	1998 A/ Units	1998 A/ Employees	1998 A/ Payroll ($1,000)	1999 B/ Units	1999 B/ Employees	1999 B/ Payroll ($1,000)
80	Health services	30,062	576,228	1,607,030	30,555	576,613	1,635,193
801	Offices and clinics of doctors of medicine	13,700	122,445	546,896	14,171	126,580	564,569
802	Offices and clinics of dentists	5,529	34,750	95,854	5,592	35,686	101,034
803	Offices and clinics of doctors of osteopathy	524	3,493	12,384	519	3,418	11,791
804	Offices of other health practitioners	5,277	29,525	76,681	5,317	27,409	67,071
805	Nursing and personal care facilities	946	84,881	143,300	1,012	86,254	148,036
806	Hospitals	466	223,274	562,958	416	221,751	572,431
807	Medical and dental laboratories	1,318	12,736	34,148	1,318	13,762	40,788
808	Home health care services	1,105	38,759	74,490	1,067	35,845	69,231
809	Miscellaneous health and allied services, NEC	1,199	26,365	60,319	1,144	25,908	60,242
82	Educational services	2,161	58,593	121,072	2,291	62,655	134,596
821	Elementary and secondary schools	606	21,341	38,990	625	22,829	42,611
822	Colleges and universities	151	21,920	52,772	156	23,022	58,377
823	Libraries	35	264	390	38	296	536
824	Vocational schools	352	4,734	10,288	360	4,927	11,426
829	School and education services, NEC	1,017	10,335	18,632	1,112	11,580	21,646
83	Social services	6,526	119,292	166,765	6,543	121,302	173,208
832	Individual and family social services	1,462	25,184	39,169	1,424	24,120	38,905
833	Job training and related services	382	11,317	17,874	342	11,385	18,816
835	Child day care services	2,642	33,848	35,755	2,725	35,643	38,281
836	Residential care	1,366	40,050	56,613	1,369	40,184	57,760
839	Social services, NEC	675	8,894	17,354	683	9,971	19,444
84	Museums, botanical and zoological gardens	192	3,673	5,963	201	3,859	6,601
841	Museums and art galleries	140	2,200	3,602	151	2,336	4,153
842	Arboreta and botanical or zoological gardens	52	1,474	2,361	50	1,524	2,448

NEC Not elsewhere classified.
A/ Revised.
B/ Preliminary.
Note: Private employment. Detail may not add to totals due to disclosure editing and/or rounding. See Tables in Section 23.00 for public employment data.

Source: State of Florida, Department of Labor and Employment Security, Bureau of Labor Market Information, "Employment and Wages" (ES-202), unpublished data.

Table 20.06. OFFICES AND CLINICS OF DOCTORS OF MEDICINE: AVERAGE MONTHLY PRIVATE REPORTING UNITS, EMPLOYMENT, AND PAYROLL COVERED BY UNEMPLOYMENT COMPENSATION LAW IN THE STATE AND COUNTIES OF FLORIDA, 1999

County	Number of reporting units	Number of employees	Payroll ($1,000)	County	Number of reporting units	Number of employees	Payroll ($1,000)
			Offices and clinics of doctors of medicine (SIC code 801)				
Florida	14,171	126,580	564,569	Levy	9	35	130
				Madison	5	31	91
Alachua	219	2,416	10,894	Manatee	191	1,862	8,161
Baker	4	13	27	Marion	209	1,796	8,530
Bay	136	1,185	5,717	Martin	102	1,095	4,563
Brevard	322	3,642	18,037	Miami-Dade	2,900	18,881	75,051
Broward	1,574	11,147	52,957	Monroe	67	348	1,338
Charlotte	132	1,036	5,203	Nassau	16	70	279
Citrus	96	843	3,419	Okaloosa	131	1,078	4,046
Clay	73	640	2,439	Okeechobee	33	255	1,030
Collier	183	1,309	7,585	Orange	732	8,629	41,462
Columbia	44	321	1,154	Osceola	104	878	3,104
De Soto	14	60	243	Palm Beach	1,260	9,808	49,582
Duval	608	8,875	40,397	Pasco	331	2,642	11,200
Escambia	185	3,325	14,842	Pinellas	889	8,724	39,858
Flagler	22	153	479	Polk	201	4,017	13,915
Franklin	6	24	69	Putnam	45	370	1,083
Gadsden	5	30	78	St. Johns	111	523	2,113
Gulf	6	33	56	St. Lucie	143	1,083	4,818
Hamilton	4	15	30	Santa Rosa	45	264	1,053
Hardee	10	64	157	Sarasota	394	3,219	15,605
Hendry	5	15	23	Seminole	239	1,944	8,346
Hernando	100	513	2,381	Sumter	6	110	433
Highlands	76	332	1,228	Suwannee	9	35	75
Hillsborough	919	8,406	37,900	Taylor	11	126	337
Holmes	10	43	120	Union	3	26	56
Indian River	131	1,287	5,587	Volusia	322	3,176	14,205
Jackson	23	159	505	Walton	13	38	91
Lake	162	1,419	5,883	Washington	9	33	91
Lee	287	4,100	19,238				
Leon	162	2,470	10,517	Multicounty 1/	115	1,353	6,287

1/ Reporting units without a fixed location within the state or of unknown county location.
Note: Private employment. Data are preliminary. Only counties for which data are disclosed are shown. Detail may not add to totals due to disclosure editing and/or rounding. See Tables 23.70, 23.71, 23.72, 23.73, and 23.74 for public employment data.

Source: State of Florida, Department of Labor and Employment Security, Bureau of Labor Market Information, "Employment and Wages" (ES-202), unpublished data.

University of Florida   **Bureau of Economic and Business Research**

Table 20.07. OFFICES AND CLINICS OF DENTISTS: AVERAGE MONTHLY PRIVATE REPORTING
UNITS, EMPLOYMENT, AND PAYROLL COVERED BY UNEMPLOYMENT COMPENSATION LAW
IN THE STATE AND COUNTIES OF FLORIDA, 1999

County	Number of reporting units	Number of employees	Payroll ($1,000)	County	Number of reporting units	Number of employees	Payroll ($1,000)
\multicolumn{8}{c}{Offices and clinics of dentists (SIC code 802)}							
Florida	5,592	35,686	101,034	Manatee	82	512	1,465
				Marion	70	506	1,160
Alachua	82	549	1,470	Martin	50	315	1,021
Bay	45	332	933	Miami-Dade	934	4,980	13,067
Bradford	7	49	111	Monroe	26	153	423
Brevard	158	1,228	3,680	Nassau	12	76	192
Broward	687	3,828	10,832	Okaloosa	64	449	986
Calhoun	4	23	57	Okeechobee	6	43	82
Charlotte	40	277	872	Orange	306	1,975	5,938
Citrus	25	174	449	Osceola	34	254	706
Clay	45	331	786	Palm Beach	545	3,022	9,839
Collier	98	538	1,788	Pasco	72	504	1,315
Columbia	9	63	193	Pinellas	376	3,000	8,488
Duval	259	2,035	5,618	Polk	109	728	2,204
Escambia	104	723	2,012	Putnam	12	99	264
Flagler	9	84	236	St. Johns	31	211	610
Gadsden	5	34	65	St. Lucie	49	346	971
Hendry	6	49	78	Santa Rosa	25	195	506
Hernando	34	384	1,041	Sarasota	183	942	2,747
Highlands	22	125	280	Seminole	127	947	2,689
Hillsborough	319	2,107	6,345	Suwannee	6	54	105
Indian River	48	301	886	Volusia	131	738	1,950
Jackson	6	39	76	Walton	6	24	42
Lake	57	413	990	Washington	5	17	22
Lee	139	915	2,894				
Leon	71	535	1,567	Multicounty 1/	24	263	551
Levy	5	33	62				

1/ Reporting units without a fixed location within the state or of unknown county location.
Note: Private employment. Data are preliminary. Only counties for which data are disclosed are
shown. Detail may not add to totals due to disclosure editing and/or rounding. See Tables 23.70, 23.71,
23.72, 23.73, and 23.74 for public employment data.

Source: State of Florida, Department of Labor and Employment Security, Bureau of Labor Market Information, "Employment and Wages" (ES-202), unpublished data.

University of Florida   **Bureau of Economic and Business Research**

Table 20.11. NURSING AND PERSONAL CARE FACILITIES AND HOSPITALS: AVERAGE MONTHLY PRIVATE REPORTING UNITS, EMPLOYMENT, AND PAYROLL COVERED BY UNEMPLOYMENT COMPENSATION LAW IN THE STATE AND COUNTIES OF FLORIDA, 1999

County	Number of reporting units	Number of employees	Payroll ($1,000)	County	Number of reporting units	Number of employees	Payroll ($1,000)
			Nursing and personal care facilities (SIC code 805)				
Florida	1,012	86,254	148,036	Leon	14	1,568	2,504
				Manatee	20	2,035	2,912
Alachua	12	851	1,374	Marion	14	1,358	2,259
Bay	12	961	1,510	Martin	9	765	1,321
Brevard	29	2,649	4,472	Miami-Dade	91	8,709	15,424
Broward	66	5,192	8,831	Okaloosa	11	886	1,374
Charlotte	12	1,290	2,017	Orange	43	4,680	8,409
Citrus	11	1,235	2,008	Osceola	14	1,202	1,879
Clay	13	911	1,641	Palm Beach	82	7,686	13,378
Collier	13	1,374	2,519	Pasco	28	1,773	2,911
Columbia	5	287	456	Pinellas	110	8,207	15,095
Duval	45	3,882	6,255	Polk	33	2,709	4,825
Escambia	12	1,300	1,900	Putnam	4	442	675
Hernando	5	506	867	St. Johns	10	678	1,088
Highlands	8	554	891	St. Lucie	8	778	1,316
Hillsborough	49	3,515	6,679	Sarasota	46	3,166	5,897
Indian River	6	812	1,218	Seminole	18	1,493	2,587
Jackson	5	453	620	Suwannee	4	641	881
Lake	14	1,305	1,959	Volusia	41	2,916	4,687
Lee	25	1,693	2,815	Multicounty 1/	20	1,203	3,725
			Hospitals (SIC code 806)				
Florida	416	221,751	572,431	Okaloosa	5	1,722	3,674
				Orange	24	19,315	49,974
Alachua	7	7,702	20,459	Osceola	5	1,550	3,937
Brevard	11	6,623	15,432	Palm Beach	34	15,400	40,063
Broward	38	11,937	29,315	Pasco	10	3,871	9,621
Duval	18	15,099	34,452	Pinellas	27	15,267	37,722
Escambia	4	6,412	15,444	Polk	6	6,639	18,083
Highlands	4	1,580	3,371	St. Lucie	7	2,170	5,715
Hillsborough	20	16,167	41,814	Santa Rosa	5	991	2,110
Lake	6	3,334	7,644	Sarasota	7	6,585	17,137
Lee	9	1,856	4,928	Seminole	7	3,054	8,070
Miami-Dade	73	37,193	110,319	Volusia	12	6,284	15,475
Monroe	4	982	2,603	Multicounty 1/	6	63	628

1/ Reporting units without a fixed location within the state or of unknown county location.
Note: Private employment. Data are preliminary. Only counties for which data are disclosed are shown. Detail may not add to totals due to disclosure editing and/or rounding. See Tables 23.70, 23.71, 23.72, 23.73, and 23.74 for public employment data.

Source: State of Florida, Department of Labor and Employment Security, Bureau of Labor Market Information, "Employment and Wages" (ES-202), unpublished data.

Table 20.14. VETERANS ADMINISTRATION MEDICAL CENTERS (VAMC): INPATIENT AND
OUTPATIENT MEDICAL AND DENTAL CARE BY VAMC IN FLORIDA
FISCAL YEAR 1997

Item	Bay Pines	Gaines-ville	Lake City	Miami	Tampa	West Palm Beach
Inpatient medical care						
Hospitals						
Average operating beds 1/ 2/	398	257	149	443	382	127
Medical 3/	211	115	117	269	238	89
Surgical	75	87	10	47	84	10
Psychiatric	112	55	22	127	60	28
Patients treated 2/ 4/	8,826	5,502	3,440	7,766	8,673	4,004
Medical 3/	5,622	3,273	2,652	4,751	5,513	2,698
Surgical	1,335	1,425	358	1,620	2,012	359
Psychiatric	1,869	804	430	1,395	1,148	947
Average daily census 5/	242	108	98	282	228	84
Nursing homes						
Patients treated in VAMC facility	458	76	425	423	792	287
Patients treated in community home 6/	429	233	77	114	336	167
State home	0	170	0	0	0	0
Domiciliaries						
Patients treated in VAMC facility	416	0	0	0	0	0
State home	0	0	277	0	0	0
Outpatient medical care						
Visits to VAMC staff	269,934	208,236	94,430	297,559	316,096	269,560
Fee basis care	62,261	6,961	3,807	7,220	183	12,301
Inpatient dental care						
Patients treated in VAMC facility	2,440	523	18,591	2,811	787	1,104
Outpatient dental care						
Visits to VAMC staff	8,524	6,888	2,713	9,153	8,630	10,037
Fee based cases completed	2,019	3	24	0	0	0

1/ Based on the number of operating beds at the end of each month for 13 consecutive months
(September 1996 through September 1997).
2/ Beds are classified according to their intended use; patients are classified according to the
classification of the beds they occupy, rather than on a diagnostic basis.
3/ Medical bed section includes medicine, neurology, intermediate care, spinal cord injury, rehabilitation medicine, and blind rehabilitation.
4/ The number of discharges and deaths during the fiscal year plus the patients remaining on
September 30, 1997, plus the number of interhospital transfers.
5/ Number of patient days during the fiscal year divided by the number of days in the fiscal year.
6/ Authorized and paid for by Veterans Administration.

Source: U.S., Department of Veterans Affairs, *Annual Report of the Secretary of Veterans Affairs,
Fiscal Year 1997.*

University of Florida   **Bureau of Economic and Business Research**

Table 20.15. HOSPITALS: NUMBER OF GENERAL, SHORT-TERM ACUTE CARE HOSPITALS AND NUMBER OF LICENSED AND ACUTE CARE BEDS IN THE STATE, AGENCY FOR HEALTH CARE ADMINISTRATION (AHCA) REGIONS AND COUNTIES OF FLORIDA, 1996

AHCA region and county	Number of hospitals	Licensed beds Total 1/	Acute care	AHCA region and county	Number of hospitals	Licensed beds Total 1/	Acute care
Florida	198	54,060	46,587	AHCA 4 (Cont.)			
				Flagler	1	81	73
AHCA 1	9	2,180	1,736	Nassau	1	260	208
Escambia	3	1,514	1,176	St. Johns	7	1,452	1,231
Okaloosa	3	432	336	Volusia	1	54	54
Santa Rosa	2	184	174	AHCA 5	21	5,484	4,769
Walton	1	50	50	Pasco	5	1,032	916
AHCA 2	14	2,001	1,735	Pinellas	16	4,452	3,853
Bay	2	529	486	AHCA 6	19	6,247	5,372
Calhoun	1	36	36	Highlands	2	321	284
Franklin	1	29	29	Hillsborough	10	3,362	2,938
Gadsden	1	51	51	Manatee	2	895	757
Gulf	1	45	45	Polk	5	1,669	1,393
Holmes	1	34	34	AHCA 7	13	5,103	4,420
Jackson	2	156	156	Brevard	4	1,183	1,116
Leon	2	950	727	Orange	6	3,323	2,818
Madison	1	42	42	Osceola	1	165	152
Taylor	1	48	48	Seminole	2	432	334
Washington	1	81	81	AHCA 8	15	4,263	3,672
AHCA 3	22	3,607	3,317	Charlotte	3	661	554
Alachua	3	1,264	1,109	Collier	1	458	381
Baker	1	25	25	De Soto	1	82	82
Bradford	1	49	49	Hendry	1	66	66
Citrus	2	299	283	Lee	5	1,536	1,393
Columbia	2	203	178	Sarasota	4	1,460	1,196
Hamilton	1	42	42	AHCA 9	21	4,820	4,219
Hernando	3	370	370	Indian River	2	472	378
Lake	3	544	500	Martin	1	336	331
Levy	1	40	40	Okeechobee	1	101	89
Marion	2	553	533	Palm Beach	15	3,396	3,035
Putnam	1	161	131	St. Lucie	2	515	386
Suwannee	1	30	30	AHCA 10	18	5,879	5,123
Union	1	27	27	Broward	18	5,879	5,123
AHCA 4	18	4,820	4,094	AHCA 11	28	9,602	8,067
Clay	1	219	175	Miami-Dade	26	9,335	7,860
Duval	8	2,808	2,407	Monroe	2	267	207

1/ Licensed inpatient beds that can be made ready and available within 48 hours. Includes acute care, psychiatric, substance abuse, rehabilitation, and neonatal intensive care beds, among others.

Note: Based on reports from 200 hospitals statewide. Reports include some teaching and specialty hospitals. For the most part, data are for general, short-term acute care hospitals offering more intensive services than those required for room, board, personal services, and general nursing care. See Glossary for definitions.

Source: State of Florida, Agency for Health Care Administration, *1999 Guide to Hospitals in Florida,* Internet site <http://www.fdhc.state.fl.us/>.

Table 20.16. HOSPITALS: DISCHARGES OF PATIENTS OF GENERAL, SHORT-TERM ACUTE CARE HOSPITALS BY SERVICE LINE IN THE STATE AGENCY FOR HEALTH CARE ADMINISTRATION (AHCA) REGIONS, AND COUNTIES OF FLORIDA, 1995 AND 1996

AHCA region and county	Total	Cardiology 1/	Gastroenterology	General surgery	Gynecology 2/	Neonatology	Neurology 3/	Oncology	Orthopedics	Other medicine 4/
Florida	1,581,982	303,054	116,740	102,844	259,716	49,272	117,880	45,468	110,942	476,066
AHCA 1	59,339	10,540	4,231	3,736	10,119	1,922	4,690	1,630	4,298	18,173
Escambia	41,710	7,876	2,747	2,675	7,151	1,624	3,384	1,420	2,885	11,948
Okaloosa	12,643	1,888	978	824	2,235	241	1,016	210	978	4,273
Santa Rosa	4,123	569	414	188	733	57	202	0	435	1,525
Walton	863	207	92	49	0	0	88	0	0	427
AHCA 2	52,817	9,082	3,980	3,234	10,369	1,540	3,963	1,002	3,272	16,375
Bay	18,326	3,343	1,526	1,131	2,895	450	1,292	389	1,390	5,910
Calhoun	254	73	0	0	0	0	0	0	0	181
Franklin	374	68	68	0	0	0	0	0	0	238
Gadsden	316	50	59	0	0	0	0	0	0	207
Gulf	393	89	104	0	0	0	0	0	0	200
Holmes	746	149	74	0	0	0	45	0	0	478
Jackson	3,640	427	319	229	1,047	45	136	50	250	1,137
Leon	26,764	4,514	1,604	1,825	6,395	1,045	2,432	533	1,632	6,784
Madison	265	34	42	0	0	0	0	0	0	189
Taylor	679	101	89	49	0	0	0	0	0	440
Washington	1,060	234	95	0	32	0	58	30	0	611
AHCA 3	126,757	24,710	10,242	8,847	16,766	2,550	9,972	3,578	9,118	40,974
Alachua	43,604	6,414	2,799	3,464	7,367	1,611	3,718	1,715	3,271	13,245
Bradford	597	139	81	0	0	0	45	0	0	332
Citrus	12,559	2,410	1,330	945	1,231	112	867	426	1,066	4,172
Columbia	5,518	1,245	706	313	551	57	278	79	131	2,158
Hamilton	405	70	64	0	0	0	35	0	0	236
Hernando	14,797	3,067	1,466	953	1,547	163	1,027	299	1,115	5,160
Lake	18,504	3,614	1,602	1,399	2,414	279	1,335	416	1,495	5,950
Levy	652	210	74	0	0	0	78	0	0	290
Marion	24,465	6,211	1,662	1,536	3,045	262	2,288	548	1,728	7,185

See footnotes at end of table.

Continued . . .

Table 20.16. HOSPITALS: DISCHARGES OF PATIENTS OF GENERAL, SHORT-TERM ACUTE CARE HOSPITALS BY SERVICE LINE IN THE STATE AGENCY FOR HEALTH CARE ADMINISTRATION (AHCA) REGIONS, AND COUNTIES OF FLORIDA, 1995 AND 1996 (Continued)

AHCA region and county	Total	Cardiology 1/	Gastroenterology	General surgery	Gynecology 2/	Neonatology	Neurology 3/	Oncology	Orthopedics	Other medicine 4/
AHCA 3 (Continued)										
Putnam	5,227	1,243	397	237	611	66	301	95	312	1,965
Suwannee	249	43	30	0	0	0	0	0	0	176
Union	180	44	31	0	0	0	0	0	0	105
AHCA 4	148,190	26,384	10,710	9,591	26,660	4,261	11,031	3,599	10,192	45,762
Baker	219	0	63	0	38	0	0	0	0	118
Clay	8,563	1,226	605	537	2,288	264	566	142	608	2,327
Duval	88,161	15,420	5,487	5,380	17,372	3,083	6,651	2,147	5,181	27,440
Flagler	1,406	279	186	110	0	0	144	36	119	532
Nassau	1,470	158	160	102	528	41	61	0	78	342
St. Johns	6,874	1,021	800	521	1,107	88	387	105	449	2,396
Volusia	41,497	8,280	3,409	2,941	5,327	785	3,222	1,169	3,757	12,607
AHCA 5	150,933	32,148	12,716	10,389	17,291	3,358	12,262	3,450	12,763	46,556
Pasco	38,433	10,713	3,564	2,616	2,458	317	3,156	821	2,818	11,970
Pinellas	112,500	21,435	9,152	7,773	14,833	3,041	9,106	2,629	9,945	34,586
AHCA 6	175,560	29,786	12,573	11,038	32,585	6,269	13,258	5,937	12,240	51,874
Highlands	10,682	1,715	1,038	693	1,186	204	733	324	770	4,019
Hillsborough	97,775	14,815	6,049	6,282	20,570	3,903	7,258	3,668	6,537	28,693
Manatee	22,219	4,494	1,908	1,574	3,341	517	2,216	471	1,873	5,825
Polk	44,884	8,762	3,578	2,489	7,488	1,645	3,051	1,474	3,060	13,337
AHCA 7	177,075	35,560	11,681	10,682	34,028	6,466	11,744	5,355	11,023	50,536
Brevard	45,965	9,850	3,755	2,598	6,379	1,341	3,789	1,339	3,308	13,606
Orange	114,070	22,514	6,805	6,864	23,401	4,739	7,187	3,677	6,748	32,135
Osceola	6,888	990	428	460	1,962	167	307	135	347	2,092
Seminole	10,152	2,206	693	760	2,286	219	461	204	620	2,703
AHCA 8	126,539	26,292	10,025	8,730	17,347	2,300	11,345	4,023	11,269	35,208
Charlotte	18,698	4,453	1,530	1,251	2,060	232	1,419	607	1,481	5,665

See footnotes at end of table.

Continued . . .

Table 20.16. HOSPITALS: DISCHARGES OF PATIENTS OF GENERAL, SHORT-TERM ACUTE CARE HOSPITALS BY SERVICE LINE IN THE STATE, AGENCY FOR HEALTH CARE ADMINISTRATION (AHCA) REGIONS, AND COUNTIES OF FLORIDA, 1995 AND 1996 (Continued)

AHCA region and county	Total	Cardiology 1/	Gastroenterology	General surgery	Gynecology 2/	Neonatology	Neurology 3/	Oncology	Orthopedics	Other medicine 4/
AHCA 8 (Continued)										
Collier	18,626	2,802	1,581	1,322	3,094	364	2,133	582	1,687	5,061
De Soto	1,991	302	163	183	566	54	132	36	0	555
Hendry	833	186	124	45	0	0	75	0	0	403
Lee	48,376	9,908	3,459	3,298	7,327	1,071	4,595	1,275	4,090	13,353
Sarasota	38,015	8,641	3,168	2,631	4,300	579	2,991	1,523	4,011	10,171
AHCA 9	162,876	31,776	11,704	10,524	24,572	4,869	12,775	5,607	12,055	48,994
Indian River	11,849	2,062	1,039	865	1,332	295	1,059	518	1,293	3,386
Martin	12,311	2,245	1,112	806	1,659	247	1,048	518	944	3,732
Okeechobee	3,511	814	364	243	42	0	270	88	201	1,489
Palm Beach	118,561	23,812	7,925	7,619	18,922	3,835	8,973	4,081	8,237	35,157
St. Lucie	16,644	2,843	1,264	991	2,617	492	1,425	402	1,380	5,230
AHCA 10	151,628	31,136	11,015	9,532	24,876	5,088	10,172	3,728	10,199	45,882
Broward	151,628	31,136	11,015	9,532	24,876	5,088	10,172	3,728	10,199	45,882
AHCA 11	250,268	45,640	17,863	16,541	45,103	10,649	16,668	7,559	14,513	75,732
Miami-Dade	244,701	44,943	17,404	15,925	44,383	10,577	16,429	7,383	13,800	73,857
Monroe	5,567	697	459	616	720	72	239	176	713	1,875

1/ Includes cardiac surgery.
2/ Includes obstetrics.
3/ Includes neurosurgery.
4/ Includes pediatrics, pulmonary medicine, urology, and vascular surgery.
Note: Data are for discharges occurring in both 1995 and 1996 and are based on reports from 200 hospitals statewide. Reports include some teaching and specialty hospitals. For the most part, data are for general, short-term acute care hospitals which offer more intensive services than those required for room, board, personal services, and general nursing care. See Glossary for definitions.

Source: State of Florida, Agency for Health Care Administration, *1999 Guide to Hospitals in Florida*, Internet site <http://www.fdhc.state.fl.us/>.

Table 20.20.   EDUCATIONAL SERVICES: ESTABLISHMENTS, EMPLOYMENT, RECEIPTS, AND PAYROLL BY KIND OF BUSINESS IN FLORIDA, 1997

NAICS code	Industry	Number of establishments	Number of employees 1/	Receipts ($1,000)	Annual payroll ($1,000)
61	Educational services	2,248	15,730	1,058,027	321,540
6114	Business schools and computer and management training	351	2,585	249,558	82,671
61141	Business and secretarial schools	26	411	16,788	6,358
61142	Computer training	151	1,154	112,093	38,830
61143	Professional and management development training	174	1,020	120,677	37,483
6115	Technical and trade schools	402	4,752	371,639	107,234
611511	Cosmetology and barber schools	89	442	17,103	6,079
611512	Flight training	98	1,758	177,659	49,294
611513	Apprenticeship training	15	26	2,333	709
611519	Other trade and technical schools	200	2,526	174,544	51,152
6116	Other schools and instruction	1,297	7,345	374,738	112,795
61161	Fine arts schools	400	1,648	65,998	17,928
61162	Sports and recreation instruction	455	2,221	125,465	40,457
61163	Language schools	39	599	34,512	8,536
61169	All other schools and instruction	403	2,877	148,763	45,874
611691	Exam preparation and tutoring	142	1,245	49,180	16,897
611692	Automobile driving schools	56	404	18,133	4,472
611699	All other miscellaneous schools and instruction	205	1,228	81,450	24,505
6117	Educational support services	198	1,048	62,092	18,840

1/ Paid employment for the pay period including March 12.
Note: The economic censuses are conducted on a 5-year cycle collecting data for years ending in 2 and 7. Data are for North American Classification System (NAICS) code 61 and may not be comparable to earlier years. See Glossary for definition.

Table 20.21.   EDUCATIONAL SERVICES: REVENUE AND EXPENDITURE FOR FIRMS EXEMPT FROM FEDERAL INCOME TAX BY KIND OF BUSINESS IN FLORIDA, 1997

(in thousands of dollars)

NAICS code	Industry	Revenue	Expenditure
61	Educational services	127,934	111,694
6114	Business schools and computer and management training	6,559	5,975
6115	Technical and trade schools	27,026	22,879
6116	Other schools and instruction	80,885	71,013
6117	Educational support services	13,464	11,827

Note: The economic censuses are conducted on a 5-year cycle collecting data for years ending in 2 and 7. Data are for North American Classification System (NAICS) code 61 and may not be comparable to earlier years. See Glossary for definition.

Source Tables 20.20 and 20.21: U.S., Department of Commerce, Bureau of the Census, *1997 Economic Census: Educational Services*, Geographic Area Series EC97S61A-FL, Issued August 1999, Internet site <http://www.census.gov/prod/ec97/97s61-fl.pdf> (accessed 26 June 2000).

University of Florida   **Bureau of Economic and Business Research**

Table 20.22. EDUCATIONAL SERVICES: ESTABLISHMENTS, EMPLOYMENT, AND PAYROLL
IN THE STATE AND COUNTIES OF FLORIDA, 1997

County	Number of establishments	Number of employees 1/	Annual payroll ($1,000)	County	Number of establishments	Number of employees 1/	Annual payroll ($1,000)
Florida	2,248	15,730	321,540	Lake	20	58	813
				Lee	41	191	3,256
Alachua	30	156	1,949	Leon	58	305	4,874
Baker	0	0	0	Levy	3	5	82
Bay	12	64	1,151	Liberty	0	0	0
Bradford	0	0	0	Madison	1	A/	(D)
Brevard	67	325	6,015	Manatee	23	341	10,583
Broward	304	2,309	42,556	Marion	15	121	1,660
Calhoun	0	0	0	Martin	18	34	668
Charlotte	14	105	3,792	Miami-Dade	340	2,412	52,852
Citrus	10	26	424	Monroe	14	63	1,064
Clay	18	120	1,829	Nassau	6	34	909
Collier	32	95	1,294	Okaloosa	24	158	3,018
Columbia	6	12	113	Okeechobee	1	A/	(D)
De Soto	0	0	0	Orange	158	1,387	35,594
Dixie	0	0	0	Osceola	19	50	1,001
Duval	102	943	19,912	Palm Beach	219	1,077	21,588
Escambia	31	166	·2,664	Pasco	21	146	2,568
Flagler	3	7	104	Pinellas	156	1,081	22,341
Franklin	0	0	0	Polk	44	348	5,637
Gadsden	4	16	322	Putnam	2	A/	(D)
Gilchrist	2	A/	(D)	St. Johns	10	35	832
Glades	0	0	0	St. Lucie	14	30	620
Gulf	0	0	0	Santa Rosa	11	21	416
Hamilton	0	0	0	Sarasota	57	246	3,447
Hardee	1	A/	(D)	Seminole	86	854	16,828
Hendry	1	A/	(D)	Sumter	3	A/	(D)
Hernando	4	11	74	Suwannee	2	A/	(D)
Highlands	0	0	0	Taylor	1	A/	(D)
Hillsborough	149	1,698	34,301	Union	0	0	0
Holmes	0	0	0	Volusia	62	384	7,063
Indian River	22	257	6,841	Wakulla	2	A/	(D)
Jackson	3	6	27	Walton	0	0	0
Jefferson	1	A/	(D)	Washington	0	0	0
Lafayette	1	A/	(D)				

(D) Data withheld to avoid disclosure of information about individual firms.
Employment range: A/ 0-19.
1/ Paid employment for pay period including March 12.
Note: The economic censuses are conducted on a 5-year cycle collecting data for years ending in 2
and 7. Data are for North American Classification System (NAICS) code 61 and may not be comparable
to earlier years. See Glossary for definition.

Source: U.S., Department of Commerce, Bureau of the Census, *1997 Economic Census: Educational
Services,* Geographic Area Series EC97S61A-FL, Issued August 1999, Internet site <http://www.census.
gov/prod/ec97/97s61-fl.pdf> (accessed 26 June 2000).

University of Florida   **Bureau of Economic and Business Research**

Table 20.27. EDUCATIONAL SERVICES: AVERAGE MONTHLY PRIVATE REPORTING UNITS EMPLOYMENT, AND PAYROLL COVERED BY UNEMPLOYMENT COMPENSATION LAW IN THE STATE AND COUNTIES OF FLORIDA, 1998 AND 1999

County	Number of reporting units	Number of employees	Payroll ($1,000)	County	Number of reporting units	Number of employees	Payroll ($1,000)
\multicolumn{8}{c}{Educational services, 1998 A/ (SIC code 82)}
Florida	2,161	58,593	121,072	Miami-Dade	353	14,077	32,914
				Monroe	11	215	427
Alachua	43	885	1,245	Nassau	7	30	39
Bay	13	164	276	Okaloosa	10	115	158
Brevard	65	1,571	3,185	Orange	164	4,109	8,566
Broward	233	7,946	17,377	Osceola	17	137	215
Charlotte	10	91	131	Palm Beach	179	4,002	8,173
Clay	14	443	967	Pasco	24	513	943
Collier	25	629	1,413	Pinellas	158	2,898	6,185
Columbia	8	53	50	Polk	43	1,942	3,104
Duval	129	3,444	6,084	Putnam	3	23	31
Escambia	42	2,070	3,149	St. Johns	16	451	845
Hillsborough	151	3,856	7,924	St. Lucie	12	182	311
Indian River	14	453	922	Santa Rosa	9	21	64
Lake	17	350	569	Sarasota	61	900	2,010
Lee	37	649	1,164	Seminole	57	1,306	2,425
Leon	48	560	889	Volusia	44	2,878	6,460
Manatee	26	361	530	Washington	3	16	11
Marion	12	214	273				
Martin	14	187	349	Multicounty 1/	56	334	1,049
\multicolumn{8}{c}{Vocational schools, 1998 A/ (SIC code 824)}
Florida	352	4,734	10,288	Miami-Dade	62	1,084	2,077
				Okaloosa	3	12	33
Alachua	8	225	323	Orange	31	491	1,362
Brevard	13	57	147	Palm Beach	36	403	774
Broward	34	638	1,238	Pasco	4	13	14
Duval	24	328	698	Pinellas	28	300	810
Escambia	7	30	74	Polk	4	54	119
Hillsborough	18	145	432	Sarasota	9	32	63
Lee	4	15	13	Volusia	11	121	217
Leon	10	54	88	Multicounty 1/	14	210	676

See footnotes at end of table.   Continued . . .

University of Florida   **Bureau of Economic and Business Research**

Table 20.27. EDUCATIONAL SERVICES: AVERAGE MONTHLY PRIVATE REPORTING UNITS EMPLOYMENT, AND PAYROLL COVERED BY UNEMPLOYMENT COMPENSATION LAW IN THE STATE AND COUNTIES OF FLORIDA, 1998 AND 1999 (Continued)

County	Number of reporting units	Number of employees	Payroll ($1,000)	County	Number of reporting units	Number of employees	Payroll ($1,000)
				Educational services, 1999 B/ (SIC code 82)			
Florida	2,291	62,655	134,596	Martin	16	226	386
				Miami-Dade	362	14,486	35,128
Alachua	48	1,005	1,408	Monroe	15	232	427
Bay	14	161	494	Nassau	7	46	68
Brevard	65	1,629	3,376	Okaloosa	11	139	193
Broward	249	8,592	19,879	Orange	171	4,427	9,831
Charlotte	11	102	163	Osceola	17	139	242
Clay	14	368	791	Palm Beach	180	4,367	9,168
Collier	28	725	1,787	Pasco	29	660	1,265
Columbia	7	44	40	Pinellas	154	3,080	6,785
Duval	133	3,525	6,873	Polk	46	2,126	3,531
Escambia	47	2,182	3,713	Putnam	3	46	55
Hernando	6	137	175	St. Johns	17	492	997
Hillsborough	171	4,626	9,169	St. Lucie	13	194	302
Indian River	17	511	1,033	Santa Rosa	9	34	105
Lake	18	387	638	Sarasota	65	982	2,187
Lee	42	715	1,295	Seminole	60	1,409	2,723
Leon	55	627	976	Volusia	49	3,012	7,248
Manatee	22	291	474	Washington	3	15	12
Marion	11	224	296	Multicounty 1/	75	321	844
				Vocational schools, 1999 B/ (SIC code 824)			
Florida	360	4,927	11,426	Leon	14	63	105
				Miami-Dade	65	1,090	2,175
Alachua	7	250	421	Okaloosa	3	21	55
Brevard	13	71	178	Orange	31	538	1,577
Broward	38	672	1,457	Palm Beach	34	540	985
Clay	3	10	22	Pinellas	22	265	891
Duval	26	374	923	Polk	4	52	125
Escambia	9	29	62	Sarasota	7	40	78
Hillsborough	21	150	426	Volusia	10	121	192
Lee	5	12	15	Multicounty 1/	15	62	148

A/ Revised.
B/ Preliminary.
1/ Reporting units without a fixed location within the state or of unknown county location.
Note: Private employment. See Table 20.05 for a list of educational services included. Only counties for which data are disclosed are shown. Detail may not add to totals due to disclosure editing and/or rounding. See tables 23.70, 23.71, 23.72, 23.73, and 23.74 for public employment data.

Source: State of Florida, Department of Labor and Employment Security, Bureau of Labor Market Information, "Employment and Wages" (ES-202), unpublished data.

University of Florida   **Bureau of Economic and Business Research**

Table 20.28. SOCIAL SERVICES: AVERAGE MONTHLY PRIVATE EMPLOYMENT COVERED
BY UNEMPLOYMENT COMPENSATION LAW BY TYPE OF SOCIAL SERVICE
IN THE STATE AND COUNTIES OF FLORIDA, 1999

County	Total (SIC 83)	Individual and family (SIC 832)	Job train-ing and vocational reha-bilitation (SIC 833)	Child day care (SIC 835)	Resi-dential care 1/ (SIC 836)	Social services NEC 2/ (SIC 839)
Florida	121,301	24,120	11,384	35,643	40,183	9,970
Alachua	2,506	292	(NA)	898	727	430
Baker	119	(NA)	(NA)	46	(NA)	(NA)
Bay	1,244	351	(NA)	422	382	30
Bradford	147	(NA)	47	54	(NA)	(NA)
Brevard	2,989	482	590	1,176	619	121
Broward	10,793	1,879	599	4,572	2,792	948
Calhoun	69	(NA)	(NA)	(NA)	(NA)	(NA)
Charlotte	651	118	34	250	240	7
Citrus	382	16	(NA)	182	179	(NA)
Clay	842	114	63	308	352	(NA)
Collier	1,571	285	41	428	778	38
Columbia	429	89	(NA)	264	(NA)	(NA)
De Soto	94	(NA)	(NA)	43	11	(NA)
Dixie	62	(NA)	(NA)	(NA)	(NA)	(NA)
Duval	7,325	1,749	611	2,502	1,718	742
Escambia	3,807	640	218	670	1,944	333
Flagler	173	76	(NA)	23	40	(NA)
Franklin	51	(NA)	(NA)	(NA)	(NA)	(NA)
Gadsden	186	(NA)	(NA)	70	32	(NA)
Gilchrist	27	(NA)	(NA)	(NA)	(NA)	(NA)
Glades	(NA)	(NA)	(NA)	(NA)	(NA)	(NA)
Gulf	(NA)	(NA)	(NA)	(NA)	(NA)	(NA)
Hamilton	33	(NA)	(NA)	(NA)	(NA)	(NA)
Hardee	211	(NA)	(NA)	113	61	(NA)
Hendry	242	(NA)	23	138	(NA)	(NA)
Hernando	565	198	(NA)	89	207	(NA)
Highlands	572	(NA)	198	140	152	(NA)
Hillsborough	9,421	2,384	641	2,772	2,887	734
Holmes	132	(NA)	(NA)	57	(NA)	(NA)
Indian River	844	243	(NA)	295	237	67
Jackson	285	159	30	94	(NA)	(NA)
Jefferson	42	(NA)	(NA)	(NA)	(NA)	(NA)
Lafayette	28	(NA)	(NA)	(NA)	(NA)	(NA)
Lake	1,569	41	(NA)	345	985	111
Lee	4,973	330	345	706	3,409	181
Leon	2,795	900	238	655	587	413
Levy	335	(NA)	(NA)	124	(NA)	(NA)
Liberty	26	(NA)	(NA)	(NA)	(NA)	(NA)

See footnotes at end of table.   Continued . . .

Table 20.28. SOCIAL SERVICES: AVERAGE MONTHLY PRIVATE EMPLOYMENT COVERED BY UNEMPLOYMENT COMPENSATION LAW BY TYPE OF SOCIAL SERVICE IN THE STATE AND COUNTIES OF FLORIDA, 1999 (Continued)

County	Total (SIC 83)	Individual and family (SIC 832)	Job training and vocational rehabilitation (SIC 833)	Child day care (SIC 835)	Residential care 1/ (SIC 836)	Social services NEC 2/ (SIC 839)
Madison	220	(NA)	(NA)	20	(NA)	(NA)
Manatee	2,215	405	(NA)	637	972	(NA)
Marion	1,488	341	324	451	361	(NA)
Martin	1,726	138	(NA)	182	1,241	(NA)
Miami-Dade	14,494	3,358	1,850	3,978	3,828	1,477
Monroe	296	106	(NA)	127	(NA)	16
Nassau	504	225	(NA)	64	(NA)	(NA)
Okaloosa	1,134	233	(NA)	532	294	(NA)
Okeechobee	419	(NA)	(NA)	150	(NA)	(NA)
Orange	5,925	1,005	529	2,209	1,539	640
Osceola	1,056	273	(NA)	299	22	177
Palm Beach	8,517	1,563	1,072	2,608	1,978	1,295
Pasco	1,449	449	64	572	340	22
Pinellas	9,430	1,966	1,622	1,843	3,519	478
Polk	2,830	411	279	963	1,103	72
Putnam	493	57	(NA)	71	240	116
St. Johns	954	194	(NA)	351	384	19
St. Lucie	1,332	246	(NA)	562	361	96
Santa Rosa	398	34	(NA)	183	139	(NA)
Sarasota	3,435	561	43	359	2,221	249
Seminole	1,699	188	228	834	437	10
Sumter	115	(NA)	(NA)	25	(NA)	(NA)
Suwannee	343	(NA)	(NA)	31	(NA)	(NA)
Taylor	55	(NA)	(NA)	(NA)	(NA)	(NA)
Union	101	(NA)	53	(NA)	(NA)	(NA)
Volusia	3,479	758	144	744	1,561	270
Wakulla	65	(NA)	(NA)	(NA)	(NA)	(NA)
Walton	383	198	(NA)	25	(NA)	(NA)
Washington	231	(NA)	(NA)	43	(NA)	66
Multicounty 3/	769	163	32	91	297	184

NEC Not elsewhere classified.
(NA) Not available.
1/ Residential social and personal care for children, the aged, and other persons with limits on ability for self-care, but where medical care is not a major concern.
2/ Includes establishments primarily engaged in community improvement and social change, such as advocacy groups, fundraising organizations (except contract or fee basis), health and welfare councils, united fund councils, community action agencies, etc.
3/ Reporting units without a fixed location within the state or of unknown county location.
Note: Private employment. Data are preliminary. Detail may not add to totals due to disclosure editing and/or rounding. See Tables 23.70, 23.71, 23.72, 23.73, and 23.74 for public employment data.

Source: State of Florida, Department of Labor and Employment Security, Bureau of Labor Market Information, "Employment and Wages" (ES-202), unpublished data.

University of Florida   **Bureau of Economic and Business Research**

Table 20.29. MUSEUMS, ART GALLERIES, BOTANICAL AND ZOOLOGICAL GARDENS: AVERAGE MONTHLY PRIVATE REPORTING UNITS, EMPLOYMENT, AND PAYROLL COVERED BY UNEMPLOYMENT COMPENSATION LAW IN THE STATE AND COUNTIES OF FLORIDA, 1999

County	Number of re-porting units	Number of em-ployees	Payroll ($1,000)	County	Number of re-porting units	Number of em-ployees	Payroll ($1,000)
Museums, art galleries, botanical and zoological gardens (SIC code 84)							
Florida	201	3,859	6,601	Monroe	10	145	249
				Okaloosa	3	60	72
Bay	6	104	91	Orange	16	440	722
Brevard	3	74	94	Palm Beach	27	440	885
Broward	17	334	601	Pinellas	10	128	269
Collier	6	61	96	Polk	4	100	164
Duval	10	269	457	St. Johns	12	199	453
Escambia	5	127	159	Sarasota	7	140	207
Hillsborough	8	469	746	Volusia	5	56	112
Miami-Dade	23	367	740				

Note: Private employment. For a list of three-digit industries included see Table 20.05. Data are preliminary. Detail may not add to totals due to disclosure editing and/or rounding. See Tables 23.70, 23.71, 23.72, 23.73, and 23.74 for public employment data.

Table 20.30. MEMBERSHIP ORGANIZATIONS: AVERAGE MONTHLY PRIVATE REPORTING UNITS EMPLOYMENT, AND PAYROLL COVERED BY UNEMPLOYMENT COMPENSATION LAW BY INDUSTRY IN FLORIDA, 1999

SIC code	Industry	Number of re-porting units	Number of em-ployees	Payroll ($1,000)
86	Membership organizations	5,928	53,962	92,061
861	Business associations	648	3,933	11,377
862	Professional membership organizations	259	2,600	8,165
863	Labor unions and similar labor organizations	515	3,217	5,829
864	Civic, social, and fraternal organizations	3,510	31,451	42,655
865	Political organizations	39	116	283
866	Religious organizations	652	7,151	11,022
869	Membership organizations, NEC	302	5,490	12,727

NEC Not elsewhere classified.
Note: Private employment. Data are preliminary. Detail may not add to totals due to disclosure editing and/or rounding. See Tables 23.70, 23.71, 23.72, 23.73, and 23.74 for public employment data.

Source for Tables 20.29 and 20.30: State of Florida, Department of Labor and Employment Security, Bureau of Labor Market Information, "Employment and Wages" (ES-202), unpublished data.

Table 20.33. PHYSICIANS: LICENSED DOCTORS OF MEDICINE AND OSTEOPATHY IN THE STATE AND COUNTIES OF FLORIDA, JULY 24, 2000

Location of licensee	Doctors of-- Medicine	Osteopathy	Location of licensee	Doctors of-- Medicine	Osteopathy
Total	41,157	3,567	Lafayette	2	0
Out-of-state	3,975	477	Lake	295	32
Foreign	117	0	Lee	741	115
Unknown	4,044	518	Leon	539	13
Alachua	1,257	24	Levy	16	2
Baker	11	1	Liberty	1	0
Bay	255	11	Madison	10	2
Bradford	11	2	Manatee	426	21
Brevard	830	59	Marion	391	29
Broward	3,355	379	Martin	274	28
Calhoun	10	0	Miami-Dade	6,025	231
Charlotte	256	29	Monroe	151	34
Citrus	181	28	Nassau	44	5
Clay	208	25	Okaloosa	282	15
Collier	422	25	Okeechobee	59	2
Columbia	83	10	Orange	1,916	150
De Soto	27	3	Osceola	187	14
Dixie	1	2	Palm Beach	2,678	255
Duval	1,956	91	Pasco	479	46
Escambia	675	33	Pinellas	2,043	350
Flagler	48	8	Polk	713	19
Franklin	10	2	Putnam	68	6
Gadsden	31	2	St. Johns	269	11
Gilchrist	3	0	St. Lucie	246	16
Glades	1	1	Santa Rosa	151	12
Gulf	13	0	Sarasota	877	70
Hamilton	4	1	Seminole	565	60
Hardee	9	1	Sumter	10	2
Hendry	18	1	Suwannee	13	0
Hernando	167	12	Taylor	16	2
Highlands	120	6	Union	15	0
Hillsborough	2,454	158	Volusia	734	84
Holmes	9	1	Wakulla	9	2
Indian River	274	22	Walton	11	3
Jackson	46	3	Washington	12	0
Jefferson	6	1			

Note: Active licenses only. Excludes delinquent active, involuntary inactive and voluntary inactive licenses.

Source: State of Florida, Department of Health, unpublished data.

University of Florida   **Bureau of Economic and Business Research**

Table 20.35. DENTISTS AND DENTAL HYGIENISTS: NUMBER LICENSED IN THE STATE
AND COUNTIES OF FLORIDA, JULY 24, 2000

Location of licensee	Dentists	Dental hygienists	Location of licensee	Dentists	Dental hygienists
Total	10,061	8,296	Lafayette	0	1
Out-of-state	480	473	Lake	74	92
Foreign	41	22	Lee	206	208
Unknown	1,449	779	Leon	104	134
Alachua	204	164	Levy	5	15
Baker	5	15	Liberty	1	0
Bay	67	80	Madison	4	2
Bradford	7	8	Manatee	103	111
Brevard	248	261	Marion	97	131
Broward	936	779	Martin	93	99
Calhoun	4	3	Miami-Dade	1,317	623
Charlotte	54	52	Monroe	37	37
Citrus	29	48	Nassau	18	31
Clay	79	103	Okaloosa	86	89
Collier	136	102	Okeechobee	9	11
Columbia	18	27	Orange	425	348
De Soto	5	3	Osceola	48	42
Dixie	3	7	Palm Beach	802	652
Duval	380	346	Pasco	87	111
Escambia	145	164	Pinellas	572	509
Flagler	19	16	Polk	137	147
Franklin	2	1	Putnam	14	17
Gadsden	13	17	St. Johns	69	62
Gilchrist	0	2	St. Lucie	62	73
Glades	0	2	Santa Rosa	35	81
Gulf	4	6	Sarasota	245	188
Hamilton	2	3	Seminole	202	206
Hardee	3	0	Sumter	6	3
Hendry	7	11	Suwannee	6	9
Hernando	38	47	Taylor	4	4
Highlands	32	30	Union	1	4
Hillsborough	481	380	Volusia	196	190
Holmes	2	2	Wakulla	1	8
Indian River	70	62	Walton	11	9
Jackson	14	20	Washington	5	8
Jefferson	2	6			

Note: Active licenses only. Excludes delinquent active, involuntary inactive and voluntary inactive licenses.

Source: State of Florida, Department of Health, unpublished data.

University of Florida   **Bureau of Economic and Business Research**

Table 20.36. HEALTH PRACTITIONERS: NUMBER LICENSED IN THE STATE AND COUNTIES
OF FLORIDA, JULY 24, 2000

Location of licensee	Chiro- practors	Optome- trists	Podia- trists	Therapists Occupa- tional	Therapists Phys- ical	Therapists Mas- sage	Nursing home adminis- trators	Psy- chol- ogists
Total	4,031	2,308	1,420	4,983	9,958	18,474	1,691	3,142
Out-of-state	721	209	128	166	415	315	67	120
Foreign	10	3	1	37	69	36	0	2
Unknown	6	334	254	467	1,429	1,515	178	199
Alachua	47	26	11	166	220	394	14	157
Baker	1	1	0	1	2	13	1	2
Bay	22	16	7	39	77	106	11	16
Bradford	2	2	0	3	1	5	4	1
Brevard	104	51	21	149	275	564	35	77
Broward	509	253	180	524	965	2,195	148	462
Calhoun	2	1	1	2	3	2	2	1
Charlotte	18	13	9	36	91	120	11	13
Citrus	20	10	5	19	48	55	18	1
Clay	19	20	4	38	62	108	20	13
Collier	60	21	12	65	120	357	22	19
Columbia	6	6	0	11	15	22	2	1
De Soto	4	3	0	4	5	10	1	3
Dixie	0	0	0	0	0	0	0	0
Duval	97	92	38	193	403	602	62	99
Escambia	46	31	14	70	120	194	22	54
Flagler	5	3	3	9	27	38	2	1
Franklin	2	0	0	1	2	4	2	0
Gadsden	3	3	0	2	5	10	6	13
Gilchrist	2	0	0	1	1	8	1	0
Glades	0	0	0	0	2	2	0	0
Gulf	0	0	0	1	5	6	1	0
Hamilton	1	0	0	0	1	3	2	0
Hardee	1	1	0	4	6	8	0	0
Hendry	4	3	0	4	5	12	1	2
Hernando	21	11	8	21	48	82	5	4
Highlands	19	6	4	23	63	36	6	4
Hillsborough	179	97	53	277	468	851	72	232
Holmes	1	1	0	0	5	6	0	0
Indian River	23	12	10	44	76	142	9	17
Jackson	3	6	0	9	12	13	5	6
Jefferson	0	0	0	3	0	7	2	0
Lafayette	0	0	0	2	1	1	1	0

See footnote at end of table.

Continued . . .

Table 20.36. HEALTH PRACTITIONERS: NUMBER LICENSED IN THE STATE AND COUNTIES
OF FLORIDA, JULY 24, 2000 (Continued)

Location of licensee	Chiro-practors	Optome-trists	Podia-trists	Therapists Occupa-tional	Therapists Phys-ical	Therapists Mas-sage	Nursing home adminis-trators	Psy-chol-ogists
Lake	34	18	13	42	80	115	23	12
Lee	109	57	29	110	263	573	36	45
Leon	35	37	8	91	163	297	18	135
Levy	3	3	0	2	3	20	1	1
Liberty	0	0	0	0	0	1	0	0
Madison	1	1	0	4	6	6	1	0
Manatee	49	29	18	108	152	274	29	22
Marion	49	20	12	56	128	166	14	24
Martin	50	19	12	41	84	218	15	21
Miami-Dade	296	210	167	498	804	1,770	88	550
Monroe	17	10	2	11	43	158	6	16
Nassau	9	6	1	7	17	52	5	3
Okaloosa	25	22	8	35	65	126	10	19
Okeechobee	4	2	3	1	6	16	2	1
Orange	132	100	33	239	451	910	78	105
Osceola	27	14	3	34	42	120	6	6
Palm Beach	409	157	144	350	693	1,911	143	261
Pasco	64	26	11	67	119	248	32	18
Pinellas	291	110	71	330	625	1,231	175	130
Polk	74	44	21	79	170	271	45	32
Putnam	4	4	2	12	26	36	1	5
St. Johns	22	11	6	39	109	161	18	25
St. Lucie	41	11	8	33	74	180	14	11
Santa Rosa	12	9	1	27	60	79	18	11
Sarasota	136	51	34	168	287	785	76	74
Seminole	74	51	24	94	207	411	29	50
Sumter	3	3	0	1	1	13	6	1
Suwannee	4	1	1	3	5	11	5	1
Taylor	2	1	1	2	1	8	1	0
Union	0	0	0	0	3	1	0	1
Volusia	90	44	22	98	210	422	58	40
Wakulla	2	0	0	0	1	13	1	0
Walton	3	1	2	7	6	25	2	3
Washington	2	1	0	3	4	4	2	0

Note: Active licenses only. Excludes delinquent active, involuntary inactive and voluntary inactive licenses.

Source: State of Florida, Department of Health, unpublished data.

Table 20.37. NURSES: LICENSED REGISTERED AND PRACTICAL NURSES IN THE STATE AND COUNTIES OF FLORIDA, JULY 24, 2000

Location of licensee	Total registered and practical nurses	Registered nurses	Practical nurses	Location of licensee	Total registered and practical nurses	Registered nurses	Practical nurses
Total	222,427	170,177	52,250	Lafayette	45	26	19
Out-of-state	6,708	6,040	668	Lake	2,761	1,918	843
Foreign	1,427	1,375	52	Lee	5,906	4,504	1,402
Unknown	17,967	15,228	2,739	Leon	3,054	2,352	702
Alachua	4,273	3,626	647	Levy	368	225	143
Baker	262	190	72	Liberty	46	19	27
Bay	2,163	1,551	612	Madison	192	96	96
Bradford	232	144	88	Manatee	3,539	2,530	1,009
Brevard	5,909	4,686	1,223	Marion	3,172	2,405	767
Broward	22,347	17,083	5,264	Martin	1,800	1,452	348
Calhoun	138	73	65	Miami-Dade	17,075	13,295	3,780
Charlotte	2,255	1,574	681	Monroe	935	841	94
Citrus	1,497	1,029	468	Nassau	569	460	109
Clay	2,076	1,648	428	Okaloosa	2,036	1,429	607
Collier	2,583	1,861	722	Okeechobee	334	207	127
Columbia	839	593	246	Orange	9,934	7,532	2,402
De Soto	347	183	164	Osceola	1,555	1,064	491
Dixie	106	67	39	Palm Beach	13,364	10,736	2,628
Duval	8,955	7,367	1,588	Pasco	4,785	3,292	1,493
Escambia	4,090	2,960	1,130	Pinellas	15,533	11,428	4,105
Flagler	725	537	188	Polk	5,441	3,715	1,726
Franklin	100	60	40	Putnam	735	437	298
Gadsden	446	273	173	St. Johns	1,545	1,187	358
Gilchrist	152	99	53	St. Lucie	2,547	1,849	698
Glades	39	23	16	Santa Rosa	1,941	1,460	481
Gulf	173	100	73	Sarasota	5,861	4,227	1,634
Hamilton	89	49	40	Seminole	4,996	3,962	1,034
Hardee	164	82	82	Sumter	297	183	114
Hendry	230	136	94	Suwannee	520	300	220
Hernando	1,895	1,316	579	Taylor	166	82	84
Highlands	1,107	751	356	Union	139	96	43
Hillsborough	12,137	9,177	2,960	Volusia	6,372	4,728	1,644
Holmes	195	105	90	Wakulla	225	137	88
Indian River	1,496	1,156	340	Walton	324	172	152
Jackson	796	485	311	Washington	264	129	135
Jefferson	133	75	58				

Note: Active licenses only. Excludes delinquent active, involuntary inactive and voluntary inactive licenses.

Source: State of Florida, Department of Health, unpublished data.

University of Florida   **Bureau of Economic and Business Research**

Table 20.38. HEALTH-RELATED RETAILERS: LICENSED DISPENSING OPTICIANS AND PHARMACISTS IN THE STATE AND COUNTIES OF FLORIDA, JULY 27, 2000

Location of licensee	Dispensing opticians	Phar- macists	Location of licensee	Dispensing opticians	Phar- macists
Total	3,271	19,675	Lafayette	0	1
NonFlorida	49	486	Lake	44	122
Unknown	117	5,994	Lee	96	331
Alachua	40	381	Leon	40	275
Baker	2	9	Levy	6	13
Bay	31	121	Liberty	0	6
Bradford	2	15	Madison	0	21
Brevard	106	323	Manatee	53	169
Broward	376	1,591	Marion	60	163
Calhoun	0	15	Martin	23	115
Charlotte	34	90	Miami-Dade	501	1,559
Citrus	20	63	Monroe	12	58
Clay	29	93	Nassau	7	23
Collier	31	175	Okaloosa	16	110
Columbia	7	37	Okeechobee	3	14
De Soto	1	14	Orange	140	781
Dixie	1	5	Osceola	12	78
Duval	97	622	Palm Beach	227	991
Escambia	34	208	Pasco	89	194
Flagler	6	27	Pinellas	204	1,101
Franklin	0	5	Polk	85	279
Gadsden	5	27	Putnam	11	33
Gilchrist	4	6	St. Johns	23	94
Glades	0	1	St. Lucie	45	103
Gulf	1	6	Santa Rosa	15	122
Hamilton	0	2	Sarasota	98	326
Hardee	1	9	Seminole	44	369
Hendry	4	13	Sumter	2	4
Hernando	30	85	Suwannee	3	19
Highlands	17	55	Taylor	1	8
Hillsborough	254	1,181	Union	0	5
Holmes	0	17	Volusia	84	342
Indian River	20	86	Wakulla	1	9
Jackson	2	34	Walton	4	18
Jefferson	1	11	Washington	0	12

Note: Active licenses only. Excludes voluntary inactive and delinquent licenses.

Source: State of Florida, Department of Health, unpublished data.

University of Florida   **Bureau of Economic and Business Research**

Table 20.40. PUBLIC LIBRARIES: OPERATING EXPENDITURE AND NUMBER OF VOLUMES IN REGIONS AND COUNTIES OF FLORIDA, FISCAL YEAR 1997-98

Area and library	Total operating expenditure (dollars)	Number of volumes 1/	Area and library	Total operating expenditure (dollars)	Number of volumes 1/
Total	276,300,704	26,517,907	Law Library	103,345	39,000
			Polk City	36,586	6,758
Miami-Dade	31,350,712	3,886,852	Polk County Historical	123,725	24,565
Broward	30,839,340	2,125,198	Winter Haven	645,524	62,699
Palm Beach Co-			Cooperative Office	229,359	(NA)
operative	24,398,471	1,561,588	Brevard	11,785,076	1,009,854
Palm Beach County	19,192,145	1,008,263	Volusia	8,469,111	659,708
Boynton Beach	1,325,242	128,315	Lee	10,179,765	832,902
Delray Beach	1,109,557	82,679	West Florida	2,568,928	295,425
Lake Park	225,585	20,459	Seminole	5,256,781	360,182
Lake Worth	387,724	72,186	Pasco	4,170,695	405,712
Palm Springs	354,545	37,610	Sarasota	5,996,658	530,125
Riviera Beach	353,700	75,684	Marion-Levy	2,827,771	281,538
West Palm Beach	1,449,973	136,392	Manatee	4,095,650	288,984
Pinellas Public Library			Leon	3,958,758	410,578
Cooperative	17,811,932	1,852,172	Alachua	7,404,802	709,463
Clearwater	4,334,430	442,601	Hialeah	1,364,438	93,584
Dunedin	1,415,359	98,446	Collier	3,801,186	299,965
Gulf Beaches	369,372	62,001	Lake	2,019,950	167,471
Gulfport	410,994	63,962	Cooper	308,902	41,064
Largo	2,084,180	207,455	Tavares	228,543	33,719
Oldsmar	394,839	27,094	Umatilia	242,538	18,690
Palm Harbor	698,381	134,206	W. T. Bland	378,343	36,896
Pinellas Park	1,055,395	79,599	Lady Lake	132,186	16,369
Safety Harbor	611,493	49,569	Fruitland Park	89,618	20,209
St. Pete Beach	426,500	42,560	Lake County System		
St. Petersburg	3,773,570	491,800	Office	639,821	524
Seminole Community	554,737	56,130	St. Lucie	2,839,420	305,965
Tarpon Springs	811,046	68,139	Northwest	2,062,431	174,277
Talking Book Library	279,699	27,860	Heartland	1,656,692	211,574
Pinellas PLC Admin/			De Soto	154,538	32,806
Answer Center	569,461	750	Hardee	126,889	34,486
Tampa-Hillsborough	15,860,958	1,366,302	Highlands	686,658	112,388
Jacksonville Library			Okeechobee	344,321	31,894
System	14,295,606	2,600,355	Heartland Co-		
Jacksonville	13,475,774	2,600,355	operative Office	344,285	(NA)
Nassau	819,832	82,644	Osceola	3,052,712	318,244
Orange	17,090,826	1,522,536	Charlotte-Glades	1,577,746	136,504
Polk	4,588,907	637,749	Okaloosa	888,851	74,497
Auburndale	212,262	42,914	Crestview-Sikes	318,356	30,350
Bartow	438,109	36,944	Mary Esther	150,546	16,104
Dr. C. C. Pearce	79,917	20,000	Niceville	262,878	28,043
Dundee	14,940	30,000	Okaloosa Co-		
Eagle Lake	37,251	13,780	operative Office	157,071	(NA)
Ft. Meade	163,130	28,595	Clay	1,462,918	163,015
Haines City	165,106	32,750	Hernando	1,635,920	207,222
Lake Alfred	57,168	24,000	Martin	2,496,529	227,258
Lake Wales	405,088	46,927	Citrus	1,925,257	137,579
Lakeland	1,737,463	201,822	St. Johns	2,209,903	204,447
Latt Maxcy	139,934	26,995	Indian River	2,803,036	269,799

See footnotes at end of table.

Continued . . .

University of Florida   **Bureau of Economic and Business Research**

Table 20.40. PUBLIC LIBRARIES: OPERATING EXPENDITURE AND NUMBER OF VOLUMES IN REGIONS AND COUNTIES OF FLORIDA, FISCAL YEAR 1997-98 (Continued)

Area and library	Total operating expenditure (dollars)	Number of volumes 1/	Area and library	Total operating expenditure (dollars)	Number of volumes 1/
Panhandle	1,013,093	101,312	Jefferson	178,767	6,097
Calhoun	157,768	451	Wakulla	161,991	7,358
Holmes	62,124	14,944	Wilderness Coast Co-		
Jackson	386,773	60,660	operative	340,723	16,642
Washington	101,994	25,257	Flagler	326,833	16,963
Panhandle Co-			Altamonte Springs	337,555	33,518
operative Office	304,434	(NA)	North Miami Beach	879,893	51,872
Monroe	1,825,492	148,139	Walton-Defuniak	289,823	55,059
Putnam	743,682	85,409	Three Rivers	489,631	40,106
Boca Raton	1,642,001	127,867	Hendry	286,466	76,485
Suwannee River	1,143,751	139,000	Oakland Park	499,368	47,363
Bruton	566,799	77,476	Winter Park	1,323,461	123,708
New River	692,943	93,803	Ft. Walton Beach	281,000	42,611
Emily Taber			Temple Terrace	535,136	64,284
Baker County	130,010	34,961	Taylor	278,191	43,773
Bradford	274,705	41,034	Eustis Memorial	577,889	74,953
Union	88,719	17,748	New Port Richey	534,409	54,018
Columbia	811,456	107,877	North Palm Beach	465,753	42,500
North Miami	848,282	99,935	Lynn Haven	141,507	18,788
Gadsden	460,032	79,396	Wilton Manors	259,183	17,985
Leesburg	768,929	114,666	Lighthouse Point	303,536	44,500
Sumter	156,805	61,402	Brockway Memorial	266,733	50,714
Bushnell	(NA)	14,342	Maitland	407,785	79,395
Coleman	(NA)	6,097	Ft. Myers Beach	682,125	58,171
E. C. Rowell	(NA)	7,358	Zephyrhills	124,973	23,749
George Nichols	(NA)	16,642	Valparaiso	109,333	19,325
Panasoffkee	(NA)	16,963	Sanibel	581,635	44,541
Wilderness Coast	773,772	80,451	Highland Beach	105,164	11,329
Franklin	92,291	14,342	Apalachicola	15,349	11,453

(NA) Not available.
1/ Includes volumes of books and bound periodicals.

Note: Libraries are omitted if they failed to report to the Division of Library Services or if they failed to meet or are not part of a system which met all of the following criteria: at least 10 hours of public service per week, a book collection of at least 2,000 volumes, at least 200 volumes purchased a year, and expenditure of at least $1,000 per year.

Source: State of Florida, Department of State, Division of Library and Information Services, *1999 Florida Library Directory with Statistics.*

University of Florida   **Bureau of Economic and Business Research**

Table 20.56. ELEMENTARY AND SECONDARY SCHOOLS: TOTAL ADMINISTRATIVE AND INSTRUCTIONAL STAFF AND DISTRIBUTION OF ADMINISTRATIVE STAFF IN THE STATE AND COUNTIES OF FLORIDA, FALL 1999

County	Total staff 1/	Total	Offi-cials admin-istra-tors mana-gers	Consul-tants/ super-visors of in-struc-tion	Prin-cipals	Assist-ant prin-cipals	Commun-ity educa-tion coordi-nators	Deans/ curri-culum coordi-nators
					Administrative staff			
Florida	163,499	9,248	2,078	555	2,627	3,340	104	544
Alachua	2,334	140	45	18	42	33	2	0
Baker	300	25	10	1	6	8	0	0
Bay	2,536	105	20	5	33	25	0	22
Bradford	343	25	8	0	8	7	0	2
Brevard	4,663	249	33	1	79	44	0	92
Broward	13,707	650	76	2	201	371	0	0
Calhoun	182	9	4	0	5	0	0	0
Charlotte	1,093	75	30	2	19	24	0	0
Citrus	1,151	78	20	5	20	33	0	0
Clay	1,969	119	40	3	28	48	0	0
Collier	2,364	143	35	29	35	27	3	14
Columbia	654	39	16	1	12	10	0	0
De Soto	341	26	12	0	5	7	0	2
Dixie	167	20	9	2	4	4	0	1
Duval	7,756	520	150	5	153	56	34	122
Escambia	3,331	170	39	19	65	46	1	0
Flagler	511	43	19	0	7	9	0	8
Franklin	117	10	6	0	4	0	0	0
Gadsden	630	60	29	6	15	3	0	7
Gilchrist	202	18	8	2	4	2	0	2
Glades	84	8	4	1	2	1	0	0
Gulf	176	14	4	1	6	3	0	0
Hamilton	178	19	10	1	6	0	1	1
Hardee	368	28	15	0	6	7	0	0
Hendry	444	36	13	2	10	11	0	0
Hernando	1,176	68	17	2	18	30	1	0
Highlands	768	50	17	3	15	15	0	0
Hillsborough	11,999	647	85	95	171	171	0	125
Holmes	276	25	10	0	7	7	0	1
Indian River	1,068	58	24	1	16	16	1	0
Jackson	617	41	13	1	16	11	0	0
Jefferson	161	18	8	2	4	3	1	0
Lafayette	83	6	3	1	2	0	0	0
Lake	2,048	117	14	6	39	38	0	20
Lee	3,855	224	49	15	66	57	0	37

See footnotes at end of table.   Continued . . .

University of Florida   **Bureau of Economic and Business Research**

Table 20.56. ELEMENTARY AND SECONDARY SCHOOLS: TOTAL ADMINISTRATIVE AND INSTRUCTIONAL STAFF AND DISTRIBUTION OF ADMINISTRATIVE STAFF IN THE STATE AND COUNTIES OF FLORIDA, FALL 1999 (Continued)

County	Total staff 1/	Administrative staff						
		Total	Officials administrators managers	Consultants/ supervisors of instruction	Principals	Assistant principals	Community education coordinators	Deans/ curriculum coordinators
Leon	2,483	142	31	10	42	59	0	0
Levy	450	37	16	2	11	7	1	0
Liberty	90	11	7	0	3	1	0	0
Madison	259	29	5	6	7	4	0	7
Manatee	2,523	138	34	6	40	56	0	2
Marion	2,663	161	28	17	44	48	6	18
Martin	1,155	69	18	2	19	25	4	1
Miami-Dade	22,600	1,371	331	56	328	614	41	1
Monroe	697	53	13	8	11	18	3	0
Nassau	673	42	15	1	15	7	0	4
Okaloosa	2,060	112	34	14	38	24	0	2
Okeechobee	459	36	14	0	10	11	0	1
Orange	10,061	475	73	44	147	207	1	3
Osceola	2,150	95	24	2	29	39	0	1
Palm Beach	10,447	497	66	20	140	271	0	0
Pasco	3,626	195	45	21	51	69	0	9
Pinellas	8,387	483	76	48	140	203	3	13
Polk	5,635	285	40	9	106	129	0	1
Putnam	970	75	31	6	19	17	0	2
St. Johns	1,417	132	57	18	26	29	0	2
St. Lucie	2,426	103	26	3	34	40	0	0
Santa Rosa	1,483	81	15	7	29	30	0	0
Sarasota	2,489	118	32	5	33	48	0	0
Seminole	3,845	189	29	0	53	92	0	15
Sumter	405	27	11	2	10	4	0	0
Suwannee	385	29	14	0	7	7	1	0
Taylor	293	26	11	3	7	4	0	1
Union	173	15	7	2	3	2	0	1
Volusia	4,507	254	44	6	74	130	0	0
Wakulla	308	27	13	1	5	4	0	4
Walton	423	29	9	2	10	8	0	0
Washington	305	29	14	2	7	6	0	0

1/ Administrative and instructional staff only as of January 25, 2000. Excludes noninstructional, non-administrative professional staff, aides, technicians, clerical/secretarial, service workers, skilled crafts workers, and unskilled laborers.
Note: Data are for public schools only. Excludes special schools.

Source: State of Florida, Department of Education, Division of Administration, Education Information and Accountability Services, *Statistical Brief: Staff in Florida's Public Schools, Fall 1999*, Series 2000-08B. Internet site <http://www.firn.edu/doe/bin00050/eiaspubs/schstf.htm> (accessed 2 May 2000).

Table 20.57. ELEMENTARY AND SECONDARY SCHOOLS: DISTRIBUTION OF INSTRUCTIONAL STAFF IN THE STATE AND COUNTIES OF FLORIDA, FALL 1999

County	Total	Teachers Elementary 1/	Teachers Secondary 2/	Exceptional student education	Guidance counselors	School social workers	School psychologists	Librarians/ audiovisual workers	Other 3/
Florida	154,251	56,044	48,569	21,682	5,285	795	1,037	2,627	18,212
Alachua	2,194	676	705	329	75	11	14	52	332
Baker	275	100	107	25	9	0	2	5	27
Bay	2,431	629	572	344	72	4	13	39	758
Bradford	318	108	101	47	9	0	3	7	43
Brevard	4,414	1,820	1,303	629	136	9	23	116	378
Broward	13,057	5,209	3,911	1,368	448	114	101	208	1,698
Calhoun	173	60	62	26	5	0	0	6	14
Charlotte	1,018	304	362	160	34	4	10	20	124
Citrus	1,073	390	333	145	35	3	7	19	141
Clay	1,850	710	598	284	70	10	12	32	134
Collier	2,221	818	680	304	121	4	17	40	237
Columbia	615	249	212	84	17	1	2	12	38
De Soto	315	119	97	38	9	2	0	5	45
Dixie	147	60	49	23	4	0	0	4	7
Duval	7,236	3,085	2,213	1,108	208	33	47	139	403
Escambia	3,161	1,149	1,039	472	99	15	12	66	309
Flagler	468	151	157	59	16	0	2	6	77
Franklin	107	45	36	12	3	0	0	4	7
Gadsden	570	216	192	64	19	3	6	15	55
Gilchrist	184	68	70	24	7	1	0	4	10
Glades	76	33	27	6	2	0	0	2	6
Gulf	162	59	61	16	5	0	2	4	15
Hamilton	159	54	51	25	4	1	1	5	18
Hardee	340	128	115	32	9	0	2	7	47
Hendry	408	171	119	52	15	0	1	9	41
Hernando	1,108	386	404	121	51	8	7	20	111
Highlands	718	250	220	117	30	4	5	16	76
Hillsborough	11,352	4,225	3,635	1,619	379	113	100	198	1,083
Holmes	251	100	100	27	8	0	1	7	8
Indian River	1,010	349	307	137	24	6	9	18	160
Jackson	576	204	192	81	25	0	2	12	60
Jefferson	143	52	48	20	5	1	0	3	14
Lafayette	77	33	27	6	1	0	0	2	8
Lake	1,931	673	586	247	80	8	12	40	285
Lee	3,631	1,187	1,188	629	115	25	27	62	398
Leon	2,341	777	708	358	79	14	12	45	348

See footnotes at end of table.   Continued . . .

University of Florida   **Bureau of Economic and Business Research**

Table 20.57. ELEMENTARY AND SECONDARY SCHOOLS: DISTRIBUTION OF INSTRUCTIONAL STAFF IN THE STATE AND COUNTIES OF FLORIDA, FALL 1999 (Continued)

County	Total	Teachers Elementary 1/	Teachers Secondary 2/	Exceptional student education	Guidance counselors	School social workers	School psychologists	Librarians/audiovisual workers	Other 3/
Levy	413	166	144	56	14	2	0	11	20
Liberty	79	26	32	10	1	0	0	2	8
Madison	230	74	88	39	4	0	0	3	22
Manatee	2,385	886	745	370	78	18	16	41	231
Marion	2,502	940	853	345	71	18	18	46	211
Martin	1,086	351	372	162	38	1	6	18	138
Miami-Dade	21,229	8,207	5,938	3,017	963	114	181	343	2,466
Monroe	644	233	201	94	15	3	6	6	86
Nassau	631	226	227	95	22	3	3	16	39
Okaloosa	1,948	764	730	196	60	2	10	42	144
Okeechobee	423	163	138	53	14	0	3	7	45
Orange	9,586	3,255	2,982	1,251	276	45	51	97	1,629
Osceola	2,055	660	676	239	68	8	19	29	356
Palm Beach	9,950	3,403	3,447	1,463	306	3	61	133	1,134
Pasco	3,431	1,135	1,037	631	125	21	23	71	388
Pinellas	7,904	2,609	2,339	1,380	238	77	59	122	1,080
Polk	5,350	2,005	1,787	677	179	10	39	112	541
Putnam	895	317	248	111	33	0	8	19	159
St. Johns	1,285	432	504	169	46	1	5	23	105
St. Lucie	2,323	636	636	234	83	8	13	36	677
Santa Rosa	1,402	495	537	182	47	4	7	30	100
Sarasota	2,371	898	740	404	50	8	13	15	243
Seminole	3,656	1,322	1,417	360	102	16	17	42	380
Sumter	378	139	125	48	11	1	0	9	45
Suwannee	356	144	133	31	13	0	0	7	28
Taylor	267	107	84	37	6	1	0	4	28
Union	158	55	61	20	6	0	0	3	13
Volusia	4,253	1,416	1,395	851	157	37	25	72	300
Wakulla	281	98	106	47	8	0	0	7	15
Walton	394	151	150	48	12	0	1	7	25
Washington	276	84	110	24	11	0	1	5	41

1/ Prekindergarten and Kindergarten through grade 5 or 6.
2/ Grades 6 through 12.
3/ Includes other teachers and nonadministrative/instructional professional staff.
Note: Data are for public schools only as of January 25, 2000. Excludes special schools.

Source: State of Florida, Department of Education, Division of Administration, Education Information and Accountability Services, *Statistical Brief: Staff in Florida's Public Schools, Fall 1999,* Series 2000-08B. Internet site <http://www.firn.edu/doe/bin00050/eiaspubs/schstf.htm> (accessed 2 May 2000).

Table 20.59. ELEMENTARY AND SECONDARY SCHOOLS: NUMBER AND AVERAGE SALARY
OF SPECIFIED DISTRICT STAFF PERSONNEL IN THE STATE AND COUNTIES
OF FLORIDA, FALL 1999

(salaries in dollars)

County	Superin-tendent salary	High school Num-ber	High school Salary	Middle/junior high school Num-ber	Middle/junior high school Salary	Elementary Num-ber	Elementary Salary	Board members Num-ber	Board members Salary
Florida	102,395	359	74,020	467	69,060	1,557	67,252	354	25,530
Alachua	109,200	6	75,869	8	61,591	24	62,673	5	28,334
Baker	82,120	1	58,226	1	53,166	3	56,717	5	20,505
Bay	97,361	4	65,028	7	63,215	19	58,794	5	26,695
Bradford	78,596	1	59,346	1	54,968	5	54,692	5	20,803
Brevard	115,486	12	68,862	15	61,836	52	58,074	5	31,299
Broward	175,000	25	85,919	21	83,264	125	77,713	9	33,810
Calhoun	77,726	1	63,600	1	58,200	1	56,900	5	19,973
Charlotte	108,211	3	73,287	4	69,209	10	67,977	5	26,305
Citrus	94,248	3	66,133	4	62,825	9	61,578	5	25,707
Clay	96,211	5	70,238	4	69,183	18	69,867	5	26,330
Collier	122,000	5	87,541	7	77,324	19	64,208	5	28,316
Columbia	88,148	2	62,196	3	60,771	7	62,356	5	22,840
De Soto	79,281	1	60,900	1	59,307	3	57,279	5	20,984
Dixie	75,359	1	54,968	1	51,956	2	54,995	5	19,946
Duval	150,000	21	69,382	28	62,969	104	60,246	7	32,653
Escambia	109,142	7	64,349	12	62,187	39	56,995	6	29,528
Flagler	89,765	1	67,500	1	49,650	3	55,150	5	22,076
Franklin	74,705	1	45,322	0	0	2	49,938	5	19,773
Gadsden	87,747	5	57,985	2	56,250	7	56,272	5	22,584
Gilchrist	85,354	2	55,445	0	0	2	53,469	5	19,942
Glades	76,677	1	54,999	0	0	1	55,795	5	19,727
Gulf	83,642	1	58,427	1	56,358	2	55,583	5	20,021
Hamilton	81,105	1	57,237	1	50,973	3	51,003	5	20,011
Hardee	80,110	1	60,594	1	57,691	4	55,128	5	20,642
Hendry	79,930	2	60,589	2	59,979	5	58,169	5	21,155
Hernando	92,752	4	63,490	4	62,333	10	60,803	5	26,062
Highlands	87,651	3	70,325	4	65,406	8	62,403	5	23,358
Hillsborough	164,999	19	79,772	36	71,108	106	67,503	7	33,539
Holmes	76,625	2	50,868	1	52,757	2	50,686	5	20,281
Indian River	120,522	2	75,804	3	69,182	10	64,121	5	25,546
Jackson	84,673	2	58,000	1	51,900	5	55,620	5	22,410
Jefferson	72,909	1	59,821	1	58,337	1	51,594	5	19,298
Lafayette	73,709	0	0	0	0	1	44,586	4	18,876
Lake	101,672	6	69,149	8	65,476	22	63,303	5	28,063
Lee	124,603	9	72,085	12	70,545	36	69,983	5	31,008
Leon	105,789	5	64,720	9	61,941	23	60,568	5	28,642

See footnote at end of table.   Continued . . .

University of Florida   **Bureau of Economic and Business Research**

Table 20.59. ELEMENTARY AND SECONDARY SCHOOLS: NUMBER AND AVERAGE SALARY
OF SPECIFIED DISTRICT STAFF PERSONNEL IN THE STATE AND COUNTIES
OF FLORIDA, FALL 1999 (Continued)

(salaries in dollars)

| County | Superin- tendent salary | Principals | | | | Elementary | | Board members | |
| | | High school | | Middle/junior high school | | | | | |
		Num- ber	Salary	Num- ber	Salary	Num- ber	Salary	Num- ber	Salary
Levy	80,476	2	53,026	1	59,059	4	54,194	5	21,300
Liberty	73,898	1	43,910	0	0	1	51,130	5	19,076
Madison	76,978	1	54,008	4	53,488	2	53,488	5	20,375
Manatee	124,765	6	74,524	7	68,139	25	65,521	5	27,744
Marion	103,480	6	78,399	7	73,701	27	67,876	5	28,551
Martin	94,865	2	73,746	4	69,649	11	68,010	5	25,903
Miami-Dade	233,047	37	89,273	51	83,469	204	81,517	9	33,683
Monroe	97,610	3	75,456	1	67,208	7	63,393	5	24,548
Nassau	95,477	3	58,561	3	57,805	9	56,044	5	22,793
Okaloosa	99,852	4	76,916	8	71,553	22	68,302	5	27,486
Okeechobee	85,000	2	66,392	3	60,893	5	57,532	5	21,486
Orange	205,900	13	77,069	26	66,625	101	66,180	5	32,983
Osceola	95,000	5	73,322	8	66,844	14	68,012	7	26,729
Palm Beach	156,279	21	78,007	26	73,027	85	68,679	5	33,810
Pasco	123,723	9	76,339	8	66,529	30	62,442	7	29,717
Pinellas	144,679	17	74,102	23	71,770	80	66,070	5	33,303
Polk	113,840	14	69,271	19	63,553	63	62,082	7	31,299
Putnam	87,065	3	66,907	4	60,903	9	60,203	6	23,747
St. Johns	94,340	3	72,036	5	62,973	13	62,263	5	25,636
St. Lucie	102,357	5	71,463	9	68,476	20	63,745	5	27,701
Santa Rosa	93,839	6	70,827	6	64,564	15	63,278	5	25,577
Sarasota	138,000	4	85,512	5	78,663	20	76,804	5	29,807
Seminole	144,091	7	76,682	13	68,576	33	64,997	5	29,987
Sumter	95,469	2	65,841	2	62,050	5	59,808	5	22,391
Suwannee	80,831	1	64,685	1	61,284	2	61,284	5	21,394
Taylor	77,911	2	55,729	1	55,725	3	54,636	5	20,621
Union	84,515	1	52,950	1	53,013	1	53,013	5	20,244
Volusia	108,930	8	73,486	10	65,738	44	61,995	5	31,075
Wakulla	85,658	1	67,750	1	61,515	3	59,160	5	20,413
Walton	82,044	2	62,172	3	60,230	4	59,259	5	21,715
Washington	77,522	2	63,982	2	57,108	2	56,579	5	20,518

Note: Data are for public schools only. The number of months worked varies from district to district. Salaries have not been adjusted for a full 12-month calendar year. Does not include special schools such as university laboratory schools.

Source: State of Florida, Department of Education, Education Information and Accountability Services, *Statistical Brief: Florida District Staff Salaries of Selected Positions, Fall 1999,* March 2000 Series 2000-09B. Internet site http://www.firn.edu/doe/eias/eiaspubs/dststfs.htm> (accessed 20 June 2000).

Table 20.60. ELEMENTARY AND SECONDARY SCHOOLS: NUMBER AND AVERAGE SALARY OF TEACHERS BY DEGREE ATTAINMENT IN THE STATE AND COUNTIES OF FLORIDA, 1999-2000

(salaries in dollars)

County	Total		Bachelor's			Master's			Specialist			Doctorate		
	Number	Average salary	Number	Percentage of total	Average salary	Number	Percentage of total	Average salary	Number	Percentage of total	Average salary	Number	Percentage of total	Average salary
Florida	145,397	36,720	88,194	60.7	33,657	51,780	35.6	40,710	3,802	2.6	48,958	1,621	1.1	47,225
Alachua	1,911	32,742	780	40.8	29,646	961	50.3	34,312	117	6.1	36,849	53	2.8	40,789
Baker	259	32,875	171	66.0	30,841	83	32.0	36,706	4	1.5	39,837	1	0.4	34,978
Bay	1,660	34,557	1,063	64.0	33,033	539	32.5	36,974	47	2.8	39,722	11	0.7	41,290
Bradford	278	32,556	185	66.5	30,831	84	30.2	36,110	6	2.2	33,199	3	1.1	38,183
Brevard	4,018	35,725	2,408	59.9	33,040	1,540	38.3	39,582	37	0.9	45,623	33	0.8	40,504
Broward	12,772	40,827	7,528	58.9	37,875	4,829	37.8	44,557	263	2.1	51,595	152	1.2	49,935
Calhoun	167	33,285	103	61.7	31,578	62	37.1	36,149	1	0.6	30,725	1	0.6	33,975
Charlotte	933	35,421	452	48.4	31,452	456	48.9	38,867	14	1.5	45,469	11	1.2	42,927
Citrus 1/	1,016	32,714	564	55.5	29,899	424	41.7	36,042	17	1.7	39,382	11	1.1	38,419
Clay	1,757	34,538	1,180	67.2	32,627	556	31.6	38,209	15	0.9	44,580	6	0.3	45,115
Collier	1,974	41,044	1,070	54.2	36,988	850	43.1	45,535	33	1.7	50,249	21	1.1	51,423
Columbia	589	33,674	378	64.2	31,185	198	33.6	37,769	7	1.2	42,328	6	1.0	45,245
De Soto	283	32,060	217	76.7	31,029	62	21.9	35,414	2	0.7	42,226	2	0.7	29,664
Dixie	151	30,600	109	72.2	28,574	38	25.2	35,728	3	2.0	35,737	1	0.7	41,070
Duval	7,050	36,116	4,612	65.4	33,823	2,342	33.2	40,311	54	0.8	45,714	42	0.6	41,516
Escambia	2,917	31,682	1,632	55.9	28,950	1,225	42.0	35,166	37	1.3	34,776	23	0.8	34,953
Flagler	420	32,474	271	64.5	30,134	144	34.3	36,504	1	0.2	45,369	4	1.0	42,672
Franklin	104	31,563	67	64.4	28,614	36	34.6	36,703	0	0.0	0	1	1.0	44,136
Gadsden	523	30,428	338	64.6	29,371	180	34.4	32,324	5	1.0	33,571	0	0.0	0
Gilchrist	182	31,801	123	67.6	30,096	55	30.2	35,358	3	1.6	34,858	1	0.5	36,634
Glades	62	35,177	43	69.4	32,445	17	27.4	40,599	2	3.2	47,848	0	0.0	0
Gulf 1/	159	31,923	106	66.7	30,152	52	32.7	35,324	0	0.0	0	1	0.6	42,886
Hamilton 1/	147	30,021	112	76.2	29,014	31	21.1	32,554	3	2.0	38,031	1	0.7	40,215

See footnotes at end of table.

Continued . . .

Table 20.60. ELEMENTARY AND SECONDARY SCHOOLS: NUMBER AND AVERAGE SALARY OF TEACHERS BY DEGREE ATTAINMENT IN THE STATE AND COUNTIES OF FLORIDA, 1999-2000 (Continued)

(salaries in dollars)

County	Total		Bachelor's			Master's			Specialist			Doctorate		
	Number	Average salary	Number	Percentage of total	Average salary	Number	Percentage of total	Average salary	Number	Percentage of total	Average salary	Number	Percentage of total	Average salary
Hardee	323	33,665	260	80.5	32,468	59	18.3	38,447	3	0.9	41,052	1	0.3	40,623
Hendry	378	34,992	282	74.6	33,445	91	24.1	39,292	4	1.1	43,801	1	0.3	44,957
Hernando	1,056	31,592	654	61.9	29,051	385	36.5	35,699	10	0.9	35,378	7	0.7	37,669
Highlands	684	34,505	459	67.1	32,363	217	31.7	38,884	2	0.3	46,188	6	0.9	36,067
Hillsborough	10,606	35,741	6,534	61.6	32,961	3,834	36.1	39,862	132	1.2	46,519	106	1.0	44,638
Holmes 1/	241	32,465	146	60.6	30,132	94	39.0	36,009	0	0.0	0	1	0.4	39,933
Indian River	853	34,996	584	68.5	32,633	220	25.8	39,049	45	5.3	45,128	4	0.5	43,091
Jackson	551	32,375	280	50.8	29,143	252	45.7	35,257	18	3.3	42,285	1	0.2	32,803
Jefferson	134	32,168	88	65.7	30,499	43	32.1	35,260	3	2.2	36,802	0	0.0	0
Lafayette	74	29,076	56	75.7	28,117	17	23.0	31,721	1	1.4	37,806	0	0.0	0
Lake	1,824	34,576	1,221	66.9	32,384	565	31.0	38,718	25	1.4	44,052	13	0.7	42,190
Lee	3,357	36,159	2,093	62.3	33,219	1,179	35.1	40,741	57	1.7	44,855	28	0.8	45,312
Leon 1/	2,097	33,343	1,086	51.8	31,041	922	44.0	35,368	55	2.6	40,558	34	1.6	40,287
Levy	390	33,827	248	63.6	32,281	133	34.1	36,821	8	2.1	32,660	1	0.3	28,295
Liberty	71	31,398	48	67.6	29,643	23	32.4	35,062	0	0.0	0	0	0.0	0
Madison	215	32,605	147	68.4	30,261	66	30.7	37,662	2	0.9	37,970	0	0.0	0
Manatee 1/	2,034	34,794	1,219	59.9	31,794	750	36.9	38,806	45	2.2	45,580	20	1.0	42,871
Marion	2,429	31,509	1,653	68.1	29,763	719	29.6	34,930	37	1.5	39,377	20	0.8	38,247
Martin	1,004	35,284	630	62.7	32,718	343	34.2	38,947	21	2.1	47,779	10	1.0	45,087
Miami-Dade	20,446	42,591	10,275	50.3	37,538	7,783	38.1	45,935	1,914	9.4	53,347	474	2.3	53,767
Monroe	600	37,663	371	61.8	35,913	223	37.2	40,533	1	0.2	46,930	5	0.8	37,682
Nassau 1/	611	34,795	389	63.7	32,591	216	35.4	38,691	4	0.7	39,373	2	0.3	33,569
Okaloosa	1,865	37,819	1,111	59.6	34,729	689	36.9	41,871	42	2.3	45,297	23	1.2	52,069
Okeechobee	414	35,051	291	70.3	32,741	117	28.3	40,399	6	1.4	42,777	0	0.0	0
Orange	9,943	33,219	6,376	64.1	31,049	3,399	34.2	36,927	92	0.9	40,690	76	0.8	40,423

See footnotes at end of table.

Continued . . .

Table 20.60. ELEMENTARY AND SECONDARY SCHOOLS: NUMBER AND AVERAGE SALARY OF TEACHERS BY DEGREE ATTAINMENT IN THE STATE AND COUNTIES OF FLORIDA, 1999-2000 (Continued)

(salaries in dollars)

County	Total		Bachelor's			Master's			Specialist			Doctorate		
	Number	Average salary	Number	Percent age of total	Average salary	Number	Percent age of total	Average salary	Number	Percent age of total	Average salary	Number	Percent age of total	Average salary
Osceola	1,891	31,897	1,220	64.5	29,531	632	33.4	35,972	23	1.2	39,759	16	0.8	40,043
Palm Beach	9,367	41,908	5,876	62.7	39,137	3,269	34.9	46,174	118	1.3	53,071	104	1.1	51,779
Pasco	3,180	33,660	2,020	63.5	31,693	1,101	34.6	36,957	32	1.0	39,332	27	0.8	39,667
Pinellas	7,628	35,860	4,744	62.2	33,784	2,712	35.6	39,041	108	1.4	42,835	64	0.8	43,166
Polk 1/	4,945	31,356	4,383	88.6	30,187	540	10.9	40,480	16	0.3	39,931	6	0.1	41,011
Putnam	800	33,783	543	67.9	31,667	245	30.6	38,093	9	1.1	41,345	3	0.4	42,060
St. Johns	1,220	33,174	749	61.4	30,634	465	38.1	37,131	0	0.0	0	6	0.5	43,566
St. Lucie	1,767	34,865	1,156	65.4	32,368	558	31.6	39,206	35	2.0	44,712	18	1.0	41,476
Santa Rosa	1,360	34,224	892	65.6	32,027	445	32.7	38,238	18	1.3	40,839	5	0.4	45,077
Sarasota	2,238	40,506	988	44.1	35,510	1,196	53.4	44,149	12	0.5	40,149	42	1.9	50,264
Seminole	3,468	35,157	1,900	54.8	31,308	1,397	40.3	39,170	111	3.2	44,957	60	1.7	45,506
Sumter	352	34,170	252	71.6	32,331	95	27.0	38,668	5	1.4	41,432	0	0.0	0
Suwannee	342	36,375	230	67.3	34,575	108	31.6	39,965	4	1.2	43,002	0	0.0	0
Taylor	242	34,052	142	58.7	31,027	89	36.8	38,158	6	2.5	38,584	5	2.1	41,438
Union 1/	139	28,924	86	61.9	27,042	51	36.7	32,120	1	0.7	27,636	1	0.7	29,056
Volusia	4,069	34,143	2,471	60.7	31,280	1,465	36.0	38,185	91	2.2	43,175	42	1.0	42,070
Wakulla	272	32,650	148	54.4	30,635	115	42.3	34,896	8	2.9	36,518	1	0.4	41,690
Walton 1/	351	30,868	249	70.9	29,543	96	27.4	33,857	4	1.1	34,750	2	0.6	44,590
Washington	234	35,898	132	56.4	32,991	98	41.9	39,625	3	1.3	39,494	1	0.4	43,607

1/ District had not negotiated a new salary schedule prior to reporting.

Note: Average salary paid to a professional on the instructional salary schedule negotiated by a Florida school district. Data were obtained from the Florida DOE Staff Database, Survey 3, February 4-11, 2000, as of April 27, 2000. Data are for public schools only and exclude special and developmental research schools.

Source: State of Florida, Department of Education, Education Information and Accountability Services, *Statistical Brief: Teacher Salary, Experience, and Degree Level, 1999-2000,* Series 2000-11B, Internet site <http://www.firn.edu/doe/bin00050/eiaspubs/teacher.htm> (accessed 18 July 2000).

Table 20.62. ELEMENTARY AND SECONDARY SCHOOLS: STUDENT-TEACHER RATIOS
AND SPECIFIED PERSONNEL PERCENTAGES AND RATIOS IN THE STATE
AND COUNTIES OF FLORIDA, 1998-99

| | FTE students per FTE teacher | | Percentage of full-time staff who are-- | | Ratio of-- | |
| | Elemen- | Second- | Teach- | Admin- | Teacher aides to teach- | Adminis- trators to teach- |
County	tary 1/	ary	ers 2/	istrators	ers 2/	ers 2/
Florida	23.44	20.73	49.45	3.47	1:4.04	1:12.18
Alachua	23.07	18.05	43.79	3.40	1:4.27	1:12.89
Baker	26.77	18.10	44.97	4.17	1:3.70	1:10.77
Bay	24.13	19.16	50.12	3.65	1:4.39	1:13.73
Bradford	20.99	17.82	50.91	4.24	1:3.70	1:12.00
Brevard	21.22	24.03	52.97	3.41	1:7.89	1:15.53
Broward	25.54	25.03	52.82	3.02	1:6.50	1:17.50
Calhoun	21.31	15.00	54.65	3.35	1:8.64	1:16.33
Charlotte	26.51	20.27	43.68	3.76	1:2.90	1:11.61
Citrus	20.49	19.33	47.51	4.03	1:4.23	1:11.80
Clay	21.11	22.25	50.25	3.76	1:6.27	1:13.36
Collier	21.79	19.37	46.38	3.41	1:2.97	1:13.59
Columbia	21.79	18.46	46.33	2.99	1:3.37	1:15.51
De Soto	22.53	18.32	46.55	4.37	1:3.14	1:10.65
Dixie	19.50	22.46	43.89	5.33	1:2.91	1:8.23
Duval	23.29	21.95	56.66	4.18	1:4.56	1:13.55
Escambia	22.42	18.41	51.03	3.43	1:5.23	1:14.87
Flagler	22.06	17.72	43.95	4.47	1:4.85	1:9.82
Franklin	17.84	19.06	50.00	5.98	1:6.57	1:8.36
Gadsden	19.24	18.85	45.86	6.08	1:3.32	1:7.54
Gilchrist	21.33	19.60	47.74	5.16	1:3.79	1:9.25
Glades	20.94	16.36	48.15	5.93	1:4.06	1:8.12
Gulf	21.22	16.66	49.46	5.05	1:5.48	1:9.78
Hamilton	21.54	18.31	39.35	5.92	1:3.09	1:6.65
Hardee	21.47	18.29	43.33	3.77	1:2.84	1:11.50
Hendry	22.98	24.38	41.20	3.90	1:2.45	1:10.57
Hernando	26.70	16.57	42.47	2.93	1:3.15	1:14.49
Highlands	24.32	21.58	44.95	3.66	1:4.20	1:12.26
Hillsborough	21.55	17.87	49.82	3.41	1:5.30	1:14.61
Holmes	18.47	15.85	50.74	4.84	1:4.54	1:10.47
Indian River	24.20	21.41	48.43	3.72	1:4.17	1:13.03
Jackson	20.10	16.51	45.64	3.64	1:3.25	1:12.55
Jefferson	20.77	17.41	41.84	6.12	1:4.10	1:6.83
Lafayette	16.56	17.61	47.22	4.86	1:3.09	1:9.71
Lake	23.72	20.49	47.24	3.40	1:4.07	1:13.88
Lee	26.45	19.01	50.41	3.71	1:5.72	1:13.58
Leon	22.52	19.52	44.78	3.48	1:3.08	1:12.86

See footnotes at end of table.   Continued . . .

Table 20.62. ELEMENTARY AND SECONDARY SCHOOLS: STUDENT-TEACHER RATIOS
AND SPECIFIED PERSONNEL PERCENTAGES AND RATIOS IN THE STATE
AND COUNTIES OF FLORIDA, 1998-99 (Continued)

County	FTE students per FTE teacher Elemen- tary 1/	FTE students per FTE teacher Second- ary	Percentage of full-time staff who are-- Teach- ers 2/	Percentage of full-time staff who are-- Admin- istrators	Ratio of-- Teacher aides to teach- ers 2/	Ratio of-- Adminis- trators to teach- ers 2/
Levy	22.14	19.66	45.08	4.66	1:3.82	1:9.66
Liberty	21.64	16.36	48.32	7.38	1:6.00	1:6.54
Madison	24.08	19.28	45.26	6.64	1:3.29	1:6.82
Manatee	23.09	20.11	45.95	3.32	1:3.46	1:13.85
Marion	22.58	20.03	43.62	3.24	1:2.69	1:13.47
Martin	24.91	17.85	46.22	3.39	1:4.05	1:13.63
Miami-Dade	24.41	25.46	52.21	3.83	1:4.89	1:13.63
Monroe	21.89	19.27	44.05	3.64	1:3.04	1:12.10
Nassau	24.78	20.57	46.30	3.45	1:3.93	1:13.43
Okaloosa	20.96	19.17	49.67	3.29	1:4.12	1:15.09
Okeechobee	21.24	20.61	43.76	3.88	1:2.24	1:11.27
Orange	23.29	18.95	48.66	2.76	1:5.02	1:17.63
Osceola	26.55	21.27	43.51	2.50	1:2.58	1:17.37
Palm Beach	24.19	19.44	50.54	3.00	1:4.11	1:16.86
Pasco	22.64	19.87	45.72	4.02	1:3.89	1:11.36
Pinellas	23.89	21.21	48.44	3.54	1:3.53	1:13.69
Polk	22.00	19.82	48.60	3.14	1:3.89	1:15.46
Putnam	23.51	19.45	41.51	4.37	1:2.92	1:9.50
St. Johns	23.34	14.43	52.00	5.81	1:5.06	1:8.95
St. Lucie	26.85	19.01	47.82	2.60	1:4.06	1:18.38
Santa Rosa	23.46	18.39	54.42	3.49	1:5.00	1:15.59
Sarasota	21.50	19.61	47.19	2.55	1:4.18	1:18.47
Seminole	23.50	19.46	52.75	3.17	1:5.31	1:16.64
Sumter	23.44	18.82	40.68	3.53	1:2.41	1:11.53
Suwannee	22.04	19.66	45.92	4.38	1:4.10	1:10.48
Taylor	19.29	19.56	45.42	4.78	1:2.85	1:9.50
Union	21.57	17.21	43.17	4.35	1:4.63	1:9.92
Volusia	22.68	19.16	46.91	3.16	1:3.34	1:14.83
Wakulla	24.49	18.31	45.47	4.80	1:3.87	1:9.48
Walton	23.27	16.24	43.80	4.13	1:2.84	1:10.59
Washington	23.05	13.27	43.91	5.79	1:3.33	1:7.58

FTE Full-time equivalent.
1/ Kindergarten through grade 6.
2/ Teachers in grades prekindergarten through grade 12 and exceptional education, primary education
specialists, and others including postsecondary vocational instructors and adult education instructors.
Note: Data are for public schools only.

Source: State of Florida, Department of Education, Division of Administration, Education Information
and Accountability Services, *Profiles of Florida School Districts, 1998-99, Student and Staff Data,* Series
2000-06, February 2000. Internet site <http://www.firn.edu.doe/bin00050/eiaspubs/profiles.htm>
(accessed 1 May 2000).

Table 20.63. ELEMENTARY AND SECONDARY SCHOOLS: ALL FUNDS REVENUE BY MAJOR SOURCE IN THE STATE AND COUNTIES OF FLORIDA, 1997-98

(in thousands of dollars, except where indicated)

County	Total all revenue receipts	Revenue per FTE student (dollars)	Federal sources Amount	Per- cent- age of total	State sources Amount	Per- cent- age of total	Local sources Amount	Per- cent- age of total
Florida 1/	15,314,451	6,338	1,145,240	7.48	7,746,017	50.58	6,423,194	41.94
Alachua	202,630	6,866	19,059	9.41	117,575	58.02	65,997	32.57
Baker	25,579	5,428	1,873	7.32	19,594	76.60	4,112	16.08
Bay	157,115	5,950	14,547	9.26	92,269	58.73	50,299	32.01
Bradford	25,938	6,183	2,068	7.97	18,200	70.17	5,671	21.86
Brevard	401,989	5,846	24,380	6.06	222,757	55.41	154,852	38.52
Broward	1,560,576	6,243	102,340	6.56	796,725	51.05	661,511	42.39
Calhoun	12,148	5,373	1,046	8.61	9,231	75.99	1,871	15.40
Charlotte	107,852	6,448	6,351	5.89	37,356	34.64	64,146	59.48
Citrus	91,567	6,116	5,987	6.54	40,783	44.54	44,797	48.92
Clay	143,869	5,362	6,812	4.73	99,549	69.19	37,509	26.07
Collier	241,904	7,639	18,390	7.60	44,116	18.24	179,398	74.16
Columbia	54,154	5,715	5,905	10.90	37,719	69.65	10,530	19.44
De Soto	30,976	6,314	3,092	9.98	20,970	67.70	6,913	22.32
Dixie	16,026	6,862	1,531	9.55	11,883	74.15	2,612	16.30
Duval	754,029	5,962	58,176	7.72	418,782	55.54	277,071	36.75
Escambia	289,426	6,157	29,627	10.24	183,294	63.33	76,505	26.43
Flagler	47,966	6,911	2,293	4.78	18,150	37.84	27,523	57.38
Franklin	9,692	6,574	1,136	11.72	3,616	37.30	4,941	50.98
Gadsden	50,374	6,081	9,047	17.96	34,532	68.55	6,795	13.49
Gilchrist	27,481	10,642	1,208	4.40	23,563	85.74	2,709	9.86
Glades	7,385	6,667	742	10.05	3,489	47.24	3,154	42.71
Gulf	14,489	5,956	1,207	8.33	7,640	52.73	5,642	38.94
Hamilton	15,777	6,852	2,225	14.10	8,615	54.60	4,937	31.30
Hardee	31,428	5,902	3,939	12.53	18,749	59.66	8,740	27.81
Hendry	56,140	7,502	6,074	10.82	37,474	66.75	12,593	22.43
Hernando	99,761	6,102	6,115	6.13	49,207	49.32	44,440	44.55
Highlands	73,694	6,549	6,499	8.82	41,514	56.33	25,680	34.85
Hillsborough	1,045,026	6,464	98,002	9.38	604,772	57.87	342,252	32.75
Holmes	36,208	9,533	2,026	5.60	31,420	86.78	2,762	7.63
Indian River	100,292	6,964	5,392	5.38	30,041	29.95	64,858	64.67
Jackson	49,744	5,863	5,526	11.11	35,606	71.58	8,612	17.31
Jefferson	12,867	6,144	1,416	11.00	9,010	70.03	2,441	18.97
Lafayette	7,022	6,637	690	9.83	5,024	71.55	1,307	18.62
Lake	162,809	5,807	11,015	6.77	90,527	55.60	61,268	37.63
Lee	369,448	6,674	26,940	7.29	123,728	33.49	218,779	59.22

See footnotes at end of table.   Continued . . .

University of Florida   **Bureau of Economic and Business Research**

Table 20.63. ELEMENTARY AND SECONDARY SCHOOLS: ALL FUNDS REVENUE BY MAJOR SOURCE IN THE STATE AND COUNTIES OF FLORIDA, 1997-98 (Continued)

(in thousands of dollars, except where indicated)

County	Total all revenue receipts	Revenue per FTE student (dol-lars)	Revenue receipts from--					
			Federal sources		State sources		Local sources	
			Amount	Per-cent-age of total	Amount	Per-cent-age of total	Amount	Per-cent-age of total
Leon	214,379	6,390	14,502	6.76	117,294	54.71	82,583	38.52
Levy	39,908	6,581	2,826	7.08	28,370	71.09	8,712	21.83
Liberty	8,410	6,631	587	6.99	6,584	78.28	1,239	14.73
Madison	20,543	5,918	2,744	13.36	15,012	73.07	2,787	13.57
Manatee	243,222	6,973	16,138	6.64	98,339	40.43	128,745	52.93
Marion	224,298	5,973	19,746	8.80	136,181	60.71	68,371	30.48
Martin	117,060	6,999	7,123	6.08	23,769	20.30	86,168	73.61
Miami-Dade	2,510,970	6,505	207,090	8.25	1,352,587	53.87	951,294	37.89
Monroe	78,214	8,165	5,226	6.68	13,080	16.72	59,909	76.60
Nassau	58,017	5,589	3,436	5.92	32,887	56.69	21,694	37.39
Okaloosa	188,501	6,154	14,944	7.93	97,746	51.85	75,812	40.22
Okeechobee	46,893	7,219	4,444	9.48	32,890	70.14	9,558	20.38
Orange	843,949	5,838	49,721	5.89	378,495	44.85	415,732	49.26
Osceola	182,624	6,193	9,051	4.96	99,882	54.69	73,692	40.35
Palm Beach	1,041,236	6,904	78,336	7.52	337,471	32.41	625,429	60.07
Pasco	281,954	6,189	21,591	7.66	164,934	58.50	95,428	33.85
Pinellas	720,687	6,197	46,067	6.39	345,503	47.94	329,117	45.67
Polk	459,744	5,793	39,994	8.70	280,195	60.95	139,555	30.35
Putnam	77,068	5,884	7,471	9.69	45,842	59.48	23,755	30.82
St. Johns	116,247	6,066	5,876	5.05	49,868	42.90	60,502	52.05
St. Lucie	186,211	6,687	16,493	8.86	82,320	44.21	87,397	46.93
Santa Rosa	138,748	6,363	9,141	6.59	94,114	67.83	35,492	25.58
Sarasota	266,379	7,363	12,705	4.77	63,012	23.65	190,662	71.58
Seminole	337,554	5,919	13,723	4.07	186,007	55.10	137,824	40.83
Sumter	33,954	5,869	3,724	10.97	22,391	65.94	7,839	23.09
Suwannee	33,360	5,483	3,016	9.04	23,770	71.25	6,574	19.71
Taylor	23,793	6,001	3,076	12.93	13,932	58.56	6,784	28.51
Union	21,778	9,376	1,056	4.85	18,837	86.49	1,886	8.66
Volusia	369,705	6,271	24,555	6.64	184,657	49.95	160,492	43.41
Wakulla	26,784	5,759	1,835	6.85	19,857	74.14	5,093	19.01
Walton	36,994	6,516	2,933	7.93	9,168	24.78	24,892	67.29
Washington	31,888	7,533	3,391	10.64	23,543	73.83	4,953	15.53

FTE Full-time equivalent.
1/ Includes special schools.
Note: Data are for public schools only.

Source: State of Florida, Department of Education, Division of Public Schools, *Profiles of Florida School Districts, 1997-98, Financial Data Statistical Report.* EIAS Series 99-15, June 1999.

Table 20.65. ELEMENTARY AND SECONDARY SCHOOLS: ALL FUNDS EXPENDITURE BY MAJOR TYPE IN THE STATE AND COUNTIES OF FLORIDA, 1997-98

(in thousands of dollars, except where indicated)

County	Total expenditure all funds	Total current expenditure	Current expenditure per FTE (dollars)	Capital outlay	Debt service
Florida 1/	15,577,977	12,846,999	5,317	1,942,654	788,324
Alachua	196,140	160,354	5,434	18,230	17,556
Baker	25,082	23,700	5,029	1,110	273
Bay	157,165	138,328	5,238	12,496	6,340
Bradford	27,128	22,200	5,292	4,672	256
Brevard	419,758	329,940	4,799	74,717	15,101
Broward	1,544,545	1,282,969	5,132	150,589	110,987
Calhoun	12,217	11,611	5,136	605	0
Charlotte	108,909	89,633	5,359	15,439	3,837
Citrus	88,842	80,208	5,357	8,479	156
Clay	153,423	125,738	4,686	24,327	3,358
Collier	274,447	182,741	5,770	50,829	40,877
Columbia	55,558	48,382	5,106	6,119	1,057
De Soto	29,038	26,343	5,370	2,007	688
Dixie	13,368	12,293	5,264	969	106
Duval	773,875	647,493	5,120	103,498	22,884
Escambia	275,128	242,816	5,166	23,918	8,394
Flagler	49,824	39,539	5,697	4,343	5,943
Franklin	9,583	8,892	6,031	386	305
Gadsden	49,067	47,442	5,727	1,463	162
Gilchrist	26,682	13,591	5,263	12,178	912
Glades	7,178	6,507	5,874	595	77
Gulf	13,959	12,770	5,249	611	579
Hamilton	16,066	14,670	6,371	1,396	0
Hardee	30,789	28,784	5,405	1,490	515
Hendry	55,176	42,331	5,657	11,000	1,845
Hernando	111,486	79,042	4,834	9,245	23,199
Highlands	70,619	63,044	5,603	5,745	1,830
Hillsborough	1,078,211	883,457	5,464	143,923	50,831
Holmes	21,190	19,846	5,225	1,126	217
Indian River	101,192	77,580	5,387	16,223	7,388
Jackson	46,799	43,514	5,129	2,642	643
Jefferson	12,813	12,130	5,792	628	54
Lafayette	6,728	5,641	5,331	522	566
Lake	165,244	137,399	4,901	22,687	5,159
Lee	403,863	315,242	5,694	59,010	29,612
Leon	221,725	177,932	5,304	31,006	12,787

See footnotes at end of table.   Continued . . .

University of Florida   **Bureau of Economic and Business Research**

Table 20.65. ELEMENTARY AND SECONDARY SCHOOLS: ALL FUNDS EXPENDITURE BY MAJOR TYPE IN THE STATE AND COUNTIES OF FLORIDA, 1997-98 (Continued)

(in thousands of dollars, except where indicated)

County	Total expenditure all funds	Total current expenditure	Current expenditure per FTE (dollars)	Capital outlay	Debt service
Levy	34,871	32,116	5,296	2,143	612
Liberty	7,017	6,645	5,240	246	125
Madison	20,394	18,885	5,440	1,088	421
Manatee	313,068	190,642	5,466	102,333	20,092
Marion	215,691	190,478	5,072	12,601	12,612
Martin	109,621	90,998	5,440	16,901	1,721
Miami-Dade	2,558,150	2,159,563	5,594	261,302	137,285
Monroe	80,458	55,836	5,829	21,053	3,569
Nassau	56,753	49,223	4,742	7,306	223
Okaloosa	205,149	154,063	5,030	36,909	14,177
Okeechobee	39,127	36,186	5,571	2,834	107
Orange	907,383	743,522	5,143	139,500	24,361
Osceola	183,599	146,058	4,953	27,422	10,118
Palm Beach	1,047,692	859,565	5,699	131,857	56,270
Pasco	287,752	241,311	5,297	31,160	15,281
Pinellas	681,750	603,144	5,186	78,144	462
Polk	453,232	409,197	5,156	31,378	12,657
Putnam	77,874	67,874	5,182	7,383	2,618
St. Johns	112,247	96,152	5,018	9,158	6,937
St. Lucie	222,080	152,056	5,461	51,967	18,056
Santa Rosa	130,603	106,655	4,891	21,449	2,498
Sarasota	252,800	215,511	5,957	26,005	11,284
Seminole	360,269	280,242	4,914	44,955	35,072
Sumter	36,010	32,730	5,658	2,666	615
Suwannee	32,758	31,617	5,197	507	634
Taylor	24,224	21,780	5,493	2,444	0
Union	20,933	13,116	5,647	7,726	91
Volusia	363,336	307,608	5,217	32,234	23,494
Wakulla	26,509	23,628	5,081	1,831	1,049
Walton	36,334	30,238	5,326	4,792	1,304
Washington	27,477	26,256	6,202	1,135	85

FTE Full-time equivalent.
1/ Includes special schools.
Note: Data are for public schools only.

Source: State of Florida, Department of Education, Division of Public Schools, *Profiles of Florida School Districts, 1997-98, Financial Data Statistical Report.* EIAS Series 99-15, July 1999.

University of Florida   **Bureau of Economic and Business Research**

Table 20.66. ELEMENTARY AND SECONDARY SCHOOLS: GENERAL FUND EXPENDITURE FOR INSTRUCTION, PUPIL PERSONNEL SERVICES, AND INSTRUCTIONAL SUPPORT SERVICES IN THE STATE AND COUNTIES OF FLORIDA, 1997-98

(in thousands of dollars)

County	Instruction	Pupil personnel services	Instructional support services	County	Instruction	Pupil personnel services	Instructional support services
Florida	7,451,118	624,682	1,364,965	Lake	79,202	7,828	15,856
				Lee	177,653	17,216	35,727
Alachua	85,770	9,049	21,322	Leon	102,049	9,432	24,701
Baker	12,410	1,692	2,847	Levy	17,839	1,622	3,294
Bay	81,681	5,364	13,516	Liberty	3,690	175	608
Bradford	12,382	785	2,054	Madison	10,750	584	2,057
Brevard	200,988	11,539	31,547	Manatee	110,668	11,474	19,789
Broward	718,438	62,538	158,198	Marion	110,935	10,945	20,496
Calhoun	6,984	349	1,166	Martin	51,264	4,677	10,479
Charlotte	50,919	5,225	10,343	Miami-Dade	1,290,851	111,574	206,288
Citrus	44,249	3,963	9,288	Monroe	30,563	2,335	5,370
Clay	74,290	6,847	14,257	Nassau	28,388	1,878	3,473
Collier	113,382	9,544	19,881	Okaloosa	90,823	5,922	15,964
Columbia	27,798	2,508	5,353	Okeechobee	19,968	2,040	4,600
De Soto	15,471	1,173	2,476	Orange	418,080	29,768	91,761
Dixie	6,733	709	1,279	Osceola	79,852	9,598	21,037
Duval	379,372	35,337	70,091	Palm Beach	526,345	27,690	70,379
Escambia	133,998	13,793	30,437	Pasco	137,443	13,552	31,642
Flagler	20,159	3,404	4,823	Pinellas	363,334	26,878	58,899
Franklin	5,246	309	528	Polk	235,130	19,396	38,422
Gadsden	25,974	1,913	5,351	Putnam	38,148	3,025	7,067
Gilchrist	7,853	670	1,373	St. Johns	56,826	5,656	10,275
Glades	3,495	319	719	St. Lucie	83,905	8,262	17,600
Gulf	7,048	503	1,186	Santa Rosa	61,160	5,150	11,079
Hamilton	7,102	1,433	2,695	Sarasota	128,439	12,564	22,640
Hardee	16,588	1,667	2,982	Seminole	168,837	12,572	24,340
Hendry	23,091	2,510	4,358	Sumter	17,663	1,100	3,856
Hernando	43,761	4,328	7,924	Suwannee	18,528	1,313	2,591
Highlands	34,860	4,343	6,913	Taylor	12,618	999	1,850
Hillsborough	497,436	41,502	92,539	Union	6,791	766	1,287
Holmes	11,616	574	1,234	Volusia	182,341	14,938	31,353
Indian River	42,055	3,324	8,925	Wakulla	12,744	1,514	2,790
Jackson	24,978	2,155	4,860	Walton	17,017	852	2,928
Jefferson	6,556	420	1,300	Washington	15,638	1,297	2,098
Lafayette	2,951	301	609				

Note: Data are for all government fund types and expendable trust funds and exclude special revenue expenditure. Data are for public schools only.

Source: State of Florida, Department of Education, Division of Public Schools, *Profiles of Florida School Districts, 1997-98, Financial Data Statistical Report.* EIAS Series 99-15, June 1999.

University of Florida   **Bureau of Economic and Business Research**

Table 20.67. ELEMENTARY AND SECONDARY SCHOOLS: OPERATING TAX MILLAGE, OPERATING TAX YIELD, ASSESSED VALUE OF NONEXEMPT PROPERTY AND ASSESSED VALUATION PER FTE STUDENT IN THE STATE AND COUNTIES OF FLORIDA, 1997-98

County	Operating tax millage	Operating tax yield ($1,000)	Assessed value of nonexempt property	
			Amount ($1,000)	Valuation per FTE student (dollars)
Florida	(X)	4,040,872	592,847,936	205,286
Alachua	7.5430	34,874	4,866,628	132,678
Baker	7.6880	2,174	297,665	53,924
Bay	7.3270	33,417	4,800,875	146,681
Bradford	7.5210	2,928	409,743	81,063
Brevard	7.1459	103,370	14,587,861	175,152
Broward	7.4460	427,616	60,451,481	211,184
Calhoun	6.7690	1,360	211,464	77,911
Charlotte	7.0340	42,427	6,349,231	312,442
Citrus	7.4240	31,791	4,507,614	237,386
Clay	7.5870	24,245	3,363,822	101,575
Collier	6.4240	119,182	19,529,076	499,812
Columbia	7.1740	6,537	959,152	81,307
De Soto	7.1490	4,566	672,340	114,807
Dixie	7.6710	1,526	209,349	67,392
Duval	7.1050	165,121	24,463,336	152,985
Escambia	7.5650	46,562	6,478,882	112,056
Flagler	7.3040	16,158	2,328,703	315,527
Franklin	6.9990	4,157	625,135	350,300
Gadsden	7.2890	4,398	635,136	64,233
Gilchrist	7.7200	1,611	219,667	68,253
Glades	7.0900	2,393	355,240	264,710
Gulf	7.0570	4,414	658,338	235,816
Hamilton	7.5690	3,468	482,301	165,286
Hardee	7.6100	5,938	821,372	128,434
Hendry	7.1140	8,224	1,216,895	134,982
Hernando	7.2510	25,777	3,742,035	191,920
Highlands	7.2290	17,274	2,515,373	174,380
Hillsborough	7.1520	199,413	29,349,684	154,279
Holmes	6.3710	1,378	227,745	50,824
Indian River	6.9750	40,817	6,159,945	337,596
Jackson	7.3650	4,995	713,869	70,116
Jefferson	7.4830	1,824	256,626	100,232
Lafayette	7.6430	856	117,869	93,737
Lake	7.1000	39,713	5,887,719	178,148
Lee	7.2450	152,695	22,185,187	322,793
Leon	7.3640	47,721	6,821,325	163,134

See footnotes at end of table.

Continued . . .

University of Florida   **Bureau of Economic and Business Research**

Table 20.67. ELEMENTARY AND SECONDARY SCHOOLS: OPERATING TAX MILLAGE, OPERATING TAX YIELD, ASSESSED VALUE OF NONEXEMPT PROPERTY AND ASSESSED VALUATION PER FTE STUDENT IN THE STATE AND COUNTIES OF FLORIDA, 1997-98 (Continued)

County	Operating tax millage	Operating tax yield ($1,000)	Assessed value of nonexempt property	
			Amount ($1,000)	Valuation per FTE student (dollars)
Levy	7.6840	5,672	776,961	100,361
Liberty	7.6300	826	113,902	76,258
Madison	7.3800	2,069	295,128	65,531
Manatee	7.0290	68,468	10,253,452	241,131
Marion	7.4650	41,105	5,796,134	125,728
Martin	7.0010	58,357	8,774,189	446,592
Miami-Dade	7.3600	570,163	81,545,000	184,020
Monroe	5.3040	39,578	7,854,664	661,385
Nassau	7.4080	15,138	2,151,002	174,244
Okaloosa	7.2830	39,851	5,759,822	159,005
Okeechobee	7.2560	6,057	878,659	104,713
Orange	7.0770	270,652	40,256,736	245,408
Osceola	7.1040	42,293	6,266,756	174,760
Palm Beach	7.0600	402,454	60,005,033	334,908
Pasco	7.1050	53,756	7,964,077	135,236
Pinellas	7.1330	225,371	33,258,494	232,610
Polk	7.4310	96,469	13,665,208	147,361
Putnam	7.0990	14,418	2,137,888	131,890
St. Johns	7.3160	38,553	5,547,054	268,678
St. Lucie	7.0430	53,136	7,941,581	224,898
Santa Rosa	7.1160	22,579	3,339,952	129,816
Sarasota	6.9470	126,251	19,130,007	433,385
Seminole	7.1560	84,698	12,458,815	180,125
Sumter	7.4250	5,277	748,123	103,812
Suwannee	7.2950	4,087	589,732	84,689
Taylor	7.2310	4,678	680,938	147,828
Union	7.6430	837	115,252	40,265
Volusia	7.1860	93,855	13,748,296	183,057
Wakulla	7.6520	2,587	355,923	62,413
Walton	7.3540	17,991	2,575,121	384,023
Washington	7.4500	2,727	385,351	94,438

FTE Full-time equivalent.
(X) Not applicable.
Note: Data are for public schools only.

Source: State of Florida, Department of Education, Division of Public Schools, *Profiles of Florida School Districts, 1997-98, Financial Data Statistical Report.* EIAS Series 99-15, July 1999.

University of Florida   **Bureau of Economic and Business Research**

Table 20.69. ELEMENTARY AND SECONDARY SCHOOLS: EXPENDITURE FOR LUNCH AND PUPIL TRANSPORTATION SERVICES IN THE STATE AND COUNTIES OF FLORIDA SCHOOL YEAR 1997-98

(in dollars)

County	Lunch services	Trans-portation services	County	Lunch services	Trans-portation services
Florida	630,939,087	537,921,693	Lake	7,266,125	6,435,551
			Lee	14,807,932	16,943,204
Alachua	8,926,653	6,987,220	Leon	7,320,624	6,881,644
Baker	1,322,617	1,236,347	Levy	1,903,979	2,061,589
Bay	7,695,091	5,410,059	Liberty	371,067	333,940
Bradford	1,077,114	982,426	Madison	1,226,027	930,174
Brevard	14,923,731	11,468,074	Manatee	10,227,750	7,251,744
Broward	51,350,964	52,912,874	Marion	11,533,849	12,010,529
Calhoun	650,436	449,767			
			Martin	4,297,750	3,752,185
Charlotte	4,975,511	3,721,686	Miami-Dade	106,465,968	66,334,570
Citrus	3,324,178	4,661,017	Monroe	3,026,726	2,720,317
Clay	5,788,290	6,573,908	Nassau	2,802,505	2,525,515
Collier	8,385,602	7,950,326	Okaloosa	6,903,062	5,429,967
Columbia	2,733,976	2,680,755	Okeechobee	2,183,536	1,667,740
De Soto	1,656,515	1,084,540	Orange	35,432,650	35,878,233
Dixie	852,171	641,437	Osceola	6,976,052	5,210,908
Duval	32,348,359	35,196,498	Palm Beach	33,648,471	22,869,054
Escambia	15,122,240	13,359,959	Pasco	12,662,226	10,432,805
Flagler	1,662,818	1,894,246	Pinellas	29,016,972	22,602,645
Franklin	506,243	303,465	Polk	27,177,683	16,104,774
Gadsden	3,414,484	2,223,650	Putnam	4,625,835	3,423,631
Gilchrist	773,251	656,994	St. Johns	3,596,617	3,570,836
Glades	314,753	283,842	St. Lucie	8,492,479	9,353,049
Gulf	662,052	593,937	Santa Rosa	5,575,268	5,994,061
Hamilton	883,757	661,319	Sarasota	8,880,560	9,606,804
Hardee	1,844,133	1,445,402	Seminole	13,125,931	12,709,111
Hendry	2,789,005	1,868,297	Sumter	2,200,130	1,523,893
Hernando	4,059,413	4,697,130	Suwannee	1,748,938	1,912,020
Highlands	3,686,349	3,352,545	Taylor	1,177,823	1,275,621
Hillsborough	46,516,898	44,878,645	Union	680,178	587,726
Holmes	1,325,935	876,047	Volusia	13,857,051	10,259,407
Indian River	4,148,841	2,667,341	Wakulla	1,281,273	1,637,060
Jackson	2,814,477	1,889,487	Walton	1,769,657	1,658,605
Jefferson	701,656	886,174	Washington	1,126,649	1,216,912
Lafayette	312,197	320,425			

Note: Data are for public schools only. Detail may not add to total due to rounding.

Source: State of Florida, Department of Education, Division of Public Schools, *Profiles of Florida School Districts, 1997-98, Financial Data Statistical Report.* EIAS Series 99-15, July 1999.

University of Florida   **Bureau of Economic and Business Research**

Table 20.74. FEDERAL AID: SPECIFIED FEDERAL HEALTH AND EDUCATION PROGRAM EXPENDITURES IN FLORIDA, OTHER SUNBELT STATES, AND THE UNITED STATES, 1999

(in millions of dollars, except where indicated)

State	Total 1/	Per capita (dollars)	Compensatory education for the disadvantaged	Medicaid	ETA employment/ training
Florida	10,811	715.42	293	4,025	261
Alabama	4,165	953.06	132	1,762	95
Arizona	4,290	897.74	113	1,445	112
Arkansas	2,504	981.59	77	1,141	63
California	32,716	987.06	935	11,503	1,165
Georgia	6,432	825.86	204	2,400	140
Louisiana	5,069	1,159.40	205	2,398	125
Mississippi	3,213	1,160.58	130	1,458	63
New Mexico	2,448	1,407.08	65	838	55
North Carolina	7,084	925.87	147	3,246	153
Oklahoma	3,191	950.24	91	1,146	83
South Carolina	3,610	929.02	81	1,810	85
Tennessee	5,742	1,047.22	130	2,778	98
Texas	16,646	830.46	674	6,830	429
Virginia	4,405	640.95	121	1,366	132
United States	274,448	1,006.44	7,550	108,569	7,116

ETA Employment and Training Administration.   1/ Includes other amounts not shown separately.
Source: U.S., Department of Commerce, Bureau of the Census, *Federal Aid to States for Fiscal Year 1999*, issued April 2000, Internet site <http://www.census.gov/prod/2000pubs/fas-99.pdf> (accessed 24 May 2000).

Table 20.75. CULTURE AND THE ARTS: STATE GRANTS TO GROUPS AND INDIVIDUALS IN THE STATE AND SPECIFIED COUNTIES OF FLORIDA, 1998-99

(in dollars)

County	Amount	County	Amount	County	Amount
Florida	28,675,095	Hardee	1,000	Nassau	15,862
Alachua	436,719	Hendry	664	Okaloosa	44,986
Bay	188,546	Hernando	1,500	Okeechobee	12,100
Bradford	733	Highlands	30,774	Orange	2,056,649
Brevard	235,539	Hillsborough	3,280,407	Osceola	15,574
Broward	2,386,955	Holmes	733	Palm Beach	1,193,229
Calhoun	32,068	Indian River	885,668	Pasco	509,816
Charlotte	14,358	Jackson	8,417	Pinellas	2,525,170
Citrus	2,272	Jefferson	8,083	Polk	828,845
Collier	1,158,507	Lafayette	2,327	Putnam	18,261
Columbia	6,000	Lake	21,397	St. Johns	12,561
De Soto	3,860	Lee	166,779	St. Lucie	999,254
Duval	978,167	Leon	548,668	Sarasota	1,346,147
Escambia	854,792	Levy	10,506	Seminole	40,374
Flagler	74,552	Madison	1,000	Sumter	4,926
Franklin	1,667	Manatee	344,490	Suwannee	32,997
Gadsden	6,750	Marion	36,788	Union	1,000
Gilchrist	1,533	Martin	74,620	Volusia	733,200
Gulf	732	Miami-Dade	6,318,793	Wakulla	13,160
Hamilton	667	Monroe	111,550	Walton	32,403

Source: State of Florida, Department of State, Division of Cultural Affairs, *1998-99 Florida Funding for Culture and the Arts,* Internet site <http://www.dos.state.fl.us/dca/99fdsum.html> (accessed 15 August 2000).

University of Florida   **Bureau of Economic and Business Research**

GOVERNMENT AND ELECTIONS

Female Voting-age Population
April 1, 1999
(percentage)

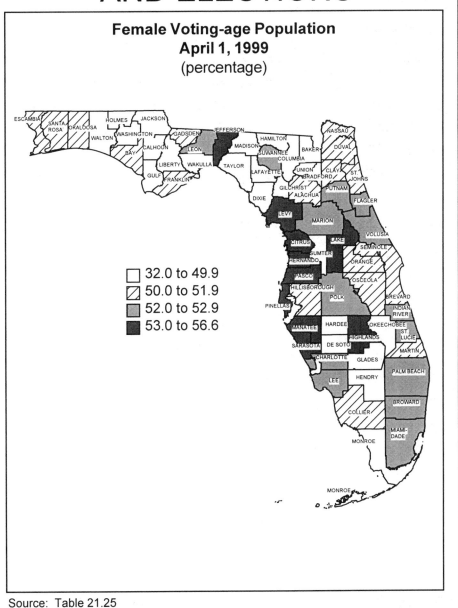

32.0 to 49.9
50.0 to 51.9
52.0 to 52.9
53.0 to 56.6

Source: Table 21.25

GOVERNMENT AND ELECTIONS

TABLES LISTED BY MAJOR HEADINGS

Table 21.01. GOVERNMENTAL UNITS: NUMBER BY TYPE IN FLORIDA AND THE UNITED STATES, 1997

Type of unit	Florida	United States
All units	1,082	87,504
Percentage change from 1992	6.7	2.9
Local government general purpose	1,081	87,453
County 1/	66	3,043
Municipal	394	19,372
Local government special purpose	621	48,409
School districts	95	13,726
Special districts	526	34,683
Single-function districts	492	31,965
Education services	8	2,251
Education 2/	4	755
Libraries	4	1,496
Social services	50	1,508
Hospitals	28	763
Health	16	686
Welfare	6	59
Transportation	17	1,404
Highways	5	721
Airports	6	476
Other 3/	6	207
Fire protection	56	5,601
Environment and housing	258	14,191
Natural resources 4/	132	6,983
Drainage and flood control	62	3,369
Soil and water conservation	61	2,449
Other	9	1,165
Parks and recreation	16	1,253
Housing and community development	105	3,469
Sewerage	2	2,004
Solid waste management	3	482
Utilities	26	3,879
Water supply	15	3,409
Other 5/	11	470
Industrial development and mortgage credit	6	215
Multiple-function	34	2,718
Natural resources and water supply	3	117
Sewerage and water supply	6	1,384
Other	25	1,217

1/ In 1968, Duval County and the City of Jacksonville consolidated to form one government, designated the City of Jacksonville. Jacksonville is counted as a municipal government, rather than as a county government, in census reporting.
2/ Primarily school building authorities.
3/ Includes parking facilities and water transport and terminals.
4/ Functions within the "natural resources" category overlap.
5/ Includes electric power, gas supply, and transit.
Note: The governments census is on a 5-year cycle collecting data for years ending in 2 and 7.

Source: U.S., Department of Commerce, Bureau of the Census, *1997 Census of Governments, Volume I, No. 1: Government Organization,* Issued August 1999, Internet site <http://www.census.gov/prod/gc97/gc97-1.pdf> (accessed 12 September 1999).

Table 21.07. LOCAL GOVERNMENTS AND PUBLIC SCHOOL SYSTEMS: NUMBER OF POLITICAL UNITS AND ELECTED OFFICIALS BY TYPE OF GOVERNMENT IN THE STATE AND COUNTIES OF FLORIDA, 1992

County	Political units			Elected officials			
	Munici-palities	School dis-tricts	Special dis-tricts	County	Munici-palities	School dis-tricts	Special dis-tricts
Florida	390	95	462	842	2,238	396	1,178
Alachua	9	2	4	15	48	5	5
Baker	2	1	3	11	10	6	5
Bay	8	2	6	14	40	6	8
Bradford	4	1	1	10	24	6	0
Brevard	15	2	15	10	84	5	28
Broward	28	2	33	11	158	7	98
Calhoun	2	1	0	12	11	6	0
Charlotte	1	1	5	14	5	5	11
Citrus	2	1	2	10	12	6	6
Clay	4	1	4	19	20	6	7
Collier	2	1	14	7	13	5	40
Columbia	2	2	3	11	10	6	5
De Soto	1	1	4	12	6	6	8
Dixie	2	1	1	11	12	5	5
Duval 1/	5	2	2	(X)	50	7	5
Escambia	2	2	5	12	16	6	10
Flagler	4	1	4	10	23	6	13
Franklin	2	1	7	11	10	6	13
Gadsden	6	1	2	11	36	6	5
Gilchrist	3	1	3	11	18	6	11
Glades	1	1	3	12	7	6	11
Gulf	2	1	2	12	10	6	5
Hamilton	3	1	2	11	16	6	5
Hardee	3	1	2	10	20	6	5
Hendry	2	1	18	10	11	6	43
Hernando	2	1	6	12	8	6	10
Highlands	3	2	6	11	19	6	21
Hillsborough	3	2	12	12	19	7	34
Holmes	5	1	3	12	29	6	0
Indian River	5	1	11	12	26	5	37
Jackson	11	2	5	13	60	6	13
Jefferson	1	1	1	10	9	6	5
Lafayette	1	1	1	13	6	6	5
Lake	14	2	4	10	76	6	3
Lee	3	2	32	10	19	5	132
Leon	1	2	5	12	5	6	5

See footnotes at end of table.   Continued . . .

Table 21.07. LOCAL GOVERNMENTS AND PUBLIC SCHOOL SYSTEMS: NUMBER OF POLITICAL UNITS AND ELECTED OFFICIALS BY TYPE OF GOVERNMENT IN THE STATE AND COUNTIES OF FLORIDA, 1992 (Continued)

County	Political units			Elected officials			
	Munici-palities	School dis-tricts	Special dis-tricts	County	Munici-palities	School dis-tricts	Special dis-tricts
Levy	7	1	3	12	39	6	10
Liberty	1	1	0	12	8	6	0
Madison	3	2	2	11	16	6	5
Manatee	6	2	18	21	40	5	36
Marion	5	2	6	10	28	6	5
Martin	4	1	6	9	22	6	15
Miami-Dade	26	2	6	36	145	7	12
Monroe	3	2	6	10	16	6	10
Nassau	3	1	4	12	19	6	12
Okaloosa	9	2	12	10	58	6	32
Okeechobee	1	1	3	11	6	5	11
Orange	13	2	15	11	73	7	21
Osceola	2	1	2	10	10	6	5
Palm Beach	37	2	39	14	204	7	104
Pasco	6	2	4	11	31	6	13
Pinellas	24	2	15	66	132	8	19
Polk	17	2	11	10	91	6	17
Putnam	5	2	4	10	28	6	5
St. Johns	3	1	9	14	17	6	38
St. Lucie	3	2	9	10	17	5	26
Santa Rosa	3	1	10	14	21	5	38
Sarasota	3	1	13	10	17	5	59
Seminole	7	2	3	11	37	5	5
Sumter	5	1	1	11	28	6	5
Suwannee	2	1	4	10	14	6	5
Taylor	1	1	1	10	5	6	0
Union	3	1	2	10	17	6	5
Volusia	14	2	13	19	75	5	15
Wakulla	2	1	1	12	10	6	5
Walton	3	1	6	10	20	6	23
Washington	5	1	3	11	48	6	5

(X) Not applicable.
1/ County-type area without any county government.
Note: School districts include community college districts. The governments census is on a 5-year cycle collecting data for years ending in 2 and 7.

Source: U.S., Department of Commerce, Bureau of the Census, *1992 Census of Governments, Volume I, No. 2: Popularly Elected Officials.*

University of Florida   **Bureau of Economic and Business Research**

Table 21.20. VOTING-AGE POPULATION: ESTIMATES BY SEX AND AGE IN FLORIDA, OTHER SUNBELT STATES, OTHER POPULOUS STATES, AND THE UNITED STATES, JULY 1, 1999

State	Total popu- lation (1,000)	Number (1,000)	Female	Aged 18 to 24	Aged 25 to 44	Aged 45 to 64	Aged 65 and over
				Percentage--			
				Persons aged 18 and over			
			Sunbelt states				
Florida	15,111	11,541	52.3	10.7	36.7	28.8	23.8
Alabama	4,370	3,304	53.0	13.3	39.6	29.9	17.2
Arizona	4,778	3,444	51.2	13.3	39.6	28.8	18.3
Arkansas	2,551	1,891	52.7	13.3	37.3	30.2	19.1
California	33,145	24,222	50.5	13.7	44.2	27.0	15.1
Georgia	7,788	5,731	52.2	13.5	44.4	28.8	13.3
Louisiana	4,372	3,182	52.9	15.1	39.2	29.9	15.8
Mississippi	2,769	2,016	53.3	15.0	39.5	28.9	16.6
New Mexico	1,740	1,244	51.5	14.2	39.3	30.5	16.1
North Carolina	7,651	5,710	52.4	12.4	41.2	29.7	16.7
Oklahoma	3,358	2,476	52.1	13.9	37.4	30.6	18.1
South Carolina	3,886	2,930	52.6	13.4	40.6	29.8	16.2
Tennessee	5,484	4,143	52.7	12.5	40.4	30.6	16.4
Texas	20,044	14,325	51.4	14.7	42.1	29.1	14.1
Virginia	6,873	5,208	51.9	12.9	43.0	29.2	14.9
			Other populous states				
Illinois	12,128	8,947	52.1	12.8	41.4	29.1	16.7
Indiana	5,943	4,414	52.3	13.1	40.5	29.6	16.8
Massachusetts	6,175	4,707	52.7	10.9	42.4	28.4	18.3
Michigan	9,864	7,303	52.2	12.7	41.0	29.5	16.8
New Jersey	8,143	6,140	52.4	11.0	41.2	29.8	18.0
New York	18,197	13,756	52.8	11.8	41.0	29.5	17.7
Ohio	11,257	8,413	52.6	12.7	39.9	29.6	17.8
Pennsylvania	11,994	9,141	52.9	11.2	38.5	29.6	20.8
United States	272,691	202,491	51.9	12.8	40.9	29.2	17.1

Note: Includes Armed Forces residing in each state.

Source: U.S., Department of Commerce, Bureau of the Census, Population Division, Population Estimates for the U.S., Regions, and States by Selected Age Groups and Sex: Annual Time Series, July 1, 1990 to July 1, 1999, released March 9, 2000, Internet site <http://www.census.gov/population/. estimates/state/st-99-09.txt> (accessed 18 May 2000).

University of Florida   **Bureau of Economic and Business Research**

Table 21.22. VOTERS: VOTING-AGE POPULATION AND REGISTERED VOTERS BY VOTING STATUS, IN FLORIDA OTHER STATES, AND THE UNITED STATES, NOVEMBER 1996

State	Voting-age population Number (1,000)	Registered to vote (percentage)	Registered voters Number (1,000)	Reported voted (percentage)
Florida	10,886	61.8	5,516	50.7
Alabama	3,139	73.8	1,744	55.6
Alaska	404	75.5	240	59.5
Arizona	3,149	58.5	1,489	47.3
Arkansas	1,843	64.4	949	51.5
California	22,871	56.1	11,079	48.4
Colorado	2,859	70.0	1,682	58.8
Connecticut	2,409	69.9	1,409	58.5
Delaware	536	64.0	293	54.7
Georgia	5,303	66.1	2,632	49.6
Hawaii	839	55.1	361	43.1
Idaho	835	68.4	502	60.1
Illinois	8,598	67.7	4,779	55.6
Indiana	4,238	68.5	2,367	55.8
Iowa	2,113	73.0	1,291	61.1
Kansas	1,823	68.9	1,129	62.0
Kentucky	2,906	69.4	1,535	52.8
Louisiana	3,098	73.4	1,915	61.8
Maine	926	81.5	626	67.7
Maryland	3,766	65.9	2,048	54.4
Massachusetts	4,560	66.7	2,569	56.3
Michigan	7,018	72.0	4,080	58.1
Minnesota	3,375	78.3	2,259	66.9
Mississippi	1,942	71.6	1,069	55.1
Missouri	3,925	75.5	2,397	61.1
Montana	649	75.1	437	67.3
Nebraska	1,181	74.1	720	61.0
Nevada	1,176	59.0	562	47.8
New Hampshire	862	71.7	518	60.1
New Jersey	5,944	63.3	3,251	54.7
New Mexico	1,213	61.7	627	51.7
New York	13,408	61.0	6,830	50.9
North Carolina	5,364	68.5	2,897	54.0
North Dakota	456	90.5	300	65.8
Ohio	8,192	68.4	4,811	58.7
Oklahoma	2,356	70.1	1,379	58.5
Oregon	2,395	72.9	1,462	61.1
Pennsylvania	8,996	65.6	4,951	55.0
Rhode Island	725	71.7	439	60.6
South Carolina	2,716	68.2	1,479	54.5
South Dakota	523	74.8	336	64.3
Tennessee	4,014	65.9	2,133	53.1
Texas	13,431	61.9	6,210	46.2
Utah	1,334	64.5	707	53.0
Vermont	434	72.0	258	59.5
Virginia	4,955	66.5	2,796	56.4
Washington	4,059	70.0	2,436	60.0
West Virginia	1,423	64.7	715	50.2
Wisconsin	3,736	77.6	2,330	62.4
Wyoming	347	71.2	230	66.2
United States	193,651	65.9	105,017	54.2

Source: U.S., Department of Commerce, Bureau of the Census, Population Division, *Current Population Reports: Voting and Registration in the Election of November 1996*, P20-504, Issued July 1998, Internet site <http://www.census.gov//prod/3/98pubs/p20-504u.pdf> (accessed 13 July 2000).

Table 21.23. VOTERS: REGISTERED VOTERS WHO REPORTED VOTING BY SEX, RACE, HISPANIC ORIGIN AND SPECIFIED AGE GROUP IN FLORIDA, OTHER STATES, AND THE UNITED STATES, NOVEMBER 3, 1996

State	Registered voters (1,000)	Reported voted (percentage) Male	Fe-male	White	Black	His-panic origin 1/	Aged 65 and over
Florida	6,727	49.6	51.6	52.7	40.5	29.0	65.1
Alabama	2,318	52.2	58.5	56.3	54.3	13.6	70.5
Alaska	305	56.3	62.6	62.3	48.6	42.6	65.3
Arizona	1,844	42.9	51.1	49.1	45.0	23.0	70.2
Arkansas	1,187	51.3	51.7	52.1	50.6	10.0	60.0
California	12,827	46.7	50.1	51.1	56.7	22.6	66.6
Colorado	2,001	57.3	60.4	60.2	39.2	38.8	68.6
Connecticut	1,685	57.2	59.7	62.6	32.6	33.3	70.7
Delaware	343	52.1	57.1	58.2	46.0	32.5	67.1
Georgia	3,506	50.1	49.2	52.3	45.6	17.9	59.5
Hawaii	463	42.5	43.6	46.6	44.8	52.2	51.2
Idaho	571	58.9	61.2	60.4	0.0	10.7	69.8
Illinois	5,819	54.7	56.4	55.4	60.2	21.3	70.6
Indiana	2,904	55.5	56.1	57.2	43.1	36.3	68.0
Iowa	1,543	61.0	61.2	63.3	44.4	27.1	71.0
Kansas	1,257	61.9	62.1	63.5	50.0	26.8	70.2
Kentucky	2,017	51.3	54.1	53.6	45.1	34.9	62.2
Louisiana	2,275	60.3	63.1	62.6	60.0	21.7	71.5
Maine	755	66.8	68.5	67.8	100.0	39.4	70.8
Maryland	2,481	53.5	55.3	54.7	56.9	40.8	57.0
Massachusetts	3,040	53.2	59.2	58.2	43.0	22.3	68.1
Michigan	5,052	55.3	60.7	58.1	63.0	39.2	71.7
Minnesota	2,644	62.9	71.0	68.1	43.9	12.3	81.8
Mississippi	1,389	54.7	55.4	59.3	48.8	27.3	65.2
Missouri	2,964	58.9	63.0	62.2	50.5	34.8	69.7
Montana	487	64.0	70.7	68.1	75.1	32.4	79.5
Nebraska	875	60.3	61.6	62.6	44.1	16.7	70.9
Nevada	694	42.2	53.4	48.6	43.0	13.4	66.0
New Hampshire	618	61.6	58.8	60.3	46.6	80.6	66.1
New Jersey	3,765	54.3	55.1	57.1	53.8	37.1	65.5
New Mexico	749	48.5	54.7	53.3	69.0	43.4	64.9
New York	8,176	49.4	52.3	55.1	42.4	28.6	63.2
North Carolina	3,673	53.0	54.9	56.4	48.7	7.7	61.9
North Dakota	412	55.5	66.1	66.4	100.0	43.6	74.6
Ohio	5,604	57.8	59.6	66.1	47.3	38.6	69.7
Oklahoma	1,652	56.6	60.1	60.8	52.0	26.7	68.5
Oregon	1,746	57.9	64.2	60.5	71.0	14.5	79.5
Pennsylvania	5,902	56.7	53.5	61.6	57.7	37.5	64.2
Rhode Island	519	59.8	61.3	62.7	26.8	25.3	72.4
South Carolina	1,851	52.0	56.6	56.2	49.9	31.2	62.4
South Dakota	391	62.6	66.0	65.6	58.5	33.7	75.3
Tennessee	2,647	53.0	53.3	52.8	56.0	9.7	65.0
Texas	8,316	44.8	47.6	46.7	47.1	27.9	58.6
Utah	861	50.6	55.4	53.9	19.9	28.8	71.2
Vermont	313	55.8	63.1	59.6	100.0	83.4	72.0
Virginia	3,294	53.9	58.7	58.5	53.3	24.8	71.5
Washington	2,840	57.8	62.2	61.0	72.1	30.2	74.0
West Virginia	921	48.8	51.4	51.6	19.3	49.6	61.7
Wisconsin	2,900	60.2	64.6	64.2	55.6	24.3	80.0
Wyoming	247	65.0	67.3	66.9	23.3	34.6	79.7
United States	127,661	52.8	55.5	56.0	50.6	26.7	67.0

1/ Persons of Hispanic origin may be of any race.

Source: U.S., Department of Commerce, Bureau of the Census, Population Division, Current Population Reports: Voting and Registration in the Election of November 1996, P20-504, Issued July 1998, Internet site <http://www.census.gov/prod/3/98pubs/p20-504u.pdf> and Internet site <http://www.census.gov/population/socdemo/voting/96cps/tab4B.txt> (accessed 13 July 2000).

Table 21.25. VOTING-AGE POPULATION: CENSUS COUNTS, APRIL 1, 1990, AND ESTIMATES
APRIL 1, 1999, BY SEX AND RACE OF PERSONS AGED 18 AND OVER IN THE
STATE AND COUNTIES OF FLORIDA

		Estimates, 1999				
			Percentage of total			
	Census		Sex		Race	
County	1990	Total	Male	Female	White	Black
Florida	10,054,095	11,892,978	47.9	52.1	86.5	11.8
Alachua	141,760	169,380	49.2	50.8	80.7	16.1
Baker	12,810	15,919	53.6	46.4	85.9	13.4
Bay	94,532	112,508	48.6	51.4	88.5	9.0
Bradford	17,087	19,876	57.2	42.8	78.8	20.2
Brevard	311,152	371,053	48.5	51.5	91.8	6.5
Broward	997,360	1,159,921	47.3	52.7	82.8	15.2
Calhoun	8,127	11,066	53.9	46.1	82.6	15.9
Charlotte	93,590	115,151	47.5	52.5	95.3	3.8
Citrus	76,980	96,094	46.8	53.2	97.6	1.8
Clay	75,330	101,513	48.8	51.2	93.2	4.6
Collier	121,474	174,964	48.2	51.8	95.9	3.4
Columbia	30,642	41,617	51.5	48.5	81.1	17.6
De Soto	18,143	21,839	53.9	46.1	82.7	16.3
Dixie	7,979	10,467	52.0	48.0	90.0	9.4
Duval	497,830	562,790	48.3	51.8	75.6	21.8
Escambia	196,088	227,353	48.9	51.1	79.4	17.5
Flagler	23,187	37,964	47.2	52.8	91.7	7.1
Franklin	6,807	8,797	48.4	51.6	89.6	9.6
Gadsden	28,845	37,183	49.0	51.0	44.3	54.7
Gilchrist	7,235	10,221	52.8	47.3	91.7	7.8
Glades	5,724	7,853	53.4	46.6	81.2	12.5
Gulf	8,655	11,218	53.8	46.3	79.2	19.6
Hamilton	7,757	11,015	57.4	42.6	62.2	37.0
Hardee	13,759	16,447	53.3	46.7	89.7	9.2
Hendry	17,614	20,939	52.0	48.0	82.7	14.7
Hernando	82,412	104,710	47.0	53.1	96.5	2.9
Highlands	55,510	66,872	46.2	53.8	92.8	6.4
Hillsborough	630,690	731,989	48.1	51.9	86.8	11.4
Holmes	11,836	14,722	52.6	47.5	91.0	7.4
Indian River	72,602	88,721	47.3	52.7	94.0	5.4
Jackson	31,022	38,822	53.4	46.6	71.9	27.0
Jefferson	8,013	10,929	43.4	56.6	61.5	37.6
Lafayette	4,191	5,491	59.0	41.0	84.2	15.2
Lake	121,614	165,013	46.9	53.1	93.2	6.2
Lee	269,118	335,235	47.5	52.6	94.3	4.9
Leon	149,007	186,191	47.5	52.5	75.4	22.5

Continued . . .

Table 21.25. VOTING-AGE POPULATION: CENSUS COUNTS, APRIL 1, 1990, AND ESTIMATES APRIL 1, 1999, BY SEX AND RACE OF PERSONS AGED 18 AND OVER IN THE STATE AND COUNTIES OF FLORIDA (Continued)

County	Census 1990	Estimates, 1999				
			Percentage of total			
			Sex		Race	
		Total	Male	Female	White	Black
Levy	19,602	26,147	46.6	53.4	89.9	9.1
Liberty	4,214	6,337	59.8	40.2	80.8	18.3
Madison	11,978	14,525	52.3	47.7	62.2	37.1
Manatee	170,868	204,478	46.7	53.3	93.3	5.9
Marion	151,424	197,160	47.1	52.9	89.4	9.6
Martin	83,024	99,892	48.1	51.9	94.7	4.6
Miami-Dade	1,465,595	1,578,816	47.4	52.6	78.1	19.9
Monroe	64,389	71,185	50.4	49.6	94.7	4.3
Nassau	31,983	42,422	48.9	51.1	91.8	7.6
Okaloosa	106,323	132,655	49.6	50.4	88.3	8.4
Okeechobee	21,521	26,361	51.5	48.5	91.1	7.5
Orange	514,989	640,962	49.1	50.9	83.5	13.7
Osceola	80,433	118,265	48.4	51.6	93.1	4.8
Palm Beach	692,775	829,061	47.2	52.8	88.8	9.9
Pasco	230,665	268,580	46.5	53.5	97.6	1.6
Pinellas	699,455	733,427	46.5	53.5	92.1	6.5
Polk	306,940	365,121	47.5	52.5	88.5	10.5
Putnam	48,414	55,078	47.8	52.3	84.3	14.8
St. Johns	65,007	90,556	48.1	51.9	93.7	5.6
St. Lucie	115,265	146,020	47.8	52.2	86.9	12.1
Santa Rosa	59,385	84,223	49.8	50.3	93.4	4.2
Sarasota	233,828	271,258	46.2	53.8	96.2	3.1
Seminole	214,314	268,571	48.6	51.5	90.8	7.1
Sumter	24,512	40,776	53.8	46.2	83.2	16.0
Suwannee	19,645	26,263	47.7	52.3	88.3	11.1
Taylor	12,272	14,936	54.2	45.8	79.4	19.1
Union	7,616	11,248	68.0	32.0	73.9	24.7
Volusia	297,236	342,277	47.7	52.3	91.6	7.3
Wakulla	10,176	15,597	51.3	48.7	87.0	12.0
Walton	21,139	32,062	50.3	49.8	91.4	6.4
Washington	12,626	16,876	51.1	48.9	81.6	15.5

Source: University of Florida, Bureau of Economic and Business Research, Population Program, *Florida Population Studies,* June 2000, Volume 33, No. 3. Bulletin No. 127.

University of Florida   **Bureau of Economic and Business Research**

Table 21.26. VOTING-AGE POPULATION: PROJECTIONS, APRIL 1, 2005, AND 2015, OF PERSONS AGED 18 AND OVER BY SPECIFIED SEX, RACE AND AGE CHARACTERISTICS IN THE STATE AND COUNTIES OF FLORIDA

County	2005 Voting-age population	2005 Percentage-- Female	2005 Race White	2005 Race Black	2005 Aged 45-64	2005 Aged 65 and over	2015 Voting-age population	2015 Percentage-- Female	2015 Race White	2015 Race Black	2015 Aged 45-64	2015 Aged 65 and over
Florida	13,232,393	51.9	86.2	12.0	33.2	23.3	15,486,267	51.7	86.0	11.9	34.4	26.1
Alachua	186,952	50.6	80.1	16.4	23.5	11.5	213,453	50.4	79.7	16.4	24.7	13.3
Baker	17,812	46.8	87.6	11.7	29.4	13.0	20,709	47.3	89.0	10.3	30.6	15.4
Bay	124,611	51.3	88.6	8.8	34.1	18.3	144,467	51.3	88.7	8.6	35.5	21.3
Bradford	21,326	43.1	80.0	19.0	31.3	17.7	23,376	43.6	81.3	17.6	31.8	20.7
Brevard	416,199	51.6	91.7	6.4	34.4	23.4	489,926	51.5	91.8	6.3	36.0	26.2
Broward	1,279,905	52.5	80.9	16.6	33.8	23.0	1,491,659	52.1	79.6	17.4	35.4	25.4
Calhoun	12,640	46.5	83.1	15.3	29.6	19.2	15,009	47.2	83.7	14.5	31.3	22.2
Charlotte	131,953	52.3	95.0	4.0	34.3	36.8	160,132	51.9	94.8	4.1	35.4	39.3
Citrus	109,873	53.0	97.6	1.8	35.0	38.9	132,917	52.5	97.6	1.7	35.5	42.2
Clay	120,016	51.2	93.0	4.7	35.8	15.0	150,739	51.3	92.9	4.7	36.3	20.1
Collier	210,915	52.0	95.9	3.4	34.7	30.8	272,733	51.9	96.0	3.3	35.5	34.7
Columbia	48,490	48.6	81.9	16.6	33.5	18.5	58,349	49.1	82.9	15.4	34.0	21.9
De Soto	24,362	45.9	82.7	16.2	30.7	25.2	27,654	46.8	83.8	15.0	31.4	28.1
Dixie	12,096	47.8	89.8	9.4	32.0	25.9	14,461	48.3	90.6	8.7	31.8	30.0
Duval	608,549	51.6	75.3	21.8	31.4	15.0	684,521	51.5	75.1	21.6	32.8	17.1
Escambia	244,590	50.9	79.0	17.6	30.7	17.0	272,887	50.8	78.7	17.5	32.0	19.1
Flagler	48,338	52.9	91.8	6.9	34.5	36.6	65,915	52.7	91.8	6.7	34.2	41.0
Franklin	9,881	52.1	90.6	8.6	41.6	28.2	11,618	52.3	91.1	8.0	39.7	35.7
Gadsden	41,610	51.0	44.6	54.1	33.4	16.1	49,098	51.1	44.8	53.3	34.7	19.4
Gilchrist	12,131	47.7	92.2	7.2	32.3	17.6	15,070	48.4	92.8	6.5	33.4	20.6
Glades	8,919	46.5	80.9	12.7	32.2	24.1	10,345	47.4	81.7	12.2	33.6	26.5
Gulf	13,309	42.3	76.4	21.9	30.7	17.6	14,770	43.2	77.8	20.3	31.9	20.2

Continued . . .

Table 21.26. VOTING-AGE POPULATION: PROJECTIONS, APRIL 1, 2005, AND 2015, OF PERSONS AGED 18 AND OVER BY SPECIFIED SEX, RACE AND AGE CHARACTERISTICS IN THE STATE AND COUNTIES OF FLORIDA (Continued)

	2005						2015					
		Percentage--						Percentage--				
			Race		Aged				Race		Aged	
County	Voting-age population	Female	White	Black	45-64	65 and over	Voting-age population	Female	White	Black	45-64	65 and over
Hamilton	12,943	42.7	62.5	36.4	29.2	14.2	15,241	44.1	63.3	35.4	30.7	17.5
Hardee	16,979	46.9	89.8	9.1	28.9	21.3	17,727	47.2	90.0	8.9	28.9	23.4
Hendry	22,939	48.2	83.6	13.8	29.8	15.6	26,149	48.5	84.5	12.9	30.7	17.5
Hernando	121,873	52.9	96.6	2.8	34.2	37.4	151,122	52.4	96.6	2.7	34.7	40.6
Highlands	74,355	53.7	93.3	5.9	29.8	44.8	86,796	53.0	93.6	5.5	30.3	47.2
Hillsborough	807,587	51.7	86.5	11.5	33.4	17.8	936,369	51.6	86.3	11.4	34.5	21.0
Holmes	16,114	47.6	90.9	7.4	32.2	20.9	18,256	48.0	91.1	7.1	32.8	24.0
Indian River	100,367	52.7	94.8	4.7	31.5	35.0	119,824	52.2	95.3	4.1	32.5	37.6
Jackson	42,804	46.1	72.0	26.7	31.9	16.6	48,208	46.4	72.6	25.9	33.3	19.3
Jefferson	12,048	56.2	64.0	35.1	34.0	19.2	13,791	55.6	65.8	33.0	34.3	23.4
Lafayette	6,596	41.2	83.8	15.5	26.2	15.6	7,858	43.0	85.2	14.1	29.1	18.0
Lake	194,465	52.9	93.8	5.6	33.2	36.2	244,100	52.6	94.1	5.2	33.8	39.6
Lee	383,683	52.4	94.3	4.9	35.3	29.8	464,965	52.0	94.2	4.8	36.5	32.9
Leon	207,761	52.3	75.3	22.3	27.9	10.0	241,019	52.2	75.5	21.7	28.7	12.6
Levy	30,185	53.2	90.7	8.2	34.0	29.3	36,817	52.8	91.3	7.5	34.2	33.1
Liberty	7,319	41.5	82.9	16.3	32.2	13.7	8,871	43.2	85.0	14.0	33.3	17.5
Madison	15,808	47.6	63.2	35.9	27.8	17.1	17,793	47.8	64.0	34.7	29.7	17.8
Manatee	228,913	52.9	93.3	5.8	33.5	32.0	269,798	52.4	93.3	5.7	34.9	34.6
Marion	228,652	52.8	89.7	9.3	33.7	32.4	281,107	52.5	89.9	8.9	34.1	36.1
Martin	112,830	51.8	95.0	4.2	32.7	33.0	134,407	51.6	95.3	3.9	34.0	35.9
Miami-Dade	1,692,954	52.3	76.5	21.1	33.5	18.1	1,898,063	52.0	75.3	21.7	34.8	19.8
Monroe	76,405	50.3	94.8	4.1	37.9	17.9	85,099	50.7	95.0	4.0	39.3	20.4
Nassau	49,485	51.1	92.6	6.7	38.4	15.4	61,665	51.2	93.3	6.0	39.0	19.4
Okaloosa	150,340	50.7	87.8	8.6	31.4	15.1	179,614	50.9	87.4	8.7	34.1	17.3

Continued . . . .

Table 21.26. VOTING-AGE POPULATION: PROJECTIONS, APRIL 1, 2005, AND 2015, OF PERSONS AGED 18 AND OVER BY SPECIFIED SEX, RACE AND AGE CHARACTERISTICS IN THE STATE AND COUNTIES OF FLORIDA (Continued)

County	2005 Voting-age population	Female	Race White	Race Black	Aged 45-64	Aged 65 and over	2015 Voting-age population	Female	Race White	Race Black	Aged 45-64	Aged 65 and over
Okeechobee	29,004	48.6	91.0	7.5	32.8	26.2	33,059	49.1	91.5	6.9	33.0	30.0
Orange	738,123	51.0	82.9	14.1	31.0	14.5	902,600	51.1	82.5	14.2	33.2	17.2
Osceola	144,249	51.5	92.9	4.9	35.5	18.1	188,316	51.4	92.8	4.9	37.1	21.7
Palm Beach	932,115	52.6	88.7	9.9	33.3	28.5	1,107,678	52.1	88.7	9.8	34.6	31.3
Pasco	296,044	53.2	97.5	1.7	31.8	37.4	343,384	52.5	97.4	1.7	32.9	39.8
Pinellas	766,108	53.0	91.7	6.7	34.3	28.7	823,532	52.3	91.4	6.9	35.5	30.9
Polk	403,043	52.4	88.7	10.2	32.7	27.0	464,767	52.2	88.8	9.9	33.4	30.2
Putnam	59,684	52.2	84.4	14.5	34.5	25.8	67,210	52.0	84.4	14.3	35.5	28.5
St. Johns	107,656	51.8	94.5	4.8	36.5	21.8	135,950	51.7	95.0	4.3	37.3	26.0
St. Lucie	168,925	52.1	87.3	11.6	34.5	27.7	206,336	51.9	87.6	11.1	35.8	30.7
Santa Rosa	100,068	50.3	93.5	4.2	33.9	16.1	126,395	50.6	93.7	4.1	35.6	20.4
Sarasota	298,554	53.5	96.3	3.1	33.8	37.7	343,957	52.8	96.3	3.0	34.4	40.9
Seminole	308,477	51.3	90.9	7.0	35.6	13.9	374,416	51.2	90.9	6.9	37.1	17.5
Sumter	49,342	46.9	84.5	14.7	31.9	29.0	63,670	48.2	86.2	12.9	32.0	34.3
Suwannee	30,383	52.1	89.4	10.0	35.2	24.7	37,025	52.1	90.1	9.2	35.1	28.5
Taylor	16,629	45.2	79.8	18.6	28.9	19.6	17,947	45.5	81.0	17.4	29.4	22.3
Union	12,968	33.8	76.5	22.1	28.2	12.0	15,069	36.4	79.4	19.2	30.5	16.3
Volusia	376,877	52.1	91.8	7.0	33.3	27.1	435,556	51.8	92.0	6.7	34.7	29.7
Wakulla	18,994	48.0	87.5	11.4	36.1	15.7	23,667	48.7	88.8	9.9	36.4	19.8
Walton	38,388	50.1	92.2	5.7	34.3	26.4	48,970	50.6	93.0	5.0	34.1	31.5
Washington	18,880	48.8	81.7	15.3	31.7	22.3	22,296	49.1	82.2	14.6	31.2	25.2

Source: University of Florida, Bureau of Economic and Business Research, Population Program, *Florida Population Studies*, June 2000, Volume 33, No. 3. Bulletin No. 127.

Table 21.30. REGISTERED VOTERS: VOTERS BY PARTY AND BY RACE IN THE STATE AND COUNTIES OF FLORIDA, FEBRUARY 14, 2000

County	Total	Democrat Total	Democrat Black	Republican Total	Republican Black	Other 1/	No party affiliation	Pre-cincts
Florida	8,282,141	3,659,294	745,436	3,282,215	48,357	150,847	1,189,785	5,845
Alachua	108,149	59,271	12,954	30,899	623	1,851	16,128	53
Baker	11,240	9,543	1,081	1,345	12	62	290	8
Bay	87,192	42,886	5,801	31,694	470	3,337	9,275	47
Bradford	12,748	9,278	1,561	2,584	60	71	815	20
Brevard	263,406	101,534	11,804	123,565	922	6,326	31,981	163
Broward	836,676	433,322	93,800	259,045	6,541	1,174	143,135	618
Calhoun	6,567	5,759	682	603	13	45	160	13
Charlotte	93,655	31,752	1,992	45,816	222	2,359	13,728	63
Citrus	77,086	32,464	1,033	31,334	72	1,594	11,694	34
Clay	79,757	23,632	2,881	44,647	534	1,216	10,262	50
Collier	113,307	27,222	1,446	66,017	139	2,717	17,351	95
Columbia	28,914	18,652	3,567	7,665	152	581	2,016	31
De Soto	14,896	9,772	1,420	3,618	66	408	1,098	15
Dixie	10,121	8,746	455	1,011	14	0	364	11
Duval	437,429	221,824	91,558	155,788	5,095	11,438	48,379	267
Escambia	170,303	80,334	23,949	68,660	1,652	3,982	17,327	108
Flagler	31,056	12,548	2,076	13,029	159	558	4,921	24
Franklin	7,143	5,829	652	953	13	37	324	8
Gadsden	24,790	21,206	12,803	2,492	307	202	890	16
Gilchrist	5,998	4,474	121	1,174	3	58	292	10
Glades	5,265	3,628	389	1,215	5	153	269	13
Gulf	9,940	7,817	1,206	1,666	46	83	374	14
Hamilton	6,685	5,813	2,045	652	65	68	152	8
Hardee	10,267	7,514	680	2,156	41	97	500	12
Hendry	15,533	9,845	1,772	4,224	109	222	1,242	22
Hernando	91,007	36,554	2,231	39,182	187	1,373	13,898	51
Highlands	50,921	21,780	2,846	22,752	202	1,282	5,107	24
Hillsborough	458,082	208,190	43,969	170,035	2,992	10,128	69,729	320
Holmes	9,706	8,296	153	1,079	5	50	281	16
Indian River	67,025	20,897	2,666	36,588	276	1,524	8,016	38
Jackson	24,850	19,552	4,999	4,143	196	201	954	27
Jefferson	7,419	5,894	2,468	1,159	32	95	271	13
Lafayette	3,857	3,525	246	250	4	0	82	5
Lake	120,687	43,588	5,318	60,007	794	2,821	14,271	84
Lee	250,568	81,411	7,214	123,564	842	4,956	40,637	150
Leon	134,584	80,311	27,463	37,869	985	2,352	14,052	94

See footnotes at end of table.   Continued . . .

University of Florida   **Bureau of Economic and Business Research**

Table 21.30. REGISTERED VOTERS: VOTERS BY PARTY AND BY RACE IN THE STATE AND COUNTIES OF FLORIDA, FEBRUARY 14, 2000 (Continued)

County	Total	Democrat Total	Democrat Black	Republican Total	Republican Black	Other 1/	No party affilia-tion	Pre-cincts
Levy	16,844	11,445	1,071	4,120	40	376	903	21
Liberty	3,454	3,243	343	156	0	6	49	8
Madison	9,718	8,223	3,061	1,229	114	84	182	11
Manatee	162,310	56,730	6,955	77,307	546	881	27,392	135
Marion	137,847	58,621	9,453	58,817	653	4,684	15,725	96
Martin	83,233	22,573	1,853	46,848	369	2,378	11,434	39
Miami-Dade	817,628	372,398	140,176	311,347	6,968	2,126	131,757	617
Monroe	48,604	19,573	1,181	18,798	124	1,750	8,483	33
Nassau	32,233	16,178	1,887	12,720	75	713	2,622	21
Okaloosa	105,766	30,673	4,521	58,964	1,335	567	15,562	48
Okeechobee	18,988	12,299	955	5,074	50	317	1,298	18
Orange	359,419	147,615	37,131	150,285	2,619	7,693	53,826	229
Osceola	84,643	35,755	2,925	30,768	338	3,393	14,727	65
Palm Beach	630,966	284,553	43,357	226,884	3,250	15,824	103,705	529
Pasco	210,067	85,600	2,313	86,260	232	525	37,682	130
Pinellas	585,500	220,149	31,077	248,869	2,356	18,725	97,757	343
Polk	233,607	110,888	21,631	91,940	1,276	3,841	26,938	163
Putnam	39,986	25,663	4,485	10,157	283	1,043	3,123	50
St. Johns	83,645	29,196	3,594	41,147	261	2,012	11,290	57
St. Lucie	113,390	47,025	10,489	44,668	563	3,911	17,786	78
Santa Rosa	71,273	27,118	1,705	35,264	186	1,683	7,208	36
Sarasota	211,567	64,710	4,343	112,173	534	3,878	30,806	144
Seminole	170,376	57,172	9,399	84,353	1,096	3,333	25,518	133
Sumter	28,544	14,048	1,880	10,615	112	526	3,355	24
Suwannee	19,555	14,169	1,922	4,107	76	806	473	16
Taylor	12,095	10,036	1,661	1,602	39	143	314	14
Union	6,089	5,284	717	624	11	28	153	11
Volusia	243,709	108,100	14,466	94,722	842	5,288	35,599	172
Wakulla	12,661	9,600	1,039	2,328	13	145	588	12
Walton	27,751	15,350	1,143	9,205	83	527	2,669	32
Washington	13,844	10,644	1,402	2,384	63	220	596	15

1/ Includes registered American Reform, Conservative, Constitution, Family Values, FL Conservative, Socialist Workers, Green, Independent, Libertarian, Natural Law, Reform, Reform Silly, Socialist Party of FL, Southern, and We the People, and registered party affiliates.
  Note: See Table 21.25 for voting-age population.

  Source: State of Florida, Department of State, Division of Elections, "County Voter Registration by Party," and "County Voter Registration by Party and Race," Internet site <http://election.dos.state.fl.us/pdf/2000voterreg/> (accessed 18 August 2000).

University of Florida   **Bureau of Economic and Business Research**

Table 21.31. VOTER TURNOUT: NUMBER REPORTED REGISTERED AND VOTED IN THE STATE AND COUNTIES OF FLORIDA, NOVEMBER 3, 1998

County	Registered voters	Voter turnout Number	Voter turnout Percentage	County	Registered voters	Voter turnout Number	Voter turnout Percentage
Florida	8,220,211	4,070,262	49.5	Lake	116,356	63,049	54.2
				Lee	242,455	125,433	51.7
Alachua	111,899	54,996	49.1	Leon	130,764	73,259	56.0
Baker	11,085	4,801	43.3	Levy	17,675	8,854	50.1
Bay	88,252	39,328	44.6	Liberty	3,511	1,601	45.6
Bradford	12,473	6,681	53.6	Madison	9,642	4,656	48.3
Brevard	285,401	150,117	52.6	Manatee	155,140	76,495	49.3
Broward	817,403	372,512	45.6	Marion	137,657	76,947	55.9
Calhoun	6,459	3,087	47.8	Martin	80,548	45,185	56.1
Charlotte	94,168	49,314	52.4	Miami-Dade	834,234	397,625	47.7
Citrus	73,110	42,598	58.3	Monroe	47,786	21,669	45.3
Clay	76,841	35,378	46.0	Nassau	30,713	16,183	52.7
Collier	108,520	60,592	55.8	Okaloosa	103,646	43,913	42.4
Columbia	29,047	12,908	44.4	Okeechobee	18,938	6,786	35.8
De Soto	14,263	6,354	44.5	Orange	353,852	180,230	50.9
Dixie	9,898	3,158	31.9	Osceola	82,923	33,132	40.0
Duval	408,175	191,905	47.0	Palm Beach	613,058	322,837	52.7
Escambia	161,187	77,569	48.1	Pasco	211,242	102,534	48.5
Flagler	29,777	18,350	61.6	Pinellas	561,353	283,157	50.4
Franklin	7,711	2,793	36.2	Polk	229,938	120,439	52.4
Gadsden	24,440	11,816	48.3	Putnam	40,961	18,847	46.0
Gilchrist	8,280	3,669	44.3	St. Johns	77,923	40,484	52.0
Glades	5,446	2,551	46.8	St. Lucie	131,806	54,686	41.5
Gulf	9,786	4,349	44.4	Santa Rosa	70,407	32,174	45.7
Hamilton	6,748	2,914	43.2	Sarasota	213,763	116,332	54.4
Hardee	10,085	4,719	46.8	Seminole	186,155	86,812	46.6
Hendry	15,905	5,958	37.5	Sumter	26,002	14,197	54.6
Hernando	92,163	47,931	52.0	Suwannee	21,111	9,314	44.1
Highlands	52,734	26,933	51.1	Taylor	12,182	5,088	41.8
Hillsborough	463,972	235,142	50.7	Union	6,037	2,697	44.7
Holmes	11,105	4,939	44.5	Volusia	252,661	123,062	48.7
Indian River	65,637	35,070	53.4	Wakulla	12,575	6,256	49.7
Jackson	24,685	12,781	51.8	Walton	25,577	12,651	49.5
Jefferson	7,823	4,853	62.0	Washington	13,300	5,716	43.0
Lafayette	3,842	1,896	49.3				

Source: State of Florida, Department of State, Division of Elections, *1998 Official General Election Returns, November 3, 1998.*

University of Florida

Bureau of Economic and Business Research

Table 21.32. ELECTION RESULTS: VOTES CAST FOR PRESIDENT AND VICE PRESIDENT
IN THE GENERAL ELECTION BY PARTY IN THE STATE AND COUNTIES
OF FLORIDA, NOVEMBER 5, 1996

County	Clinton and Gore (Demo-crat)	Dole and Kemp (Repub-lican)	Perot and Choate (Reform)	County	Clinton and Gore (Demo-crat)	Dole and Kemp (Repub-lican)	Perot and Choate (Reform)
Florida	2,546,870	2,244,536	483,870	Lake	29,750	35,089	8,813
				Lee	65,692	80,882	18,389
Alachua	40,144	25,303	8,072	Leon	50,058	33,914	6,672
Baker	2,273	3,684	667	Levy	4,938	4,299	1,774
Bay	17,020	28,290	5,922	Liberty	868	913	376
Bradford	3,356	4,038	819	Madison	2,791	2,195	578
Brevard	80,416	87,980	25,249	Manatee	41,835	44,059	10,360
Broward	320,736	142,834	38,964	Marion	37,033	41,397	11,340
Calhoun	1,794	1,717	630	Martin	20,851	28,516	5,005
Charlotte	27,121	27,836	7,783	Miami-Dade	317,378	209,634	24,722
Citrus	22,042	20,114	7,244	Monroe	15,219	12,021	4,817
Clay	13,246	30,332	3,281	Nassau	7,276	12,134	1,657
Collier	23,182	42,590	6,320	Okaloosa	16,434	40,631	5,432
Columbia	6,691	7,588	1,970	Okeechobee	4,824	3,415	1,666
De Soto	3,219	3,272	965	Orange	105,513	106,026	18,191
Dixie	1,731	1,398	652	Osceola	21,870	18,335	6,091
Duval	112,258	126,857	13,844	Palm Beach	230,621	133,762	30,739
Escambia	37,768	60,839	8,587	Pasco	66,472	48,346	18,011
Flagler	9,583	8,232	2,185	Pinellas	184,728	152,125	36,990
Franklin	2,095	1,563	878	Polk	66,735	67,943	14,991
Gadsden	9,405	3,813	938	Putnam	12,008	9,781	3,272
Gilchrist	1,985	1,939	841	St. Johns	16,713	27,311	4,205
Glades	1,530	1,361	521	St. Lucie	36,168	28,892	8,482
Gulf	2,480	2,424	1,054	Santa Rosa	10,923	26,244	4,957
Hamilton	1,734	1,518	406	Sarasota	63,648	69,198	14,939
Hardee	2,417	2,926	851	Seminole	45,051	59,778	9,357
Hendry	3,882	3,855	1,135	Sumter	7,014	5,960	2,375
Hernando	28,520	22,039	7,272	Suwannee	4,479	5,742	1,874
Highlands	14,244	15,608	3,739	Taylor	3,583	3,188	1,140
Hillsborough	144,223	136,621	25,154	Union	1,388	1,636	425
Holmes	2,310	3,248	1,208	Volusia	78,905	63,067	17,319
Indian River	16,373	22,709	4,635	Wakulla	3,054	2,931	1,091
Jackson	6,665	7,187	1,602	Walton	5,341	7,706	2,342
Jefferson	2,543	1,851	393	Washington	2,992	3,522	1,287
Lafayette	829	1,166	316	Absentees 1/	902	1,212	94

1/ Absentees counted per: Division of Elections Rule 1S-2.013. These votes are included in state
totals but not in county detail.
Note: Excludes other candidates.

Source: State of Florida, Department of State, Division of Elections, *1996 Official General Election
Returns, November 5, 1996.*

University of Florida   **Bureau of Economic and Business Research**

Table 21.33. ELECTION RESULTS: VOTES CAST FOR UNITED STATES SENATOR, NOVEMBER 8, 1994 AND NOVEMBER 3, 1998, AND FOR GOVERNOR AND LIEUTENANT GOVERNOR, NOVEMBER 3, 1998 IN THE STATE AND COUNTIES OF FLORIDA

| | United States Senator 1/ | | | | Governor/Lieutenant Governor--1998 B/ | |
| | 1994 A/ | | 1998 | | Jeb | Buddy |
County	Connie Mack (R)	Hugh E. Rodham (D)	Bob Graham (D)	Charlie Crist (R)	Bush/ Frank Brogan (R)	MacKay/ Rick Dantzler (D)
Florida	2,895,200	1,210,577	2,436,407	1,463,755	2,191,105	1,773,054
Alachua	35,723	19,740	38,611	14,917	23,812	29,343
Baker	4,010	1,185	2,586	2,082	3,268	1,326
Bay	29,885	7,951	21,050	17,739	26,759	12,017
Bradford	5,124	1,905	4,000	2,531	4,349	2,113
Brevard	121,019	37,177	84,304	62,687	88,251	57,896
Broward	219,370	170,539	276,632	81,822	137,494	225,010
Calhoun	2,515	926	2,112	894	1,796	1,191
Charlotte	38,693	12,980	26,470	21,640	29,197	18,885
Citrus	29,884	10,528	24,764	17,431	23,347	17,750
Clay	28,614	5,561	15,763	19,223	26,585	8,261
Collier	47,974	10,688	22,536	35,957	41,688	16,981
Columbia	9,223	3,303	7,638	4,984	7,698	4,863
De Soto	4,547	1,667	3,656	2,489	3,711	2,296
Dixie	2,080	1,178	1,979	1,088	1,855	1,209
Duval	134,072	50,415	104,640	71,653	111,716	74,016
Escambia	60,370	17,175	39,763	36,624	50,325	24,956
Flagler	9,946	4,891	10,677	7,345	9,779	8,326
Franklin	2,709	1,107	1,780	928	1,536	1,203
Gadsden	5,598	5,311	9,733	1,890	4,028	7,269
Gilchrist	2,629	970	2,315	1,283	2,097	1,408
Glades	1,882	819	1,672	781	1,382	1,044
Gulf	3,826	1,449	2,751	1,467	2,579	1,670
Hamilton	1,825	976	2,027	816	1,550	1,277
Hardee	3,974	1,292	2,539	2,058	2,631	1,938
Hendry	4,325	1,563	4,023	1,828	3,582	2,270
Hernando	34,727	14,653	27,620	19,035	25,441	20,592
Highlands	19,688	6,396	14,083	11,551	15,781	10,186
Hillsborough	168,720	67,109	125,790	102,638	127,686	101,038
Holmes	3,800	1,069	3,114	1,641	3,082	1,680
Indian River	28,263	7,969	16,745	16,177	21,767	12,011
Jackson	8,659	3,756	8,818	3,747	7,328	4,774
Jefferson	2,493	1,566	3,708	979	1,970	2,585
Lafayette	1,599	406	1,225	644	1,263	582
Lake	46,359	13,181	35,210	26,610	38,250	22,975
Lee	103,187	30,201	65,504	55,681	78,816	43,077
Leon	47,243	26,194	55,744	16,941	31,455	41,153
Levy	6,304	2,524	5,634	3,114	4,733	3,899
Liberty	1,352	513	1,142	437	962	602
Madison	3,102	1,573	3,300	1,236	2,228	2,155
Manatee	60,863	20,263	42,366	33,216	46,490	29,316

See footnotes at end of table.   Continued . . .

Table 21.33. ELECTION RESULTS: VOTES CAST FOR UNITED STATES SENATOR, NOVEMBER 8, 1994 AND NOVEMBER 3, 1998, AND FOR GOVERNOR AND LIEUTENANT GOVERNOR, NOVEMBER 3, 1998 IN THE STATE AND COUNTIES OF FLORIDA (Continued)

County	United States Senator 1/				Governor/Lieutenant Governor--1998 B/	
	1994 A/		1998		Jeb Bush/ Frank Brogan (R)	Buddy MacKay/ Rick Dantzler (D)
	Connie Mack (R)	Hugh E. Rodham (D)	Bob Graham (D)	Charlie Crist (R)		
Marion	15,518	7,607	39,903	31,656	43,960	31,219
Martin	51,032	17,073	24,551	18,897	27,466	17,053
Miami-Dade	245,803	143,047	272,534	75,900	200,801	181,724
Monroe	34,986	9,603	13,363	7,600	11,630	9,424
Nassau	11,594	3,512	8,105	7,647	10,894	4,692
Okaloosa	40,330	7,390	17,689	25,828	33,844	9,732
Okeechobee	4,790	2,118	4,452	2,204	3,644	2,917
Orange	128,915	46,223	107,771	69,595	104,652	73,709
Osceola	24,112	8,516	19,121	12,915	19,841	12,383
Palm Beach	195,964	117,166	218,622	81,804	126,450	184,468
Pasco	76,901	30,624	58,337	40,460	54,588	45,252
Pinellas	233,140	83,762	158,703	114,899	150,293	126,212
Polk	91,915	31,248	69,530	48,539	69,506	47,951
Putnam	13,420	6,461	12,159	6,484	10,828	7,800
St. Johns	26,912	4,975	20,190	19,803	27,942	11,984
St. Lucie	96,345	29,277	33,748	20,332	29,099	24,675
Santa Rosa	68,643	19,280	14,366	17,370	24,089	7,650
Sarasota	27,043	7,291	63,174	49,184	69,829	44,252
Seminole	37,992	15,928	46,805	39,092	54,738	31,331
Sumter	7,817	2,785	7,869	5,770	8,036	5,746
Suwannee	7,016	1,907	5,641	3,526	5,916	3,206
Taylor	4,271	1,513	3,423	1,599	2,926	2,078
Union	2,083	679	1,650	1,029	2,056	641
Volusia	84,804	38,268	75,490	46,222	64,544	57,229
Wakulla	4,417	1,678	4,593	1,541	3,361	2,659
Walton	8,727	2,439	6,467	5,704	8,355	3,891
Washington	4,534	1,538	3,736	1,841	3,550	2,033
Overseas Military absentees	0	0	391	510	(X)	(X)

(R) Republican.
(D) Democrat.
(X) Not applicable.
A/ Does not include 220 write-in votes.
B/ Does not include 282 write-in votes.

1/ Absentee ballots counted per: Division of Elections Rule 1S-2.013. These votes are included in state but not in county detail in 1998.
Correction: Data for Governor/Lieutenant Governor were erroneously switched in the previous *Abstract*.

Source: State of Florida, Department of State, Division of Elections, *1998 Elections: Official General Election Returns, November 3, 1998,* and previous edition.

University of Florida   **Bureau of Economic and Business Research**

Table 21.35. FEMALE OFFICIALS: WOMEN IN STATE LEGISLATURES IN FLORIDA
AND THE UNITED STATES, 2000

Area	Total legislators	Women legislators			
		Number	Percentage of total	Senate	House
Florida	160	38	23.8	7	31
United States	7,424	1,670	22.5	396	1,274

Source: Center for the American Woman and Politics (CAWP), Eagleton Institute of Politics, Rutgers University (copyright). Internet site http://www.cawp.rutgers.edu/pdf/stleg.pdf> (accessed 26 June 2000)

Table 21.36. BLACK OFFICIALS: BLACK ELECTED OFFICIALS BY OFFICE IN FLORIDA, THE SOUTH
AND THE UNITED STATES, JANUARY 1996 AND 1997

Office	Florida		South 1/		United States	
	1996	1997	1996	1997	1996	1997
Total	(NA)	218	(NA)	6,307	8,545	8,658
U.S. and state legislatures 2/	(NA)	41	(NA)	990	606	1,286
City and county offices 3/	(NA)	146	(NA)	3,858	5,023	5,062
Law enforcement 4/	(NA)	32	(NA)	579	994	999
Education 5/	(NA)	15	(NA)	1,225	1,922	1,966

1/ Includes Alabama, Arkansas, Delaware, District of Columbia, Florida, Georgia, Kentucky, Louisiana, Maryland, Mississippi, North Carolina, Oklahoma, South Carolina, Tennessee, Texas, Virginia, and West Virginia.
2/ Includes elected state administrators.
3/ County commissioners, councilmen, mayors, vice mayors, aldermen, regional officers, and others.
4/ Judges, magistrates, constables, marshals, sheriffs, justices of the peace, and others.
5/ Members of state education agencies, college boards, school boards, and others.

Source: Joint Center for Political and Economic Studies, Washington, DC, *Black Elected Officials: A Statistical Summary, 1993-1997,* annual (copyright).

Table 21.37. HISPANIC OFFICIALS: HISPANIC ELECTED OFFICIALS BY OFFICE IN FLORIDA
THE SOUTH, AND THE UNITED STATES, SEPTEMBER 1994

Office	Florida	South	United States
Total	64	2,298	5,459
State executives and legislators, including U.S. representatives	16	61	199
County and municipal officials	33	1,059	2,197
Judicial and law enforcement	12	410	651
Education and school boards	3	768	2,412

Source: U.S., Department of Commerce, Bureau of the Census, *Statistical Abstract of the United States, 1999.*

University of Florida   **Bureau of Economic and Business Research**

Table 21.42. COMPOSITION OF CONGRESS AND STATE LEGISLATURES: NUMBER OF UNITED STATES REPRESENTATIVES, SENATORS AND STATE LEGISLATORS BY PARTY AFFILIATION, SPECIFIED YEARS 1991 THROUGH 1997

	Florida				United States			
Year 1/	Demo-crats	Repub-licans	Demo-crats	Repub-licans	Demo-crats	Repub-licans	Demo-crats	Repub-licans
	U.S. represent-atives		U.S. senators		U.S. represent-atives		U.S. senators	
1991	9	10	1	1	267	167	56	44
1993	10	13	1	1	258	176	57	43
1994	10	13	1	1	257	176	56	44
1995	8	15	1	1	204	230	47	53
1996	8	15	1	1	197	236	46	53
1997	8	15	1	1	197	236	46	53
	State represent-atives		State senators		State represent-atives		State senators	
1992	71	49	20	20	3,186	2,223	1,132	799
1994 A/	63	57	19	21	2,817	2,603	1,021	905
1996	59	61	17	23	2,886	2,539	998	931
1997	59	61	17	23	2,886	2,539	998	931

A/ Status as of December 7, 1994.
1/ U.S. representative and senator data refer to the beginning of the first session. State legislative data refer to election years.
Note: Excludes vacancies and persons classified as Independents.

Source: U.S., Department of Commerce, Bureau of the Census, *Statistical Abstract of the United States, 1999.* 1992, 1994, and 1996 National Conference of State Legislatures, Denver, CO, unpublished data, (copyright).

Table 21.43. APPORTIONMENT: MEMBERSHIP IN THE UNITED STATES HOUSE OF REPRESENTATIVES FOR FLORIDA AND THE UNITED STATES 1840 THROUGH 1990

Census of--	Florida	United States	Census of--	Florida	United States
1840	A/ 1	232	1930	5	435
1850	1	237	1940	6	435
1860	1	243	1950	8	437
1870	2	293	1960	12	435
1880	2	332	1970	15	435
1890	2	357	1980	19	435
1900	3	391	1990	23	435
1910	4	435			

A/ Assigned after apportionment.
Note: Total membership includes representatives assigned to newly admitted states after the apportionment acts. Population figures used for apportionment purposes are those determined for states by each decennial census.
Source: U.S., Department of Commerce, Bureau of the Census, *1990 Census Profile: Population Trends and Congressional Apportionment,* No. 1, March 1991.

University of Florida   **Bureau of Economic and Business Research**

COURTS AND LAW ENFORCEMENT

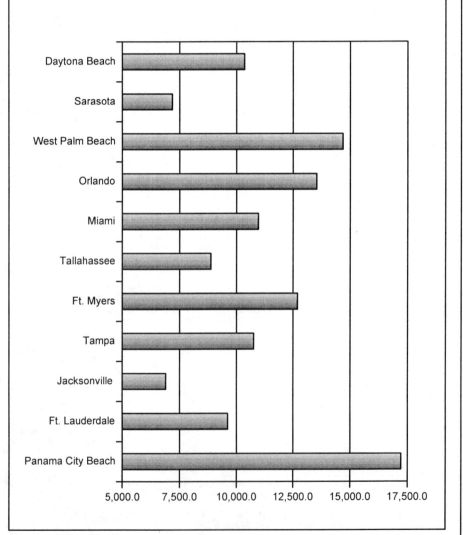

Crime Rates in Specified Florida Cities, 1999
(rates per 100,000 population)

Daytona Beach	
Sarasota	
West Palm Beach	
Orlando	
Miami	
Tallahassee	
Ft. Myers	
Tampa	
Jacksonville	
Ft. Lauderdale	
Panama City Beach	

5,000.0 7,500.0 10,000.0 12,500.0 15,000.0 17,500.0

Source: Table 22.03

SECTION 22.00
COURTS AND LAW ENFORCEMENT

TABLES LISTED BY MAJOR HEADINGS

University of Florida   **Bureau of Economic and Business Research**

TABLES LISTED BY MAJOR HEADINGS

Table 22.01. CRIMINAL OFFENSES AND RATES: CRIME INDEX OFFENSES BY TYPE OF OFFENSE IN FLORIDA, 1994 THROUGH 1999

Item	Total index of- fenses 1/	Violent crime				Nonviolent crime		
		Mur- der	Forc- ible sex	Rob- bery	Aggra- vated as- sault	Bur- glary	Larceny	Motor ve- hicle theft
Number of index offenses 2/								
1994	1,130,875	1,152	13,413	45,263	98,007	233,006	617,195	122,839
1995	1,078,619	1,030	12,259	42,142	94,777	213,050	605,751	109,610
1996	1,079,623	1,077	12,942	41,643	95,688	219,056	605,448	103,769
1997	1,073,757	1,014	13,224	40,703	95,860	214,894	599,190	108,872
1998	1,025,100	966	12,702	36,130	89,875	202,559	578,774	104,094
1999	934,349	856	12,583	31,996	83,424	180,785	532,462	92,243
Percentage change from previous year								
1994	1.3	-2.9	-2.5	-5.2	-1.1	-5.0	3.8	7.2
1995	-4.6	-10.6	-8.6	-6.9	-3.3	-8.6	-1.9	-10.8
1996	0.1	4.6	5.6	-1.2	1.0	2.8	-0.1	-5.3
1997	-0.5	-5.8	2.2	-2.3	0.2	-1.9	-1.0	4.9
1998	-4.5	-4.7	-3.9	-11.2	-6.2	-5.7	-3.4	-4.4
1999	-8.9	-11.4	-0.9	-11.4	-7.2	-10.7	-8.0	-11.4
Rate per 100,000 population								
1994	8,148.2	8.3	96.6	326.1	706.2	1,678.9	4,447.0	885.1
1995	7,623.1	7.3	86.6	297.8	669.8	1,505.7	4,281.1	774.7
1996	7,491.3	7.5	89.8	289.0	664.0	1,520.0	4,201.1	720.0
1997	7,298.1	6.9	89.9	276.6	651.5	1,460.6	4,072.5	740.0
1998	6,833.8	6.4	84.7	240.9	599.1	1,350.4	3,858.4	693.9
1999	6,098.1	5.6	82.1	208.8	544.5	1,179.9	3,475.1	602.0
Percentage change from previous year								
1994	-0.7	-4.8	-4.4	-7.0	-3.0	-6.9	1.7	5.1
1995	-6.4	-12.3	-10.4	-8.7	-5.1	-10.3	-3.7	-12.5
1996	-1.7	2.7	3.7	-3.0	-0.9	0.9	-1.9	-7.1
1997	-2.6	-7.7	0.1	-4.3	-1.9	-3.9	-3.1	2.8
1998	-6.4	-6.7	-5.8	-12.9	-8.0	-7.5	-5.3	-6.2
1999	-10.8	-13.2	-3.0	-13.3	-9.1	-12.6	-9.9	-13.2

1/ The crimes selected for use in the index are chosen based on their serious nature, their frequency of occurrence, and the reliability of reporting from citizens to law enforcement agencies. The Crime Index is used as a basic measure of crime.

2/ Actual offenses known to law enforcement officers, not the number of persons who committed them or number of injuries they caused.

Note: Rates may not add to totals due to rounding. Percentage changes calculated by the Bureau of Economic and Business Research.

Source: State of Florida, Department of Law Enforcement, *Crime in Florida: 1999 Annual Report,* and previous editions, Internet site <http://www.fdle.state.fl.us/index.asp> (accessed 25 April 2000).

University of Florida   **Bureau of Economic and Business Research**

Table 22.02. CRIMINAL OFFENSES AND RATES: CRIME INDEX OFFENSES, CRIME RATES, AND OFFENSES CLEARED IN THE STATE AND COUNTIES OF FLORIDA, 1999

County	Crime index offenses			Crime rate per 100,000 population		Offenses cleared 4/ (percentage)
	Total 1/	Violent 2/	Nonviolent 3/	1999	Percentage change 1998 to 1999	
Florida	934,349	128,859	805,490	6,098.1	-10.8	22.4
Alachua	16,023	2,055	13,968	7,409.5	-18.3	16.3
Baker	543	81	462	2,481.8	-17.5	37.4
Bay	7,195	742	6,453	4,792.9	-18.4	36.2
Bradford	977	174	803	3,831.4	-0.9	31.4
Brevard	22,702	3,670	19,032	4,781.4	-6.1	21.6
Broward	84,842	9,718	75,124	5,693.0	-13.4	24.7
Calhoun	114	16	98	807.5	-64.4	36.8
Charlotte	3,218	212	3,006	2,352.8	-19.8	27.4
Citrus	2,903	416	2,487	2,526.6	-12.7	28.7
Clay	4,768	459	4,309	3,414.7	-8.4	41.3
Collier	9,967	1,357	8,610	4,537.0	-9.2	20.7
Columbia	3,306	582	2,724	5,849.9	-3.5	26.5
De Soto	1,323	296	1,027	4,652.2	-15.3	22.5
Dixie	497	70	427	3,687.5	-14.2	23.3
Duval	52,319	7,560	44,759	6,858.4	-10.8	21.9
Escambia	14,425	2,288	12,137	4,782.6	-12.3	31.4
Flagler	1,172	116	1,056	2,552.8	-20.5	27.0
Franklin	385	25	360	3,541.2	-23.6	10.4
Gadsden	1,886	406	1,480	3,663.7	-20.4	36.3
Gilchrist	394	54	340	2,939.0	32.3	26.4
Glades	407	52	355	4,124.9	6.6	16.0
Gulf	444	107	337	3,082.7	4.4	54.3
Hamilton	419	76	343	2,914.6	-23.9	26.5
Hardee	1,094	101	993	4,842.0	-2.6	22.7
Hendry	1,595	210	1,385	5,220.6	-28.2	16.7
Hernando	5,113	749	4,364	4,013.6	11.5	26.6
Highlands	3,737	387	3,350	4,605.5	-17.6	26.3
Hillsborough	74,017	11,257	62,760	7,650.3	-4.9	22.3
Holmes	196	41	155	1,037.1	-44.6	34.7
Indian River	5,042	519	4,523	4,601.3	-11.4	23.2
Jackson	1,490	369	1,121	3,012.0	31.0	34.8
Jefferson	344	101	243	2,384.9	-38.6	52.0
Lafayette	26	17	9	373.5	-23.1	100.0
Lake	8,667	2,014	6,653	4,251.4	-1.9	29.9
Lee	20,663	2,634	18,029	4,953.8	-3.3	27.6
Leon	16,967	2,627	14,340	7,139.9	-8.8	33.2

See footnotes at end of table.   Continued . . .

Table 22.02. CRIMINAL OFFENSES AND RATES: CRIME INDEX OFFENSES, CRIME RATES, AND OFFENSES CLEARED IN THE STATE AND COUNTIES OF FLORIDA, 1999 (Continued)

County	Crime index offenses Total 1/	Vio- lent 2/	Nonvio- lent 3/	Crime rate per 100,000 population 1999	Per- centage change 1998 to 1999	Offenses clear- ed 4/ (per- cent- age)
Levy	1,894	401	1,493	5,669.3	1.7	30.3
Liberty	123	27	96	1,528.3	-10.1	46.3
Madison	1,133	134	999	5,771.2	10.5	21.4
Manatee	13,922	2,064	11,858	5,411.8	-3.4	15.5
Marion	11,864	1,952	9,912	4,756.4	-2.2	43.7
Martin	4,550	489	4,061	3,744.4	-8.6	24.0
Miami-Dade	193,412	27,781	165,631	9,094.5	-10.9	17.1
Monroe	3,117	352	2,765	3,581.5	-51.2	21.2
Nassau	2,680	383	2,297	4,670.5	16.4	29.4
Okaloosa	5,000	563	4,437	2,784.1	-25.5	31.3
Okeechobee	1,437	268	1,169	4,046.8	218.1	27.9
Orange	70,624	9,974	60,650	8,344.8	-4.3	22.1
Osceola	10,575	1,169	9,406	6,719.6	-7.0	25.6
Palm Beach	75,295	8,795	66,500	7,224.7	-14.9	15.9
Pasco	13,944	1,597	12,347	4,270.8	-9.3	21.3
Pinellas	52,067	7,613	44,454	5,793.1	-8.5	25.0
Polk	27,230	3,008	24,222	5,736.2	-26.4	20.3
Putnam	4,392	748	3,644	6,026.1	1.9	47.5
St. Johns	4,476	560	3,916	3,928.4	-7.2	32.5
St. Lucie	8,488	1,475	7,013	4,541.3	-17.1	27.5
Santa Rosa	2,843	415	2,428	2,524.2	-32.2	32.2
Sarasota	12,581	1,323	11,258	3,968.8	-12.4	22.4
Seminole	15,344	1,913	13,431	4,332.7	-2.7	22.8
Sumter	1,288	294	994	2,534.3	-17.2	32.6
Suwannee	1,400	229	1,171	4,071.4	-12.5	25.1
Taylor	874	153	721	4,406.1	-6.7	25.2
Union	147	55	92	1,062.7	-14.9	83.0
Volusia	22,568	3,276	19,292	5,288.7	-14.4	21.8
Wakulla	700	160	540	3,390.2	-8.4	36.4
Walton	1,003	102	901	2,478.6	-21.3	34.3
Washington	198	28	170	893.7	79.7	68.7

1/ Actual offenses known to law enforcement officers, not the number of persons who committed them or number of injuries they caused.
2/ Includes murder, forcible sex, robbery, and aggravated assault.
3/ Includes breaking and entering (burglary), larceny, and auto theft.
4/ Clearance of an offense occurs when an offender is identified, charged, and taken into custody, or occasionally when some element beyond law enforcement control precludes formal charges against the offender.
Note: Data are aggregates of offenses reported to municipal, county, and state law enforcement agencies and campus police departments. Percentage changes calculated by Bureau of Economic and Business Research.

Source: State of Florida, Department of Law Enforcement, *Crime in Florida: 1999 Annual Report,* and previous editions, Internet site <http://www.fdle.state.fl.us/index.asp> (accessed 25 April 2000).

Table 22.03. CRIMINAL OFFENSES AND RATES: CRIME INDEX OFFENSES AND CRIME RATES IN THE STATE, COUNTIES, CITIES, AND SPECIFIED AREAS OF FLORIDA, 1999

Area	Number of index offenses 1/	Crime rate per 100,000 popu- lation	Area	Number of index offenses 1/	Crime rate per 100,000 popu- lation
Florida	934,349	6,098.1	Brevard (Continued)		
			Palm Bay	3,573	4,515.3
Alachua	16,023	7,409.5	Rockledge	667	3,351.1
Sheriff's office	6,208	6,370.1	Satellite Beach	243	2,365.0
Alachua	452	7,168.9	Titusville	2,352	5,615.4
Archer	168	11,570.3	West Melbourne	525	5,351.7
Gainesville	7,638	7,532.2	Melbourne Airport	1	(X)
Hawthorne	150	10,760.4	State agencies	1	(X)
High Springs	198	5,020.3			
Micanopy	78	12,111.8	Broward	84,842	5,693.0
Newberry	48	1,845.4	Sheriff's office	5,934	4,633.6
Waldo	17	1,620.6	Coconut Creek	1,220	3,084.4
Santa Fe Community			Cooper City	674	2,346.0
College	55	(X)	Coral Springs	3,918	3,506.9
University of Florida	1,009	(X)	Dania	1,580	8,549.8
State agencies	2	(X)	Deerfield	2,062	4,021.9
			Davie	3,878	5,742.7
Baker	543	2,481.8	Ft. Lauderdale	14,309	9,605.2
Sheriff's office	542	2,477.3	Hallandale	2,437	7,735.5
State agencies	1	(X)	Hillsboro Beach	36	2,050.1
			Hollywood	9,743	7,632.0
Bay	7,195	4,792.9	Lauderdale by the Sea	79	2,080.0
Sheriff's office	2,748	3,633.4	Lauderdale Lakes	1,488	5,339.1
Cedar Grove	93	2,857.1	Lauderhill	3,082	6,091.4
Lynn Haven	295	2,305.4	Lighthouse Point	228	2,141.9
Mexico Beach	84	8,061.4	Margate	1,800	3,548.4
Panama City	2,515	6,657.5	Miramar	2,690	4,928.3
Panama City Beach	891	17,220.7	North Lauderdale	1,284	4,293.9
Parker	130	2,557.0	Oakland Park	2,962	10,490.2
Springfield	427	4,562.5	Parkland	231	1,747.5
Florida State University			Pembroke Park	465	9,719.9
Panama City	12	(X)	Pembroke Pines	4,373	3,641.4
			Plantation	5,012	6,231.2
Bradford	977	3,831.4	Pompano Beach	6,578	8,841.0
Sheriff's office	507	2,628.6	Sea Ranch Lakes	29	4,707.8
Lawtey	67	9,410.1	Sunrise	5,023	6,405.8
Starke	403	7,772.4	Tamarac	1,427	2,722.6
			Weston	651	1,531.0
Brevard	22,702	4,781.4	Wilton Manors	886	7,511.7
Sheriff's office	7,119	3,607.5	Seminole Indian Reservation	371	(X)
Cocoa	1,724	9,515.4	Port Everglades	82	(X)
Cocoa Beach	1,102	8,637.0	Ft. Lauderdale		
Indialantic	141	4,749.1	International AP	148	(X)
Indian Harbour Beach	119	1,483.1	State agencies	162	(X)
Melbourne	5,064	7,164.2			
Melbourne Beach	61	1,858.1	Calhoun	114	807.5
Melbourne Village	10	1,612.9	Blountstown	114	4,574.6

See footnotes at end of table.　　　　　　　　　　　　　　　　Continued . . .

University of Florida　　　　　　　　**Bureau of Economic and Business Research**

       Florida Statistical Abstract 2000

Table 22.03. CRIMINAL OFFENSES AND RATES: CRIME INDEX OFFENSES AND CRIME RATES
IN THE STATE, COUNTIES, CITIES, AND SPECIFIED AREAS
OF FLORIDA, 1999 (Continued)

Area	Number of index offenses 1/	Crime rate per 100,000 popu- lation	Area	Number of index offenses 1/	Crime rate per 100,000 popu- lation
Charlotte	3,218	2,352.8	Escambia (Continued)		
Sheriff's office	2,890	2,347.2	University of West Florida	108	(X)
Punta Gorda	328	2,403.6	State agencies	9	(X)
Citrus	2,903	2,526.6	Flagler	1,172	2,552.8
Sheriff's office	2,361	2,279.7	Sheriff's office	1,070	2,723.0
Crystal River	334	7,634.3	Flagler Beach	100	2,202.2
Inverness	208	2,990.2	State agencies	2	(X)
Clay	4,768	3,414.7	Franklin	385	3,541.2
Sheriff's office	4,129	3,317.0	Sheriff's office	385	5,826.3
Green Cove Springs	290	5,420.6			
Orange Park	349	3,560.5	Gadsden	1,886	3,663.7
			Sheriff's office	766	2,324.5
Collier	9,967	4,537.0	Greensboro	12	1,916.9
Sheriff's office	8,812	4,437.1	Gretna	38	1,322.2
Naples	1,150	5,453.6	Havana	184	10,132.2
State agencies	5	(X)	Midway	27	2,022.5
			Quincy	855	10,753.4
Columbia	3,306	5,849.9	State agencies	4	(X)
Sheriff's office	1,946	4,215.6			
Lake City	1,355	13,089.3	Gilchrist	394	2,939.0
State agencies	5	(X)	Sheriff's office	326	2,709.4
			Trenton	68	4,949.1
De Soto	1,323	4,652.2			
Sheriff's office	774	3,527.8	Glades	407	4,124.9
Arcadia	548	8,433.4	Sheriff's office	407	4,124.9
State agencies	1	(X)			
			Gulf	444	3,082.7
Dixie	497	3,687.5	Sheriff's office	374	3,629.3
Sheriff's office	410	3,593.7	Port St. Joe	70	1,708.2
Cross City	87	4,204.9			
			Hamilton	419	2,914.6
Duval	52,319	6,858.4	Sheriff's office	317	2,987.8
Atlantic Beach	611	4,486.4	Jasper	101	4,764.2
Baldwin	99	6,226.4	State agencies	1	(X)
Jacksonville	49,601	6,897.9			
Jacksonville Beach	1,520	7,220.9	Hardee	1,094	4,842.0
Neptune Beach	308	4,098.5	Sheriff's office	694	4,339.4
Jacksonville Port Authority	53	(X)	Bowling Green	121	6,722.2
University of North Florida	121	(X)	Wauchula	244	6,853.9
State agencies	6	(X)	Zolfo Springs	35	2,820.3
Escambia	14,425	4,782.6	Hendry	1,595	5,220.6
Sheriff's office	10,947	4,549.5	Sheriff's office	1,041	4,303.8
Pensacola	3,256	5,338.2	Clewiston	553	8,689.5
Pensacola Junior College	105	(X)	State agencies	1	(X)

See footnotes at end of table.   Continued . . .

University of Florida   **Bureau of Economic and Business Research**

Table 22.03. CRIMINAL OFFENSES AND RATES: CRIME INDEX OFFENSES AND CRIME RATES
IN THE STATE, COUNTIES, CITIES, AND SPECIFIED AREAS
OF FLORIDA, 1999 (Continued)

Area	Number of index offenses 1/	Crime rate per 100,000 population	Area	Number of index offenses 1/	Crime rate per 100,000 population
Hernando	5,113	4,013.6	Lake	8,667	4,251.4
Sheriff's office	4,536	3,794.1	Sheriff's office	4,675	3,831.8
Brooksville	577	7,360.6	Clermont	491	5,541.1
			Eustis	489	3,250.0
Highlands	3,737	4,605.5	Fruitland Park	123	4,042.1
Sheriff's office	2,116	3,374.1	Groveland	100	3,913.9
Avon Park	579	7,093.9	Howey-in-the-Hills	6	727.3
Lake Placid	155	10,977.3	Lady Lake	194	1,484.7
Sebring	887	10,015.8	Leesburg	1,482	9,485.4
			Mascotte	123	4,705.4
Hillsborough	74,017	7,650.3	Mount Dora	604	6,663.7
Sheriff's office	37,800	6,086.4	Tavares	288	3,331.0
Plant City	2,536	8,938.7	Umatilla	84	3,342.6
Tampa	32,016	10,761.5	State agencies	8	(X)
Temple Terrace	703	3,416.9			
Tampa International			Lee	20,663	4,953.8
Airport	440	(X)	Sheriff's office	11,314	4,233.1
University of South Florida	501	(X)	Cape Coral	2,985	3,085.0
State agencies	21	(X)	Ft. Myers	5,978	12,700.8
			Sanibel	197	3,276.8
Holmes	196	1,037.1	Florida Gulf Coast		
Sheriff's office	178	1,107.8	University	15	(X)
Bonifay	18	635.8	Lee County Airport	171	0.0
			State agencies	3	0.0
Indian River	5,042	4,601.3			
Sheriff's office	3,249	4,603.6	Leon	16,967	7,139.9
Fellsmere	74	2,846.2	Sheriff's office	2,672	2,903.5
Indian River Shores	53	1,899.6	Tallahassee	12,905	8,862.7
Sebastian	565	3,597.1	Capitol Police	177	(X)
Vero Beach	1,099	6,137.3	Florida A & M		
State agencies	2	(X)	University	410	(X)
			Florida State		
Jackson	1,490	3,012.0	University	773	(X)
Sheriff's office	936	2,551.6	State agencies	30	(X)
Cottondale	19	1,630.9			
Graceville	95	3,525.1	Levy	1,894	5,669.3
Marianna	398	5,965.2	Sheriff's office	1,023	3,808.1
Sneads	40	1,774.6	Cedar Key	57	7,412.2
State agencies	2	(X)	Chiefland	401	19,676.2
			Inglis	44	3,228.2
Jefferson	344	2,384.9	Williston	369	15,543.4
Sheriff's office	195	1,695.1			
Monticello	148	5,068.5	Liberty	123	1,528.3
State agencies	1	(X)	Sheriff's office	123	1,528.3
Lafayette	26	373.5	Madison	1,133	5,771.2
Sheriff's office	26	373.5	Sheriff's office	719	4,719.7

See footnotes at end of table.   Continued . . .

University of Florida

Table 22.03. CRIMINAL OFFENSES AND RATES: CRIME INDEX OFFENSES AND CRIME RATES IN THE STATE, COUNTIES, CITIES, AND SPECIFIED AREAS OF FLORIDA, 1999 (Continued)

Area	Number of index offenses 1/	Crime rate per 100,000 popu- lation	Area	Number of index offenses 1/	Crime rate per 100,000 popu- lation
Madison (Continued)			Miami-Dade (Continued)		
Greenville	39	3,931.5	North Bay Village	326	5,322.5
Madison	375	11,010.0	North Miami	4,867	9,674.4
			North Miami Beach	2,424	6,554.5
Manatee	13,922	5,411.8	Opa-Locka	2,549	16,471.7
Sheriff's office	9,430	5,118.6	Pinecrest	971	5,426.4
Bradenton	3,387	6,943.1	South Miami	1,102	10,449.5
Bradenton Beach	76	4,475.9	Sunny Isles	947	6,609.0
Holmes Beach	202	3,980.3	Surfside	331	7,642.6
Longboat Key	169	2,524.3	Sweetwater	336	2,348.0
Palmetto	657	6,098.6	Virginia Gardens	58	2,546.1
State agencies	1	(X)	West Miami	263	4,485.8
			Florida International		
Marion	11,864	4,756.4	University	461	(X)
Sheriff's office	5,975	3,011.0	Miami-Dade public schools	2,723	(X)
Belleview	252	7,074.7	State agencies	111	(X)
Dunnellon	138	7,467.5			
Ocala	5,499	12,063.2	Monroe	3,117	3,581.5
			Sheriff's office	3,116	5,251.8
Martin	4,550	3,744.4	State agencies	1	(X)
Sheriff's office	3,531	3,353.2			
Jupiter Island	8	1,426.0	Nassau	2,680	4,670.5
Sewalls Point	21	1,164.7	Sheriff's office	1,968	4,233.1
Stuart	983	7,099.5	Fernandina Beach	711	6,528.9
State agencies	7	(X)	State agencies	1	(X)
Miami-Dade	193,412	9,094.5	Okaloosa	5,000	2,784.1
Metro-Dade	91,534	8,216.2	Sheriff's office	2,892	2,423.0
Aventura	3,058	13,412.3	Crestview	709	4,974.7
Bal Harbour	147	4,549.7	Ft. Walton Beach	978	4,400.3
Bay Harbor Islands	140	3,034.9	Niceville	252	2,108.1
Biscayne Park	67	2,207.6	Shalimar	36	5,454.6
Coral Gables	3,407	8,109.6	Valparaiso	131	1,950.6
El Portal	179	7,203.2	State agencies	2	(X)
Florida City	1,167	18,880.4			
Golden Beach	30	3,550.3	Okeechobee	1,437	4,046.8
Indian Creek	4	7,547.2	Sheriff's office	1,120	3,683.2
Hialeah	14,922	7,065.3	Okeechobee	312	6,115.3
Hialeah Gardens	926	5,185.1	State agencies	5	(X)
Homestead	3,590	13,470.9			
Key Biscayne	170	1,754.6	Orange	70,624	8,344.8
Medley	268	31,162.8	Sheriff's office	39,283	7,000.9
Miami	40,048	10,965.9	Apopka	1,739	7,652.7
Miami Beach	14,359	15,273.6	Eatonville	130	5,227.2
Miami Shores	974	9,577.2	Edgewood	118	8,183.1
Miami Springs	857	6,446.0	Maitland	464	4,614.2
Miccosukee	96	(X)	Oakland	40	4,728.1

See footnotes at end of table.   Continued . . .

University of Florida   **Bureau of Economic and Business Research**

Table 22.03. CRIMINAL OFFENSES AND RATES: CRIME INDEX OFFENSES AND CRIME RATES
IN THE STATE, COUNTIES, CITIES, AND SPECIFIED AREAS
OF FLORIDA, 1999 (Continued)

Area	Number of index offenses 1/	Crime rate per 100,000 popu- lation	Area	Number of index offenses 1/	Crime rate per 100,000 popu- lation
Orange (Continued)			Palm Beach (Continued)		
Ocoee	1,555	6,836.4	Wellington	1,107	3,540.0
Orlando	24,995	13,537.2	West Palm Beach	11,913	14,683.5
Windermere	24	1,331.9	Florida Atlantic University	267	(X)
Winter Garden	657	4,864.9	Palm Beach County		
Winter Park	1,281	5,130.8	School Board	1,119	(X)
University of Central Florida	319	(X)	State agencies	90	(X)
State agencies	19	(X)			
			Pasco	13,944	4,270.8
Osceola	10,575	6,719.6	Sheriff's office	11,186	3,806.5
Sheriff's office	5,481	5,600.6	Dade City	716	11,614.0
Kissimmee	4,064	9,852.6	New Port Richey	1,084	7,387.2
St. Cloud	1,015	5,557.7	Port Richey	302	11,143.9
State agencies	15	(X)	Zephyrhills	653	7,191.6
			State agencies	3	(X)
Palm Beach	75,295	7,224.7			
Sheriff's office	26,646	5,599.4	Pinellas	52,067	5,793.1
Atlantis	100	5,858.2	Sheriff's office	11,049	3,938.0
Belle Glade	1,873	11,058.6	Belleair	70	1,701.5
Boca Raton	3,243	4,633.3	Belleair Beach	24	1,112.1
Boynton Beach	4,958	8,936.1	Belleair Bluffs	39	1,780.8
Delray Beach	5,009	9,347.1	Clearwater	6,920	6,635.9
Greenacres City	1,493	5,830.0	Dunedin	1,200	3,353.7
Gulf Stream	17	2,381.0	Gulfport	887	7,412.1
Highland Beach	75	2,157.0	Indian Rocks	184	4,326.4
Hypoluxo	137	9,042.9	Indian Shores	170	4,453.8
Juno Beach	122	4,202.6	Kenneth City	247	5,645.7
Jupiter	1,640	4,834.2	Largo	3,072	4,493.1
Jupiter Inlet Colony	2	480.8	Madeira Beach	411	9,797.4
Lake Clarke Shores	92	2,516.4	North Redington Beach	35	2,928.9
Lake Park	711	10,375.0	Oldsmar	511	4,383.3
Lake Worth	3,388	10,855.8	Pinellas Park	2,984	6,622.4
Lantana	764	8,705.6	Redington Beach	43	2,651.1
Manalapan	16	5,047.3	Safety Harbor	424	2,460.5
Mangonia Park	615	44,792.4	St. Petersburg	21,078	8,685.2
North Palm Beach	546	4,339.5	St. Petersburg Beach	695	7,151.7
Ocean Ridge	60	2,915.5	Seminole	364	3,743.7
Pahokee	448	6,332.2	South Pasadena	277	4,718.9
Palm Beach	258	2,657.1	Tarpon Springs	972	4,721.2
Palm Beach Gardens	2,117	6,122.6	Treasure Island	345	4,690.7
Palm Beach Shores	137	13,211.2	Pinellas County		
Palm Springs	508	4,970.7	Campus Police	23	(X)
Riviera Beach	4,427	15,255.0	University of South Florida	23	(X)
Royal Palm Beach	998	5,187.1	St. Petersburg-Clearwater		
South Bay	243	7,288.5	Airport	12	(X)
South Palm Beach	19	1,275.2	State agencies	8	(X)
Tequesta	137	2,674.7			

See footnotes at end of table.   Continued . . .

University of Florida

Bureau of Economic and Business Research

Table 22.03. CRIMINAL OFFENSES AND RATES: CRIME INDEX OFFENSES AND CRIME RATES IN THE STATE, COUNTIES, CITIES, AND SPECIFIED AREAS OF FLORIDA, 1999 (Continued)

Area	Number of index offenses 1/	Crime rate per 100,000 popu- lation	Area	Number of index offenses 1/	Crime rate per 100,000 popu- lation
Polk	27,230	5,736.2	Sarasota (Continued)		
Sheriff's office	12,779	4,272.6	University of South Florida	46	(X)
Auburndale	935	9,676.1	State agencies	5	(X)
Bartow	1,472	9,692.5			
Davenport	84	3,958.5	Seminole	15,344	4,332.7
Ft. Meade	271	4,964.3	Sheriff's office	5,212	2,965.2
Frostproof	131	4,614.3	Altamonte Springs	2,143	5,316.6
Haines City	1,081	7,814.1	Casselberry	1,321	5,342.3
Lake Alfred	187	4,869.8	Lake Mary	413	4,040.3
Lake Hamilton	152	13,160.2	Longwood	624	4,440.7
Lake Wales	1,246	12,297.7	Oviedo	816	3,623.9
Lakeland	6,798	8,773.1	Sanford	4,121	11,040.3
Mulberry	231	6,928.6	Winter Springs	693	2,371.7
Winter Haven	1,854	7,124.7	State agencies	1	(X)
State agencies	9	(X)			
			Sumter	1,288	2,534.3
Putnam	4,392	6,026.1	Sheriff's office	813	1,949.2
Sheriff's office	2,626	4,516.8	Bushnell	123	4,829.2
Crescent City	179	9,808.2	Center Hill	42	5,419.4
Palatka	1,575	14,484.1	Webster	49	5,697.7
Welaka	12	2,023.6	Wildwood	257	6,254.6
			State agencies	4	(X)
St. Johns	4,476	3,928.4			
Sheriff's office	3,160	3,259.8	Suwannee	1,400	4,071.4
St. Augustine	1,087	8,571.9	Sheriff's office	819	2,950.7
St. Augustine Beach	192	4,444.4	Live Oak	579	8,733.0
Florida School Deaf			State agencies	2	(X)
and Blind	36	(X)			
State agencies	1	(X)	Taylor	874	4,406.1
			Sheriff's office	349	2,768.1
St. Lucie	8,488	4,541.3	Perry	525	7,263.4
Sheriff's office	2,181	3,342.5			
Ft. Pierce	3,926	10,223.7	Union	147	1,062.7
Port St. Lucie	2,350	2,822.7	Sheriff's office	147	1,062.7
State agencies	31	(X)			
			Volusia	22,568	5,288.7
Santa Rosa	2,843	2,524.2	Sheriff's office	6,459	3,503.6
Sheriff's office	2,268	2,302.3	Daytona Beach	6,741	10,354.5
Gulf Breeze	189	3,053.8	Daytona Beach Shores	295	9,983.1
Milton	384	4,842.4	DeLand	2,329	12,495.3
State agencies	2	(X)	Edgewater	565	3,052.9
			Holly Hill	1,055	9,268.2
Sarasota	12,581	3,968.8	Lake Helen	84	3,253.3
Sheriff's office	8,322	3,660.3	New Smyrna Beach	991	5,327.1
Sarasota	3,711	7,183.7	Orange City	735	11,484.4
Venice	457	2,376.3	Ormond Beach	1,486	4,171.8
Sarasota/Bradenton Airport	40	(X)	Ponce Inlet	43	1,703.0

See footnotes at end of table.

Continued . . .

University of Florida   **Bureau of Economic and Business Research**

Table 22.03. CRIMINAL OFFENSES AND RATES: CRIME INDEX OFFENSES AND CRIME RATES
IN THE STATE, COUNTIES, CITIES, AND SPECIFIED AREAS
OF FLORIDA, 1999 (Continued)

Area	Number of index offenses 1/	Crime rate per 100,000 popu- lation	Area	Number of index offenses 1/	Crime rate per 100,000 popu- lation
Volusia (Continued)			Walton	1,003	2,478.6
Port Orange	1,013	2,237.1	Sheriff's office	806	2,306.0
South Daytona	576	4,318.8	DeFuniak Springs	197	3,572.7
Volusia County Beach					
Patrol	195	(X)	Washington	198	893.7
State agencies	1	(X)	Sheriff's office	107	592.4
			State agencies	91	2,223.3
Wakulla	700	3,390.2			
Sheriff's office	700	3,390.2			

(X) Not applicable.
1/ Actual offenses known to enforcement officers. Index offenses include murder, forcible sex, robbery, aggravated assault, burglary, larceny, and auto theft.

Note: The data reflected in this table are by geographic jurisdiction and are not intended to depict an individual law enforcement agency's activity. Sheriff's office totals include the activity occurring within those incorporated jurisdictions who do not report directly to the Uniform Crime Reporting (UCR) program. County totals reflect all UCR activity occurring within that county. State agencies are listed only for counties with state agency activity.

Source: State of Florida, Department of Law Enforcement, *Crime in Florida: 1999 Annual Report,* Internet site <http://www.fdle.state.fl.us/index.asp> (accessed 25 April 2000).

University of Florida   **Bureau of Economic and Business Research**

Table 22.04. CRIMINAL OFFENSES: ADULT AND JUVENILE ARRESTS BY OFFENSE AND BY SEX, IN FLORIDA, 1999

Offense	Total all ages	Adult arrests			Juvenile arrests		
		Total	Male	Female	Total	Male	Female
Total	897,679	766,343	617,146	149,197	131,336	100,189	31,147
Murder	741	661	588	73	80	67	13
Forcible sex offenses	4,222	3,421	3,347	74	801	781	20
Forcible rape	2,274	1,906	1,882	24	368	362	6
Forcible sodomy	455	309	297	12	146	140	6
Forcible fondling	1,493	1,206	1,168	38	287	279	8
Robbery	9,628	7,006	6,377	629	2,622	2,412	210
Aggravated assault	40,017	32,892	25,234	7,658	7,125	5,147	1,978
Burglary	27,716	17,460	15,839	1,621	10,256	9,389	867
Larceny	90,805	62,796	41,281	21,515	28,009	17,680	10,329
Motor vehicle theft	12,970	8,278	7,176	1,102	4,692	3,892	800
Manslaughter	90	84	70	14	6	4	2
Kidnap/abduction	1,059	979	927	52	80	69	11
Arson	662	360	271	89	302	247	55
Simple assault	83,479	67,169	53,478	13,691	16,310	10,935	5,375
Drug arrests	141,719	126,630	104,463	22,167	15,089	13,348	1,741
Bribery	69	65	53	12	4	4	0
Embezzlement	899	800	462	338	99	49	50
Fraud	11,271	10,596	7,004	3,592	675	432	243
Counterfeit/forgery	5,530	5,244	3,479	1,765	286	190	96
Extortion/blackmail	292	248	221	27	44	39	5
Intimidation	8,283	6,880	5,849	1,031	1,403	1,120	283
Prostitution/commercialized sex	14,548	14,252	10,360	3,892	296	258	38
Nonforcible sex offenses	4,116	3,780	3,439	341	336	320	16
Stolen property buy/ receive/possess	5,419	4,708	3,989	719	711	619	92
Driving under influence	57,715	57,234	46,766	10,468	481	348	133
Destruction/damage/vandalism	6,777	3,884	3,258	626	2,893	2,526	367
Gambling	931	827	775	52	104	103	1
Weapons violations	8,293	6,384	5,908	476	1,909	1,653	256
Liquor law violations	31,120	28,811	25,106	3,705	2,309	1,758	551
Miscellaneous	329,308	294,894	241,426	53,468	34,414	26,799	7,615

Note: A person is counted each time he/she is arrested or summoned; therefore, arrest counts do not reflect the specific number of persons arrested since one individual may be arrested several times for the same or different crimes.

Source: State of Florida, Department of Law Enforcement, *Crime in Florida: 1999 Annual Report,* Internet site <http://www.fdle.state.fl.us/index.asp> (accessed 25 April 2000).

University of Florida   **Bureau of Economic and Business Research**

Table 22.06. DOMESTIC VIOLENCE OFFENSES: NUMBER AND RELATIONSHIP OF THE VICTIM TO THE OFFENDER IN FLORIDA, 1999

Primary offense	Total	Per-centage change from 1998	Arrests	Relationship of victim to offender	
				Spouse	Parent
Total	126,044	-5.5	63,410	35,570	10,498
Criminal homicide	186	-2.1	104	63	9
Manslaughter	13	-40.9	12	0	0
Forcible sex offenses	2,584	-7.9	934	189	112
Forcible rape	1,186	-17.6	493	157	44
Forcible sodomy	409	-0.5	150	16	9
Forcible fondling	989	3.6	291	16	59
Aggravated assault	23,414	-6.9	13,396	5,250	2,005
Aggravated stalking	241	-2.4	142	96	8
Simple assault	94,765	-4.7	47,632	28,007	7,907
Threat/intimidation	4,378	-9.1	1,048	1,773	451
Simple stalking	463	-31.2	142	192	6

	Relationship of victim to offender (Continued)				
	Child	Sibling	Other family	Cohab-itant	Other
Total	9,883	9,168	7,951	40,700	12,274
Criminal homicide	37	8	13	46	10
Manslaughter	7	1	3	2	0
Forcible sex offenses	768	301	619	279	316
Forcible rape	306	93	241	161	184
Forcible sodomy	104	82	108	43	47
Forcible fondling	358	126	270	75	85
Aggravated assault	2,529	2,115	1,792	6,922	2,801
Aggravated stalking	9	0	5	77	46
Simple assault	6,364	6,537	5,189	32,239	8,522
Threat/intimidation	159	199	305	1,030	461
Simple stalking	10	7	25	105	`118

Source: State of Florida, Department of Law Enforcement, *Crime in Florida: 1999 Annual Report,* Internet site <http://www.fdle.state.fl.us/index.asp> (accessed 25 April 2000).

Table 22.08. CRIME RATES: PROPERTY AND VIOLENT CRIME RATES IN FLORIDA
AND THE UNITED STATES, 1989 THROUGH 1998

(rates per 100,000 population)

	Florida			United States		
Year	All crime	Property crime 1/	Violent crime 2/	All crime	Property crime 1/	Violent crime 2/
1989	8,804.5	7,695.1	1,109.4	5,741.0	5,077.9	663.1
1990	8,810.8	7,566.5	1,244.3	5,820.3	5,088.5	731.8
1991	8,547.2	7,362.9	1,184.3	5,897.8	5,139.7	758.1
1992	8,358.2	7,151.0	1,207.2	5,660.2	4,902.7	757.5
1993	8,351.0	7,145.0	1,206.0	5,484.4	4,737.6	746.8
1994	8,250.0	7,103.2	1,146.8	5,373.5	4,660.0	713.6
1995	7,701.5	6,630.6	1,071.0	5,275.9	4,591.3	684.6
1996	7,497.4	6,446.3	1,051.0	5,086.6	4,450.1	636.5
1997	7,271.8	6,248.2	1,023.6	4,930.0	4,318.7	611.3
1998	6,886.0	5,947.4	938.7	4,615.5	4,049.1	566.4

1/ Includes burglary, larceny-theft, and motor vehicle theft.
2/ Includes murder, forcible rape, robbery, and aggravated assault.
Note: Some data may be revised.

Source: U.S., Department of Justice, Federal Bureau of Investigation, *Crime in the United States,*
1998, Internet site <http://www.fbi.gov/ucr/Cius_98/98crime/98cius17.pdf> (accessed 25 April 2000),
and previous editions.

Table 22.09. CAPITAL PUNISHMENT: PRISONERS UNDER SENTENCE OF DEATH BY RACE, SEX
AND HISPANIC ORIGIN IN FLORIDA, THE SOUTH, AND THE UNITED STATES,
DECEMBER 31, 1997 AND 1998

	Florida		South 1/		
Item	Number	Percentage of United States	Number	Percentage of United States	United States
Prisoners under sentence of death on 12-31-97 A/	367	11.0	1,828	54.9	3,328
Changes during 1997					
Received under death sentence	25	8.8	186	65.3	285
Removed from death row 2/	16	17.2	64	68.8	93
Executed	4	5.9	55	80.9	68
Prisoners under sentence of death on 12-31-98	372	10.8	1,895	54.9	3,452
White	241	12.6	1,045	54.8	1,906
Black	131	8.8	827	55.7	1,486
Women	4	8.3	26	54.2	48
Hispanic origin 3/	43	13.7	152	48.4	314

A/ Revised.
1/ Includes Alabama, Arkansas, Delaware, Florida, Georgia, Kentucky, Louisiana, Maryland, Mississippi,
North Carolina, Oklahoma, South Carolina, Tennessee, Texas, and Virginia.
2/ Excludes executions. Includes suicide, murder, and death by natural causes.
3/ Persons of Hispanic origin may be of any race.

Source: U.S., Department of Justice, Bureau of Justice Statistics, *Bureau of Justice Statistics Bulletin:*
Capital Punishment, 1998, Internet site <http://www.ojp.usdoj.gov/bjs/bjs/abstract/cp98.htm>
(accessed 10 December 1999).

University of Florida   **Bureau of Economic and Business Research**

Table 22.10. PRISONERS: NUMBER UNDER JURISDICTION OF STATE OR FEDERAL
CORRECTIONAL AUTHORITIES IN FLORIDA AND THE UNITED STATES
DECEMBER 31, 1996 THROUGH JULY 30, 1999

Item	1996	1997	1998 A/	1999 B/
Florida				
Total prisoners	63,763	64,713	66,280	68,599
Percentage change from previous year	-0.2	1.5	2.4	3.5
Prisoners sentenced to more than a year	63,746	(NA)	(NA)	(NA)
Per 100,000 resident population	439	443	445	453
United States				
Total prisoners	1,180,520	1,219,776	1,277,502	1,333,561
Percentage change from previous year	5.0	3.3	4.7	4.4
Prisoners sentenced to more than a year	1,138,187	(NA)	(NA)	(NA)
Per 100,000 resident population	427	436	452	468

(NA) Not available.
A/ Revised.   B/ Preliminary.
Note: Data for 1996 and 1997 are for December 31 through June 30.   Data for 1998 and 1999 are
for July 1 through June 30, and are not comparable to earlier years.

Source: U.S., Department of Justice, Bureau of Justice Statistics, *Bureau of Justice Statistics Bulletin:
Prison and Jail Inmates at Midyear 1999*, Internet site <http://www.ojp.usdoj.gov/bjs/abstract/
pjim99.htm> (accessed 25 April 2000), and previous editions.

Table 22.11. POPULATION UNDER CRIMINAL SENTENCE: INCARCERATED INMATES AND
OFFENDERS UNDER COMMUNITY SUPERVISION OF THE FLORIDA DEPARTMENT
OF CORRECTIONS, JUNE 30, 1995 THROUGH 1999

Type of supervision	1995	1996	1997	1998	1999
Under supervision, total	198,048	201,944	207,624	211,013	218,939
Incarcerated offenders	61,992	64,333	64,713	66,280	68,599
Male	58,497	60,782	61,282	62,768	64,966
White	23,658	25,437	26,048	26,731	27,818
Black	33,586	34,123	34,014	34,778	35,824
Other	1,253	1,222	1,220	1,259	1,324
Female	3,495	3,551	3,431	3,512	3,633
White	1,494	1,551	1,470	1,504	1,587
Black	1,998	1,977	1,860	1,891	1,894
Other	3	23	101	117	152
Community supervision	136,056	137,611	142,911	144,733	150,340
Probation	93,723	98,420	102,136	103,918	108,354
Felony	90,879	95,183	98,726	100,409	104,552
Misdemeanor	1,362	1,674	1,703	1,770	1,877
Administrative	1,482	1,563	1,707	1,712	1,708
Sex offender	(NA)	(NA)	(NA)	27	217
Drug offender probation	6,332	7,857	9,921	11,628	12,348
Community control	14,692	14,465	14,605	13,895	14,540
Pretrial intervention	7,793	7,813	8,339	8,355	8,560
Post-prison release	(NA)	9,056	7,910	6,937	6,538
Parole	2,838	2,747	2,524	2,456	2,373
Other 1/	10,667	6,309	5,386	4,481	4,165

(NA) Not available.
1/ Includes conditional, control, supervised community, conditional medical, and other post-prison
releases.
Source: State of Florida, Department of Corrections, *1998-99 Annual Report,* Internet site <http://
www.dc.state.fl.us/pub/annual/9899/stats/> (accessed 27 April 2000), and previous editions.

University of Florida   **Bureau of Economic and Business Research**

Table 22.12. POPULATION UNDER CRIMINAL SENTENCE: INCARCERATED OFFENDERS AND OFFENDERS UNDER COMMUNITY SUPERVISION OF THE FLORIDA DEPARTMENT OF CORRECTIONS BY PRIMARY OFFENSE, JUNE 30, 1999

| | Incarcerated offenders | | Community supervision | | | | |
| | Total | Admitted 1998-99 | Total 1/ | Proba-tion 2/ | Commu-nity control | Condi-tional release | Parole |
Primary offense							
Total	68,599	23,762	150,340	120,702	14,540	3,661	2,373
Murder, manslaughter	10,430	1,002	2,520	1,659	165	159	503
First degree murder	5,098	361	426	232	30	32	121
Second degree murder	3,946	332	898	496	38	64	292
Third degree murder	118	25	68	51	6	2	9
Other homicide	50	5	65	30	4	0	31
Manslaughter	752	184	699	546	50	50	45
DUI manslaughter	466	95	364	304	37	11	5
Sexual offenses	7,518	1,616	8,722	7,360	897	242	142
Capital sexual battery	2,407	298	1,162	1,049	76	25	8
Life sexual battery	1,261	103	277	212	19	23	23
First degree sexual battery	888	163	1,112	982	73	20	35
Second degree sexual battery	546	147	681	539	83	39	18
Other sexual battery	195	4	67	35	2	0	30
Lewd, lascivious behavior	2,221	901	5,423	4,543	644	135	28
Robbery	10,317	2,221	5,116	3,192	596	878	407
With weapon	7,073	1,271	2,606	1,554	298	415	320
Without weapon	3,054	894	2,455	1,593	292	462	84
Home invasion	190	56	55	45	6	1	3
Violent personal offenses	8,113	3,207	22,847	19,147	2,160	681	140
Home invasion, other	2	1	5	3	0	0	1
Carjacking	417	147	107	73	21	10	3
Aggravated assault	705	443	4,451	3,873	372	66	45
Aggravated battery	2,878	1,061	5,326	4,323	595	320	25
Assault and battery on law enforcement officers	979	461	2,784	2,237	261	150	5
Other assault and battery	103	63	498	433	36	4	1
Aggravated stalking	107	54	568	490	67	0	2
Resisting arrest with violence	378	239	1,834	1,518	175	72	0
Kidnapping	1,456	233	900	699	104	41	31
Arson	370	138	740	614	88	8	11
Abuse of children	257	110	2,143	1,753	178	3	4
Leaving accident, injury/death	97	59	931	805	95	2	1
DUI, injury	195	95	545	468	73	1	2
Other violent offenses	169	103	2,015	1,858	95	4	9
Burglary	12,288	4,332	14,786	11,464	1,865	704	213
Burglary of structure	2,513	1,315	7,245	5,787	799	246	91
Burglary of dwelling	6,013	2,183	4,288	3,127	692	298	77
Armed burglary	1,964	401	938	665	171	70	16
Burglary with assault	1,712	371	1,012	783	121	84	19
Other burglary/trespass	86	62	1,303	1,102	82	6	10

See footnotes at end of table.

Continued . . .

Table 22.12. POPULATION UNDER CRIMINAL SENTENCE: INCARCERATED OFFENDERS AND OFFENDERS UNDER COMMUNITY SUPERVISION OF THE FLORIDA DEPARTMENT OF CORRECTIONS BY PRIMARY OFFENSE, JUNE 30, 1999 (Continued)

| Primary offense | Incarcerated offenders | | Community supervision | | | | |
	Total	Admitted 1998-99	Total 1/	Proba-tion 2/	Commu-nity control	Condi-tional release	Parole
Theft, forgery, fraud	4,799	2,906	38,630	32,265	2,648	242	216
Other grand theft	996	652	16,672	13,996	978	52	99
Grand theft, automobile	1,015	663	2,935	2,432	279	55	25
Stolen property	1,749	852	3,875	3,185	492	77	27
Forgery, uttering and counterfeiting	405	279	4,453	3,674	341	24	35
Worthless checks	80	54	2,828	2,336	150	3	4
Fraudulent practices	294	187	6,292	5,289	259	12	20
Other theft, property damage	260	219	1,575	1,353	149	19	6
Drugs	11,439	6,477	41,056	31,237	4,733	544	606
Sale/purchase/manufacturing	6,815	3,814	15,109	11,620	2,013	380	246
Trafficking	2,387	823	2,015	1,513	274	30	152
Other possession	2,237	1,840	23,932	18,104	2,446	134	208
Weapons	1,743	789	4,535	3,681	449	133	31
Discharging	295	148	920	753	125	17	5
Possession	1,448	640	3,562	2,884	321	116	25
Other weapons offenses	0	1	53	44	3	0	1
Other offenses	1,936	1,212	11,912	10,529	1,003	78	98
Escape	925	431	1,225	963	141	56	31
DUI, no injury	321	248	1,554	1,379	144	5	23
Traffic, other	295	298	5,102	4,530	553	4	3
Racketeering	162	58	368	329	29	2	3
Pollution/hazardous materials	2	2	167	145	2	1	0
Other offenses	231	175	3,496	3,183	134	10	38
Data unavailable	16	0	216	168	24	0	17

DUI Driving under the influence.
1/ Includes pretrial intervention, control releases, and other post-prison releases not shown separately.
2/ Includes drug offender probation.

Source: State of Florida, Department of Corrections, *1998-99 Annual Report*, Internet site <http://www.dc.state.fl.us/pub/annual/9899/stats> (accessed 27 April 2000).

University of Florida   **Bureau of Economic and Business Research**

Table 22.13. PRISONERS: LENGTH OF SENTENCE, CLASS OF FELONY, AGE, MEDICAL CLASSIFICATION, EDUCATIONAL LEVEL, LITERACY SKILLS LEVEL, AND PRIOR COMMITMENTS BY RACE AND SEX OF OFFENDER IN FLORIDA
JUNE 30, 1999

Item	Total	White		Black		Other	
		Male	Female	Male	Female	Male	Female
Length of sentence (years)							
Total	68,599	27,818	1,587	35,824	1,894	1,324	152
Average 1/	15.3	15.8	9.7	15.4	8.1	17.8	8.4
Median 1/	8.0	8.1	4.0	9.0	4.0	10.0	5.0
1 year or less	5	3	0	2	0	0	0
1 to 5	26,360	10,492	948	13,232	1,178	422	88
6 to 10	13,461	5,536	251	7,047	352	242	33
11 to 15	7,741	3,072	132	4,216	139	165	17
16 to 24	5,885	2,253	83	3,328	84	136	1
25 to 30	3,793	1,505	29	2,128	41	85	5
31 to 50	2,528	983	27	1,445	25	48	0
51 years or more	1,120	435	11	639	8	27	0
Life/death	7,699	3,536	106	3,783	67	199	8
Data unavailable	7	3	0	4	0	0	0
Class of felony 2/							
Capital	4,029	2,150	82	1,613	47	131	6
Life felony	5,433	2,054	60	3,070	75	166	8
First degree, life	4,084	1,537	65	2,331	67	76	8
First degree	15,752	6,410	312	8,253	367	344	66
Second degree	26,848	10,667	616	14,216	859	454	36
Third degree	10,981	4,454	448	5,449	464	139	27
Misdemeanor	3	0	0	2	1	0	0
Data unavailable	1,469	546	4	890	14	14	1
Current age (years)							
Average age	34	35	36	33	34	34	34
Median age	33	34	35	32	34	33	34
16 and under	136	32	1	100	0	3	0
17	351	107	6	221	11	4	2
18	836	265	4	533	21	13	0
19	1,478	598	14	797	40	27	2
20	1,915	712	23	1,114	31	32	3
21	2,084	835	27	1,126	50	40	6
22 to 24	6,821	2,486	108	3,928	158	127	14
25 to 29	11,763	4,418	239	6,573	292	224	17
30 to 34	12,112	4,656	333	6,423	424	239	37
35 to 39	12,203	4,912	346	6,242	434	238	31
40 to 44	8,786	3,598	271	4,484	242	171	20
45 to 49	5,024	2,267	101	2,420	118	105	13
50 to 54	2,589	1,370	61	1,063	37	54	4
55 to 69	2,242	1,388	46	732	34	39	3
70 and over	251	171	7	63	2	8	0
Data unavailable	8	3	0	5	0	0	0
Medical grade classification 3/							
Unrestricted	37,756	14,666	902	20,239	1,117	733	99
Minimum	23,584	10,025	471	12,062	533	449	44
Moderate	5,801	2,454	150	2,895	171	124	7
Severe	925	465	36	372	37	14	1
Data unavailable	533	208	28	256	36	4	1

See footnotes at end of table.   Continued . . .

Table 22.13. PRISONERS: LENGTH OF SENTENCE, CLASS OF FELONY, AGE, MEDICAL CLASSIFICATION, EDUCATIONAL LEVEL, LITERACY SKILLS LEVEL, AND PRIOR COMMITMENTS BY RACE AND SEX OF OFFENDER IN FLORIDA JUNE 30, 1999 (Continued)

Item	Total	White		Black		Other	
		Male	Female	Male	Female	Male	Female
Tested education grade level 4/							
Median grade level	7	9	10	6	6	6	7
1	1,374	277	4	1,003	43	43	4
2	4,136	841	37	2,934	201	115	8
3	5,092	1,079	48	3,609	242	101	13
4	4,749	1,097	63	3,298	200	81	10
5	6,538	1,854	122	4,203	243	105	11
6	6,163	1,955	132	3,737	242	83	14
7	4,708	1,702	112	2,669	136	81	8
8	5,264	2,132	122	2,814	112	78	6
9	6,621	3,126	225	3,007	142	99	22
10	4,508	2,473	159	1,754	58	59	5
11	3,078	1,793	114	1,061	57	46	7
12	7,602	5,446	333	1,648	74	92	9
Data unavailable	8,766	4,043	116	4,087	144	341	35
Tested literacy skill levels 4/							
Median skill level	7	9	10	6	6	6	7
Less than basic literacy (1.0-3.9)	10,602	2,197	89	7,546	486	259	25
Basic literacy skills (4.0-8.9)	27,422	8,740	551	16,721	933	428	49
Functional literacy skills (9.0-12.9)	21,809	12,838	831	7,470	331	296	43
Data unavailable	8,766	4,043	116	4,087	144	341	35
Prior DC commitments							
None	34,603	16,843	1,144	14,658	974	848	136
One	14,022	5,368	255	7,706	409	275	9
Two	8,771	2,770	105	5,533	245	114	4
Three	5,478	1,556	61	3,668	141	50	2
Four	3,030	723	14	2,187	79	26	1
Five	1,529	331	8	1,159	26	5	0
Six	721	148	0	553	16	4	0
Seven	274	54	0	215	3	2	0
Eight	119	17	0	102	0	0	0
Nine or more	43	5	0	37	1	0	0
Data unavailable	9	3	0	6	0	0	0

DC Department of Corrections.
1/ Sentence lengths of 50 years or longer, life, and death were calculated as 50 years.
2/ Primary offense.
3/ Medical grades are assigned to inmates by health care professionals based primarily on general physical stamina, mental health, and functional capacity.
4/ Most recent Tests of Adult Basic Education (TABE) scores.

Source: State of Florida, Department of Corrections, *1998-99 Annual Report*, Internet site <http://www dc.state.fl.us/pub/annual/9899/stats> (accessed 27 April 2000).

Table 22.14. POPULATION UNDER CRIMINAL SENTENCE: INCARCERATED OFFENDERS AND OFFENDERS UNDER COMMUNITY SUPERVISION BY COUNTY OF COMMITMENT OR SUPERVISION AND BY RACE IN THE STATE AND COUNTIES OF FLORIDA, JUNE 30, 1999

County	Incarcerated offenders				Community supervision 1/			
	Total	White	Black	Other races	Total 2/	White	Black	Other races
Florida	68,599	29,405	37,718	1,476	150,300	94,548	53,116	2,636
Alachua	952	256	691	5	2,428	1,067	1,356	5
Baker	72	40	32	0	217	158	58	1
Bay	1,358	797	547	14	2,967	2,227	709	31
Bradford	144	63	79	2	266	175	91	0
Brevard	1,736	898	818	20	4,311	3,018	1,257	36
Broward	7,686	2,702	4,879	105	15,237	8,460	6,394	383
Calhoun	85	35	50	0	122	87	35	0
Charlotte	375	259	111	5	966	831	127	8
Citrus	221	178	42	1	874	787	76	11
Clay	410	249	156	5	802	699	94	9
Collier	529	336	182	11	1,528	1,285	215	28
Columbia	476	224	251	1	1,192	800	389	3
De Soto	123	53	67	3	291	205	86	0
Dixie	82	49	33	0	284	212	72	0
Duval	4,495	1,275	3,182	38	6,002	2,875	3,050	77
Escambia	2,138	857	1,265	16	4,065	2,338	1,681	46
Flagler	96	46	50	0	328	249	78	1
Franklin	57	29	28	0	146	106	40	0
Gadsden	418	36	378	4	1,060	207	835	18
Gilchrist	39	27	12	0	90	80	9	1
Glades	33	15	17	1	64	53	9	2
Gulf	73	40	32	1	188	121	66	1
Hamilton	86	33	51	2	310	119	191	0
Hardee	105	52	43	10	249	204	41	4
Hendry	129	49	70	10	347	189	112	46
Hernando	368	246	115	7	1,153	1,020	126	7
Highlands	341	174	156	11	658	443	207	8
Hillsborough	6,351	2,644	3,502	205	13,293	7,835	5,167	291
Holmes	81	69	11	1	196	179	16	1
Indian River	385	172	209	4	828	592	231	5
Jackson	294	127	164	3	545	333	209	3
Jefferson	111	23	88	0	196	50	146	0
Lafayette	24	16	8	0	79	61	18	0
Lake	537	260	270	7	1,683	1,217	430	36
Lee	1,146	579	534	33	2,694	1,884	781	29
Leon	1,273	290	977	6	3,877	1,437	2,424	16

See footnotes at end of table.

Continued . . .

University of Florida

Bureau of Economic and Business Research

Table 22.14. POPULATION UNDER CRIMINAL SENTENCE: INCARCERATED OFFENDERS
AND OFFENDERS UNDER COMMUNITY SUPERVISION BY COUNTY OF COMMITMENT
OR SUPERVISION AND BY RACE IN THE STATE AND COUNTIES
OF FLORIDA, JUNE 30, 1999 (Continued)

County	Incarcerated offenders				Community supervision 1/			
	Total	White	Black	Other races	Total 2/	White	Black	Other races
Levy	92	43	48	1	523	393	130	0
Liberty	34	16	17	1	86	63	21	2
Madison	122	27	93	2	351	100	249	2
Manatee	985	523	429	33	2,318	1,590	670	58
Marion	966	450	500	16	2,993	1,931	1,015	47
Martin	481	197	275	9	911	696	211	4
Miami-Dade	9,160	3,233	5,524	403	16,455	8,679	7,254	522
Monroe	543	328	202	13	1,567	1,305	245	17
Nassau	139	76	62	1	320	253	65	2
Okaloosa	552	290	255	7	1,866	1,387	471	8
Okeechobee	175	92	74	9	622	523	82	17
Orange	3,767	1,572	2,044	151	9,049	5,135	3,689	225
Osceola	636	398	211	27	1,457	1,165	212	80
Palm Beach	3,096	1,195	1,833	68	7,290	4,651	2,348	291
Pasco	970	778	164	28	2,671	2,468	172	31
Pinellas	4,580	2,167	2,369	44	10,225	7,029	3,133	63
Polk	2,736	1,495	1,199	42	5,695	3,949	1,706	40
Putnam	470	208	257	5	889	586	299	4
St. Johns	323	272	50	1	990	682	300	8
St. Lucie	866	431	422	13	2,205	1,335	859	11
Santa Rosa	933	469	446	18	762	677	82	3
Sarasota	438	209	226	3	2,171	1,685	473	13
Seminole	1,025	338	676	11	2,722	1,915	772	35
Sumter	143	65	76	2	419	291	126	2
Suwannee	198	87	107	4	633	431	197	5
Taylor	188	73	115	0	442	278	163	1
Union	60	23	36	1	103	67	36	0
Volusia	1,586	827	745	14	3,942	2,815	1,095	32
Wakulla	85	56	29	0	285	216	68	1
Walton	110	84	26	0	558	469	85	4
Washington	114	71	40	3	244	181	62	1
Interstate	186	109	62	15	(NA)	(NA)	(NA)	(NA)
Data unavailable	11	5	6	0	(NA)	(NA)	(NA)	(NA)

(NA) Not available.
1/ Felony and misdemeanor probation, community control, pretrial intervention, control release, parole, and other supervision.
2/ Includes data not distributed by race.

Source: State of Florida, Department of Corrections, *1998-99 Annual Report,* Internet site <http://www.dc.state.fl.us/pub/annual/9899/stats/> (accessed 27 April 2000), and unpublished data.

Table 22.15. COUNTY DETENTION FACILITIES: AVERAGE DAILY INMATE POPULATION
AND INCARCERATION RATES IN THE STATE AND COUNTIES OF FLORIDA
1997 THROUGH 1999

County	Average daily population 1/			Percentage change		Incarceration rate 2/		
	1997	1998	1999	1997-1998	1998-1999	1997	1998	1999
Florida	47,540	50,813	50,873	7.0	0.1	3.3	3.5	3.4
Alachua	717	816	806	12.4	-1.2	3.6	3.9	3.8
Baker	83	92	109	31.3	18.5	4.1	4.4	5.2
Bay	812	930	953	17.4	2.5	5.9	6.4	6.5
Bradford	130	133	153	17.7	15.0	5.3	5.3	6.0
Brevard	964	1,062	1,123	16.5	5.7	2.2	2.3	2.4
Broward	4,176	4,559	4,673	11.9	2.5	3.1	3.2	3.2
Calhoun	23	27	28	21.7	3.7	1.9	2.1	2.1
Charlotte	181	213	221	22.1	3.8	1.4	1.6	1.7
Citrus	282	285	311	10.3	9.1	2.7	2.6	2.8
Clay	167	257	239	43.1	-7.0	1.4	2.0	1.8
Collier	639	665	615	-3.8	-7.5	3.4	3.3	2.9
Columbia	258	270	291	12.8	7.8	5.2	5.0	5.3
De Soto	116	120	112	-3.4	-6.7	4.3	4.4	4.0
Dixie	66	79	82	24.2	3.8	5.3	6.1	6.2
Duval	2,704	2,727	2,749	1.7	0.8	3.8	3.7	3.6
Escambia	1,356	1,433	1,433	5.7	0.0	4.8	4.9	4.8
Flagler	76	88	74	-2.6	-15.9	2.0	2.1	1.7
Franklin	88	83	88	0.0	6.0	8.6	7.9	8.2
Gadsden	136	141	154	13.2	9.2	3.0	2.8	3.0
Gilchrist	21	25	33	57.1	32.0	1.8	2.0	2.5
Glades	26	31	27	3.8	-12.9	3.0	3.2	2.7
Gulf	34	34	40	17.6	17.6	2.5	2.4	2.8
Hamilton	75	70	61	-18.7	-12.9	6.1	5.1	4.3
Hardee	101	102	120	18.8	17.6	4.4	4.5	5.3
Hendry	131	144	151	15.3	4.9	4.4	4.8	5.0
Hernando	302	344	337	11.6	-2.0	2.5	2.8	2.7
Highlands	200	275	271	35.5	-1.5	2.6	3.5	3.4
Hillsborough	2,981	3,241	3,173	6.4	-2.1	3.3	3.5	3.4
Holmes	34	24	24	-29.4	0.0	2.0	1.4	1.3
Indian River	386	438	429	11.1	-2.1	3.9	4.2	4.0
Jackson	244	245	217	-11.1	-11.4	5.3	5.0	4.4
Jefferson	25	21	36	44.0	71.4	1.9	1.5	2.5
Lafayette	21	28	29	38.1	3.6	3.3	4.0	4.1
Lake	602	584	599	-0.5	2.6	3.4	3.1	3.1
Lee	1,061	1,120	1,131	6.6	1.0	2.8	2.8	2.8
Leon	993	979	977	-1.6	-0.2	4.6	4.3	4.2
Levy	103	95	94	-8.7	-1.1	3.5	3.0	2.9
Liberty	13	14	15	15.4	7.1	1.9	1.8	1.9

See footnotes at end of table.   Continued . . .

University of Florida   **Bureau of Economic and Business Research**

Table 22.15. COUNTY DETENTION FACILITIES: AVERAGE DAILY INMATE POPULATION
AND INCARCERATION RATES IN THE STATE AND COUNTIES OF FLORIDA
1997 THROUGH 1999 (Continued)

	Average daily population 1/			Percentage change		Incarceration rate 2/		
				1997-	1998-			
County	1997	1998	1999	1998	1999	1997	1998	1999
Madison	87	83	72	-17.2	-13.3	4.8	4.3	3.7
Manatee	1,032	1,258	1,170	13.4	-7.0	4.4	5.2	4.7
Marion	1,240	1,227	1,135	-8.5	-7.5	5.5	5.2	4.7
Martin	429	500	496	15.6	-0.8	3.8	4.3	4.2
Miami-Dade	7,716	7,321	6,860	-11.1	-6.3	3.8	3.5	3.3
Monroe	557	585	547	-1.8	-6.5	6.7	6.9	6.4
Nassau	123	109	103	-16.3	-5.5	2.5	2.1	1.9
Okaloosa	291	437	444	52.6	1.6	1.8	2.6	2.5
Okeechobee	160	186	187	16.9	0.5	4.8	5.3	5.3
Orange	3,343	3,636	4,124	23.4	13.4	4.4	4.5	5.0
Osceola	529	679	712	34.6	4.9	3.9	4.7	4.8
Palm Beach	2,351	2,536	2,549	8.4	0.5	2.4	2.5	2.5
Pasco	535	599	606	13.3	1.2	1.8	1.9	1.9
Pinellas	2,181	2,465	2,457	12.7	-0.3	2.5	2.8	2.8
Polk	1,646	1,746	1,783	8.3	2.1	3.7	3.8	3.8
Putnam	205	211	197	-3.9	-6.6	2.9	3.0	2.8
St. Johns	279	480	331	18.6	-31.0	2.9	4.5	3.0
St. Lucie	780	907	863	10.6	-4.9	4.5	5.1	4.7
Santa Rosa	221	300	346	56.6	15.3	2.3	2.9	3.2
Sarasota	678	682	730	7.7	7.0	2.2	2.2	2.3
Seminole	812	967	936	15.3	-3.2	1.3	2.9	2.7
Sumter	122	125	144	18.0	15.2	3.4	2.8	3.0
Suwannee	99	175	185	86.9	5.7	3.3	5.3	5.5
Taylor	120	105	122	1.7	16.2	6.6	5.5	6.3
Union	15	18	16	6.7	-11.1	1.2	1.4	1.2
Volusia	1,389	1,372	1,452	4.5	5.8	3.4	3.3	3.5
Wakulla	137	148	153	11.7	3.4	8.1	7.9	7.7
Walton	93	112	118	26.9	5.4	2.8	3.1	3.1
Washington	43	53	57	32.6	7.5	2.2	2.6	2.7

1/ Average annual figures based on monthly data.
2/ Per 1,000 population based upon self-reports of county total population as well as county inmate population.
Note: Data are collected monthly from the 67 county jail systems statewide from January 1, 1996 through December 31, 1998. Data for some months in some counties were not available and were not included in the annual averages. The high increase in inmate population and incarceration rates in some of the counties is the result of holding a large portion of the inmate population for the U.S. Marshal and the contracting of bedspace.

Source: State of Florida, Department of Corrections, Bureau of Planning, Research, and Statistics, *Florida County Detention Facilities: 1999 Annual Report*, and previous editions, Internet site <http://www.dc.state.fl.us/pub/jails/annual/1999/table2.html> (accessed 24 April 2000).

University of Florida   **Bureau of Economic and Business Research**

Table 22.16. RECIDIVISM: STANDARD RECIDIVISM RATES OF PRISONERS BY AGE AT RELEASE, JANUARY 1, 1993 TO JULY 31, 1999

Item	Rates 1/	Under 18	18 to 24	25 to 34	35 to 49	50 to 59	Over 59
Release year	30.1	47.5	35.3	31.8	25.8	12.7	8.5
Fiscal 1993-94	30.3	48.7	35.4	31.8	24.6	12.0	12.1
Fiscal 1994-95	30.4	48.9	36.2	31.7	25.0	14.1	10.6
Fiscal 1995-96	32.4	56.2	36.9	34.9	27.2	14.6	8.1
Fiscal 1996-97	29.3	43.8	35.2	30.9	25.9	11.0	4.2
Race and sex	30.1	47.5	35.3	31.8	25.8	12.7	8.5
White male	23.9	43.2	28.7	26.8	19.2	8.6	6.0
Black male	35.5	51.3	40.4	36.2	31.5	18.3	15.0
White female	23.2	(NA)	26.5	26.4	19.0	7.0	0.0
Black female	26.0	(NA)	26.7	28.2	22.9	13.9	(NA)
Other male	21.7	(NA)	26.8	21.4	16.9	12.0	(NA)
Education grade	30.1	47.5	35.3	31.8	25.8	12.7	8.5
1 - 3.9	35.1	62.9	45.2	36.8	30.3	14.5	10.3
4 - 8.9	32.4	44.2	38.0	33.3	27.5	14.6	10.5
9 - 11.9	27.3	45.9	30.5	29.0	22.1	11.4	4.5
12 and over	23.1	38.9	25.2	25.2	20.2	7.3	0.0
Prior recidivism	30.1	47.5	35.3	31.8	25.8	12.7	8.5
None	28.9	47.4	34.4	30.4	24.2	11.8	8.2
1	46.2	(NA)	51.9	47.2	43.0	25.3	22.1
2 or more	51.1	(NA)	43.3	49.8	52.5	(NA)	(NA)
Offense type	30.1	47.5	35.3	31.8	25.8	12.7	8.5
Violent	23.3	(NA)	31.3	24.8	16.3	6.0	4.1
Property	35.0	51.7	36.0	36.8	32.2	21.1	17.2
Drugs	32.3	55.3	40.0	33.4	28.3	15.7	13.1
Other	31.2	55.0	40.7	33.2	26.0	13.2	40.4
Time in prison	30.1	47.5	35.3	31.8	25.8	12.7	8.5
1 to 12 months	30.8	48.0	34.6	31.4	26.9	15.6	14.6
1+ to 2 years	31.5	47.1	36.4	32.8	26.7	14.0	11.4
2+ to 3 years	30.8	50.7	35.8	32.4	26.3	15.0	9.4
3+ to 4 years	29.8	(NA)	35.1	31.2	26.2	14.1	12.8
4+ to 5 years	29.5	(NA)	33.4	33.5	25.2	4.9	5.6
5 years or more	24.2	(NA)	30.2	28.5	22.0	6.9	3.5
Release custody	30.1	47.5	35.3	31.8	25.8	12.7	8.5
Close	36.6	55.5	44.5	36.4	29.1	14.9	10.6
Medium	30.3	52.1	35.9	32.8	25.9	10.3	6.6
Minimum	28.9	41.0	32.7	30.5	25.3	14.1	10.3
Type of disciplinary reports	30.1	47.5	35.3	31.8	25.8	12.7	8.5
None	24.5	42.1	29.2	26.5	22.0	10.3	7.8
No major	24.7	42.8	29.3	26.6	22.3	10.8	8.1
No violent	26.8	43.4	31.3	28.7	23.9	11.7	8.3
1 to 2 total	30.6	49.6	34.0	31.7	27.4	17.4	8.7
1 to 2 major	31.9	47.7	35.6	33.0	28.1	17.1	7.7
1 to 2 violent	35.8	50.9	38.5	36.1	32.4	19.5	6.7

(NA) Not available.
1/ For all age groups.
Note: The standard recidivism rate is defined at two years after prison release. A recidivist is an inmate who, after release from prison, commits a new offense that results in a commitment to the Department of Corrections. Repeat offenders who return to prison for a technical violation of supervision are not counted.

Source: State of Florida, Department of Corrections, *Recidivism Report: Inmates Released from Florida Prisons*, December 1999, Internet site <http://www.dc.state.fl.us/pub/recidivism/standard.html> (accessed 24 April 2000).

University of Florida   **Bureau of Economic and Business Research**

Table 22.20. JUVENILE DELINQUENCY: CASES AND YOUTHS REFERRED FOR DELINQUENCY BY MOST SERIOUS OFFENSE IN FLORIDA, 1997-98 AND 1998-99

Offense	Cases received			Youths referred		
	1997-98	1998-99	Change	1997-98	1998-99	Change
Felonies	58,511	56,808	-2.9	43,391	43,096	-0.7
Murder/manslaughter	94	115	22.3	94	111	18.1
Attempted murder	140	86	-38.6	136	80	-41.2
Sexual battery	920	813	-11.6	888	786	-11.5
Other sex offenses	720	834	15.8	621	770	24.0
Armed robbery	1,241	1,065	-14.2	1,150	987	-14.2
Other robbery	1,821	1,688	-7.3	1,668	1,538	-7.8
Arson	568	628	10.6	550	595	8.2
Burglary	17,907	16,263	-9.2	14,214	12,814	-9.8
Auto theft	5,139	4,537	-11.7	3,237	2,957	-8.6
Grand larceny	4,311	4,693	8.9	3,087	3,499	13.3
Receiving stolen property	349	366	4.9	207	237	14.5
Concealed firearm	604	436	-27.8	469	334	-28.8
Aggravated assault/battery	8,603	11,164	29.8	6,698	8,498	26.9
Forgery	446	613	37.4	310	475	53.2
Nonmarijuana drug	4,690	4,846	3.3	3,054	3,212	5.2
Marijuana	1,284	1,654	28.8	939	1,221	30.0
Escape	795	642	-19.2	344	276	-19.8
Resisting arrest with violence	711	549	-22.8	423	342	-19.1
Shooting/throwing missile	1,116	1,293	15.9	785	991	26.2
Traffic offenses	97	184	89.7	44	93	111.4
Other	6,955	4,339	-37.6	4,473	3,280	-26.7
Misdemeanors	89,907	81,897	-8.9	58,113	54,319	-6.5
Assault/battery	21,164	20,377	-3.7	14,479	14,164	-2.2
Prostitution and other sex offenses	196	364	85.7	136	263	93.4
Petty larceny	5,562	7,323	31.7	3,314	5,256	58.6
Shoplifting	24,408	18,092	-25.9	18,940	13,842	-26.9
Receiving stolen property	51	14	-72.5	28	6	-78.6
Concealed weapon	778	613	-21.2	473	395	-16.5
Disorderly conduct	2,866	5,652	97.2	1,672	3,461	107.0
Vandalism	4,256	3,634	-14.6	2,534	2,219	-12.4
Trespassing	8,130	6,771	-16.7	3,797	3,315	-12.7
Loitering and prowling	2,335	1,947	-16.6	1,040	883	-15.1
Nonmarijuana drug	2,808	3,354	19.4	1,935	2,338	20.8
Marijuana	5,580	5,797	3.9	3,319	3,586	8.0
Alcohol-related offenses	2,890	2,856	-1.2	2,039	2,116	3.8
Violation of game laws	130	131	0.8	113	100	-11.5
Resisting arrest without violence	3,107	3,195	2.8	1,233	1,369	11.0
Unauthorized use of a car	16	4	-75.0	5	2	-60.0
Other	5,630	1,773	-68.5	3,056	1,004	-67.1
Other delinquency	25,485	14,782	-42.0	5,612	4,244	-24.4
Contempt	3,157	1,436	-54.5	589	423	-28.2
Violation of ordinance	70	858	1,125.7	39	506	1,197.4
Traffic	59	148	150.8	33	86	160.6
Interstate compact	313	257	-17.9	243	211	-13.2
Nonlaw violation of community control or furlough	8,433	6,794	-19.4	1,601	1,462	-9
Case reopened	5,783	910	-84.3	1,653	456	-72.4
Prosecution previously deferred	5,696	3,051	-46.4	1,193	851	-28.7
Transfer from other county	1,974	1,328	-32.7	261	249	-4.6

Note: Data for 1997-98 are revised. Percentage change from 1997-98.

Source: State of Florida, Department of Juvenile Justice, Bureau of Data and Research, *Profile of Delinquency Cases and Youths Referred at Each Stage of the Juvenile Justice System, 1994-95 Through 1998-99*, Internet site <http:/www.djj.state.fl.us/rnd/mr/2000-1/> (accessed 28 April 2000).

Table 22.21. JUVENILE DELINQUENCY: CASES AT VARIOUS STAGES OF THE JUVENILE JUSTICE SYSTEM BY AGE, RACE, AND SEX IN FLORIDA, 1998-99

			Disposition	
		Dis-	Non-	
Item	Received	posed 1/	judicial	Judicial
Total	153,487	145,551	74,640	80,184
0-9	2,119	2,097	1,539	631
10	1,881	1,785	1,161	719
11	3,683	3,495	2,060	1,617
12	8,327	8,048	4,422	4,095
13	15,204	14,686	7,660	7,963
14	22,596	22,002	11,068	12,382
15	29,171	27,969	13,805	16,121
16	33,649	31,615	15,945	17,728
17	34,410	31,559	16,166	17,416
18 and over	2,447	2,295	814	1,512
White male	66,992	64,085	32,882	35,567
Black male	47,116	43,923	20,593	26,759
Other male	1,086	1,038	566	523
White female	22,394	21,393	12,421	9,732
Black female	15,525	14,751	7,947	7,467
Other female	369	353	227	131
Unknown	5	8	4	5

		Disposition (Continued)		
		Placed		Trans-
		on		ferred
	Referred	community	Commit-	to adult
	to JASP	control	ments 2/	court
Total	16,520	31,999	13,292	5,043
0-9	533	231	13	2
10	404	299	39	1
11	623	745	147	1
12	1,216	1,816	543	11
13	1,926	3,491	1,379	36
14	2,563	5,209	2,388	164
15	2,906	6,450	3,288	488
16	3,199	6,911	3,101	1,493
17	3,054	6,407	2,266	2,617
18 and over	96	440	128	230
White male	7,633	15,170	5,687	2,001
Black male	3,795	9,443	5,378	2,636
Other male	140	218	89	27
White female	3,012	4,056	1,171	180
Black female	1,884	3,046	958	198
Other female	55	62	9	1
Unknown	1	4	0	0

JASP Juvenile Alternative Services Program.
1/ Placement in detention during the interim between arrest and case disposition.
2/ Placement in commitment programs ranging from day-treatment programs for less serious offenders to secure training schools and boot camps for more serious offenders.
Note: Since not all charges are always disposed in the same way, some duplication may exist.

Source: State of Florida, Department of Juvenile Justice, Bureau of Data and Research, *Profile of Delinquency Cases and Youths Referred at Each Stage of the Juvenile Justice System, 1994-95 Through 1998-99*, Internet site <http://www.djj.state.fl.us/rnd/mr/2000-1/> (accessed 28 April 2000).

Table 22.22. JUVENILE DELINQUENCY: YOUTHS REFERRED FOR DELINQUENCY TO THE JUVENILE JUSTICE SYSTEM BY AGE IN THE STATE AND COUNTIES OF FLORIDA, 1998-99

County	0-9	10	11	12	13	14	15	16	17	18 and over
Florida	1,833	1,493	2,712	5,765	9,896	14,163	18,196	21,903	23,881	1,817
Alachua	30	23	46	112	148	198	224	303	348	34
Baker	5	3	6	12	12	21	27	30	36	2
Bay	34	20	30	53	119	163	212	304	432	16
Bradford	3	3	4	11	9	15	30	26	37	1
Brevard	50	44	89	189	368	471	604	674	754	44
Broward	125	119	222	500	885	1,265	1,604	1,843	2,013	118
Calhoun	3	2	0	2	5	7	12	19	14	1
Charlotte	2	6	12	25	49	58	82	100	142	10
Citrus	17	11	9	27	59	85	89	118	103	3
Clay	41	25	31	67	98	165	191	231	225	16
Collier	24	17	41	83	133	207	253	318	309	14
Columbia	9	5	18	27	60	76	100	121	137	6
De Soto	9	5	9	12	19	25	31	52	53	3
Dixie	0	0	1	4	6	15	15	13	21	0
Duval	35	53	124	283	496	796	1,015	1,194	1,295	60
Escambia	37	29	44	122	205	279	376	465	522	80
Flagler	5	7	6	17	26	37	56	68	83	7
Franklin	3	1	1	2	5	8	8	20	25	1
Gadsden	2	3	4	18	28	51	68	78	113	3
Gilchrist	1	3	3	10	13	20	15	19	26	3
Glades	4	2	0	4	4	2	8	9	8	1
Gulf	2	1	3	6	3	8	12	12	22	2
Hamilton	4	2	2	7	7	9	11	16	17	5
Hardee	9	2	7	9	23	28	39	47	43	8
Hendry	4	1	9	28	37	49	66	71	87	5
Hernando	7	10	21	33	65	58	107	105	119	10
Highlands	14	15	14	46	55	68	92	107	138	12
Hillsborough	144	125	232	460	707	1,101	1,442	1,762	1,853	186
Holmes	0	0	0	3	6	4	12	18	24	1
Indian River	10	6	14	45	72	72	135	156	139	10
Jackson	7	2	5	15	24	30	36	54	54	2
Jefferson	1	0	2	2	3	6	13	24	25	3
Lafayette	0	0	0	2	0	4	1	5	1	0
Lake	49	32	46	79	166	214	271	287	283	10
Lee	30	24	50	100	213	311	394	491	636	44
Leon	27	28	55	113	166	215	260	320	391	11
Levy	8	1	2	10	22	21	41	45	46	5

See footnote at end of table.   Continued . . .

Table 22.22. JUVENILE DELINQUENCY: YOUTHS REFERRED FOR DELINQUENCY TO THE JUVENILE
JUSTICE SYSTEM BY AGE IN THE STATE AND COUNTIES
OF FLORIDA, 1998-99 (Continued)

County	0-9	10	11	12	13	14	15	16	17	18 and over
Liberty	0	0	0	4	1	5	5	4	8	1
Madison	7	3	9	15	12	12	27	26	32	2
Manatee	53	46	67	114	197	255	310	400	374	66
Marion	61	35	72	129	185	267	343	380	362	24
Martin	25	21	46	45	89	112	114	169	209	20
Miami-Dade	118	116	221	599	1,099	1,677	2,250	2,735	2,736	181
Monroe	3	4	5	14	36	59	60	82	103	9
Nassau	11	5	13	21	42	45	62	87	88	2
Okaloosa	15	8	18	49	77	151	285	308	371	42
Okeechobee	2	3	11	20	48	63	69	88	101	2
Orange	120	88	152	326	551	883	1,101	1,260	1,434	105
Osceola	28	29	57	83	136	159	198	274	325	21
Palm Beach	91	92	179	343	685	824	970	1,165	1,217	104
Pasco	14	18	33	80	140	230	290	328	354	23
Pinellas	186	140	210	400	607	856	1,030	1,211	1,240	80
Polk	111	79	137	244	400	621	715	837	902	83
Putnam	15	18	15	40	74	105	112	140	155	7
St. Johns	11	13	18	44	58	90	123	171	185	9
St. Lucie	45	28	47	108	139	185	253	294	289	24
Santa Rosa	5	4	16	34	88	97	132	178	185	14
Sarasota	30	17	43	82	128	189	284	352	435	49
Seminole	41	28	45	123	244	301	407	526	592	43
Sumter	4	4	5	11	25	40	61	84	60	3
Suwannee	2	4	7	16	31	30	28	46	51	5
Taylor	1	1	7	13	14	14	25	21	28	3
Union	5	1	2	4	5	4	7	7	12	1
Volusia	55	46	97	222	355	496	642	757	894	90
Wakulla	7	3	1	11	17	31	50	53	50	1
Walton	0	0	2	5	23	29	35	47	48	9
Washington	1	2	2	2	5	14	9	16	17	0
Unknown	8	4	5	12	22	37	54	54	78	10
Out-of-state	3	3	8	14	47	120	193	278	372	47

Note: The number of youths referred is determined by counting only the most serious offense for which
a youth is charged during the fiscal year. This differs from the number of cases received in that the most
serious offense on any given date is counted as one case. Therefore, the same youth may be referred for
additional offenses on different dates throughout the year, resulting in more than one case received.

Source: State of Florida, Department of Juvenile Justice, Bureau of Data and Research, *Profile of
Delinquency Cases and Youths Referred at Each Stage of the Juvenile Justice System, 1994-95
Through 1998-99*, Internet site <http:/www.djj.state.fl.us/rnd/mr/2000-1/> (accessed 28 April 2000).

Table 22.23. JUVENILE DELINQUENCY: YOUTHS REFERRED FOR DELINQUENCY TO THE JUVENILE JUSTICE SYSTEM BY SEX AND RACE IN THE STATE AND COUNTIES OF FLORIDA, 1998-99

County	Total	Per-cent-age change from 1997-98	Male White	Male Black	Male Other	Female White	Female Black	Female Other	Un-known
Florida	101,659	-5.1	45,139	27,231	796	17,074	11,105	309	5
Alachua	1,466	3.5	451	577	7	178	249	4	0
Baker	154	17.6	70	38	1	24	21	0	0
Bay	1,383	21.5	785	206	26	272	85	9	0
Bradford	139	-10.9	62	31	2	28	15	1	0
Brevard	3,287	3.9	1,788	543	34	668	244	10	0
Broward	8,694	-5.0	3,022	3,368	89	1,070	1,129	16	0
Calhoun	65	3.2	42	7	0	9	7	0	0
Charlotte	486	-18.9	305	40	2	130	9	0	0
Citrus	521	-0.8	361	20	3	130	5	2	0
Clay	1,090	2.2	665	112	12	251	45	5	0
Collier	1,399	5.0	802	179	7	321	89	1	0
Columbia	559	15.3	270	114	5	114	53	3	0
De Soto	218	-17.4	99	54	0	39	26	0	0
Dixie	75	-17.6	44	7	0	15	9	0	0
Duval	5,351	-7.2	1,679	2,055	66	644	875	32	0
Escambia	2,159	3.6	728	747	41	316	312	15	0
Flagler	312	-0.3	168	55	5	59	25	0	0
Franklin	74	-16.9	40	9	0	19	6	0	0
Gadsden	368	-18.2	27	239	1	10	91	0	0
Gilchrist	113	28.4	87	3	0	22	1	0	0
Glades	42	13.5	22	7	2	9	1	1	0
Gulf	71	-34.3	45	14	0	9	3	0	0
Hamilton	80	-9.1	16	38	0	9	17	0	0
Hardee	215	-4.0	138	23	0	43	10	1	0
Hendry	357	15.2	195	73	8	60	17	4	0
Hernando	535	-7.1	376	46	0	93	17	3	0
Highlands	561	2.9	263	113	0	112	72	1	0
Hillsborough	8,012	-6.2	3,330	2,258	40	1,425	935	23	1
Holmes	68	-41.9	56	0	0	11	1	0	0
Indian River	659	0.6	328	135	0	135	60	1	0
Jackson	229	-3.4	101	70	3	29	26	0	0
Jefferson	79	-16.8	19	39	0	3	18	0	0
Lafayette	13	-38.1	4	6	0	1	2	0	0
Lake	1,437	-1.6	745	335	4	237	116	0	0
Lee	2,293	3.0	1,172	404	12	501	202	2	0
Leon	1,586	-7.7	541	599	9	183	253	1	0
Levy	201	-12.2	112	47	0	28	14	0	0

See footnote at end of table.   Continued . . .

University of Florida   **Bureau of Economic and Business Research**

Table 22.23. JUVENILE DELINQUENCY: YOUTHS REFERRED FOR DELINQUENCY TO THE JUVENILE JUSTICE SYSTEM BY SEX AND RACE IN THE STATE AND COUNTIES OF FLORIDA, 1998-99 (Continued)

County	Total	Per-cent-age change from 1997-98	Male White	Male Black	Male Other	Female White	Female Black	Female Other	Un-known
Liberty	28	-12.5	22	1	0	3	2	0	0
Madison	145	-1.4	31	86	0	12	16	0	0
Manatee	1,882	-3.8	979	363	4	375	158	3	0
Marion	1,858	-7.0	960	368	4	373	150	3	0
Martin	850	8.0	456	153	19	153	60	9	0
Miami-Dade	11,732	-10.5	4,322	4,389	63	1,376	1,557	24	1
Monroe	375	-25.3	233	46	3	74	19	0	0
Nassau	376	0.8	219	56	0	82	19	0	0
Okaloosa	1,324	3.4	704	179	25	310	87	19	0
Okeechobee	407	19.7	241	53	3	91	17	2	0
Orange	6,020	-6.2	2,274	1,898	47	942	830	27	2
Osceola	1,310	2.7	702	168	11	339	87	3	0
Palm Beach	5,670	-6.2	2,142	1,955	27	773	758	15	0
Pasco	1,510	-6.7	1,033	93	9	342	30	3	0
Pinellas	5,960	-8.4	2,792	1,329	92	1,063	657	27	0
Polk	4,129	-4.2	1,995	957	19	697	456	5	0
Putnam	681	-3.0	301	199	5	92	83	1	0
St. Johns	722	7.3	406	107	0	143	65	1	0
St. Lucie	1,412	1.1	600	407	4	227	172	2	0
Santa Rosa	753	16.6	520	53	8	157	13	2	0
Sarasota	1,609	-6.8	881	254	9	358	104	3	0
Seminole	2,350	4.3	1,198	397	19	521	206	9	0
Sumter	297	-4.5	115	98	0	55	29	0	0
Suwannee	220	-8.7	112	48	2	37	20	1	0
Taylor	127	-19.6	68	31	0	16	12	0	0
Union	48	-5.9	29	7	0	9	3	0	0
Volusia	3,654	-4.6	1,850	681	30	786	300	7	0
Wakulla	224	-1.3	138	24	0	52	10	0	0
Walton	198	0.5	136	13	2	40	6	1	0
Washington	68	-26.9	38	8	0	19	3	0	0
Unknown	284	1036.0	118	85	5	43	30	3	0
Out-of-state	1,085	-53.1	566	114	7	307	86	4	1

Note: The number of youths referred is determined by counting only the most serious offense for which a youth is charged during the fiscal year. This differs from the number of cases received in that the most serious offense on any given date is counted as one case. Therefore, the same youth may be referred for additional offenses on different dates throughout the year, resulting in more than one case received.

Source: State of Florida, Department of Juvenile Justice, Bureau of Data and Research, *Profile of Delinquency Cases and Youths Referred at Each Stage of the Juvenile Justice System, 1994-95 Through 1998-98*, Internet site <http:/www.djj.state.fl.us/rnd/mr/2000-1/> (accessed 28 April 2000).

University of Florida   **Bureau of Economic and Business Research**

Table 22.24. JUVENILE DELINQUENCY: YOUTHS COMMITTING VIOLENT FELONY OFFENSES BY TYPE OF OFFENSE IN THE STATE, DEPARTMENT OF JUVENILE JUSTICE SERVICE DISTRICTS, AND COUNTIES OF FLORIDA, 1998-99

District and county	Total 1/ Number	Total 1/ Per-centage change from 1997-98	Murder 2/	Sex offense	Robbery	Assault	Resisting arrest with violence	Shoot or throw a deadly missile
Florida	14,103	13.2	191	1,556	2,525	8,498	342	991
District 1	491	21.2	5	70	48	319	25	24
Escambia	298	8.4	1	35	34	195	16	17
Okaloosa	100	25.0	4	15	8	62	7	4
Santa Rosa	66	57.1	0	12	6	45	0	3
Walton	27	237.5	0	8	0	17	2	0
District 2	476	-1.4	5	62	58	319	16	16
Bay	105	16.7	0	12	11	71	6	5
Calhoun	5	-16.7	0	1	0	3	0	1
Franklin	13	8.3	0	2	0	10	1	0
Gadsden	89	8.5	3	8	19	54	3	2
Gulf	8	-42.9	0	4	1	3	0	0
Holmes	4	-33.3	0	1	0	3	0	0
Jackson	30	36.4	0	6	1	22	0	1
Jefferson	11	-52.2	0	1	1	8	0	1
Leon	156	23.8	1	19	20	109	3	4
Liberty	2	-60.0	0	1	0	1	0	0
Madison	17	-45.2	0	4	3	9	1	0
Taylor	12	-57.1	1	0	1	7	1	2
Wakulla	17	-34.6	0	3	1	13	0	0
Washington	7	-41.7	0	0	0	6	1	0
District 3	564	29.7	6	78	71	348	9	52
Alachua	257	36.7	4	35	41	149	4	24
Bradford	25	13.6	0	6	4	14	0	1
Columbia	81	84.1	0	8	6	55	3	9
Dixie	9	28.6	0	0	1	7	0	1
Gilchrist	13	160.0	0	4	0	9	0	0
Hamilton	17	0.0	1	0	1	12	0	3
Lafayette	5	0.0	0	1	1	3	0	0
Levy	29	0.0	0	2	0	21	2	4
Putnam	94	6.8	1	14	13	62	0	4
Suwannee	20	0.0	0	4	2	13	0	1
Union	14	40.0	0	4	2	3	0	5
District 4	1,028	21.4	9	158	164	636	15	46
Baker	36	500.0	0	5	0	29	1	1
Clay	90	2.3	0	20	10	49	1	10
Duval	768	19.3	7	124	140	460	11	26
Nassau	43	16.2	1	2	3	32	0	5
St. Johns	91	26.4	1	7	11	66	2	4
District 5	969	-1.0	14	106	154	591	28	76
Pasco	219	65.9	3	31	34	122	8	21
Pinellas	750	-11.5	11	75	120	469	20	55
District 6	1,324	13.8	19	153	235	812	21	84
Hillsborough	1,063	9.1	14	93	215	657	16	68
Manatee	261	38.1	5	60	20	155	5	16

See footnotes at end of table.

Continued. . .

University of Florida

Bureau of Economic and Business Research

Table 22.24. JUVENILE DELINQUENCY: YOUTHS COMMITTING VIOLENT FELONY OFFENSES BY TYPE OF OFFENSE IN THE STATE, DEPARTMENT OF JUVENILE JUSTICE SERVICE DISTRICTS, AND COUNTIES OF FLORIDA, 1998-99 (Continued)

District and county	Total 1/ Number	Percentage change from 1997-98	Murder 2/	Sex offense	Robbery	Assault	Resisting arrest with violence	Shoot or throw a deadly missile
District 7	1,710	24.5	21	190	206	1,129	41	123
Brevard	418	24.0	3	64	39	262	8	42
Orange	844	19.5	9	75	127	567	23	43
Osceola	170	58.9	3	24	13	112	2	16
Seminole	278	24.7	6	27	27	188	8	22
District 8	701	30.1	12	86	115	428	12	48
Charlotte	40	-13.0	0	2	1	30	2	5
Collier	154	41.3	3	21	17	101	3	9
De Soto	41	41.4	2	4	12	20	0	3
Glades	6	100.0	0	0	0	5	0	1
Hendry	71	129.0	1	5	8	48	2	7
Lee	210	38.2	5	23	51	115	3	13
Sarasota	179	5.9	1	31	26	109	2	10
District 9	970	16.6	12	79	208	563	27	81
Palm Beach	970	16.6	12	79	208	563	27	81
District 10	1,272	8.0	12	114	313	675	52	106
Broward	1,272	8.0	12	114	313	675	52	106
District 11	2,332	-4.6	53	149	681	1,261	36	152
Miami-Dade	2,292	-4.5	53	143	677	1,238	36	145
Monroe	40	-11.1	0	6	4	23	0	7
District 12	438	15.6	3	58	53	290	13	21
Flagler	39	21.9	0	5	5	26	2	1
Volusia	399	15.0	3	53	48	264	11	20
District 13	654	19.8	12	98	48	410	12	74
Citrus	48	2.1	2	8	3	30	2	3
Hernando	87	77.6	0	17	8	47	0	15
Lake	236	16.3	5	46	20	129	6	30
Marion	227	15.8	0	21	16	168	3	19
Sumter	56	9.8	5	6	1	36	1	7
District 14	564	32.4	5	84	75	342	16	42
Hardee	28	64.7	0	3	5	19	0	1
Highlands	53	26.2	2	8	4	31	2	6
Polk	483	31.6	3	73	66	292	14	35
District 15	511	46.4	2	60	66	323	17	43
Indian River	69	30.2	1	13	12	40	2	1
Martin	123	80.9	1	5	18	75	3	21
Okeechobee	52	48.6	0	12	7	29	1	3
St. Lucie	267	38.3	0	30	29	179	11	18

1/ The number of youths referred is determined by counting only the most serious offense for which a youth is charged during the fiscal year. This differs from the number of cases received in that the most serious offense on any given date is counted as one case. Therefore, the same youth may be referred for additional offenses on different dates throughout the year.
2/ Includes attempted murder and manslaughter.

Source: State of Florida, Department of Juvenile Justice, Bureau of Data and Research, *Profile of Delinquency Cases and Youths Referred at Each Stage of the Juvenile Justice System, 1994-95 Through 1998-99*, Internet site <http://www.djj.state.fl.us/rnd/mr/2000-1/> (accessed 28 April 2000).

Table 22.30. VICTIM SERVICES: CRIMES COMPENSATION TRUST FUNDS RECEIPTS
IN THE STATE, JUDICIAL CIRCUITS, AND COUNTIES OF FLORIDA
FISCAL YEAR 1998-99

(rounded to thousands of dollars)

Judicial circuit and county	Total	Court cost 1/	Other 2/	Judicial circuit and county	Total	Court cost 1/	Other 2/
Florida	20,106	16,833	3,273	Circuit 8 (Cont.)			
				Levy	20	28	-8
Circuit 1	650	805	-155	Union	0	3	-3
Escambia	346	430	-85	Circuit 9	1,346	1,489	-143
Okaloosa	124	151	-27	Orange	1,203	1,336	-134
Santa Rosa	141	172	-31	Osceola	143	153	-9
Walton	39	52	-13	Circuit 10	875	995	-119
Circuit 2	557	682	-124	Hardee	65	82	-17
Franklin	19	26	-8	Highlands	64	80	-16
Gadsden	108	116	-8	Polk	747	833	-86
Jefferson	15	17	-2	Circuit 11	1,511	1,845	-334
Leon	383	483	-101	Miami-Dade	1,511	1,845	-334
Liberty	5	5	-1	Circuit 12	587	691	-104
Wakulla	28	33	-5	De Soto	32	39	-7
Circuit 3	235	285	-50	Manatee	228	265	-37
Columbia	82	98	-16	Sarasota	327	386	-59
Dixie	16	22	-6	Circuit 13	1,373	1,531	-158
Hamilton	27	27	0	Hillsborough	1,373	1,531	-158
Lafayette	7	8	-1	Circuit 14	524	645	-121
Madison	10	12	-3	Bay	392	478	-86
Suwannee	62	78	-16	Calhoun	7	9	-1
Taylor	33	40	-7	Gulf	22	26	-4
Circuit 4	1,474	1,737	-264	Holmes	41	50	-9
Clay	172	193	-21	Jackson	43	57	-14
Duval	1,214	1,438	-224	Washington	20	26	-6
Nassau	88	106	-19	Circuit 15	712	878	-166
Circuit 5	640	863	-223	Palm Beach	712	878	-166
Citrus	84	129	-45	Circuit 16	224	282	-58
Hernando	91	115	-24	Monroe	224	282	-58
Lake	153	187	-34	Circuit 17	1,333	1,504	-171
Marion	280	387	-107	Broward	1,333	1,504	-171
Sumter	32	45	-13	Circuit 18	1,054	1,210	-156
Circuit 6	1,294	1,656	-362	Brevard	592	687	-96
Pasco	243	287	-44	Seminole	463	523	-60
Pinellas	1,051	1,369	-318	Circuit 19	582	699	-117
Circuit 7	707	898	-191	Indian River	144	173	-29
Flagler	47	61	-14	Martin	184	222	-39
Putnam	58	82	-24	Okeechobee	48	59	-10
St. Johns	118	168	-49	St. Lucie	206	245	-39
Volusia	485	588	-103	Circuit 20	941	1,150	-209
Circuit 8	213	262	-50	Charlotte	123	141	-18
Alachua	145	177	-32	Collier	330	389	-59
Baker	20	22	-2	Glades	24	28	-4
Bradford	17	20	-3	Hendry	55	68	-13
Gilchrist	11	13	-2	Lee	409	524	-115

1/ Mandatory court cost is $50 per conviction of which the court clerk retains $1.
2/ Includes surcharges, offense, interest, restitution, subrogation, refunds, and other receipts.

Source: State of Florida, Office of the Attorney General, Division of Victim Services, *Annual Report, 1998-1999.*

Table 22.31. VICTIM SERVICES: VICTIM COMPENSATION AWARDS AND AMOUNT
OF BENEFITS PAID IN THE STATE, JUDICIAL CIRCUITS, AND COUNTIES
OF FLORIDA, FISCAL YEAR 1998-99

Judicial circuit and county	Number of awards	Benefits awarded (dollars)	Judicial circuit and county	Number of awards	Benefits awarded (dollars)
Florida	7,684	16,574,564	Circuit 8 (Continued)		
			Levy	36	30,537
Circuit 1	252	548,786	Union	8	9,910
Escambia	99	225,369	Circuit 9	385	714,079
Okaloosa	90	193,990	Orange	331	634,564
Santa Rosa	49	85,386	Osceola	54	79,515
Walton	14	44,041	Circuit 10	303	655,705
Circuit 2	131	287,609	Hardee	8	10,876
Franklin	11	8,151	Highlands	29	129,918
Gadsden	25	66,648	Polk	266	514,911
Jefferson	7	16,676	Circuit 11	889	2,795,337
Leon	68	153,477	Miami-Dade	889	2,795,337
Liberty	5	7,544	Circuit 12	250	641,832
Wakulla	15	35,113	De Soto	4	13,016
Circuit 3	127	234,657	Manatee	140	373,254
Columbia	55	71,033	Sarasota	106	255,562
Dixie	7	16,932	Circuit 13	484	1,364,319
Hamilton	11	39,830	Hillsborough	484	1,364,319
Lafayette	6	2,493	Circuit 14	203	439,527
Madison	11	14,418	Bay	121	314,801
Suwannee	27	76,846	Calhoun	3	11,051
Taylor	10	13,105	Gulf	5	15,089
Circuit 4	951	1,761,020	Holmes	15	7,848
Clay	84	151,853	Jackson	43	64,014
Duval	849	1,581,590	Washington	16	26,724
Nassau	18	27,577	Circuit 15	467	1,033,745
Circuit 5	297	413,530	Palm Beach	467	1,033,745
Citrus	52	74,481	Circuit 16	64	135,350
Hernando	24	45,118	Monroe	64	135,350
Lake	44	57,867	Circuit 17	465	1,006,384
Marion	160	227,193	Broward	465	1,006,384
Sumter	17	8,871	Circuit 18	374	622,593
Circuit 6	630	1,501,803	Brevard	238	439,235
Pasco	102	179,250	Seminole	136	183,358
Pinellas	528	1,322,553	Circuit 19	428	615,184
Circuit 7	337	658,711	Indian River	187	171,310
Flagler	21	53,914	Martin	55	78,344
Putnam	56	75,731	Okeechobee	31	60,316
St. Johns	96	119,881	St. Lucie	155	305,214
Volusia	164	409,185	Circuit 20	330	740,158
Circuit 8	317	404,235	Charlotte	23	65,146
Alachua	229	307,137	Collier	140	280,930
Baker	7	22,295	Glades	5	12,844
Bradford	22	24,342	Hendry	10	11,586
Gilchrist	15	10,014	Lee	152	369,652

Note: Victim compensation claims are processed for financial assistance to crime victims for lost income (lost wages, disability, and loss of support), funeral expenses, and reimbursement of other out-of-pocket and treatment expenses directly related to a crime injury.

Source: State of Florida, Office of the Attorney General, Division of Victim Services, *Annual Report, 1998-1999.*

Table 22.50. HATE CRIMES: HATE-MOTIVATED CRIMES BY TYPE OF OFFENSE AND BY MOTIVATION IN FLORIDA, 1993 THROUGH 1998

Offense and motivation	1993	1994	1995	1996	1997	1998
Offenses, total	313	283	183	212	160	203
Crimes against persons	238	206	119	148	117	125
Percentage of total	76.0	72.8	65.0	69.8	73.1	61.6
Assaults	175	153	91	105	84	88
Percentage of total	55.9	54.1	49.7	49.5	52.5	43.3
Motivation						
Race/color	227	198	128	156	113	127
Percentage of total	72.5	70.0	69.9	73.6	70.6	62.6
Religion	31	29	23	26	18	27
Percentage of total	9.9	10.2	12.6	12.3	11.3	13.3
Ethnicity	29	28	17	24	7	21
Percentage of total	9.3	9.9	9.3	11.3	4.4	10.3
Sexual orientation	26	28	15	6	22	28
Percentage of total	8.3	9.9	8.2	2.8	13.8	13.8

Note: A hate crime is an act committed or attempted by one person or group against another person or group, or their property, that in any way constitutes an expression of hatred toward the victim based on his or her personal characteristics. It is a crime in which the perpetrator intentionally selects the victim based on one of the following characteristics: race, color, religion, ethnicity, ancestry, national origin, or sexual orientation.

Source: State of Florida, Office of the Attorney General, *Hate Crimes in Florida, January 1, 1998 through December 31, 1998,* Internet site <http://legal.firn.edu/justice/> (accessed 15 August 2000).

Table 22.51. LAWYERS: NUMBER AND MEMBERS IN GOOD STANDING OF THE FLORIDA BAR BY SECTION IN FLORIDA, JULY 1, 2000

Section	Number of members	Section	Number of members
Members in good standing, total	61,014	Members in sections (Continued)	
Florida	49,531	Administrative	1,028
Out-of-state	11,315	Practice, management, and	
Foreign	168	technology	892
		Labor and employment	1,992
Members in sections, total	26,347	International	860
Tax	1,934	Entertainment, arts, and	
Real property, probate	7,559	sports	784
Trial	6,385	Health	1,232
Business	4,089	Public interest	310
General	1,827	Governmental	946
Family	3,172	Elder	1,516
Local government	1,297	Out-of-state	1,199
Workers' compensation	1,628	Appellate practice	1,099
Criminal	2,192	Equal opportunites law	110
Environmental and land use	1,746		

Source: The Florida Bar, release from the Records Department, July 1, 2000.

University of Florida   **Bureau of Economic and Business Research**

Table 22.52. LAWYERS: MEMBERS IN GOOD STANDING OF THE FLORIDA BAR IN THE STATE
AND COUNTIES OF FLORIDA, JULY 1, 2000

County	Number of members	County	Number of members
Total	61,014	Lafayette	2
Out-of-state	11,315	Lake	234
Foreign	168	Lee	837
Alachua	742	Leon	2,627
Baker	10	Levy	33
Bay	233	Liberty	2
Bradford	23	Madison	12
Brevard	792	Manatee	426
Broward	6,377	Marion	389
Calhoun	4	Martin	378
Charlotte	148	Miami-Dade	11,266
Citrus	94	Monroe	263
Clay	115	Nassau	43
Collier	722	Okaloosa	243
Columbia	79	Okeechobee	28
De Soto	24	Orange	3,731
Dixie	5	Osceola	123
Duval	2,384	Palm Beach	4,742
Escambia	651	Pasco	290
Flagler	42	Pinellas	2,607
Franklin	16	Polk	710
Gadsden	47	Putnam	76
Gilchrist	9	St. Johns	225
Glades	2	St. Lucie	266
Gulf	11	Santa Rosa	74
Hamilton	9	Sarasota	1,034
Hardee	11	Seminole	584
Hendry	23	Sumter	21
Hernando	106	Suwannee	37
Highlands	72	Taylor	18
Hillsborough	4,233	Union	3
Holmes	9	Volusia	832
Indian River	247	Wakulla	26
Jackson	30	Walton	41
Jefferson	22	Washington	12

Source: The Florida Bar, release from the Records Department, July 1, 2000.

Table 22.55. LEGAL SERVICES: AVERAGE MONTHLY PRIVATE REPORTING UNITS, EMPLOYMENT
AND PAYROLL COVERED BY UNEMPLOYMENT COMPENSATION LAW
IN THE STATE AND COUNTIES OF FLORIDA, 1999

County	Number of reporting units	Number of employees	Payroll ($1,000)	County	Number of reporting units	Number of employees	Payroll ($1,000)
			Legal services (SIC code 81)				
Florida	12,925	67,538	319,471	Lee	248	1,307	4,722
				Leon	335	2,389	12,296
Alachua	165	833	2,749	Levy	9	15	29
Baker	4	12	22	Madison	4	14	40
Bay	76	352	1,175	Manatee	116	597	2,153
Bradford	7	21	42	Marion	128	555	1,809
Brevard	256	1,008	3,961	Martin	97	597	2,255
Broward	1,762	7,615	34,646	Miami-Dade	3,032	15,629	84,382
Charlotte	45	249	1,009	Monroe	78	212	643
Citrus	33	156	429	Nassau	15	47	131
Clay	36	135	353	Okaloosa	101	364	1,055
Collier	211	1,032	4,498	Okeechobee	7	34	66
Columbia	23	93	299	Orange	822	6,369	31,361
De Soto	8	23	70	Osceola	39	101	241
Duval	546	3,660	18,779	Palm Beach	1,280	6,376	32,770
Escambia	184	1,178	5,454	Pasco	114	488	1,525
Flagler	12	40	117	Pinellas	724	3,188	12,515
Franklin	5	9	12	Polk	198	1,157	4,610
Gadsden	14	31	75	Putnam	23	72	170
Gulf	6	19	46	St. Johns	49	157	486
Hardee	6	18	31	St. Lucie	77	305	1,088
Hendry	8	19	43	Santa Rosa	18	103	334
Hernando	31	97	220	Sarasota	335	1,634	7,320
Highlands	31	140	349	Seminole	173	496	1,592
Hillsborough	868	6,417	33,516	Sumter	10	18	31
Holmes	4	10	12	Suwannee	10	28	65
Indian River	76	341	1,598	Volusia	260	1,065	3,659
Jackson	10	28	53	Walton	11	29	39
Jefferson	6	10	28				
Lake	97	413	1,322	Multicounty 1/	70	159	987

1/ Reporting units without a fixed location within the state or of unknown county location.
Note: Private employment. These data include establishments which are engaged in offering legal
advice or services and which are headed by a member of the Bar. Data are preliminary. Only counties
for which data are disclosed are shown. Detail may not add to totals due to disclosure editing and/or
rounding. See Tables 23.70, 23.71, 23.72, 23.73, and 23.74 for public employment data.

Source: State of Florida, Department of Labor and Employment Security, Bureau of Labor Market Information, "Employment and Wages" (ES-202), unpublished data.

University of Florida   **Bureau of Economic and Business Research**

GOVERNMENT FINANCE AND EMPLOYMENT

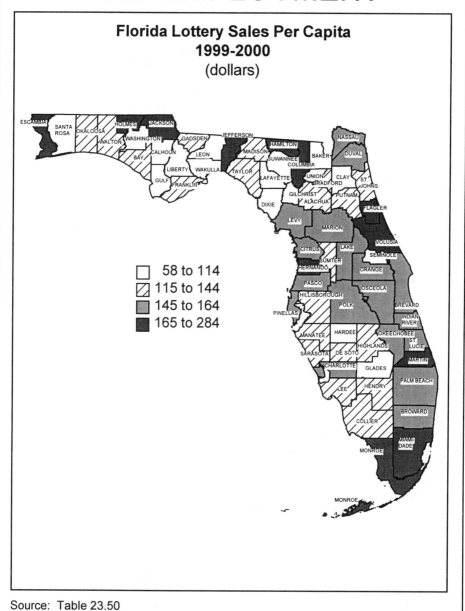

Florida Lottery Sales Per Capita
1999-2000
(dollars)

Legend:
- 58 to 114
- 115 to 144
- 145 to 164
- 165 to 284

Source: Table 23.50

TABLES LISTED BY MAJOR HEADINGS

TABLES LISTED BY MAJOR HEADINGS

HEADING

PAGE

University of Florida   **Bureau of Economic and Business Research**

Table 23.07. FEDERAL GOVERNMENT FINANCE: EXPENDITURE BY AGENCY AND BY SPECIFIED PROGRAM IN FLORIDA AND THE UNITED STATES, FISCAL YEAR 1998-99

(in thousands of dollars)

Item	Florida	United States
Total expenditure	64,671,311	1,191,549,212
Grants and other payments to state and local governments, total	10,810,960	274,448,288
Department of Agriculture	869,936	18,717,928
Agricultural Marketing Service	16,660	463,360
Cooperative State Research Service--Education and Extension Service	12,705	538,063
Extension activities	9,660	398,553
Research and education activities	3,045	139,510
Farm Service Agency	72	2,053
Food and safety inspection service	0	37,345
Food and nutrition service	792,249	16,298,836
Child nutrition programs	477,794	8,680,080
Commodity assistance program	5,126	137,156
Food stamp program	113,851	3,392,390
Needy families	6,582	145,124
Special supplemental food program (WIC)	188,896	3,944,086
Forest Service	3,056	342,209
Payments to states and counties	1,440	270,178
State and private forestry	1,616	67,012
Natural Resources Conservation Service	719	51,299
Rural development activities	44,475	984,763
Water systems and waste disposal systems grants	12,096	379,368
Rental assistance payments	21,885	532,912
Department of Commerce	28,792	756,979
Economic Development Administration	8,393	368,114
National Oceanic and Atmospheric Administration	19,396	359,345
National Telecommunications and Information Administration	1,003	27,942
Corporation for Public Broadcasting	9,848	250,468
Department of Defense 1/	162	159,370
Department of Education	1,021,054	22,767,588
Office of Bilingual Education and Minority Language Affairs	28,913	305,640
Office of Educational Research and Improvement	6,728	300,325
Office of Special Education and Rehabilitative Services	402,852	7,416,657
Office of Vocational and Adult Education	68,150	1,433,218
Office of Elementary and Secondary Education	434,601	10,912,433
Office of Postsecondary Education	79,810	2,399,315
Department of Energy	2,564	181,488
Environmental Protection Agency	95,128	3,223,430
Equal Employment Opportunity Commission	893	29,849
Federal Emergency Management Agency	168,941	2,693,233
Disaster relief	163,526	2,421,796
Department of Health and Human Services	5,825,280	148,566,374
Administration for Children and Families	1,382,578	32,703,418
Child care and development	134,563	3,172,096
Child support enforcement	105,393	1,887,275
Children and family services (headstart)	211,080	5,491,812
Family preservation and support	11,937	245,713

See footnotes at end of table.   Continued . . .

University of Florida   **Bureau of Economic and Business Research**

Table 23.07. FEDERAL GOVERNMENT FINANCE: EXPENDITURE BY AGENCY AND BY SPECIFIED PROGRAM IN FLORIDA AND THE UNITED STATES, FISCAL YEAR 1998-99 (Continued)

(in thousands of dollars)

Item	Florida	United States
Grants to state and local governments (Continued)		
Department of Health and Human Services (Continued)		
Administration for Children and Families (Continued)		
Foster care and adoption assistance	156,869	4,706,375
Low-income home energy assistance	35,152	1,175,190
Refugee and entrant assistance	38,766	296,417
Social services block grant	105,037	1,992,710
Temporary assistance to needy families (TANF)	577,153	13,653,356
Other	6,628	82,474
Administration on Aging	53,132	863,608
Center for Disease Control and Prevention	14,674	491,891
Health Care Financing Administration (Medicaid)	4,024,883	108,569,022
Health Resources and Services Administration	259,722	3,835,386
Indian Health Service	673	77,781
Substance Abuse and Mental Health Administration	89,618	2,025,268
Department of Housing and Urban Development	1,054,629	30,348,022
Fair housing and equal opportunity	1,627	30,950
Community development and planning	207,421	5,568,964
Housing programs	845,581	24,748,108
Public housing programs	746,081	21,795,578
Home ownership assistance	52,456	1,367,705
Institute for Museum and Library Services	6,858	151,553
Department of Interior	18,972	2,599,114
National Park Service	822	39,350
Department of Justice	296,751	4,871,264
Department of Labor	265,255	7,308,688
Bureau of Labor Statistics	2,983	71,863
Employment and Training Administration	260,507	7,115,713
Older American programs	66	97,478
State unemployment insurance and employment service operations	111,523	3,315,060
Workforce Investment Act	145,087	3,436,091
Welfare to work program	3,831	267,084
National Foundation on the Arts and the Humanities	773	29,910
Neighborhood Reinvestment Corporation	1,982	63,650
Social Security Administration supplemental security income	3,014	51,218
State Justice Institute	38	6,896
Department of Transportation	1,085,345	29,522,568
Federal Aviation Administration	73,034	1,564,911
Federal Highway Administration	787,467	23,103,338
Federal Transit Administration	211,601	4,569,247
Department of the Treasury	42,454	208,163
Department of Veterans Affairs	12,291	432,453
Expenditure for salaries and wages	7,834,920	177,278,501
Department of Defense	3,421,695	70,412,959
Military	2,261,363	42,035,098
Active	2,088,587	37,216,740
Inactive	172,776	4,818,358
Civilian	1,160,332	28,377,861
Army	268,059	22,640,471
Navy	1,875,022	25,696,372
Air Force	1,203,656	17,787,992

See footnotes at end of table.   Continued . . .

Table 23.07. FEDERAL GOVERNMENT FINANCE: EXPENDITURE BY AGENCY AND BY SPECIFIED
PROGRAM IN FLORIDA AND THE UNITED STATES, FISCAL YEAR 1998-99 (Continued)

(in thousands of dollars)

Item	Florida	United States
Expenditure for salaries and wages (Continued)		
Department of Defense (Continued)		
Other defense civilian	74,958	4,288,124
Nondefense agencies	4,413,225	106,865,542
Agriculture	80,115	4,373,958
Commerce	44,721	2,233,634
Education	350	283,591
Energy	84	1,103,384
Environmental Protection Agency	5,125	1,153,870
Federal Deposit Insurance Corporation	4,709	526,998
Federal Emergency Management Agency	5,749	261,557
General Services Administration	5,386	765,997
Health and Human Services	11,669	3,388,723
Housing and Urban Development	14,438	595,904
Interior	53,348	3,093,755
Justice	341,155	6,649,039
Labor	19,284	886,412
National Aeronautics and Space Administration	115,048	1,256,652
Postal Service	2,418,911	47,322,049
Small Business Administration	5,375	254,358
Social Security Administration	102,442	3,080,252
State Department	8,319	575,450
Transportation	338,375	5,448,261
Treasury	268,003	7,272,658
Veterans affairs	542,674	9,500,302
Other nondefense	27,945	6,658,080
Direct payments for individuals for retirement and disability	37,386,160	523,449,666
Retirement and disability retirement insurance payments	76,651,743	1,060,434,399
Social Security payments	28,857,201	415,194,346
Retirement insurance payments	19,325,795	254,592,577
Survivors insurance payments	4,719,681	77,843,099
Disability insurance payments	3,155,354	54,426,651
Supplemental security income payments	1,656,371	28,332,019
Federal retirement and disability benefits	6,279,964	75,664,343
Civilian	2,997,966	44,585,606
Military	3,281,998	31,078,737
Veterans benefits	1,548,800	21,000,323
Payments for service connected disability	1,124,345	14,607,085
Other benefit payments	424,455	6,393,238
Other	700,195	11,590,654
Other than for retirement and disability	22,163,650	328,336,332
Medicare	17,101,933	208,648,401
Hospital insurance payments	9,806,635	129,827,775
Supplementary medical insurance payments	7,295,298	78,820,626
Excess earned income tax credits	1,734,247	26,319,231
Unemployment compensation	631,262	19,430,578
Food stamp payments	820,235	15,877,668
Housing assistance	414,211	9,868,985
Agricultural assistance	103,927	21,314,938
Federal employees life and health insurance	523,804	11,766,927
Other	834,030	15,109,604

See footnotes at end of table.   Continued . . .

Table 23.07. FEDERAL GOVERNMENT FINANCE: EXPENDITURE BY AGENCY AND BY SPECIFIED PROGRAM IN FLORIDA AND THE UNITED STATES, FISCAL YEAR 1998-99 (Continued)

(in thousands of dollars)

Item	Florida	United States
Procurement contracts	8,639,271	216,372,757
Department of Defense	6,764,215	133,775,555
Army	1,244,707	30,787,689
Navy	1,768,430	37,554,681
Air Force	3,364,568	35,451,238
Army Corps of Engineers	97,137	2,971,972
Other defense	289,373	27,009,975
Nondefense agencies	1,875,056	82,597,202
Agriculture	15,668	3,154,433
Commerce	7,421	1,091,654
Education	599	693,404
Energy	3,867	15,585,954
Environmental Protection Agency	1,220	1,066,198
Federal Emergency Management Agency	489	288,271
General Services Administration	193,295	6,915,309
Health and Human Services	56,730	4,148,427
Housing and Urban Development	4,717	773,354
Interior	10,998	1,074,600
Justice	66,247	3,180,099
Labor	46,454	1,090,588
National Aeronautics and Space Administration	550,215	10,937,050
Postal Service 2/	680,865	13,320,013
Small Business Administration	113	37,654
Social Security Administration	3,027	458,480
State Department	4,208	945,417
Transportation	53,189	2,697,051
Treasury	13,622	3,280,480
Veterans Affairs	110,830	2,575,378
Other nondefense	51,241	9,049,467

1/ Includes salaries, wages, and compensation, such as housing allowances; distribution based on duty station.
2/ Actual outlays for contractual commitments. Figures do not reflect federal government expenditures.
Note: Expenditures classified as "other" may not be specified in the table and are contained in the totals for major expenditure categories.

Source: U.S., Department of Commerce, Bureau of the Census, *Federal Aid to States for Fiscal Year 1999,* issued April 2000, Internet site http://www.census.gov/prod/2000pubs/fas-99.pdf> and *Consolidated Federal Funds Report for Fiscal Year 1999, State and County Areas*, issued April 2000, Internet site <http://www.census.gov/prod/2000pubs/cffr-99.pdf> (accessed 24 May 2000).

Table 23.08. FEDERAL GOVERNMENT FINANCE: DIRECT EXPENDITURE BY TYPE IN THE UNITED STATES AND IN THE STATE AND COUNTIES OF FLORIDA, FISCAL YEAR 1998-99

(in thousands of dollars, except where indicated)

County	Total	Procure-ment	Grants	Wages and salaries	Retirement and disability	Other direct payments
United States 1/	1,539,906	216,373	294,469	177,279	523,450	328,336
Florida	87,214,874	8,639,271	11,190,873	7,834,920	37,386,160	22,163,650
Alachua	1,038,641	55,681	277,534	143,473	371,529	190,424
Baker	73,438	564	15,044	2,479	40,164	15,188
Bay	1,211,349	155,954	66,688	277,623	440,567	270,518
Bradford	96,285	758	15,273	7,029	48,700	24,525
Brevard	4,132,023	1,616,403	128,358	333,092	1,555,335	498,835
Broward	6,375,792	191,211	476,627	386,597	3,115,868	2,205,489
Calhoun	56,465	350	16,265	1,111	24,356	14,383
Charlotte	776,706	5,539	21,962	13,497	512,018	223,691
Citrus	635,779	3,038	23,198	10,429	419,748	179,366
Clay	467,288	8,058	21,957	18,161	344,851	74,260
Collier	893,240	9,181	76,360	30,426	559,620	217,653
Columbia	272,377	6,507	40,676	41,452	131,018	52,724
De Soto	118,144	640	17,451	2,970	57,907	39,176
Dixie	67,072	199	7,672	962	44,616	13,624
Duval	4,901,471	656,836	483,877	1,415,335	1,575,947	769,476
Escambia	2,189,962	171,364	210,496	655,062	867,237	285,803
Flagler	246,390	5,690	9,071	5,413	180,621	45,595
Franklin	50,977	339	8,013	1,217	25,167	16,242
Gadsden	215,177	3,122	71,994	5,986	85,390	48,686
Gilchrist	45,691	313	5,143	1,151	27,551	11,534
Glades	27,997	957	3,227	461	17,451	5,900
Gulf	74,958	199	17,713	758	36,150	20,138
Hamilton	52,437	412	14,026	1,510	24,840	11,649
Hardee	84,914	625	17,960	2,732	39,996	23,601
Hendry	105,729	1,562	24,501	4,174	46,429	29,063
Hernando	845,309	4,887	45,894	15,591	545,386	233,551
Highlands	504,961	4,954	34,857	13,044	308,217	143,890
Hillsborough	4,436,270	308,130	629,756	684,823	1,919,819	893,742
Holmes	104,778	1,611	28,408	2,884	47,387	24,488
Indian River	645,923	12,943	34,743	18,396	395,380	184,460
Jackson	264,522	2,494	71,236	27,906	103,909	58,977
Jefferson	80,157	474	37,895	1,498	26,088	14,202
Lafayette	22,123	2,637	4,830	711	8,906	5,040
Lake	1,145,827	13,902	64,490	25,506	758,850	283,079

See footnote at end of table.   Continued . . .

Table 23.08. FEDERAL GOVERNMENT FINANCE: DIRECT EXPENDITURE BY TYPE IN THE UNITED STATES AND IN THE STATE AND COUNTIES OF FLORIDA, FISCAL YEAR 1998-99 (Continued)

(in thousands of dollars, except where indicated)

County	Total	Procure-ment	Grants	Wages and salaries	Retirement and disability	Other direct payments
Lee	2,031,570	29,328	113,339	96,010	1,258,253	534,641
Leon	2,974,313	46,998	2,221,074	90,940	426,659	188,641
Levy	148,257	1,076	18,353	4,154	87,641	37,033
Liberty	30,496	608	12,191	1,590	11,175	4,932
Madison	97,260	512	36,129	2,193	38,426	20,001
Manatee	1,143,744	25,583	66,433	56,927	691,403	303,397
Marion	1,325,660	48,719	127,733	33,904	811,324	303,980
Martin	658,345	18,950	28,209	14,526	418,484	178,177
Miami-Dade	10,358,747	316,103	2,645,851	1,017,933	3,277,012	3,101,848
Monroe	480,607	68,473	30,494	92,697	169,849	119,094
Nassau	244,415	8,389	20,622	52,842	124,624	37,938
Okaloosa	1,764,352	457,478	60,470	480,381	642,827	123,196
Okeechobee	162,002	2,360	17,614	3,739	85,525	52,765
Orange	4,791,665	1,760,587	418,334	376,109	1,535,397	701,238
Osceola	480,509	10,353	53,803	14,296	267,771	134,286
Palm Beach	6,887,817	1,617,578	445,118	290,344	2,907,877	1,626,900
Pasco	1,695,485	11,595	118,347	36,967	950,162	578,415
Pinellas	5,493,874	638,588	294,658	323,849	2,752,409	1,484,370
Polk	1,983,002	37,225	267,474	72,497	1,149,310	456,496
Putnam	346,952	1,861	69,234	7,044	179,556	89,255
St. Johns	559,019	71,062	58,276	22,635	300,540	106,505
St. Lucie	945,134	14,047	70,716	26,447	583,091	250,834
Santa Rosa	560,760	42,663	71,748	58,497	309,164	78,687
Sarasota	1,986,038	19,810	81,324	46,721	1,272,971	565,212
Seminole	1,087,284	39,309	113,583	80,522	621,295	232,575
Sumter	242,335	9,889	19,509	41,735	119,284	51,918
Suwannee	163,726	1,330	23,543	6,372	92,252	40,229
Taylor	107,915	23,659	17,047	1,874	42,763	22,571
Union	32,966	517	7,815	959	15,981	7,694
Volusia	2,169,555	63,709	198,540	69,181	1,279,953	558,173
Wakulla	64,925	1,264	9,083	3,186	36,597	14,795
Walton	396,454	1,642	16,972	251,992	93,086	32,762
Washington	114,329	469	33,229	2,397	51,468	26,766
Undistributed	3,425,184	0	380,813	0	75,014	2,969,357

1/ Rounded to millions of dollars.

Source: U.S., Department of Commerce, Bureau of the Census, *Consolidated Federal Funds Report for Fiscal Year 1999, State and County Areas,* issued April 2000, Internet site <http://www.census.gov/prod/2000pubs/cffr-99.pdf> (accessed 24 May 2000).

University of Florida   **Bureau of Economic and Business Research**

Table 23.15. DEFENSE CONTRACTS: AWARDS AND PAYROLL IN FLORIDA, OTHER SUNBELT STATES, OTHER POPULOUS STATES, AND THE UNITED STATES, SPECIFIED FISCAL YEARS ENDING SEPTEMBER 30, 1996 THROUGH 1998

(in millions of dollars)

State	Contract awards 1/			Payroll 2/		
	1995-96	1996-97	1997-98	1995-96	1996-97	1997-98
Florida	5,863	6,394	5,464	6,670	6,910	6,716
Alabama	1,838	2,107	2,202	2,183	2,150	2,450
Arizona	2,911	1,977	3,003	1,865	1,919	1,842
Arkansas	249	191	217	730	764	721
California	18,230	18,477	17,401	12,332	12,396	11,479
Georgia	3,966	3,950	3,690	4,332	4,090	4,585
Louisiana	1,078	1,759	1,241	1,333	1,283	1,198
Mississippi	1,912	1,431	1,352	1,301	1,277	1,214
New Mexico	676	512	833	1,168	1,129	1,074
North Carolina	1,421	1,110	1,004	4,259	4,062	4,078
Oklahoma	771	751	921	2,172	2,085	2,190
South Carolina	1,012	919	969	2,263	2,127	2,267
Tennessee	1,137	1,211	1,216	1,072	924	1,050
Texas	8,819	7,411	7,980	8,383	8,070	8,343
Virginia	9,563	11,188	12,871	11,356	10,544	10,441
Illinois	1,256	1,248	1,285	1,988	2,073	2,059
Indiana	1,552	1,721	1,649	1,022	867	775
Massachusetts	4,675	4,910	4,245	843	866	816
Michigan	1,241	1,101	1,065	764	805	812
New Jersey	2,564	3,016	2,661	1,419	1,589	1,451
New York	3,501	3,178	3,062	1,688	1,675	1,703
Ohio	2,733	2,676	2,472	2,337	2,256	2,131
Pennsylvania	3,687	3,039	3,318	2,218	2,213	2,146
United States	109,408	106,561	109,385	99,794	97,296	97,378

1/ State data include net value of contracts over $25,000 for military awards for supplies, services, and construction.
2/ Data are estimates and cover active duty military and direct hire civilian personnel, including Army Corps of Engineers.
Note: Data refer to awards in year specified and to state in which prime contractor is located. Expenditure may extend over several years and work may be performed by a subcontractor in another state.

Source: U.S., Department of Commerce, Bureau of the Census, *Statistical Abstract of the United States, 2000,* and previous editions.

Table 23.20. VETERANS' ADMINISTRATION: VETERAN POPULATION AND VETERANS' ADMINISTRATION (VA) EXPENDITURE BY PROGRAM IN THE STATE AND COUNTIES OF FLORIDA, FISCAL YEAR 1998-99

County	Veteran population	Total	Compensation and pension	Readjustment and vocational rehabilitation	Insurance and indemnities	Construction medical services and related costs 1/
Florida	1,652,328	2,858,393	1,552,188	102,600	178,762	1,024,844
Alachua	17,928	252,719	21,237	4,084	1,908	225,491
Baker	1,649	5,318	4,679	437	201	0
Bay	18,284	37,775	33,248	2,508	2,020	0
Bradford	3,003	4,242	3,767	150	325	0
Brevard	61,082	88,291	76,811	4,416	7,063	0
Broward	129,448	121,484	101,313	5,067	15,104	0
Calhoun	1,511	1,949	1,719	86	144	0
Charlotte	26,261	24,428	21,469	391	2,567	0
Citrus	23,658	7,476	5,098	160	2,218	0
Clay	16,436	21,176	17,836	1,599	1,741	0
Collier	25,614	10,347	7,621	144	2,583	0
Columbia	5,552	14,282	6,481	142	600	7,060
De Soto	2,930	1,783	1,443	7	333	0
Dixie	1,817	2,874	2,669	16	188	0
Duval	68,501	106,775	85,466	12,781	8,528	0
Escambia	32,621	70,150	58,469	7,027	3,890	764
Flagler	7,032	1,387	718	4	665	0
Franklin	1,310	1,626	1,455	30	141	0
Gadsden	2,658	4,990	4,411	248	331	0
Gilchrist	1,155	2,094	1,888	71	135	0
Glades	1,126	1,202	1,058	13	131	0
Gulf	1,363	2,507	2,249	101	157	0
Hamilton	970	1,967	1,816	47	103	0
Hardee	1,860	2,076	1,838	27	211	0
Hendry	1,881	2,079	1,840	34	204	0
Hernando	26,876	26,201	23,288	485	2,429	0
Highlands	14,905	13,756	12,104	268	1,384	0
Hillsborough	92,140	394,848	110,684	8,559	10,624	264,981
Holmes	1,722	5,132	4,811	116	206	0
Indian River	21,584	15,658	13,323	391	1,944	0
Jackson	4,066	7,372	6,601	292	479	0
Jefferson	1,079	1,952	1,755	71	126	0
Lafayette	606	1,211	1,094	49	68	0
Lake	26,927	23,147	19,523	771	2,853	0

See footnote at end of table.

Continued . . .

University of Florida   **Bureau of Economic and Business Research**

Table 23.20. VETERANS' ADMINISTRATION: VETERAN POPULATION AND VETERANS'
ADMINISTRATION (VA) EXPENDITURE BY PROGRAM IN THE STATE AND COUNTIES
OF FLORIDA, FISCAL YEAR 1998-99 (Continued)

County	Veteran popula- tion	Total	Compensa- tion and pension	Readjust- ment and vocational rehabil- itation	Insur- ance and indem- nities	Construc- tion medi- cal services and related costs 1/
			Expenditure ($1,000)			
Lee	60,881	51,315	43,570	1,610	6,135	0
Leon	20,767	22,287	15,960	4,166	2,161	0
Levy	4,129	5,742	5,130	173	439	0
Liberty	635	1,079	982	26	70	0
Madison	1,391	2,361	2,128	72	161	0
Manatee	35,473	32,948	28,520	807	3,621	0
Marion	32,517	13,388	9,840	93	3,454	0
Martin	22,162	16,304	14,006	263	2,035	0
Miami-Dade	91,759	307,994	82,985	5,368	11,458	208,184
Monroe	13,496	12,673	10,901	340	1,432	0
Nassau	5,089	5,969	5,081	278	611	0
Okaloosa	21,797	60,486	51,705	6,278	2,502	0
Okeechobee	4,073	4,635	4,110	95	429	0
Orange	83,917	98,975	81,335	8,876	8,765	0
Osceola	15,433	3,517	1,921	33	1,562	0
Palm Beach	128,008	208,351	85,676	2,750	12,871	107,054
Pasco	65,896	56,426	48,493	1,938	5,995	0
Pinellas	123,771	347,461	122,941	3,955	13,881	206,683
Polk	52,108	58,953	51,036	2,126	5,791	0
Putnam	9,416	4,455	3,332	82	1,040	0
St. Johns	12,246	11,026	9,203	485	1,338	0
St. Lucie	21,814	25,071	21,807	856	2,408	0
Santa Rosa	11,225	23,474	19,775	2,414	1,285	0
Sarasota	51,433	42,972	36,806	907	5,259	0
Seminole	37,987	75,468	65,931	5,597	3,941	0
Sumter	5,548	19,314	13,696	433	557	4,627
Suwannee	2,887	6,820	6,304	176	340	0
Taylor	1,697	2,545	2,260	82	204	0
Union	1,099	1,314	1,136	44	133	0
Volusia	57,805	36,636	29,391	978	6,266	0
Wakulla	1,659	2,676	2,328	152	196	0
Walton	6,253	10,283	9,302	406	575	0
Washington	2,402	5,202	4,812	151	240	0

1/ Includes administrative.

Source: U.S., Veterans' Administration, Internet site <http://www.va.gov//about_va/history/expend.htm>.

University of Florida   **Bureau of Economic and Business Research**

Table 23.29. STATE GOVERNMENT FINANCE: REVENUE, EXPENDITURE, DIRECT EXPENDITURE INDEBTEDNESS, AND CASH AND SECURITY HOLDINGS IN FLORIDA, 1998

Item	Total ($1,000)	Percentage change 1997 to 1998	Per capita 1/ (dollars)
Revenue, total	51,751,884	24.9	3,470
General revenue	36,780,333	7.3	2,466
Intergovernmental	8,301,851	0.1	557
Taxes	22,521,069	6.8	1,510
General sales	12,923,644	7.1	866
Selective sales	4,004,285	-0.2	268
License taxes	1,451,319	5.9	97
Corporation net income	1,271,261	3.1	85
Other taxes	2,870,560	19.8	192
Current charges	2,079,808	10.4	139
Miscellaneous	3,877,605	28.4	260
Utility	5,343	2.2	0
Insurance trust	14,966,208	109.4	1,003
Expenditure, total	39,214,010	4.7	2,629
Intergovernmental	12,537,431	5.4	841
Direct	26,676,579	4.4	1,788
Current operation	18,993,077	6.6	1,273
Capital outlay	3,325,318	6.0	223
Insurance benefits and repayments	2,482,895	-8.9	166
Assistance and subsidies	836,943	-14.6	56
Interest on debt	1,038,346	14.8	70
Exhibit: salaries and wages	7,014,591	-5.1	470
Expenditure, total	39,214,010	4.7	2,629
General expenditure	36,662,429	5.8	2,458
Intergovernmental	12,537,431	5.4	841
Direct	24,124,998	6.0	1,617
General expenditure by function			
Education	12,594,739	8.6	844
Public welfare	8,159,979	6.1	547
Hospitals	502,081	-8.9	34
Health	1,840,385	-0.5	123
Highways	3,254,239	3.0	218
Police protection	337,665	5.6	23
Correction	1,931,914	4.5	130
Natural resources	1,067,914	-3.2	72
Parks and recreation	133,437	-10.0	9
Governmental administration	1,671,987	8.9	112
Interest on general debt	1,038,346	14.8	70
Other and unallocable	4,129,743	4.7	277
Utility	68,686	-14.5	5
Insurance trust	2,482,895	-8.9	166
Debt at end of fiscal year	16,969,289	5.9	1,138
Cash and security holdings	77,359,658	18.3	5,186

1/ Based on U.S. Bureau of the Census population estimates.

Source: U.S., Department of Commerce, Bureau of the Census, Internet site <http://www.census.gov/ftp/pub/govs/state/09stfl.txt> (accessed 12 June 2000).

University of Florida   **Bureau of Economic and Business Research**

Table 23.31. STATE TREASURER'S REPORT: BALANCE SHEET FOR FISCAL YEAR 1998-99

(in dollars)

Item	Assets
Currency and coins	300,000.00
Unemployment compensation investments 1/	2,152,412,206.76
Deferred compensation assets 2/	1,232,031,851.84
Demand accounts 3/	284,526,689.92
Consolidated revolving account 4/	537,755.43
Total cash, receivables, and other assets	3,669,808,503.95
Certificates of deposit accounts	1,883,825,000.00
State-owned investments	10,063,817,590.06
Total investments held in custody of the Treasurer 5/	11,947,642,590.06
Total assets	15,617,451,094.01

	Liabilities
General revenue fund	1,591,622,950.75
Trust fund 6/	10,790,730,919.85
Working capital fund	550,156,315.40
Budget stabilization fund	786,890,000.00
Total four funds	13,719,400,186.00
Adjustments 7/	35,487,850.38
Due to special purpose investments 8/	629,993,450.36
Due to deferred compensation participants 2/	1,232,031,851.84
Due to consolidated revolving account agency participants 4/	537,755.43
Total liabilities	15,617,451,094.01

1/ Represents U.C. benefit funds invested by the federal government and due from the U.S. Treasury-Unemployment Trust Fund.

2/ All assets are held in the Deferred Compensation Trust Fund for the exclusive benefit of participants and their beneficiaries. Of the plan assets, $99,482,241.97 are Statutory Valuation Reserves.

3/ Represent "Per Reconciled Cash Balance" of $342,678,858.19 as of June 30, 1999 with receipted items in transit of $60,686,869.33 and disbursed items in transit of $2,534,701.06 which nets to $58,152,168.27. These items have cleared the bank but have not been posted to the state ledger. The total bank deposit figure does not include $38,011,591.00 held in clearing and/or revolving accounts outside the Treasury.

4/ The amount due to agency participants in the Consolidated Revolving Account as of June 30, 1999 is $5,098,456.45. Of this amount $537,755.43 is in a financial institution account and $4,560,701.02 is invested in Special Purpose Investment Accounts.

5/ Includes purchased interest in the amount of $1,109,502.39.

6/ Includes $6,194,196,082.66 earning interest for the benefit of trust funds, unemployment trust fund balance of $2,152,412,206.76, and the remaining balance of $2,444,122,630.43 earning interest for general revenue.

7/ Represents a $78,902.57 posting discrepancy within the Comptroller's records and $35,408,947.81 interest not yet receipted to state accounts.

8/ Represents Treasurer's Special Purpose Investment Accounts held in the Treasurer's custody and interest due to those accounts. Treasurer's Special Purpose Investment Accounts are investments on behalf of state agencies with funds outside the Treasurer's Cash Concentration System and other statutorily created entities.

Note: Total market value of all securities held by Treasury $11,842,997,131.18.

Source: State of Florida, *Annual Report of the State Treasurer for the Fiscal Year Ending June 30, 1999.*

Table 23.40. STATE GOVERNMENT FINANCE: REVENUE, EXPENDITURE, AND CHANGE IN FUND BALANCE BY FUND TYPE IN FLORIDA, FISCAL YEAR 1998-99

(in thousands of dollars)

| | | Fund type | | |
| | | Governmental | | |
Item	Total 1/	General	Special revenue	Expendable trust
Beginning fund balance, July 1, 1998	15,215,428	3,314,841	6,129,845	2,735,168
Revenue, total	41,517,724	17,185,824	19,791,326	2,056,423
Taxes 2/	24,045,086	16,775,179	6,248,493	654,222
Licenses and permits	955,328	61,021	831,791	0
Fees and charges	4,021,194	170,229	2,044,432	543,276
Grants and donations	10,314,947	208	9,817,906	120,614
Investment earnings	1,121,716	101,178	224,961	495,953
Fines, forfeits, and judgments	291,115	1,805	181,160	108,125
Flexible benefits contributions	183,745	0	58,630	119,440
Refunds	466,137	76,204	382,486	6,459
Other	118,456	0	1,467	8,334
Expenditure, total	38,435,017	14,925,937	18,782,345	1,288,569
Current				
Expenditures	1,787,291	0	0	0
Economic opportunities, agriculture and employment	1,871,259	58,255	963,523	849,481
Public safety	2,525,988	1,984,975	517,643	23,370
Education	9,403,180	6,575,047	2,738,619	89,514
Health and social concerns	12,796,494	4,230,621	8,565,639	234
Housing and community development	190,336	7,020	183,316	0
Natural resources and environmental management	596,885	182,273	414,612	0
Recreational and cultural opportunities	152,182	61,834	90,348	0
Transportation	795,059	113	794,196	750
Government direction and support services	4,699,368	1,746,118	2,598,898	324,706
Capital outlay	2,545,395	76,469	1,912,548	396
Debt service				
Principle retirement	410,314	2,699	2,477	0
Interest and fiscal charges	661,266	513	526	118
Excess (deficiency) of revenue over expenditure	3,082,707	2,259,887	1,008,981	767,854
Other financing sources (uses)	-770,175	-2,074,574	-133,750	-12,973
Excess (deficiency) of revenue and other financing sources over expenditure and other financing uses	2,312,532	185,313	875,231	754,881
Change in reserve for inventories	14,827	8,509	6,318	0
Ending Fund Balance, June 30, 1999	18,754,864	3,527,548	6,878,464	4,832,880

1/ Total presented only to facilitate financial analyses. Includes fund types and account groups that use differing bases of accounting, restricted and unrestricted amounts, and interfund transactions which have not been eliminated. Excludes community water management districts, community college and university direct-support organizations, transportation/expressway authorities, and other component units.
2/ Florida levies neither a personal income tax nor an ad valorem tax on real or tangible personal property. Taxes are, however, the principal means of financing state operations.

Source: State of Florida, Office of the Comptroller, *Florida Comprehensive Financial Report*, Fiscal Year Ended June 30, 1999, Internet site <http://www.dbf.state.fl.us/cafr99html/opercd-gv.html> (accessed 14 April 2000).

University of Florida   **Bureau of Economic and Business Research**

Table 23.41. STATE GOVERNMENT FINANCE: TAX COLLECTIONS BY TYPE OF TAX COLLECTED IN FLORIDA AND THE UNITED STATES, FISCAL YEAR 1997-98

| Type of tax | Florida | | United States 1/ | |
	Amount ($1,000)	Per capita 2/ (dollars)	Amount ($1,000)	Per capita 2/ (dollars)
Total	22,513,115	1,509.33	474,990,564	1,760.69
Property	984,694	66.02	10,661,670	39.52
Sales and gross receipts	16,927,461	1,134.85	227,404,841	842.94
General sales	12,923,644	866.43	156,061,702	578.49
Selective sales	4,003,817	268.42	71,343,139	264.45
Alcoholic beverage	565,188	37.89	3,767,473	13.97
Amusement	(X)	(X)	2,130,240	7.90
Insurance premium	376,212	25.22	9,150,229	33.92
Motor fuels	1,496,717	100.34	28,330,413	105.01
Pari-mutuels	60,061	4.03	405,298	1.50
Public utilities	634,213	42.52	8,792,973	32.59
Tobacco products	467,050	31.31	7,746,662	28.72
Other	404,376	27.11	11,019,851	40.85
License	1,443,838	96.80	29,682,659	110.03
Alcoholic beverages	29,917	2.01	302,257	1.12
Amusement	8,742	0.59	299,858	1.11
Corporation	120,796	8.10	6,127,611	22.71
Hunting and fishing	13,899	0.93	1,037,831	3.85
Motor vehicle	832,095	55.79	13,672,480	50.68
Motor vehicle operators	111,057	7.45	1,260,931	4.67
Public utility	28,130	1.89	358,560	1.33
Occupation and business	289,627	19.42	6,179,621	22.91
Other	9,575	0.64	443,510	1.64
Other taxes	3,157,122	211.66	207,241,394	768.20
Individual income	(X)	(X)	161,249,928	597.72
Corporation net income	1,271,261	85.23	31,108,628	115.31
Death and gift	577,530	38.72	6,940,007	25.73
Documentary and stock transfer	1,238,609	83.04	3,544,117	13.14
Severance	69,722	4.67	4,158,897	15.42
Other, NEC	(X)	(X)	239,817	0.89

NEC Not elsewhere classified.
(X) Not applicable.
1/ Excludes the District of Columbia and territories.
2/ Per capita amounts are based on a Bureau of the Census estimate of 14,916,000 in Florida and 269,775,000 in the United States.

Source: U.S., Department of Commerce, Bureau of the Census, Internet site <http://www.census.gov/govs/statetax/98tax.txt> (accessed 17 August 2000).

University of Florida　　　　　　　　　　　　**Bureau of Economic and Business Research**

Table 23.43. STATE GOVERNMENT FINANCE: SALES AND USE TAX COLLECTIONS BY TRADE CLASSIFICATION IN FLORIDA, FISCAL YEARS 1997-98 AND 1998-99

(amounts rounded to thousands of dollars)

Group	1997-98	1998-99	Per-centage change
All classifications, total	12,944,937	13,858,158	7.1
Food and beverage group	1,728,074	1,832,820	6.1
Grocery stores	565,546	609,140	7.7
Meat markets	1,391	1,360	-2.2
Seafood dealers	1,033	1,126	9.0
Vegetables and fruit markets	3,298	3,300	0.1
Bakeries	6,807	7,444	9.3
Delicatessens	9,091	13,494	48.4
Candy, confectionery, concession stands	27,802	27,858	0.2
Restaurants, lunchrooms, catering services	990,061	1,039,231	5.0
Taverns, night clubs, bars, liquor stores	123,045	129,867	5.5
Apparel group	392,807	425,099	8.2
Clothing stores	324,452	350,407	8.0
Shoe stores	62,774	65,398	4.2
Hat shops	5,581	9,294	66.5
General merchandise group	1,879,748	1,953,623	3.9
Department stores	807,213	812,149	0.6
Variety stores	435,116	426,132	-2.1
Drug stores	135,233	124,813	-7.7
Jewelry, leather, and sporting goods	160,673	153,220	-4.6
Feed, seed, fertilizer stores	6,125	7,169	17.1
Hardware, paints, and machinery	124,378	130,043	4.6
Farm implements and supplies	23,234	26,722	15.0
General merchandise stores	141,283	226,061	60.0
Second-hand stores, antique shops, flea markets	25,828	26,420	2.3
Dry goods stores	20,664	20,894	1.1
Automotive group	2,497,095	2,729,107	9.3
Motor vehicle dealers, trailers, campers	1,979,472	2,181,832	10.2
Auto accessories, tires, and parts	154,310	163,865	6.2
Filling and service stations, car wash	61,779	67,090	8.6
Garage and repair shops	169,664	171,126	0.9
Aircraft dealers	22,232	20,962	-5.7
Motorboat and yacht dealers	109,638	124,231	13.3
Furniture and appliances group	885,696	1,024,271	15.6
Furniture stores, new and used	272,422	299,132	9.8
Household appliances, dinnerware, etc.	87,300	102,983	18.0
Store and office equipment	150,813	168,587	11.8
Music stores, radios, and televisions	375,161	453,569	20.9
Lumber, builders, and contractors group	701,959	795,923	13.4
Building contractors	36,944	43,770	18.5
Heating and air conditioning	35,713	37,937	6.2
Electrical and plumbing	79,857	88,115	10.3
Decorating, painting, and papering	42,920	48,831	13.8
Roofing and sheet metal	11,660	13,067	12.1
Lumber and building materials	494,866	564,202	14.0
General classification group	4,854,392	5,087,669	4.8
Hotels, apartment houses, etc.	595,811	633,083	6.3
Auctioneers and commission dealers	36,746	37,464	2.0
Barber and beauty shops	41,000	41,751	1.8
Book stores	48,368	52,127	7.8
Cigar stands and tobacco shops	4,881	5,227	7.1

Continued . . .

Table 23.43. STATE GOVERNMENT FINANCE: SALES AND USE TAX COLLECTIONS BY TRADE CLASSIFICATION IN FLORIDA, FISCAL YEARS 1997-98 AND 1998-99 (Continued)

(amounts rounded to thousands of dollars)

Group	1997-98	1998-99	Per-centage change
General classification group (Continued)			
Florists	18,516	19,396	4.8
Fuel dealers, L.P. gas dealers	26,611	25,153	-5.5
Funeral directors monuments	3,681	3,168	-13.9
Scrap metal and junk yards	3,248	3,198	-1.6
Itinerant vendors	19,130	21,128	10.4
Laundry, cleaning services, alterations	12,111	13,594	12.2
Machine shops and foundries	13,619	14,708	. 8.0
Horse, cattle, and pet dealers	66,458	65,712	-1.1
Photographers, photo supplies, art galleries	55,953	56,192	0.4
Shoe repair shops	2,612	3,043	16.5
Storage and warehousing	10,736	10,733	0.0
Gift, card, and novelty stores, taxidermy	118,398	122,215	3.2
Newsstands	3,401	3,451	1.5
Social clubs and associations	28,098	29,279	4.2
Industrial machinery equipment	204,964	197,563	-3.6
Admissions	262,809	292,077	11.1
Holiday season vendors, Christmas trees	771	758	-1.7
Rental of tangible property	235,743	269,717	14.4
Fabrication and sales of cabinets, etc.	58,518	64,068	9.5
Manufacturing and mining	352,230	366,659	4.1
Bottlers (beer and softdrinks)	9,134	10,625	16.3
Pawn shops	6,600	7,162	8.5
Communications	590,640	634,586	7.4
Transportation	17,663	16,799	-4.9
Graphic arts and printing	103,333	108,610	5.1
Insurance, banking, information services, etc.	14,046	13,813	-1.7
Sanitary and industrial supplies	28,623	29,562	3.3
Packaging materials and paper boxes	8,957	8,756	-2.2
Repair of tangible personal property	67,053	72,473	8.1
Advertising	21,158	21,332	0.8
Topsoil, clay, sand, and fill dirt	21,583	24,326	12.7
Trade stamp redemption centers	31	45	44.1
Nurseries and landscaping	29,960	32,130	7.2
Vending machines	23,313	25,990	11.5
Importing and exporting	13,731	14,949	8.9
Medical, dental, surgical, hospital supplies	43,053	45,147	4.9
Wholesale dealers	313,061	348,416	11.3
Schools and educational institutions	4,238	4,015	-5.3
Office space and commercial rentals	704,740	760,573	7.9
Parking lots, boat docking, and storage	19,627	21,534	9.7
Utilities, electric or gas	284,839	292,969	2.9
Dual users of special fuels	1,100	1,054	-4.2
Public works, government contractors	5,589	5,238	-6.3
Flea market vendors	8,310	7,981	-4.0
Carnival concessions	484	595	22.9
Other professional services	4,111	6,902	67.9
Other personal services	94,972	100,701	6.0
Other industrial services	8,162	7,837	-4.0
Commercial fisherman	102	119	17.3
Miscellaneous	181,764	111,967	-38.4

Source: State of Florida, Department of Revenue, Internet site <http://sun6.dms.state.fl.us/dor/tables/f101999.html> (accessed 15 June 2000).

University of Florida   **Bureau of Economic and Business Research**

Table 23.45. STATE GOVERNMENT FINANCE: TAX COLLECTIONS BY OR WITHIN COUNTIES
BY TYPE OF TAX COLLECTED IN THE STATE AND COUNTIES OF FLORIDA
FISCAL YEAR 1998-99

County	Total 1/	Sales and use taxes	Motor vehicle tags	Pari-mutuel wagering taxes
Florida	14,377,426,679	13,858,158,449	A/ 460,626,292	58,641,938
Alachua	151,608,423	146,895,732	4,712,691	0
Baker	6,799,864	6,203,829	596,035	0
Bay	138,654,017	134,756,247	3,897,770	0
Bradford	11,057,715	10,376,872	680,843	0
Brevard	315,285,125	303,209,200	11,880,711	195,214
Broward	1,379,081,119	1,335,638,006	33,126,355	10,316,758
Calhoun	4,020,981	3,725,116	295,865	0
Charlotte	91,921,758	88,127,258	3,794,500	0
Citrus	59,442,550	56,386,145	3,056,405	0
Clay	83,792,240	77,144,940	3,555,266	3,092,034
Collier	267,780,001	260,523,721	7,256,280	0
Columbia	36,931,903	35,494,442	1,437,461	0
De Soto	13,191,297	12,324,381	866,916	0
Dixie	3,279,518	2,913,045	366,473	0
Duval	721,320,191	699,499,349	19,215,598	2,605,244
Escambia	223,193,497	216,035,281	6,828,322	329,894
Flagler	20,439,279	19,103,454	1,335,825	0
Franklin	5,505,706	5,246,138	259,568	0
Gadsden	13,887,763	13,076,924	810,839	0
Gilchrist	2,745,690	2,380,263	365,427	0
Glades	1,534,687	1,346,434	188,253	0
Gulf	4,440,461	4,102,520	337,941	0
Hamilton	6,151,506	5,886,439	265,067	0
Hardee	9,553,819	8,826,699	727,120	0
Hendry	17,278,922	15,906,596	1,372,326	0
Hernando	57,776,622	54,755,933	3,020,689	0
Highlands	44,316,403	41,919,136	2,397,267	0
Hillsborough	1,016,536,659	983,443,321	27,527,048	5,566,290
Holmes	4,746,675	4,329,173	417,502	0
Indian River	90,935,822	87,810,155	3,125,667	0
Jackson	21,332,487	20,231,642	1,100,845	0
Jefferson	5,258,973	4,238,753	621,982	398,238
Lafayette	1,270,254	1,105,789	164,465	0
Lake	120,124,548	114,547,261	5,577,287	0
Lee	410,071,761	396,339,423	11,889,120	1,843,218
Leon	183,350,581	178,211,612	5,138,969	0
Levy	15,411,881	14,329,462	1,082,419	0

See footnotes at end of table.   Continued . . .

University of Florida   **Bureau of Economic and Business Research**

Table 23.45. STATE GOVERNMENT FINANCE: TAX COLLECTIONS BY OR WITHIN COUNTIES
BY TYPE OF TAX COLLECTED IN THE STATE AND COUNTIES OF FLORIDA
FISCAL YEAR 1998-99 (Continued)

County	Total 1/	Sales and use taxes	Motor vehicle tags	Pari- mutuel wagering taxes
Liberty	1,412,307	1,238,314	173,993	0
Madison	5,089,676	4,678,732	410,944	0
Manatee	192,743,471	174,040,812	18,702,659	0
Marion	181,132,915	173,769,448	7,281,843	81,624
Martin	118,050,852	114,125,416	3,925,436	0
Miami-Dade	1,686,254,316	1,612,008,124	60,479,672	13,766,520
Monroe	121,264,784	118,857,249	2,407,535	0
Nassau	35,879,468	34,431,554	1,447,914	0
Okaloosa	140,622,457	136,128,274	4,494,183	0
Okeechobee	19,606,442	18,479,242	1,127,200	0
Orange	1,372,290,507	1,346,612,848	25,677,659	0
Osceola	148,363,502	144,446,460	3,917,042	0
Palm Beach	1,031,113,015	994,980,452	27,643,839	8,488,724
Pasco	171,328,630	162,086,130	9,242,500	0
Pinellas	716,715,397	689,584,707	21,208,632	5,922,058
Polk	348,484,352	334,123,149	14,361,203	0
Putnam	32,685,101	30,954,253	1,730,848	0
St. Johns	88,197,383	83,161,643	3,458,400	1,577,340
St. Lucie	100,054,837	95,340,175	4,650,271	64,391
Santa Rosa	42,350,515	39,512,244	2,838,271	0
Sarasota	294,661,891	284,980,993	9,200,442	480,456
Seminole	323,205,152	311,853,029	9,252,880	2,099,243
Sumter	16,051,865	14,720,881	1,330,984	0
Suwannee	15,208,751	14,256,844	951,907	0
Taylor	11,893,789	11,399,802	493,987	0
Union	2,964,515	2,630,306	334,209	0
Volusia	298,487,155	286,261,501	10,832,374	1,393,280
Wakulla	5,886,786	5,386,081	500,705	0
Walton	35,481,859	34,661,262	820,597	0
Washington	7,284,395	6,447,455	442,528	394,412
Out-of-state	1,148,722,905	1,147,308,451	1,414,454	0
Other	103,879,987	63,301,927	A/ 40,578,060	0

A/ Includes refunds.
1/ Does not include gasoline taxes.

Source: Column 2, State of Florida, Department of Revenue, Internet site <http://sun6dms.state.fl. us/dor/tables/f91999.html> (accessed 22 August 2000); Column 3, State of Florida, Department of High- way Safety and Motor Vehicles, Division of Motor Vehicles, *Revenue Report, July 1, 1998-June 30, 1999*; Column 4, State of Florida, Department of Business and Professional Regulation, Division of Pari-Mutuel Wagering, *68th Annual Report for the Fiscal Year Ending on June 30, 1999*.

Table 23.46. STATE GOVERNMENT FINANCE: GASOLINE TAX COLLECTIONS
IN FLORIDA, FISCAL YEARS 1969-70 THROUGH 1998-99

Fiscal year	Gallons sold	Tax rate (cents)	Tax collected 1/ (dollars)
1969-70	3,054,891,901.3	7	213,842,433.12
1970-71	3,341,148,943.8	7	233,880,426.09
1971-72	3,685,131,310.5	7/8	291,484,318.30
1972-73	4,080,699,270.9	8	326,454,941.67
1973-74	4,157,754,572.7	8	332,617,165.82
1974-75	4,243,123,105.1	8	339,449,848.41
1975-76	4,326,195,422.0	8	346,095,633.76
1976-77	4,483,397,014.2	8	358,671,761.14
1977-78	4,721,812,693.4	8	377,745,015.47
1978-79	4,961,448,003.1	8	396,915,840.25
1979-80	4,765,935,970.1	8	381,274,877.61
1980-81	4,681,857,035.4	8	374,548,562.90
1981-82	4,746,090,470.3	8	379,687,237.63
1982-83	4,686,388,610.8	5.7/8/9.7	387,286,074.47
1983-84	4,709,246,332.0	5.7/8/9.7	455,678,899.26
1984-85	4,739,366,278.0	5.7/9.7	458,188,999.77
1985-86	5,003,004,954.0	5.7/9.7	483,953,518.77
1986-87	5,493,474,844.7	5.7/9.7	484,754,881.20
1987-88	5,869,584,946.8	5.7/9.7	569,328,353.84
1988-89	5,995,884,170.5	5.7/9.7	581,596,538.65
1989-90	6,087,306,071.0	5.7/9.7	590,082,229.69
1990-91	5,985,729,187.8	9.7/10.9/11.2	653,943,345.04
1991-92	6,065,182,815.5	9.7/10.9/11.2/11.6	689,690,791.78
1992-93	6,279,687,903.2	9.7/10.9/11.2/11.6/11.8	723,722,832.76
1993-94	6,451,928,258.1	10.9/11.2/11.6/12.1	765,014,400.64
1994-95	6,560,589,349.5	11.6/11.8/12.1/12.3	802,201,952.42
1995-96	6,780,173,415.7	12.3/12.5	830,748,648.21
1996-97	6,832,487,453.1	12.5/12.8	861,169,355.99
1997-98	7,017,565,750.3	12.8/13.0	903,343,661.76
1998-99	7,291,963,115.1	13.0/13.1	948,325,667.05

1/ Includes collection fees.
Note: Some data may be revised.

Source: State of Florida, Department of Revenue, *Report of Fuel Tax Collections and Distributions, Fiscal Year 1994-95,* and unpublished data.

University of Florida　　　　　　　　　　　　　　**Bureau of Economic and Business Research**

Table 23.48. STATE FUNDS TO LOCAL GOVERNMENT: DISTRIBUTION OF SHARED TAXES
BY THE FLORIDA DEPARTMENT OF REVENUE TO COUNTY AND CITY GOVERNMENTS
BY MAJOR SOURCE IN THE STATE AND COUNTIES OF FLORIDA
FISCAL YEAR 1998-99

(rounded to thousands of dollars)

County	Total DOR distri- bution	Half-cent sales tax distributed to-- County govern- ments	Half-cent sales tax distributed to-- City govern- ments	Emer- gency and supple- mental	Revenue sharing County	Revenue sharing Munici- pal	County tax on motor fuel
Florida	1,860,733	773,718	385,646	6,500	419,620	205,139	70,111
Alachua	22,859	7,995	5,488	0	5,326	3,033	1,018
Baker	1,820	487	130	309	518	117	260
Bay	19,663	7,203	5,367	0	3,872	2,398	822
Bradford	2,090	698	236	195	588	183	190
Brevard	46,212	15,707	12,141	0	10,152	6,245	1,967
Broward	188,226	53,260	69,284	0	30,979	29,367	5,336
Calhoun	1,181	270	79	209	309	99	215
Charlotte	13,370	7,345	728	0	4,336	208	753
Citrus	9,400	4,697	483	0	3,435	241	544
Clay	12,154	6,257	846	0	4,078	367	606
Collier	33,294	20,063	3,579	0	7,673	685	1,293
Columbia	5,725	2,705	577	0	1,647	267	528
De Soto	2,479	902	255	140	725	185	272
Dixie	1,187	229	47	234	323	92	262
Duval 1/	106,610	60,708	3,577	0	23,160	16,093	3,072
Escambia	32,005	16,117	3,763	0	9,301	1,567	1,257
Flagler	3,452	1,479	254	160	1,219	50	290
Franklin	1,193	329	155	79	265	99	266
Gadsden	4,223	877	330	886	1,166	593	371
Gilchrist	979	195	33	251	318	40	142
Glades	954	102	19	240	233	40	319
Gulf	1,271	246	139	227	303	123	233
Hamilton	1,275	402	136	29	349	116	242
Hardee	2,055	599	209	216	561	198	272
Hendry	2,977	1,066	393	0	802	219	498
Hernando	9,578	4,719	310	0	3,796	185	567
Highlands	7,263	3,075	776	0	2,326	476	611
Hillsborough	132,630	63,668	26,377	0	30,131	8,637	3,816
Holmes	1,483	322	89	322	422	113	216
Indian River	12,587	5,740	2,342	0	3,147	791	568
Jackson	4,563	1,318	538	419	1,185	543	559
Jefferson	1,272	309	74	220	347	73	250
Lafayette	640	87	15	164	159	34	181
Lake	18,122	6,873	3,596	0	4,888	1,774	990
Lee	52,939	24,936	10,762	0	12,310	3,220	1,711
Leon	26,156	9,136	7,103	0	5,765	3,191	961

See footnotes at end of table.   Continued . . .

University of Florida   **Bureau of Economic and Business Research**

Table 23.48. STATE FUNDS TO LOCAL GOVERNMENT: DISTRIBUTION OF SHARED TAXES
BY THE FLORIDA DEPARTMENT OF REVENUE TO COUNTY AND CITY GOVERNMENTS
BY MAJOR SOURCE IN THE STATE AND COUNTIES OF FLORIDA
FISCAL YEAR 1998-99 (Continued)

(rounded to thousands of dollars)

County	Total DOR distri- bution	Half-cent sales tax distributed to-- County govern- ments	City govern- ments	Emer- gency and supple- mental	Revenue sharing County	Munici- pal	County tax on motor fuel
Levy	3,058	1,024	295	178	874	207	480
Liberty	747	99	20	148	167	40	273
Madison	1,738	334	99	354	452	145	355
Manatee	25,529	11,952	3,804	0	7,302	1,426	1,045
Marion	25,917	12,942	2,962	0	7,386	1,128	1,498
Martin	15,735	9,247	1,407	0	4,106	356	620
Miami-Dade	272,153	94,095	54,357	0	57,017	59,343	7,341
Monroe	15,592	7,244	3,577	0	3,013	832	926
Nassau	5,447	2,475	720	0	1,567	282	403
Okaloosa	20,024	8,517	4,115	0	4,904	1,576	912
Okeechobee	3,341	1,461	234	0	1,031	176	439
Orange	166,736	88,613	34,682	0	32,126	7,783	3,532
Osceola	20,289	9,190	4,107	0	4,583	1,372	1,037
Palm Beach	135,905	54,431	36,348	0	28,847	12,381	3,897
Pasco	26,776	13,386	1,496	0	9,868	762	1,263
Pinellas	101,423	33,314	29,870	0	21,193	14,110	2,937
Polk	50,449	21,250	9,371	0	13,060	4,387	2,382
Putnam	5,672	2,255	532	0	1,997	395	493
St. Johns	12,229	6,527	1,120	0	3,491	421	670
St. Lucie	15,893	4,771	3,959	0	3,912	2,408	842
Santa Rosa	7,644	3,201	473	0	2,961	302	707
Sarasota	39,179	19,570	6,342	0	10,080	1,989	1,199
Seminole	43,048	17,876	10,757	0	9,583	3,665	1,166
Sumter	3,689	1,093	266	491	1,098	248	493
Suwannee	3,111	1,061	251	256	934	251	358
Taylor	2,159	718	330	0	499	203	408
Union	939	193	57	252	238	82	116
Volusia	43,892	13,192	13,101	0	8,986	6,802	1,811
Wakulla	1,563	473	19	244	550	19	257
Walton	5,190	2,646	593	0	1,191	222	537
Washington	1,778	442	153	277	488	160	258

DOR Department of Revenue.
1/ Duval County is the consolidated city of Jacksonville.
Note: Detail may not add to totals due to rounding.

Source: State of Florida, Department of Revenue, Internet site <http://sun6.dms.state.fl.us/dor/
tables/> (accessed 15 June 2000).

University of Florida   **Bureau of Economic and Business Research**

Table 23.50. STATE LOTTERY: SALES IN THE STATE AND COUNTIES OF FLORIDA
FISCAL YEARS 1994-95 THROUGH 1999-2000

(rounded to thousands of dollars)

County	1994-95	1995-96	1996-97	1997-98	1998-99	1999-2000
Florida	2,303,486	2,117,085	2,159,669	2,130,848	2,178,590	2,324,386
Alachua	25,103	23,734	24,166	24,284	25,504	25,957
Baker	2,501	2,303	2,262	2,028	2,087	2,107
Bay	24,939	21,866	21,868	21,096	20,414	20,543
Bradford	3,422	3,152	3,193	3,267	3,489	3,602
Brevard	71,821	68,880	70,103	68,942	69,612	72,568
Broward	231,817	209,958	213,034	207,230	211,506	235,014
Calhoun	1,312	1,227	1,180	1,140	1,332	1,320
Charlotte	19,528	17,900	18,906	19,564	19,418	20,472
Citrus	16,784	15,713	16,279	16,810	16,918	17,894
Clay	13,114	12,353	12,911	13,051	13,491	14,315
Collier	24,182	22,357	23,401	23,875	24,545	27,326
Columbia	8,790	8,424	8,796	8,983	9,233	9,386
De Soto	3,105	2,858	2,848	2,933	3,199	3,390
Dixie	1,305	1,348	1,326	1,236	1,367	1,358
Duval	115,885	106,516	109,163	108,724	111,775	114,160
Escambia	72,207	62,131	62,689	59,833	60,165	62,168
Flagler	6,397	6,234	6,417	6,512	7,202	7,966
Franklin	1,629	1,442	1,487	1,520	1,510	1,416
Gadsden	7,593	6,671	6,763	6,757	7,042	7,070
Gilchrist	932	1,152	1,306	1,151	1,090	1,165
Glades	953	907	689	687	684	674
Gulf	1,739	1,551	1,590	1,533	1,593	1,550
Hamilton	8,521	4,892	3,990	3,569	3,187	3,092
Hardee	2,238	1,982	2,024	2,117	2,167	2,203
Hendry	4,629	4,122	4,291	4,079	4,282	4,399
Hernando	20,285	19,531	20,858	20,197	20,377	21,235
Highlands	10,879	9,821	10,047	9,970	10,014	10,219
Hillsborough	128,350	117,034	119,728	118,182	124,084	132,611
Holmes	6,031	5,556	5,529	5,754	5,646	5,373
Indian River	15,783	14,626	14,953	15,714	16,698	17,722
Jackson	19,368	15,299	14,446	13,858	13,649	13,046
Jefferson	5,432	3,379	2,739	2,522	2,705	2,604
Lafayette	444	413	453	394	382	406
Lake	28,555	27,696	29,716	30,509	31,116	33,305
Lee	52,317	49,074	50,732	51,615	51,989	56,222
Leon	25,641	21,986	22,503	21,993	22,656	23,332

See footnote at end of table.   Continued . . .

Table 23.50. STATE LOTTERY: SALES IN THE STATE AND COUNTIES OF FLORIDA
FISCAL YEARS 1994-95 THROUGH 1999-2000 (Continued)

(rounded to thousands of dollars)

County	1994-95	1995-96	1996-97	1997-98	1998-99	1999-2000
Levy	5,191	5,024	4,909	4,798	5,029	5,285
Liberty	831	691	822	739	786	758
Madison	3,507	2,761	2,932	2,830	2,702	2,595
Manatee	33,011	29,786	30,189	30,523	30,906	33,476
Marion	38,014	35,354	37,627	37,093	39,024	40,376
Martin	18,486	17,284	18,281	18,867	19,567	21,372
Miami-Dade	375,442	354,696	351,789	335,938	344,388	375,979
Monroe	14,049	13,320	13,907	13,478	13,655	14,663
Nassau	16,425	11,390	10,386	9,899	9,319	8,784
Okaloosa	25,640	22,545	22,545	21,565	21,184	22,095
Okeechobee	5,644	5,136	5,307	5,220	5,305	5,633
Orange	118,085	110,784	116,775	118,570	121,586	128,338
Osceola	24,215	22,785	24,084	24,274	24,236	25,589
Palm Beach	151,562	140,687	142,100	142,599	145,398	157,669
Pasco	48,002	44,548	46,521	46,448	47,431	50,457
Pinellas	139,180	127,057	129,920	129,071	130,214	140,246
Polk	69,925	63,533	66,542	66,286	67,662	70,806
Putnam	11,468	10,675	10,662	10,166	10,313	10,520
St. Johns	13,397	12,391	12,721	12,741	12,922	13,723
St. Lucie	28,718	26,251	25,921	26,663	27,776	30,318
Santa Rosa	11,399	10,691	11,184	10,712	10,834	11,350
Sarasota	40,452	36,372	36,732	36,173	37,413	41,483
Seminole	35,889	33,927	35,898	35,939	37,620	40,043
Sumter	5,474	5,076	5,473	5,402	5,349	5,852
Suwannee	3,782	3,601	3,727	3,521	3,591	3,596
Taylor	2,751	2,463	2,584	2,594	2,803	2,810
Union	1,177	1,058	1,117	1,115	1,168	1,188
Volusia	67,907	63,640	66,693	65,970	68,211	72,415
Wakulla	2,112	1,895	1,984	2,014	2,090	2,104
Walton	6,267	5,712	5,965	6,147	6,059	5,800
Washington	1,950	1,867	1,988	1,867	1,923	1,872

Note: Data are unaudited gross sales amounts.

Source: State of Florida, Department of the Lottery, unpublished data.

University of Florida   **Bureau of Economic and Business Research**

Table 23.52. TOBACCO LICENSES: NUMBER OF LICENSES ISSUED IN THE STATE
AND COUNTIES OF FLORIDA, FISCAL YEARS 1997-98 AND 1998-99

County	1997-98	1998-99 Total	Per-cent-age change	Issued with alcoholic beverage license	County	1997-98	1998-99 Total	Per-cent-age change	Issued with alcoholic beverage license
Florida	29,949	28,617	-4.4	24,059	Lake	342	347	1.5	312
					Lee	825	792	-4.0	697
Alachua	336	319	-5.1	278	Leon	372	363	-2.4	324
Baker	44	41	-6.8	38	Levy	92	84	-8.7	78
Bay	432	397	-8.1	343	Liberty	18	19	5.6	15
Bradford	51	46	-9.8	40	Madison	46	40	-13.0	36
Brevard	881	805	-8.6	707	Manatee	412	409	-0.7	349
Broward	2,660	2,510	-5.6	2,089	Marion	444	438	-1.4	393
Calhoun	36	32	-11.1	25	Martin	240	227	-5.4	206
Charlotte	202	191	-5.4	159	Miami-Dade	4,769	4,653	-2.4	3,481
Citrus	207	191	-7.7	169	Monroe	462	414	-10.4	341
Clay	184	180	-2.2	166	Nassau	133	112	-15.8	101
Collier	430	420	-2.3	369	Okaloosa	322	305	-5.3	274
Columbia	140	130	-7.1	120	Okeechobee	98	92	-6.1	83
De Soto	53	53	0.0	49	Orange	1,672	1,658	-0.8	1,370
Dixie	36	36	0.0	34	Osceola	392	372	-5.1	312
Duval	1,471	1,402	-4.7	1,203	Palm Beach	1,894	1,811	-4.4	1,523
Escambia	582	528	-9.3	467	Pasco	511	508	-0.6	454
Flagler	85	85	0.0	77	Pinellas	1,844	1,708	-7.4	1,474
Franklin	50	45	-10.0	39	Polk	835	799	-4.3	702
Gadsden	119	111	-6.7	92	Putnam	153	147	-3.9	130
Gilchrist	23	22	-4.3	19	St. Johns	236	240	1.7	210
Glades	26	23	-11.5	22	St. Lucie	318	323	1.6	288
Gulf	39	39	0.0	35	Santa Rosa	150	138	-8.0	120
Hamilton	48	44	-8.3	36	Sarasota	531	504	-5.1	434
Hardee	38	39	2.6	33	Seminole	489	481	-1.6	438
Hendry	95	89	-6.3	79	Sumter	87	83	-4.6	72
Hernando	173	168	-2.9	150	Suwannee	64	65	1.6	56
Highlands	134	133	-0.7	120	Taylor	65	60	-7.7	55
Hillsborough	1,968	1,840	-6.5	1,497	Union	22	23	4.5	15
Holmes	54	49	-9.3	42	Volusia	887	860	-3.0	737
Indian River	219	200	-8.7	169	Wakulla	53	48	-9.4	45
Jackson	122	116	-4.9	96	Walton	125	115	-8.0	95
Jefferson	44	40	-9.1	34	Washington	48	41	-14.6	34
Lafayette	16	14	-12.5	9					

Source: State of Florida, Department of Business and Professional Regulation, Division of Alcoholic Beverages and Tobacco, unpublished data.

University of Florida   **Bureau of Economic and Business Research**

Table 23.53. ALCOHOLIC BEVERAGE LICENSES: NUMBER OF LICENSES ISSUED BY TYPE OF LICENSE IN THE STATE AND COUNTIES OF FLORIDA, LICENSE YEAR OCTOBER 1, 1998 THROUGH SEPTEMBER 30, 1999

		Type of license						
County	Total	Clubs enter-tain-ment and tracks 1/	Package sales only 2/	Package and on-premises sales 3/	Dis-tribu-tors 4/	Manu-factur-ers 5/	Import/export 6/	Broker sales agent (BSA)
Florida	36,286	1,564	16,612	9,837	8,169	40	54	10
Alachua	431	11	222	87	111	0	0	0
Baker	44	2	32	6	4	0	0	0
Bay	503	16	208	144	135	0	0	0
Bradford	52	2	33	11	6	0	0	0
Brevard	1,185	61	484	360	278	1	0	1
Broward	3,634	101	1,610	1,028	887	3	4	1
Calhoun	29	0	20	9	0	0	0	0
Charlotte	306	27	122	73	84	0	0	0
Citrus	268	26	117	78	47	0	0	0
Clay	215	12	117	44	42	0	0	0
Collier	728	64	236	234	194	0	0	0
Columbia	144	7	93	21	23	0	0	0
De Soto	67	5	28	23	11	0	0	0
Dixie	42	0	26	11	5	0	0	0
Duval	1,598	57	834	415	286	4	1	1
Escambia	670	25	329	133	183	0	0	0
Flagler	124	8	41	52	23	0	0	0
Franklin	60	1	27	15	17	0	0	0
Gadsden	100	1	70	18	11	0	0	0
Gilchrist	22	0	14	1	7	0	0	0
Glades	34	2	16	7	9	0	0	0
Gulf	50	2	22	17	9	0	0	0
Hamilton	42	0	29	13	0	0	0	0
Hardee	43	0	28	15	0	0	0	0
Hendry	102	7	54	27	14	0	0	0
Hernando	242	20	109	73	40	0	0	0
Highlands	198	19	100	44	35	0	0	0
Hillsborough	1,924	72	975	408	465	3	1	0
Holmes	46	0	36	10	0	0	0	0
Indian River	323	30	145	80	68	0	0	0
Jackson	114	0	90	24	0	0	0	0
Jefferson	42	2	30	7	3	0	0	0
Lafayette	11	0	8	3	0	0	0	0
Lake	440	27	227	103	82	1	0	0
Lee	1,172	84	454	331	300	3	0	0
Leon	435	11	218	94	112	0	0	0
Levy	109	6	62	23	17	1	0	0
Liberty	15	0	11	4	0	0	0	0
Madison	45	1	31	13	0	0	0	0
Manatee	564	27	243	165	128	1	0	0

See footnotes at end of table.   Continued . . .

Table 23.53. ALCOHOLIC BEVERAGE LICENSES: NUMBER OF LICENSES ISSUED BY TYPE OF LICENSE IN THE STATE AND COUNTIES OF FLORIDA, LICENSE YEAR OCTOBER 1, 1998 THROUGH SEPTEMBER 30, 1999 (Continued)

County	Total	Clubs entertainment and tracks 1/	Package sales only 2/	Package and on-premises sales 3/	Distributors 4/	Manufacturers 5/	Import/export 6/	Broker sales agent (BSA)
Marion	537	26	286	140	85	0	0	0
Martin	390	39	146	124	81	0	0	0
Miami-Dade	4,965	92	2,302	1,638	893	2	36	2
Monroe	631	29	202	202	197	1	0	0
Nassau	145	7	76	30	32	0	0	0
Okaloosa	445	28	177	112	128	0	0	0
Okeechobee	110	10	62	27	11	0	0	0
Orange	1,907	50	868	467	518	2	2	0
Osceola	454	16	202	126	110	0	0	0
Palm Beach	2,546	122	1,055	673	685	0	8	3
Pasco	606	52	297	146	111	0	0	0
Pinellas	2,146	89	923	562	566	2	2	2
Polk	982	49	549	203	169	12	0	0
Putnam	155	10	83	33	29	0	0	0
St. Johns	351	25	138	102	85	1	0	0
St. Lucie	440	25	253	95	67	0	0	0
Santa Rosa	156	0	107	49	0	0	0	0
Sarasota	859	58	279	287	235	0	0	0
Seminole	625	29	293	146	156	1	0	0
Sumter	89	6	55	17	11	0	0	0
Suwannee	71	1	52	18	0	0	0	0
Taylor	67	3	41	11	12	0	0	0
Union	14	0	11	0	3	0	0	0
Volusia	1,155	53	472	336	294	0	0	0
Wakulla	63	3	34	15	11	0	0	0
Walton	164	6	67	46	44	1	0	0
Washington	40	0	31	8	0	1	0	0

1/ Beer, wine, and/or all alcoholic beverages sold in clubs (including bottle clubs), civic and performing arts centers, at race tracks and from golf carts. Licenses included in this category are: 11C, 11CS, 11PA, 12RT, 14BC, and GC.

2/ Beer, wine, and/or all alcoholic beverages sold by the package only. Licenses included in this category are 1APS, 2APS, 3APS, 3BPS, 3CPS, and 3PS.

3/ Beer, wine, and/or all alcoholic beverages to consume on premises and by the package. Establishments with three are more bars (such as hotels) are included. Licenses included in this category are: 1COP, 2COP, COP, and 3M.

4/ Distributors of beer, wine, and/or liquor (including wine distributed to churches). Licenses included in this category are: 4COP, 5COP, 6COP, 7COP, 8COP, JDBW, and KLD.

5/ Manufacturers of beer, wine, and/or liquor. Licenses included in this category are: AMW, BMWC, CMB, CMBP, DD, and ERB.

6/ Licenses included in this category are: IMPR and MEXP.

Source: State of Florida, Department of Business and Professional Regulation, Division of Alcoholic Beverages and Tobacco, *Number and Series of Beverage Licenses Issued by County,* October 1999.

Table 23.54. PARI-MUTUEL WAGERING: PERFORMANCES, ATTENDANCE, AND REVENUE BY TYPE OF EVENT IN FLORIDA, FISCAL YEARS 1994-95 THROUGH 1998-99

| | | Number of-- | | Pari-mutuel | Revenue |
Item	Days	Per-form-ances	Paid attendance	handle (dollars)	to state (dollars)
All tracks and frontons					
1994-95	4,845	6,681	10,285,062	1,582,305,874	93,536,408
1995-96	4,692	6,616	9,403,703	1,525,851,211	88,788,492
1996-97	4,773	6,697	8,579,944	1,592,442,941	71,827,554
1997-98	4,969	6,800	7,679,823	1,609,182,244	66,928,766
1998-99	4,604	6,231	3,621,059	1,611,699,224	58,614,939
Thoroughbred tracks					
1994-95	379	379	1,789,908	516,739,403	14,503,157
1995-96	380	380	1,678,460	533,743,649	15,341,989
1996-97	371	371	1,516,959	618,139,522	13,994,221
1997-98	373	373	1,354,380	670,026,874	14,578,415
1998-99	372	372	800,801	723,336,651	12,733,644
Harness tracks					
1994-95	195	195	418,225	74,200,943	1,609,622
1995-96	176	176	368,770	66,139,058	1,450,038
1996-97	187	187	367,816	93,430,598	2,067,898
1997-98	188	188	330,681	106,383,512	2,271,704
1998-99	176	176	24,533	104,021,815	2,185,425
Greyhound tracks					
1994-95	3,045	4,240	5,897,749	800,744,617	67,797,851
1995-96	2,963	4,204	5,395,716	745,215,792	63,310,564
1996-97	3,040	4,278	4,923,047	716,043,639	48,642,211
1997-98	3,141	4,364	4,356,082	682,101,586	43,821,658
1998-99	3,052	4,247	2,172,642	655,571,620	41,402,630
Jai Alai frontons					
1994-95	1,226	1,867	2,179,180	190,620,911	9,625,778
1995-96	1,173	1,856	1,960,757	180,752,712	8,685,901
1996-97	1,175	1,861	1,772,122	164,829,182	7,123,224
1997-98	1,267	1,875	1,638,680	150,670,272	6,256,989
1998-99	1,004	1,436	623,083	128,769,138	2,293,240

Note: These data represent the distribution of revenue derived from pari-mutuel performances and do not represent the total revenue received by the Division of Pari-Mutuel Wagering. Excluded are such items as licenses, fees, escheated tickets, charity, scholarship performances, and other miscellaneous items.

Source: State of Florida, Department of Business and Professional Regulation, Division of Pari-Mutuel Wagering, *68th Annual Report for the Fiscal Year Ending on June 30, 1999.*

University of Florida   **Bureau of Economic and Business Research**

Table 23.58. STATE RETIREMENT SYSTEM: MEMBERSHIP, PAYROLL, CONTRIBUTIONS ANNUITANTS, AND BENEFITS IN FLORIDA, JUNE 30, 1999

System	Active member- ship 1/	Annual payroll 1/ ($1,000)	Accu- mulated contri- butions 1/ ($1,000)	Annu- itants	Annual benefits Total paid ($1,000)	Annual benefits Average (dol- lars)
Total	591,916	17,445,161	255,196	172,117	1,981,064	(X)
Average salary (dollars)	(X)	29,472	(X)	(X)	11,510	11,510
Florida retirement system	1,066	17,388,169	144,632	161,850	1,864,489	(X)
Regular members	530,405	15,134,977	134,186	150,295	1,647,992	10,965
Senior management members	1,323	111,126	1,622	412	14,450	35,074
Special risk members	54,683	1,955,900	6,472	9,835	163,696	16,644
Administrative support	186	7,390	105	86	1,749	20,345
Elected official class members	1,834	127,790	2,247	1,222	36,600	29,951
Renewed membership	2,419	50,986	0	(X)	(X)	(X)
Teachers retirement system	1,026	55,947	109,885	6,744	100,232	14,863
Survivors' benefits	(X)	(X)	(X)	965	1,815	1,881
State and county officers and employees retirement system	40	1,045	679	2,449	12,813	5,232
Highway patrol pension trust fund	0	0	0	88	1,256	14,280
Judicial retirement system	0	0	0	21	456	21,736

(X) Not applicable.
1/ Excludes DROP participants.

Table 23.59. STATE RETIREMENT SYSTEM: ANNUITANTS AND BENEFITS BY AGE OF RETIREMENT IN FLORIDA, JUNE 30, 1999

Retirement age	Retirees Number	Retirees Annualized benefits (dollars)	Joint annuitants Number	Joint annuitants Annualized benefits (dollars)
Total	154,852	1,836,994,139	16,307	142,574,513
Under age 40	619	4,119,335	184	1,975,878
40-44	1,347	9,232,148	322	2,026,812
45-49	4,667	42,611,013	931	5,817,814
50-54	16,285	216,544,168	1,833	14,784,582
55-59	32,975	436,962,546	2,915	26,807,021
60-64	62,009	721,690,345	4,441	41,053,235
65-69	29,900	333,913,242	2,637	22,256,917
70-74	5,441	58,962,600	554	5,142,276
75-79	1,319	10,922,342	142	1,005,112
80-84	255	1,858,437	42	207,523
85 and over	35	177,958	14	60,274
Member deceased	0	0	2,292	21,437,062

Note: Annuitants include all retired persons or survivors of retired persons who are receiving monthly benefits. Does not include 965 persons receiving monthly benefits from the survivors' benefit trust fund or the 750 annuitants under various general revenue pensions.

Source for Tables 23.58 and 23.59: State of Florida, Department of Management Services, Division of Retirement, *Florida Retirement System: July 1, 1998-June 30, 1999 Annual Report*, Internet site <http://www.frs.state.fl.us/frs/public/annual/ar9899.pdf> (accessed 4 August 2000).

University of Florida   **Bureau of Economic and Business Research**

Table 23.60. STATE RETIREMENT SYSTEM: ADDITIONS, DEDUCTIONS, AND BALANCES OF THE FLORIDA RETIREMENT SYSTEM, FISCAL YEARS 1997-98 AND 1998-99

(in dollars)

Item	1997-98	1998-99
Additions, total	18,148,000,468	14,743,060,791
Pension contributions, total	3,250,750,499	3,167,556,372
State	822,792,644	801,537,048
Nonstate	2,362,119,072	2,301,446,724
Employee	30,424,037	30,866,462
Transfers from other funds	35,414,746	33,706,138
Net investment income	14,878,079,864	11,543,620,268
Net appreciation in fair value of investments	12,767,560,207	9,106,130,867
Interest income	1,273,775,028	1,473,031,875
Dividends	770,375,519	894,884,776
Net real estate operating income	183,133,202	216,443,788
Other investment income	3,263,006	6,430,042
Less investment expense	120,027,098	153,291,080
Net income from security lending	19,170,105	31,884,151
Deductions, total	1,765,006,371	2,348,194,013
Benefit payments	1,736,525,978	2,314,669,713
General revenue fund	6,223,598	6,757,506
Refunds of contributions	2,713,434	2,602,340
Administrative expenses	19,013,539	23,461,659
Property dispositions	15,687	23,312
Depreciation expense	514,135	679,483
Net increase	16,382,994,097	12,394,866,778
Net assets		
Beginning of year	67,363,539,188	83,746,533,285
Adjustment to beginning balance	0	0
End of year	83,746,533,285	96,141,400,063

Table 23.61. STATE RETIREMENT SYSTEM: RETIREMENT TRUST FUND BALANCES OF THE FLORIDA RETIREMENT SYSTEM, FISCAL YEARS 1997-98 AND 1998-99

(in dollars)

Trust fund	1997-98	1998-99
Total	83,855,887,951	96,278,891,129
Florida Retirement System	83,746,533,285	96,141,400,063
Institute of Food and Agricultural Sciences (IFAS)		
Supplemental Retirement Program	11,685,278	12,531,213
Health Insurance Subsidy	61,918,546	89,387,087
State University System (SUS)		
Optional Retirement Program	428,406	247,936
Senior Management Service Optional		
Annuity Program	0	0
General revenue appropriation	0	0
Police Officers and Firefighters' Premium Tax Trust Fund	35,322,436	35,324,830

Source for Tables 23.60 and 23.61: State of Florida, Department of Management Services, Division of Retirement, *Florida Retirement System: July 1, 1998-June 30, 1999 Annual Report*, Internet site <http://www.frs.state.fl.us:/frs/public/annual/ar9899.pdf> (accessed 4 August 2000).

University of Florida   **Bureau of Economic and Business Research**

Table 23.70. FEDERAL GOVERNMENT: AVERAGE MONTHLY EMPLOYMENT COVERED
BY UNEMPLOYMENT COMPENSATION LAW BY INDUSTRY, IN FLORIDA, 1999

SIC code	Industry	Number of employees
01-99	All industries	120,290
43	U.S. postal service	46,107
53	General merchandise stores	3,709
54	Food stores	904
59	Miscellaneous retail	25
594	Miscellaneous shopping goods stores	5
596	Nonstore retailers	19
61	Nondeposit credit institutions	129
63	Insurance carriers	68
65	Real estate	53
70	Hotels, rooming houses, camps, and other lodging places	1,006
702	Rooming and boarding houses	692
704	Organization hotels and lodging houses, on membership basis	313
79	Amusement and recreation services	2,337
80	Health services	12,697
801	Offices and clinics of doctors of medicine	969
806	Hospitals	11,727
83	Social services	10
84	Museums, art galleries, and botanical and zoological gardens	14
87	Engineering, accounting, research, management, and related services	831
89	Services, NEC	496
91	Executive, legislative, and general government, except finance	1,714
92	Justice, public order, and safety	7,256
921	Courts	1,845
922	Public order and safety	5,411
93	Public finance, taxation, and monetary policy	4,996
94	Administration of human resource programs	3,045
941	Administration of educational programs	12
943	Administration of public health programs	48
944	Administration of social, human resource, and income maintenance programs	2,398
945	Administration of veterans' affairs, except health and insurance	588
95	Administration of environmental quality and housing programs	1,576
951	Administration of environmental quality programs	1,323
953	Administration of housing and urban development programs	253
96	Administration of economic programs	7,858
961	Administration of general economic programs	825
962	Regulation and administration of transportation programs	3,039
963	Regulation and administration of communications, electric, gas, and other utilities	10
964	Regulation of agricultural marketing and commodities	1,757
965	Regulation, licensing, and inspection of miscellaneous commercial sectors	484
966	Space research and technology	1,743
97	National security and international affairs	25,461
971	National security	23,741
972	International affairs	1,719

NEC Not elsewhere classified.
Note: Data are preliminary. Detail may not add to totals due to disclosure editing and/or rounding.

Source: State of Florida, Department of Labor and Employment Security, Bureau of Labor Market Information, "Employment and Wages" (ES-202), unpublished data.

University of Florida   **Bureau of Economic and Business Research**

Table 23.72. STATE GOVERNMENT: AVERAGE MONTHLY EMPLOYMENT COVERED BY UNEMPLOYMENT COMPENSATION LAW BY INDUSTRY IN FLORIDA, 1999

SIC code	Industry	Number of employees
01-99	All industries	208,343
08	Forestry	1,149
16	Heavy construction other than building construction-- contractors	7,002
61	Nondeposit credit institutions	80,590
73	Business services	142
79	Amusement and recreation services	1,509
80	Health services	5,452
82	Educational services	69,116
821	Elementary and secondary schools	782
822	Colleges, universities, professional schools, and junior colleges	68,187
823	Libraries	147
83	Social services	4,311
832	Individual and family social services	553
836	Residential care	3,758
84	Museums, art galleries, and botanical and zoological gardens	60
91	Executive, legislative, and general government, except finance	6,384
911	Executive offices	557
912	Legislative bodies	1,432
919	General government, NEC	4,395
92	Justice, public order, and safety	48,751
921	Courts	1,939
922	Public order and safety	46,812
93	Public finance, taxation, and monetary policy	4,609
94	Administration of human resource programs	39,763
941	Administration of educational programs	1,269
943	Administration of public health programs	30,443
944	Administration of social, human resource, and income maintenance programs	7,700
945	Administration of veterans' affairs, except health and insurance	351
95	Administration of environmental quality and housing programs	5,193
951	Administration of environmental quality programs	4,967
953	Administration of housing and urban development programs	227
96	Administration of economic programs	14,644
961	Administration of general economic programs	113
962	Regulation and administration of transportation programs	5,423
963	Regulation and administration of communications, electric, gas, and other utilities	409
964	Regulation of agricultural marketing and commodities	2,935
965	Regulation, licensing, and inspection of miscellaneous commercial sectors	5,764
97	National security and international affairs	260

NEC Not elsewhere classified.
Note: Data are preliminary. Detail may not add to totals due to disclosure editing and/or rounding.

Source: State of Florida, Department of Labor and Employment Security, Bureau of Labor Market Information, "Employment and Wages" (ES-202), unpublished data.

University of Florida   **Bureau of Economic and Business Research**

Table 23.73. LOCAL GOVERNMENT: AVERAGE MONTHLY EMPLOYMENT COVERED BY UNEMPLOYMENT
COMPENSATION LAW BY INDUSTRY IN FLORIDA, 1998 and 1999

SIC code	Industry	Number of employees 1998 A/	1999 B/
01-99	All industries	608,053	624,856
07	Agricultural services	1	1
16	Heavy construction other than building construction contractors	4	3
41	Passenger transportation	1,282	1,341
44	Water transportation	27	30
45	Transportation by air	1,382	1,454
47	Transportation services	39	45
49	Electric, gas, and sanitary services	6,339	6,105
491	Electric services	3,046	2,778
492	Gas production and distribution	195	200
493	Combination electric and gas, and other utility services	1,421	1,441
494	Water supply	353	358
495	Sanitary services	1,324	1,222
497	Irrigation systems	(NA)	106
57	Furniture and home furnishings	(NA)	3
62	Security and commodity brokers and services	7	9
63	Insurance carriers	82	4
637	Pension, health, and welfare funds	3	4
639	Insurance carriers, NEC	79	(NA)
65	Real estate	2,108	2,130
651	Real estate operators (except developers) and lessors	(NA)	125
653	Real estate agents and managers	(NA)	2,005
73	Business services	72	69
734	Services to dwellings and other buildings	37	36
737	Computer programming, data processing, and other computer-related services	35	33
75	Automotive repair services, and parking	154	149
79	Amusement and recreation services	846	955
792	Theatrical producers (except motion picture), bands, orchestras, and entertainers	76	109
794	Commercial sports	357	402
799	Miscellaneous amusement and recreation services	414	445
80	Health services	33,910	32,296
805	Nursing and personal care facilities	509	555
806	Hospitals	33,177	31,533
808	Home health care services	224	207
82	Educational services	324,135	338,046
821	Elementary and secondary schools	292,003	306,531
822	Colleges, universities, professional schools, and junior colleges	31,501	30,864
823	Libraries	632	652

See footnotes at end of table.   Continued . . .

University of Florida   **Bureau of Economic and Business Research**

Table 23.73. LOCAL GOVERNMENT: AVERAGE MONTHLY EMPLOYMENT COVERED BY UNEMPLOYMENT COMPENSATION LAW BY INDUSTRY IN FLORIDA, 1998 and 1999 (Continued)

SIC code	Industry	Number of employees	
		1998 A/	1999 B/
83	Social services	5	47
832	Individual and family services	(NA)	27
833	Job training and vocational rehabilitation services	(NA)	20
86	Membership organizations	162	173
861	Business associations	2	2
864	Civic, social, and fraternal associations	158	169
869	Membership organizations, NEC	2	2
87	Engineering, accounting, research, management and related services	1	1
89	Services, NEC	47	48
91	Executive, legislative, and general government, except finance	184,563	186,946
911	Executive offices	538	445
912	Legislative bodies	59,613	60,509
913	Executive and legislative offices combined	123,993	125,557
919	General government, NEC	420	435
92	Justice, public order, and safety	40,606	42,301
921	Courts	7,765	7,977
922	Public order and safety	32,842	34,324
93	Public finance, taxation, and monetary policy	5,857	6,013
94	Administration of human resource programs	237	224
943	Administration of public health programs	24	27
944	Administration of social, human resource, and income maintenance programs	208	193
945	Administration of veterans' affairs, except health and insurance	5	4
95	Administration of environmental quality and housing programs	5,390	5,621
951	Administration of environmental quality programs	4,066	4,202
953	Administration of housing and urban development programs	1,324	1,418
96	Administration of economic programs	796	845
961	Administration of general economic programs	28	22
962	Regulation and administration of transportation programs	746	801
964	Regulation of agricultural marketing and commodities	16	16
965	Regulation, licensing, and inspection of miscellaneous commercial sectors	6	6

NEC Not elsewhere classified.
(NA) Not available.
A/ Revised.
B/ Preliminary.
Note: Detail may not add to totals due to disclosure editing and/or rounding.

Source: State of Florida, Department of Labor and Employment Security, Bureau of Labor Market Information, "Employment and Wages" (ES-202), unpublished data.

Table 23.74. GOVERNMENT EMPLOYMENT: AVERAGE MONTHLY EMPLOYMENT COVERED BY UNEMPLOYMENT COMPENSATION BY LEVEL OF GOVERNMENT IN THE STATE AND COUNTIES OF FLORIDA, 1998 AND 1999

County	1998 A/			1999 B/		
	Federal	State	Local	Federal	State	Local
Florida	120,280	206,362	608,052	120,290	208,343	624,855
Alachua	2,909	26,246	9,930	2,890	26,676	10,032
Baker	70	1,658	810	72	1,632	833
Bay	3,044	1,187	5,575	3,048	1,181	5,702
Bradford	37	1,460	945	39	1,476	957
Brevard	5,566	2,308	17,046	5,467	2,274	17,384
Broward	7,040	7,878	64,818	7,255	7,220	66,991
Calhoun	24	460	474	25	448	489
Charlotte	259	744	4,033	280	699	4,262
Citrus	195	392	3,204	201	407	3,357
Clay	325	438	4,098	322	423	4,328
Collier	581	782	7,629	628	843	8,035
Columbia	1,054	1,614	2,244	1,043	1,676	2,274
De Soto	54	1,716	1,049	56	1,675	1,055
Dixie	17	469	554	16	456	555
Duval	17,261	7,209	25,959	16,583	7,184	26,300
Escambia	7,006	4,821	11,213	6,814	4,848	11,758
Flagler	90	159	1,712	95	161	1,721
Franklin	23	235	410	23	246	410
Gadsden	117	3,461	1,713	122	3,366	1,775
Gilchrist	28	492	554	30	495	567
Glades	11	32	326	10	35	336
Gulf	15	539	590	14	664	598
Hamilton	33	688	685	33	734	703
Hardee	49	599	1,111	51	575	1,102
Hendry	111	631	1,723	110	615	1,679
Hernando	291	604	4,171	292	604	4,248
Highlands	293	392	3,146	297	391	3,166
Hillsborough	11,166	15,503	42,176	11,217	15,697	40,590
Holmes	60	524	771	57	510	763
Indian River	344	555	3,847	361	554	3,598
Jackson	497	2,806	2,639	509	2,884	2,678
Jefferson	28	385	536	30	409	566
Lafayette	14	389	235	15	376	241
Lake	504	1,196	6,845	519	1,171	7,422
Lee	1,829	3,723	19,492	1,918	3,783	19,979
Leon	1,693	40,345	10,794	1,691	41,311	10,929
Levy	75	353	1,367	77	367	1,399
Liberty	48	433	281	49	428	297
Madison	50	509	931	49	506	977
Manatee	1,148	988	8,858	1,159	983	9,050

See footnotes at end of table.

Continued . . .

University of Florida   **Bureau of Economic and Business Research**

Table 23.74. GOVERNMENT EMPLOYMENT: AVERAGE MONTHLY EMPLOYMENT COVERED BY UNEMPLOYMENT COMPENSATION BY LEVEL OF GOVERNMENT IN THE STATE AND COUNTIES OF FLORIDA, 1998 AND 1999 (Continued)

County	1998 A/			1999 B/		
	Federal	State	Local	Federal	State	Local
Marion	650	2,153	11,316	690	2,116	11,633
Martin	281	865	3,825	290	852	3,960
Miami-Dade	18,342	18,218	99,263	18,379	18,228	100,240
Monroe	1,273	782	3,921	1,271	764	3,982
Nassau	604	266	2,130	599	265	2,326
Okaloosa	6,546	970	6,230	6,513	996	6,355
Okeechobee	75	490	1,232	75	478	1,281
Orange	7,320	11,513	36,691	7,342	11,758	38,306
Osceola	254	573	6,231	271	629	6,637
Palm Beach	5,730	8,446	38,687	5,585	8,407	43,153
Pasco	653	1,304	10,005	681	1,351	10,392
Pinellas	6,031	4,619	30,344	6,144	4,605	32,476
Polk	1,415	4,401	20,531	1,430	4,522	20,436
Putnam	158	583	3,835	155	578	3,917
St. Johns	405	1,332	3,995	420	1,373	4,139
St. Lucie	485	1,325	7,385	528	1,374	7,671
Santa Rosa	811	850	3,681	827	882	3,728
Sarasota	829	1,656	9,484	891	1,658	9,436
Seminole	1,407	897	11,668	1,489	884	12,146
Sumter	779	751	1,275	789	768	1,293
Suwannee	121	293	1,226	127	296	1,241
Taylor	36	514	916	37	539	995
Union	18	1,882	471	19	1,905	474
Volusia	1,266	3,438	15,747	1,298	3,499	15,997
Wakulla	73	415	815	79	445	853
Walton	171	612	1,397	157	616	1,486
Washington	43	962	1,229	51	975	1,169
Multicounty 1/	517	1,299	(NA)	554	1,447	(NA)
Out-of-state 2/	(NA)	(NA)	(NA)	205	271	(NA)

(NA) Not available.
A/ Revised.
B/ Preliminary.
1/ Reporting units without a fixed location within the state or of unknown county location.
2/ Employment based in Florida, but working out of the state or country.
Note: Detail may not add to totals due to rounding.

Source: State of Florida, Department of Labor and Employment Security, Bureau of Labor Market Information, "Employment and Wages" (ES-202), unpublished data.

University of Florida   **Bureau of Economic and Business Research**

Table 23.75. STATE AND LOCAL GOVERNMENT: OPTIONAL GAS TAX RATES AND COLLECTIONS IN THE STATE AND COUNTIES OF FLORIDA, FISCAL YEAR 1998-99

County	Esti-mated gallons (1,000)	Total collec-tions ($1,000)	Service charge 1/ ($1,000)	County	Esti-mated gallons (1,000)	Total collec-tions ($1,000)	Service charge 1/ ($1,000)
Florida	7,291,963	506,868	30,412	Lake	97,297	6,588	395
				Lee	210,503	14,271	856
Alachua	102,859	6,794	408	Leon	108,867	7,186	431
Baker	13,973	982	59	Levy	19,557	1,421	85
Bay	84,920	5,668	340	Liberty	3,103	302	18
Bradford	14,033	941	56	Madison	10,523	1,777	107
Brevard	222,307	15,016	901	Manatee	105,662	7,336	440
Broward	724,590	47,694	2,862	Marion	142,447	10,984	659
Calhoun	5,643	466	28	Martin	64,986	4,327	260
Charlotte	74,963	5,197	312	Miami-Dade	865,112	58,845	3,531
Citrus	50,007	3,284	197	Monroe	55,993	3,557	213
Clay	61,418	4,030	242	Nassau	26,472	2,043	123
Collier	107,621	7,088	425	Okaloosa	91,048	4,907	294
Columbia	43,085	3,431	206	Okeechobee	24,967	1,902	114
De Soto	8,989	714	43	Orange	474,943	33,828	2,030
Dixie	6,340	497	30	Osceola	98,308	6,821	409
Duval	367,230	27,386	1,643	Palm Beach	455,885	30,443	1,827
Escambia	137,345	9,531	572	Pasco	138,818	9,587	575
Flagler	20,410	1,434	86	Pinellas	367,085	23,792	1,427
Franklin	6,488	386	23	Polk	230,233	18,220	1,093
Gadsden	25,687	2,541	152	Putnam	34,833	2,434	146
Gilchrist	5,025	353	21	St. Johns	65,949	5,138	308
Glades	3,804	305	18	St. Lucie	94,407	6,792	408
Gulf	4,935	340	20	Santa Rosa	55,519	3,648	219
Hamilton	10,660	749	45	Sarasota	145,477	9,576	575
Hardee	10,599	853	51	Seminole	158,175	10,197	612
Hendry	20,080	1,290	77	Sumter	35,394	3,925	235
Hernando	56,948	4,096	246	Suwannee	22,481	1,783	107
Highlands	37,029	2,842	170	Taylor	12,339	837	50
Hillsborough	475,173	33,931	2,036	Union	4,230	382	23
Holmes	9,308	661	40	Volusia	212,727	13,751	825
Indian River	54,939	4,253	255	Wakulla	10,771	756	45
Jackson	30,498	2,804	168	Walton	28,420	2,174	130
Jefferson	9,576	863	52	Washington	10,648	745	45
Lafayette	2,304	176	11				

1/ Six percent charge imposed on collections for state general revenue fund.
Note: Detail may not add to totals because of rounding.

Source: State of Florida, Department of Revenue, Internet site <http://sun6.dms.state.fl.us/dor/tables/f91999.html> (accessed 15 June 2000), and unpublished data.

Table 23.76. STATE AND LOCAL GOVERNMENT: EMPLOYMENT BY FUNCTION AND PAYROLL
OF STATE AND LOCAL GOVERNMENTS IN FLORIDA AND THE UNITED STATES
MARCH 1999

Item	Florida State and local	Florida State only	United States State and local	United States State only
Full-time equivalent employees, all functions	733,590	179,654	14,708,602	4,043,265
General administration	62,392	24,997	1,001,943	361,805
Financial	21,822	7,049	370,520	163,609
Central	13,012	1,812	257,514	53,796
Judicial and legal	27,558	16,136	373,909	144,400
Police protection	53,387	3,991	849,063	98,239
Police with powers of arrest	36,001	2,208	638,305	59,153
Other police protection	17,386	1,783	210,758	39,086
Fire protection	19,851	A/	289,590	A/
Correction	45,736	31,872	678,178	457,185
Streets and highways	23,177	10,310	543,337	247,209
Air and water transportation	4,130	1	51,653	7,551
Airports	2,880	A/	38,823	2,939
Water transport	1,250	1	12,830	4,612
Public welfare	18,237	12,455	485,835	224,109
Health	23,516	17,996	393,650	169,371
Hospitals	34,799	5,969	952,301	415,771
Social insurance administration	3,781	3,781	93,426	93,426
Solid waste management	6,863	A/	109,176	1,745
Sewerage	8,631	A/	122,878	1,489
Parks and recreation	17,041	1,080	238,325	32,937
Housing and community development	4,410	A/	119,061	A/
Natural resources	12,324	7,724	182,297	146,984
Public utilities	22,017	523	448,239	34,138
Water supply	9,924	A/	156,023	844
Electric power	5,157	A/	78,214	5,468
Gas supply	820	A/	10,805	A/
Transit	6,116	523	203,197	27,826
Education	338,600	48,525	7,564,775	1,541,501
Elementary and secondary schools	267,739	A/	5,765,345	44,861
Higher education	68,795	46,459	1,701,596	1,398,806
Other education	2,066	2,066	97,834	97,834
Libraries 1/	4,836	A/	115,980	546
State liquor stores	(X)	(X)	6,918	6,918
Other and unallocable	29,862	10,430	461,977	202,341
March payroll, total ($1,000)	2,016,220	530,526	43,762,637	12,561,997

(X) Not applicable.
A/ Local government only.
1/ United States totals include state government amounts for some states.

Source: U.S., Department of Commerce, Bureau of the Census, "1999 Public Employment Data State
and Local Governments" and "State Government Employment Data, March 1999," Internet site <http://
www.census.gov/govs/apes/> (accessed 4 August 2000).

University of Florida   **Bureau of Economic and Business Research**

Table 23.77. LOCAL GOVERNMENT: EMPLOYMENT AND PAYROLL BY SPECIFIED FUNCTION IN THE STATE AND COUNTIES OF FLORIDA, MARCH 1997

County	Total	Total 1/	Education	Public welfare	Health and hospitals	Highways	Public safety 2/	Environment and housing 3/	Government administration	Utilities	March payroll ($1,000)	Average earnings 4/ (dollars)
Florida	631,590	543,525	287,037	5,293	37,147	13,487	65,016	35,069	35,541	21,114	1,358,677	2,549
Alachua	10,474	8,678	4,932	82	200	125	999	499	669	487	19,560	2,319
Baker	860	691	538	3	9	24	24	27	26	11	1,406	2,071
Bay	7,880	6,634	3,570	4	1,378	246	537	292	311	91	14,679	2,261
Bradford	1,283	906	616	0	13	23	64	27	74	33	1,680	1,847
Brevard	18,160	15,688	8,366	102	960	475	1,819	1,221	1,123	391	34,996	2,280
Broward	65,689	55,161	24,295	307	8,002	965	7,558	3,644	3,687	2,335	154,379	2,885
Calhoun	503	425	294	3	0	28	20	9	40	3	862	2,070
Charlotte	4,304	3,687	1,947	29	20	174	554	148	375	139	8,063	2,202
Citrus	3,957	2,941	1,903	23	33	117	254	89	260	47	6,217	2,164
Clay	4,133	3,890	2,718	3	11	144	437	124	220	44	8,376	2,166
Collier	7,785	6,758	3,596	19	169	123	1,066	537	663	136	17,145	2,570
Columbia	2,390	2,034	1,421	3	20	81	158	64	143	26	3,972	1,963
De Soto	1,080	957	619	3	2	63	97	44	46	16	1,862	1,961
Dixie	569	480	366	1	18	28	4	33	20	2	811	1,700
Duval	27,996	23,788	13,445	127	320	574	3,002	1,113	1,350	1,927	64,594	2,744
Escambia	11,889	9,925	6,357	194	152	230	889	584	388	275	21,160	2,143
Flagler	1,555	1,235	934	4	40	59	40	40	37	12	2,289	1,870
Franklin	492	438	222	0	0	7	12	8	11	16	799	1,842
Gadsden	1,738	1,590	1,135	1	22	91	125	49	86	37	3,249	2,059
Gilchrist	543	421	337	0	0	3	3	1	4	2	789	1,878
Glades	317	285	139	3	13	22	24	13	48	2	566	1,993
Gulf	655	555	307	2	12	25	67	65	45	11	1,153	2,108
Hamilton	693	652	385	1	15	32	42	22	35	7	1,278	1,965

Continued . . .

See footnotes at end of table.

Table 23.77. LOCAL GOVERNMENT: EMPLOYMENT AND PAYROLL BY SPECIFIED FUNCTION IN THE STATE AND COUNTIES OF FLORIDA, MARCH 1997 (Continued)

County	Total	Employment Full-time equivalent Total 1/	Edu- cation	Public welfare	Health and hosp- itals	High- ways	Public safety 2/	Environ- ment and hous- ing 3/	Govern- ment adminis- tration	Utili- ties	March payroll ($1,000)	Average earn- ings 4/ (dollars)
Hardee	1,145	1,001	735	2	12	61	42	46	52	15	1,849	1,862
Hendry	1,560	1,428	847	2	204	61	6	61	26	15	2,680	1,882
Hernando	4,292	3,912	1,998	2	14	102	420	124	367	61	8,476	2,175
Highlands	3,020	2,568	1,607	7	40	110	230	73	216	31	5,430	2,148
Hillsborough	40,849	37,347	19,204	622	4,497	827	3,881	2,683	2,554	797	90,257	2,443
Holmes	703	611	478	0	0	3	10	33	5	5	1,155	1,920
Indian River	3,801	3,555	1,611	7	87	215	534	347	181	269	8,426	2,410
Jackson	2,907	2,416	1,439	155	404	84	104	45	47	14	4,959	2,094
Jefferson	542	461	318	6	7	40	26	25	21	4	806	1,754
Lafayette	272	241	170	0	12	11	7	6	21	0	430	1,784
Lake	6,435	5,478	3,220	12	52	169	687	285	380	148	11,768	2,193
Lee	19,782	16,564	7,038	212	4,351	432	1,727	1,042	664	213	41,611	2,593
Leon	13,081	9,973	5,322	46	180	454	1,017	614	979	580	23,940	2,483
Levy	1,397	1,293	891	0	11	89	89	37	51	13	2,436	1,925
Liberty	259	225	173	0	5	18	0	3	15	11	430	1,935
Madison	1,129	895	561	1	113	33	54	31	50	13	1,774	1,993
Manatee	8,756	8,166	4,422	61	203	217	929	617	448	348	17,684	2,178
Marion	8,772	7,572	4,942	11	17	233	969	382	409	153	15,381	2,040
Martin	3,841	3,357	1,912	4	81	112	484	110	290	85	7,469	2,247
Miami-Dade	100,994	87,062	40,785	1,800	9,888	1,058	11,135	6,925	5,202	4,165	265,222	3,182
Monroe	4,511	4,229	1,729	0	487	61	528	174	425	422	10,245	2,436
Nassau	2,011	1,806	1,192	1	50	62	182	75	116	1	3,826	2,144
Okaloosa	6,771	5,770	3,844	5	67	225	557	308	237	267	12,431	2,195
Okeechobee	1,663	1,429	1,061	10	0	41	140	16	49	19	2,937	2,122

See footnotes at end of table.

Continued . . .

Table 23.77. LOCAL GOVERNMENT: EMPLOYMENT AND PAYROLL BY SPECIFIED FUNCTION IN THE STATE AND COUNTIES OF FLORIDA, MARCH 1997 (Continued)

| County | Total | Employment Full-time equivalent | | | | | | | | | March payroll ($1,000) | Average earnings 4/ (dollars) |
		Total 1/	Education	Public welfare	Health and hospitals	Highways	Public safety 2/	Environment and housing 3/	Government administration	Utilities		
Orange	39,781	33,139	18,580	597	185	875	3,535	2,775	2,380	1,664	78,201	2,405
Osceola	6,361	5,478	3,195	38	20	235	620	308	395	289	11,965	2,208
Palm Beach	41,482	34,775	16,497	282	504	824	5,396	2,379	2,561	1,230	93,465	2,722
Pasco	8,445	7,965	6,256	0	22	32	764	111	426	37	16,182	2,051
Pinellas	33,635	28,611	14,897	134	163	659	3,793	2,620	2,337	1,328	71,007	2,511
Polk	18,120	16,728	9,568	191	305	537	1,921	926	1,266	989	35,494	2,138
Putnam	3,859	3,477	2,037	2	55	103	211	92	111	722	7,593	2,204
St. Johns	6,836	5,568	2,055	0	100	96	332	234	247	58	12,230	2,234
St. Lucie	8,421	7,451	4,828	17	6	236	878	377	391	182	16,810	2,275
Santa Rosa	3,718	3,062	2,178	3	11	125	216	81	248	44	6,532	2,160
Sarasota	11,434	10,853	4,110	11	2,655	327	1,643	603	510	356	29,280	2,724
Seminole	11,487	10,211	6,269	10	117	354	1,403	675	840	167	25,085	2,502
Sumter	1,689	1,479	820	2	64	19	159	61	154	15	2,712	1,900
Suwannee	1,310	1,128	706	0	0	63	88	55	43	37	2,353	2,114
Taylor	1,051	872	542	1	33	8	98	43	79	16	1,686	1,962
Union	493	395	330	0	8	10	0	15	6	0	698	1,787
Volusia	16,202	13,890	8,474	115	76	453	2,185	928	858	253	29,645	2,151
Wakulla	881	715	547	4	18	1	56	6	30	3	1,409	1,992
Walton	1,472	1,309	729	6	52	139	108	57	99	17	2,380	1,825
Washington	1,475	1,241	478	0	562	14	57	8	94	8	2,441	1,989

1/ Includes "other" and unallocable employment.
2/ State total includes Corrections.
3/ State total includes natural resources.
4/ Average March earning of full-time equivalent employees.

Source: U.S., Department of Commerce, Bureau of the Census, *1997 Census of Governments, Volume 3, Public Employment: Compendium of Public Employment, 1997*, Issued March 2000, Internet site <http://www.census.gov/prod/gc97/gc973-2.pdf> (accessed 26 June 2000).

Table 23.81. COUNTY FINANCE: REVENUE AND EXPENDITURE AND PER CAPITA AMOUNTS
IN THE STATE AND COUNTIES OF FLORIDA, FISCAL YEARS
1995-96 AND 1996-97

	Revenue				Expenditure			
	Total ($1,000)		Per capita (dollars)		Total ($1,000)		Per capita (dollars)	
County	1995-96	1996-97	1995-96	1996-97	1995-96	1996-97	1995-96	1996-97
Florida	21,209,643	21,912,409	1,472	1,489	19,789,861	20,591,540	1,373	1,400
Alachua	198,580	166,047	982	798	196,757	160,819	973	773
Baker	14,710	15,919	710	753	14,525	15,503	701	733
Bay	138,630	125,135	975	865	130,106	115,386	915	798
Bradford	14,955	16,474	599	653	16,170	17,139	647	679
Brevard	334,531	335,104	743	732	342,316	339,409	760	741
Broward	1,879,163	1,768,868	1,350	1,242	1,626,288	1,776,718	1,168	1,248
Calhoun	10,304	9,166	824	712	10,552	8,217	844	638
Charlotte	187,121	198,594	1,445	1,512	168,630	199,237	1,302	1,517
Citrus	124,133	81,577	1,151	742	119,029	80,416	1,103	731
Clay	106,461	129,463	849	1,012	95,732	122,251	763	956
Collier	288,574	325,575	1,495	1,628	299,854	295,794	1,553	1,479
Columbia	45,271	52,532	861	979	41,254	49,133	785	915
De Soto	22,895	24,439	857	898	24,532	24,106	918	885
Dixie	13,211	13,795	1,048	1,058	13,726	13,760	1,089	1,055
Duval 1/	2,205,284	2,977,319	3,027	4,015	1,731,056	2,367,201	2,376	3,192
Escambia	224,887	219,228	785	753	216,726	207,906	757	714
Flagler	40,970	42,937	1,049	1,042	41,677	42,793	1,067	1,039
Franklin	11,997	13,549	1,156	1,291	10,437	11,714	1,006	1,116
Gadsden	29,230	27,939	631	562	27,946	26,532	603	533
Gilchrist	11,020	12,568	907	1,003	10,096	11,630	831	928
Glades	12,395	12,697	1,317	1,316	11,919	12,440	1,266	1,289
Gulf	12,857	12,812	949	908	12,834	14,127	948	1,002
Hamilton	16,491	15,538	1,228	1,133	15,858	15,260	1,181	1,113
Hardee	27,875	17,167	1,238	765	27,327	26,739	1,213	1,191
Hendry	33,439	34,074	1,109	1,124	32,800	33,277	1,088	1,098
Hernando	111,145	124,619	927	1,021	108,665	112,180	906	919
Highlands	58,907	61,661	755	775	56,046	29,261	719	368
Hillsborough	1,476,821	1,434,503	1,621	1,545	1,439,549	1,325,753	1,580	1,427
Holmes	8,037	7,627	462	433	7,467	7,729	429	439
Indian River	130,148	143,637	1,273	1,373	116,381	137,256	1,139	1,312
Jackson	27,611	30,157	568	611	25,693	32,366	528	655
Jefferson	10,639	10,459	776	748	10,600	10,582	773	757
Lafayette	5,547	6,349	791	907	5,945	6,613	848	944
Lake	110,085	114,305	604	607	104,584	107,883	574	573
Lee	806,166	730,419	2,101	1,853	841,330	768,140	2,193	1,948

See footnotes at end of table.   Continued . . .

University of Florida   **Bureau of Economic and Business Research**

Table 23.81. COUNTY FINANCE: REVENUE AND EXPENDITURE AND PER CAPITA AMOUNTS
IN THE STATE AND COUNTIES OF FLORIDA, FISCAL YEARS
1995-96 AND 1996-97 (Continued)

	Revenue				Expenditure			
	Total ($1,000)		Per capita (dollars)		Total ($1,000)		Per capita (dollars)	
County	1995-96	1996-97	1995-96	1996-97	1995-96	1996-97	1995-96	1996-97
Leon	167,296	185,905	755	816	162,745	165,543	734	727
Levy	27,015	27,419	880	868	25,466	25,843	830	818
Liberty	7,232	8,918	972	1,159	7,169	9,271	964	1,205
Madison	14,376	15,366	767	807	14,142	13,698	754	720
Manatee	333,086	338,627	1,407	1,403	300,034	322,276	1,267	1,335
Marion	145,046	162,284	633	684	139,751	156,882	610	661
Martin	174,777	184,307	1,527	1,584	176,506	161,890	1,542	1,391
Miami-Dade	5,106,402	4,858,389	2,499	2,346	4,963,124	4,695,667	2,429	2,268
Monroe	195,537	198,270	2,334	2,340	176,526	178,641	2,107	2,108
Nassau	48,867	52,498	956	995	42,993	48,524	841	920
Okaloosa	138,176	145,242	836	849	114,205	142,662	691	834
Okeechobee	32,015	35,770	952	1,029	32,754	32,170	974	926
Orange	1,174,535	1,272,641	1,511	1,584	1,156,953	1,211,081	1,488	1,507
Osceola	264,308	227,500	1,892	1,582	243,908	215,977	1,746	1,502
Palm Beach	1,491,642	1,587,803	1,519	1,582	1,497,496	1,622,280	1,525	1,616
Pasco	253,900	270,734	819	857	246,844	262,787	796	832
Pinellas	945,808	997,390	1,073	1,123	890,420	923,375	1,010	1,040
Polk	295,324	370,942	652	808	278,020	306,391	614	668
Putnam	65,676	63,709	934	907	66,776	58,655	950	835
St. Johns	125,705	133,172	1,236	1,257	123,983	129,473	1,219	1,222
St. Lucie	144,310	132,114	822	738	133,121	134,024	759	748
Santa Rosa	84,794	77,926	861	761	76,748	76,522	779	748
Sarasota	378,833	429,158	1,239	1,380	361,831	412,320	1,183	1,326
Seminole	352,361	322,929	1,071	957	316,953	301,139	963	892
Sumter	32,716	35,252	806	795	38,344	33,169	945	748
Suwannee	40,117	30,042	1,277	904	39,926	30,576	1,271	920
Taylor	26,285	30,251	1,382	1,577	24,212	29,420	1,273	1,534
Union	7,555	8,113	580	619	7,837	7,337	602	560
Volusia	306,045	318,221	752	769	300,926	285,533	739	690
Wakulla	19,592	20,680	1,087	1,108	19,014	20,647	1,055	1,106
Walton	45,822	44,564	1,335	1,235	41,423	38,144	1,207	1,057
Washington	14,398	14,022	729	697	12,952	14,353	656	714

1/ Duval County is the consolidated city of Jacksonville.
Note: Per capita figures computed using Bureau of Economic and Business Research April 1, 1996 and 1997 population estimates.

Source: State of Florida, Department of Banking and Finance, Office of the Comptroller, Internet site
<http://localgovserver.dbf.state.fl.us/>.

Table 23.83. COUNTY FINANCE: REVENUE BY SOURCE OF COUNTY GOVERNMENTS IN FLORIDA
FISCAL YEAR 1996-97

(rounded to thousands of dollars)

County	Total	Taxes and impact fees	Federal grants	State and other govern-ments	Charges for services	Fines and forfeits	Other sources and transfers
Florida	21,912,409	6,635,148	656,600	1,795,524	6,268,576	149,625	6,406,936
Alachua	166,047	65,387	1,521	18,231	23,633	1,884	55,391
Baker	15,919	5,030	884	3,072	1,721	206	5,005
Bay	125,135	42,249	514	15,245	29,003	1,477	36,646
Bradford	16,474	5,499	542	2,823	2,249	328	5,032
Brevard	335,104	129,515	5,071	45,060	107,222	3,037	45,199
Broward	1,768,868	546,203	34,069	128,854	466,757	11,424	581,561
Calhoun	9,166	2,637	1,696	2,247	259	94	2,232
Charlotte	198,594	77,560	1,072	16,339	67,629	795	35,199
Citrus	81,577	40,009	1,324	13,059	13,941	717	12,527
Clay	129,463	44,035	20	14,110	9,486	1,266	60,547
Collier	325,575	117,972	2,267	33,288	87,662	3,911	80,475
Columbia	52,532	18,094	1,050	6,692	5,476	809	20,411
De Soto	24,439	9,459	25	3,255	2,558	200	8,941
Dixie	13,795	4,088	2,547	2,535	849	199	3,577
Duval 1/	2,977,319	398,057	34,955	169,788	1,142,181	11,571	1,220,767
Escambia	219,228	102,946	8,430	35,519	40,157	2,403	29,773
Flagler	42,937	18,621	252	5,504	5,296	256	13,007
Franklin	13,549	4,888	392	2,644	939	210	4,477
Gadsden	27,939	9,468	169	5,314	1,983	512	10,493
Gilchrist	12,568	3,557	1,839	1,947	1,128	104	3,992
Glades	12,697	4,240	588	2,250	1,081	460	4,077
Gulf	12,812	5,053	334	2,364	1,065	172	3,825
Hamilton	15,538	5,499	653	2,814	1,564	254	4,754
Hardee	17,167	6,742	132	3,827	1,115	365	4,985
Hendry	34,074	13,368	501	4,525	5,018	438	10,225
Hernando	124,619	52,486	32	10,880	27,954	848	32,420
Highlands	61,661	32,756	159	10,373	6,352	801	11,220
Hillsborough	1,434,503	481,644	53,993	124,462	255,247	2,735	516,421
Holmes	7,627	2,848	1,421	2,412	587	23	337
Indian River	143,637	69,853	1,912	11,671	37,584	1,037	21,581
Jackson	30,157	11,010	1,318	5,755	3,660	351	8,063
Jefferson	10,459	4,701	716	2,313	811	281	1,637
Lafayette	6,349	1,844	36	1,958	389	86	2,035
Lake	114,305	51,107	1,487	15,759	25,060	1,779	19,114

See footnotes at end of table.   Continued . . .

University of Florida   **Bureau of Economic and Business Research**

Table 23.83. COUNTY FINANCE: REVENUE BY SOURCE OF COUNTY GOVERNMENTS IN FLORIDA FISCAL YEAR 1996-97 (Continued)

(rounded to thousands of dollars)

County	Total	Taxes and impact fees	Federal grants	State and other govern-ments	Charges for services	Fines and forfeits	Other sources and transfers
Lee	730,419	176,689	9,290	70,818	234,811	2,505	236,305
Leon	185,905	78,672	2,765	20,845	20,319	1,385	61,919
Levy	27,419	11,037	185	4,455	2,495	339	8,907
Liberty	8,918	1,448	225	2,396	651	177	4,021
Madison	15,366	5,453	474	2,932	1,040	1,026	4,440
Manatee	338,627	97,754	1,903	39,384	133,226	1,979	64,381
Marion	162,284	77,992	678	26,331	24,356	2,382	30,545
Martin	184,307	84,690	1,216	18,669	38,118	2,138	39,476
Miami-Dade	4,858,389	1,237,942	342,369	252,438	1,916,995	26,358	1,082,286
Monroe	198,270	83,685	13,600	16,704	35,176	4,418	44,687
Nassau	52,498	22,789	388	5,257	11,941	579	11,543
Okaloosa	145,242	28,611	4,049	17,632	40,901	116	53,933
Okeechobee	35,770	12,850	1,309	5,179	4,104	505	11,823
Orange	1,272,641	494,434	22,616	133,942	250,199	12,156	359,295
Osceola	227,500	89,173	529	17,737	24,082	797	95,182
Palm Beach	1,587,803	481,456	28,909	99,494	381,348	10,396	586,200
Pasco	270,734	110,878	7,046	29,418	69,377	1,221	52,795
Pinellas	997,390	322,280	11,970	68,458	260,566	6,879	327,237
Polk	370,942	133,862	9,955	49,834	72,263	4,317	100,710
Putnam	63,709	24,979	241	7,137	9,906	588	20,857
St. Johns	133,172	52,592	1,068	14,043	31,199	1,409	32,861
St. Lucie	132,114	67,115	2,289	18,090	27,993	2,457	14,170
Santa Rosa	77,926	33,317	486	10,720	22,696	1,058	9,650
Sarasota	429,158	179,555	4,277	37,454	113,643	2,786	91,444
Seminole	322,929	145,552	4,732	32,159	46,597	3,352	90,538
Sumter	35,252	12,145	1,608	4,807	3,447	1,060	12,184
Suwannee	30,042	9,314	729	6,356	2,930	500	10,213
Taylor	30,251	9,116	32	5,206	14,482	250	1,165
Union	8,113	2,043	239	2,025	381	73	3,352
Volusia	318,221	125,147	13,700	35,622	86,813	4,010	52,929
Wakulla	20,680	5,866	1,626	3,916	2,653	356	6,261
Walton	44,564	22,914	3,238	6,669	5,273	708	5,762
Washington	14,022	5,369	938	2,506	983	309	3,916

1/ Duval County is the consolidated city of Jacksonville.
Correction: Data presented in the previous *Abstract* were for fiscal year ending 1996, not fiscal year 1996-97 as shown.

Source: State of Florida, Department of Banking and Finance, Office of the Comptroller, Internet site <http://localgovserver.dbf.state.fl.us/>.

University of Florida   **Bureau of Economic and Business Research**

Table 23.84. COUNTY FINANCE: EXPENDITURE BY FUNCTION OF COUNTY GOVERNMENTS
IN FLORIDA, FISCAL YEAR 1996-97

(rounded to thousands of dollars)

County	Total	General govern- ment	Public safety	Physical and eco- nomic environ- ment	Trans- porta- tion	Human services cultural and re- creation	Debt service and other uses and interfund transfers
Florida	20,591,540	2,764,046	3,852,665	3,445,248	2,481,868	2,476,422	5,571,291
Alachua	160,819	32,365	48,940	9,698	11,637	5,479	52,700
Baker	15,503	2,246	4,129	1,601	2,568	713	4,246
Bay	115,386	22,513	32,241	29,628	6,115	5,784	19,107
Bradford	17,139	3,036	3,588	1,618	1,282	728	6,887
Brevard	339,409	82,749	66,008	54,482	34,529	43,494	58,147
Broward	1,776,718	190,369	335,410	196,883	197,221	264,845	591,990
Calhoun	8,217	1,130	1,929	1,033	1,290	477	2,358
Charlotte	199,237	36,190	42,366	39,059	17,677	14,127	49,817
Citrus	80,416	25,687	19,970	2,856	11,994	7,630	12,280
Clay	122,251	26,011	25,088	7,023	11,323	6,721	46,085
Collier	295,794	49,139	72,963	54,427	26,954	24,228	68,083
Columbia	49,133	5,315	10,423	6,947	3,514	2,358	20,576
De Soto	24,106	3,636	6,009	2,040	1,877	874	9,670
Dixie	13,760	1,737	2,947	1,501	3,387	354	3,835
Duval 1/	2,367,201	271,666	261,624	764,258	214,343	169,695	685,614
Escambia	207,906	45,577	66,238	18,278	42,750	10,355	24,709
Flagler	42,793	9,004	9,320	1,863	7,288	2,461	12,858
Franklin	11,714	1,777	3,234	1,010	1,112	695	3,887
Gadsden	26,532	5,062	6,095	1,249	3,299	2,072	8,755
Gilchrist	11,630	2,100	3,180	1,196	801	362	3,990
Glades	12,440	2,462	3,234	1,083	1,469	416	3,777
Gulf	14,127	2,878	2,843	1,539	2,386	696	3,785
Hamilton	15,260	2,266	3,932	1,977	1,781	744	4,560
Hardee	26,739	4,048	5,143	1,280	2,735	1,186	12,347
Hendry	33,277	5,964	8,364	3,330	3,577	1,530	10,513
Hernando	112,180	20,594	32,943	12,828	10,239	6,023	29,552
Highlands	29,261	9,180	1,237	8,446	9,006	46	1,346
Hillsborough	1,325,753	179,371	222,010	170,933	73,309	176,539	503,590
Holmes	7,729	1,637	1,849	1,336	1,812	376	718
Indian River	137,256	23,261	41,016	29,553	11,893	13,292	18,241
Jackson	32,366	5,074	6,753	1,910	6,830	2,402	9,396
Jefferson	10,582	1,384	3,034	2,260	1,562	398	1,943
Lafayette	6,613	1,066	2,120	607	530	256	2,035
Lake	107,883	23,049	30,514	13,714	11,934	7,353	21,318

See footnotes at end of table.   Continued . . .

University of Florida   **Bureau of Economic and Business Research**

Table 23.84. COUNTY FINANCE: EXPENDITURE BY FUNCTION OF COUNTY GOVERNMENTS
IN FLORIDA, FISCAL YEAR 1996-97 (Continued)

(rounded to thousands of dollars)

County	Total	General govern- ment	Public safety	Physical and eco- nomic environ- ment	Trans- porta- tion	Human services cultural and re- creation	Debt service and other uses and interfund transfers
Lee	768,140	131,971	116,655	70,691	156,939	48,863	243,021
Leon	165,543	31,147	38,694	16,414	14,976	10,871	53,441
Levy	25,843	4,231	7,596	1,499	3,291	1,031	8,194
Liberty	9,271	1,286	1,241	1,075	1,080	129	4,460
Madison	13,698	1,793	3,524	1,781	1,859	555	4,185
Manatee	322,276	72,880	64,165	67,522	30,558	28,414	58,737
Marion	156,882	31,216	50,771	11,520	25,931	11,048	26,395
Martin	161,890	32,174	46,302	24,456	10,762	20,216	27,980
Miami-Dade	4,695,667	303,328	735,580	878,672	848,601	1,081,666	847,820
Monroe	178,641	29,384	52,939	25,249	10,111	20,957	40,002
Nassau	48,524	8,148	11,112	8,090	6,550	2,018	12,607
Okaloosa	142,662	27,721	22,713	23,942	11,971	6,744	49,572
Okeechobee	32,170	5,283	8,547	2,383	2,109	2,717	11,131
Orange	1,211,081	142,394	252,812	152,705	101,244	87,152	474,774
Osceola	215,977	31,337	43,566	20,358	27,214	13,125	80,377
Palm Beach	1,622,280	255,619	296,386	234,892	164,546	123,890	546,947
Pasco	262,787	51,221	57,359	45,668	25,024	16,455	67,060
Pinellas	923,375	162,947	193,044	129,796	64,751	59,409	313,427
Polk	306,391	72,083	92,557	43,547	31,808	24,781	41,615
Putnam	58,655	14,169	13,913	5,591	3,203	2,810	18,969
St. Johns	129,473	20,450	27,816	17,916	9,677	12,767	40,847
St. Lucie	134,024	37,208	32,109	13,398	22,131	15,974	13,204
Santa Rosa	76,522	16,668	37,585	3,704	7,365	4,650	6,551
Sarasota	412,320	63,719	93,625	75,591	44,052	35,368	99,963
Seminole	301,139	46,472	67,731	44,181	49,194	12,449	81,111
Sumter	33,169	4,685	6,751	3,983	3,057	1,135	13,558
Suwannee	30,576	5,242	5,775	3,814	3,408	2,603	9,733
Taylor	29,420	1,024	1,588	2,461	5,182	13,727	5,436
Union	7,337	845	1,372	1,098	613	350	3,059
Volusia	285,533	46,548	67,395	49,019	44,741	35,683	42,146
Wakulla	20,647	2,875	5,301	3,987	1,213	1,162	6,108
Walton	38,144	5,871	6,924	11,933	6,395	1,869	5,152
Washington	14,353	2,564	2,523	867	2,287	1,121	4,991

1/ Duval County is the consolidated city of Jacksonville.
Correction: Data presented in the previous *Abstract* were for fiscal year ending 1996, not fiscal year
1996-97 as shown.

Source: State of Florida, Department of Banking and Finance, Office of the Comptroller, Internet site
<http://localgovserver.dbf.state.fl.us/>.

University of Florida   **Bureau of Economic and Business Research**

Table 23.85. MUNICIPAL FINANCE: REVENUE AND EXPENDITURE PER CAPITA, PERSONAL
SERVICES EXPENDITURE, AND BONDED INDEBTEDNESS OF CITY GOVERNMENTS
SERVING A 1997 POPULATION OF 45,000 OR MORE IN FLORIDA
FISCAL YEAR 1996-97

City	Revenue Total ($1,000)	Revenue Per capita (dollars)	Expenditure Total ($1,000)	Expenditure Per capita (dollars)
Jacksonville 1/	2,977,319	4,261	2,367,201	3,388
Miami	863	2	542	1
Tampa	893,734	3,072	628,100	2,159
St. Petersburg	550,474	2,280	486,385	2,015
Hialeah	258,927	1,251	189,294	914
Orlando	644,128	3,652	462,740	2,624
Ft. Lauderdale	481,341	3,205	314,945	2,097
Tallahassee	670,259	4,766	570,185	4,054
Hollywood	260,599	2,060	195,924	1,549
Clearwater	296,342	2,837	227,874	2,181
Pembroke Pines	114,520	1,100	105,312	1,011
Coral Springs	131,474	1,277	106,242	1,032
Gainesville	317,153	3,176	288,123	2,885
Miami Beach	416,124	4,478	325,742	3,505
Cape Coral	140,455	1,560	117,346	1,303
West Palm Beach	209,106	2,621	169,917	2,130
Port St. Lucie	97,227	1,247	87,113	1,117
Plantation	121,644	1,571	99,321	1,282
Palm Bay	66,211	871	61,682	812
Sunrise	173,974	2,310	136,294	1,810
Lakeland	385,480	5,122	355,953	4,729
Pompano Beach	222,958	3,003	117,669	1,585
Boca Raton	199,349	2,913	162,227	2,371
Melbourne	92,858	1,364	80,561	1,184
Largo	61,622	906	62,469	918
Daytona Beach	118,392	1,846	100,801	1,572
Davie	81,380	1,317	55,450	897
Pensacola	197,756	3,264	167,114	2,758
Deltona	19,253	329	14,365	246
Delray Beach	125,712	2,376	96,046	1,815
Boynton Beach	113,450	2,169	84,636	1,618
Sarasota	162,228	3,161	108,581	2,116
Tamarac	60,616	1,193	44,878	884
North Miami	101,379	2,012	78,066	1,549
Lauderhill	40,867	814	33,008	658
Miramar	58,029	1,159	45,395	907
Margate	42,001	842	41,118	824
Deerfield Beach	85,275	1,727	60,112	1,217
Bradenton	76,382	1,591	59,216	1,233
Ft. Myers	138,958	2,987	127,758	2,746

1/ Consolidated Duval County.
Note: Per capita figures computed using Bureau of Economic and Business Research April 1, 1997
population estimates.

Source: State of Florida, Department of Banking and Finance, Office of the Comptroller, Internet site
<http://localgovserver.dbf.state.fl.us/>.

University of Florida   **Bureau of Economic and Business Research**

Table 23.86. MUNICIPAL FINANCE: REVENUE BY SOURCE OF CITY GOVERNMENTS
SERVING A 1997 POPULATION OF 45,000 OR MORE IN FLORIDA
FISCAL YEAR 1996-97

(rounded to thousands of dollars)

City	Total	Taxes and impact fees	Federal grants	State and other govern- ments	Charges for services	Fines and for- feits	Other sources and trans- fers
Jacksonville 1/	2,977,319	398,057	34,955	169,788	1,142,181	11,571	1,220,767
Miami	863	206	53	36	77	3	488
Tampa	893,734	151,469	20,519	46,188	177,335	4,359	493,865
St. Petersburg	550,474	96,150	7,220	45,936	159,154	2,395	239,620
Hialeah	258,927	69,955	12,057	16,571	53,225	0	107,118
Orlando	644,128	130,358	13,695	70,048	138,022	1,988	290,016
Ft. Lauderdale	481,341	98,469	18,771	16,649	120,432	4,546	222,473
Tallahassee	670,259	48,709	15,255	11,887	339,880	1,909	252,619
Hollywood	260,599	55,775	3,190	17,254	78,955	2,483	102,941
Clearwater	296,342	54,120	2,463	13,830	97,309	1,932	126,688
Pembroke Pines	114,520	52,010	987	7,806	27,797	1,265	24,655
Coral Springs	131,474	40,301	522	7,651	23,656	1,259	58,085
Gainesville	317,153	23,943	5,955	10,731	203,262	1,582	71,680
Miami Beach	416,124	95,291	6,102	23,586	70,056	6,533	214,556
Cape Coral	140,455	33,107	1,401	9,191	33,715	1,432	61,609
West Palm Beach	209,106	54,388	5,161	11,825	70,949	1,270	65,512
Port St. Lucie	97,227	24,714	1,259	4,470	27,156	519	39,110
Plantation	121,644	33,324	62	6,082	32,448	832	48,896
Palm Bay	66,211	25,091	632	5,977	17,004	381	17,126
Sunrise	173,974	41,119	1,269	6,481	55,126	595	69,383
Lakeland	385,480	21,285	3,811	11,815	222,915	906	124,748
Pompano Beach	222,958	91,270	2,257	12,849	57,075	2,639	56,867
Boca Raton	199,349	53,993	2,986	14,118	38,099	1,346	88,807
Melbourne	92,858	24,993	890	5,490	34,897	909	25,679
Largo	61,622	21,556	1,766	10,939	7,264	480	19,617
Daytona Beach	118,392	26,888	2,306	7,172	50,965	1,118	29,944
Davie	81,380	28,052	982	4,274	13,602	1,019	33,451
Pensacola	197,756	28,054	7,098	7,596	54,556	637	99,814
Deltona	19,253	10,169	0	3,676	3,707	138	1,563
Delray Beach	125,712	33,355	1,498	5,688	35,931	638	48,602
Boynton Beach	113,450	28,914	279	7,554	31,272	186	45,246
Sarasota	162,228	34,076	1,822	5,375	47,817	1,141	71,997
Tamarac	60,616	17,653	28	3,773	19,554	403	19,204
North Miami	101,379	17,874	565	5,361	29,263	913	47,404
Lauderhill	40,867	13,512	439	4,378	13,965	236	8,337
Miramar	58,029	20,767	596	3,600	18,323	600	14,143
Margate	42,001	17,463	201	4,678	15,466	601	3,591
Deerfield Beach	85,275	20,229	418	4,309	23,250	1,189	35,879
Bradenton	76,382	15,484	1,883	5,938	20,089	229	32,759
Ft. Myers	138,958	37,236	8,555	5,523	37,562	789	49,293

1/ Consolidated Duval County.

Source: State of Florida, Department of Banking and Finance, Office of the Comptroller, Internet site
<http://localgovserver.dbf.state.fl.us/>.

University of Florida   **Bureau of Economic and Business Research**

Table 23.87. MUNICIPAL FINANCE: EXPENDITURE BY FUNCTION OF CITY GOVERNMENTS SERVING A 1997 POPULATION OF 45,000 OR MORE IN FLORIDA, FISCAL YEAR 1996-97

(rounded to thousands of dollars)

City	Total	General govern- ment	Public safety	Physical and eco- nomic envi- ronment	Trans- porta- tion	Human ser- vices, cultur- al, and recrea- tion	Debt service 1/
Jacksonville 2/	2,367,201	271,666	261,624	764,258	214,343	169,695	685,614
Miami	542	164	121	46	21	44	146
Tampa	628,100	37,477	152,690	149,121	32,989	39,947	215,877
St. Petersburg	486,385	83,569	83,965	94,700	16,226	84,061	123,864
Hialeah	189,294	42,883	48,312	66,264	7,512	11,925	12,398
Orlando	462,740	84,031	92,197	83,867	62,303	48,975	91,366
Ft. Lauderdale	314,945	48,393	86,032	83,516	13,657	25,041	58,306
Tallahassee	570,185	37,039	46,930	229,921	63,314	20,888	172,093
Hollywood	195,924	56,921	59,958	37,738	12,977	6,778	21,553
Clearwater	227,874	48,535	36,838	73,320	14,543	20,203	34,435
Pembroke Pines	105,312	14,777	33,320	26,626	5,083	16,365	9,141
Coral Springs	106,242	19,384	25,256	11,948	4,317	13,140	32,197
Gainesville	288,123	24,690	29,063	169,651	12,293	5,544	46,883
Miami Beach	325,742	55,663	68,237	82,310	15,225	39,989	64,318
Cape Coral	117,346	14,461	22,562	34,385	11,391	8,743	25,804
West Palm Beach	169,917	14,013	40,935	50,266	7,698	11,316	45,689
Port St. Lucie	87,113	6,630	10,981	46,374	5,048	6,238	11,842
Plantation	99,321	17,545	26,786	21,234	2,364	8,560	22,832
Palm Bay	61,682	6,290	16,332	10,610	10,698	2,356	15,396
Sunrise	136,294	14,487	28,260	31,998	2,914	14,575	44,060
Lakeland	355,953	26,943	26,978	188,929	29,104	23,267	60,731
Pompano Beach	117,669	28,985	39,785	32,642	3,400	7,486	5,371
Boca Raton	162,227	19,629	29,892	37,373	13,677	14,188	47,467
Melbourne	80,561	9,437	19,169	20,441	15,098	6,296	10,120
Largo	62,469	11,949	17,894	20,139	1,304	8,261	2,923
Daytona Beach	100,801	17,851	24,147	32,049	7,509	11,258	7,987
Davie	55,450	8,993	21,554	4,811	3,105	4,640	12,347
Pensacola	167,114	18,045	22,734	35,427	14,024	11,463	65,421
Deltona	14,365	2,583	5,806	3,079	2,002	781	114
Delray Beach	96,046	16,469	25,723	20,491	5,008	9,668	18,688
Boynton Beach	84,636	16,750	20,199	21,312	1,347	9,492	15,535
Sarasota	108,581	23,817	22,947	30,294	5,529	8,904	17,090
Tamarac	44,878	11,482	12,559	11,950	1,552	1,804	5,530
North Miami	78,066	34,370	10,147	21,463	2,168	5,302	4,615
Lauderhill	33,008	5,868	11,249	9,015	845	3,306	2,726
Miramar	45,395	2,862	18,663	11,844	1,002	2,983	8,042
Margate	41,118	4,085	15,983	12,072	1,036	2,836	5,106
Deerfield Beach	60,112	9,681	13,689	21,647	1,813	4,031	9,251
Bradenton	59,216	6,388	8,878	13,576	1,765	4,890	23,719
Ft. Myers	127,758	13,179	20,673	33,033	4,326	10,066	46,481

1/ Includes other uses and interfund transfers.
2/ Consolidated Duval County.

Source: State of Florida, Department of Banking and Finance, Office of the Comptroller, Internet site <http://localgovserver.dbf.state.fl.us/>.

University of Florida   **Bureau of Economic and Business Research**

Table 23.89. PROPERTY VALUATIONS: NET ASSESSED VALUES OF REAL, PERSONAL, AND RAILROAD PROPERTY IN FLORIDA, JANUARY 1, 1963 THROUGH 1999

(amounts rounded to thousands of dollars)

Year	Total Amount	Percentage change from previous year	Real property Amount	Percentage of total	Personal property Amount	Percentage of total	Railroad and private car lines Amount	Percentage of total
1963	19,210,827	4.67	16,890,665	87.92	2,152,967	11.21	167,195	0.87
1964	23,994,036	24.90	21,140,438	88.11	2,674,478	11.14	179,121	0.75
1965	29,760,016	24.03	26,233,082	88.15	3,321,356	11.16	205,578	0.69
1966	36,253,654	21.82	31,943,021	88.11	4,036,480	11.13	274,153	0.76
1967	40,606,927	12.01	35,154,260	86.57	5,162,026	12.71	290,640	0.72
1968	42,060,610	3.58	36,637,166	87.10	5,125,541	12.19	297,903	0.71
1969	45,180,722	7.42	39,697,479	87.86	5,187,897	11.48	295,346	0.66
1970	51,247,667	13.43	45,066,274	87.94	5,915,000	11.54	266,393	0.52
1971	59,967,320	17.01	51,822,900	86.42	7,845,286	13.08	299,134	0.50
1972	67,053,619	11.82	56,610,767	84.43	10,134,332	15.11	308,520	0.46
1973	82,146,275	22.51	69,936,535	85.14	11,870,966	14.45	338,774	0.41
1974	107,894,309	31.34	92,979,953	86.18	14,570,730	13.50	343,627	0.32
1975	120,558,360	11.74	103,460,245	85.82	16,690,698	13.84	407,417	0.34
1976	128,700,512	6.75	109,217,279	84.86	19,072,710	14.82	410,523	0.32
1977	139,650,757	8.51	118,232,881	84.66	20,925,041	14.98	492,835	0.35
1978	151,271,654	8.24	129,382,344	85.53	21,393,945	14.14	495,365	0.33
1979	159,642,320	5.53	135,705,468	84.38	24,422,967	15.30	513,884	0.32
1980	187,750,045	17.61	164,755,192	87.75	22,480,384	11.97	514,470	0.27
1981	237,140,341	26.31	211,148,696	89.04	25,579,874	10.79	411,772	0.17
1982	272,997,005	15.12	244,424,808	89.53	28,194,359	10.53	377,839	0.14
1983	298,583,050	9.37	266,304,607	89.19	31,858,923	10.67	419,519	0.14
1984	323,647,775	8.39	288,392,562	89.11	34,820,448	10.76	434,765	0.13
1985	356,061,973	10.02	317,508,051	89.17	38,100,514	10.70	453,408	0.13
1986	385,126,891	8.16	343,168,089	89.11	41,389,766	10.75	569,036	0.15
1987	417,508,830	8.41	372,504,470	89.22	44,326,033	10.62	678,327	0.16
1988	446,103,804	6.80	398,216,681	89.27	47,192,039	10.58	695,085	0.16
1989	485,766,305	8.90	434,583,860	89.46	50,554,052	10.41	628,394	0.13
1990	524,248,524	7.92	469,498,829	89.56	54,114,754	10.32	634,941	0.12
1991	553,456,777	5.57	496,581,168	89.72	56,260,942	10.17	614,667	0.11
1992	560,820,605	1.33	501,638,271	89.45	58,586,918	10.45	595,416	0.11
1993	570,341,544	1.70	509,360,697	89.31	60,380,135	10.59	600,712	0.11
1994	595,216,496	4.36	530,408,830	89.11	62,835,320	10.56	1,972,345	0.33
1995	623,757,999	4.80	556,091,584	89.15	67,006,163	10.74	660,252	0.11
1996	652,462,117	4.60	580,555,689	88.98	71,217,716	10.92	688,712	0.11
1997	691,235,598	5.94	616,179,520	89.14	74,069,860	10.72	986,218	0.14
1998	736,334,987	6.52	658,425,719	89.42	77,005,107	10.46	904,162	0.12
1999	792,002,081	7.56	709,696,964	89.61	81,359,589	10.27	945,529	0.12

Note: Net assessed value is total assessed or just value less nontaxable value of property having a classified use value. Classified use value is the value at which agricultural land and certain privately owned park and recreation land is assessed for tax purposes. The "highest and best" use principle is relaxed and assessment is based on current use only. Some data may be revised.

Source: State of Florida, Department of Revenue, *Florida Property Valuations and Tax Data, December 1999*, Internet site <http://sun6.dms.state.fl.us/dor/property/99FLpropdata.pdf> (accessed 26 May 2000).

University of Florida   **Bureau of Economic and Business Research**

Table 23.90. PROPERTY VALUATIONS: ASSESSED AND TAXABLE VALUES BY CATEGORY
OF REAL PROPERTY IN FLORIDA, JANUARY 1, 1998 AND 1999

(rounded to thousands of dollars)

Category	Just value 1/		Taxable value 2/	
	1998	1999	1998	1999
Total 3/	769,129,097	823,921,736	552,787,321	593,665,189
Residential	355,698,029	385,820,278	274,281,896	296,186,201
Vacant	25,336,205	26,626,165	24,961,312	26,027,924
Single-family	330,361,823	359,194,113	249,320,583	270,158,277
Mobile homes	12,040,224	13,341,502	6,595,530	7,417,763
Multifamily	35,699,603	38,305,794	33,965,664	36,399,078
9 units or less	13,526,012	14,250,371	12,201,321	12,790,145
10 units or more	22,173,591	24,055,423	21,764,343	23,608,933
Condominiums	98,550,791	105,508,723	82,811,267	88,838,401
Cooperatives	3,408,692	1,912,632	2,490,157	1,470,022
Retirement homes	1,797,046	1,790,562	1,568,507	1,514,716
Commercial	104,357,704	112,465,314	102,651,332	110,691,750
Vacant	8,555,067	9,149,897	8,392,104	8,989,167
Improved	95,802,637	103,315,417	94,259,227	101,702,583
Industrial	25,099,413	26,677,047	24,694,996	26,253,277
Vacant	2,579,709	2,649,313	2,505,841	2,580,882
Improved	22,519,704	24,027,733	22,189,155	23,672,395
Agricultural	37,096,413	38,322,039	9,125,807	9,427,032
Institutional	20,045,868	21,239,645	4,998,901	5,319,164
Government	63,397,288	65,939,414	590,290	611,186
Leasehold	1,780,980	2,373,727	816,047	1,258,221
Miscellaneous	4,436,223	4,585,164	3,053,204	3,172,540
Nonagricultural	5,598,498	5,517,090	5,103,938	5,061,280

1/ The value of property for tax purposes as determined by the elected county property appraiser.
Value is determined at the highest and best use of property, except for special classes provided for in
Florida Statutes.
2/ The value against which millage rates are applied to compute the amount of tax levied. Total taxable
value makes up the ad valorem tax base for units of government in Florida.
3/ Totals include centrally assessed values not shown elsewhere.

Source: State of Florida, Department of Revenue, *Florida Property Valuations and Tax Data, December
1999*, Internet site <http://sun6.dms.state.fl.us/dor/property/99FLpropdata.pdf> (accessed 26 May 2000).

University of Florida   **Bureau of Economic and Business Research**

Table 23.91. PROPERTY VALUATIONS: ASSESSED, EXEMPT, AND TAXABLE VALUES
OF REAL PROPERTY IN THE STATE AND COUNTIES OF FLORIDA
JANUARY 1, 1998 AND 1999

(rounded to thousands of dollars)

County	Just values 1/ 1998	Just values 1/ 1999	Exempt and immune values 1998	Exempt and immune values 1999	Taxable values 2/ 1998	Taxable values 2/ 1999
Florida	769,223,110	825,142,972	202,364,923	209,540,889	552,726,274	594,844,397
Alachua	8,743,488	9,317,830	4,103,116	4,207,615	4,424,109	4,790,892
Baker	680,133	717,428	456,724	466,050	218,717	236,387
Bay	6,875,320	7,541,464	2,511,118	2,564,146	4,335,327	4,847,077
Bradford	700,591	728,212	373,872	379,680	324,775	340,636
Brevard	21,861,466	22,806,401	8,077,757	8,135,542	13,415,043	14,150,281
Broward	76,059,597	81,186,881	15,568,108	16,087,287	58,714,098	63,180,482
Calhoun	379,586	391,809	214,878	221,073	160,101	164,632
Charlotte	7,980,140	8,578,159	1,781,919	1,857,947	6,028,108	6,397,315
Citrus	4,705,351	5,026,928	1,528,326	1,583,795	3,086,118	3,303,612
Clay	4,822,619	5,184,637	1,556,604	1,605,689	3,176,040	3,426,384
Collier	24,421,971	28,368,450	3,662,017	4,028,163	20,304,972	23,271,327
Columbia	1,740,546	1,841,830	853,439	896,764	842,815	900,656
De Soto	1,417,511	1,485,278	828,757	832,731	586,087	638,775
Dixie	457,677	470,261	272,883	279,326	182,574	187,853
Duval	32,260,338	34,193,390	9,641,655	9,935,635	21,670,377	23,006,705
Escambia	11,046,577	11,314,784	5,098,046	5,166,513	5,438,473	5,714,893
Flagler	3,004,559	3,192,599	734,876	784,105	2,264,685	2,382,386
Franklin	1,539,393	1,625,214	866,887	874,623	641,069	716,841
Gadsden	1,067,194	1,122,970	570,527	569,678	486,686	537,293
Gilchrist	509,995	521,743	323,832	322,375	181,485	195,275
Glades	922,909	941,271	611,930	620,212	310,353	320,292
Gulf	869,307	1,086,201	445,635	511,930	417,761	523,490
Hamilton	478,264	494,353	253,794	267,484	223,178	225,631
Hardee	1,523,595	1,572,693	1,004,834	1,019,139	514,451	540,419
Hendry	2,353,765	2,417,184	1,457,618	1,424,708	895,802	990,860
Hernando	5,026,183	5,288,124	1,682,028	1,742,142	3,332,944	3,509,121
Highlands	3,248,708	3,580,436	1,105,060	1,317,647	2,138,391	2,255,733
Hillsborough	38,338,369	41,379,146	11,138,328	11,350,397	26,262,027	28,722,314
Holmes	500,639	573,991	301,979	350,411	188,851	202,004
Indian River	8,072,476	8,662,683	2,166,367	2,225,079	5,864,580	6,328,961
Jackson	1,458,431	1,506,276	808,941	824,053	608,505	632,174
Jefferson	738,457	749,836	537,215	539,944	197,779	206,770
Lafayette	7,670,282	8,348,378	172,769	177,888	92,191	96,026
Lake	267,008	276,542	2,207,717	2,319,217	5,394,789	5,942,687
Lee	27,264,639	29,347,986	5,273,969	5,393,387	21,669,298	23,421,079
Leon	11,829,615	12,318,757	5,133,073	5,167,944	6,490,852	6,887,901

See footnotes at end of table.   Continued . . .

University of Florida   **Bureau of Economic and Business Research**

Table 23.91. PROPERTY VALUATIONS: ASSESSED, EXEMPT, AND TAXABLE VALUES
OF REAL PROPERTY IN THE STATE AND COUNTIES OF FLORIDA
JANUARY 1, 1998 AND 1999 (Continued)

(rounded to thousands of dollars)

County	Just values 1/		Exempt and immune values		Taxable values 2/	
	1998	1999	1998	1999	1998	1999
Levy	1,292,902	1,342,015	596,885	612,651	684,272	716,589
Liberty	552,080	540,701	480,469	465,422	63,171	67,319
Madison	522,184	614,216	295,645	365,726	225,057	246,673
Manatee	12,707,450	13,519,212	2,878,668	2,969,344	9,542,871	10,149,832
Marion	9,241,625	9,835,275	3,657,858	3,786,076	5,385,034	5,782,611
Martin	10,046,737	10,836,862	2,235,819	2,313,084	7,693,515	8,276,955
Miami-Dade	101,605,438	108,467,175	21,947,691	22,270,416	77,593,227	83,197,550
Monroe	11,283,345	12,968,724	3,143,747	4,007,024	7,930,604	8,644,547
Nassau	2,798,472	3,106,418	733,240	786,926	2,000,420	2,223,577
Okaloosa	8,361,621	9,057,191	2,275,780	2,356,610	5,891,037	6,435,422
Okeechobee	1,419,765	1,448,369	667,257	676,313	747,275	766,307
Orange	49,049,453	52,539,502	11,617,302	12,191,286	37,043,348	39,780,215
Osceola	8,554,894	9,585,403	2,469,475	2,911,176	6,065,186	6,638,572
Palm Beach	73,956,471	79,026,240	14,529,990	14,832,262	58,236,593	62,228,527
Pasco	10,904,978	12,087,492	3,603,996	3,795,689	7,167,543	7,838,655
Pinellas	42,355,438	44,382,706	10,845,942	10,974,123	30,601,978	32,049,130
Polk	14,780,659	15,365,515	4,877,190	4,956,497	9,815,883	10,325,837
Putnam	2,291,076	2,398,473	930,297	956,888	1,336,239	1,404,805
St. Johns	7,704,793	8,966,583	1,731,506	1,885,252	5,755,043	6,614,045
St. Lucie	8,726,736	9,143,435	2,508,462	2,590,752	6,176,596	6,491,767
Santa Rosa	5,013,223	5,425,960	1,648,330	1,800,682	3,175,634	3,396,081
Sarasota	23,801,300	25,931,541	4,136,116	4,392,160	18,921,228	20,458,782
Seminole	15,011,582	16,164,430	3,013,284	3,062,836	11,843,554	12,824,067
Sumter	1,297,878	1,528,838	626,070	675,948	671,460	832,301
Suwannee	1,025,277	1,060,799	545,324	555,875	446,698	473,231
Taylor	862,329	882,133	463,892	467,929	394,904	410,773
Union	600,828	680,284	497,294	571,578	100,018	104,961
Volusia	17,616,841	18,533,951	4,661,174	4,802,028	12,687,207	13,328,707
Wakulla	723,110	753,826	380,717	390,330	319,259	345,105
Walton	3,654,844	4,139,803	722,596	743,030	2,835,755	3,283,903
Washington	623,079	649,774	316,311	324,654	292,259	312,386

1/ The value of property for tax purposes as determined by the elected county property appraiser before deduction of exemptions and immunities. Value is determined at the highest and best use of property, except for special cases provided for in Florida Statutes.
2/ The value against which millage rates are applied to compute the amount of tax levied. The tax base of a unit of local government also includes the taxable value of personal property and centrally assessed property.
Note: Data for 1999 are revised.

Source: State of Florida, Department of Revenue, *Florida Property Valuations and Tax Data, December 1999*, Internet site <http://sun6.dms.state.fl.us/dor/property/99FLpropdata.pdf> (accessed 26 May 2000).

University of Florida   **Bureau of Economic and Business Research**

Table 23.92. PROPERTY VALUATIONS AND TAXES: ASSESSED, EXEMPT, AND TAXABLE VALUES, MILLAGE RATES, AND TAXES ON MUNICIPAL REAL, PERSONAL, AND RAILROAD PROPERTY IN THE STATE, COUNTIES, AND SELECTED MUNICIPALITIES OF FLORIDA, 1999

(rounded to thousands of dollars, except where indicated)

County and municipality 1/	Total assessed value	Exemption value Homestead	Other 2/	Taxable Value	Operating millage rate	Taxes
Florida TMP	447,598,759	39,462,122	72,906,106	335,230,532	5.1220	1,717,062
Alachua TMP	6,884,347	525,651	3,550,286	2,808,410	4.9870	14,005
Gainesville	6,117,881	414,392	3,313,041	2,390,448	4.9416	11,813
Baker TMP	155,622	24,554	40,204	90,864	3.3211	302
Bay TMP	4,291,858	491,058	772,405	3,028,395	2.4443	7,402
Panama City	1,790,067	190,391	455,900	1,143,777	5.0000	5,719
Bradford TMP	243,799	35,880	77,191	130,728	3.7385	489
Brevard TMP	12,721,380	1,867,848	1,834,224	9,019,309	4.9726	44,849
Cocoa	618,775	86,193	168,640	363,942	4.1321	1,504
Melbourne	3,309,458	410,512	622,129	2,276,817	4.5228	10,298
Palm Bay	2,596,656	521,233	248,163	1,827,260	7.1742	13,109
Rockledge	884,383	140,752	143,630	600,001	5.5590	3,335
Titusville	1,549,118	262,475	269,674	1,016,969	5.7735	5,871
Broward TMP	82,032,202	8,842,382	5,257,656	65,932,164	5.1801	341,532
Coconut Creek	1,992,166	305,619	190,317	1,496,229	5.3901	8,065
Cooper City	1,359,965	196,544	112,752	1,050,669	6.2820	6,600
Coral Springs	5,614,062	548,678	311,591	4,753,793	4.0238	19,128
Dania	1,277,449	101,885	168,835	1,006,729	6.1000	6,141
Davie	3,832,103	392,652	486,781	2,952,670	6.0089	17,742
Deerfield Beach	3,673,135	454,575	208,895	3,009,665	6.2278	18,744
Ft. Lauderdale	14,843,845	828,408	2,039,032	11,976,405	5.5664	66,665
Hallandale	1,759,607	227,478	78,702	1,453,427	6.9870	10,155
Hollywood	7,326,032	814,355	843,060	5,668,617	6.2999	35,712
Lauderdale Lakes	874,304	147,973	83,079	643,251	4.9500	3,184
Lauderhill	1,612,555	280,891	75,601	1,256,063	5.6000	7,034
Margate	1,963,832	380,636	90,137	1,493,058	7.0881	10,583
Miramar	2,598,543	361,253	198,158	2,039,133	6.9226	14,116
North Lauderdale	796,201	150,640	68,167	577,393	5.0365	2,908
Oakland Park	1,573,841	142,745	176,553	1,254,543	5.2059	6,531
Pembroke Pines	6,289,969	909,254	399,732	4,980,983	3.9034	19,443
Plantation	5,348,121	538,294	402,766	4,407,060	3.7500	16,526
Pompano Beach	5,721,672	454,457	480,308	4,786,907	4.7811	22,887
Sunrise	3,942,694	545,267	380,469	3,016,958	6.3250	19,082
Tamarac	2,402,691	497,240	101,968	1,803,482	5.4900	9,901
Weston	3,231,993	256,917	116,950	2,858,126	1.5235	4,354
Calhoun TMP	79,498	15,836	17,088	46,573	1.3787	64
Charlotte TMP	1,570,778	124,610	198,060	1,248,109	2.9565	3,690
Citrus TMP	659,591	68,186	133,342	458,063	5.9400	2,721
Clay TMP	823,442	99,464	159,338	564,639	3.6982	2,088
Collier TMP	10,945,575	280,790	1,202,036	9,462,749	1.3664	12,930
Naples	7,132,841	167,719	998,306	5,966,816	1.1800	7,041
Columbia TMP	561,357	47,547	171,470	342,339	3.5516	1,216
De Soto TMP	226,370	30,479	70,337	125,553	8.6287	1,083
Dixie TMP	58,574	11,074	22,676	24,824	4.2850	106

See footnotes at end of table.

Continued . . .

Table 23.92. PROPERTY VALUATIONS AND TAXES: ASSESSED, EXEMPT, AND TAXABLE VALUES, MILLAGE RATES, AND TAXES ON MUNICIPAL REAL, PERSONAL, AND RAILROAD PROPERTY IN THE STATE, COUNTIES, AND SELECTED MUNICIPALITIES OF FLORIDA, 1999 (Continued)

(rounded to thousands of dollars, except where indicated)

County and municipality 1/	Total assessed value	Exemption value Homestead	Other 2/	Taxable Value	Oper- ating mill- age rate	Taxes
Duval TMP	9,481,427	786,417	2,710,883	5,984,128	6.1725	36,937
Jacksonville	6,920,418	511,920	2,383,802	4,024,695	7.4711	30,069
Beach	1,276,838	130,707	154,399	991,732	3.9071	3,875
Escambia TMP	2,888,082	372,723	645,649	1,869,710	5.0088	9,365
Pensacola	2,848,197	365,272	635,911	1,847,014	5.0570	9,340
Flagler TMP	455,749	47,967	76,563	331,219	2.9927	991
Franklin TMP	275,669	40,698	65,819	169,152	5.4606	924
Gadsden TMP	530,784	79,554	218,562	232,668	1.8769	437
Gilchrist TMP	66,549	11,731	20,111	34,707	0.2937	10
Glades TMP	45,512	7,652	13,379	24,481	4.1720	102
Gulf TMP	392,765	36,965	58,148	297,652	4.9470	1,472
Hamilton TMP	103,460	16,127	28,511	58,823	4.0525	238
Hardee TMP	208,584	37,135	77,064	94,384	5.8205	549
Hendry TMP	443,670	46,911	136,244	260,514	4.3505	1,133
Hernando TMP	443,779	27,378	173,155	243,246	7.4673	1,816
Highlands TMP	752,921	94,399	146,531	511,992	7.0098	3,589
Hillsborough TMP	21,558,314	1,831,711	5,073,386	14,653,217	6.3140	92,520
Plant City	1,383,788	150,669	214,294	1,018,825	4.7000	4,788
Tampa	19,097,023	1,564,145	4,772,407	12,760,470	6.5390	83,441
Temple Terrace	1,077,503	116,897	86,685	873,921	4.9100	4,291
Holmes TMP	127,525	19,874	36,648	71,004	0.0597	4
Indian River TMP	3,728,393	286,783	401,277	3,040,333	2.3724	7,213
Sebastian	672,166	125,942	61,864	484,360	5.0000	2,422
Vero Beach	1,734,819	113,554	275,257	1,346,008	2.1425	2,884
Jackson TMP	437,318	70,007	143,818	223,493	2.1912	490
Jefferson TMP	81,789	14,322	17,515	49,951	9.2482	462
Lafayette TMP	22,898	4,516	6,933	11,449	2.0000	23
Lake TMP	4,063,566	570,265	637,406	2,855,894	4.4472	12,701
Eustis	588,843	86,964	95,261	406,618	5.2374	2,130
Leesburg	883,925	82,851	201,558	599,516	4.5000	2,698
Lee TMP	11,637,738	952,760	1,130,342	9,554,636	4.6294	44,232
Cape Coral	5,022,883	707,443	383,096	3,932,344	6.8478	26,928
Ft. Myers	2,683,307	150,570	593,319	1,939,418	5.7816	11,213
Leon TMP	10,283,317	625,234	4,440,218	5,217,865	3.2000	16,697
Tallahassee	10,283,317	625,234	4,440,218	5,217,865	3.2000	0
Levy TMP	373,229	53,840	39,789	279,600	3.4603	968
Liberty TMP	25,845	4,357	10,284	11,204	3.0000	34
Madison TMP	117,829	20,544	24,293	72,992	6.4762	473
Manatee TMP	4,501,587	406,175	512,128	3,583,283	2.9038	10,405
Bradenton	2,175,103	276,787	283,804	1,614,512	3.2000	5,166
Marion TMP	2,735,393	259,559	444,900	2,030,933	5.2548	10,672
Ocala	2,490,365	221,364	415,918	1,853,083	5.2743	9,774
Martin TMP	2,761,362	108,159	494,114	2,159,090	3.7043	7,998
Miami-Dade TMP	63,249,643	3,947,194	8,220,672	50,081,777	7.4600	373,608
Aventura	3,615,849	193,859	57,085	3,364,904	2.2270	7,494
Coral Gables	6,540,606	244,191	703,530	5,592,886	5.5000	30,761

See footnotes at end of table.   Continued . . .

Table 23.92. PROPERTY VALUATIONS AND TAXES: ASSESSED, EXEMPT, AND TAXABLE
VALUES, MILLAGE RATES, AND TAXES ON MUNICIPAL REAL, PERSONAL, AND
RAILROAD PROPERTY IN THE STATE, COUNTIES, AND SELECTED
MUNICIPALITIES OF FLORIDA, 1999 (Continued)

(rounded to thousands of dollars, except where indicated)

County and municipality 1/	Total assessed value	Exemption value Homestead	Exemption value Other 2/	Taxable Value	Operating millage rate	Taxes
Miami-Dade TMP (Cont.)						
Hialeah	6,966,964	815,589	904,007	5,247,368	7.4810	39,256
Hialeah Gardens	575,040	78,879	51,196	444,965	7.3270	3,260
Homestead	919,446	77,738	236,639	605,069	8.5000	5,143
Miami	19,110,297	1,016,977	4,705,435	13,387,884	10.9000	145,928
Miami Beach	9,089,393	350,022	1,081,526	7,657,845	8.6980	66,608
North Miami	1,792,410	227,408	278,089	1,286,912	9.0380	11,631
North Miami Beach	1,506,676	194,997	196,882	1,114,797	8.4035	9,368
Opa-locka	515,387	38,819	73,602	402,965	9.8000	3,949
Pinecrest	2,105,096	115,446	205,400	1,784,251	2.1000	3,747
Monroe TMP	7,176,675	155,124	2,926,662	4,094,889	3.2357	13,250
Key West	5,627,320	96,599	2,842,701	2,688,021	3.7912	10,191
Nassau TMP	1,231,787	84,604	336,901	810,283	6.2549	5,068
Okaloosa TMP	4,824,901	427,937	616,014	3,780,949	2.8917	10,933
Ft. Walton Beach	1,025,873	129,341	169,755	726,778	4.9700	3,612
Okeechobee TMP	249,380	27,628	41,634	180,119	5.4399	980
Orange TMP	29,392,672	1,391,504	6,940,909	21,060,259	3.9999	84,240
Apopka	1,169,605	144,456	143,218	881,931	3.7619	3,318
Ocoee	1,165,864	149,717	136,831	879,315	4.0000	3,517
Orlando	16,311,606	717,572	5,775,002	9,819,033	6.0666	59,568
Winter Park	2,543,530	157,578	384,758	2,001,193	3.8160	7,637
Osceola TMP	2,612,920	264,568	558,688	1,789,665	4.4500	7,964
Kissimmee	1,947,708	153,668	469,816	1,324,224	4.5453	6,019
St. Cloud	665,212	110,899	88,872	465,441	4.1790	1,945
Palm Beach TMP	52,825,480	3,718,024	5,259,832	42,847,624	5.3353	228,603
Belle Glade	350,853	41,904	102,983	205,966	8.9800	1,850
Boca Raton	10,855,689	520,843	1,244,567	9,090,279	3.2293	29,355
Boynton Beach	3,163,287	401,968	285,783	2,475,535	8.2409	20,401
Delray Beach	3,969,640	386,562	413,254	3,169,824	7.6500	24,249
Greenacres City	912,160	165,335	48,472	698,353	6.1272	4,279
Jupiter	3,803,645	285,324	450,178	3,068,142	2.3814	7,306
Lake Worth	1,073,593	150,713	194,239	728,641	11.0839	8,076
Palm Beach Gardens	4,248,823	252,008	482,989	3,513,826	4.3497	15,284
Riviera Beach	2,023,758	137,535	365,105	1,521,118	8.9970	13,685
Royal Palm Beach	961,484	153,516	99,155	708,813	6.5377	4,634
Wellington	2,370,567	222,719	165,557	1,982,290	2.2500	4,460
West Palm Beach	6,096,296	380,599	1,306,652	4,409,046	8.8368	38,962
Pasco TMP	1,604,430	202,231	318,616	1,083,583	6.2256	6,746
Pinellas TMP	33,760,387	4,030,898	3,877,659	24,851,830	5.1933	129,062
Clearwater	6,655,350	622,988	1,128,884	4,903,479	5.5032	26,985
Dunedin	1,798,380	261,924	376,363	1,160,093	4.1166	4,776
Largo	2,667,511	359,245	310,266	1,997,999	3.4000	6,793
Pinellas Park	2,212,800	300,541	195,127	1,717,132	5.0788	8,721
Safety Harbor	934,144	134,216	141,420	658,509	3.4018	2,240
St. Petersburg	11,347,620	1,550,425	1,904,510	7,892,685	7.4235	58,591
Tarpon Springs	1,120,526	143,472	162,459	814,595	5.2041	4,239

See footnotes at end of table.   Continued . . .

Table 23.92. PROPERTY VALUATIONS AND TAXES: ASSESSED, EXEMPT, AND TAXABLE VALUES, MILLAGE RATES, AND TAXES ON MUNICIPAL REAL, PERSONAL, AND RAILROAD PROPERTY IN THE STATE, COUNTIES, AND SELECTED MUNICIPALITIES OF FLORIDA, 1999 (Continued)

(rounded to thousands of dollars, except where indicated)

County and municipality 1/	Total assessed value	Exemption value Homestead	Other 2/	Taxable Value	Oper- ating mill- age rate	Taxes
Polk TMP	7,481,475	876,298	1,677,490	4,927,686	4.3608	21,489
Bartow	523,553	81,558	153,756	288,239	1.7820	514
Lakeland	3,858,007	381,937	991,846	2,484,225	2.9950	7,440
Winter Haven	1,183,979	132,006	237,067	814,906	6.3250	5,154
Putnam TMP	650,111	72,040	229,707	348,363	7.0392	2,452
St. Johns TMP	1,192,710	100,673	251,150	840,887	5.3012	4,458
St. Lucie TMP	5,275,920	787,221	739,293	3,749,405	4.8342	18,125
Ft. Pierce	1,645,823	156,647	478,567	1,010,610	7.3305	7,408
Port St. Lucie	3,599,544	626,093	259,672	2,713,778	3.9400	10,692
Santa Rosa TMP	910,421	86,849	271,037	552,534	2.1071	1,164
Sarasota TMP	9,732,148	633,118	1,646,105	7,452,925	3.0997	23,102
North Port	926,844	164,605	99,309	662,930	4.8000	3,182
Sarasota	4,998,714	294,798	1,192,148	3,511,769	2.9601	10,395
Venice	1,717,661	129,965	270,882	1,316,815	3.4060	4,485
Seminole TMP	8,978,015	1,010,352	657,114	7,310,549	4.7508	34,731
Altamonte Springs	2,221,813	174,946	117,597	1,929,269	4.4224	8,532
Casselberry	915,605	127,804	44,450	743,352	4.8000	3,568
Oviedo	1,173,146	165,424	67,892	939,830	4.9950	4,694
Sanford	1,533,409	165,876	239,336	1,128,197	6.7900	7,660
Winter Springs	1,253,086	209,415	70,691	972,981	3.5495	3,454
Sumter TMP	208,820	35,289	23,985	149,546	3.5077	525
Suwannee TMP	162,670	29,883	36,514	96,273	4.6420	447
Taylor TMP	266,903	37,551	75,372	153,981	4.7300	728
Union TMP	59,068	8,125	22,849	28,094	2.1494	60
Volusia TMP	15,414,265	2,152,509	1,734,708	11,527,048	4.6127	53,171
Daytona Beach	3,304,471	290,227	658,694	2,355,550	6.1168	14,408
DeLand	976,277	90,645	234,794	650,838	5.7870	3,766
Deltona	1,938,417	497,600	91,380	1,349,438	4.1980	5,665
Edgewater	589,101	139,476	35,673	413,952	5.9500	2,463
New Smyrna Beach	1,541,902	162,767	136,389	1,242,746	5.1336	6,380
Ormond Beach	2,196,010	267,199	200,128	1,728,683	2.7927	4,828
Port Orange	1,706,034	314,070	156,645	1,235,319	4.4851	5,541
Wakulla TMP	111,287	17,750	48,930	44,606	1.1433	51
Walton TMP	235,403	37,043	51,450	146,910	4.2551	625
Washington TMP	191,820	28,585	52,829	110,406	4.9361	545

TMP Total municipal property.
1/ Only municipalities with a 1999 population of 15,000 or more are shown. Refer to the source for data for other municipalities.
2/ Includes governmental, institutional, and miscellaneous other exempt properties.

Source: State of Florida, Department of Revenue, *Florida Property Valuations and Tax Data, December 1999*, Internet site <http://sun6.dms.state.fl.us/dor/property/99FLpropdata.pdf> (accessed 26 May 2000).

University of Florida   **Bureau of Economic and Business Research**

Table 23.93. COUNTY MILLAGE: AD VALOREM MILLAGE RATES IN THE COUNTIES OF FLORIDA, JANUARY 1, 1999

County	Total county-wide millage	County government Oper-ating millage	County government Debt service millage	District school board Oper-ating millage	District school board Debt service millage	Other mill-age 1/
Alachua	22.1080	8.7500	0.0200	8.7060	2.2500	2.3820
Baker	21.7694	8.8500	0.0000	9.1860	0.0000	3.7334
Bay	14.6300	5.6620	0.0000	6.9180	2.0000	0.0500
Bradford	19.6524	10.0000	0.0000	9.1610	0.0000	0.4914
Brevard	15.2961	4.1781	0.0000	7.1710	2.0000	1.9470
Broward 2/	17.3663	6.8947	0.6463	8.6740	0.4543	0.6970
Calhoun	16.1180	10.0000	0.0000	6.0680	0.0000	0.0500
Charlotte	14.5071	4.7141	0.0000	6.6260	2.5100	0.6570
Citrus	17.9678	7.7410	0.0000	6.9430	2.0000	1.2838
Clay	18.4965	8.9885	0.0000	7.0260	2.0000	0.4820
Collier	11.8633	3.5058	0.0000	7.7600	0.0000	0.5975
Columbia	19.7384	8.7260	0.0000	6.1230	2.7600	2.1294
De Soto	18.3980	8.4800	0.0000	9.3010	0.0000	0.6170
Dixie	19.8114	10.0000	0.0000	9.3200	0.0000	0.4914
Duval	20.6781	10.7618	0.0243	8.6910	0.6750	0.5260
Escambia	17.8170	8.7560	0.0000	9.0110	0.0000	0.0500
Flagler	15.6107	5.2500	0.2677	8.8400	0.7270	0.5260
Franklin	14.5410	6.7290	0.0000	7.7620	0.0000	0.0500
Gadsden	20.0220	10.0000	0.0000	8.9720	0.0000	1.0500
Gilchrist	19.5864	10.0000	0.0000	7.0950	2.0000	0.4914
Glades	19.0160	10.0000	0.0000	6.7220	1.5970	0.6970
Gulf	15.0203	7.0883	0.0000	7.8820	0.0000	0.0500
Hamilton	19.1904	9.6670	0.0000	9.0320	0.0000	0.4914
Hardee	19.1380	8.7500	0.0000	9.1510	0.0000	1.2370
Hendry	22.0090	10.0000	0.0000	6.8120	2.0000	3.1970
Hernando	19.5744	8.5704	0.1000	7.0030	3.4790	0.4220
Highlands	18.7690	8.5000	0.0000	6.9550	2.0000	1.3140
Hillsborough	18.0022	7.5968	0.1854	8.7710	0.3000	1.1490
Holmes	16.9920	9.0000	0.0000	5.9420	2.0000	0.0500
Indian River	14.4651	4.0855	0.2396	8.6140	1.0000	0.5260
Jackson	15.4375	8.6875	0.0000	6.7000	0.0000	0.0500
Jefferson	18.3684	10.0000	0.0000	6.8270	1.0000	0.5414
Lafayette	19.6714	10.0000	0.0000	7.1800	2.0000	0.4914
Lake	14.4595	4.7333	0.0000	8.7420	0.0000	0.9842
Lee	15.5825	5.4875	0.0000	8.9410	0.0000	1.1540
Leon	18.4900	8.5800	0.0000	8.7780	1.0820	0.0500

See footnotes at end of table.   Continued . . .

Table 23.93. COUNTY MILLAGE: AD VALOREM MILLAGE RATES IN THE COUNTIES
OF FLORIDA, JANUARY 1, 1999 (Continued)

County	Total county-wide millage	County government Oper-ating millage	County government Debt service millage	District school board Oper-ating millage	District school board Debt service millage	Other mill-age 1/
Levy	19.0394	9.0000	0.0000	7.1280	2.0000	0.9114
Liberty	19.2010	10.0000	0.0000	9.1510	0.0000	0.0500
Madison	18.9634	9.6830	0.0000	8.7890	0.0000	0.4914
Manatee	17.1601	7.4594	0.3010	8.6070	0.0000	0.7927
Marion	16.4640	6.1500	0.0000	7.8320	2.0000	0.4820
Martin	15.7687	5.5630	0.5880	6.6020	2.0000	1.0157
Miami-Dade 2/	17.0100	5.8090	0.8160	8.6540	0.9900	0.7410
Monroe	12.3997	5.1056	0.0000	5.6550	0.0000	1.6391
Nassau	16.2951	6.7321	0.0000	9.0810	0.0000	0.4820
Okaloosa	12.4824	4.4604	0.0000	7.9720	0.0000	0.0500
Okeechobee	19.3375	8.0000	0.5865	7.1540	2.0000	1.5970
Orange	14.3204	5.2264	0.0000	8.6120	0.0000	0.4820
Osceola	16.4615	5.9945	0.0000	6.8040	2.4660	1.1970
Palm Beach	16.1742	4.6000	0.3456	8.5870	0.4560	2.1856
Pasco	18.7010	8.5700	0.0000	6.8940	2.8150	0.4220
Pinellas	16.8242	6.5010	0.0000	8.6660	0.0000	1.6572
Polk	17.4710	7.9770	0.0000	9.0720	0.0000	0.4220
Putnam	18.7730	8.4000	0.0000	8.9670	0.9240	0.4820
St. Johns	16.3120	6.0610	0.2470	8.6160	0.5820	0.8060
St. Lucie	20.8664	7.5794	0.0000	9.0250	0.0000	4.2620
Santa Rosa	15.1250	6.9720	0.0000	8.1030	0.0000	0.0500
Sarasota	14.1164	4.3858	0.0882	5.9450	2.5920	1.1054
Seminole	15.1389	4.9989	0.1170	6.7850	2.7560	0.4820
Sumter	20.0230	10.0000	0.0000	9.3030	0.0000	0.7200
Suwannee	16.3804	9.0500	0.0000	6.8390	0.0000	0.4914
Taylor	17.0174	8.0760	0.0000	8.4500	0.0000	0.4914
Union	20.4854	10.0000	0.0000	7.4940	2.0000	0.9914
Volusia	16.8160	6.3730	0.0000	8.7400	1.1770	0.5260
Wakulla	20.0720	10.0000	0.0000	8.5120	1.5100	0.0500
Walton	14.6950	6.2980	0.0000	8.3470	0.0000	0.0500
Washington	19.1710	10.0000	0.0000	7.1210	2.0000	0.0500

1/ Includes county government special service districts and independent special service districts.
2/ Proposed millage used.

Source: State of Florida, Department of Revenue, *Florida Property Valuations and Tax Data, December 1999*, Internet site <http://sun6.dms.state.fl.us/dor/property/99FLpropdata.pdf> (accessed 26 May 2000).

Table 23.94. LOCAL GOVERNMENT FINANCE: AD VALOREM TAXES IN THE STATE AND COUNTIES OF FLORIDA, JANUARY 1, 1999

(in millions, rounded to hundred thousands of dollars)

County	Total taxes levied Amount	Percentage change 1998-1999	Municipal taxes	County taxes Total	County-wide County government Operating levy	County government Debt service	District school board Operating levy	District school board Debt service	Special service districts	Independent service districts	Less than county-wide County government special services districts	Independent special services districts
Florida	14,293.8	5.6	1,740.8	11,086.0	4,195.6	176.2	5,317.6	797.7	36.0	563.0	201.7	459.5
Alachua	147.2	4.8	14.0	120.8	48.9	0.1	37.5	23.7	0.0	10.6	0.0	2.7
Baker	7.0	3.8	0.3	6.7	2.8	0.0	2.3	0.6	A/	1.0	0.0	0.0
Bay	93.7	9.7	7.4	82.4	31.7	0.0	39.1	11.3	0.0	0.4	2.5	0.9
Bradford	9.7	2.2	0.5	8.9	4.7	0.0	4.3	0.0	0.0	0.0	0.0	0.2
Brevard	306.4	0.9	44.2	233.8	63.8	0.0	140.3	0.0	21.7	8.0	1.1	1.0
Broward	1,757.1	4.8	335.7	1,228.6	484.7	47.5	611.9	31.9	0.0	52.5	11.2	181.5
Calhoun	3.6	-1.3	A/	3.6	2.2	0.0	1.3	0.0	0.0	A/	0.0	0.0
Charlotte	116.9	3.1	3.7	96.7	32.8	0.0	60.1	3.6	0.0	0.3	0.0	4.5
Citrus	94.5	4.0	2.7	88.1	37.9	0.0	34.0	9.8	1.6	4.7	2.2	1.5
Clay	74.9	8.2	2.1	72.8	35.4	0.0	27.6	7.9	0.0	1.9	0.0	0.0
Collier	340.8	7.4	12.9	290.1	85.7	0.0	189.7	0.0	0.9	13.9	0.0	21.2
Columbia	24.0	72.3	1.2	22.8	10.1	0.0	10.3	0.0	0.2	2.3	0.0	0.0
De Soto	14.7	5.9	1.1	13.6	6.3	0.0	6.9	0.0	0.0	0.5	0.0	0.0
Dixie	5.6	6.7	0.3	4.5	2.3	0.0	2.1	0.0	0.0	0.1	0.0	0.0
Duval	588.8	2.8	6.9	559.6	281.0	0.7	188.0	75.1	0.0	14.8	0.0	6.9
Escambia	144.2	4.4	9.7	130.4	63.8	0.0	66.2	7.0	0.0	0.4	0.0	0.8
Flagler	44.3	0.1	1.0	40.2	13.5	0.7	17.6	0.0	0.0	1.4	2.3	0.3
Franklin	12.2	8.4	0.9	11.0	5.1	0.0	5.9	0.0	0.0	A/	0.0	0.0
Gadsden	15.4	11.3	0.4	15.0	7.5	0.0	6.7	0.0	0.7	A/	0.0	0.0
Gilchrist	5.3	8.7	A/	5.0	2.6	0.0	1.8	0.5	0.0	0.1	0.2	0.0
Glades	7.4	1.3	0.1	7.2	3.8	0.0	2.6	0.6	0.0	0.2	0.0	0.1

Continued . . .

See footnote at end of table.

Table 23.94. LOCAL GOVERNMENT FINANCE: AD VALOREM TAXES IN THE STATE AND COUNTIES OF FLORIDA, JANUARY 1, 1999 (Continued)

(in millions, rounded to hundred thousands of dollars)

County	Total taxes levied — Amount	Total taxes levied — Percentage change 1998-1999	Municipal taxes	County taxes — Total	County-wide — County government — Operating levy	County-wide — County government — Debt service	County-wide — District school board — Operating levy	County-wide — District school board — Debt service	County-wide — Special service districts	County-wide — Independent service districts	Less than county-wide — County government special services districts	Less than county-wide — Independent special services districts
Gulf	13.0	5.8	1.5	11.3	5.3	0.0	5.9	0.0	0.0	0.0	0.2	0.0
Hamilton	10.5	0.2	0.2	10.3	5.2	0.0	4.8	0.0	0.0	0.3	0.0	0.0
Hardee	17.0	1.4	0.5	16.5	7.3	0.0	8.1	0.0	0.0	1.1	0.0	0.0
Hendry	31.3	8.2	1.1	30.0	13.2	0.4	12.3	0.0	0.0	4.5	0.0	0.1
Hernando	88.3	3.6	1.8	80.5	35.2	0.0	28.8	14.3	0.0	1.7	0.0	1.0
Highlands	52.2	4.3	3.6	46.9	22.8	0.0	18.7	5.4	0.0	0.0	0.0	1.7
Hillsborough	872.0	5.9	93.1	628.5	264.6	7.9	305.5	10.4	0.0	40.0	21.2	27.5
Holmes	4.5	7.4	A/	4.5	2.3	0.0	1.5	0.5	0.0	0.1	0.0	0.0
Indian River	135.2	3.8	7.2	97.5	28.6	1.7	60.3	7.0	0.0	0.0	14.6	10.1
Jackson	12.9	-1.3	0.5	12.1	6.8	0.0	5.2	0.0	0.0	A/	0.3	0.0
Jefferson	5.6	0.9	0.5	5.1	2.8	0.0	2.2	0.0	0.0	A/	0.0	0.0
Lafayette	2.6	2.7	A/	2.5	1.3	0.0	0.9	0.3	0.0	A/	0.0	0.0
Lake	121.9	6.3	12.7	97.4	33.3	0.0	60.7	0.0	0.0	3.5	1.6	10.2
Lee	525.7	-8.1	45.0	383.0	138.6	0.0	225.8	0.0	0.0	18.6	0.0	50.3
Leon	159.6	3.6	16.7	142.9	66.3	0.0	67.8	8.4	0.0	0.5	0.0	0.0
Levy	17.3	0.8	1.0	15.7	7.8	0.0	6.2	1.7	0.0	0.0	0.0	0.6
Liberty	2.3	4.9	A/	2.3	1.1	0.0	1.1	0.0	0.0	A/	0.0	0.0
Madison	6.9	5.5	0.5	6.4	3.3	0.0	3.0	0.0	0.0	0.2	0.0	0.0
Manatee	217.7	4.1	10.4	200.7	87.2	3.5	77.3	23.4	0.0	9.3	0.0	0.6
Marion	139.5	2.9	10.7	107.1	41.2	0.0	46.1	19.8	0.0	0.0	1.4	0.0
Martin	184.0	4.7	8.0	154.1	53.9	5.7	64.0	19.4	0.0	11.0	0.0	3.9
Miami-Dade	2,272.1	4.7	427.2	1,561.1	540.7	78.6	792.5	90.7	0.0	58.7	0.0	0.0
Monroe	132.9	-0.2	13.2	110.0	46.3	0.0	37.1	14.2	0.0	12.4	0.0	0.0

See footnote at end of table.

Continued . . .

Table 23.94. LOCAL GOVERNMENT FINANCE: AD VALOREM TAXES IN THE STATE AND COUNTIES OF FLORIDA, JANUARY 1, 1999 (Continued)

(in millions, rounded to hundred thousands of dollars)

County	Total taxes levied Amount	Total taxes levied Percentage change 1998-1999	Municipal taxes	County taxes Total	County-wide County government Operating levy	County-wide County government Debt service	County-wide District school board Operating levy	County-wide District school board Debt service	County-wide Special service districts	County-wide Independent service districts	Less than county-wide County government special services districts	Less than county-wide Independent special services districts
Nassau	48.9	9.4	5.1	42.6	17.6	0.0	18.5	5.2	0.0	1.3	0.0	0.6
Okaloosa	104.3	4.0	10.9	87.1	31.1	0.0	55.6	0.0	0.0	0.3	A/	5.8
Okeechobee	19.4	3.6	1.0	17.7	7.8	0.6	7.0	2.0	0.0	0.4	0.0	0.7
Orange	911.0	4.3	84.5	648.6	244.9	0.0	403.6	0.0	0.0	0.0	0.9	33.8
Osceola	133.1	5.7	8.0	118.9	45.2	0.0	51.3	18.6	3.8	0.0	0.0	5.2
Palm Beach	1,436.3	4.2	228.9	1,091.4	310.3	23.3	444.5	165.7	0.0	147.5	114.1	2.0
Pasco	190.5	8.9	6.7	170.2	78.0	0.0	62.7	25.6	0.8	3.8	8.8	4.8
Pinellas	816.4	4.6	133.0	611.7	234.6	0.0	316.6	0.0	0.0	59.7	0.0	27.4
Polk	279.9	0.8	21.5	247.4	115.7	0.0	102.6	29.0	0.0	0.0	0.0	11.1
Putnam	45.7	1.9	2.5	41.0	18.8	0.0	20.1	2.1	0.0	0.0	0.0	1.1
St. Johns	128.3	10.1	4.5	116.9	43.5	1.8	42.8	23.2	0.0	5.8	4.3	1.9
St. Lucie	196.4	5.9	18.1	171.0	62.1	0.0	54.9	19.1	3.8	31.1	2.6	0.0
Santa Rosa	59.6	3.3	1.2	57.9	26.5	0.0	31.1	0.0	0.0	0.2	0.0	0.5
Sarasota	334.3	4.8	23.1	309.3	96.1	1.9	130.2	56.8	2.4	21.8	0.0	1.5
Seminole	271.1	5.3	34.7	217.1	71.7	1.7	94.2	42.6	0.0	6.9	0.0	0.0
Sumter	20.9	20.2	0.5	19.7	10.2	0.0	9.5	0.0	0.0	0.0	0.0	0.7
Suwannee	12.8	5.2	0.6	12.3	6.0	0.0	5.9	0.0	0.0	0.3	0.0	0.0
Taylor	13.8	1.6	0.7	12.4	5.9	0.0	6.1	0.0	0.0	0.4	0.7	0.0
Union	2.9	3.3	A/	2.8	1.4	0.0	1.0	0.0	0.0	0.1	0.0	0.0
Volusia	355.7	3.0	53.2	252.6	95.7	0.0	131.3	17.7	0.0	7.9	11.1	31.6
Wakulla	9.4	12.4	A/	9.3	4.2	0.0	3.6	1.5	0.0	A/	0.0	0.0
Walton	55.9	10.4	0.6	52.0	22.4	0.0	29.4	0.0	0.0	0.2	0.2	3.1
Washington	8.6	2.2	0.5	8.0	4.2	0.0	3.0	0.8	0.0	A/	0.0	0.0

A/ Less than $100,000.
Source: State of Florida, Department of Revenue, *Florida Property Valuations and Tax Data, December 1999*, Internet site <http://sun6.dms. state.fl.us/dor/property/99FLpropdata.pdf> (accessed 26 May 2000).

Table 23.95. LAND USE: ASSESSED VALUE AND PROPORTION OF LAND BY USE IN THE STATE AND COUNTIES OF FLORIDA, 1999

County	Residential Value (million dollars)	Residential Per-cent-age of total value	Commercial Value (million dollars)	Commercial Per-cent-age of total value	Industrial Value (million dollars)	Industrial Per-cent-age of total value	Agricultural Value (million dollars)	Agricultural Per-cent-age of total value	Institutional Value (million dollars)	Institutional Per-cent-age of total value	Miscellaneous 1/ Value (million dollars)	Miscellaneous 1/ Per-cent-age of total value
Florida	526,920.07	67.9	112,488.15	14.5	26,668.84	3.4	10,575.15	1.4	21,226.16	2.7	78,268.91	10.1
Alachua	4,492.24	53.3	1,033.24	12.3	156.30	1.9	228.12	2.7	237.59	2.8	2,273.08	27.0
Baker	203.56	38.7	32.31	6.1	7.59	1.4	99.51	18.9	13.97	2.7	169.34	32.2
Bay	4,517.57	65.3	921.41	13.3	120.99	1.7	77.60	1.1	156.45	2.3	1,120.67	16.2
Bradford	323.92	60.3	50.97	9.5	10.34	1.9	77.95	14.5	21.33	4.0	52.52	9.8
Brevard	13,908.34	63.0	2,673.89	12.1	524.50	2.4	89.80	0.4	660.05	3.0	4,207.66	19.1
Broward	57,097.16	72.4	11,188.13	14.2	3,704.68	4.7	106.51	0.1	1,571.74	2.0	5,246.90	6.6
Calhoun	111.94	42.7	22.32	8.5	4.21	1.6	84.82	32.3	7.89	3.0	31.12	11.9
Charlotte	6,477.16	80.8	789.14	9.8	102.88	1.3	78.20	1.0	183.53	2.3	382.01	4.8
Citrus	3,306.29	69.5	532.28	11.2	33.70	0.7	39.44	0.8	137.57	2.9	709.10	14.9
Clay	3,503.64	73.2	587.26	12.3	90.19	1.9	70.42	1.5	156.35	3.3	376.89	7.9
Collier	20,923.20	79.0	2,652.80	10.0	375.93	1.4	258.95	1.0	482.05	1.8	1,791.96	6.8
Columbia	743.63	49.6	204.96	13.7	38.49	2.6	147.22	9.8	46.80	3.1	318.76	21.3
De Soto	395.16	42.9	83.24	9.0	11.87	1.3	281.58	30.6	26.30	2.9	121.98	13.3
Dixie	169.15	51.1	15.15	4.6	3.57	1.1	72.82	22.0	4.09	1.2	66.14	20.0
Duval	18,904.23	58.6	5,961.34	18.5	2,091.13	6.5	98.74	0.3	1,362.98	4.2	3,833.74	11.9
Escambia	5,739.45	53.8	1,223.61	11.5	274.89	2.6	73.37	0.7	360.03	3.4	2,990.48	28.0
Flagler	2,333.72	77.6	252.85	8.4	34.03	1.1	47.61	1.6	51.88	1.7	288.65	9.6
Franklin	694.06	46.5	65.85	4.4	12.06	0.8	11.42	0.8	21.76	1.5	688.12	46.1
Gadsden	505.33	53.5	66.26	7.0	41.77	4.4	128.42	13.6	36.19	3.8	166.95	17.7
Gilchrist	176.36	54.8	10.83	3.4	5.21	1.6	84.01	26.1	8.18	2.5	37.09	11.5
Glades	188.93	36.8	44.44	8.7	3.78	0.7	128.88	25.1	7.76	1.5	139.83	27.2
Gulf	471.36	55.2	32.10	3.8	27.67	3.2	28.51	3.3	22.40	2.6	272.24	31.9
Hamilton	124.85	37.8	28.80	8.7	53.48	16.2	68.28	20.7	6.26	1.9	48.63	14.7

See footnote at end of table.

Continued . . .

Table 23.95. LAND USE: ASSESSED VALUE AND PROPORTION OF LAND BY USE IN THE STATE AND COUNTIES OF FLORIDA, 1999 (Continued)

County	Residential Value (million dollars)	Residential Percentage of total value	Commercial Value (million dollars)	Commercial Percentage of total value	Industrial Value (million dollars)	Industrial Percentage of total value	Agricultural Value (million dollars)	Agricultural Percentage of total value	Institutional Value (million dollars)	Institutional Percentage of total value	Miscellaneous 1/ Value (million dollars)	Miscellaneous 1/ Percentage of total value
Hardee	216.67	26.8	49.91	6.2	12.86	1.6	258.50	32.0	26.22	3.2	243.49	30.1
Hendry	481.25	32.9	114.67	7.8	66.51	4.5	467.55	31.9	25.16	1.7	308.98	21.1
Hernando	3,709.50	73.9	508.05	10.1	75.68	1.5	87.98	1.8	134.36	2.7	507.34	10.1
Highlands	1,944.54	60.1	410.21	12.7	48.04	1.5	332.23	10.3	165.89	5.1	332.82	10.3
Hillsborough	24,045.91	61.7	6,847.58	17.6	1,757.29	4.5	457.44	1.2	1,361.25	3.5	4,509.93	11.6
Holmes	149.44	38.3	26.00	6.7	4.51	1.2	120.95	31.0	22.55	5.8	67.13	17.2
Indian River	5,710.08	73.5	935.01	12.0	145.52	1.9	167.59	2.2	223.51	2.9	591.13	7.6
Jackson	531.05	45.6	122.52	10.5	31.17	2.7	169.58	14.6	65.67	5.6	244.03	21.0
Jefferson	100.48	31.1	26.74	8.3	2.96	0.9	137.86	42.6	13.70	4.2	41.81	12.9
Lafayette	52.52	33.0	3.75	2.4	1.00	0.6	69.78	43.8	6.47	4.1	25.62	16.1
Lake	5,874.05	72.9	841.92	10.5	169.02	2.1	244.37	3.0	233.25	2.9	693.11	8.6
Lee	21,739.18	77.6	3,407.58	12.2	599.75	2.1	150.58	0.5	627.23	2.2	1,491.07	5.3
Leon	6,107.10	52.2	1,655.65	14.1	209.06	1.8	98.10	0.8	272.29	2.3	3,359.43	28.7
Levy	586.57	55.6	99.15	9.4	9.31	0.9	177.22	16.8	24.90	2.4	157.95	15.0
Liberty	55.07	14.7	4.52	1.2	2.07	0.6	31.41	8.4	6.66	1.8	275.79	73.4
Madison	163.55	41.0	29.81	7.5	11.60	2.9	127.30	31.9	19.81	5.0	46.83	11.7
Manatee	9,224.12	73.5	1,503.15	12.0	424.70	3.4	276.47	2.2	341.66	2.7	778.79	6.2
Marion	5,354.80	62.1	975.65	11.3	322.02	3.7	446.13	5.2	241.27	2.8	1,277.34	14.8
Martin	7,536.55	75.3	1,000.17	10.0	212.46	2.1	183.76	1.8	193.32	1.9	883.80	8.8
Miami-Dade	68,558.66	65.7	17,155.49	16.4	6,187.50	5.9	494.72	0.5	2,713.98	2.6	9,297.57	8.9
Monroe	7,100.23	56.0	1,875.77	14.8	94.14	0.7	0.03	0.0	199.21	1.6	3,411.26	26.9
Nassau	1,996.84	69.2	345.92	12.0	87.31	3.0	140.34	4.9	70.36	2.4	244.16	8.5
Okaloosa	6,139.64	71.0	1,025.06	11.9	106.38	1.2	65.09	0.8	178.16	2.1	1,132.71	13.1
Okeechobee	633.08	58.6	128.94	11.9	12.96	1.2	138.11	12.8	32.55	3.0	134.99	12.5
Orange	27,651.62	54.6	13,506.28	26.7	2,019.96	4.0	287.39	0.6	1,648.41	3.3	5,534.41	10.9

See footnote at end of table.

Continued . . .

Table 23.95. LAND USE: ASSESSED VALUE AND PROPORTION OF LAND BY USE IN THE STATE AND COUNTIES OF FLORIDA, 1999 (Continued)

County	Residential Value (million dollars)	Residential Percentage of total value	Commercial Value (million dollars)	Commercial Percentage of total value	Industrial Value (million dollars)	Industrial Percentage of total value	Agricultural Value (million dollars)	Agricultural Percentage of total value	Institutional Value (million dollars)	Institutional Percentage of total value	Miscellaneous 1/ Value (million dollars)	Miscellaneous 1/ Percentage of total value
Osceola	5,189.85	63.6	1,843.42	22.6	125.73	1.5	169.12	2.1	237.96	2.9	594.91	7.3
Palm Beach	57,635.82	76.5	9,324.89	12.4	1,713.19	2.3	783.52	1.0	1,535.01	2.0	4,379.51	5.8
Pasco	8,287.55	75.4	1,459.93	13.3	160.76	1.5	195.78	1.8	308.62	2.8	578.53	5.3
Pinellas	29,768.99	69.3	6,193.02	14.4	1,571.87	3.7	15.37	0.0	1,859.59	4.3	3,562.65	8.3
Polk	8,877.73	61.6	1,907.07	13.2	739.45	5.1	470.76	3.3	495.02	3.4	1,922.68	13.3
Putnam	1,402.25	64.0	182.45	8.3	85.04	3.9	62.03	2.8	89.54	4.1	370.81	16.9
St. Johns	6,243.20	77.8	838.73	10.4	86.23	1.1	89.50	1.1	236.69	2.9	532.43	6.6
St. Lucie	5,881.13	69.6	881.06	10.4	200.26	2.4	194.59	2.3	162.98	1.9	1,126.18	13.3
Santa Rosa	3,771.26	76.4	387.20	7.8	50.61	1.0	116.84	2.4	112.28	2.3	496.86	10.1
Sarasota	19,238.89	78.3	2,889.08	11.8	506.82	2.1	52.19	0.2	731.09	3.0	1,161.43	4.7
Seminole	11,667.83	74.2	2,731.75	17.4	556.20	3.5	24.51	0.2	271.95	1.7	468.42	3.0
Sumter	847.54	67.5	126.48	10.1	23.16	1.8	124.23	9.9	12.64	1.0	121.30	9.7
Suwannee	415.19	52.2	61.57	7.7	13.86	1.7	170.87	21.5	37.03	4.7	96.71	12.2
Taylor	287.03	44.7	54.51	8.5	61.97	9.7	107.99	16.8	23.80	3.7	106.28	16.6
Union	67.04	29.4	8.63	3.8	3.73	1.6	67.21	29.5	5.32	2.3	75.91	33.3
Volusia	12,595.96	73.8	2,230.55	13.1	380.87	2.2	152.63	0.9	595.05	3.5	1,117.19	6.5
Wakulla	384.30	56.9	34.12	5.1	9.66	1.4	45.76	6.8	8.43	1.2	192.87	28.6
Walton	3,132.69	80.5	226.21	5.8	20.45	0.5	109.45	2.8	47.54	1.2	353.75	9.1
Washington	252.07	48.2	34.83	6.7	15.97	3.1	110.17	21.1	24.60	4.7	85.18	16.3

1/ Includes lease hold interests, utilities, mining, petroleum and gas lands, subsurface rights, right-of-ways, submerged lands, sewage disposal, borrow pits, wastelands, outdoor recreational/park lands, and governmental lands.

Source: State of Florida, Department of Revenue, unpublished data. Compiled by Armasi, Inc.

ECONOMIC INDICATORS AND PRICES

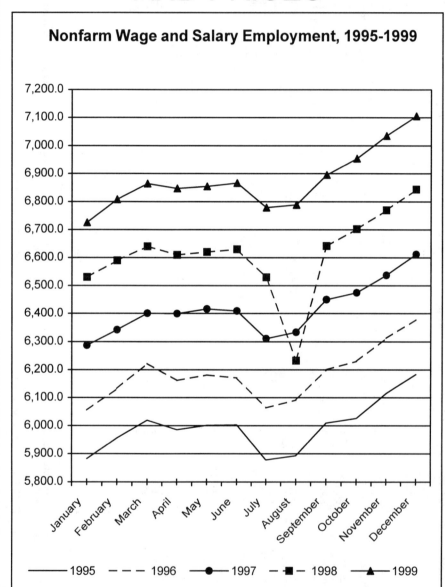

Nonfarm Wage and Salary Employment, 1995-1999

Legend: 1995, 1996, 1997, 1998, 1999

Source: Table 24.12

SECTION 24.00
ECONOMIC INDICATORS AND PRICES

TABLES LISTED BY MAJOR HEADINGS

University of Florida **Bureau of Economic and Business Research**

Table 24.12. ECONOMIC INDICATORS: SPECIFIED INDICATORS OF THE FLORIDA ECONOMY
JANUARY 1994 THROUGH DECEMBER 1999

(not adjusted for seasonal variation)

Month and year	Unemployment rate	Nonfarm wage and salary employment 1/ (1,000)	Sales and use tax collections 2/	Month and year	Unemployment rate	Nonfarm wage and salary employment 1/ (1,000)	Sales and use tax collections 2/
1994				**1997**			
January	7.3	5,657.6	915.6	January	5.2	6,286.7	1,089.7
February	6.5	5,724.8	796.5	February	4.6	6,342.0	973.9
March	6.4	5,788.3	841.4	March	4.5	6,400.7	1,016.1
April	6.4	5,799.2	931.2	April	4.6	6,399.7	1,097.4
May	6.5	5,801.7	845.3	May	4.6	6,416.3	1,022.7
June	7.0	5,806.5	825.0	June	5.0	6,409.3	1,031.0
July	7.2	5,708.6	832.8	July	5.0	6,310.7	1,008.9
August	6.9	5,713.7	813.0	August	4.9	6,333.6	1,038.2
September	6.8	5,828.0	825.8	September	5.0	6,450.2	1,016.2
October	6.3	5,836.3	822.1	October	4.7	6,474.8	1,009.7
November	6.0	5,947.6	841.7	November	4.6	6,536.8	1,041.3
December	5.5	5,979.9	913.8	December	4.1	6,612.1	1,087.4
1995				**1998**			
January	6.1	5,882.0	991.7	January	4.9	6,530.4	1,217.4
February	5.3	5,956.2	856.1	February	4.3	6,589.5	1,064.7
March	5.1	6,019.9	898.1	March	4.2	6,639.8	1,082.1
April	5.1	5,986.0	962.1	April	4.3	6,609.8	1,170.7
May	5.3	6,001.2	887.5	May	4.2	6,619.6	1,121.1
June	5.8	6,003.2	906.2	June	4.5	6,629.4	1,087.3
July	5.8	5,877.9	902.0	July	4.4	6,529.8	1,130.1
August	5.7	5,893.1	871.1	August	4.4	6,232.3	1,081.6
September	5.9	6,009.9	878.1	September	4.4	6,641.5	1,032.3
October	5.5	6,026.6	878.1	October	4.2	6,702.3	1,047.3
November	5.3	6,114.7	893.9	November	4.1	6,769.8	1,105.8
December	4.9	6,182.7	993.5	December	3.6	6,843.6	1,166.0
1996				**1999**			
January	5.6	6,055.8	1,034.9	January	4.3	6,726.1	1,312.5
February	5.0	6,132.1	936.6	February	3.8	6,807.9	1,147.3
March	4.8	6,222.1	1,004.7	March	3.7	6,863.8	1,171.4
April	4.8	6,161.1	1,035.9	April	3.8	6,847.0	1,312.7
May	4.9	6,180.8	971.0	May	3.7	6,854.2	1,191.8
June	5.4	6,170.5	963.0	June	4.0	6,866.1	1,159.3
July	5.4	6,063.3	933.0	July	3.9	6,778.7	1,214.6
August	5.2	6,091.3	940.7	August	3.9	6,788.7	1,170.7
September	5.4	6,200.3	945.5	September	4.0	6,895.2	1,123.9
October	5.1	6,230.4	915.4	October	3.9	6,954.2	1,148.4
November	4.9	6,312.2	984.9	November	3.9	7,035.4	1,162.8
December	4.5	6,379.1	1,038.6	December	3.4	7,105.1	1,267.8

1/ Data are for employment covered by unemployment compensation.
2/ Data are in millions, rounded to thousands of dollars.
Note: Some data are revised.

Source: State of Florida, Department of Labor and Employment Security, Internet site <http://lmi.floridajobs.org/> (accessed 23 June and 18 August 2000), and State of Florida, Department of Revenue, Internet site <http://sun6.dms.state.fl.us/dor/tables/f9199.html> (accessed 23 June 2000).

Table 24.14. GROSS STATE PRODUCT: ESTIMATES IN FLORIDA, OTHER SUNBELT STATES
OTHER POPULOUS STATES, AND THE UNITED STATES, SPECIFIED YEARS
1987, 1992, AND 1994 THROUGH 1997

(in millions of current dollars)

State	1987	1992	1994	1995	1996	1997
			Sunbelt states			
Florida	205,211	280,220	321,700	338,651	360,271	380,607
Alabama	60,527	79,604	89,327	94,948	98,474	103,109
Arizona	58,849	78,278	95,360	103,638	111,911	121,239
Arkansas	32,236	43,810	50,364	53,144	56,111	58,479
California	619,518	825,193	875,965	918,928	966,778	1,033,016
Georgia	117,029	159,299	185,982	200,152	214,436	229,473
Louisiana	76,069	89,748	103,880	112,497	117,633	124,350
Mississippi	33,660	43,302	50,751	53,748	55,757	58,314
New Mexico	22,818	31,949	40,885	41,004	42,571	45,242
North Carolina	115,737	160,579	182,268	193,635	203,485	218,888
Oklahoma	48,165	60,807	65,957	68,335	72,690	76,642
South Carolina	53,073	70,945	80,684	85,137	88,343	93,259
Tennessee	80,924	109,047	127,852	134,489	138,761	146,999
Texas	302,373	424,521	484,099	515,866	554,726	601,643
Virginia	120,740	161,020	178,788	188,002	198,560	211,331
			Other populous states			
Illinois	230,199	298,747	336,867	353,639	370,430	393,532
Indiana	91,350	122,097	141,358	147,383	154,227	161,701
Massachusetts	139,012	165,325	185,988	195,664	207,256	221,009
Michigan	166,298	201,635	240,645	247,725	259,201	272,607
New Jersey	175,137	232,881	255,777	266,702	279,238	294,055
New York	420,379	526,235	565,161	589,506	621,188	651,652
Ohio	192,429	245,726	276,742	292,076	303,569	320,506
Pennsylvania	204,691	269,900	296,781	312,252	322,845	339,940
United States	4,649,993	6,133,012	6,868,041	7,231,814	7,629,503	8,103,234

Source: U.S., Department of Commerce, Bureau of Economic Analysis, Economics and Statistics
Administration, Internet site <http://www.bea.doc.gov/bea>.

University of Florida   **Bureau of Economic and Business Research**

Table 24.15. GROSS STATE PRODUCT: ESTIMATES OF GROSS STATE PRODUCT (GSP) BY COMPONENT AND MAJOR INDUSTRIAL GROUP IN FLORIDA, SPECIFIED YEARS 1977 THROUGH 1997

(in millions of dollars)

Item	1977	1982	1987	1992	1995	1996	1997
Components of GSP							
Total	66,073	124,965	205,211	280,220	338,651	360,271	380,607
Compensation	38,223	72,891	119,440	163,133	194,874	206,359	219,155
Indirect business taxes and nontax liability	6,038	10,680	19,065	29,096	34,952	36,819	38,169
Other gross state product	21,812	41,394	66,707	87,990	108,825	117,093	123,283
GSP by major industry							
Farms	1,510	2,679	3,385	3,875	3,250	3,678	3,573
Agriculture forestry, and fisheries	2,125	3,622	5,069	6,273	6,011	6,610	6,691
Mining	546	1,867	847	798	825	993	1,027
Construction	3,441	7,378	12,430	12,243	15,672	17,381	17,876
Manufacturing	7,056	13,735	21,175	24,650	27,743	28,164	29,108
Durable goods	3,603	8,015	12,600	13,939	15,377	15,635	16,208
Nondurable goods	3,453	5,719	8,575	10,711	12,366	12,529	12,900
Transportation, communications, and public utilities	6,794	12,052	18,588	25,193	30,771	32,426	33,388
Wholesale trade	4,951	8,569	13,668	19,382	24,388	26,665	28,533
Retail trade	7,790	13,892	23,966	31,122	37,714	40,354	42,487
Finance, insurance, and real estate	12,552	25,273	43,502	59,574	73,521	78,819	83,763
Services	10,652	21,731	39,716	63,045	79,873	84,672	91,196
Government	10,166	16,846	26,251	37,939	42,134	44,186	46,538
Federal civilian	1,788	2,923	4,163	6,194	6,566	7,160	7,454
Federal military	1,785	2,955	4,433	5,269	4,506	4,992	5,308
State and local	6,593	10,969	17,655	26,475	31,062	32,034	33,776

Note: Data for earlier years are revised. See Appendix for discussion of Gross State Product (GSP) estimates.

Source: U.S., Department of Commerce, Bureau of Economic Analysis, Regional Economic Information System, Internet site <http://www.bea.doc.gov/bea/>.

Table 24.20. BUILDING PERMIT ACTIVITY: PRIVATE RESIDENTIAL HOUSING UNITS AUTHORIZED BY BUILDING PERMITS IN FLORIDA AND THE UNITED STATES, 1988 THROUGH 1999

Month	1988	1989	1990	1991	1992	1993
Florida						
Annual total 1/	170,597	164,985	126,347	95,308	102,022	115,103
January	11,786	13,582	14,982	7,141	7,103	7,438
February	12,243	13,404	9,318	7,025	6,974	8,604
March	15,721	14,163	12,228	7,485	9,707	9,810
April	13,935	14,593	12,314	8,697	8,870	10,226
May	14,918	17,165	11,836	9,986	8,093	10,893
June	19,255	17,454	12,078	9,773	9,776	11,052
July	13,523	11,756	11,113	9,372	9,853	10,118
August	15,656	13,657	10,667	8,063	8,009	10,119
September	14,614	12,393	8,700	7,246	8,689	11,517
October	13,578	12,754	8,622	7,440	8,972	8,940
November	13,239	11,483	8,592	6,378	7,337	9,333
December	12,911	11,279	6,933	8,458	8,887	12,875
United States						
Annual total	1,455,623	1,338,423	1,110,766	948,794	1,094,933	1,199,063

	1994	1995	1996	1997	1998	1999
Florida						
Annual total 1/	128,602	122,903	124,318	133,990	148,603	164,722
January	11,166	9,940	9,743	9,863	10,712	13,676
February	9,962	8,166	9,376	9,209	9,713	12,537
March	12,164	10,677	9,856	12,207	12,284	14,188
April	11,766	9,686	11,069	11,212	11,447	13,367
May	11,658	10,038	11,174	11,185	11,512	11,654
June	12,077	11,208	10,603	11,798	12,980	14,802
July	11,825	10,101	10,904	12,561	13,653	14,136
August	13,369	10,577	11,889	10,272	14,307	15,342
September	12,136	10,368	11,280	11,785	11,272	12,113
October	11,002	9,266	9,895	12,103	13,640	13,700
November	10,284	9,891	9,088	8,517	12,027	10,697
December	10,483	9,668	8,798	9,662	11,306	14,214
United States						
Annual total	1,371,637	1,332,549	1,433,670	1,441,136	1,612,260	1,663,533

1/ Annual total reflects revisions not distributed to months.

Note: To arrive at state totals, data for metropolitan areas (MSAs and PMSAs) were taken from reports submitted by all places within these areas. Estimates for nonmetropolitan areas in Florida and the United States were based on a sample of the data; 17,000 places for 1988 through 1993 and 19,000 for 1994 through 1999. See Glossary for metropolitan area definitions and see map at the front of the book for area boundaries.

Source: U.S., Department of Commerce, Bureau of the Census, *Housing Units Authorized by Building Permits*, Series C-40, Internet site <http://www.census.gov/const/www.C40/table2.html> (accessed 8 May 2000).

University of Florida   **Bureau of Economic and Business Research**

Table 24.30. GROSS AND TAXABLE SALES: SALES REPORTED AND SALES AND USE TAXES
COLLECTED BY THE DEPARTMENT OF REVENUE IN FLORIDA, 1966 THROUGH 1999

(sales and taxes rounded to dollars)

Year	Gross sales	Taxable sales	Net sales taxes paid	Number of reports
1966	22,070,877,464	10,052,183,902	292,635,382	1,848,519
1967	23,523,783,328	10,738,028,301	314,139,054	1,868,644
1968	28,188,063,900	13,361,484,763	467,573,056	2,102,650
1969	33,441,677,220	16,246,816,932	616,919,658	2,324,350
1970	36,834,259,466	18,339,123,013	681,920,445	2,394,366
1971	41,255,223,174	20,272,358,516	784,708,762	2,528,429
1972	49,280,284,464	23,884,881,400	947,086,120	2,508,097
1973	59,294,867,904	28,264,125,745	1,136,864,712	2,495,557
1974	65,887,520,411	29,785,250,309	1,216,071,766	2,689,313
1975	66,764,958,864	29,329,230,180	1,197,020,925	2,845,986
1976	73,791,141,256	32,215,852,176	1,323,271,879	2,962,711
1977	82,783,600,222	36,274,024,296	1,500,074,880	2,788,578
1978	98,227,927,655	43,640,280,027	1,816,192,620	2,844,083
1979	114,373,759,327	50,555,056,774	2,074,119,153	3,005,717
1980	136,318,330,861	58,177,097,809	2,383,348,768	3,177,162
1981	156,619,282,052	66,750,301,522	2,691,772,260	3,214,217
1982	161,796,458,854	66,663,022,175	3,143,878,949	3,451,004
1983	168,492,566,327	73,906,494,761	4,035,324,107	3,632,967
1984	195,758,800,411	84,639,051,288	4,498,315,417	3,735,161
1985	210,089,814,330	89,673,013,371	4,874,199,447	3,887,677
1986	223,601,586,263	98,612,192,144	5,304,286,552	4,249,174
1987	259,753,403,821	113,379,458,921	6,053,620,606	5,054,411
1988	277,485,847,435	119,103,871,758	7,299,532,184	5,115,463
1989	289,076,440,275	122,788,168,387	7,834,635,188	5,101,085
1990	303,464,877,632	127,283,343,961	8,242,720,563	5,177,182
1991	310,147,685,581	126,648,591,209	8,181,744,259	5,505,665
1992	330,770,069,551	135,959,144,438	8,778,486,852	5,747,984
1993	360,267,713,516	150,592,943,893	9,582,751,878	6,091,241
1994	385,110,859,523	159,956,354,846	10,008,966,792	5,837,879
1995	423,309,073,509	171,551,704,651	10,975,746,043	5,644,615
1996	451,908,747,292	182,117,956,958	11,461,071,670	5,569,872
1997	480,333,681,982	196,353,235,291	12,326,816,327	5,456,337
1998	495,076,575,334	208,234,872,534	13,071,502,379	6,199,782
1999	538,986,640,384	226,636,112,442	14,207,915,429	5,093,050

Note: These sales were reported to the Department of Revenue for the 5 percent regular sales tax, the 5 percent use tax, and the 3 percent vehicle and farm equipment sales tax from January to December of each year. The sales occurred, for the most part, from December of the previous year through November of the posted year. In February 1988 the regular sales and use tax increased to 6 percent; this increase is reflected in the collections from March 1988. These data are not comparable with retail sales figures reported by the Bureau of the Census because of differences in definitions of retailers and retail sales. At various times, changes in the rate of the taxes or in the items to be taxed or excluded have been made. Data prior to 1993 are unaudited and are not comparable to later years. Some data are revised.

Source: State of Florida, Department of Revenue, unpublished data. Data from 1987 to present are prepared by the University of Florida, Bureau of Economic and Business Research.

University of Florida   **Bureau of Economic and Business Research**

Table 24.72. CONSUMER AND PRODUCER PRICE INDEXES: ANNUAL AVERAGES AND PERCENTAGE CHANGES FOR ALL URBAN CONSUMERS INDEX AND PRODUCER PRICE INDEX IN THE UNITED STATES, 1982 THROUGH 1999

| | Consumer prices 1/ | | | | | |
| | All items | | Commodities | | Services | |
Year	Index	Per-centage change	Index	Per-centage change	Index	Per-centage change
1982	96.5	6.2	97.0	4.1	96.0	9.0
1983	99.6	3.2	99.8	2.9	99.4	3.5
1984	103.9	4.3	103.2	3.4	104.6	5.2
1985	107.6	3.6	105.4	2.1	109.9	5.1
1986	109.6	1.9	104.4	-0.9	115.4	5.0
1987	113.6	3.6	107.7	3.2	120.2	4.2
1988	118.3	4.1	111.5	3.5	125.7	4.6
1989	124.0	4.8	116.7	4.7	131.9	4.9
1990	130.7	5.4	122.8	5.2	139.2	5.5
1991	136.2	4.2	126.6	3.1	146.3	5.1
1992	140.3	3.0	129.1	2.0	152.0	3.9
1993	144.5	3.0	131.5	1.9	157.9	3.9
1994	148.2	2.6	133.8	1.7	163.1	3.3
1995	152.4	2.8	136.4	1.9	168.7	3.4
1996	156.9	3.0	139.9	2.6	174.1	3.2
1997	160.5	2.3	141.8	1.4	179.4	3.0
1998	163.0	1.6	141.9	0.1	184.2	2.7
1999	166.6	2.2	144.4	1.8	188.8	2.5

| | Producer prices 2/ | | | | | |
| | All commodities | | Farm products | | Industrial commodities | |
Year	Index	Per-centage change	Index	Per-centage change	Index	Per-centage change
1982	100.0	2.0	100.0	-4.9	100.0	2.7
1983	101.3	1.3	102.4	2.4	101.1	1.1
1984	103.7	2.4	105.5	3.0	103.3	2.2
1985	103.1	-0.6	95.1	-9.9	103.7	0.4
1986	100.2	-2.8	92.9	-2.3	99.9	-3.7
1987	102.8	2.6	95.5	2.8	102.6	2.7
1988	106.9	4.0	104.9	9.8	106.3	3.6
1989	112.2	5.0	110.9	5.7	111.6	5.0
1990	116.3	3.7	112.2	1.2	115.8	3.8
1991	116.5	0.2	105.7	-5.8	116.5	0.6
1992	117.2	0.6	103.6	-2.0	117.4	0.8
1993	118.9	1.5	107.1	3.4	119.0	1.4
1994	120.4	1.3	106.3	-0.7	120.7	1.4
1995	124.7	3.6	107.4	1.0	125.5	4.0
1996	127.7	2.4	122.4	14.0	127.3	1.4
1997	127.6	-0.1	112.9	-7.8	127.7	0.3
1998	124.4	-2.5	104.6	-7.4	124.8	-2.3
1999	125.5	0.9	98.4	-5.9	126.5	1.4

1/ 1982-84 = 100.
2/ 1982 = 100.
Note: Due to changes in the methodology used to computer the Consumer Price Index, caution should be used when comparing data for 1998 and following years to previous data. See Appendix for discussion of consumer and producer price indexes.

Source: U.S., Department of Labor, Bureau of Labor Statistics, *CPI Detailed Report,* January 2000, and Internet site <http://stats.bls.gov/ppihome.htm> (accessed 22 June 2000).

University of Florida   **Bureau of Economic and Business Research**

Table 24.73. CONSUMER PRICE INDEXES: INDEXES BY COMMODITY IN THE UNITED STATES
1998 AND 1999

(1982-84 = 100, except where indicated)

Index expenditure category and commodity	Relative importance December 1999	Annual average index 1998	Annual average index 1999	Per-centage change 1998 to 1999
Wage earners and clerical workers index (CPI-W), all items	100.0	159.7	163.2	2.2
All urban consumers index (CPI-U), all items				
Expenditure category				
All items	100.0	163.0	166.6	2.2
All items (1967 = 100)	(NA)	488.3	499.0	(X)
Food and beverages	16.3	161.1	164.6	2.2
Food	15.3	160.7	164.1	2.1
Food at home	9.6	161.1	164.2	1.9
Cereals and bakery products	1.5	181.1	185.0	2.2
Meats, poultry, fish, and eggs	2.5	147.3	147.9	0.4
Dairy and related products	1.1	150.8	159.6	5.8
Fruits and vegetables	1.4	198.2	203.1	2.5
Nonalcoholic beverages and beverage materials	1.0	133.0	134.3	1.0
Other food at home	2.0	150.8	153.5	1.8
Sugar and sweets	0.4	150.2	152.3	1.4
Fats and oils	0.3	146.9	148.3	1.0
Other foods	1.3	165.5	168.9	2.1
Other miscellaneous foods 1/	0.3	102.6	104.9	2.2
Food away from home	5.7	161.1	165.1	2.5
Other food away from home 1/	0.2	101.6	105.2	3.5
Alcoholic beverages	1.0	165.7	169.7	2.4
Housing	39.6	160.4	163.9	2.2
Shelter	30.2	182.1	187.3	2.9
Rent of primary residence	7.0	172.1	177.5	3.1
Lodging away from home	2.4	109.0	112.3	3.0
Owners' equivalent rent of primary residence 2/	20.5	187.8	192.9	2.7
Tenants' and household insurance 1/	0.4	99.8	101.3	1.5
Fuels and utilities	4.7	128.5	128.8	0.2
Fuels	3.8	113.7	113.5	-0.2
Fuel oil and other fuels	0.3	90.0	91.4	1.6
Gas (piped) and electricity	3.5	121.2	120.9	-0.2
Water and sewer and trash collection services 1/	0.9	101.6	104.0	2.4
Household furnishings and operations	4.7	126.6	126.7	0.1
Household operations 1/	0.9	101.5	104.5	3.0
Apparel	4.7	133.0	131.3	-1.3
Men's and boys' apparel	1.3	131.8	131.1	-0.5
Women's and girls' apparel	1.9	126.0	123.3	-2.1
Infants' and toddlers' apparel	0.3	126.1	129.0	2.3
Footwear	0.8	128.0	125.7	-1.8
Transportation	17.5	141.6	144.4	2.0
Private transportation	16.1	137.9	140.5	1.9
New and used motor vehicles 1/	7.7	100.1	100.1	0.0
New vehicles	4.8	143.4	142.9	-0.3

See footnotes at end of table.   Continued . . .

University of Florida   **Bureau of Economic and Business Research**

Table 24.73. CONSUMER PRICE INDEXES: INDEXES BY COMMODITY IN THE UNITED STATES
1998 AND 1999 (Continued)

(1982-84 = 100, except where indicated)

Index expenditure category and commodity	Relative importance December 1999	Annual average index 1998	Annual average index 1999	Per- centage change 1998 to 1999
All urban consumers index (CPI-U) (Continued)				
Expenditure category (Continued)				
Used cars and trucks	1.9	150.6	152.0	0.9
Motor fuel	3.2	92.2	100.7	9.2
Gasoline (all types)	3.1	91.6	100.1	9.3
Motor vehicle parts and equipment	0.5	101.1	100.5	-0.6
Motor vehicle maintenance and repair	1.6	167.1	171.9	2.9
Public transportation	1.4	190.3	197.7	3.9
Medical care	5.8	242.1	250.6	3.5
Medical care commodities	1.3	221.8	230.7	4.0
Medical care services	4.5	246.8	255.1	3.4
Professional services	2.9	222.2	229.2	3.2
Hospital and related services	1.4	287.5	299.5	4.2
Recreation 1/	6.0	101.1	102.0	0.9
Video and audio 1/	1.7	101.1	100.7	-0.4
Education and communication 1/	5.4	100.3	101.2	0.9
Education 1/	2.7	102.1	107.0	4.8
Educational books and supplies	0.2	250.8	261.7	4.3
Tuition, other school fees, and childcare	2.5	294.2	308.4	4.8
Communication 1/	2.7	98.7	96.0	-2.7
Information and information processing 1/	2.5	98.5	95.5	-3.0
Telephone services 1/	2.3	100.7	100.1	-0.6
Information and Information processing other than telephone services 3/	0.2	39.9	30.5	-23.6
Personal computers and peripheral equipment 1/	0.1	78.2	53.5	-31.6
Other goods and services	4.7	237.7	258.3	8.7
Tobacco and smoking products	1.3	274.8	355.8	29.5
Personal care	3.5	156.7	161.1	2.8
Personal care products	0.7	148.3	151.8	2.4
Personal care services	1.0	166.0	171.4	3.3
Miscellaneous personal services	1.5	234.7	243.0	3.5
Commodity and service group				
Commodities	42.1	141.9	144.4	1.8
Food and beverages	16.3	161.1	164.6	2.2
Commodities less food and beverages	25.8	130.5	132.5	1.5
Nondurables less food and beverages	14.9	132.6	137.5	3.7
Apparel commodities	4.7	133.0	131.3	-1.3
Nondurables less food, beverages, and apparel	10.2	137.4	146.0	6.3
Durables	10.9	127.6	126.0	-1.3
Services	57.9	184.2	188.5	2.5
Rent of shelter 2/	29.9	189.6	195.0	2.8
Tenants' and household insurance 1/	0.4	99.8	101.3	1.5

See footnotes at end of table.   Continued . . .

University of Florida   **Bureau of Economic and Business Research**

Table 24.73. CONSUMER PRICE INDEXES: INDEXES BY COMMODITY IN THE UNITED STATES
1998 AND 1999 (Continued)

(1982-84 = 100, except where indicated)

Index expenditure category and commodity	Relative importance December 1999	Annual average index 1998	Annual average index 1999	Percentage change 1998 to 1999
Commodity and service group (Continued)				
Services (Continued)				
Gas (piped) and electricity	3.5	121.2	120.9	-0.2
Water and sewer and trash colleciton services 1/	0.9	101.6	104.0	2.4
Household operations 1/	0.9	101.5	104.5	3.0
Transportation services	6.9	187.9	190.7	1.5
Medical care services	4.5	246.8	255.1	3.4
Other services	10.8	216.9	223.1	2.9
Special indexes				
All items less food	84.7	163.4	167.0	2.2
All items less shelter	69.8	157.2	160.2	1.9
All items less medical care	94.2	158.6	162.0	2.1
Commodities less food	26.8	132.0	134.0	1.5
Nondurables less food	15.9	134.6	139.4	3.6
Nondurables less food and apparel	11.2	139.2	147.5	6.0
Nondurables	31.2	146.9	151.2	2.9
Services less rent of shelter 2/	28.0	191.8	195.8	2.1
Services less medical care services	53.4	178.4	182.7	2.4
Energy	7.0	102.9	106.6	3.6
All items less energy	93.0	170.9	174.4	2.0
All items less food and energy	77.7	173.4	177.0	2.1
Commodities less food and energy commodities	23.4	143.2	144.1	0.6
Energy commodities	3.4	92.1	100.0	8.6
Services less energy	54.4	190.6	195.7	2.7
Purchasing power of the consumer dollar:				
1982-84 = $1.00	(NA)	0.614	0.600	(X)
1967 = $1.00	(NA)	0.205	0.200	(X)

(NA) Not available.
(X) Not applicable.
1/ Indexes on a December 1997 = 100 base.
2/ Indexes on a December 1982 = 100 base.
3/ Indexes on a December 1988 = 100 base.
Note: See Appendix for explanation of CPI-W and CPI-U.

Source: U.S., Department of Labor, Bureau of Labor Statistics, *CPI Detailed Report*, January 2000.

University of Florida   **Bureau of Economic and Business Research**

Table 24.74. CONSUMER PRICE INDEXES: INDEXES FOR ALL URBAN CONSUMERS BY CATEGORY AND COMMODITY IN MIAMI-FT. LAUDERDALE AND TAMPA-ST. PETERSBURG-CLEARWATER FLORIDA, ANNUAL AVERAGE 1999

Expenditure category and commodity	Miami-Ft. Lauderdale 1999	Miami-Ft. Lauderdale Change 1/	Tampa-St. Petersburg-Clearwater 1999	Tampa-St. Petersburg-Clearwater Change 1/
All items	162.4	1.2	140.6	2.3
Food and beverages	171.0	1.2	137.7	3.0
Food	171.3	1.1	136.8	3.2
Food at home	169.3	1.6	136.0	3.2
Food away from home	176.2	0.6	137.2	2.5
Alcoholic beverages	168.8	2.5	141.4	1.0
Housing	155.2	1.1	135.3	2.3
Shelter	164.0	1.4	145.7	2.5
Renters of primary residence	152.9	1.1	140.7	2.5
Owners' equivalent rent of primary residence 2/	164.8	1.4	150.0	2.0
Fuel and other utilities	115.8	-1.9	120.1	0.3
Fuels	105.7	-2.2	111.0	0.2
Gas (piped) and electricity	104.7	-2.2	110.7	0.1
Electricity	102.5	-2.4	109.3	-0.1
Utility natural gas service	162.4	1.6	170.0	5.3
Household furnishings and operations	162.5	1.9	116.1	2.7
Apparel	138.2	-9.1	148.2	2.8
Transportation	148.8	3.2	126.3	1.7
Private transportation	148.7	3.3	126.8	1.2
Motor fuel	109.8	10.2	121.0	8.1
Gasoline (all types)	109.2	10.5	119.1	8.1
Medical care	231.3	1.8	191.9	-0.1
Recreation 3/	99.2	-1.1	100.6	0.2
Education and communication 3/	102.0	1.5	99.5	0.1
Other goods and services	203.3	6.7	192.6	8.1
Commodity and service group				
All items	162.4	1.2	140.6	2.3
Commodities	154.2	0.8	129.5	2.8
Commodities less food and beverages	142.6	0.5	124.5	2.6
Nondurables less food and beverages	134.6	1.2	144.9	5.0
Durables	154.6	-0.3	100.5	-0.2
Services	169.9	1.4	151.0	1.8
Special aggregate indexes				
All items less medical care	158.6	1.2	137.3	2.4
All items less shelter	161.8	1.1	138.8	2.1
Commodities less food	144.0	0.6	125.9	2.5
Nondurables	154.2	1.2	141.0	3.9
Nondurables less food	137.2	1.3	144.8	4.6
Services less rent or shelter	183.5	1.5	154.5	1.0
Services less medical care services	163.7	1.4	146.1	2.1
Energy	106.1	3.8	115.4	3.8
All items less energy	168.6	1.0	142.6	2.1
All items less food and energy	168.0	1.0	143.8	1.9

1/ Percentage change from 1997 to 1998.
2/ Indexes on a November 1982 = 100 base for Miami-Ft. Lauderdale.
3/ Indexes on a December 1997 = 100 base.
Note: The Miami-Ft. Lauderdale and Tampa-St. Petersburg-Clearwater areas are two of several metropolitan areas for which a consumer price index is issued bimonthly.

Source: U.S., Department of Labor, Bureau of Labor Statistics, *CPI Detailed Report,* January 2000.

Table 24.75. PRODUCER PRICE INDEXES: INDEXES BY STAGE OF PROCESSING, BY DURABILITY OF PRODUCT, AND BY COMMODITY IN THE UNITED STATES, ANNUAL AVERAGES 1997, 1998, AND 1999, AND JUNE 2000

(1982 = 100, not seasonally adjusted)

Item	Annual average			June 2000 A/
	1997	1998	1999	
All commodities	127.6	124.4	125.5	133.3
By stage of processing				
Crude materials for further processing	111.1	96.8	98.2	121.9
Intermediate materials, supplies, etc.	125.6	123.0	123.2	129.7
Finished goods 1/	131.8	130.7	133.0	138.4
Finished consumer goods	130.2	128.9	132.0	138.8
Capital equipment	138.2	137.6	137.6	138.5
By durability of product				
Durable goods	133.9	132.6	132.2	133.2
Nondurable goods	122.9	118.6	120.5	132.5
Manufactures, total	130.7	129.0	130.1	135.7
Durable manufactures	133.5	132.6	132.4	133.4
Nondurable manufactures	127.6	125.2	127.6	137.3
Farm products, processed foods and feeds	127.0	122.7	120.3	122.6
Farm products	112.9	104.6	98.4	99.8
Foods and feeds, processed	134.0	131.6	131.1	133.9
Industrial commodities	127.7	124.8	126.5	135.3
Chemical and allied products	143.6	143.9	144.2	152.2
Fuels and related products and power	86.1	75.3	80.5	105.3
Furniture and household durables	130.8	131.3	131.7	132.7
Hides, skins, and leather products	154.2	148.0	146.0	149.7
Lumber and wood products	183.8	179.1	183.6	178.5
Machinery and equipment	125.9	124.9	124.3	124.1
Metals and metal products	131.8	127.8	124.6	127.9
Nonmetallic mineral products	133.2	135.4	138.9	143.0
Pulp, paper, and allied products	167.9	171.7	174.1	185.4
Rubber and plastics products	123.2	122.6	122.5	124.5
Textile products and apparel	122.6	122.9	121.1	121.0
Transportation equipment 1/	141.6	141.2	141.8	142.9
Motor vehicles and equipment	132.7	131.4	131.7	131.7

A/ Preliminary.
1/ Includes data for items not shown separately.
Note: See Appendix for discussion of producer price indexes.

Source: U.S., Department of Labor, Bureau of Labor Statistics, Internet site <http://stats.bls.gov/sahome.html#PPI> (accessed 23 June 2000).

University of Florida   **Bureau of Economic and Business Research**

Table 24.76. ENERGY PRICES: NATURAL GAS, ELECTRICITY, FUEL OIL, AND GASOLINE PRICES
U.S. CITY AVERAGE AND MIAMI-FT. LAUDERDALE, FLORIDA, JUNE 1999 THROUGH MAY 2000

(in dollars)

Month and year	Piped gas per 40 therms		Electricity per 500 kilowatt-hours		#2 fuel oil per gallon--	All types gasoline per gallon	
	U.S. city average	Miami-Ft. Lauderdale	U.S. city average	Miami-Ft. Lauderdale	U.S. city average	U.S. city average	Miami-Ft. Lauderdale
1999							
June	30.131	47.586	45.994	42.493	0.845	1.204	1.230
July	30.440	48.452	46.298	42.493	0.857	1.244	1.263
August	30.823	49.439	46.235	42.493	0.877	1.309	1.317
September	31.752	50.533	46.267	42.493	0.939	1.334	1.365
October	31.574	50.533	45.736	42.493	0.976	1.329	1.393
November	32.369	50.770	45.378	42.493	1.018	1.319	1.401
December	31.585	49.098	45.375	42.493	1.088	1.353	1.448
2000							
January	31.664	50.733	45.207	41.645	1.189	1.356	1.455
February	31.823	51.617	45.542	41.645	1.614	1.422	1.500
March	31.710	51.278	45.598	41.645	1.359	1.594	1.625
April	32.055	51.963	45.524	41.645	1.286	1.561	1.635
May 1/	32.715	52.599	45.509	41.645	1.263	1.552	1.614

1/ Preliminary.

Source: U.S., Department of Labor, Bureau of Labor Statistics, *CPI Detailed Report,* monthly releases.

Table 24.77. ELECTRICITY PRICES: COST PER KILOWATT-HOUR OF ELECTRICITY BY CLASS
OF SERVICE OF THE FLORIDA ELECTRIC UTILITY INDUSTRY, 1986 THROUGH 1998

(in cents)

Year	Total	Residential	Commercial	Industrial	Other public authorities
1986	7.23	7.98	6.83	5.74	7.06
1987	7.06	7.91	6.45	5.03	10.34
1988	7.04	7.80	6.71	5.31	6.81
1989	7.05	7.74	6.58	5.51	8.20
1990	7.03	7.77	6.82	5.10	6.92
1991	7.15	7.89	6.88	5.29	6.95
1992	6.90	7.75	6.41	5.36	6.59
1993	7.21	7.99	6.43	6.18	7.37
1994	6.95	7.78	6.33	5.56	6.43
1995	7.04	7.76	6.42	5.42	9.06
1996	7.19	8.00	6.65	5.52	6.85
1997	7.18	8.07	6.63	5.42	6.73
1998	6.99	7.89	6.21	5.61	6.46

Note: Cost by class of service is defined as revenue by class of service/kilowatt-hour consumption by class of service. Some data may be revised.

Source: State of Florida, Public Service Commission, Division of Research and Regulatory Review, *Statistics of the Florida Electric Utility Industry, 1998*.

University of Florida   **Bureau of Economic and Business Research**

Table 24.78. INDUSTRIAL AND COMMERCIAL FAILURES: NUMBER IN FLORIDA AND NUMBER AND LIABILITIES IN THE UNITED STATES, 1993 THROUGH 1998

	Florida		United States		Failures
Year	Business starts	Fail- ures 1/	Business starts	Num- ber 1/	Current li- abilities 2/ ($1,000,000)
1993	(NA)	5,091	166,154	86,133	47,756
1994	13,997	3,609	188,387	71,558	28,978
1995	12,344	2,906	168,158	71,194	37,284
1996	12,299	2,676	170,475	71,931	29,569
1997	13,032	2,597	166,740	84,342	24,802
1998	13,029	2,047	155,141	71,857	23,868

(NA) Not available.

1/ Includes firms discontinuing following assignment, voluntary or involuntary petition in bankruptcy, attachment, execution, foreclosure, etc.; voluntary withdrawals from business with known loss to creditors; also enterprises involved in court action, such as receivership and reorganization or arrangement which may or may not lead todiscontinuance; and business making voluntary compromise with creditors out of court.

2/ Liabilities exclude long-term publicly held obligations; offsetting assets are not taken into account.

Source: Dun & Bradstreet Corporation, Murray Hill, NJ, *A Decade of Business Starts,* monthly, and *Business Failure Report,* annual, (copyright).

Table 24.79. PRICE LEVEL INDEX: RELATIVE WEIGHTS ASSIGNED TO SELECTED ITEMS PRICED FOR THE FLORIDA PRICE LEVEL INDEX, 1999

Item	Number of items	Weight	Item	Number of items	Weight
Apparel	17	5.426	Housing (Continued) Electricity		
Food	32	17.907	500 kilowatt-hours		1.638
Cup of coffee		1.245	1,000 kilowatt-hours		1.638
Hamburger lunch		4.442	Hotel-motel rate 1/		1.046
Soft drink, served		1.245	House purchase price		22.737
			Nonlocal phone service 1/		1.294
Health, recreation, and			Residential phone service		1.193
personal services	25	13.877	Residential water service		1.027
Bowling		1.551	Property taxes		1.195
College tuition 1/		1.402			
Extraction		1.041	Transportation	14	18.115
Filling		1.041	Auto insurance		
Movie rental		1.035	Liability		1.387
			Physical damage		1.387
Housing	30	44.675	Auto repair charge		1.779
Air conditioning seasonal			Chevrolet Cavalier		3.830
inspection		1.026	Ford Escort		3.830
Apartment rent, monthly		5.201	Gasoline, unleaded self-service		3.002

1/ Items which have a constant price for all counties.

Note: Items weighted one percent or more are included. See also note on Table 24.80 and discussion under this section in the Appendix.

Source: State of Florida, Department of Education, Office of Education Planning, Budgeting, and Management, *The 1999 Florida Price Level Index*, Internet site <http://www.firn.edu/doe/bin00047/> (accessed 5 April, 2000).

University of Florida   **Bureau of Economic and Business Research**

Table 24.80. PRICE LEVEL INDEX: RELATIVE WEIGHTS ASSIGNED TO SELECTED ITEMS PRICED
FOR THE FLORIDA PRICE LEVEL INDEX, 1999

(population-weighted state average = 100)

| County | Florida Price Level Index | | Food | Housing | Apparel | Transpor-tation | Health recrea-tion, and personal services |
	Index	Rank among coun-ties					
Alachua	94.24	30	99.20	88.87	98.87	97.14	98.25
Baker	90.78	55	100.97	82.04	93.13	99.78	91.18
Bay	95.03	23	107.33	90.50	93.46	97.47	89.91
Bradford	90.45	58	98.20	82.72	89.21	98.85	93.05
Brevard	97.60	13	99.71	95.36	97.56	98.84	99.85
Broward	106.91	2	101.20	110.93	104.69	103.19	107.89
Calhoun	87.81	66	97.68	80.72	89.06	96.19	85.03
Charlotte	94.31	29	98.30	90.67	92.62	96.06	98.22
Citrus	90.59	57	99.39	84.65	91.67	94.63	91.14
Clay	95.01	24	98.10	90.46	96.25	99.60	98.16
Collier	100.09	8	99.83	99.97	101.25	97.06	104.07
Columbia	91.21	51	102.11	85.03	88.47	97.32	88.60
De Soto	91.53	49	101.51	85.62	86.25	98.28	89.46
Dixie	91.26	50	99.52	85.24	94.54	92.92	94.90
Duval	97.01	14	98.60	94.24	102.05	99.83	97.78
Escambia	93.84	36	96.92	87.50	101.77	98.59	99.63
Flagler	94.17	32	100.36	89.31	97.22	97.33	95.34
Franklin	95.57	21	103.35	91.80	98.04	99.50	90.80
Gadsden	91.73	46	100.16	84.23	90.01	95.87	98.18
Gilchrist	90.88	54	103.57	82.14	95.38	94.07	94.36
Glades	94.11	33	100.57	88.96	95.03	96.94	96.93
Gulf	91.70	48	105.01	86.08	92.69	96.42	84.77
Hamilton	89.59	62	100.50	83.40	94.29	95.00	85.22
Hardee	90.62	56	98.13	84.63	98.80	95.35	89.68
Hendry	94.22	31	100.80	87.35	92.41	97.76	101.99
Hernando	91.71	47	97.35	86.79	88.60	98.51	91.51
Highlands	93.22	38	97.74	88.65	93.93	95.80	97.27
Hillsborough	100.48	7	99.95	102.65	96.56	100.48	96.24
Holmes	90.17	60	104.40	81.35	92.05	96.16	89.41
Indian River	96.64	15	99.32	92.19	102.58	97.81	102.59
Jackson	87.80	67	97.75	81.14	86.54	96.55	84.02
Jefferson	93.85	35	101.34	86.00	98.29	99.08	98.97
Lafayette	90.99	53	105.43	83.32	92.43	95.07	89.15
Lake	94.48	28	101.95	92.01	94.83	94.53	91.85
Lee	96.59	16	102.31	90.46	98.01	99.10	103.46
Leon	95.74	20	100.09	89.74	99.88	98.77	102.35
Levy	91.93	44	107.89	83.93	95.61	94.51	90.12
Liberty	89.65	61	101.87	80.91	94.75	96.73	88.85

See footnote at end of table.   Continued . . .

University of Florida   **Bureau of Economic and Business Research**

Table 24.80. PRICE LEVEL INDEX: RELATIVE WEIGHTS ASSIGNED TO SELECTED ITEMS PRICED
FOR THE FLORIDA PRICE LEVEL INDEX, 1999 (Continued)

(population-weighted state average = 100)

County	Florida Price Level Index		Food	Housing	Apparel	Transpor- tation	Health recrea- tion, and personal services
	Index	Rank among coun- ties					
Madison	91.15	52	99.42	84.05	94.79	96.53	93.22
Manatee	99.27	10	101.94	98.75	112.60	96.68	95.80
Marion	93.30	37	106.02	86.67	94.51	94.93	93.67
Martin	98.39	12	98.26	97.00	105.64	100.76	97.16
Miami-Dade	106.84	3	100.33	111.30	110.87	107.34	100.28
Monroe	107.78	1	106.58	116.09	98.35	97.48	101.12
Nassau	92.71	39	97.00	88.57	97.13	97.08	92.29
Okaloosa	94.49	27	101.20	90.40	97.88	95.71	94.99
Okeechobee	93.94	34	99.07	89.83	103.08	98.16	90.87
Orange	99.21	11	100.75	98.39	88.64	98.54	104.17
Osceola	95.52	22	99.38	90.78	112.00	96.98	96.67
Palm Beach	105.62	4	97.02	110.37	99.29	103.41	107.86
Pasco	96.36	17	99.39	93.44	101.95	96.99	98.16
Pinellas	103.34	5	98.14	108.86	96.99	98.20	102.54
Polk	95.93	19	101.48	94.14	88.11	95.92	96.73
Putnam	91.88	45	102.11	85.45	90.29	97.14	91.50
St. Johns	96.10	18	97.52	94.83	94.05	98.53	95.69
St. Lucie	94.58	26	99.08	91.94	105.69	97.63	88.81
Santa Rosa	91.99	43	96.39	87.36	94.84	97.01	92.62
Sarasota	100.57	6	101.02	102.29	101.30	94.97	101.56
Seminole	100.00	9	102.20	99.38	95.83	96.25	105.02
Sumter	88.57	64	98.44	81.49	92.65	94.00	88.29
Suwannee	89.10	63	95.06	84.24	88.01	94.51	89.27
Taylor	92.52	41	104.23	85.57	95.88	98.92	88.59
Union	90.24	59	98.54	82.12	96.67	97.27	92.28
Volusia	94.75	25	98.06	92.03	101.33	95.68	94.94
Wakulla	92.59	40	100.14	83.92	99.76	97.84	99.05
Walton	92.05	42	101.09	86.91	103.21	96.24	86.27
Washington	88.15	65	99.81	81.36	88.07	95.67	83.67

Note: The Florida Price Level Index is a set of numbers which reflects the price level in each county relative to population-weighted statewide average (100 for each category) for a particular point in time, August, 1999. It measures price level differences from place to place in contrast to the consumer price index prepared by the U.S. Bureau of Labor Statistics, which measures price level changes from month to month. The basis for these comparisons is one of fixed standard of living which represents the consumption pattern of a typical wage earner or clerical worker. The index measures in each county the relative cost of living by this standard. See Table 24.79 for relative weights of items priced.

Source: State of Florida, Department of Education, Office of Education Planning, Budgeting, and Management, *The 1999 Florida Price Level Index*, Internet site <http://www.firn.edu/doe/bin00047/> (accessed 5 April, 2000).

Table 24.85. CONSUMER CONFIDENCE INDEX: TOTAL INDEX AND COMPONENTS OF THE FLORIDA CONSUMER CONFIDENCE INDEX BY MONTH, JULY 1997 THROUGH JUNE 2000

(1996 = 100)

			Index component				
Year	Month	Index 1/	Current person-al 2/	Future person-al 3/	U.S. one year 4/	U.S. five years 5/	House-hold pur-chases 6/
1997	7	100.00	90.00	106.00	104.00	85.00	116.00
	8	100.00	88.00	103.00	106.00	83.00	118.00
	9	101.00	92.00	106.00	105.00	84.00	117.00
	10	102.00	93.00	106.00	106.00	86.00	117.00
	11	100.00	95.00	103.00	101.00	85.00	114.00
	12	99.00	91.00	107.00	103.00	83.00	111.00
1998	1	104.00	98.00	106.00	104.00	87.00	123.00
	2	106.00	100.00	108.00	108.00	93.00	123.00
	3	106.00	96.00	106.00	112.00	92.00	125.00
	4	106.00	98.00	108.00	110.00	91.00	123.00
	5	107.00	98.00	107.00	112.00	94.00	123.00
	6	103.00	100.00	106.00	104.00	84.00	121.00
	7	104.00	98.00	106.00	104.00	89.00	122.00
	8	101.00	93.00	107.00	96.00	85.00	122.00
	9	97.00	91.00	105.00	88.00	85.00	118.00
	10	96.00	93.00	104.00	83.00	80.00	117.00
	11	100.00	94.00	103.00	98.00	85.00	121.00
	12	97.00	92.00	104.00	90.00	80.00	121.00
1999	1	104.00	96.00	104.00	105.00	90.00	125.00
	2	108.00	99.00	109.00	113.00	93.00	127.00
	3	107.00	101.00	110.00	113.00	89.00	124.00
	4	103.00	96.00	105.00	101.00	88.00	124.00
	5	105.00	97.00	110.00	105.00	90.00	122.00
	6	104.00	100.00	106.00	98.00	88.00	124.00
	7	106.00	97.00	108.00	110.00	93.00	121.00
	8	102.00	95.00	107.00	99.00	88.00	123.00
	9	105.00	99.00	105.00	103.00	94.00	122.00
	10	101.00	95.00	108.00	96.00	87.00	119.00
	11	103.00	94.00	109.00	104.00	93.00	113.00
	12	104.00	102.00	106.00	109.00	93.00	110.00
2000	1	107.00	98.00	106.00	116.00	94.00	122.00
	2	110.00	107.00	109.00	111.00	99.00	124.00
	3	102.00	100.00	103.00	98.00	92.00	118.00
	4	106.00	100.00	103.00	107.00	97.00	120.00
	5	106.00	102.00	107.00	101.00	96.00	122.00
	A/ 6	106.00	100.00	105.00	104.00	101.00	121.00

A/ Preliminary.
1/ Based on a monthly telephone survey of approximately 1,000 randomly selected Florida households. Compiled from survey responses giving views of personal financial and general business conditions.
2/ Personal financial conditions at time of survey as compared to previous year.
3/ Personal financial conditions anticipated a year from time of survey.
4/ U.S. business conditions anticipated a year from time of survey.
5/ U.S. business conditions anticipated five years from time of survey.
6/ Perception that the time of survey is a good time to buy major household items.

Source: University of Florida, Bureau of Economic and Business Research, Survey Program, *Florida Economic and Consumer Survey,* July 2000.

STATE
COMPARISONS

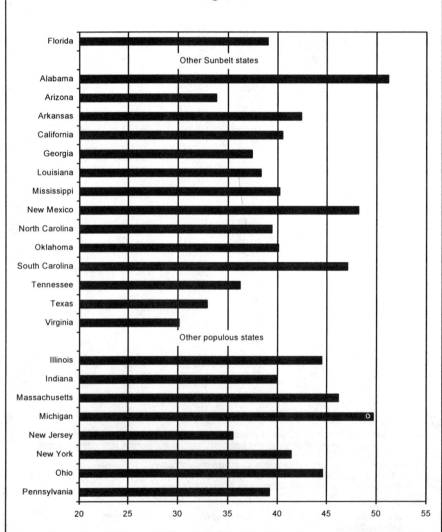

Percentage of Voting-age Population
Voting in 1998

Florida	39
	Other Sunbelt states
Alabama	51
Arizona	34
Arkansas	42
California	40
Georgia	37
Louisiana	38
Mississippi	40
New Mexico	48
North Carolina	39
Oklahoma	40
South Carolina	47
Tennessee	36
Texas	33
Virginia	30
	Other populous states
Illinois	44
Indiana	40
Massachusetts	46
Michigan	49
New Jersey	35
New York	41
Ohio	44
Pennsylvania	39

Source: Table 25.10

SECTION 25.00
STATE COMPARISONS

TABLES LISTED BY MAJOR HEADINGS

Table 25.01. SOCIAL STATISTICS AND INDICATORS: POPULATION CHARACTERISTICS OF FLORIDA OTHER SUNBELT STATES, OTHER POPULOUS STATES, AND THE UNITED STATES

State	Total April 1 1990 (1,000)	Total (1,000)	Rank among states	Percent-age of population aged 65 and over	Persons per square mile of land area	Per-centage change 1990 to 1999
			Sunbelt states			
Florida	12,938	15,111	4	18.1	280.2	16.8
Alabama	4,040	4,370	23	13.0	86.1	8.2
Arizona	3,665	4,778	20	13.2	42.0	30.4
Arkansas	2,351	2,551	33	14.2	49.0	8.5
California	29,811	33,145	1	11.0	212.5	11.2
Georgia	6,478	7,788	10	9.8	134.5	20.2
Louisiana	4,222	4,372	22	11.5	100.4	3.6
Mississippi	2,575	2,769	31	12.1	59.0	7.5
New Mexico	1,515	1,740	37	11.5	14.3	14.8
North Carolina	6,632	7,651	11	12.5	157.0	15.4
Oklahoma	3,146	3,358	27	13.4	48.9	6.8
South Carolina	3,486	3,886	26	12.2	129.0	11.5
Tennessee	4,877	5,484	16	12.4	133.0	12.4
Texas	16,986	20,044	2	10.1	76.5	18.0
Virginia	6,189	6,873	12	11.3	173.6	11.0
			Other populous states			
Illinois	11,431	12,128	5	12.3	218.2	6.1
Indiana	5,544	5,943	14	12.5	165.7	7.2
Massachusetts	6,016	6,175	13	13.9	787.9	2.6
Michigan	9,295	9,864	8	12.4	173.6	6.1
New Jersey	7,748	8,143	9	13.6	1,097.6	5.1
New York	17,991	18,197	3	13.4	385.3	1.1
Ohio	10,847	11,257	7	13.3	274.9	3.8
Pennsylvania	11,883	11,994	6	15.8	267.6	0.9
United States	248,791	272,691	(X)	12.7	77.1	9.6

Population Estimates, July 1, 1999 A/

See footnotes at end of table.   Continued . . .

University of Florida   **Bureau of Economic and Business Research**

Table 25.01. SOCIAL STATISTICS AND INDICATORS: POPULATION CHARACTERISTICS OF FLORIDA OTHER SUNBELT STATES, OTHER POPULOUS STATES, AND THE UNITED STATES (Continued)

	Population (Continued)					
	Estimates, July 1, 1999 A/ (Continued)					
	Age (1,000)					
State	Under 5	5-17	18-24	25-44	45-64	65 and over
			Sunbelt states			
Florida	952	2,618	1,236	4,238	3,325	2,742
Alabama	291	775	440	1,307	989	568
Arizona	386	949	460	1,365	991	629
Arkansas	178	483	251	706	572	361
California	2,499	6,424	3,319	10,707	6,548	3,648
Georgia	580	1,477	774	2,543	1,653	761
Louisiana	314	876	481	1,247	953	501
Mississippi	202	550	302	795	582	335
New Mexico	131	364	176	489	379	200
North Carolina	534	1,407	709	2,352	1,694	955
Oklahoma	233	649	343	926	759	449
South Carolina	253	702	393	1,189	875	473
Tennessee	367	974	520	1,674	1,268	681
Texas	1,640	4,080	2,100	6,034	4,174	2,016
Virginia	451	1,214	673	2,241	1,519	775
			Other populous states			
Illinois	878	2,304	1,143	3,705	2,603	1,496
Indiana	414	1,115	576	1,787	1,308	743
Massachusetts	392	1,076	513	1,996	1,338	860
Michigan	655	1,906	928	2,995	2,157	1,224
New Jersey	543	1,460	673	2,532	1,827	1,108
New York	1,214	3,227	1,619	5,644	4,063	2,430
Ohio	740	2,104	1,065	3,359	2,487	1,501
Pennsylvania	712	2,140	1,025	3,515	2,702	1,899
United States	18,942	51,257	26,011	82,748	59,191	34,540

See footnotes at end of table.

Continued . . .

University of Florida

Bureau of Economic and Business Research

Table 25.01. SOCIAL STATISTICS AND INDICATORS: POPULATION CHARACTERISTICS OF FLORIDA OTHER SUNBELT STATES, OTHER POPULOUS STATES, AND THE UNITED STATES (Continued)

State	Population (Continued)					
	Median age July 1 1999 A/	Projections, July 1, 2025 (1,000)				Living in metro-politan areas 1996 B/
		Race			Hispanic origin 1/	
		White	Black	Other		
		Sunbelt states				
Florida	38.7	16,541	3,556	610	4,944	92.9
Alabama	36.0	3,780	1,364	80	63	67.7
Arizona	34.5	5,599	285	527	2,065	87.6
Arkansas	36.0	2,536	468	52	67	48.3
California	33.6	36,388	3,426	9,471	21,232	96.6
Georgia	34.0	6,282	3,322	268	346	68.5
Louisiana	34.1	3,145	1,849	140	227	75.2
Mississippi	33.7	1,939	1,162	40	39	35.3
New Mexico	34.5	2,192	89	332	1,241	56.7
North Carolina	35.5	6,824	2,244	283	210	66.8
Oklahoma	35.8	3,166	433	457	245	60.2
South Carolina	35.5	3,174	1,402	67	81	69.6
Tennessee	36.2	5,332	1,223	111	104	68.0
Texas	33.0	22,089	3,871	1,224	10,230	84.2
Virginia	35.4	5,951	1,973	543	538	77.9
		Other populous states				
Illinois	35.2	10,504	2,176	760	2,275	84.1
Indiana	35.4	5,811	615	119	243	71.7
Massachusetts	36.5	5,694	655	553	934	96.1
Michigan	35.5	8,011	1,705	362	431	82.4
New Jersey	37.0	6,815	1,721	1,024	1,861	100.0
New York	36.4	13,813	4,048	1,969	4,309	91.8
Ohio	36.1	9,805	1,660	280	319	81.1
Pennsylvania	37.9	10,716	1,530	437	639	84.6
United States	35.5	262,222	47,539	25,288	58,925	79.9

(X) Not applicable.
A/ Provisional.
B/ Population in Metropolitan Statistical Areas July 1, as defined through June 30, 1996, as a percentage of resident population. See Glossary for definition.
1/ Persons of Hispanic origin may be of any race.

Source: Columns 1-17, U.S., Department of Commerce, Bureau of the Census, Internet site <http://www.census.gov/population/www/> (accessed 23 August 2000); Column 18, U.S., Department of Commerce, Bureau of the Census, *Statistical Abstract of the United States, 1999.*

Table 25.02. SOCIAL STATISTICS AND INDICATORS: HOUSING CHARACTERISTICS OF FLORIDA OTHER SUNBELT STATES, OTHER POPULOUS STATES, AND THE UNITED STATES

	Housing					New privately-owned units permitted 1999 A/ (1,000)
	Households, July 1, 1998				Persons per house-hold	
		Age of householder (percentage)				
State	Total	15-44	45-64	65 and over		
			Sunbelt states			
Florida	5,881	40.8	30.5	28.7	2.48	163.1
Alabama	1,663	44.7	32.9	22.5	2.56	19.3
Arizona	1,762	46.9	31.2	21.9	2.60	64.0
Arkansas	970	43.0	32.6	24.3	2.56	11.7
California	11,446	49.5	31.2	19.3	2.79	135.0
Georgia	2,843	50.5	32.5	16.9	2.63	91.0
Louisiana	1,599	46.0	33.6	20.5	2.66	17.2
Mississippi	997	45.1	32.5	22.5	2.68	12.3
New Mexico	632	46.4	33.5	20.3	2.70	9.6
North Carolina	2,883	46.5	32.4	21.1	2.54	84.3
Oklahoma	1,288	44.5	32.8	22.7	2.52	13.3
South Carolina	1,441	45.4	33.5	21.0	2.58	35.7
Tennessee	2,100	45.4	33.7	20.9	2.52	38.1
Texas	7,113	50.0	32.2	17.8	2.71	144.9
Virginia	2,579	48.4	33.0	18.6	2.55	53.0
			Other populous states			
Illinois	4,438	46.2	32.5	21.3	2.65	52.5
Indiana	2,231	46.3	32.5	21.2	2.57	40.9
Massachusetts	2,349	45.5	31.7	22.8	2.52	18.5
Michigan	3,693	46.2	32.6	21.2	2.60	52.6
New Jersey	2,957	43.1	34.0	22.9	2.69	32.2
New York	6,766	43.9	33.7	22.4	2.61	41.5
Ohio	4,285	45.2	32.5	22.4	2.55	55.8
Pennsylvania	4,593	41.5	32.3	26.2	2.54	40.9
United States	101,041	46.2	32.4	21.5	2.61	1,640.2

A/ Based on a sample of 19,000 permit-issuing places. Data are unadjusted.

Source: U.S., Department of Commerce, Bureau of the Census, Population Division, *Estimates of Housing Units, Households, Households by Age of Householder, and Persons per Household: July 1, 1998*, released December 8, 1999, Internet site <http://www.census.gov/population/estimates/housing/sthuhh1.txt>, and *New Privately Owned Housing Units Authorized Unadjusted Units for Regions, Divisions, and States, December 1999 Year-to-date*, Internet site <http://www.census.gov/const/C40/Table2/t2yu9912.txt> (accessed 18 May 2000).

University of Florida   **Bureau of Economic and Business Research**

Table 25.03. SOCIAL STATISTICS AND INDICATORS: VITAL STATISTICS CHARACTERISTICS
OF FLORIDA, OTHER SUNBELT STATES, OTHER POPULOUS STATES
AND THE UNITED STATES

State	Rates, 1999 Live births 1/	Births to teenage mothers 2/	Rates, 1998 Deaths 1/	Suicides 3/	Mar-riages 1/	Di-vorces 1/
			Sunbelt states			
Florida	13.0	55.5	1,060.4	14.6	9.3	5.4
Alabama	14.2	65.5	1,009.9	13.1	11.5	6.0
Arizona	17.0	70.5	820.4	17.2	8.1	5.5
Arkansas	14.4	70.8	1,083.8	13.6	15.1	6.1
California	15.6	53.5	694.8	10.5	5.9	(NA)
Georgia	16.3	65.4	790.7	10.8	7.8	4.7
Louisiana	15.3	65.4	923.3	11.0	9.6	(NA)
Mississippi	15.4	73.0	1,011.8	12.0	7.5	4.7
New Mexico	15.6	69.0	743.1	17.1	7.7	4.6
North Carolina	14.9	61.0	901.0	11.4	8.5	4.9
Oklahoma	14.6	61.6	1,013.8	14.1	7.7	6.0
South Carolina	14.2	60.4	907.9	11.7	10.8	3.8
Tennessee	14.2	64.3	983.6	13.7	14.9	6.4
Texas	17.3	70.9	721.7	10.8	9.6	(NA)
Virginia	13.9	43.5	801.7	12.2	9.5	4.4
			Other populous states			
Illinois	15.0	53.2	867.4	8.6	7.0	3.4
Indiana	14.5	53.3	906.5	11.8	5.9	(NA)
Massachusetts	13.1	30.8	898.6	8.2	6.4	2.7
Michigan	13.5	42.6	867.5	9.9	6.7	4.0
New Jersey	14.0	34.6	882.5	7.2	6.0	3.1
New York	14.2	38.5	861.7	7.5	6.4	2.5
Ohio	13.4	48.1	944.7	9.9	7.6	4.1
Pennsylvania	12.1	36.9	1,055.7	11.4	6.2	3.2
United States	14.5	51.1	864.7	11.3	8.3	3.5

(NA) Not available.
1/ Rate per 1,000 persons.
2/ Rate per resident female population aged 15-19 years.
3/ Rate per 100,000 persons.
Note: Birth, marriage, and divorce rates are preliminary; death rates are final. Birth and death rates are by place of residence and exclude nonresidents of the United States and members of the armed forces abroad. Marriage and divorce rates are by place of occurrence. Divorce rates include annulments.

Source: U.S., Department of Health and Human Services, National Center for Health Care Statistics, Centers for Disease Control and Prevention, *National Vital Statistics Report*, Volume 47 and 48, various issues, Internet site http://www.cdc.gov/nchs/products/pubs/pubd/nvsr/nvsr.htm> (accessed 23 August 2000).

University of Florida   **Bureau of Economic and Business Research**

Table 25.04. SOCIAL STATISTICS AND INDICATORS: HEALTH STATISTICS CHARACTERISTICS
OF FLORIDA, OTHER SUNBELT STATES, OTHER POPULOUS STATES
AND THE UNITED STATES

State	Community hospital beds 1998 A/	Nursing home resident rate 1998 B/	Active physi- cians 1998 C/	Enrollees in managed care, 1997 (percentage) Medi- care	Medi- cade	Persons without health care coverage 1998 (percentage)
			Sunbelt states			
Florida	3.3	221.9	24.3	23.8	65	17.5
Alabama	3.9	363.4	19.4	5.0	71	17.0
Arizona	2.3	218.7	21.3	35.4	85	24.2
Arkansas	3.9	462.3	18.9	2.1	56	18.7
California	2.3	265.9	23.7	38.9	46	22.1
Georgia	3.3	442.1	20.6	2.4	76	17.5
Louisiana	4.1	551.2	23.6	11.0	5	19.0
Mississippi	4.7	394.5	16.2	0.5	40	20.0
New Mexico	2.0	294.1	21.0	18.0	80	21.1
North Carolina	3.1	366.7	22.3	1.4	69	15.0
Oklahoma	3.3	441.6	19.6	6.8	50	18.3
South Carolina	3.0	339.6	20.1	1.0	4	15.4
Tennessee	3.8	458.9	23.9	1.5	100	13.0
Texas	2.9	385.4	20.4	11.7	25	24.5
Virginia	2.6	340.7	23.4	3.5	60	14.1
			Other populous states			
Illinois	3.3	458.6	25.8.	8.9	13	15.0
Indiana	3.3	496.8	19.6	3.2	58	14.4
Massachusetts	2.7	462.0	38.4	19.1	63	10.3
Michigan	2.8	316.0	25.9	2.2	68	13.2
New Jersey	3.2	358.9	30.6	11.4	59	16.4
New York	3.8	370.8	37.1	14.4	30	17.3
Ohio	3.1	485.0	25.1	9.9	28	10.4
Pennsylvania	3.7	387.5	31.5	20.2	68	10.5
United States	3.1	373.6	25.5	14.5	54	16.3

A/ Beds per 1,000 civilian population.
B/ Nursing home residents (all ages) per 1,000 resident population 85 years of age and over.
C/ Nonfederal physicians per 10,000 civilian population.

Source: U.S., Department of Health and Human Services, National Center for Health Care Statistics Centers for Disease Control and Prevention, *Health United States, 2000, with Adolescent Health Chart-book,* Internet site <http://www.cdc.gov/nchs/data/hus00.pdf> (accessed 23 August 2000).

Table 25.05. SOCIAL STATISTICS AND INDICATORS: EDUCATION CHARACTERISTICS OF FLORIDA OTHER SUNBELT STATES, OTHER POPULOUS STATES, AND THE UNITED STATES

State	Enrollment rate fall 1998 A/	Average salary of teachers 1998-99 ($1,000)	Receipts 1998-99 (million dollars)	Current ex- penditure per pupil in ADA 1998-99 (dollars)	College enrollment, 1997 B/ Number (1,000)	Minority (percentage)
			Sunbelt states			
Florida	80.4	35.9	16,732	6,203	658	32.8
Alabama	94.8	35.8	3,979	4,818	219	26.9
Arizona	94.8	35.0	4,849	4,918	293	25.9
Arkansas	94.4	32.4	2,436	5,545	112	18.8
California	93.4	45.4	37,573	5,462	1,958	47.5
Georgia	96.3	39.7	9,715	6,296	306	30.7
Louisiana	87.5	32.5	5,082	5,757	219	32.4
Mississippi	90.6	29.5	2,942	4,658	131	32.8
New Mexico	88.6	32.4	2,137	5,429	109	45.0
North Carolina	90.1	36.1	8,546	6,272	374	25.1
Oklahoma	96.5	31.1	3,778	5,593	177	20.9
South Carolina	94.1	34.5	4,917	8,005	178	26.4
Tennessee	93.4	36.5	4,661	5,579	250	19.2
Texas	98.3	35.0	28,415	6,475	969	37.0
Virginia	93.9	37.5	6,697	6,550	365	24.9
			Other populous states			
Illinois	87.6	45.6	15,239	6,404	726	28.4
Indiana	89.3	41.2	8,401	7,207	296	11.1
Massachusetts	90.4	45.1	7,529	7,854	413	17.4
Michigan	90.8	48.2	16,882	8,139	550	17.3
New Jersey	87.9	51.2	12,663	10,420	326	29.4
New York	88.6	49.4	29,885	9,786	1,024	30.7
Ohio	87.7	40.6	14,932	6,816	537	13.6
Pennsylvania	84.9	48.5	15,344	7,716	588	14.3
United States	91.4	40.6	348,548	6,734	14,502	26.0

ADA Average daily attendance.

A/ Public elementary and secondary school enrollment, fall 1997, as a percentage of persons 5-17 on July 1, 1998.

B/ Preliminary. Excludes students taking courses for credit by mail, radio, or TV, and students in branches of U.S. institutions operated in foreign countries.

Source: U.S., Department of Commerce, Bureau of the Census, _Statistical Abstract of the United States, 2000,_ and National Education Association, Washington, DC, Estimates of School Statistics Database (copyright).

Table 25.06. SOCIAL STATISTICS AND INDICATORS: PERSONAL FINANCES AND INCOME AND WEALTH AND PHYSICAL CHARACTERISTICS OF FLORIDA, OTHER SUNBELT STATES, OTHER POPULOUS STATES, AND THE UNITED STATES

State	Personal finances			Income and wealth		
	Average revenue of electricity sold 1999 A/ (cents)	Life insurance in force 1998 (million dollars)	State gasoline tax rate December 31, 1998 (cents per gallon)	Median family income 1998 B/ (dollars)	Persons in poverty 1998 (percentage)	Average adjusted gross income 1998 C/ (dollars)
			Sunbelt states			
Florida	7.8	727,545	13.0	52,581	13.1	42,252
Alabama	7.2	211,962	18.0	51,156	14.5	35,364
Arizona	8.2	183,668	18.0	49,397	16.6	41,278
Arkansas	7.3	101,270	18.6	44,471	14.7	32,655
California	10.5	1,520,594	18.0	55,209	15.4	46,645
Georgia	7.0	455,298	7.5	55,989	13.5	41,707
Louisiana	6.6	186,518	20.0	49,037	19.1	34,829
Mississippi	6.8	105,578	18.4	43,907	17.6	31,056
New Mexico	9.0	72,539	18.9	43,829	20.4	32,727
North Carolina	7.9	444,511	22.3	54,331	14.0	38,953
Oklahoma	6.6	126,922	17.0	47,436	14.1	34,073
South Carolina	7.6	190,634	16.0	52,111	13.7	35,487
Tennessee	6.4	312,674	20.0	50,310	13.4	37,586
Texas	7.3	957,139	20.0	51,148	15.1	41,063
Virginia	7.4	464,617	17.5	60,860	8.8	45,623
			Other populous states			
Illinois	8.7	742,465	19.0	61,672	10.1	47,186
Indiana	7.2	286,095	15.0	55,284	9.4	39,649
Massachusetts	10.7	407,280	21.0	68,958	8.7	51,812
Michigan	8.5	478,974	19.0	59,019	11.0	43,641
New Jersey	10.9	583,170	10.5	70,983	8.6	54,210
New York	13.4	1,089,033	22.7	57,142	16.7	49,149
Ohio	8.7	635,062	22.0	60,169	11.2	38,621
Pennsylvania	8.4	664,364	25.9	58,507	11.3	41,376
United States	8.1	14,471,448	D/ 19.1	56,061	12.7	42,917

(NA) Not available.
A/ Average revenue per kilowatt-hour sold to residences.
B/ Median income for 4-person families.
C/ Preliminary data from a sample of individual income tax forms.
D/ Average rate.

Source: Column 1, U.S., Department of Energy, Energy Information Administration, Internet site <http://www.eia./doe.gov/cneaf/electricity/epm/epmt53.txt> (accessed 24 August 2000); Column 2, American Council of Life Insurance, *Life Insurance Fact Book, 1999*; Column 3, U.S., Department of Transportation, Federal Highway Administration, *Highway Statistics, 1998*; Column 4, U.S., Department of Commerce Bureau of the Census, Internet site <http://www.census/gov/hhes/income/4person.html> (accessed 13 June 2000); Column 5, U.S., Department of Labor, Bureau of Labor Statistics, Internet site <http://ferret.bls.census.gov/macro/031999/pov/new25_001.htm> (accessed 13 June 2000); Column 6, U.S., Department of the Treasury, Internal Revenue Service, *Statistics of Income: SOI Bulletin, Spring 2000*.

Table 25.07. SOCIAL STATISTICS AND INDICATORS: EMPLOYMENT CHARACTERISTICS OF FLORIDA OTHER SUNBELT STATES, OTHER POPULOUS STATES, AND THE UNITED STATES

State	Labor force participation rate, 1998 A/ Male	Labor force participation rate, 1998 A/ Female	Annual average unemployment rate, 1998 A/ Male	Annual average unemployment rate, 1998 A/ Female	Average annual pay 1997 B/ (dollars)	Average weekly earnings for manu-facturing 1998 C/ (dollars)
			Sunbelt states			
Florida	70.2	55.1	4.0	4.6	28,143	494.49
Alabama	72.0	56.9	3.4	5.1	27,035	526.26
Arizona	73.0	56.5	3.8	4.5	29,317	512.68
Arkansas	68.9	56.9	5.5	5.6	24,422	481.64
California	75.1	58.1	5.9	6.0	35,349	583.11
Georgia	77.4	63.1	4.0	4.4	30,873	521.25
Louisiana	69.9	56.6	5.3	6.2	26,905	657.73
Mississippi	69.7	54.6	4.9	5.9	23,822	461.73
New Mexico	71.0	57.6	6.4	5.9	25,716	488.58
North Carolina	74.3	59.9	3.1	3.9	28,107	505.12
Oklahoma	72.4	57.3	4.2	4.9	25,122	524.10
South Carolina	74.2	60.1	3.4	4.2	26,151	453.48
Tennessee	72.5	59.2	4.0	4.4	28,457	507.50
Texas	78.8	60.2	4.3	5.5	31,512	533.31
Virginia	75.7	60.1	2.3	3.7	31,384	566.89
			Other populous states			
Illinois	76.3	61.5	4.4	4.5	34,704	588.70
Indiana	77.2	61.5	3.0	3.2	29,107	654.65
Massachusetts	74.8	63.4	3.8	2.8	37,787	598.08
Michigan	75.5	59.8	4.2	3.5	34,542	808.35
New Jersey	74.7	59.1	4.6	4.6	(NA)	628.42
New York	71.4	55.8	5.4	5.8	40,678	571.03
Ohio	73.5	59.8	4.4	4.0	30,395	697.55
Pennsylvania	72.8	56.4	4.8	4.5	31,582	592.72
United States	74.9	59.8	4.4	4.6	31,908	580.05

See footnotes at end of table.

Continued . . .

University of Florida   **Bureau of Economic and Business Research**

Table 25.07. SOCIAL STATISTICS AND INDICATORS: EMPLOYMENT CHARACTERISTICS OF FLORIDA OTHER SUNBELT STATES, OTHER POPULOUS STATES, AND THE UNITED STATES (Continued)

State	Con-struc-tion	Manu-fac-turing	Whole-sale and retail trade	Finance insurance and real estate	Serv-ices	Govern-ment
			Percentage distribution of nonagricultural employment, 1999 D/			
			Sunbelt states			
Florida	5.3	7.1	25.0	6.5	36.8	14.1
Alabama	5.4	19.2	23.2	4.8	23.8	18.3
Arizona	7.2	9.8	23.7	6.5	31.5	16.1
Arkansas	4.4	22.1	23.0	4.0	23.7	16.4
California	4.9	13.8	22.9	5.9	31.3	16.0
Georgia	5.1	15.4	24.9	5.2	27.4	15.2
Louisiana	6.8	9.9	23.4	4.5	27.5	19.5
Mississippi	4.8	21.2	21.9	3.7	23.4	19.8
New Mexico	6.0	5.8	23.4	4.5	28.9	24.7
North Carolina	5.8	20.8	22.6	4.8	25.7	15.7
Oklahoma	4.0	12.6	23.1	5.0	28.5	19.3
South Carolina	6.2	18.8	24.0	4.5	24.4	17.2
Tennessee	4.6	19.0	23.5	4.9	26.8	14.6
Texas	5.8	11.9	23.8	5.7	28.4	16.8
Virginia	5.8	11.6	22.0	5.4	31.8	17.9
			Other populous states			
Illinois	4.2	16.1	22.6	6.8	30.4	13.9
Indiana	5.0	23.2	23.7	4.8	24.5	13.6
Massachusetts	3.7	13.4	22.8	7.0	35.9	12.9
Michigan	4.2	21.6	23.5	4.6	27.4	14.7
New Jersey	3.6	12.1	23.4	6.6	32.6	14.8
New York	3.7	10.6	20.2	8.9	34.6	17.1
Ohio	4.3	19.6	24.0	5.5	28.0	13.9
Pennsylvania	4.2	16.7	22.4	5.8	32.5	12.7
United States	6.1	17.8	28.8	7.4	37.7	19.5

(NA) Not available.

A/ Percentage of civilian noninstitutional population of each specified group in the civilian labor force. Includes persons 16 years old and over.

B/ Data are for workers covered by state and federal unemployment insurance programs and are preliminary.

C/ Average weekly earnings of production workers on manufacturing payrolls.

D/ Does not include mining and transportation, communications, and public utilities.

Source: Columns 1-4, U.S., Department of Labor, Bureau of Labor Statistics, *Geographic Profile of Employment and Unemployment, 1998*, Internet site <http://www.bls.gov/opub/gp/pdf/gp98_12.pdf> (accessed 24 August 2000); Col 5, U.S. Department of Labor, Bureau of Labor Statistics, *News: Average Annual Pay by State and Industry 1998*; Columns 6-12, U.S., Department of Labor, Bureau of Labor Statistics, *Employment and Earnings*, May 2000.

University of Florida   **Bureau of Economic and Business Research**

Table 25.08. SOCIAL STATISTICS AND INDICATORS: MANUFACTURING AND AGRICULTURAL CHARACTERISTICS OF FLORIDA, OTHER SUNBELT STATES, OTHER POPULOUS STATES AND THE UNITED STATES

	Manufacturing			Agriculture		
		Rank	Per-centage		Farm cash receipts 1998 A/	
	Jobs won/lost 1997 to 1999	among states in em-ployment	change in gross state product	Farm acreage	Amount (million	Rank among
State	(1,000)	1999	1987-97	1999 B/ (1,000)	dollars)	states
			Sunbelt states			
Florida	-4.2	13	74.3	10,400	6,762	9
Alabama	-11.8	19	70.4	9,200	3,283	25
Arizona	4.0	29	106.0	27,500	2,368	29
Arkansas	-0.3	25	81.4	14,650	5,422	12
California	8.8	1	66.7	27,800	24,616	1
Georgia	10.5	11	96.1	11,200	5,454	11
Louisiana	-2.8	31	63.5	8,150	1,891	33
Mississippi	3.1	26	73.2	11,400	3,454	23
New Mexico	-3.9	45	98.3	44,700	1,950	32
North Carolina	-31.0	8	89.1	9,300	7,164	8
Oklahoma	3.0	32	59.1	34,000	3,900	20
South Carolina	-17.9	21	75.7	4,850	1,511	36
Tennessee	-8.5	12	81.7	11,900	2,216	31
Texas	1.7	3	99.0	130,500	13,206	2
Virginia	-9.4	18	75.0	8,600	2,328	30
			Other populous states			
Illinois	-16.7	5	71.0	27,700	7,742	6
Indiana	13.3	9	77.0	15,500	4,885	15
Massachusetts	-14.5	16	59.0	570	507	44
Michigan	11.6	4	63.9	10,400	3,480	22
New Jersey	-15.1	14	67.9	830	828	39
New York	-27.8	7	55.0	7,800	3,146	26
Ohio	-4.1	2	66.6	14,900	4,973	14
Pennsylvania	-7.3	6	66.1	7,700	4,175	18
United States	-243.0	(X)	74.3	947,340	196,761	(X)

(X) Not applicable.
A/ Includes net commodity credit loans.
B/ As of June 1.

Source: Columns 1, 2, U. S., Department of Labor, Bureau of Labor Statistics, *Employment and Earnings*, May 2000; Column 3, U.S., Department of Commerce, Bureau of Economic Analysis, Internet site <http://www.bea.doc.gov/bea/regional/gsp/gspsum_c.htm>; Columns 4-6, U.S., Department of Agriculture, Economic Research Service, Internet sites <http://usda.mannlib.cornell.edu/reports/nassr/other/zfl-bb/fmno0200.txt> and <http://www.ers.usda.gov/briefing/farmincome/firkdmu.htm> (accessed 14 July 2000).

Table 25.09. SOCIAL STATISTICS AND INDICATORS: SOCIAL INSURANCE AND WELFARE CHARACTERISTICS OF FLORIDA, OTHER SUNBELT STATES, OTHER POPULOUS STATES, AND THE UNITED STATES

State	Persons in the federal food stamp program 1999 A/ (1,000)	Average weekly state unemployment benefits, 1998 (dollars)	Workers' compensation payments, 1998 (million dollars)	Average medicaid benefits per recipient (dollars)	Temporary assistance for needy families (TANF) recipients 1998	Average monthly social security benefits 1998 B/ (dollars)
			Sunbelt states			
Florida	819	205	2,208	3,059	246	741.70
Alabama	346	152	615	2,877	52	672.90
Arizona	233	149	419	455	100	746.30
Arkansas	210	188	161	3,519	31	662.30
California	1,804	154	7,374	2,355	1,909	742.00
Georgia	514	180	808	2,558	172	692.00
Louisiana	463	148	365	3,131	122	656.30
Mississippi	232	146	235	2,825	45	633.50
New Mexico	144	169	117	2,569	78	666.40
North Carolina	435	207	766	3,403	162	701.90
Oklahoma	221	189	520	3,285	58	699.50
South Carolina	251	174	484	3,090	52	695.90
Tennessee	425	174	518	2,073	149	690.50
Texas	1,255	208	1,465	2,893	346	700.00
Virginia	282	183	591	3,123	94	709.30
			Other populous states			
Illinois	767	227	1,687	4,131	449	775.90
Indiana	255	201	439	4,625	117	768.40
Massachusetts	205	261	641	5,332	166	745.20
Michigan	515	235	1,367	3,169	309	784.30
New Jersey	346	266	955	6,634	182	819.80
New York	1,464	206	2,557	6,770	862	780.20
Ohio	552	215	2,335	4,189	320	746.50
Pennsylvania	704	238	2,448	4,575	346	764.80
United States	15,729	200	41,705	3,681	7,826	730.50

A/ Average monthly participants. Federal fiscal year ending September 30.
B/ Data are for December 1999 and include retired workers, disabled workers, survivors, and children.

Source: Columns 1-5, U.S., Department of Commerce, Bureau of the Census, *Statistical Abstract of the United States, 2000,* and previous edition; Column 6, U.S., Department of Health and Human Services, Social Security Administration, *Social Security Bulletin: Annual Statistical Supplement, 2000,* Internet site <http://www.ssa.gov/statistics/Supplement/2000/html/t5k1.htm> (accessed 25 August 2000).

Table 25.10. SOCIAL STATISTICS AND INDICATORS: ELECTION AND PUBLIC SAFETY
CHARACTERISTICS OF FLORIDA, OTHER SUNBELT STATES, OTHER POPULOUS
STATES, AND THE UNITED STATES

State	Elections			Public safety		
	Percent-age of voting-age pop-ulation voting in 1998	Women in state leg-islatures 2000 (per-centage)	Hispanic elected officials 1994 A/	Adults on probation per 100,000 resident adults 1999	Police officers per 10,000 persons 1996 B/	Hate crime offenses 1998
			Sunbelt states			
Florida	39.0	23.8	64	2,533	26	202
Alabama	51.2	7.9	0	1,264	23	0
Arizona	33.8	35.6	341	1,657	23	322
Arkansas	42.4	14.1	2	1,612	23	3
California	40.5	25.8	796	1,372	22	2,116
Georgia	37.4	19.5	0	5,368	26	40
Louisiana	38.3	16.7	12	1,104	37	16
Mississippi	40.2	12.6	0	618	21	3
New Mexico	48.2	27.7	716	907	24	40
North Carolina	39.4	18.2	0	1,841	23	53
Oklahoma	40.1	10.1	1	1,131	22	74
South Carolina	47.1	10.6	0	1,534	23	114
Tennessee	36.2	16.7	0	967	23	63
Texas	32.9	17.7	2,215	3,121	25	378
Virginia	30.1	16.4	0	616	28	203
			Other populous states			
Illinois	44.5	25.4	881	1,501	32	379
Indiana	40.0	18.0	8	2,399	19	54
Massachusetts	46.2	26.0	1	983	29	491
Michigan	49.7	24.3	8	2,341	21	427
New Jersey	35.5	15.8	37	2,095	35	813
New York	41.4	21.3	83	1,335	39	778
Ohio	44.6	20.5	4	2,198	21	233
Pennsylvania	39.2	12.6	8	1,298	21	217
United States	41.9	22.5	5,459	1,864	25	9,235

(NA) Not available.
A/ Persons of Hispanic origin may be of any race.
B/ Based on estimated resident population as of July 1.

Source: Column 1, U.S., Department of Commerce, Bureau of the Census, Internet site <http://www.
census.gov/population/socdemo/voting/cps1998/tab04.txt> (accessed 28 August 2000); Column 2,
Center for the American Woman and Politics (CAWP), Eagleton Institute of Politics, Rutgers University,
Women in State Legislatures, 2000, Internet site <http://www.cawp.rutgers.edu/pdf/stleg.pdf> (accessed
26 June 2000); Columns 3, 5, U.S., Department of Commerce, Bureau of the Census, *Statistical Abstract
of the United States, 1999*; Column 4, U.S., Department of Justice, Bureau of Justice Statistics, *Bureau
of Justice Statistics Bulletin: Probation and Parole in 1999*, Internet site <http://www.ojp.usdoj.gov/
bjs/abstract/pp99pr.htm> (accessed 28 August 2000); Column 6, U.S., Department of Justice, Federal
Bureau of Investigation, *Hate Crime Statistics, 1998*, Internet site <http://www.fbi.gov/ucr/98hate.pdf>
(accessed 28 August 2000).

Table 25.11. SOCIAL STATISTICS AND INDICATORS: GOVERNMENTAL EXPENDITURE CHARACTERISTICS OF FLORIDA, OTHER SUNBELT STATES, OTHER POPULOUS STATES, AND THE UNITED STATES

State	Federal government expenditure per capita, 1995-96 (dollars)					
	Total	Educa-tion	Public welfare	Health and hospitals	Highways	Police protec-tion
			Sunbelt states			
Florida	4,220.33	1,251.86	512.71	417.44	318.07	210.69
Alabama	3,881.40	1,356.53	553.81	697.47	268.51	117.51
Arizona	3,827.89	1,388.54	592.87	188.60	280.36	175.46
Arkansas	3,457.76	1,260.58	632.26	349.00	327.79	101.14
California	4,750.38	1,373.95	756.12	480.51	200.81	226.13
Georgia	4,167.94	1,516.42	638.02	516.71	279.04	136.74
Louisiana	4,226.94	1,298.96	683.82	612.55	295.49	156.70
Mississippi	3,861.15	1,343.69	591.66	586.57	366.47	105.51
New Mexico	4,564.01	1,525.88	683.22	463.25	489.54	164.77
North Carolina	3,958.99	1,397.14	625.97	568.93	262.18	136.28
Oklahoma	3,523.20	1,370.81	492.95	371.25	286.11	121.66
South Carolina	4,064.94	1,429.89	692.03	721.56	195.63	121.12
Tennessee	3,754.68	1,198.89	708.72	482.87	279.98	123.98
Texas	3,783.23	1,456.43	535.52	411.25	267.91	134.96
Virginia	3,915.39	1,501.51	492.52	286.38	339.12	136.40
			Other populous states			
Illinois	4,300.76	1,436.07	745.40	307.60	304.04	192.30
Indiana	3,774.07	1,577.38	554.85	350.59	251.03	106.25
Massachusetts	5,044.27	1,322.22	948.69	461.93	374.67	183.18
Michigan	4,526.32	1,797.14	705.45	430.54	246.30	152.25
New Jersey	5,260.67	1,824.77	888.24	253.04	322.47	225.00
New York	6,609.23	1,812.44	1,377.41	677.57	326.88	254.04
Ohio	4,104.01	1,488.26	707.38	338.39	252.44	154.25
Pennsylvania	4,237.82	1,495.12	817.97	266.14	246.20	143.90
United States 1/	4,483.33	1,503.52	729.33	417.72	298.14	168.43

See footnotes at end of table. Continued . . .

University of Florida **Bureau of Economic and Business Research**

Table 25.11. SOCIAL STATISTICS AND INDICATORS: GOVERNMENTAL EXPENDITURE
CHARACTERISTICS OF FLORIDA, OTHER SUNBELT STATES, OTHER POPULOUS
STATES, AND THE UNITED STATES (Continued)

State	Federal government expenditure per capita, 1998-99 (dollars)					
	Total	Grants to state and local govern- ments	Salaries and wages	Direct payments to indivi- duals 1/	Pro- cure- ments	Other
			Sunbelt states			
Florida	5,771.52	740.57	518.48	2,474.06	571.71	1,466.70
Alabama	6,127.34	1,059.94	640.25	2,262.69	845.89	1,318.56
Arizona	5,641.99	949.53	556.95	1,982.52	1,000.69	1,152.30
Arkansas	5,342.55	1,024.64	437.27	2,279.07	182.97	1,418.60
California	5,009.78	1,097.29	535.02	1,529.22	778.25	1,070.01
Georgia	5,035.15	866.88	807.84	1,700.88	661.26	998.28
Louisiana	5,577.33	1,195.75	495.18	1,809.38	609.92	1,467.09
Mississippi	5,955.28	1,223.47	613.50	2,042.98	700.46	1,374.87
New Mexico	7,805.42	1,580.58	946.28	2,023.18	2,259.41	995.96
North Carolina	4,865.86	994.41	689.49	1,945.50	267.92	968.55
Oklahoma	5,714.25	962.09	822.09	2,160.72	497.18	1,272.17
South Carolina	5,361.45	998.20	628.26	2,081.30	653.73	999.97
Tennessee	5,629.00	1,075.95	495.64	2,022.73	824.35	1,210.33
Texas	4,888.59	916.47	588.59	1,571.90	723.53	1,088.10
Virginia	8,415.97	690.95	1,753.27	2,250.19	2,770.94	950.62
			Other populous states			
Illinois	4,603.75	872.85	494.71	1,732.95	286.96	1,216.28
Indiana	4,514.32	791.84	331.78	1,860.28	373.86	1,156.56
Massachusetts	6,121.78	1,431.25	472.68	1,899.93	931.68	1,386.25
Michigan	4,447.75	989.89	297.29	1,839.20	209.34	1,112.04
New Jersey	4,960.77	891.71	441.92	1,894.27	516.51	1,216.35
New York	5,594.92	1,586.55	413.33	1,868.32	372.20	1,354.52
Ohio	4,731.62	910.96	385.63	1,922.94	400.44	1,111.65
Pennsylvania	5,790.22	1,095.60	452.19	2,265.61	494.73	1,482.09
United States 2/	5,555.20	1,062.29	639.53	1,888.34	780.56	1,184.47

1/ Retirement and disability.
2/ Average.
Note: Some data are preliminary.

Source: U.S., Department of Commerce, Bureau of the Census, Internet site <http://www.census.gov/
ftp/pub/govs/state/98states.xls> (accessed 12 June 2000), and *Consolidated Federal Funds Report:
for Fiscal Year 1999, State and County Areas,* Issued April 2000, Internet site <http://www.census.gov/
prod/2000pubs/cffr-99.pdf> (accessed 24 May 2000).

Table 25.12. SOCIAL STATISTICS AND INDICATORS: GEOGRAPHY AND CLIMATE CHARACTERISTICS OF FLORIDA, OTHER SUNBELT STATES, OTHER POPULOUS STATES, AND THE UNITED STATES

State	Total area 1990 (square miles)	Land area 1990 (per-centage)	Developed nonfederal land 1992 A/ (per-centage)	Climate 1/ Average annual days with rainfall .01 inch or more 2/	Climate 1/ Heating degree days 3/	Climate 1/ Cooling degree days 3/
			Sunbelt states			
Florida	59,928	90.0	5.1	116	1,434	2,551
Alabama	52,237	97.2	2.2	122	1,702	2,627
Arizona	114,006	99.7	1.5	36	1,350	4,162
Arkansas	53,182	97.9	1.4	105	3,155	2,005
California	158,869	98.2	5.4	35	1,458	727
Georgia	58,977	98.2	3.3	116	2,991	1,667
Louisiana	49,651	87.7	1.9	115	1,513	2,655
Mississippi	48,286	97.2	1.5	109	2,457	2,215
New Mexico	121,598	99.8	0.9	61	4,425	1,244
North Carolina	52,672	92.5	3.9	112	3,457	1,417
Oklahoma	69,903	98.2	2.0	83	3,669	1,859
South Carolina	31,189	96.5	2.0	110	2,649	1,966
Tennessee	42,146	97.8	2.4	107	3,082	2,118
Texas	267,277	98.0	9.0	79	2,407	2,803
Virginia	42,326	93.6	2.4	114	3,963	1,348
			Other populous states			
Illinois	57,918	96.0	3.4	125	6,536	762
Indiana	36,420	98.5	2.3	126	5,615	1,014
Massachusetts	9,241	84.8	1.4	127	5,641	678
Michigan	96,705	58.7	4.0	135	6,569	626
New Jersey	8,215	90.3	1.7	113	5,169	826
New York	53,989	87.5	3.3	121	4,906	1,096
Ohio	44,828	91.4	3.9	137	5,708	797
Pennsylvania	46,058	97.3	3.7	117	4,954	1,101
United States	3,717,796	95.1	100.0	(X)	(X)	(X)

(X) Not applicable.
A/ Includes urban and built-up areas in units of 10 acres or greater, and rural transportation.
1/ Data are for a major city in each state.
2/ Period of record through 1998.
3/ Sums of the negative departures of the daily temperature from 65 degrees Fahrenheit. Period of record through 1998.

Source: U.S., Department of Commerce, Bureau of the Census, *Statistical Abstract of the United States, 2000,* and previous edition.

University of Florida   **Bureau of Economic and Business Research**

APPENDIX. EXPLANATORY NOTES AND SOURCES

SECTION 1.00. POPULATION

EXPLANATORY NOTES. A series of intercensal population estimates for the 1990s appears in Table 1.20. Extreme caution must be exercised when deriving annual changes from successive estimates. Calculating such changes can lead to inaccurate conclusions regarding population growth, especially for small places. The best base of any estimate of population change is generally the most recent census enumeration.

Counties and municipalities are legal and political entities, but from a sociological point of view the community of which a person considers himself or herself to be a part may not correspond to such an entity. Terms like "Greater Jacksonville" or "the Miami area" are used to indicate the real community. People do not hesitate to cross city or county limits or even state lines to work, to buy or sell, or to seek cultural, medical, recreational, or social services. For this reason, the U.S. Office of Management and Budget has designated areas known as Metropolitan Statistical Areas (MSAs). An MSA is a geographic area with a large population nucleus together with adjacent communities having a high degree of economic and social integration with that nucleus. These areas were designated as Standard Metropolitan Statistical Areas (SMSAs) before January 1983. New MSA standards for the next decade are expected to be published before December 31, 2000.

Generally an area qualifies for recognition as an MSA in one of two ways: if there is a city of at least 50,000 population or an urbanized area of at least 50,000 with a total metropolitan population of at least 100,000. An MSA may include a single county or several counties that have close economic and social ties to a central city or urban area. In metropolitan complexes of one million or more population, separate component areas (previously MSAs) are defined if specified criteria are met. Such areas are designated Primary Metropolitan Statistical Areas (PMSAs) and any area containing PMSAs is designated as a Consolidated Metropolitan Statistical Area (CMSA).

In Florida, MSAs are defined in terms of entire counties. Population living in MSAs may be referred to as the metropolitan population. Nineteen MSAs were designated in Florida effective June 1983 and a twentieth was designated in June 1984. The two areas redefined as PMSAs together comprise the Miami-Ft. Lauderdale CMSA. On December 31, 1999, new MSA designations went into effect nationally. Florida's MSAs remained the same as those defined in 1992 (see map on page vi). Table 1.65 contains population figures for Florida's current MSAs.

Agencies of the state government have grouped counties into different districts. There are eleven planning districts, each containing several counties that have common interests and needs for planning community development. A map on page 49 shows the counties by planning districts. Florida Department of

Health districts are mapped on page 257, water management districts are on page 276, National Weather Station offices are on page 282, and crop-reporting district boundaries are on page 332.

SOURCES. The Census of Population taken once every ten years by the U.S. Bureau of the Census provides basic statistics about population. Selected Florida data from the 1990 census are included in this *Abstract.* Table 1.19 contains a historical population series for counties beginning with the 1940 census.

At the back of this volume is an index of the most recent census information appearing in previous editions. In 1994, the Bureau of Economic and Business Research (BEBR), University of Florida, published a collection of county 1990 census data titled *1990 Census Handbook - Florida.* This volume also includes some 1980 data for comparison and information on how to use census data, primary census sources, and census definitions.

In addition to the decennial censuses, the Census Bureau issues a series of *Current Population Reports*, known as P-Series. These contain national, regional, and sometimes state population statistics resulting from periodic surveys, special censuses, and cooperative estimation and projection efforts between the individual states and the Census Bureau. Many of these reports can be found on the Census Bureau's worldwide web Internet site, www.census.gov/.

Between census years, estimates of the population of the state, counties, and municipalities of Florida are made by the BEBR Population Program. These are released annually in *Florida Estimates of Population.*

The *Abstract* contains estimates and projections of population by age, race, and sex. Benchmark data are from the 1990 census. The age, race, and sex estimates and projections are developed by BEBR and released in the *Florida Population Studies* series. New Hispanic origin population estimates for Florida and its counties are presented on Table 1.36. BEBR also provides unpublished median age, projections, and elderly population statistics and data on total net migration and migration of persons aged 65 and over to Florida. Voting-age population estimates and projections are presented in Section 21.00.

Data on veterans are from the U.S. Department of Veterans Affairs in Washington, which releases reports on the age, location, and period of service of veterans. Financial information about veterans at the county level can be found in Section 23.00. Data on immigrants are from the U.S. Immigration and Naturalization Services. Data on state-to-state and intercounty migration in Tables 1.74, 1.75, and 1.76 are from the Internal Revenue Service. The Florida Department of Children and Families provides homeless population figures in the publication *Annual Report on Homeless Conditions in Florida* and data on refugees entering Florida on their website; www.state.fl.us/cf_web/.

SECTION 2.00. HOUSING

SOURCES. The decennial Census of Housing is taken simultaneously with the Census of Population and provides basic information about people in their living arrangements. Extensive data from the 1990 Census of Housing can be found in previous *Abstracts* (refer to the census index at the back of this volume) and in the *1990 Census Handbook - Florida.*

The Census Bureau also releases statistics compiled on subjects from the decennial or special censuses and surveys such as the American Housing Survey. Estimates of housing units and households in every state are now published on the Internet and appear in Table 2.01. American Housing Survey data on homeownership rates in Table 2.02 are from the Census Bureau's *Housing Vacancies and Homeownership Annual Statistics* and are also available on the Internet.

The Bureau of Economic and Business Research (BEBR), University of Florida, makes annual estimates of the number of households and average household size for intercensal years. These are published in the series, *Florida Population Studies.*

Four agencies of the State of Florida provide information relating to housing. The Office of Education Budget and Management, Department of Education provides prices of average housing by county and the Florida Price Level Index, which includes a housing component. The Florida Agency for Health Care Administration publishes data on the number of nursing homes, licensed beds, and room rates in the *Guide to Nursing Homes in Florida* on their Internet site; www.floridahealthstat.com/. The Division of Hotels and Restaurants of the State Department of Business and Professional Regulation publishes statistics on apartment houses, rooming houses, and licensed lodgings. The Department of Highway Safety and Motor Vehicles annually publishes the number of tags sold to owners of mobile homes and recreational vehicles in *Revenue Report.*

Data on home sales and median sales prices in metropolitan areas are provided in unpublished form by the Florida Association of Realtors and the University of Florida's Real Estate Research Center.

SECTION 3.00. VITAL STATISTICS AND HEALTH

EXPLANATORY NOTES. Vital statistics usually include data on births, infant deaths, abortions, teenage pregnancies, illegitimate births, marriages, divorces, annulments, and deaths by cause. Also included in this section are indicators of child well-being. For births and deaths, "resident" is the term indicating births or deaths among residents of a specified area regardless of where the event occurred. "Recorded" is the term used to identify births or deaths occurring in a specified area regardless of the usual residence of the person counted. The birth and death figures in this section are resident data. Marriages and dissolutions of marriage are reported by place of occurrence. Cases of Human Immunodeficiency Virus (HIV) and Acquired Immunodeficiency Syndrome (AIDS) in Table 3.28 are diagnosed cases and reported cases. There is a time lag—occasionally as much as several years—between diagnosis of a case according to national Centers for Disease Control criteria and the case's entry into the Florida Department of Health's AIDS Reporting System.

SOURCES. The Public Health Statistics Section of the Department of Health is the principal source of vital statistics data for Florida and its counties. Data are released monthly in *Vital News* and later accumulated in an annual report, *Florida Vital Statistics.*

Statistics on HIV and AIDS are available from the Division of Disease Control of the Florida Department of Health in a quarterly report of cumulative data, *The Florida HIV/AIDS, STD, and TB Surveillance Report,* and are available on their website; www.doh.state.fl.us. Data on child and teen deaths, children affected by divorce, and reports of maltreatments are used with permission from a copyrighted biennial publication, *Florida's Children at a Glance: The 1999 Statewide and County Update* produced by the University of South Florida, Louis de la Parte Florida Mental Health Institute, and the Florida Center for Study of Children's Futures. The Florida Department of Children and Families reports cases of elder abuse in *Adult Abuse Reports by County* on its website; www.state.fl.us/cf_web/.

SECTION 4.00. EDUCATION

EXPLANATORY NOTES. In census counts and estimates of population, persons of Hispanic origin are considered to be of any race. The Florida Department of Education, on the other hand, reports persons of Hispanic origin as a separate racial category. Some duplication of data results when persons of Hispanic origin are summed with race data. Therefore, totals are not complete unless persons of Hispanic origin are included. Every effort has been made to individually note the differences on the education tables where this occurs.

SOURCES. The principal sources of information on public and private elementary and secondary education in Florida are provided by the Florida Department of Education. Resources include the annual *Profiles of Florida School Districts*, reports from the Bureau of Education Information and Accountability Services of the Division of Administration, various *Statistical Briefs* released by both the Division of Administration and the Division of Public Schools, other publications, and unpublished data. Many of the reports and much of the data, including information on dropout and graduation rates, high school completers, and test results can now be found on the Department's Internet site; www.firn.edu/doe/. High School Competency Test (HSCT) and Florida Comprehensive Assessment Test (FCAT) scores are presented in new Tables 4.77 and 4.79. Readiness for college data are available in *Readiness for Postsecondary Education* on the Internet.

School-age population is available in unpublished form from the Bureau of Economic and Business Research. Enrollment information about the State University System is available in the *Fact Book* published by the Florida Board of Regents and is available on the Internet. The Office of Educational Research and Improvement of the National Center for Education Statistics, U.S. Department of Education publishes accredited colleges and universities enrollment data every two years in the *Directory of Postsecondary Institutions*. Data on public community colleges come from reports of the Florida Community College System, Florida Department of Education.

Data on the extent of public and private education, exceptional programs, the level achieved by the pupils, and the availability and enrollments of schools, colleges, and universities are all included in Section 4.00. Employment and finances of educational institutions and data on educational services are in Section 20.00. Additional information on the public funding of education is in Section 23.00.

SECTION 5.00. INCOME AND WEALTH

EXPLANATORY NOTES. The earnings components of personal income are allocated on a place-of-work basis. These earnings are converted to a place-of-residence basis by means of a residence adjustment factor. Property income and transfer payments are then added to earnings, resulting in total income on a place-of-residence basis. This conversion is illustrated in Table 5.14. The first basis, earnings by place of work, is useful in the analysis of the income structure of a given area in terms of industrial markets and purchasing power. Expressed per capita, the latter basis, earnings by place of residence, is an indicator of living standards and welfare level. See Section 9.00 for estimates of farm income.

The Bureau of Economic Analysis (BEA) recently reclassified government employee retirement plans covering federal civilian, military, and state and local government employees, which resulted in a raise in personal income. Changed were the amount of employer contributions (added to other labor income), dividend and interest received by these plans (added to personal dividend income and personal interest income), and personal contributions (no longer included in personal contributions for social insurance). A complete discussion of these changes and other revisions to state personal income may be found in "Comprehensive Revision of State Personal Income" online at www.bea.gov/bea/regional/articles/0600spi/maintext.htm.

Families and unrelated individuals are classified as being above or below the poverty level by comparing their calendar-year money income to an income cutoff or "poverty threshold." The income cutoffs vary by family size, number of children, and age of the family householder or unrelated individual. Poverty status is determined for all families (and, by implication, all family members). Poverty status is also determined for persons not in families, except for inmates of institutions, members of the Armed Forces living in barracks, college students living in dormitories, and unrelated individuals under 15 years old.

The poverty thresholds are revised annually to reflect changes in the Consumer Price Index. The poverty threshold for a family of four in 1999 was $17,028, as shown on Table 5.46. Poverty thresholds are computed on a national basis only. No attempt has been made to adjust these thresholds for regional, state, or other local variations in the cost of living.

The Statistics of Income series data published by the U.S. Internal Revenue Service are based on the tax-defined concept, adjusted gross income (AGI), which excludes certain types of income. Caution should be exercised in comparing these data over time as annual changes in tax law will continue to affect the definition of AGI.

SOURCES. One source for income data is the U.S. Internal Revenue Service. Data such as income sources, tax deductions, and credits are from statistical samplings of individual tax returns and are reported in the series *Statistics of Income.*

Florida household income data by household size and income class are based on results from the Florida Economic and Consumer Survey, Bureau of Economic and Business Research (BEBR), University of Florida.

The source for statistics on personal income in Florida is the U.S. Department of Commerce, Bureau of Economic Analysis (BEA). The BEA has made comprehensive estimates of personal income, by type and industrial source, covering all metropolitan areas and counties in the nation for selected years from 1969 through 1998. Annual estimates are published in *Survey of Current Business.* State and county data published in this *Abstract* are from the BEA's Regional Economic Information System (REIS) CD-ROM for June 2000.

University of Florida   **Bureau of Economic and Business Research**

Updated estimates of national poverty thresholds are published annually in the *Statistical Abstract of the United States* and can be found on the Internet. Poverty thresholds based on money income and median household income, the number of poor persons, and children living in poverty are published annually by the U.S. Bureau of the Census on their website; www.census.gov/hhes/.

The income of military retirees appears in the Department of Defense publication, *DOD Statistical Report on the Military Retirement System.*

SECTION 6.00. LABOR FORCE, EMPLOYMENT, AND EARNINGS

EXPLANATORY NOTES. Tables of employment and payroll devoted to individual industries and nonprofit organizations are presented in this section and in other sections of the *Abstract.* Data are defined by the State Unemployment Insurance Program and are often termed "covered employment" or "ES-202" data. Any firm or nonprofit establishment whose employees are covered by state and federal unemployment laws must submit monthly reports on the number of persons on its payroll and the amount employees were paid. The data generated from these reports provide useful measures of the impact of various industries, firms, or other organizations on the economies of the state and its counties. The Bureau of Labor Market Information of the Florida Department of Labor and Employment Security compiles these statistics and recently began publishing the data on the Internet; http://lmi.floridajobs.org/. Many tables in this *Abstract* include revised data for 1998 along with figures for 1999.

Covered employment data include most employed persons in Florida, but certain workers are specifically excluded from coverage. These are some agricultural and domestic employees, self-employed workers, and elected officials. Among the excluded self-employed are such occupations as insurance or real estate agents whose earnings are from commissions. Certain nonprofit organizations such as churches may elect to participate in the program.

Also missing from the tables are data for the state or counties in which there were so few units that the information for an individual establishment might be made public or estimated by competitors. In these instances and when one firm in a specific category or county has 80 percent of the employment of all the business in that category or county, no data are reported. Often data may be undisclosed at the level of the county or 3-digit SIC industry group but are reported in aggregate at the state level. Disclosure guidelines adopted by the Department of Labor and Employment Security in keeping with federal rules prevent publication of reporting units and employment ranges for undisclosed establishments.

The derivation and meaning of SIC codes are briefly discussed in the Preface and the Glossary, which lists the major industrial groups and codes. Table 6.03 presents data for all covered employees by industry and Tables 6.04 and 6.05 present employment data by county. Tables in various sections present state and county data by major industries and industry sub-groupings, such as Tables 12.50, 12.51, 12.52, and 12.53, 13.36 and 13.37, etc. Detailed public employment data for governments appear in Section 23.00.

SOURCES. The basis of statistics on the employment status of the population is a monthly Current Population Survey (CPS) conducted by the U.S. Bureau of the Census and detailed data (e.g., employment by occupation, labor force status by age, race, sex) are available from the decennial censuses. The U.S. Bureau of Labor Statistics (BLS) publishes monthly data from the CPS in *Employment and Earnings* and other related publications listed below. The Bureau of Labor Market Information (LMI), Department of Labor and Employment Security of the State of Florida has the responsibility of preparing estimates of employment status following procedures developed in cooperation with the U.S. Bureau of Labor Statistics. LMI publishes information about Florida, its counties, metropolitan areas, and cities in *Florida Labor Force Summary*, and releases special reports on small counties. Different samples are used to prepare these sets of employment and unemployment estimates. *Florida Industry and Occupational Employment Projections* is published annually by LMI.

The U.S. Bureau of Labor Statistics (BLS) compiles statistics and publishes data on nonagricultural employment in Florida and its metropolitan areas. BLS publishes much of its data on the Internet at http://stats.bls.gov. Longstanding BLS publications such as the monthly *Employment and Earnings* and annual *Geographic Profile of Employment and Unemployment,* and the series of bulletins or releases entitled *News* may also be found online.

The U.S. Equal Opportunity Commission publishes the occupational distribution data in *Job Patterns for Minorities and Women in Private Industry* and the U.S. Bureau of Economic Analysis provides data on proprietors and wage and salary workers. Farm employment data appear in Section 9.00.

SECTION 7.00. SOCIAL INSURANCE AND WELFARE

EXPLANATORY NOTES. For purposes of managing state-administered public assistance programs, the state has been divided into fifteen Department of Health districts; a map showing these districts appears on page 257.

SOURCES. Four public assistance programs—for the aged, the blind, the permanently and totally disabled, and dependent children—are administered by the state but are financed in part by the federal government in grants to states under the Social Security Act. The principal source of state and national data on these programs is the U.S. Department of Health and Human Services, Social Security Administration. Published Social Security Administration reports such as the *Social Security Bulletin, OASDI Beneficiaries by State and County,* and *SSI Recipients by State and County* and related unpublished data may be found on the Internet; www.ssa.gov/.

Historical average weekly wages and unemployment insurance contribution and disbursement data are provided by the Florida Department of Labor and Employment Security (FDLES). Data on nonfatal occupational injuries and illnesses by industry in the state are found in the FDLES Division of Safety publication *Occupational Injuries and Illnesses in Florida* online; www.fdles.state.fl.us/.

The Health Care Financing Administration in the U.S. Department of Health and Human Services provides unpublished statewide Medicare enrollment and payment data. The principal source of Medicaid eligibility, recipient, and expenditure data for Florida and its counties is the Florida Agency for Health Care Administration.

The Florida Department of Health furnishes unpublished Aid to Families with Dependent Children (AFDC) statistics and publishes food stamp data in *Florida Food Stamp Program Participation Statistics.*

SECTION 8.00.   PHYSICAL GEOGRAPHY AND ENVIRONMENT

SOURCES. The Geography Division of the Bureau of the Census, U.S. Department of Commerce provides revised data on the land and water area of the state and counties of Florida based on TIGER mapping files from the 1990 Census of Population and Housing.

Solid waste data are published by the Bureau of Solid and Hazardous Waste, Florida Department of Environmental Protection in the annual report *Solid Waste Management in Florida;* www.dep.state.fl.us/.

Data on water use are collected by the United States Geological Survey, five water management districts in the state, and the Florida Department of Environmental Regulation. A map of the water management districts with district headquarters is on page 276. Some figures are obtained from utilities and information on agricultural irrigation is collected by the Institute of Food and Agricultural Sciences at the University of Florida and the Florida Department of Agriculture and Consumer Services. Water-use data were compiled from these various sources by the U.S. Geological Survey, Water Resource Division in cooperation with the Florida Department of Environmental Protection.

Tables in this section containing information relating to temperature, precipitation, and other climatic phenomena present data supplied by the National Environmental Satellite, Data, and Information Service of the National Oceanic and Atmospheric Administration (NOAA), U.S. Department of Commerce. Their publications are issued both annually and monthly under the title, *Climatological Data: Florida.* A map of the National Weather Station Offices located throughout the state is on page 282. Hurricane data are published in periodic NOAA technical memoranda found on their Internet site, www.nhc.noaa.gov/.

The Division of Air Resources Management, Florida Department of Environmental Protection publishes information on air pollution in the report *Comparison of Air Quality Data with the National Ambient Air Quality Standards* on the Internet; www.dep.state.fl.us./air/.

SECTION 9.00.   AGRICULTURE

EXPLANATORY NOTES. Since 1840 a Census of Agriculture has been taken every five years. Congress authorized agricultural censuses to be taken in 1978 and 1982 to coincide with the quinquennial economic censuses. After 1982, the agricultural census again reverted to a five-year cycle to be taken in years ending in "2" and "7." An index at the back of this book lists recent census tables appearing in previous *Abstracts*.

The *1997 Census of Agriculture* released the first geographical area data about Florida from the 1997 economic censuses and gave us our first glimpse of how the 1997 census categories differ form those used in earlier censuses. Census tables are based on the recently implemented North American Industry Classification System (NAICS). This revised system of classifying establishments by economic activity replaces the Standard Industrial Classification (SIC) system. See the Glossary for a definition and for a listing of industrial categories.

As defined since the 1978 census, a farm is "any place from which $1,000 or more of agricultural products were sold or normally would have been sold during the census year." Because data for selected items are collected from a sample of operators, the results are subject to sampling variability. Dollar values have not been adjusted for changes in price levels between census years.

When comparisons are made between Florida and other states, the other states selected either have a similar climate (the southern tier of Sunbelt states) or produce similar crops (citrus in Arizona and California, sugarcane in Hawaii and Louisiana, etc.).

SOURCES. Timely and detailed data on farm receipts, income, taxes, and value of farm marketings are provided in tables based on annual publications of the U.S. Department of Agriculture, *Agricultural Statistics*, online at www.usda.gov/ nass/pubs/ and from the Department's Economic Research Service, Internet site www.econ.ag.gov/. The U.S. Department of Commerce, Bureau of Economic Analysis provides additional farm income data, some of which also appears in Section 5.00.

NAICS data primarily covering characteristics of farms and farm operators are from the *1997 Census of Agriculture* published by the U.S. Department of Commerce, Bureau of the Census.

Agricultural employment information comes from the Bureau of Economic Analysis, U.S. Department of Commerce and from the Bureau of Labor Market Information, Florida Department of Labor and Employment Security. (See discussion under Section 6.00 of this Appendix.) The Florida Department of Business and Professional Regulation has data on veterinarians licensed in the state.

Water-use data for agricultural irrigation are from the U.S. Geological Survey. (See discussion under Section 8.00 of this Appendix). The Agricultural Stabilization and Conservation Service, U.S. Department of Agriculture provides state and county estimates of nonresident alien ownership of agricultural land in their publication *Foreign Ownership of U.S. Agricultural Land* at Internet site, www.econ.ag.gov/.

Information about citrus production, cash receipts, other crop cultivation, and livestock is from the Florida Agricultural Statistics Service, Florida Department of Agriculture and Consumer Services; www/nass.usda.gov/fl/. A map of counties in crop-reporting districts appears on page 332. A complete series of crop estimates for the state dating back to 1919 is available from the reporting service upon request. The Florida Department of Citrus provides unpublished information on orange juice sales.

SECTION 10.00 FORESTRY, FISHERIES, AND MINERALS

SOURCES. Forestry employment and payroll data come from the Bureau of Labor Market Information, Florida Department of Labor and Employment Security, as does similar information for fishing and mining. (See discussion under Section 6.00 of this Appendix.) The Division of Forestry of the Florida Department of Agriculture and Consumer Services provides data on the harvest of forest products. The Forest Service, U.S. Department of Agriculture publishes data on national forests in *Land Areas of the National Forest System*.

The Marine Fisheries Information System, Florida Department of Natural Resources provides unpublished data on fish landings. The National Marine Fisheries Service of the National Oceanic and Atmospheric Administration, U.S. Department of Commerce publishes data on fishery products, plants, and cooperatives in its annual *Fisheries of the United States*. Table 19.45 in Section 19.00 gives information on the number of commercial boats registered in the state and counties of Florida.

Basic data about mineral production are from *The Minerals Yearbook*, published by the U.S. Geological Survey, Department of the Interior, Internet site, http://minerals.er.usgs.gov/, and the *1997 Economic Census: Mining* published by the U.S. Bureau of the Census and based on the newly-defined NAICS system (see the discussion in Section 9.00 of this Appendix and the Glossary) at www.census.gov/.

SECTION 11.00. CONSTRUCTION

SOURCES. Statistics on building construction activity and characteristics of that industry (SIC codes 15-17) are in this section. Table 11.01 provides construction industry data based on the NAICS industry classification system (see the discussion in Section 9.00 of this Appendix and the Glossary) published online in the *1997 Economic Census: Construction* by the U.S. Bureau of the Census at www.census.gov/prod/ec97/. Additional information about NAICS and all available *1997 Economic Census* publications may be found on the U.S. Bureau of the Census website; www.census.gov/epcd/www.econ97.html/.

The principal sources of building permit data for Florida are the Bureau of Economic and Business Research (BEBR), University of Florida, and the U.S. Bureau of the Census. BEBR publishes monthly and annual summaries on the type and value of building permits for construction issued by local administrative offices throughout Florida in *Building Permit Activity in Florida*. BEBR compiles, and makes available in unpublished form, data on construction starts. Building permit data and mobile home data for states can be found on the Census Bureau's website on the Internet at www.census.gov/.

Data on employment and payrolls are supplied by the Bureau of Labor Market Information, Florida Department of Labor and Employment Security. (See discussion under Section 6.00 of this Appendix.)

SECTION 12.00. MANUFACTURING

SOURCES. The U.S. Bureau of the Census conducts a complete count of manufactures every five years as part of its comprehensive economic census. New table 12.05 depicts manufacturing industry data by kind of business based on the recently-developed NAICS industry classification system (see the discussion in Section 9.00 of this Appendix and the Glossary) published online in the *1997 Economic Census: Manufacturing* by the U.S. Bureau of the Census at www.census.gov/prod/ec97/. Census data for counties are updated in Table 12.06. NAICS codes 31-33 represents the manufacturing industry and data for establishments, employment, and annual payroll are presented.

In addition to the 5-year censuses, the Bureau of the Census also conducts, in intervening years, a sample survey called the *Annual Survey of Manufactures*. Data from the *Survey* for specified metropolitan areas are found at the beginning of the chapter.

The Bureau of Labor Market Information of the Florida Department of Labor and Employment Security provides data on the number of units, employees, and payroll for manufacturing establishments based on the Standard Industrial Classification system. Major industry divisions for manufacturing are found in SIC codes 20-39. A number of industries are detailed in tables in this section and many include county breakdowns.

Unpublished data on the value of Florida products are made available by the Research Department, Enterprise Florida, Inc. and may be found online at www.floridabusiness.com/.

SECTION 13.00. TRANSPORTATION

SOURCES. The U.S. Department of Transportation provides data on roads and highways, tax receipts, bridges, and vehicles in *Highway Statistics*, a publication of the Federal Highway Administration. Information about licenses, drivers of motor vehicles, and motor vehicle registrations comes from the Florida Department of Highway Safety and Motor Vehicles. The same department publishes accident data in *Florida Traffic Crash Facts* (www.hsmv.state.fl.us/) and automobile tag and revenue data in *Revenue Report*.

Every five years the Bureau of the Census conducts an economic census that includes transportation. Table 13.01 provides establishment, employment, revenue, and annual payroll data from the *1997 Economic Census: Transportation and Warehousing* based upon the NAICS industry classification system (see the discussion in Section 9.00 of this Appendix and the Glossary). An index at the back of the book lists tables from recent previous censuses appearing in earlier editions of *Abstract*.

Employment and payroll figures for all modes of transportation except interstate railroads are supplied by the Bureau of Labor Market Information, Florida Department of Labor and Employment Security. Interstate railroads are not included because their employees are not covered by the same unemployment law as workers in other industries.

Data on miles of track in the state's rail system are from the Rail Office, Florida Department of Transportation publication, *Florida Rail System Plan*.

Water transportation (SIC code 44) includes both the movement of vessels through Florida waterways and the volume of commodities shipped into and out of Florida ports. The authorities of the various ports in the state have supplied data on their activities. Enterprise Florida, Inc. furnished unpublished data on exports and imports through Florida customs districts.

Unpublished air traffic information comes from the Federal Aviation Administration of the U.S. Department of Transportation's Internet site; www.apo.data.faa.gov/. Data on aircraft pilots appears in the publication *U.S. Civil Airmen Statistics* and is available on the Internet; www.api.hq.faa.gov/airmen/.

SECTION 14.00. COMMUNICATIONS

EXPLANATORY NOTES. Newspaper publishing and other print media (SIC code 27) are considered to be manufacturing by the U.S. Bureau of the Census as well as the Office of Management and Budget, which establishes the Standard Industrial Classification. Since newspapers, periodicals, and books compete with electronic media in providing communications, data are repeated in this section. Table 12.50 in Section 12.00 shows newspapers as a component of the manufacturing industry. Also included in Section 14.00 are data on telephones (SIC code 481), radio and television broadcasting (SIC code 483), and cable and other pay TV services (SIC code 484).

SOURCES. The U.S. Bureau of the Census conducts an economic census in years ending in 5 and 7. Data recently released from the 1997 census include statistics on the information industry; a new census category based upon the NAICS industry classification system (see the discussion in Section 9.00 and the Glossary). New tables at the beginning of chapter 14.00 highlight this change and include establishment, employment, revenue, and annual payroll data for the information industry.

Postal revenue data are provided by the U.S. Postal Service. The Florida Public Service Commission supplies data on telephone companies servicing Florida in the *Annual Report* and in *Statistics of Florida Telecommunications Companies.* Employment and payroll data are from the Bureau of Labor Market Information, Florida Department of Labor and Employment Security. (See discussion under Section 6.00 of this Appendix.)

SECTION 15.00. POWER AND ENERGY

SOURCES. Data in this section have been selected to describe the status of the electric, gas, and sanitary service industries, and the consumption and production of electricity, gas, gasoline, fuel oil, and nuclear power. Energy information is supplied in various publications by the Energy Information Administration, U.S. Department of Energy or on the Internet at www.eia.doe.gov/.

Data on the utilities industry by kind of business and by metropolitan areas from the *1997 Economic Census: Utilities* based on the NAICS classification system (see the discussion in Section 9.00 and the Glossary) are shown in new tables 15.01 and 15.02.

Major sources of data on electrical energy in Florida are published by the Florida Public Service Commission in the *Annual Report* and *Statistics of the Florida Electric Utility Industry.* Natural gas statistics for the state are also found in the Commission's *Annual Report* and on the Energy Information Administration, U.S. Department of Energy website, www.eia.doe.gov/, or in *Natural Gas Annual.* Data on nuclear power plants are furnished by the U.S. Bureau of the Census in the *Statistical Abstract of the United States.*

The Oil and Gas Section of the Florida Department of Environmental Protection provided crude oil and natural gas data. The Florida Department of Community Affairs (DCA) publishes the *Florida Motor Gasoline and Diesel Fuel Report* (www.dca.state.fl.us/). The DCA also compiles and provides information from U.S. Department of Energy published and unpublished data on energy consumption, pricing, and production along with state and county data on motor fuel consumption. Another source of state motor fuel data is *Highway Statistics,* published by the Federal Highway Administration.

The Bureau of Labor Market Information of the State Department of Labor and Employment Security supplies information on employment and payroll in the utility industry. (See discussion under Section 6.00 of this Appendix.)

Information on consumer prices of energy as measured by the Consumer Price Index is reported in Section 24.00.

SECTION 16.00. WHOLESALE AND RETAIL TRADE

SOURCES. Data from the *1997 Economic Census: Wholesale Trade* and *1997 Economic Census: Retail Trade* are featured in several tables of this section. An index of recent previous census tables appearing in earlier *Abstract*s is at the back of this edition. Wholesale and retail trade industries are grouped according to the new NAICS industry classification system explained in Section 9.00 of this Appendix and in the Glossary. Number of establishments, employment, payroll, and sales, payroll and expenses are presented where possible by kind of business and by county in which the establishments are located. All *1997 Economic Census* publications may be found online at the U.S. Bureau of the Census website www.census.gov/prod/ec97/epcd/www/econ97.html/.

Covered employment and payroll information by kind of business and county comes from the Bureau of Labor Market Information (LMI), Florida Department of Labor and Employment Security. (See the discussion under Section 6.00 of this Appendix.) Since there are some differences in coverage and classification, LMI figures are not necessarily comparable with those from the economic censuses conducted by the Bureau of the Census every five years.

The Florida Department of Revenue is the source for information on sales reported by firms in connection with the sales and use tax laws. In addition to the data presented in this section, printouts of county gross and taxable sales by business category are available from the Bureau of Economic and Business Research (BEBR), University of Florida on a subscription basis. These business categories vary in coverage and classification from the Bureau of the Census figures. Data on retail sales tax collections may be found in Table 23.43. A time series of gross and taxable sales is in Table 24.30.

Health professionals who operate at the retail level and are required to have a license such as dispensing opticians or pharmacists are reported by the Florida Department of Health. These data are presented in Section 20.00.

SECTION 17.00. FINANCE, INSURANCE, AND REAL ESTATE

EXPLANATORY NOTES. Industries covered in this section are those SIC codes numbered 60 through 67, including banking and other credit agencies, establishments dealing in securities and commodities, insurance and real estate offices, and investment firms.

SOURCES. The U.S. Bureau of the Census recently released geographic area series data from the *1997 Economic Census: Finance and Insurance* for Florida. New tables at the front of section 17.00 depict the finance and insurance industry by kind of business based on the NAICS classification system (See Glossary).

University of Florida   **Bureau of Economic and Business Research**

Historical and recent summaries of banking data for Florida may be found in the *Annual Report of the Division of Banking,* published by the state Office of the Comptroller. Another major source of banking data is the Federal Deposit Insurance Corporation (FDIC), which issues *Statistics on Banking* and *Bank* and *Thrift Branch Office Data Book: Summary of Deposits.*

Figures on number of establishments, employment, and payroll for banking and credit, insurance, real estate and investment industries come from the Florida Department of Labor and Employment Security, Bureau of Labor Market Information. (See the discussion in Section 6.00 of this Appendix.)

Data on homeowner and rental vacancy rates are from the Bureau of the Census, U.S. Department of Commerce annual publication *Housing Vacancies and Homeownership Annual Statistics,* on the Internet; www.census.gov/hhes/.

A basic source of information on activities of insurance companies in Florida is the *Florida Department of Insurance Annual Report.* Data on life insurance are from the American Council of Life Insurance, *Life Insurance Fact Book.*

The Florida Department of Business and Professional Regulation furnishes unpublished information about licensed persons who handle real estate transactions.

SECTION 18.00.   PERSONAL AND BUSINESS SERVICES

EXPLANATORY NOTES. The Standard Industrial Classification System lists services from SIC code 70 to SIC code 89. A county-level aggregate of establishments with these codes appears in Table 18.28. Other tables in this section based on the establishments covered by the unemployment insurance law show data on personal services (SIC code 72), business services (SIC code 73), automotive repair, services, and parking (SIC code 75), miscellaneous repair services (SIC code 76), engineering, accounting, research, management and related services (SIC code 87), private household services (SIC code 88), and services not elsewhere classified (SIC code 89). Information about establishments with other service SIC codes are to be found in Sections 19.00, 20.00, and 22.00.

Data on specified industries from the *1997 Economic Census: Administrative and Support and Waste Management and Remediation Services* are reported in new tables at the front of this section. These tables present data according to the recently-developed NAICS industry classification system. An explanation of the system appears in the Glossary and in Section 9.00 of this Appendix. An index of recent previous census tables appearing in earlier *Abstract*s is at the back of this edition.

SOURCES. Data on establishments, employment, and payroll of service establishments whose employees are covered by the unemployment insurance law are provided by the Bureau of Labor Market Information, Florida Department of Labor and Employment Security. (See the discussion under Section 6.00 of this Appendix.)

Many service establishments are operated by professional individuals who are licensed by the state. Data on these professionals have been supplied from the Florida Department of Business and Professional Regulation. Information on health, educational, and cultural services is reported in Section 20.00.

SECTION 19.00. TOURISM AND RECREATION

EXPLANATORY NOTES. Estimates of the number of tourists entering Florida by automobile are made by Florida's Visit Florida using traffic counts and information from welcome stations. Tourist arrivals by air are based on arrivals at major airports. Individual visitors are interviewed on a randomly selected basis about expenditures and length of stay. Sample results are expanded to the total visitor population.

    SOURCES. New tables from the recently published economic census conducted by the U.S. Bureau of the Census appear in the front of this chapter. Data from the *1997 Economic Census: Arts, Entertainment, and Recreation,* and *1997 Economic Census: Accommodation and Foodservices* based on the NAICS industry classification system (See the discussion in Section 9.00 of this Appendix and the Glossary) are provided. These publications may be located on the Internet at www.census.gov/prod/ec97/epcd/www/econ97.html/.

    Visit Florida issues reports of tourist information in an annual report, *Florida Visitor Study.* The Transportation Statistics Office of the Florida Department of Transportation records traffic counts at strategic highway locations around the state. Data on tourist facilities (hotels, motels, and food service establishments) that are regulated by the Division of Hotels and Restaurants of the Florida Department of Business and Professional Regulation are available from the department's *Master File Statistics.* The Florida Department of Revenue provides information on the gross and taxable sales of businesses. Some businesses have been classified for purposes of presenting data in this section as "tourist- and recreation-related" businesses. The Department of Revenue also provides information on the tourist-development or local option tax collected in several counties on its Internet site; sun6.dms.state.fl.us/dor/.

    Data on employment in tourist- and recreation-related industries come from the Bureau of Labor Market Information, Florida Department of Labor and Employment Security. (See discussion under Section 6.00 of this Appendix.)

    Boats registered by county statistics are provided by the Bureau of Vessel Titles and Registrations, Florida Department of Highway Safety and Motor Vehicles in *Vessels Registered in Florida.* Data on recreational boating and personal watercraft accidents are from the Office of Waterway Management, Division of Law Enforcement, Florida Department of Environmental Protection and are available online in *Florida Boating Accident Statistics,* http://fcn.state.fl.us/fwc/law/. The Recreation and Parks Management Information System, Florida Department of Environmental Protection issues information on the nature, size, and popularity of state parks. Data on national parks in Florida were taken from the *National Park Service Statistical Abstract,* published on the Internet by the National Park Service, U.S. Department of the Interior at www2.nature.nps.gov/stats/.

SECTION 20.00. HEALTH, EDUCATION, AND CULTURAL SERVICES

    SOURCES. The U.S. Bureau of the Census conducts an economic census every five years in years ending in 2 and 7. Data from the 1997 census pertaining to health, social assistance, and educational services can be found in two economic census publications; *1997 Economic Census: Health Care and Social Assis-*

tance and *1997 Economic Census: Educational Services.* The 1997 census uses the recently developed NAICS industry classification system explained in the Glossary.

Data on employment are from the covered employment and payroll figures supplied by the Bureau of Labor Market Information, Florida Department of Labor and Employment Security. (See discussion under Section 6.00 of this Appendix.)

Information on physicians, dentists, nurses, opticians, pharmacists, and other licensed health service practitioners and professionals comes from the Florida Department of Health. General, short-term acute care hospital data are from the Florida Agency for Health Care Administration publication *Guide to Hospitals in Florida.* Data on veterans' hospitals come from the U.S. Department of Veterans Affairs, *Annual Report of the Secretary of Veterans Affairs.*

Library information is supplied by the Division of Library and Information Services, Florida Department of State in *Florida Library Directory with Statistics.*

Educational establishment information comes from the Florida Department of Education in *Profiles of Florida School Districts, Statistical Briefs,* and unpublished data sources. Much of the data can be found on the Internet; www.firn.edu/doe/.

Federal aid data are published by the U.S. Bureau of the Census in *Federal Aid to States* and are on the Internet; www.census.gov/. Information on arts grants to Florida groups and individuals by county is from *Florida Funding for Culture and the Arts* issued by the Division of Cultural Affairs, Florida Department of State and may be found online at www.dos.state.fl.us/.

SECTION 21.00. GOVERNMENT AND ELECTIONS

SOURCES. Every five years since 1957, the U.S. Bureau of the Census has conducted a Census of Governments. This census covers four major subject areas: governmental organization, taxable property values, public employment, and governmental finances. Table 21.01 presents information from the first volume of the 1997 census about governmental units by type in Florida and the United States. Other volumes from the 1997 census are scheduled to be released throughout 2000. Table 21.07 shows numbers of local governments and elected officials in Florida in 1992 by county and by type of government. An index of recent census tables appearing in previous *Abstract*s is at the back of this edition.

The Division of Elections in the Florida Department of State provides information on registered voters, voter turnout, and numbers of votes cast in given elections in *Official General Election Results.*. The U.S. Bureau of the Census provides voting-age population estimates for states on their Internet site; www.census.gov/. Estimates and projections on state and county voting-age population, released annually by the Bureau of Economic and Business Research (BEBR), University of Florida, appear in tables 21.25 and 21.26.

Several private sources have granted permission to include data in this section. The Joint Center for Political and Economic Studies publishes the annual *Black Elected Officials: A Statistical Summary.* Information on the composition of state legislatures is available in the *Statistical Abstract of the United States* and from the National Conference of State Legislatures in copyrighted unpublished data. Data on female officials may be found in copyrighted information releases from the

Center for the American Woman and Politics, Eagleton Institute of Politics, Rutgers University on the Internet; www.rci.rutgers.edu/~cawp/.

Apportionment data are from the Bureau of the Census, U.S. Department of Commerce *1990 Census Profile: Population Trends and Congressional Apportionment.*

SECTION 22.00. COURTS AND LAW ENFORCEMENT

EXPLANATORY NOTES. Data on criminal offenses are subject to certain limitations. Many crimes are not reported to law enforcement agencies and hence are not counted in preparing crime statistics. Victims may report crimes to prosecuting authorities rather than to law enforcement agencies or for various reasons may not report at all.

An additional factor to consider when studying crime rates in Florida is the presence of large numbers of tourists. The crime rates in this section are based on resident population. When adjustments are made for the tourist presence, the crime rate in Florida drops.

SOURCES. The principal source of data on crimes and criminals in Florida is *Crime in Florida*, the annual report of the Florida Department of Law Enforcement (FDLE), other FDLE unpublished data, and on the Internet; at www.fdle.state.fl.us/.

Other sources on the criminal justice system include publications of two divisions of the U.S. Department of Justice: the annual *Crime in the United States* (www.fbi.gov/) from the Federal Bureau of Investigation, and reports and bulletins from the Bureau of Justice Statistics (www.ojp.usobj.gov/bjs/).

Data on county jails are from *Florida County Detention Facilities* issued by the Bureau of Planning, Research, and Statistics in the state Department of Corrections, Internet site www.dc.state.fl.us/. Prison and prisoner information is made available by the Department of Corrections in its *Annual Report.* New table 22.16 presents recidivism data from *Inmates Released From Florida Prisons* published on the Department's website.

Juvenile delinquency data are from the Bureau of Data and Research, Florida Department of Juvenile Justice, *Profile of Delinquency Cases and Youths Referred at each Stage of the Juvenile Justice System*, on the Internet; www.djj.state.fl.us/.

Victim compensation data are from the *Annual Report* of the state Division of Victim Services, Office of the Attorney General, which also publishes *Hate Crimes in Florida* on the Internet, http://legal.firn.edu/justice/.

Legal services data are furnished by the Florida Bar and the Bureau of Labor Market Information, Florida Department of Labor and Employment Security.

SECTION 23.00. GOVERNMENT FINANCE AND EMPLOYMENT

EXPLANATORY NOTES. A number of tables in the Health, Education, and Cultural Services section (20.00) contain data on property valuations, revenue, expenditure, and taxes for education by public agencies. In Section 19.00, Table 19.54 provides figures on the tourist-development/local option tax and Table 19.70 provides information about tax collections from tourist- and recreation-related businesses.

Although the official records of the Comptroller are used by the Bureau of the Census in its compilations on state and local government finances, the Bureau of the Census has found it necessary at times to classify and present the government financial statistics in terms of its own system of uniform concepts and categories rather than according to the diverse terminology and structure of individual governments. This procedure explains the differences that may be found between similar data from the two sources.

Public government employment data by industry and county are from the Bureau of Labor Market Information (BLMI), Florida Department of Labor and Employment Security.

SOURCES. The U.S. Bureau of the Census publishes a number of annual series and increasingly is publishing data on the Internet; www.census.gov/. Users should contact the bureau for a list of current publications. Two sources for government expenditure data published online are *Federal Aid to States* and *Consolidated Federal Funds Report*. The census also conducts a Census of Governments every five years, coincident with the economic censuses. (An index of recent census tables in previous *Abstracts* appears at the end of this book).

Veterans' Administration expenditures are published on the Internet; www.va.gov/.

Official records and reports of the Comptroller of the State of Florida comprise the basic source of information about government finances in Florida and are published in the *Florida Comprehensive Financial Report* and in unpublished form. Other State of Florida sources of data on government finances and employment include the Department of Revenue (http://sun6.dms.state.fl.us/dor/), *Florida Property Valuations and Tax Data*; the Department of Business and Professional Regulation, data on pari-mutuel wagering and beverage and tobacco licenses; Department of the Lottery for ticket sales; the Department of Highway Safety and Motor Vehicles for motor vehicle licenses; *Annual Report of the State Treasurer*, the Bureau of Labor Market Information on employment and payroll; the Division of Retirement, *Annual Report* (www.dos.state.fl.us/); and the Florida Department of Banking and Finance (http://localgovserver.dbf.state.fl.us/). Some state publications are no longer being produced due to recent governmental reorganization. Users are encouraged to search government agency websites on the Internet.

The Florida Department of Revenue annually reviews the ad valorem tax rolls submitted by county property appraisers and Armasi, Inc., compiles data from the tax rolls, making the data available with software that displays data geographically by county. Table 23.95 presents assessed land use values by county summarized by Armasi, Inc., from the Department of Revenue files.

SECTION 24.00. ECONOMIC INDICATORS AND PRICES

EXPLANATORY NOTES. Tables in the first twenty-three sections of the *Abstract* are primarily cross-sectional or "snapshot" portrayals of a set of circumstances or a situation existing at any one time. Because many readers are interested in charting trends over time, most tables in Section 24.00 contain data over several years.

Consumer price indexes are developed by the Bureau of Labor Statistics (BLS) of the U.S. Department of Labor and appear in the monthly *CPI Detailed Report* and on Internet site http://stats.bls.gov/. The BLS publishes two indexes: one reflecting the buying habits of all urban households (CPI-U) and one reflecting the buying habits of urban wage earners and clerical workers (CPI-W). Both indexes are comparable with historical CPI figures; the index for all urban households is used in tables in this section (except for the entry of the CPI-W index in Table 24.73). The CPI-U is based on information reflecting the buying habits of about 80 percent of the U.S. population and represents all urban residents, including professional workers, the self-employed, the poor, the unemployed, and retired persons. Not included are persons living outside urban areas, farm families, persons in military services, and those in institutions. The Bureau of Labor Statistics issues a bimonthly CPI for the Miami-Ft. Lauderdale CMSA and Tampa-St. Petersburg-Clearwater MSA. (See Table 24.74.)

Both the CPI-U and the CPI-W use updated expenditure weights based on data tabulated from the consumer expenditure surveys. Also, the rental equivalence measures of home ownership costs in both the CPI-U and the CPI-W were improved to better represent both owners' and renters' shelter costs.

The series of producer prices appears in Tables 24.72 and 24.75. According to the BLS, the series measures the average changes in prices received in primary markets of the United States by producers of commodities in all stages of processing. The sample used for calculating the indexes contains nearly 2,800 commodities and about 10,000 quotations selected to represent the movement of prices of all commodities produced in the agriculture, forestry, fishing, mining, manufacturing, gas, electric, and all public utilities sectors.

The *Florida Price Level Index* (FPLI) is prepared by the Office of Education Budget and Management, Florida Department of Education. The FPLI measures relative price levels across counties. Items representative of the expenditure categories used by the BLS in the CPI are surveyed in each county. Table 24.79 shows the relative weights of selected items in the survey; Table 24.80 compares the index and sub-indexes for major items across counties. Section 15.00 contains additional information on energy prices.

The Bureau of Economic Analysis, U.S. Department of Commerce introduced estimates of Gross State Product (GSP) by state, by component, and by industry for each state for the period 1936-1986. GSP is the gross market value of goods and services attributable to labor and property located in the state. It is the state counterpart to national Gross Domestic Product (GDP). These estimates are available on CD-ROM from the Regional Economic Information System and online at www.bea.doc.gov/.

SOURCES. Extensive series of economic indicators for the United States, Florida, and its counties are maintained in the BEBR Data Base, Bureau of Economic and Business Research, University of Florida. Data surveying consumer confidence is presented in the BEBR monthly publication, *Florida Economic and Consumer Survey.*

The Bureau of Labor Statistics, U.S. Department of Labor prepares consumer and producer price indexes and publishes them in detailed monthly reports and on the Internet; http://stats.bls.gov/.

The Department of Revenue of the State of Florida has data on sales and use tax collections. The Department of Labor and Employment Security provided employment data.

The International Trade Administration, U.S. Department of Commerce reports building permit activity in the states on the Internet; www.census.gov/. Table 24.20 presents data from current and previous editions of this publication back to 1988.

Data on new incorporations and failures of industrial and commercial establishments shown in Table 24.78 are available by permission from the copyrighted reports, *A Decade of Business Starts* and *Business Failure Report*, published by Dun & Bradstreet.

The Florida Public Service Commission provides electricity price data in *Statistics of the Florida Electric Utility Industry.*

SECTION 25.00. STATE COMPARISONS

SOURCES. Both economic and noneconomic factors are listed in this section to permit the reader to compare aspects of life in Florida to similar living conditions in other Sunbelt and populous states. There are numerous sources for these tables, most of which have been discussed in previous sections. The *Statistical Abstract of the United States* published by the Bureau of the Census is a primary source as is census bureau information on the Internet; www.census.gov/. Sources not previously mentioned are the Bureau of the Census, *Estimates of Housing Units and Households of States;* U.S. Department of Health and Human Services, *National Vital Statistics Report* and *Health United States with Adolescent Health Chartbook;* and U.S. Federal Bureau of Investigation, *Hate Crime Statistics.*

SUMMARY OF SOURCES

STATE SOURCES. Most of the state publications are available free of charge from the agency issuing the report. Supplies are frequently limited and sometimes requests cannot be honored unless they come from other state agencies. Increasingly, publication reproductions and/or unpublished data can be retrieved from the Internet. The state has a system of state depository libraries, coordinated by the Division of Library Services, Florida Department of State, R.A. Gray Building, Tallahassee. All state agency publications are supposed to be on file in depository libraries or available for interlibrary loan. The reference departments of most libraries are willing to answer questions about data in these publications if the requests are not too time-consuming. The Florida Division of State Library Services issues a monthly and annual summary of state agency publications called *Florida Public Documents.*

Depository libraries of the State of Florida include the public libraries of Bay, Broward, and Orange counties, Cocoa, Jacksonville, Miami Beach, Miami-Dade, Ocala, St. Petersburg, Tampa-Hillsborough, and West Palm Beach. University libraries designated as depositories are those at Central Florida, Florida Atlantic, Florida (Gainesville), Florida International, Florida State, Miami, North Florida, South Florida, West Florida, Jacksonville, and Stetson. The State Library of Florida in the R.A. Gray Building in Tallahassee also is a depository.

FEDERAL SOURCES. Some federal reports are available without charge from the agency issuing the information, but most federal publications must be purchased from the Superintendent of Documents, U.S. Government Printing Office (GPO), Washington, D.C. 20402 (phone 202/783-3238) or from a local Government Printing Office bookstore. Publications purchased from the GPO must be prepaid. As noted throughout this edition, agencies are making use of the Internet to provide easy access to publications and free data to users. The *Statistical Abstract of the United States* is similar in purpose to the *Florida Statistical Abstract* and much more comprehensive. Readers interested in information about the nation, its regions, and states are referred to it.

The federal government also maintains a system of depository libraries in all fifty states, usually the same libraries as state depositories. The University of Florida is designated as a regional depository library and is required to receive and retain one copy of all depository government publications made available to depository libraries either in print or on microfiche. Many of the libraries listed above as state depositories are also federal depositories and some are not listed. Refer to the annual directory printed by the University of Florida Libraries, *Federal Document Depositories and Resource Information for Florida and Puerto Rico.*

PRIVATE SOURCES. A number of private agencies and associations issue publications or reports which have been used in this and recent editions of *Abstract*. Some are copyrighted and have been used with permission. Several have additional information which can be obtained for a fee.

American Council of Life Insurance, Washington, D.C.
Center for the American Woman and Politics (CAWP), Eagleton Institute of Politics, Rutgers University
Dun & Bradstreet Corporation, New York, New York
Enterprise Florida, Inc., Orlando, Florida
Federal Deposit Insurance Corporation, Washington, D.C.
Florida Association of Realtors
Louis de la Parte Florida Mental Health Institute, University of South Florida
Joint Center for Political and Economic Studies, Washington, D.C.
National Conference of State Legislatures, Denver, Colorado
National Education Association, Washington, D.C.

COMPUTER TAPES. The University of Florida Library in Gainesville maintains an extensive collection of information about Florida in books and files and on computer tapes. All the data from the population, housing and economic censuses can be accessed from their computer tapes. Data from the 1990 census and the Bureau of Labor Statistics are also available on CD-ROM. Many agencies make data available through the Internet worldwide computer network; this source may eventually replace many printed publications.

BUREAU PUBLICATIONS. The Bureau of Economic and Business Research (BEBR) at the University of Florida can supply a variety of detailed information about Florida:

Florida Estimates of Population. Intercensal estimates of the population of Florida, its counties, cities, and unincorporated areas. Also includes components of population change and density figures. Published annually. A summary of census results is published in census years.

Florida Population Studies. Bulletins providing information on age, race, and sex components of Florida's population, household numbers and average household size, projections of population, discussions of estimation and projection methodology, and other topics related to population. Published three times a year.

Special Population Reports. 1995 estimates of Hispanic population with age and sex detail is the most recent of these four releases. Also include revised 1980-90 population estimates by county, an evaluation of population projection errors for Florida counties and an evaluation of 1990 population estimation. Published periodically.

Florida and the Nation. Comparison statistics and ranked data for Florida, the other 49 states, and the United States.

The Florida Long-term Economic Forecast. A two-volume long-range economic forecast of income, employment, construction, and population for the State of Florida, its metropolitan areas, and counties. Volume One focuses on the state and MSAs and Volume Two on the state and counties. Published annually.

Florida County Rankings. At-a-glance ranked data for more than 400 current data topics for all Florida counties, with a state comparison for each topic and pertinent data maps.

Florida County Perspectives. Individual ranking reports for each of Florida's 67 counties in the same categories used in *Florida County Rankings*, with historical data summaries.

Building Permit Activity in Florida. Monthly comparisons with year-to-date data, with an annual summary, of the value and number of units permitted in the state, counties, cities, and unincorporated areas of Florida.

The Economy of Florida. Twenty-three experts explore the many sectors of Florida's economy, including international trade, telecommunications, regions, health care, the labor market, housing, banking, military bases and defense manufacturing, and tourism.

1990 Census Handbook: Florida. Over 600 pages of census information for Florida, its counties, congressional districts and most populous cities and comparisons of Florida with the other forty-nine states.

Gross and taxable sales information. Printouts of sales information from the Florida Department of Revenue reports of gross and taxable sales for the sales and use taxes. Available by county and by kind-of-business category. Issued monthly and annually.

Florida Economic and Consumer Survey. Monthly survey data on Florida consumers' confidence in the national and local economies, buying plans, personal financial condition, and special topics.

BEBR Monographs. In-depth analyses of topics relevant to an understanding of the Florida economic and business climate. Issued periodically. Current titles include *Population Projections: What Do We Really Know?*; *Local Government Economic Analysis Using Microcomputers*; *Cuban Immigration and Immigrants in Florida and the United States: Implications for Immigration Policy*; *Urban Development Issues: What is Controversial in Urban Sprawl?*; *Preparing the Economic Element of the Comprehensive Plan*; *Concurrency Management Systems in Florida: A Catalog and Analysis*; and *The Economic Impact of Local Government Comprehensive Plans.*

BEBR Data Base. A computerized data management system containing extensive economic data for the United States, Florida, and all counties. Provides PC access to current and historical data for Florida, any of its counties and Metropolitan Statistical Areas, and for the United States. Continuously updated.

University of Florida   **Bureau of Economic and Business Research**

Migration releases. Based on data collected by the U.S. Bureau of the Census and Internal Revenue Service these BEBR-prepared reports include state and county migration flows with age, sex, and race detail. Updated as data becomes available.

For pricing and ordering information, please contact:
    Bureau of Economic and Business Research
    University of Florida
    P. O. Box 117145
    221 Matherly Hall
    Gainesville, Florida 32611-7145
    Phone: (352) 392-0171 ext. 219   FAX: (352) 392-4739
    The Internet: http://www.bebr.ufl.edu
    E-mail: info@bebr.ufl.edu

GLOSSARY

ALIEN. Person who is not a citizen of the United States whether or not he/she is a resident, legally or illegally.

AMERICAN INDIAN, ESKIMO, OR ALEUT POPULATION. See Race.

ANCESTRY. A person's nationality group, lineage, or the country in which the person or the person's parents or ancestors were born before their arrival in the U.S. Different from other indicators of ethnicity, such as country of birth and language spoken in home and is a separate characteristic from race.

ASIAN OR PACIFIC ISLANDER POPULATION. See Race.

BLACK POPULATION. See Race.

BUSINESS ESTABLISHMENT. A commercial enterprise.

CHILDREN. Sons and daughters classified as "own child of householder," including stepchildren and adopted children, who have never been married and are under age 18.

CIVILIAN LABOR FORCE. See Labor Force.

CLASS OF WORKERS. Private wage and salary workers who work for a private employer for wages, salary, commission, tips, pay-in-kind, or at price rates. Private employers include churches and other nonprofit organizations. Also includes persons who consider themselves self-employed but who work for corporations where in most cases these persons own or are a part of a group that owns controlling interest in the corporation.
Government workers who work for a governmental unit, regardless of the activity of the particular agency.
Self-employed workers who work for profit or fees in their own unincorporated business, profession, or trade, or who operate a farm. Includes owner-operators of large stores and manufacturing establishments, as well as small merchants, independent craft-persons and professionals, farmers, peddlers, and other persons who conduct enterprises of their own.
Unpaid family workers who work without pay on a farm or in a business operated by a person to whom they are related by blood or marriage.

COLLEGE STUDENTS. See Residency.

COMMUNITY HEALTH PURCHASING ALLIANCE (CHPA). Authorized by the 1993 Florida legislature to assist members of the alliance in securing the highest quality health care at the lowest possible price. Membership is voluntary and available primarily to businesses that have 50 or fewer employees. CHPAs are state-chartered, not-for-profit, private purchasing organizations and have exclusive territories.

COMMUTE. Travel back and forth regularly, usually between place of residence and place of work.

CONSOLIDATED METROPOLITAN STATISTICAL AREA (CMSA). A large metropolitan complex with a population over one million in which individual metropolitan components, Primary Metropolitan Statistical Areas (PMSAs), have been defined.

CONSUMER PRICE INDEX (CPI). A measure of the average level of prices over time in a fixed market collection of goods and services. The index is intended to represent prices of most items and services that people purchase in daily living, and is calculated to represent purchases by urban wage earners and clerical workers or by all urban consumers.

CONTRACT RENT. See Rent.

COUNTY. An administrative subdivision of a state; a local government organization and political jurisdiction authorized and designated by a state's constitution or statutes.

DROPOUT. A student over the age of compulsory school attendance (16) who has voluntarily removed himself from the school system before graduation; or who has not met attendance requirements; or who has withdrawn from school but has not transferred to another public or private school or enrolled in any other educational program; or has withdrawn from school due to hardship without official granting of such withdrawal; or is not eligible to attend school because of reaching the maximum age for an exceptional student program.

EARNINGS. Sum of wage and salary income and net income from farm and non-farm self-employment. Reported before deductions for personal income taxes, social security, bond purchases, union dues, and other deductions.

EDUCATIONAL ATTAINMENT. Years of school completed.

EMPLOYED PERSONS. All civilians 16 years of age and over that work at all as paid employees for an employer, or in their own business or profession, on their own farm, or who work 15 hours or more as unpaid workers in an enterprise operated by a family member and all those temporarily absent from their jobs due to such factors as illness or vacation (during a given reference week).

ENERGY. The ability to do work; can exist in many forms such as chemical, light, heat, etc.
Primary energy is energy available from conversion of original fuel rather than from a secondary form such as electricity.

Renewables are energy sources that can be used continuously or regenerated quickly such as wind, sunlight, wood, and solid waste.

FAMILY HOUSEHOLD. A householder and one or more other person(s) living in the same household who are related to the householder by birth, marriage, or adoption. All persons in a household who are related to the householder and are regarded as members of his or her family.

FAMILY HOUSEHOLD INCOME. See Income.

FARM. For the 1990 census, property of one acre or more where $1,000 or more of agricultural products were sold from the property in 1989.

FARM POPULATION. See Rural farm population.

FIRM. A business organization or entity consisting of one or more establishment(s) under common ownership or control; a commercial partnership of two or more persons.

GENERAL, SHORT-TERM ACUTE CARE HOSPITAL. Establishment that offers services more intensive than those required for room, board, personal services, and general nursing care. Offers facilities and beds for use beyond 24 hours by individuals requiring diagnosis, treatment, or care for illness, injury, deformity, infirmity, abnormality, disease, or pregnancy. Regularly makes available at least clinical laboratory services, diagnostic radiology services, and treatment facilities for surgery, medical, or obstetrical care, or other definitive medical treatment of similar extent.

GROSS STATE PRODUCT (GSP). The gross market value of the goods and services attributable to labor and property located in a state.

GROUP QUARTERS. All persons not living in households are classified by the Census Bureau as living in group quarters—institutional and noninstitutional. Institutional group quarters are all institutions offering care or custody, e.g., prisons, mental hospitals, nursing homes, juvenile institutions. Noninstitutional quarters include workers' dormitories, monasteries, convents, large rooming houses or boarding houses or communes having at least ten persons unrelated to the resident who maintains the living quarters. Noninstitutional quarters also cover certain living arrangements regardless of the number or relationship of the people in the unit such as military barracks, college dormitories, missions and emergency shelters for the homeless. Data on the homeless also include visible in street locations or predesignated street sites, (e.g., bridges, parks, bus depots) where the homeless congregate.

HISPANIC ORIGIN. Persons who classified themselves in one of the Hispanic-origin categories listed on the census questionnaire—Mexican, Puerto Rican, Cuban, or other Spanish/Hispanic origin. This latter category includes those whose origins are from Spain or the Spanish-speaking countries of Central or South America, or the Dominican Republic, or they are Hispanic-origin persons identifying themselves generally as Spanish, Spanish-American, Hispanic, Latino, etc. Origin can be viewed as the ancestry, nationality group, lineage or country in which the person or person's parents or ancestors were born before their arrival in the U.S. Persons of Hispanic origin may be of any race. Households and families are classified by the Hispanic origin of the householder.

HOMELESS POPULATION. See Group quarters.

HOMEOWNER VACANCY RATE. The proportion of the homeowner inventory which is vacant for sale. Rates are computed by dividing the vacant year-round units for sale only by the sum of the number of owner-occupied units, vacant year-round units sold but awaiting occupancy, and vacant year-round units for sale only.

HOMEOWNER VACANCY RATE. The proportion of the homeowner inventory which is vacant for sale. Rates are computed by dividing the vacant year-round units for sale only by the sum of the number of owner-occupied units, vacant year-round units sold but awaiting occupancy, and vacant year-round units for sale only.

HOUSEHOLD. The person or persons occupying a housing unit. Designation of a household as "family" or "nonfamily" is based on the householder. If the household has family members of the householder, then it is classified as a family household. If the householder is an individual unrelated to other household members, lives alone, or is living in group quarters (not institutionalized), then the household is classified as a nonfamily household.

HOUSEHOLD INCOME. See Income.

HOUSEHOLDER. Person, or one of the persons, in whose name the home is owned or rented and who is listed in column one of the census questionnaire. If there is no such person in the household, any adult household member could be designated as "householder."
Family householder is a householder living with one or more person(s) related to him or her by birth, marriage, or adoption.
Nonfamily householder is a householder living alone or with nonrelatives only.

HOUSING UNIT. A house, an apartment, a group of rooms, or a single room occupied as a separate living quarters, or if vacant, intended for occupancy as a separate living quarters.
Occupied housing unit is the usual place of residence of the person or group of persons living there at the time of the census enumeration, or the unit from which the occupants are only temporarily absent (away on vacation, etc.).
Owner-occupied housing unit is one in which the owner or co-owner lives, whether the unit is owned without lien or mortgaged.

Renter-occupied unit is any unit not classified as owner-occupied, including a unit rented for cash rent or one occupied without payment of cash rent.

Vacant housing unit has no one living in it at the time of census enumeration, unless the occupants are only temporarily absent. May be classified as "seasonal and migratory," or "year-round." Seasonal unit is intended for occupancy during only certain seasons of the year. Migratory unit is held for occupancy for migratory labor employed in farm work during crop season. Year-round vacant unit is available or intended for occupancy at any time of the year.

IMMIGRANTS. Aliens admitted for legal permanent residence in the United States, including persons who may have entered as nonimmigrants or refugees, but who subsequently changed their status to that of a permanent resident.

INCOME. The amount of money or monetary equivalent received during a specified time period in exchange for work performed, sale of goods or property, or from profits made on financial investments.

Adjusted gross income is a tax-defined concept of income. Certain kinds of income such as some portion of capital gains, social security, and in-kind transfer payments are excluded and certain types of expenses such as some trade and business expenses, alimony payments, and contributions to individual retirement plans are deducted.

Family household income and nonfamily household income are compiled by summing and treating as a single amount the money income of all family or nonfamily household members aged 15 and over.

Household income includes the money income of the householder and all other persons aged 15 and over in the household, whether related to the householder or not. Because many households consist of only one person, average household income is usually less than average family income.

Interest, dividend, or net rental income includes interest on savings or bonds, dividends from stockholdings or membership in associations, net royalties, and net income from rental of property to others and receipts from boarders or lodgers.

Labor income is an item generally used for various types of supplemental earnings in cash and in kind.

Mean income is the amount obtained by dividing the total income of a particular statistical universe by the number of units in that universe.

Median income is the amount that divides the income distribution into two equal groups, one having incomes above the median and the other having incomes below the median. For households, families, and unrelated individuals the median income is based on the distribution of the total number of units including those with no income. The median for persons is based on persons with income.

Money income is an income definition of the Census Bureau. It is the sum of amounts reported separately for wage and salary income; net nonfarm self-employment income; net farm self-employment income; interest, dividend, net royalty or rental income; social security or railroad retirement income;

public assistance or welfare income; unemployment compensation; alimony; veterans' payments; and all other income. Not included are monies received from the sale of property owned by a recipient; the value of income "in-kind" from food stamps, public housing subsidies, medical care, employer contributions for pensions, etc.; withdrawal of bank deposits; money borrowed; tax refunds; exchanges of money between relatives living in the same household; gifts and lump-sum inheritances, insurance payments, and other types of lump-sum receipts.

Personal income is an income definition of the Bureau of Economic Analysis. It is the sum of current income received by persons from all sources and is measured before deduction of personal contributions to social insurance programs and income and other personal taxes. It is reported in current dollars and includes the following categories of earnings: private and governmental wages and salaries; labor income; farm and nonfarm proprietors' income; property income; and government and business transfer payments, but excludes transfers among persons. (Also, includes some nonmonetary income such as estimated net rental values—to owner—of owner-occupied homes, and the value of services furnished without payment, and food and fuel produced and consumed on farms.)

Disposable personal income is personal income less personal tax and nontax payments. Personal taxes include income, estate, gift, personal property and license taxes. Nontax payments include fines and penalties, tuition, and donations.

Property income is net rental income, dividends, and interest.

Proprietors' income is net income of owners of unincorporated businesses (farm and nonfarm, with the latter including the income of independent professionals).

Public assistance income includes three items: supplementary security income payments made by federal or state welfare agencies to low-income persons aged 65 or over, blind, or disabled; aid to families with dependent children; and general assistance. Separate payments received for hospital or other medical care are excluded.

Social security income includes social security pensions and survivors' benefits and permanent disability insurance payments made by the Social Security Administration prior to deductions. Medicare reimbursements are not included.

INMATES OF INSTITUTIONS. See Group quarters.

INTEREST, DIVIDEND, OR NET RENTAL INCOME. See Income.

LABOR FORCE. Includes the civilian labor force, which comprises all civilians in the noninstitutional population 16 years and over classified as "employed" or "unemployed" and members of the Armed Forces stationed in the United States.

MANUFACTURED HOUSING. Any prefabricated dwelling such as a mobile home or modular housing.

MANUFACTURING ESTABLISHMENT. An enterprise usually consisting of a single physical location where raw materials are transformed into new products.

MARITAL STATUS. Classification refers to the status of persons aged 15 and over at the time of census enumeration. Couples who live together (unmarried persons, common-law marriages) were allowed to report the marital status they considered the most appropriate. Persons reported as separated are those living apart because of marital discord, with or without a legal separation. Persons in common-law marriages are classified as now married, except separated if they consider this category most appropriate; persons whose only marriage has been annulled are classified as never married; persons married at the time of enumeration (including those separated), widowed, or divorced are classified as ever married. Persons whose current marriage has not ended by widowhood or divorce are classified as now married. This category includes married persons whose spouse may have been (1) temporarily absent for such reasons as travel or hospitalization; (2) absent, including all married persons living in group quarters, employed spouses living away from home or in an institution, or absent in the Armed Forces; and (3) those who are separated.

MARKET VALUE. Amount a seller reasonably expects to obtain in a market for commodities, merchandise, services, or whatever is being sold.

MEDICAID. A jointly funded state and federal health care program for low-income persons. States establish their own eligibility criteria and may set benefits above the minimum established by federal law.

MEDICARE. Federal health insurance program for people aged 65 and over. Also covers (since 1973) eligible disabled persons of any age and persons with chronic kidney disease.

METROPOLITAN POPULATION. Population living inside Metropolitan Statistical Areas (MSAs) or Consolidated Metropolitan Statistical Areas (CMSAs).

METROPOLITAN STATISTICAL AREA (MSA). A geographic area with a large population nucleus together with adjacent communities, which has a high degree of economic and social integration with the nucleus. An MSA may include entire counties and generally has a city of at least 50,000 population or an urbanized area of at least 50,000 with a total metropolitan population of at least 100,000. This term replaces the term Standard Metropolitan Statistical Area, which was used prior to January 1983. See map at front of the book for list of counties in MSAs.

MOBILE HOME. Movable dwelling, ten or more feet wide and thirty-five or more feet long (a movable dwelling of less than these dimensions is considered to be a travel trailer or a motor home), designed to be towed on its own chassis and without need of a permanent foundation. Does not include prefabricated or modular housing, travel trailers, and other self-propelled vehicles such as motor homes. Mobile homes or trailers to which one or more permanent rooms have been added or built are classified by the Census Bureau as single-unit, detached housing.

MILITARY PERSONNEL. See Labor force and Residency.

MILL. Unit of monetary value equal to 1/1000 of a U.S. dollar.

MILLAGE RATE. Tax rate stated in mills where one mill produces one dollar of tax for every $1,000 of taxable property.

MONEY INCOME. See Income.

MUNICIPALITY. Political subdivision within which a municipal corporation has been established to provide a general local government for a specific population concentration in a defined area. In Florida, municipalities may be called cities, towns, or villages and have been established either by special acts of the legislature or by general law.

NAICS. Abbreviation of North American Industry Classification System.

NONFAMILY HOUSEHOLDER. See Householder.

NONMETROPOLITAN POPULATION. Population living outside of metropolitan areas (as defined by the U.S. Office of Management and Budget).

NONPUBLIC SCHOOL. See Private school.

NONRELATIVES. Any persons in the household not related to the householder by birth, marriage, or adoption. Includes roomers, boarders, partners, roommates, paid employees, wards, and foster children.

NORTH AMERICAN INDUSTRY CLASSIFICATION SYSTEM (NAICS). System for classifying industrial establishments by type of economic activity which replaces the Standard Industrial Classification System. It is a production-oriented system developed jointly by Mexico's Instituto Nacional de Estadística, Geografía e Informática, Statistics Canada, and the United States Office of Management and Budget. NAICS was designed to provide new comparability in statistics about business activity across North America and to be consistent with the United Nations' International Standard Industrial Classification for certain high-level groupings. NAICS identifies new emerging technology industries and reorganizes industries into more meaningful sectors, particularly expanding the services industries. NAICS groups the economy into 20 broad sectors, up from the 10 divisions of the SIC system. For more details, conversion tables and related products available on the subject go to www.census.gov/ and search for "NAICS" or "North American Industry Classification System." The major industry groups and their NAICS codes are as follows:

Agriculture, forestry, fishing, and hunting (11)
Mining (21)
Utilities (22)
Construction (23)
Manufacturing (31-33)
Wholesale trade (42)
Retail trade (44-45)
Transportation and warehousing (48-49)
Information (51)
Finance and insurance (52)
Real estate and rental and leasing (53)
Professional, scientific, and technical services (54)
Management of companies and enterprises (55)
Administrative and support and waste management and remediation
    services (56)
Education services (61)
Health care and social assistance (62)
Arts, entertainment, and recreation (71)
Accommodation and food services (72)
Other services (except Public administration) (81)
Public administration (92)

OCCUPATIONAL LICENSING. . Required operational licenses for professional persons who operate at the retail level such as dispensing opticians or pharmacists.

OCCUPIED HOUSING UNIT. See Housing unit.

OWNER-OCCUPIED HOUSING UNIT. See Housing unit.

PER CAPITA. A per capita (per person) figure is defined by taking the total for
some item (e.g., government expenditures, income) and dividing it by the
number of persons in the specified population.

PERSONAL INCOME. See Income.

PERSONS PER FAMILY. Number of persons living in families divided by the
number of families.

PERSONS PER HOUSEHOLD. Number of persons living in households divided
by the number of households.

PLACE OF BIRTH. For census enumeration, the mother's usual state or country
of residence at the time of birth. Native-born persons are those born in the
U.S., Puerto Rico, or an outlying area of the U.S. Includes a small number of
persons born at sea or in a foreign country but with at least one American
parent. Foreign-born persons are those not classified as native born.

PLACE OF WORK. Geographic location at which workers carry out their occupational activities.

POVERTY STATUS. In census publications, based on a definition developed by the Social Security Administration in 1964 and revised by a federal interagency committee in 1969 and 1980. Defined by income levels that (depending on family or household size) describe a family or household as being in extreme want of necessities. Income cutoffs or poverty thresholds used by the Bureau of the Census to determine the poverty status of families and individuals are defined by family size and by presence and number of family members aged 18 and under. Unrelated individuals and two-person families are differentiated by age of householder. If total income of a family or individual is less than the corresponding threshold, the family or individual is classified as below the poverty level. Poverty thresholds are adjusted annually to allow for changes in the cost of living as reflected in the Consumer Price Index and are computed on a national basis only. The poverty index is based on money income and does not take into account noncash benefits, such as food stamps, Medicaid, and public housing. Differences in poverty thresholds based on farm-nonfarm residence have been eliminated. Nonfarm thresholds now apply to all families. Beginning in 1987, poverty thresholds are based on revised processing procedures and are not directly comparable with prior years.

POVERTY THRESHOLD. See Poverty status.

PRIMARY METROPOLITAN STATISTICAL AREA (PMSA). A Metropolitan Statistical Area which is part of a larger urban complex with a population over one million and is designated as a Consolidated Metropolitan Statistical Area (CMSA).

PRIVATE SCHOOL. Any individual, association, co-partnership, or corporation which designates itself an education center and which includes kindergarten or a higher grade below college level. Primarily supported by private funds.

PROPERTY INCOME. See Income.

PROPRIETORS' INCOME. See Income.

PUBLIC ASSISTANCE INCOME. See Income.

PUBLIC SCHOOL. Any school controlled and supported primarily by a local, state, or federal agency.

RACE. In census enumeration, reflects self-identification by respondents and does not necessarily denote a scientific definition of biological stock. American Indian, Eskimo, or Aleut includes persons who are classified in one of these specific categories or who entered the name of a specific Indian tribe.

Asian or Pacific Islander includes persons who indicated their race as Japanese (also Nipponese and Japanese American), Chinese (also Cantonese, Tibetan, Chinese American, Taiwanese, and Formosan), Cambodian, Hmong, Filipino, Korean, Thai, Vietnamese, Asian Indian, Hawaiian, Guamanian, Samoan, Laotian, or entered responses classified as other Asian or other Pacific Islander.

Black includes those who indicated their race as Black or Negro, or who classified themselves as African American, Afro-American, Jamaican, Black Puerto Rican, West Indian, Haitian, or Nigerian.

White includes those who indicated their race as "white," as well as persons who entered a response such as Canadian, German, Italian, Arab, Near Easterner, Lebanese, or Polish.

The other race category includes all persons not listed in the race categories described above. Persons reporting in the "other race" category and providing write-in entries such as multiracial, multiethnic, mixed, interracial, Wesort, or Spanish/Hispanic origin group (such as Mexican, Cuban, or Puerto Rican) are included here.

RENT. Contract (cash) rent is the monthly rent agreed to, or contracted for, regardless of any furnishings, utilities, fees, meals, or services that may be included. For vacant units, it is the monthly rent asked at the time of enumeration. In some tabulations, contract rent is presented for all renter-occupied housing units, as well as for "specified renter-occupied" housing units and for "specified vacant-for-rent" housing units which include renter units except one-family houses or mobile homes on 10 or more acres. Respondents were asked to exclude any rent paid for additional units or for business premises. Gross rent is the contract rent plus the estimated average monthly cost of utilities if these are paid by the renter. Renter units occupied without payment of cash rent are shown separately as no cash rent.

RENTAL VACANCY RATE. The proportion of the rental inventory which is vacant for rent. Rates are computed by dividing the vacant year-round units for rent by the sum of the number of renter-occupied units, vacant year-round units rented by awaiting occupancy, and vacant year-round units for rent.

RENTER-OCCUPIED HOUSING UNIT. See Housing unit.

RESIDENCY. The place where a person lives and sleeps most of the time is the usual residence. It may not be the person's legal or voting residence. College students are considered residents of the community in which they live while attending college. Military personnel (persons in the Armed Forces) are counted as residents of the area in which their installations are located. Persons staying only temporarily away from their usual residence (e.g., migrant workers, vacationers) are considered to have a usual home elsewhere in which they are counted for census purposes.

RETAIL TRADE. Businesses primarily engaged in selling merchandise for personal, household, or farm consumption.

RURAL FARM POPULATION. Only in rural areas and includes all persons living on places of one acre or more from which at least $1,000 worth of agricultural products were sold during 1989.

RURAL POPULATION. Population not classified as urban.

SCHOOL DISTRICT. A political organization and jurisdiction that supports and administers local public schools. There is an independent school district in each Florida county and there are 28 community college districts in the state.

SCHOOL MEMBERSHIP (ENROLLMENT). Cumulative number of students registered during a school year.

SERVICE INDUSTRIES. Establishments primarily engaged in rendering a wide variety of services to individuals and to business establishments.

SIC. Abbreviation of Standard Industrial Classification.

SOCIAL SECURITY INCOME. See Income.

SPANISH ORIGIN. See Hispanic origin.

SPECIAL DISTRICT. A local government entity established to provide one or more specific function(s) such as fire protection, public transit, water management, libraries, or hospitals. About one-third of Florida's special districts have taxing power.

STANDARD INDUSTRIAL CLASSIFICATION SYSTEM (SIC). Industrial classification system for classifying establishments by type of economic activity. Developed and published in a manual by the Executive Office of the President, Office of Management and Budget, and revised and published in 1987 (which supersedes the 1972/77 edition). Major industries are assigned two-digit SIC codes: 01 through 99; subdivisions are classified by three- and four-digit codes. The major industry groups and their SIC codes are as follows:
> Agriculture (01, 02, 07)
> Forestry and fisheries (08, 09)
> Mining (10-14)
> Construction (15-17)
> Manufacturing (20-39)
> Transportation, communications, and public utilities (40-49)
> Wholesale trade (50-51)
> Retail trade (52-59)
> Finance, insurance, and real estate (60-67)
> Services (70-89)
> Public administration (91-97)
> Nonclassifiable establishments (99)

An example of SIC coding is the construction industry, which is divided into major group SIC 15, "building construction—general contractors and operative builders"; group SIC 16, "heavy construction other than building construction"; and group SIC 17, "construction—special trade contractors." Group 15 is in turn divided into group 152, "general building contractors, residential buildings," group 153, "operative builders," and 154, "general building contractors, nonresidential buildings." Group 152 is subdivided into 1521, "general contractors, single-family houses," and 1522, "general contractors, residential buildings, other than single-family."

TENURE OF HOUSING UNIT. See Housing unit.

TRANSFER PAYMENTS. General disbursements to persons for which they do not render current services. These include payments by government and business to individuals and nonprofit institutions.

UNEMPLOYED PERSONS. All civilians 16 years of age and over who do not work and who actively seek employment, and who are available to work except for temporary illness (during a given reference week).

UNRELATED INDIVIDUAL. Householder living alone or with nonrelatives or household member who is not related to the householder by blood, marriage, or adoption, or person living in group quarters who is not an inmate of an institution.

URBAN POPULATION. Comprises all persons living in urbanized areas and in places (incorporated and unincorporated) of 2,500 or more inhabitants outside urbanized areas.

URBANIZED AREA. Incorporated place and adjacent densely settled surrounding area that together have a minimum population of 50,000.

VACANT HOUSING UNIT. See Housing unit.

WHITE POPULATION. See Race.

WHOLESALE TRADE. Establishments primarily engaged in selling merchandise to retailers, to institutions, to industrial, commercial, and professional users, or to other wholesalers.

WORKERS. See Labor force and Class of workers.

WORKERS' COMPENSATION. State-administered medical care payments and income maintenance. Benefits are granted for work-caused disability, illness, injury, or death.

INDEX OF CENSUS TABLES

The U.S. Bureau of the Census conducts various censuses at regular intervals. This index lists tables that include data from the most recent of these censuses published in the 1990 through 1998 editions of the *Florida Statistical Abstract.* Only tables that cite Census publications and/ or Census Summary Tape Files (STF) as the primary source are listed here. The Bureau of the Census is used frequently as a secondary source on tables throughout the *Abstract.* The user is encouraged to refer to the index at the back of the book for aid in locating additional census-related data. No tables from the 1999 edition are included here. A more complete index of census tables may be found in *Abstracts* from 1994 and earlier. Users are also directed to the *1990 Census Handbook - Florida* published in 1994 by the Bureau of Economic and Business Research. It contains the most-used state and county data from the decennial census.

CENSUS OF AGRICULTURE
(Conducted approximately every 5 years)

AREA AND DEMOGRAPHIC CHARACTERISTIC INCLUDED	CENSUS YEAR	FLORIDA STATISTICAL ABSTRACT YEAR	TABLE
FLORIDA, STATE ONLY			
SPECIFIED CHARACTERISTICS	1987-1997	1994-1999	9.34
STATE AND COUNTIES			
CHARACTERISTICS OF OPERATORS	1987	1990-1993	9.38
DITTO	1992	1994-1995	9.38
DITTO	1992-1997	1997-1999	9.39
FARM ACREAGE BY USE	1987	1990-1992	9.36
DITTO	1992-1997	1994-1999	9.36
FARMS, SIZE, AND VALUE OF LAND AND BUILDINGS	1987-1997	1994-1999	9.35
MARKET VALUE OF AGRICULTURAL PRODUCTS SOLD	1987-1992	1994	9.37
DITTO	1992-1997	1995-1999	9.38

CENSUS OF GOVERNMENTS
(Conducted every 5 years)

AREA AND DEMOGRAPHIC CHARACTERISTIC INCLUDED	CENSUS YEAR	FLORIDA STATISTICAL ABSTRACT YEAR	TABLE
FLORIDA AND UNITED STATES			
NUMBER OF GOVERNMENTAL UNITS BY TYPE	1987	1990-1993	21.01
DITTO	1992-1997	1994-1999	21.01
STATE AND COUNTIES			
NUMBER AND TYPE OF GOVERNMENT UNIT	1987	1990-1994	21.07
DITTO	1992	1995-1999	21.07
SCHOOL SYSTEMS	1987	1990-1994	21.07
DITTO	1992	1995-1999	21.07

CENSUS OF HOUSING
(Conducted every 10 years)

AREA AND DEMOGRAPHIC HARACTERISTIC INCLUDED	CENSUS YEAR	FLORIDA STATISTICAL ABSTRACT YEAR	TABLE
FLORIDA, SELECTED STATES, AND UNITED STATES			
UNITS IN STRUCTURE, PERCENTAGE AND MEDIAN VALUE			
OF OCCUPIED UNITS	1990*	1992-1994	25.01
STATE AND COUNTIES			
MOBILE HOMES BY HOUSING CHARACTERISTICS	1990	1992-1995	2.35
OCCUPIED HOUSING UNITS AND PERCENTAGE OWNER-			
AND RENTER-OCCUPIED	1990*	1992-1994	2.06
DITTO..............	1990*	1995	2.06
OCCUPIED HOUSING UNITS BY NUMBER OF UNITS IN			
STRUCTURE BY TENURE	1990	1992-1994	2.08
OCCUPIED HOUSING UNITS BY RACE AND HISPANIC ORIGIN OF			
HOUSEHOLDER	1990	1992-1994	2.07
BY TENURE	1990	1992-1994	2.07
OWNER-OCCUPIED HOUSING UNITS BY VALUE	1990*	1992-1995	2.09
RENTER-OCCUPIED HOUSING UNITS BY AMOUNT OF RENT	1990	1992-1994	2.10
DITTO..............	1990	1995	2.11
TOTAL, VACANT AND OCCUPIED HOUSING UNITS, AND			
VACANCY RATES	1990*	1991-1993	2.01
DITTO..............	1990*	1994-1995	2.02
TYPE AND PURPOSE OF FUEL USED	1990	1992-1994	15.05

CENSUS OF MANUFACTURES
(Conducted every 5 years)

AREA AND DEMOGRAPHIC CHARACTERISTIC INCLUDED	CENSUS YEAR	FLORIDA STATISTICAL ABSTRACT YEAR	TABLE
STATE AND SMSAS			
CHARACTERISTICS	1972-1982	1990	12.01
DITTO.............................	1972-1987	1991-1997	12.01
DITTO.............................	1987-1992	1998-1999	12.01
ESTABLISHMENTS, EMPLOYMENT, VALUE ADDED BY			
MANUFACTURE, AND NEW CAPITAL EXPENDITURE	1972-1982	1990	12.01
DITTO.............................	1972-1987	1991-1997	12.01
DITTO.............................	1987-1992	1998-1999	12.01
VALUE ADDED BY MANUFACTURE	1972-1982	1990	12.01
DITTO.............................	1972-1987	1991-1997	12.01
DITTO.............................	1987-1992	1998-1999	12.01
STATE AND COUNTIES			
ESTABLISHMENTS, EMPLOYMENT, VALUE ADDED BY			
MANUFACTURE, VALUE OF SHIPMENTS, AND NEW			
CAPITAL EXPENDITURE	1987	1991-1994	12.06
DITTO.............................	1992	1997-1999	12.06

*1990 Census of Population and Housing.

University of Florida   **Bureau of Economic and Business Research**

*1990 Census of Population and Housing.

University of Florida   **Bureau of Economic and Business Research**

CENSUS OF POPULATION (CONTINUED)
(Conducted every 10 years)

AREA AND DEMOGRAPHIC CHARACTERISTIC INCLUDED	CENSUS YEAR	FLORIDA STATISTICAL ABSTRACT YEAR	TABLE
STATE, COUNTIES, AND MUNICIPALITIES			
INCOME, PER CAPITA	1980-1990*	1992-1995	5.45

CENSUS OF RETAIL TRADE
(Conducted approximately every 5 years)

AREA AND DEMOGRAPHIC CHARACTERISTIC INCLUDED	CENSUS YEAR	FLORIDA STATISTICAL ABSTRACT YEAR	TABLE
STATE AND COUNTIES			
WHOLESALE AND RETAIL TRADE, SALES	1987	1990-1992	16.06
DITTO..	1992	1995-1999	16.06
FLORIDA, STATE ONLY			
ESTABLISHMENTS, SALES, AND NUMBER OF UNINCORPORATED BUSINESSES BY KIND OF BUSINESS	1987	1990-1994	16.12
ESTABLISHMENTS, SALES, AND PAYROLL BY KIND OF BUSINESS	1992	1995-1999	16.12
ESTABLISHMENTS, SALES, AND SALES PER ESTABLISHMENT	1939-1987	1990-1994	16.11
DITTO..	1948-1992	1995-1999	16.11

CENSUS OF SERVICE INDUSTRIES
(Conducted every 5 years)

AREA AND DEMOGRAPHIC CHARACTERISTIC INCLUDED	CENSUS YEAR	FLORIDA STATISTICAL ABSTRACT YEAR	TABLE
FLORIDA, STATE ONLY			
ESTABLISHMENTS AND RECEIPTS BY KIND OF BUSINESS	1982-1987	1991-1994	18.01
ESTABLISHMENTS, RECEIPTS, AND PAYROLL BY KIND OF BUSINESS	1987	1991-1994	18.02
DITTO..	1987-1992	1995-1999	18.01
HEALTH, EDUCATIONAL, AND SOCIAL SERVICES BY KIND OF BUSINESS, NUMBER OF ESTABLISHMENTS AND RECEIPTS	1982-1987	1991-1992	20.01
HEALTH, EDUCATIONAL, AND SOCIAL SERVICES BY KIND OF BUSINESS, NUMBER OF ESTABLISHMENTS, RECEIPTS, AND PAYROLL	1987-1992	1995-1999	20.01
HEALTH, EDUCATIONAL, AND SOCIAL SERVICES, ESTABLISHMENTS AND RECEIPTS BY TAX STATUS	1987	1991-1992	20.02

University of Florida   **Bureau of Economic and Business Research**

CENSUS OF WHOLESALE TRADE
(Conducted approximately every 5 years)

AREA AND DEMOGRAPHIC CHARACTERISTIC INCLUDED	CENSUS YEAR	FLORIDA STATISTICAL ABSTRACT YEAR	TABLE
FLORIDA, STATE ONLY			
ESTABLISHMENTS, SALES, AND SALES PER ESTABLISHMENT	1948-1987	1990-1993	16.01
DITTO	1958-1987	1994	16.01
DITTO	1963-1992	1995	16.01
DITTO	1967-1992	1996-1999	16.01
BY SIC CODE	1987	1990-1994	16.02
DITTO	1992	1995-1999	16.02
STATE AND COUNTIES			
WHOLESALE AND RETAIL TRADE, SALES	1987	1990-1992	16.06
DITTO	1992	1995-1999	16.06

CENSUS OF MINERAL INDUSTRIES
(Conducted approximately every 5 years)

AREA AND DEMOGRAPHIC CHARACTERISTIC INCLUDED	CENSUS YEAR	FLORIDA STATISTICAL ABSTRACT YEAR	TABLE
FLORIDA, STATE ONLY			
CHARACTERISTICS OF MINERAL INDUSTRIES	1992	1999	10.60

CENSUS OF TRANSPORTATION, COMMUNICATIONS, AND PUBLIC UTILITIES
(Conducted approximately every 5 years)

AREA AND DEMOGRAPHIC CHARACTERISTIC INCLUDED	CENSUS YEAR	FLORIDA STATISTICAL ABSTRACT YEAR	TABLE
FLORIDA, STATE ONLY			
ESTABLISHMENTS, REVENUE AND ANNUAL PAYROLL BY KIND OF BUISNESS	1992	1999	13.01

University of Florida   Bureau of Economic and Business Research

University of Florida   **Bureau of Economic and Business Research**

University of Florida   **Bureau of Economic and Business Research**

Counties--Continued
  Schools, public elementary and secondary--
    Continued
      Revenue, 598
      Salaries, 591
      Staff, 587, 589, 593, 596
      Taxes and property valuations, 603
      Testing, 138, 139, 140
  Schools, public secondary, testing, 141
  Schools, vocational, 574
  Security and commodity brokers, 509
  Services, 527
  Soap, detergents, and cleaning preparations;
    perfumes, cosmetics, and other toilet
    preparations, manufacturing, 394
  Social Security, 251, 254
  Social services, 576
  Solid waste, 270, 272
  Soybeans, 333
  Stone, clay, glass and concrete products,
    manufacturing, 396
  Sugarcane, 334
  Supplemental Security Income (SSI), 259
  Taxes, tourist-development, 549
  Telecommunications, 442
  Telephone communications, 442
  Textile mill products, manufacturing, 390
  Tobacco, 334
    Licenses, 692
  Tobacco products, manufacturing, 390
  Tourist facilities, 550
  Tourists, 540
  Transfer payments, 206
  Transportation and public utilities, 416
  Transportation services, 418
  Unemployment, 232
  Veterans, 677
  Veterinarians, 294
  Voter registration, 622
    Party and race, 620
  Voter turnout, 622
  Wastewater treatment, 281
  Water area, 268
  Water transportation, 418
  Water use, 277, 279, 324
  Wholesale trade, 472, 478
County government. See Government, local.
Credit institutions, nondepository, 219, 504,
  509, 698
Credit intermediation and related activities, 497
Credit unions, 503
Crime, 631, 632, 634, 643
  Arrests, 641
  Detention facilities, 651
  Domestic violence, 642
  Hate, 664

Crime--Continued
  Juvenile delinquency, 654, 655, 656, 658, 660
  Victim compensation, 662, 663
Cropland, foreign-owned, 321
Crops (See also Agricultural production, crops and
  individual commodities):
  Acreage harvested, 309, 335
  Acreage planted, 335
  Cash receipts, 306, 307, 315, 320
  Market value, 316
  Production and value, 335
Cubans, refugees, 75
Cucumbers, 307, 315, 324, 335
Customs districts activity, 428

D

Dairy:
  Cash receipts, 315
  Production, 338
Daytona Beach. See Cities and Metropolitan
  areas.
De Soto County. See Counties.
Deaths, 758
  Accidental, 109
  Boating, 543, 544
  Cause, 108, 109
  Child and teen, 110
  Infant, 102
  Motor vehicle, 422, 423, 425
    Alcohol-related, 425
  Race, 91, 102, 106, 109
  Sex, 109
  Suicides, 109, 758
Defense contracts, 676
Defense, Department of, 670
Democrats, 620, 627
Dental hygienists, licensed, 580
Dentists:
  Licensed, 580
  Offices, 561
  Offices and clinics, 565, 698, 700
Depository institutions, 219, 504, 508
Detention facilities, 651
Detergents. See Soap, detergents, and cleaning
  preparations; perfumes, cosmetics, and other
  toilet preparations manufacturing.
Disability, 251, 255, 259
  Income, 205
  Medicare beneficiaries, 249, 250
Dissolutions of marriage. See Divorces.
Dividends, 159
Divorces, 114, 758
Dixie County. See Counties.
Doctors. See Physicians.
Domestic violence, 642

University of Florida   **Bureau of Economic and Business Research**

University of Florida   **Bureau of Economic and Business Research**

University of Florida   **Bureau of Economic and Business Research**

University of Florida   **Bureau of Economic and Business Research**

University of Florida   **Bureau of Economic and Business Research**

University of Florida   **Bureau of Economic and Business Research**

University of Florida   **Bureau of Economic and Business Research**